SOCIAL WORK PRACTICE

SOCIAL WORK PRACTICE
A Critical Thinker's Guide

Eileen Gambrill

New York   Oxford
OXFORD UNIVERSITY PRESS
1997

OXFORD UNIVERSITY PRESS

Oxford New York
Athens Auckland Bangkok Bogotá Bombay
Buenos Aires Calcutta Cape Town Dar es Salaam Delhi
Florence Hong Kong Istanbul Karachi
Kuala Lumpur Madras Madrid Melbourne
Mexico City Nairobi Paris Singapore
Taipei Tokyo Toronto

and associated companies in

Berlin Ibadan

Library of Congress Cataloging-in-Publication Data
Gambrill, Eileen D., 1934–
Social work practice : a critical thinker's guide / Eileen
Gambrill.
p.   cm.
Includes bibliographical references and index.
ISBN 0-19-511332-2
1. Social service—United States.   2. Social case work—United
States.   3. Social workers—United States.   I. Title.
HV91.G325   1997
361.3'2—dc20   96-31313
                                                                CIP

3 5 7 9 8 6 4 2
Printed in the United States of America
on acid-free paper

CONTENTS

PROLOGUE

Joe is employed by a local outreach program for the homeless. Clients do not come to him, he goes to them. He spends much of his time talking and offering help to people who live on the streets, although sometimes it is weeks or months before anyone with whom he speaks takes him up on any of his offers of help. Lilly, a 28-year-old homeless woman, is typical of the people he sees. She has used cocaine for many years, supports herself through prostitution, and has been HIV positive for the past two years. Joe often wonders whether he is really helping anyone. As one of my students said to me, "No one prepared me for the kind of clients I met in my work with the homeless." Joe works together with other social workers in an advocacy group to increase the availability of low-cost housing for homeless families.

Jennifer works for a local community advocacy group, helping people with common concerns form coalitions. She spends a lot of time getting to know both community residents and the staffs of both the public and private community agencies. Jennifer helps the residents plan how to achieve their goals and, then, helps them to implement and evaluate the results. She also keeps in touch with politicians and advocacy groups. Her work requires her to make many decisions, such as which people to approach first, how to approach them, how to win over reluctant participants, and how persistent she should be.

Tanya is employed in the emergency response unit of her city's child protective services. She investigates claims of child abuse and neglect and decides what action to take. Her decision must be based on only one or two interviews, which is one of the frustrating aspects of her job. If she believes there is cause for concern, she refers the family to a worker in another unit in the agency. Tanya's caseload is large, and she has little time to linger over the details that ideally she should know before making a decision. Now that Tanya has worked for two years on this unit, she is thinking of requesting a change to a unit that provides ongoing services to families. She is currently working with a group interested in establishing neighborhood service centers in low-income areas.

The goal of these centers would be to prevent problems such as child maltreatment and delinquency.

Barbara is the administrator of an inner-city homeless shelter for families in New York City, which houses about 60 families. She supervises a large staff and is responsible for the day-to-day running of the center. She and her staff have to decide when to enforce the rules and when not to. Running this center requires balancing the rights of people to do whatever they feel like doing and the rights of others to be protected from harm and abuse, not always an easy task. As in so many social work jobs, resources are scarce. In Barbara's case, this means that there are always more people who need housing than can be accommodated, requiring her staff to choose who will receive shelter and who will not. Limited counseling and material aid are provided by a community support program that is run by a local hospital. Barbara spends some of her free time writing proposals to the city's board of supervisors to fund more low-cost housing.

Ahnan works in a day care center for emotionally disturbed boys and girls between the ages of 12 and 18. His responsibilities include planning and carrying out treatment programs for each resident. He must decide when to use observation to gather information, when and how to observe relevant exchanges, and how to evaluate his effectiveness. He and the other staff work closely together, holding weekly meetings during which they review each resident's progress in all areas (e.g., school, peer relationships, family relationships). Ahnan also helps run the weekly family-counseling groups with the residents' parents. Ahman enjoys these groups the most. He worries about some of the parents' lack of involvement, but his greatest frustration are those staff who do not adhere to agreed-on programs.

Maria works at a center in San Francisco that provides medical services to the homeless. Because she previously worked in a large metropolitan hospital with middle-class clients, it took her a while to get used to such a vastly different clientele. Many people do not keep their appointments, and she has no way of getting in touch with them, since most have no telephones. Many of her clients are IV-drug users and have contracted AIDS. One night a week she visits a homeless shelter for families where she and a nurse offer help with medical and other concerns. A major part of Maria's job is to help clients obtain practical services they need.

Gail works in a hospice and visiting nurses agency that offers in-home help to clients who are gravely ill. Many of her clients have AIDS; others are terminally ill with cancer. She visits them at home, assesses their needs, and provides whatever help she can to address them, including helping them understand and meet their financial obligations. She also offers help to her clients' caregivers. She spends some of her free time working with an organization lobbying for national health care coverage. Every day, Gail sees what happens to people with no health care insurance: some of them spend their last days worrying about how they will pay their medical bills. She must make many decisions each day including decisions about time scheduling (how to plan her day), about what information to gather, and what service methods to use. Should Mr.

Vincent be referred to a support group for HIV-positive clients? Should she suggest to Mrs. Martin that she attend a bereavement group? Does Mr. Kander need home help and, if so, how much? What's the best way to tell parents that their son is dying of AIDS? What's a good way to approach a potential service provider who has refused to supply needed resources? What can she do when needed services are not available? Gail struggles with many ethical decisions. Should she report a client's income that has not been declared? What should she do about a colleague who fails to visit clients as promised? What should she do about a client's threat to commit suicide?

Marie works in an old-age home. Her responsibilities include helping the residents communicate more effectively with their relatives and the staff. For example she may help a resident get in touch with their relatives and plan how to enhance the quality of their exchanges. The residents usually do not come to her with concerns; rather, Marie usually has to take initiative and discover what they would like, such as more frequent social contacts, answers to medical questions, and financial planning. Observing who does what, when, and to whom gives her opportunities to improve the quality of the residents' lives. For example, when she first arrived at the center, she noticed that many of the residents looked bored and depressed. She checked this out by talking to residents and staff. They confirmed her observations. She involved residents in planning recreational activities and group meetings. Marie makes scores of decisions each day. Some involve ethical dilemmas. For example, should she contact the only living child of an elderly resident who is dying, even though this resident has asked her not to do so? Does she have a right (or obligation) to try to involve bored, depressed residents in social and recreational activities, even though they have not asked to be included? What should she do about a staff member who makes nasty remarks about and patronizes the residents? How can she determine whether she is helping her clients?

Marie enjoys her work. She likes the freedom to choose what she does every day, and she gets great pleasure from enhancing the quality of the residents' lives. Not all the staff are open to her ideas and suggestions. Some think she coddles the residents. Perhaps her biggest worry is the lack of resources to provide services. Additional staff are needed, but little money is available for programming. She is working together with the residents and administrators to establish an ombudsperson program to mediate conflicts between administrators and residents.

Robert works in the employee assistance program of a large metropolitan hospital. He established this program and is proud of the unit that now includes three full-time social workers. He offers services to staff who seek his help with problems like depression, concerns about needle sticks (being stuck by a needle with blood from an AIDS patient), marital problems, problems between employees and supervisors, and substance abuse problems. Confidentiality is a key concern. Not even the supervisors of staff members who seek his help are informed about their visits, and his office is off-site to protect confidentiality. He makes decisions about what assessment methods to use, whether to involve significant others such as a partner of a client who worries about contracting AIDS, and what methods to use to help clients. Robert tries to keep up with new methods by attending each year a couple of carefully selected workshops in areas of special interest to his clients, such as substance abuse and stress management. He enjoys the varied nature of his job, and he has an excellent grasp of what social workers can offer and has improved the reputation of the social worker's role among staff in this large hospital. His main complaint is that there aren't enough staff to provide services, which puts extra pressure on Robert and his fellow social workers.

These examples of social workers' everyday work illustrate the variety of clients that social workers see and the different functions of social work described in Chapter 1: helping, social reform, and social control. As you read this book, you will see that these three functions of social work often conflict. The examples highlight the central role of decision making in social work at all levels. This includes deciding how to assess problems, what service methods to use, and how to evaluate progress. Critical thinking attitudes, knowledge, and skills that will help you make sound decisions are described throughout this book. The examples also highlight the social aspect of social work, the importance of developing positive working relationships with colleagues, other professionals, clients, and administrative staff. Lastly, the examples illustrate the scarcity of resources that social workers and their clients often confront.

INTRODUCTION TO THIS BOOK

Social Work Practice: A Critical Thinker's Guide provides a practice model built around the everyday decisions social workers make—both those who offer direct services to clients and/or those who function as case managers (arrange, coordinate, and monitor services provided by others). It is a contextual practice model in which the reciprocal interactions between individuals and their environments are emphasized. The personal is related to the political throughout, including the very definition of problems. I wrote this book because there is a need for a social work text that candidly addresses the controversial issues and problems in social work and offers practice guidelines that considers them. Problems include ignoring practice-related research that could be of value to clients, overlooking uncertainty in decision making, disregarding problems of concern to clients, forcing unwanted "services" on clients, and not acknowledging harm done in the name of helping. This book draws heavily on social science knowledge and integrates this knowledge around everyday practice decisions so that both clients and social workers will gain the benefits of available knowledge: clients by receiving effective methods (those likely to succeed in attaining outcomes they value) and social workers in having the professional satisfaction of offering high quality services. It is assumed that the value of practice beliefs and methods are best assessed through their success in helping clients. Topics that are often ignored are emphasized including hidden forms of coercion cloaked in professional jargon and the importance of critically examining background knowledge concerning problems addressed.

Unique features include chapters on knowledge (what it is and how to get it), critical thinking, involving clients, and handling challenging social situations such as expressing unpopular opinions.

Material is organized around key practice decisions such as deciding what problems to focus on, how to define them, what data to gather, how to combine material, how to select service methods and how to assess progress. Common errors in making different kinds of decisions are noted drawing on literature in social psychology, problem solving and decision making. Detailed assessment, intervention, and evaluation guidelines are described as well as a discussion of underlying assumptions and related controversies that will help you to use a *planful* approach in your work that offers the benefits of corrective feedback regarding service outcomes. The interrelationship among assessment, intervention, and evaluation is highlighted.

This book is for social workers who want to think critically about what they do, why they do it, and what outcomes result from services offered. It is for students who want to dig beneath the surface of popular beliefs about what is best. The purpose of thinking critically about these topics is to increase the likelihood that clients receive services that enhance the quality of their lives. Although some texts emphasize the importance of reflection, this text emphasizes the importance of critical reflection—a critical appraisal of points of view no matter what their source. Only by discovering our errors can we move forward and learn how to be better problem solvers. Practice decisions based on questionable criteria such as tradition (what's usually done), popularity (what most people do), or newness (what's the latest method) may harm rather than help clients and victimize rather than empower them. The uncertainties and conflicting interests involved in making practice decisions are highlighted and guidelines are suggested to maximize the likelihood of offering high quality services. Advantages of the problem-focused practice model described include keeping concerns of clients clearly in view, creatively searching for resources including client assets, and an emphasis on *functional* knowledge—information that decreases uncertainty about how to help clients. Major emphases include respecting individual differences (including cultural ones); recognizing the role of environmental factors in contributing to problems; empowering clients by offering them real influence over the quality of their lives; offering clients effective methods; and evaluating service outcomes in an ongoing manner so that timely changes in practices, programs, and policies can be made. Step-by-step assessment, intervention, and evaluation guidelines are described as well as valuable interpersonal skills.

There are two different ways to approach this book. Which is better depends on how soon you have to begin working with clients. One of the odd characteristics of social work education is that students often must start working with clients before they are prepared to do so. If this applies to you, you could start with Chapter 9 and work back over the background knowledge chapters when you have time. The questions at the end of each chapter will help you to review your knowledge, skills, and outcomes achieved. You may find it helpful to review these sections before reading the chapters.

ACKNOWLEDGMENTS

I owe a debt to all those who have cared enough and have had the courage to raise questions regarding claims of effectiveness about what helps people. We share an appreciation of criticism as the route to knowledge. I have drawn liberally on practice-related scientific literature as well as the questions, frustrations, and occasions for celebration of clients, seasoned practitioners, and students. I gratefully acknowledge the help of the University of California library system. In particular I want to thank Lora Graham and Craig Alderson at the School of Social Welfare Library. I thank all those who have provided encouragement while this book was in preparation including David Estrin (a former editor) and Richard Dangel who provided valuable feedback on some earlier chapter drafts. Thanks also to Leonard Gibbs and Tomi Gomory for their keen interest in critical appraisal and its value in the helping professions. I also want to thank Gioia Stevens and production editor Karen Shapiro of Oxford University Press. Some of the material in Chapter 18 is based on *Taking Charge of Your Social Life* (written with Cheryl Richey). Thanks is extended to Sharon Ikami for her consistent good will and excellent word processing skills. Lastly, I want to acknowledge the continued support of Gail Bigelow.

PART

I

GETTING ORIENTED

CHAPTER 1

Social Work: An Introduction

OVERVIEW

This chapter offers a bird's-eye view of the profession of social work and suggests a philosophy of practice for increasing the likelihood of providing services clients value. The context of social work as well as its major functions are described. Recurrent themes and controversies are highlighted.

You Will Learn About

- Social work and social welfare.
- Range of concerns addressed.
- The advantages and disadvantages of being a social worker.
- The functions of social work and social welfare.
- Social work as a profession.
- A philosophy of practice.

SOCIAL WORK AND SOCIAL WELFARE

Social welfare refers to the laws, programs, and services designed to provide benefits to people who require assistance in meeting their basic needs (Karger & Stoesz, 1994). Universal welfare programs (e.g., social security) offer benefits to people in all income classes, whereas selective programs are designed solely for the poor. Popple and Leighninger (1993) organize all social welfare services under three kinds of dependency, which they define as the inability to

carry out expected social roles, such as that of parent or employee. These include the following:

1. Services for people who are economically dependent, including cash support programs, for example, Aid to Families with Dependent Children (AFDC), Supplemental Security Income (SSI), and in-kind programs such as Medicaid and Medicare, subsidized housing, and food stamps.

2. Services for people who are dependent because

they are unable to fulfill roles as defined by themselves. Such assistance includes mental health services, family counseling, employment services, socialization services, and information and referral services.

3. Services for people who are dependent because they have not fulfilled roles as defined by others. These include probation and parole, child and adult protective services, and involuntary mental health services.

The term *welfare* is often associated with being poor. However, if it includes not paying full value for services/products and governmental aid, it provides benefits for the nonpoor as well. Examples of corporate welfare include subsidies and tax breaks for the mining, aerospace, agricultural, high-tech, and finance industries. Corporate welfare also includes supporting tobacco farmers and spending taxpayers' money to build roads in national forests that ease the way for private firms to gather timber.

Social work practice is carried out in both public and private agencies and includes direct services to individuals, families, groups, and communities, as well as administration, management, and policy analysis (see Exhibit 1.1). Local, state, and federal governments fund public agencies that offer services mandated by legislation. Public agencies often purchase services from private agencies, which may be either corporate for-profit organizations or nonprofit voluntary agencies; many agencies are designed especially for particular groups. Social work and social welfare are concerned with decisions about how resources should be distributed—how much money should be spent on which programs and who should make those decisions. These choices are influenced by values and beliefs regarding individual responsibility, how free people are to influence the quality of their lives, and the obligation of the state to its citizens. Decisions about how resources should be distributed reflect differences of opinion about problems and how to address them.

Social workers offer services for a broad range of circumstances, such as crises (e.g., sudden illness or death); alcohol or drug abuse; lack of hous-

EXHIBIT 1.1
Examples of Public and Private Agencies

AIDS Help & Prevention Plan
AIDS Legal Referral Panel
Alameda County Department of Social Services
Alameda County Probation Department
Asian Women's Shelter
Bay Area Information Referral System
Bayview Hunters Point Adult Day Health Center
Big Brothers/Big Sisters
Catholic Social Services
Center for Families in Transition
Center for Southeast Asian Refugee Resettlement
Children's Hospital, Social Service Dept.
Chinatown Youth Center
Coming Home Hospice
Community Board
Deaf Counseling, Advocacy & Referral Agency
East Bay Elder Abuse Consortium
Easter Seal Society
Eden Psychiatric Day Treatment Center
Emergency Services Network
Family Service Agency
Gay Rescue Mission
Gay Youth Community Coalition of the Bay Area
Health Care for the Homeless
Independent Living Resources
Japanese American Senior Center
Jewish Family and Children's Services
Korean Community Service Center
La Clinica de la Raza
Legal Aid Society
Marin Community Mental Health Services
On Lok Senior Health Services
Parent–Infant Neighborhood Center
Refugee Women's Programs
Suicide Prevention & Crisis Intervention
Teenage Pregnancy & Parenting Project
Travelers Aid Society
United Way of the Bay Area
Urban Indian Child Resource Center
Volunteers of America

ing, money, food, or medical care; transitions such as retirement; and interpersonal problems such as parent–child or marital conflict and child and elder abuse. Problems may require attention because they disrupt role performance (like that of parent). Examples of such problems are depression, anxiety, and stress from chronic poverty, illness, or disability. Conflicts with or a lack of responsiveness from agency personnel may be a problem as well. Refugees may seek help establishing a new life in the United States. Crack-addicted babies and children and adults with AIDS may need assistance.

Limited funding for welfare programs requires difficult decisions about service priorities. The goals of social work identified by the National Association of Social Workers in 1981 are still relevant today (see Exhibit 1.2). Social workers work with both poor and middle-class people and offer services to both the homeless and families who abuse or neglect their children. They work in medical and psychiatric hospitals, old-age homes, community mental health centers, employee assistance programs, probation departments, and group homes for troubled (or troubling) adolescents. Social workers can even be found in veterinary clinics (e.g., helping people who have recently lost a pet).

THE ADVANTAGES AND DISADVANTAGES OF BEING A SOCIAL WORKER

Being a social worker has many advantages. One is that you get paid to help others. An interest in helping others draws many to social work. The benefits of helping are suggested in the quotes below, from hospice staff and volunteers:

> One day my young patient with AIDS greeted me at the door with "I've been waiting anxiously for you to get here. I really need the ray of sunshine and good cheer you always impart when you come to see me.

I look forward to each of your visits." And with that he gave me a big hug. It really made my day, and I felt good about everything all day long—good and bad.

> One special note from a family read: "You made a difference to all of us. What could have been a terrible time for our family turned into something special. We have never been so close. Thank you." (Larson, 1993, p. 21)

Altruism (helping others with little regard for our own benefit) provides benefits to the helper as well as the helped.

A second advantage of social work is that you can continue to learn throughout your career. You may, for example, become better at identifying problems of concern to your clients. A third advantage is flexibility in moving from one social work job to another. Many social workers who start out offering direct services move on to supervisory and administrative positions, or they transfer from one area of practice (working with the homeless) to another (working in a hospital with drug-addicted babies and their families). Some social workers combine a private practice with employment in a public or private agency. Another advantage is helping to prevent injustices and misery (see the later discussion of the social reform functions of social work).

EXHIBIT 1.2
Goals of Social Work

Goal	Goal	Goal	Goal
To enhance problem-solving, coping, and developmental capacities.	To link people with resources, services, and opportunities.	To promote effective and humane service systems.	To develop and improve social policy.
Functions	Functions	Functions	Functions
Assessing Detecting/identifying Supporting/assisting Advising/counseling Advocating/enabling Evaluating	Referring Organizing Mobilizing Negotiating Exchanging Brokering Advocating	Administration and management development Supervision Coordination Consultation Evaluation Staff development	Policy analysis and development Policy advocacy

One disadvantage of being a social worker is that you will probably not get rich (see Gibelman & Schervich, 1996). Many social workers supplement their salaries through private practice and consultation. Another disadvantage is that social workers sometimes are associated in the mind of the public with the disadvantaged and deviant persons with whom many work (Fineman, 1985). You can counter this possible stigma by developing pride as a social worker based on offering high quality services.

THE FUNCTIONS OF SOCIAL WORK AND SOCIAL WELFARE

A historical and contextual view of social work and social welfare suggests three major functions: (1) relief of psychological distress and material need, (2) social control (e.g., maintaining social order and discipline, regulating the labor market), and (3) social reform (altering conditions related to psychological distress and material need). Recognizing these different, often conflicting functions will help you to understand the paradoxes in the field (such as statements of good intent not accompanied by action) and to identify resources and obstacles to helping clients. The ideas of Charity Organization Societies (COSs) and Settlement Houses that were imported from England to the United States, emphasized these three functions to different degrees. Although in both, there was a concern with eliminating poverty, they embodied quite different views of its causes. The COSs stressed individual responsibility. Friendly visitors visited the poor in their homes and listened and offered advice. The distribution of cash payments was discouraged. Mary Richmond who was in charge of a COS, believed that it was important to identify the specific skills involved in providing charity to the poor. Her famous book, *Social Diagnosis* was published in 1917. Those who worked in Settlement Houses pointed to environmental factors as the causes of poverty (e.g., unemployment, lack health services, poor quality housing).

Relief of Psychological Distress and Material Need

In a broad sense, social welfare helps people to function effectively in their social environment. This includes providing for basic survival needs (adequate nutrition, clothing, shelter, and medical care) and creating opportunities to enhance psychological well-being and social productivity (Federico, 1990, p. 25). The preamble of the new draft of the NASW Code of Ethics states that "the primary mission of the social work profession is to enhance human well-being and help meet basic human needs of all people with particular attention to the needs and empowerment of people who are vulnerable, oppressed and living in poverty" (1996). Helping clients may involve enhancing clients' knowledge and skills, as well as helping them obtain needed resources.

Societies throughout history have offered aid for practical problems such as a lack of money, need for medical attention, shelter, food, and clothing (Morris, 1986). Recent decades brought more organized services, a change from volunteer to paid staff, the view of many resources as rights rather than privileges, and use of social services by the middle class both to provide material aid and to relieve psychological distress. Cloward and Epstein (1965) see the expansion of entitlements and the increased demand for services by the middle class as leading to the neglect of those who most need help and to a corresponding disinterest in environmental change. The responsibility for providing services has increasingly shifted from public agencies to private enterprises (Kamerman & Kahn, 1989).

Social Reform

From the earliest days of social work, many social workers have stressed the need for social reform, believing that the lack of food, housing, employment, and educational and recreational opportunities—not the unworthiness of individual persons—was responsible for social problems. Jane Addams founded Hull House in Chicago in 1889. By 1911 there were hundreds of settlement houses in the United States. Settlement workers, who daily encountered environmental deprivation, emphasized reform. They also had a social control function. For example, settlement house staff socialized new immigrants into American customs, including ways of dressing (e.g., not wearing a "babushka"). Charity organizations also have been interested in pursuing social change:

> And especially in the way of social reform can such a society exercise its greatest influence. It can insist on open spaces in the city for the recreation of the poor. . . . It can prevent cruelty to children; preserve the dependent and neglected children from evil surroundings; it can institute "country weeks," and insure the prompt payment of wages. (McCulloch, 1880, speaking for the Associated Charities).

Gradually, private channels for relief to the poor, such as charity organizations were replaced by official public channels, such as departments of public welfare, which offered a wide range of services. For example, the Public Welfare Department of Dayton, Ohio, took responsibility for recreation, charity, correctional and reformatory institutions, disease control, and health needs. Individual distress was viewed as the concern of all people. D. Frank Garland (1916), the director of public welfare in Dayton, described the purpose of his department as "based on the principle that the welfare of all is the ultimate goal of the community. . . . For example, . . . [l]oss of employment is frequently due, not to the indifference of the individual workman, but to great industrial crises, or combinations and conditions in which workmen are allowed no vote" (Garland, 1916, p. 310).

The Depression of the 1930s greatly increased the number and range of social workers' clients, and emphasized the close connection between economic conditions and personal problems and the need for legislation on a broad level. President Franklin D. Roosevelt's New Deal legislation transferred the funding of social services from the private sector to the public. The Social Security Act was passed in 1935. Some people believed that the new services were offered because of political reasons as well as humanitarian purposes to reduce discontent, win elections, and to maintain the social system substantially unchanged.

Social reform served many functions, including gaining political advantage over opponents (Katz, 1989). Some of these reform efforts served the needs of businesses (to protect and expand markets) and professional groups more effectively than the needs of those groups for which they were supposedly designed. Katz suggested that in order to secure low-paid workers, fast-food chains lobby legislators to pass bills requiring welfare women (even those with young children) to work.

History shows that social reform has always been a struggle:

> If there is no struggle there is no progress. Those who profess to favor freedom, and yet depreciate agitation, are men who want crops without plowing up the ground. They want rain without thunder and lightning. They want the ocean without the awful roar of its many waters. This struggle may be a moral one; or it may be a physical one; or it may be both moral and physical; but it must be a struggle. Power concedes nothing without a demand. It never did and it never will. Find out just what people will submit to, and you have found the exact amount of injustice and wrong which will be imposed upon them; and these will continue until they are resisted with either words or blows, or with both. The limits of tyrants are prescribed by the endurance of those whom they oppress. (Frederick Douglass, Letter to an abolitionist associate, 1849)

Social workers and many others advocated working hard to remedy inequities and to create a more just environment for all citizens. Unions also sought equality of opportunity and tried to improve working conditions. Their efforts were often followed by violent attacks on union members (Boyer & Morais, 1994). Social work clients changed from supplicants to demonstrators and lobbyists, demanding help as a right. The lobbying efforts of elderly citizens brought about the indexing of Social Security under the Nixon administration. In the late 1960s, students in many schools of social work protested the social service agencies' lack of commitment to their clients. Then during the 1980s, the individual change model and calls for professionalism rose to the fore, and the student protests and interest in courses on community organization ebbed.

Social Control

Social control is another function of social work and social welfare. It refers to encouraging adherence to social norms and minimizing, eliminating, or normalizing deviant behavior. Functions include protecting citizens from harm and reaffirming standards of morality (Conrad & Schneider, 1992, p. 7). Examples of informal social control are internalized beliefs and norms and influence in face-to-face exchanges such as ridicule, praise, and ostracism. Examples of formal social control are laws and regulations and actions by governmental representatives such as police and social workers.

Mimi Abramowitz argues that since the colonial times, social welfare policies have treated women differently based on the extent to which their lives conformed to certain family ethics (1988, pp. 3–4). Institutions concerned with social control include the educational, social welfare, criminal justice, and medical systems and the mass media. Leslie Margolin (in press) contends that social work in public agencies is engaged mainly in political surveillance-keeping track of marginal and common people in their homes. Social workers are integrally involved in defining problems and deciding what should be done about them: what is healthy (good) or unhealthy (bad). It is they who investigate and keep records (Margolin, in press). Indeed, an ever lengthening list of behaviors are defined as mental illness requiring the help of "experts." The social control influences of social workers can be seen in their roles as probation and parole officers and as child protection workers when they remove children from neglectful or abusive parents, in protective services for the elderly when they arrange for conservatorship, and in mental health agencies when they recommend hospitalization. An interest in social control is reflected in concerns on the part of "friendly visitors" in the Charity Organization Societies to distinguish between those who deserve aid and those who do not.

a discrimination must be made between those who are helpless from misfortune and those whose misery arises from their own default; and that to aid the willingly idle man or woman, or anyone who can help himself, is in the highest degree hurtful to the person aided and to society at large. Its [Charity's] more immediate duty has been to extend aid to that class of worthy and industrious poor, who, by reason of sickness, accident, loss of employment or of property, have fallen temporarily behind, and to rescue them from permanent pauperism by timely assistance; to extend a helping hand to widows with dependent children, to aged and infirm people partly able to help themselves, to single women when work suddenly ceases; and, above all, to so do this [in a way] to prevent the injurious and wasteful results of indiscriminate giving. (M'Cagg, 1879, pp. 147)

Katz argues that welfare has often been designed "to promote social order by appeasing protest or disciplining the poor" (1989, p. 33). A policy's social control function is not necessarily obvious. The language of caring and nurturance may obscure manipulative and coercive practices (Margolin, in press; Szasz, 1994).

Some people contend that social work helps maintain a capitalistic economic system by containing dissatisfaction of disadvantaged and oppressed groups such as poor inner-city residents. They argue that a major function of social work is to keep the economy working smoothly by controlling those with limited access to resources and providing a labor force (Galper, 1975). George and Wilding (1984) suggest that social services contribute to political stability in five ways:

1. Through apparent efforts to alleviate problems that might result in serious discontent and that could be used to criticize the current economic and political structure.

2. By defining social problems as caused by individual, family, or group factors rather than by structural and economic factors. A case approach to problems obscures political and economic causes and encourages a fragmented view. Clients' problems are dealt with one at a time (education, health, housing) and are delegated to a different group of professionals.

3. By promoting values and behaviors that support political stability. Schools reward conformity, effort, and achievement and downplay conflict in economic and social life and sources of inequity (Merelman, 1975). Medical sociologists and anthropologists describe ways in which health care systems support the prevailing cultural values (e.g., Lock, 1993).

4. By supporting authority and related hierarchical systems (e.g., keeping clients waiting for long periods in drab waiting rooms). The educational system helps legitimate inequality (hierarchy) by claiming to provide equal opportunity. Then if someone is not successful, the fault is with the individual (Tapper & Salter, 1978).

5. By replacing class conflict with group conflict. Funds for services are allotted by group (elderly, at-risk infants, the homeless), thereby obscuring the shared underclass status of many clients and the political and economic conditions contributing to this status.

All five factors decrease the likelihood of political protest.

Controversial Issues

A moment's reflection on the different functions of social work highlights the potential for conflicts and contradictions. The goal of social control may compete with that of helping clients. This is a common dilemma in child welfare settings in which workers are mandated both to protect children and to help parents who have harmed (and may continue to harm) their children. Social control aims are often disguised as concerns about helping clients as can be seen from a history of institutionalized psychiatry (see for example Szasz, 1994). Negotiating the optimal balance between individual freedom and the protection of others has been the subject of treatises both small and large.

Conflicting goals lead to different opinions about how problems should be addressed. Some people believe that welfare programs are too extensive, that they encourage dependence on government aid and get in the way of individual re-

sponsibility. Some critics want to eliminate welfare altogether. Many believe that the programs developed during President Lyndon Johnson's War on Poverty were misguided. In his controversial book *Losing Ground* (1984), Charles Murray argues that the social policies of the 1960s and 1970s principally involved the transfer of funds from some groups of poor people to other groups of poor people and harmed the very people they were designed to help. In *The Economics of Wealth and Poverty* (1986), Gordon Tullock observes that money is redistributed mainly from some middle-class groups to other middle-class groups, with the only justification being that the recipients want the money. He argues that based on what people do rather than what they say they do and value, they really are not all that charitable. Some scholars claim that American welfare has always been inadequate, cruel, and irrational, pointing out that social welfare expenses make up a much smaller percentage of the United States' gross national product than they do in other wealthy nations and that resistance to social welfare is greater in this country (e.g., Katz, 1989). They note too that America is the only Western democracy that does not have national health insurance. One of four children in this country is living either in poverty or on the poverty line. Many scholars see social welfare programs as focusing on the symptoms of inadequate social conditions rather than on the conditions that create the problems (e.g., Piven & Cloward, 1993). For example, if the unemployment rate among urban inner-city black youth were not so high, crime and drug use might not be so prevalent in this population.

Some people believe that social workers have no business doing psychotherapy, that it distracts them from helping clients build communities (Specht, 1990; Specht & Courtney, 1994). Others contend that psychotherapy is a legitimate role of social work (Wakefield, 1988, 1992). Whether it is or is not depends on how psychotherapy is defined and on beliefs about the purpose of social work and social welfare. As always, a key question is who profits and who loses from a particular point of view. Exploring who benefits and who loses from a belief, policy, or procedure will reveal mismatches between words (intent) and outcome. Exploring who profits and who loses from a belief, policy, or procedure will often bear surprising results. For example, Leroy Pelton (1989) sees the child welfare system's focus on investigation, blame, and subsequent child removal as diverting attention from the problems of poverty and its effects on children and from making fundamental changes in our social, economic, and public welfare systems.

SOCIAL WORK AS A PROFESSION

Certain occupations—such as social work—have been transformed into professions, which Abbott defines as "exclusive occupational groups applying somewhat abstract knowledge to particular cases" (1988, p. 8). According to Greenwood, a profession has the following attributes: (1) a systematic body of theory, (2) professional authority, (3) the sanction of the community, (4) a code of ethics, and (5) a professional culture (1957). Professionals are expected to offer certain services in a competent manner. All professions claim special knowledge and skills to help clients achieve certain ends. This knowledge supposedly makes those with relevant degrees "experts" in solving certain kinds of problems. The Council on Social Work Education, formed in 1952, serves as an accrediting body for schools of social work. Degrees in social work are the bachelor's, the master's, and the doctorate. There are 416 social work education programs in the United States (see Ginsberg, 1995). B.S.W. degrees are offered by 392, M.S.W. degrees by 122, and Ph.D. degrees by 52. Although the bachelor's degree is the entry-level social work degree, many positions require a master's degree as well as a state license. Master's degree programs often are divided into problem-area specializations (e.g., mental health, aging, children and families, and health) and service-level specializations (e.g., direct practice with individuals, families, or groups and management and administration). Social work doctoral programs are for students who wish to do research or to teach or who want advanced practice knowledge and skills.

The National Association of Social Workers (NASW) was founded in 1955. It holds conferences and publishes a monthly periodical (*NASW News*) and five journals, including *Social Work*, which is distributed to all members. In 1970 social workers with a B.S.W. degree were permitted to become full members of NASW. Other social work organizations include the National Association of Black Social Workers (NABSW), National Association of Puerto Rican Social Service Providers (NAPRSSP), and National Indian Social Worker Association (NISWA). As of 1995, NASW had 153,000 members (Gibelman & Schervich, 1996). Its functions include "promoting the professional development of its members, establishing and maintaining professional standards of practice, advancing sound social policies, and providing other services that protect its members and enhance their professional stature" (Barker, 1987, p. 104). NASW established the Academy of Certified Social Workers (ACSW) in 1962, whose members must have an M.S.W. or doctorate from an accredited school, two years of supervised field time or 3,000 hours of part-time practice experience. A candidate must also submit three professional references and pass the ACSW examination. Membership in NASW is required for admission and continued participation. NASW also maintains a National Register of Clinical Social Workers and offers a diplomate in clinical social work to eligible applicants.

The Role of Professions in a Society

In addition to providing help with certain kinds of problems, professions have political and economic functions and interests. "No matter how disinterested its concern for knowledge, humanity, art, or whatever, the profession must become an interest group to at once advance its aims and to protect itself from those with competing aims. On the formal associations level, professions are inextricably and deeply involved in politics" (Friedson, 1973, pp. 29–30). The public mental health system is a huge industry consuming about $29 billion a year of taxpayers' money (Manderscheid & Sonnenschein, 1993). Recognizing the political and economic functions of professions helps account for their vague codes of ethics (e.g., they serve both a public relations and an ideological role) and exaggerated claims of expertise and success (to gain public and legislative support), which can be seen in the ongoing battles to protect and expand their "turf" (e.g., between psychologists and psychiatrists).

Professional status is not necessarily based on demonstrations of effectiveness (Goode, 1960). This is true of social work as well as other professions such as medicine. For example, midwifery was officially discredited at the beginning of the twentieth century when it was replaced by obstetric care, even though midwives had lower rates of stillbirths and puerperal sepsis than did the (male) physicians (Ehrenreich & English, 1973). The evolution of professions is a result of their interrelationships and these interrelationships are influenced by the manner in which different occupational groups control their knowledge and skills. Abbott (1988) offers a fascinating account of how different professions redefine problems and tasks in order to ward off "interlopers" and enlarge their jurisdiction to new problems (see also the discussion of the medicalization of deviance in Chapter 7). For example, Abbott notes that "psychiatrists in the twenties tried to seize control over juvenile delinquency, alcoholism, industrial unrest, marital strife, and numerous other areas" (p. 23). Understanding how the professions work (how they develop, what constraints influence them) will help you to work toward changes that will improve services within your professional organization.

Controversial Issues

Not all social workers thought professionalization was a good idea. Many staff in the newly developed public agencies "saw in professionalism a defense of status, not of skills and proficiency" (Ehrenreich, 1985, p. 113). They attempted to develop a practice model that gave the environment a central role and contended that the concern with professionalism distracted social workers from community organizing and client advocacy and toward individual treatment approaches. Another controversy is whether credentials (e.g., licenses,

degrees) protect clients. In *House of Cards: Psychology and Psychotherapy Built on Myth* (1994), Dawes argues that licensing gives the public only the illusion of protection, but does serve the economic interests of professionals. Based on research showing that nonprofessionals are as successful as professionals in helping clients with a variety of problems, he argues that possession of a degree or "experience" does not ensure a unique domain of knowledge or a unique degree of success in helping people. That is, credentials may not be accompanied by a track record of success in resolving certain kinds of problems. Authors such as Peter Breggin (1991) and Thomas Szasz (1987) argues that professional helpers often harm rather than help, by unnecessarily depriving people of their freedom (e.g., locking them up in mental hospitals), undermining their ability to help themselves (e.g., only an expert can help), and injuring them in the name of helping (e.g., causing irreversible damage by using neuroleptics).

Indeed, as a result of professional intervention, the presenting complaints may get worse or losses may occur that would not otherwise. For example, in a comparison of intensive services provided by social workers to elderly clients and the usual agency procedures, it was found that mortality was higher in the group receiving the former (Blenkner, Bloom, & Nielson, 1971). Studies of decision making in professional contexts reveal a variety of common errors, such as incorrectly defining problems (e.g., missing physical causes) and selecting ineffective or harmful treatments (e.g., Kassirer & Kopelman, 1991). Studies of decision making in child welfare show the effects of *ratcheting* (adhering to a particular point of view despite evidence that it is wrong) and *templating* (inappropriately applying correlational data to individual clients (Howitt, 1992). Peter Breggin suggests that "the mental health problems, led by psychiatry, have rushed into the void left by the default of the family, the schools, the society, and the environment" (1991, p. 275). He notes that blaming child victims of neglectful or abusive histories by diagnosing, drugging and hospitalizing them "takes the pressure off the parents, the family, the school, and the society" (p. 275).

THE IMPORTANCE OF
A HISTORICAL PERSPECTIVE

A historical view, whether of a profession, policy, agency, community, problem, group, family or individual lends a depth of understanding that may otherwise not be possible. It reveals misguided beliefs and actions as well (e.g., *The March of Folly* by Barbara Tuchman, 1985). It illustrates the power of words and ideas to sway others and to wield influence in ways that may limit freedom and inflict harm. Consider the successful use of propaganda in pre-World War II Germany. Patterns of discrimination may emerge as well as the ideologies that mask them. For instance, studies of the history of housework highlight the role of economic profit in influencing household work (Oakley, 1976). A historical perspective can help us to avoid false paths and be wary of potential harmful consequences and coercion involved in pursuing grand untested proposals for change (utopias) rather than pursuing small scale changes. Without "the long view," you may mistakenly assume there has been (and is) agreement about what is best, what is true. You may discover that ideas that you now accept as self-evident did not exist or were rejected as misguided in other times. Concepts you may view as central may not be present in other cultures. An historical perspective combined with valuing critical discussion can help us to free ourselves from prejudice and error and to view our ideas not as inherent or self-created, but as influenced by the particular culture that surrounds us.

A historical view allows us to judge how far a field has advanced, stayed the same, or regressed. Do we know more today than we did a decade ago about how to help the unemployed, the homeless, families that abuse and neglect children, or people who drink too much? In his provocative essay "The End of Social Work" (1997), David Stoesz argues that social work as a profession has failed to make the transition to the postindustrial era, as indicated by the erosion of private practice and public social services. History highlights the shifting balances in the profession regarding reform and control goals. A historical perspective will help us to recognize old functions in new guises, such as the traditional role of the social worker as the middle person between the rich and the poor, reflected in the competing interests between control and reform. Being familiar with the history of a profession will help you to recognize recurrent debates (e.g., how to classify people, the effects of welfare on the work ethic, and government's obligation to those in need). It will help you to recognize continuities between current approaches and past trends. For example, the emphasis on the role of the environment in creating and maintaining problems reflects a long term theme in social work that has ebbed and flowed over the years.

The Value of a Global Perspective

A global perspective reveals how events in one part of the world affect what happens in other locales. A global perspective often reveals that what we assume to be universally true is not, that what we take for granted as moral and ethical ways of behaving are not similarly viewed in other cultures and countries, and that what is viewed as a problem differs in different societies. The service systems of various countries differ; for example, Canada and Britain have had national health insurance for decades. Karl Popper (1994) views cultural clashes as essential to knowledge development. (To explore international social work further, see, for example, Hokenstad, Khinduka and Midgley, 1992.)

A PHILOSOPHY OF PRACTICE

Is a professional someone who applies special knowledge in a framework that honors the ethical codes of that profession? Is it someone who has had success in helping clients achieve outcomes they value and/or someone who has successfully completed a M.S.W. degree in social work and is licensed? Is it someone with all these characteristics? Different beliefs about what it means to be a professional influence how helpers act in their everyday exchanges with clients. Some characteristics are more likely than others to avoid harm and increase the likelihood of helping. This is why a philosophy of practice is important. Philosophy is the study of what is right to do and believe and on what basis beliefs and actions should be selected. *Webster's New World Dictionary* (1988) defines philosophy as "a particular system of principles for the conduct of life." Many philosophers believe that philosophy is relevant to everyone because life requires making decisions that involve moral and ethical issues.

> All men and all women are philosophers. If they are not conscious of having philosophical problems, they have, at any rate, philosophical prejudices. Most of these are theories which they take for granted: they have absorbed them from their intellectual environment or from tradition. Since few of these theories are consciously held, they are prejudices in the sense that they are held without critical examination, even though they may be of great importance for the practical actions of people, and for their whole life. (Popper, 1992, p. 179)

John Dewey (1933) emphasized philosophy as criticism, as thinking reflectively and carefully about questions and issues.

The Importance of a Philosophy of Practice

The purpose of a philosophy of practice is to increase the likelihood that clients receive effective service and are not harmed. It will help you to act consistently in accord with goals you value and can provide a source of renewal from the challenges of practice in a time of scarce resources. The hallmarks suggested guided my selection of content in this book. The first three (responsibility for decisions, enhancing personal welfare, and avoiding harm) are key ones from which the others follow. These others have three interrelated sources: (1) what logically follows from the first three (e.g., valuing truth over ignorance and prejudice), (2) what we know about problem solving (e.g., criticism of ideas is invaluable), and (3) what we know about common errors in professional decision making (e.g., not basing decisions on data, ignoring the gap between personal beliefs and available problem-related knowledge). Many of these criteria are not included in the Code of Ethics of the National Association of Social Workers.

1. Professionals are responsible for the decisions they make. Professionals are assumed to be uniquely qualified to provide certain kinds of services, and professional codes of ethics highlight responsibilities to provide competent services. Taking responsibility for decisions is basic to accountability to clients. Many social workers I talk to, students as well as experienced social workers, tell me they do not make decisions. But they do, and only by accepting responsibility for them are they likely to honor their ethical obligations to their clients.

2. Services help clients and their significant others attain outcomes they value. Three possible outcomes of professional contact are: (a) clients acquire valued outcomes; (b) clients are worse off than before; and (c) there is no change. This hallmark emphasizes the distinction between a feeling of helping and being helped (e.g., of feeling empowered and actually being empowered). It highlights the importance of achieving both aims. The NASW Code of Ethics lists service as its first value: "Social workers' primary goal is to help people in need and to address social problems." Focusing on helping clients attain outcomes they value will help us to avoid getting sidetracked into pursuing fine-sounding (perhaps utopian) but impossible aims. "I stress a practical approach: the combating of evils, of avoidable suffering and of avoidable lack of freedom (by contrast with promises of a heaven on earth)" (Popper, 1992, p. 90). Clients' interests must be balanced against the right of others to be protected from harm and to pursue the goals that they value. Protecting some clients may require taking away opportunities from others, such as the opportunity to abuse or neglect children or adults.

3. Clients are not harmed. Enhancing the welfare of clients entails avoiding harm. The history of the helping professions is partly a history of harm done in the name of helping (e.g., Szasz, 1994; Valenstein, 1986). For instance, adolescents may be institutionalized for the treatment of substance abuse, even though there is no evidence that institutionalization is effective (Schwartz, 1989).

Or rather than creating an environment in which residents can acquire skills that improve the quality of life, residential settings may create counter-habilitative conditions (Favell & McGimsey, 1993; Meinhold & Mulick, 1990). The history of the helping professions shows that caring is not enough to protect people from harm and to maximize the likelihood that they will receive help. Intent to "do good" focuses on the values and beliefs of the "helper" rather than the freedom, values, and constitutional rights of the clients. Decisions made involve balancing the risks and benefits of doing something (offering a "service") against the risks and benefits of doing nothing. Professionals often assume that they must act, and clients often expect action. It is easy to act and to assume that this is best when it may not be.

4. Use of the least restrictive methods. Avoidance of harm and provision of help requires attention to the restrictiveness of methods. Restrictiveness refers to the removal of freedom and the use of unpleasant methods. Institutionalizing clients is more restrictive than working with them in their communities. Future as well as current outcomes of different courses of action should be considered when gauging restrictiveness. For example, not using a temporary restrictive plan may result in much more restrictiveness in the future (e.g., continued institutionalization).

5. Clients (or their representatives) are fully informed and involved in decisions. Clients have a right to be involved in decisions that affect their lives. This highlights the importance of fully informing clients about recommended methods as well as alternatives and their risks, benefits, and costs. Honoring this guideline encourages a collaborative relationship in which both helpers and clients have responsibilities and share in decisions made. Professionals have an obligation to be candid about lack of resources and alternatives. They have an obligation to clearly describe any coercive elements or practice such as investigatory aims. They have an obligation not to mislead clients. Sharing data about degree of progress with clients involves clients as informed participants in making decisions about what to do next.

6. Professionals have problem-related knowledge and skills. The claimed possession of specialized knowledge and skills is the basis on which professionals claim certain rights not extended to people who are not professionals. Professionals thus have an ethical obligation to be informed about what theories have been critically tested related to the goals that they and their clients pursue. The NASW Code of Ethics calls for social workers to base their practice on "empirically based knowledge, relevant to social work and social work ethics" (1995, p. 20). (Unfortunately, the code adds the adjective recognized, which connotes reliance on consensus and authority rather than critical testing.) The importance of background knowledge to making sound decisions and resolving problems is highlighted in the literature on problem solving and professional decision making. Chapters in Part 2 of this book describe such background knowledge.

7. Practice decisions are well reasoned. The reasoning that professionals use is more than a personal matter. Social workers' influence on their clients' lives and their obligation to help and not to harm obligates them to think critically about practice-related assumptions and make well-reasoned decisions. Karl Popper (1994) argues that relying on unexamined claims about what is true reflects an arrogance that is at odds with a compassion for others. Practitioners differ in the criteria on which they base claims. Avoidable errors often occur because of reliance on questionable criteria, such as anecdotal experience to evaluate the accuracy of claims. Well-reasoned decisions are those for which sound arguments can be made. For example, claims relied on have survived risky predictions and are compatible with and informed by empirical data describing relationships between behavior and specific environmental changes.

8. Truth is valued over certainty, ignorance, and prejudice. Making well-reasoned decisions requires valuing truth over ignorance and prejudice.

If professionals are obligated to help clients and avoid harm, they must value "truth, the search for truth, the approximation to truth through the critical elimination of error, and clarity" (Popper, 1994, p. 70). Karl Popper (1994) defines truth as the correspondence of statements with facts. If a community organizer says, "I helped this community," this statement should correspond with the facts (e.g., residents report that they have been helped because there is a new park, a new recreation center, a citizens' advisory center, and a day care center for toddlers). Valuing truth highlights the vast extent of our ignorance about the world. As Popper notes, we all are equal in our vast ignorance. "It is important never to forget our ignorance. We should therefore never pretend to know anything, and we should never use big words. What I call the cardinal sin . . . is simply talking hot air, professing a wisdom we do not possess" (Popper, 1992, p. 86). We have "the obligation never to pose as a prophet" (p. 206). But the "prophet motive" (Jarvis, 1990) is difficult to resist, given the public's interest in soothsayers and prophets.

9. Critical discussion and testing of claims is valued. Valuing truth over prejudice and ignorance entails critically testing claims and conclusions. Only through criticism can we discover our errors. This is essential for learning how to do better in the future. Critical discussion with oneself as well as with others is necessary for making well-informed decisions and valuing truth over certainty, ignorance, and prejudice. Principles that Karl Popper highlights as the basis of every rational discussion are as follows:

1. The principle of fallibility: perhaps I am wrong and perhaps you are right. But we could easily both be wrong.

2. The principle of rational discussion: we want to try, as impersonally as possible, to weigh up our reasons for and against a theory: a theory that is definite and criticizable.

3. The principle of approximation to the truth: we can nearly always come closer to the truth in a discussion which avoids personal attacks. It can help us to achieve a better understanding; even

in those cases where we do not reach an agreement. (Popper, 1992, p. 199)

10. Decisions are data based as well as theory based. Respecting individual differences, valuing truth over ignorance and prejudice, and making well-reasoned decisions requires basing practice decisions on data as well as theory when this is necessary to help clients and evaluate outcomes. Guesses about the causes of problems should be checked against data gathered in real-life settings when this is necessary to help clients. For example, only by collecting detailed observational data in real-life, problem-related settings may informed guesses be made about the causes of problem-related behaviors and circumstances. Only then may the unique circumstances of an individual client be understood. Collecting data on a client's progress provides a guide for practice decisions (e.g., plans can be changed as necessary). This allows us to discover whether we are helping, harming, or having no effect. It allows clients to find out whether the quality of their lives has improved, remained the same, or diminished. Anthony Flew (1985) contends that the sincerity of our interest in helping clients is reflected in the efforts we make to find out whether we do help them. Compassion for the trouble of others requires finding out if we did help.

11. Individual differences are valued and respected. Only by attending to individual differences can we clarify our clients' problems and make informed decisions about whether we can offer any help and, if so, what kind. Without a respect for individual differences, we may make incorrect assessments and miss opportunities to help clients. Labeling people ignores the uniqueness of each client's behavior and the circumstances in which it occurs. It is deeply disrespectful of their unique individual variability. It obscures our unique happiness and miseries and their individual contexts. In obscuring individual patterns of variability and related contingencies, we forgo a source of assessment information that may provide the only route to informed guesses about the functions of behaviors that result in helping clients attain outcomes they value such as more positive parent-child exchanges. Respect for individual differences requires challenging biases and stereotypes and building on clients' strengths. It requires allowing clients discretion in how hard to work to achieve their goals. Barbara Simon (1994) contends that paternalism slips in when practitioners work harder than their clients to remedy situations.

12. Self-knowledge that contributes to making well-reasoned practice decisions is sought and used. Only if professionals critically examine their problem-solving styles and the influences on them, including fears and vested interests, can they take the corrective steps needed to enhance their success in helping clients and avoiding harm. Raymond Nickerson (1986) views self-knowledge as one of three kinds of knowledge required for sound reasoning. Others include domain-specific knowledge and performance skills. Self-knowledge

includes accurate description of gaps between personal knowledge (e.g., your current assumptions about a problem such as poverty) and the available domain-specific knowledge.

13. Words correspond to actions. Only if values are acted on are they meaningful. This will require a correspondence between values, words and actions. If a social worker claims to value informed consent, a review of her interviews with clients should show that she fully informs her clients about alternative plans and clearly describes to them the criteria she relies on to recommend plans (e.g., tradition—what the agency usually offers, popularity, newness, or scientific—results of critical tests of claims). Likewise, if a social worker says he builds on his clients' assets, a review of his work should show that he helps them identify personal assets that can be used to pursue desired outcomes.

SUMMARY

Throughout time, some people have needed help, and others have offered it. Social workers provide help for a broad range of problems, including child and adult abuse and neglect; material concerns such as a lack of food, clothing, or housing; parent–child conflicts, chronic illness, and disability; and loneliness and depression. The struggle to establish social work as a profession was hard fought. As with other professions, schools were created, a national organization formed, a code of ethics developed, and licensing laws passed. Social work gradually changed from using volunteers who worked with the poor to paying staff to provide services to both poor and middle-class persons. Not everyone welcomed professionalization; some viewed it as drawing attention away from the need for social reform and as contributing to the welfare of professionals rather than clients.

Social work is carried out in a political, social, and economic context that shapes the definition of problems and their proposed resolutions. The history of social work reflects the strains in the profession between reform and control and between individual and community. The different functions of social work and social welfare inevitably lead to controversies about what these functions should be and help explain the problems that continue to plague social work, such as relying on ideology instead of evidence to support claims of effectiveness and a control function mixed with a preference for helping within a voluntary context. The purpose of the social services is to help clients, yet the services offered may contribute to inequalities that perpetuate problems. Social control goals can be seen in the efforts to distinguish between the deserving and undeserving poor and in social workers' decisions about what is acceptable and what is deviant behavior. Those characteristics of professionals that protect the welfare of their clients include a focus on helping and avoiding harm, respecting individual differences, fully informing clients, taking responsibility for decisions made, and making well-reasoned decisions.

REVIEWING WHAT YOU KNOW

1. Describe the difference between social welfare and social work.
2. Identify the major functions of social work and social welfare.
3. Give examples of the control functions of social welfare.
4. Discuss some of the controversial issues regarding the different functions of social work and social welfare.
5. Describe the attributes of a profession.
6. Describe controversial issues concerning professionalization.
7. Discuss the value of having a philosophy of practice.
8. Discuss the relationship of valuing truth over ignorance and prejudice to helping clients and avoiding harm.

SUGGESTED ACTIVITY

Review the characteristics of professionals described in this chapter and check those you also value. If you disagree with any, explain why and add others that you consider important, also offering a well-reasoned argument for why you believe this.

CHAPTER 2

Clients and Services

OVERVIEW

This chapter describes a contextual view of helper–client exchanges that assumes that both parties influence each other and in turn are influenced by their task environment (e.g., management practices in an agency and public policies that affect agency practice). I discuss the effects of earlier help-seeking efforts on later ones and other variables that influence services, such as the beliefs, goals, and expectations of both clients and helpers. In particular, I emphasize the cultural diversity of clients and its implications.

You Will Learn About

- The route to the agency.
- Helping as a social influence process.
- The clients' beliefs, expectations, and goals.
- The helpers' beliefs, expectations, and goals.
- Social policy and agency influences.
- The cultural diversity of clients.
- Barriers to cross-cultural helping and remedies for them.

THE ROUTE TO THE AGENCY

Social workers see an unrepresentative sample of all those individuals who have a certain behavioral or emotional pattern or confront certain experiences. For example, only some people with relationship or drinking problems see social workers. Only some people who commit crimes are caught, prosecuted, and found guilty and thus meet a probation or parole officer. Seeking help from an agency may be preceded by seeking help from friends or relatives (see Exhibit 2.1). On the other hand, people may be reluctant to talk to friends or relatives because of their involvement in problems, fears about how they will react, and concerns about confidentiality, indebtedness, and negative impressions. Some people ask the advice of clergy, elders, indigenous healers, and even hairdressers and bartenders. Strategies these helpers' use may be the same as those used by professional helpers, such as offering support, listening, suggesting alternatives, and sharing personal experiences.

Clients may find out about social services through relatives or friends, the Yellow Pages, radio, or television. Or other professionals may refer clients. Requesting help from a social service agency may be a last resort. It may be viewed as a sign of weakness or immaturity or as a negative reflection on the family.

Clients, Applicants, and Resisters

A *client* is defined as someone who makes an explicit agreement with a social worker about the purpose of their work together. Most people who come to social service agencies are not clients. Some are *applicants* who request something, such as a teacher who seeks help with a "hyperactive" child. Applicants may become clients. Many people social workers see are reluctant participants. They are people who have had their freedom limited against their will, such as parents suspected of child abuse, youths or adults on probation, and residents of mental hospitals. They may ask only to be let alone. Helen Harris Perlman calls such individuals "resisters." "They come unwillingly, dragging their feet and their spirit, feeling coerced, robbed of their free will by other persons or conditions they oppose. Sometimes they want help, but not the kind that is to be had or not the kind under the conditions to be required" (1979, p. 115). They may deny that there is a problem, blame others, and be antagonistic. Resisters may become clients when, for example, a parent whose children have been removed may agree to participate in a plan to regain custody of her children. Social workers often act

as though they are working with a client when in fact they are talking to an applicant or a resister, that is, someone with whom they do not have an agreement to work together toward an agreed on goal. They may not understand why this person does not do what they recommend, failing to realize that he or she never actually agreed to do so. If you have trouble involving your clients (e.g., they don't complete agreed-on tasks), check to see whether you have an agreement to work toward a goal.

Previous Contacts with Professionals

People's previous help-seeking experiences influence how they respond when they go to an agency and also what they expect from future meetings. Prior experiences are not always satisfactory. Clients who have encountered rude or insensitive professionals may be hostile or reserved, expecting more of the same. Negative or unhelpful experiences may make them unwilling to seek further help.

> All those &%$@**# did was ask dumb questions and take our money. They never gave us any help at all! When they told us that we might as well put him in an institution because he would never be able to count money or even talk, I sort of lost my mind. I was so sad that I was in a fog for about a week. Then I heard a voice inside me telling me that I would have to do the job by myself. (Kozloff, 1979, p. 17)

HELPING AS A SOCIAL INFLUENCE PROCESS

Helpers and clients influence each other. Therefore, if we want to understand the helping process, we must explore the transaction (i.e., the interactions) between helpers and clients and the context in which it occurs. Jerome Frank states that research has not altered his earlier view of helping as an interpersonal process in which the helper's beliefs, values, and optimism overcome the client's demoralization and offer hope (see Frank & Frank, 1991). Studies of helping highlight the social in-

EXHIBIT 2.1
Examples of Help-Seeking Efforts Before Seeking Help from Professionals

THE GREEN FAMILY

Mrs. Ryan, age 89, had been living for six years with her son-in-law (Mr. Green), her daughter, and their two teenage children. This arrangement was made when Mr. Ryan died. Since her daughter and her family had an extra room in their home and since Mrs. Ryan wanted to live with them, they had all agreed that this would be a good plan. Now, six years later, Mr. and Mrs. Green were not so sure any longer this arrangement was a good idea. They felt that Mrs. Ryan was becoming an increasing burden. The help she had provided, such as straightening up after dinner and cleaning, decreased as her health became more fragile owing to a heart condition. And as the children became older and more able to care for themselves, her babysitting services were no longer of benefit to the family. As the children advanced into their teens, value differences between Mrs. Ryan and her grandchildren became accentuated. She was appalled, for example, at the TV shows they watched and was shocked about their open discussion of birth control and the possibility of what might be done if the daughter became pregnant. At first, Mrs. Ryan had expressed her differences of opinion, but since this seemed to result in conflict and hard feelings, she had increasingly withdrawn from discussions and spent more and more time in her room. The Greens were very concerned about this state of affairs. They did not seem able to help Mrs. Ryan and their children achieve a more satisfying means of discussing their differing values, and they were torn between their loyalty to their children and their loyalty to Mrs. Ryan. The increased care that Mrs. Ryan required was an additional burden on the Greens, both of whom worked full time. The Greens also worried about what they would do if Mrs. Ryan had another heart attack, one that left her with substantial disabilities. How would they then care for her? They were worried about the financial burden this might entail, as funds were not overly plentiful in the household. Mrs. Green was a practical nurse, and her husband worked as a truck driver in a nearby lumber company. They were in their early fifties.

The Greens had many discussions between themselves about what to do. Should they bring up the possibility of Mrs. Ryan's entering a home for the elderly that was located about twenty miles away? Wouldn't it be better to make arrangements now rather than wait until Mrs. Ryan became more feeble and more of a burden to the household? They had also sought the opinion of a couple with whom they were good friends. The couple had advised them to act now rather than later, that is, to place Mrs. Ryan in the home. They talked to the minister of their church, even though they went to church only sporadically. He suggested that they talk with Mrs. Ryan. But they did not take the minister's advice, since they thought she would feel that they did not want her and would insist on moving out. They went to the library and took out a couple of books on living with old people to try to find suggestions.

None of these efforts seemed to help matters. Finally, Mrs. Green decided that she would talk to the social worker at the hospital and ask her advice. The social worker referred the Greens to a local service for the elderly.

THE LAKELAND FAMILY

For the past year, Mr. and Mrs. Lakeland had been having difficulty with their 14-year-old son. In addition to Brian, two other children lived in the home, a girl aged 11 and an older brother aged 18. Brian would not follow his parents' instructions, would often tease his sister and the dog, and would disappear without telling his parents where he was going. The parents also had received many complaints about his behavior from the school authorities—that he got into fights at school and was failing in many subjects.

Mrs. Lakeland had spoken with her mother about their problems with Brian, and she suggested that "time would work things out." However, time did not seem to be working things out, and the Lakelands grew increasingly restive about their relationship with Brian and his relationships with others, including his interaction with the family dog, since Brian's teasing was beginning to take a cruel cast: he would twist the dog's tail or kick him. The Lakelands sought the help of their family doctor, who had been seeing Brian since Brian was 4 years old. At this time he had been diagnosed as having epilepsy. Brian was supposed to take medication twice a day, and this seemed to control his seizures if he remembered to take it, which was another problem; Brian often forgot to take his medication. It was because of this diagnosis of epilepsy that the Lakelands had extended extra leeway to Brian in terms of his behavior. They felt that "he couldn't help himself as much as the other children." Dr. Bernard, the physician, suggested that the parents be very firm with Brian and place strict limits on his behavior. They did this; that is, they "laid down the law" to Brian, told him that he was not to tease the dog anymore, was to take his medication every day, was to mind his parents, and so forth—or else. "Or else" was left simply to imply that they would take other steps. This seemed to have an effect for a day or two, and then the situation became even worse. Brian threatened his father with a knife when one evening right after supper, Mr. Lakeland had demanded that he stop teasing his sister and the dog.

Mrs. Lakeland decided to contact the Family Service Agency. She knew about this agency, since she passed it on her way to work every day. She thought that maybe they would be able to offer the family some help.

JULIE

Julie had never thought she would get pregnant. She thought that she had timed everything right and that there would be no chance. But here she was, pregnant at age 15. What would she do? She became so upset every time she tried to think about it that it was hard for her to see clearly the possible alternatives and their advantages and disadvantages, let alone decide among them. Should she have the baby or not? If she did, what would she do with it? Would her parents keep it? Should she have the baby and give it up for adoption? What would she do about school? If she had an abortion, where would she go for it? Who would find out? Would she be able to have more children if she had an abortion? Would it hurt a lot? What would her parents say and do? She knew how strict her parents were about their religion and how much against abortion they were. Whom could she talk to? If she talked to a friend, even her best friend, wouldn't she tell others and wouldn't her mother find out? Where could she go for help? She didn't even want to share her predicament with her boyfriend. He would think she was dumb for getting pregnant. After all, she had told him it was safe.

Still she had to do something. Time was passing, and she knew that if she were going to have an abortion, it should be done within the first three months.

EXHIBIT 2.1 (*continued*)

Maybe the laboratory where she had had the pregnancy test would know about someone to talk to. She remembered that she had seen a notice on the bulletin board when she was there about some service. She decided that she would go back to the laboratory and look of the address.

---

fluence process that takes place even in "nondirective" approaches (Bergin & Garfield, 1994; Truax, 1966). Helpers reinforce some behaviors, ignore others, and punish still others. In turn, clients influence the helpers' behavior. The subtlety of these social influence processes (they may not be obvious) does not remove the fact that they do not occur. Jurjevich (1974) argues that this subtlety allows helpers to misuse their power, to the detriment of their clients.

Prior help-seeking experiences as well as the match between the helpers' and clients' goals influence what occurs. Client goals include obtaining help with problems, preserving self-respect, limiting invasions of privacy, satisfying needs for dependence and nurturance, and seeking assurance that nothing is wrong. The social worker's goals include establishing and maintaining an area of expertise, using expertise, making money, demonstrating competence, and serving others. The possibility of mismatches has led some investigators to describe helper–client interactions as *problematic social situations* (Stone, 1979, p. 46). Waitzkin describes exchanges between physicians and patients as "micropolitical situations" in which the control of information reinforces the power relations that parallel those in the broader society, especially those concerning social class, gender, race, and age (1991, p. 54). Cultural differences between clients and helpers may increase the likelihood of miscommunication.

Although the transactional model may seem reasonable, some professionals neither subscribe to it nor act on it. Instead, they may blame lack of client participation on their clients, overlooking their responsibility to do what they can to increase participation. They may take too much responsibility, thereby neglecting their clients' responsibilities and rights to make their own choices (how or if to participate). With many problems such as homelessness, lack of medical services, unemployment and lack of day care, client participation is a moot point since even maximal participation would not succeed in attaining needed resources.

CLIENTS' BELIEFS, EXPECTATIONS, AND GOALS

Clients' goals and beliefs regarding their problems, what services will be offered, and what results are likely also influence the helping process. Clients have certain expectations about what will happen in and result from their meetings with social workers, and the extent to which they match those of their helpers will affect the outcome (see Exhibit 2.2). Ignoring or misunderstanding client expectations may result in premature drop out. Some clients may be helped in one meeting (Talmon, 1990). Others may drop out because they do not feel helped and believe that further visits would be a waste of time, money, and effort.

Beliefs About Problems

Clients assume different degrees of responsibility for their problems, and also the solutions. A client may approach the social worker as an outsider who will join him in blaming family members for his problems. Or the client may feel depressed and hopeless because she does not have the material resources she needs. According to the *moral model*, a person is responsible for both his or her problems and their solution. This model contrasts with a *medical or disease model*, in which the client is assumed to be responsible for neither the problem nor its solution (Brickman et al., 1982). In the *compensatory model*, the client is viewed as being re-

EXHIBIT 2.2
Clients' Expectations

JULIE

As Julie approaches the agency, she has a last-minute wish to turn around and go home. What will happen? What will she have to tell the social worker? Will the social worker want to know all the details of her sexual relations with her boyfriend? Won't the social worker think Julie is stupid for not taking more precautions? Will she jump on her for thinking about having an abortion? Will she jump on her for wanting to have her child and raising it herself? Here she is at the door. She can always say she feels sick and leave.

Julie arrives at the door of the agency and goes inside. A woman is sitting at a desk, says hello in a pleasant manner, and asks Julie if she can help her. Julie tells her she has an appointment. The woman says "fine" and asks her if she has been there before. Julie says "no" and begins to feel like going home. The woman at the desk says, "Could you please fill in the information on this form? It will just take you a minute." This request bothers Julie. She starts to wonder again if they will tell her mother. She looks at the form and sees that it just calls for some very basic information: her age, year in school, address, and phone number. She completes the form and sits down in the waiting room. She asks herself again for about the thousandth time—what do I want to do? And the same thought comes to her. I want to have an abortion. She cannot imagine herself taking care of a baby right now.

THE LAKELAND FAMILY

The interview with the social worker has been set for 7 P.M. to accommodate the Lakelands, both of whom work. As they think about the upcoming interview, they become uneasy. Maybe this mess is all their fault. Maybe they have not done a good job as parents. Maybe it is because they both work full time. Maybe Brian has epilepsy because he fell when he was 2, and Mr. Lakeland should should have caught him before he hit his head. And what is there new to try? They already tried being firm with Brian; they tried putting him on medication. But he won't take it. Maybe the social worker will get him to take this. Maybe she will lay down the law to Brian, and he will begin acting like a human being.

Brian reluctantly agreed to accompany his parents on the visit to the social worker. He dreads this. Every time he sees his counselor at school, all he (the counselor) does is yell at him. "Why can't you be like all the other students? What's the matter with you? Why don't you take your medication?" He does do some nasty things—but they are fun, and they really don't hurt anyone. Why can't anybody else see that? The social worker probably won't see it either. Well, he'll go along, but he's not going to admit that he is the bad guy in all this. If his parents treated him better, none of this would happen. They're always talking about what a goody-goody his older brother is in college and all of that. Why don't they just leave him alone? He (Brian) gets so made at his father sometimes.

sponsible for the solution but not the problem. According to the *enlightenment model*, a person is responsible for the problem but not its solution.

Clients' Expectations About Services and Outcomes

Clients may not know what to expect, or they may have preconceived notions about the type of social worker who can help them. The less familiar the clients are with the services offered, the more important it is to describe the services carefully. Many clients prefer a direct approach, in which the social worker offers advice and guidance in a respectful collaborative exchange (see for example, Davis and Proctor, 1989, for reviews of research on ethnicity and preferred service patterns). This advice and guidance may not be provided by professionals, however. Significant others—such as an elder in a Native American group or an older brother in a Chinese family—may be the adviser. The greater the cultural differences between helpers and clients are, the greater the need to attend to differences that may affect the helping process. People on probation or parole may view social workers as disliked and feared authorities who will or can limit their freedom and interfere in their lives.

Clients have preconceived ideas about the kind of person who can help them. A client may believe that only someone who has had similar experiences can be of help; thus an elderly widow may believe that only another elderly widow can appreciate her loss. In their study of helpers and clients, Mayer and Timms (1970) found that clients expected workers to agree with their view of the solution and to help change the situation. They were puzzled and surprised at the workers' emphasis on talking, their failure to take a stand against an offending significant other, their interest in exploring the clients' past, their focus on feelings, and their interest in them rather than in the people the clients considered responsible for the problems. Social workers attributed their clients' reluctance to engage in expected behaviors to their resistance to acknowledging their role in creating their own problems. The most satisfied clients were those who requested material aid and—received it (see also Maluccio, 1979).

Clients may expect their problems to be resolved quickly, even when this is unlikely.

> I had been so unhappy for so long that when my mother suggested I go to the agency I thought, "Wow! I'll be all fine and cured!" . . . So . . . when I first went in there, I went with this kind of illusion that there was this Good Fairy who was going to wave the magic wand and I'd just be so happy and peaceful! . . . Well, it took me a couple of months to realize that the counselor wasn't a Good Fairy. Oh, she was just a nice lady to talk with. . . . She gave me time to talk about myself and after a while I began to feel better . . . but it didn't happen overnight. (Maluccio, 1979, pp. 55–56)

Or clients may not believe that their problems can be solved. The helper's skill in creating positive expectations is part of the success of all forms of help, psychological as well as medical (Skrabanek & McCormick, 1992; Frank, & Frank, 1991).

Clients' Expectations About How They Will Be Evaluated

A client who complains about a family member may worry that the social worker will think that he has contributed to the problem. He may worry that a social worker of a different race or ethnicity will not be sympathetic or be able to understand his concerns. The norms for asking for certain types of aid in the community in which a client lives affect expectations. For example, in some communities, seeking counseling is viewed as a sign of personal deficiency. Asking for material aid may be hard, even though the client may have a legal right to such aid.

HELPERS' BELIEFS, EXPECTATIONS, AND GOALS

Helpers also have beliefs, expectations, and goals. Their evaluation of clients is influenced by the attributions they make about their behavior. Lack of client participation may be attributed to personality characteristics of clients, overlooking environmental causes and the fact that change is difficult.

Social workers also have beliefs about what behaviors are appropriate, what causes a particular behavior, whether and how that behavior can be changed, and how much responsibility their clients have. Consider two different social workers who may interview Julie:

> Mrs. Kulp works at a family service agency. Most of the clients she sees have problems with their children, but occasionally she interviews unwed teenagers. She is scheduled to talk to Julie the next day. As the time for the interview approaches, the following thoughts drift through her mind: Another unwed teenager. I just don't understand why they have such loose moral values. Imagine having intercourse at that age! Teenagers should have to face up to the consequences of their actions. But because the agency's policy is to explore alternatives with young unwed mothers, I guess I'll have to do this. I hope Julie isn't thinking of having an abortion!

> Mrs. Landis works at the same agency. As the time for her appointment with Julie approaches, she thinks: Why doesn't this community provide better family-planning services for teenagers? If better services were available, there would not be as many unwanted pregnancies. I wonder what Julie will want to do. Even if she has decided on an alternative, I'll encourage her to at least take a look at other possibilities so that she will be aware of all the available options.

These two workers' different attitudes may influence how they act when they interview Julie as well as the options they offer to her and how they describe them. Social workers often predict outcomes in advance, and these judgments influence how they will act. Expectations of failure may result in less effort (Houts & Galante, 1985).

Research suggests that the helpers' reactions are influenced by their views of the ease with which people become involved in a helping relationship, their motivation for change, how predictable their behavior is, and their estimates of how much a client will benefit from assistance (Wills, 1978). Some research has found that helpers' views are less favorable than laypersons' are. Professionals tend to focus on negative traits and this focus increases with increasing experience (Wills, 1978):

"Experience produces an increased emphasis on negative characterological aspects, particularly an increased perception of maladjustment, and a less generous view of clients' motivation for change" (Wills, 1978, p. 981). Are professionals' views more accurate? Research shows that they are not: "In general, there is no difference in judgmental accuracy between professionals and lay persons" (p. 981). The best way to guard against the negative effects of expectations is to be aware of and question them. It is the unexamined assumption that often causes the most mischief. The emphasis on environmental circumstances related to problems clients confront, including unequal educational, housing, health, and recreational opportunities should protect social workers from this negative bias.

THE INFLUENCE OF THE PROFESSION

Each profession claims to have special skills in responding to certain kinds of complaints, and each uses a certain ideology to justify its actions and assure the public that it is working in its best interests (e.g., the ideology of doing good). The ideology used to support claims and the technologies used in their service influence the services clients receive. In his brilliant study of the professions, Abbott (1988) described the delicate balance between clarity and obscurity that is needed to maintain professional jurisdiction over certain kinds of problems. If the methods used to identify and resolve certain problems are clear, people with fewer or no credentials may usurp problem areas from the domain of professionals. Leslie Margolin (in press) argues that many professionals mystify not only their clients (as to their real purpose) but also themselves about the covert functions of social work. He views home visits, interviewing, record keeping, and record sharing as technologies used to justify taking actions that affect clients "for their own good." Professionals may be responsible for blocking policies and practices that in fact protect clients. In regard to the abuse of children, consider the position of some of the leaders of the American Professional Society on the abuse of children (which consists of 5,000 child protective workers) against taping interviews with children in sex abuse cases, which is routine in countries such as Britain and Canada, to guard against improper, incorrect inferences. What is important is to look candidly at what social workers do and do not do, so that you will not mystify yourself or your clients about hidden sources of influence (e.g., investigating rather than helping them).

SOCIAL POLICY AND AGENCY INFLUENCES

Agencies have policies concerning what services they provide, who is eligible to receive them, and what fees (if any) are charged (see Exhibit 2.3). In turn, the agencies' programs and procedures are influenced by public policies and federal, state, and county regulations and funding. How services are organized affects clients. Some scholars argue that the investigative/coercive and helping/supportive roles that characterize child welfare services are incompatible (e.g., Lindsey, 1994). Commercialization of services has increased in many service sectors, including the nursing home industry. Public services are often contracted out to private agencies. Policies and practices may benefit staff rather than clients.

Even the manner of the agency's receptionist—whether it is curt and cold or warm and welcoming, and respectful of cultural differences—can influence how people respond. One study showed that the receptionist at a social service agency could discourage a client by withdrawing her advocacy activities (Hall, 1974, p. 125). The physical characteristics of waiting rooms affect clients. Are educational brochures available describing the agency's services? Are play materials available for children? Preferred practice frameworks decide which services will be provided and thus the outcomes achieved. For example, a study comparing the effectiveness of psychodynamic, individually oriented child therapy and structural family therapy found that although both were effective in reducing the behavioral and emotional problems of Hispanic youth and in improving the psychodynamic ratings of child functioning, family functioning deteriorated with individual child therapy (Szapocznik et al., 1989).

The Technology Used and the Criteria Used to Select It

Agencies use different service methods and rely on different criteria to select them. Stephen Fawcett and his colleagues define social technology as "a

EXHIBIT 2.3
Describing Your Agency

1. What are your agency's goals?
2. What services are offered to what clients in what geographical area? Do the services provided reach those in need?
3. What are the agency's funding sources? How do they influence the services provided?
4. How well does the staff (e.g., in regard to ethnicity, age, sexual orientation, gender) match the clients? Discuss the implications of the degree of match.
5. Who are the gatekeepers in your agency, and how do they affect the delivery of service?
6. Describe the waiting room in your agency. How could it be made more welcoming?
7. What service methods does your agency rely on, and how do they affect clients (e.g., in regard to recording systems, practice methods)?
8. What criteria are used to select service methods, and what are their implications for clients?
9. How does your agency track the quality of the services offered and their outcomes? Do these methods provide an accurate picture?
10. What training opportunities are provided to staff; what is their quality; and how are their outcomes evaluated?
11. What is your agency's administrative style, and how does it affect the services that your clients receive?
12. Describe your agency's specific policies, programs, and practices that enhance the provision of services.
13. Describe specific policies, programs, and practices that detract from the quality of services provided to clients.
14. What external groups influence the services offered by your agency?
15. Describe your agency's links with other agencies.
16. At this time, what changes in your agency are most needed to enhance its provision of services?

replicable set of procedures that is designed to produce an effect on socially important behaviors of
relevant participants under a variety of real-life
conditions" (1984, p. 147). Some agencies focus on
"people-change" technologies; others, on "envi-
ronmental-change" technologies. Some focus on
processing people (giving them labels and referring
them elsewhere). (See Exhibit 2.4.)

Exhibit 2.4 provides an opportunity to review
the service methods used in your agency. You are
more likely to discover creative uses of both new
and old technologies if you make it a habit to ask,
"How could I use this with _____?"

Clients often need a number of services. The
term *case management* refers to the arrangement,
coordination, and evaluation of services offered to
an individual or family. Case managers often are
responsible for screening potential clients, assessing their needs, developing service plans, linking
clients with needed resources, and monitoring and
evaluating the services provided (see Exhibit 2.5).
Effective case management often requires a continuum of care levels that match the client's need
and that help maintain his or her independence (see
Exhibit 2.6). (The term *case management* also can
have a negative meaning, referring to the speedup
of work and the lowering of service quality because
of monetary concerns. For example, a key responsibility of discharge planners in a hospital is to get
patients out of the hospital as quickly as possible.)

Agencies differ in criteria relied on to choose
service methods. Technology related to problems
addressed may be more or less developed and critically tested, and agencies draw on tested methods
to different degrees. The same kind of methods may
be offered to all clients, regardless of their suit-
ability. For example, when asked why she was using play therapy for a 6-year-old Chinese American
boy referred because he was not following instructions at school or home, the social worker answered, "That's what the agency offers."

Tradition may not offer the best guidelines.
Leslie Margolin (in press) suggests that in the early
part of the century, social workers used the technologies of the telephone, the case record, and the
interview to gain and maintain a power position in
relation to their clients. He suggests that they used

the techniques of friendliness, an expressed interest in doing good, and an apparent absence of self-
interest to gain entry into the once private homes
of the poor, where they could collect information
that was not necessarily related to concerns of
clients. They also kept case records on clients to
which they could refer to justify their decisions.
The biographies in these records might have been
incomplete and inaccurate. Clients did not have access to them; today, many clients still do not. (For
arguments for and against giving clients access to
their records, see Gelman, 1997; Winchester-Vega,
1997.) The telephone was used to pass on information in records to other social workers, again
without allowing clients to make corrections.

CLIENTS' CULTURAL DIVERSITY

Social work in the United States is practiced in a
diverse society. Patterns of behavior in different
groups may overlap to a large or small degree depending on past and present shared contingencies.
Everyone has a culture (see Glossary in Appendix
2-A). We all grow up in a particular social environment that shapes and maintains our behavior.
Each individual has a unique identity. This is influenced by dominant cultural values and practices
(e.g., the media) as well as by unique family experiences, geographical setting (e.g., rural/urban/
suburban), and generation. Identity may change
over time. We may go through different stages in
forming our identity, such as accepting the dominant cultural values and then rejecting them and accepting what is viewed as best from different perspectives (Helms, 1990). Different cultures create
and maintain certain patterns of behavior and values. Culture is passed on in part by language, the
arts, and other symbols.

Not all people value Individualism and competition for status and recognition; rather, the family
and community may be at the top of the list.
Likewise, the self-exploration valued in Western
culture may be considered by others as a cause of
problems. Some parents may encourage children
who are experiencing problems to think more about
their family and less about themselves. For in-

EXHIBIT 2.4
Reviewing the Technology Your Agency Uses and the Criteria for Selecting It

A. What are the main service methods that your agency's staff uses?

___ Case management	___ Skill training	___ Community development
___ Support	___ Brokering	___ Social action
___ Outreach	___ Advocating	___ Other _____
___ Recording	___ Education	_____
___ Crisis Intervention	___ Insight development	

B. Check those factors that affect your agency's choice of technology.

___ Funding	___ Scientific	___ Personal preferences of staff
___ Staff knowledge and training	___ Popularity	___ Administrative decisions
___ Staff time	___ Tradition	___ Other _____
___ Staff hired	___ What seems interesting	_____

C. Please answer the following using a scale of 1 (not at all), 2 (a little), 3 (a fair amount), 4 (a great deal), 5 (best that could be):

1. Technology used is state-of-the art (best that can be given available knowledge).	1	2	3	4	5
2. Fidelity of methods used is high.	1	2	3	4	5
3. Fidelity[a] of methods used is routinely reviewed.	1	2	3	4	5
4. Each staff member receives feedback each month on fidelity of methods used.	1	2	3	4	5
5. Staff select service methods based on their demonstrated track record of success in helping clients achieve valued outcomes.	1	2	3	4	5
6. Technology used is updated every six months based on related empirical literature.	1	2	3	4	5
7. Staff at all levels welcome questions about service methods used.	1	2	3	4	5
8. Client feedback regarding the effects and acceptability of methods used is regularly collected and reviewed.	1	2	3	4	5
9. Staff have training required to provide services they offer with maximal effectiveness.	1	2	3	4	5

[a]Fidelity refers to the degree to which service methods match those that maximize likelihood of success.

stance, the autonomy of the individual is less valued in Japanese than in Western culture; instead, social connectedness and endurance are emphasized (DeVos, 1985). The wishes of European Americans to be fully informed about their health status and to participate actively in decisions about life support are not shared by all other groups. Although 69% of European Americans believe that a patient should be told of a terminal diagnosis, only 35% of Korean Americans agree (Mydans, 1995; *New York Times*, September 13, 1995, p. A-13).

Cultural adaptation refers to a graadual change in behavior toward prevailing cultural patterns. *Cultural change* may result from the intrusion of outsiders or a gradual change in values and behavior within a group. *Cultural relativism* refers to the belief that a culture should be evaluated in terms of its own standards. And *acculturation* is the integration of one's original values, traditions, and behaviors with those of the prevailing culture. A person's rate of acculturation is influenced by the length of residence in the new country, income, educational level, age, and language. People who belong to two cultures may feel marginal in both (i.e., not feel fully a part of either). Diane de Anda suggests that the following factors influence the degree of "bicultural" socialization and nature of exchanges with the dominant group:

• Degree of commonality between the cultures regarding norms, values, beliefs, and perceptions, including conceptual style and problem-solving approach.

EXHIBIT 2.5
Example: Case Management With the Frail Elderly

The case manager in this example works for a nonprofit senior citizens' center that is primarily funded by state and federal funds. She is assigned to the long-term care unit, and carries a caseload of approximately 100 clients. As part of the program evaluation, she was asked to keep a diary of what happened during a typical day. The following are excerpts from her diary:

Wednesday, 7:30 A.M. Arrived early to catch up on previous day's paperwork. Organized documents from eight cases from past two days, including two new care plans and five medical reports.

8:00–8:10 A.M. Mrs. Garcia, a seventy-nine-year-old woman, called. She was distraught over a letter received from the Social Security office, thinking it meant her benefits would be cut off. Explained that it was a form letter, indicating a routine change, not affecting the amount of her check. Knowing that she is often forgetful and has a hearing problem, made a note to make home visit tomorrow to be certain she understands what was said.

8:10–8:30 A.M. Met with Jim from In-Home Support Services. Mr. Thomas, a ninety-three-year-old man, had fallen last night and was in Mercy Hospital. Homemaker had found him when she arrived at 7:00 this morning. He is not expected to live. Homemaker is very upset. Called his daughter and will plan to meet her at hospital later this morning.

8:30–9:30 A.M. Staff meeting regarding ten clients discharged from City Hospital with inadequate discharge plans. Discussed how to work better with discharge planners from hospitals since this situation continues to be a problem. As I left meeting, another case manager told me that my client, Mrs. Hannibal, had refused to let the home health nurse into her apartment.

9:30–9:45 A.M. Called Mrs. Hannibal, but no one answered the phone. Called the emergency assistance program to meet me at her apartment.

9:45–10:00 A.M. Drove to Mrs. Hannibal's apartment. No one answered, so got manager to let me in. Mrs. Hannibal was very paranoid, had been drinking, threw bottle at me and screamed that "no one is going to get me out of here. I'll never go to a home. I'll die first." Worked with emergency assistance staff to get Mrs. Hannibal calmed down. She is a sixty-seven-year-old widow. She goes in and out of the hospital every two months. Has a severe drinking problem.

10:00–11:00 A.M. Arrived at Mercy Hospital. Met Mr. Thomas's daughter. She was in tears, saying it was all her fault, that if he had been living with her this would have never happened. Talked with her regarding fact that her father had wanted to live alone, that this had been his choice. Contacted hospital social worker to work with daughter.

11:15–12:00 A.M. Back to office. Wrote up visits to Mrs. Hannibal and Mr. Thomas. Called two new referrals and set up appointments to do assessments tomorrow. Received call from Mrs. Roman, age eighty-three. She is very lonely and wondered when I would be seeing her. Her husband died last week and she is crying. Has no family. Assured her I would be by to see her on Friday.

Source: F. E. Netting, P. M. Kettner, & S. L. McMurty (1993), *Social work macro practice* (pp. 10–12). New York: Longman.

EXHIBIT 2.6
Continuum of Long-Term Care Services by Category

In-Home Services

Outreach	Homemaker and chore services
Information and referral	Household repair services
Comprehensive geriatric assessment	Personal care
	Home-delivered meals
Emergency response system	Home health
	In-home high-technology therapy
Companionship/friendly visiting	Hospice
Telephone reassurance	
Caregiver respite services	

Community-Based Services

Case management	Adult care homes
Transportation	Shared housing
Senior centers	Congregate housing
Senior discount programs	Wellness and health promotion clinics
Recreational activities	
Caregiver support groups	Geriatric assessment clinics
Self-help groups	Physician services
Counseling	Adult day care
Foster homes	Mental health clinics
	Outpatient clinics

Institutional Services

Alcohol and drug treatment	Swing beds
Rehabilitation	Skilled nursing care
Psychiatric care	Extended care

Source: F. E. Netting, P. M. Kettner, & S. L. McMurty (1993), Social work macro practice (Table 5.4, p. 100). New York: Longman.

- Availability of cultural translators, mediators, and models.

- Amount and type (e.g., positive or negative) of feedback provided by each culture in relation to efforts to encourage normative behaviors.

- Degree of bilingualism.

- Degree of dissimilarity in physical appearance from the majority culture (e.g., skin color, facial features) (1984, p. 102).

Common Classifications

An important part of any culture is the classifications common to it. In the United States, we currently live in a culture that emphasizes differences in race, ethnicity, and class. Other common classifications are based on gender, sexual orientation, age, and physical ability. The classifications we use frame our thinking.

For instance, ethnicity is a common classification (see Appendix 2A). The term *American Indian* or *Native American* refers to the North American native peoples. Values common to many Native Americans include sharing, cooperation, harmony with nature, and noninterference with others. American Indians often view themselves as an extension of the tribe, in which older people are respected and valued. The importance of the extended family thus should suggest to social workers the value of meeting with Native American clients in their homes so that significant others can participate. Storytelling is often used to encourage change. Direct confrontation is considered rude and inappropriate. Respect is shown by the avoidance of direct eye contact. And firm handshakes are out of place with Native American clients.

The term *Asian American* covers many groups, including Chinese, Filipinos, Japanese, Koreans, Asian Indians, Vietnamese, Cambodian, Laotian, Khmer, and Hmong (Ho, 1987). Differences among individuals in these groups are related to different acculturation patterns, different geographical regions, and different socioeconomic status, family experiences, and reason for immigration. Characteristics shared by many Asian Americans include deference to authority, emotional restraint, clear roles and hierarchical family structure and an orientation to the family and extended family (Tsui & Schultz, 1985). Chinese Americans are the fastest-growing group of Asian Americans in the United States, and many of their values have Confucian, Taoist, and Buddhist roots. Very generally, Buddhists believe that we can transcend suffering by avoiding desire or attachment to this world. They believe that living a virtuous life will eliminate desire and that this consists of following the Eightfold Path: "right views, right thought, right speech, right conduct, right livelihood, right effort, right mindfulness, and right meditation" (Lynch & Hanson, 1992, p. 188). Confucian ideals include loyalty, selfless friendship, filial piety, and a duty to country and family. Certain obligations, responsibilities, and privileges are believed to accompany each family role (father, mother, son, daughter).

Compared with European Americans, Asians have a more holistic view of health that includes social, physical, psychological, and cultural factors. Inner conflicts are often expressed in the form of physical complaints. A focus on psychological factors may be embarrassing. Focused, structured, short-term intervention is preferred over more nondirective counseling. Helpers are expected to be active and to offer solutions. Japanese culture values implicit over explicit nonverbal communication. Here too, respect for elders is emphasized, and self disclosure to strangers will seem foreign and inappropriate. Those in subordinate positions are expected to show submissive behaviors such as remaining silent, not asking questions.

As with other groups, African Americans and their families vary widely in their histories, values, and socioeconomic status. Most African Americans are descendants of West Africans who were brought to this country as slaves. Many people believe that it is because of their long history of slavery, followed by continued discrimination, that African Americans are overrepresented in the prison population, unemployment rate, and juvenile delinquency rate. Concerns about racism can be detected in many blacks' distrust of white social workers and sensitivity to signs of racism and disregard. African Americans raised in the inner city may speak black English, which uses more nonverbal cues, shorter sentences, and less elaboration than white English does. Such differences may lead to misinterpretations or negative stereotypes.

The term *Latino* is preferred by many persons from Mexico, Puerto Rico, Cuba, and Central American and Latin American countries who live in the United States. Here too, the various groups have different norms, values, and communication styles. In general, cooperation is preferred to competition. Traditional Latino families are patriarchal, thus having the father as the primary authority figure. Here, too, different generations confront different problems in language, strain between cultures, and intergenerational conflicts.

Class differences refer to differences in economic opportunities, resources, and occupations or positions. Styles of interaction among working-class people vary in certain ways compared with styles of interaction among middle-class people. Research suggests that lower-class clients are offered inferior forms of service and receive diagnoses of psychopathology more often than do clients of higher economic status (review in Davis & Proctor, 1989).

The role of economic advantage is highlighted in a report on developmental differences among children in three kinds of families: welfare families, working-class families, and professional families (Hart & Risley, 1995). The investigators studied language development in the children in these three groups during their first three years in relation to the learning experiences provided by their parents. The average "number of words children heard per hour was 2,150 in the professional families, 1,250 in the working-class families, and 620 in the welfare families" (p. 132). Only relative economic advantage related to the differences, not race or ethnicity, gender, firstborn, secondborn, and so on.

Gender refers to biological difference, and sexual identity pertains to learned patterns of behavior that result from social and cultural expectations. Women's and men's socialization experiences differ as a result of cultural practices and beliefs, though not necessarily in the ways frequently assumed (see Exhibit 2.7). Differences in gender-based experiences can be seen at a very early age, as demonstrated in studies of the different ways that parents respond to boy and girl infants and that elementary school teachers respond to boys and girls. Carol Tavris (1992) argues that women have to be bicultural, to have two styles of talking. That is, when women are with other women, they are assertive, but when they are with men, women use a passive style of talking, which includes more "tag statements" (e.g., "Do you think so?") and hesitations.

Clients also differ in their sexual orientation. Despite research showing that persons who are gay or lesbian can be just as effective parents and can fulfill other social roles just as well as heterosexuals can, both professionals and laypeople often

EXHIBIT 2.7
Do Men and Women Differ?

Where the differences aren't	Where the differences are
Attachment, connection	Care-taking
Cognitive abilities	Communication
Verbal, mathematical,[a]	Interaction styles
reasoning, rote	Uses of talk
memory, vocabulary,	Power differences
reading,[b] etc.	Emotions
Dependency	Contexts that produce them
Emotions	Forms of expression
Likelihood of feeling	"Feminization of love"
them	"Feminization of distress"
Empathy	Employment, work opportunities
Moods and "moodiness"	Health and medicine
Moral reasoning	Medication and treatment
Need for achievement	Longevity differences
Need for love and	Income
attachment	Life-span development
Need for power	Effects of children
Nurturance[c]	Work and family sequence
Pacifism, belligerence	Life narratives
(e.g., depersonalizing	Power and status at work, in
enemies)	relationships, in society
Sexual capacity, desire,	Reproductive experiences
interest	Reproductive technology and its
Verbal aggressiveness,	social/legal consequences
hostility	"Second shift": housework, child
	care, family obligations
	Sexual experiences and concerns
	Violence, public and intimate
	Weight and body image

Source: C. Tavris (1992). The mismeasure of women *(p. 196).* New York: Simon & Schuster.
[a]Males excel at highest levels of math performance; in general population, females have slight advantage.
[b]Males are more susceptible to some verbal problems. However, many alleged sex differences seem to be an artifact of referral bias: More boys are *reported* for help than girls, but there are no sex differences in the *actual* prevalence of dyslexia and other reading disabilities.
[c]As a capacity; in practice, women do more of the actual care and feeding of children, parents, relatives, friends.

pathologize and stigmatize them. Gay and lesbian young people confront unique risks, as shown by the fact that they account for 30% of all adolescent suicides. Differences in sexual orientation usually are not visible, thereby creating special problems (e.g., the ability to "pass" and the tendency to hide one's sexual orientation because of potential negative reactions). Violence and attempts to pass laws mandating discrimination against gay/lesbian individuals highlight the strains that confront gay/lesbian people. Lesbian and gay people may be put

into situations where they have to defend their sexuality when their goal is to deal with a relationship problem, "come out" on the job or with family and friends, or handle some situation unrelated to their sexuality. Questions such as the following may help heterosexual people understand how this feels:

- What do you think caused your heterosexuality?
- When and how did you first decide you were heterosexual?
- Is it possible your heterosexuality is just a phase you will grow out of?
- Is it possible your heterosexuality stems from a neurotic fear of people of the same sex? Maybe you just need a positive gay experience?
- Heterosexuals have histories of failures in gay relationships. Do you think you may have turned to heterosexuality because of a fear of rejection?
- To whom have you disclosed your heterosexual tendencies? How did they react?
- Why must you heterosexuals be so blatant, making a public spectacle of your heterosexuality? Can't you just be what you are and keep it quiet?

People who live at a certain time (different cohorts) have different experiences that create unique ways of viewing the world. Some older people are discriminated against because of their age, as are recent refugees because of their immigrant status. There also are regional differences; that is, growing up in New York City is quite different from growing up on a farm in Nebraska. People hold different religious beliefs. Physical disabilities may create unique challenges and needs, such as wheelchair access to transportation. Harlan Lane (1992) argues that deaf people have a distinct culture (e.g., sign language). Although some differences are readily observable, others are not. For example, physical illness may or may not be accompanied by observable indicators.

THINKING CRITICALLY ABOUT MULTICULTURALISM

Thinking critically about beliefs requires raising questions about views, including "politically correct" ones. It calls for distinguishing between what is simply asserted as true and what is suggested as accurate based on a critical evaluation of claims and concepts. Here too, in the area of multiculturalism, we can find helpers imposing their values on clients, relying on pseudoscience, making false claims, or using empty words (e.g., Ortiz de Montellano, 1992). Here too, we should examine the soundness of classifications and theories. Common assumptions that require examination include the following:

- Gender, class, race, and ethnicity are reasonable categories (e.g., there is greater variation among people in different categories than within each group).
- Better services are provided by helpers who match clients (e.g., in race, ethnicity, gender, or sexual orientation).
- Multicultural knowledge enhances services.
- In order to offer services to different groups, different knowledge is required.
- Emphasizing cultural differences does more good than harm.
- The less frequent use of mental health services by minority clients deprives them of valuable and needed services.
- All clients want to increase their "critical consciousness" of how their personal problems are affected by economic, political, and social factors.

One myth is that cultural clashes are new, but this is not so. Karl Popper (1992) suggests that cultural clashes resulted in the discovery by the Greeks of critical discussion as a way to gain knowledge. Social workers have always confronted cultural clashes. Another myth is that only certain people or groups have a culture. Everyone has a culture.

OVERCOMING BARRIERS

Barriers to cross-cultural helping and suggested ways to address them are discussed in the section that follows (also see Exhibit 2.8).

1. Become informed about and take actions to reduce discrimination and oppression. A familiarity with research documenting the prevalence of discrimination will help you appreciate the unequal hands that some people are dealt. Without understanding the effects of oppression and discrimination on creating and maintaining problems, you may make incorrect assumptions about their causes. Discriminatory policies and procedures (institutional discrimination) are often the most difficult to identify because they are the "taken-for-granted" background in which we carry out our everyday activities. Work together when concerning others to reduce discriminatory practices and policies that restrict opportunities for certain groups. You may help your clients become more aware of the political, social, and economic factors contributing to their problems. That is, you may raise their critical consciousness (Freire, 1973). You may help clients to realize that "change in our individual situation is often critically dependent on wider structural alterations fought for collectively" (Brookfield, 1995).

2. Reinforce positive alternatives to prejudicial statements and actions. When confronted with discriminatory practices and prejudiced behavior, you have choices about how and whether to respond. Your actions will be influenced by your goals. Possible goals may be to

- Put the offender in his place.
- Straighten him out.
- Let him know that you are not going to put up with _____.
- Reeducate him.
- Work together with others to reduce prejudice and discrimination.

Your goals may differ depending on the situation. You may lose an opportunity to win over and reeducate an offender in your rush to bring prejudiced remarks to his attention. Consider S. Andhil Fineberg's (1949) example of a woman who attended a dinner party at which another woman made a racist remark. On their way home, her partner asked why she did not "call her" on her remark.

EXHIBIT 2.8
Barriers and Remedies Related to Cross-Cultural Helping

Barrier	Remedy
1. Discriminatory and oppressive policies and practices.	1. Take appropriate steps with concerned others to identify and alter related practices and policies. This should be preceded by a contextual assessment to discover leverage points for change.
2. A focus on punishing prejudicial statements and actions rather than reinforcing positive ones.	2. Reinforce positive alternatives to prejudice; reeducate, win over.
3. Biases, prejudices, and stereotypes.	3. Identify and alter them.
4. Lack of knowledge about a group's history, norms, expectations, and values and individual differences within it.	4. Become informed.
5. Lack of communication skills required to negotiate differences.	5. Acquire needed skills (e.g., active listening, empathy).
6. Lack of facility in client's language.	6. Learn the language; use translators; hire bilingual staff.
7. Fear of differences.	7. Value differences as opportunities to forward understanding.
8. Uncritical acceptance of common classifications (e.g., Asian, white, black).	8. Critically evaluate common classifications and their consequences.
9. Organizational barriers (e.g., service patterns based on beliefs, values, and norms that conflict with clients').	9. Involve other concerned professionals in identifying and changing dysfunctional procedures and policies.
10. Confounding personal and political goals and the pursuit of knowledge.	10. Don't confuse personal and political agendas and the pursuit of knowledge. Be honest about personal and political agendas. Evaluate the evidence for claims.
11. Not recognizing our shared humanness (e.g., of problems, potentials. Relying on stereotyped categories (e.g., race, ethnicity).	11. Recognize shared humannness and experiences.
12. A belief that empathy is enough to help others.	12. Combine empathy with related actions.

The woman replied that she did not think that the woman was really prejudiced and that she had bigger plans for her—to reeducate her and to get her actively involved in an antiracist organization—which she was able to do. We may accomplish more by reinforcing alternative positive behaviors than by punishing undesired behaviors.

3. Identify and neutralize biases, prejudices, and stereotypes. A bias is an emotional leaning to one side in regard to a person, group, or issue: a prejudice is a negative, preconceived judgment that is not supported by fact and that results in unequal treatment (see Appendix 2A). What are your biases and stereotypes regarding different groups or problems? How do they affect your practice decisions? We often seek data consistent with our biases and prejudices and ignore contradictory evidence. Critically examining assumptions is a key characteristic of reflective helpers. Prejudice is more likely when

- Two groups are competing with each other.
- A contact is unpleasant, involuntary, and tense.
- A group's prestige or status decreases as a result of contact.
- The members of a group or the whole group feel mistreated and frustrated.
- One group's moral or ethnic standards are objectionable to another group.
- The members of a group are of lower status or are lower in any relevant characteristics compared with those of the majority group. (see Amir, 1969, p. 338)

Prejudice does not always result in discrimination. Prejudices are often based on stereotypes. A *stereotype* refers to responding to a person as if he or she were a member of a group and, in so doing, overlooking differences between the individual and the group. Stereotypes often are caricatures of supposed group traits. For example, if you believe that all Mexican American husbands expect to make all important decisions, you may incorrectly assume this about a Mexican American couple who prefer to make decisions together.

Familiarity with a group does not always increase understanding and liking. Gender discrimination is prevalent in all socioeconomic classes. Violence toward gays and lesbians has increased (Comstock, 1991). Efforts to legislate discrimination against gay and lesbian people attest to the pervasiveness of homophobia in our society. Beliefs related to racism include the following:

- The belief that there are well-defined and distinctive ethnic groups and races.
- The belief that racial mixing lowers biological quality.
- The belief that some races are superior to others.
- The belief that some groups are naturally prone to criminality, sexual looseness, or dishonest business practices.
- The belief that the "superior" races should rule and dominate the "inferior" races.
- The belief that there are temperamental differences among races.

Familiarity with research documenting the prevalence of biases, prejudices, and stereotypes and their effects will help you to appreciate their pervasiveness and the seriousness of their consequences. Biases and stereotypes are not figments of an overly active imagination (as some might have us believe). Racist attitudes and actions are rife. An attitude can be defined as holding certain beliefs about certain individuals and being predisposed to act toward them in certain ways. Attitudes and behaviors may not be closely related. Literature describing efforts to alter attitudes toward certain groups (e.g., people with disabilities, gay/lesbian people, people of certain ethnic groups) suggests that altering attitudes may be slow going perhaps because programs address only one of multiple interlinked contingency systems that influence attitudes (e.g., the individual level) leaving in place contingencies at other lev-

els (e.g., cultural practices) that maintain certain attitudes.

4. Learn about and be attentive to cultural differences. Individually tailor your services to each client's unique circumstances, expectations, values, and customs to the extent to which this adds to rather than detracts from helping clients and avoiding harm. This may require understanding the meaning in different cultures of certain nonverbal behaviors. Consider, for example, the meaning of the following nonverbal behaviors to people with Filipino roots:

- Beckoning someone with an index finger is a sign of contempt. Instead, indicate "come here" by waving the fingers of one hand closed together with the palm down, facing inward.
- Raising the eyebrows means "No."
- Men or boys (as well as women or girls) may hold hands in public; this gesture has no sexual implications. However, physical contact with members of the opposite sex is to be avoided in public.
- Never shows anger in public. People are expected to control their emotions and must avoid direct confrontation.
- Filipinos often smile when upset or embarrassed.
- Filipinos may laugh at a crucial point in a meeting as an indication that they are giving their most important message. (see Lynch & Hanson, 1992, p. 296)

Information about refugees' experiences when leaving their country of origin and their difficulties in adjusting to a new culture may be important to obtain. Challenges refugees and immigrants confront in their new homeland include an unfamiliar language, new customs and values, a lack of work opportunities, and scarce low-cost housing (Berry, 1991).

You might assume that a client who is reluctant to make decisions without consulting family members is excessively dependent, when in fact her wish reflects the norms and values of her culture. Cultures also have different norms regarding expressiveness. Whereas helpers may expect their clients to discuss openly their feelings and problems, the clients may be reluctant to share their personal feelings and experiences with strangers. Overlooking cultural differences may result in inaccurately viewing clients as inhibited and/or repressed. Assertion training that emphasizes the open expression of feelings is not appropriate for all clients.

You may be able to win your client's trust by candidly discussing the differences between the two of you. Think of a scale ranging from 0 (no cultural differences) to 10 (great differences) in relation to the degree of match between any two people. The higher up the scale one goes, the more important the relevant cultural knowledge, open-mindedness, and skills in negotiating differences will be. (Seek useful training opportunities, and consult other sources for further details about multicultural counseling and the history, language, and culture of different groups, such as Green, 1992; Healy, 1995; Lum, 1992; Lynch & Hanson, 1994; Ponterotto, Casas, Suzuki, & Alexander, 1995; Sue & Sue, 1990; Harrison, Wodarski, & Thyer, 1992.)

5. Acquire and use skills in negotiating differences. Knowledge of cultural differences will be of little value if this is not accompanied by skills and values that encourage its use. Use the communication skills described in Chapter 12 (e.g., active listening and empathy) to put your knowledge about differences to good use. Respect for each client's individuality will help you avoid imposing your values on clients. Sue and Sue (1990) suggest that "qualities such as respect and acceptance of the individual, positive regard, understanding the problem from the individual's perspective, allowing the client to explore his or her own values, and arriving at an individual solution are core qualities that may transcend cultures" (Sue & Sue, 1990, p. 187). I would go further and say that these aspects of service *should* transcend culture. Become aware of your own communication styles and how they influence others, and alter those that get in the way.

6. Acquire or arrange for needed language skills. If you work with clients who do not speak your language, learn their language, use translators, or encourage your agency to hire bilingual staff members. It's hard enough to communicate when we do speak each other's language (see Exhibit 2.9). Seek clarification when you are unsure what a client means. Misunderstandings may lead to incomplete or incorrect views of problems and result in selecting ineffective or harmful service options.

7. Value culture clashes. We tend to like people who are similar to ourselves and to fear differences. The greater the differences are, the greater our fears may be. Cultural differences are often regarded as negative, as hampering communication and resulting in stress and misunderstanding. But such differences may be not only valuable but also essential to resolve shared problems and to advance knowledge (Popper, 1994).

> Culture is the widening of the mind and of the spirit.
>
> Jawaharal Nehru

8. Critically evaluate common classifications and their effects. Classifications are based on certain presumed characteristics. For example, someone may think of herself as black, white, a lesbian, or a senior citizen. Think carefully about common classifications (e.g., race, ethnicity). Are they sound? Do they do more good than harm? How do you know? Although many people in a group may share a certain history, they may do so in different ways and with different outcomes. It is easy to assume that the categories used to classify people are inevitable and correct when in fact they may be neither.

Perhaps we all would benefit from classifying people in relation to the quality of their altruistic contributions (their citizenship) or their environmental caring (contribution to rather than denigration of the environment). Yheudi Webster argues that categories such as race and gender are social classifications used to limit opportunities for certain kinds of people (those who are poor, dark skinned, and female). He believes that categories such as gender, class, race, and ethnicity perpetu-

EXHIBIT 2.9
Example of the Importance of Language Differences

A Latina mother from Central America gave birth to a female child with a stomach disorder that the teaching hospital was having difficulty diagnosing. The child could not eat normally and had to be tube fed. The mother's first two children, ages 4 and 2, had been born healthy. The child remained in the hospital for over 2 months; assessment indicated that the child would have long-term medical difficulties.

It was expected that the mother would visit frequently so that she could learn the complicated feeding procedures, since the child's discharge from the hospital was imminent. The mother would agree to visitation schedules so one of the staff could instruct her. However, she would typically miss two visits out of three. The staff felt she was not bonding with the child since visitation had always been infrequent.

A social worker was asked to take on the case and to attend a staffing with the multidisciplinary team and the mother. Staff members spoke in English about the mother, noting that they felt there were potential child abuse issues present in view of her lack of participation. They described the mother as uncaring and unnurturing.

Review by the bilingual/bicultural social worker uncovered the following: (1) the mother, although she had lived in the United States for 5 years, had few friends and no relatives in the area, was a single parent, and had no one who could provide child care for her two other children, as well as no money to pay for child care; and (2) she lived more than an hour's distance from the hospital, in a rural area where bus transportation was infrequent and meant several bus transfers. The mother related to the social worker that lack of child care and money kept her from visiting her daughter. It was painful for her not to be able to see her daughter more often. Also, when she did come, the nurses acted very cold with her and she felt unwanted, and disrespected by staff. Moreover, instructions were often in Spanish that was hard for her to follow; she had made mistakes in trying to learn the complicated feeding instructions, resulting in her feeling incompetent as a mother.

The interventionist explained these considerations to the staff. The staff asked why the mother had not told them of her problems. The mother answered in Spanish that no one had ever asked her. Intervention by the social worker included educating the staff about this mother's embarrassment about her poverty, and her lack of education and communication skills, as well as her reticence in interacting with professionals. Child care and transportation were obtained and further monitoring noted no child abuse present.

Source: M. E. Zuniga (1992). Families with Latino roots. In E. W. Lynch & M. J. Hanson (Eds.), Developing cross-cultural competence (p. 170). Baltimore: Paul H. Brookes.

ate discrimination and oppression by encouraging classifications that do not accurately define the group's variablity and that the very notions of "black" and "white" people as classifications are self-defeating and dangerous political myths. He emphasizes *racialization* (rather than race) referring to race as a distinguishing characteristic be-

cause of political and social interests (see the discussion of racial, ethnic, and class theories of social problems in Chapter 7).

Some writers suggest that a focus on cultural groups allows us to avoid the responsibility and effort required to make our own reasoned moral judgments (Finkielkraut, 1995). That is, we may fall back on a general classification, such as sexual orientation, as a reason for our beliefs or actions, rather than thinking things through for ourselves. We may say, "I'm Asian. That's what we believe." In this way, we may become "subservient" to a "culture" that may not really exist because it contains so many distinct subcultures. Use your critical thinking skills to examine the inferences on which common classifications are based and the effects of such classifications. Classifications have consequences. Uncritical acceptance of common ones may result in thinking less of a person because he or she is in a certain category or setting ourselves apart as better. In either case we set ourselves apart from others which may obscure our shared humanness.

9. Remove organizational barriers. Western-style mental health and psychotherapy may be foreign to some of your clients. Many clients prefer more structured approaches that address economic, educational, vocational, and material needs. Examine both your agency and interagency relationships, and identify changes that could be made to enhance services, such as hiring bilingual staff (e.g., Rogler, Malgady, Giuseppe, & Blumenthal, 1987). Work with colleagues who share your concerns, and select one or two changes to pursue systematically. You should be aware of the formal and informal communication channels in your agency and among agencies, as well as the internal and external influences on agency policies and practices.

10. Don't confound personal and political agendas and the search for truth. We all have political and personal agendas—interests we would like to advance—and it is easy to confuse them with the pursuit of truth. Community organizers may claim, "We need money for more recreation centers. We know that this will decrease crime," even though they may have no evidence that such centers will decrease crime. Instead, they should say: "We will test whether they do affect crime." Confounding political agendas and evidentiary concerns obscures what is known and what is not, making it more difficult to think critically about issues. It would be better if people were honest about what has been critically tested and what has not. Advantages include highlighting the need to test claims and discovering the actual effects of programs.

11. Attend to our shared humanness. Emphasizing cultural differences prevents us from recognizing shared problems and experiences and may decrease our empathy for others. It may preclude our forming the broad-based coalitions we need in order to make changes valued by many people, regardless of their race, gender, ethnicity, sexual orientation, age, or physical ability. Yheudi Webster believes that classifications such as race, class, and ethnicity should be abandoned because they perpetuate the consciousness of difference that underlies "dehumanization" (p. 264) and that social problems should be classified as human problems (see Chapter 7). It is human beings who are discriminated against and oppressed. In this human-centered theory, human beings are viewed as the victims of deficient government and corporate policies.

12. Don't be satisfied with empathy. In his passionate book *The Night Is Dark and I Am Far from Home* (1990), Jonathan Kozol suggests that we often confuse an empathy for others' plights with doing something to help them. That is, we use caring as an indication that we are doing something to relieve misery and injustice when, in fact, we are doing nothing.

SUMMARY

Only some people with certain kinds of problem seek aid from social service agencies. Those who do typically pursue other options first, such as talking to friends and relatives. It may be difficult to find out where to go for different kinds of aid, and it is the agency's responsibility to make its services known and to integrate them with those of other agencies. The expectations and goals of both clients and social workers, eligibility requirements, time limits, and preferred practice frameworks influence the services clients receive. Cultural differences influence whose help is sought, what are viewed as problems, what causes are favored to account for them, and what methods and outcomes are preferred. Western-style service approaches are not appropriate for all clients.

Barriers to helping include the service providers' prejudices and stereotypes and a lack of knowledge about or respect for cultural differences. An uncritical acceptance of questionable classifications such as race may get in the way of recognizing common human needs and individual differences related to problems and resolutions. Lack of communication skills needed to negotiate differences and lack of language facility may present obstacles. Barriers suggest ways to overcome them (e.g., to learn about differences that help you work effectively with clients, to become aware of your biases and stereotypes and change dysfunctional service delivery systems).

EXPLORING YOUR EXPECTATIONS, VALUES, AND BELIEFS

1. Imagine that you need money and are on your way to the local welfare office to ask for aid. Describe your thoughts and feelings. Complete the following items:
   a. People who ask for financial help are _____.
   b. Giving financial aid to people is _____.
2. Whom do you seek help from when you have a problem? Give two examples, and explain why you would consult this person.
3. Did you ever seek help for a problem? If not, what are your reasons?
4. Do you have any biases that might affect how you would react to Julie? (see the case example in this chapter). Complete the following:
   • Abortion is _____.
   • People who have abortions are _____.
   • If I had an unplanned pregnancy, I would _____.
5. Would you have any biases about Mrs. Ryan if the Greens consulted you? (see the description in this chapter). Complete the following statements:
   a. People over 75 are usually _____.
   b. If an elderly relative wanted to live with me, I would _____.
   c. If I were over 75, I would _____.
6. Describe one of your "differences" that you are willing to discuss and how it has affected your life.
7. Select a problem that some people confront and examine the correspondence between what you feel and think (empathy) and what actions you would take to resolve this problem.

REVIEWING YOUR COMPETENCIES

Reviewing What You Know

1. Describe some of the reasons why people may not seek help either from service agencies or informal sources.

2. Distinguish among resisters, applicants, and clients.
3. Describe helpers' expectations and goals, and explain why they are important to consider.
4. Describe clients' expectations and goals and the factors that influence them.
5. Describe the characteristics of Western-style mental health agencies and how they may differ from what some clients may expect or value.
6. Give examples of "blaming the victim" that result from stereotypes and prejudice.
7. Give examples of content knowledge that may help you in working with different kinds of clients.
8. Explain what a culture is.
9. Discuss the problems with classifying people by race, class, or ethnicity.

Reviewing What You Do

1. A review of audiotaped or videotaped interviews shows that you are sensitive to differences among clients, applicants, and resisters. You
   a. Discuss the resisters' feelings and possible objections.
   b. Do not respond in kind to hostile or negative comments.
   c. Use a range of methods to "engage" people (see Chapter 11).
   d. Do not act as if you are working with a client when the person is an applicant or a resister.
2. You clarify expectations about what will occur.
3. Your language and the helping methods you select reflect your sensitivity to individual differences.
4. You are not judgmental.
5. You seek information about your clients' expectations and desired outcomes.
6. Given a case example, you can describe cultural differences that you should consider.
7. You can identify sources of discrimination and oppression that may be related to certain kinds of problems.
8. Given a case example, you can identify your biases and stereotypes.

Reviewing Results

1. Applicants and resisters become clients.
2. Clients achieve desired outcomes.

APPENDIX 2A   GLOSSARY

Acculturation: The integration of the values, behaviors, and traditions of a dominant culture with those of another.

Assimilation: The blending of the culture of one group with that of another. By adopting the customs, beliefs, and norms of the dominant culture, a group loses its unique identity.

Bias: Partiality shown in relation to an individual or group.

Bicultural: Being a part of two or more different cultures.

Class: Differences in economic opportunities, resources, and certain occupations or positions. Education, occupation, income, and relationship to the means of production determine social class.

Class theory of social relations: An appeal to economic differences to account for social problems.

Cultural pluralism: The existence of many cultures in a region. Certain groups maintain their own social structure, values, and patterns of behavior. This term is also used to reflect the values of harmonious relationships among groups and a lack of discrimination and dysfunctional competition for resources.

Culture: The values and beliefs and related social contingencies that guide a group's conduct, passed on from one generation to another. A culture includes language, values, religious beliefs and customs, art forms, and patterns of social relationships.

Discrimination: "Differential treatment of individuals on the basis of their social category by people or the institutional policies they create and enforce" (Jones, 1986, p. 289). Discriminatory actions deprive certain persons or groups of valued opportunities. The unfair treatment of one group over another.

Ethnic identity: A person's particular values, traditions, and behaviors that are assumed to be based on cultural differences related to ancestry, national origin, or religion.

Ethnicity: An identity and sense of belonging assumed to be based on cultural differences in values, attitudes, customs, and rituals related to a common ancestry, national origin, or religion. People who are part of a particular ethnic group often believe that they are different from other groups in important ways. An ethnic group is assumed to "differ from a racial group, which is defined with references to anatomical similarities" (Webster, 1992, p. 14).

Ethnic theory of social relations: Reliance on ethnic differences to account for social relations.

Ethnocentrism: Reliance on the cultural practices in one's ethnic group as a central reference point.

Genocide: The systematic killing of members of a particular group with the intention of eliminating the whole group.

Marginality: Being a part of different groups without fully being part of either. An example is a client with an invisible (not observable) illness.

Minority group: A group of persons with unequal access to power that is considered by the majority group to be in some way unworthy of sharing power equally and that is stigmatized in terms of assumed inferior traits or characteristics (Mindel & Habenstein, 1981, p. 7–8). This term is often applied to women and the aged, even though these groups do not represent a numerical minority.

Oppression: The discriminatory treatment of an individual or group based on (for example) gender, age, or sexual orientation.

Prejudice: "A faulty generalization from a group characteristic (stereotype) to an individual member of the group, irrespective of either (1) the accuracy of the group stereotype, or (2) the applicability of the group characterization to the individual in question" (Jones, 1986, p. 288).

Race: In a biological sense, an isolated inbreeding group with a unique genetic makeup. As a social construction, race is based on racialization.

Race relations: Racialized social relations.

Racialization: Racial categorization, the racialization of social relations.

Racism: Feelings of superiority to another group. Negative views of the cultural differences of different racial groups. Racism may be overt or covert, individual or institutional (e.g., the inequitable distribution of services to certain groups).

Racial theory of social relations: A combination of racial classification (reliance on anatomical, biological, or genetic criteria to form distinct populations) and racial causation (the imputation of a determining status to racial attributes in the explanation of behavior) (Webster, 1992). The victimization of nonwhites by whites and the uniqueness of each race's immigrant experiences is emphasized.

Segregation: Confinement of a group to particular areas (geographical/institutional).

CHAPTER 3

Values, Ethics, and Obligations

Overview

This chapter provides an overview of practice-related ethical concerns. The relationship between values and ethics is discussed and key social work values and related ethical principles are described. Increasing knowledge and skills that give clients real (rather than illusory) options to enhance the quality of their lives and involving them in decisions is emphasized. Issues related to competence, confidentiality, and informed consent are reviewed. The relationship between ethics and ideology is discussed and examples of clashing ideologies given. Thinking critically about practice decisions is suggested as a valuable guide. Additional discussion of ethical concerns related to assessment, deciding on service plans, and evaluating outcome is included in chapters dealing with these topics.

You Will Learn About

- Values and ethics.
- Critical thinking and discussion as a guide.
- Serving and avoiding harm as key principles.
- Self-determination, empowerment, and respect as key values.
- Informed consent.
- Ethical concerns and legal regulations regarding confidentiality.
- Ethical issues related to competence.
- Ethical issues related to selection of outcomes and service plans.
- Other ethical concerns.
- The importance of knowledge about legal regulations and resources.
- Liability (bases for lawsuits and how to avoid them).

- What clients can do about illegal or unethical behavior on the part of professionals.
- Ethics and ideology.
- Concerns about the fox guarding the chickens.
- Encouraging ethical behavior.

VALUES AND ETHICS

Values can be defined as the social principles, goals, or standards held by an individual, group, or society (see Exhibit 3.1). Values state preferences regarding certain goals and how to attain them. They are used to support decisions at many different levels (e.g., policy, agency practices, helper decisions). The preamble to the code of ethics of the National Association of Social Workers (NASW) states, "The mission of the social work profession is rooted in a set of core values. These core values, embraced by social workers throughout the profession's history, are the foundation of social work's unique purpose and perspective (1996). Core values emphasized are (1) service, (2) social justice, (3) dignity and worth of the person, (4) importance of human relationships, (5) integrity, and (6) competence. Ethical issues are moral-value issues suggesting that some ways of acting are bad, good, wrong, or right. Related differences of opinion are at the heart of different points of view about the "best way to live," the most moral way to behave toward others, and how to structure society. A society's values are reflected in its ethical principles and related actions. Some of these values stress ensuring fairness for the least advantaged individuals in the society. Utilitarian values emphasize pursuing the greatest good for the greatest number of people.

Ethical Dilemmas

Ethical dilemmas are those in which two or more principles or values conflict or when it is difficult or impossible to be faithful to an ethical principle. For example, should people who have repeatedly assaulted others and caused serious injury and/or loss of life be paroled, even though there is a high probability that they will continue such actions?

Here, self-determination and protecting others from harm are in conflict. The factors to consider include

1. The client's interests.
2. The interests and rights of other involved parties such as family members or victims.
3. The professional code of ethics.
4. The social worker's personal values.
5. The agency's policy.
6. Legal regulations.

No wonder reaching decisions agreeable to all interested parties is difficult (or impossible)! "Practitioners are asked to solve problems every day that philosophers have argued about for the last two thousand years and will probably debate for the next two thousand. Inevitably, arbitrary lines have to be drawn and hard cases decided" (Dingwall, Eekelaar, & Murray, 1983, p. 244). The prescribed action may be legally mandated.

Legal issues concern legislated rights or obligations, which may or may not be possible to act on. For example, parents may have a legal right to educate their children at home but not be able to do so because of insufficient funds. Some rights are both moral and legal, such as the right to free speech. They conform to a standard of behavior and also are legally mandated.

CRITICAL THINKING AND DISCUSSION AS A GUIDE

Ethical choices involve assigning values to different options after reviewing the likely results of each. Those people who favor critical thinking stress its importance in arriving at ethical decisions (e.g., Baron, 1985; Brookfield, 1987; Popper, 1992;

EXHIBIT 3.1
Ethical Principles of the NASW Code of Ethics

VALUE I: *SERVICE*

Ethical Principle: *Social workers' primary goal is to help people in need and to address social problems.*
Social workers elevate service to others above self-interest. Social workers draw on their knowledge, values, and skills to help people in need and to address social problems. Social workers are encouraged to volunteer some portion of their professional skills with no expectation of significant financial return (pro bono service).

VALUE II: *SOCIAL JUSTICE*

Ethical Principle: *Social workers challenge social injustice.*
Social workers pursue social change, particularly with and on behalf of vulnerable and oppressed individuals and groups of people. Social workers' social change efforts are focused primarily on issues of poverty, discrimination, and other forms of social injustice. These activities seek to promote sensitivity to and knowledge about oppression, and cultural ethnic diversity. Social workers strive to ensure equality of opportunity, access to needed information, services, and resources, and meaningful participation in decision making for all people.

VALUE III: *DIGNITY AND WORTH OF THE PERSON*

Ethical Principle: *Social workers respect the inherent dignity and worth of the person.*
Social workers treat each person in a caring and respectful fashion, mindful of individual differences and cultural and ethnic diversity. Social workers promote clients' socially responsible self-determination. Social workers seek to enhance clients' capacity, and opportunity to change and to address their own needs. Social workers are cognizant of their dual responsibility to clients and to the broader society. They seek to resolve conflicts between clients' interest and the broader society's interests in a socially responsible manner consistent with the values, ethical principles, and ethical standards of the profession.

VALUE IV: *IMPORTANCE OF HUMAN RELATIONSHIPS*

Ethical Principle: *Social workers recognize the central importance of human relationships.*
Social workers understand that relationships between and among people are an important vehicle for change. Social workers engage people as partners in the helping process. Social workers seek to strengthen relationships among people in a purposeful effort to promote, restore, maintain, and enhance the well-being of individuals, families, social groups, organizations, and communities.

VALUE V: *INTEGRITY*

Ethical Principle: *Social workers behave in a trustworthy manner.*
Social workers are continually aware of the profession's mission, values, ethical principles, and ethical standards, and practice in a manner consistent with them. Social workers act honestly and responsibly and promote ethical practices on the part of the organizations with which they are affiliated.

EXHIBIT 3.1 (*continued*)

VALUE VI: *COMPETENCE*

Ethical Principle: *Social workers practice within their areas of competence and develop and enhance their professional expertise.*
Social workers continually strive to increase their professional knowledge and skills and to apply them in practice. Social workers should aspire to contribute to the knowledge base of the profession.

Source: National Association of Social Workers (1996), Code of ethics (pp. 5–6). Silver Spring, MD: NASW.

1994). Valuing critical inquiry will encourage you to prefer truth to ignorance and prejudice, to ferret out your biases, and to think carefully about your responsibilities and the degree of match between what you say you value and what you actually do. As with all decisions, they may have unintended and unwanted consequences. Critical discussion of different options may help to catch and avoid some of these. Critical discussion (e.g., seeking clarity, questioning assumptions, and considering different perspectives) will help you to identify involved participants at different levels and their interests (e.g., clients, significant others, the agency, community) and the possible consequences of different options. Ask yourself the following questions:

- What exactly is the issue (e.g., what resources are involved? Freedom? Money)?

- Who is involved and in what ways?

- What are alternate options?

- What are the likely consequences of each for those who may be affected?

- What may be the unintended consequences of each option?

- What grounds would best serve as a guide (e.g., equity in resource distribution, reduction of misery)?

- What changes could be made at what levels (individual, family, community, agency, service system) to honor ethical principles?

You may encourage your clients to consider both the future and the immediate consequences of dif-

EXHIBIT 3.2
Thinking Critically About an Ethical Dilemma

Select an ethical dilemma related to social work practice that you have encountered or know about.

1. Describe the dilemma.
2. Note how the following are involved and may conflict:
   Client's interests (this may be a community or group).
   Interests of involved others.
   Agency policies/interests (e.g., obligation to colleagues).
   Legal regulations (as relevant).
   Professional code of ethics (note values that conflict).
3. Describe possible courses of action (or inaction), including their feasibility and the likely consequences of each to involved parties.
4. Select the option you think is best.
5. Explain your reasons for selecting this option. Place your argument in diagram form (see Chapter 6). Is this a well-reasoned argument?
6. Indicate how much you relied on each of the following in reaching your decision.

	Not at All	A Little	Somewhat	A Great Deal
Critical reflection	___	___	___	___
Discussions with other staff	___	___	___	___
Professional literature	___	___	___	___
Discussions with my supervisor	___	___	___	___
Discussions with an administrator	___	___	___	___
Discussions with agency's legal consultant	___	___	___	___
Professional code of ethics	___	___	___	___
My own moral standard	___	___	___	___
Discussions with friends	___	___	___	___

ferent courses of action. For example, programs designed to enhance adolescents' decision-making skills encourage them to consider both the future and the immediate consequences of risk behaviors (e.g., smoking, unprotected sexual intercourse) (Baron, & Brown, 1991). Honoring the code of inquiry in Chapter 6 Appendix C will increase the likelihood of making ethical decisions. That is, you will be more likely to consider other points of view and the consequences of each option. You will be more likely to discover competing interests and spot questionable appeals and arguments that if acted on would harm clients. Exhibit 3.2 provides an opportunity to critically review an ethical concern.

Thinking critically about practice issues will also help you discover unrecognized concerns and balance the advantages and disadvantages of acting versus not acting (see Exhibit 3.3). It will help you distinguish between legitimate and illegitimate uses of power. In regard to the use of power, Thomas Szasz, in *Cruel Compassion* (1994), as well as his other books, argues that clients' rights

are routinely infringed on by a coercive psychiatry that imposes unwanted treatment on children and adults, even though there is no evidence that it is effective. The influence of professionals is not always obvious. In fact, the more subtle it is (e.g., an unrecognized social influence), the more controlling it may be, precisely because it is not noticed.

SERVING AND AVOIDING HARM AS KEY PRINCIPLES

The first value listed in the 1996 draft of the NASW Code of Ethics is service, which also is cited in the philosophy of practice described in Chapter 1. The related ethical principle can be seen in Exhibit 3.1. The code states that: social workers are encouraged to elevate service to others above self-interest; and social workers' primary responsibility is to promote the well-being of clients. This call to elevate service to others above one's own self-interest implies that self-interest is bad and is possible to ignore. But self-interest is quite different from selfishness;

EXHIBIT 3.3
Failing to Act

Just as we may act when we should not because not doing so results in more harm than good, we may fail to act when this results in more harm than good. Research suggests that we often overlook ethical concerns related to *not* acting (omissions) (Baron, 1994). This exercise provides an opportunity for you to consider the consequences of an omission.

Situation: _____

_____

Omission (what was not done): _____

_____

Consequences: _____

_____

Discussion: _____

_____

Suggestions for discussion:

1. Would you act differently in the future? If so, what would you do, and why?
2. What factors influenced your decision (e.g., agency policy, feared risks)?
3. Can you think of other examples of failing to act when you think you should have acted?
4. What could be done to prevent omissions that limit opportunities to help clients?

indeed, self-interest is critical to survival. Calling on social workers to ignore self-interest implies that they are better than other human beings (a dangerous belief) and that good intentions are sufficient to help clients.

Avoiding Harm as a Corollary of Serving

Some procedures designed to protect people may have the opposite effect; consider, for example, the juvenile court system, which stripped juveniles of the basic rights available to adults (In re Gault, 387 U.S. 1, 87 S. Ct. 1428 L.ED. and 527 1967). Harm includes removing valuable opportunities, locking people up against their will, stigmatizing them by means of negative diagnostic labels, and not fully informing clients, with the result that they make decisions they otherwise would not make. Consider the hundreds of allegations that a government report made concerning treatments for head injuries:

> Unethical marketing (e.g., lying to the families of people suffering recent brain injuries and pressure tactics to gain access to hospital records of patients with substantial insurance).
>
> Bad care. Patients who said they were promised intensive therapy report finding quadriplegic children unattended, having lain for hours or days in vomit or feces. Others said their children's condition seriously deteriorated from neglect.
>
> Expensive rehabilitation programs that admit and keep patients who cannot benefit from them, simply to garner insurance payments. One researcher found that for an average nine-month stay, patients were charged $106,000 for treatment not justified by the results. Patients released after less than six months did just as well, the researcher found.
>
> Companies instructing medical staff members to file false or misleading reports of patient progress to insurance companies. (Kerr, 1992a, p. A1)

Both consumer groups and scholars like Peter Breggin (1991) and Thomas Szasz (1994) have pointed out the coercion in the "helping" professions.

SELF-DETERMINATION AND EMPOWERMENT AS KEY VALUES

Self-determination refers to a belief that people should be allowed to arrange their lives in accord with their preferences. Stephen Fawcett and his colleagues define empowerment as the process of gaining some control over those events, outcomes, and resources important to an individual or group (1994, p. 472), for example, enhancing neighborhood residents' influence on programs, policies, and practices that affect them. Lorraine Gutierrez defines empowerment as "a process of increasing personal, interpersonal, or political power so that individuals can take action to improve their life situations" (1990, p. 149). Self-determination and empowerment involve giving clients real (rather than merely perceived) influence over the quality of their lives and involving clients in making decisions that affect them. They require a candid recognition and discussion of any coercive aspects of contact between social workers and clients. Focusing on outcomes that clients value (whenever they do not compromise the rights of others) respects self-determination. Clearly describing goals and methods (including their risks and benefits as well as alternative options) and any coercive aspects of meetings (including unapparent negative consequences dependent on the amount of participation) provides a degree of self-determination that contrasts with the pursuit of vague goals and the use of vaguely described methods (see also later discussion of informed consent). Leslie Margolin (in press) contends that social work's current concerns for empowerment are due to its need to atone for past excesses of controlling clients in the name of helping them (see for example Ryan, 1976). He suggests that current discussions of empowerment in social work are yet another way in which social workers in the public social services disguise investigatory and judgmental aims. That is, they say the right thing, but an examination of what they do with what results reveals quite a different picture. He suggests that the very notion that social workers can empower clients places power firmly in the hands of social workers—they give it to clients.

Feeling Free and Being Free

It may not be evident when self-determination (choice) has been compromised. Only when we clarify such vague terms as *self-determination* and understand how our behavior is influenced by our environments (some of which we create by our behavior) can we discover how "free" we are and how we can expand our freedom. Only then can we see whether the freedom we feel matches our actual freedom and whether what we have freely chosen is really what our culture has socialized us to value (Skinner, 1971). Consider women who have breast augmentations. Is this a free choice? Or is it encouraged by hidden influences such as a society's standards of beauty? Values and norms (e.g., regarding ideal weight and breast size, what kinds of cars are status symbols) are socially constructed; we are not born with them.

Constraints Imposed by Being an Agent of the State

In the public social services, conflicts between individual rights and state's rights (as reflected in legislation and public policies) compromise the self-determination of both social workers and clients. Social workers who work in public agencies work as social agents, not as clients' agents. That is, they are obligated to carry out the policies of the agencies in which they work, and their duties are structured by institutional arrangements. They are not free agents to pursue the broad call to provide service to clients, as in the NASW Code of Ethics. Social workers are mediators between their clients' needs and the constraints imposed by policy (for example, regarding resources). Russell Hardin argues that professional ethics in public agencies are "the ethics of the role holders in institutions" (1990, p. 528), not the ethics emphasized in the NASW Code of Ethics, which primarily concern the individual relationship between clients and social workers.

The NASW Code of Ethics states that "a social worker's responsibility to the larger society or specific legal obligations may on limited occasions [actually, there are many occasions] supersede loyalty owed clients, and clients should be so advised."

The NASW Code of Ethics states that: "Social workers may limit clients' right to self-determination when, in the social workers' professional judgement, clients' actions or potential actions pose a serious, foreseeable, and imminent risk to themselves or others." Overlooking constraints may result in misleading both ourselves and our clients about what we can offer and how effective it is likely to be. For instance, social workers may invade their clients' privacy and interfere in their family life (e.g., remove children from the care of their parents) and confine people against their will (e.g., for psychiatric evaluation). The law views these intrusions as necessary on the grounds that they further interests of social importance (e.g., protect children from neglect or abuse).

Constraints Posed by a Lack of Resources

You cannot empower your clients if you yourself are not empowered (i.e., do not have the resources needed). The degree to which you can "empower" your clients thus depends partly on the extent to which your knowledge, skills, and other resources match what is needed to help clients attain outcomes they value. Accurately estimating this match is one of the important ways you take responsibility for your decisions. You may refer clients elsewhere if you do not have the needed knowledge and skills or resources.

You cannot inform your clients about problem-related influences if you are not aware of them yourself. An understanding of interlinked contingencies among different levels (e.g., how a public policy affects options) will help you to identify constraints to and opportunities for helping clients. Clearly describing desired outcomes and related contingencies will help you to estimate accurately what you can accomplish, given current constraints and resources, and help you avoid unrealistic paths and false promises.

RESPECT FOR THE INHERENT DIGNITY AND WORTH OF EACH PERSON

Social workers have stressed the importance of respecting their clients' dignity and uniqueness. The

NASW Code of Ethics calls on social workers to "respect the inherent dignity and worth of the person," to "engage people as partners in the helping process," and to "promote conditions that encourage respect for cultural and social diversity within the United States and globally" (see Exhibit 3.1). Respect requires honesty (fully informing clients), involving clients and significant others in making decisions that affect their lives, giving clients in similar circumstances a similar quality of services, and using service methods that are most likely to result in outcomes clients value with due consideration for possible risks, discomfort, and client preferences. Respect for clients requires acting and speaking in considerate ways, whether or not you are in their presence. Respect involves identifying and supporting the clients' strengths and avoiding unnecessary and/or harmful pathologizing. For instance, professionals sometimes assume that people labeled *schizophrenic* cannot make decisions for themselves, an assumption that is likely to result in coercive interventions that ride roughshod over self-determination (Szasz, 1994). This is especially questionable when there is no evidence that forced intervention is effective.

Selecting assessment, intervention, and evaluation methods based on the following criteria shows respect for clients: (1) there is evidence that the methods can achieve what they purport to achieve (i.e., they are effective); (2) they are acceptable to clients and significant others; (3) they do not harm clients, significant others, or other parties; (4) they help clients attain outcomes they value; (5) they are the least intrusive; (6) they build on the clients' assets; and 7) helpers have the required competencies to use them effectively. Respect requires attending to individual differences that will influence the outcome of service, which may involve recognizing and considering differences in ethnicity, race, sex, sexual orientation, age, class differences, and physical and intellectual capabilities. Sue and Sue (1990) suggest that culturally sensitive helpers

- Respect cultural differences, believing that other cultures are as valuable and legitimate as their own.
- Are aware of their values and biases and how these may affect their clients.

- Are comfortable with differences between themselves and their clients and do not see them as deviant. But they do not deny differences.
- Correctly identify situations in which a client should be referred to someone of his or her own race or culture.
- Acknowledge their own stereotypes and beliefs that may interfere with helping.

Concerns for respect and serving call on social workers to "behave in a trustworthy manner." Value 5 in the 1996 Code of Ethics is called integrity. Trust and integrity imply predictability, a correspondence between what you say and what you do, meaning that clients can count on you to do what you say you will do.

INFORMED CONSENT

Integral to informed consent is the competence to offer it, and the extent to which it is offered voluntarily and is informed (see also the previous discussion of self-determination). Being informed requires adequate information. Requirements include the following:

- An absence of coercion and undue influence.
- A description of anticipated costs to both clients and significant others.
- The capability of clients to provide consent.
- A clear and complete explanation, in the client's native language and at his or her level of comprehension, of suggested aims and methods, including their purposes.
- A description of possible discomforts and risks (including effects on the client's job, family, independence).
- A description of hoped-for benefits.
- A description of alternative service methods and their potential goals and benefits (e.g., the extent to which each has been critically tested and found to be useful, ineffective, or harmful).
- An offer to answer any questions.
- Informing clients that they are free to withdraw their consent and discontinue their participation at any time.

Research shows that informed consent requirements are usually not followed (see for example, Lidz et al., 1984). Although statutory and regulatory policy require psychiatrists to disclose the risks of neuroleptic medication (e.g., of tardive dyskinesia), a study of 540 psychiatrists from 94 state and county mental hospitals in 35 states found that only 54% of psychiatrists told their patients about the possibility (Kennedy & Sanborn, 1992) (Tardive dyskinesia is an irreversible neurological condition characterized by involuntary muscular movements.) In public agencies such as protective service units for children, clients have no control over the intrusion of social workers into their lives. Clients should be fully informed about the potential consequences of different degrees of participation. The NASW Code of Ethics calls on social workers to describe accurately their personal qualifications (including competence) to their clients, agencies, and the public.

Your knowledge (e.g., about alternative procedures) limits the extent to which you can provide informed consent. That is, if you don't know about "what's out there," you cannot inform your clients. What if clients refuse to give their consent? Should you help parents acquire more effective parenting skills even if their child doesn't agree? Comparing current and future risks and benefits to all affected parties of different options and involving all participants in making decisions will guard your clients' interests. You also should consider the consequences of inaction as well as action. For example, refusing to help if one party does not agree to participate may allow an intolerable situation to continue or worsen.

Ethical issues come to the fore when clients cannot give informed consent. Clients labeled *mentally ill* may be (incorrectly and unethically) assumed to be unable to make their own decisions, and so decisions may be made for them. This assumption of "lack of agency" (the inability to make decisions) lies behind the intrusive methods that have been used in psychiatry since the beginning of this profession's history (e.g., Szasz, 1994). Special safeguards are required to increase the likelihood that the objectives pursued and the methods used are in the client's interest while also protecting society's interests in preventing harm to others. The approval and ongoing surveillance of all programs by a board—composed of a concerned representative of the client, laypeople not associated with the service setting, experts in the procedures used, and a representative of the institution can be used as a safeguard for institutionalized residents. Advance directives such as living wills also protect clients' wishes.

ETHICAL CONCERNS AND LEGAL REGULATIONS REGARDING CONFIDENTIALITY

Confidentiality refers to professional ethics that regulate against disclosure of information about a client without the client's permission. This differs from *privileged communication*, which refers to legal rights that (under certain circumstances) protect clients from having their communications revealed in court without their permission (Watkins, 1989). If information must be shared because of legal requirements, (e.g., the duty to report suspected child abuse and neglect), clients should be so informed. The duty to warn includes suspected institutional maltreatment of residents by staff. Some of the concern about the confidentiality of records is due to undocumented negative material in records. Such material should not be there in the first place. Talking about clients to friends, family, and acquaintances is unethical. "Bad mouthing" clients by name in informal staff get-togethers may create a negative set toward clients by other staff and is equally unacceptable.

Waivers of Privileged Communication

In Tarasoff v. Regents of the University of California (1974, 17, Cal 2d 425), the parents of a young woman who was murdered sued the regents because a university psychologist did not tell the woman that his client intended to kill her. The plaintiffs argued that the psychologist had an obligation to warn the woman of his client's intent. They won their case. (For a recent update of related cases, see Kagle & Kopels, 1994; also Knapp & Van de Creek, 1987). The many grounds for waivers of privileged communication illustrate the limits of confidentiality, which include the following:

- The client waives her privilege.
- The client introduces privileged material into the litigation.
- The social worker is called to testify in a criminal case.
- A client sues his counselor.
- A client commits or threatens a criminal act.
- A patient threatens suicide.
- A client threatens to harm his therapist.
- A minor is involved in criminal activity.
- Child abuse or neglect is suspected.
- A client is using certain types of drugs.
- A client's condition is alleged to make his employment hazardous to others.
- The court orders a professional examination.
- It is assumed that involuntary hospitalization is needed for the client's protection.
- The client dies.
- A professional needs to collect fees for services rendered.
- Information is learned outside the service relationship.
- Information is shared in the presence of a third person.
- The federal government needs certain information.
- It is assumed that emergency action is needed to save the client's life.
- It is assumed that legal action is needed to protect a minor.
- A presentence investigation report is prepared.
- The professional is employed in an agency or institution.
- A social worker is employed in a military setting.
- Claims are filed for life and accident insurance benefits. (adapted from Wilson, 1978, pp. 111–133)

Does a social worker have a duty to warn significant others who are at risk of contracting AIDS because of their sexual involvement with a client who has AIDS in cases in which the client has not shared this information with his or her partner? Some argue that the social worker does have an obligation to warn those at risk (Reamer, 1992). Others argue that the obligation to protect confidentiality overrides the "duty to warn" (Gelman, 1992).

Courts have allowed material from confidential psychotherapy sessions to be used as evidence in trials in cases in which the confidentiality of the client–therapist relationship has been ruled as no longer applying because the therapist exercised his or her "duty to warn" a third party of threats made by a client (see In Court: "Duty to Warn" v. Confidentiality, *NASW News*, July 1990, p. 16). For example, in 1982 a former client set fire to his social worker's home, killing her husband and leaving the social worker badly burned. The accused never denied the act and told a court-appointed defense therapist of his intent to kill the social worker's brother as well as other persons. The potential victims were informed at the therapist's request, and the therapist's testimony was used in evidence during the murder trial.

ETHICAL ISSUES RELATED TO COMPETENCE

One of the six key values in the new draft of the NASW Code of Ethics calls for workers to "practice within their areas of competence and develop and enhance their professional expertise." The Code of Ethics also recommends that social workers "provide services and represent themselves as competent only within the boundaries of their education, training, license, certification, consultation received, supervised experience, or other relevant professional experience" (1.04). They "should accept responsibility or employment only on the basis of existing competence or the intention to acquire the necessary competence" (4.01). The code does not specify the criteria to be used to assess proficiency or competence. The code of ethics further advises social workers to "critically examine and keep current with emerging knowledge relevant to social work" and "fully use evaluation and research evidence in their professional practice" (5.02). "When generally reconized standards do not exist with respect to an emerging area of practice, social workers should exercise careful judgment and take responsible steps—including appropriate education, training, consultation and supervision to ensure the competence of their work and protect clients from harm" (1.04c). Further, the code calls on social workers to "work toward the maintenance and promotion of high standards of practice" (5.01), but it does not mention the criteria to be used to determine whether social workers have reached these practice ideals.

Incompetence may be related to a lack of required skills and knowledge, faulty ethical judgments (either intentional or due to ignorance), or personal impairment (the social worker may have a substance abuse problem or be overworked). High caseloads, insufficient resources, and inadequate training and supervision increase the likelihood of a social worker's inadequate handling of cases, the results of which are sometimes described in daily newspapers. (e.g., a child already known to have been abused is killed by his biological parents).

Accountability and Competence

To some social workers, accountability means having their clients' best interests at heart, ensuring their self-determination, and respecting them. Such vague language allows great leeway in actions and outcomes, some of which may not be in the clients' best interests. John Kunkel, for example, argues that projects that "are simply designed to do good," without delineating *specific* goals and without regard to learning principles and behavioral procedures, are practically guaranteed to be unsuccessful and to "do evil" (1970, p. 315).

In the practice model described here, it is assumed that accountability requires offering services that are most likely to help clients attain outcomes they value (when acceptable to clients), focusing on objectives that enhance the quality of clients' lives, and evaluating progress in an ongoing manner using valid measures and sharing the results with clients. This kind of accountability requires accurate estimates of the degree to which your

knowledge and skills match what is needed to help clients, informing them about mismatches, and referring them to other sources when available. My students tend to overestimate their competence to provide certain kinds of services (e.g., social skills training, parent training) and to underestimate the domain-specific knowledge and skills available. Clients rarely know that their helper is not adequately trained or supervised. If more competent help is not available, you can offer to work with clients, with their full knowledge of the limits of your expertise.

The NASW Code of Ethics calls for social workers to "monitor and evaluate policies, the implementation of programs and practice interventions" (5.02). (It does not call for social workers to share this information with clients.) Ongoing monitoring based on valid progress measures allows timely case management decisions and keeps clients informed about degree of progress. This kind of accountability is important for both practical and ethical reasons. A concern for accountability highlights the importance of attending to process (what is done) as well as outcome (what is achieved). *Procedural fidelity* refers to the match between how a method should be implemented for maximal effect and how it actually is implemented. Increasing attention is being given to this match as research accumulates showing that how a method is carried out influences outcome.

Ethical Issues Related to Selection of Outcomes

Ethical practice requires involving clients in selecting outcomes, forming a clear agreement about what specific outcomes will be pursued, considering the interests of all involved parties, and focusing on *functional* objectives (those that improve the quality of clients' lives) (see also the earlier discussion of respect and informed consent). Vague statements such as "enhance social functioning" or "empower clients" may obscure different views of what to focus on as well as outcomes that do the opposite (e.g., decrease empowerment). Only when related objectives are clearly described can differences of opinion be discerned.

In victimless crime, there would seem to be no ethical or principled basis on which professionals should impose treatment on an unwilling client (Szasz, 1987). Are there any circumstances that do ethically warrant unwanted change attempts? Some argue that there are. For example, Robinson contends that "individuals presented for treatment . . . for reasons of having physically harmed others can lay no moral claim on the right not to be changed" (1974, p. 236). (The right to be different in terms of physically harming others is a separate issue from the question of whether society has a right to force such persons to accept treatment.) Others argue that criminal behavior should be handled by the criminal justice system but that this does not warrant coerced "treatment" (e.g., Szasz, 1994). Professionals who have authority over people in a supervisory or monitoring role (e.g., in child welfare departments and institutional settings) should be especially vigilant to make sure they have a legitimate reason for intervening (e.g., to protect children from physical abuse).

ISSUES RELATED TO CASE RECORDS

Clients should be informed about who will have access to their records and under what circumstances access will be granted (see also the section on confidentiality). Access may be legally mandated. Sheldon Gelman (1997) makes a persuasive argument for giving clients access to their records, suggesting that this will improve record keeping, increase accountability to clients, and is essential to self-determination (e.g., making informed decisions) and a democratic society. Giving clients access to their records would allow them to correct errors and help to equalize the power differences between helpers and clients. (For a contrasting view, see Winchester-Vega, 1997.) Such access is vital if you accept Margolin's (in press) view that the case record is the main way in which social workers create biographies that are used to justify their main aims of investigating, classifying, and judging clients. The confidentiality of others mentioned in records should be protected. Clients should have an opportunity to challenge items in

their records and either have them removed or insert rebuttals. And, the clients' permission should be obtained before sharing case-record data with others, unless such sharing is legally required.

The NASW Code of Ethics calls for social workers to "include sufficient and timely documentation in records to facilitate the delivery of services and to ensure continuity of services provided to clients in the future" (8.04). That is, records should facilitate the coordination and evaluation of services. The importance of records was highlighted in Whitree v. New York State (290 N.Y.S. 2d. 486 [ct. Claims] 1968), in which the records' inadequacy was cited as the reason that a client was held in a mental hospital for 12 years. The court held that the inadequate records hindered the development of treatment plans. Including negative material that is irrelevant to the provision of service and fudging records to protect service providers are examples of unethical recording practices. (For further discussion of the purposes of record keeping, both explicit and implicit, see Kagle, 1991; Margolin, in press).

ETHICAL AND LEGAL ISSUES
RELATED TO SEXUAL CONDUCT

The NASW Code of Ethics explicitly prohibits sexual activities with current clients, "whether such contact is consensual or forced" (p. 11). It also states that "social workers should not engage in sexual activities or sexual contact with former clients because of the potential for harm to the client" (p. 12). Questions here are, What is a "former client"? Over what duration of time should this be extended? Consider a community organizer who may work with scores of "clients." According to California law, "any kind of sexual contact, asking for sexual contact, or sexual misconduct by a psychotherapist with a client is illegal as well as unethical (Business and Professional Sections 726 and 4982 k). *Sexual contact* means touching another person's intimate part (sexual organ, anus, buttocks, groin, or breast). *Touching* means physical contact with another person, either through the person's clothes or directly with the person's skin (Section 728).

OTHER ETHICAL CONCERNS

Other ethical issues concern employer/employee relationships, conflicts between loyalties to colleagues and clients, and agency policies and procedures that hinder service. Between 1979 and 1987, 292 cases were filed with NASW Chapter Committees on Inquiries on which records were available (Berliner, 1989). Ninety-six were sustained. Many complaints involved personnel violations such as alleged unfair dismissal or gender discrimination. Conduct as a social worker and ethical responsibility to colleagues, organizations, the profession, or society accounted for between 25 to 28% each.

Conflicts may occur between obligations to employers and responsibilities to clients. For example, an agency policy may conflict with providing high-quality services to clients. Or services may be compromised by complex forms, long waiting times, and the shift from one worker to another. The NASW Code of Ethics advises social workers to "avoid unwarranted negative criticism of colleagues with clients or with other professionals. Unwarranted negative criticism may include demeaning comments that refer to colleagues' level of competence or to individuals' attributes, such as race, ethnicity, natural origin, color, sex, sexual orientation, age, marital status, political belief, religion, or mental or physical disability" (2.01, b). Given the code's recommendation to social workers to take action when they have good reason to believe that a colleague is engaged in incompetent practice, I assume that this is warranted criticism.

Ethical and Legal Issues Related to Policy and Planning

Policy decisions involve defining what should be as well as what is. Agency administrators help to create policy by their day by day decisions. Key ethical dilemmas in public agencies (and in health services) involve decisions about allocating (scarce) resources. Moral dilemmas that may arise include: (1) personal obligations (e.g., compared with the state's obligation), (2) responsibility to different communities, (3) obligations across generations, and (4) collective responsibilities (e.g., of

groups). Reamer (1990) views ethical issues related to social planning as one of three main areas of ethical concerns in social work practice. Some of the unfortunate events in child welfare, such as children dying at the hands of their foster or biological parents, result from a lack of funds for required services, including supervisory visits. Many community based group homes for adults have closed because of inadequate state funding for quality programs. Residents may then be institutionalized at an even greater cost to taxpayers and also lose their independence. Many clients need a variety of resources that will require coordination among different agencies. Consider drug-exposed infants, for whom the essential services may include medical treatment, respite and nursing care, and early intervention to prevent or address developmental delays, to name but a few.

Burton Gummer (1996) argues that the NASW Code of Ethics is mainly concerned with direct service providers and their interactions with their clients. He argues that the code is silent on the hard decisions that social workers must make about how to distribute scarce resources. He believes that the code is remiss in not providing guidelines for problems of concern to managers, such as how to allocate scarce resources. He notes that a professional code of ethics presumes that other attributes of a profession are in place (e.g., a service ethic, a knowledge base, specialized training, and independent, discretionary decisions) and points out that these attributes are missing in the public social services in which helpers are responsible mainly to agency mandates and not to individual clients. Public policies typically allow considerable discretion by administration and line staff.

Russell Hardin contends that a major role, for example, of doctors today is to mediate conflicts between society and the patient about how to distribute scarce resources (1990, p. 536). He highlights the "costs to new professionals from a code of ethics that so neglects the greatest range of actual cases of difficult moral choices they will face on the job" (p. 540). Gummer (1996) suggests that frameworks for evaluating public officials such as Wilbern's (1984) levels of public morality apply to social work administrators as well, since both bear the responsibility of implementing public social policies. The first three (basic honesty and conformity to the law, conflicts of interest, and service orientation and procedural fairness) concern the administrator's moral responsibilities. The other three (the ethics of democratic responsibility, public policy determination, and compromise and social integration) concern the ethics of decisions and actions. He argues that most codes of ethics deal only with personal morality.

Critical appraisal of proposed policies as well as ongoing evaluation of their effects are necessary to detect unwanted consequences at an early point and take timely corrective action (Magee, 1985).

Ethical Issues Related to Professional Organizations

The new draft of the NASW Code of Ethics calls on social workers to "work toward the maintenance and promotion of high standards" (5.01) and "to uphold and advance the values, ethics, knowledge, and mission of the profession," including "responsible criticism of the profession" (though this is not defined). Professionals are ethically bound to work together to achieve the highest quality of services for the greatest number of clients at the least cost. Clearly they do not always do so. The interest in expanding and protecting markets may compete with such aims. There are intense struggles and considerable funds are spent by professional organizations to maintain and/or expand their turf.

In 1989, only after a long struggle by both psychologists and social workers, did Congress pass legislation to include psychologists and social workers in the Medicare programs. Who is to be allowed to provide services in health maintenance organizations (HMOs) is a hard-fought issue. Citing the maintenance of health care standards as a reason to exclude certain professional groups may mask the less altruistic goal of protecting and expanding special interests. Readers of professional newsletters may be "taken in" by attacks on other professional groups and, as a result, may be less willing to try to understand the contributions of other professionals and to work cooperatively with them. Competing for clients is ethically questionable when it results in unnecessarily intrusive care

(e.g., hospitalization or prolonged stays in residential centers), lower-quality care, higher costs, or the withholding of needed care.

KNOWLEDGE OF LEGAL REGULATIONS AND RESOURCES

You should be familiar with the legal regulations that pertain to your clients and refer them to helpful sources as needed for further information. Because legal regulations often differ from state to state, you must find out what regulations apply to your state. You can keep up with current information about recent legal developments in particular areas by reviewing relevant sources such as *Youth Law News*. The American Civil Liberties Union publishes handbooks for older persons, crime victims, women, single people, gays and lesbians, prisoners, young people, and students. Legislation concerning clients' rights has increased. Classic decisions include Wyatt v. Stickney (344 F. Supp. 387 [M.D. Ala. 1972]), which states that clients have a right to adequate staff and to an individualized intervention program with a timetable for achieving specific objectives, as well as the identification of criteria for the release of clients to less restrictive environments and for their discharge. Juveniles' right to treatment was upheld in the Morales v. Turman case (383 F. Supp. 53 [E.D. Tex. 1974]). The right to treatment in the least restrictive alternative favors community settings. This court, as well as others, called for periodic progress reviews. Children as well as adults have a right to refuse treatment.

P.L. 94-142 (the Education for All Handicapped Children's Act) states that all children have a right to education, regardless of their mental or physical disability. This act calls for an individualized education program (IEP) for each handicapped child between the ages of 3 and 21; to "the maximum extent appropriate," handicapped children are "mainstreamed" (educated with children who are not handicapped); parents or guardians participate in the formation of educational plans; parents receive prior written notice whenever there is a proposed change or referral to initiate a change in the child's educational placement by school authorities; and when a complaint is received, parents should have an opportunity for an impartial due process hearing.

You should also be familiar with public laws that you and your clients could appeal to gain assistance. For example, Part H of the Education for the Handicapped Act (EHA) added in 1986 (authorized by Public Law 99-457) provides technical and financial assistance to help states develop interagency programs of early intervention. This could be drawn on to provide services to drug-exposed children (Morrow, 1990).

Testifying in Court

You may be required to testify in court in regard to civil commitment, child custody, or the termination of parental rights. Court appearances will be less stressful if you prepare for them. The best defense in court is sound practice, including adequate records and selection of methods based on what practice-related research suggests is effective (Besharov, 1985). An *expert witness* is one who is recognized or qualified by the court to offer certain kinds of opinions. The agreement to be an expert witness carries both responsibilities and risks. You should not agree to be an expert witness in areas in which you are not competent. Claims of competence (expertise) may (and should) be tested in court. Knowing that it is impossible to predict what someone will do in the future (in contrast to stating what has been found in general) should caution you to refrain from making unwarranted predictions (Ceci & Bruck, 1995; Dawes, 1994a). Be sure to consider possible conflicts of interest when deciding whether to be a witness. For example, in a custody dispute, a social worker may be asked to offer testimony about a child's feelings about her parents. If one of the parents is a client of the social worker, the social worker's testimony may be biased in the client's favor.

LIABILITY

Liability has become an increasing concern in social work as the number of law suits against individual social workers and social service agencies

has increased. There are four elements in the definition of malpractice: (1) a helper–client relationship was established; (2) the helper's conduct fell below an acceptable standard; (3) the helper's breach of duty was the proximate cause of an injury; and (4) the client sustained an injury (Rosswell, 1988). Injuries may be defined as a worsening of symptoms; the appearance of new problems; a misuse of counseling (e.g., encouraging unnecessary dependency on the social worker), taking on tasks that clients are not ready for, resulting in failure or other negative effects such as becoming disillusioned with counseling; and treatment-induced (iatrogenic) loss of a job, divorce, emotional harm, suicide, defamation of character, or abandonment (premature termination). Besharov (1985) believes that most social workers underestimate the extent of their liability. Supervisors may not realize that they may be liable for the negligence of those they supervise.

Varieties of Malpractice Claims

Many malpractice claims concern the selection of assessment and intervention methods (e.g., incorrect service, improper death of client or other, suicide of client, incorrect or incomplete assessment, and poor results). Half the claims of incorrect "diagnosis" made under NASW's insurance policy alleged that medical sources of problems were overlooked. Not seeking expert advice when it is needed and not referring clients to specialists when problems exceed the limits of one's competence may result in a lawsuit. Some lawsuits are based on a violation of clients' civil rights, such as an alleged failure to notify foster parents of the imminent removal of a child from their care and the failure to offer them a hearing or priority in an adoption decision. Alleged breaches of professional behavior, such as not being available when needed and not completing service once it has been started, also have been the basis of lawsuits. (Clients should be able to see another professional when their social worker is not available, and this substitute individual is required to have the requisite skills.) Alleged sexual contact is a common ground for malpractice claims.

Steps you can take to reduce your legal vulnerability are as follows:

- Be aware of the existence and nature of professional liability;

- Adhere to legal and administrative requirements;

- Maintain agency and professional standards of conduct and performance;

- Keep complete records;

- Ensure financial protection [e.g., malpractice insurance];

- Involve law enforcement agencies in child protective efforts.

- Be sensitive to high-risk situations; and

- Advocate for improved services and legal reform. (Besharov, 1985, p. 167).

As Besharov notes, "Good practice is the best defense" (1985 p. 168).

Agencies may be held responsible for failing to protect workers from assault by clients. Failure to provide adequate care in residential settings continues to receive attention. Suits claiming the neglect of residents (in contrast to active abuse) were won in Mississippi against a nursing home run by the nation's largest nursing home chain, and damages were awarded to the families of residents whose last years of life were diminished by neglect. The dollar amounts included

> $50,000 for leaving Mrs. Berryhill in her own excrement; $25,000 for verbal abuse of her by the staff, $15,000 for not bathing Mr. Bolian, $15,000 for keeping him in a smelly room, $60,000 for failing to give him the physical therapy he needed. . . . The jury further found that Beverly Enterprises' failure to provide good care was so "willful, wanton, malicious or callous" as to merit another $125,00 in punitive damages to each claimant. (Lewin, 1990, p. A1)

The National Senior Citizens Law Center, a nonprofit advocacy group in Washington, D.C., estimates that such negligence affects residents in 60% of the nation's nursing homes. Inadequate monitoring or intrusive interventions such as unnecessary confinement may result in lawsuits against social workers and social service agencies.

WHAT CAN CLIENTS DO ABOUT UNETHICAL OR ILLEGAL BEHAVIOR?

Clients may seek your advice about alleged ethical lapses in professional conduct. What should you suggest? What are your options? What are the clients' options? How can someone know when the lack of success or negative effects are a result of professional incompetence? Although this may be easy in some cases, it may not be in others, because of the consumers' lack of knowledge (e.g., about alternative methods). The tendency of laypersons to view professionals as experts complicates the situation.

The first step may be for the client to talk to the social worker, his or her supervisor, or an ombudsperson, if one is available. A complaint could be lodged with an agency administrator or referring source. The client could request another social worker. Clients can obtain information and guidance about unethical or illegal professional behavior from state licensing boards, professional associations or sexual assault/crisis centers. Final resorts include filing a lawsuit in civil court or taking criminal action (filing a complaint with local law enforcement authorities) (Hare-Mustin, Marecek, Kaplan, & Liss-Levinson, 1979, p. 14). Concerns about the emotional drains of conflict and fears about the loss of confidentiality or retribution may prevent clients from taking action. Or they may believe that complaining is useless because "nothing will happen." They may be unwilling to "make a fuss" or to "bother" people. They may not know how to make a complaint and what to do if it is ignored. Other obstacles include a lack of transportation or the required fees and an inability to read or write or to describe one's complaints clearly. Clients may be reluctant to persevere if their initial efforts fail. The potential problems awaiting those who lodge complaints underscores the importance of consumer rights and advocacy groups.

Residents of institutional settings should be fully informed of their rights; social workers in such settings should consider this one of their responsibilities. McDermott (1989) described the organization of a nursing home resident's campaign to inform staff and residents of resident rights, including access to information, privacy (closing bedroom doors, expecting staff to knock before entering), access to the community, dignified treatment, and participation in decision making regarding bedtime, menus, and activities. (Note that some require clarification, for example, "dignified treatment.") Residents' rights councils should be established in all institutional settings. Allowing elderly clients to take part in decision making has been shown to prolong life and enhance well-being (Langer & Rodin, 1976; Schultz, 1976).

Does Licensing Protect Consumers?

Do professional licenses protect clients from harm or mediocre practice? Does passing the test required to become a licensed social worker mean that someone is competent? If so, in what areas? What is the correlation between test scores and helping clients achieve outcomes they value? Robyn Dawes (1994a) argues that licensing psychotherapists gives the public a false sense of assurance that they will receive competent expert services that cannot be provided by lower-paid service providers. He notes that a review of psychotherapy research shows that credentialing (e.g., licensing) and experience are not related to success.

Blowing the Whistle

What should you do if you have evidence that a fellow social worker is offering incompetent services? Would you first talk to this person? If this did not help, would you discuss your concerns with your supervisor or with an agency administrator? If these steps failed, would you contact your agency's board of directors or "go public"? The NASW Code of Ethics (1996) states that "social workers who have direct knowledge of a social work colleague's incompetence should consult with that colleague and assist that colleague in taking remedial actions" (2.08). If the colleague "has not taken adequate steps to address the incompetence," he or she "should take action through appropriate channels established by employing agencies, NASW licensing and regulatory bodies, and

other professional organizations." The code also calls for social workers to "defend and assist colleagues who are unjustly charged with unethical conduct."

Agencies and professions may try to block attempts to expose their workers' incompetence by claiming that confidential client information was (or would be) revealed by the "whistle-blower." It may be assumed that loyalty to one's profession requires hiding one's "dirty linen." Even in cases in which all agree that the service was inadequate and clients were harmed, the exposure of incompetent practice may result in negative sanctions against the whistle-blower (Glazer & Glazer, 1989). It is hoped that legislation drafted to protect whistle-blowers will prevent this. For example, there is now legislation to protect whistle-blowers in the military from receiving unfair or inappropriate "mental health evaluations" or involuntary commitment for the treatment of "mental health problems."

ETHICS AND IDEOLOGY

Ethical principles often rest on ideologies. *Ideology* has been defined as "a systematic body of ideas which emerge from and justify a state of society or a political program" (Bynum, Browne, & Porter, 1985, p. 199). The term *ideology* can be used in a descriptive sense to refer to a system of beliefs or practices or in a persuasive sense to refer to efforts to advance a belief system (Thompson, 1987). In the latter sense, it is used to justify and explain a certain way of acting, by providing "vocabularies of motive" (Mills, 1959). Karl Popper (1994) defines ideology as beliefs that are not open to critical discussion.

Different ideologies suggest different answers to ethical questions, creating different views about the world and our place in it as well as about the role of professions and different kinds of "self-knowledge" (what we think we know about ourselves). Ideology is used to influence how issues and problems are framed and what actions people take. Politicians, advertisers, and professional organizations spend great amounts of money to encourage ideologies that support their vested interests.

Ideology in the form of slogans ("We do it for you") is often used as a substitute for thinking. Critically examining ideologies may reveal that although they may appear to forward humanitarian aims, they instead forward beliefs and actions that harm people. Only by looking beyond the surface can we discover the consequences of an ideology.

Recognizing Ideology

One way to recognize ideology is by its appeal to authority to support claims, as in "Dr. Z. says that. . . ." If an instructor expects you to believe what he says simply because he said it, he is being ideological. Karl Popper would say that he is imprisoned by his beliefs rather than using theory (guesses about what may be true) to suggest hypotheses about what may or may not be true and then noting the need to test them critically. Other indicators include impatient or defensive reactions when questioned. Ideological statements often have a "slogan" quality, such as "We know social work is effective." The "pronouncement" nature of such claims, unaccompanied by recognizing the need to examine them critically, reveals their ideological nature. In addition, ideological statements are usually general rather than specific. Exactly what actions are called for may be vague, as in the statement "Humanistic practice guards clients' rights." What is humanistic practice? What are the rights referred to? What criteria will be used to determine whether the rights are indeed being guarded?

Another way to recognize ideological statements is by their emotional appeal. They play on our fears, anger, and self-interest to encourage certain ways of behaving and thinking (e.g., donate money, vote for a certain candidate, seek a certain kind of therapy). Ideology and propaganda are related. *Propaganda* refers to efforts to encourage people to act in certain ways based on as little critical thought as possible (Ellul, 1965). Both ideology and propaganda have an interest in persuading not through rational discussion but through emotion. Both play on our emotions and encourage emotional reasoning. We are often unaware of the emotive effects of language and so may act uncritically on statements that sound appealing (e.g., "We

believe in citizen participation") but may not represent reality (there may be none). Ideological statements also play on our reluctance to raise questions for fear of appearing ignorant, difficult, or disloyal. Scientific theories that become entrenched (not open to critical testing and discussion) become ideologies.

Uses and Misuses of Ideology

Ideologies can maintain commitment in difficult times. For instance, the professional ideology of "doing good" can provide solace when social workers are hard pressed by excessive caseloads. However, ideologies may compromise services and maintain or increase economic and social inequities by providing false assurances. Awareness of majority ideologies and the ways they may be imposed on minority groups is important in challenging prejudice and related discriminatory patterns of behavior. The ideology of individualism, for example, emphasizes individual rights. However, many people view rights without the resources to act on them as a cruel hoax. Ideological statements may be made to hide reality (e.g., certain consequences of a policy). Statements that appear to support an equality that benefits everyone (e.g., "We believe in individual freedom") may instead forward an economic system that excludes millions from sharing its benefits. Appeals to social justice may refer to efforts to impose unwanted political and economic systems on everyone. Relying on ideology (e.g., appealing to professional values and good intent) in place of critical discussion is ethically questionable if this diminishes the quality of services that clients receive. For example, if we uncritically accept the view that professionals do only good, we will lose opportunities to discover when they do harm or seek aims that do not favor the clients' interests.

John Ehrenreich argues that the Progressive Era ideology of the professional middle class that social problems could be viewed as technical problems solvable by "scientific" management (i.e., delivered by middle-class managers) furthered middle-class interests, often at the cost of making working conditions less appealing to those managed (the working class) (1985, p. 134). Demott (1990) argues that even before the turn of the century, prevailing elite ideology described the key division in American society not as that between rich and poor, but as that between industrious and idle, virtuous and vicious, community-minded and selfish. Leslie Margolin argues that it is because social work's overall look and feel is non-exclusionary and non-divisive, that it is able to create and reinforce popular beliefs about who is worthy and who is not (in press).

Ideological Clashes

Ethical dilemmas often reflect ideological clashes. Some common ones are highlighted in the sections that follow.

Pessimistic and Optimistic Ideologies. Some beliefs about life emphasize our passivity and view the environment as inherently hostile and unknowable. Karl Popper (1992) refers to these as *pessimistic ideologies. Optimistic ideologies* are quite different. Here it is believed that we can discover knowledge about the world, hard as it may be to do so. Karl Popper suggests that "over-optimism about the power of reason . . . an over-optimistic expectation concerning the outcome of a discussion" (1994, p. 44) may be responsible for a pessimistic ideology. The contextual perspective described in this book embraces an optimistic perspective that reflects what we know so far about the interaction among genes, organisms, and their environments. Here, we are viewed as active participants in the creation of our environments. This view highlights the interaction between our actions and our environments and opportunities to create new environments (e.g., cultural practices that benefit all citizens).

Service and Professional Ideologies. Service and professional ideologies may clash. The ideology of service emphasizes the importance of serving clients, but the need of a professional organization to reconcile differences among diverse groups in its own membership requires compromises (Friedson, 1986) (e.g., between calls for us-

ing methods that have been found to help clients [they have been critically tested] and protecting professional discretion). "The professional association tends more to provide services to their members than to exercise control over their ethical or technical work behavior" (Friedson, 1986, p. 187). Claims made by professional organizations about the unique qualifications of social workers to offer certain services are often overstated, reflecting one of the functions of professional ideology—to maintain and expand its turf. That is, more knowledge and skills and a wider jurisdiction are claimed than are warranted by critical discussion and testing (Friedson, 1973).

A perusal of just about any professional journal reveals a cornucopia of overstated claims about what is known. A key function of professional claims of knowledge is to gain public and legislative support for that profession. Reliance on ideology obscures the need to critically test claims of effectiveness. Indeed, to protect the profession's reputation, its members may try to prevent or discredit whistle-blowers who expose ineffective or harmful practices.

Professional, Personal, and Bureaucratic Ideologies. Promoting service and justice is emphasized by the National Association of Social Workers. Most social work practice is carried out in organizations, and the bureaucratic ideology and the policies they reflect may conflict with both service (e.g., caseloads may be too high, and supervision may be poor) and professionals' interests in maintaining control over their work. (See also the earlier discussion of constraints imposed by being an agent of the state.) Benson suggests that "to a bureaucratic elite, the only acceptable ideologies among their staff are those that support organizational purposes" (1967, p. 197).

The functions of bureaucratic ideology include maintaining a smoothly running agency, implementing agreed-on policies, and staying out of trouble. Management may set requirements that are viewed as an encroachment on professional discretion. Line staff typically identify with the clients, whereas administrators focus on "getting the work done." Social workers may have an ideology independent of that of both their profession and the agencies in which they work, which may result in clashes between administrators and employees who set their own goals. Consequently, a welfare worker may learn "how to break the rules, to lie, cheat, to forge or destroy documents in the interest of the client" (Benson, 1967, p. 161). Administrators may appeal to professional ideology for bureaucratic purposes. Protests by line staff about large caseloads and poor supervision may be answered by the administration with "We are committed to serving clients and expect staff to use their professional skills to manage caseloads."

Capitalistic and Socialistic Ideologies. The ideology of capitalism assumes that free enterprise (the open market, unrestricted competition) is the most effective economic system and that people have a right to unlimited gain. The emphasis on individualism is part and parcel of the ideology of capitalism (Bellah, Madsen, Sullivan, Swidler, & Tipton, 1985). Each person is assumed to be able to control his or her own destiny, fashion his or her own lifestyle, and take responsibility for his or her own problems. Such an ideology stresses individual liberties and rights and idealizes the "self-made" man (or woman).

The ideology of socialism regards the economic inequalities in a capitalistic society as unjust. Socialism sees the good of all people as critical and pays particular attention to conflicts of interest among classes. The ideology of individualism and the economic ideology of which it is a part (capitalism) are considered responsible for creating and maintaining economic inequities and encouraging the inappropriate use of psychological approaches with clients who have material and social support needs. Some people suggest that the recognition of shared interests among economically disadvantaged groups is obscured by ideologies that "balkanize" the working class (thereby setting groups such as poor African Americans and poor whites against each other), that political and economic inequities limiting the extent to which people can be "self-made" are ignored or downplayed, and that the limits of self-determination are obscured by vague statements asserting its ease or accomplish-

ment. Radical and structural theories of social work embrace a socialistic ideology (Clark & Asquith, 1985), in which social problems are assumed to be largely due to political and economic factors.

Social Justice or Psychotherapy. The NASW Code of Ethics emphasizes the social justice mission of social work on "behalf of individuals and groups of vulnerable or oppressed people" (see Exhibit 3.1). The code advises social workers to "act to prevent and eliminate domination, exploitation, and discrimination against any person, group, or class on the basis of race, ethnicity, national origin, color, age, religion, sex, sexual orientation, marital status, political belief, mental or physical disability, or any other preference, personal characteristic, or status" (p. 24). The code also calls on social workers to "engage in social and political actions that seek to ensure that persons have equal access to the resources, employment, services, and opportunities that they require to meet their basic human needs and to develop fully" (p. 24).

Can social workers achieve these lofty aims? Can we ensure these outcomes? F. A. Hayek (1976) views the belief in social justice as "the gravest threat to most other values of a free civilization" (p. 67) and contends that there is no agreement on standards to evaluate the extent to which there is social justice. Therefore, some people must impose their standards on others. He argues that the belief in social justice "has lured men to abandon many of the values which in the past have inspired the development of civilization" (p. 67), that this goal is unattainable, and that striving for it creates undesirable consequences such as further limiting personal freedom. Anyone advocating "social justice" as a goal must provide a sound counterargument to Hayek's arguments.

People differ as to whether they believe psychotherapy has a legitimate role in social work. Wakefield (1992) argues that it helps people maximize their potential and that this is a legitimate aim of social work. Others argue that psychotherapy does not have a legitimate role in social work (e.g., Specht & Courtney, 1994). Feminist writers criticize individually based psychotherapy for overlooking social causes of problems (e.g., Kantrowitz & Ballou, 1992; Lerman, 1992). They contend that humanistic ideologies emphasizing authenticity, self-actualization, meaningful human relationships, being in touch with one's inner feelings, expanding one's awareness, and using cognitive–behavioral methods, ignore structural factors related to problems, including unequal opportunities for men and women. (See also Tavris, 1992.)

The first clarification needed is a definition of psychotherapy. Unless we know the domain of helping efforts to which this term refers, we cannot be sure what we are talking about. Shouldn't our purpose guide our selection of methods? What are the problems with which social work should be concerned? Only when we have answered this question, can we wisely choose the best methods to address them. When confronted with a specific individual, family, group, organization, or community experiencing real-life problems, we can ask, given this problem, what service methods are most likely to be effective?

Mental Illness and Contextual Ideologies. The ideology of mental illness assumes that personal troubles often reflect illnesses requiring treatment by experts. Although individuals are supposedly not blamed for their problems in this model, they indeed are often forced to accept treatment they do not want. Some scholars contend that the ideology of mental illness is used to deprive people of their freedom and liberty by labeling them as mentally ill and forcing treatment on them (e.g., Szasz, 1994). Environmental causes are often ignored or downplayed, and instead, biological and psychological causes are emphasized. Client dependency is encouraged by assuming that experts are needed to "treat" an ever lengthening list of "mental disorders." In contrast, contextual perspectives emphasize the role of environmental factors in creating and maintaining personal troubles and social problems, including status differences in who receives stigmatizing labels (e.g., schizophrenic) and unwanted "treatment."

Other Ideologies. Legal ideologies emphasize rights. Biological ideologies emphasize physical causes (see Chapter 7). Cultural ideologies under-

score the role of cultural factors in understanding behavior.

The ideology of the nuclear family sees the nuclear family as providing the optimal setting for raising children. Adequate families are those that are self-sufficient and relatively free from social pressures. The nuclear family is the ideal, and families that deviate from it are looked down on and receive fewer resources. Many have argued that the ideology of "doing good" masks the coercive nature of child welfare services (e.g., Margolin, in press). Sarri and Finn (1992) note for example the "civilizing mission" that shaped 19th- and early 20th-century federal policy toward Native Americans. "Through the boarding school system, thousands of Native American children were separated from their families, communities and cultures; social control was imposed in the name of education" (p. 224).

CAN THE FOX GUARD THE CHICKENS?

The history of the helping professions shows that there are problems with any profession guarding the competency of their members. The reasons include self-interest and the tendency of professionals to define problems within a particular framework. History shows that it is professionals who may get in the way of fully informing clients about the negative side effects of "treatments." Consider, for example, the barriers that physicians place in the way of informing patients about the negative effects of neuroleptic medication (e.g., tardive dyskinesia) (Brown & Funk, 1986). Wexler (1990) contends that the child welfare system injures the very children it is supposed to protect.

Because most helpers are rarely observed while interacting with their clients, their behavior is known mainly by indirect means such as reports in staff meetings and case records. The variability of behaviors in relation to particular ethical concerns is not known, and the NASW Code of Ethics, including the 1995 draft, generally is vague about what behaviors are involved in what situations. Vague descriptions and the lack of visibility of processes and outcomes allow professionals to mystify their services beyond what is or can be offered and, in addition, may conceal negative outcomes.

The Need for Limits on Professional Discretion

The history of the helping professions highlights the need for limits on professional discretion in choosing (1) objectives (involving clients in decisions and fully informing them), (2) service plans (emphasizing acceptable plans that are least intrusive and restrictive and most effective and efficient), and (3) evaluation methods (tracking clear, relevant progress indicators). Economic, judicial, and legislative pressures have been necessary to increase professional accountability. It is not unusual for lawsuits to be brought against residential institutions or for state-licensing agencies to warn an agency of policies and practices that harm clients. Lawsuits have been filed against many public child welfare agencies for failing to implement procedural guidelines legislated to protect children. In one such case, the court that reviewed the foster care placement of a disabled child and the services offered held that the agency had not made reasonable efforts to provide either preventive or reunification services to the family, because

1. The family was not formally referred to parenting classes, identified as a critical service, until nine months after the child was removed from the home.
2. The agency was too slow in providing family and marital counseling and offered no adequate explanation for why it had not offered intensive family counseling from the outset.
3. The agency's efforts to arrange a medical appointment for the mother to determine if she needed medication superseded and interfered with the provision of necessary individual counseling for the mother.
4. The agency failed to provide frequent and appropriate visitation, because it did not attempt unsupervised, extended, overnight and weekend visits which the court deemed entirely appropriate.

5. The child's medical exam was not to be considered a reunification service, as it was not given for other than routine purposes. (*Matter of a Child*, no. 88178, 1986) (see Shotton, 1990, p. 2)

The potential for professional abuse of power highlights the importance of regulations requiring a clear description of the reasons why clients must have any part of their freedom curtailed and strict limitations of grounds for doing so. The greater the potential influence over clients, the greater the need for constraints on professional behaviors to ensure that clients receive requested services in a manner that does not intrude on their rights. Advances have been made in many areas. No longer can children be denied a right to education by being suspended from school because of vague complaints that they are a management problem. The exact nature of the offending behaviors must be described in writing, and the parents and the child have a right to this information. Guidelines for specific standards of practice already exist in some areas, such as the institutional care of developmentally disabled clients, and are described in legislation (see also Exhibit 3.4). Many states have specific written guidelines limiting the use of aversive methods in institutional settings. However, written guidelines and legislation are not enough to protect clients from harm and to ensure service quality (Hannah, Christian, & Clark, 1981). Contingencies must be arranged that support programs, policies, and practices that guard client's interests. Consumers of services must help to define the limits of professional discretion (Lenrow & Cowden, 1980). Many consumer interest groups have been created to give people valuable information about the efficiency, effectiveness, and intrusiveness of different methods. The Public Citizen's Health Research Group publishes material for consumers (e.g., *Health Letter*), as do the state boards that regulate professional practice. A client bill of rights is shown in Exhibit 3.5.

Obstacles to Increasing Ethical Practice

The emphasis on the sanctity of professional opinion and the assumption that professionals "do

EXHIBIT 3.4
Position Statement on a Clients' Rights to Effective Behavioral Treatment

The Association for Behavior Analysis issues the following position statement on clients' rights to effective behavioral treatment as a set of guiding principles to protect individuals from harm as a result of either the lack or the inappropriate use of behavioral treatment.

The Association for Behavior Analysis, through majority vote of its members, declares that individuals who receive behavioral treatment have a right to:

1. *A therapeutic physical and social environment:* Characteristics of such an environment include but are not limited to: an acceptable standard of living, opportunities for stimulation and training, therapeutic social interaction, and freedom from undue physical or social restriction.

2. *Services whose overriding goal is personal welfare:* The client participates, either directly or through authorized proxy, in the development and implementation of treatment programs. In cases where withholding or implementing treatment involves potential risk and the client does not have the capacity to provide consent, individual welfare is protected through two mechanisms: Peer Review Committees, imposing professional standards, determine the clinical propriety of treatment programs; Human Rights Committees, imposing community standards, determine the acceptability of treatment programs and the degree to which they may compromise an individual's rights.

3. *Treatment by a competent behavior analyst:* The behavior analyst's training reflects appropriate academic preparation, including knowledge of behavioral principles, methods of assessment and treatment, research methodology, and professional ethics; as well as practical experience. In cases where a problem or treatment is complex or may pose risk, direct involvement by a doctoral-level behavior analyst is necessary.

4. *Programs that teach functional skills:* Improvement in functioning requires the acquisition of adaptive behaviors that will increase independence, as well as the elimination of behaviors that are dangerous or that in some other way serve as barriers to independence.

5. *Behavioral assessment and ongoing evaluation:* Pretreatment assessment, including both interviews and measures of behavior, attempts to identify factors relevant to behavioral maintenance and treatment. The continued use of objective behavioral measurement documents response to treatment.

6. *The most effective treatment procedures available:* An individual is entitled to effective and scientifically validated treatment; in turn, the behavior analyst has an obligation to use only those procedures demonstrated by research to be effective. Decisions on the use of potentially restrictive treatment are based on consideration of its absolute and relative level of restrictiveness, the amount of time required to produce a clinically significant outcome, and the consequences that would result from delayed intervention.

Source: This statement is an abbreviated version of a report by the Association for Behavior Analysis, Task Force on the Right to Effective Behavioral Treatment (See R. Van Houten [chair], S. Axelrod, J. S. Bailey, J. E. Favell, R. M. Foxx, B. A. Iwata, and O. I. Lovaas). Journal of Applied Behavior Analysis, 21(1988):381–384.

good," are sincere, and engage in ethical behavior are obstacles to identifying hidden sources of power that repress rather than help clients and to identifying clear standards of practice and arranging monitoring and incentive systems to support them. Some of the reasons for the vagueness of ethical codes lie in their political and economic functions (e.g., to provide evidence of good intentions and ideals and to avoid excluding constituencies from certain activities (Ceci & Bruck, 1995, p. 284; Daniels, 1973; Margolin, in press). It is in the interest of professionals to be vague about goals, procedures, and outcomes if clients and other interested parties would object if they were clearly described. The following statement made 20 years ago is still true today:

Most institutions protect themselves by assuring a lack of information. In virtually any public institu-

tion, the goals are too imprecise to serve as a safeguard against which to judge the workings of the institution. It is impossible to tell by whom important decisions will be made, when they will be made, and what factors will be weighed in the process. Once a decision is made, it is impossible to trace its impact, good or bad. There is not only no feedback within the institution, but also no communication of objective data to the public. (Martin, 1975, pp. 97–98)

Some people argue that this vagueness benefits clients, that it allows professionals to define goals and negotiate value conflicts in ways that would not be possible if specific codes existed. However, the history of the helping professions shows that this flexibility often works against rather than for clients. Only when general terms such as respect and empowerment are clearly defined and related

EXHIBIT 3.5
Client Bill of Rights

You have the right to
- Receive respectful services that will be helpful to you.
- Refuse a particular type of service or end a service without obligation or harassment.
- A safe environment free from sexual, physical, and emotional abuse.
- Report unethical and illegal behavior by a helper.
- Ask questions about services.
- Request and receive full information about the helper's professional qualifications, including licensure, education, training, experience, specialization, and limitations.
- Have, before beginning, written information about fees, method of payment, insurance reimbursement, number of sessions, substitutions (in cases of vacation and emergencies), and cancellation policies.
- Refuse electronic recording but to request it if you wish.
- Refuse to answer any question or disclose any information you choose not to reveal.
- Know the limits of confidentiality and the circumstances when a helper is legally required to disclose information to others.
- Know if there are supervisors, consultants, students, or others with whom your situation will be discussed.
- Request and, in most cases receive, a summary of your file, including your diagnosis, your progress, and type of treatment.
- Request the transfer of a copy of your file to any helper or agency you choose.
- Receive a second opinion at any time about services.
- Request that the therapist inform you of your progress.

Source: Sacramento: California State Department of Consumer Affairs (1990). Adapted from Professional Therapy Never Includes Sex (p. 16).

actions are taken do values become meaningful to clients: "a value has small worth except as it is moved, or is movable, from believing into doing, from verbal affirmation into action" (Perlman, 1976, p. 381). Vague descriptions of goals, procedures, and outcomes provide "a shield for the practitioner," which is not always in the best interests of clients (Rothman, 1980, p. 145). Vague ethical standards offer an illusion of agreement. They provide a false reassurance that professionals agree on what actions should be taken in given situations and act accordingly. Vague standards obscure areas of disagreement and allow a range of discretion that may not be in the clients' best interests. We need more descriptive studies of ethical dilemmas that arise in everyday practice from the point of view of all involved parties (clients, significant others, social workers, administrators, supervisors) and how they are handled. We should develop clear decision-making guidelines related to specific dilemmas. Each should have a level of detail that permits the identification of the potential consequences of different options to those persons involved.

ENCOURAGING ETHICAL BEHAVIOR

If ethical behavior is to occur, it must be supported. Use your observation and contingency analysis skills to discover opportunities to encourage ethical practices, programs, and policies in your agency (see Chapter 8). Established standards of practice and monitoring and contingency systems that support them increase the likelihood that clients will receive high-quality services. Highlighting ethical issues both in work and educational settings will increase awareness of ethical concerns. Periodic reviews by supervisors, administrators, and/or review panels may help ensure that clients are fully informed and are offered services likely to address their problems.

Agencies are obligated to encourage ethical practice by clearly describing expected actions in given situations, by monitoring the quality and outcome of service provided, and by designing and maintaining training programs and incentive systems that maximize the quality of service (e.g., LaVigna, Willis, Schaull, Abedi, & Sweitzer, 1994). This requires a greater "visibility of practice" regarding what helpers do, rather than what they say they do and to what effect. Administrators and supervisors should review randomly selected interviews to identify opportunities for improvement in the ethical decisions made. They could monitor selected cases to ensure that:

- Problems of concern to clients are focused on when feasible and ethical.
- Client assets are supported and strengthened.
- Clear service agreements exist (see Chapter 10).
- Clients and significant others are informed participants in the selection of goals and procedures, and review of progress.

- Clear, relevant progress indicators are tracked.
- Valid assessment, intervention, and evaluation methods are used.
- The least intrusive and restrictive and most acceptable procedures are selected.
- Creative, energetic, and informed efforts are made to acquire needed resources.

Time may have to be put aside for the staff to discuss ethical concerns as a staff and should be, if they affect clients' lives.

What Are Your Obligations?

It is meaningful to discuss ethical values and actions only if we are free to make decisions. Many social workers, seasoned as well as students, tell me that they do not make any decisions. Their reasons include "I don't have sufficient resources"; "I don't have time"; "My supervisor makes the decisions"; and "I'm regulated by agency policy." Some of my students tell me that "I just do assessments that I pass on to my supervisor who makes the decisions." In fact, you cannot get through an hour at work without making decisions. Taking responsibility for the decisions you make is a hallmark of professionals and essential to ethical practice. Examples of practice-related decisions are given in Chapter 6 and are noted throughout this book. Accepting responsibility for decisions is a burden. It is also a freedom—a freedom to exercise what discretion is available in the best interests of your clients. Not taking responsibility leaves you powerless, helpless, unaccountable to your clients and unlikely to recognize social control aims masked as "doing good." It takes away what freedom you do have (and some people argue that we have some freedom in making decisions, even in dire circumstances. Consider the different contingencies in taking and not taking responsibility for practice decisions.

How much responsibility falls on your shoulders for your agency's programs, policies, and practices? Is it ethically acceptable to work in an agency that you know is offering ineffective or harmful services? Social workers often do not have

EXHIBIT 3.6
Consequences for Assuming or Denying Responsibility for Practice Decisions

Assuming responsibility for your decisions	People can blame me for poor decisions. I can blame myself for poor decisions. I can praise myself for good decisions. Others can praise me for good decisions. I am burdened by responsibility for my decisions.
Denying you make decisions	No one, including clients, can blame me for poor decisions. No satisfaction in tasks/outcomes achieved. I feel helpless/alienated/controlled by fate/others. I can't blame myself for poor decisions. I am not burdened by responsibility for making decisions.

the resources needed to help clients. How much responsibility should you take for this state of affairs? What should you do if the resources missing are your own domain-specific knowledge and skills (e.g., you do not have the knowledge and skills needed to help a parent acquire positive parenting skills)? Who or what is responsible for this (you, your educational program, your agency, or all of these)? What should you do if you work in an agency that routinely transforms clients' goals into other goals that may not benefit the clients or may even harm them? What is your responsibility here? These are hard questions that you should consider to avoid fooling yourself or your clients about what can be achieved (grandiosity) or overlooking the options that do exist (an inaccurate sense of helplessness).

You may believe that good intentions are what matters most in helping clients and avoiding harm. Only if you transform this belief into a guess about what may be true (or false) and test it can you examine its accuracy (e.g., by carefully evaluating outcomes). Only by being softhearted (compassionate and caring), as well as hard-headed (clarifying and critically evaluating assumptions), and competent (in possession of knowledge and skills required to address problems) will you have the best chance of helping clients and avoiding harm. Ask yourself, "Would I be satisfied with compassion alone on the part of my physician?" Does your answer reflect a double standard—art for them and science for me?

Handling Discrepancies Between Ideals and Realities

Perhaps in no other profession than in social work is there a greater contrast between the loftiness of service ideals and the stark realities of daily practice in the limited help that can be offered: "Their jobs [especially in the public social services] force them to see what ignorance, poverty, disease and destitution can do. They are forced to deal with social reality at its worst" (Benson, 1967, p. 193). Social workers must try daily to resolve problems whose fundamental causes lie outside their field. "In attempting to apply the highest ideals to the most resistant realities, the social welfare worker frequently feels trapped, frustrated, and helpless. How he responds to such situations determines his future

and his character as a social welfare worker" (p. 97). Unless you develop skills to cope with mismatches between ideals and realities, you may fall into habits that harm clients, such as pretending that you are competent to offer certain services when you are not, denying that you make any decisions, congratulating yourself for success even when you have had none, offering clients empty promises, or applying rules and regulations in a rigid manner that disregards their needs. You may focus on "interesting" problems, overlooking your client's needs. You may deny rather than examine dilemmas created by conflicting loyalties. You may overlook coercive aspects of practice and make decisions "for your clients' own good" rather than allowing them to make their own decisions. Keeping your purpose in view (e.g., to achieve outcomes that your clients value and to avoid harm), critically reviewing assumptions (your own as well as those of others), and taking responsibility for your decisions will help you make ethical decisions.

SUMMARY

Ethical practice requires considering the competing interests involved in practice decisions: legal regulations, clients' interests, the interests of involved others, professional codes of ethics, agency policy, and personal values. Only when ethical concerns are clarified will competing interests be revealed. Critical thinking is suggested as a guide to making ethical decisions. Inherent in critical discussion and thinking is considering opposing views and basing decisions on well-reasoned judgments in which the interests of all involved parties are considered. Ethical and legal issues arise in selecting objectives, service plans, and evaluation methods. Informed consent, confidentiality, and working within the limits of one's competence are other ethical concerns. Respect for clients requires building on their strengths, offering them effective methods, avoiding stereotyping and pathologizing them, and talking to and about clients in a polite manner. It means offering clients real (rather than merely perceived) influence over the quality of their lives and individually tailoring methods to each client's unique characteristics. Self-determination requires involving clients in decisions made and ensuring informed consent. Accountability requires focusing on objectives that make a real difference in the lives of clients, monitoring progress and sharing the results with clients, and being willing to have one's work observed in order to assess the quality of services offered.

Ethical issues and ideologies (beliefs and accepted values of particular groups) are closely related. Ideological clashes—often at the heart of ethical dilemmas in social work—include those between service and professional ideologies and between bureaucratic and service ideologies. Ideologies may obscure the real sources of influence and prevent the correction of policies or procedures that harm rather than help clients. Continuous vigilance is necessary to protect clients' rights; good intentions and verbal statements of caring are not enough.

REVIEWING YOUR COMPETENCIES

Reviewing What You Know

1. Describe the key ethical principles in the NASW Code of Ethics.
2. Describe the characteristics of ethical dilemmas.
3. Identify those factors that should be considered when thinking about ethical issues.
4. Describe the role of critical thinking in making ethical decisions.
5. Identify the kinds of harms to clients that may result from not recognizing hidden sources of power in social work practice.
6. Explain why professional codes of ethics are vague.
7. Describe the requirements of informed consent.
8. Identify ethical issues related to competence.
9. Describe the components of accountability.
10. Distinguish between privileged communication and confidentiality.
11. Describe common waivers of privileged communication.
12. Discuss the social worker's role as an agent of the state and how this may conflict with being an agent of the client.
13. Identify the ethical and legal concerns related to case records.
14. Describe the indicators of respect for clients.
15. Discuss the problems of professional organizations in monitoring the work of practitioners.
16. Identify the major legal regulations related to your area of practice. What are recent laws? What effects will they have?
17. Discuss the relationship between ethical practice and client empowerment.
18. Describe the four elements in the definition of malpractice.
19. Give examples of grounds for malpractice.
20. Describe steps you can take to reduce your vulnerability to malpractice lawsuits.
21. Describe clients' options when confronted with unethical or illegal behavior by professionals.
22. Describe the relationship between ethics and ideology.
23. Explain what is meant by the term *ideology*.
24. Identify the indicators of ideology.
25. Describe the functions of ideology.
26. Discuss common ideological clashes in social work.
27. Identify ethical concerns in agency policies and procedures.
28. Identify ethical issues related to social and public policies.

Reviewing What You Do

1. Given specific examples, you correctly identify ethical issues and legal constraints.
2. You can describe the specific steps you can take in your work setting to address specific ethical concerns. You can clearly describe the concerns and identify leverage points for change as well as constraints and resources (e.g., regarding who will benefit and who will lose from proposed changes).
3. You demonstrate critical thinking values, knowledge, and skills in discussing ethical issues (see Chapter 6).
4. You recognize ideological statements.
5. You explain to your clients the limits of confidentiality.
6. You take the appropriate steps to ensure your clients' informed consent.
7. You offer your clients effective methods.
8. You take appropriate steps to alter unethical agency policies and procedures.
9. You take appropriate steps to alter unethical public and social policies.
10. You provide accurate information to your clients about their legal rights.

Reviewing Results

1. Legal regulations are honored.
2. Clients receive services that enhance the quality of their lives.
3. The services offered enhance clients' knowledge and skills.
4. Unethical agency policies and practice are changed.
5. Unethical social and public policies are changed.

P A R T

II

BACKGROUND KNOWLEDGE

CHAPTER 4

Thinking About Knowledge and How to Get It

OVERVIEW

Professionals are assumed to have unique knowledge. This chapter introduces you to different views of knowledge and how to get it. Questionable as well as sound criteria for evaluating knowledge claims are described and you are encouraged to explore your views on this important topic. The importance of self-directed learning skills is emphasized.

You Will Learn About

- Different approaches to knowledge.
- Criteria used to evaluate knowledge claims.
- Scientific criteria.
- Questionable criteria.
- The importance of learning how to learn skills.
- The importance of reviewing your beliefs about learning.
- Ethical issues.

The philosophy of practice described in Chapter 1 highlights the importance of thinking about knowledge and how to get it. Explore your views by answering the questions in Exhibit 4.1. The assumption that professionals have certain knowledge and competencies is emphasized in this philosophy as well as the importance of making well-reasoned decisions and valuing truth over prejudice and ignorance. This implies that there is some knowledge for professionals to master, that some decisions are better reasoned than others, and that there is a difference among truth, prejudice, and ignorance. A concern for helping and not harming implies that certain decisions are better than others. The closer the match is between the knowledge you have and knowledge you need to help clients (or to correctly determine that you cannot), the more likely you are to help clients and avoid harm.

EXHIBIT 4.1
Reviewing Your Beliefs About Knowledge

Please circle the numbers in the columns that best describe your responses.

	SA	A	N	D	SD	
1. Since we can't know anything for sure, we really don't know anything.	1	2	3	4	5	_____
2. Since our beliefs influence what we see, we can't gather accurate knowledge about our world.	1	2	3	4	5	_____
3. It's good not to be too skeptical because anything is possible.	1	2	3	4	5	_____
4. We can't be certain of anything.	1	2	3	4	5	_____
5. Everything is relative; all ways of knowing are equally true.	1	2	3	4	5	_____
6. Criticism (critical discussion and testing) provides a valuable route to knowledge.	1	2	3	4	5	_____
7. Some things can't be demonstrated scientifically.	1	2	3	4	5	_____
8. Scientific reasoning and data are of no value in planning social policy and social action.	1	2	3	4	5	_____
9. I rely on my personal experience to support claims and conclusions.	1	2	3	4	5	_____
10. Science is a way of thinking developed by white male Western Europeans that does not apply to other cultures.	1	2	3	4	5	_____
11. I rely on the experts to know what's true.	1	2	3	4	5	_____
12. It is apparent without elaborate observations that cigarette smoking is associated with cancer.	1	2	3	4	5	_____
13. It's important for professionals to have sound reasons for their decisions.	1	2	3	4	5	_____
14. The opinions of 10 million qualified and reputable physicians or other professionals are of no value unless they are based on scientific evidence.	1	2	3	4	5	_____
15. Just because a famous person makes a claim (e.g., Freud) doesn't mean it is accurate.	1	2	3	4	5	_____
16. It usually is best to go along with what other people accept as true.	1	2	3	4	5	_____
17. Tradition provides a sound guide for assessing the accuracy of claims.	1	2	3	4	5	_____
18. Newness provides a sound guide for assessing the accuracy of claims.	1	2	3	4	5	_____
19. Manner of presentation provides a sound guide for assessing the accuracy of claims.	1	2	3	4	5	_____
20. Testimonials provide a sound guide for assessing the accuracy of claims.	1	2	3	4	5	_____
21. Case examples provide a sound guide for assessing the accuracy of claims.	1	2	3	4	5	_____
22. Good intentions provide a sound guide for assessing the accuracy of claims.	1	2	3	4	5	_____
23. What a person or his or her associates are like provides a sound guide for assessing the accuracy of claims.	1	2	3	4	5	_____
24. Empirical research has little to offer to social workers.	1	2	3	4	5	_____
25. Some things are so obvious that it is pointless to go through the drawn-out procedure of experimentation or observation.	1	2	3	4	5	_____
26. It is obvious that any type of psychotherapy will help people more than no psychotherapy at all.	1	2	3	4	5	_____
27. It is always better to take for truth the things that learned and educated people say because none of us really has the time to check things out.	1	2	3	4	5	_____
28. I am convinced that there are spaceships from outer space by the very fact that stories about them keep cropping up again and again.	1	2	3	4	5	_____
29. Before we can conclude that a new drug or treatment is helpful, we must first ascertain the course of the problem without any treatment at all.	1	2	3	4	5	_____
30. Professionals have an obligation to critically evaluate claims of effectiveness no matter who makes them.	1	2	3	4	5	_____

Key: SA = strongly agree; A = agree; N = neutral; D = disagree; SD = strongly disagree.

DIFFERENT APPROACHES TO KNOWLEDGE

The question, What is knowledge? has been of concern to philosophers throughout the ages. Given that we are all philosophers in making scores of decisions each day about how to act and how to solve problems, we too must consider this question. Karl Popper suggests that we do not know more today than we did thousands of years ago, because solving some problems only creates new ones. For example, medical advances have created new problems, such as overpopulation. Some people believe that nothing can be known "for sure." (This is assumed in science.) But does that mean we don't know anything? Can you jump from a high window without harm or walk through walls? Others argue that because we know nothing for sure, we really know nothing. We should follow out the logic of each position. For example the clear success of scientific methods in hundreds of areas shows that all methods are not equally effective in testing knowledge claims. If we know nothing, then what is the rationale for professional education? Exhibit 4.2 offers responses to the view that we know nothing.

Raymond Nickerson (1986) defines knowledge as information that decreases uncertainty about how to achieve a certain outcome. We can ask: "What knowledge will help us to solve problems clients confront (e.g., elder abuse, a need for reliable respite care)?" Studies of the development of assumptions about knowledge (e.g., what can be known and what cannot, how we can know, and how certain we can be in knowing) suggest a scale ranging from the belief that we can know reality with certainty by direct observation, to the view

that there is never certainty and that we must critically appraise and synthesize information from multiple sources (Kitchener, 1986). Karl Popper (1992) defines knowledge as problematic and tentative guesses about what may be true. It results from selective pressures from the real world in which our guesses come into contact with the environment through a process of trial and error (Munz, 1985). Knowledge serves different functions, only one of which is to encourage the growth of knowledge. For example Munz (1985) suggests that the function of false knowledge (beliefs that are not true and that are not questioned) is to maintain social bonds among people by protecting shared beliefs from criticism (the growth of knowledge). This may be necessary to encourage cooperation in a group. Cultures often thrive because of false knowledge. Such cultures "are doubly effective in promoting social behavior because, not being exposed to rational criticism, they enshrine emotionally comforting and solidarity-producing attitudes" (pp. 283–284). This view suggests that the growth of knowledge can only take place in certain circumstances (i.e., cultures)—those in which alternative views are entertained and all views are subject to criticism, that is, in an environment in which rationality is valued and practiced (see

EXHIBIT 4.2
Responses to Some Beliefs About Knowledge

Beliefs	Critique
There are things we just can't know.	It depends on whether a belief can be put into a testable form. Many claims can be investigated through observation and experimentation.
It's not good to be skeptical because anything is possible.	Skepticism is not synonymous with closed mindedness—quite the opposite. Being skeptical encourages rather than discourages a search for alternative possibilities.
Scientists/researchers don't know everything.	Scientists would be the first to agree. However, just because we don't know everything does not mean we don't know anything.
Some things can't be proved scientifically.	Science deals with only certain kinds of questions (those that are testable). However, many claims that some people believe are untestable can be put into a testable form.
We can't be certain of anything.	Even if this is the case, some beliefs have survived more rigorous testing than have others.
Human behavior and the mind are mysterious things.	Just because something is mysterious does not mean that it can't be explored.
Everything is relative.	Is this so? Can you walk through the walls in your home? Are there no moral guidelines for our behavior?

Source: Based on W. Gray (1991), Thinking critically about New Age ideas. Belmont, CA: Wadsworth.

EXHIBIT 4.3
Examples of Practice-Related Claims

A professor tells you: "Some people who have a problem with alcohol can learn to be controlled drinkers; abstinence is not required for all people." Do you believe her simply because she says so? If not, what other information should you seek, and why?

Your supervisor says, "Refer the client to the Altona Family Service Agency. They know how to help these clients." Would you take her advice? What questions are relevant here?

An advertisement for a residential treatment center for youth claims: "We've been successfully serving young people for more than 50 years." Would this convince you? If not, what kind of evidence would you seek, and why?

An article you read states that "grassroot community organization is not effective in alienated neighborhoods." What questions would you raise?

Glossary in Appendix 4A). Only in this way do beliefs confront the environment.

EVALUATING KNOWLEDGE CLAIMS

The most important decisions you will make in your career concern the criteria you use to evaluate the accuracy of theories and claims of effectiveness. Which criteria you decide to use influence your selection of assessment, intervention, and evaluation methods. Consider the statements in Exhibit 4.3. Your beliefs about these claims will influence your actions. *Theories* are conjectures (guesses) about what may be true. We always have theories. "There is no pure, disinterested, theory-free observation" (Popper, 1994, p. 8). We are influenced by our evolutionary history in how we see and react to the world as well as by the culture in which we have grown up. We see what we expect to see, as discussed in Chapter 5 (see also the later discussion of objectivity).

You will encounter many competing theories in your career. How will you choose among them? How will you select those most likely to be of value in helping clients attain outcomes they value? Because our theories influence our decisions, they are important to examine. Exhibit 4.4 shows some

of the differences between everyday and scientific theories.

Avoiding Harm in the Name of Helping

If you rely on false claims or theories, your clients may be harmed rather than helped; you may create false hopes; harm rather than help clients; and miss the opportunity to use effective methods. Consider Emma Eckstein, one of Sigmund Freud's patients (Masson, 1984). He attributed her complaints of stomach ailments and menstrual problems to masturbation. Freud's colleague Fleiss recommended a nose operation, based on his belief that the sexual organs and the nose were connected. Eckstein's subsequent pain and suffering then were attributed to her psychological deficiencies. The real cause was a large wad of dressing left in her nose by mistake.

Consider the many claims of effectiveness regarding intervention based on qualitative data (e.g., anecdotal case reports), that were later shown to be false, based on controlled research findings. For example, the findings of controlled—in contrast to qualitative—studies of the effects of facilitated communication (a method alleged to help nonverbal people talk) "have been consistently negative indicating that FC is neither reliably replicable nor valid when produced" (Jacobson, Mulick, & Schwartz, 1995, p. 754). These controlled studies showed that the communication alleged to be from previously nonverbal people was actually determined by the facilitators.

We rely on different criteria in different situations to evaluate claims. For example social workers rely on criteria such as intuition, testimonials, and case examples when making decisions about their clients, but want their physicians to rely on the results of controlled experimental studies and a demonstrated track record of success based on data collected systematically and regularly when making decisions about a serious medical problem that affected them (Gambrill & Gibbs, 1996). Shouldn't what is good for the goose be good for the gander? Let's take a closer look at the different criteria for evaluating claims.

QUESTIONABLE CRITERIA

Decisions that get in the way of helping clients may be made because of lack of knowledge about the limitations of commonly accepted criteria for evaluating the accuracy of claims. Questionable criteria such as popularity, testimonials, newness, or tradition do not provide sound grounds on which to accept claims, often because they consider only part of the picture (e.g., only examples that support a belief; other examples include manner of presentation and anecdotal experience; see Exhibit 4.5). Before reading the next section, review your answers to the items in Exhibit 4.1 to explore which criteria you use.

Authority

The source of the fallacy of authority is the mistaken assumption that status is correlated with accuracy. Appeals based on authority can be recognized by the assertion of a claim (e.g., play therapy is the best method to use with acting-out children) based solely on the someone's status or position, with no reference to empirical studies that provide evidence (Gibbs, 1991). Let us say that Ms. Sommers, a case manager for the elderly, tells her supervisor that she referred Mr. Rivers to the

EXHIBIT 4.4
Differences Between Lay and Scientific Theories (Guesses)

Lay Theories	Scientific Themes
Implicit (tacit, unspecified assumptions).	Explicit, clearly described, allowing criticism.
Often ambiguous and inconsistent, mutually incompatible views are held often unknowingly.	Consistent, not mutually contradictory.
Seek verification, and rely on induction (accumulation of evidence).	Seek falsification since no amount of evidence that all extroverts are sociable can prove this is so. Hunches must be tested.
Beliefs are often based on correlations confusing cause and effect.	Less likely to assume causality from correlational data through use of experimental procedures.
Content oriented (describe types and categories).	Exploratory and process oriented; alter events to test accuracy of predictions.
Focus on the individual (internal psychological causes) and tend to overlook environmental causes. Laypeople tend to be psychologists rather than sociologists (recognizing societal and structural causes).	Focus more on external (environmental causes).
Hold many minitheories (guesses) for specific events; use narrow-band theories; add "ad hoc" guesses as needed to account for unexpected findings.	Rely on a few concepts or broad principles that can account for a wide range of behavior; use broad-band theories; discard a theory as false when it cannot account for findings that another theory can account for.
Not based on trustworthy data (this does not necessarily mean they are wrong).	Based on critical thinking and discussion by many different people.

Source: Adapted from Adrian Furnham (1988), *Lay theories: Everyday understanding of problems in the social sciences* (pp. 2–7). New York: Pergamon.

EXHIBIT 4.5
Questionable Criteria for Evaluating Knowledge Claims

Criteria	Example
Authority (what do the "experts" say?)	"If Freud said it, it must be true."
Popularity (argument ad populum)	"Eighty percent of social workers use.... I'm going to use it too."
Manner of presentation	"She gave a convincing talk. I'm going to use her methods."
Experience	"I've seen five clients and used facilitated communication successfully with all of them."
Tradition	"That's the way we have always done it. We should continue to use these methods."
What's new	"Its the latest thing. We should try it, too."
Uncritical documentation	Accepting a claim based on vague, undocumented evidence.
Case examples	You present a vivid case example to support a claim. "I used narrative therapy with my client, and she improved dramatically.
Testimonials	"I believe it works because Mrs. Rivera said she tried it and it helped.
Characteristics of the person (ad hominem)	"She presents a good argument, but look at the school she graduated from."
Good intentions	In response to a question from a client about an agency's effectiveness you say: "We really care about our clients."
What makes sense	I think bioenergetics works. It makes sense.
Intuition	I just knew that support groups will be best.
Entertainment value	This is a fascinating account of depression. I think it is correct.
Emotional reactions	I trust my feelings when making decisions.

Montview Nursing Home because Dr. Lancaster told her that this home provides excellent services—even though Dr. Lancaster offered no evidence that it does. Appeals to authority are a common social persuasion strategy. For example, cereal companies often use famous baseball players to tout the many benefits of their cereals. Appeals to unfounded authority also are common in the professional literature, such as citing a famous person to support a claim when in fact he or she has not conducted any critical tests of the claim.

Popularity and Numbers

Popularity and numbers refer to the acceptance of claims simply because many people accept them. For instance, an agency may decide to adopt psychoanalytic methods because many other agencies use these methods. Here, too, the question is whether there is any evidence that popular methods are effective. Consider the increasing use of residential care for adolescents alleged to have substance abuse and psychiatric problems. Schwartz (1989) argues that there is no evidence that such programs are effective, even though huge sums of

money are spent on them. A reliance on popularity is similar to a reliance on consensus (what most people think). But what most people think may not be correct.

Tradition

Tradition (what has been done in the past) may be appealed to to support claims. For example, when asked why she was using genograms, a social worker may answer, "That's what our agency has used for the past five years." Advertisers often note how long their product has been sold, suggesting that this establishes its effectiveness. Because a method has been used for many years does not mean it is effective. In fact, it may be harmful. Consider how long the practice of bloodletting lasted. Some practice guidelines are based on what social workers say they do and what they believe is important to outcome. Testing as well as guessing call for systematic exploration to determine how well verbal reports match what actually happens and whether what helpers think is important to outcome in fact has any relationship to it.

Newness

Newness (the latest method) is often appealed to as in "We are using the new coaddiction model with all our clients." Simply because something is new or innovative does not mean it is effective. After all, everything was new at some time.

Manner of Presentation

We are often persuaded that a claim is correct by the confident manner in which it is presented. This fallacy occurs when (1) a speaker or writer claims that something is true of people or that a method is effective; (2) persuasive interpersonal skills are used (e.g., building the self-esteem of audience members, joking); and (3) the effectiveness of the method is not addressed (Gibbs, 1991). Being swayed by the style of presentation underlies persuasion by the material's entertainment value. How interesting is a practice view? Does it sound profound? Does it claim to empower clients? Here, too, the question is whether there is any evidence for the claims made.

Good Intentions

We may accept claims of effectiveness because we believe that those who make them have good intentions, that they want to help clients. But good intentions and services that help clients do not necessarily go together, as a history of the professions shows.

What Makes Sense

You may have read that expressing anger in frustrating situations is helpful in getting rid of your anger. This may make sense to you. But is it true? In fact, the research on anger suggests that it does not have this happy effect (see Averill, 1982; Tavris, 1989). Explanations always "make sense" to the person who accepts them. "People's thinking is logical if seen on its own premises" (Renstrom, Andersson, & Marton, 1990, p. 556). Whether these premises are accurate is another question. What about common sense? This may re-

fer to cultural maxims and shared beliefs or shared fundamental assumptions about the social and physical world (Furnham, 1988). One problem here is that different maxims often give contradictory advice.

Testimonials

Testimonials are reports by people who have used a product or service that that product or service is effective. For example, someone who has attended Alcoholics Anonymous may say, "I tried it and it works." The testimonial is a variant of the case example fallacy and is subject to the limitations of case examples in offering evidence for a claim. Testimonials may include detailed vivid descriptions of the method used, the distressing state of affairs prior to its use, and the positive results. Testimonials are widely used in advertising. The problem with testimonials is not that the report about an individual's personal experience with a given method is not accurate, but the further step of making a claim that this experience means that the method works.

Case Examples

In the case example fallacy, conclusions about many clients are made based on a few unrepresentative examples. The case example fallacy involves faulty generalization. What may be true in a few cases may not be at all true of many other cases. Gibbs (1991) gives three reasons why case examples so readily snare the unwary: (1) the detailed description of case examples has considerable emotional appeal, especially in comparison to the dull data from large representative samples that may be reported in the literature; (2) social workers become immersed in the details of a particular case and forget that what may be true of this case may be quite untrue of others; and (3) cases that "prove the point" can always be found. Case examples are easy to remember because they have a storylike quality. Extreme examples often are selected, also making them easy to remember, even though they are unrepresentative of other cases.

Attacking (or Praising) the Person (Ad Hominem Appeals)

Rather than address a person's argument related to a claim, the person making the claim may be attacked or praised. For example, you may suggest that an advocacy group should be made up of community residents because they already have had experience with advocacy and are eager to work together. Then another staff member may respond "But how can you say this? You haven't completed your training program yet." Rather than addressing your argument, he is commenting on your education. (This example illustrates that ad hominem appeals may function as diversions—an attempt to sidetrack people.)

Entertainment Value

Some claims are accepted simply because they are interesting, even though interest value does not indicate accuracy.

Emotional Appeals

When evaluating claims, we are easily swayed by our emotions, and politicians and advertisers take advantage of this. They may appeal to our self-pity, self-esteem, fears, and self-interest. Vivid testimonials and case examples play on your emotions. For example, a TV commercial for an alcohol treatment center may show an unkempt, depressed man with a drinking problem and describe the downward spiral allegedly caused by drinking, including the loss of job and family. We may then see him in the Detox Treatment Center, which is clean and whose staff seem caring and concerned. Next we see our client shaved, well dressed, employed, and looking happy and healthy. Words, music, and pictures may contribute to the emotive effect. Because of the commercial's emotional appeal, we may overlook the absence of evidence for the effectiveness of the Detox Treatment Center.

Experience

Professionals often appeal to their anecdotal experiences to support claims of effectiveness. (Relying on documented track record of success is quite different, as they offer a systematic record or experimental evidence.) A social worker may state, "I know cognitive behavioral methods are most effective with depressed clients because they are effective with my clients." Experience in everyday practice and beliefs based on this are the key source of what is known as *practice wisdom*. Although anecdotal experience (practice wisdom) does provide an important source of "guesses" about what is effective, it is not a sound basis for evaluating claims of effectiveness.

Problems with Learning from Experience. The key problem with relying on experience as a guide to what is accurate is the lack of comparison (Dawes, 1988). An interest in comparison is a hallmark of scientific thinking. Our experience is not a sound guide because it is often restricted and biased (see Exhibit 4.6). For example, a child welfare worker may assume that few child abusers stop abusing their children because she sees those who do not stop abusing their children more than those who do stop. Her experience with this biased sample result in incorrect inferences about the recurrence of child abuse (i.e., an overestimate). When

EXHIBIT 4.6

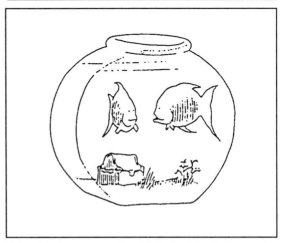

"If I'm right in my guess that this is the Atlantic, then we're the biggest fish in the world."

Source: Used with permission of Richard Guindon.

relying on experience we may not recognize that conditions have changed; that what worked in the past may no longer work in the present. For example, Western style mental health services may not be appropriate for many clients. In addition we tend to recall our successes and forget our failures. That is, we tend to selectively focus on our "hits." Unless we have kept track of both our hits and our misses we may arrive at incorrect conclusions. We tend to be overconfident of our beliefs perhaps because of our interest in predicting what happens in our world. This interest can encourage an illusion of control in which we overestimate how much control we really have. Also, as Dawes (1988) points out, we tend to create our own experience. If we are friendly, others are likely to be friendly in return. If we are hostile, others are likely to be hostile. Dawes (1988) refers to this as "self-imposed bias in our own experience" (p. 106).

Another problem with relying on experience concerns the biased nature of our memory of what happened. We tend to remember what is vivid, which often results in biased samples. We often alter views about the past to conform to current moods or views. We don't know what might have happened if another sequence of events had occurred. Overlooking this, we may unfairly praise or blame ourselves (or someone else). A social worker might say, "If only I had focused more on the teenager, Mario and his mother would have returned for a second interview." But maybe if he had concentrated more on the teenager, Mario would have walked out of the first interview. As Dawes (1988) observes out, experience lacks comparison.

Relying on experience opens us to accepting irrelevant causes. We may assume that mental illness results in homelessness because many homeless people are mentally ill. But does it? Our tendency to look for causes encourages a premature acceptance of causes that may lead us astray. So experience, while honing skills in many ways, may also have negative effects such as a reluctance to consider new ideas and an unwarranted overconfidence in the extent to which we can help clients. Indeed, one advantage of being a novice is a greater willingness to question beliefs. With all

these concerns about learning from experience, then, what should we do? As Dawes reminds us, we cannot go around conducting controlled experiments. We can, however, be cautious about generalizing from the past and present to the future. "In fact, what we often would do is to learn how to avoid learning from experiences" (1988, p. 120).

Intuition

Intuition is another criterion used to evaluate the accuracy of claims. Someone may ask, "How did you know that this method would be effective?" The answer may be: "My intuition." *Webster's New Collegiate Dictionary* (1988) defines intuition as "the direct knowing or learning of something without the conscious use of reasoning." The view that intuition involves a responsiveness to information that although not consciously represented, yields productive insights, is compatible with the differences that Dreyfus and Dreyfus (1986) found between experts and novices, one of which was that experts rely on "internalized" rules that they no longer may be able to describe. No longer remembering where we learned something encourages attributing solutions to "intuition." When asked what made you think that "Y" service would be effective, your answer may be, "Intuition." When asked to elaborate, you may offer sound reasons reflecting your knowledge of content and appropriate inference rules. That is, you used far more than uninformed hunches. Jonathan Baron defines intuition as "an unanalyzed and unjustified belief" (1994, p. 26) and argues that beliefs based on intuition may be either sound or unsound. He notes that therefore, basing beliefs on intuition may have consequences that harm people.

Although both intuition and experience may be a valuable source of ideas about what may be true, they are not a good guide to their accuracy. Relying on intuition or what "feels right" is ethically questionable when other grounds, including a critical examination of intuitive beliefs, will result in better-reasoned decisions. Intuition cannot show which method is most effective in helping clients; a different kind of evidence is required for this. Relying on intuition often means that we use only some of the information relevant to a decision. Moreover, decisions based on intuition are likely to be inconsistent. But this inconsistency may not be evident because no one keeps track of the decisions made, the grounds for making them, and their outcomes. We may not be aware of our inconsistent reliance on values and rules that we think are important. The greater the number of factors that must be considered in arriving at a well-reasoned decision and the more that is known about the relevance of considering them, the less likely is intuition to offer the best guide for decisions. Attributing judgments to "intuition" decreases the opportunities to teach practice skills; one has "it" but doesn't know how or why "it" works. If you ask your supervisor, "How did you know to do that at that time," and she says, "My intuition," this will not help you learn what to do.

Uncritical Documentation

Simply because something appears in print does not mean that it is true. Consider many of the claims in newspapers such as the *National Enquirer*. Similarly, just because a claim is accompanied by a reference is not a good reason for assuming that it is accurate. Unless the report describes the evidence for this statement, it is uncritical documentation. For all we know, this statement could be merely someone's uninformed opinion. Always ask, How do we know?

SCIENCE AND SCIENTIFIC CRITERIA

Our concern for helping and not harming clients obliges us to critically evaluate our assumptions about what is true and what is false, as well as their consequences. Relying on scientific criteria offers a way to do so. In 1991 the Council on Social Work Education called for social work curricula to be based on a scientific framework.

Misunderstandings and Misrepresentations

Surveys show that most people do not understand the basic characteristics of science (Miller, 1987;

also see Exhibit 4.7). Misunderstandings about science may result in ignoring this problem-solving method and the knowledge it has generated to help clients enhance the quality of their lives. Misunderstandings and misrepresentations of science are so common that D. C. Phillips, a philosopher of science, entitled his latest book *The Social Scientist's Bestiary: A Guide to Fabled Threats to and Defenses of Naturalistic Social Science* (1992). Even some academics confuse logical positivism (discarded by scientists long ago) and science as we know it today. Science is often misrepresented as a collection of facts or as referring only to controlled experimental studies. Many people confuse science with pseudoscience, bogus science, and scientism (see the Glossary in Appendix 4A). Some people protest that science is misused. Saying that a method is bad because it has been or may be misused is not a cogent argument. Anything can be misused including social work services. Some people believe that critical reflection is incompatible with passionate caring. Reading the writings of any number of scientists, including Loren Eiseley, Carl Sagan, Karl Popper, and Albert Einstein, should quickly put this false belief to rest. Consider a quote from Karl Popper: "I assert that the scientific way of life involves a burning interest in objective scientific theories—in the theories in themselves, and in the problem of their truth, or their nearness to truth. And this interest is a *critical* interest, an *argumentative* interest" (1994, p. 56).

Far from reinforcing myths about reality, as some claim (e.g., Karger, 1983, p. 204), science is

EXHIBIT 4.7
Misconceptions About Science

There is a search for final answers.
Intuitive thinking has no role.
It is assumed that science knows, or will soon know, all the answers.
Objectivity is assumed.
Chance occurrences are not considered.
Scientific knowledge is equivalent to scientific thinking.
The accumulation of facts is the primary goal.
Linear thinking is required.
Passion and caring have no role.
There is one kind of scientific method.
Unobservable events are not considered.

likely to question them. This is one reason that the fear of science is as old as science itself (White, 1896). Many scientific discoveries, such as Charles Darwin's theory of evolution, clashed with (and still does) some religious views of the world. Consider the church's reactions to the discovery that the earth was not the center of the universe. Only after 350 years did the Catholic church agree that Galileo was correct in stating that the earth revolves around the sun. All sorts of questions that people may not want raised may be raised such as: "Does this residential center really help residents? Would another method be more effective? Does what I'm doing really help clients? How accurate is my belief about _____?" An accurate understanding of science will help you distinguish among helpful, trivializing, and bogus uses. Bogus uses may create and maintain views of problems and proposed solutions that leave unchanged or decrease the quality of life for clients (Scheper-Hughes & Lovell, 1987).

What Is Science?

Science is a way of thinking about and investigating the accuracy of assumptions about the world. It is a process for solving problems in which we learn from our mistakes. Science rejects a reliance on authority (e.g., pronouncements by highly placed officials or professors) as a route to knowledge. Authority and science are clashing views of how knowledge can be gained.

There are many ways to do science and many philosophies of science. The terms *science* and *scientific* are sometimes used to refer to any systematic effort—including case studies, correlational studies, and naturalistic studies—to acquire information about a subject. All methods are vulnerable to certain kinds of error, which must be considered when evaluating the data they generate. Nonexperimental approaches to understanding include natural observation, as in ethology (the study of animal behavior in real-life settings), and correlational methods that use statistical analysis to investigate the degree to which events are associated. These methods are of value in suggesting promising experiments as well as when events of interest

cannot be experimentally altered or if doing so would destroy what is under investigation.

The view of science presented here, critical rationalism, is one in which the theory-laden nature of observation is assumed (i.e., our assumptions influence what we observe) and rational criticism is viewed as the essence of science (Miller, 1994; Phillips, 1987, 1992; Popper, 1972). Popper's view of science can be summed up in four steps: (1) we select a problem; (2) we try to solve it by proposing a theory as a guess about what may be true; (3) we critically discuss and test our theory, and (4) which always reveals new problems. Creative, bold guesses about what may be true are essential to the development of knowledge, especially those guesses that can be refuted; that is, you can find out whether they are false. This view of science emphasizes the elimination of errors by means of criticism: "Knowledge grows by the elimination of some of our errors, and in this way we learn to understand our problems, and our theories, and the need for new solutions" (Popper, 1994, p. 159). The growth of knowledge is not in accuracy of depiction or certainty but in an increase in universality and abstraction (Munz, 1985). That is, a better theory can account for a wider range of events. Concepts are assumed to have meaning and value, even though they are unobservable.

Scientific Statements Are Refutable/Testable

The scientific tradition is the tradition of criticism (Popper, 1994, p. 42). Karl Popper considers the critical method to be one of the great Greek inventions. Scientific statements are those that can be tested (they can be refuted). Consider the question, How many teeth are in a horse's mouth? You could speculate about this, or you could open a horse's mouth and look inside. If an agency for the homeless claims that it succeeds in finding homes for applicants within 10 days, you could accept this claim at face value or systematically gather data to see whether this claim is true.

The essence of science is creative, bold guessing and rigorous testing in a way that offers accurate information about whether a guess (conjecture or theory) is correct (Asimov, 1989). Popper argues that "the growth of knowledge, and especially of scientific knowledge, consists of learning from our mistakes" (1994, p. 93). Science is concerned with knowledge that can be pursued through the consideration of alternatives. It is assumed that we can discover approximations to the truth by means of rational argument and critical testing of theories and that the soundness of an assertion is related to the uniqueness and rigor of the relevant critical tests. A theory should describe what cannot occur as well as what can occur. If you can make contradictory predictions based on a theory, it cannot be tested. If you cannot discover a way to test a theory, it is not falsifiable. Testing may involve examining the past as in Darwin's theory of evolution. Some theories are not testable (falsifiable). There is no way to test them to find out if they are correct. Psychoanalytic theory is often criticized on the grounds that it cannot be falsified, that contradictory hypotheses can be drawn from the theory. As Karl Popper points out, irrefutability is not a virtue of a theory, but a vice. Theories can be falsified only if specific predictions are made about what can happen and also about what cannot happen.

Justification Versus Falsification. Many people accept a justificationist approach to knowledge development, focusing on gathering support for (justifying, confirming) claims and theories. Let's say that you see 3,000 swans, all of which are white. Does this mean that all swans are white? Can we generalize from the particular (seeing 3,000 swans, all of which are white) to the general, that all swans are white? Karl Popper (and others) contend that we cannot discover what is true by means of induction (making generalizations based on particular instances) because we may later discover exceptions (swans that are not white). (In fact, black swans are found in New Zealand.) Popper maintains that falsification (attempts to falsify, to discover the errors in our beliefs) by means of critical discussion and testing is the only sound way to develop knowledge (Popper, 1992; 1994). Confirmations of a theory can readily be found if one looks for them. Popper also uses the criterion of falsifiability to demark what is or could be scientific knowledge from what is not or could not be.

For example, there is no way to refute the claim that "there is a God," but there is a way to refute the claim that "assertive community outreach services for the severely mentally ill reduces substance abuse." We could, for example, randomly distribute clients to a group providing such services and compare those outcomes with those of clients receiving no services or other services. Although we can justify the selection of a theory by its having survived more risky tests concerning a wider variety of hypotheses (not been falsified), compared with other theories that have not been tested or that have been falsified, we can never accurately claim that this theory is "the truth." We can only eliminate false beliefs.

Some Tests Are More Rigorous Than Others

Some tests are more rigorous than others and so offer more information about what may be true or false. Compared with anecdotal reports, experimental tests are more severe tests of claims. Unlike anecdotal reports, they are carefully designed to rule out alternative hypotheses about what may be true and so provide more opportunities to discover that a theory is not correct. Making accurate predictions (e.g., about what service methods will help a client) is more difficult than offering after-the-fact accounts that may sound plausible (even profound) but provide no service guidelines. Theories differ in the extent to which they have been tested and in the rigor of the tests used. The question raised will suggest the research method required to explore it (Gambrill, 1995a). Every research method is limited in the kinds of questions it can address successfully. Purpose will suggest the kinds of evidence needed to test different kinds of claims. Thus, if our purpose is to communicate the emotional complexity of a certain kind of experience (e.g., the death of an infant), then qualitative methods may be needed (e.g., detailed case examples, thematic analyses of journal entries, open-ended interviews at different times).

The Search for Patterns and Regularities

It is assumed that the universe has some degree of order and consistency. This does not mean that unexplained phenomena or chance variations do not occur or are not considered. For example, chance variations contribute to evolutionary changes (Lewontin, 1991; 1994). And uncertainty is assumed. Since a future test may show an assumption to be incorrect, even one that is strongly corroborated (has survived many critical tests), no assertion can ever be proved. This does not mean that all beliefs are equally sound; some have survived more rigorous tests than have others (Asimov, 1989).

Parsimony

An explanation is parsimonious if all or most of its components are necessary to explain most of its related phenomena. Unnecessarily complex explanations may get in the way of detecting relationships between behaviors and related events. Consider the following two accounts:

1. Mrs. Lancer punishes her child because of her own unresolved superego issues related to early childhood trauma. This creates a negative disposition to dislike her oldest child.
2. Mrs. Lancer hits her child because this temporarily removes his annoying behaviors (he stops yelling) and because she does not have positive parenting skills (e.g., she does not know how to identify and reinforce acceptable behaviors).

The second account suggests specific behaviors that could be altered. It is not clear that concepts such as "unresolved superego issues" and "negative disposition" yield specific guidelines for altering complaints.

Scientists Strive for Objectivity

"What we call scientific objectivity is nothing else than the fact that no scientific theory is accepted as dogma, and that all theories are tentative and are open all the time to severe criticism—to a rational, critical discussion aiming at the elimination of errors" (Popper, 1994, p. 160). Basic to objectivity is the critical discussion of theories (eliminating errors through criticism). The theory-laden nature of

observation is assumed (see Glossary in Appendix 4A). Observation is always selective (influenced by our theories, concepts). Scientists are often wrong and find out that they are wrong by testing their predictions. In this way, better theories (those that can account for more findings) replace earlier ones. Science is conservative in its insisting that a new theory account for previous findings. (For critiques of the view that advancing knowledge means abandoning prior knowledge, see Phillips, 1987). Science is revolutionary in its calling for the overthrow of previous theories shown to be false, but this does not mean that the new theory has been established as true.

Although the purpose of science is to seek true answers to problems (statements that correspond to facts), this does not mean that we can have certain knowledge. Rather, we may say that certain beliefs (theories) have (so far) survived critical tests or have not yet been exposed to them. And some theories have been found to be false. An error "consists essentially of our regarding as true a theory that is not true" (Popper, 1992, p. 4). We can avoid error or discover it by doing all that we can to discover and eliminate falsehoods (p. 4).

A Skeptical Attitude

Scientists are skeptics. They question what others view as fact or "common sense." They ask for arguments and evidence. They do not have sacred cows.

> Science . . . is a way of thinking. . . . [It] invites us to let the facts in, even when they don't conform to our preconceptions. It counsels us to consider hypotheses in our heads and see which ones best match the facts. It urges on us a fine balance between no-holds-bared openness to new ideas, however heretical, and the most rigorous skeptical scrutiny of everything—new ideas and established wisdom. (Sagan, 1990, p. 265)

Scientists and skeptics seek criticism of their views and change their beliefs when they have good reason to do so. Skeptics are more interested in arriving at accurate answers than in not ruffling the feathers of supervisors or administrators.

Other Characteristics

Science deals with specific problems that can be solved (that can be answered with the available methods of empirical inquiry). For example, is intensive in-home care for parents of abused children more effective than the usual social work services? Is the use of medication to decrease depression in elderly people more (or less) effective than cognitive-behavioral methods? Examples of unsolvable questions are, Should punishment ever be used in raising children? Are people inherently good or evil? Saying that science deals with problems that can be solved does not mean, however, that other kinds of questions are unimportant or that a problem will remain unsolvable. New methods may be developed that yield answers to questions previously unapproachable in a systematic way. Scientific knowledge is publicly reviewed by a community. Science is collective. Scientists communicate with one another, and the results of one study inform the efforts of other scientists.

ANTISCIENCE

Antiscience refers to rejection of scientific methods as valid. For example, some people believe that there is no such thing as privileged knowledge, that is, that some is more sound than others. Typically such views are not related to a particular real-life problem and to a candid appraisal of the results of different ways of solving a problem. That is, they are not problem focused allowing a critical appraisal of competing views. Antiscience is common in academic settings (Gross & Levitt, 1994) as well as in the popular culture (e.g., John Burnham, *How Superstition Won and Science Lost*, 1987). Many people confuse science, scienticism, and pseudoscience, resulting in an antiscience stance (see Glossary in Appendix 4A). We must value truth, the search for truth, the approximation to truth through the critical elimination of error, and clarity (Popper, 1994, p. 70) in order to overcome the influence of other values (e.g., trying to appear profound by using obscure words or jargon; see also the discussion of obstacles to critical thinking in Chapter 6).

THE DIFFERENCE BETWEEN SCIENCE AND PSEUDOSCIENCE

The term *pseudoscience* refers to material that makes sciencelike claims but provides no evidence for them (see Bunge, 1984). Pseudoscience is characterized by a causal approach to evidence (weak evidence is accepted as readily as strong evidence is; see Exhibit 4.8). A critical attitude—which Karl Popper (1972) defines as a willingness and commitment to open up favored views to severe scrutiny—is basic to science, distinguishing it from pseudoscience. Indicators of pseudoscience include irrefutable hypotheses and a reluctance to revise beliefs even when confronted with relevant criticism. It makes excessive (untested) claims of contributions to knowledge. Results of a study may be referred to in many different sources until they achieve the status of a law without any additional data being gathered. Richard Gelles calls this the "Woozle Effect" (1982, p. 13). Pseudoscience is a billion-dollar industry. Products include self-help books, "subliminal" tapes, and call-in advice from "authentic psychics," who have no evidence that they accomplish what they promise (Beyerstein, 1990; Druckman & Bjork, 1991; Leahey & Leahey, 1983). Pseudoscience can be found in all fields, including multiculturalism (e.g., Oritz De Montellano, 1992).

The terms *science* and *scientific* are often used to increase the credibility of a view or approach, even though no evidence is provided to support it. The term *science* has been applied to many activ-

EXHIBIT 4.8
Hallmarks of Pseudoscience

Discourages critical examination of claims/arguments.
The trappings of science are used without the substance.
Relies on anecdotal evidence.
Is not self-correcting.
Is not skeptical.
Equates an open mind with an uncritical one.
Falsifying data are ignored or explained away.
Relies on vague language.
Is not empirical.
Produces beliefs and faith but not knowledge.
Is often not testable.
Does not require repeatability.

See, for example, Bunge, 1984; Gray, 1991.

ities in social work that in reality have nothing to do with science. Examples are "scientific charity" and "scientific philanthropy." The misuse of appeals to science to sell products or encourage certain beliefs is a form of propaganda. Prosletizers of many sorts cast their advice as based on science. They use the ideology and "trappings" of science to pull the wool over our eyes in suggesting critical tests of claims that do not exist. Classification of clients into psychiatric categories lends an aura of scientific credibility to this practice, whether or not there is any evidence that it is warranted or that it is helpful to clients (Kirk & Kutchins, 1992a).

QUACKERY

Quackery refers to the promotion and marketing, for a profit, of untested, often worthless and sometimes dangerous, health products and procedures, by either professionals or others (Jarvis, 1990; Young, 1992). Advertisers, both past and present, use the trappings of science (without the substance) to encourage consumers to buy products (Pepper, 1984). Indicators of quackery include the promise of quick cures, the use of anecdotes and testimonials to support claims, privileged power (only the great Dr. _____ knows how to _____), and secrecy (claims are not open to objective scrutiny). Natale (1988) estimated that in 1987 Americans spent $50 million on subliminal tapes, even though there is no evidence that they offer what they promise (Druckman & Bjork, 1991). For every claim supported by sound evidence, there are scores of bogus claims in advertisements, newscasts, films, TV, newspapers, and professional sources, making it a considerable challenge to resist their lures. Reasons suggested by William Jarvis (1990) for why some professionals become quacks include the profit motive (making money) and the prophet motive (enjoying adulation and discipleship resulting from a pretense of superiority).

FRAUD

Fraud is the intentional misrepresentation of the effect of certain actions (e.g., taking a medicine to alleviate depression) to persuade people to part with something of value (e.g., money). It does this by means of deception and misrepresentation (Miller & Hersen, 1992). Indeed, fraud is so extensive in some areas that special organizations have been formed and newsletters written to help consumers evaluate claims (e.g., *Health Letter* published by the Public Citizens Research Group). Fraudulent claims (often appealing to the trappings of science) may result in overlooking effective methods or being harmed by remedies that are supposed to help.

REVIEWING YOUR EDUCATIONAL ENVIRONMENTS

The aim of a professional education is to provide the values, knowledge, and skills required to address problems focused on. First, we should stop and ask: What is education? What does it mean to be a well-educated professional? What do well-educated social work students value and do? How do they reason? How do they handle conflicting interests (e.g., social control and helping clients attain outcomes they value) and competing claims of effectiveness? There is an extensive literature in education and philosophy that can help us think about these questions. One distinction is between education on the one hand and schooling and indoctrination on the other. You can use Exhibit 4.9 to review your social work program. Education is conjecture based rather than belief based. It is rationally based rather than authority based. That is, all claims, no matter who makes them, are subject to critical testing and discussion. It is contextual rather than parochial. It is self-corrective.

Education should broaden rather than narrow understanding, encourage well-reasoned beliefs, and increase success in attaining valued goals. Differences between education and schooling/indoctrination highlight the emphasis on students learning to think critically for themselves in the former rather than relying on authority as in the latter. Education requires presenting alternative views on subjects discussed, providing arguments for claims or positions, accurately describing opposing

EXHIBIT 4.9
Education Compared With Schooling and Indoctrination

Education	Schooling/Indoctrination
Conjecture based.	Belief based.
Rationally based; guesses are critically tested; errors are readily conceded.	Authority based.
Contextual (sensitive to context).	Parochial.
Critical reflection (assumptions are rigorously tested).	Uncritical reflection.
Honors standards such as clarity, relevance, breadth, and depth.	Narrow, vague, superficial.
Falsification based (ask: How can I rigorously test my assumption?; How can I falsify this conjecture?).	Justification based (ask, How can I support my claims?).
Problem focused (on removing complaints of clients and significant others).	Professionally focused (on what professionals want or find entertaining).
Self-corrective.	Not self-corrective.
Problem seeking.	Problem hiding.
Students learn to think for themselves to be "reasonable and exercise good judgment while remaining cautious and open minded" (Lipman, 1991, p. 145).	Insistence on being conventional; conforming in thought and action.
A high percentage of functional content (content that helps social workers help their clients).	A high percentage of inert content.
Integrated.	Fragmented (e.g., in relation to field and class or interrelated levels of intervention).
Data are used to critically test and correct theory.	Guess and guess again.
Concepts and theories are clearly described.	Concepts/theories remain vague.
Discordant views are welcomed.	Discordant views are punished (e.g., ridiculed) or ignored (e.g., censored).
Assume that the essence of education is critical inquiry.	Assume that the essence of education is a well-stocked and conforming mind.
View knowledge as tentative.	View knowledge as certain.
Students are active, critical inquirers.	Students are passive.

E. Gambrill (1996), Thinking critically about social work education. Address to annual program meeting, Council on Social Work Education, Washington, DC, February 16.

points of view, questioning accepted views, and offering sound reasons for doing so. Knowledge is viewed as tentative, ambiguous, and hard to get. Both students and instructors are critically reflective (not just reflective) and reasonable. Understanding is emphasized, rather than memorizing. The interest is in educating minds, not in training memories (Perkins, 1992). Discordant points of view have a quite different fate in education compared to indoctrination. They are welcomed in the former and punished or censored in the latter. A teaching evaluation for exploring the degree to which your instructors provide an educational climate can be found in *Critical Thinking for Social Workers: A Workbook* (Gibbs & Gambrill, 1996).

Only a percentage of relevant knowledge that could be presented will be during your education as a social worker. In addition, small or large amounts of inert content [information that is not accompanied by procedural (how to) knowledge] and irrelevant content will be offered. Educators may not base their teaching on instructional methods known to be helpful in acquiring knowledge and skills (Gagne, 1987). (Components of effective skill training programs are described in Chapter 21.) One study shows that on average, students have only three opportunities each year to observe a staff member interview a client (Barth & Gambrill, 1984). The better your learning and critical thinking skills (see Chapter 6) are, the more likely you will discover "what's missing" (e.g., alternative views and helpful facts). For example, you could ask instructors: Are there alternative explanations that allow more accurate prediction and result in more effective plans? Does anyone disagree with this view?

> The function of education is to teach one to think intensively and to think critically.
> Martin Luther King, Jr., *What manner of man*, c. 1958.

Cultivate Helpful Beliefs About Learning

Acquiring a thorough knowledge of a subject usually requires time, effort, and a willingness to examine our assumptions. "The problem of producing an expert may be not so much in selecting someone who has special capability, but to create and maintain the motivation needed for long-continued training" (Chi, Glaser, & Farr, 1988, p. xxxv). Effective learners believe that knowing and understanding are products of their own efforts and intellectual processes. They believe they have control over how much they learn. Beliefs that promote learning include the following: (1) effort and persistence are required to gain knowledge; (2) we can gain knowledge and solve many problems if we make the effort; (3) knowledge is not certain; (4) we can acquire knowledge by thinking critically for ourselves, not just by relying on authorities (Nickerson, 1988–1989); and (5) "the growth of knowledge depends entirely on the existence of disagreement" (Popper, 1994, p. 34).

Beliefs like "If I don't understand right away, I never will" and "Conflict is bad and should be avoided" are obstacles to learning. Let's say that you believe that "you are master of your fate" and that your instructor presents empirical evidence suggesting that environmental factors influence behavior. There is a conflict here. One useful step is to recognize that part of learning is dealing with the conflict of ideas. Ask yourself, "Can I offer a well-reasoned argument for my point of view that is compatible with what is known and that is stronger than the arguments for other views?" Learning requires hard work; clarifying and understanding other points of view require time and effort.

Critically Assess Your Practice Values, Knowledge, and Skills

You are more likely to continue to learn your career if you critically examine your career values, skills, and knowledge. Helping clients may require

gaining new knowledge and skills and winnowing out misleading beliefs and skills that are not useful. Basic to this process is a willingness to challenge what you believe and do, viewing theories and skills as tools to be judged by their value in helping clients. Your beliefs will affect how easy it is to understand new concepts. They may be more or less compatible with new perspectives. Many beliefs are implicit rather than explicit, making the task more difficult. You cannot very well alter a belief you don't know you have.

Cultivate Valuable Learning Skills

You will learn more if you use an active learning style, in which you question what you read, summarize points, look for alternative explanations, seek specific examples of general statements, and ask questions such as "How could this be applied?"; "Is this useful?" Question the "obvious" to avoid premature closure and routinized ways of acting (a mindless approach) that may harm rather than help your clients. Effective and creative thinkers are open to new possibilities; they critically evaluate their beliefs. They do not think there is anything wrong with being undecided, changing their mind, or questioning authorities (Weisberg, 1986). Differences between deep and superficial learning approaches include the following:

The deep approach involves:

- The intention to understand.
- Actively engaging with content.
- Relating concepts to everyday experience.
- Relating new ideas to previous knowledge.
- Relating evidence to conclusions.
- Examining an argument's logic.

The surface approach involves:

- Focusing on completing assignments.
- Memorizing information.
- Failing to distinguish principles from examples.
- Treating a task as an external imposition.

- Focusing on discrete elements without integrating them.
- Not thinking about your purpose or situation. (Entwistle, 1987, p. 16)

Reviewing how much you understand about what you hear or read and relating new ideas to practice increase learning. Learning requires challenging what you do and think—asking questions such as "Are there other explanations?" Our tendency to seek material that confirms our views and to ignore contradictory material highlights the importance of active learning.

Take advantage of steps known to be helpful when learning a skill: (1) clear description of skills required to attain valued outcomes, including intermediate steps (designing a learning hierarchy); (2) assessment of pre-training competency levels (baselines); and (3) design of an individually tailored training program using model presentation, rehearsal, and feedback. Learn to be your own best critic (i.e., a constructive one, as all critics should be), and arrange prompts (cues) and positive feedback for valued behaviors (see Chapter 22).

Take Advantage of Useful Material and Training Opportunities

Effective practice requires updating your knowledge and skills. You will need skills to gain access to helpful material, as well as values and strategies to help you to ferret out biases and misconceptions. You can discover promising assessment, intervention, and evaluation options by reading practice-related literature. Too many helpers believe too soon that no more information is available that offers valuable planning guidelines or that more does exist but there is no time to find it. Whether you find useful material depends on your learning skills and knowing what to look for and where to look and having clear objectives. Focus on content that decreases uncertainty about how to help clients.

Reviews evaluating the cumulative findings in an area are helpful. Learn how to evaluate the quality of reviews or seek the advice of someone whose evaluations are sound. Collections of abstracts are another source of information (e.g., *Social Work Abstracts, Psychological Abstracts*), as are handbooks such as the *Handbook of Family Violence* (Van Hasselt, Morrison, Bellack, & Hersen, 1987) and the *Handbook of Behavior Therapy in Education* (Witt, Elliott, & Gresham, 1988). University continuing-education programs and conventions of professional organizations offer courses and workshops. Although research on continuing education indicates that the effects of training programs are often modest (see Eisenberg, 1986), effective learning skills increase the likelihood of learning and using new knowledge on the job. Your agency should provide needed training programs or refer staff to them (e.g., LaVigna et al., 1994). Ideally, you should have access to interactive computer programs designed to enhance valuable competencies based on formats known to enhance learning. Effective information retrieval skills are also necessary. You can file material by problem, keeping useful assessment forms, resources available, and procedural descriptions in each file.

Be Critical. Critical thinking values and skills will help you to distinguish the wheat from the chaff whether reading, listening or thinking (see Chapter 6). We tend to be impressed with material that is high sounding and unintelligible, even though difficulty may be unrelated to (or negatively correlated with) informative value (see the classic example by Naftulin, Ware & Donnelly, 1973). Armstrong (1980) suggests we spend more time trying to understand obtuse compared to clear content and rationalize our investment by believing that the material is worthwhile. Questions to keep in mind include the following:

1. Is the content potentially relevant? If so, in relation to what outcomes?
2. Is relevant literature referred to?
3. Are concepts clearly defined?
4. Is the derivation of concepts from a theory clear and appropriate?
5. Can the variables be altered in practice situations?

6. Are the data collection methods clearly described?

7. Are measures valid and reliable?

8. Is the study design clearly described?

9. Is the study design adequate? (For example, are needed control groups included? Were subjects randomly selected and distributed to groups?)

10. Are the data collection methods free of sample bias?

11. Are the intervention methods clearly described (who, what, where, when, how long, etc.)?

12. Is there any evidence that the service was offered as planned?

13. Is it likely that the intervention caused the changes? Are alternative explanations likely?

14. Were the changes impressive?

15. Is the data analysis appropriate?

16. Were there any negative effects?

17. Are follow-up data available?

18. Can the findings be generalized to other situations?

Be Charitable. "The principle of charity requires that we look for the best, rather than the worst, possible interpretation of the material we are studying" (Scriven, 1976, p. 71). Unless you are charitable as well as critical, you may overlook valuable material. Make it a habit to look beyond labels (e.g., behavioral, psychoanalytic) to the value of the content.

Getting the Most Out of Supervision

The quality of your supervision will influence what you learn. Field experiences often, if not typically, do not include the detailed guidance and feedback required for learning (experience alone does not necessarily improve performance) (Dawes, 1988). Some of the questions to raise are

• How informed is your supervisor about empirically based assessment, intervention, and evaluation methods related to the problems addressed?

• How effective is your supervisor as a teacher and coach?

• To what extent are educational formats used that contribute to learning (e.g., Gagne, 1985, 1987)?

• How dependable is your supervisor in giving you agreed-on supervision?

• How often does your supervisor give you feedback based on direct observation of your work (e.g., on a community task force) or review of audio or videotapes of your exchanges with clients?

You will get more out of supervision if you identify specific competencies you want to acquire, describe intermediate steps between current and desired performance levels, request information, seek clarification, and offer positive feedback for valued supervisory behaviors (for more details, see Drury, 1984; Kadushin, 1992). Both Hawthorne (1975) and Kadushin (1968) describe "games" that supervisors and the supervised play. Well-designed quality assurance programs pay careful attention to identifying, monitoring, and providing supportive contingencies for valued supervisory behaviors (LaVigna et al, 1994; McClanahan & Krantz, 1993). They are characterized by "feedback reciprocity," in which feedback is offered not just down the line (e.g., from supervisor to line staff) but also up the line (e.g., from line staff to supervisors).

SUMMARY

Thinking about knowledge and how to get it is vital to being a responsible professional interested in helping clients and not harming them. The history of the helping professions shows that professionals can harm as well as help. Some social workers rely on authority—that is, what high-status people say—as a guide. Others rely on popularity or tradition (what's usually done). These criteria do not provide sound guides about accuracy. A falsification (in contrast to justification) approach to knowledge will help you to counter the tendency to search only for data that confirm your views and to ignore data that do not. This requires searching for alternative hypotheses through critical testing or discussion. Based on what you learn from this criticism, you may make better guesses in the future (i.e., those that are closer to the truth). Sound criteria include well-reasoned arguments and critical tests that suggest that one option is more likely than another to result in valued outcomes. Effective learning skills include being both a critical and a charitable consumer. You are more likely to acquire additional knowledge and skills if you take an active approach to what you read or hear and believe that you can influence how much you learn.

REVIEWING YOUR COMPETENCIES

Reviewing What You Know

1. Give examples of harm to clients as a result of actions based on unfounded claims.
2. Describe a relativist view of knowledge and the conclusions that follow from it.
3. Describe a scientific approach to knowledge.
4. Define science.
5. List five common misconceptions about science.
6. Discuss the difference between science and pseudoscience.
7. Explain why the word *proof* should be avoided (though not, however, as applied to mathematics).
8. Describe the advantages of a falsification approach to knowledge, compared with a justification approach.
9. Give examples of negative effects on clients of a justification approach to knowledge.
10. Discuss why parsimonious explanations are important.
11. Give an example of the use of scientific problem solving (e.g., testing a claim of effectiveness).
12. Discuss the assertion that there is no such thing as objectivity.
13. List some of the indicators of quackery.
14. Give examples of appeals to authority.
15. Give examples of the use of testimonials, and describe their limitations in evaluating claims.
16. Give examples of appeals to tradition and popularity.
17. Give examples of ad hominem arguments, and explain why they provide questionable grounds for evaluating claims.
18. Discuss the differences between education and indoctrination/schooling.
19. Discuss the statement "No evidence will sway the true believer."
20. Describe helpful beliefs about learning.
21. Describe the difference between active and passive learning.

Reviewing What You Do

1. You ask questions that permit sound appraisal of the accuracy of claims.
2. Your written and spoken communications show that you are a charitable yet critical consumer of the professional literature.
3. Your selection of practice methods shows that you can distinguish between pseudoscience and science.
4. You rely on sound rather than questionable criteria when making practice decisions. (See for example Exercise 1 in Gibbs & Gambrill, 1996).
5. A review of your written and spoken communications shows that you understand the differences between the accuracy of a belief and the intensity with which it is held.
6. You ask questions that help you evaluate what you read in the professional literature.
7. You find scientific research related to problems of concern to your clients and creatively and correctly apply the findings to your work with your clients.
8. You accurately describe your skill levels in relation to specific service goals.
9. You accurately evaluate the extent to which your social work programs provide an education rather than indoctrination.
10. You accurately critique the instructional soundness of educational programs (e.g., determine whether they enhance learning).
11. You are not "taken in" by slick human service advertisements that use testimonials and other weak appeals.

Reviewing Results

1. Your practice skills increase each year, as determined by a review of the methods you use and the service goals you achieve.

APPENDIX A   GLOSSARY

Antiscience: Rejection of scientific methods as valid.

Critical discussion: "Essentially a comparison of the merits and demerits of two or more theories (usually more than two). The merits discussed are, mainly, the *explanatory power* of the theories . . . the way in which they are able to solve our problems of explaining things, the way in which the theories cohere with certain other heavily valued theories, their power to shed new light on old problems and to suggest new problems. The chief demerit is inconsistency, including inconsistency with the results of experiments that a competing theory can explain" (Popper, 1994, pp. 160–161).

Cynicism: A negative view of the world and what can be learned about it.

Eclecticism: The view that we should adopt whatever theories of methodologies are useful in inquiry, no matter what their source and without undue worry about their consistency.

Empiricism: The position that all knowledge (usually excluding that which is logical or mathematical) is in some way "based on" experience. Adherents of empiricism differ markedly over what the "based on" amounts to—"starts from" and "warranted in terms of" are, roughly, at the two ends of the spectrum of opinion (Phillips, 1987, p. 203).

False knowledge: Beliefs that are not true and that are not questioned (Munz, 1985).

Falsification approach to knowledge: The view that we can discover only what is false, not what is true.

Hermeneutics: "The discipline of interpretation of textual or literary material, or of meaningful human actions" (Phillips, 1987, p. 203).

Justification approach to knowledge: The view that we can discover the truth by seeking support for our theories.

Knowledge: Problematic and tentative guesses about what may be true (Popper, 1992, 1994); "guess work disciplined by rational criticism" (1992, p. 40). Criticism is "the crucial quality of knowledge" (Munz, 1985, p. 49).

Logical positivism: The main tenet of logical positivism is the verifiability principle of meaning: "Something is meaningful only if it is verifiable empirically (i.e., directly, or indirectly, via sense experiences) or if it is a truth of logic or mathematics" (Phillips, 1987, p. 204). The reality of theoretical entities is denied.

Nonjustificationist epistemology: The view that knowledge is not certain. It is assumed that although some claims of knowledge may be warranted, no warrant is so firm that it is not open to question (see Karl Popper's writings).

Paradigm: "A theoretical framework that influences the problems that are regarded crucial, the ways these problems are conceptualized, the appropriate methods of inquiry, the relevant standards of judgement, etc." (Phillips, 1987, p. 205).

Phenomenology: "The study of, in depth, of how things appear in human experience" (Phillips, 1987, p. 205).

Postmodernism: Disputes assumptions of science and its products. All grounds for knowledge claims are considered equally questionable (see for example, Rosenau, 1992; Munz, 1992).

Postpositivism: The approach to science that replaced logical positivism decades ago (see for example, Phillips, 1987, 1992).

Pseudoscience: Material that makes sciencelike claims but provides no evidence for them.

Quackery: The promotion of products and procedures known to be false or which are untested for a profit (Pepper, 1984).

Rationality: An openness to criticism. "A limitless invitation to criticism is the essence of rationality" (Munz, 1985, p. 50). Rationality consists of making mistakes and eliminating error by natural selection (p. 16).

Relativism: Relativists "insist that judgments of truth are always relative to a particular framework or point of view" (Phillips, 1987, p. 206). This point-of-view prevents criticism from outside a closed circle of believers.

Science: A process designed to develop knowledge by critically discussing and testing theories.

Scientific objectivity: Scientific objectivity is solely the critical approach (Popper, 1994, p. 93). It is based on mutual rational criticism in which high standards of clarity and rational criticism are valued (Popper, 1994, p. 70). See also Critical discussion.

Scientism: A term used "to indicate slavish adherence to the methods of science even in a context where they are inappropriate" and "to indicate a false or mistaken claim to be scientific" (Phillips, 1987, p. 206). Scientism refers to the view that "authority should be conferred upon knowledge and the knower, upon science and the scientists, upon wisdom and the wise man, and upon learning and the learned" (Popper, 1992, p. 33).

Skepticism: A provisional approach to claims; the careful examination of all claims.

Theory: Myths, expectations, guesses, and conjectures about what may be true. A theory always remains hypothetical or conjectural. "It always remains guesswork. And there is no theory that is not beset with problems" (Popper, 1994, p. 157).

Theory ladenness (of perception): "The thesis that the process of perception is theory-laden in that the observer's background knowledge (including theories, factual information, hypotheses, and so forth) acts as a 'lens' helping to 'shape' the nature of what is observed" (Phillips, 1987, p. 206).

Truth: "An assertion is true if it corresponds to or agrees with, the facts (Popper, 1994, p. 174). We can never be sure that our guesses are true. "Though we can never justify the claim to have reached truth, we can often give some very good reasons, or justifications, why one theory should be judged as nearer to it than another" (Popper, 1994, p. 161).

CHAPTER 5

A Problem-Focused Model Based on Critical Inquiry

OVERVIEW

This chapter describes a problem-focused practice model based on critical inquiry that grounds professional decisions on client concerns and draws on related literature concerning problem solving and decision making. Helping clients, like life itself, involves solving problems. Problem-solving phases and related decisions are described as are obstacles to making sound decisions. Being forewarned is being prepared. If you are aware of obstacles and know how to avoid them, you and your clients are more likely to succeed in attaining outcomes clients value.

You Will Learn About

- Advantages of grounding practice on client concerns.
- The relationship between problems and decisions.
- What we know about problem solving.
- Barriers to problem-solving.

ADVANTAGES OF GROUNDING PRACTICE AND CLIENT CONCERNS

A problem-focused model based on critical inquiry will help you to fulfill the hallmarks of professionals described in the philosophy of practice in Chapter 1. Clients, whether individuals, families, groups, organizations, or communities, have real-life problems. Clients may need concrete services such as housing, food, or health care. Family caregivers of elderly relatives may need respite care and information about different kinds of resources. Residents of an inner-city neighborhood may need guidance in how to influence the agenda of local board meetings. A person with a developmental disability may need help locating a job. Analyzing social issues often involves trying to solve social problems such as unemployment, lack of health care, and violence. We are all engaged in problem solving on an everyday basis. Karl Popper views problem solving as our primal activity, one needed for our very survival. He views evolution as the history of problem solving. Based on our trial solutions we eliminate certain errors and are confronted with new problems. Asking "What problem am I trying to solve?" will help you to avoid unpromising directions and activities such as getting caught up in how to define words. A problem focus grounds practice activities on outcomes of concern to clients (see Exhibit 5.1). Always the question would be, "Will this perspective or action help me to help my clients by, for example, considering alternative views?" Focusing on problems of concern to clients and/or significant others in no way implies that client strengths are overlooked. This incomplete approach and its undesirable effects (e.g., blaming clients for their problems and overlooking environmental causes) are critiqued throughout this book. It would be a poor problem solver indeed who did not take advantage of personal and environmental resources.

The problem-focused model described emphasizes the importance of critically reviewing assumptions and drawing on the scientific literature to inform practice decisions including material concerning problem solving, critical thinking, and professional decision making. This literature describes the errors we tend to make regardless of our intelligence and steps we can take to avoid them to maximize problem-solving success. It highlights the importance of considering the context in which problems occur including constraints that limit options. A problem focus highlights key decisions involved across all service levels and common questions, actions, needed resources, and common errors in different problem-solving phases. It grounds practice in the details of real-life concerns. This kind of grounding is needed to critically test guesses about what knowledge is helpful. Medicine has taken the lead in exploring the value of problem-focused education (see, for example, Barrows, 1994). A problem focus encourages a community of inquiry in which different approaches to problems are critically reviewed—a community in which we recognize the many ways we fool ourselves and are fooled by others. It highlights that we are all equal in our vast ignorance and emphasizes the value of clashing points of view out of which new knowledge may emerge if critically explored in an atmosphere of mutual respect and keen interest in other points of view. It serves as a guide to how precise we have to be. Sir Karl

EXHIBIT 5.1
Advantages of a Problem-Focused Practice Model

1. Grounds educational and professional activity on problems of concern to clients.
2. Evaluates effectiveness by the degree to which outcomes clients value are achieved and outcomes that harm clients are minimized.
3. Encourages use of knowledge about problem solving.
4. Emphasizes the value of criticism.
5. Emphasizes the value of functional knowledge (that which decreases uncertainty about how to attain valued outcomes).
6. Emphasizes the importance of assessment of knowledge, skills, and values.
7. Discourages irrelevant activities/discussion.
8. Discourages the active promotion of ignorance/pseudoscience/quackery.
9. Helps you to deal constructively with uncertainty and less-than-hoped-for success.
10. Is useful in discovering the level of precision/knowledge/skills/time required to solve a problem.
11. Helps us to discover which problems we can solve and which ones we cannot solve.
12. Encourages generalization of values, knowledge, and skills (e.g., from class to field).
13. Highlights how ethical principles apply to particular cases.
14. Encourages contextual understanding (e.g., links between personal problems and social issues).
15. Emphasizes the importance of resources and their allocations in problem solving.
16. Emphasizes the importance of learning-how-to-learn skills.
17. Forges closer links between field and class.
18. Forges closer links between different parts of the curriculum (research, practice, policy, management practices, and ethics).
19. Encourages a focus on education in contrast with indoctrination.

Popper (1994) suggests that we should never be more precise than we have to be when trying to solve problems. For example, why bother collecting more detailed information about the circumstances of a homeless family if this will be of no value whatsoever in helping this family (even in offering support as a listener)?

THE RELATIONSHIP BETWEEN PROBLEMS AND DECISIONS

Problems involve gaps between some current and desired state of affairs. Solving problems requires making decisions about the reasons related to gaps between current and desired situations and what

plans are most promising to close them (see Exhibit 5.2). This is true whether you are considering a social policy, helping a community gain better services, helping family members resolve disagreements, or working with depressed single parents. A major purpose of this book is to increase your awareness of the decisions you make so that you make decisions that are most likely to result in outcomes clients value. You and your clients decide how to define problems (e.g., is lack of a job due to lack of job skills and/or limited employment opportunities), who to involve, what data to collect and how to gather it, how to evaluate the accuracy of data gathered, and how to integrate it. You make decisions about what causes to focus on, what outcomes to select, what plans are most promising, and

EXHIBIT 5.2
Decision Making Map

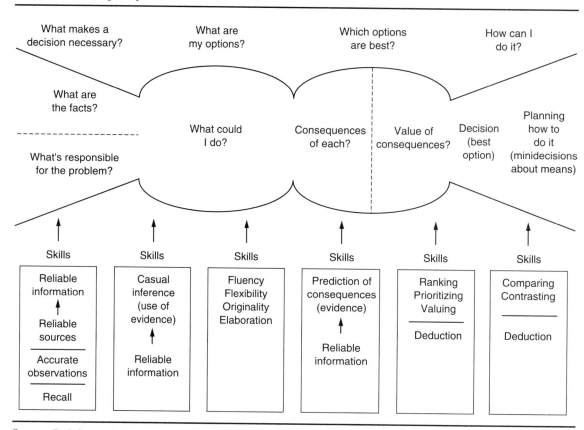

Source   R. J. Swartz & D. N. Perkins (1990). *Teaching thinking: Issues and approaches* (p. 158). Pacific Grove, CA: Critical Thinking Press.

how to evaluate progress. Decisions include moment-to-moment ones about what to say next. Different decisions and problems involve different levels and kinds of uncertainty and conflicting interests and may require different kinds of information. Decisions may guide behavior well or poorly in relation to outcomes clients value.

Decisions and Options (Menus)

Decision making requires making choices among different (often competing) courses of action (Rachlin, 1989). You may have to decide whether lack of concrete resources is related to lack of information, poor marketing of services, policies restricting resource access, lack of skills needed to attain resources, or beliefs that interfere with accepting help. The way you and your clients frame gaps between current and desired circumstances will influence decisions. For example, our decisions tend to be more extreme when they are posed in terms of possible losses rather than gains (Slovic, Fischhoff, & Lichtenstein, 1982). You and your clients may have to decide whether to seek valued outcomes through efforts of the client alone or to involve other clients with similar concerns in a joint effort. The list of options (the "menu") related to a decision differ in number, variety, and whether they include feasible options that will help clients to attain outcomes they value. Exhibit 5.3 illustrates decisions you will make and options you may consider. Cultural differences may influence the attractiveness of different options.

Lists of options (menus) differ in their "noise level" (number and vividness of irrelevant and misleading options). Misleading items may be included (those that will take you and your clients in unhelpful directions). For example, invalid standardized scales that do not measure what they presume to measure may be relied on. This decreases the likelihood of understanding problems and selecting effective plans. It may mislead both you and your clients about the nature of problems and related circumstances. You may, for example, incorrectly attribute the cause of problems to psychological characteristics of the client and overlook environmental causes. Valuable options may be missing. When I

ask students what sources of data they draw on they often list client self-report, reports from significant others, other professionals' opinions, the results of standardized paper and pencil tests (another form of self-report), and case records in which data from one or more of these sources are described. Observation in role-play or real-life settings and self-monitoring (clients or significant others collect data in real-life settings) are rarely mentioned. If these methods would increase the likelihood of understanding problems and selecting effective plans, then this list of options is incomplete.

Valuable options may be included but not be possible to pursue, perhaps because of limited resources. This may make it impossible to close the gap between current and desired circumstances. You and your clients may be forced to rely on some modest approximation. For example, rather than helping community members to organize to improve the quality of their neighborhood you may have to settle for the more modest goal of helping residents to make their homes more secure from crime because of lack of funds. Low potential to close gaps (resolve problems) presents unique challenges to social workers and their clients. Your background knowledge (your beliefs about what is useful) and skills in carrying out involved tasks (e.g., helping community members participate effectively in board meetings) will influence success.

What Is a Good Decision?

As Jonathan Baron (1994) points out, the whole point of good thinking is to increase the probability of good outcomes (true conclusions). A good outcome is one that the decision maker likes. Good decision makers "do the best they can with what is knowable." Clearly this is not always done. Herek, Janis, and Huth (1989) examined the thinking of U.S. presidents (and their advisers) in making decisions related to international crises. They noted the following indicators of defective decision making based on a review of historical records:

1. Gross omissions in surveying alternatives (inadequate search for possibilities).

EXHIBIT 5.3
Examples of Decisions and Options

Decision	Options (examples)	Decision	Options (examples)
What kind of problem it is	Lack of concrete resources Lack of information Lack of skills Emotional/affective Lack of social support Interpersonal (between people) Within the person Decision problem Transition problem Culture conflict Discrimination/oppression Group process Community problem Service system problem Public and social policy problem	How to integrate data	Sequentially review data Try to examine all data at once Rely on intuition Use an "expert" computer-based program Consult the professional literature
What theory to draw on	Psychoanalytic Cognitive Family systems Social learning Life span developmental Contextual	What to do if you do not have resources to help clients attain outcomes they value	Offer support Refer elsewhere Help clients form self-help advocacy groups "Problem shift" (focus on another area) Pretend you do and forge ahead
What to explore to find out what kind of problem it is	Psychological characteristics Biological factors Family environment Community influences Cultural differences Material circumstances Recent events Service system Public and social policies Political, social, and economic influences	What intervention level(s) to focus on	Individual Family Community Service system Public and social policy
How to explore (i.e., what kinds of assessment data to rely on)	Self-report in interview Standardized tests Self-monitoring Observation in role plays Observation in real life Physiological measures Case records	How to evaluate progress	Your opinion Self-report of clients Self-report by significant others Standardized questionnaires Observation of behavior in role play Observation of behavior in problem-related real-life settings Archival records Pre-post data Review of data collected following service
How to evaluate claims	Rely on common sense Authority Manner of presentation (e.g., confidence with which views are expressed) Intuition Tradition Consensus (what most people believe) Testimonials/case examples Anecdotal experience Systematically collected data regarding degree of success Scientific criteria (e.g., critical tests of claims)	How to encourage generalization and maintenance of positive outcomes	Train and hope Involve significant others Focus on behaviors of value to clients in real-life Focus on behaviors that will continue to be reinforced in real-life settings Shift to naturally occurring schedules of reinforcement Provide relapse training

2. Gross omissions in surveying objectives (inadequate search for goals).

3. Failure to examine major costs and risks of the preferred choice (inadequate search for evidence).

4. Selective bias in processing information (biased interpretation).

Studies of decision making in professional contexts reveal a variety of common errors such as incorrect definition of problems (e.g., missing physical causes) and selection of treatments that are ineffective or harmful (see, for example, Kassirer & Kopelman, 1991). Many of these errors occur because of reliance on questionable criteria for evaluating the accuracy of claims.

WHAT WE KNOW ABOUT PROBLEM SOLVING

There is a rich literature on problem-solving lying in many different fields (see, for example, Voss, 1989). Literature on problem solving indicates that:

- Problem definition is a critical phase.
- Creative as well as critical thinking is required.
- We readily fall into a number of "intelligence traps."
- Experts organize knowledge in a different way than novices and approach problems from a more abstract level.
- Some ways of structuring problems are better than others.
- Jumping to conclusions (deciding on one option too soon) and overlooking promising alternatives are common errors.
- Ability to learn from experiences is important (not experience per se).
- The rules of thumb (strategies) we use influence our success.
- We may have the tools (skills and knowledge) required to solve problems but not use them.
- Monitoring progress is important (e.g., to catch false directions).

- Both problem-related knowledge and self-knowledge influence success.
- Beliefs about what knowledge is and how to get it influence success.
- Errors of both omission and commission occur.
- How we allocate our resources influences success (e.g., time spent in overall planning).
- We can learn to become better problem solvers.

Successful compared to unsuccessful problem solvers think more about their thinking. They critically review their assumptions and reasoning. They are their own best critics. They ask questions about the accuracy of data. They ask: What evidence supports this claim? Has it been critically tested? With what results? Are there plausible alternative views?

Problem Solving Is Uncertain

Defining problems and making decisions in the helping professions is an uncertain activity. Uncertainty may concern: (1) the nature of the problem; (2) the outcomes desired; (3) what is needed to attain valued outcomes; (4) likelihood of attaining outcomes; and (5) measures that will best reflect degree of success. The requirements of a rational model of problem solving and decision making in which we estimate the probability that each alternative will yield hoped-for outcomes, assign values to different options, and select the alternative with the greatest value are often impossible to satisfy. Information about options may be missing, and accurate estimates of the probability that different alternatives will result in desired outcomes may be unknown. We work under environmental constraints such as time pressures. Preferences may change in the very process of being asked about them. Problems that confront clients (e.g., lack of housing or day care) are often difficult ones that challenge the most skilled of helpers. They are often unstructured and untidy (Adams, 1986). Rarely is all relevant information available, and it is difficult to integrate different kinds of data. Knowledge may be available but not used.

Poorly defined problems may have a variety of

solutions. Even when a great deal is known, this knowledge is usually in the form of general principles that do not allow specific predictions about individuals (Dawes, 1994a). For example, even though 62% of convicted rapists rape again when released from prison, this does not allow you to accurately predict whether a particular person will rape again if released. You can only appeal to the general information. Physicians usually work in a state of uncertainty about the true state of the patient (Sox, Blatt, Higgins, & Marton, 1988, p. 6). They can only estimate the probability that a client has a certain illness. We are willing to (and must often) settle for less than the best. We often *satisfice* (select the first minimally acceptable plan) rather than search for an optimal alternative.

Creativity and Intuition Play an Important Role

Successful problem solvers draw on their creative talents to discover options for solving problems.

> The scientist and the artist, far from being engaged in opposed or incompatible activities, are both trying to extend our understanding of experience by the use of creative imagination subjected to critical control, and so both are using irrational as well as rational faculties. Both are exploring the unknown and trying to articulate the search and its findings. Both are seekers after truth who make indispensable use of intuition. (Magee, 1985, p. 68–69)

Styles, attitudes, and strategies associated with creativity include:

- Readiness to explore and to change.
- Attention to problem finding as well as problem solving.
- Immersion in a task.
- Restructuring of understanding.
- A belief that knowing and understanding are products of one's intellectual efforts.
- Withholding of judgment.
- An emphasis on understanding.
- Thinking in terms of opposites.

- Valuing complexity, ambiguity, and uncertainty combined with an interest in finding order.
- Valuing feedback but not deferring to convention and social pressure.
- Recognizing multiple perspectives on a topic (based on Greeno, 1989; Nickerson, Perkins, & Smith, 1985; Weisberg, 1986).

Domain-Specific Knowledge and Skills Are Important

Content knowledge includes facts, concepts, principles, and strategies that contribute to problem solving. Procedural knowledge includes the skills required to implement content knowledge. Let's say that you have been asked to help homeless people form self-help groups. What facts may be important to know? What theories and concepts will be helpful? What skills do you need to use this knowledge effectively? Studies of decision making among physicians highlight the importance of knowledge of content related to problems. The "possession of relevant bodies of information and a sufficiently broad experience with related problems to permit the determination of which information is pertinent, which clinical findings are significant, and how these findings are to be integrated into appropriate hypotheses and conclusions" were foundation components related to competence in clinical problem solving (Elstein et al., 1978, p. x–xi). As Nickerson (1988) points out, "The importance of domain-specific knowledge to thinking is not really debatable. To think effectively in any domain one must know something about the domain and, in general, the more one knows the better" (p. 13). Research in problem solving shows that knowledge that could be helpful may remain unused (inert). We may not remember what we know or transfer useful strategies from one area to another. Perhaps we never knew or understood useful facts, concepts, principles, or strategies in the first place. Content knowledge without performance skills to put this into use remains unused. This is known as the "parroting problem"; we can describe what should be done to solve a problem but cannot put this knowledge into effect.

Problem Solving Involves Different Interrelated Phases

We can draw on what is known about problem solving to refine the phases suggested by John Dewey (1933) in his discussion of reflective thinking: (1) identify and clarify problems; (2) identify promising options; (3) evaluate options; (4) select the best one and try it out; and (5) evaluate the results. Less-than-hoped-for results suggest a fifth step "try again" (circle back through prior stages). Questions, actions, resources needed, and common errors in different problem-solving phases can be seen in Exhibit 5.4. Initial steps influence later ones like water flowing through smaller and smaller filters unless you use "debugging" strategies to avoid this effect. Many of the errors shown reflect a confirmatory bias (seeking only data that support favored views). Imagine that you are a community organizer in a low-income neighborhood and believe that new immigrants moving into the neighborhood are the least likely to become active in community advocacy efforts. Because of this belief you may concentrate your attention on long-term residents. As a result, new resident immigrants are ignored with the consequences that they are unlikely to become involved. This will strengthen your original belief.

Defining Problems Is a Critical Phase

Problem definition (clarifying and deciding how to structure a problem) is a critical step in problem solving. Vague definitions get in the way of identifying related behaviors and the circumstances in which they occur. Different theories involve different problem spaces (i.e., how a problem is represented). Consider homelessness. This could be viewed as: (1) the client's own fault (he is lazy); (2) a family problem (relatives are unwilling to help); (3) due to a lack of low-cost housing; (4) a problem with service integration (services are not integrated); (5) due to a "mental disorder"; (6) a result of our basic economic structure (e.g., unskilled jobs have decreased); and (7) discrimination based on racial prejudice. Experts pay more attention to problem definition and structure problems at a deeper (more abstract) level compared to novices who tend to accept problems as given (Voss, 1989). For example, experts in physics tend to sort problems in relation to abstract laws and principles, whereas novices sort problems in relation to surface structure (i.e., concepts directly stated in the problem). Experts in applied behavior analysis use their knowledge of general principles of behavior to identify contingencies related to behaviors of concern (associations between behaviors and what happens right before and after (see Chapter 8). Only by clarifying and redefining (restructuring) a problem may it be solved, or may you discover that there is no solution (see Exhibit 5.5). Creative (bold guesses) and contextual (integrative) thinking will often be needed to describe the "problem space" accurately (structure the problem in a way that yields a solution). Only in this way are we likely to discover the interrelationship among different problem-related levels of influence (e.g., individual, family, community, agency, service system). Only by helping a client to make use of his or her strengths may valued outcomes be attained. This constructional approach is a hallmark of the contextual view described in this book.

> A problem well stated is a problem half solved.
> —Charles F. Kettering

We Tend to Make Certain Kinds of Errors

Studies of decision making in professional contexts reveal a variety of common errors such as incorrect definitions of problems (e.g., missing physical causes) and selection of treatments that are ineffective or harmful (see, for example, Breggin, 1991; Kassirer & Kopelman, 1991). Studies of decision making in child welfare show the effects of *ratcheting* (persisting with a point of view in spite of evidence that it is wrong) and templating (inappropriately applying correlational data to individual clients) (Howitt, 1992). We tend to make rapid decisions with little thought or reflection and in some instances this may work fine. However, critical thinking may be needed to make sound decisions and solve problems. Only through critical inquiry

EXHIBIT 5.4
Problem-Solving Phases and Related Questions, Actions Needed Resources and Common Errors

Step	Questions	Actions	Needed Resources	Common Errors
1. Clarify the problem	What kind of problem is it? Who is involved? How does it affect clients and significant others? What would happen if nothing were done? What are influential contingencies? What is the base rate? What solutions have been attempted to what effect? Do attempted solutions make problems worse? What are clients' and significant others' points of view about the problems and how they can be solved?	Gather data Evaluate accuracy of data Accurately assess the gap between personal and available problem-related scientific knowledge Fill in the gap as needed (e.g., read relevant scientific literature).	Problem-related domain-specific knowledge (e.g., base rate) Time and materials needed for assessment Access to relevant environments (e.g., homes, classrooms) Knowledge about accurate assessment methods and skills in using them with success	Jump to conclusions (overlook alternative views) Seek to justify views rather than critically evaluate them Ignore environmental causes Gather irrelevant data Underestimate available problem-related scientific knowledge Overestimate personal problem-related knowledge Rely on invalid data (e.g., small biased samples) Disregard conflicting evidence Stereotyping
2. Search for solutions	What are options? How feasible is each? How likely is it that each will result in desired outcomes? What resources are needed to address problems at different interrelated levels? What resources could be ? created What resources are available at different levels What constraints must be considered?	Review alternatives Assess the likely success of each Review and seek resources Identify constraints	Domain-specific knowledge (e.g., about problem-related factors) Access to information about resources See also items listed under step 1	Overlook options (e.g., to rearrange environmental cues and consesequences) Look only for data that confirm your assumptions Overlook constraints Overlook resources Not revising views based on new information See other items under Step 1

	Questions	Tasks	Resources	Common errors
3. Decide on a plan	Can you provide help needed? What plan is least costly and most likely to be successful, and most acceptable to clients? How likely is it to be successful? Should you refer?	Integrate data collected; Review soundness of arguments for different plans; Review feasibility of plans	Knowledge, resources, and skills required to implement plans with the fidelity needed for success	Overlook promising options; Overlook constraints; Don't fully inform clients about options and their advantages and disadvantages
4. Implement plans	Can the plan be implemented? With what fidelity can you implement it?	Arrange requisites needed; Fill in gaps in content and procedural knowledge and skills	Knowledge, resources, and skills required to implement plans with the fidelity	The "dilution" effect (i.e., offer ineffective version of plans); Do not arrange for corrective feedback about outcome
5. Evaluate results	How can outcome be accurately assessed with the least cost? Was plan implemented with fidelity? Have we succeeded? If so, how can gains be maintained? If not, what should we do next?	Select relevant, sensitive, feasible outcome measures; Design a monitoring procedure; Collect ongoing data regarding outcome; Alter plans as necessary in accord with degree of progress	Knowledge and skills related to evaluation and troubleshooting	Use vague outcome measures; Use inaccurate measures; Do not gather both subjective and objective measures; Post-hoc fallacy (assume that because there was a change, your services were responsible); Overlook harmful effects; Not revising plans as needed based on outcome data.
6. Try again?	Can the plan be implemented more effectively? Should we circle back to assessment? Is another plan likely to be successful? Can constraints be addressed?	Circle back to assessment— check problem structuring; Proceed through other phases	Time, troubleshooting skills	Give up too soon; Fail to critically examine favored views

EXHIBIT 5.5
Problem-Solving Flow Chart

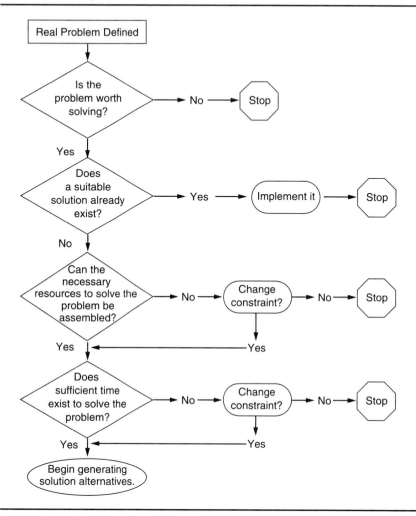

Source   H. S. Folger & S. E. LeBlanc (1995), *Strategies for creative problem solving* (p. 51). Englewood Cliffs, NJ: Prentice Hall.

may we avoid errors we are prone to make *no* matter what our intelligence (Perkins, 1995). Many errors occur because of reliance on questionable criteria such as anecdotal experience to evaluate the accuracy of claims as discussed in Chapter 4.

In errors of commission we *do* something that decreases the likelihood of discovering valuable options. We may:

• Look only for data that confirm our beliefs.

• Jump to conclusions.

• Stereotype people or theories.

• Assume that correlation reflects causation.

• Prematurely discard a valuable opinion.

In errors of omission we fail to do something, which decreases the likelihood of discovering valuable options. We may:

- Not question initial assumptions.
- Ignore the role of environmental causes.
- Overlook cultural differences.
- Overlook client assets.

These two kinds of errors are interrelated. For example, jumping to conclusions (an error of commission) can occur only if you do not question your initial assumptions (an error of omission). These errors may result in:

- Errors in description (e.g., assuming a client was abused as a child when she was not). This involves misclassification.
- Errors in estimating covariations (e.g., assuming all people who were abused as children abuse their own children).
- Errors in identifying causal relationships (e.g., assuming that abuse as a child is responsible for abuse of one's own children later).
- Errors in prediction (e.g., incorrectly predicting that participation in parenting classes will prevent a parent from abusing her children in the future).

Common defaults in thinking emphasized by David Perkins (1995) include:

- *Hasty thinking:* Impulsive and mindless; we don't reflect on what we think or do.
- *Narrow thinking:* Tendency to think in narrow context; we overlook the "big picture" (e.g., my-side bias).
- *Fuzzy thinking:* Imprecise, unclear; we overlook key differences; we do not question vague terms (e.g., support, strength).
- *Sprawling thinking:* Wandering aimlessly in a disorganized manner without integrating; we bounce from one view to another without ever deciding on an overview (p. 153).

They occur because of a lack of attention to planning, monitoring, and questioning. Consider the Barnum effect. This refers to people accepting vague personality descriptions about themselves that could be true of just about anybody.

We Learn Through Our Mistakes

Mistakes are inevitable and provide valuable learning opportunities. Failures and mistakes (less-than-hoped-for success) offer information that may yield better guesses next time around. They help us to learn about the nature of the problem (Popper, 1994).

> But the approach to truth is not easy. There is only one way towards it, the way through error. Only through our errors can we learn; and only he will learn who is ready to appreciate and even to cherish the errors of others as stepping stones towards truth, and who searches for his own errors: who tries to find them, since only when he has become aware of them can he free himself from them. (Popper, 1992, p. 149)

Unavoidable mistakes are those that could not have been anticipated. They occur despite taking advantage of problem-related knowledge and critical thinking skills (in spite of making and acting on reasoned judgments). You may have worked with caregivers of an elderly relative to identify activities the relative enjoys but find that they do not function as reinforcers. Even though you and your clients do your best to identify reinforcers, you cannot know whether particular events will function as reinforcers until you try them out. Avoidable mistakes are mistakes that could have been avoided by thinking more critically about assumptions and their possible consequences. They may occur because of faulty decision-making styles (e.g., jumping to conclusions) and/or agency policies and procedures that interfere with sound decision making (an autocratic style). One of your greatest challenges in becoming a successful problem solver is reappraising the value of mistakes. We are often taught to hide rather than reveal them. Hiding them makes it less likely that they will be corrected in the future.

We Discover How to Do Better Through Criticism

Only through seeking feedback about the outcomes of our decisions and critically evaluating our ideas can we advance our understanding of problems;

"we can do better only by finding out what can be improved and then improving it . . . critical comments from others, far from being resented, is an invaluable aid to be insisted on and welcomed" (Magee, 1985, p. 37). It is better to critically review a plan before it is put into effect than to discover foreseeable flaws after the fact. Critical discussion and testing of ideas are both invaluable in discovering errors so we can improve our guesses.

We Can Become Better Problem Solvers

The good news is that we can learn to become better problem solvers (see Exhibit 5.6). We can learn how to allocate our resources such as planning time wisely. We can become familiar with barriers to problem solving and develop skills for avoiding them. We can acquire critical thinking values, knowledge, and skills that contribute to problem solving and decision making. These are described throughout this book. We can become

more aware of how we think, as described in Chapter 6. The term *metacognitive* refers to awareness of and influence over our reasoning process (e.g., monitoring our thinking by asking questions such as "How am I doing?" "Is this correct?" "How do I know this is true?" "What are my biases?" "Is there another way to approach this problem?" "Do I understand this point?"). These questions highlight the importance of *self-correction* in problem solving. Related behaviors can be thought of as self-governing processes (strategies we use to guide our thinking). They can help us to use effective approaches to problem solving and to avoid common intellectual traps. Increasingly metacognitive levels of thought include: (1) Tacit: Thinking without thinking about it; (2) Aware: Thinking and being aware that you are thinking; (3) *Strategic:* Organizing our thinking by using strategies that enhance its efficacy; and (4) *Reflective:* Reflecting on our thinking (pondering how to proceed and how to improve) (Swartz & Perkins, 1990, p. 52).

EXHIBIT 5.6
Components of Effective Problem Solving

---

1. Recognize that a problem exists. Questions: What kind of a problem is it? How is it played out at different system levels (individual, family, community, society)? At what level (if any) can it be resolved and how?
   Consider full problem (e.g., interrelated system levels).
   Question the obvious.
   Use multiple representations of the problem space (including visual ones).
2. Select steps required to solve a problem (order steps).
   Carefully review data at hand.
   Avoid snap judgments.
   Sift out relevant from irrelevant data.
   Combine and compare information effectively.
   Use a variety of cues.
   Simplify goals.
   Redefine goals.
   Check to see that steps selected follow a natural or logical order.
3. Resource allocation (planning *how* to spend time).
   Spend time on high-level planning.
   Make use of prior knowledge in planning and allocating resources.
   Be flexible and willing to change plans and resource allocation.
   Be on the lookout for new kinds of resources.
4. Monitor adequacy of solution.
   Beware of "justification of effort" effects.
   Avoid impulsiveness.
   Seek external feedback.
   Be open to, but evaluative of, external feedback.

Source: Adapted from J. Sternberg (1986), Intelligence applied: Understanding and increasing your intellectual skills. *San Diego: Harcourt Brace Jovanovich.*

BARRIERS TO PROBLEM SOLVING

Barriers to problem solving are discussed in the following sections. Being forewarned is being prepared (see Exhibit 5.7).

Knowledge Is Limited

Our ignorance is vast. Witte, Witte, & Kerwin (1994) offer a course on medical ignorance at the University of Arizona Medical School to highlight the importance of knowing what is not known when making decisions. Overlooking what is not known encourages attitudes (e.g., overconfidence) and problem-solving styles (e.g., jumping to conclusions) that may get in the way of helping clients or delude clients that help is at hand when it is not. We often do not know the true prevalence of a behavior or its natural history. The probabilities of different outcomes given certain interventions may be unknown. Every source of information has a margin of error that may be small or large. We often don't know how great the range of error is or if it is random or biased. In the approach to knowledge presented in this book (critical rationalism), it is assumed that nothing is ever proven. However, theories (guesses about what is true) differ in the extent to which they have survived critical tests and in the range of situations to which they can be applied with success, and these differences can be used to select options. As Isaac Asimov (1989) notes, it is unlikely that we will find out in the next 500 years that the world is really cube shaped, or shaped like a donut with a hole in the middle.

Information Processing Barriers

We can consider only so much information at one time. The consequences of this include: (1) selective perception (we don't necessarily see what's there); (2) sequential (rather than contextual) processing of information; (3) reliance on "heuristics" (strategies) to reduce effort (e.g., vivid case examples); and (4) faulty memory (our memory is inaccurate). All may interfere with problem solving. We tend to disregard data that do not support preferred beliefs and assign exaggerated importance to

data that do support our beliefs. Strategies that we use with success in solving some problems may work against us in other situations.

Memory as Reconstructive. We rely on our memory when processing and organizing data. Research shows that memory is a "reconstructive process." With the passage of time, proper motivation, certain questions, or the introduction of interfering facts, memory may change (Ceci & Bruck, 1995; Loftus & Ketcham, 1994). We tend to recall our successes and overlook our failures. This is one reason "intuition" may lead us astray. False memories can be created through biased interviewing methods (Ceci & Bruck, 1995; Ofshe & Watters, 1994). Simply being asked a question repeatedly can result in memories of events that did not happen (Ceci & Bruck, 1993, 1995). Our memories change in accord with our stereotypes. Consider a study in which subjects were read a description of some events in a woman's life (Gahagan, 1984, p. 93). Some subjects were told later that the woman had met a lesbian and had started a homosexual relationship with her. Other subjects were told that she met a man and initiated a relationship with him. A third group received no information about sexual relationships. A week later, all participants were asked to recall details of the woman's earlier life. Subjects who were told that she had initiated a homosexual relationship showed strong distortion effects in their recall in accord with stereotypes about "typical characteristics of lesbians" (p. 93).

Memory may be imperfect because events were not accurately noted in the first place. Even if we accurately observed a sequence of events, our memory of these events may not remain accurate. Although some details may be accurately recalled, we may make up events to fill in gaps in our memory, to create what seem to be "logical sequences" of actions. We then imagine that we really saw these events. We may thus have artificial memories. The illusion of having a memory of an event can be created by including inaccurate descriptive data in a question. For example, studies have been conducted in which subjects watched a car accident and later received new information about the acci-

EXHIBIT 5.7
Barriers to Problem Solving

1. Limited Knowledge Is Available
    Little is known about the prevalence of a problem.
    Little is known about the causes of a problem.
    Little is known about what methods will be most effective in solving a problem.
2. Information Processing Barriers
    We can only consider so many different kinds of data at one time.
    Our memory is often inaccurate.
    We process information sequentially rather than contextually.
    We rely on misleading "rules" to simplify tasks (see section on cognitive biases).
3. Task Environment
    Reliance on questionable criteria to evaluate claims.
    Lack of resources (e.g., time, services, money).
    Value on winning rather than learning.
    Lack of cooperation among colleagues.
    Autocratic bosses (value only their own ideas).
    Overvalue of tradition (as preferable to change).
    Taboo topics (e.g., questioning claims of effectiveness).
    Distractions (constant interruptions).
    Time pressures.
    Reluctance to examine the results of policies, programs, and practices.
    Autocratic decision-making style.
4. Motivational blocks
    Value winning over discovering approximations to the truth.
    Vested interest in an outcome.
    Interest in predicting our environment.
    Cynicism.
5. Emotional Blocks
    Fatigue.
    Anger.
    Anxiety.
    Low tolerance for ambiguity.
    Inability to "incubate."
    Lack of zeal.
    Appeal of vivid material.
6. Perceptual Blocks
    Defining problem too narrowly (e.g., overlooking environmental causes).
    Overlooking alternative views.
    Stereotyping.
    Judging rather than generating ideas.
    We see what we expect to see.
7. Intellectual Blocks
    Reliance on questionable criteria to evaluate claims.
    Failure to think critically about beliefs.
    Inflexible use of problem-solving strategies.
    Lack of accurate information.
    Limited use of problem-solving languages (e.g., words, equations, illustrations, models).
    Arrogance.
8. Cultural Blocks
    Disdain for intellectual rigor.
    Valuing John Wayne thinking (strong pro/con positions with little reflection).
    Fear that the competition of ideas would harm the social bonding functions of false beliefs (see Chapter 4).
9. Expressive Blocks
    Inadequate skill in writing and speaking clearly.
    Social anxiety.

Source: Adapted from J. L. Adams (1986). Conceptual blockbusting: A guide to better ideas (3rd ed.). Reading, MA: Addison-Wesley.

dent and then changed their description (Loftus, 1979). Events may be forgotten because of interference from similar memories. High anxiety interferes with remembering events. It decreases attention to detail so that events may not be noticed. Drugs and alcohol also affect memory. Methods explored to "jog memory" include multiple probes, use of different question forms, hypnosis, and monetary incentives (Loftus & Ketcham, 1994).

The Task Environment

Decisions are influenced by the environment in which they are made including popular approaches to defining problems and evaluating the accuracy of claims (see Chapter 4). Funding patterns influence services available. Pressure to conform may result in poor decisions. In "Why I Do Not Attend Case Conferences," Meehl (1973) describes a tendency to reward anything anybody says, "gold and garbage alike." Time pressures and distractions decrease the care with which we acquire and process data and may encourage a mindless approach in which we make decisions with little thought (Langer, 1989). Agencies differ in the extent to which they encourage a culture of thoughtfulness in which critical inquiry is valued (see Exhibit 5.8). Autocratic administra-

EXHIBIT 5.8
Evaluating the Culture of Thoughtfulness in Your Agency

Please circle the numbers in the columns that best describe your responses.					
Statements Describing Actions in Your Work Environment	SD	D	N	A	SA
1. The purposes of discussions are clearly described.	1	2	3	4	5
2. Alternative views on issues are sought.	1	2	3	4	5
3. Alternative views are considered carefully.	1	2	3	4	5
4. Evidence against as well as for favored views is sought.	1	2	3	4	5
5. Key terms are clearly defined.	1	2	3	4	5
6. Behaviors of interest are clearly described, with specific examples given.	1	2	3	4	5
7. Questions are clearly stated.					
8. People identify assumptions underlying their beliefs.	1	2	3	4	5
9. Implications of proposed options are clearly described.	1	2	3	4	5
10. Getting at the "truth" is valued over "winning" an argument.	1	2	3	4	5
11. People are never punished for introducing ideas that differ from those favored by a group.	1	2	3	4	5
12. Criticisms of an argument focus on important points and are made without sarcasm or put-downs.	1	2	3	4	5
13. When available and relevant, research data are cited in support of statements and related sources are noted; appropriate documentation is provided.	1	2	3	4	5
14. Inferences made are compatible with what is known about behavior.	1	2	3	4	5
15. Group leaders/administrators do not rely on unsupported pronouncements about what is best.	1	2	3	4	5
16. Beliefs and actions are well reasoned (based on acceptable, relevant, and sufficient evidence).	1	2	3	4	5
17. The buddy-buddy system (agreement based on friendship rather than the cogency of a view) is discouraged.	1	2	3	4	5
18. Participants do not interrupt each other.	1	2	3	4	5
19. People take responsibility for describing the reasons for their beliefs/actions.	1	2	3	4	5
20. People change their mind when there is good reason to do so.	1	2	3	4	5
21. Participants thank others who point out errors in their thinking.	1	2	3	4	5
22. Reliance on questionable criteria is avoided (e.g., unfounded authority, tradition, anecdotal experience).*	1	2	3	4	5
23. Diversionary tactics are avoided (e.g., red herring, angering an opponent).*	1	2	3	4	5
24. Evasive tactics are avoided (e.g., changing the topic).*	1	2	3	4	5

*You could determine the rate per minute of informal fallacies during a discussion.
Key: SD = strongly disagree; D = disagree; N = neutral; A = agree; SA = strongly agree.
Source: L. Gibbs & E. Gambrill (1996), Critical thinking for social workers: A workbook (pp. 221–222). Thousand Oaks, CA: Pine Forge Press.

tors may squelch critical discussion and testing of claims about services.

Personal Blocks

Some barriers to problem solving are self-imposed (see Exhibit 5.9). The accuracy of our beliefs about the problems we confront affects our success as problem solvers, as do our beliefs about ourselves (e.g., whether we think we can make a difference). Research concerning learning and problem solving emphasizes the importance of background knowledge. This refers to the assumptions that we bring to a question. They may help us to solve problems, make sound decisions, and understand new concepts, or they have the opposite effects—they get in the way of solving problems and learning. Only if you are aware of your assumptions—only if you can see them in the clear daylight, can you critically examine them. Motivational barriers include vested interests in a certain outcome and lack of interest in a problem. We may believe that sincerity is enough to protect clients from harmful or inef-

fective services when it is not. Professionals as well as clients and those who care about them are eager to help clients and thus may be vulnerable to false claims about the effects of untested service methods. Emotional barriers include fear of making mistakes and a low tolerance for uncertainty. We may fear taking risks or feel helpless in the face of great need.

> Many people fear nothing more than to take a position which stands out sharply and clearly from the prevailing opinion. The tendency of most is to adopt a view that is so ambiguous that it will include everything and so popular that it will include everybody.
> —Rev. Martin Luther King, Jr.

Lack of knowledge may get in the way of offering clients valuable options. Our beliefs about behavior may have little overlap with what is known about behavior based on systematic investigation. Let's say you are working with a child labeled "autistic" and know little about autism. Your domain-specific knowledge will differ considerably compared to a well-trained professional who specializes in this area. Perceptual blocks such as stereotyping may get in the way of accurately defining a problem or discovering related causes.

Intellectual barriers include inflexible use of problem-solving strategies that result in getting caught in "loops." Focusing on justifying our beliefs rather than on critiquing them is a major obstacle. Only if we critically evaluate beliefs and actions, including our most cherished views, can we discover flaws in our thinking and prejudices that may get in the way of helping clients. Self-criticism is essential to problem solving. We may use rules inconsistently. Making the obscure less obscure requires time, effort, and skill. Without values and attitudes that foster critical thinking time may not be taken or effort made. A preoccupation with finding *the* cause of a problem can be a barrier rather than asking *how* behaviors or events can be altered to attain desired outcomes (Feinstein, 1967). Complete Exhibit 5.10 to explore your problem-solving style.

EXHIBIT 5.9
Why Intelligent People Fail (Too Often)

1. Lack of motivation
2. Lack of impulse control
3. Lack of perseverance
4. Capitalizing on the wrong abilities
5. Inability to translate thought into action
6. Lack of product orientation
7. Task completion problems and lack of follow through
8. Failure to initiate
9. Fear of failure
10. Procrastination
11. Misattribution of blame
12. Excessive self-pity
13. Excessive dependency
14. Wallowing in personal difficulties
15. Distractibility and lack of concentration
16. Spreading oneself too thick or too thin
17. Inability to delay gratification
18. Inability or unwillingness to see the forest from the trees
19. Lack of balance between critical, analytical thinking, and creative, synthetic thinking
20. Too little or too much self-confidence

Source: R. J. Sternberg (1987), Teaching intelligence: The application of cognitive psychology to the improvement of intellectual skills. In J. B. Baron & R. J. Sternberg (Eds.), Teaching thinking skills: Theory and practice (pp. 212–213). New York: W. H. Freeman.

EXHIBIT 5.10
Exploring Your Problem-Solving Style

Please circle the numbers in the columns that best indicate your degree of agreement with each statement.

	SD	D	N	A	SA
1. I go to the original sources for basic information.	1	2	3	4	5
2. When my first efforts fail, I try again.	1	2	3	4	5
3. I seek out points of view that differ from my own.	1	2	3	4	5
4. I arrange a way to see if I have resolved problems I tackle.	1	2	3	4	5
5. I welcome criticism of my views.	1	2	3	4	5
6. If I can't solve a problem right away, I assume it's not solvable.	1	2	3	4	5
7. I break up complex problems into subproblems.	1	2	3	4	5
8. I consider constraints that affect the potential to solve problems.	1	2	3	4	5
9. I challenge my initial assumptions about how a problem could be solved.	1	2	3	4	5
10. I consider alternative ways to approach a problem.	1	2	3	4	5
11. I get frustrated when I can't solve problems rapidly.	1	2	3	4	5
12. I usually accept the first option I can think of.	1	2	3	4	5
13. I consider the consequences of each alternative.	1	2	3	4	5
14. I carefully review arguments against as well as for different options.	1	2	3	4	5
15. I enjoy working on difficult problems.	1	2	3	4	5
16. I take time to clearly describe problems before seeking solutions.	1	2	3	4	5
17. I consider the "big picture" when thinking about problems and options.	1	2	3	4	5
18. I critically assess the accuracy and completeness of my problem-related background knowledge.	1	2	3	4	5
19. I am not afraid of admitting it when I don't know something.	1	2	3	4	5
20. I change my mind when I have good reason to do so.	1	2	3	4	5
21. I like to probe deeply into issues, to find out "what's really going on."	1	2	3	4	5
22. I tend to go along with what other people think and want.	1	2	3	4	5
23. I seek out other people's ideas.	1	2	3	4	5
24. I usually rely on intuition to test my guesses about what may happen.	1	2	3	4	5
25. I enjoy taking risks.	1	2	3	4	5
26. I welcome critical evaluation from others about my ideas.	1	2	3	4	5
27. I critically review my preferred options.	1	2	3	4	5

Key: SD = strongly disagree; D = disagree; N = neutral; A = agree; SA = strongly agree.

COGNITIVE BIASES THAT INFLUENCE PROBLEM SOLVING

Nisbett and Ross (1980) suggest that we often make judgmental errors (incorrect choices) because we rely on "heuristics" (cognitive shortcuts, rules of thumb, strategies). These may be in the form of implicit or explicit rules (if ___, then ___). Although these shortcuts may often serve us well, they may also result in errors. Nisbett and Ross (1980) suggest that many cognitive biases are related to two "heuristics": availability and representativeness (see also Plous, 1993).

Availability

We often rely on what's available (e.g., a preferred practice theory or a vivid example). Biases related to availability are shown in Exhibit 5.11. The accessibility of events/concepts in our perception, memory, or imagination influences our decisions (Tversky & Kahneman, 1973). We structure problems based on past experiences. We see what we think we will see, and we seek information that is consistent with our preconceived notions and disregard conflicting evidence. We focus on items that are easy to recognize and rely on readily recalled

EXHIBIT 5.11
Examples of Bias Related to Availability

Availability   Influence by the accessibility of data. For example, we may judge the probability of an event by how easy it is to recall or imagine it.

Preconceptions and preferred practice theories	Influence by our assumptions about behavior/people.
Vividness	Concrete and salient data stand out more and are given more weight than are abstract data (e.g., statistical reports), or events that do not occur.
Behavior confirmation	We seek data that confirm our favored views and ignore contradictory data.
Anchoring and insufficient adjustment	Influence by initial judgments or data and underadjustment of these based on new information.
Recency effects	Influence by data seen, heard, or read most recently.
Frequency, familiarity, imaginability	Influence by how easy it is to imagine an event, by how familiar we are with it, or how often we see, hear, or think about it.
Fundamental attribution error	Attributing behavior to personal characteristics and overlooking environmental influences (the former are often more vivid).
Resources available	Basing decisions on resources available rather than client need.
Emotional influences	Influence by our mood or feelings about a person/event.
Motivational influences	Influence by our preferences for certain outcomes.
Illustory correlation	Incorrect assumption that two or more variables co-vary.

Source: Based on R. Nisbett & L. Ross (1980), Human inference: Strategies and shortcomings of social judgment. *Englewood Cliffs, NJ: Prentice-Hall. See also A. Tversky & D. Kahneman (1974), Judgment under uncertainty: Heuristics and biases. Science, 185, 1124–1131.*

examples. Let's say that one of your clients has a substance-abuse problem and that you recently went to a workshop on self-esteem. This "schema" or concept (self-esteem) is readily available in your thoughts. You may associate self-esteem with your client's problems and believe that low self-esteem is mainly (or partly) responsible for this person's substance abuse. The client in the interview is more vivid than his or her home and neighborhood, which you may not see. Vivid case examples are easy to recall and crowd out data that, although less vivid, may be more informative. Behaviors such as hitting and yelling are more vivid compared to polite requests and following instructions.

Availability influences our judgments about causal relationships (Kahneman & Tversky, 1973). For example, observers tend to attribute the cause of other people's behavior to characteristics of the person rather than to situational factors (Batson, O'Quinn & Pych, 1982). The "actor's" behavior is more noticeable compared to more static situational events. Many factors that are *not* correlated with the frequency of an event influence how important it seems such as how visible it is, how vivid it is, and how easily it can be imagined (that is, how available it is). We tend to overestimate the prevalence of illnesses that receive a great deal of me-

dia attention such as cancer and underestimate the prevalence of illnesses that receive little media attention such as diabetes (Slovic, Fischhoff, & Lichtenstein, 1982).

The Influence of Preconceptions and Preferred Theories. The impact of preconceptions is one of the better demonstrated findings of twentieth-century psychology" (Nisbett & Ross, 1980, p. 67). Consider the classic study in which teachers were told that certain children in their classroom did very well on a nonverbal intelligence test that predicts intellectual blooming (Rosenthal & Jacobson, 1968). These children showed superior gains over the next eight months. Actually, they were randomly selected. Many similar studies show that if teachers have low expectations about students, the students will perform poorly, and if they have high expectations, the students will perform well. Differences in expectations create different interactions. For example, teachers pay greater attention to students for whom they have high expectations (see Rosenthal 1994). Our expectations alter what we do and do not attend to as suggested in Exhibit 5.12. For example, if you are not aware that you have a preconception that people 85 years old are "over the hill," you may focus on an elderly client's deficiencies and overlook her assets. You may overlook environmental factors related to her concerns (such as reactions of significant others). Our preconceptions and theories affect which concepts and beliefs are available. They influence what events we notice or inquire about. These theories are more available compared to others.

Preconceptions can lead to incorrect inferences when a theory: (1) is held on poor grounds (there is not adequate reason to believe it is relevant); (2)

> Concepts may be informative, misleading, or irrelevant

is used unconsciously; or (3) it preempts examination of the data (Nisbett & Ross, 1980, p. 71). We may hold theories that have no empirical support as dearly as theories that do. We may be unaware of preconceptions that influence our decisions. We

may not critically evaluate the accuracy of our beliefs. The more ambiguous the data, the more preconceptions influence assumptions. Much of our understanding of the world is theory-based rather than data-based; our interpretations are inferences based on guesses about what may be true. Overconfidence in a theory increases the likelihood of biased preconceptions. We are particularly likely to be overconfident of our judgments about people. Only if you critically examine your assumptions may you discover flaws in your thinking and discover better options.

The generation as well as the retrieval of data may be biased by preconceptions. Our beliefs about the causes associated with a problem may result in a selective inquiry during assessment. Practitioners who are psychoanalytically oriented search for different types of data compared to those who use a cognitive-behavioral practice model (Kopta, Newman, McGovern, & Sandrock, 1986).

EXHIBIT 5.12
The Preconceived Notion

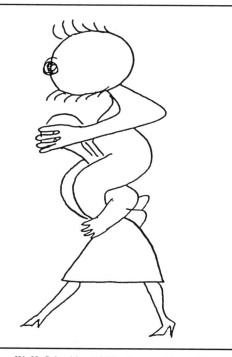

Source: W. H. Schneider (1965), *Danger: Men talking.* New York: Random House.

Vividness. The vividness or concreteness of material influences how available it is. However, "The vividness of information is correlated only modestly, at best, with its evidential value" (Nisbett & Ross, 1980, p. 60). We are often influenced by vivid case examples. Such biased selection (*attempted proof by selected instances*) may result in incorrect judgments. Vivid material is more likely to be remembered and is thus more likely to influence the collection, organization, and interpretation of data.

Emotional interest, the extent to which content provokes imagery and is concrete, and its sensory, temporal, or spatial proximity contribute to vividness. If a suspected murderer is called a "vicious killer" we may more readily believe that he was responsible for alleged crimes. The heavy impact of negative exchanges in relationships that are basically positive is thought to be due to the fact that positive exchanges become the expected background in such relationships. They are taken for granted; they are less vivid (Rook, 1984a). Events that do not take place are not as vivid (Nisbett & Ross, 1980). This type of information tends to be overlooked when it can be crucial. Sherlock Holmes solved a case based on the fact that a dog

did not bark at an intruder. Both clinicians and researchers tend to ignore areas in which parents of
developmentally disabled children cope well
(Jacobson & Humphrey, 1979; Kazak & Marvin,
1984). A search for nonobvious factors may reveal
overlooked causes.

> Vision is the art of seeing things invisible.
> —Jonathan Swift

Vivid information can be misleading, especially when duller but more informative material
is not considered. Helpers often discount statistical information by citing a single case that supposedly contradicts this information. Testimonials
are often employed to support claims as in "I've
tried it. It works." Helpers often appeal to their
personal experience: "I have seen this in my own
practice" (see list of practitioner fallacies in
Exhibit 4.5). The greater vividness of case examples compared to statistical data may explain why
research reports are often of little interest to
helpers. A vivid case example, unless it is known
to be typical, ought to be given little weight in
making decisions. It rarely warrants the inferential weight assigned to it. You should certainly
give less weight to a single example than to relevant statistical data.

Behavioral Confirmation. We tend to seek and
overweigh evidence that supports our beliefs and
to ignore and underweigh contrary evidence. We
try to justify (confirm) our assumptions rather than
to falsify them (test them as rigorously as possible). Consider the study by Snyder and Swann
(1978) in which students were asked to test the hypothesis that a person was either an extrovert or an
introvert. Those who believed he was an extrovert
asked questions that prompted data in support of
their view. Students who tested the assumption that
the person was an introvert selected questions that
would prompt answers supporting this view. Both
created a self-fulfilling prophecy. Studies of medical reasoning show that overinterpretation is a
common error. This refers to assigning new information to favored hypotheses rather than exploring
alternative accounts that more effectively explain

data or remembering this information separately
(Elstein et al., 1978).

These confirmatory biases are also seen in the
hundreds of studies of interviewer biases. A single
hypothesis is pursued (e.g., that a child's behavior
is a result of sexual abuse) and an alternative hypothesis (e.g., that he has not been so abused) ignored. As a result many false allegations of sexual
abuse have occurred (Ceci & Bruck, 1995). Social
workers often assign labels to clients based on the
*Diagnostic and Statistical Manual of Mental
Disorders* (1994). These labels may result in a selective search for data that confirm the label.
Contradictory data may be ignored. We use different standards to criticize opposing evidence than to
evaluate supporting evidence. Data that provide
some support for and against views increase confidence for holders of both views (Lord, Ross, &
Lepper, 1979). This confirmation bias influences
judgment in all phases of work with clients: defining problems, deciding on causes, and selecting service plans.

Anchoring and Insufficient Adjustment. We
tend to believe in initial judgments, even when we
are aware that the knowledge we have access to has
been arbitrarily selected (e.g., by the spin on a
roulette wheel). Adjustments from initial values are
usually inadequate. We often form impressions of
clients quickly (Houts & Galante, 1985). For example, helpers make assumptions about clients'
manageability and treatability that may influence
what questions they ask and what methods they
consider (Wills, 1978, 1982). Helpers differ in the
impressions they form of the very same client.
Nisbett and Ross (1980) attribute primacy effects
to our tendency to generate theories that bias the
interpretation of data. These effects are encouraged
by premature commitment to one assumption and
insufficient revision of beliefs, as well as the tendency to believe (often falsely) in the consistency
of behavior across different situations. One way to
avoid anchoring effects is to consider an alternative estimate at another extreme.

Recency Effects. We are also influenced by recency—what we last see or hear. You may attend

a workshop on child abuse and as a result suspect child abuse more readily in families. This too is a kind of influence based on availability.

Representative Thinking: Misuse of Resemblance Criteria

We often make judgments based on the degree to which a characteristic seems to be representative of (resemble or be similar to) another characteristic or schema (theory) (Tversky & Kahneman, 1974). Biases related to representativeness can be seen in Exhibit 5.13. We have beliefs about what types of causes are associated with certain effects. We often assume that causes resemble their effects when this may not be so. This heuristic involves the application of resemblance or "goodness of fit" criteria to practice decisions such as classifying clients into certain diagnostic categories, deciding on the causes of problems, and predicting what clients will do. Representative thinking is mainly an associative process in which the associations we have with a certain characteristic (such as African-American or homosexual) influence our judgments (client characteristic → schema → inference). Overestimating the relationship between abuse as a child and abuse of one's own children reflects reliance on resemblance criteria. Consider some other examples:

- Foxes have remarkable lungs. Therefore, the lungs of a fox will remedy asthma.

- Turmeric (which is yellow) will cure jaundice.
- Unwillingness to discuss "homosexual feelings" reflects excessive interest in them. (Here and in the next two examples we see the assumption of opposites.)
- A generous action reflects underlying stinginess.
- Permissiveness when raising children leads to radicalism as adults.

The problem is, similarity is *not* influenced by a number of factors we should consider: (1) whether a person/object belongs in a certain group; (2) the probability that an outcome was a result of a particular cause; and (3) the probability that a process will result in a certain outcome. Reliance on representative thinking may yield incorrect beliefs about the degree to which: (1) outcomes reflect origins; (2) instances are representative of their categories; and (3) antecedents are representative of consequences. Associative thinking may occur unnoticed (automatically, mindlessly) unless we question our assumptions, search for alternative possibilities, and review the quality of evidence. We "are far more confident than is warranted in [our] ability to judge the plausibility of specific cause-effect relationships based on superficial resemblance of features" (Nisbett & Ross, 1980, p. 117). Causes and effects may bear little or no resemblance to one another. Reliance on representativeness results in errors, because we use clues that

EXHIBIT 5.13
Biases Related to Reliance on Representativeness

Representativeness   Misuse of resemblance criteria. Influence by the similarity of events (e.g., the probability of an event is estimated by how closely it resembles a population).

Ignoring sample size	We tend to overlook nonrepresentativeness of data (it may not reflect population characteristics).
Stereotyping	Treating a description as if it represents all the individuals in a group (when it does not).
Overconfidence	Excessive belief in the accuracy of our judgments.
Reliance on consistency	Search for consistent rather than informative data.
Overlooking regression effects	Forgetting that extreme scores return to mean levels.
Ignoring base-rates	We tend to overlook prevalence of a behavior/event in a population
Ignoring predictive validity	Overlooking questionable validity of the data we rely on in making judgments (e.g., predictions).
Misconceptions	Inaccurate belief that events are related when they are not (e.g., the belief that a series of heads in a coin toss means that the next toss will be a tail).

Note: Some sources of error are discussed in later chapters.

do not accurately predict an outcome. For example, we may incorrectly assume that because a homeless child is similar to another client we just saw, similar causes are involved. We often use superficial resemblance to make inferences about causes. Other schemas (views) that may be far more likely are *not* considered. (For readers who want to pursue this further, see Appendix 5A.)

Ignoring Sample Size. Social workers deal with samples of behavior. Helpers often rely on small samples of self-report data gathered in an interview (a sample from one source). These samples may be biased and therefore misleading. Assessing the representativeness of samples to a population is a key helping skill. How likely is it that a sample (e.g., of behaviors, thoughts, or feelings) accurately represents the population from which it is drawn? How likely is it that what you see during one hour in a residential center accurately reflects the usual pattern of interaction between staff and residents? Relying on similarity when making judgments about the extent to which a sample is representative of a population may result in incorrect estimates.

Stereotyping. We have biases about certain groups, individuals, or behaviors that influence our judgments. Stereotypes are a kind of preconception. They influence what we do and what we believe. They save us time. We don't have to think about all the ways in which a client may not fit our conception. Stereotypes can be set up remarkably quickly. For example, children told that a visitor to their school was clumsy resulted in many of the children holding him responsible for knocking over a cake (when in fact he had not) (Leichtman & Ceci, 1995).

Stereotyping is an incorrect assessment of variability, "a set of people who are labeled as belonging to a given group is presumed to be more homogeneous than is in fact the case" (Holland, Holyoak, Nisbett, & Thagard, 1986, p. 245). It is a false estimate of the complexity of a group. The *fallacy of stereotyping* (Scriven, 1976, p. 208) consists of treating a description as if it represents all the individuals in a group of which it may (or may not) be a fairly typical sample. We tend to overestimate the variability of in-groups (groups of which we are a member). Thus, we might generalize too little from knowledge of a sample of in-group members on some dimension about which we have little information. We tend to *under*estimate the degree of variability in "out-groups" (groups of which we are not a member). For example, people who are *not* gay or lesbian may *under*estimate the degree of variability among people who are gay or lesbian. On the other hand gay men and lesbians may overestimate the degree of variability of gay or lesbian people. *Under*estimating the variability of groups with which we are *not* familiar results in believing that we learn more (than we in fact do) from experience with one member of that group. If you have never before met a Native American, you may be inclined to make greater generalizations about what all Native Americans are like than if you have met many. If you have met many Native Americans from only one of the hundreds of different tribes you may underestimate the degree of variability of behavior, values, and norms in other tribes. If we underestimate the degree of variability we may lose a chance to identify clues about what a person is like or may do in certain situations. If we search only for evidence that supports a stereotype, we may miss alternative accurate accounts. For example, Ceci and Bruck (1995) note that "Failure to test an alternative to a pet hunch can lead interviewers to ignore inconsistent evidence and to shape the contents of the interview to be consistent with their own beliefs" (p. 80).

RELYING ON QUESTIONABLE CRITERIA TO EVALUATE CLAIMS

Problems may remain unsolved because we rely on questionable criteria to evaluate claims about what is accurate. We may, for example, rely on tradition, or popularity, or authority (see Chapter 4). Review Exhibit 4.5 and become familiar with these misleading criteria for evaluating the accuracy of claims (see also Appendix 5B). Focusing on service goals will help you to choose wisely among different criteria. For example, if your goal is to discover the causes of a client's complaint, rely on sources that provide accurate data.

IS A THOUGHTFUL APPROACH TO PROBLEM SOLVING ALWAYS NEEDED?

Thoughtful problem solving requires clear description of problems and related factors and outcomes, review of resources and obstacles, selection and implementation of plans likely to succeed in attaining valued outcomes, and "trying again" as necessary based on feedback about progress. The purpose of a systematic approach is to increase the likelihood of solving problems. Thus, ideally, this approach should be used whenever it is needed to reveal promising options. However, there will be times when shortcuts can be taken with no loss. For example, many different options may be available to solve a problem. Here, little time may be needed for you and your clients to make a choice. If you cannot use a systematic approach when needed, you could offer support or refer clients elsewhere if other agencies provide needed services. You could forge ahead anyway, pretending you have what you

need. Problems here are misleading clients and yourself about what can be accomplished.

Slowing Down to Speed Up

Practice questions may been puzzling or intractable because we move too fast in describing the details of a situation. For example, a social worker may say that a client is reluctant to participate in setting up a plan. He or she may fail to describe how the client came to the agency. This vital information is often skipped over. Perhaps the social worker does not have a client (someone with whom there is a clear agreement to work toward certain outcomes) but a resister (someone present against his or her will) or an applicant (someone who wants something from an agency). Often the original problem as well as what would occur if the problem were solved is vague. We can often answer questions by going more slowly (laying a firm foundation) rather than by going too fast.

SUMMARY

Helping clients involves making decisions. The problems you will confront will usually be unstructured ones in which there are differences of opinion about how success should be evaluated and in which alternatives may be unknown or not possible. No matter what our intelligence, we are likely to fall into common intelligence traps unless we develop values, knowledge, and skills that help us avoid them. Personal blocks to problem solving include emotional barriers such as fear of taking risks and motivational barriers (vested interests in certain outcomes). Environmental blocks include noisy offices and time pressures and autocratic decision-making styles. Cultural blocks include a professional culture that punishes those who ask questions about dubious claims of effectiveness. We are subject to a variety of cognitive biases such as looking only for data that support our beliefs and being influenced by available data or beliefs. The good news is that we can become more effective problem solvers. We can learn how to avoid errors that get in the way of helping clients attain outcomes they value and avoiding harm.

REVIEWING YOUR COMPETENCIES

Reviewing What You Know

1. Describe the advantages of a critically reflective problem-focused practice model.
2. Discuss the relationship between problem solving and decision making.
3. Describe some of the major research findings regarding problem solving.

4. Describe the role of creativity in problem solving.
5. Give examples of incorrect problem structuring and its potential harmful effects on clients.
6. Discuss the role of resource allocation in problem solving.
7. Describe common errors in problem solving.
8. Discuss the influence of rules (heuristics) in problem solving and decision making.
9. Describe the availability bias and give examples of this bias in social work.
10. Describe the representative bias and give examples of this bias in social work.
11. Give examples of the influence of stereotypes.
12. Describe personal barriers to problem solving and discuss why they pose a barrier.
13. Describe environmental barriers to problem solving and describe why they function as barriers.
14. Discuss the role of mistakes in learning.
15. Describe common errors of omission in decision making.
16. Compare the criteria you use to make practice decisions with those you use to make decisions about your own health.

Reviewing What You Do

1. You identify practitioner fallacies in a given case example and accurately describe why they are of concern.
2. You recognize cognitive biases in practice examples.
3. You avoid common errors in problem solving.
4. You accurately recognize when nothing can be done to resolve a problem.

Reviewing Results

1. Problems are solved.
2. You make effective use of available information.

APPENDIX 5A.   AVOIDING ERRORS CAUSED BY REPRESENTATIVE THINKING

Representative thinking is an association process in which some characteristic "triggers" an associated theory, belief, or schema. An example given by Howitt (1992) is assuming that a man abused his stepson because there is a correlation between being a stepfather and abuse of children. You can draw on rules of probability theory to avoid errors caused by representative thinking. Consider the example of a college admissions committee reviewing applicants given by Dawes (1988). One applicant was outstanding in all areas; however, she misspelled a word on her application. One committee member believed that this indicated that she was dyslexic and her application was denied. Let's call misspelling a word c and the associated schema (dyslexia) the symbol S. We can then ask about *conditional* probabilities: What is the probability of c given S or S given c? The probability that members of S have characteristic c $[p(c|S)]$ *is* likely.

People with dyslexia often do misspell words. However, the probability that the characteristic c implies membership in S (dyslexia) is given by the conditional probability $p(S|c)$ (the probability that people with characteristic c are members of S), which is the *inverse* of $p(c|S)$. As Dawes points out, it is true that misspelling is a characteristic of dyslexia. However, probably many more students cannot spell certain words who are *not* dyslexic than who are dyslexic.

Thus, "The basic problem with making probability judgments on the basis of representative characteristics is that the schema accessed [dyslexia] may in fact be *less* probable, given the characteristic, than one not accessed when the schema not accessed has a much greater *extent* in the world than the accessed one" (p. 70). The number of people who are *not* dyslexic is much larger than the number of people who are dyslexic. The problem is that when a schema (i.e., dyslexia) is accessed (considered), the actual extent of the class is usually not, resulting in faulty decisions. As Dawes points out, representative thinking does not distinguish between the probability of c given S and the probability of S given c. Most associations are *not* symmetric.

Consider another example. It is often said that smoking marijuana leads to heroin use. Let's call smoking marijuana c and heroin use S. Thus, this assumption can be written $p(c|S)$. What *should* be considered is $p(S|c)$. Venn diagrams can be used to represent conditional probabilities (the ratio of the area in the overlap to the area in the large circle) (see Exhibit 5.14). This illustrates the nonsymmetric nature of conditional probabilities. You cannot simply reverse them. The probability that marijuana smokers also use heroin is much smaller than the probability that heroin users smoke marijuana. Can you apply this analysis to the stepparent "template" mentioned in the first paragraph?

EXHIBIT 5.14
Hypothesized Venn diagram of pot smokers
and hard drug users

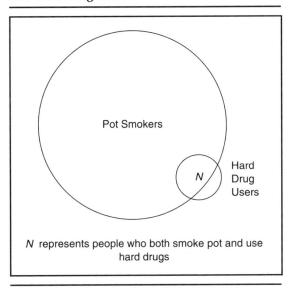

N represents people who both smoke pot and use hard drugs

Source: R. M. Dawes (1988), *Rational choice in an uncertain world* (p. 82). San Diego: Harcourt Brace Jovanovich.

APPENDIX 5B. A CATALOG OF FAULTY INFERENCES

1. *Fallacy of representativeness.* Assuming that two or more things or events are related simply because they resemble each other.

   Foxes have remarkable lungs. Therefore the lungs of a fox will remedy asthma.

2. *Irrelevant conclusion.* A conclusion is irrelevant to the reasoning that led to it.

   I don't think Mr. Jones abused his child. He acts like a normal father; he even spends time on the weekend repairing his car.

3. *Fallacy of division.* Assuming that what is true of the whole is necessarily true of each individual part of the whole.

   Staff at the Mixer Community Mental Health Center are psychoanalytically oriented. Mary M., who works there, is psychoanalytically oriented.

4. *Fallacy of labeling.* Labeling yourself or others when the label is unjustified by the circumstances, or when the label is inappropriately used as a reason for behavior or lack of behavior (Sternberg, 1986, p. 96).

   You have worked hard to help a client to little avail. You say to yourself "I'm a failure."

5. *Hasty generalization.* Considering only exceptional cases and generalizing from those cases to a rule that fits only those exceptions.

   Bill and a friend were discussing the director of their agency. Bill said, "He is a total failure because he has not increased funding for our agency."

6. *Overlooking the role of chance.* Assuming that an outcome due entirely to chance is related to skill.

   My next baby must be a boy. We've had five girls.

7. *Personalization.* Assuming you are the cause of some event for which you were not primarily responsible or taking personally a statement that is not directed toward you.

   A client failed to keep an agreement that you believe he could have kept. You say to yourself, "It's my fault."

8. *Magnification/minimization.* Magnifying our negative characteristics or mistakes or minimizing our positive characteristics or accomplishments.

   Mrs. Silvers (a supervisor) congratulated Max on his success with his client. He said "Oh, it's really not a big thing."

9. *Fallacy of composition.* Assuming that what is true of parts of a whole is true of the whole.

   Jane is behaviorally oriented. Therefore staff at her agency are behaviorally oriented.

10. *"Should" statements (e.g., "I must do this," "I should feel that," "They should do this")* are fallacies when they are used as the sole reason for behavior.

    A supervisor tells her staff: "You should evaluate your practice."

Source: Based on Robert J. Sternberg (1986), Intelligence applied: Understanding and increasing your intellectual skills *(pp. 94–105). San Diego: Harcourt Brace Jovanovich.*

11. *False cause*. Relying on the mere fact of coincidence or temporal succession to identify a cause.

    John worked in a large office. He applied for a promotion, but a woman received it. He said to himself, "It's clear that the woman was promoted and not me because she is a woman."

12. *Invalid disjunction* (either/or-ing). Considering only two solutions when there are more than two that should be considered.

    We must either hospitalize him or leave him to wander the streets.

13. *Fallacies based on availability*. Accepting the first explanations for an event that occurs to you without considering other, less obvious or readily available explanations.

    I can see he is an angry man by how he acts in the office. I think he is guilty of abusing his wife.

14. *Argument from ignorance*. Assuming that something is true simply because it has not been shown to be false, or that it is false simply because it has not been shown to be true.

    You don't have any proof that your method works. Therefore I don't think it does.

15. *Mental filter*. Picking out some small aspect of a situation (often a negative one) and focusing on that one small aspect so that the "bigger picture" is ignored. All events are viewed through the filter of one aspect of the situation.

    I just don't like the way my director dresses.

16. *Emotional reasoning*. Using our emotions or feelings as evidence of a truth.

    This is true because I feel it is true.

17. *Appeal to authority*. Arguing that a claim is true based purely on an authority's status with no reference to evidence.

    Dr. Monston said. . . .

18. *Argumentation ad populum*. Assuming that "if everyone else thinks this way, it must be right." Appeal to popularity.

    Everyone is using this new method. I think we should use it too.

19. *Argumentum ad hominem*. Attacking or praising some aspects of a person's character, lifestyle, race, religion, sex, and so on, as evidence for (or against) a conclusion, even when these circumstances are irrelevant to the situation being examined.

    He has a point. But look at how he is dressed.

20. *Inference by manner of presentation (how believable is this person?).*

    She gave a convincing talk. I'm going to use her methods.

21. *Appeal to experience.*

    I've seen thirty clients and used x successfully with all of them. It works!

22. *Appeal to tradition.*

    That's the way we have always done it. We should continue to use these methods.

23. *Influence by testimonials.*

    I believe it works because Mrs. Rivera said she tried it and it helped.

24. *Appeal to newness.*

    It's the latest thing. We should try it too.

25. *Assume hard headed therefore hard hearted.*

    She can't really care about her clients if she spends that much time questioning our agency's methods.

26. *Assume that good intentions result in good services (e.g., protect clients from harm.*

    In response to a question from a client about an agency's effectiveness, you say: "We really care about our clients."

27. *Weak documentation.*

    Accepting a claim based on vague, undocumented evidence.

CHAPTER 6

Critical Thinking

Critical thinking is suggested as a guide to practice decisions, and related values, attitudes, knowledge, and skills are described. As Karl Popper points out, "There are always many different opinions and conventions concerning any one problem or subject-matter. This shows that they are not all true. For if they conflict, then at best only one of them can be true" (1994, p. 39). The relationship between science and critical thinking is discussed and the costs and benefits of critical thinking are reviewed. Barriers are noted and remedies suggested.

You Will Learn About

- The hallmarks of critical thinking.
- Related values, skills, and knowledge.
- Critical thinking and scientific reasoning.
- The benefits of critical thinking and discussion.
- The costs of critical thinking.
- Reviewing your beliefs about knowledge.

HALLMARKS OF CRITICAL THINKING

The term *reflection* is becoming increasingly popular. But as Steven Brookfield notes, "Reflection is not by definition critical" (1995, p. 8). Critical thinking is a unique kind of purposeful thinking in which we use standards such as clarity. Critical thinking involves the careful examination and evaluation of beliefs and actions in order to arrive at well reasoned ones (see Exhibit 6.1). It is

Clear versus unclear
Precise versus imprecise
Specific versus vague

EXHIBIT 6.1
Characteristics of Critical Thinking

1. It is purposeful.
2. It is responsive to and guided by *intellectual standards* (relevance, clarity, depth, and breadth).
3. It supports the development of *traits* of intellectual humility, integrity, perseverance, empathy, and self-discipline.
4. The thinker can identify the *elements of thought* present in thinking about a problem, such that logical connections are made between the elements and the problem. Critical thinkers routinely ask the following questions:
   What is the purpose of my thinking (goal/objective)?
   What precise question (problem) am I trying to answer?
   Within what point of view (perspective) am I thinking?
   What concepts or ideas are central to my thinking?
   What am I taking for granted, what assumptions am I making?
   What information am I using (data, facts, observation)?
   How am I interpreting that information?
   What conclusions am I coming to?
   If I accept the conclusions, what are the implications? What would the consequence be if I put my thoughts into action?
   For each elements, the thinker considers standards that shed light on the effectiveness of her thinking.
5. It is *self-assessing* (self-critical), *and self-improving* (self-corrective). The thinker assesses her thinking, using appropriate standards. If you are not assessing your thinking, you are not thinking critically.
6. *There is an integrity to the whole system.* The thinker is able to critically examine her thought as a whole and to take it apart (consider its parts as well). The thinker is committed to be intellectually humble, persevering, courageous, fair and just. The critical thinker is aware of the variety of ways in which thinking can become distorted, misleading, prejudiced, superficial, unfair, or otherwise defective.
7. It *yields a well-reasoned answer.* If we know how to check our thinking and are committed to doing so, and we get extensive practice, then we can depend on the results of our thinking being productive.
8. It is responsive to the social and moral imperative to argue from opposing points of view and to *seek and identify weakness and limitations in one's own position.* Critical thinkers are aware that there are many legitimate points-of-view, each of which (when thought through) may yield some level of insight.

Source: R. Paul (1993), Critical thinking: What every person needs to survive in a rapidly changing world *(Rev. 3rd Ed.). (pp. 22–23). Santa Rosa, CA: Foundation for Critical Thinking.*

Accurate versus inaccurate
Relevant versus irrelevant
Consistent versus inconsistent
Logical versus illogical
Deep versus superficial
Broad versus narrow
Complete versus incomplete
Significant versus trivial
Adequate (for purpose) versus inadequate
Fair versus biased or one sided (Paul, 1993, p. 63).

Critical thinking involves clearly describing and taking responsibility for our claims and arguments, critically evaluating our views no matter how cherished, and considering alternative views. "One cannot tell truth from falsity, one cannot tell an adequate answer to a problem from an irrelevant one, one cannot tell good ideas from trite ones—unless they are presented with sufficient clarity" (Popper, 1994, p. 71). This means paying attention to the process of reasoning (how we think), not just the product. Consider the statements in Chapter 4, Exhibit 4.3. If you carefully examined these using the preceding standards, you thought critically about them. Critical thinking encourages us to examine the context in which problems occur (e.g., to connect private troubles with public issues), to view questions from different points of view, to identify and question our assumptions, and to consider the possible consequences of different beliefs or actions (see list of Socratic questions in Appendix 6A).

Critical thinking and scientific reasoning are closely related. Both provide a way of thinking about and testing assumptions that is of unique value in problem solving. Consider, for example, the advances in medicine, transportation, computer technology, astronomy, and helping people with developmental disabilities, depression, and anxiety. Both critical thinking and scientific reasoning use reasoning for a purpose (i.e., to solve a problem), relying on standards such as clarity, relevance, and accuracy. Both regard criticism as essential to forward understanding, and both encourage us to challenge our assumptions, consider opposing views, and check our reasoning for errors. Both are anti-authoritarian.

RELATED VALUES, SKILLS, AND KNOWLEDGE

Values, skills and knowledge related to critical thinking are discussed in the next sections. Exhibit 6.2 shows key differences between critical and uncritical thinkers.

Values, Attitudes, and Styles

Critical thinking is independent thinking—thinking for oneself. Critical thinkers question what others view as self-evident: They ask:

- How do I know this claim is true?
- Who presented it as accurate? Are vested interests involved? How reliable are these sources?

- Are the facts presented correct?
- Have any facts been omitted?
- Is there any reliable evidence that a claim is true? Have any critical tests been performed? If so, were they relatively free of bias? Have the results been replicated? How representative were the samples used?
- Are there other promising points of view? Have these been tested?

Critical thinkers are skeptics rather than believers. That is, they are neither gullible (believing anything people say, especially if it agrees with their own views) nor cynical (believing nothing and having a negative outlook on life). This was nicely illustrated by Susan Blackmore in her keynote address at the 1991 annual meeting of CSICOP (Committee for the Scientific Investigation of Claims of the Paranormal) when she presented what she described as her favorite slide (a question mark) between slides of a sheep (illustrating gullibility) and a goat (illustrating cynicism). Cynics look only for faults. They have a contemptuous distrust of all knowledge. Skeptics (critical thinkers)

EXHIBIT 6.2
Differences Between Critical and Uncritical Thinkers

	Critical Thinkers	Uncritical Thinkers
General traits	Values criticism.	Avoids critical appraisal.
	Welcomes problematic situations and is tolerant of ambiguity.	Searches for certainty and is intolerant of ambiguity.
	Is self-critical; looks for alternative possibilities and goals; seeks evidence on both sides.	Is not self-critical and is satisfied with first attempts.
	Is reflective and deliberative; searches extensively when appropriate.	Is impulsive, gives up prematurely and is overconfident of the correctness of initial ideas.
	Values rationality.	Denigrate rationality; argues that thinking carefully won't help; overvalues intuition as a source of tested knowledge.
Goals	Is deliberative in discovering goals.	Is impulsive in discovering goals.
	Revises goals when necessary.	Does not revise goals.
Possibilities	Is open to multiple possibilities and considers alternatives.	Prefers to deal with limited possibilities; does not seek alternatives to an initial possibility.
	Is deliberative in analyzing possibilities.	Is impulsive in choosing possibilities.
Evidence	Uses evidence that challenges favored possibilities.	Ignores evidence that challenges favored possibilities.
	Searches for evidence against possibilities that are initially strong, or in favor of those that are weak.	Searches only for evidence that that favors strong possibilities.

Source: A. A. Glattborn & J. Baron (1991), The good thinker. In A. L. Costa (Ed.), Developing minds: A resource book for teaching thinking (rev. ed.). (Vol. 1). (p. 65). Alexandria, VA: Association for Supervision and Curriculum Development.

value truth and seek approximations to it through critical discussion and the testing of theories. Criticism is viewed as essential to forward understanding.

Key intellectual traits suggested by Richard Paul are shown in Exhibit 6.3. Critical thinking involves using related knowledge and skills in everyday life and acting on the results (Paul, 1993). It requires flexibility and a keen interest in discovering mistakes in our thinking. Truth (accuracy) is valued over "winning" or social approval. Values and attitudes related to critical thinking include open-mindedness, an interest in and respect for the opinion of others, a desire to be well informed, a tendency to think before acting, and curiosity. It means being fair-minded, that is, accurately de-

scribing opposing views and critiquing both preferred and less preferred views using the same rigorous standards.

Critical thinking encourages intellectual modesty rather than pomposity, by emphasizing the importance of our being aware of what we don't know. It discourages arrogance, the assumption that we know better than others or that our beliefs should not be subject to critical evaluation. As Popper emphasized, "In our infinite ignorance we are all equal" (Popper, 1992, p. 50). These attitudes reflect a belief in and respect for the intrinsic worth of all human beings, for valuing learning and truth without self-interest, and a respect for opinions that differ from one's own (Nickerson, 1988–1989, p. 507). They also highlight the role of affective com-

EXHIBIT 6.3
Examples of Valuable Intellectual Traits

Intellectual autonomy: Analyzing and evaluating beliefs on the basis of reason and evidence.

Intellectual civility: Taking others seriously as thinkers, treating them as intellectual equals, granting respect and full attention to their views, an interest in persuading rather than browbeating. It is distinguished from verbally attacking others, dismissing them, or stereotyping their views.

Intellectual confidence in reason: Confidence that in the long run one's own higher interests and those of humankind will best be served by giving the freest play to reason—by encouraging people to come to their own conclusions through a process of developing their own reasoning skills; form rational viewpoints, draw reasonable conclusions, persuade each other by reason and become reasonable people despite the many obstacles to doing so. Confidence in reason is developed through solving problems though reason, using reason to persuade, and being persuaded by reason. It is undermined when we are expected to perform tasks without understanding why, or to accept beliefs on the sole basis of authority or social pressure.

Intellectual courage: Critically assessing viewpoints regardless of negative reactions. To figure things out for ourselves, we must not passively and uncritically "accept" what we have "learned." It takes courage to be true to our own thinking, to tolerate ambiguity, and to face ignorance and prejudice in our own thinking. Examining cherished beliefs is difficult, and the penalties for non-conformity are often severe.

Intellectual curiosity: An interest in deeply understanding, figuring things out, and in learning. When we lack passion for figuring things out, we tend to settle for incomplete or incoherent views.

Intellectual discipline: Thinking guided by intellectual standards (e.g., clarity and relevance). Undisciplined thinkers neither know or care when they come to unwarranted conclusions, confuse distinct ideas, or ignore pertinent evidence. It takes discipline to keep focused on the intellectual task at hand, locate and carefully assess evidence, to systematically analyze and address questions and problems, to honor standards of clarity, precision, completeness, and consistency.

Intellectual empathy: Putting ourselves in the place of others to genuinely understand them and recognize our egocentric tendency to identify truth with our views. Indicators include accurately presenting the viewpoints and reasoning of others and reasoning from assumptions other than our own.

Intellectual humility: Awareness of the limits of one's knowledge, sensitivity to bias and prejudice and limitations of one's viewpoint. No one should claim more than he or she actually knows. It does not imply spinelessness or submissiveness. It implies lack of pretentiousness, boastfulness, or conceit, combined with insight into the strengths and weaknesses of the logical foundations of one's views.

Intellectual integrity: Honoring the same standards of evidence to which one holds others, practicing what one advocates, and admitting discrepancies and inconsistencies in one's own thought and action.

Intellectual perseverance: The pursuit of accuracy despite difficulties, obstacles, and frustration; adherence to rational principles despite irrational opposition of others; recognition of the need to struggle with confusion and unsettled questions over time to achieve understanding. This trait is undermined when others provide the answers, or do your thinking for you.

Source: R. Paul (1993), Adapted from Critical thinking: What every person needs to survive in a rapidly changing world *(Rev. 3rd Ed.). (pp. 470–472). Santa Rosa, CA: Foundation for Critical Thinking.*

ponents, such as a tolerance for ambiguity, differences of opinion, and empathy for others. Critical reflection stresses the value of self-criticism. It prompts question such as Could I be wrong? Have I considered alternative views? Do I have sound reasons to believe that this plan will help this client?

Related Skills and Knowledge

Problem solving, decision making, creative thinking, and critical thinking use similar kinds of knowledge and skills, including accurately weighing evidence and arguments, identifying assumptions, and recognizing contradictions (see Exhibit 6.4). As discussed in Chapter 5, we often fail to solve problems not because we are not intelligent but because we fall into intelligence traps (jump to conclusions). This highlights the value of acquiring strategies that avoid these "defaults" in thinking.

In addition to content knowledge, we need performance skills. For example, knowing the pitfalls to be avoided in observing the interaction between clients and significant others (e.g., students and teachers) will not be useful without the skills to avoid them. Critical thinking skills are not a substitute for problem-related knowledge. For example, you may need specialized knowledge to evaluate the plausibility of premises related to an argument. Consider the following example:

- Depression always has a psychological cause.
- Mr. Draper is depressed.
- Therefore the cause of Mr. Draper's depression is psychological in origin.

Even though the logic of this argument is sound, the conclusion may be false, as the cause of Mr. Draper's depression could be physiological. The more that is known about a subject that can decrease uncertainty about what decision is best, the more important it is to be familiar with this knowledge.

Nickerson (1986) suggests self-knowledge as one of the three forms of knowledge central to crit-

EXHIBIT 6.4
Examples of Critical Thinking Skills

Clarify problems.
Identify significant similarities and differences.
Recognize contradictions and inconsistencies.
Refine generalizations and avoid oversimplifications.
Clarify issues, conclusions, or beliefs.
Analyze or evaluate arguments, interpretations, beliefs, or theories.
Identify unstated assumptions.
Clarify and analyze the meanings of words or phrases.
Use sound criteria for evaluation.
Clarify values and standards.
Detect bias.
Distinguish relevant from irrelevant questions, data, claims, or reasons.
Evaluate the accuracy of different sources of information ("evidence").
Compare analogous situations; transfer insights to new contexts.
Make well-reasoned inferences and predictions.
Compare and contrast ideals with actual practice.
Discover and accurately evaluate the implications and consequences of a proposed action.
Evaluate one's own reasoning process.
Raise and pursue root or significant questions.
Make interdisciplinary connections.
Analyze or evaluate actions or policies.
Explore thoughts underlying feelings and feelings underlying thoughts.
Design and carry out critical tests of concepts, theories, and hypotheses.
Compare perspectives, interpretations, or theories.
Evaluate perspectives, interpretations, or theories.

Source: Based on R. H. Ennis (1987), A taxonomy of critical thinking dispositions and abilities. In J. B. Baron and R. J. Sternberg (Eds.), Teaching thinking skills: Theory and practice. New York: Freeman. Richard Paul (1993), Critical thinking: What every person needs to survive in a rapidly changing world. Santa Rosa, CA: Foundation for Critical Thinking.

ical thinking (in addition to knowledge of content related to a topic and critical thinking skills). Without self-knowledge, content and performance knowledge may remain unused. Three of the nine basic building blocks of reasoning that Paul suggested (ideas and concepts drawn on, whatever is taken for granted, and the point of view in which one's thinking is embedded), concern background beliefs that influence how we approach problems. Self-knowledge includes familiarity with resources and limitations of reasoning processes in general, knowledge of our personal style of thinking (e.g., the strategies we use), and personal obstacles (e.g., stereotypes that bias what we see) (see Chapter 2).

THE BENEFITS OF CRITICAL THINKING

Benefits of critical thinking are described next (also see Exhibit 6.5).

EXHIBIT 6.5
Benefits of Critical Thinking

You Will Be More Likely To

Clearly describe problems.
Discover problem-related resources and constraints.
See the connection between private troubles and public issues; think contextually.
Focus on outcomes related to clients' complaints.
Accurately assess the likelihood of attaining outcomes.
Make valuable contributions at case conferences (e.g., identify flawed arguments, suggest alternative views).
Correctly identify the degree of precision required to solve problems.
Select programs and policies that address problems with a minimum of dysfunctional side effects.
Make accurate predictions.
Select effective plans.
Accurately assess the effects of policies, programs, and plans.
Make timely changes in plans, programs, and policies that have unintended negative effects.
Use resources (e.g., time) wisely.
Respect and have empathy for others.
Continue to learn and to enhance learning skills.

Because You Will

Recognize the vital role of criticism in problem solving and decision making.
Discover false consciousness and mystifications.
Participate more actively in creating your environments.
Ask questions with a high payoff value (they decrease uncertainty about how to attain valued outcomes).
Discover contradictions between what you say and what you do.
Select effective service methods.
Recognize mistakes in thinking.
Use mistakes and less-than-hoped-for success as learning opportunities.
Recognize propaganda, pseudoscience, quackery, and fraud.
Communicate effectively.
Avoid cognitive biases.
Identify and remove personal obstacles to problem solving (e.g., excessive concern with social approval, self-censorship).
Take active steps to create and maintain a community of inquiry.
Be less likely to "sell out" (act in ways that do not support your values).
Be task focused.

Clearly Describe Problems and Discover Related Factors

Critical thinking encourages you to think contextually, to consider the big picture, and to connect personal troubles to social issues. Its value is in deepening your understanding of issues and selecting well-reasoned beliefs and actions. You will be less likely to offer vague incomplete accounts of problems. Only by considering the interlinked contingencies related to a problem can you and your clients accurately define it and estimate the degree to which it is solvable and if so, how. Many problems confronting clients are not solvable by social workers (e.g., lack of well-paying unskilled jobs, poor-quality education, and lack of health care for all residents).

Thinking critically will help you to avoid vague problem descriptions (e.g., he is aggressive, she has a mental disorder) that get in the way of discovering options. If you don't know what the problem is, you won't be able to solve it or to find out whether it has been solved. Critical thinking will guide you to be only as precise as you have to be to do the best that can be done under given circumstances. "Clarity is an intellectual value in itself; exactness and precision, however, are not" (Popper, 1992, p. 50).

Discover False Consciousness and Mystification

False consciousness and mystification refer to beliefs that obscure or distort, rather than reveal, what is true about the world, such as who benefits from certain ideologies, programs, practices, and policies. Many people believe in will power (Furnham, 1988), but they don't stop and ask: What is will power? Where does it "come from"? How does relying on will power help me address complaints? Who's making money from encouraging me to believe in will power?

We could ask the same questions about self-esteem. Who benefits from emphasizing "self-esteem" as a cause of problems? Who loses? We could argue that federal, state, and county governments save millions of dollars by attributing young people's less than hoped-for academic and job performance to their low self-esteem rather than providing education, housing, employment, health care, and recreation that provide the successful experiences on which self-esteem is grounded. Although appeals to self-esteem and will power may sound informative and as though they give us control over our fates, they seldom provide specific guidelines to achieving change. If we can identify the environmental and personal causes of our problems, we will be in a better position to offer our clients real (rather than merely perceived) influence over the quality of their lives. And we are more likely to discover connections between private troubles and social issues.

Critical thinking is an antidote to mystification. It can help us avoid actions and beliefs that diminish opportunities to help clients (see Exhibit 6.6). Many scholars, although vastly disparate in many or even most of their views, emphasize empowerment through self-education (e.g., Friere, 1973; Popper, 1994; Skinner, 1953). A key part of this education (this self-emancipation through knowledge) is the critical appraisal of accepted beliefs. This self-education will help you avoid censorship and deception, whether your own or that encouraged by others in ways and with results that you dislike. Steven Brookfield argues that reflection becomes critical when it has two purposes: (1) to understand how considerations of power undergird, frame, and distort educational processes and interactions; and (2) to question assumptions and practices that seem to make our lives easier but actually work against our own best long-term interests (1995, p. 8). He highlights the value of critical reflection in the "illumination of power" (p. 9).

In *Under the Cover of Kindness: The Invention of Social Work* (in press), Leslie Margolin argues that social workers mystify themselves about their motives and actions by continually emphasizing their essential goodness and services and that this mystification hides power over clients and self-interest. He argues that knowledge about clients is used to attain power over their lives and suggests that "it is social work's very rejection of political motive that makes it so politically effective." The more immune that social work is to criticism, the less able clients are to resist its ministrations (p. 11). Margolin contends that social workers rou-

EXHIBIT 6.6
Hypnotic Effect of One's Own Words

Source: W. H. Schneider (1965), *Danger: Men talking.* New York: Random House.

tinely convert clients' expressed needs (what they say they want) to a minute examination of them (what they are like, what their homes are like). He suggests that the great achievement of social workers during this century was gaining access to the privacy of the homes of the poor and that they used (and still do today) seductive and manipulative ways to do this (e.g., "the hostess technique"—a friendly demeanor to hide underlying investigative and judgmental roles).

Discourage the Active Promotion of Ignorance

Currently, ignorance is actively promoted in social work in a number of ways. One is through censorship (e.g., telling students not to read outside of social work; not presenting arguments against popular points of view, such as those questioning the concept of mental illness (Boyle, 1990; Szasz, 1994). Previous literature may be ignored. For example, descriptions of the "strengths perspective rarely mention the constructional approach described in *Social Casework: A Behavioral Approach* by Schwartz and Goldiamond (1975). Another way that ignorance is actively promoted is through punishment (e.g., ridiculing the questioning of popular views) (see also the discussion of pseudoscience, quackery, and fraud in Chapter 4).

Participate More Actively in Creating Your Environments

Many writers highlight the emancipating quality of critical thinking and argue that such reasoning is essential to a democracy (e.g., Baron, 1994; Brookfield, 1987, 1995; Friere, 1993; Paul, 1993). Thinking critically will help you recognize obstacles to your taking any responsibility for the quality of service offered by your agency. Such obstacles may be pressures to conform and to obey authorities as well as identifying with authorities, so becoming an authoritarian yourself (Nelson-Jones, 1987, p. 74). Brookfield emphasizes that "one fundamental purpose of encouraging adults to become critical thinkers is to help them feel a sense

of personal connection to wider happenings" (1987, p. 53).

Critical thinking will help you avoid the extremes of helplessness and hopelessness and grandiosity in your professional life. Grandiosity refers to excessive claims of effectiveness (e.g., claiming success, even though no one has cared enough to evaluate it. David Stoesz (1997) notes how seldom social workers take collective action to protest the increasingly diminished resources that compromise services. And too seldom do they blow the whistle on scandalous conditions.

Increase Your Self-Awareness

Self-awareness and critical inquiry go hand in hand. Both encourage contextual awareness—exploring how past and present environments influence what you do, value, and believe and how, in turn, you influence your environments. Critical thinking will help you discover false voices—beliefs you have accepted without critical thought which, on reflection, you find problematic. "Voices" are not necessarily true, nor are they necessarily ours (e.g., accepted after careful review).

> Those who counsel people to accept themselves uncritically lead them into the very trap they claim to be helping them to avoid, the trap of dependence on others. . . . The only way for people to become individuals is to . . . carefully examine the self they have taken for granted, identifying the influences society has had on them, evaluating those influences against some reasonably objective standard, and deciding which ones they will strengthen and which ones they will combat. (Ruggiero, 1988, p. 57)

Critical thinking helps free us from the prisons of unexamined views that limit our vision. It encourages us to examine the perspective within which we reason and the effect of our own cultural experiences in developing them. It can help us identify our "logical vulnerabilities," that is, topics or positions to which we have a strong initial reaction in one direction that prevents critical inquiry (Seech, 1993). Thinking carefully about problems and possible ways to solve them helps us detect contradictions between what we do and what we say we value. It teaches us to be aware of how our emotions affect our beliefs and actions (Salovey & Turk, 1988). Appendix 6B provides an opportunity for you to explore the extent to which you are a critical thinker.

Evaluate All Claims and Arguments

Making decisions involves suggesting and evaluating arguments in favor of believing or doing one thing rather than another. Consider the following:

- I think her own abuse as a child caused this parent to mistreat her children. We know that a past history of being abused leads to later aggressive behavior. And this parent denies that she abused her child.

- If Constance developed insight into her past relationships with her father, she would understand how she contributed to the problems in her own marriage.

- If he could get money to establish a community service agency, our neighborhood would have fewer problems.

The term *argument* is used here to refer to a form of inquiry in which we examine beliefs and actions, not to a conflict between two or more people. An argument "is a group of statements, one or more of which (the premises) support or provide evidence for another (the conclusion)" (Damer, 1995, p. 4). Argument is an essential form of inquiry. It provides a way to evaluate the accuracy of different views. For example, if different theories are contradictory, they both cannot be true. Claims asserted with no reasons for them are opinions, not arguments. An example is "I think games are best to use in activity groups." People use different criteria to evaluate claims and arguments (see Chapter 4).

What Is a Good Argument? An argument is aimed at suggesting the truth or demonstrating the falsity of a claim. "A good argument . . . offers reasons and evidence so that other people can make

up their minds for themselves" (Weston, 1992, p. xi). As Sir Karl Popper emphasizes:

> Victory in a debate is nothing, while even the slightest clarification of one's problem—even the smallest contribution made towards a clearer understanding of one's own position or that of one's opponent—is a great success. A discussion which you win but which fails to help you to change or to clarify your mind at last a little should be regarded as a sheer loss. (1994, p. 44)

A key part of an argument is the claim, conclusion, or position put forward. A second is the reasons or premises offered to support the claim. Indicator terms such as *therefore*, *because*, *thus*, and *so* often precede the premises for a claim. Premises can be divided into grounds and warrants. Grounds refer to the data or evidence offered to support the conclusions. Warrants concern the justification for the connection between the grounds and the claim. The grounds and their warrants should be acceptable, relevant and sufficient (see Appendix 6C). Let's say a teacher consults a school psychologist about a hard-to-manage student. The psychologist tells the teacher that the student is hyperactive and should be placed on medication because this has been found to decrease hyperactivity. What is the psychologist's conclusion? What is the premise? To what warrants does the psychologist appeal (e.g., an assumption that hyperactivity has a physical cause)? Do alternative accounts (rival hypotheses) suggest a different conclusion (e.g., a poorly designed curriculum that does not match the student's skills and knowledge, so he is bored)? (For practice in identifying rival hypotheses, see Huck & Sandler, 1979.)

Logic, in the narrow sense, is concerned with the form or validity of deductive arguments. "It provides methods and rules for restating information so as to make what is implicit explicit" (Nickerson, 1986, p. 7). Critical inquiry also requires skill in establishing the relevance of data to an argument. It requires raising questions such as "What's the likelihood that this claim is true given this evidence?" For instance, if a client hears voices, is he schizophrenic? Logic is not helpful in deciding that a client who complains of fatigue and headaches should be seen by a physician to determine whether these complaints have a physical basis.

The general rules for constructing arguments are (1) clearly identify the premises and conclusion; (2) present your ideas in a natural order; (3) use reliable premises; (4) use specific, concrete language; (5) avoid loaded terms; and (6) stick to one meaning for each term (Weston, 1992, p. v). You could use an outline form:

Premise 1: _____
Premise 2: _____
Conclusion: _____
_____

Be sure to separate the inferences and evidence and avoid overstating inferences. Review your argument for fallacies, and search for alternative accounts. Can you make a strong "rebuttal argument" against your position?

The accuracy of a conclusion does not necessarily indicate that the reasoning used to reach it was sound. For example, errors in the opposite direction may have canceled each other out. Likewise, the lack of evidence for a claim does not mean that it is incorrect (nor does it keep people from believing it). Assigning the proper weight to different kinds of evidence is an important part of analyzing an argument. People often use "consistency" to support their beliefs (e.g., degree of agreement among different sources of data). A helper may say that Mrs. X is depressed because she has a past history of depression. An assertion should be consistent with other beliefs. Self-contradictory views should not knowingly be held. However, two or more assertions may be consistent with each other but yield little or no insight into the soundness of an argument. Thus, saying that A (a history of "depression") is consistent with B (alleged current "depression") is saying only that given A, it is possible to believe B.

Recognize Informal Fallacies

A fallacy is a mistake in thinking, "a violation of one of the criteria of a good argument" (Damer,

1995, p. 24). A valid argument is one whose premises, if true, offer good or sufficient grounds for accepting a conclusion. Thus, an argument may be unsound for one of three reasons:

(1) There may be something wrong with its logical structure.

- All mental patients are people.
- John is a person.
- Therefore John is a mental patient.

(2) It may contain false premises.

- All social workers are competent.
- Mrs. Landis is a social worker.
- Therefore Mrs. Landis is competent.

(3) It may be irrelevant or circular.

- Kicking the dog is a sign of aggression.
- Brian kicks his dog.
- Therefore Brian has an aggressive personality.

The last two kinds are *informal* fallacies. They have a correct logical form but are still incorrect. Fallacies result in defective arguments (e.g., the premises may not provide an adequate basis for a conclusion). A premise may be unacceptable or irrelevant or provide insufficient support. Most fallacies are informal (see Damer, 1995; Engel, 1994; Kahane, 1995; Thouless, 1974). They concern the content of arguments rather than their form. These are essentially irrelevant appeals (such as judging the soundness of a position by the confidence with which it is stated) in which the wrong point is supported or premises that are not relevant to an issue are used to support a conclusion. There are many kinds of informal fallacies. Anthony Weston (1992) considers the two greatest fallacies to be drawing conclusions based on too little evidence (e.g., generalizing from incomplete information) and overlooking alternatives.

In the fallacy of "begging the question," a statement appears to address the facts but does not. Variants of question begging include the use of alleged certainty and circular reasoning. Vacuous guarantees (e.g., "It works") may be offered or an assumption made that because a condition ought to be, it is. Some informal fallacies overlook the facts, as in a "sweeping generalization" in which a rule or assumption that is valid in general is applied to a specific example for which it is not valid. Consider the assertion that parents who were abused as children abuse their own children. In fact, many do not. Other informal fallacies distort facts or positions, as in "straw person arguments" in which a position that is significantly different from the one presented is attacked. Diversions such as trivial points, irrelevant objections, or emotional appeals may be used to direct attention away from an argument's main point. Emotional reasoning is another common fallacy. For example, we may be influenced by appeals to pity, fear, or self-interest (such as enhancing self-esteem). Some fallacies work by creating confusion, such as a feigned lack of understanding and excessive wordiness that obscures arguments. "Either–oring" is a common fallacy. That is, we incorrectly assume there are only two options when in fact there are many. This fallacy of the false dilemma prevents us from discovering other options. If you are aware of these common informal fallacies, you will be better able to detect bogus claims and faulty arguments.

Some informal fallacies could also be classified as social psychological persuasion strategies. They work through our emotions rather than through the thoughtful consideration of a claim. For example, we like to please people we like and may be reluctant to question claims they make. Influences based on liking (e.g., the "buddy–buddy syndrome") or fear may prevent us from making well-reasoned decisions in case conferences (e.g., Dingwall, Eekelar, & Murphy, 1983; Meehl, 1973). People may try to pressure us into maintaining a position by telling us that we must do so in order to be consistent with our prior beliefs or actions—as if we could not (or should not) change our minds. Or they may appeal to fears about scarcity (if you don't act now, a valuable opportunity will be lost). Learn how to recognize and counter these persuasion strategies (e.g., Cialdini, 1993).

Recognize Propaganda

We can persuade people (including ourselves) through either well-reasoned arguments or questionable approaches, such as relying on manner of presentation or appeals to emotions (pity, fear, hate, attraction). The purpose of propaganda is to encourage beliefs and actions with the least thought possible (Ellul, 1965). Its purpose is not to inform but to persuade. Propagandists take advantage of informal fallacies. They encourage mistakes in thinking by trying to persuade us through irrelevant emotional appeals (to pity, anger, or fear) and ad hominem arguments (attacking those who disagree with them, rather than addressing their arguments). Propagandists may misrepresent their position (tell only part of the truth) or rely on slogans and putdowns. Human services advertisements often rely on propaganda methods such as vivid case examples (Gibbs & Gambrill, 1996). Many examples can be found in *Social Work*, especially for residential care centers for adolescents. Critical thinking skills, values, and knowledge will help you spot propaganda in human services advertisements (e.g., reliance on testimonials).

Communicate Effectively

Effective communication is a vital practice skill. Clear language is important, whether speaking or writing. David Perkins (1992) uses the term the "language of thoughtfulness" to highlight its role in critical thinking. Clear communication requires use of a language (English, Spanish, French) in accord with agreed-on meanings. The degree to which a "culture of thoughtfulness" exists is reflected in the language used. To the gullible, obscurity heightens the appearance of profoundness; indeed, Armstrong (1980) found that clear writing was viewed as less profound than obscure writing. If terms are not clarified, confused discussions may result because of the assumption of "one word, one meaning." Vague terms that may vary in their definitions include *abuse*, *aggression*, and *addiction*. Technical terms may be carelessly used, resulting in "bafflegarb" or "psychobabble"—words that sound informative but are not.

Karl Popper argues that "critical reason is the only alternative to violence so far discovered" and that it is the duty of intellectuals to "write and speak in clear simple language" (which requires hard work) in order to replace violence with critical discussion (Popper, 1994, p. 69). This view conflicts with what Popper calls "the cult of incomprehensibility, or imprecise and weak sounding language," and also with the common habit of stating "the utmost trivialities in high-sounding language" (p. 71).

We often misuse speculation (assume that what is can be discovered merely by thinking about it). Using a descriptive term as an explanation offers an illusion of understanding. For example, a teacher may state "Ralph is aggressive," and when asked, "How do you know?" she may say, "He hits other children." If then asked why she thinks Ralph does this, she may reply, "Because he is aggressive." This goes around in a circle. It is a pseudoexplanation.

A knowledge of fallacies related to the use of language and a care in using it should improve the quality of your judgments. Both professionals and intellectuals have a special responsibility to write and speak clearly. Clients will not understand obscure jargon or garbled sentences. Critical thinking can be valuable in making organized presentations at staff meetings and case conferences. This will help you to organize information logically and carefully, consider your goals, and consider alternatives. Disagreements often concern how a word is to be used (for example, what is empowerment?). One way to get sidetracked in problem solving is to become caught up in defining words rather than critically testing theories by making risky predictions and testing them. Karl Popper argues that a preoccupation with definition will lead only to an endless regression to other words. What is needed are bold guesses about the nature of a problem, combined with critical discussion and a testing of related arguments. Like scientists, professional helpers are concerned with finding real solutions to real problems. "Our aim should not be to analyze meanings, but to seek for interesting and important truths; that is, for true theories" (Popper, 1992, p. 178).

Avoid Cognitive Biases

Thinking carefully about claims will help you to avoid the cognitive biases described in Chapter 5. Guidelines that you can use to avoid these sources of error are discussed in this chapter as well as later chapters.

Have Greater Empathy for Others and Ourselves

Critical thinking encourages intellectual empathy and contextual understanding, both of which encourage empathy for ourselves and others. Understanding the context of behavior will encourage empathic rather than judgmental reactions, even when confronted with challenging situations that "push your buttons." Valuing truth means having a sincere interest in understanding other points of view. We know we may be (and often are) wrong. Kuhn (1970) argues that we cannot talk fruitfully (learn from one another) if we have different frameworks. In *The Myth of the Framework* (1994), Karl Popper argues that what is important are theories and problems, not frameworks. He points out that we share many problems, regardless of our particular frameworks.

Recognize Pseudoscience, Fraud, and Quackery

Thinking critically about claims and arguments will help you detect pseudoscience, fraud, and quackery and avoid their influence (see the discussion in Chapter 4).

OBSTACLES TO AND COSTS OF CRITICAL THINKING

Thinking critically has both costs and obstacles.

Costs

The costs of critical thinking include forgoing the comfortable feeling of "certainty" and the time and hard work required to clearly describe what you believe and to understand different views (Gambrill, 1990). You must abandon intellectual arrogance and instead accept intellectual responsibility. No longer will you be able to say, "Well that's just what I think should be done" without taking responsibility for providing an argument for your position and a rebuttal to other views. No longer can you rely on unfounded authority, anecdotal experiences, or case examples to support your views. Relativists will have to examine contradictions between their views (all knowledge claims are equally valid) and their actions (e.g., driving cars, flying in planes). (For an excellent critique of postmodernism, see Munz, 1992.) Acquiring practice knowledge and skills takes time and effort and often requires abandoning favored beliefs.

The sheer quantity of potentially relevant material is a problem that is aggravated by lack of agreement about criteria to use to select knowledge (see Chapter 4). Valuable criteria for selecting material include relevance (how useful it is to achieving service goals), feasibility (how I can use it) and the range of situations to which it can be applied (Rothman & Thomas, 1994). Learning a new language and new concepts and letting go of old ones may result in the loss of a valued "believer group" (Munz, 1985). You may fall into the "sunk costs error" (continuing to invest in one option because of previous "investments" in it, even though it looks like a loser). The best option here is to cut your losses by not "throwing good money after bad."

Obstacles

Obstacles to critical thinking include the prevalence of uncritical thinking; social, political, and economic interests; and a disdain for intellectual rigor.

The Prevalence of Uncritical Thinking. Thinking critically about claims is not valued by many groups and individuals. To the contrary, they may try to obscure reality by relying on propaganda methods and appealing to pseudoscience. (See discussion of the functions of false knowledge in

Chapter 4.) Phillips (1992) argues that raising questions about "truth" has the taboo quality today that talking about sex had in Victorian times. We are surrounded by pseudoscience and propaganda, making it a continuous challenge to resist their allure (e.g., Ellul, 1965; Pratkanis & Aronson, 1991).

Professional ideology poses an obstacle if it interferes with the critical appraisal of claims (Margolin, in press). Burnham (1987) argues that one reason that superstition won and science lost in the United States is the media's role in presenting content in fragmented bits and pieces. The media, pop psychology (such as New Age material), and professional journals often present incomplete accounts of problems. Feelings and thoughts are often more vivid than environmental causes. It is easy to overlook environmental circumstances that contribute to these thoughts and feelings. Incomplete analyses of problems contribute to ignoring the bigger picture and obscure the complexity of issues. We may read "Crack-addicted mother kills baby." The focus is on the mother's addiction. Little or nothing may be said about her impoverished life circumstances, both past and present, and related economic and political factors. The media often suppress information and mystify rather than clarify problems (e.g., see Jenson, 1994—*Censored: The News That Didn't Make the News and Why*). Millions watch talk shows like Oprah Winfrey's and Geraldo's and are influenced by claims based on personal opinion and manner of presentation (e.g., the confidence with which people speak). For instance, in a show on bullying, an "expert" emphasized that bullies have low self-esteem and that is why they bully others. In fact, research shows that bullies do not have low self-esteem (Olweus, 1993). Fewer and fewer organizations control the mass media (Bagdikian, 1992). This decreases exposure to alternative points of view.

Work settings differ in the extent to which they value critical inquiry. They may provide no incentives for arriving at well-reasoned beliefs and actions. Access to new material may be difficult because of busy schedules that allow no time off for reading. Teachers and supervisors may not model the intellectual virtues associated with critical inquiry such as selecting methods based on empirical evidence of what is helpful in attaining outcomes clients value. Teachers may encourage a relativistic position, in which anything goes, or view students as passive receptacles into which they pour "knowledge." Although clear writing is a responsibility of intellectuals and those who write about practice, you will often find obscurantism in its place. Terms may be unclear. Practice methods or implications may not be clearly spelled out or candid statements made about the lack of critical testing of claims.

> I lead a life where I hardly have time to think.
> —Nelson Mandela, *Higher than Hope*, 1991

Social, Political, and Economic Factors. Concerns about protecting vested interests (e.g., economic gain and power) may loom much larger than concerns about helping people and "telling the truth." The mental health industry is big business and there is sharp competition for clients in many areas of practice. Politics thrive on polarization. "So we have behaviorists on the one hand, mentalists on the other, each camp believing the other to be naive, stupid, and occasionally downright evil" (Schnaitter, 1986, p. 265). Social, political, and economic factors are partly responsible for the fragmentation of psychology and social work and the ambivalence about what criteria to use to accept "knowledge." In *The Mismeasure of Women*, Carol Tavris gives many examples of how stereotypes influence research. The efforts of professional organizations such as the National Association of Social Workers (NASW) to protect turf, acquire funds, and enhance the positive image of social workers compete with measured, accurate descriptions of what social work can and has achieved. Careers are advanced by new "discoveries," new modes of therapy, encouraging a proliferation of untested therapies, each claiming success. Millions of dollars are spent each year on products such as subliminal tapes, despite the absence of evidence that they deliver what they promise (Druckman & Bjork, 1991). Competing values and goals may be an obstacle. Not all helpers

give first priority to the goals of enhancing the personal welfare of clients and avoiding harm. Goals that compete with these include maintaining status by appearing more expert than is the case (perhaps even to yourself).

Courage Is Required. It takes courage to challenge accepted beliefs, especially when held by "authorities" who do not value a culture of thoughtfulness in which alternative views are welcomed and arguments critically evaluated. To those who uncritically embrace a "doing good ideology," asking that verbal statements of compassion and caring be accompanied by evidence of helping, may seem disloyal or absurd. To the autocratic and powerful, raising questions threatens their power to simply "pronounce" what is and is not without taking responsibility for presenting well-reasoned arguments and involving others in decisions. Even when you ask questions tactfully, people may feel threatened, and their feelings may be hurt. Other people may become defensive, hostile, or angry when you question what they say—even when you do so with courtesy and intellectual empathy. Socrates was sentenced to death because he questioned other people's beliefs (See Plato's Apology). Without emotion management skills for handling negative reactions to critical inquiry (your own as well as that of others), you may have a lapse of spirit and may not challenge fuzzy thinking. The skills described in Chapter 13 will help you to develop a "thick skin" where you need it to offer the best to clients. Evolutionary history highlights the powerful role of status. Thus the social work student who questions a professor, supervisor, administrator, or physician may be viewed as a threat rather than as a source of additional ideas. An understanding of social hierarchies and how ranking maintains them will help you view such reactions in their historical and biological context. This evolutionary view will help you not to take things personally. It links our lives to the entire span of animal and human development (Gilbert, 1989).

It takes courage to question our beliefs and candidly examine their accuracy, especially if you do not usually do so. Unless you have grown up in an environment in which critical thinking was valued and modeled, you may feel personally attacked when someone disagrees with or questions what you say. You may have to unlearn part of what you have learned. "Many participants in a rational, that is, a critical, discussion find it particularly difficult that they have to unlearn what their instincts seem to teach them (and what they are taught, incidentally, by every debating society); that is, to win" (Popper, 1994, p. 44).

Personal Characteristics. Our willingness to suspend disbelief and to rush from one task to another, leaving no time to think carefully, also are obstacles. Vincent Ruggiero (1988) lists the following obstacles:

1. Disdain for intellectual rigor. "Solving problems, making decisions, and evaluating issues is hard work and requires an active approach, perseverance in the face of difficulty and confusion, and refusal to settle for easy answers" (p. 55). As Ruggiero notes, we are accustomed to being passive spectators and to being entertained, whereas learning requires action and may not always be entertaining. Anti-intellectualism is alive and well in academia as well as elsewhere (e.g., Gross & Levitt, 1994).

2. Misconceptions about oneself. Ruggiero refers to "the romantic notion that the self is effectively insulated from the influences of society" (1988, p. 56). We are encouraged to look within to discover our values as if we have carefully chosen them when we may never have carefully thought about them. As Ruggiero notes, the influence others have on us in childhood precedes for years our ability to reflect on this. We uncritically absorb much during our early development from our parents, peers, and the mass media.

3. Misconceptions about the truth. This includes the "view that truth is entirely subjective . . . people create their own truth and whatever they accept as true is 'true for them'" (Ruggiero, 1988, p. 58). If one kind of thinking were as good as another, we would not do much of what we do, in-

cluding designing planes that stay in the air and cars that work well. Ruggiero argues that relativeness strips ideas of their interest. All are the same.

> It undermines curiosity and wonder, robs students of sensitivity to problems, and makes relevant data indistinguishable from irrelevant and promising approaches indistinguishable from unpromising, thereby paralyzing creativity and leaving minds mired in subjectivity. If one idea is as good as another, there is no good reason for students to subject their ideas to critical scrutiny and no purpose in the discussion of issues other than to stroke one's vanity (1988, p. 59).

4. Confusion about values. Misconceptions about the truth result in confusion about values. If truth is relative, how can we compare values? Acceptance of moral relativism makes it impossible to judge. If one truth is as good as another, we cannot say which actions are morally correct and which are not. However as Ruggiero observes, not judging is itself a form of judgment that may permit injustices to continue. "Both relativism and absolutism are extreme positions which should be rejected" (1988, p. 61).

5. Basing beliefs on feelings. We often base our beliefs on what we "feel"—our emotional reactions. This encourages uncritical acceptance of actions and beliefs.

6. Intellectual insecurity results from the other five obstacles.

> Because of their disdain for intellectual rigor, many students are uncomfortable when problems and issues are not solved quickly and easily. Because they harbor a misconception about self, they are unprepared to deal with positions that differ from their own and so are ill at ease with dialogue. Because they harbor a misconception about truth, they are not ready to support their views and are nervous and sometimes belligerent when asked to do so. Because they are confused about values, they are defensive when discussions about values arise. Because they are in the habit of basing their belief on feelings, accepted uncritically, they can do little more than assert their views and thus are intimidated by reasoned discourse (Ruggiero, 1988, p. 64).

Information-Processing Factors. The way we acquire and process information influences our judgments. We tend to seek data that confirm our views and to overlook those that do not. This tendency will be an obstacle to becoming informed unless you develop skills to counter it. We are influenced by cognitive biases and tend to fall into certain intelligence traps such as not exploring alternative views (see Chapter 5). Use helpful questions and tools to counter the misleading effects of availability and resemblance criteria (see Chapter 5). "John Wayne reasoning" discourages critical thinking. David Perkins uses this term to describe those who prefer clear-cut black-and-white views to a reflective exploration of pros and cons (1995, p. 129).

REDUCING THE COSTS AND INCREASING THE BENEFITS OF CRITICAL THINKING

Steps you can take to reduce the costs and increase the benefits of critical thinking are described in the next section.

Remember What's at Stake

Keep in mind that your clients benefit or suffer as a result of your beliefs and actions. Concentrating on helping clients attain outcomes they value will give you the courage and focus you need to use your critical thinking skills. And keep in mind that your professional code of ethics lists service first. This will help you not to take things personally and to keep your purpose clearly in view: to help clients achieve outcomes they value and to avoid harm. It will help you have the courage and take the time needed (when available) to question what should be questioned. Although rapid intuitive thinking may suffice in some situations, at other times critical thinking may be needed to make well-reasoned decisions. Focusing on service goals will avoid "cognitive load bottleneck" (Perkins, 1995, p. 169) because you will focus on gathering information that reduces uncertainty about how to help clients.

Allocate Your Resources Wisely

You won't have time to think carefully about all the decisions you make. When working with clients confronting a crisis, you must work fast. You may have a caseload that makes it impossible to carefully plan services. You will have to decide how much time and effort to devote to what particular decisions. Like it or not, many social workers have to "triage" problems in terms of how much resources to devote to which ones. This problem doesn't go away by not thinking about it. Rather, by not thinking about it, you may fail to take corrective steps. As your skills increase, you may be able to help clients resolve some problems more swiftly or recognize more quickly that the problem cannot be solved. You can also work together with your colleagues to change policies and practices that limit service options.

View Criticism as Essential to Learning and Problem Solving

The purpose of education is to expand our horizons—to challenge accepted views, to consider new ones, to acquire well-reasoned ways to evaluate beliefs, and to replace mystification with understanding. Many scholars suggest that we cannot learn unless there is conflict. Never put your "whole self" on the line when threatened by a question or disagreement (e.g., think you are "stupid," slow, uninformed). It is precisely when you feel attacked (but in reality may be confronted with a good question asked in a respectful manner) that you can use your philosophy of practice as a guide to choose wisely among competing goals (e.g., to discover the most accurate account rather than to "win" an argument).

When a critical discussion of your views reveals flaws, you may feel disappointed, uncertain, anxious, or angry. Perhaps a Buddhist perspective on feelings will help you not allow these momentary negative feelings to keep you from pursuing higher goals (to help clients by discovering approximations to what may be true). Thinking critically about your goals, actions, and values will involve you in the fascinating if arduous task of deciding for yourself how life should be lived and social work should be practiced. You will raise questions about the source of your values. You will look around the world and back into the recent and distant past to test your assumptions. Questioning the accuracy of your judgments will help you to pay attention to the uncertainty involved in making decisions and to shift from being a "believer" who does not question their beliefs to a "questioner." Rather than saying, "I believe there is such a thing as mental illness," you might say, "I think the evidence suggests that there is such a thing as mental illness." This focuses attention on related evidence.

Value Errors as Learning Opportunities

One of your greatest challenges will be to change your attitude toward errors. Feedback is an essential part of learning. If you are not making mistakes, you are probably not learning. The outcomes of your actions provide valuable feedback. Did you achieve what you had hoped? Could you have been more successful? If so, how? Mistakes are inevitable, and you can learn from them. This is explicitly recognized in professions such as medicine (Bosk, 1979). Only by making and recognizing your mistakes can you make better guesses about what difficulties you may have in solving a problem. Failures provide an opportunity to do better in the future. "The growth of knowledge always consists in correcting earlier knowledge. . . . Settled knowledge does not grow" (Popper, 1994, p. 156). Popper contends that there "is only one way of learning to understand a problem which we do not yet understand—and that is to try and solve it and fail. . . . Our failure hopefully provides information about where the difficulties lie and we can use this information to make better tests in the future" (pp. 157–158). So by criticizing our efforts, "we learn more and more about our problem: we learn where its difficulties lie" (p. 158).

Pay Attention to What You Don't Know

If problem-related knowledge will help your clients attain valued outcomes, it is important to estimate accurately your current knowledge and, if it is lacking, to fill in the gaps. In their course on medical ignorance at the University of Arizona School of Medicine, Witte and his colleagues (1994) stress the importance of attending to what you don't know. You can use Venn diagrams to estimate knowledge needed, what is available, and how much of this you know. Keep in mind that most guesses (theories) about what is true are wrong (see, for example, any history of science or medicine). As Socrates stated, "I know that I know almost nothing, and hardly this."

Plan Time-outs for Critical Reflection

In the everyday world of practice, you may not have time for critical reflection; you may have to act and reflect later. Keep track, in a critical thinking log, of exchanges, decisions, or questions you want to review, and consider them later when you have time. The points you note become topics for staff meetings, and if they affect the quality of services, they should be discussed. Stay informed by seeking out sources that present alternative perspectives for accepted views. Ask: What's missing? Have there been any critical tests of this claim? Are there other points of view? Otherwise you may be lulled into accepting dubious claims and faulty arguments.

Review Your Beliefs About What Knowledge Is and How to Get It

As discussed in Chapter 4, our beliefs about knowledge and how it can be acquired affect how we think and what we learn. It is thus important to examine them.

Practice

Practice is important to learning all skills, including critical thinking. You can practice critical thinking when thinking, reading, writing, listening or speaking. Scores of opportunities will arise each day, in work-related contexts, and also when reading the newspaper, listening to the radio or watching television, or talking to your friends. Look for books containing useful exercises (e.g., Gibbs & Gambrill, 1996; Huck & Sandler, 1979). I ask my students to keep a critical thinking log. This allows them to think about interesting ideas and questions later. You might want to note agency decisions that you should think about (e.g., how to ration scarce resources), arguments in favor of different points of view on a question of interest, or relationships between ideas.

Use Helpful Maxims and Questions

Helpful maxims include the following:

- Focus on service goals.
- Search for alternative views.
- Pay attention to environmental variables.
- Be suspicious of vivid material.
- Look for material that is both true and informative.
- Pay attention to uncertainty.
- Get the whole picture.
- Watch your language.

- Beware of personally relevant data.

Some helpful questions are the following:

- What's missing? What's wrong with this picture?
- What are my assumptions?
- Is there evidence against my point of view? (See Exhibit 6.7.)
- How extensive is my ignorance of domain-specific knowledge and skills?
- How can I test my predictions?
- What's the relative frequency?
- Is it a question of fact (Data can be gathered to answer it.)
- Where did the sample come from? (This question will help you avoid decisions based on biased samples.)
- Are my metaphors misleading?
- What about the other three cells? (see Chapter 17.)
- Have I thought carefully enough about this decision?
- Given this evidence, what's the likelihood that this claim is accurate?

EXHIBIT 6.7
Evaluating Inferences About a Behavior

Behavior: _____

Inference	Supporting evidence	Counterevidence
1. _____	a. _____	a. _____
_____	b. _____	b. _____
	c. _____	c. _____
2. _____	a. _____	a. _____
_____	b. _____	b. _____
	c. _____	c. _____
3. _____	a. _____	a. _____
_____	b. _____	b. _____
	c. _____	c. _____

Which inference has survived the most critical tests? _____

Take Advantage of Visual Representations

Take advantage of visual tools that can help you and your clients clarify problems and related factors (e.g., Mattaini, 1993a). You can use decision trees, flowcharts, or Venn diagrams. You can use concept maps to explore your assumptions related to a concept (i.e., to identify your associations with this concept). You and your clients can use balance sheets to guide your decision making in complex situations (Eddy, 1990).

Take Advantage of Available Knowledge

Take advantage of information that decreases uncertainty related to practice decisions. For example, knowing that 40% of the alleged cases of sexual abuse are false should caution you not to jump to the conclusion that claims of abuse are always true. And knowing that interviewer bias is common should remind you to question other helpers' reports. Keep in mind that correlational research concerning the relationship between a symptom (e.g., depression) and an outcome (e.g., a suicide attempt) does not permit you to predict what a particular client will do.

Take Advantage of Helpful Distinctions

Distinctions that will help you critically evaluate different views of problems and their causes are described next.

Truth and Credibility. Credible statements are those that are possible to believe. As Dennis Phillips (1992) points out, just about anything may be credible (believable). This does not mean it is true. Thus the distinction between truth and credibility is an important one. History shows that often what once seemed credible was false (the belief that tuberculosis was inherited) and what once seemed incredible was true (e.g., people could fly in airplanes). Accounts are often accepted when they "make sense," even though there is no evidence that they are accurate. Only by testing our guesses can we evaluate their soundness.

Reasoning and Truth. Reasoning does not necessarily yield the truth. "An assertion is true if it corresponds to or agrees with the facts" (Popper, 1994, p. 174) (also see the Glossary in Appendix 4A). "People who are considered by many of their peers to be reasonable people often do take, and are able to defend quite convincingly, diametrically opposing positions on controversial matters" (Nickerson, 1986, p. 12). However, effective reasoners are more likely than are ineffective reasoners to prefer theories that are closer to the truth. Some beliefs (guesses) are better (closer to the truth) than are others.

Widely Accepted Versus Well Supported. What is widely accepted is not necessarily accurate. For example, many people believe in the influence of astrological signs (i.e., their causal role is widely accepted). However, some would argue that there is no evidence that they influence behavior (Dean, 1986–1987).

A Feeling That Something Is True and Whether It Is True. People often use their "feelings" as a criterion to accept or reject possible causes. A "feeling" that something is true may not (and often does not) correspond with what is true. Not making this distinction helps to account for the widespread belief in many questionable causes, such as astrological influences (Dean, 1987). Basing actions and beliefs on feelings discourages a careful examination of their soundness, and in professional contexts, this may result in decisions that do not benefit clients.

Bias/Propaganda/Point of View. Bias refers to an emotional leaning to one side. Biased people may or may not be aware of their biases. Propaganda refers to strategies designed to encourage action with the least thought possible (Ellul, 1965). Examples of propaganda tactics are appealing to emotions or authority, presenting only one side of an argument, and deflecting criticism by attacking the critics' motives. Propagandists are aware of their interests and often disguise them. People with a point of view are aware of their interests but describe their sources and do not use propaganda devices. Their statements and questions encourage rather than discourage critical review, as they state their views clearly so that they can be examined critically. People with a point of view are open to clarifying their statements when asked to do so. (For further discussion, see Pratkanis & Aronson, 1991.)

Beliefs, Facts, Opinions, and Reasoned Judgments. One definition of a belief is that it is a statement (guess/inference/assumption) that can be shown to be false. If I say, "Play therapy helps children overcome anxiety," I can test this to find out whether it is accurate. There is no way to test certain beliefs, such as whether there is a God. Belief

implies a commitment, a reluctance to criticize a view. Commitment and criticism are clashing approaches (Bartley, 1984). Facts can be defined as beliefs that have been critically evaluated and/or tested. *Facts* are capable of falsification, whereas beliefs may not be. *Opinions* are statements of preferences and values. It does not make sense to consider opinions as true or false, because people have different preferences, as in the statement: "I prefer cognitive explanations for behavior." This differs from the claim "What people say to themselves influences their behavior," because we can gather evidence to find out if this statement is accurate. Reasoned judgments consist of sound arguments based on good evidence.

SUMMARY

Critical thinking can help you make well-reasoned practice decisions and avoid misleading directions and bogus claims. It will help you discover alternative views and avoid false prophets. Another benefit of critical thinking is reaching moral decisions in which you consider the interests of all involved parties and act as you think you should. Critical thinking requires a careful examination of the evidence related to beliefs and a fair-minded consideration of alternative views. Scientific reasoning and critical thinking are closely related. Both value clarity, critical discussion, and the testing of assumptions. Critical thinking encourages us to reflect on how we think and why we hold certain beliefs. It requires an acceptance of well-reasoned conclusions even when they are not our preferred ones. Critical thinkers question what others take for granted. They challenge accepted beliefs and ways of acting. They ask questions such as Have there been any critical tests of your claim? Could there be another explanation? Raising such questions often requires courage. Valuing the search for approximations to the truth will help you honor related intellectual virtues such as accurately representing disliked as well as favored points of view. Many of the costs of not thinking carefully about beliefs and actions are hidden, such as false assumptions that may result in doing harm in the name of doing good. Curiosity may languish when we accept vague, oversimplified accounts that obscure the complexity of issues and give the illusion of understanding but offer no guidelines for helping clients. Complaints may continue because causes remain hidden.

Critical discussion is not the norm in our society, and it is not in the interests of many groups to reveal the lack of evidence for claims made and policies recommended; fuzzy thinking is the oppressor's friend. Keeping your eye on your goal—to help clients—will provide a firm grounding for courage to question assumptions.

REVIEWING YOUR COMPETENCIES

Reviewing What You Know

1. Discuss the value of critical inquiry for social work.
2. Describe the hallmarks of critical thinking and discussion.
3. Describe the components of critical inquiry.
4. Explain the difference between a cynic and a skeptic (critical thinker).
5. Identify your sources of "logical vulnerability" (see the section on increasing self-awareness).
6. Describe the relationship between critical thinking and scientific reasoning.
7. Explain what is meant by the term *propaganda*.
8. Describe the parts of an argument.
9. Give examples of the influence of language on practice decisions.
10. Identify reasoning errors in the following statements:
    a. That may be true, but the last five clients I saw did not show this behavior.
    b. If this is what nursing homes are like, I don't look forward to getting old.
    c. All I know is that the alcoholics we see here never recover.
    d. I just don't understand it. We know that Mrs. Jones is a schizophrenic, but she doesn't act like one.

Reviewing What You Do

1. You can accurately diagram practice-related arguments and identify flaws in them.
2. You can identify vague terms.
3. You ask questions that are valuable in assessing the accuracy of claims.
4. You can explain what critical thinking and discussion is so that a person who does not understand this acquires this knowledge.
5. Observation of your work demonstrates that you value intellectual virtues inherent in critical inquiry.
6. You welcome opportunities to examine the accuracy of your beliefs (e.g., welcome constructive criticism), as shown in discussions with colleagues and clients.
7. You listen carefully to other people's ideas.
8. You correctly describe both preferred and opposing views on topics discussed.
9. You recognize the connection between private troubles and public issues.
10. You can accurately identify fallacies in practice-related material (e.g., begging the question).
11. You thank others for pointing out flaws in your arguments.
12. You review your assumptions when given new information.
13. You clearly identify assumptions related to your argument.
14. You rely on valid sources of evidence when making decisions.
15. You identify and overcome personal obstacles to critical thinking.
16. You reinforce behaviors associated with critical thinking in your educational and work environments.

Reviewing Results

1. Your practice actions and beliefs are well reasoned.
2. You make ethical decisions.
3. Agency culture moves closer to a one of thoughtfulness.

APPENDIX 6A. A TAXONOMY OF SOCRATIC QUESTIONS

Questions of Clarification

- What do you mean by _____?
- What is your main point?
- How does _____ relate to _____?
- Could you put that another way?
- Is your basic point _____ or _____?
- What do you think is the main issue here?
- Let me see if I understand you; do you mean _____ or _____?
- How does this relate to our discussion (problem, issue)?
- What do you think John meant by his remark? What did you take John to mean?
- Jane, would you summarize in your own words what Richard has said? . . . Richard, is that what you meant?

- Could you give me an example?
- Would this be an example: _____?
- Could you explain that further?
- Would you say more about that?
- Why do you say that?

Questions That Probe Assumptions

- What are you assuming?
- What is Karen assuming?
- What could we assume instead?
- You seem to be assuming _____. Do I understand you correctly?
- All of your reasoning depends on the idea that _____. Why have you based your reasoning on _____ rather than _____?
- You seem to be assuming _____. How would you justify taking this for granted?
- Is it always the case? Why do you think the assumption holds here?
- Why would someone make this assumption?

Questions That Probe Reasons and Evidence

- What would be an example?
- How do you know?
- Why do you think that is true?

- Are these reasons adequate?
- Why did you say that?
- What led you to that belief?

Source: R. Paul (1992), Critical thinking: What every person needs to survive in a rapidly changing world (Rev. 2nd Ed.). (pp. 367–368). Santa Rosa, CA: Foundation for Critical Thinking.

- Do you have any evidence for that?
- What difference does that make?
- What are your reasons for saying that?
- What other information do we need?
- Could you explain your reasons to us?
- But is that good evidence to believe that?
- Is there reason to doubt that evidence?
- Who is in a position to know if that is so?
- What would you say to someone who said _____?
- Can someone else give evidence to support that response?
- By what reasoning did you come to that conclusion?
- How could we find out whether that is true?

- How does that apply to this case?
- What would change your mind?

Questions about Viewpoints or Perspectives

- You seem to be approaching this issue from _____ perspective. Why have you chosen this rather than that perspective?
- How would other groups/types of people respond? Why? What would influence them?
- How could you answer the objection that _____ would make?
- What might someone who believed _____ think?
- Can/did anyone see this another way?
- What would someone who disagrees say?
- What is an alternative?
- How are Ken's and Roxanne's ideas alike? Different?

Questions That Probe Implications and Consequences

- What are you implying by that?
- When you say _____, are you implying _____?
- But if that happened, what else would happen as a result? Why?
- What effect would that have?
- Would that necessarily happen or only probably happen?
- What is an alternative?
- If this and this are the case, then what else must also be true?
- If we say that *this* is unethical, how about *that*?

Questions About the Question

- How can we find out?
- What does this question assume?

- Is this the same issue as _____?
- How would _____ put the issue?

- Would _____ put the question differently?   • Why is this question important?
- How could someone settle this question?
- Can we break this question down at all?
- Is the question clear? Do we understand it?
- Is this question easy or hard to answer? Why?
- Does this question ask us to evaluate something?
- Do we all agree that this is the question?
- To answer this question, what questions would we have to answer first?
- I'm not sure I understand how you are interpreting the main question at issue.

APPENDIX 6B.   ARE YOU A CRITICAL THINKER?

	SD	D	N	A	SA
1. I think it is important to examine the accuracy of my beliefs.	1	2	3	4	5
2. I make it a habit to critically evaluate claims of effectiveness, my own as well as those that others make.	1	2	3	4	5
3. I can readily spot questionable claims.	1	2	3	4	5
4. I often discover that something I believe is correct.	1	2	3	4	5
5. I am grateful to people who point out flaws in my thinking.	1	2	3	4	5
6. It is important to examine the accuracy of claims about what helps clients.	1	2	3	4	5
7. I actively search for evidence against my assumptions.	1	2	3	4	5
8. It's embarrassing for me to admit that I have been wrong.	1	2	3	4	5
9. I like to discuss controversial issues with people who disagree with me.	1	2	3	4	5
10. Changing my mind is a sign of weakness.	1	2	3	4	5
11. People don't respect me if they ask me to support my claims with evidence.	1	2	3	4	5
12. Professionals should base their decisions on well-reasoned arguments.	1	2	3	4	5
13. Learning something from a discussion is more important than winning an argument.	1	2	3	4	5
14. I take responsibility for clearly explaining the reasons for my views.	1	2	3	4	5
15. I welcome criticism of my views.	1	2	3	4	5
16. I often say "I could be wrong."	1	2	3	4	5
17. I take responsibility for evaluating the consequences of actions I propose.	1	2	3	4	5
18. I seek only data that support my point of view.	1	2	3	4	5
19. I take responsibility for clarifying vague statements I make.	1	2	3	4	5
20. I change my mind when I have good reason to do so.	1	2	3	4	5
21. I thank others for pointing out errors in my thinking.	1	2	3	4	5
22. I become defensive when others question my claims/statements.	1	2	3	4	5

Key: SD = strongly disagree, D = disagree, N = neutral, A = agree, SA = strongly agree.

APPENDIX 6C. A CODE OF CONDUCT FOR EFFECTIVE RATIONAL DISCUSSION

The Fallibility Principle

Each participant should acknowledge the possibility that none of the positions presented deserves acceptance and that, at best, only one is true or the most defensible position.

The Truth-Seeking Principle

Each participant should be committed to searching for the truth or at least the most defensible position on the issue. Therefore, you should be eager to examine alternative positions, look for insights in the positions of others, and allow other participants to present arguments for or raise objections to any position held with regard to any disputed issue.

The Burden of Proof Principle

The burden of proof for any position usually rests on the person who presents it. If and when someone asks, the proponent should provide an argument for that position.

The Principle of Charity

The argument presented for any position should be one that can be reconstructed into a commonly accepted or standard argument form. If an argument is reformulated by a challenger, it should be expressed in the strongest possible version consistent with the arguer's original intention. If there is any question about that intention or about implicit parts of the argument, the arguer should be given the benefit of doubt in the reformulation.

The Clarity Principle

The formulations of all positions, defenses, and challenges should be free of any kind of linguistic confusion and clearly separated from other positions and issues.

The Relevance Principle

The person who presents an argument for or challenges a position should offer only those reasons or questions that are directly related to the merit of the position at issue.

The Acceptability Principle

The person who presents an argument for or challenges a position should attempt to use premises or reasons that are mutually acceptable to the participants or that at least meet standard criteria of acceptability.

Source: Adapted from T. E. Damer (1995), Attacking faulty reasoning: A practical guide to fallacy-free arguments *(3rd ed.). (pp. 172–186). Belmont, CA: Wadsworth.*

The Sufficient Grounds Principle

The person who presents an argument for or challenges a position should attempt to provide reasons that are sufficient in number, kind, and weight to support the conclusion.

The Rebuttal Principle

The person who presents an argument for or challenges a position should attempt to provide effective responses to all serious challenges or rebuttals to the argument or position at issue.

The Resolution Principle

An issue should be considered resolved if the proponent for one position successfully defends that position by presenting an argument that uses relevant and acceptable premises that are sufficient in number, kind, and weight to support the acceptance of the premises and the conclusion and provides an effective rebuttal to all serious challenges to the argument or position at issue. Unless you can demonstrate that these conditions have *not* been met, you should accept the conclusion of the successful argument. In the absence of a successful argument for any one position, you are obligated to accept the position supported by the best of the good or nearly successful arguments presented.

The Suspension of Judgement Principle

If no position comes close to being successfully defended, or if two or more positions seem to be defended with equal strength, you should, in most cases, suspend judgment about the issue. If practical considerations require an immediate decision, you should weigh the relative risks of gain or loss connected with the consequences of suspending judgment and decide the issue on those grounds.

The Reconsideration Principle

If a good argument for a position is subsequently found to be flawed in a way that raises *new* doubts about the merit of that position, you are obligated to reopen the issue for further consideration and resolution.

CHAPTER 7

Competing Views of Problems and Their Causes

OVERVIEW

This chapter highlights the importance of understanding the context in which social work practice takes place, including competing views of problems and their causes. The contextual nature of problem definition is discussed and ongoing controversies are noted. Theories of behavior are described together with the implications of different views. The importance of distinguishing among facts, concepts, and evaluations is highlighted and guidelines are suggested for reviewing theories (guesses about what may be accurate). A developmental–contextual model is suggested that attends to multiple levels of analysis.

You Will Learn About

- Professionals as problem definers.
- Distinguishing among facts, concepts, and evaluations.
- Problems as deviance.
- The importance of understanding the politics of problem definition.
- Ongoing controversies.
- Theories of behavior.
- A developmental–contextual model.
- Thinking critically about theories.
- Different levels of abstraction.

PROFESSIONALS AS PROBLEM DEFINERS

The goal to help clients resolve problems sounds straightforward. However, considering the other functions of social welfare and social work (social control and social reform) suggests that problem definition is not so clear cut. As you become immersed in the everyday world of practice, it is easy to forget about the economic, political, and social context in which personal and social problems are defined and reacted to. You may forget that definitions change in accord with popular ideas of the times and may forget to ask who benefits and who loses from a particular definition. Many scholars argue that professionals are involved not so much problem-solving as problem-setting (e.g., Schon, 1987). The assumptions underlying different functions of social work are based on different beliefs about human nature (Why people do what they do, how they change, if they can change). For example, social reform efforts emphasize political, economic, and social conditions (e.g., the quality of education). Problems and the approaches to them are institutionalized in an organizational structure. Social welfare agencies address problems in ways that reflect underlying assumptions about problems and their causes. Practice is carried out in the context of currently accepted social and public policies that given patterns of behavior are problems and certain remedies are appropriate. Who should receive welfare, how much, when, and for how long are vigorously debated. Are parents who mistreat their children bad people who should be imprisoned or overburdened people who should be helped? Are they themselves victims of the inequitable distribution of employment, housing, and education opportunities? Who is hurt by current definitions? Who gains? Recognizing the links between definitions of problems reflected in current policies and practices will help you identify options for and constraints on helping clients.

THE IMPORTANCE OF UNDERSTANDING THE POLITICS OF PROBLEM DEFINITION

Without a contextual understanding of problems, you may miss the relationship between the personal and the political (Mills, 1959). You may accept problem definitions that limit opportunities to help clients. Without a contextual understanding, it is easy to fall into "blaming clients" and focusing on "changing them" or giving them a rationale for their plights rather than altering the environmental conditions related to their problems. Thinking critically about problems and proposed remedies commits you to the hard work and courage required to question popular assumptions and examine underlying points of view. Clarifying and critically examining basic assumptions is a key component of critical thinking. Recognizing underlying goals and points of view is not easy. They are often implicit rather than explicit. They may be part of the basic social fabric and related belief systems in which we live, perhaps unquestioned or even unrecognized. They may be deliberately suppressed. Related facts and figures may be suppressed or distorted (see the yearly publication *Censored: The News That Didn't Make the News and Why*). Raising questions about accepted views of a profession, organization, supervisor, professor, or agency may be met with attempts to evade questions or discredit (or cajole) those who raise questions.

There are great stakes in how problems are framed, and people with vested interests devote considerable time, money, and effort to influence what others believe. "Problem crusaders" (people with a particular interest in a particular view of a problem) forward particular definitions. Economic interests influence problem definition. Problem definition is influenced by professionals' interest in maintaining and gaining power, status, and economic resources as well as by differences of opinion about what makes one explanation better than another. Profit making is the key aim of for-profit and many (supposedly) not-for-profit service enterprises. Residential psychiatric facilities for youth and nursing homes are multimillion-dollar businesses. The concern for profit rather than service is reflected in the mistreatment (e.g., unneeded hospitalization) of clients in order to make money.

Different Problem Definitions Have Different Consequences

Different ways of defining problems have different consequences. Thomas Szasz (1987, 1994) argues that many people who injure others and are labeled mentally ill have committed criminal offenses and should be treated accordingly. Others believe that many criminals are mentally ill and should receive psychiatric care. Throughout history, poverty has been variously viewed as a crime, a personal limitation, or a reflection of discrimination and oppression (social injustice). Views about problems and their causes affect who receives aid and who does not as well as what is offered and the spirit in which it is offered. Defining behaviors as indicators of mental illness results in quite different consequences than does defining them as criminal. A moralistic definition of problems encourages the belief that people with these problems are bad people who deserve whatever ill fate awaits them, including "justified" punishment or enforced "treatment."

Feminist scholars and advocates have been in the vanguard in emphasizing the relationship between personal problems and social issues (the personal and the political). Understanding the context in which problems occur provides opportunities to destigmatize clients. Tavris (1992) argues that there has been a turning away from the environmental context of personal problems in the current focus on individual characteristics (e.g., past history of abuse, low self-esteem). This is not to say that individual past histories are not important. It is to say that contextual factors such as gender role expectations comprise a part of individual histories (see also, McGrath, Keita, Strickland, & Russo, 1993). Service models that focus on altering the behavior of battered women so that their partners will stop abusing them encourage the view that women can control the behavior of their abusive partners if they change their own behavior. Does this mean that these women are responsible for the behavior of those who batter them? Focusing on the victim discounts the social

roots of wife abuse (e.g., norms that support male dominance over women; see Gilbert, 1994). A study of 6,000 sheltered women revealed that access to resources permitting independent living (e.g., transportation, child care, and a source of income after leaving the shelter) was the best predictor of whether a woman would remain away from her abusive partner (Gondolf & Fisher, 1988).

PROBLEM DEFINITION AS CONTROVERSIAL

People have different opinions about what a problem is, who and what is responsible for it, and how it can be resolved (see Exhibit 7.1). Consider what is known as *compulsive gambling.* Some people believe that this is a disease, whereas others view it as a learned behavior maintained by a complex reinforcement schedule. Spirited controversies continue about the prevalence of stranger abduction of children and sexual assault against women. Some scholars argue that some state of affairs becomes a social problem when an objective state exists. Others believe that social problems are socially constructed. They argue that although certain needs of the sick, poor, elderly, and very young have been recognized throughout the centuries, they have been defined differently at different times and receive more or less attention at different times. One of the ongoing debates concerns the extent to which peo-

EXHIBIT 7.1
Proposed Causes for Problems

Moral: They are due to moral deficiencies of individuals.

Psychiatric/medical: It is assumed that problems result from a disease (mental illness) that may have a biochemical and/or constitutional base.

Psychological: Problems result from individual characteristics such as differences in personality traits. These may unfold in stages. Examples include psychodynamic, developmental, and cognitive models.

Social interactional: Problems result from the interaction between personal characteristics and social experiences. This includes social learning theory.

Sociological/cultural: Problems result from social/cultural characteristics (e.g., disorganization, contingency patterns, socioeconomic status, discrimination).

Ecological/contextual: Both personal and environmental factors are considered including social, political, and economic conditions. This includes systems models and radical behavioral theory.

Philosophical/moral (humanistic, hermeneutic linguistic, phenomenological/existential, and moral/legal). An example of a moral/legal cause is the argument that mental illness is rare and that many behaviors (e.g., assault) labeled as indicators of mental illness should be criminalized or considered to be one's own business (e.g., suicide, drug use) and decriminalized and demedicalized.

ple are responsible for their own problems: whether to locate the source of problems in the people who have them and to focus on changing individuals and families and/or to examine related environmental causes and pursue environmental reform. If someone drinks too much, is homeless, is unemployed, is this "her fault"? Do environmental conditions such as high unemployment, poor quality education, and lack of low-cost housing contribute to these problems? Moral definitions of problems are alive and well (e.g., lack of individual responsibility). Moral principles may be based on (1) common sense (what appears to be self-evident); (2) revelation (communication of values by a transcendent power); (3) socialization (learning society's values), or (4) moral reasoning (we must reason out what is right and wrong). They may emphasize (1) utility (greatest good for the greatest number); (2) beneficence, love, charity; (3) justice (fair play—all rules apply equally; just deserts—a belief that there should be some equivalence between behavior and rewards or punishment); or (4) equality (equal obligations and rights). The freedom to choose is a foundation requirement of moral behavior.

DEVIANCE AS A PROBLEM

From a purely descriptive point of view deviance refers to the variability of behavior (the range of behaviors that occur, their form, variety, and timing). Variability of behavior is a key factor in evolutionary history, and it is essential to creativity. Some variations in behavior are labeled as problems, such as child and elder abuse. A *positivistic view* of deviance dominates many helping efforts. It is assumed that deviance is definable in a straightforward manner as behavior not within permissible conformity to social norms (beliefs about expected behaviors in given situations that are part of a known and shared consensus). This view typically searches for causes in physiology and/or the psyche. Questions focused on are, "Why do they do it?" and "How can we make them stop?"

In an *interactional view* of deviance, moral or right behavior is considered to be socially constructed (not given) relative to actors, context, and historical time (see Exhibit 7.2). Social problems are viewed as "constructed" in accord with cultural, political, and economic considerations (e.g., Berger & Luckman, 1966; Conrad & Schneider, 1992;

EXHIBIT 7.2
Some Important Views and Concepts

Deviance as a problem	Variations in behavior that are negatively defined or condemned in a society.
Interactional view	Deviance is an ascribed status. It involves the classification of behavior, persons, situations, and things into categories of condemnation and negative judgment which are constructed and applied successfully to some members of a social community by others. The essence of deviance is not the actors' behaviors but is "a quality attributed to such persons and behaviors by others."
Positivistic view	Deviance is inherent in particular kinds of behavior.
Medicalization of deviance	The expansion of medicine as an agent of social control.
Politics	"How control and power are gained, shared, abdicated, protected, abused and delegated" (Brookfield, 1987, p. 164). "Process by which decisions are made, wealth is distributed, services are regulated, justice is maintained, and minority interests are protected" (p. 164).
Social control	Means by which society secures adherence to social norms. The greatest power comes from having the authority to define certain behaviors, persons or things as "deviant." They "define the problem (e.g., as deviance), designate what type of problem it is, and indicate what should be done about it" (Conrad & Schneider, 1992, p. 8).
Social problem	A condition/behavior of people or their environment that is viewed as undesirable.
Social policy	Social policy involves the definition of social problems and decisions about how to approach them.

Source: Based on P. Conrad & J.W. Schneider (1992), Deviance and medicalization: From badness to sickness. *Philadelphia: Temple University Press; and S.D. Brookfield (1987),* Developing critical thinkers: Challenging adults to explore alternative ways of thinking and acting. *(San Francisco: Jossey-Bass).*

Lemert, 1967; Scheff, 1984; Spector & Kitsuse, 1987). "A social problem is a putative condition or situation that (at least some) people label a 'problem' in the arenas of policy discourse and action, defining it as harmful and framing its definition in particular ways" (Hilgartner & Bosk, 1988, p. 70).

The interactional view assumes the following:

- Deviance is universal but there are no universal forms of deviance.
- Deviance is a social definition, not a property inherent in any particular kind of behavior. Views of deviance are integrally related to morality (beliefs about what is right or wrong).
- Social groups create roles and enforce their definitions through judgments and social sanctions.
- Deviance is contextual; that is, what is labeled as deviant varies in different social situations.
- Defining and sanctioning deviance involves power.

What is viewed as right (or wrong) is the product of certain people making claims based on their particular interests, values, and views. Deviance becomes defined as actions or conditions regarded as inappropriate to or in violation of certain powerful groups or conventions. Those who have more power are usually more successful in creating and imposing rules and sanctions on those who are less powerful.

Changing Views

Many behaviors once condemned as sinful were later considered crimes and are now defined as medical or psychological problems. The changing ways in which certain behaviors have been viewed supports a contextual view of deviance. For instance, only when women gained more political and economic independence was greater attention given to battered women. Advances in knowledge often force changes in how people view a problem. For example, it had been assumed that tuberculosis was inherited because people who lived together tended to "get it." When the bacillus responsible for tuberculosis was isolated, people were no longer blamed for developing it. Changing ideas about what is and what is not mental illness illustrate the consensual nature of psychiatric diagnoses. Homosexuality was defined as a mental illness until 1973, when the American Psychiatric Association, under pressure from gay and lesbian advocacy groups and bitter infighting, decided that it was not.

Problems have careers. You could take any pattern of behavior (e.g., drug use, delinquency) and explore the different ways it has been viewed. Consider masturbation. At one time it was thought to be responsible for an enormous range of problems, including mental retardation (see Szasz, 1970). Cultural values, common metaphors, as well as political and economic pressures, influence the decisions we make about problems. In the past, housewives who wanted to work were often regarded as pathological (Oakley, 1976). The metaphors used to describe problems influence how we view them and what solutions we propose. Consider the "war on drugs." This metaphor may encourage use of force against those who sell and use drugs as well as feelings of "us against them" (see Exhibit 7.3 for a historical note; for critiques of crime and drug policies, see Szasz, 1995; Walker, 1994).

The Medicalization of Deviance

Physicians have been very successful in forwarding medical definitions for problems, as illustrated by the lengthening list of behaviors viewed as signs of mental illness requiring the help of experts. Professional experts set the rules for what is and what is not "normal." The number of listings in the 1994 *Diagnostic and Statistical Manual* of the American Psychiatric Association continues to increase (from 80 in 1980 to more than 300 in 1994). The coffers of helping professionals grow rich from the medicalization of problems. Aren't problems an inescapable part of life? Great literature throughout the ages highlights life's trials and tribulations (e.g., Unamuno, 1972). Don't we, as Thomas Szasz argues, trivialize and stigmatize them by viewing them as psychological problems? In the *Mismeasure of Women* (1992), Carol Tavris suggests that labels such as *dependent personality dis-*

EXHIBIT 7.3
Historical Note

The belief that Satan causes disliked behavior or attributes is an ancient one. Magicians were viewed as active agents of dethroned gods (devils), and many people who practiced magic promoted the belief that they had supernatural powers (White, 1993/1896). Christianity forbade the practice of magic, and the fourth-century Holy Roman emperor Constantine decreed that offenders be buried alive. From ancient times, society has distinguished between good and bad magic: Good magic could be used to cure diseases and protect crops, whereas bad magic was used for evil purposes such as bringing bad luck to others. In the Middle Ages when Christianity was at its height in Europe "the terror of magic and witchcraft took complete possession of the popular mind" (White, 1993/1896, p. 383). Women were the principal targets of this persecution. During the Inquisition, not believing in magic was grounds for punishment, as it implied also not believing in Satan and thus God.

order which are most often given to women, punish women for fulfilling expected roles. She contends that we should examine the conditions in society that result in so many women showing these characteristics and alter them. She argues that expected gender roles and unequal educational and job opportunities contribute to many troubles women confront. Women often accept society's definition of problems and label themselves in ways that obscure their options. For example, a woman may inaccurately view her low-paid job as a result of her low self-esteem. Natural biological changes such as menopause are viewed as needing the help of experts to negotiate. The influence of culture is often overlooked. For example, during menopause, Japanese women are apt to complain of stiff shoulders, whereas Western women complain of hot flashes (Lock, 1993). Japanese women attribute little importance to the end of menstruation, seeing it as a normal part of aging.

The Language of Problem Definition

The words we use influence how we think about problems and behaviors. Labels and classifications (e.g., black, white, race, ethnicity) have significant policy implications and thus warrant careful analysis. Consider the widespread use of medical language: healthy/unhealthy, wellness/sickness, health/disease. Language and the ideology it reflects play

a key role in obscuring economic differences. For instance, both working-class and upper-middle-class people are often labeled as middle class, creating the illusion that most people belong to the middle class (Gans, 1980). Many problems created in part by inequities in housing, job opportunities, education, health care, and the court system, are treated as separate from one another, which makes it difficult to detect shared causes (Demott, 1990). DeMott contends that differences in economic circumstances are daily translated into other terms including moral differences. What is major becomes minor or is ignored as peripheral. Complexities are obscured. Child maltreatment is viewed as "to be expected" among the poor and therefore is treated with indifference and apathy. If it's "their" fault, what responsibility do we have to do anything about it? The metaphor of war, as in the "war against drugs" makes it easier to use violent means against "them" (e.g., seizing property, killing). Here, too, societal factors related to drug use are obscured.

CONTROVERSIES

Controversies include the relative importance attributed to biological, psychological, and environmental factors and how the "environment" is defined. Views that emphasize the interaction among genes, organisms, and their environments differ in how reciprocal these relationships are assumed to be and in the range of environmental events considered.

What System Levels to Focus On

The search for explanations reflects a shifting balance between a focus on individual characteristics (e.g., biological or psychological) and environmental causes (e.g., social reinforcement patterns). Theories of practice and of behavior differ in what they include in "the environment," ranging from political, social, and economic influences to a narrower focus on the influence of family relationships. One option points to the individual as the source of problems and the key to their resolution (see Exhibit 7.4). Let's call this level 1, the individual focus. For example, in trait approaches, individual or psychological processes are focused on. Biological and/or early experiences, especially in childhood, are regarded as causes of stable personality qualities that are more or less independent of current environments. Modern-day versions of trait views include some genetic theories and psychoanalytic theory, with its emphasis on the enduring influence of early childhood development. Between 1917 and 1929, a vocal minority of social workers embraced Freudian theory, despite the absence of evidence that this would be useful in helping clients attain outcomes they valued.

This view encouraged a focus on individual

pathology as the cause of human maladies. It emphasized unconscious, instinctual drives and the enduring influence of early childhood experiences. Inherent in a psychoanalytic framework is the assumption that observable problems are only the outward signs of some underlying process, which must be altered to bring about lasting change. Some social work scholars suggest that social workers turned to individually focused methods because altering environmental conditions was so difficult or impossible. The emphasis on psychological/individualistic ideologies, the stress on the power of positive thinking (Meyer, 1988) and the "self-made man" (Wyllie, 1954), the idea that people can better themselves through their own efforts (if they wanted to), focuses attention on the individual.

A second option (level 2) includes an interest in families. Considerable attention is given to the family in social work. It is viewed as a key interpersonal context in which behavior develops and is maintained. In level 3, social groups and community characteristics are also considered, such as quality of housing, transportation, and recreational settings. Social groups may include self-help groups and social advocacy groups. A fourth option (level 4, contextual or ecological) includes attention to service systems and the factors that influence them such as political, economic, and social factors and related values. Confining attention to levels 1 and 2 may result in incomplete assessment and selection of ineffective services. The wide variety of services that may be needed to help clients is suggested in the referrals made in a program for runaway and homeless youth (Rothman, 1991):

Counseling and individual treatment (74%)
Health service (55%)
Housing and placements (50%)
Family counseling (44%)
Educational services (31%)
Sex information (26%)
Vocational services (20%)
Legal services (15%)
Substance abuse services (9%)

Perhaps the most common mismatch is using level 1 services for problems that require level 3 or 4 so-

EXHIBIT 7.4
Different Levels of Focus

Level 1
Individual focus on the person
Level 2
Individual and family
Level 3
Individual, family, social groups, and community
Level 4
Individual, family, social groups, community, organizations, and service systems and the political, economic, and social factors that influence them

lutions. Some scholars suggest that it is the emphasis on the individual as the cause of problems that is responsible for the overrepresentation of the poor, minorities, and other oppressed groups in institutional settings. William Ryan (1976) argues that policies that focus on changing individuals or families ignore related political, economic, and social factors and, in effect, "blame the victim." Consider, for example, the focus on the "alcoholic" rather than on the economic factors that foster substance abuse, including the multimillion-dollar advertising industry. Golden-berg believes that an ideology that encourages people to view problems as the result of personal deficiencies is one of four factors that make up and encourage oppression. He defines oppression as "a state of continual marginality and premature obsolescence." Other factors are

- Containment, which restricts and narrows the scope of possibilities (e.g., a reservation).
- Expendability, which assumes that specific groups are expendable and replaceable without loss to society.
- Compartmentalization, which prevents people from living an integrated lifestyle (e.g., little relationship between life interests and work) (1978, p. 3).

The Relationship Between Inside and Outside

Different views of problems and related behaviors are based on different assumptions about the interaction among genes, organisms, and their environments (Lewontin, 1994). These range from a view in which inside (genes) and outside (the environment) are rigidly separated as in the incorrect belief that genes cause behavior, to the view that environmental factors are all important. Lewontin notes that both Darwin and Mendel rigidly separated the inside (e.g., genes) from the outside (environment), but in opposite ways. Darwin argued that the causes of variation in organisms were inside and the causes of the selection of variations were outside (in the environment). Lewontin argues that this separation between the outside and the inside is not compatible with what we know about the interactions among genes, organisms, and environments. This reveals a close relationship among our genes, our environments, our actions, and those around us. "The evolution of organisms is a co-evolution of organism and environment. Just as there is no change in the world that does not change organisms, so there is no change in organisms that does not change the world (Lewontin, 1995, p. 44). This is not to say that the view that genes cause behavior or the view that environmental variables cause behavior might not be correct under some circumstances, as Lewontin notes. It is to say that under most circumstances, both views will be wrong. Not only is there a complex interaction (e.g., in relation to the environmental order of events), but in addition, there is a great deal of "developmental noise" (unknown sources of variation) within an organism. As he notes, this does not mean that everything is connected in a holistic sense, in which we cannot find ruptures or a lack of connections. Nor does it imply that there are no critical points at which small changes may make a big difference.

Construction or Adaptation

In *Inside and Outside: Gene, Environment and Organism* (1994), R. C. Lewontin highlights the importance of examining the "metaphors" we use to think about behavior, such as potential, fitness, development, and adaptation. Lewontin contends that common metaphors such as *potential* and *innate capacity* are wrong. "There are differences among genotypes, with different consequences in different environments, but there is no way in general over environments, to rate these innate or intrinsic properties from 'bad' to 'good,' 'high' to 'low' 'small' to 'big.' There is complete environmental contingency" (1994, p. 19). Furthermore we play a great role in creating our environments. Lewontin argues that we must rid ourselves of the metaphor of adaptation, the view that organisms are adapting to a fixed world and either they adapt or they do not (p. 32). He notes that the metaphor of adaptation implies that there is an autonomously determined world to which we change in order to fit. But how do we know what "problems" confront organisms?

This is a particularly difficult question in fields such as evolutionary biology. How do we know what particular characteristic of an organism yielded a solution to a problem? He argues that we can only guess at the environment of an organism. Each organism creates and exists in "a set of micro habitats" in which it spends its time and so we can only guess at what the organism's problems may be. Moreover, an organism has a multitude of problems (pp. 33–34). He argues that there is no stability in the world. He views metaphors of stability, harmony, and balance of nature as ideological inventions characteristic of a particularly insecure time in the history of the Western world (p. 47).

Lewontin contends that based on what little we know about genes, organisms, and environments, a more accurate metaphor is that of construction. "If we want to understand evolution, we must understand it as construction because the actual situation is that organisms make their own environments. They define them. They create them. They change them. They interpret them. There are powerful causal pathways that go from organism to what we call 'environment' " (1994, p. 36). He contends that only through careful observation of organisms in their environment can we discover their environments. He gives the example of the use of different parts of his garden by different birds. What is the "environment" to one differs dramatically from what it is for others. "There is an external world but there is no single environment out there" (p. 38).

Discrimination and Oppression as Causes

Historical, sociological, and psychological research shows that discrimination and oppression based on skin color, gender, sexual orientation, and physical ability are everyday realities (e.g., Davidio & Gaertner, 1986). William Goode highlights the roles of stereotyping and discrimination in what he calls "subversion (any special, additional efforts people make in order to get more prestige than their achievements would otherwise elicit, or less disesteem; or to prevent others from getting the respect they would otherwise get or to cause others to receive disesteem they would otherwise not receive" (1978, p. 212). The quality of education provided

in many inner-city schools is scandalously poor, and dropout rates are high, especially among poor and minority students. Many students who do graduate are unable to read, which greatly limits their employment options. Some argue that poverty has become increasingly a gender issue. Others believe it always has been so (Abramovitz, 1988). Gibbs and her colleagues (1988) contend that the lack of educational and employment opportunities for young African-American men is related to their overrepresentation in the juvenile justice system. Epidemiological data indicate higher coronary heart disease, morbidity, and mortality rates among poor and minority groups (Rene, 1987).

Mirowsky and Ross (1989) explored the relationship between psychological distress (depression and anxiety) and social factors and concluded that half of all symptoms of depression can be attributed to social factors. The proportion of severe distress attributed to social factors was even more striking: socioeconomically disadvantaged persons experience 83.9% of all severe distress. They argue that there is no evidence that patterns of social distress reflect genetic or biochemical abnormalities. They believe that lack of control over negative events may result in biochemical changes (see Exhibit 7.5). Biochemical changes may enter the picture at different points (e.g., reduced opportunity or sense of control). Such change may partly account for symptoms and may be a result of social factors.

> The patterns of distress reflect the patterns of autonomy, opportunity, and achievement in America. The realities of socio-economic status—amount of education, type of employment or lack of it, family income—have a profound influence on a person's sense of control. Minority status is associated with a reduced sense of control partly because of lower levels of education, income, and employment, and partly because for members of minority groups, any given level of achievement requires greater effort and provides fewer opportunities" (Mirowsky & Ross, 1989, p. 16).

The Lapse of Individual Responsibility as a Cause

There is no doubt that oppression and discrimination exist, that some people are deprived of options

EXHIBIT 7.5
A Suggested Relationship Between Social Conditions and Psychological Distress

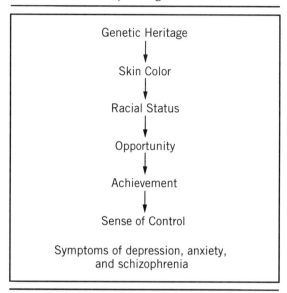

Genetic Heritage

↓

Skin Color

↓

Racial Status

↓

Opportunity

↓

Achievement

↓

Sense of Control

↓

Symptoms of depression, anxiety,
and schizophrenia

Source: Based on J. Mirowsky & C. E. Ross (1989), *Social causes of psychological distress* (p. 178). New York: Aldine de Gruyter.

they value because of some ascribed or acquired characteristic. We are dealt uneven hands at birth. Some of us are luckier than others. But are discrimination and oppression the principal causes of social and personal problems? Competing with this is the view that lack of individual initiative and responsibility is mainly responsible for or contribute to problems. For example, Sykes (1993) argues that we have become a nation of victims using past difficult experiences as excuses to continue wallowing in self-sorrow. A counterargument to those who believe that structural factors such as a capitalistic economy are largely responsible for problems like poverty (which in turn lead to crime and violence) is that most poor people do not engage in crime and violence. This view emphasizes the role of choice in making decisions and living with the results of these choices. Existential viewpoints emphasize our responsibility for our decisions, no matter what the circumstances. For example, Victor Frankl suggests that each person is responsible for

the fulfillment of the specific meaning of her or his own life (1967). He contends that no matter what our circumstances are (even if we are in a concentration camp), we cannot escape choosing among possibilities. He views this responsibility as the essence of human existence (Frankl, 1969). In her book *The Empowerment Tradition in American Social Work* (1994), Barbara Simon cautions social workers to avoid the paternalism reflected in working harder than their clients to resolve problems or to enhance the clients' skills. "To ask and keep asking clients for an investment and renewal of their hard work and commitment is to communicate respect and hope" (1994, p. 26).

THEORIES OF BEHAVIOR (GUESSES ABOUT WHAT MAY BE TRUE)

Problems involve behaviors. Some behaviors occur too much, too seldom, at the wrong time, or with the wrong intensity. Elected politicians may refuse to see representatives of community action groups. Recreation centers may not admit certain minority group members. Employers may discriminate against certain kinds of applicants. These theories (guesses about what may be true) differ in a number of ways (see Exhibit 7.6), such as in the degree to which they are molded by the particular time and place in which they developed. For example, scholars argue that Victorian culture influenced psychoanalytic theory. They differ in their scope—the range of species, people, and kinds of behavior to which they apply. For example, evolutionary theory embraces all life-forms, thereby connecting us with the other species of mammals and the rest of nature.

Different practice theories have been influenced by different theories of behavior. Psychosocial practice is influenced by psychoanalytic theory. Behavioral practice is based on behavioral theory. A medical illness model dominates practice in many areas, focusing on the individual as the source of problems. The client is viewed as having an illness in need of a diagnosis and treatment. Many social workers accept a disease model of alcohol abuse, even though researchers agree that

EXHIBIT 7.6
Ways in Which Theories of Behavior Differ

Degree to which behavior is viewed as knowable.

Goals pursued (e.g., explanation and interpretation alone, understanding based on prediction and influence, political interests).

Criteria accepted to evaluate claims (e.g., tradition, consensus, authority, scientific, critical testing).

Range of problems addressed with success (inclusiveness/scope).

Causal importance attributed to psychological factors (e.g., feelings/thoughts).

Causal importance attributed to biological characteristics (e.g., genetic and/or brain differences).

Attention devoted to evolutionary influences.

Importance attributed to developmental stages.

Range of environmental factors considered (e.g., family, community, society).

Importance attributed to past experiences.

Degree of optimism about how much change is possible.

Degree to which critical testing of claims is possible and valued. (Some guesses are not falsifiable; you cannot find out whether they are accurate.)

Degree of empirical support (evidence for and against a theory).

Ease with which service guidelines can be developed.

Degree to which a theory accounts for and is compatible with related knowledge.

Note: The terms *explanations*, *theory*, and *guess* are used interchangeably.

there is no evidence that substance abuse is a disease (Fingarette, 1988). Some people believe that behavior is endlessly malleable and is due to cultural and social variations. Different beliefs include:

- Genetic determinism: The belief that all behavior is due to genetic differences.

- Cultural determinism: The belief that all behavior is a result of social conditions.

- Radical environmentalism: The belief that behavior is solely influenced by environmental factors.

- Integrative (contextual): The belief that both biological, psychological and environmental variables influence behavior.

Psychological theories focus on the individual. Sociological theories focus more broadly on social structure. Different views of behavior have differ-

ent consequences in relation to how people are treated. A given view may be used to pursue certain goals even if it is not believed. For example, William Goode notes that "in class relations derogatives can also be a nationally chosen program, a propaganda technique, by which one presents oneself or one's group as honorable and another as worthy of denigration—in order to justify a planned victimization. One can do this without at all believing the accusations made" (1978, p. 367). There is general agreement that behavior varies, that it is influenced by a variety of variables, and that it can be analyzed at different levels (e.g., physiological, psychological, sociological). Integrative views consider multiple levels of causality.

Genetic Explanations

Currently there is a renaissance of interest in searching for genetic markers for physical and psychological signs and symptoms. Sociobiologists emphasize reproductive success as the main determinant of the development of traits and social strategies and assume that behavior is influenced mainly by genetic differences (Wilson, 1975). Critics of sociobiology claim that ideology is used to legitimize current patterns of inequality as a biological inevitability. They contend that the biological and the social are neither separable, nor antithetical, nor alternatives, but complementary (see Lewontin, 1991). Some argue that genotype (genetic makeup) can never be separated from phenotype (visible characteristics that result from the interaction between the genotype and the environment), because both the environment and random developmental factors affect how genotype is expressed (Lewontin, 1994). People with a common genetic history often share a similar environmental history. Even, when a genetic influence is found, it may account for only a small portion of the variance in understanding a problem or behavior. Although many people accept the findings of twin studies purporting to show a strong hereditary component to developing schizophrenia, others do not, pointing out methodological flaws (Boyle, 1990; Lewontin, Rose, & Kamin, 1984). From a helping point of view, a key question is: "Can influential characteristics be altered to help clients achieve desired outcomes?" (See also the earlier discussion of inside and outside.)

Biomedical Explanations

Biophysical or biomedical explanations are used to account for a broad range of behaviors. Factors focused on may include biochemical changes, brain damage, and genetic differences. Evolutionary influences can be viewed as a kind of biophysical explanation if they are mediated through anatomical, physiological, and genetic characteristics. Biochemical/pharmaceutical approaches to altering behavior have increased. Proponents of this view assume, for example, that certain behaviors are related to too much or too little of certain biochemical substances. Malnutrition, hypoglycemia, and allergic reactions are associated with hyperactivity, learning disabilities, and mental retardation. Beliefs that "something in the blood" or "something in the food" is related to mental illness have a long history and are reflected in current treatments, some of which are of dubious value (Skrabanek, 1990). The finding of biochemical abnormalities related to certain behavior patterns only establishes that abnormalities in biochemistry are present, not that they cause the behavior. Biochemical changes may result from stress caused by limited opportunities due to discrimination, (see Exhibit 7.5). Biophysical characteristics may or may not be related to evolutionary processes.

Physical abnormalities in the brain are often assumed to be responsible for certain kinds of mental illness as well as hyperactivity and explosive temper. Another kind of biophysical explanation assumes that brain damage causes a "disorder." Here, too, even when brain damage can be detected, it does not necessarily indicate that it causes any particular behavior. Additional problems with these kinds of explanations include limited intervention knowledge and predictive validity.

> To say that Rachel can't walk, talk or feed herself because she is retarded tells us nothing about the conditions under which Rachel might learn to perform these behaviors. For [someone] to explain Ralph's failure to sit down on the basis of hyperactivity caused by brain damage does not provide any useful information about what might help Ralph learn to stay in his seat. Even apparently constitutional differences in temperament are so vulnerable to environmental influences as to provide only limited information about how a child is apt to behave under given conditions. (Alberto & Troutman, 1990, p. 9).

The premature acceptance of biophysical explanations will interfere with discovering alternative explanations that yield intervention knowledge. Alberto and Troutman (1990) argue that biophysical explanations give teachers excuses not to teach. It is not that such explanations are not accurate but that they often are incomplete. For instance, environmental factors may also be important. (For a critique of biological approaches to deviant behavior, see Boyle, 1990; Gorenstein, 1992.)

Developmental Explanations

The term *development* refers to "the process of continual change during the lifetime of an organism" (Lewontin, 1995, p. 121). There is an "unfolding" metaphor associated with it emphasizing the role of internal characteristics. Developmental accounts describe differences and related factors at different ages (e.g., childhood, adolescence, adulthood, and old age) and/or speculate about such differences. Knowledge about developmental norms and transitions that occur at different ages in different cultures may be valuable in discovering risks and opportunities, when planning for smooth transitions (e.g., from adolescent to adulthood), and predicting the likelihood of success. For example, divorce or separation may initiate a sequence of changes, such as loss of social support, that produce other changes, such as increased sadness and irritability, that in turn may compromise parenting skills (see for example, Patterson & Forgatch, 1990).

Although it is generally accepted that development is contingent on environment, there is disagreement about the relative importance of (1) genetically or physically determined processes, (2) environmental conditions, and (3) the actions of the

EXHIBIT 7.7
An Overview of a Developmental Model of Chronic Antisocial Behavior

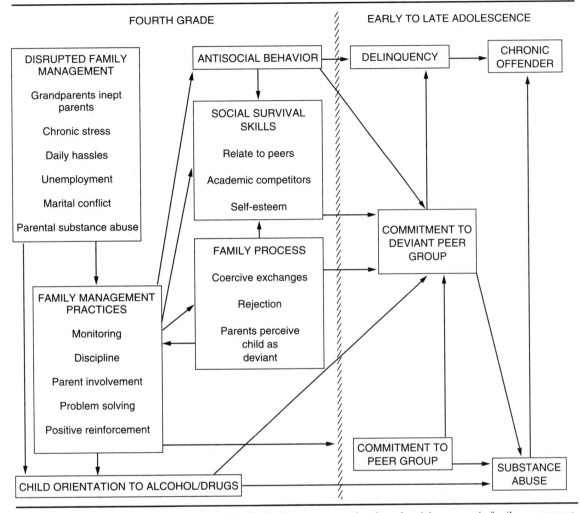

Source: L. Bank, G. R. Patterson, & J. B. Reid (1987), Delinquency prevention through training parents in family management. *Behavior Analyst, 10,* 77.

organism and those around it. Development is often described as a series of stages, as in Freud's theory. Core beliefs about the self and others are assumed to be related to early childhood experiences and people may become fixated at a certain stage, resulting in abnormal development. Developmental theories of moral development have also been described (Gilligan, 1982; Kohlberg & Lickona, 1986). In complex developmental views, social learning variables are considered as

well as the effects of earlier stages on later ones (see Exhibit 7.7).

Some argue that what are viewed as developmental changes in fact reflect changing environments. Variables such as age and social class are "marker variables" that correlate with many problems but do not explain them or provide service guidelines (Baer, 1984, 1987). The similarities of circumstances for many people at a given age in a society may lead one to assume (incorrectly) that biological development is responsible, overlooking the role of similar contingencies. In a contextual perspective it is assumed that people confront different tasks in different environments at different times and may respond to similar situations in different ways. For example, although some women experience the "empty nest syndrome" when their grown children leave home, many do not. Acceptance of a stage theory of development may get in the way of identifying environmental factors that can be rearranged. That is, it may be incorrectly assumed that a person "is stuck" in a given stage and there is nothing to do but wait for time to pass. Some scholars suggest that acceptance of Piagetian stages resulted in withholding valuable learning experiences from children, on the grounds that they were "not ready."

Cognitive Explanations

What sets us apart from the other species of mammals is our enormous cognitive potentials. In cognitive explanations, a causal role is attributed to thoughts. There is an interest in identifying and altering mental events such as expectations, schemas (views of the self and world), moods, and attributions. There is no doubt that people differ in what they say to themselves and that certain kinds of thoughts are correlated with certain kinds of overt behaviors. For example, people who are effective in social situations attend to different social cues and say different things to themselves during social exchanges than do people who are not as effective (see the review in Gambrill, 1995b). Depressed compared to nondepressed college students attribute negative outcomes to personal, unchangeable, global causes and positive outcomes to environmental, changeable, specific causes (Seligman, Abramson, Semmel, & Van Baeyer, 1979). Seligman (1975) suggests that people who are depressed have developed a learned helplessness and so make little or no effort to gain valued outcomes. (See also Peterson, Maier & Seligman, 1993.) Cognitive accounts differ in their answers to (and interest in) the question, "Where do thoughts come from?" Other questions are, Do thoughts function in a causal role? Are they re-sponsible for behaviors and feelings? Do they serve a mediating role in which they function as parts of "chains of behavior," with thoughts being one kind of behavior? For example, you may think about an upcoming exam, feel anxious, and then study. Do thoughts serve both functions?

Behavioral Explanations

In behavioral views, actions, thoughts, and feelings are considered to be largely a function of a person's learning history. Varied social histories result in a wide range of behavior. Biochemical and genetic influences are assumed to play a role; however, their interaction with learning variables is emphasized. In addition, different species have their own "biological boundaries" on learning. Behavior that may seem quite bizarre typically serves adaptive functions, but only when contingencies of reinforcement (relationships between behaviors and their consequences) are clarified may they become apparent. In this way, behavior always "makes sense." An emphasis on the role of learning in developing and maintaining behavior and a rejection of a "disease model" of mental illness, decreases the likelihood of imposing negative labels on clients. Variations in behavioral views reflect different assumptions about the causes of behavior and what intervention should focus on (e.g., thoughts and/or environmental factors), and also different preferred methodologies (the intensive study of individuals or the study of group differences).

Applied Behavior Analysis. Behavior analysis involves the systematic investigation of variables that influence behavior. Applied behavior analysis involves the application of findings from the experimental analysis of behavior to concerns of social importance (Baer, Wolf, & Risley, 1968, 1987). It is assumed that most behaviors are learned through interaction with the environment, that behavior is selected by its consequences. Research has repeatedly illustrated that it is possible to have reliable influence over behavior by systematically varying associated antecedents and consequences. It is this research that yielded the principles of behavior described in Chapter 8. Applied behavior

EXHIBIT 7.8
Loneliness in a Retirement Home

Behavioral questioning revealed that one of the indicators of complaints of loneliness was receiving few letters (Goldstein & Baer, 1976). The next question was, "What behaviors of whom were responsible for that low rate?" (Baer, 1982, p. 285). An examination of letters written by residents revealed that residents who complained of receiving few letters were punishing letter writing (e.g., they reproached their correspondents for not writing). The residents were prompted to write nonreproachful letters to relatives or old friends who rarely or never wrote to them. A nonreproachful letter including at least one question requiring an answer was modeled, and the next several letters written by the elderly residents were read and the content commented on before they were mailed. Within a very few tries, residents wrote nonreproachful, nonaccusatory letters. They now wrote about their daily lives, happenings of interest, and memories of past experiences with their correspondents. The residents were coached to include self-addressed, stamped envelopes in their letters, with comments explaining that they wanted to make replying easy. These changes in letter writing were made in a multiple baseline design, across three residents. "In perfect response to the staggered timing of that design, the three complainers began to receive prompt replies to their letters, almost tripling their average rate of receiving letters. Furthermore, they began to receive letters from new correspondents. This led them to begin writing to yet other potential correspondents and to receive prompt answers, accomplishing still higher rates of letters received—and letters to answer. All this activity filled time in otherwise often empty days. That behavior change and its snowballing effects were accompanied by a thorough absence of complaints about loneliness". (Baer, 1982, p. 286)

analysts have taken a leading role in developing and evaluating programs of benefit to a wide range of clients, including students at all levels of education, people with developmental disabilities, people with chronic pain, the unemployed, the elderly, parents, and children.

As used here, the term *applied* refers to the extent to which a behavior is socially important. *Behavior* refers to what people do. Behavior—and the translation of problems into behaviors that if changed would resolve them—is of central interest (see Exhibit 7.8). *Analytic* requires "a believable demonstration of the events that can be responsible for the occurrence or nonoccurrence of that behavior" (Baer, Wolf, & Risley, 1968, p. 94). "The analytic challenges for anyone who deserves to be called an 'applied behavior analyst' are (1) to restate the complained-of problem in behavioral terms; (2) to change the behaviors indicated by that restatement; and then (3) to see whether changing

them has decreased the complaining response" (Baer, 1982, p. 284). The analysis of behavior has been achieved when you can influence it in predicted ways.

The effects of altering a given variable are tracked on an ongoing basis. It is assumed to be just as important to carefully measure behavior in real-life settings such as classrooms, organizations, and groups as it is in laboratory settings. The social validity of outcomes is emphasized; that is, services must improve the behavior focused on in a *socially significant way.* Significant others such as teachers, parents, or residential staff are included in assessing the value of service. Another characteristic of this framework is a concern with generalization. Are positive outcomes maintained? Do they occur in other environments or involve other behaviors? The hallmarks of applied behavior analysis offer important safeguards for clients: the goals focused on must be of direct concern to clients, and success must be measured in terms of real-life gains.

Radical Behaviorism. There are different kinds of behaviorism which are often confused (e.g., Zuriff, 1986). Radical behaviorism is the philosophy related to applied behavior analysis as well as a theoretical account of behavior. It "is the attempt to account for behavior solely in terms of natural contingencies—either contingencies of survival, contingencies of reinforcement, or contingencies of social evolution" (Day, 1983, p. 101). Culture is viewed "as the contingencies of social reinforcement maintained by a group" (Skinner, 1987, p. 74). "It is the effect on the group, not the reinforcing consequences for individual members, that is responsible for the evolution of culture" (p. 54). Pursuit of a "science of behavior" is a basic goal. It is not claimed that a radical behavioral perspective is the only scientific psychology, but it is contended that a scientific approach is most likely to yield knowledge about behavior and how it can be altered in comparison with other approaches.

Radical behaviorism is perhaps more misunderstood and misrepresented and attracts more objections than any other perspective in psychology (Todd, 1992; Todd & Morris, 1983). One of the oddest objections is that it ignores the meaning of events. In fact, attention is devoted to discovering the unique individual meanings of events (their functions) through a detailed exploration of the relationships between behavior and related cues and consequences. Misunderstandings result in ignoring this framework, which has been applied to help a wide range of clients attain outcomes they value such as participating more effectively on community board meetings, obtaining employment, and maintaining independent living arrangements.

The term "*radical behaviorism*" is so named because it represents a sharp break with earlier forms such as John Watson's methodological behaviorism. Not only are private events such as thoughts and feelings not dismissed, they are viewed as behaviors that themselves require an explanation (traced to their environmental, evolutionary, and/or physiological origins) (see Hayes & Brownstein, 1987, for further discussion). Private events (such

as thoughts and feelings) are believed to operate as elements in chains that begin with observable environmental events and end with observable responses (Baer, 1982, p. 278). Both thoughts and feelings may play a mediating role in chains of behavior. An example that Don Baer gives is using an algorithm for determining the square root of a real number. Once we memorize the algorithm, we can apply it to relevant problems. The algorithm mediates correct answers. So one could say (given that this algorithm is essential to solving square root problems) that this response (the algorithm) is causal to solving square root problems. Here, *mediate* implies an intermediate relation.

Behaviorists argue that the environmental contingencies associated with feelings, expectations, moods, or "states of mind" often remain unknown in cognitive accounts of behavior. To understand thoughts and feelings, we would have to explore past and present environmental histories. Feelings can be used as clues to contingencies (relationships between behavior and environmental events). For example, keeping a daily log of what happens before and after feelings of anger may reveal related punishing contingencies (e.g., criticism by a supervisor). Our experiences with others result in different feelings about them. We like people who offer us positive consequences, such as praise and respect, and dislike those who offer us negative consequences, such as insults and ridicule. Family members' emotions and attitudes about one another indicate who is being punished and reinforced and who is doing the punishment and reinforcement. The advantage of viewing thoughts and feelings as behaviors is that they cannot as readily be inaccurately presumed to be the sole causes of behavior. They themselves are behaviors in need of explanation.

Social Learning Theory (SLT). Social learning theory underlies cognitive-behavioral methods (Bandura, 1986). As in radical behaviorism, a reciprocal interaction is assumed between people and their environments (i.e., we both influence and are influenced by our environment). SLT accepts cognitive explanations in contrast to applied behavior analysis and behavioral approaches emphasizing changes in our learning histories as explanatory. It is assumed that we present a important part of our environment through our expectations, goals, and standards. Thoughts are considered to play an important role in the complex processes that affect attention and in the degree to which different kinds of interventions are effective. Observational learning is given a key role. This refers to acquisition of new behavior by observing modeled behavior. Bandura argues that cognitive mediation is required for the delayed performance of observed behavior. Group experiments are typical in social learning theory, in contrast to functional, process-oriented, intensive study of single cases. Both applied behavior analysis and cognitive-behavioral approaches emphasize careful evaluation of results, relying on observable outcomes. If this focus were lost, efforts would fall outside what would be considered a behavioral perspective.

Racial, Ethnic, and Class Theories of Social Problems and Relations

Racial differences are often appealed to as key in understanding social relations in the United States, including victimization (see Exhibit 7.9). Discrimination and oppression based on skin color is a past and present reality. Problems are viewed as ethnic, not racial, in an ethnic theory of social relations. It is assumed that solutions must address cultural stereotyping and ethnocentrism. A class analysis of social relations categorizes people according to their economic characteristics. Policies, behavior, and

problems are viewed as shaped by economic interests, market forces, and relationships to the means of production. (In a racial theory, socioeconomic conditions are viewed as racial and as requiring racial explanations.) The United States is the most economically stratified of all industrial countries. Economic inequality has increased; the gap in income between the bottom one fifth and the top one fifth has widened (Holmes, 1996). Certain physical illnesses such as the incidence of cancer are higher in low-education and low-income groups, regardless of race (Boring, Squires, & Heath, 1992).

Are race, ethnicity, and class sound classifications? Are there greater differences among different races, ethnic groups, and classes than within them? Is there some essence that all members of a group share? What is a white person? What is an Asian person? Are there more differences within a category (e.g., black, white) than between them? There has been a great genetic intermingling among peoples of different ethnicities and races. Attempts to categorize people into different races based on clear differences have repeatedly failed (no clear dividing lines emerged). Gender is a complex classification with many overlaps at different levels of analysis (biological, social, and psychological). Do racial, ethnic, or class theories provide a satisfactory explanation of social relations? Does race or ethnicity imply a certain cultural experience? We speak of black and white cultures as if they existed. But aren't there thousands of different "African-American experiences"? What is an ethnic group? For example, aren't there scores of different Asian-

EXHIBIT 7.9
A Typology of Social Theories

	Racial	Ethnic	Class	Human-centered
Criteria of classification	Anatomical	Cultural	Economic	Species
Causation	Race and racism	Ethno-centrism	Capitalism	Reasoning
Objects of victimization	Races	Non-WASPs	Working class	All human beings
Stratification	Racial power	WASP hegemony	Class structure	Universal insecurity
Proof structure	Reality	Reality	Reality	Logical rules
Conflict resolution	Racial reforms	Acculturation	Socialist revolution	Educational reforms

Source: Yenudi Webster (1992), The racialization of America (p. 37). New York: St. Martin's Press.

American groups? Is there an equation of culture and ethnicity (or culture and race)? Is race, ethnicity, religion, or language an adequate basis for culture? Can there be many cultures in one? Can one person be a member of more than one culture? Don't we overlook individual differences by classifying diverse experiences on the basis of one characteristic? Sociologists and biologists agree that no basis can be found for racial classification: "anatomical criteria such as skin color, facial form and hair type cannot be decisive as means of demarcating racial types, for there are different gradations of each of these characteristics" (Webster, 1992, p. 47). (See also Katz, 1995.) The populations of India, Pakistan, and Indonesia do not fit the threefold classification of Caucasoid, Mongoloid, and Negroid. The number of races suggested vary from 3 to 113. Races identified are phenotypically distinct within one set of criteria, but not in another. They are often genetically indistinguishable.

Yehudi Webster views racial classification as part of a racial theory of social relations in which persons are racially classified and their biological and moral attributes are viewed as explanations of their behavior and historical developments. He argues that racial ethnic descriptions focus on selected anatomical and cultural differences for moral–political purposes (1992). By assigning themselves to a race by virtue of their skin color, some humans initiated the racialization of themselves and others. Racial classification was initiated as a justification for certain political and economic decisions and arrangements. He argues that the view that certain physical differences imply a racial identity is propagated by social scientists, governmental institutions, and the media. He contends that social scientists generally justify the use of terms such as *race*, *ethnicity*, and *class* with reference to a reality that is itself a product of the dissemination of racial, ethnic, and class theory. Once persons are racially classified, there is no escaping the implications of racial motives (e.g., racism). Webster views racial classification itself as racism. (He notes that *racism* refers to many things, including "a belief system or ideology, discriminatory policies and behavior, theories of genetic in-

feriority, and socioeconomic inequality" [1992, p. 241].)

Webster argues that racial and ethnic descriptions of events are "forms of propaganda, an indoctrination into a conviction that U.S. society has different racial and ethnic groups that are locked in a relationship of domination/oppression" (1992, p. 13). He suggests that the continued daily use of racial categories racialize our experiences. He points out that the government, social scientists, and the media daily saturate us with the alleged validity of categories based on race, ethnicity, and class, which he considers bogus categories that do more harm than good (i.e., they underplay our shared humanness and, in so doing, make it easier for us to dehumanize others). Some of our most inspiring leaders such as Martin Luther King also emphasized our shared humanness.

A CONTEXTUAL VIEW

A contextual view highlights the interaction between people and their environments. It directs attention to *both* personal and environmental characteristics and emphasizes the mutual influence of people and their environments (Smith & Thelen, 1993). It emphasizes that the environment differs for each person. The terms "contextual" and "ecological" are used interchangeably here. Ecological models are contextual and historical. Our environments can be viewed as multiple interlinked ecological levels, each of which holds certain risks and provides certain opportunities (see Exhibit 7.10). The competencies and values we develop and the environments we create for ourselves are related to these risks and opportunities as well as by what we bring to them and how others respond.

Each ecological level involves unique contingencies for an individual and may influence other levels. Consider youth who are "turned off" to learning because of punishing educational experiences and the potential consequences of this. Research suggests that recurrent depression may cause changes in the brain that in turn influence affect (see discussion of Robert Post's research in

EXHIBIT 7.10
A Summary of the Ecology of Sociocultural Risk and Opportunity

Ecological Level	Definition	Examples	Issues Affecting Children
Microsystem	Situations in which the child has face-to-face contact with influential others	Family, school, peer group, church.	Is the child regarded positively? Is the child accepted? Is the child reinforced for competent behavior? Is the child exposed to enough diversity in roles and relationships? Is the child given an active role in reciprocal relationships?
Mesosystem	Relationships between micro-systems; the connections between situations.	Home/school, home/church, school/neighborhood.	Do settings respect each other? Do settings present basic consistency in values?
Exosystem	Settings in which the child does not participate but in which significant decisions are made affecting the child or adults who do interact directly with the child.	Parents' place of employment, school board, local government, parents' peer group.	Are decisions made with the interests of parents and children in mind? How well do supports for families balance stresses for parents?
Macrosystem	"Blueprints" for defining and organizing the institutional life of the society.	Ideology, social policy, shared assumptions about human nature, the "social contract."	Are some groups valued at the expense of others (e.g., sexism, racism)? Is there an individualistic or a collectivistic orientation? Is violence a norm?

Source: J. Garbarino (1992), Children and families in the social environment *(2nd ed.) (p. 30). New York: Aldine de Gruyter.*

Holden, 1991). In addition, research concerning both social and personal problems suggests that usually many interlinked contingencies are involved (e.g., Mirowsky & Ross, 1989). Consider child maltreatment (see Exhibit 7.11). Why is it that one-third of all adolescent suicides involve gay or lesbian youth when they represent only 10% of the population? Could homophobia (irrational hatred or fear of gay and lesbian people) and the resulting discrimination be the cause? Societal tolerance of violence as well as accepted gender roles contribute to the battering of women. Overlooking these important influences yields an incomplete view of the causes of observed behaviors and environments.

The Advantages of a Contextual Model

A contextual view highlights the influences we have (and could have) over our environments. It emphasizes the importance of attending to individ-

ual differences. A contextual perspective highlights developmental opportunities for growth and preventative options for avoiding or muting risk factors that limit opportunities. For example, providing information and enhancing skills may prevent problems associated with transitions such as marriage, birth of a child, or retirement. It draws attention to problems with such commonly accepted metaphors as adaptation (in emphasizing the challenge of understanding exactly what a person's "environment" is and what problems may be within it). It reminds us that change on one level can be used to create opportunities on another. For example, gaining and maintaining paid employment for clients with developmental disabilities may require enhancing their social and vocational skills as well as persuading employers to offer them jobs. If it is not possible to work on one level, it may be possible to work on another. If teachers refuse to participate in programs to help their students, peers may be involved or students "empowered" by en-

EXHIBIT 7.11
Possible Etiological Factors in a Contextual Model of Child Abuse Neglect

A. Predisposing individual factors
  Exposure to violence

B. The family environment
  1. Characteristics of the child
    Prematurity
    Temperament
    Unwanted pregnancy
    Aversive cry

  2. Characteristics of parent(s)
    Lack of effective parenting skills
    Inappropriate expectations
    Ineffective problem-solving skills
    Lack of friendship skills
    Depression, substance abuse
    Low frustration tolerance
    Health problems
    Child viewed as appropriate target of abuse
    Believes in value of severe punishment

  3. Interaction between parent(s) and child
    Mismatch in preferred interaction styles
    High rates of threats, demands, and complaints
    Low frequency of affectional and supportive behavior

  4. Role of other family members
    Marital conflict
    Low resourcefulness in face of material hardship

  5. Other characteristics of the home
    Disorganization
    Little opportunity for privacy
    Unwanted intrusion from visitors
    High density of people

C. Community factors
    Lack of respite or day care
    Lack of social support
    Lack of public transportation
    High crime rate
    Few settings for positive exchanges
    Few recreational options

D. Social norms
    Tolerance of violence
    Acceptance of physical punishment to discipline children

E. Public policies regarding
    Funds for education
    Funds for low-cost housing
    Funding for community organization
    Funding for health care

hancing their social influence skills. In his work with runaway youths, Jack Rothman (1991) notes that in 48% of the cases, options other than working with parents must be found. Efforts to attain needed resources from agencies through cooperative means may fail, whereas social action may succeed. Appreciation of the connections between personal problems and social conditions will help you avoid victim blaming (focusing on psychological or biological characteristics and overlooking environmental influences). A feminist perspective has been valuable in pointing out macrolevel influences on women's risks and opportunities (see Tavris, 1992). Without a contextual understanding of problems, including those caused by professionals themselves (e.g., giving clients psychiatric labels that limit rather than broaden their options), you will lose opportunities to help your clients. The preamble of the draft of the NASW Code of Ethics states, "Fundamental to social work is attention to the environmental forces that create, contribute to, and address problems in living" (1996).

A contextual framework encourages you to keep in mind that what are defined as social problems may disguise social conflict and competing efforts to control resources. For example, what is viewed as a "racial problem" may reflect disagreements about opportunities open to African-Americans. Overlooking macrolevel influences may result in overestimating what can be accomplished at the individual and family levels. On the other hand, considering only organizational, community, and societal influences may result in not recognizing the contribution of individual characteristics to problems, such as a lack of effective communication skills. Contextual models are historical. They involve looking at the past as well as the present and future. A contextual approach encourages us to consider the origin of our values and goals. It encourages us to examine the context in which we develop our values rather than to accept them as given. Only by viewing problems and possible solutions in both a historical and a contextual perspective are we likely to discover variables that influence problems and opportunities for preventing and resolving them. People's actions create social changes that in turn influence their behavior and the behavior of others. Review a problem that interests you by following the guidelines in Exhibit 7.12.

A historical view will avoid mistaken beliefs that result from "cohort centrism" (e.g., assuming that people who live at a given time age in the same way). *Cohort effects* refer to those changes in society at a particular historical time that affect people. *Cohort centrism* is responsible for the mistaken assumption that differences found in cross-sectional studies (e.g., in physical health) show that age was responsible for them (Riley, 1988). In fact, people in a given cohort may change biologically, psychologically, and socially in quite different ways. Different cohorts influence social change in different ways. To get some practice in thinking contextually, see Exhibit 7.13.

Why Isn't a Contextual View Used More Often?

There are many reasons that a contextual view may not be used. It may not be possible to implement plans based on a contextual view or even to gather the information required. Some approximation may have to be used. Social workers as well as clients may be disempowered (e.g., not have the resources needed to attain valued goals). Chronic

lack of resources may create a helplessness and hopelessness, a giving up on working together with clients to increase resources at whatever system level is needed. A contextual view is inherently political. It emphasizes the involvement of value judgments and conflicting interests in the very definitions of problems. It emphasizes the importance of understanding contingencies and the power relationships they represent. A contextual assessment may show a need to work at the community, service system, and policy levels. Not only may this require greater resources compared to working with individuals and families, it may threaten vested interests and create opposition. Consider the negative reactions of legislators and politicians to presenting data to elected officials concerning a bill on child passenger safety and the provision of subsidized "lifeline" utility rates for low-income families (Fawcett, 1991). Contextual preventive efforts can be expensive, and so public officials may ignore or suppress information reflecting problems' social, economic, and political causes. Competing interests result in considerable foot-dragging, even with successful programs. Staff may not have required knowledge or skills. They may not know how to think and act contextually, that is, to connect the personal and the political. They may prefer working with individuals and families on a psychological or family level, ignoring other levels of influence. Psychological models of

EXHIBIT 7.12
Thinking About a Social Problem

Select a problem such as depression, homelessness, elder abuse, or poverty, and answer the following questions:
1. Exactly what is the problem? Clearly describe related behaviors (e.g., their form and frequency) and/or other indicators (e.g., income below certain levels, lack of low-cost housing). Have indicators accepted changed over time?
    What is known about the prevalence of related circumstances and/or behaviors?
    What is known about their variability (e.g., do they differ in different groups, times, or settings)?
    Do people agree on whether the selected indicators reflect a problem? If not, what are key differences?
2. What causes were commonly accepted in the past for this problem?
3. What causes are now proposed (e.g., genetic differences, moral lapses, discrimination/oppression) in professional and lay sources (e.g., mass media)? What is known about correlated factors?
4. What are the consequences of each view? Who loses and gains from each account?
5. What guesses about causes have been critically tested? Which one(s) in what way(s), and what are the findings?
6. What point of view do you think is most useful in understanding this problem? On what criteria do you base your choice?
7. Can your preferred view account for related empirical findings?
8. Do vested interests and/or discrimination influence how the problem is defined and remedies proposed? If so, how? Do they influence the definition of related behaviors or circumstances as a problem rather than as an asset or a basic constitutional right? Are political or personal agendas confounded with scientific ones? If so, in what ways? Give examples.

EXHIBIT 7.13
Relating Individual Problems to Social Issues

A. Presenting problem: a family's homlessness
B. Related structural factors
   1. Economic _____
   _____
   _____
   _____
   _____
   _____

   2. Social/cultural/values/norms: _____
   _____
   _____
   _____
   _____
   _____

   3. Political: _____
   _____
   _____
   _____
   _____
   _____

   4. Cohort effects: _____
   _____
   _____
   _____
   _____
   _____

   5. Service system: _____
   _____
   _____
   _____
   _____
   _____

problems dominate the media, making contextual models less vivid and available. Questioning accepted values and practices takes time and effort as well as courage and an interest in thinking things out for yourself. It requires digging beneath the surface of fine sounding words and asking: What is actually done? Who says this is good or bad? On what grounds? Who benefits from a view? Who loses?

A contextual approach highlights both our opportunities and responsibilities for creating the environments in which we live. Taking responsibility can be a burden. This is suggested by the many ways in which we try to escape from freedom (Fromm, 1963), for example, through being constantly busy. There are many ways to "step out" (Kozol, 1990). We may feel overwhelmed, especially if we are told that we are different from all other human beings in placing services to others before self interest (see NASW ethical principles in Chapter 3). You will have to balance caring with a realistic appraisal of what you can do.

THINKING CRITICALLY ABOUT THEORIES

Theories are guesses about what may be true. You will come across many theories in the course of your career. As discussed in Chapter 4, there are competing views of how to evaluate their accuracy. Sir Karl Popper, considered by many thoughtful people to be the greatest twentieth-century philosopher, suggests criteria for selecting theories that are especially pertinent to professions dedicated to helping people. One is a theory's *potential refutability:* Can you determine whether it is false? Is it falsifiable? Popper argues that we can only eliminate false beliefs in our search for knowledge (see Chapter 4). A second criterion is whether a theory has *survived rigorous tests* and in the variety of tests it has survived (its *scope*). Theories that are broad in scope yield many testable hypotheses and can be applied successfully to a range of problems. New theories should account for all previous findings and more (Popper, 1994). In this sense, progress is both conservative (a new theory must account for prior findings) and revolutionary (it replaces earlier theories).

Theories should be *logically consistent.* That is, they should not contain contradictory predictions, for if they do, they cannot be tested. *Parsimony* (simplicity) is another valuable characteristic of a theory. The rule of parsimony calls for choosing the simplest explanation, which is useful in avoiding unnecessary concepts that can be misleading.

Applicability is especially important in professions. From an ethical and practical point of view, the bottom line is whether theories (guesses about what may be true) are useful in helping clients attain valued outcomes. Are they helpful in clarifying problems, identifying related factors, and selecting effective services? Relying on theories that do not offer practice knowledge may result in excuses not to help clients. Although selection of a theory can be justified by having survived more risky tests concerning a wider variety of hypotheses than other theories, it can never accurately be claimed to be "the truth." All knowledge is conjectural. Another theory, broader in scope, may override earlier ones.

Avoiding the Prisons of Frameworks (Theories)

We often think within a belief system or framework, rather than about it. We may assume that a feminist, behavioral, or multicultural framework, is best. This is quite different from proposing a theory or hypothesis about what may be true or false and then critically evaluating our guesses (e.g., searching for alternative views). If we do not critically evaluate our theories (assumptions), they function as prisons that limit our vision rather than as tools to discover what is false (Popper, 1994). Keep in mind that most theories about what is true are wrong (see, for example, any history of science or medicine). As Socrates said, "I know that I know almost nothing, and hardly this." A theory believed too soon stifles further inquiry. If our questions are answered, why look further? Those who are opposed to what Popper calls the myth of the framework "will welcome a discussion with a partner who comes from another world, from another framework for it gives them an opportunity to discover their so far unfelt chains, to break these chains, and thus to transcend themselves" (1994, p. 53).

THE VALUE OF TRANSLATION AND INTEGRATION SKILLS

We often associate the word *translation* with translating words and sentences in one language into those of another. Other kinds of translation skills contribute to problem-solving, especially in professions such as social work, in which problems are often complex and causes varied and intertwined. To discover options, we may have to translate concepts from one discipline into those of another or combine them in a way that yields a more comprehensive whole and does not contain contradictory assumptions. We may have to translate among theories in one discipline or translate across professions. Each profession and discipline has a certain way of thinking about topics addressed. A psychologist may approach a problem of homelessness from a different point-of-view than an economist, biologist, anthropologist, or sociologist does. Each discipline has a related domain of knowledge that may overlap with other domains to different degrees. Translation is required even among those who speak the same language. What does a client mean when she says, "My neighbors are driving me crazy"? Does her meaning of "crazy" match yours? Recognizing the need for translation is a vi-

EXHIBIT 7.14
Distinguishing Among Empirical, Conceptual, and Evaluative Statements
Concerning Social Problems

	Empirical Statement	Conceptual Statement	Evaluative Statement
Definition of terms	A statement of fact based on observations that can be confirmed or disconfirmed by the observations of others.	A general idea that indicates hypothetical relationships between things or categories.	A value judgment indicating what is desirable or undesirable.
Related terms sometimes used interchangeably	Evidence, facts, factual information, descriptive statement, statistics.	Theoretical statement, abstraction, causal model, paradigm.	Normative statement, moral statement, opinion, values, ideology.
Illustrative statements from social problems:			
Juvenile delinquency	The first juvenile court was established in Chicago, Illinois, in 1899.	The weaker the attachment between parents and child, the greater the likelihood of delinquent behavior.	The innocence of youth is best served by a juvenile court that keeps youngsters away from hardened criminals.
Poverty	In 1990, 31.5 million persons, or 12.8% of the U.S. population were below the official poverty line.	Limited education contributes to poverty, but poverty, in turn, contributes to limited education. Therefore, limited education is both a cause and effect of poverty.	Most welfare goes to support people who are lazy or have loose morals.
Race relations	During the past several years, unemployment rates for blacks and whites indicate a consistent ratio of 2 to 1. In other words, blacks are disproportionately unemployed.	Insecure and frustrated persons in a majority group are more likely to form negative images of persons in minority groups.	Many white Americans are hypocrites who believe in equality but refuse to vote for qualified black candidates.

Source: P. L. Baker, L. E. Anderson, & D. S. Dorn (1993), Social problems: A critical thinking approach *(p. 66). Belmont, CA: Wadsworth.*

tal first step. As Alfred Kadushin noted long ago, the "assumption of ignorance" increases the likelihood that you hear and understand what others say.

Different Levels of Abstraction

We can discuss problems and related behaviors and causes at different levels of abstraction, ranging from the concrete (e.g., "He does not follow any of his teacher's instructions") to the abstract (e.g., "He is hyperactive"). It is important to distinguish among three kinds of statements in thinking about problems: (1) factual (did a father assault his child?), (2) conceptual (why did he do it), and (3) evaluative (was it right or wrong?) (see Exhibit 7.14). Questions of fact (what is) and explanation (why it is) differ from those of values (what should be) and definitions (meaning questions). As we

move from facts to theories, we become more removed from concrete data. What is useful depends on our purpose. If we think we know what "the facts are" but do not (because we are being too vague about events of interest), we may make faulty decisions. We may confuse descriptions (what occurs) and inferences (guesses about why it occurs).

If you want to clearly describe what people do, a concrete level is needed. Let's say that you believe that your supervisor does not speak to you in a "respectful manner." What is a "respectful manner"? What does your supervisor do or not do (and when and where) that relates to respect? This example illustrates the key role of classification in thinking about behavior. You must decide what behaviors to include in the category "disrespectful." Considering different levels of abstraction will help you distinguish between theoretical concepts and how they are measured. Consider anxiety. This complex concept is a key one in some theories of behavior. What is anxiety? How should (or can) this be measured? Do measures used accurately represent the theoretical concepts?

SUMMARY

Professionals are integrally involved in problem definition. The context in which problems are defined and services are created influence what problems are addressed and how. Behaviors once viewed as sins, were later viewed as crimes and are now viewed as symptoms of mental illness. It is easy to lose sight of the consensual nature of what is defined as a problem. It is easy to take "what is" as the way they should be or inevitably are. Controversies related to problem definition include what is viewed as a problem, what its related causes are, and what remedies are proposed. People have different beliefs about the causes of problems and how they can be resolved and prevented. Biological, psychological, and sociological accounts (or some mix thereof) may be drawn on. Different points of view have different ways of approaching problems. In professions, perspectives that offer leverage in helping clients are of unique interest. The question "Will this theory help me help my clients?" is a key one.

REVIEWING YOUR COMPETENCIES

Reviewing What You Know

1. Describe the role of professionals in defining problems.
2. Identify controversial issues in problem definition.
3. Discuss deviance as variations in behavior that contribute to evolutionary change and adaptation.
4. Describe an interactional view of deviance.
5. Describe "the medicalization of deviance" and give an example.
6. Identify different system levels that may be focused on to understand problems, and discuss how they may affect one another.
7. Give empirically based examples of the relationships between social conditions and psychological distress.
8. Describe sound criteria for evaluating the usefulness of a theory (guess about what may be true).
9. Distinguish among facts, concepts, explanations, beliefs, and evaluative statements related to a problem that interests you.
10. Describe and critique racial, ethnic, and class theories of social problems and relations.

Reviewing What You Do

1. You ask questions about problems that forward understanding of them.
2. You can critique different kinds of explanations for behavior.

3. You can accurately describe different kinds of views of problems in the professional literature and media and identify underlying assumptions.

Reviewing Results

1. You select theories (guesses about what may be true) that are helpful in resolving client complaints.

Behavior: Background Knowledge

OVERVIEW

This chapter introduces you to what has been learned about the complex interactions between behavior and its consequences. We know more today about how our behavior is influenced by our environments, both past and present. Understanding these influences will help you (1) identify environmental influences related to behaviors of interest, (2) select appropriate intervention levels (e.g., individual, family, group, organization, community, state), (3) recognize incomplete accounts of problems, and (4) accurately assess the likelihood that valued outcomes can be attained given the current circumstances.

You Will Learn About

- Why a chapter on behavior is included in a book on practice.
- Contingencies: their variety and importance.
- Antecedents: their variety and importance.
- Motivation and emotion.
- Variables that influence operant learning.
- Respondent behavior.
- Evolutionary influences on behavior.

A CONTEXTUAL APPROACH

A contextual approach highlights the reciprocal interactions between our behavior and the environment. The greater our understanding of the context in which problems occur, the more likely we are to identify what is needed to attain related outcomes. We can draw on what has been found about the relationships between our behavior and the environment to understand the situations clients confront.

This knowledge provides guidelines for gathering information about problem-related behavior. It has been successfully applied to help a wide variety of clients, including people with depression, anxiety, and developmental disabilities; the unemployed; community residents who want more influence over their environment; and parents who want to enhance their parenting skills. Without this knowledge, you and your clients may overlook environmental factors related to problem-related behaviors and potentials for change. Without it you may skim the surface of what seems to be obvious (perhaps influenced by the vividness of data), missing key environmental influence (e.g., effects of laws and public policies).

WHY A CHAPTER ON BEHAVIORAL PRINCIPLES IS INCLUDED IN A BOOK ON PRACTICE

Doesn't a discussion of behavioral principles belong in a book on human behavior and development rather than in a book on social work practice? My answer is that it belongs in both, for four reasons. First is the fundamental attribution error. We tend to overlook environmental causes and attribute behavior to personality characteristics. Environ-mental influences that maintain behavior are often less vivid and thus are easy to overlook. This error may result in incomplete accounts of problems that result in incorrectly attributing problems to clients' personal characteristics. Our feelings and thoughts are readily accessible to us and thus are readily viewed as causes. It is easy to overlook less vivid but influential environmental influences. These are individual and cultural differences in the balance between attention to environmental and psychological variables (see Krull & Erickson, 1995). Shweder and Bourne (1982) suggest that non-Western people may be culturally primed to see context and social relationships as a necessary condition for behavior, compared with Westerners, who may be culturally primed to search for abstract summaries of the autonomous individual. Being familiar with envi-

ronmental influences on behavior should decrease the likelihood of focusing on "fixing" people and overlooking opportunities to help clients to alter deficient environments.

The second reason is that the transfer of knowledge is a key problem (knowledge developed in one situation may not be used in others in which it would be of value). Including this material here may help you integrate and transfer knowledge about behavior to practice situations. A third reason is that the principles of behavior described in this chapter are empirically based (i.e., they describe relationships between behavior and environmental events that have been found through systematic exploration). Beliefs about the causes of behavior must be reviewed in light of these findings, just as those who wish to construct flying machines must consider empirical findings about gravity. One of the key differences between experts and novices is domain-specific knowledge—experts know more than novices and their knowledge is integrated in a more abstract manner (Ericsson & Smith, 1991). Incorrect beliefs about behavior may result in incomplete or inaccurate views of problems. A fourth reason is that this knowledge is not always covered in texts on social work.

Why This Knowledge Is So Often Ignored and Misrepresented

Knowledge about contingencies of reinforcement is often ignored and misrepresented, even though it has been used successfully to help clients with many different kinds of problems (Todd, 1992; Wyatt, 1990). Why is this? There are five reasons. (See also the discussion of myths and misconceptions about rearranging contingencies in Chapter 22.)

1. A Focus On Feelings and Personality Traits As Causes of Behavior.   In everyday life we often attribute behavior to feelings, as in "He hit her because he was angry." This is an incomplete account. We must go on to ask: Where do these feelings come from? Where do personality traits come from? What are they? Saying "that he hit his wife because he was angry" does not explain why he was angry. Both the behavior (hitting his wife) and the emotion (anger) may be the result of environmental contingencies yet to be described. Perhaps in the past his wife complied with his requests after he hit her; that is, in the past, hitting his wife may have been reinforced. Consider another example. Let's say that a social worker writes in her record, "Mrs. Jones tried to kill herself because she felt lonely and believed that no one cared about her." Why did she feel lonely? What's going on in her life that produced these feelings, thoughts, and the suicide attempt? These accounts stop too soon because they do not identify the contingencies (the relationships between behavior and environmental factors) related to feelings, thoughts, and behavior. Feelings and thoughts are vivid, thus readily available to regard as causes of behavior. Environmental changes are often less vivid, and so are easily overlooked.

2. Those Who Create and Maintain Influential Contingencies Benefit From Obscuring Them. Those who create and maintain contingencies that influence our behavior, such as those who create government policies and the laws to enforce them often benefit from mystifying both the source of influence and their effects. For example, officials may say, "We're doing it for you" when, a careful analysis of the contingencies reveals that they are "doing it for themselves" in relation to the main beneficiaries. (See also the discussion of critical thinking as a demystifying process in Chapter 6.) Ignorance of political, social, legal, and economic consequences may be bliss for those who create and maintain these consequences but loss for those whom they affect.

We often confuse feeling free with being free (Skinner, 1971). Simply because we feel free does not mean that we are not influenced by our environments. Consider a comment from John Kunkel's *Society and Economic Growth:*

> It is evident that the behavioral perspective of development includes political phenomena as important determinants of both the replication and modification

of behavior. The explanation of "apathetic peasants," for example, will lead the investigator from the study of the various contingencies that maintain "apathetic" activities through community power structures, officials, and land owners to the operation of regional and national governments. How much more comfortable and inoffensive are the implications of a psychodynamic perspective! Here "apathy" is assumed to be due to some characteristics of the internal state, and the investigator is led into the study of personality and child-raising practices. While the psychodynamic approach recognizes that governments affect development, it minimizes both their positive and detrimental roles. But peasant mentality, authoritarian personalities, and innate traditionalism can serve as convenient scapegoats for the slow pace of development only as long as the psychodynamic perspective holds sway. With the rise of a behavioral perspective, a new series of often uncomfortable questions arises: "what activities in the population do governmental operations maintain?" "why does the government not shape different behavior patterns?" and "what changes in government operations are required if the behavior of peasants and others is to be modified?" (1970, p. 277).

Appealing to personality traits of individuals to account for problems allows the creators of influential contingencies to blame others less powerful.

3. Understanding Behavioral Principles Takes Time and Effort. Acquiring a working knowledge of the principles of behavior requires careful study. Many social workers choose not to take the time to acquire this knowledge. This can be seen in the many misrepresentations of the behavioral perspective in the social work literature. (For accurate descriptions, see Cooper, Heron, & Heward, 1987; Malott, Whaley, & Malott, 1993; Martin & Pear, 1996; Michaels, 1993; Sulzer-Azaroff & Mayer, 1991; Sundel & Sundel, 1993).

4. Antiscience. Our knowledge of behavioral principles is the result of systematic research over many years. The experimental analysis of behavior reflects a scientific approach to understanding behavior. Guesses about what may be true or false are tested and the prevalence of antiscience both in academic and in everyday life is robust, as discussed in Chapter 4.

5. The Mistaken Belief That Being Guided by Behavioral Principles Allows No Room For Influencing Our Lives. Behavioral principles describe the relationships that have been found between our behavior and what happens before and after. We can influence our environments by rearranging what happens before and after. Thus, far from decreasing our influence over our environments, a knowledge of behavioral principles offers additional options for changing our environments.

6. A Search For Magical Cures. Problems can seem overwhelming. Consider youth violence and child abuse. It is tempting to search for easy answers rather than do the hard work necessary to understand the multiple interlinked contingencies related to problems.

CONTINGENCIES: THEIR VARIETY AND IMPORTANCE

Contingencies are relationships between behavior and related cues and consequences. Depending on what happens after our behavior, we are more or less likely to repeat that behavior in similar situations in the future. Depending on what happens after our behavior (its consequences), behavior may be established, maintained, decreased, or increased. Decades of research in both applied and laboratory settings show that our behavior is influenced by its consequences. If you reveal an error you have made to your supervisor and she tells you, "You did the right thing to tell me" and works with you to correct it, you may tell her about other errors in the future. On the other hand if your supervisor severely criticizes you, you may be less likely to reveal errors again. A *contingency* is the complete description of a specific operant. It includes a definition of the range of behaviors that will result in a specific consequence and the situations in which that consequence influences the future probability

of the behavior. The term *operant* refers to a class of behaviors, all of which have the same effect on the environment (see the Glossary in Appendix 8A). A child may get his mother's attention by yelling, by tugging on her clothes, or by hitting his brother. He may do so only in certain situations—those in which he has been reinforced for such behavior in the past. The concept of the operant highlights the fact that different forms of behavior can have the same function. The components of an operant are influenced by cultural practices.

Contingency analysis is a valuable tool for exploring contexts. It can help you discover personal and environmental factors related to problems. A contingency analysis will often reveal that changes are needed at many different interrelated levels to resolve a problem. Consider the many different parties and influences at many different levels involved in successful pressures on the tobacco industry. Anthony Biglan (1996) argues that change efforts were successful (e.g., laws regarding smoking were changed) because the involved parties (1) shared a common verbal analysis about the effects of smoking and its causes, (2) held overlapping memberships in organizations, (3) held joint meetings, and (4) had ample funding. Contingencies related to behavior may be quite complex and may be discovered only by carefully observing behavior in real-life settings. Discovering the contingencies related to behaviors of interest may require a fine-grained analysis. Consider children and their families. "Child behavior is functional [affects others] at the micro-social level [the child's unique environment] and theory building [guesses about what may be maintaining problem-related behaviors] at a minimum, needs to focus on understanding processes that are actually formative to the [unique] response styles children display in various settings" (Dishion, Patterson, & Kavanagh, 1992, p. 277). Exhibit 8.1 describes contingencies affecting families, and Exhibit 8.2 illustrates the many influences on families. A contingency analyses will often reveal "*perverse incentives*", incentives that work against positive change and maintain unwanted behaviors. Consider the incentive structure suggested by Caplow (1994) of the war on drugs.

EXHIBIT 8.1
Contingencies Affecting Families

For more than two decades, Gerald Patterson and his colleagues studied inter-action patterns in families that produce antisocial children. Their research shows that children and parents actively participate in creating their family environ-ments shaping antisocial children. Parenting behavior has been found to be a key factor in doing so. A child learns his or her interpersonal style in the family.

The coercion process begins with something that is intrinsically normal, a rather high level of child noncompliance and continued employment of aversive behaviors that are maintained because they work (escape conditioning). The par-ents fail both in teaching the prosocial behaviors that would replace the coer-cive ones, and they also fail to use effective discipline strategies for the deviant behaviors that do occur. The process moves out of control when the frequencies of these coercive behaviors reach very high levels (Chamberlain & Patterson, 1995, p. 213).

This research shows that parenting practices, including noncontingent reac-tions and low supervision and involvement are important in creating antisocial children (see also, Biglan, Lewin & Hops, 1990; Dishion, Patterson, & Kavanagh, 1992). "Noncontingent means that their reactions are not significantly correlated with what the child is doing. For example, if the child behaves in a prosocial fashion, the mother is no more likely to react in a positive, interested, support-ive fashion than if the child is being neutral or deviant" (Chamberlain & Patterson, 1995, p. 212). Coercive behaviors common in families with antisocial children include:

1. *Punishment acceleration*, in which parents' reprimands accelerate aggressive behavior.
2. *Crossover*, in which a family member responds with negative behavior to pos-itive behavior of another.
3. *Counterattacks*, in which negative behavior of one family member is re-sponded to with negative behavior by another family member.
4. *Continuance*, in which family members continue to behave in a negative way, regardless of how others behave.

Families in turn are influenced by their environment including employment op-portunities and the quality of education for children. The media daily depict vi-olent acts. Mothers of aggressive children behave more aggressively toward their children on days when they have unpleasant exchanges with people outside the family (Wahler, 1980).

To young people, especially minority males, it offers:

- More sexual opportunities than they can obtain any other way

- More money than they can expect to earn any other way

- More respect from peers and from strangers than they can obtain any other way

- Easy access to drugs, weapons, cars and other lux-ury goods

- An exciting and glamorous way of life.

To law enforcement agents, it offers:

- Opportunities for personal and collective advance-ment

EXHIBIT 8.2

The Relation Among Family Management Practices, Crises, and Antisocial Child Behavior

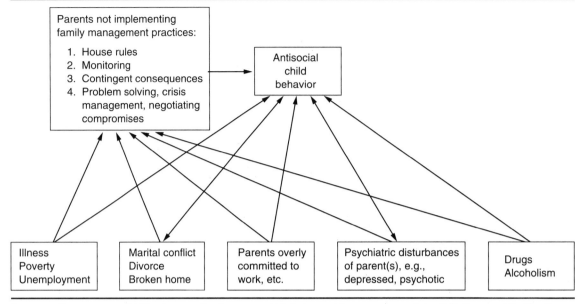

Source: G. R. Patterson (1982), *Coercive family process: Vol. 3. A social learning approach* (p. 217). Eugene, OR: Castalia.

- An inexhaustible supply of suspects
- Opportunities for illicit profit
- Easy access to drugs, weapons, cars and other luxury goods
- An exciting and glamorous way of life

To professional criminals and criminal organizations, it offers:

- Larger profits than are available from any other kind of criminal activity
- Opportunities for organizational development
- Opportunities for manipulating the justice system

To the farmers in exotic lands who grow opium, coca and marijuana for export to the United States, it offers:

- More profit than they can obtain from any legal crop (1994, pp. 99–100)

Consider also the consequences suggested by a student in reference to a pregnant immigrant seeking prenatal care in the first trimester (S− =

punishing consequences, S+ = positive consequences):

S+ = Confirmation of pregnancy (can be S− if the woman wants to deny the pregnancy).

S+ = Promise of medical attention to help ensure healthy outcome.

S− = Might find a problem with the pregnancy.

S− = Costs involved (of visit, transportation, wages lost).

S+ = Individual attention to woman.

S− = Medical system often depersonalizing, sometimes humiliating.

S− = Many taboos in regard to undressing in front of men, and many physicians are male.

S− = Language barriers.

S+ = Advice about diet and care of self.

S− = This advice might not be culturally sensitive.

S− = Long wait for an appointment or long hours in waiting room.

S+ = Contact with other pregnant women (in waiting room or groups).

S− = Unfamiliar technological devices and practices.

S− = Difficulty in obtaining child care or leaving work.

Some contingencies are remote, that is, they will not occur until some future time. For example, even if you do not exercise, you may not have heart trouble for decades—a remote consequence. Other contingencies are immediate; that is, they have an immediate effect on the future probability of our behavior. Some contingencies are natural, such as falling off your bike if you tip too far to one side. Others are *arbitrary*; that is, they are arranged by other people, such as government officials. Still others are *self-arranged*, such as your giving yourself a special treat for reading a chapter in this book. We often must arrange contingencies at different system levels to support valued behaviors, because natural related contingencies are remote, aversive, or inconsequential. Consider the interlinked contingencies related to the use of seat belts (see Exhibit 8.3). Contingencies at one level (e.g., individual, family, group, community, city, nation) influence those at other levels. Consider the influence of social and public policies on funding patterns for services that in turn influence individual citizens.

Chains of Behavior

A given behavior is usually part of a sequence, or *chain*, of behaviors. We artificially extract from this sequence one reaction that is called problematic. For example, a client may tell you that he often feels angry. He may feel angry after he has not asked for what he wants in a series of exchanges at work and at home. Clients often describe their exchanges with others as a trichotomy of events that starts with another person's behavior. They describe behavior patterns in a way that minimizes their own contribution (Watzlawick, Beavin, & Jackson, 1967). A husband may say in response to his wife's complaint that he is rude, "If you didn't nag me, I wouldn't have to tell you to shut up." He may not mention what he does (or does not do) before his wife starts to "nag" him. Perhaps he ig-

nored his wife's friendly attempts to start a conversation.

Cultures and Contingencies

Differences in cultural norms and values reflect different reinforcement histories. For example, one group may ignore a behavior that to another group may be the occasion for a gang fight. "Behavior is the joint product of (i) the contingencies of survival responsible for the natural selection of the species and (ii) the contingencies of reinforcement responsible for the repertoires acquired by its members, including (iii) the special contingencies maintained by an evolved social environment" (Skinner, 1981, p. 502). Cultural practices (not individual persons) survive over time as a result of natural selection by differential consequences. (What is beneficial for the individual or culture may not necessarily benefit the species.) Sigrid Glenn (1991) defines a cultural practice as "a set of interlocking contingencies of reinforcement in which the behavior and behavioral products of each participant function as environmental events with which the behavior of other individuals interact" (1991, p. 10). For each cultural practice we can ask, Who is involved? What are related antecedents and consequences? How do different practices at different levels influence one another? Cultural practices affect our behavior, and we in turn affect cultural practices. A cultural practice may survive or disappear depending on its outcome. Different cultures create different learning histories as a result of different social reinforcement patterns.

Cultural contingencies influence how we interpret physiological and psychological events (Angel & Thoits, 1987). Events have different meanings (influences on thoughts, feelings, and behavior) for different people because of unique histories in particular groups. Being born at a particular historical time (e.g., during the Vietnam War) creates unique influences on behavior known as *cohort differences*. We can examine contingencies at different levels (individual, family, group, organization, legislation, policy), including their interrelationships. This verbal analysis can help us understand who benefits and who loses from a certain policy or program.

EXHIBIT 8.3
The Performance–Management Model of Cultural Change

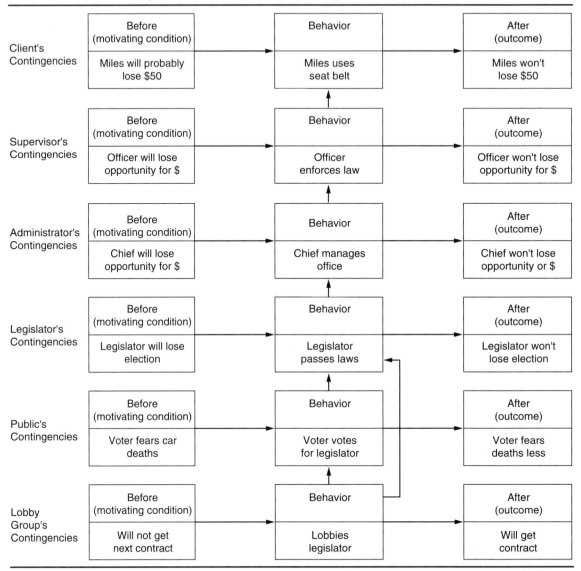

Source: R. W. Malott (1994), *Rule-governed behavior, self-management, and performance management* (p. 54). Kalamazoo, MI: Department of Psychology, Western Michigan University.

REINFORCEMENT

Behavior may be established or maintained by either positive or negative reinforcement. Positive and aversive influences differ in important ways and are accompanied by different emotions.

Positive reinforcement is associated with positive feelings, a decreased likelihood of aggression, and an increased likelihood of offering positive consequences to others. Aversive control, which involves both punishment and negative reinforcement, is associated with negative feelings such as anger, an increased likelihood of responding aggressively to others, and a decreased likelihood of offering positive consequences to others. Aversive events increase aggression, whether or not the aggression is reinforced, as described later in the discussion on punishment.

Positive Reinforcement

The term *positive reinforcement* refers to a procedure in which an event is presented following a behavior and there is an increase in the future likelihood of that behavior (see Exhibit 8.4). The definition of positive reinforcement has two parts: a procedure (a behavior is followed by the presentation of an event) and an effect on behavior (the probability that the behavior will occur in the future on similar occasions is increased). If you do a favor for a friend and she thanks you, you are more likely to do another favor for her in the future. If a teenager steals a car, has a great ride, and receives admiration from his friends for his "feat," he is more likely to steal another car in the future.

The term *positive reinforcement* refers to a procedure, whereas the term *positive reinforcer* refers to an event that, when presented contingent on a behavior, increases the future likelihood of that behavior. Positive reinforcers please people and are accompanied by positive feelings. "We call them pleasant and the behaviors they reinforce pleasure. They please even when they are accidental ('happy' first meant 'lucky')" (Skinner, 1988, p. 178). Reinforcement may be contingent on a low rate of behavior. For example, a teacher may praise a student only if the student talks out of turn less than twice a day. Or a high rate of behavior may be re-

inforced. Some reinforcers are on a limited hold; they are available only until a certain time. Driving to a restaurant will be reinforced only if you arrive before closing time.

Most reinforcers are *conditioned*, or *secondary*, *reinforcers*, in contrast to *primary reinforcers*, such as food, which functions as reinforcers without any prior learning history. Positive *conditioned reinforcers* often are events that consistently precede contact with other positive reinforcers. If a parent's smile is repeatedly associated with food and physical contact, the smile will become a conditioned reinforcer for an infant and may then increase the behavior that it follows. An event may also assume a reinforcing function by being associated with the removal of negative events. Money and approval acquire their function as reinforcers by being paired with things that are already reinforcing. Conditioned reinforcers such as money and approval that are paired with a variety of reinforcers become *generalized reinforcers* capable of maintaining a range of behaviors independent of particular states of deprivation. Attention and affection "are conditioned reinforcers which maintain behavior because they are discriminative stimuli for future behavior in other chains of performances leading ultimately to other reinforcers. The approval of one's friends, for example, makes possible their acceptance and issuance of invitations for social occasions . . . and so forth" (Ferster, Culbertson, & Boren, 1975, p. 381).

Because of different learning histories, an event that functions as a reinforcer for one person may not do so for another. We each have a unique reinforcer profile, a list of events that function as reinforcers. Thus, reinforcers are known not by their

---

EXHIBIT 8.4
Some Procedures and Their Effects on Behavior

Procedure	Effect on Behavior	
	Behavior Increases	Behavior Decreases
An event is presented following a behavior.	Positive reinforcement	Punishment
An event is removed following a behavior.	Negative reinforcement	Punishment
What usually happens no longer does so.	Prior punishment	Operant extinction

physical characteristics but by their functional effects, and so an event that functions as a reinforcer in one situation may not do so in another. Significant others, such as parents, spouses, or teachers, often assume that what is reinforcing for them is also reinforcing for those with whom they interact (their significant others). This may not be so. Such events could, however, be developed as reinforcers. For example, a teacher's approval could be established as a reinforcer by pairing it with events or items that already function as a reinforcer. On the other hand, because of similar learning histories in a given society, the same reinforcer may have identical functions for many people. Some reinforcers are substitutable; they may satisfy the same or similar needs. Other reinforcers are not.

Negative Reinforcement

Behavior can be established and maintained by preventing, reducing, or removing unpleasant events following its performance. We repeat not only those behaviors that result in pleasurable consequences but also those that remove annoying or painful events (see Exhibit 8.4). If the sun is shining in your eyes and you pull down a shade that removes the glare, your behavior is maintained by negative reinforcement (getting rid of something annoying). Tantrums may be maintained by escaping from or avoiding difficult tasks, especially if socially acceptable forms of escape are not available (Iwata, 1987). The definition of negative reinforcement includes two parts: the description of a procedure (the removal of an event contingent on a behavior) and a behavioral effect (the subsequent increase in the future probability of the behavior). Like positive reinforcers, aversive stimuli generate a variety of physiological reactions. In both positive and negative reinforcement, actions are followed by a change in the environment. In the former, something is presented, and in the latter, something is removed. Both procedures increase the future probability of behavior, and both involve contingencies (relationships between behavior and the environment).

Negative reinforcement is involved in both avoidance and escape behavior. Avoidance behavior is maintained by the removal of anticipated unpleasant events, for example, not starting a conversation with someone because of fear of rejection. Escape behavior is maintained by the removal of a negative event that is already present, for example, ending a conversation with someone who is abusive. Much of our everyday behavior is maintained by negative reinforcement (the removal of aversive or negative events). Aversive events are often used to influence others. For example, people may present unpleasant events to a person, such as critical comments, until that person performs some desired behavior, at which time the events (critical comments) are removed, as illustrated in the example of the child asking for candy. Our society relies heavily on negative reinforcement: Most of our laws function by means of negative reinforcement. We act in accordance with the law to avoid imprisonment. Consider also religious proscriptions. We avoid an unpleasant afterlife by acting piously in this life. Many advertising campaigns are based on hoped for negative reinforcement effects, such as using a certain deodorant to avoid social rejection. Negative reinforcement plays a role in maintaining aversive behavior in families (see Exhibit 8.1). Aggression by family members is often negatively reinforced by a decrease in the frequency of aggressive behaviors by other family members.

As with positive reinforcers, classifying an event as a negative reinforcer depends on its effects on behavior. We cannot tell for sure whether an event will function as a negative reinforcer until we arrange its removal following a behavior and see whether the behavior increases in the future. Aversive events function as reinforcers when they are decreased in intensity or ended. If a child nags his mother to buy a candy bar, repeating over and over, "Buy me a candy bar," the mother may finally buy one, resulting in removal of nagging. Her behavior succeeds in removing an unpleasant event. When the mother and her son are next in a store, her son might again ask her to buy him a candy bar, since he received one in the past. The mother, because he was quiet after she bought him candy in the past, will be more likely to again do so. (Her child will be more likely to whine on similar occasions in the future since he was reinforced for whining.) Just as there are many different kinds of events that may function as positive reinforcers, there are many different kinds of events that may function as negative reinforcers, including social ones (disapproval, criticism), undesired tasks (cleaning), and negative self-statements ("I'm really stupid"). Most are conditioned reinforcers; their reinforcing effects are required through learning. Just as what functions as a positive reinforcer may vary from person to person depending on his or her unique learning history, what may function as a negative reinforcer may also vary as a function of past history. The same factors that are important with positive reinforcement (immediacy, amount, schedule, and frequency) are important with negative reinforcement.

Natural contingencies involving negative reinforcement (moving out of the sun on a hot day) differ in important ways from socially imposed ones—a parent's request to a child to pick up his toys may carry an implied threat of an unpleasant event for noncompliance. Natural contingencies usually allow a range of behaviors that will remove an unpleasant event. For example, to escape the sun's heat, you could find a shady spot, go inside, or use an umbrella. Socially arranged contingencies are often more controlling in requiring a particular behavior (e.g., apologizing). Behavior that is under the control of natural contingencies benefits the person. The controller is often the beneficiary in socially imposed contingencies.

Superstitious Conditioning

Some behaviors are maintained by the accidental pairing of a behavior and a consequence. This is known as *superstitious conditioning*. For instance, carrying a lucky charm may be followed by an absence of a feared event, thus increasing the tendency to carry this around.

> A: "Why do you carry that lucky charm?"
> B: "To keep lions away."
> A: "That's crazy, there aren't any lions around here."
> B: "See!"

Superstitious conditioning may be responsible for some ineffective parenting practices. That is, parents may make inaccurate attributions about the causes of a child's behavior because of accidental reinforcement. Such superstitious beliefs may hinder the discovery of real contingencies. Because you think you "know the answer" you may not consider alternative possibilities. Can you think of any behaviors of your own that may be maintained by superstitious conditioning?

Punishment

Consequences may also decrease behavior. If behavior is followed by an aversive event (punishment) or by the removal of a positive reinforcer (response cost), or is no longer followed by reinforcing events (operant extinction), it will decrease in frequency. If a child's request for a cookie results in a slap from his mother (an aversive event) or if the mother consistently ignores his requests (no longer attends to them, that is, operant extinction), he will eventually make fewer requests. Drivers who are caught speeding and receive a fine (response cost) may be less likely to speed in the future. Thus, what happens after a behavior may make it more or less likely in the future. Punishment is a procedure in which an aversive event is presented after a behavior and there is a subsequent decrease in that behavior. The definition includes two factors, the description of a procedure and an effect on behavior. In order to determine whether an event is a punishing one, a contingency must be arranged and the future probability of behavior observed. Aversive events should be distinguished from punishment. There are many types of aversive events, including withholding reinforcement (extinction), removing a positive reinforcer (response cost), and presenting an aversive event contingent on a behavior (punishment). The same variables that influence the effectiveness of reinforcement also influence the effectiveness of punishment, including the immediacy with which a negative event follows a behavior, the intensity of this event, and the schedule of punishment.

Punishment is an inescapable part of life. We

learn through both punishing consequences and positive consequences. For example, if we don't watch where we are going, we will fall when learning to ride a bike, so we learn not to lean too far to one side. Leaning too far to one side is punished by falling, whereas maintaining a straight position is reinforced by avoiding unpleasant falls. This illustrates the close relationship between punishment and negative reinforcement. To arrange for the negative reinforcement of a behavior, a negative event must be presented that can be removed contingent on behavior. This event is presented after some preceding behavior (or its lack) and functions as a punishing event for that behavior.

Punishment is widely used in everyday life to influence the behavior of others. The mother who slaps her child, the supervisor who tells you that your reports are bad, and the teacher who sends a child to the principal's office—all hope to change behavior. They hope for an increase in desired behaviors and/or a decrease in undesired behaviors. The supervisor hopes to increase good report writing and decrease bad report writing. The mother hopes to increase polite verbal behavior and to decrease rude back talk. However, all too often, desirable alternatives are not identified and reinforced. Rather, people often attempt to prod others into acting in expected ways by punishing behavior (or its lack) and removing this contingent on compliance. A mother may stop nagging her daughter to do the dishes when the daughter finally gets up and does them. Power differentials between people (e.g., between parents and children, or teachers and students) make it possible for the more powerful to coerce behavior from the less powerful by threatening some aversive event or the withdrawal of some privilege for failure to comply. There is usually something readily at hand to remove. The threat is removed contingent on compliance. Use of punishment is encouraged by its immediate (but often temporary) effects, lack of skill in the use of positive methods of influence, and a low tolerance for disliked behaviors.

Disadvantages of Punishment. Behavioral researchers have taken the lead in identifying the negative effects of punishment (e.g., Azrin & Holtz,

1966). Noncontingent aversive events increase both the probability of aggressive behavior and behavior reinforced by the opportunity to engage in aggressive behavior. Both elicited and operant aggression may result. The former refers to aggressive reactions that have no influence on the probability of further punishment. For example, if a monkey is shocked in a chamber, he will attack a tennis ball in the chamber, even though this action will in no way influence the probability of future shocks. Consider how this might apply to violence in families. In *operant aggression*, behavior does influence the probability of further punishment. For example, a potential victim may punch a bully, who then retreats. Aversive events are more likely to suppress prosocial and neutral behaviors than aggressive behaviors perhaps because they tend to encourage aggressive behavior (Biglan, Lewin, & Hops, 1990). Abuse, was found to predict aggressiveness even after factors such as social class, family disruption, and exposure to spousal violence were controlled.

Modeling aggressive behavior is another disadvantage of punishment. The person delivering the punishment serves as a model for aggressive behaviors such as hitting and yelling. Physically abusing children increases the likelihood that they will develop aggressive behavior, perhaps because effective ways of relating to others are not established. An example of a parent without a clue regarding this is the father who strikes his child saying, "I told you not to hit your brother." Another disadvantage is that the punisher may be avoided. For example, if parents often punish their children, the children may avoid them, and so the parents will have less influence on the children's behavior using positive means.

Neutral cues that are present when punishment is delivered may acquire aversive properties by being paired with punishing events. At a future time, these cues may elicit emotional responses, resulting in avoidance behaviors. If the punishment is intense, the probability of a variety of behaviors, including desirable ones, may be lessened. For example, if parents severely punish sexual exploration in young children, the children may avoid all sexual behavior in the future—appropriate as well as inappropriate. If a negative event serves as a cue for a positive reinforcer to follow, the presentation of negative events may increase the frequency of undesired behaviors. For example, if a mother is affectionate to her child only after she beats him, the behaviors that lead to the beatings may increase. (Since in these instances, there is no decrease in behavior, these relationships between behavior and its consequences cannot accurately be called punishment procedures.) The discomfort involved in punishment is unpleasant for the recipient, and permission to use punishment allows one to do so from anger.

Punishment teaches only what not to do and leaves the development of desirable behaviors to chance. It does not eliminate reinforcement for inappropriate behavior. Neither does it undo any damage caused by such behavior. If behavior is punished in a situation that differs from those in which a decrease in response is hoped for, changes may be confined to the original context in which the punishment occurred. Creativity and persistence often are required to persuade significant others—such as teachers, parents and staff members—to use positive rather than coercive methods.

Response Cost

Response cost involves the contingent removal of a positive reinforcer following a behavior. Access to reinforcers is removed contingent on behavior. Like operant extinction and the use of punishment, response cost, by definition, results in a decrease in behavior. Unlike extinction, this procedure involves a contingency (a relationship between behavior and its consequences). Some reinforcer that is already being sampled (such as watching television), some opportunity or privilege that is normally available (such as use of the car on the weekend), or some reinforcer that has been accumulated (such as money) is removed contingent on a behavior or its absence (e.g., not doing chores). Removing the opportunity to visit a friend because of stealing or being fined 10 points for not completing a chore are examples of the use of response cost. In everyday life, punishment is often combined with response cost, as when a par-

ent tells a child she must help with the dishes because she teased her sister. If doing the dishes deprives the child of opportunities to engage in pleasurable activities, it is aversive in and of itself. That is, response cost as well as punishment is involved. Only by using threats of monetary fines for infractions (response cost) and threats of imprisonment (punishment) may companies alter practices that many people believe to be dangerous.

Extinction

If behavior is no longer followed by reinforcing events, it will decrease in frequency. If a mother consistently ignores a child's requests he will eventually make fewer of them. In operant extinction, there is no longer any contingency between a behavior and the reinforcer that followed it in the past. The schedule on which the behavior was reinforced influences how rapid this decrease will be (see the later discussion of schedules). If a behavior has been reinforced on a continuous schedule, there may be an initial increase in the frequency and intensity of the behavior when reinforcement is withheld. However, this usually is followed by a decrease. For example, if a child's rude requests have typically been granted and then such behavior is consistently ignored, the child may at first shout even louder and more often. The decrease in behavior will be more gradual, and an initial increase in behavior is less likely if behavior has been maintained on an intermittent schedule of reinforcement. The initial increase in behavior that usually occurs when an extinction procedure is used can be avoided by providing positive reinforcement for alternative behaviors. Note that for an extinction procedure to be in effect, the behavior must occur without being reinforced and there must be a resultant decrease in behavior over the long term.

Nonreward (e.g., extinction) creates emotional effects similar to those of punishment. Jeffrey Gray (1987) views these as so similar that he defines anxiety in terms of both frustration (nonreward) and punishment. Both increase arousal and attention and behavioral inhibition. This helps explain the intense reactions to social rejection, which may include nonreward as well as punishment of social behaviors. Nonreward may occur when previous behaviors have not been reinforced and also when they have been reinforced, as in extinction.

THE ROLE OF ANTECEDENTS

Our behavior is influenced by what happens before it, mainly (but not totally) because it is reinforced in particular circumstances (see Exhibit 8.5). A given change in the environment (stimulus) may have a variety of functions (influences on behavior). Consider Mrs. R., who seeks help because of

a fear of cars that prevents her from accepting a job in which she has to drive. We can ask: "What functions do cars have at this point? First, they serve as eliciting stimuli for anxiety. When Mrs. R. thinks of cars or approaches them, she starts to sweat and becomes tense. Second, cars are a cue for avoidance behavior. Mrs. R. avoids riding in cars and avoids being around them as much as possible. Third, cars function as *negative reinforcers*; that is, they reinforce behavior that removes or avoids them. So cars function as (1) eliciting stimuli for sweating and muscle tension, (2) discriminative cues for avoidance behavior, and (3) negative reinforcers for escape and avoidance behaviors.

EXHIBIT 8.5
A Contingency Diagram Analyzing Criminal Activities by Members of Youth Gangs

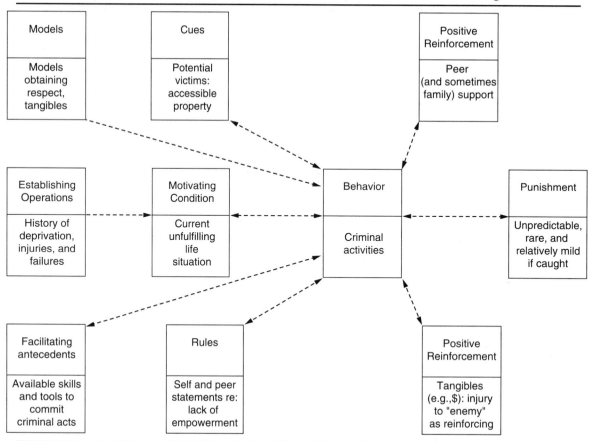

Source: M. A. Mattaini (1993), *More than a thousand words: Graphics for clinical practice* (p. 243). Washington, DC: National Association of Social Workers.

Successful intervention would reverse these functions (e.g., cars would cue approaching behavior in relevant situations). Rearranging antecedents (e.g., planning positive activities for children) is a valuable option for increasing positive exchanges and avoiding unpleasant ones between parents and children. Consider the parent who brings toys that a child likes to play with on a long plane trip, compared with the parent who does not prepare in this way.

Occasions for Behavior

Most of our behavior is reinforced only in certain situations and is therefore associated only with certain stimuli. Antecedents acquire influence over our behavior because of their association with behavior and its consequences. For example, we ask certain kinds of questions of others only in certain kinds of situations, such as "How do you feel?" or "How are you?" We are more likely to perform behavior in situations in which it has been reinforced in the past and are less likely to perform behavior in situations in which it has been punished or has not been reinforced. Thus, antecedent events acquire influence over behavior through their association with reinforcing events.

Suppose that Mr. Smith typically adjourns to the living room and reads the paper after dinner and that earlier in the marriage has wife attempted to initiate a conversation with him at this time and received only a "humm" or a rattle of the paper. She probably no longer tries to initiate conversations with him during this time, since her efforts were not reinforced in this situation. Her husband's reading the paper in the living room after dinner is a cue that attempts to make conversation will not be reinforced. But if Mrs. Smith's attempts are successful when her husband puts the paper down, this may be a cue for initiating a conversation.

Most of our behavior consists of *discriminated operants*, behaviors that occur only in certain situations (those in which they are reinforced). An antecedent event that increases the probability of a behavior is called a *discriminative stimulus* (S^D). (A *stimulus* is defined as any change in the environment that can influence behavior.) Those stim-

uli signaling that a behavior will probably not be reinforced are called s deltas ($S\Delta s$). A discrimination can be established by reinforcing a behavior in one situation and not reinforcing it in other situations (i.e., differential reinforcement). A discrimination has been established when there is a high rate of a behavior in one situation and a low rate in all other situations. Establishing appropriate discriminations is a key aspect of developing effective repertoires. For example, people who do not do well in social situations such as meeting people and making friends may not perceive (notice) signs of friendliness by others and so not initiate conversations. Social skills training may include helping clients learn how to recognize such clues (see Chapter 22).

Inappropriate or inadequate discriminations are often involved in presenting problems. Examples include continuing to drink alcohol even when signs of intoxication are evident or a student's incorrect assumption that a teacher's facial expressions indicate disapproval. It is not unusual for children to be well behaved in school but difficult to manage at home or vice versa, reflecting different contingencies of reinforcement in the different settings. Parents may reinforce annoying behaviors at home (and not reinforce desired behaviors), whereas the teacher may reinforce desired behaviors and ignore unwanted behaviors. The teacher thus becomes a cue for desired behaviors because she reinforces them; the parents become a cue for undesired behaviors because they reinforce them and ignore desired behaviors.

Antecedent events that are similar to those present during learning will elicit or occasion similar behaviors. If a person slows down when he sees a police car in back of him, he may also have this reaction when he spots cars that are similar to police cars. This is known as *stimulus generalization* and occurs with both operant and respondent behavior. Situational factors that are not related to whether a behavior is reinforced but that are usually present may affect behavior if these change radically. The term *response generalization* refers to the fact that behaviors that are similar to a behavior that is reinforced will also tend to increase in future probability. If you reinforce a friend for telling particular types of jokes, he may tend to tell you similar jokes. Generalization across time is of major importance in the helping professions (Do valued outcomes persist?)

Establishing Operations

If we want to increase the frequency of certain behaviors, we must arrange relevant establishing (motivating) conditions. *Establishing operations* alter the effectiveness of other events as forms of reinforcement and evoke the type of behavior that has been reinforced in the past by those events (Michaels, 1993, p. 78). The first effect is described as *reinforcer establishing.* The second is referred to as an *evocative effect.* Examples of establishing operations include food deprivation and painful stimulation. Food deprivation increases the effects of food reinforcers and increases behaviors that result in access to food. Painful stimulation makes the reduction of pain a powerful reinforcer and also evokes behaviors that previously ended pain. Establishing operations "motivate" behavior (see also the later section on motivation).

Necessary and Facilitating

Necessary and facilitating refer to personal and environmental characteristics that influence how easy it is to carry out a behavior. For example, we are not capable of certain acts (e.g., levitating). Problem-solving styles and nutrition may affect the probability of behavior; for instance, the availability of certain items and contexts (weapons, isolated spots, alcohol, drugs) may increase the likelihood of assaults (see Exhibit 8.5). Behavior may also be influenced by events removed in time. Wahler (1980) calls these "setting" events. For example, a child may have had a very upsetting day with her teacher and be irritable at home later in the day. You may have had a frustrating drive to work and feel irritable when seeing your first client.

Models

The influence of behavior by observing others is known as *observational learning.* By observing oth-

ers, we may learn new skills. Observing what happens to others may inhibit or disinhibit behavior (Bandura, 1986). Concerns are often raised about the prevalence of models of violent behavior in movies, TV, and newspapers. If a model's behavior is followed by punishing consequences, we are less likely to engage in that behavior. On the other hand, if their behavior is followed by positive consequences, we are more likely to engage in the behavior. If a student sees another classmate get caught cheating, he may be less likely to cheat himself. But if he sees a fellow student get away with cheating, he may be more likely to cheat. Emotional responses can be conditioned or extinguished simply by observing what happens to other people. A child's fear of thunderstorms may be related to his mother's fear reactions on such occasions. Watching someone approach a feared object increases the probability that someone who fears such objects will approach it (Bandura, Blanchard, & Ritter, 1969). Finally, watching others may facilitate behavior (cue behavior that is not subject to inhibitory processes). For example, if we smoke, we may smoke more when we are around others who smoke.

VERBAL INFLUENCES

Human beings are unique in the development of complex verbal repertoires that influence behavior in a variety of ways. Verbal behavior includes talking, thinking, imagining, and writing. It is our main source of communication and a key source of influence. Verbal behavior is *socially* mediated; that is, it is largely developed and maintained by the behavior of other people. Parents ask children, "Why did you do that?" "Why don't you like it?" and so on. Thus, children's verbal repertoires are created by adults. Verbal behavior may have all the functions other kinds of behavior may have (e.g., cue overt behavior, elicit emotional reactions, and function as reinforcers). For example, research shows that our feelings and behavior are affected by what we say to ourselves (Bandura, 1986).

Verbal behavior acquires its influence over our actions because of its association with certain consequences. Instructional control (by either others or ourselves) is created through individual learning histories. Instructions given by others are effective by influencing self-instructions (what we say to ourselves).

> By behaving verbally, people cooperate more successfully in common ventures. By taking advice, heeding warnings, following instructions, and observing rules, they profit from what others have already learned. Ethical practices are strengthened by codifying them in laws, and special techniques of ethical and intellectual self-management are devised and taught. Self-knowledge or awareness emerges when one person asks another such a question as "What are you going to do?" or "Why did you do that?" (Skinner, 1981, p. 502)

Rule-Governed Behavior

Rule-governed behavior is behavior influenced by descriptions of contingencies (e.g., in a book or lecture). A book on bowling may state: "If you hold your arm steady, you will get a strike." "We tend to follow a rule because previous behavior in response to similar verbal stimuli has been reinforced" (Skinner, 1969, p. 148). One reason we follow rules is to escape from or avoid aversive events. For example, studying for final examinations may be maintained by ending self-blame, guilt, or anxiety (negative reinforcement). Rules can be learned quickly, are valuable if contingencies are complex or unclear, and make it easier to profit from similarities between contingencies (Skinner, 1974, p. 125). For example, many contingencies are remote, such as the relationship between smoking cigarettes and developing lung cancer. Competing contingencies often are present (e.g., pleasing others while also pursuing personal goals). "Correspondence training" is used to increase the match between what people say they will do and what they actually do (e.g., Deacon & Konarski, 1987). Describing contingencies that work is just as important as describing those that do not. Rules provide a way to understand how self talk influences behavior. A rule functions as a discriminative stimulus and, as such, can be effective as part of a set of contingencies. The links between verbal and overt behavior underscore the importance of assessing the role of self-statements in problems (see Chapter 16).

Rule-Based Learning

Rule-based learning is based on a description of contingencies, and so it differs from contingency-shaped learning, which is based on direct experience (Skinner, 1969). The effects of rule-based contingencies depend on the extent to which they accurately describe what is likely to happen. Reading the descriptions of a contingency in this book (If you do x, y will occur) will generally not be as effective in developing skilled behavior as are learning experiences in which direct feedback is used to shape behavior. Rule-governed behavior is more variable. Descriptions of contingencies may or may not be accurate. For example, the likelihood of unpleasant consequences may be greatly exaggerated, as when a client has an excessive fear of social disapproval. Rules often are incomplete. Neither the consequences related to behaviors of interest nor the cues may be described. Rules may not reflect real-life contingencies and so result in punishing consequences (Poppen, 1989). Consider self-statements such as "Everyone should like me." We may overgeneralize or attend to only part of a situation (focus on negative outcomes and ignore positive ones). Excessive rule following that decreases sensitivity to real-life contingencies is a common side effect of verbal influence (Hayes, Kohlenberg, & Melancon, 1989).

Lately, a great deal of attention has been given to "equivalence classes" (Hayes, 1989). These are classes of events that may differ in form but are linked by a common learning history. This linking may occur through verbal associations (verbal stimuli associated with events) created by unique learning histories. What on the surface may seem to be unrelated may be related by a common association based on a unique learning history. For example, based on his learning history, a man may equate his wife's expressing an opinion with disrespect to him and may then feel he has a right to hit her. That is, he equates expressing an opinion and disrespect.

MOTIVATION

Motivational variables are related to the different reinforcing effectiveness of environmental events. *Motivation* can be viewed as a relationship between a set of operations (e.g., deprivation of a reinforcer such as social approval) and their effects on behavior (increased persistence in overcoming obstructions and increased resistance to extinction). As discussed earlier in this chapter, establishing operations (e.g., deprivation of water) influence motivational conditions (conditions of our body or environment) that influence our motivational level (sensitivity to reinforcement) (Malott, Whaley, & Malott, 1993, p. 159). Defining motivation in this way provides guidelines for understanding and altering behavior. For example, antecedents related to behaviors can be identified and changed. Identifying problem-related contingencies will help you and your clients understand the motivation for them (their meanings) (e.g., Exhibits 8.3 and 8.5).

EMOTIONS

Emotion can also be viewed as a relationship between certain antecedent conditions (an abrupt stimulus change such as experiencing an intense pleasant or unpleasant event) and their effects on behavior (Millenson & Leslie, 1979). Here, too, the reinforcing value of events and general activity level are altered. Characteristics of emotion identified by Paul Ekman (1994) include the following: (1) presence in other primates, (2) distinctive physiology, (3) commonalities universals in antecedent events, (4) quick onset, (5) brief duration, (6) automatic appraisal, and (7) unbidden occurrence. Some emotions have a distinctive universal signal.

Large changes in the schedule or amount of reinforcement or punishment are usually accompanied by emotional reactions or a disruption of ongoing behavior. If a teacher severely criticizes a child, the child may have difficulty continuing to work. If a person gets a call while reading a magazine informing him that he has just won a $5,000 trip for his jingle about Crispy Cracky cereals, he is unlikely to continue reading the magazine. Just as a large change in the amount of a reinforcer or aversive event can alter behavior, so can a large change in the schedule of reinforcement. This, too, is likely to create emotional effects that disrupt be-

havior, such as when a companion who supported most of another person's behavior dies. High levels of emotion decrease our skill in making discriminations. High levels of stress may result in emotional effects that decrease parents' skills in identifying specific desired behaviors to reinforce on the part of their children. There is a rich and fascinating literature on the origins and functions of emotions (Ekman & Davidson, 1994; Lewis & Haviland, 1993).

An evolutionary view highlights the communication and survival functions of emotions. One of the main functions of emotion is mobilizing us to deal quickly with environmental threats (e.g., from predators). We appraise events as harmful or beneficial. An anatomical perspective highlights the role of our "reptilian" brain in our emotions. For example, Paul MacLean notes that the two older functions of our brain "lack the capacity for verbal communication with the parts of the human brain accounting for speech" (1993, p. 67). This has important implications for the potential of higher-level cognitive influences on our emotions (see also Gilbert, 1989). In a review of research related to fear and anxiety for example, Ohman writes:

> Responses of fear and anxiety originate in an alarm system shaped by evolution to protect creatures from impending danger. This system is biased to discover threat, and it results in a sympathetically dominated response as a support of potential flight or fight. This response system can be triggered from three different levels of information processing, the first two of which are inaccessible to introspection. The first level concerns a direct link to an arousal system from elementary feature detectors geared to respond to biologically relevant threats. Thus, the arousal system becomes collaterally and automatically activated with the activation of further information-processing stages, whose functioning may be influenced by the arousal. The second level concerns a schema-driven nonconscious bias to discover threat in the environment, which delivers information to conscious perception, but has no effect or only a weak effect on physiological arousal. The third level concerns the direct effect of expectancy and physiological arousal on the cognitive–interpretive activity resulting in perceived threat (1993, pp. 529–530).

The emotions and accompanying behaviors common to a culture depend on the basic forms of social organization that are favored. In competitive, power-based groups, fear and appeasement are common. In cooperative reassurance-based groups, playfulness, problem-solving, and sharing are common (Gilbert, 1989) (see also the later discussion of respondent behaviors). Studies of emotions show that women compared to men "display more warmth, happiness, shame, guilt, fear, and nervousness which are related to affiliation, vulnerability and self consciousness and are consistent with women's lower social status and power, lower physical aggression, and their traditional gender roles, including child caretaking and social bonding, which necessitates being able to read the emotional signals of others" (Brody & Hall, 1993, p. 452). In their discussion of anger and hostile interactions, Elizabeth Lemerise and Kenneth Dodge note that "the extent to which a society recognizes and values sadness is related to the society's views about aggression, about individual versus collective responsibility, and about activity versus passivity" (1993, p. 556). They note that Tahitians find danger in sadness because it is associated with fatigue and the lack of drive. Tahitians do not see sadness as an emotion and do not have a word for it. They consider it not as "felt by the self, but rather is the result of an outside difficulty that subdues the self" (p. 554).

VARIABLES THAT INFLUENCE OPERANT LEARNING

A knowledge of variables that influence operant learning will help you and your clients design effective service programs. These variables include timing, magnitude, frequency, and schedule of reinforcement. *Timing* refers to the period of time between a behavior and the presentation of a reinforcer. For maximum effect, a reinforcer should immediately follow the behavior. Excessive delays are one of the principal errors made in using reinforcement. *Frequency* refers to how often a behavior is reinforced; *magnitude* refers to how much of a reinforcer is offered; and *quality* refers to the

reinforcing potential of one event relative to others. Although awareness of the relationship between behavior and its consequences facilitates learning, it is not essential. Many contingencies influence our behavior that we either cannot identify or misidentify (Baron, 1994; Nisbett & Ross, 1980; Plous, 1993). We may learn about contingencies through direct experience (contingency-shaped behavior) or what we hear or read (rule-governed behavior). Beliefs about rule-governed contingencies are less likely (compared with contingency-shaped behavior) to accurately reflect contingencies (relationships between our behavior and environmental changes). Beliefs about a contingency may override the effects of real-life contingencies. Consistency refers to the use of an established schedule. If schedules vary a great deal, developing new behaviors may be more difficult.

Schedule of Reinforcement

The *schedule of reinforcement* refers to the particular pattern that describes the relationship between a behavior and its consequences. Different schedules produce different patterns of behavior.

Why It Is Important to Know About Scheduling Effects. Understanding schedules of reinforcement is important because they influence the rate of behavior, its maintenance, and its resistance to extinction (how difficult it is to decrease a behavior). Consider the "addictive" effects of variable ratio schedules of reinforcement in gambling. Scheduling effects are often overlooked, resulting in serious assessment errors. Sudden changes in response requirements may disrupt behavior. Children have different histories in terms of how much output has been required before reinforcement in a given situation. If a teacher requires the same output for all children, those who are not accustomed to this requirement will not meet her expectations. The teacher may label such children as lazy or unmotivated (she may "blame the victim"), when in fact environmental factors are responsible (a change in the schedule of reinforcement). This teacher may refer these children to a social worker because of "lack of motivation," not realizing that she must arrange the motivating conditions for the children's behavior by offering schedules of reinforcement that match each child's unique reinforcement history. She could then provide new histories by gradually changing the requirements. Transitions such as retirement usually involve changes in reinforcement schedules, which may account for some of the changes in behavior and emotions occurring at such times. Behaviors that are maintained on "thin schedules" of reinforcement are especially likely to be disrupted by punishment that would otherwise have little effect.

Schedule changes may result in attack (e.g., when a schedule is thinned and reinforcement is given less often) or changes in the frequency of other behaviors such as water drinking (Epling & Pierce, 1988). Such behaviors are called *adjunctive behaviors.* Examples are time-filling behaviors such as idle conversation, habits such as nail-biting, smoking, hand washing, self-stimulating rituals, manic episodes, and rage outbursts (Foster, 1978). A further influence of schedules is shown by the effects of preceding schedules on later ones.

Different Kinds of Schedules and Their Effects on Behavior.
Some behavior is followed by the same reinforcer on every occasion (a *continuous schedule* of reinforcement). If your favorite coffee shop always opens at 9 A.M. on Tuesdays, walking to this shop to get some coffee at that time will always be reinforced. Most behavior is maintained on an *intermittent schedule* (a consequence does not follow every instance of a behavior). For example, only on some occasions do you hit the jackpot when you pull a slot machine handle. The advantages of intermittent reinforcement include its value in maintaining behavior and resistance to extinction (a behavior persists longer when reinforcement is no longer provided).

There are two main types of intermittent schedules. In *ratio schedules*, either a fixed or variable number of behaviors are required before a consequence occurs. Such schedules usually produce high performance rates. An example of a fixed-ratio schedule is piecework production in a factory. In a *fixed-ratio schedule*, a pause in responding typically occurs after reinforcement, followed by a fairly steady rate of behavior until the next reinforcer occurs. Difficulty in starting a new project (e.g., a new term paper) may reflect the pause in responding that occurs in fixed-ratio schedules. Emotional reactions, such as anxiety, are more likely to disrupt behavior maintained on fixed-ratio schedules in which there are long pauses after reinforcement, than with behaviors on variable-ratio schedules in which small response requirements are occasionally reinforced.

Pulling the lever on a slot machine is an example of a *variable-ratio schedule*. This schedule generates behaviors that have a high stable rate and are difficult to decrease. In fixed-ratio schedules, the higher the ratio, the higher the rate of behavior (one reinforcement for every 10 behaviors is a higher ratio than one reinforcer for every five). In a variable-ratio schedule, the higher the average ratio (the average number of behaviors required before a reinforcer follows), the higher the rate of behavior will be. Parents who reinforce undesirable behaviors on high-ratio schedules ensure a high rate of this behavior.

In *interval schedules*, behavior is reinforced only after a fixed or variable amount of time has passed. The first behavior that occurs after a certain time interval is reinforced. Behaviors that occur before this are not reinforced. Waiting for a bus that arrives only on the hour is an example of a fixed-interval schedule. Interval schedules differentially reinforce low rates of behavior, whereas ratio schedules differentially reinforce high rates of behavior. An example of a behavior on a variable-interval schedule is a child's request for an ice cream cone when the mother buys one only when she thinks enough time (which is variable) has passed since the child last had one. Variable-interval schedules create behaviors that occur at a low rate and are difficult to decelerate. A low rate results because the reinforcement is not dependent on response output. Many factors influence the rate of behavior on interval schedules (Ferster, Culbertson, & Boren, 1975). For example, if the behavior is very strong, such as waiting for an ambulance, there may be a fairly steady output of behavior, such as looking in the direction in which the ambulance is to approach, even though it is not due to arrive for a set period of time. When a variable schedule is used, it is more difficult to decrease behavior. Parents who try to decrease behavior by no longer reinforcing it often do this for only a certain period of time. That is, they provide periodic reinforcement that will create behavior that is difficult to decrease. Occasional reinforcement may maintain behavior.

Complex Schedules. In everyday life, reinforcement is often available for more than one response from more than one source. Many behaviors, each of which is on a certain schedule of reinforcement, may compete with one another. For example, an elementary school student may receive reinforcement from his peers for making funny faces and concurrently receive criticism from his teacher for getting the incorrect answer on a problem. In *concurrent schedules*, two or more schedules are in effect independently and at the same time for two or more different behaviors. The *matching law* refers to the finding that we tend to match our behaviors in choice situations to the rate of reinforcement for each choice (McDowell, 1988). This provides valuable guidelines for altering behavior. We can increase valued behaviors by enriching their schedules of reinforcement while decreasing or holding constant reinforcement for other behaviors. Some schedules combine both a response and an interval requirement. For example, a teacher may require a certain number of problems to be completed and evaluate the students' progress after a certain amount of time has passed. She is using a *conjunctive schedule*. Different schedules of reinforcement may be in effect for the same behavior in different situations. For example, saying "How are you?" to some people you know may always be reinforced by a friendly response, but this may not be true for other people.

RESPONDENT BEHAVIOR

Respondent behaviors include those that involve the autonomic nervous system, such as heart rate and blood pressure, whereas operants (behavior that "operates" on or influences the environment) involve the skeletal muscles (walking, running). We usually associate respondent behaviors with involuntary reactions and operants with voluntary behaviors. Examples of respondent reactions are an increased heart rate before going on stage to give a speech, sweaty palms before a test, and goose pimples on a chilly day. Respondent behavior plays a key role in many problems, including depression, anxiety, chronic pain, aggression, and child abuse. Some events (unconditioned stimuli) elicit behavior without any previous learning.

> The ability to respond automatically to certain stimuli is part of the genetic endowment of each organism. Such behaviors function as protection against certain harmful stimuli (e.g., pupil contraction in bright light) and help regulate the internal economy of the organism (e.g., changes in heart rate and respiration in response to temperature and activity levels); these responses evolved through natural selection because of their survival value to the species. (Cooper, Heron, & Heward, 1987, p. 19).

Respondent learning involves pairing neutral events with cues that already elicit a given reaction. Ivan Pavlov (1927), a famous physiologist who won a Nobel Prize for his studies of digestion in dogs, spent the major part of his career investigating conditioned reflexes. Stimuli that affect behavior only after being paired with events that already elicit a response are known as *conditioned stimuli*. For example, only after an experience of painful drilling at a dentist's office may approaching the office cause discomfort. In higher order respondent conditioning, neutral events become conditioned stimuli by being paired with conditioned stimuli. Knowledge of respondent learning can help you understand the complex interactions between respondent and operant behavior (e.g., between anxiety and avoidance reactions). The placebo effect can be viewed as a conditioned response (Adler, 1988). The "placebo effect is a favorable response to the act of treatment rather than the treatment itself" (Jarvis, 1990, p. 9); cues associated with receiving a certain treatment may result in effects associated with that treatment.

Variables That Influence Respondent Learning

Classical conditioning is complex in the associations that may be formed. The characteristics of conditioned and unconditioned stimuli as well as physical relationships among them influence whether a conditioned response is acquired. Prior learning history influences later experiences through preexisting associations. Recent discussions of Pavlovian (respondent) conditioning emphasize the overlap between cognitive and conditioning influences. The associations formed are influenced by the "net" of associations related to a particular stimulus, including inhibitory and excitatory associations (Rescorla, 1988). Thus classical conditioning entails much more than the establishment of single associations between specific cues. Consider the "blocking" effect that one stimulus may have on another. That is, conditioning to a particular stimulus may be prevented by previous conditioning to another event. There are biological boundaries and specific differences in the particular responses that can be associated with particular stimuli. We are biologically prepared to experience certain kinds of reactions in certain kinds of situations. Our evolutionary history influences emotional reactions such as anger, panic attacks, social anxiety, and shyness (Gilbert, 1989; Trower, Gilbert, & Sherling, 1990). Neutral events that are paired with aversive stimuli become conditioned aversive stimuli. The avoidance of such events is reinforcing.

The intensity of the unconditioned stimulus (US) relative to other background events and the number of pairings (up to a point) between it and a neutral stimulus influence the effects of pairing a neutral event with a conditioned or unconditioned stimulus. A single pairing may result in a conditioned response as in long-lasting taste aversions to particular kinds of food. Conditioned taste aversions are a concern when patients undergo treatments that induce nausea, such as chemotherapy for cancer. A third variable is the time between the presentation of the neutral and conditioned stimulus. With humans, close contiguity between two events is not necessarily required because of the influential role of thoughts (e.g., reminders about contingencies) (Rescorla, 1988). Contiguity between events may not produce an association, and failure to arrange contiguity does not preclude associative learning. Even *backward conditioning* (presentation of the unconditioned event before the neutral one) may be effective with humans, whereas it usually is not with animals.

The intensity of the eliciting stimulus affects the magnitude and latency of respondent reactions. In general, the greater the intensity of the eliciting stimulus and the shorter the time period between its presentation and the occurrence of a response (the shorter the latency), the greater the magnitude of the response. Intensity is influenced by preexisting associations. With conditioned responses, the likelihood of a reaction, its magnitude, and its latency are related to the degree of similarity of an event (or complex events) to the one (or those) present during conditioning. Thus, in the example of the dentist's office, the probability and magnitude of conditioned reactions on future occasions will be influenced by the similarity of the events presented on the next visit to those originally present. Is the dentist wearing the same white coat? Is the client again there to have a cavity filled? Thoughts about feared events will influence reactions. What is similar depends on the events associated with a stimulus (see the discussion of stimulus equivalence).

Respondent extinction involves repeated presentation of an event without pairing this with events with which it has typically been associated in the past. For example, a child may be gradually exposed to speaking in front of adults, thus avoiding the anxiety reactions usually experienced when his mother tried to force him to speak. As extinction progresses, the magnitude of the reaction decreases, and the latency between the presentation of the conditioned stimulus and the conditioned response increases. Empirical research on anxiety suggests that exposure to feared events is the principal factor in the success of anxiety reduction methods (Barlow, 1988; Marks, 1987).

Counterconditioning involves pairing an event with a response that is incompatible with the reaction typically elicited. For example, in systematic desensitization based on relaxation, feared events are presented in a context of relaxation. This procedure may be carried out symbolically (relevant events are imagined) or in vivo (events are actually presented). The goal is to associate a different response (relaxation) with feared events. If effective, this procedure will alter the function of a stimulus from one that elicits unpleasant emotional reactions and occasions avoidance behavior (e.g., leaving a situation) to one that elicits pleasant or neutral reactions and occasions approach behavior. For example, a client who is afraid of elevators and who avoids them before seeking help will feel comfortable when around elevators and will get on them if you are successful. A counterconditioning procedure may also be used to change an event from one that elicits pleasant reactions and cues approach behavior (e.g., smoking) to one that elicits unpleasant reactions and cues avoidance behavior.

The Interaction Between Respondent and Operant Behaviors

In the past, a wide separation was made between respondent and operant behavior in terms of their controlling variables; respondent behavior was thought to be influenced mainly by antecedents (what happens before the behavior), and operant behavior, mainly by its consequences (what happens after behavior). We now know that the difference between these two types of reactions—whether they can be influenced by their consequences—has been exaggerated. Heart rate, blood pressure, and a range of other responses can be brought under operant control. That is, they can be influenced by what happens after they occur (e.g., see books on behavioral medicine). Both respondents and operants are involved in most reactions and chains of behavior. Seeing a lover after a long absence, for instance, may elicit warm feelings and cue greeting behaviors. Thus, the same event may elicit respondent reactions and occasion operant behaviors. Each person may have a different pattern of responses in a situation.

Different response systems may or may not be related, depending on the unique learning history of each person: (1) overt behavior (e.g., avoidance of crowds and verbal reports, descriptions of anxiety, (2) cognitions (thoughts about crowds), and (3) physiological reactions (increased heart rate).

Physiological reactions such as a rapid heart beat may or may not accompany verbal reports of fear or avoidance of related situations. Thoughts may or may not trigger anxiety reactions, depending on the person's learning history. Failure of a reaction to follow the principles of respondent behavior should be a signal that other factors are involved, such as reinforcement from significant others or that eliciting events (those that result in the response) have not been identified. A respondent reaction should be observed every time the eliciting stimulus is presented, given that other factors are held constant. In contrast, we speak of operant behavior as being emitted—the antecedents (SDs as establishing operations) set the occasion on which a behavior is likely to be reinforced.

EVOLUTIONARY INFLUENCES

We have a history both as individuals and as species. Both histories influence what environments we create and their risks and opportunities. It is easy to lose sight of the fact that we carry anatomical, physiological, and psychological characteristics related to our evolutionary history. This history influences biological selection (some living beings are more likely to survive), behavioral selection (we act on the environment and are affected by the consequences), environmental selection (through our behaviors we create our own unique environments), and cultural selection (patterns of behavior in a network of individuals). Variability of behavior is a key building block of evolutionary theory. Variations followed by positive consequences or the removal of negative consequences are likely to recur in the future. Those that are followed by the removal of positive consequences or the presentation of negative ones are less likely to reoccur. There is a complex interaction among biological, behavioral, and cultural selection. Behavior changes over time for an individual, family, and culture in accord with changes in contingencies. This happens not only over someone's lifetime but also over the evolutionary history of a species. Goals and related social strategies may change, such as care eliciting (recruiting help and life sustaining resources), caregiving, competition (power seeking), and cooperation (sharing). We learn about our world through our interactions in it with other people, other species, and our physical environment. That is, we evolve in certain ways depending on our experiences. In this sense, we are "embodied theories" about what works and has worked in the past (what has solved problems we confront) (Munz, 1985). Karl Popper views evolution as the history of problem solving for a species.

Evolutionary psychology is "the attempt to understand normal social motives as products of the process of evolution by natural selection" (Daly & Wilson, 1988, p. ix). Contingencies consist of relationships between behavior and their consequences and antecedents. Contingencies critical to our survival in early times may now hamper rather than help us. For instance, we seem to have difficulty decreasing our use of punishment, with all the negative consequences of relying on coercion (Sidman, 1989). Paleopsychology emphasizes the importance of archaic biological roots on complex human behavior. An evolutionary perspective adds a historical dimension to understanding aggression and caregiving in society, as well as what Paul Gilbert (1989) refers to as "defeat states" such as depression and the experiences that may be responsible. Threats to survival and ecological imbalances are just as important today as they were millions of years ago, and phylogenetic carryovers influence our behavior, especially our emotions in certain situations (e.g., when we are threatened). Threats occur both from outside organized groups (e.g., predators, strangers) and within them (from dominant individuals). Both social and nonsocial defense systems evolved over time. The defense system is essentially concerned with the avoidance of all forms of threat, injury and attack. It is a self-protective system with attentional, evaluative, affective and behavioral components designed to protect the animal" (Gilbert, 1989, pp. 42–43). The nonsocial defense system evolved to defend against predators. This includes (1) hypersensitivity to sensory data; (2) rapid increases in arousal—startle, alertness; and (3) rapid, unpredictable movements, as in rapid flight, freezing, and automatic aggression. Once initiated, it tends to be controlled inter-

nally. You can see the potential relevance of such reactions to human behavior (e.g., panic attacks and aggression). (See also Gilbert, 1993.)

Paul Gilbert (1989) argues that social defense systems evolved in order to facilitate interaction within species (e.g., to regulate control over territory, allow breeding) and to protect against predators (e.g., parents act to reduce physical dangers to their offspring). There also are social and nonsocial safety systems. Gilbert suggests that social signals (such as smiling) evolved to facilitate cooperative behavior. Cooperative behavior can be viewed as an evolutionary adaptation designed to permit caregiving to infants who cannot defend themselves. Defense and safety systems interact. For example, anxiety may result because of an increase in fear or a loss of safety. "Defeat states" are assumed to be involved in depression, whereas submissive behavior reflects anxiety. Consider battered women who are habitually forced into a submissive role (Gilbert, 1994).

Reassurance or Threat: Different Modes of Group Interaction

Group organization requires close proximity and thus special processes to regulate behavior. Gilbert highlights the role of ranking in regulating social interaction. For example, "in order for a lower-ranking animal not to be chased away, injured or even killed, the lower rank must be able to send signals of submission which inhibit the attack of the more dominant animal (Gilbert, 1989, p. 46). In what he calls the hedonic mode, behavior is regulated by the exchange of reassuring signals.

> The social structure is one of *mutual dependence* rather than (as in the agonic mode) *mutual defensiveness.* Whereas in the agonic mode arousal tends to be high (e.g., with braced readiness) and priming of self-protective behaviors, the hedonic mode maintains arousal at lower levels. It facilitates increased proximity to others and deactivates defensive behaviors which would otherwise be aroused by close proximity. This allows for a safer exploration of the social environment without a major preoccupation with potential threat from within the social domain (Gilbert, 1989, p. 52).

Rather than submissive appeasement, reassurance signals are offered (e.g., hugging, sharing). Exploration, problem solving, and cooperative behavior are characteristics of the hedonic mode seen among chimpanzees. The absence of threat signals reduces defensive reactions and increases trust. The response to predator threat is a group one rather than an individual one. In the hedonic mode, prestige depends on the ability to control positive (rather than defensive) attention of others. Prestige may be measured by the amount of positive attention that others direct toward an individual.

An evolutionary perspective gives us a view of human nature that builds on cross-cultural work. It can help us answer the question "What is human nature?" Understanding evolutionary influences on human behavior may help us understand how to shift further toward a society regulated by caring and cooperation. An appreciation of the evolutionary roots of human behavior allows us to realistically view the potential for change. For example, the evolutionary functions of status hierarchies (ranking) suggest how difficult it will be to alter the reinforcing value of status and dominance. Karen Pryor (1984) suggests that some people use punishment to control others in order to assert their dominance (their rank). Here, too, it is important to examine the soundness of commonly accepted but incorrect metaphors, such as the view of evolution as a ladder or cone leading to human beings as the pinnacle of success. Stephen Jay Gould (1995) notes that these misleading images of evolution continue to constrain our vision.

SUMMARY

The unique relationships between behavior and its consequences result in unique reinforcement histories, which vary from person to person and culture to culture. Human behavior is complex, and each person's repertoire is different. Patterns of social interaction and the accompanying emotional reactions that evolved over millions of years continue to influence our behavior, although to be sure, these are modified by higher-order cognitive processes. Natural selection through differential biological, behavioral, and cultural consequences influences our behavior and the cultural practices we create and maintain. Both immediate and remote contingencies affect behavior, and they often are difficult to identify. Some contingencies, such as punishment and response cost, decrease behavior, whereas others, such as positive and negative reinforcement, increase behavior. The cues associated with reinforcement (or its absence) acquire influence over behavior through this association. Thus, both antecedents and consequences affect our behavior. Verbal behavior (talking, thinking, imagining, writing) has a variety of influences on behavior as a result of past and current contingencies of reinforcement. The principles related to respondent conditioning offer valuable information about emotional reactions. Knowledge about the complex interactions between behavior and environmental changes provides a valuable tool for clarifying the context in which problems occur and for discovering options for helping clients enhance the quality of their lives.

REVIEWING YOUR COMPETENCIES

Reviewing What You Know

1. Describe different kinds of behavior.
2. Define the term *contingency*, and gives examples.

3. Distinguish between respondent and operant behavior, and give examples.
4. Define the term *operant*.
5. Define *operant conditioning*, and give examples.
6. Discuss the role of the variability of behavior in the "selection of behavior."
7. Distinguish between the form and the function of behavior, and give examples.
8. Define *positive reinforcement*, and give an example.
9. Define *negative reinforcement*, and give an example.
10. Describe the difference between positive and negative reinforcement.
11. Describe how positive and negative reinforcement are similar.
12. Explain what is meant by the statement "reinforcers are relative," and give examples.
13. Discuss the role of negative reinforcement in families.
14. Define two types of punishment, and give an example of each.
15. Describe the disadvantages of using punishment.
16. Define and give examples of operant extinction.
17. Describe the difference between punishment and operant extinction.
18. Distinguish between punishment and response cost.
19. Discuss the differences between positive and aversive control in relation to their effects.
20. Describe variables that influence operant learning.
21. Explain why schedules of reinforcement are important.
22. Describe how a discrimination is established and the criteria used to determine if one has been established.
23. Describe different kinds of changes that may be achieved through model presentation.
24. Explain what is meant by "establishing operations," and give examples.
25. Distinguish between rule-governed and contingency-shaped behavior and explain why this is an important distinction.
26. Identify the variables that influence respondent learning.
27. Give some examples of the influence of antecedents to behavior.
28. Describe some of the effects of our evolutionary history on our behavior.
29. Define the term "*behavior chain*", and give examples. Explain why chains of behavior are important to consider during assessment and intervention.
30. Describe three functions a stimulus may have, and give an example of each.
31. Mr. L. reports that he has a severe fear of cars. He goes out of his way to avoid the sight and sound of cars. Cars have acquired three functions as stimuli. What are they?
32. Define the term *stimulus generalization*, and gives examples.
33. Define the term *response generalization*, and give examples.
34. Describe different causes of a low frequency of a behavior in a given situation.

Reviewing What You Do

1. You identify consequences that function as reinforcers.
2. You can teach someone the meaning of "contingency management."
3. You can correctly apply behavioral principles to problems of concern to clients at many different levels (communities, organizations, groups, families, and individuals).

Reviewing Results

1. Given specific examples, you can describe and implement feasible, well-designed plans to alter behavior.

APPENDIX 8A   GLOSSARY

Avoidance behavior: Behavior maintained by delaying, preventing, or minimizing aversive events.

Behavior: What people do, acting on or having commerce with the outside world. In radical behaviorism, thoughts and feelings are viewed as behaviors.

Behavior chain: A sequence of responses, each associated with a particular cue and reinforcer.

Concurrent contingencies: Multiple, perhaps competing consequences in a given context.

Contingency: An association between a behavior and its related cues and consequences.

Contingency management: Rearranging contingencies between a behavior and related cues and consequences that results in a change in behavior and the conditions that influence behavior.

Cultural practice: "A set of interlocking contingencies of reinforcement in which the behavior and behavioral products of each participant function as environmental events" which influence the behavior of other individuals (Glenn, 1991, p. 10).

Culture: Practices characteristic of a group and their associated interrelated contingencies.

Culture clash: Differences in norms, values, beliefs, and related contingency systems.

Culture shock: Feeling of confusion and anxiety as a result of being in a new environment (e.g., accustomed behaviors may no longer be reinforced).

Discrimination: A high rate of a particular behavior in one situation and a low rate in all others.

Discriminative stimulus: A cue that signals the availability of reinforcement if a behavior occurs.

Ecological niche: A particular environment that creates particular behaviors and in turn is affected (altered) by them.

Ecology: The study of the interrelationships between organisms and their environments.

Eliciting stimulus: A cue that elicits a respondent behavior.

Equivalence class: Classes of events that may differ in form but are linked because of our learning history. (See for example, Sidman, 1994.)

Escape behavior: Behavior maintained by removing aversive events.

Establishing operation: An event, such as deprivation or pain that alters the reinforcer effectiveness of some events and evokes the type of behavior reinforced by those events in the past.

Extinction: A procedure in which the usual reinforcement for a behavior is withheld, resulting in a decrease in the probability of that behavior in the future.

Generalization: The occurrence of a behavior in situations in which it was not learned.

Imitation: The duplication of a behavior that is modeled.

Interlinked: Contingencies that influence one another at different contingency system levels (individual, group, family, organization, community, society).

Learning: Any relatively enduring change in behavior as a result of experience.

Matching law: When two behaviors are available (they are current), the relative rate of each and the time spent in each are a function of the relative rate of reinforcement for the two behaviors (McDowell, 1988).

Metacontingency: Dependence between a cultural practice and its outcome for a group (Glenn, 1991).

Model presentation: Displaying an example of behavior.

Negative reinforcement: A procedure in which an event is removed following a behavior and there is a future increase in the probability of that behavior in similar circumstances.

Negative reinforcer: A stimulus that increases behavior that removes it and decreases behavior that results in its presentation.

Operant: A class of behaviors, all of which have a similar effect on the environment.

Operant behavior: Behavior maintained by its consequences.

Operant learning: The selection of behavior by its consequences.

Positive reinforcement: A procedure in which an event is presented following a behavior and there is an increase in the future probability of the behavior in similar circumstances.

Positive reinforcer: A stimulus that increases behavior that it follows and decreases behavior when it is removed contingent on that behavior.

Punishment: A procedure in which an event is presented following a behavior and there is a decrease in the future probability of the behavior.

Respondent behavior: Behavior elicited by antecedent stimuli.

Respondent learning (also known as classical conditioning): The process by which neutral stimuli acquire the ability to elicit respondents through their association with stimuli that elicit a response.

Respondent extinction: The conditioned or unconditioned stimulus is no longer paired with a stimulus, resulting in the CS gradually ceasing to elicit a CR.

Response cost: A procedure in which an event is removed following a behavior and there is a decrease in the future probability of the behavior.

Rule governed behavior: Behavior influenced by verbal descriptions of contingencies.

Schedule of reinforcement: The pattern of reinforcement related to a behavior.

Self-efficacy: The belief that one can perform a task or fulfill role expectations.

Shaping: The reinforcement of successive approximations to a desired behavior.

Social control: Contingencies that regulate behavior by means of norms, laws, rules, and regulations.

Social exchange theory: A theory or behavior emphasizing the costs and benefits of interacting with another person or group.

Socialization: The social influence process by which behavior and values are shaped and maintained.

Stimulus: Any aspect of the environment that can be distinguished; any condition, event, or change in the physical world (inside or outside the body). Examples include people, places, things, light, sound, and odors.

PART

III

GETTING STARTED

CHAPTER 9

Contextual Assessment

OVERVIEW

The chapter describes contextual strengths-oriented guidelines for clarifying problems and identifying related factors. A more detailed procedural guide is presented in Chapter 10, and additional guidelines for assessing families, group, organizations, and communities are given in Chapters 23 and 24. A multilevel contingency analysis will often be required to clarify problems and discover related factors. Without it, you may end up with what Pacey (1983) calls one-half technology—attending to just part of the problem which, in addition to not resolving it, may create unwanted side effects. Assessment knowledge and skills are needed to provide direct services and, also if you are a case manager and coordinate services provided by others, so that you select those most likely to be of value to clients.

You Will Learn About

- What's involved.
- What's at stake.
- The difference between diagnosis and assessment.
- Making assessment of value to clients.
- Characteristics of contextual assessment.
- Important distinctions.
- Sources of influence that should be reviewed.
- Thinking critically about labels.

WHAT'S INVOLVED

Assessment involves five major interrelated tasks: (1) identifying problems, (2) clarifying problems, (3) detecting the characteristics of clients and their environments that influence problems, (4) interpreting and integrating the data collected, and (5) selecting outcomes to focus on (Nay, 1979). This lays the groundwork for suggesting plans to resolve problems. This phase is an ongoing process in which theories (guesses) are altered as needed in response to new information. A broad contextual scan of problem-related factors should point to particular areas requiring more detailed review. Assessment should indicate how likely it is that outcomes of interest can be attained. The possibility may be slim when needed resources are not available or when the environment cannot be rearranged.

Assessment should indicate what factors influence clients' options, make demands on them, or create discomfort (see Exhibit 9.1). Consider a client who is said to neglect her child because of her heroin addiction. A contextual analysis requires detailed information about the pattern of heroin use (assuming that the parent does use heroin and that this does interfere with her parenting), including high-risk situations (those in which she is likely to use heroin) and low-risk situations (those in which she is unlikely to use heroin). It also requires a clear description of "neglect" and related factors. Detailed information is needed about the mother's parenting skills and the personal and environmental factors that affect them (e.g., a belief in the value of severe physical punishment, an abusive partner,

Exhibit 9.1
Characteristics That May Be Related to a Problem at Different System Levels

Level 1: Individual	
____ Health	____ Vocational skills
____ Developmental	____ Self-management skills
____ Temperament	____ Reinforcer profile
____ Intelligence	____ Acculturation level
____ Problem-solving skills	____ Cultural background
____ Social skills	

Level 2: Family	
____ Problem-solving skills	____ Extended family network
____ Family composition	____ Living space
____ Income	____ Goals and values
____ Cultural norms	____ Cultural conflicts
____ Interaction patterns	

Level 3: Community	
____ Recreational opportunities	____ Accessibility of services (e.g., medical, legal)
____ Crime rate	____ Cultural diversity
____ Educational resources	____ Social support available
____ Physical environment	____ Transportation available
____ Cultural norms	

Level 4: Service System	
____ Services provided	____ Eligibility rules
____ Problem definitions favored	____ Favored intervention methods
	____ Links with other agencies

Level 5: Societal	
____ Cultural diversity	____ Emphasis on consumerism
____ Tolerance for violence	____ Patterns of discrimination
____ Programs funded	____ Expected gender roles
____ Economic inequities	____ Media (e.g., diversity of points of view readily available)
____ Options for influencing policy	

no money for needed medical services, and her alleged heroin use). What parenting skills does the mother possess? Which are absent? What factors interfere with the use of positive parenting skills? What environmental factors are related to both her heroin use and the quality of her parenting, such as poverty and policies that do not hold fathers responsible for contributing financially to the care of their children?

Decisions must be made about what data to collect, how to gather them, and how to organize them (see Exhibit 5.3). Let's say that you work in a student counseling center and a young woman is referred to you because she is having trouble studying and is receiving failing grades. What data will be useful in clarifying complaints and related factors? Will you focus on her study habits? Will you explore her "self-esteem"? Will you explore her current life circumstances, including her financial resources and significant others? Will you consider cultural differences that may be related to her concerns? How will you translate "trouble studying" and "receiving failing grades" into specific outcomes that, if attained, will resolve the problem? What knowledge and skills will you use to avoid accounts that result in selection of ineffective methods? Your theories about behavior and how it is maintained and can be changed will influence what data you gather.

Assessment frameworks differ in what is focused on as discussed in Chapter 7. History suggests that some approaches are more successful than others. For example, trying to assess people by examining the bumps on their heads was not very fruitful. However, for decades many people believed it was useful. Focusing solely on personal characteristics may result in "psychologizing" rather than helping clients. The complexity of many problems highlights the value of a multilevel contextual analysis.

WHAT'S AT STAKE?

Although decisions typically must be made on the basis of incomplete data, without a sound assessment framework, interviews may drift, opportuni-

ties to gather useful data may be lost, and assessment may be incomplete, resulting in selecting ineffective or harmful plans (see Exhibit 9.2). Clients may be referred to agencies that offer poor-quality services. Here, as well as in other phases of work with individuals, families, groups, organizations, or communities, specialized knowledge may be required and critical thinking skills needed to weigh the accuracy of evidence and soundness of viewpoints.

Common Errors

An accurate assessment will avoid three interrelated errors: (1) focusing on irrelevant outcomes, (2) offering inaccurate and incomplete causal analyses, and (3) choosing ineffective or harm-inducing (iatrogenic) service plans. Examples of incomplete assessment include the following:

- Problem-related behaviors are not clearly described.
- Cultural factors are overlooked.
- The functions of behaviors of interest are unknown (e.g., related environmental consequences such as reactions by significant others are not identified).
- Related setting events and antecedents are not identified.
- The client's strengths are ignored.
- Positive alternatives to undesired behaviors are not identified.
- Baseline data are not available (e.g., description of the severity of behaviors, thoughts, or feelings prior to intervention).
- Related physical characteristics of the environment are overlooked.
- Higher-level contingencies (e.g., loss of financial aid) are overlooked.

Inaccurate or incomplete accounts may occur because attention is too narrowly focused on one source (e.g., thoughts). Related environmental contingencies may be overlooked. Objectives may be selected prematurely. Common sources of error

Exhibit 9.2
An Example of Incomplete Assessment

John, a social work student, works in a crisis center. One of the clients to whom he provides ongoing services is a 46-year-old African–American woman, Mrs. K., who lives in a "satellite" home for psychiatric patients. Her 12-year-old daughter lives with her in the home. Mrs. K. had what was called an "acute psychotic episode," which led to a short hospitalization and her current residence in the community care home. John decided to focus on decreasing Mrs. K's "sense of shame." No information was provided about the condition that precipitated the "acute psychotic break"; the whereabouts of her relatives (including her three other children); her assets, work, medical, and educational history; or a description of the changes she wanted in her life. The student had never visited the home where she lived (and was not sure his supervisor would approve of his visiting), had never seen Mrs. K. and her daughter together, and had no contact with Mrs. K.'s other children. John also had no information about what was happening in her life at the time of the "acute psychotic episode" or what had been happening over the past 10 years.

Obtaining an overview of Mrs. K.'s problems and desired outcomes as well as relevant historical data, and additional information about her current life revealed a fuller picture of this woman and her situation that called into question the focus on shame. Mrs. K., who was originally presented as a debilitated, problem-ridden, psychiatric patient with few assets, was discovered to be a woman who had raised four children (three of whom lived close by but with whom she had no contact) and had held a responsible job for 15 years. She was in good health, had many interpersonal skills, and enjoyed being around people. She loved her children and was concerned about creating a good environment for her youngest child, who lived with her. The problems of concern to her were improving her relationship with her youngest daughter, getting along better with the people in the community home, and decreasing negative thoughts about herself. Mrs. K. was a woman with many potential assets, including relatives with whom she could cultivate positive contacts.

This example of incomplete assessment is not unusual; it is common even among second-year master's degree students with whom I have worked. Often, as in this case, premature closure results in selection of a negative outcome (decreasing shame) rather than a positive one (e.g., increasing enjoyable exchanges with significant others).

---

that result in inaccurate or incomplete definitions of problems and their analysis are

- Vague descriptions.
- Hasty assumptions about causes.
- Failure to search for alternative accounts.
- Speculating when data collection is called for (e.g., observation in real-life settings).
- Confusing the form and function of behavior.

- Using uninformative labels.
- Confusing motivational and behavior deficits.
- Focusing on pathology and overlooking assets.
- Collecting irrelevant material.
- Relying on inaccurate sources of data.
- Being misled by first impressions.
- Being mislead by the client's superficial resemblance to another client in the past.

Hasty, incomplete assessment may result in selecting outcomes that are not of concern to clients or do not address contingencies that must be altered in order to achieve desired outcomes. You may accept an incomplete account because, you attribute behaviors of concern to other behaviors. A teacher may attribute poor academic performance to low self-esteem because a student often "puts herself down" (has a high frequency of negative self-statements). This assessment is incomplete. Factors related to both self esteem and negative thoughts (e.g., past history of punishment in academic settings as well as current punishing consequences provided by the teacher) have not been identified. The *fundamental attribution* error is made when behavior is attributed to characteristics of the individual, overlooking the role of environmental causes.

Assessment may reveal that service should not focus on the person presented as "the problem" but, rather, on significant others who maintain undesired behaviors by reinforcing them and by failing to reinforce valued behaviors. Understanding their role may call for a restructuring of how a problem is defined. For example, rather than "personal" problems such as depression, agoraphobia, and drinking, resulting in marital discord, the association may be the reverse (Jacobson, Holtzworth-Munroe, & Schmaling, 1989). That is, marital discord may result in these problems.

THE DIFFERENCE BETWEEN DIAGNOSIS AND ASSESSMENT

The term *diagnosis* was borrowed from medicine, in which a physician makes a diagnosis of a patient's condition and then recommends a treatment based on this diagnosis. Observed behavior is used as a sign of more important underlying processes, typically of a pathological nature. A staff member in a mental hospital may say that "Mr. Smith tries to hit the staff members and spits on them." When asked for an explanation, he may say, "Mr. Smith is mentally ill." Assessment differs from diagnosis in a number of ways. Assessment encourages the description of: *processes* rather than the study of

conditions. For example, rather than describing a client as anxious, a contextual assessment requires the description of the context in which the anxiety occurs and the patterns of related behaviors that occur over time. "A fitting metaphor is the motion picture rather than the still photograph" (Peterson, 1987, p. 30). Observable behaviors are not used as signs of something more significant but as important in their own right as samples of relevant behaviors. Behavior is considered to be related to identifiable environmental or personal events (e.g., thoughts).

Assessment requires a clear description of problem-related behaviors and a search for associated setting events, cues, and consequences. Trait labels (e.g., aggressive personality) are not used, since they do not offer information about what people do in specific situations and what specific factors affect their behavior. Attributing the cause of problems to character traits ("She's just lazy") or to thoughts or feelings, increases the likelihood of "pseudoexplanations" (circular explanations that are not helpful). You may say "She is lazy" referring to the fact that she does not complete her homework. When, asked, "Why doesn't she complete her homework?" you may say, "She is lazy."

What About Person–Environment Fit?

The concept of person–environment fit has been suggested as a key one in social work. Problems are viewed, as mismatches between environmental and personal characteristics. Examples include lack of a ramp allowing persons in wheelchairs to enter buildings and lack of information needed by clients to obtain food stamps. One advantage of this view is the clear recognition that the environment rather than the client may require change. But do mismatches always create problems? Don't people adapt to less than ideal conditions? Consider an elderly person living alone who tells the social worker that she is satisfied with the few social contacts she has, which may indeed be true. But it also may be true that she has adapted to (learned to be happy with) a lean schedule of social contacts and would be happier if she had more. Rachlin (1980) argues that we feel happiness and sadness when we move from one level of reinforcement to another and that when we "get used to" a new level, we may be as happy as we were with a richer one. Not all problems are revealed by mismatches. For example, clients may not complain about discrimination or oppression they experience. The very term "raising one's consciousness" reflects a concern to identify causes of unhappiness that are not apparent.

MAKING ASSESSMENT OF VALUE TO CLIENTS

Assessment frameworks should be instrumental (help clients achieve valued outcomes). It is not very useful to carry out an assessment that offers few, if any, guidelines for resolving problems (or for discovering that they cannot be resolved given current resources). You can make assessment of value by helping people to clearly describe desired outcomes and related factors. If problems remain vague (a teacher does not identify what she means by a student's "aggressiveness" or a supervisor does not identify what she means by staff's poor caregiving skills), it will be difficult or impossible to identify specific problem-related behaviors and associated causes. If maintaining conditions are not identified, plans may be misdirected. Focus on collecting data that decrease uncertainty about how to attain outcomes clients value. Collecting irrelevant data wastes time and money and increases the likelihood that you and your clients will be misled by irrelevant material.

Assessment should offer clients more helpful views of their problems, a more helpful vocabulary for describing problems and options, and a model of how to break down a problem into manageable parts (Stuart, 1980). Another way to make assessment of value is to attend to client assets; to help clients to identify what they like about themselves and significant others, what is going well in their lives, and what they can contribute. Assessment frameworks are more likely to be useful if they take advantage of what is known about factors related to problems and about the accuracy of different kinds of data.

Social Workers as Consultants

The values, attitudes, and methods involved in a contextual practice framework reflect a consultant model in which you help clients by making use of professional values, attitudes, knowledge, and skills. You use your knowledge and skills to help clients enhance the quality of their lives (Bergan & Kratchowill, 1990). This model is compatible with the indirect methods often relied on in social work. That is, you often help mediators (e.g., parents, teachers, residential or agency staff) acquire new knowledge and skills to address problems with their significant others (e.g., children, students, residents, or other staff). This model was aptly described by Tharp and Wetzel (1969). Potential sources of support for mediators include the person with the presenting problem, the other people they see, and the consultant (you). The term *consultation* highlights the collaborative nature of helping relationships, including the joint decision-making process that is ideally involved in practice. Clients and significant others participate in deciding whether to share or collect data, whether to carry out assignments, what plans are suitable, and whether they are satisfied with outcomes of service. You can and should do your best to encourage helpful actions, but clients and significant others play a key role in what results.

CHARACTERISTICS OF A CONTEXTUAL ASSESSMENT

The characteristics of a contextual assessment are the following:

1. Individually tailored assessment (each person, group, family, organization, or community is viewed as unique).
2. A preference for testing inferences.
3. A focus on the clients' assets rather than their deficiencies.
4. A focus on the present.
5. An emphasis on contingencies on interrelated system levels.
6. A preference for observation (seeing for yourself).

7. A clear description of problems and desired outcomes.

8. A clear description of assessment methods.

9. The use of valid assessment methods.

10. A close relationship between assessment and intervention.

A contextual framework decreases the likelihood of errors, such as focusing on people's deficiencies rather than their strengths, neglecting environmental causes and resources, and focusing on outcomes that will not resolve problems. A contextual assessment encourages a broad review of resources that may reveal leverage points that would otherwise be overlooked.

An Individually Tailored Assessment

Individualized assessment does not mean you focus on individuals as the locus of problems. It means that whether individuals, families, groups, communities, or organizations are involved, a careful assessment is required, including an understanding of each person's unique environment including the functions of problem-related behaviors (Wolpe, 1986). This includes an assessment of the client's motivation. Why should clients and/or significant others participate? What objections might they have? (see Chapter 11). Although social workers talk a lot about the importance of "starting where the client is" and respecting individual differences (including cultural differences), they often do not do so (see Exhibit 9.3). For example, detailed information about behaviors of concern and related circumstances based on observation in real-life settings may not be collected even when it is feasible and ethical to do so. Individualized assessment avoids the *patient uniformity myth* in which individuals, families, groups, or organizations are mistakenly assumed to be similar

EXHIBIT 9.3
Contextual Assessment: Honored in Words and Ignored in Practice

Alessi (1988) points out that behavior and learning problems in school may be associated with one or more of five broad areas: (1) the child may be misplaced in the curriculum, or the curriculum may contain faulty teaching routines; (2) the teacher may not be using effective teaching and/or behavior management practices; (3) the principal and other school administrators may not be using effective school management practices; (4) the parents may not be providing the home-based support necessary for effective learning; and (5) the child may have physical and/or psychological problems that may be contributing to the learning problems (see Alessi (1988) for supporting references).

To find out whether school psychologists consider these multiple influences, Alessi asked several groups of school psychologists (about 50 in each), in different areas of the country, whether they agreed that each of these five factors played a primary role in a given school learning or behavior problem. They almost always agreed. He then asked for the number of cases each psychologist had examined in the past year to determine the source of learning problems. The answer was about 120. Rounding this to 100 and multiplying by 50 yielded about 5,000 cases studied by the group in the past year. Next, Alessi asked how many of their psychological reports concluded that the referred problem was due primarily to one of these factors. For curriculum factors, inappropriate teaching practices, and school administrative factors, the answer was none. For the parent and home factors, the answer ranged from 500 to 1,000 (10 to 20%). When he asked how many of their reports concluded that child factors were primarily responsible for the referred problem, the answer was 100%

(Kiesler, 1966; Wolpe, 1986). Indicators of this myth are

- Speculating about the causes of problems without checking beliefs against data gathered in real-life settings.
- Using vague labels and description of problems.
- Stereotyping (talking about clients as if they were no different from other members of a group)

An individualized assessment requires attention to cultural differences that may be related to problems and potential resolutions.

A Preference for Testing Inferences

Unexamined speculation may result in acceptance of incomplete or incorrect accounts of problems. Consider a social worker who saw a family because the mother was concerned about her 10-year-old child's behavior at school. The social worker believed that the child's "misbehavior" in class occurred because the mother's boyfriend had left her and the child was upset about it. The social worker did not observe the child in the classroom or obtain any information about her academic progress. I asked the social worker when the boyfriend had left the mother, and she said he left 8 months before the problems at school started. According to the mother, the child's problems at school started in the last month. The social worker reported that because the child was no longer worried about the boyfriend's leaving (this change was not explained) and because classroom behavior was no longer a problem (no evidence was provided for this claim), she decided not to work on the problem that had brought the mother to the clinic but to offer her supportive counseling for herself.

What are some of the inferences here? One is that the child was indeed misbehaving in class. This inference should have been tested for its accuracy by observing the child in her classroom. Since the social worker never observed the child in the classroom, we don't know whether or not this was true (or if this child misbehaved any more or less often than did other children in the class). Speculation

was relied on when observation was called for. Untested speculation can get in the way of translating problems into outcomes that, if achieved, would resolve problems. For example, if you limit your source of information to a teacher's report about an "unmanageable child," you may mistakenly assume that (1) the child's behavior is unmanageable; (2) it is worse than that of the other children in the classroom; and (3) the causes of behavior can be discovered by relying on the reports of significant others (e.g., teachers). This is a classic example of "working in the dark." Another inference is that the child misbehaved in the classroom because the mother's boyfriend had left. There is little evidence on which to base this and some counterevidence as well (the time lapse between the boyfriend's leaving and the start of the alleged misbehavior). Parsimonious accounts that involve limited inferences (they are closely tied to concrete data) are easier to test than those that include many, perhaps conflicting, theories.

An Emphasis on Clients' Assets Instead of Deficiencies

There is an emphasis on helping clients acquire knowledge and skills that increase their opportunities for reinforcement in real life settings. Arthur Schwartz (a social worker) and Israel Goldiamond (a psychologist) combined their efforts to create guidelines for a strength-oriented practice framework (*Social Casework: A Behavioral Approach* (1975). Repertoires of interest may be related to fulfilling roles (e.g., parent, husband, wife, daughter, employee). Consider adult children caring for an elderly relative in their home. Valued behaviors include reinforcing independent behaviors on the part of the elderly relative, providing opportunities for recreation and social contacts, arranging time-outs from caregiving responsibilities, planning shared positive events among family members, and constructive problem solving to address concerns that arise. Emphasizing the construction of repertoires has many advantages. First, you are less likely to pathologize people. Second, it encourages you to search for positive alternatives to unwanted behaviors, especially those that are functional (enhance opportunities for reinforcement in real-life contexts) (Meyer & Evans, 1989). Increasing alternative positive behaviors is often the most effective way to decrease unwanted behavior (Goldiamond, 1984). Third, attending to clients' assets helps them focus on their strengths and to use them to pursue valued outcomes.

Focus Is on the Present

There is a focus on present concerns and related factors. The biopsychosocial approach favored in social work emphasizes current problems and circumstances. This is also true of ego psychological and behavioral approaches. The circumstances in which a reaction originally developed, such as a fear of crowds, may be different from those that currently maintain this fear. Perhaps the fear is now maintained by attention from significant others and by the avoidance of disliked tasks such as shopping. Understanding problems often requires an overview of the client's current life, including relationships with significant others, employment, physical health, recreational activities, and community and material resources such as housing and income. What is the client's typical day like? Does she like her work? Does she have any friends? How is her physical health? Whom does she live with? Are the circumstances in any of these areas related to desired outcomes?

What About Past History? Although all practice perspectives recognize the role of past history in influencing thoughts, feelings, and behavior, they differ in how much attention is given to the past and what is focused on (e.g., feelings, thoughts, or actual experiences). More traditional psychoanalytic practice devotes greater emphasis to helping people understand (gain insight into) their past experiences and the relationship of these experiences to their present behavior. In a behavioral perspective past history is assumed to be reflected in current behavior, feelings, thoughts. The influence of the past is suggested by research in many areas (this does not mean that later change is not possible). For instance, antisocial behavior by children and adolescents is related to an early childhood history

of neglect and family conflict (Rutter, 1989). Information about the past allows you and your clients to view current events in a more comprehensive context (Wolpe, 1990). Major areas include medical history, educational and work history, significant relationships, family history, and developmental history. Helpful coping skills may be discovered by finding out what clients have tried in the past to resolve problems. You may discover valuable information about possible reinforcers or unusual social histories related to problems.

Demographic indicators reflecting past behavior and social competence, such as work history and marital status, are better predictors of future behavior than are personality tests or clinical judgments (Dawes, 1994a; Mischel, 1968). The more that past situations resemble current ones, the more informative data about the past may be in predicting future behavior. Knowledge about past contingencies may be of value when it is difficult to identify current maintaining factors and may be helpful in predicting future problems (keeping in mind that current maintaining conditions may differ from those present when a behavior was established). Although effective intervention does not require discovering a problem's historical causes (e.g., Barlow, 1988), understanding how problems began may clarify the origins of behaviors of interest. New ways of viewing past events may be helpful.

Information about the past may encourage clients to alter present behaviors and increase understanding of current reactions. A client with low self-esteem may understand how past discrimination based on gender or race resulted in limited opportunities for mastery experiences. Helping clients to understand the effects of the political on the personal is a key in feminist counseling both past and present. A client may be willing to learn and use positive communication skills if she sees how negative reactions resulted in the loss of valued consequences in the past. Disadvantages of excessive focus on the past include offering clients an excuse for not addressing problems and slowing down progress in removing complaints. Excessive attention to past troubles may create pessimism about the future and encourage rationalizations and excuses that get in the way of solving problems.

Furthermore, the clients' descriptions of past events may not be accurate.

Contingencies Are of Interest

A contingency analysis involves describing the context in which problems occur (i.e., the relationships between behavior *in real-life settings* and what happens right before and after), including alternative behaviors that, if increased, would compete successfully with undesired behaviors. For example, rather than focusing directly on undesired behavior (e.g., eating and binging), Israel Goldiamond (1984) helped a client take advantage of naturally competing activities, such as enriching her social life. This kind of nonlinear analysis often reveals effective ways to resolve problems.

Considerable advances have been made in some areas in identifying problem-related contingencies. For example, assessment protocols have been developed to identify the cues and consequences related to the self-injurious behavior of children (Luiselli, Matson, & Singh, 1992). This is truly *"starting where the client is."* Discovering options for attaining valued outcomes may require a multilevel contingency analysis of agencies and residential settings, including supervisory and administrative practices. This will often reveal competing contingencies that interfere with attainment of valued goals. Some of the myths and misconceptions about contingency analysis are as follows:

- It's easy.
- I can do it sitting in my office.
- Thoughts and feelings are not considered.
- It dehumanizes people.
- The helper–client relationship is not important.

The interest in behavior and related circumstances calls for the translation of problems into observable behaviors and the discovery of options for rearranging the environment.

A *descriptive analysis* involves identification of problem-related behaviors and associated setting events, antecedents, and consequences. Helpful questions to ask when trying to identify influential variables are, What does this behavior communicate? What is its "meaning"? Behaviors have a communication function. They communicate a desire for or a dislike of something. Accurate description of contingencies will help you select effective methods to change them. For example, the methods required to decrease self-injurious behavior will differ depending on whether this behavior is maintained by positive reinforcement (e.g., attention from adults) or negative reinforcement (e.g., escape from difficult tasks). An accurate description will help you avoid victim blaming (attributing the cause of problems to the client when the causes lie in the environment). Accounts that do not include a description of problem-related environmental contingencies are incomplete ones that may interfere with the discovery of options. A *functional analysis* requires demonstration that certain antecedents and/or consequences influence behaviors of interest. This involves the systematic variation of selected variables (e.g., certain consequences), noting changes that occur.

The focus on contingencies has a number of implications for assessment. One is observing people in real-life contexts when it is feasible, ethical, and necessary to do so to clarify problems and their causes. A second is an emphasis on collecting information about individuals. Information about group differences do not offer precise information about what people do in specific situations and what cues and consequences influence their behavior, although it may offer clues about how an individual may react. Clients are encouraged to recognize and alter the role they play in maintaining problems. For example, teachers and parents often reinforce behaviors they complain about. If you play a role in creating and maintaining problems, you can play a role in resolving them. This is not to say that clients can alter societal conditions related to their problems. Clearly the homeless are in no position to change conditions related to their plight such as shortages of affordable housing. It is to encourage you to give clients as much influence as possible over the quality of their lives. Achieving community and societal change will require efforts at many levels, including community organizing, coalition building, and seeking changes in legislation.

The Importance of Consequences. The consequences that follow behavior affect its future probability. (See chapter 5.) A contingency analysis often reveals that desired behaviors are ignored and undesired ones are reinforced. Studies of residential centers show that contingencies often are counterhabilitative rather than habilitative; they discourage independence and client engagement (Meinhold & Mulick, 1990). Policies and procedures may contribute to the neglect and abuse of residents (Favell & McGimsey, 1993). Significant others may not realize that they are maintaining the very behaviors they complain about through the consequences they offer (e.g., attention). That is, what they believe are positive reinforcers may have the opposite effect (punish behavior).

Different Kinds of Consequences. Behavior is affected by many kinds of consequences, including reactions from significant others, changes in the physical environment, and physiological changes. Consider test anxiety. The term *anxiety* may refer to physiological changes (increased heart rate), to related thoughts (worries about failure), and/or to behaviors (avoidance of test situations). Taking a test may be followed by negative self-statements (thoughts), increased muscle tension (physical changes), and social consequences (parents calling and saying, "I hope you did as well as your brother did.") An alternative set of consequences might be positive self-statements for a job well done or anticipation of a high grade; a friend suggesting, "Let's go out on the town tonight and celebrate"; and a pleasant tiredness from a job well done.

The sum total of consequences that follow a behavior has been called the *reinforcing event* (Tharp & Wetzel, 1969). This may be mostly positive, mostly negative, or balanced. Behaviors are often followed by more than one change in the environment. For example, drinking alcohol may be followed by increased physical relaxation (a positive consequence) and a decrease in anxiety-provoking thoughts (the removal of a negative event). Discovering the function of a behavior (its effects on the environment) may be difficult when it is followed by both punishment and reinforcement. In these instances, strong behavior may be observed

Exhibit 9.4
Consequences of School Attendance

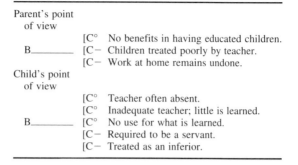

Parent's point of view		
	[C°	No benefits in having educated children.
B_____	[C−	Children treated poorly by teacher.
	[C−	Work at home remains undone.
Child's point of view		
	[C°	Teacher often absent.
	[C°	Inadequate teacher; little is learned.
B_____	[C°	No use for what is learned.
	[C−	Required to be a servant.
	[C−	Treated as an inferior.

only indirectly because it is displayed in only indirect forms (Ferster, 1972). You may, for example, want to talk to someone you are attracted to but approach the person indirectly because of a fear of rejection. Drawing a diagram of consequences related to behaviors of interest may be useful when exploring contingencies. Consider the example of school attendance described by Kunkel (1970, p. 147). The diagram in Exhibit 9.4 shows that there are no positive consequences for attendance (C+). There are negative consequences (C−) and often a lack of any effects (C°). No wonder school attendance was low in this community!

The Importance of Antecedents. Behaviors tend to occur in the situations in which they are reinforced. Cues associated with reinforcement increase the probability of behaviors reinforced in their presence, whereas cues associated with punishing consequences (i.e., behavior is punished in their presence) decrease the probability of behaviors punished in their presence. Brian found that when the dog began to snarl, he might get bitten (see example in Exhibit 2.1). When this happened, he stopped teasing the dog. Snarling was a cue that continued teasing may result in a nasty bite. We usually say hello only when there is someone present. Their presence is the antecedent for saying hello. An elderly resident of a retirement home may snap at the staff when she is asked to carry out a task that is too difficult for her. Disliked reactions may occur because a person is uncomfortable or bored or is asked to do something with little notice

Reviewing Antecedents

One hour before examination.	A^-	
Thoughts of failure.	A^-	Anxiety
A nervous roommate who also has exams.	A^-	
Reassurance by a friend.	A^+	

Supervisor seems in a good mood.	A^+	
All important work has been completed.	A^+	Asking supervisor for the rest of the afternoon off.
It is near the end of the day.	A^+	
Worry that you will be considered undependable.	A^-	

or in an unpleasant way. In these instances, altering antecedents (sometimes other people's behavior) may correct the problem. One goal of assessment is to identify antecedents that influence behaviors of interest.

Like consequences, antecedents have a variety of sources. If you are relaxed during written examinations, you may think about past successes, share reassurances with a friend, and feel rested after a good night's sleep. If you are anxious, you may anticipate failing (cognitive cue), have had a telephone call from your parents reminding you how important it is to pass the exam (social cue), and be tired from staying up all night (physiological cues). We may make past or future events current by thinking about them, and they in turn influence what we do, feel, and think. The sum total of antecedents related to a behavior can be termed

the *antecedent event.* This may increase or decrease the probability of the behavior in the future.

Identify high-risk situations for problematic behaviors. Common antecedents for disruptive behavior of developmentally disabled children and youth can be seen in Exhibit 9.5. Notice that some are demand-based (disruptive behavior occurs when an instruction or demand is given and succeeds in getting rid of unwanted tasks). What are low-risk situations (those in which problematic behavior rarely occurs)?

Rearranging antecedents (stimulus control) is one way to change behavior (see Chapter 22). *Setting events* are a kind of antecedent that are closely associated with a behavior but are not in the immediate situation in which behaviors of interest occur. For example, because of an unpleasant exchange with his teacher before coming home,

Exhibit 9.5
Examples of Antecedents of Disruptive Behavior

People	Places	Social Interactions
Specific staff	Novel places	Refusal of a request
New staff	On the bus	Given an instruction
Staff changes	School rooms	Requests to transition
Parent(s)	At work	Provocation by peers
Doctors	In the community	Peers' disruptive behavior
Specific peers	Bathrooms	Difficulty communicating
Female staff		Peers receiving attention
		Presentation of a task

Medical	Self-Created	Ecology/Atmosphere
Pre- and postseizure	After self-stimulation	Crowds
During illness	Moodiness	Noise
Drug side effects	Withdrawal	Absence of schedule
Prior to menses	Agitated behavior	Personal space violation

Source: C. Schrader & M. Levine (1994), PTR: Prevent, teach and reinforce *(Chapter 2, p. 3). San Rafael, CA: Behavioral Counseling and Research Center.*

a child may respond angrily to a request by his parents. The setting event alters the likelihood of certain reactions in later situations.

Clear Description of Problems and Outcomes

Only if complaints and related setting events, antecedents, and consequences are clearly described can they be translated into specific changes that result in their removal. A focus on vague problems may prevent the discovery of related factors. And if outcomes are not clearly described, it will be difficult to determine the actual frequency of behaviors of interest or to assess progress. The specific referents to which clients refer when using a vague term such as *uncooperative, immature,* or *aggressive* may differ. One person may define aggressive behavior as hitting, shoving, or slapping, whereas another may include verbal responses such as yelling, shouting, and name-calling. Adults who are thought by many people to have been abused as children (e.g., they were beaten with straps and locked in closets for long periods) may not define this as abuse. They may say, "I was bad" or "I deserved it." Exhibit 9.6 gives examples of clearly described outcomes, and Exhibit 9.7 shows examples of presenting problems, their referents, and related outcomes.

Focus on outcomes that succeed in removing complaints. Some outcomes can be identified early on, such as the need for a different kind of housing, creation of a local neighborhood mediation board, day care for children, or a homemaker. Additional information will be required to identify specific outcomes related to many problems.

A Preference for Observation

An interest in clearly describing problem-related behaviors and the circumstances in which they occur as well as a preference for limited testable inferences highlight the value of observing behaviors in problem-related contexts. Discovering the unique functions of behaviors of interest may require observation in real-life settings. Self report often offers incomplete or inaccurate account of behaviors and related circumstances. Complement armchair speculation with real-life exploration (seeing for yourself) when this is needed for understanding problems. Always ask: "Are my speculations of value in helping clients?"

Clear Description of Assessment Methods

Clear description of assessment methods fulfills one of the conditions for informed consent. If you clearly describe your methods, your colleagues will

Exhibit 9.6
Examples of Outcomes at Different Levels of Intervention

Level	Examples
Individual	Increase parenting skills. (e.g. giving clear instructions, and offering positive feedback for accomplishments). Increase daily number of planned activities from zero to five.
Family	Increase weekly time spent in shared activities from 0 to 2 hours a week. Hold a 1-hour problem-solving session each week.
Group	Increase number of positive comments exchanged among group members from none to two for each group member. Increase percentage of group members who complete assignments. Increase leadership skills (e.g., suggest agenda items, refocus discussion on topics of interest).
Organization	Increase weekly positive comments given by supervisors to staff for valued behaviors from zero to two. Increase number of people who offer valuable suggestions at case conferences.
Community	Increase the percentage of residents involved in local planning from 5 to 20. Establish a neighborhood mediation board by December 30. Increase percentage of parents who attend parent–teacher meetings at school. Increase percentage of youth who help elderly residents with chores.
Service system	Increase percentage of agreed-on reports received on time. Increase positive feedback to staff for specific behaviors that contribute to service delivery. Increase percentage of successful referrals (those that result in receipt of requested service).

Exhibit 9.7
Examples of Presenting Problems, Specific Referents, and Desired Outcomes

Presenting Problem	Specific Referents	Desired Outcomes
My 14-year-old daughter is uncontrollable.	She stays out beyond curfew time.	Return home by agreed on time.
	She calls me names.	Discuss issues without name-calling.
Loneliness (80-year-old male).	No one ever visits me at home.	Have one person visit each week.
	I never speak to anyone on the phone.	Have three telephone conversations per week.
	I never go to the senior center.	Visit the senior center for 1 hour once a week.
Lack of participation at community-board meetings.	I don't say anything.	Offer three elaborated opinion statements at each board meeting
Children have no proper care.	Children are left by themselves for 3 hours when they return from school.	Arrange care for children between return from school and the time parent finishes work.

be able to duplicate those that are successful, and your supervisors will be able to offer you better feedback. Clear description makes it possible to accumulate information about what works.

Use of Valid Methods

Assessment is more likely to be informative if you rely on methods that provide accurate information. This will require familiarity with the scientific literature concerning assessment methods. Self-report may not reflect what occurs in real life, and observers may be biased. Validity is a concern in any kind of assessment, however, the nature of the concern is different in sign and sample approaches. In a *sign approach* to assessment, behavior is used as a sign of some entity (e.g., a personality trait) at a different level. The concern is with vertical validity. Is the sign an accurate indicator of the underlying trait? In a *sample approach* different levels (e.g., behavior and personality dispositions) are not involved. Questions here are: (1) Does self-report provide an accurate account of behavior and related circumstances? (2) Does behavior in role play reflect behavior in real life? (3) Do changes achieved remove complaints? (4) Different kinds of validity are discussed in Chapter 14.

A Close Relationship Between Assessment and Intervention

Assessment should offer guidelines for selecting plans. It should help you and your clients discover

"leverage points" for attaining valued outcomes. It should indicate (1) those objectives that must be reached to resolve the problem, (2) what must be done to achieve them, (3) how the objectives can be pursued most effectively, and (4) the probability of attaining them, given current resources and options.

IMPORTANT DISTINCTIONS

Three important distinctions are discussed in this section: (1) form and function, (2) motivational and behavior deficits, and (3) response inhibition and behavior deficits. Overlooking these may result in selection of ineffective plans.

Form and Function

The form of a behavior (its topography) does not indicate its function (why the behavior occurs). Identical forms of behavior may be maintained by different contingencies. Someone might run down the street because he is being chased by someone (whom you cannot see because he has not yet rounded the corner), because he enjoys running, or because he is hungry and lunch is waiting for him at home. Thus, running may be maintained by either positive or negative reinforcement or both. A client may drink alcohol to avoid worrying about unpaid bills, because he enjoys the resulting relaxed feeling, because it upsets his mother and he enjoys her discomfort, or for all these reasons. A child saying the word *toast* might be reading a word, or she may be hungry and this prompts her to say *toast* because this produced food on previous occasions. Or she might be telling her parents that there is no toast (Ferster, Culbertson, & Boren, 1975). Just as the same behavior may have different functions, different behaviors may have identical functions. Saying the word *toast*, banging on the table, or throwing cereal all may be maintained by attention from parents; that is, all three behaviors may belong to the same response class, or operant. A behavioral analysis includes a description of behaviors of concern as well as evidence that specific antecedents and consequences affect them; thus it requires both a functional and a descriptive analysis.

Motivation Versus Behavior Deficits

When someone does not know how to perform a given behavior, he has a *behavior deficit.* When someone knows how to perform a behavior but is not reinforced on an effective schedule or is punished, she has a *motivation deficit.* If a desired behavior does not occur, its absence may point to either a behavior or a motivation deficit. Motivation and behavior deficits can be distinguished by arranging the conditions for the performance of a behavior. A client could be asked to role-play behaviors of interest and also asked whether she uses similar behaviors in other situations. If she does engage in desired behaviors in other situations, then she has a motivational deficit. If a client can perform a behavior if he is paid $500 to do so, motivation is the problem.

The distinction between motivational and behavioral deficits is important because different intervention methods are usually called for. Altering a motivational deficit requires rearranging contingencies, but there is no need to establish a behavior, although prompts such as verbal instructions may be needed. If a behavior deficit is the problem, then new behaviors must be established, perhaps by model presentation or shaping (see Chapter 21).

Motivation deficits are often mistaken for behavior deficits. A teacher may say that a student does not know how to do addition problems, or a husband may say that his wife does not know how to talk to him about his work. The student and the wife may not use these behaviors because they are not reinforced.

Response Inhibitions Versus Behavior Deficits

Emotional reactions may interfere with desired behavior. For example, a client may not initiate conversations, not because he does not know how to, but because of social anxiety. Role playing can be used to find out whether required skills are available. If they are, then interfering factors can be sought (e.g., anxiety, lack of knowledge about when to use skills, lack of reinforcement and/or punishment). A disruption of behavior may suggest that the behaviors were easily disruptable to begin with. Anxiety, for example, "is not so much a thing of itself as it is a general condition of a larger repertoire" (Ferster, 1972, p. 6). If the behaviors were better maintained through positive consequences, a punishing consequence could not disrupt them so easily.

SOURCES OF INFLUENCE THAT SHOULD BE REVIEWED

A contextual assessment requires a review of both personal and environmental factors that may influence problems and options. Possible influences include other peoples' actions, the physical environment, tasks and materials, physiological changes, thoughts, genetic differences, and developmental factors. Material and community resources and related political, economic, and social conditions also affect options.

Social and Public Policy

A contextual assessment calls for attention to the relationship between personal problems and public issues. The values and norms in a society and conflicts about them are reflected in the social and public policies that influence what resources are available. For example the lack of low-cost housing is partly responsible for the increase in homeless families. Keeping these higher-level contingencies in mind should help you avoid incorrect accounts of problems.

Other People

Problems clients confront may require a cultural change because problem-related behaviors are influenced by people at many different system levels. Consider Exhibit 8.3, which describes contingencies related to wearing seat belts. We can see that our behavior is affected by many system levels. You may be able to influence only some related contingency levels. It is important to see the big picture to avoid inaccurate estimates of what can be accomplished. How do significant others such as family members view a problem, and what will they gain or lose if outcomes proposed are achieved? Attention from others may become an important maintaining factor for behavior, even though it was not involved in an initial reaction. For example, a woman may become anxious when she is away from home. Her family members may respond with sympathy and support, which may increase her reports of fear, especially if she receives little attention at other times.

Family members may not recognize their role in maintaining problem-related behaviors. Brian's parents were unaware of how their reactions helped maintain Brian's behaviors that they found annoying. That is, they attended to (reinforced) him when he teased the dog and ignored him when he played nicely with the dog. Brian, in turn, influenced his parents' behavior. Staff in residential settings are often unaware that they reinforce behaviors they complain about. They may ignore "sane" behaviors that are not troublesome and reinforce "crazy" behaviors with attention (Paul & Lentz, 1977). Supervisors who complain about line staff's behavior may not realize that they ignore desired behaviors. Current life circumstances will influence whether significant others can participate effectively. Mrs. Lakeland's full-time job, coupled with running a household in which the children shouldered few chores, left her tired and, in her words, "more likely to fly off the handle." Her husband worked full time on one job and three nights a week on another to help his older son pay for college.

The Physical Environment

The influence of the physical environment is often overlooked. Brian did not have a room of his own and had no place where he could work on his hobbies without being interrupted. Physical arrangements in residential and day care settings influence behavior. Unwanted behaviors may be encouraged by available materials. For example, toys may distract children from educational tasks. Temperature changes, crowding, and noise level affect behavior. Increasing physical space can reduce aggressive behavior of severely handicapped persons (Rago, Parker, & Cleland, 1978). The characteristics of the community in which clients live influence problems and options. Children who live in poor-quality environments (e.g., little play space, industrial neighborhoods, littered streets) are less satisfied with their lives, experience more negative emotions, and have more restricted and less positive friendships compared with children who live in higher-quality settings (Homel & Burns, 1989). The frequency of nonaccidental injuries to children is related to their home's physical condition, which in turn is related to socioeconomic status (Pelton, 1989). Hazards in the rundown housing in which many poor families live include lead poisoning and unprotected windows. Poor people have fewer options in dealing with potential hazards. They may not be able to afford baby sitters or bars on windows. Board-and-care operators may crowd residents into small rooms, provide few if any social opportunities, and fail to make needed repairs. Shelters for the homeless may be more dangerous than the streets for those they claim to shelter.

Tasks and Activities

The kind of task we confront influences behavior. In such cases, focus may be on altering the task environment. Behaviors of concern may occur because of boredom or excessive demands. For example, there is a relationship between tasks children confront and injurious behavior (Luiselli,

Matson, & Singh, 1992). Assessing the quality of the curriculum as this may influence behaviors is important in classrooms.

Biophysical Factors

Overlooking physical causes may result in incorrect inferences about the causes of problems. For instance, certain kinds of illness are associated with psychological changes. Examples are hyperthyroidism in a young refugee woman referred by an internist because of anxiety; an orange-sized (and curable) meningioma in a middle-aged refugee woman referred by a family physician with a diagnosis of depression; and pellagra in a refugee teacher who suddenly became socially withdrawn, confused, and silly (Westermeyer, 1987). Environmental pollutants and nutritional deficiencies may affect health and behavior, and a lack of sleep may lower our ability to solve problems. Hormonal changes associated with menopause may result in mood changes that may be mistakenly attributed to psychological causes. On the other hand, psychological changes may be mistakenly attributed to hormonal changes. For example, a coworker may incorrectly attribute disliked behavior to premenstrual tension.

Chronic health problems increase with age. Health problems are a major concern for clients with AIDS. A physical examination should be required whenever physiological factors may be related to a problem (e.g., seizures, depression, fatigue, or headaches). Explore adequacy of nutrition and coffee, alcohol, or drug intake. Drugs, prescribed or not, may influence how clients appear and behave. Fetal alcohol syndrome and drug-affected infants have received increasing attention (for further discussion, see Hollandsworth, 1990).

Thoughts: What We Say to Ourselves

Thoughts may function as cues in chains of behavior and may contribute to problems such as anxiety, anger, and depression (for more details, see Chapter 16). A depressed client may have a high frequency of negative self statements and a low frequency of positive self statements. The thoughts and feelings we have in a situation are related to our past and current experiences in that situation and in those that are similar or associated in some way. A causal role may be mistakenly attributed to thoughts because the histories related to their development as well as current related contingencies are ignored. It is not that an explanation that attributes the cause of problems to thoughts is wrong; it is that such accounts are incomplete. A change in thoughts and feelings often occurs as a result of behavior changes. You can examine the role of thoughts (such as self-instructions) by varying certain ones and determining the effects on behaviors of interest.

What About Feelings?

Feelings, mood states, and affects such as depression, anxiety, and anger may be presented as a problem or be related to other problems. For example, a parent's depression may be related to her neglect of her child. The absence of certain feelings may be a problem, such as not liking one's children or not having empathy for harm caused to others. People differ in the range of emotions they experience, their intensity, and the situations in which they occur. What is appropriate in specific circumstances is influenced by cultural norms. Different people express their feelings in different ways. Just because someone does not cry when a relative dies does not mean she does not care. Find out what situations aggravate feelings of concern and what situations lessen them. This will suggest changes in thoughts, behaviors, and/or environmental circumstances that may alter feelings.

Theories of behavior differ in whether causal status is given to feelings and in the variables believed to account for feelings (e.g., early childhood experiences, past and current contingencies). Changing feelings will not make up for a lack of skills required to attain a valued outcome or rearrange related environmental contingencies. Here, too, as with thoughts, it is not that attributing the cause of problems to feelings is wrong, it is that the account is incomplete. The relative importance of behaviors, thoughts, affect, and physiological responses may have implications for selection of plans. For example, if social anxiety is mainly related to muscle tension, relaxation training may be called for. If it is mainly cued by negative self-statements such as "I bet I'll be a flop again," cognitive restructuring combined with exposure to feared situations may be the best option. If it is related to a lack of effective social skills, social skills training may be required.

Cultural Differences

Cultural differences in values and norms may influence the problems clients confront, preferred communication styles, and service options. Norms for behavior differ in different groups. These differences involve far more than race and ethnicity. They include differences related to gender, physical abilities, sexual orientation, geographical region, religion, and age. Cultural differences may be reflected in preferred problem-solving styles and beliefs about the causes of problems. Lack of knowledge about differences may result in incorrect assumptions about the cause of problems and differences of opinion about whether a behavior is a problem.

A client's degree of acculturation is important to assess. Differences in degree of acculturation among family members may create strains in families. De Anda (1984) suggests that the interaction of ethnic minority clients with mainstream culture is influenced by the following:

- Degree of overlap between cultures (regarding norms, values, beliefs, perceptions, and related contingencies).

- Availability of "cultural translators, mediators, and models."

- Nature of contingencies.

- Overlap between the conceptual style and problem-solving approach of the minority individual and the prevalent styles of the majority culture.

- Degree of bilingualism.

- Similarity in physical appearance to that of the majority culture (e.g., skin color, facial features).

Level of acculturation influences dropout rate, level of stress, attitude toward helpers, and the process

and goals that are appropriate (Sue & Sue, 1990). Some standardized assessment instruments have been developed to assess acculturation (see Sue & Sue, 1990). Knowledge of problems faced and preferred communication styles of different generations will be valuable.

Developmental Considerations

Knowledge about required tasks and related behaviors at different ages and life transitions can be helpful in making decisions. Knowledge of typical behavior at different times (developmental norms) offers information about the prevalence of a behavior. This information can be used to "normalize" behavior (help clients realize that reactions they believed to be unusual or abnormal are typical). For example, an adolescent may think that there is something wrong with him because he masturbates. The prevalence of masturbation among youth of his age calls for normalization of this concern. A parent may believe that his child is doomed to a career of crime because he was caught stealing. The parent may not know that many children steal some object at some time. (This is not to say that nothing should be done to discourage stealing.) Information about changes that are common in different life-cycle phases (e.g., parenthood, retirement) can help in preventive planning (e.g., offering support groups for people nearing retirement or for couples about to have their first child). Knowledge about the hierarchical nature of some developmental tasks (i.e., some behaviors must be learned before others) may inform case planning.

THINKING CRITICALLY ABOUT LABELS

Psychiatric labels have been applied to an ever-increasing variety of behaviors viewed as mental disorders (see also the discussion of the medicalization of deviance in Chapter 7). The fourth edition of the *Diagnostic and Statistical Manual of Mental Disorders* (*DSM-IV*) (1994) of the American Psychiatric Association contains hundreds of diagnostic categories. Psychiatric labels are required for third party reimbursement.

Research suggests that professional education increases the use of negative labels and attentiveness to clients' negative characteristics (Batson, O'Quin, & Pych, 1982). We should think critically about labels and ask: When are they helpful? When are they irrelevant? When are they misleading or harmful? Do they offer guidelines about how to help clients? What are underlying assumptions? Are they reasonable? For example, what is a "disorder"? Is there such an entity as schizophrenia? How do we know? Is there such a thing as "mental illness"? Social workers use labels in two main ways. One is as a shorthand term to refer to a cluster of specific behaviors. The term *hyperactive* may refer to the fact that a student often gets out of his seat and talks out of turn in class. Labels are also used as diagnostic categories that are supposed to indicate the cause of the problem and suggest remedies. For example, a teacher may conclude that a child has an attention deficit disorder because he has difficulty concentrating on assigned tasks and sitting in his seat and assume that he should be medicated (e.g., take Ritalin). Notice the circularity here:

Observed Behavior	Inference	Reasons for Inference
Does not work on assigned tasks.	Attention deficit disorder.	Does not work on assigned tasks.
Often gets out of his seat.		Often gets out of his seat.

This label is based on the two observed behaviors, and no such underlying condition may exist. If this is the case, a descriptive term is used as a pseudoexplanatory term. The use of labels in this manner can be frustrating, since although it may seem that more is known, no additional information is available.

Problems with Psychiatric Labels

People differ in their beliefs about the usefulness of diagnostic labels such as *borderline personality*. In *The Selling of DSM* (1992a), Kirk and Kutchins (both social workers) document the problems with this system—such as the consensual nature of what is included (agreement among individuals is relied on rather than empirical criteria), lack of agreement about what label to assign clients (poor reliability), and lack of association between a diagnosis and indications of what plans will be effective (see Exhibit 9.8). They discuss the role of political and economic considerations in the creation and "selling" of the *DSM* (see also Kirk & Kutchins, 1992a, 1994).

Some writers argue that psychiatric classification systems trivialize human problems in living and encourage blaming victims for their plights rather than examining the social circumstances that are often responsible. Diagnostic labeling implies the need for specialists to help people with their problems. As more and more behaviors are assigned a label, the mental health industry can grow ever greater (see also McReynolds, 1989). Key conceptual questions such as "What is mental illness?" "and What is a disorder?" are glossed over. For a quarter of a century, Thomas Szasz has contended that there is no such thing as mental illness. Some people believe, however, that there is convincing evidence that a disorder called schizophrenia exists and has a biological cause (Torrey, 1995). Others present cogent arguments against these beliefs (Boyle, 1990). Some scholars argue that the concept of mental disorder is culturally relative (e.g., Kirmayer, 1994). Others argue that it is not (Wakefield, 1994). In *The Mismeasure of Woman* (1992), Tavris contends that labels newly included

Exhibit 9.8
Problems with Psychiatric Labels

Are typically vague, resulting in low reliability.
Lack validity.
Do not offer information about how to resolve problems.
Are often used for reasons that benefit professionals rather than clients (reimbursement, creation of an aura of expertise).
Pathologize clients.
Are based on shifting consensual grounds.
Cut off search for environmental causes.
Are used for social control purpose.
May encourage unwanted behavior argued by labeling theorists, (e.g., Scheff, 1984).

in the *DSM-IV* (1994) continue to misdirect attention away from political, social, and economic conditions related to expected gender roles and toward supposed individual deficiencies (see Exhibit 9.9). Many scholars argue that labels such as "mental illness" are used for social control purposes and often result in harming rather than helping people (e.g., Szasz, 1994). Consider labels such as *drapetomania* (an irresistible propensity to run away). This "disease" was rampant among slaves in the South in the last century.

"Categories and labels are powerful instruments for social regulation and control, and they are often employed for obscure, covert, or hurtful purposes: to degrade people, to deny them access to opportunity, to exclude 'undesirables' whose presence in some way offends, disturbs familiar custom, or demands extraordinary effort" (Hobbs, 1975, p. 11). Status offenders are labeled as mentally ill and are confined, without due process, to inpatient psychiatric and chemical dependency units of private hospitals (Schwartz, 1989). (The term "*status offender*" refers to youths who fall under juvenile court jurisdiction because of conduct prohibited only because of their juvenile status, e.g., disobedience, curfew violations, running away, and truancy.) Ira Schwartz (1989) argues that reasons for this trend include insurance policies favoring inpatient care, widespread advertising describing residential treatment centers, lack of community-based services for status offenders who cannot be confined in juvenile correctional institutions, and too many hospital beds. He refers to this relabeling of typical teenage behavior as mental illness as "the medicalization of defiance." Howitt (1992) contends that labels given to clients often obscure lapses in agency services that create problems (e.g., via false assumptions due to uncritical thinking). Many social workers believe there are serious misuses of the *DSM*, including assigning an inappropriate diagnosis simply for reimbursement reasons (Kirk & Kutchins, 1988).

Labels are stigmatizing. They say too little about positive attributes, potential for change, and change that does occur and too much about presumed negative characteristics and limits to change. People labeled are often regarded as if they possess only

Exhibit 9.9
The All-American Game: Name What's Wrong with Women!

Source: C. Tavris (1994), The illusion of science in psychiatry. Skeptic, 2, 79.

the characteristics of a category (e.g., "schizo-phrenic").

> Few options for change are generated by an assessment that regards Mary to be an "inadequate personality." ... [T]his kind of diagnosis doesn't indicate what needs to be changed. The vagueness of the label can prevent us from knowing when that label is no longer deserved or appropriate. It will be difficult for Mary to prove her labelers wrong. If we deal with the specifics of the children being clean, going to the doctor if they have earaches, and receiving proper nutrition, the directions for change become clear. It will also be clear to everyone when the problems are resolved. (Kinney, Haapala, & Booth, 1991, p. 86)

Negative labels often do not reflect changes that take place. That is, even though changes may be made, the same label (e.g., "developmentally disabled") may be applied to a client. Labels often provide an illusion of understanding. You may think you know more about how to help a client (or discover that you cannot), but in fact know nothing more about the client's concerns, the factors related to them, and how to attain desired outcomes (see earlier discussion of circular accounts). Accepting a label may prematurely close off consideration of promising options. Labels that limit exploration do not have to be fancy ones like *hyperactive* or *paranoid*; they can be everyday ones like "*old lady.*" The tendency to use an either/or classification system (people either have or do not have something, e.g., being an alcoholic or not) obscures varied individual patterns that may be referred to by a term.

Although they may sound sophisticated, too often labels offer few if any guidelines about what to do to resolve problems. Neither trait nor diagnostic labels offer enough detail about what people do in specific situations and what personal and environmental events influence their behavior to be of value in clarifying problems and related factors. The individual variability of behavior is overlooked, resulting in lost opportunities to discover unique relationships between a client's behavior and his or her environments. Dispositional attributions shift attention away from observing what people do in specific situations to speculating about what they have done. General predictions about a person based on tiny samples of behavior in one context are not likely to be accurate, especially when behaviors of interest occur in quite different situations.

Within labeling theory, the label itself is considered to be partially responsible for deviant acts (Scheff, 1984). For example, applying labels such as *delinquent* or *shy* may encourage behaviors that match this label and hinder change. A client who has trouble making friends may think of himself as shy and may use this label as an excuse not to initiate conversations. An adolescent labeled *delinquent* may begin to think of himself as a "delinquent" and so engage in other acts compatible with this label. Labeling is viewed as a behavior that varies from culture to culture, from person to person, and from time to time. This point-of-view is very different from a psychiatric one, in which there is a search for a correct diagnostic label for a client. In the former instance, there is a concern that labeling will encourage deviant behavior and result in ignoring clients' strengths and environmental causes of problems.

A contextual assessment takes a very different approach. It includes a clear description of complaints and related factors and a description of what a person can do and cannot do, what he or she can learn to do, and what is expected of him or her, as well as environmental factors that influence problem-related behaviors (Hobbs, 1975, p. 105). This kind of assessment often reveals that environmental deficiencies contribute to problems (e.g., a lack of recreational opportunities, a lack of day care, low wages).

Helpful Labels

Labels that are instrumental (i.e., they point to effective plans or indicate accurately that there are no effective options) are helpful. Recognizing signs of pathology is important if this increases understanding of what can be accomplished and how. Some elderly clients do have dementia. Labels can normalize clients' concerns. Parents who have been struggling to understand why their child is developmentally slow may view themselves as failures. Recognizing that their child has a specific kind of developmental disability that accounts for this can be a relief. Failing to use labels may prevent clients from receiving appropriate help. Consider the Japanese custom of labeling clients as *neurasthenic* to protect them and their relatives from the social stigma associated with mental illness. Munakata (1989) suggests that the use of such a "disguised diagnosis" given to the pilot was responsible for the 1982 crash of an airliner in Tokyo. The pilot, who had hallucinations and delusions at the time of the crash, had a history of psychiatric problems.

What About the P-I-E System?

The National Association of Social Workers helped fund the development of a new classification system, Person-In-Environment (PIE) (Karls & Wandrei, 1994). Although its creators argue that it is useful, others believe that the same concerns that apply to the *DSM* apply as well to P-I-E (e.g., a lack of validity).

ASSESSING THE RISK OF SUICIDE AND ABUSE

Social workers are legally required to report suspected child abuse. This includes physical abuse, sexual molestation, and inattention to physical needs, such as inadequate supervision. As important as it is to detect abuse when it is present, it also is important not to falsely accuse people of abuse. False allegations create havoc in families (Howitt, 1992).

You should be familiar with the risk factors related to suicide (e.g., depression, a preformed plan, prior attempts). This is not to say that you can prevent suicide; indeed, there is no evidence that suicide can be prevented (Hillard, 1995). In fact, research suggests that hospitalizing suicidal adolescents to prevent their committing suicide increases the risk. The identification of risk factors is based on correlational research that does not allow you to predict what any one person will do (Dawes, 1994a). You can, however, take steps to decrease risk (e.g., offer support, discuss related concerns, offer hope). Scholars disagree about hospitalizing "suicidal" people against their will to pre-

vent suicide. Some argue that not only is this unethical—it can't be done (i.e., be used to prevent suicide) (e.g., Gomory, 1997; Szasz, 1994).

PROBLEMS VARY IN THEIR COMPLEXITY

Problems vary in their complexity. Questions to ask when exploring complexity include the following:

- Will achieving valued outcomes have negative as well as positive effects?
- Are contexts available that will facilitate change?
- Do significant others and clients have required knowledge and skills?
- Are problems interlinked?
- Are needed resources available?

Significant others may lack needed skills, have interfering beliefs, or be threatened by proposed changes. A parent may lack verbal statements of praise that her children find reinforcing. A problem may be linked to other areas that must be addressed, such as a lack of vocational skills. A grandparent may visit a family and reinforce a child's annoying behavior. Staff may complain about the "dependency" of residents, not realizing that they themselves encourage and maintain dependent behaviors. They may oppose a plan in which independent behaviors will be reinforced, viewing this as bribery. Attempts to resolve problems may create more problems. Distinguishing between problems and efforts to resolve them will help you and your clients avoid confusing the results of attempting solutions and the effects of the original concern (Watzlawick, Weakland, & Fisch, 1974). Limited resources (such as day care, vocational training programs, recreational centers, high-quality educational programs, parent training programs) and limited influence over environmental contingencies often pose an obstacle. For example, you may have little influence over teachers who do not know how to plan effective curricula or to encourage valued behaviors by means of positive change methods. Discriminatory policies and practices may stand in the way. Expected role behaviors may limit change. For example, a father may view child rearing as totally his wife's responsibility. You may have little influence over inadequate housing or access to crack cocaine that contributes to a parent's neglect of a child. Agency policies and practices and the physical characteristics of the environment affect options. The lack of coordination among services may limit access to needed resources. Clients may receive fragmentary, overlapping, or incompatible services.

SUMMARY

Assessment should indicate the likelihood of attaining valued outcomes. This may be slim because needed resources are not available or because related environmental or personal characteristics cannot be altered. Assessment should be of value to clients and significant others by offering some immediate benefits, such as hope and concrete help. It is an ongoing process in which decisions are altered as necessary in response to new information. A contextual analysis should indicate the levels of intervention required to attain valued outcomes (individual, family, group, community, agency, service system, policy). Characteristics of a contextual assessment include use of methods that are likely to offer accurate data, a preference for observation and clear description, and avoidance of appeals to personality traits and dispositions as causal agents. Complaints are translated into observable behaviors that, if changed, will remove them. This may involve behaviors of service providers as well as those of clients and significant others. There is an interest in understanding the function of behaviors. What do problem-related behaviors communicate?

Assessment methods should be individually tailored to each client and include a search for client assets and material and community resources and consideration of cultural differences as they relate to desired outcomes, and proposed resolutions. This framework avoids blaming clients for their problems, relying on stigmatizing labels that are not useful, and offering incomplete accounts that ignore environmental causes. A procedural guide for carrying out a contextual assessment is described in the next chapter.

REVIEWING YOUR COMPETENCIES

Reviewing What You Know

1. Describe the basic characteristics of a contextual assessment framework.
2. Describe the differences between a sign (diagnostic) and a sample (assessment) approach.
3. Describe common assessment errors that result in incomplete or incorrect problem analyses.
4. Describe the difference between a descriptive and a functional analysis.
5. Give an example of a pseudoexplanation.
6. Describe four ways assessment can be of value to clients.
7. Explain why significant others are important to include in assessment, and give examples.
8. Give examples of the difference between motivation and behavior deficits.

9. Give examples of the difference between topographic and functional descriptions of behavior.
10. Describe what is meant by "the client uniformity myth."
11. Describe the differences between a constructional and a deficiency approach to helping.
12. Discuss the role of past history in a contextual assessment.
13. Describe the disadvantages of focusing on the past.
14. Describe the limitations of psychiatric labels and give examples.
15. Describe the difference between setting events and antecedents.
16. Accurately describe different kinds of contingencies and their effects on behavior.
17. Give examples of the influence of the physical environment on behavior.
18. Discuss the roles of thoughts and feelings in different practice perspectives.
19. Discuss the relationship between behavior deficits and behavior surfeits (behaviors that occur too often).
20. Give examples of inadequate and inappropriate stimulus control.
21. Give examples of inadequate or inappropriate reinforcing functions.

Reviewing What You Do

1. You can review a case example and accurately critique it from a contextual strengths-oriented assessment perspective.
2. You can review a case example and accurately describe the kinds of information you would need from a contextual strengths-oriented assessment perspective.
3. You can review a case example and accurately describe the ratio of helpful to irrelevant data.
4. You clearly describe problems and their outcomes.
5. You identify related environmental factors related to problems, including setting events, antecedents, and consequences.
6. You involve significant others in assessment.
7. You identify personal assets and environmental resources.
8. Your inferences about the causes of problems are supported by sound evidence.
9. You avoid noninstrumental labels.
10. You focus on appropriate systems levels (e.g., individual, family, group, agency, community, societal).

Reviewing Results

1. Clients form more helpful views of their problems.
2. Clients report that assessment was helpful.
3. Clients increase their problem-solving skills.
4. The plans selected resolve clients' problems.

CHAPTER 10

Beginning: A Procedural Guideline

OVERVIEW

Social work practice has beginnings, middles, and endings. This chapter describes decisions, tasks, and accompanying skills involved in the beginning phase. Goals and related skills in initial interviews include offering introductory information, developing a collaborative working relationship, identifying a mutually agreeable purpose, and encouraging positive expectations. The value of gathering an overview of problems/desired outcomes and setting priorities are described, as are the advantages of clear service agreements. Guidelines are offered for clarifying problems and related factors and selecting objectives. A careful assessment will help you tailor your decisions to the unique characteristics and circumstances of each client (individual, family, group, organization, or community). Your success will be related to the "goodness of fit" between these characteristics and what is offered.

You Will Learn About

- A problem-solving guide.
- Culturally sensitive practice.
- Initial interviews.
- Obtaining an overview of problems/desired outcomes.
- Criteria for establishing priorities.
- Cultivating helpful views of problems.
- Identifying objectives and related circumstances.
- Encouraging a collaborative set.
- Forming service agreements.
- Handling crisis situations.

A PROBLEM-SOLVING GUIDE

Helping clients can be approached as a series of problem-solving tasks related to the questions shown in Exhibit 10.1. Initial meetings set the stage for later ones and influence whether or not there will be later meetings. Many decisions, tasks, and accompanying skills in the beginning stages are common to all levels of service with a wide variety of problems and clients. Examples are (1) describing services, (2) clarifying what will be expected of clients and what clients can expect from you, (3) clarifying problems and identifying related factors, (4) selecting problem-related outcomes to focus on, (5) offering timely concrete help, (6) involving significant others, and (7) identifying resources and obstacles. You and your clients will have to decide whether you can offer any help; what outcomes to pursue; what behaviors, thoughts, feelings, or environmental factors are related to these outcomes; whom to involve in the assessment; what settings to explore; and what referrals to make (if

any). Knowledge about human behavior and development will be valuable in making these decisions.

Complaints should be translated into objectives that if achieved would solve the problem (Baer, 1982). Valued outcomes may involve the behavior of service providers as well as significant others and clients. If you are a successful broker and advocate for your clients, you influence the "gate-keepers" of resources needed by your clients. Find out why complaints are made at this time and what would happen if nothing were done (unless this is obvious). What has been tried, to what effect? Do any positive consequences result from problems? What negative effects occur? That is, what benefits and costs are involved, both to clients and significant others, both currently and in the future? What benefits would result if changes were made? Would anything change for the worse? Is there any overarching contingency that will make it difficult to attain outcomes that clients value? For example, a client who wants to keep her Supplementary

EXHIBIT 10.1
Assessment: Questions and Reasons for Asking Them

Question	Rationale
What's the problem?	Clear problem definition increases the likelihood of selecting relevant outcomes and identifying related factors. This also helps you to assess the likelihood of attaining outcomes.
What does it communicate?	Provides information about functions the problem may serve (e.g., prevention of worse problems, lack of skill or knowledge, interest in certain reinforcers).
Who is affected by the problem and how are they affected?	Provides information about who to involve and who may help or hinder change efforts.
Why now?	Offers clues about related factors, possible obstacles, and sources of help.
What would happen if nothing were done?	Helpful in understanding how problems influence overall short and long term functioning.
How will I know if the problem is solved? What would be different?	Identifies specific outcomes related to complaints and specific criteria to use to assess progress.
Who and/or what influences the problem? (What makes it worse? What makes it better?)	Provides information about related contingencies.
What efforts have been made to resolve the problem? What happened?	Offers data about options and the effects of attempted resolutions; provides opportunities to support helpful options.
What obstacles must be overcome?	Assess feasibility of attaining outcomes and helpful in planning intervention.
What resources are needed? What resources are available?	Assess feasibility of achieving outcomes and helpful in planning what to do.
What could be done to prevent the problem from recurring?	Provides information about how to prevent problems in the future.

EXHIBIT 10.2
A Problem-Solving Guide

Preparation

1. Prepare (see Chapter 11).
2. Offer crisis services as needed. Get an overview of desired problems/outcomes.

Engagement and Exploration

3. Decide on priorities and whether you can provide services. If not, refer clients elsewhere as needed.
4. Develop a collaborative helping relationship.
5. Describe problem-related behaviors and the context in which they occur (e.g., related setting events, antecedents, and consequences). Gather baseline data if possible.
6. Review resources and obstacles.
7. Organize and interpret data.

Syntheses

8. Select problem-related objectives (outcomes to focus on).
9. Form a clear service agreement.

Intervention

10. Select plans.

Implementation

11. Implement plans.

Evaluation

12. Evaluate outcome.
13. Alter plans as needed.
14. Arrange additional maintenance plans as needed.
15. Monitor outcome.
16. End.

Follow-up

17. Follow up.

Security Income benefits (SSI) may also want to overcome her depression, but if she did, she would lose this source of income. Clients must be *involved*—encouraged to discuss personally relevant topics and to move from the general to the specific. Both voluntary and involuntary clients are more likely to participate in helpful ways if you focus on outcomes they value. Your tasks include providing support and reassurance, maintaining focus, and helping clients and significant others to clearly describe problem-related goals and associated factors.

A contextual assessment framework suggests the problem-solving agenda in Exhibit 10.2 (Gambrill, Thomas, & Carter, 1971; Thomas & Walter, 1973). These guidelines can be used to an-

swer the questions in Exhibit 10.1. In practice, steps often overlap and do not necessarily occur in the order shown. In some settings, such as outreach services for the homeless and psychiatric emergency centers, your contacts with clients may be sporadic, with little opportunity to work systematically. You will have to vary your actions in accord with what the client wants and what you can provide. Assessment should precede decisions about plans unless a crisis is at hand. If there is a crisis (a situation requiring immediate attention), exploring why it occurred so that future crises can be avoided may have to take second place.

INITIAL INTERVIEWS/EXCHANGES

Although initial exchanges with clients may be in the form of an interview in many settings, in others it may not. For example, in outreach services to the homeless, encounters may be by chance and be sporadic. There are different kinds of interviews, including assessment interviews (e.g., determining people's eligibility for certain services). Objectives of initial interviews are to

- Establish rapport and increase client comfort.
- Offer support and encouragement.
- Describe the agency's services.
- Offer concrete, material help.
- Form a collaborative relationship.
- Gather a profile of problems/desired outcomes.
- Determine if service can be provided.
- Arrange conditions for continuance or discontinuance.
- Help clients to clearly describe problems and explore how they may be resolved.
- Reach an agreement about outcomes to pursue.

In some agencies, intake workers refer clients to staff, who provide ongoing services. If this is the case, clients should be informed about this so that they will be prepared to meet someone new on their next visit. Interviews should be goal directed. Multiple purposes may be served by any one exchange, such as providing concrete help and information, making a decision (e.g., whether an applicant meets eligibility requirements), and offering support. With resisters, the purpose of the interview might be to explore how you could help them as well as meet goals imposed by other sources, such as the court.

Your tasks include arranging a distraction-free environment, guiding the focus of interviews, and avoiding interviewer biases, making the exchange as comfortable as possible. Interviewer biases include the following (Ceci & Bruck, 1995):

• Repeating a question *within* an interview which may encourage clients to report events that did not occur.

• Stereotype induction: interviewer transmits a negative view of a person or event to a client (e.g., telling a child that a suspect "does bad things").

• Searching only for confirmatory evidence for favored assumptions.

Draw on your interviewing skills to encourage clients to share needed material, explore concerns, and identify personalized goals (steps clients can take to resolve problems) (Carkhuff & Anthony, 1979). Relationship skills of value in helping clients move from sharing, exploring, and understanding to acting are described in Chapters 12 and 13. The greater burden for being courteous and considerate and effectively handling cultural differences falls on you. This will require not taking negative or rude behavior "personally" (it gets under your skin and/or you react in kind). Stay focused on service goals. Decide on mutually understood, feasible, acceptable goal(s) for each interview. Use language that is clear and intelligible to clients, and personalize your comments and questions (e.g., use examples from their lives). (See Exhibit 20.3.)

Whenever possible, end interviews on an upbeat. For example, reaffirm your agreement to work together to achieve agreed-on outcomes, encourage positive expectations, review what has been accomplished, and support clients' assets. People's lives are made up of more than their problems.

EXHIBIT 10.3
Example of a Beginning Interview

Mr. and Mrs. Lakeland consulted a social worker, Mr. Colvine, about problems with their son Brian, aged 14. This exhibit continues the description of the Lakeland family presented in Chapter 2. Most of the reflective and paraphrasing statements have been omitted to save space. One of Mr. Colvine's goals was to help his clients feel at ease. Other goals were to find out what changes family members wanted and to gather information about how these could be achieved. Notice the focus on the present and the interest in clearly describing problems and outcomes and related setting events, antecedents, and consequences. Brian and his parents were on time for their first interview with Mr. Colvine. Brian looked sullen, and his parents seemed anxious. They fidgeted in their seats. Brian had a scowl on his face, did not look at his parents, and sat apart from them.

MR. COLVINE: (To all three clients.) Could you tell me about your family? Who lives at home, for example?

MR. LAKELAND: Well, my wife and I, our oldest son Bob, Brian, and his little sister Joan. Joan's only 11, and Bob is 18. Oh, yes, we also have a dog. (He glares at Brian, who continues to look down at the floor.) We have a good life. We shouldn't be having this trouble.

MR. COLVINE: Is there anything else you would like to tell me about your family?

MR. LAKELAND: We both (looks at his wife) work hard to stay ahead of the game. My wife works full time too, and I have a part-time job three nights a week. We need the extra money for Bob, since he just started college. He is really a smart boy.

MR. COLVINE: Is this the first time you have sought help with the family problems?

MRS. LAKELAND: No, we saw a social worker at another agency 2 years ago about Brian. We were having trouble with him then. She was nice to talk to, and we kept on going, since we didn't want to show disrespect. But she didn't help us much.

MR. COLVINE: What did the social worker suggest?

MRS. LAKELAND: She said we should learn to talk to each other and listen to each other and wanted to see the whole family together. We did talk, but it didn't seem to change anything at home.

MR. COLVINE: Was there any other time you sought help?

MR. LAKELAND: Yes, we also went to see our doctor, and he said that we should be real strict with Brian and get him to take his medication. We were strict for a while, but then things just returned to their usual miserable state.

MR. COLVINE: I would like to find out what changes you would like to see in your family. This will help me know how I can be of help to you. Brian, let's start with you. What changes would you like to see in your family?

BRIAN: Gee, I don't know. Why don't you ask them? (He points to his parents.)

MR. COLVINE: I'll also be asking your father and mother what changes they would like to see, but I want to know what changes you would like, too. Could you give me one example?

BRIAN: Well, you could get them off my back.

MR. COLVINE: Could you give me an example of what happens when they "are on your back"?

BRIAN: Sure, they nag me all the time; don't do this, do that. It's really a pain.

MR. COLVINE: Could you tell me what was happening the last time they asked you to do something?

BRIAN: Yeah, just today. I was playing with the dog, and they said to cut it out. I wasn't hurting anyone.

MR. COLVINE: Can you tell me what you were doing?

BRIAN: I was picking him up by his tail. He really likes this. (Brian smirks, and his parents look at him in disgust, and with an air of helplessness, they sigh.)

MR. COLVINE: Can you think of another example of when your parents are "on your back"?

BRIAN: They're on my back all the time—take my medication, have good table manners, don't tease my sister, get better grades. They're always threatening me, too—we'll send you away.

MR. COLVINE: OK. That's helpful. Now I'd like you to describe something that your parents do that you like. Think back over the past week.

BRIAN: (Looks at his parents.) Well . . . (pause) they try their best. (Silence.)

MR. COLVINE: Think back over the past week, Brian. Give me an example of something either your Dad or Mom did that you liked.

BRIAN: Well, Dad took me around to collect the money for my papers.

MR. COLVINE: How about your Mom?

BRIAN: (Looks at his mother.) Gee, that's hard (he grins). (His mother rolls her eyes upward.) Well, she told me she liked my new haircut yesterday.

MR. COLVINE: OK, Brian. We'll come back to you in a minute. Mr. Lakeland, could you tell me what changes you would like to see in the family?

(*continued*)

EXHIBIT 10.3 (*continued*)

MR. LAKELAND: (Pause.) Well, things seem to be getting out of hand lately with Brian. We've always had trouble with him. You know he is epileptic and has to take medication. He often forgets to take this. He never did too well in school, but lately his grades have been getting really bad. But I guess what really concerns us most is that he is getting more violent. He threatened to hit his mother the other day and threatened to throw a knife at me last week. Things are getting out of hand. I don't know how much longer we can go on like this.

MR. COLVINE: I can see that you are concerned about what is happening in your family, and I hope that we can work together and see that some changes can be made. It sounds like changes you would like are for Brian to take his medication regularly, for him not to physically threaten you or your wife, and for him to get better grades in school.

BRIAN: I was just kidding.

MRS. LAKELAND: No, you were not.

MR. LAKELAND: Yes, and mainly to mind us, do what we say.

MR. COLVINE: Now, Mr. Lakeland, give me an example of something you like about Brian. What are some of the things he does that you like?

MR. LAKELAND: He helps me in the yard. He is pretty good, too, about delivering the papers on his route. Sometimes I have to keep reminding him to get up. But after he is up, he usually gets right out there. He doesn't always remember to collect the money though, and that's a problem.

MR. COLVINE: Let's keep focused on the positives right now. It seems that there are a number of things that Brian does that you like. And how about you, Mrs. Lakeland? What changes would you like to see in the family?

MRS. LAKELAND: My husband has picked out the big ones. It really bothers me when he talks nasty to me.

MR. COLVINE: Could you give me an example?

MRS. LAKELAND: Well, yesterday when I asked Brian to take out the garbage, he said, "Do it yourself, bitch." (Mrs. L. looks like she is going to cry, and Brian looks very sheepish.)

MR. COLVINE: Does he talk to you that way very often, Mrs. Lakeland?

MRS. LAKELAND: No, but it really hurts me and makes me mad when he does.

MR. COLVINE: I can see that it is upsetting to you. (Pause.) Can you think of anything else?

MRS. LAKELAND: Not really.

MR. COLVINE: Mrs. Lakeland, what are some things that Brian does that you like?

MRS. LAKELAND: Well, I really don't feel that he means to be so bad. I think he just gets beside himself. He can be nice at times.

MR. COLVINE: Could you give me an example?

MRS. LAKELAND: Well, he brought me some flowers for my birthday last week. He helps his father with the yard work sometimes.

MR. COLVINE: What else does he do that you like?

MRS. LAKELAND: Sometimes he makes a special dessert for the family, one that is also his favorite. (She smiles for the first time.) He lets Bob help him with his homework sometimes.

MR. COLVINE: Brian, you said that you would like your parents to "get off your back." Are there any other changes you would like to see in your family?

BRIAN: Well, yeah, I'd like to have my own work space. I have no place to work on my models. My stuff always gets pushed out of the way.

MR. COLVINE: OK. Let's note that down too. (He writes this change under the column "Changes Brian would like.") Is there anything else?

BRIAN: (Pause.) No, nothing I can think of.

MR. COLVINE: (To the parents.) What have you done to try to change Brian's behavior?

MR. LAKELAND: We've tried everything. We tried to talk to him, and that didn't work. We tried to punish him by removing privileges, and that didn't work. He just seemed to get madder. We talked to our doctor, and he said to be firm with Brian. That worked for about a day. Nothing seems to work, and things seem to be getting worse.

MRS. LAKELAND: Nothing we have tried has had any effect.

MR. COLVINE: Well, we will try to find some ways that will be helpful. I can see that you are discouraged about how things are now. It is frustrating to try to make things better and not be as successful as you would like. (The Lakelands nod in agreement.)

MR. COLVINE: Brian, what have you tried to change your parents' behavior?

BRIAN: Are you kidding? You can't change them. They're old stick-in-the-muds.

MR. COLVINE: But what have you tried?

BRIAN: I tried to tell them I just forget. But they don't believe me.

MR. COLVINE: Have you tried anything else?

BRIAN: No, what's the use?

MR. COLVINE: (Pause.) I'd like to find out a bit more about what happens when things get really bad at home. Can you tell me about a recent incident?

MRS. LAKELAND: How about when he threatened to hit me. He said, "I'm going to punch you" and raised his fist to me.

MR. COLVINE: Were you present too, Mr. Lakeland?

MR. LAKELAND: Yes, and Brian's older brother and his sister were there, too.

MR. COLVINE: OK. What was going on before he threatened you?

MRS. LAKELAND: We were having dinner, and Brian was teasing his little sister. He was calling her "Cutsy," which she hates, and making fun of her new haircut. She started to cry, she was so upset. I twice asked Brian to stop this, and he just kept on. Then I finally shouted at him that if he didn't stop, he was to leave the table. That's when he threatened me.

MR. COLVINE: Then what did you do?

MR. LAKELAND: I told him that he better not threaten his mother, and I told him to leave the table and go up to his room. Instead, he went out of the house and slammed the door.

MR. COLVINE: Brian, is this how you would describe what happened?

BRIAN: They just kept nagging me. I was just having some fun. (Mr. Colvine obtains specific descriptions of three other incidents that occurred at home, including what happened right before and right after each one.)

MR. COLVINE: Brian, what other things do your parents do that you like?

BRIAN: Well, Dad takes me fishing once in a great while, but not very often. Mom makes my favorite dishes sometimes. She's not such a bad mother. (He smiles.) But they sure do nag me.

MR. COLVINE: Is there anything else you can think of, Brian?

BRIAN: They used to stick up for me when I got into trouble at school, but now they just think I'm always in the wrong.

MR. COLVINE: Could you give me an example?

(continued)

EXHIBIT 10.3 (*continued*)

> BRIAN: Sure, last week I got kicked out of my math class for no reason and sent to the principal's office. They called my Mom at work the next day to complain about me. They (points to his parents) didn't even stick up for me.
>
> MR. COLVINE: What do you mean, Brian?
>
> BRIAN: They didn't even let me give my side of the story.
>
> MR. COLVINE: (To the parents.) Is this how you see the situation?
>
> MRS. LAKELAND: I guess I did get upset. I hate to be bothered at work and just tried to get off the phone. When I saw Brian later, I did hop on him.
>
> MR. COLVINE: We'll get back to this topic later, too. Let me get a better idea of what your family is like. When was the last time you did something as a family, all of you did something together?
>
> MRS. LAKELAND: (Looks at her husband.) I can't remember. Can you, Bill?

Offering Introductory Information

If clients are not familiar with services available, one of your tasks will be to describe them. You can allay concerns about what to expect by informing clients about services available, fees (if any), time limits, mutual responsibilities, and the approach that will be used. This will help to demystify what may occur and take the client "off the hook" in being expected to talk right away. Clients are more likely to participate in helpful ways if they understand the rationale for and activities involved in assessment. You can ease the transition into the interview by small talk (a brief discussion of a neutral topic) unless this is inappropriate because of the urgency of a problem or client anxiety or anger. You could note that initial discomfort is common. You could gather some basic descriptive information to put the client at ease, even though this is already available. Sometimes, novice interviewers are so nervous themselves that they forget basic amenities such as helping clients feel physically comfortable, for example, by suggesting that they take off their jacket (see Appendix 10A).

An introductory statement offers an opportunity to establish your role in guiding the helping process and to clarify expectations (see Exhibit 10.4). Ambiguous statements of purpose may increase client anxiety about what will happen especially with nonvoluntary clients. Checking client expectations provides an opportunity to correct misunderstandings. Correcting misconceptions and encouraging

helpful views is often a gradual process. Be honest about your agenda, and describe the limits on confidentiality. You may postpone introductory information if clients are eager to talk. Or, you may suggest that it will be helpful to first describe what you can offer, especially if clients seem to misunderstand this. Introductory statements may not be necessary if clients are familiar with the agency's services.

GATHER A PROFILE OF PROBLEMS/DESIRED OUTCOMES

One helpful way of proceeding is to first get an overview of problems and/or desired outcomes (assuming that one problem does not take precedence) (Gambrill, Thomas, & Carter, 1971). This will help you and your client discover interrelationships among valued outcomes and to set priorities. If additional concerns emerge later, they can be added and priorities changed as needed. If several family members are present, ask each one to identify desired outcomes and to indicate their importance. Use your knowledge of cultural norms to decide whom to ask first. For example, if the father is viewed as the authority in a family, he may be insulted if you speak first to his wife or children. Encourage clients and significant others to talk to one another (if this is culturally appropriate). You may have to prompt clients to do this: "Maria, could you tell John what changes you would like." Then if Maria starts to talk to you, prompt her to speak

EXHIBIT 10.4
Examples of Introductory Statements

1. Let me tell you about our agency and some of the things that will happen in our work together. We'll make a tentative agreement today about how many times we will see each other. I know that it's difficult for you to come to the agency, and we could have some of our meetings in your home if this would be convenient for you. I'd like to meet your other children so I can get a picture of your whole family. Today we'll identify changes that each of you here today would like to make in your family and then we'll have a better idea of what other information we'll need to see how these can be accomplished. I'd like you to focus on present concerns—changes that you would like to see right now. I'll be asking you to do some homework between sessions. These tasks won't take up much of your time, and they will be very valuable in our work together. This will allow us to make use of time between our meetings.

If anything comes up and you cannot make a meeting, please give me 24 hours' notice. If I have to rearrange a meeting, I'll give you at least 24 hours' notice. As we discussed on the phone, your fee for each session will be _____. This is payable _____. We'll have periodic telephone contact with each other between sessions, but there will be no additional fee for these contacts. I'll be helping you this morning to identify what changes each of you would like in your family.

2. An example of an introductory statement about a parent-training program follows. Responsibilities of the parents are highlighted, skills they will learn are noted as well as the need to alter old beliefs and habits, and benefits of the program are described. Note the positive spirit of this statement and the attention to the parents' feelings.

Basically, we are here so that together we can help you to take charge of your children's future. We will help you to learn and to use important skills for planning, running, and keeping track of a home-educational program which may change your children in a big way. Make no mistake about it, though. This means learning new skills on your part. It may even mean changing some basic ideas of yours and some habitual ways in which you deal with your children, yourselves, and with other people.

... Your kids do a lot of things that are driving you up the wall and that do, or will, get your children into trouble and keep them from enjoying many of the good things in life. We can teach you how to reduce and replace those problem behaviors with behaviors that are helpful for your children to learn and do, which are considered appropriate, normal, some of which may even be expected or demanded if your child is to have a place in this society.

The second reason you should be involved in this program has to do with the relationship between home and school. Even if your children are in a terrific program and are learning all kinds of things, that does not mean that they are going to do any of them, or do them well, in the home. You have to learn some of the skills your kids' teachers have, if it is a good program, or else a lot of the progress they are making in school may have no effect on your child at home. On the other hand, if you are not satisfied with your children's school program, this program teaches you not only how to provide your children with a partial substitute, but how to evaluate your children's school program and

(continued)

EXHIBIT 10.4 (*continued*)

to make important comments on how it can be improved. In fact, imagine what a group of motivated and skillful parents could do to help change the school programs their children are in!

And, if your children are not even in a program anywhere, you certainly need to learn how to teach your children in the home.

Third, many of you have said that you've had a rough time getting help over the years. And you may be pretty bitter as a result of your experiences. Well, we can't make excuses for others, but the truth is that many people and many facilities have just not been geared to meet your needs and the needs of your children. Some, as you know, have not seemed to be interested in the particular problems of your kids.

But things have been changing and can be changed even more. One benefit of this Program, then, is that it can help to prepare your children for evaluations because, as you know, if your children are screaming their heads off or do not pay attention, it is hard to pinpoint their strengths and weaknesses. In addition, we can help you to use available services such as physicians or speech therapists, and to seek outside help when it is needed.

Finally, the Program will help you to establish networks between families, so that you all can maintain your efforts and home programs, and can help others to do what you will have learned.

Source: M. A. Kozloff (1979), A program for families of children with learning and behavior problems *(pp. 152–153). New York: Wiley.*

to John. Exhibit 10.5 describes the problems of concern to Brian and his parents, and Exhibit 10.6 illustrates a profile concerning a homeless client, which was prepared by Joe Neifert, one of my students. His client, a 28-year-old African American woman, reported being homeless since the age of 20 and had no identified family or relatives. She had never been employed. Note that room is included on the profile to indicate who labels a given area as a problem and who has the problem. This offers valuable information about degree of agreement about problems/outcomes. Teachers, social workers, the school nurse, and parents all may note problems with a youth, none of which he considers a problem. Problem solving in organizations and communities will involve a wider variety of interested parties compared to working with individuals and families. Here, too, getting an overview of problems of concern to different groups, understanding different points-of-view about why they occur and how they can be solved, and describing attempted solutions and their effects provide valuable assessment information.

Encourage clients to focus on *present* concerns/desired outcomes. Obtain specific examples of each, including a description of related situation(s), who has the concern, and who would like to see changes. You may discover desired outcomes by asking questions like How would you like your life to be different? How would we know if we were successful? Use prompts as needed (e.g., "Is there anything else that concerns you right now?"). You and your clients can then review information noted to decide which areas to focus on first. Areas listed may be interrelated.

Coach clients to think in terms of desired outcomes rather than problems (see Exhibit 10.7). You may need more information to identify specific problem-related outcomes (see Chapters 14 and 15). Helping clients clearly describe problems and related factors is a key practice skill. Clients may describe problems in vague terms like "everything is a mess," "he's impossible," "we can't talk," or "he is always that way." They may use general metaphors such as "He is smothering me." Help them identify specific related behaviors to which

EXHIBIT 10.5
Problem/Outcome Profile

Case: Lakeland
No.: 1
Worker(s): Colvine

Problem Number	Label	Who Labels	Who has Problem	Date Noted	Examples	Situational Context	Desired Outcome
1	No respect.	Mrs. L.	Brian	10/13	1. Calls Mrs. L. a grouch. 2. Refers to Mrs. L. as "she" rather than as "Mother."	1. In evening. 2. No particular context other than Mrs. L.'s presence.	Refer to Mrs. L. as "Mother." Decrease negative labels for Mrs. L.
2	Mean to dog.	Both parents	Brian	10/13	Holds radio in dog's ear; plays too roughly; holds dog's head between knees.	Mainly in the evening.	Pet dog gently. Do not hold dog "against his will." (criterion—struggling to get away).
3	"Not appreciative" re: sister.	Mrs. L.	Brian	10/13	Does not say "thank you" when Joan does something for him.	At home.	Thank his sister when she does something for him.
4	Teases Joan.	Both parents	Brian	10/13	Plugs transistor into her ear when she does not want it; punches her.	When she is around.	Decrease hitting; do not force her to do things.
5	Not home on time.	Both parents	Brian	10/13	Comes in later than 3:30 on days when could be home by 3:30.	Weekdays.	Come straight home from school, arriving home at 3:30.
6	Not enough time spent with Joan.	Mrs. L.	Brian	10/13	Rarely plays games with her.	When Joan is home.	Spend more time with Joan.
7	Does not follow instructions; argumentative.	Both parents	Brian	10/13	Make bed; turn radio down; go to bed; come to dinner table; stop playing roughly with Charlie.	At home.	Follow instructions; complete agreed-on chores.
8	Does not sit at dinner table.	Mrs. L.	Brian	10/13		Fridays or late school days are excluded.	Sit at dinner table with rest of family except Friday and late school days.

(continued)

EXHIBIT 10.5 (*continued*)

Problem Number	Label	Who Labels	Who has Problem	Date Noted	Examples	Situational Context	Desired Outcome
9	Parents don't do what they say they will.	Brian	Both parents	10/13	Mr. L. does not take trips as promised; Mrs. L. doesn't give what she promises, didn't start bank account when promised.	Something else comes up, or fatigue prevents follow-through.	Parents keep their promises.
10	Nagging.	Brian	Parents	10/13	Parents ask him to do something many times.	At home.	Ask him to do something only once.
11	Brian leaves house without telling parents where he is going.	Parents	Brian	10/13		After school.	Leave note or inform someone when leaving house; indicate when will be back.
12	Brian does not straighten room daily.	Parents	Brian	10/13	Bed not made, clothes thrown on floor.	At home.	Make bed, hang clothes up, put dirty clothes in hamper each morning.
13	Brian does not clean room on weekend.	Parents	Brian	10/13	Does not vacuum, dust, change bed.	At home.	Brian will vacuum and dust his room each Saturday and change sheets on bed.
14	Not allowed in store by himself.	Brian	Brian	10/13		Caught but not prosecuted for shoplifting.	Be allowed to go to store by himself.
15	Does not always take medication (for control of epilepsy).	Parents	Brian	10/13	Did not take medication and had seizures.	Taking pills at school makes him late for class.	Take medication three times a day (morning, afternoon, and evening).

16	Won't take tranquilizers.	Parents	Brian	10/13	Refuses to take tranquilizers.	Brian says tranquilizers make him sleepy.	Take tranquilizers as recommended by doctor (note—check whether needed).
17	Physical assaults on family member.	Parents	Brian	10/13	During argument with parents threatened to throw a knife at Mr. L.	At home after dinner.	Do not physically assault or threaten family members.
18	Rough physical interaction with a family member.	Parents	Brian	10/13	Pushes sisters or parents when talking to them.	At home when disagreement occurs or when "playing."	Do not push or shove any family member, even "in play."
19	Brian does not come home when told in evening.	Parents	Brian	10/13	Returns home an hour or two later than agreed.	Evenings.	Return home at agreed-on time.
20	Mrs. L. is a grouch.	Brian	Mrs. L.	10/13	Doesn't do any work when comes home; always asking children to do things for her.	When Mrs. L. comes home.	Mrs. L. will smile more when she comes home from work; do chores and not ask children to do things she can do herself.
21	Poor grades.	Parents	Parents, Brian	10/13	Gets C's, D's, and F's.	School.	Get more B's and C's.

EXHIBIT 10.6
Problem Profile of a 28-Year-Old Homeless Woman

Problem Number	Label	Who Labels	Who Has Problem	Date Noted	Examples	Situational Context	Desired Outcome
1.	Chronic drug use (cocaine)	Society, staff at services, client	Client	11/95	Smokes crack cocaine daily.	Smokes crack in the North area of Berkeley.	To enter recovery and stop using drugs/cocaine.
2.	Prostitution.	Police, society, client	Client	11/95	Client prostitutes herself for money and crack cocaine.	Client regularly is assaulted and abused. Client does not inform her clients that she is HIV positive.	Practice safe sex. Stop being a prostitute to prevent future abuse.
3.	Does not treat her HIV.	Staff	Client	11/95	When client gets ill, she rarely takes her antibiotics and other meds. Decompensates to the point that she ends up in the county hospital.	Client feels she will die from AIDS, so she does not treat it. Continually ill.	Get client to follow a medical and health plan.
4.	Unprotected & uninformed sex.	Staff, client	Client, society	11/95	Public health concern when client has sex with drug users to get money and/or drugs. Client does this at least 4 to 5 times a week.	Client normally has unprotected sex. She does not inform her partners that she is HIV positive.	Practice safe sex. Inform partners she is HIV positive before they engage in sexual activities.
5.	Living outdoors	Staff, society	Client	11/95	Being homeless for 8 years, has negatively affected the client's health. She does not want to live indoors.	Homeless people in Berkeley are exposed to easy access to drugs and being physically abused.	Get client to be housed on a consistent basis.
6.	People do not like me.	Client	Client	11/95	Her prostitution clients abuse her. People on the street take her drugs and money.	Prostitution sets up the client to be a victim.	Discontinue drug use, prostitution, and seek healthy environment. People should be nice to me.
7.	Don't have enough money.	Client	Client	11/95	Don't have enough money to buy food and drugs that I want.	I spend my general relief in a week. No money left for the rest of the month.	County should give me more money.

Source: *J. Neifert (1995), School of Social Welfare, University of California at Berkeley.*

EXHIBIT 10.7
Differences Between Presenting Problems and Desired Outcomes

Presenting Problems	Desired Outcomes
Vague	Specific
Stated in negative terms	Stated in positive terms
Viewed in noninstrumental ways[a]	Instrumental
Seem impossible to alter	Personalized (indicate how client may change situation)
Not measurable	
Not observable	
Do not point to an agenda	Measurable
	Observable
	Suggest an agenda (initial and intermediate steps)

[a]No information is offered about how to achieve valued outcomes.

these terms refer as well as the context in which they occur (what happens right before and after them). You might ask: "What would you do differently if you were not depressed?" The reply might be: "I would go out more, not sit around the house."

DECIDE ON PRIORITIES

Reach a clear mutual agreement about the focus of contact as soon as possible. Otherwise, interviews may drift, and opportunities to help clients may be lost. Agreeing on priorities will involve reviewing the problem profile, finding out the client's priorities, and identifying areas that are interlinked (e.g., a client with a drinking problem who also wants to find a job may first have to stop drinking). Criteria to consider include the following:

1. Annoyance level to significant others and/or clients.

2. Urgency or danger.

3. Interference in the client's life.

4. Ease in attaining the outcome.

5. Likelihood of early progress.

6. Centrality of the concern in a complex of problems.

7. Cost of the intervention (e.g., time, money, energy).

8. Ethical acceptability

9. Likelihood that gains will be maintained.

10. Possible consequences if concern is resolved.

With some clients, a high-priority outcome, such as the need for housing, is clear right away, and you and your client can concentrate on that. Often, there is an overarching goal such as deciding where to live, getting out of a detention facility, or reunifying children with their biological parents who have been removed by the court. This overarching goal provides the focus of your work. Objectives required to achieve it must then be identified. For example, objectives that must be met to return a child in foster care to her biological parents may include increasing positive parenting skills and arranging supervisory care of children. This distinction between goals and objectives is useful in reminding you and your clients that many objectives may have to be attained to reach a goal.

If there are many different problems (or many objectives related to a goal), it may not be possible to pursue all of them at once. Focus on those of greatest concern. Baseline data may reveal that a behavior is less (or more) frequent than a client thought. Considering the importance of a problem in relation to the client's overall functioning will suggest priorities. For example, unless a client stops drinking, he may lose his job. Some behaviors pose a serious threat to clients or significant others. Problems are often interrelated. For example, Brian's concern about his parents' "nagging" was related to his behaviors that annoyed his parents. If there is more than one client, find out about each person's preferences. The following questions will help you and your clients understand the effects of a problem:

- What do problem-related behaviors (or their lack) communicate?

- What would happen if nothing were done?

- What does the problem prevent the client from doing?

Selecting outcomes that are easy to attain has been suggested as a criterion because this will pro-

vide early success. Skills learned in handling easier problems may be of value with more difficult
ones. This criterion must be balanced against annoyance value. Both criteria can be considered by
selecting concerns with the highest annoyance
value and pursuing them in small steps, each of
which has a high probability of being achieved.
Outcomes that are not likely to be achieved should
usually not be chosen. However, at times such outcomes may have to be pursued because of court involvement or the client's wishes. For example, a
child may have been removed from his parents'
custody on grounds of neglect, and one condition
for his return may be his parents' not using drugs.
If the parents want their child back and if more
drug-free days is a court requirement, this objective may have to be pursued, even though there may
be little hope of success.

Some outcomes are likely to occur in the natural course of events and so may not warrant intervention. A parent may complain that her 4-year-
old son wets his bed at night. Many 4-year-old boys
wet their bed at night, and most stop without any
special intervention. This does not mean, however,
that steps should not be taken to decrease bed wet-
ting, especially if the parents respond adversely to
the child because of it.

You may reframe problems as reactions that are
typical in certain situations. A client who has recently lost a spouse may believe that she is abnormal because she cries often: She may not be aware
that crying is typical in the grieving process.
Information about developmental norms and common reactions in given situations will help you decide whether behaviors are typical in certain circumstances and whether they are "time limited."

DECIDE WHETHER SERVICES CAN BE PROVIDED

An overview of problems and desired outcomes
will indicate whether the services you can offer
match those desired. If there is a match, then the
conditions for continuance can be discussed (e.g.,
forming a service agreement). If you do not have
the knowledge or skills required to offer help, do

not have the authority or resources to do so, or have
biases that might get in the way, you may have to
refer the client elsewhere. You will have to assess
your background knowledge in relation to the services needed. Only when you clarify problems and
related contingencies may it be obvious that little
leverage is possible in attaining outcomes clients
value.

Make Referrals as Needed

Brokering (linking clients to needed resources) is
a key helper role. Making effective referrals requires matching the client's interests and characteristics to available resources. Effective referrals
involve gaining an agency's agreement to see a person, encouraging people to keep appointments, and
offering benefits for the client through having the
client receive the service (Miller, Pruger, & Clark,
1979). The following steps will be helpful (see also
Mathews & Fawcett, 1981):

1. Clearly describe desired outcomes.
2. Identify helpful formal and informal resources.
3. Describe relevant resources to the client and
   how they may help.
4. Find out if the client is interested in using the
   resource.
5. If so, assess the client's motivation and capacity to contact the resource.
6. Offer help based on the assessment in item 5.
7. Follow up to find out whether the client did seek
   the services recommended and what happened.

Clients are more likely to keep an appointment
at another agency if it is arranged beforehand. Clear
description of desired outcomes will make it easier to choose useful referrals. If your agency does
not maintain an up-to-date file of resources, develop your own. Include information about services
that each agency offers as well as data about their
track record in helping clients with particular problems. Agencies differ in practice methods preferred, attention to evaluation, and obstacles that
clients confront when seeking services (e.g., long
waiting lists and complex forms). Use your knowl-

edge about obstacles to prepare clients for them, or use other agencies. You may have to accompany a client to an agency and advocate in her behalf (try to convince staff that they are eligible for service). Following up on referrals will let you know how successful your efforts have been and provide information about the need for better linkages with, within, or among agencies.

ENCOURAGE A COLLABORATIVE WORKING RELATIONSHIP

A collaborative framework involves *working with* clients as well as clients working with significant others to achieve outcomes of mutual interest (significant others are people who influence the clients' behavior). In a collaborative relationship, both parties have responsibilities. You and your clients *work together* to achieve desired outcomes. You can encourage this by

- Focusing on goals and objectives valued by clients and significant others.
- Seeking feedback from clients about suggested procedures.
- Supporting clients' assets.
- Responding to clients' suggestions and feedback.
- Agreeing on assignments that will be carried out between meetings both for clients and social workers.

When significant others are involved, encourage the view that they as well as clients will work together to achieve agreed-on outcomes—if this is culturally appropriate (Jacobson & Margolin, 1979). You can do this by seeing clients and significant others together and suggesting assignments that highlight how they influence each other's behavior. If significant others refuse to participate, you may have to work with the client alone (e.g., Thomas, & Ager, 1993). Seeing clients and significant others together offers opportunities to observe how they interact. An excessive focus on forming a collaborative relationship is not appropriate if clients have quite different expectations about what

will occur. Identify hesitations, unrealistic expectations, and fears clients have so that you can address them at an early point (see Chapter 11). Ignoring such reactions may result in lost opportunities to overcome obstacles and waste time setting up agreements that are not really agreements, or clients may "drop out."

Encourage Trust and Rapport

Establishing a collaborative working relationship requires trust and mutual respect. Showing concern for a person's troubles will encourage rapport and trust. Be sure to listen attentively to what is said (see Chapter 12). You don't have to agree with people to understand their perspective. Clients may be hostile, rude, aggressive, or sullen. The more vulnerable they feel, the more negative they may be. Dislike does not preclude empathy. A contextual analysis of a client's life circumstances will help you understand the unique situations that confront each client. There are always two (or more) sides to a story. As Leroy Pelton (1989) notes, parents who abuse their children are often victims themselves—victims of impoverished childhoods, second-class educations, poor health care, chaotic living conditions due to lack of resources, dangerous housing (poor wiring, broken toilets and furnaces), and no cushion of money or social support in times of need. Another way to encourage liking is to keep in mind that family members usually do care about one another (Kinney, Haapala, & Booth, 1991). Their motivation and intentions are usually positive. A review of more than 800 instances of child abuse indicated that 87% were in the context of parents trying to discipline their children (Kadushin & Martin, 1981). The parents' intent was not to abuse their children. Husbands who batter their wives often believe that their actions will improve their relationship.

People who seek or are referred for help may be ambivalent about the time and effort that may be involved. They may worry about whether they will be helped or can trust a stranger, how they will be evaluated, and what they will have to reveal. Involuntary clients such as parents alleged to have abused their children or elderly clients in need of

EXHIBIT 10.8
Helping Clients Feel at Ease

CONSULTANT: Well, I'm glad to see you Mr. and Mrs. Blake. (Parents are offered and take a seat at a comfortable distance from consultant. If parents seem tense or shy, the consultant encourages a little ice-breaking small talk about the weather, about a funny incident at the child's school, or some encouraging developments in the child's education, and possibly offers them coffee or a soft drink.)

PARENTS: (Return greeting and participate in small talk.)

CONSULTANT: (Makes sure to smile at parents as they indicate that they are more at ease; for example, when parents smile at consultant or settle into their chairs.) This is our first meeting. And it may be the first of some valuable meetings to come. I think we can get a lot done together.

CONSULTANT: (Smiles and speaks softly.) It's natural to feel a bit uneasy. I sometimes get butterflies too, when I first meet parents. I don't know how they feel about things. And, you know, some parents have gotten so little help, that they may not have much trust in new people who offer them help. And I don't blame them at all. If I were you, I wouldn't trust me, at least not yet! (Anticipates possible distrust or hostility of parents toward professionals. Remains alert for any movements indicating parents' agreement, such as a smile, nod of the head, or a settling into a more comfortable position, and reinforces such movements by smiling.)

Source: M. A. Kozloff (1979), A program for families of children with learning and behavior problems *(pp. 61–62). New York: Wiley. Reprinted by permission of the publisher.*

protective care may be angry about unwanted intrusions into their privacy that they view as unnecessary. Identifying and focusing on goals clients value will encourage participation. For example, clients may want to prevent their children from being taken away from them or to have children who have been removed to be returned. This does not mean that they will take part in agreed-on ways. This remains to be seen. However, you can increase the likelihood that clients will participate by being a trustworthy, friendly, competent, and empathic (see Exhibit 10.8).

Be Honest

It is important to be honest with clients, for both practical and ethical reasons. For instance, withholding bad news may create more worry. If a medical social worker withholds information, the client may reach even more alarming conclusions about what is wrong. Social workers in public agencies sometimes have hidden agendas—goals that are not shared with clients. A child welfare worker may secretly hope that a parent who has neglected her child will not show up for visits so that a petition for abandonment can be filed. Potential consequences of participation or its lack should be candidly discussed in a supportive manner (see also the later section on service agreements). Any involuntary pressures on clients and their feelings about this should be recognized and ways in which meetings might benefit clients explored. Examples of what you could say are

• "I know you didn't come here of your own free will and that you may be angry about being here."

• "You probably don't feel like seeing me, but . . ."

• "I think there are some ways I can be of help."

If feelings are brought out into the open, you can explore what might be accomplished within the present constraints. You may have to discuss certain topics even if it is uncomfortable for clients.

CLEARLY DESCRIBE PROBLEMS
AND THEIR CONTEXT

Clarifying problems and their context is a key assessment task. Without this, the specific changes needed to attain valued outcomes will remain a mystery. Explain this to clients so they understand your interest in clearly describing outcomes and related factors. You may have to observe behavior in real-life settings to discover behaviors of concern, desired alternatives, and related antecedents and consequences. Only if the *function(s)* of behaviors of concern (their meanings) are understood, can plans be soundly based. Basing plans on a functional analysis is now mandated by law for special education students in California (Positive Behavioral Intervention Regulations, California Department of Education, 1993).

Find out what clients refer to when they use vague terms such as *lack of communication, van-*

dalism, and *assault.* People often have different meanings for the same words. What specific behaviors, thoughts, or feelings occur too often, too seldom, at the wrong time, or in the wrong place? Ask questions that focus on behavior and related events, such as

- Can you give me an example?
- What was going on when this occurred?
- Could you describe the most recent time this happened?
- Are there things he doesn't do that are related to ____?

When you have one example, seek others until you have identified the referents to which a general term refers. If you assume that you and the client share the same referents for vague terms, you will not ask such questions and may be biased by stereotypes. This untested assumption may get in the way of clarifying problems. Use *what, who, when,* and *where* questions rather than *why* questions (see Exhibit 10.9). For example, if your client says he

---

EXHIBIT 10.9
Case Example of a Beginning Interview with a Teacher

CONSULTANT: (1) Jody, what are your general concerns regarding Candy's behavior? (2) In very general terms, tell me about her behavior.

CONSULTEE: She is a very complicated child. She has had quite a difficult background. Mainly, I guess it's her adjustment to her new home, her adjustment to the new class situation, and being able to get along with her peer group.

CONSULTANT: (3) OK.

CONSULTEE: All of these things are based on what has been happening to her in the past.

CONSULTANT: (4) As far as adjustment to her classroom situation is concerned, what are some of the things you are talking about?

CONSULTEE: Her behavior is inappropriate in that she has a hard time staying in her seat. She has a hard time knowing when to speak out and when not to. She does a lot of blurting out of things when she shouldn't. She has been taking things from other children but wants very much to be their friend and to be my friend.

CONSULTANT: (5) The general area then appears to be social, getting along with other children.

(continued)

EXHIBIT 10.9 (*continued*)

CONSULTEE: Right. Rather than academics.

CONSULTANT: (6) Academic behavior is not uppermost in your mind?

CONSULTEE: She does quite well.

CONSULTANT: (7) In the area of social concerns, it would be adjustment to the classroom situation, staying in the seat, speaking at appropriate times, and taking things from others that are the concerns you have about her social behavior.

CONSULTEE: She just doesn't know how to go about getting along with other people. There are a lot of little things that happen that cause her not to be liked by the other children. Yet, they are trying, in part, to overlook things. She doesn't seem to be willing to try to work things out by herself, nor does she seem to understand what is necessary. She just seems to go down her own little path.

CONSULTANT: (8) So that the major goals that you have, or the direction that you would like to move in, is for her to be able to get along better with others and to adjust to the classroom situation better. (9) You see those as two separate areas: adjusting to the classroom and getting along better with others?

CONSULTEE: Separate, yes. But it is important to work on them together.

CONSULTANT: (10) As far as getting along better with others is concerned, what are some of the things you would like her to do?

CONSULTEE: I would like for her to learn to understand others. What are some of the necessary social skills she needs to have? She needs to know when children want to be her friend. She often puts the children in a position where she demands this friendship. When she doesn't get it, she turns kind of vengeful instead of trying to figure out what she is going to do in order to get them to be her friend.

CONSULTANT: (11) All right, she demands friendship, and (12) what exactly does she do in these kinds of situations?

CONSULTEE: When she is wanting to have friends?

CONSULTANT: (13) Yes.

CONSULTEE: She will pull at them physically, handle them in trying to get them away from other children. She often trys to give things to the children and then expects them to turn around and be her friend because she has given something to them. She trys to get up and be by a particular person at a time when she shouldn't be out of her seat. The other child knows that what is going on is wrong and tries to ignore it or tells her to sit down or something. She still stays right there.

CONSULTANT: (14) Then, in getting along with peers, it is to know when she is with friends not to demand their friendship or to get them away from other children or to try to bribe them into being her friend, but to understand the ways in which she can get other children to like her. (15) Is that right?

CONSULTEE: Yes.

CONSULTANT: (16) In the area of adjustment to the classroom, what are some of the skills that you would like her to have?

CONSULTEE: I would like her to stay in her seat when it is the appropriate time to be in her seat. I would like her to listen when I say, "Please go sit down," rather than have to get to the point that I am having to get mad at her. I don't like to get to that point. She won't listen at first. She won't listen a second time and so on. I would like her to raise her hand instead of just blurting out in class. These are the main things she needs to work on, I think.

CONSULTANT: (17) Our two major areas of concern are getting along with other children and adjusting to the classroom situation. (18) Which of these areas would you want to concentrate on?

CONSULTEE: I think working on the classroom behavior. I think that if that can begin to come around, the children would in turn understand and like her better.

CONSULTANT: (19) Under classroom behavior, what do you want to work on first? (20) You mentioned staying in her seat, listening when spoken to, and raising her hand to be called on. (21) Which of those would you like to work on first?

CONSULTEE: I would like to work on the one that I think we could remedy the fastest and easiest so that the other things could come around. So I would say following directions.

CONSULTANT: (22) The situation we would like her to follow directions in is in the classroom. (23) Is there any particular time?

CONSULTEE: During direct teaching time. During the time that they do independent work. I think it would be mostly when it is teacher-directed.

CONSULTANT: (24) So, whenever you are doing direct teaching to the group, you would like her to follow whatever directions you give to the group?

CONSULTEE: No. Wait a minute. I think I want to change that. I would say, actually, that we have the most trouble in between subjects, while we are changing over, when we are changing the activity or something. That is when she has the hardest time.

CONSULTANT: (25) So, whenever you are changing from one activity to another and you give a direction to the class, you would like her to follow the direction immediately. (1) Would you be able in the next few days, until I get back here on Tuesday, to keep track of how many times you give a direction and it is not followed by her? (2) It could simply be just keeping a running tally during these times.

CONSULTEE: Shall I keep track of what the specific direction is?

CONSULTANT: (3) If you can, because there may be one type of direction that she is not following rather than another. (4) The type of direction and whether she follows it would be a simple thing. (5) Record every time you give a direction and whether she follows it so we have a percentage.

CONSULTEE: OK. Sure.

CONSULTANT: (6) Then, our goal is to get her to adjust to the classroom, (7) and our first step is to get her to follow directions. (8) Once we have helped that, we can concentrate on staying in her seat and that sort of thing.

CONSULTEE: I think that is good.

CONSULTANT: (9) Can we get together, then, next Tuesday, look at the data, and go from there?

CONSULTEE: Yes. This same time?

CONSULTANT: (10) Fine. (11) Thanks.

Source: *J. R. Bergan & T. R. Kratchowill (1990),* Behavioral consultation and therapy *(pp. 307–310). New York: Plenum.*

is an alcoholic, find out the referents for this term so that you can understand what this person means. What specific behaviors (or their absence) are referred to? Helpful questions are, What do you drink? How much do you drink? How often do you drink? Where do you drink? The client may not be able to clearly describe behaviors of concern and related circumstances. Terms that refer to emotions, such as *anxiety* and *anger*, must be clarified; each person may refer to somewhat different reactions when using such words. Useful questions include: How do you know when you are anxious? What do you do when you are anxious? You may have to observe clients in real-life settings to identify problem-related behaviors and associated cues and consequences. You could use the coding system developed by John Bergan and Thomas Kratchowill (1990) to review interview content.

Asking people why something occurs presumes that they know the answer. This can be frustrating to clients, since they probably do not know, but since the question was asked, it seems that they should know the answer. Instead, ask "What happens when . . ." or "How do you know that. . . ?" Why questions encourage uninformative motivational accounts. A student may say, "I'm just lazy," or "I'm just shy." Such statements are often offered as explanations for problems. They may be used as excuses not to change. Why questions are useful in discovering a client's point-of-view about the causes of a problem and how they can be resolved. For example, a teacher may believe that a student's "out-of-control" behavior is due to a poor home environment. She may not realize that she reinforces the very behaviors she complains about. You may help her understand the role she plays via your questions.

Descriptions should refer to observable characteristics of behavior or the environment. They should be easy to accurately repeat and paraphrase. Boundary conditions should be clear so that behaviors to be included and excluded can be readily distinguished. Examples of clearly defined behaviors are snacking (eating between meals) and initiating a conversation (a verbal exchange lasting at least 3 minutes), introducing agenda items at a local citizen board meeting, and thanking others for their contributions to team meetings. Examples of vague terms are *aggressive*, *unmanageable*, *sad*, *insecure*, *anxious*, *depressed*, and *overly dependent*. Ask: Would people agree on its occurrence based on this description? If the answer is no, further clarification is necessary. Try to select behaviors that have a definite beginning and end, such as offering opinions at citizen board meetings, following instructions, requesting help when needed, and initiating conversations. Discourage use of vague negative labels such as shy or aggressive. General labels get in the way of discovering specific behaviors and related causes. When possible, obtain a sample of the behaviors of concern and the context in which they occur by observing relevant behaviors in role plays or real-life.

Identify Positive Alternatives and Related Contingencies

Clients often present desired changes in negative terms, such as "being less miserable" or "feeling less nervous." Find out what they would *do* if they were less miserable or less nervous. Possible questions are, How could you know if you were less miserable? What would you do differently? What would you do more often? What would you do less often? Focus on increasing positive alternatives to the behaviors complained about. Relying first on positive intervention programs is now mandated for special education students in the State of California (Positive Behavioral Intervention Regulations, 1993). Understanding the *communicative functions* of problem-related behaviors will help you identify positive alternatives. For example, children's noncompliance and "out-of-control" behavior in class may be maintained by getting rid of unwanted demands (e.g., tasks that are too difficult). Identifying positive alternatives may require observation in real-life settings. Clients often have difficulty describing behaviors they want to see more of, because they focus on behaviors they dislike. So many unpleasant exchanges may have taken place between family members that they become negative scanners of each other's behavior, attending only to disliked reactions. Helpful questions are, What does he do that you like? What would you like him to do? The answer to the first question sometimes is, "Nothing." Most clients need help in identifying specific behaviors to be increased as well as approximations to them. You could ask clients what an ideal friendship or child would be like (when relevant) and then identify specific behaviors related to general terms. You may discover problem-related objectives by asking a client what she would do if he behaved in a way opposite to that complained about. You could ask a child, "What would your teacher do if he liked you?" Be careful not to impose your assumptions on clients.

Some positive alternatives become obvious once disliked behaviors have been noted. Two behaviors may be physically incompatible in that they cannot be performed at the same time: a child cannot sit in his seat and run around the room at the same time. In other instances, competing behaviors may be more difficult to identify. Here, locate those behaviors that are functionally incompatible with undesired reactions. This requires searching for behaviors and circumstances that are not correlated with problematic behavior. Agency staff may no longer complain after implementing a quality assurance program that involves them in its planning. A child may not cry while playing with other children. If so, play could be increased to decrease crying. A woman may not feel depressed when working or talking to friends. These behaviors could be encouraged to decrease depression. When desired behaviors are identified, you can explore how contingencies could be altered to increase them. Examples of positive counterparts of problematic behavior are

- Praising staff (criticizing them).
- Following instructions (not following instructions).
- Talking with roommate for 5 minutes when entering the house after work (not communicating).
- Sharing toys (not keeping toys to self).
- Initiating conversations (avoiding people).

When low-frequency behaviors, such as occasional school vandalism or fire setting, are of concern, identify and reinforce behaviors that are function-

ally incompatible with them. For example, Patterson and Reid guessed that a youth's occasional fire setting was related to low rates of positive reinforcement for desired behaviors at school, at home, and on the playground. Their intervention centered on increasing reinforcement of such behaviors in these contexts (Patterson & Reid, 1970). This is another example of the nonlinear approach often required to address concerns (see also Goldiamond, 1984).

Describe the Context in Which Problems Occur

Clients often overgeneralize. They may not be accustomed to identifying specific *behaviors-in-situations*. They may not realize that behaviors of concern occur only in certain situations. For example, a parent may say that her daughter is always out of control or that she feels angry all the time. Behavior usually varies in accordance with the presence or absence of certain events. A child may wet her bed only at home and never when she visits friends or relatives. Point out that behavior often differs in different situations. No one is always shy or always aggressive. You can review data collected highlighting situational variations. Helpful questions in identifying antecedents and consequences are

- When does this usually occur?
- What's going on when this happens?
- Are there any times when this does not occur?
- Does this happen at certain times of the day more than others?
- What happens right afterward?
- What happens right before?
- Are there some things that make it worse (or better)?

For example, Brian's leaving the house without telling his parents where he was going was usually preceded by what he described as "their nagging." Leaving the house resulted in getting rid of the "nagging" and so was negatively reinforced. Brian's parents positively reinforced many behaviors they complained of and failed to attend to desired behaviors, such as playing ball with the dog, helping his sister with her homework, and offering to help around the house. They did not intend to reinforce these behaviors, however; the effects of our behavior often do not match our intentions.

Focus on behavior and surrounding environmental cues and consequences—what occurs in what situations and how others respond before and after behaviors of concern. Find out what happens in real life. What situations increase the likelihood of behaviors of concern? What situations make them less likely? Questions such as When did this start? may offer clues about environmental changes related to problems. What we do and think influence what we feel, and so it is helpful to identify actions and thoughts along with environmental factors that influence feelings. We can use feelings as clues about who has (or is believed to have) influence over important consequences. Use the information you have gained to complete a contingency analysis chart (see Exhibit 8.5). You can review this in relation to resources at hand (see Chapter 16) to evaluate your options.

Obtain an Overview of Current Life Circumstances and Past History

Find out what the client's life is like in major areas (e.g., work, family, friends, material resources, recreational interests). What is a typical week like? What are housing conditions like? Without an overview of a client's current real-life circumstances, you may overlook factors related to problems, for example, important contingencies that maintain behaviors of interest. Information about the nature of a person's thoughts will indicate the contribution of dysfunctional beliefs and expectations. Knowledge about conditions often related to particular problems and about cultural differences and developmental norms will be useful. Differences in acculturation may be related to family problems.

Past history is pertinent to review when exploring the present leaves questions unanswered or when a review of the past suggests patterns that are helpful to point out. For example, an organization's current problems may be related to its history.

Organizations, like people, have histories. A parent's low self-esteem may be related to a past history of "put-downs" throughout childhood and adolescence. Work history is important to review when employment is a concern. Structured interview schedules have been developed to obtain a "psychosocial history" and to gather information about specific problems. Examples of content reviewed in schedules are demographic data and current living arrangements, educational history, marital history, work history and current financial circumstances, and physical illnesses and current physical symptoms.

Collect Baseline Data When Possible

A *baseline* is a measure of how often a behavior occurs before intervention. This allows comparison of the frequency (or duration, intensity, or latency) of a behavior (or thought, or feeling) before intervention with the frequency after intervention. Information about antecedents and consequences related to behaviors of concern and desired alternatives is often collected at the same time. Baseline data provide valuable information about the severity of problems and their context and a comparative point for you and your clients to track degree of progress. For instance, a second-grade teacher may complain that a student's misbehavior is worse than that of any other students in her class. Observation may indicate that this student's rate of annoying behaviors (talking out of turn, getting out of his seat) is no higher than that of other students. Baseline data may be collected by clients, or they may already be available (e.g., frequency of arrests). The data gathered by Brian and his parents revealed a high frequency of noncompliance by Brian right before and during dinner when the entire family was present. His noncompliance was much lower when only Brian and his parents were at home. For a week, Julie kept track of the times she was free from worrisome thoughts about her decision. Mrs. Landis gave her an index card divided into 1-hour periods for each day. Julie put a check mark in each 1-hour period during which she did not worry. She also wrote down in a small diary what she worried about. Julie's record indicated that she was better able to deal with intrusive thoughts at school than when she was at home with her parents or on weekends. Because behavior often differs in different situations, you should gather baseline data in all problem-relevant situations if possible, if this is needed to understand problems and/or determine baseline levels so that progress can be reviewed.

The skills required for gathering and using baseline data include (1) identifying specific behaviors, thoughts, or feelings; (2) selecting feasible methods to monitor them; and (3) summarizing data. If a behavior occurs only in certain contexts (such as the classroom), collect it only there. With low-frequency behaviors or when it is necessary to intervene immediately, you may rely on a *prebaseline* (an estimate of the current frequency of a behavior). When low-frequency behaviors are of concern, identify related behaviors that occur frequently. For example, stealing a car may only happen once every 6 weeks, but criticism from parents and teachers may occur every day as well as a lack of praise for desired behavior. Praise for desired behaviors can be offered often each day. Explosive anger on the part of an administrator may occur only once a month but situations in which she does not say what she wants may occur several times each workday.

ENCOURAGE HELPFUL VIEWS OF PROBLEMS AND THEIR CAUSES

Find out how clients view concerns and possible solutions. Placing yourself in other people's "shoes" will help you understand their viewpoints. What have clients and significant others tried to resolve problems? Beliefs about problems and their causes are reflected in our attempted solutions. Attempted solutions may create more problems and be an obstacle to change (Watzlawick, Weakland, & Fisch, 1974). If you understand your client's point of view, you will be in a better position to suggest solutions that are compatible with this or to discuss the advantages of other views. (People who insist that you do not understand their perspective—when you do—may mistakenly

equate understanding and agreement.) Understanding a viewpoint does not mean that you agree with it—or that it is accurate. Help clients view problems in instrumental ways that show what can be done to solve them. If a client says: "If only my Uncle George had not drunk himself to death, I wouldn't be miserable today," point out that since there is no way time can be turned back and Uncle George cured of his drinking, this offers no clues about how to resolve current problems.

Coach clients to think in terms of desired outcomes related to problems. Help them discover *personalized objectives* (steps *they* can take to resolve concerns). To identify these, clients may have to understand their own role in relation to the problem. For example, a caregiver of an elderly homebound relative who complains about her "endless talking" may not realize that she supports this behavior by attentively listening to her. This problem can be reframed from the caregiver's view that the elderly woman is to blame, to a view that people influence one another and thus the caregiver can do something to change disliked behaviors (e.g., reinforce desired alternatives). This new view increases her influence over her environment. Avoid pathological labels, and encourage clients to view concerns as *problems-in-living*. This will help reduce any sense of stigma clients may feel. This does not mean problems should be minimized or ignored. It does mean questioning clients' views of themselves as sick or pathological for having problems. Clients may accept society's definition of problems as being one's own fault. They may have little or no awareness that their troubles are related to political, social, and economic ideologies and policies that influence the quality of their neighborhoods and schools and their access to health care and employment.

Clients may agree to participate after they understand how current patterns of behavior work against them. Many people get caught up in the "reinforcement trap." That is, they give in (reinforce) annoying behavior, gaining temporary respite at the cost of increasing the probability of annoying behavior in the future. Overgeneralizations such as "it will never change" or "he's always that way" can be challenged by collecting data showing they are inaccurate. For example, a parent may learn from data she collects that the child she describes as "never minding" does follow some instructions.

Decrease Blame and Negative Labels

Clients may blame themselves or others for their troubles. Blame encourages defensiveness and fear and gets in the way of identifying *personalized goals*, steps that the complainer can take to make positive changes. There are a number of ways to nudge clients toward less negative views of themselves or significant others, including the use of interviewing skills such as paraphrasing and suggesting other views (see Chapter 12). When appropriate, "normalizing" concerns helps clients realize that their complaints are not unusual. You could point out that 5,000 other people have also lost their jobs because of recent business closures in a community, that complaints about lack of communication between adolescents and their parents are common, that fears about having cancer when one has certain symptoms are not unusual.

IDENTIFY SPECIFIC OUTCOMES TO FOCUS ON

After you and your clients have decided on priorities (what to focus on first), you then can identify specific related objectives that describe

- What behaviors are to occur.
- With what frequency, duration, or intensity.
- In what situations.
- When they are to occur.
- Who is to display them.
- Intermediate steps.

Examples of clear objectives are as follows:

- Form a citizens review board in 3 months.
- Identify clear criterion referenced performance standards for staff within 6 months.
- Each weekday after school, spend one-half hour talking about your child's work.
- Return greetings (say hi or hello, look at the person, smile).
- Attend school 4 days a week.
- Within 1 week, sign up for food stamp program.
- Wear an orthodontic device during all waking hours.

Objectives should be achievable, relevant (related to the problems focused on), and measurable. Relevance can be determined by asking, Will meeting these objectives solve this problem? Moving from vague problems to clear relevant objectives usually requires gathering data from a variety of sources.

Clearly describing problems and related factors will help clients move from vague goals that do not offer information about how to attain them, to *specific*, *relevant* objectives (see Exhibit 10.10). A clear description of objectives ensures that you and your clients understand the purpose of your contacts, guides the selection of plans, and allows you to judge whether resources are available (e.g., your skills) to offer needed services. Objectives will often involve changes in the environment, such as altering how significant others respond, gaining needed resources, and creating significant others. Explain the purposes of identifying specific objectives with a minimum of jargon and a maximum of clarity. These include making sure objectives are relevant to problems focused on, selecting effective plans, evaluating progress, avoiding sidetracks, and identifying intermediate steps.

Plan an Agenda

An agenda includes description of baseline levels, intermediate steps, and desired outcomes. Exam-

EXHIBIT 10.10
Examples of Objectives

The Lakeland Family

Changes Mr. and Mrs. Lakeland wanted.

1. Brian would treat the family dog respectfully: pet the dog gently if he touches him, not pick him up by the tail, not kick the dog.
2. Brian would take his medication (three times each day—morning, afternoon, and evening).
3. Tell his parents (or leave a note) where he was going when he left the house and planned to be away for more than 1 hour.
4. Address his mother politely (not call his mother negative names, such as "old bag").
5. Not physically threaten his parents.
6. Get better grades in school (a C+ average), and complete homework assignments on time.
7. Reach agreements with Brian in a positive way. (Each person would have a chance to state his or her wishes, and all would be responsible for suggesting possible solutions, identifying their advantages and disadvantages, and reaching compromises.)
8. Brian would take out the garbage each evening within 1 hour after dinner and cut the grass once a week in the spring, summer, and fall (or shovel snow in winter).

Changes Brian desired:

1. His father would help him collect the money for his paper route once a month.
2. His father would take him fishing once a month.
3. His parents would not "nag" him (they would ask him to do something only once).
4. His brother Bob would help him with his homework twice a week.
5. To solve conflicts with his parents in a positive way (see above).
6. A "special dinner" (something he chose) cooked by his mother once a week.
7. His parents to be "nicer to him" (to say more positive things to him).
8. He would get along better at school (his teachers would not yell at him as much).

Mrs. Ryan and the Greens

Outcomes Mrs. Ryan wanted:

1. Have more contact with other people.
2. Take a 30-minute walk every day.
3. Write six letters a week.
4. Have more family conversations.
5. Do more chores around the house (dust every third day, clean the kitchen counters each day, and vacuum once a week).

Outcomes the Greens wanted:

1. Gain information about the aging process.
2. Have some time to themselves.
3. Gain information about Medicare.

Joint outcomes:

1. Decide where Mrs. Ryan will live.
2. Share their feelings constructively.

Julie

Desired outcomes:
1. Decide whether to have an abortion or to have her baby.
2. Decide whether to involve her parents in this decision.
3. Learn how to avoid future pregnancies.
4. Decide how to handle the situation with her boyfriend.
5. Not worry about this decision all the time.

---

ples of baseline levels and desired outcomes are as follows:

Baseline Levels	Objectives
1. Zero assignments completed per week.	1. All assignments completed each week.
2. Zero initiations of conversations. (A conversation is more than a greeting and at least 1 minute in length.)	2. Four conversations initiated per week.
3. Five temper tantrums per day.	3. Zero tantrums per day.
4. Five criticisms of staff a day.	4. Zero criticism of staff; praise staff three times a day.

The first two examples involve behaviors to be increased. Examples 3 and 4 involve behaviors to be decreased. The goal may be to stabilize a variable behavior or to vary a stable behavior. For instance, a woman may seldom visit places where she can start conversations, so the goal may be to visit such places more regularly. Or she may always use the same remark to initiate conversations, so the goal may be to vary what she says. Another goal may be to maintain a behavior at its current level (e.g., help an elderly client maintain her current frequency of daily social contacts, help an administrator maintain her current level of positive feedback (verbal praise, letters of appreciation) for valued staff behaviors).

You may also have to identify *intermediate behaviors* (behaviors that lie between what the client is now doing (baseline levels), and desired outcomes). Intermediate steps may involve gradually increasing or decreasing the frequency of the same behavior or introducing different behaviors. A task analysis may be required to discover related behaviors (see Chapter 15). The description of initial, intermediate, and desired objectives provides a step-by-step agenda. Each step should be clearly described (require a minimum of interpretation), including specific criteria that will be used to assess performance. For example, if *neatness* is used to assess written records, clearly define what this means. To what does "neat" refer?

Resolving a problem often involves pursuit of many objectives. Let's say a teacher complains that

a 6-year-old is unmanageable. This vague term may refer to behavior surfeits, such as shouting in class or hitting other students, as well as a lack of desired behaviors, such as not completing assignments, not following instructions, and not playing cooperatively with peers. The objectives might be to increase assignments completed on time from zero to all assigned, increase instructions followed from 25 to 80%, and increase time spent in cooperative play with peers during free time from 10 to 60%. A series of intermediate steps may have to be pursued to achieve each objective. It may be necessary to identify levels of correctness and neatness, and to clearly describe desired social behaviors. Even when the objective is to increase a behavior that already exists, this may have to be done gradually. If the aim is to increase homework assignments completed from 1 per week to 15 per week, the intermediate steps might be 2 assignments, 4, 6, and so on. Clear description of approximations to desired outcomes will make it easy to identify and to reinforce these.

Guidelines for Selecting Objectives and Goals

Focus on outcomes that are important to clients and significant others. People won't be interested in pursuing outcomes that do not interest them. Select objectives that involve changing the circumstances related to concerns. This will require distinguishing between *indirect* and *direct* methods. For example, a direct approach to altering eating patterns would be to focus on eating. An indirect approach would focus on the conditions related to problematic eating patterns, such as boredom. Indirect approaches are generally more effective than direct approaches. Consider Jenny, a college student who wanted to lose weight. She had moved to San Francisco 4 months ago, had no friends there, and could not find a job. She ate when she was home alone. Rather than focusing directly on eating, boredom, lack of friends, lack of a job, and negative self-statements were addressed.

Since the most effective way to decrease undesired reactions is to increase desired alternatives, pick objectives that involve increasing desired behaviors, thoughts, or feelings. Focus on the construction of repertoires rather than their elimination. A client may learn to replace worrisome thoughts with task-focused self-statements. Caregivers can be encouraged to focus on and reinforce behaviors they want to see more often.

The *relevance-of-behavior rule* emphasizes selecting behaviors that will continue to be reinforced after services end (Ayllon & Azrin, 1968). Objectives should involve behaviors and situations that are *functionally significant* for clients, that "make a difference" in the client's life. Selecting objectives that result in benefits for clients and significant others in real-life settings requires a clear description of the contexts in which new behaviors will take place and anticipation of possible consequences of new ways of acting. The call for functional significance is legally mandated for some populations. Consider the regulations mandating that educational services be appropriate for the needs of handicapped students. "Behavioral interventions" are designed to give people greater access to a variety of community settings, social contacts, and public events and to ensure individuals' their right to placement in the least restrictive educational environment as outlined in that person's IEP (individual education plan) (Positive Behavioral Intervention Regulations, 1993, p. 2). Materials used are functional if they are a part of nonclassroom (or training) situations or are used by nonhandicapped persons of the same age group as the student in a nonclassroom setting (Reid, Parsons, McCarn, Green, Phillips, & Schepis, 1985). There is an emphasis on chronological age appropriateness, functional utility, and community integration in selecting objectives. Functionality (relevance-of-behavior) is a key characteristic all objectives should share. Studies of attitudes toward handicapped students have found that seeing students engage in integrated, age-appropriate functional activities increases perceived competence (Bates, Morrow, Pancsofar, & Sedlak, 1984). This rule is often violated. For example, staff in residential settings may focus on behaviors that benefit them rather than the residents. Staff may offer unneeded help that erodes independent self-care behaviors because it is easier for them (i.e., residents would take longer to complete tasks themselves).

A Five-Step Approach

Mager (1972) has identified five steps in the process of goal analysis. *Step 1* entails writing down the goal, using whatever words seem reasonable, no matter how vague. *Step 2* involves writing down the things that someone would say or do if they attained the goal. Relevant questions here are, What will I accept as evidence that the goal has been achieved? How would someone know if he saw a person who had achieved the goal? People who represent the goal (e.g., good parents) could be identified and relevant behaviors noted. Be sure to include positives (what a person would do or say) as well as omissions (what she would not do or say). For example, perhaps a good parent would

Positives	Negatives
Take children for required medical checkups.	Do not hit children
Feed children a balanced diet.	Do not leave children unsupervised.
Dress children properly.	Do not allow husband to abuse children.
Keep children clean.	
Provide appropriate play opportunities.	Do not call children names like "stupid."
Use instructions effectively.	

Step 3 involves going back over the list and tidying up. As Mager points out, there are bound to be "a number of fuzzies" (1972, p. 53). There may also be redundancies and items that describe procedures rather than outcomes. Remove items that describe *procedures* (e.g., attend parenting class). The task at this point is to identify *outcomes*, not to describe how to attain these. Other examples of process goals are joining Alcoholic Anonymous, attending a drug treatment program, and seeing a psychotherapist for 6 months. None of these describes the desired outcomes (ways in which a person should be different) after the program. Describe the specific outcomes hoped for as a result of suggested procedures. Cross out duplications, and place terms that are still vague on separate pages for further analysis.

Step 4 involves further clarification. Exactly what is intended for each performance? For example, *effectively* must be clearly defined in the statement "uses instructions effectively." *Step 5* consists of scanning objectives to make sure they are clear. Are all relevant behaviors identified? Could the clients act in ways that would match your description but would not be helpful in attaining desired outcomes? For example, a goal of "attend school more often" could be met by going to school 3 days a week rather than 1. What may be desired is for a student to go to school 5 days a week. If fuzzies are found, performance criteria are not yet complete. Have you clearly described the situations in which behaviors are expected? Have you set a frequency or duration criterion? Scan objectives along ethical dimensions also. Will achieving objectives benefit both the client and significant others? Will there be any negative effects if the outcomes are attained?

The first steps encouraged should be the closest approximations to desired outcomes that are comfortable and achievable. If a "lonely" client wants to meet more people, a first step may be to locate promising places to meet people (i.e., to gain information). The next may be to visit one or two places a week and start one conversation while there. Others might be arranging future meetings and introducing more personal topics (Gambrill & Richey, 1988). Each step should be described in specific terms that require a minimum of interpretation. Progress with initial steps provides guidelines for moving on to more advanced ones.

Selecting Objectives as a Negotiation Process

Deciding on goals and objectives involves a process of negotiation between you and your clients, applicants, or resisters. It is better to select too few than too many outcomes to pursue, so that those of most concern are addressed. Agreement may not be possible because of ethical objections you may have. You may be reluctant to pursue a goal that concerns someone else without that person's involvement. If significant others refuse to participate, you will have to decide whether it is practical and ethical to proceed without their involvement. Let's say a teacher refers a 7-year-old to you because of his "out-of-control behavior" in class. The teacher may expect you to remove this child from class and to work with him individually.

Observation in the classroom may reveal that the teacher provokes out-of-control behaviors and does not reinforce desired behaviors. If you cannot involve this teacher, you will have to decide whether outcomes can be attained without his participation. Perhaps you could persuade the child's parents to offer reinforcement at home for behaviors at school. Or you could help the student learn how to prompt more positive feedback for desired classroom behaviors (see the classic study by Graubard, Rosenberg, & Miller, 1971).

If family members or others differ in what they want or clients cannot decide what they want, the agreed-on goal could be to help them reach a decision (Stein, Gambrill, & Wiltse, 1978; Stuart, 1980). This goal could be pursued when parents and children cannot decide whether they want to live together again or when an elderly client is trying to decide whether to move from her apartment to a sheltered living condition. You might work with community residents to help them to decide on priorities. (See chapter 24.) Exhibit 10.11 provides a checklist for reviewing objectives.

Common Errors

One common error is focusing on outcomes that are the consequences of behavior change rather than on the changes required to achieve these results (Stuart, 1980). For example, improving family life will be a result of changes in the behaviors of family members. Objectives should refer to these behaviors (thoughts or feelings), not to their indirect consequences (e.g., improvement in family life). Vagueness is a common error (pursuing outcomes such as increasing communication, enhancing caregiving, decreasing abuse, providing support). Stating objectives negatively (in terms of not doing something) is another error (e.g., not being rude, not getting upset). It does not indicate exactly what should occur. Whenever possible, describe objectives in positive terms. Identify what could be done more often to achieve desired outcomes (e.g., increase polite requests, remain calm). This allows you and your clients to rely on positive methods to achieve valued outcomes (e.g., positive reinforcement). Focusing on personal characteristics and

EXHIBIT 10.11
Checklist for Reviewing Objectives

	0	1	2	3
____ 1. They are specific (i.e., clearly described).	0	1	2	3
____ 2. They address the clients' concerns (if achieved, they will resolve problems).	0	1	2	3
____ 3. An agreement has been made to pursue them.	0	1	2	3
____ 4. They build on the clients' assets.	0	1	2	3
____ 5. They are personalized (they offer clients and significant others influence in achieving desired outcomes).	0	1	2	3
____ 6. They are attainable.	0	1	2	3
____ 7. They focus on behaviors that will continue to be reinforced after service ends.	0	1	2	3
____ 8. They focus on increasing positive alternatives to unwanted behaviors.	0	1	2	3
____ 9. They offer both immediate and long-term benefits to clients and significant others.	0	1	2	3
____10. Intermediate steps are identified.	0	1	2	3
____11. Progress will be easy to assess.	0	1	2	3
____12. They provide the most effective way to resolve concerns.	0	1	2	3
____13. Achieving objectives will not result in negative consequences for clients, significant others, or society.	0	1	2	3
____14. If achieved, they will prevent future problems.	0	1	2	3

Key: 0 = not at all, 1 = somewhat, 2 = mostly, 3 = completely. Scores may range from 0 to 42.

overlooking environmental factors related to desired outcomes is a common error.

Disregarding the relevance-of-behavior rule is another common error (focusing on objectives that do not really make a difference to clients in real life). Defining the problem to be time spent in an activity rather than identifying specific behaviors or outcomes also is common. Spending more time at a task does not necessarily result in a greater amount of a desired product. If "increasing study time" is accepted as a goal, the client may spend more time "studying" (perhaps sitting with a book in hand), but there may be no improvement in comprehension. Help clients select outcomes that refer to specific behaviors or their products. Avoid process goals (e.g., complete a parenting course), and focus on outcome goals (e.g., give clear instructions to children). Teaching a parent better parenting skills describes how the goal is to be reached, not what is to be achieved. Try to avoid this confusion of means and ends.

SERVICE AGREEMENTS

Service agreements describe the goals and conditions of service. Written agreements encourage helpers and clients to be specific about goals, re-lated objectives, and mutual responsibilities and help prevent hidden agendas—objectives that are not shared. The term *agreement* is preferable to *contract* because the latter implies a legal status that service agreements do not possess. Service agreements contain the following information:

• Overall goal (if relevant).

• Objectives that must be achieved to attain this goal.

• Consequences if objectives are or are not met.

• Responsibilities of participants.

• Time limits.

• Signatures of participants.

Written agreements are especially important when working with involuntary clients in clarifying expectations and responsibilities and possible consequences if they are not fulfilled.

Forming a service agreement involves a negotiation process between you and your clients in which objectives and mutual responsibilities are clarified. Your responsibilities include providing competent services, describing fees (if any) and procedures as well as prospects for success, and identifying protections assured to clients, such as

EXHIBIT 10.12
Service Agreement with W. Family

This agreement is between _____, child welfare worker for _____ County, and Louise and Stewart W., parents of Steven W., who is a dependent of the _____ County Juvenile Court.

Both parents want Steven returned home on a trial basis, and Steven agrees with this goal. _____ agrees to recommend a trial visit if both parents participate in a program to accomplish the following objectives:

1. Increase the frequency with which the children complete household chores (see attached).
2. Decrease Mr. W.'s alcohol consumption to two or fewer drinks per day (see attached).
3. Increase Mrs. W's free time from zero to 2 hours per week.
4. Visit Steven in accord with the attached schedule.

Failure to participate in this program will result in a statement to the court that in the opinion of the worker, a trial visit is not feasible at the present time.

The contract is in effect for ninety (90 days), beginning _____ and ending _____.

Signed:

_____
Stewart W. (father)

_____   _____
Louise W. (mother)   Child Welfare Worker

Source: Adapted from T. J. Stein, E. D. Gambrill, & K. T. Wiltse (1978), Children in foster care: Achieving continuity of care (p. 231). New York: Praeger.

confidentiality. The clients' responsibilities include sharing needed information, carrying out agreed-on assignments, and keeping appointments except when emergencies arise. Specific times to evaluate progress should be described in the agreement as well as the criteria that will be used to measure success. Exhibit 10.12 shows a service agreement drawn up by a social worker and parents who wanted their child returned to their care. A goal is identified as well as objectives and the consequences if these are not attained.

Agreements should focus on goals selected by the clients. Clients will have little interest in working toward aims they do not want and value. (Also, you cannot agree to pursue goals you believe are unethical, such as helping a person become a better shoplifter, or are unattainable, such as securing the release of a prisoner in a week.) Some social workers object to allowing clients to select the overall goal, on the grounds that if the goal were attained, it would be a "bad outcome." Or they may ask, "How do you know the goal can be achieved?" Agreeing on a goal is only a first step. The specific objectives required to meet the goal must be identified and met. Both you and your clients (and perhaps the court) participate in selecting objectives

so that a "bad outcome" should not result if they are met. Identifying a goal gives direction to your work together, but it does not guarantee that it will be reached.

Agreements may be formed at different points during assessment. Agreements written during the early stages of assessment describe expectations relevant to work with all clients and describe the conditions required to gather needed data about others (e.g., home visits). The results of assessment can be included in agreements written after assessment has been completed. Agreements can be amended as needed as additional information is gathered. Specific plans related to each objective can be described in writing in attachments to the main contract. Mutual signing of the agreement highlights that both parties have responsibilities, that these should be clear, and that progress will be reviewed at agreed-on times. Signing the agreement may increase the clients' commitment to participate. If clients are reluctant to do so, explore the reasons for their refusal. If this reflects a reluctance to sign anything, work can proceed as usual. If it stems from a lack of commitment to pursue agreed-on goals, additional discussion may be needed about the basis for your work together.

Be Clear

Vague agreements are unfair to both clients and social workers. Statements such as "use reasonable discipline" or "work cooperatively with parents" are vague. Process objectives such as "participate in counseling" should be accompanied by a clear description of the specific objectives hoped for as a result of participation. What would a client do differently at the end of the class compared with the start? Participation in a program does not necessarily mean that anything has been achieved. Although initial agreements may contain vague descriptions of objectives related to an overall goal (such as deciding where someone will live), as assessment progresses, specific related objectives and plans to achieve them should be clearly described.

Decide on Time Limits

Time limits may be suggested by agency policy, clients, the court, or practice-related literature. Time limits are a key part of managed health care. Separate time limits may be selected for an overall goal (e.g., returning a child from foster care to his biological parents) and for attaining objectives necessary to reach this goal (e.g., locating a two-bedroom apartment in 3 months). A client may be willing to pursue a time-limited goal but not a long-range one. Overextending the length of service may have negative effects by suggesting that problems are greater than people thought. A study of clients seen at Kaiser-Permanente clinics found that short-term treatment was more effective than long-term treatment for 85% of the clients and that long-term treatment produced negative effects for 5 to 6% of clients (Cummings, 1977).

The Pros and Cons of Written Service Agreements

Some writers argue that agreements should be used only between equal partners, which does not apply to social workers and clients, especially involuntary clients. Others (including me) believe that service agreements help protect and inform clients by encouraging clarity of objectives and consequences

depending on whether these are met. This view highlights the importance of clearly describing goals and objectives as well as mutual responsibilities and consequences. Service agreements help identify legitimate areas of exploration and those that are out of bounds. As with any other practice tool, they will not always be appropriate. Using vague service agreements in a routinized, mechanical fashion is a waste of time and provides only an illusion of agreement about focus and methods.

SELECT PROGRESS INDICATORS

Help clients identify relevant, clear progress indicators. If objectives are clear, it will be easier to identify specific, relevant progress indicators. Questions such as "How would you know if we were successful?" are helpful here. Be sure to select measures that are meaningful to clients. This will require involving them in decisions made. Selecting measures that accurately reflect outcomes also is important. Self-report may not be a sound guide. Different people (e.g., children, peers, parents, teachers) perceive change differently and may report change even when there is none (see Patterson, Dishion & Chamberlain, 1993). These authors suggest that different people may be influenced by different biases. Guidelines for evaluation are discussed in Chapter 19.

CULTURALLY SENSITIVE PRACTICE

Differences in race, age, gender, ability, ethnicity, or sexual orientation between you and your clients may require specialized knowledge and skills to ensure that lack of knowledge, biases and stereotypes on your part do not get in the way. In Thailand—a Buddhist nation that encourages children's inhibition, peacefulness, politeness, and deference and discourages aggression—children and adolescents are referred for clinic treatment more often for "overcontrolled syndrome" (fearfulness, sleep problems, and somaticizing) (Weisz, Suwanlert, Chaiyasit, & Walter, 1987). In the United States, where independence, competitiveness, and differentiation from the family are emphasized, children and adolescents are referred more often for "undercontrolled syndrome" (disobedience, fighting, and arguing). An American social worker might inappropriately pathologize a Thai child referred for "overcontrolled behavior." Efforts to reassure clients that you can be of help, even though you are of a different race, culture, age, ethnicity, or sexual orientation, may not always work out well. Time may be needed to establish trust and to encourage clients to discuss personal matters with a stranger. Taking time to get acquainted is especially important when a rapid task focus would be viewed as unpleasant and abrupt. Consider an example given by Lewis and Ho regarding a Native American family:

> The Redthunder family came to the school social worker's attention when teachers reported that both children had frequently been tardy and absent in the past weeks. Since the worker lived near Mr. Redthunder's neighborhood she volunteered to transport the children back and forth to school. Through this process she became acquainted with the entire family, especially with Mrs. Redthunder. The worker sensed that there was much family discomfort and that a tumultuous relationship existed between Mr. and Mrs. Redthunder. Instead of probing into their personal and marital affairs, the worker let Mrs. Redthunder know that she was willing to listen should the woman need someone to talk to. Mrs. Redthunder broke into tears one day and told the worker about her husband's problem of alcoholism and their deteriorating marital relationship. Realizing Mr. Redthunder's position of respect in the family and his resistance to outside interference, the social worker advised Mrs. Redthunder to take her family to visit the minister, a man whom Mr. Redthunder admired. The Littleaxe family, who were mutual friends of the worker and the Redthunder family, agreed to visit the Redthunders more often. Through those frequent but informal family visits, Mr. Redthunder obtained a job. He drank less and spent more time with his family." (1975, p. 381).

There are hundreds of tribes with different values, language, cultural norms, and preferred communication styles. Viewing each client as an individual will make you less likely to stereotype others. If you cannot overcome interfering reactions, refer clients elsewhere if possible. If this is not possible, then it is your responsibility to overcome your personal biases and stereotypes.

Most guidelines recommended for working with different groups are important for all clients. Consider the suggestions by Sue and Sue for working with African American clients. Only the first two pertain to clients of a different ethnicity or race:

- Find out how the client feels about working with someone from a different ethnic group.
- If appropriate, discuss issues related to racial identity and associated personal conflicts.
- Identify client expectations.
- Describe what will occur and find out whether clients believe this process will be useful.
- Describe the limits of confidentiality.
- Explore the history of the problem, the client's views of causes, and outcomes valued.
- Gather information about the family.
- Identify strengths of clients and significant others. What resources are available? What problems have been successfully handled?
- Identify factors related to problems.
- Establish mutually agreed-on goals.
- Discuss how goals will be pursued.
- Discuss the number of sessions required to achieve outcomes and the responsibilities of the helper and client.
- Find out whether the client thinks you can work together. If not, explore other options. (1990, p. 225)

Most guidelines suggested for working with Asian immigrants and refugees also are appropriate for all clients.

- Use restraint when gathering information.
- Prepare clients by engaging in role preparation.
- Focus on problems of concern to clients and help clients decide on their goals.

- Identify material needs (e.g., food, money, and shelter). Provide information on services and help in filling out forms and dealing with agencies.
- Consider intergenerational conflicts. (see Sue & Sue, 1990, pp. 199–200)

Other items listed also pertain to many clients:

- The helper should not ask too many questions because of the norm against sharing private matters with outsiders.
- Take an active and directive role.
- Service should be time limited, focus on resolution of problems, and deal with the present or immediate future.

CRISIS INTERVIEWS

Social workers often provide help in crisis situations (concerns that require immediate attention). Perhaps a family has been evicted and must find housing immediately. A crisis can be defined as a situation that temporarily overwhelms a person's coping skills. Situational crises include natural disasters, assaults, loss of a job, or the sudden death of relative. Maturational crises include life changes such as the birth of a child, divorce, or retirement. A crisis may be accompanied by an openness to change. This possibility underscores the importance of providing timely services. Relieving distress and helping clients recapture previous levels of functioning may require a more directive approach than usual (e.g., recommending some immediate action). Finding out why the crisis occurred (if it is not obvious) and planning how to prevent future ones (if possible) may temporarily take a back seat to pursuing more immediate goals. Providing support and encouraging positive expectations are important tasks.

Child-welfare workers have been criticized for having a crisis mentality—going from crisis to crisis rather than carrying out systematic case planning. To the extent to which problems are inaccurately labeled as a crisis and prevent systematic planning, such a work style is dysfunctional both to clients and to social workers: to clients in that problems may not be resolved; to social workers in that they feel buffeted about by circumstances beyond their control. If something is presented as a crisis, ask, "Is it something that precludes systematic attention to other concerns?" (For a more detailed discussion of working with clients confronting a crisis, see Dixon, 1987; Gilliland & James, 1993; Hoff, 1995).

SUMMARY

Common tasks in beginning work with individuals, families, groups, organizations, and communities include identifying and clarifying problems and related factors, supporting assets, offering support, and deciding whether help can be provided. The interview is a typical setting for initial meetings. If ongoing services are to be offered, or arranged, and monitored, other tasks include reaching a mutual agreement on the focus of contact, gathering information about factors related to desired outcomes, forming helpful views of concerns, selecting outcomes to focus on, and encouraging positive expectations. Special attention should be given to identifying and supporting the clients' strengths. Moving from vague to clear descriptions of outcomes and related factors and from dysfunctional to instrumental views of concerns is usually a gradual process. A written service agreement is helpful in clarifying expectations and responsibilities. Indicators of success are that clients receive needed help, complete agreed-on tasks, and/or seek out and obtain help from referral sources.

REVIEWING YOUR COMPETENCIES

Reviewing What You Know

1. Describe specific steps you can take to increase the client's comfort during interviews.
2. Explain what is meant by role induction and its purpose.
3. Describe the information that should be offered to clients in introductory statements.
4. Explain what is meant by a collaborative set and how it can be encouraged.
5. Describe the advantages of getting an overview of problems/desired outcomes.
6. Give examples of questions that are helpful in clarifying problems.
7. Describe criteria for establishing priorities.
8. Distinguish between goals and objectives, and give examples of each.
9. Describe the characteristics of clear objectives and give examples.
10. Identify common errors in identifying objectives.
11. Identify the "fuzzies" in the following list and items that refer to a process outcome:
    a. Attend parent training program.
    b. Improve housing and financial status.
    c. Develop nurturing skills.
    d. Make child improve behavior.
    e. Visit doctor once a week.
12. Describe important characteristics of written service agreements and their rationale.
13. Explain the purposes of gathering baseline data, and give an example of a baseline.
14. Describe the differences between direct and indirect problem-solving approaches, and give examples.
15. Describe cultural differences that should be considered in the beginning stages of work with clients.
16. Describe common errors that are made in beginning interviews.

Review What You Do

1. You normalize problems as appropriate.
2. You offer effective introductory statements (see Appendix 10A).
3. You involve resisters in useful exchanges.
4. You identify intermediate steps related to valued outcomes.
5. You and your clients select objectives that meet the criteria in Exhibit 10.11.
6. You form a collaborate set with your clients.
7. You attend to cultural differences when deciding how and when to involve significant others.
8. You gather helpful information.
9. You include problem/outcome profiles in your case records.
10. You form written service agreements, when appropriate, that clearly describe objectives and mutual expectations.

11. You can accurately critique written service agreements.
12. You rely on communication styles that are compatible with those of your clients.
13. You encourage instrumental views of problems.
14. You identify relevant, feasible progress indicators.
15. You gather relevant historical information and descriptive data about the client's current life circumstances.
16. You identify specific problem-related outcomes to focus on.
17. You identify both environmental and personal problem-related factors.
18. Your interviews reflect a clear, agreed-on focus.
19. You encourage clients to identify what is going well in their lives.
20. You note and support clients' assets.
21. You collect baseline data when possible.
22. You encourage positive expectations.
23. You can distinguish between vague and clear objectives.
24. A high percentage of your comments and questions during interviews concern behaviors in situations and planning.
25. You can accurately critique a beginning interview.

Reviewing Results

1. Clients receive needed help.
2. Clients keep subsequent appointments.
3. Clients report that meetings were helpful.
4. Useful information is shared.
5. Specific assignments are agreed on.
6. Assignments are completed.
7. Clients seek out and benefit from referral sources.
8. Clients feel more hopeful.

APPENDIX 10A   INITIAL INTERVIEW CHECKLIST

1. *Social Amenities*
   _____ Greet the person.
   _____ See that clients are as comfortable as possible.
   _____ Recognize any difficulties that clients may have had in attending the interview.
   _____ Speak in a friendly and respectful manner; do not be hostile, sarcastic, or condescending.
   _____ Recognize any coercion concerning clients' presence.

2. *Offer Introductory Information Agency's Services*
   _____ Number, frequency, and length of interviews.
   _____ Overview of service framework (e.g., focus on current concerns, involvement of significant others).
   _____ Description of other types of contacts that may be involved (e.g., home visits).
   _____ Fees (if any).
   _____ Purpose of initial meeting.

Responsibilities of Clients

_____ Keep scheduled appointments.

_____ Provide 24-hour notice when an appointment must be canceled.

_____ Paid agreed-on fees (if any).

_____ Collect data concerning progress.

_____ Share difficulties that occur.

Your Responsibilities

_____ Keep scheduled appointments.

_____ Maintain confidentiality.

_____ Arrange for feedback concerning progress.

_____ Clearly describe procedures and the reasons for them.

_____ Offer effective services.

_____ Enhance motivation.

3. *Encourage a Collaborative Relationship*

_____ Include significant others in initial interview.

_____ Emphasize clients' responsibility to participate.

_____ Seek feedback and suggestions from clients.

_____ Check clients' understanding as needed.

_____ Support valuable suggestions by clients and validate their feedback.

_____ Anticipate hesitations.

4. *Get Information (additional interviews will be required to complete some items)*

_____ Draw up a profile of outcomes and concerns for each person.

_____ Establish priorities.

_____ Find out why people sought help at this time.

_____ Find out what would happen if the problem were ignored.

_____ Identify specific behaviors, thoughts, and feelings to be increased, decreased, varied, stabilized, or maintained.

_____ Obtain relevant historical information.

_____ Identify antecedents, consequences, and setting events that influence concerns.

_____ Get an overview of clients' current life.

_____ Determine expectations.

_____ Determine clients' and significant others' views of concerns and solutions.

_____ Identify specific problem-related outcomes.

_____ Find out what efforts have been made to attain desired outcomes and what resulted.

_____ Identify immediate and future consequences of achieving desired outcomes, both for clients and significant others.

_____ Identify personal assets and environmental resources.

_____ Identify potential obstacles and ways to overcome them.

_____ Collect prebaseline information.

_____ Assess motivation.

_____ Identify relevant and practical progress indicators.

5. *Be of Help*

_____ Provide support.

_____ Help clients identify what is going well.

_____ Identify personalized, achievable problem-related outcomes.

_____ Encourage positive expectations.

_____ Offer more helpful views of concerns.

_____ Help clients enhance their problem-solving skills.

_____ Provide needed services.

6. *Arrive at Joint Decisions*

_____ Agree on focus of contact.

_____ Make an explicit verbal or written service agreement.

_____ Select helpful assignments.

_____ Arrange next meeting.

_____ Make appropriate referrals as necessary.

CHAPTER 11

Engaging Clients

OVERVIEW

This chapter describes steps you can take to engage clients in collaborative working relationships. Client participation can be viewed as a set of behaviors, such as completing agreed-on tasks, which like any other behaviors, are influenced by the circumstances in which they occur. A contextual approach requires attending to both personal and environmental factors that influence participation, including the transaction between helpers and clients, the helper's knowledge and skills, and the agency context.

You Will Learn About

- Thinking critically about client participation.
- Factors that influence participation.
- Steps you can take to enhance participation.
- Preparing for interviews as a way to enhance participation.
- Ethical issues.

THINKING CRITICALLY ABOUT CLIENT PARTICIPATION

Lack of participation is not a mystery and it is not something that should be blamed on clients. Rather, it is an occasion to examine what can be done to increase it. Considering obstacles from the client's point of view will help you respond effectively.

Lack of participation is often blamed on clients. Terms such as "compliance" and "resistance" focus attention on the client. In a contextual view the influence of the helper and the match between helpers and clients, as well as agency characteristics, are considered. This view offers many options for increasing participation that respect and involve clients as colleagues. It highlights the importance of recognizing the boundaries between your responsibilities (to do the best that is possible under the circumstances) and the clients' responsibilities (to work toward objectives they say they want to pursue). It also emphasizes the importance of candidly recognizing coercive aspects that surround exchanges between you and your clients. Many clients are not in your office by choice. Either they have been forced to come or are subject to unwanted restrictions you may impose. Examples of the former are parents alleged to have abused their children and elderly clients under conservatorship. An example of the latter is staff who hospitalize a client they view as suicidal against the person's wishes. In either case there is actual or potential coercion that may affect the clients' participation in two main ways. Clients may participate but only because they are goaded into it by avoidance of even more disliked or feared potential consequences. Or they may not participate in hoped-for ways. In either instance, informed consent and respect for clients calls for candid recognition of coercive aspects.

You may jump to the conclusion that nothing can be done because the client is "nonvoluntary." Don't let a label (*nonvoluntary*) get in your way when seeking a solution. As always, it is important to question your assumptions. Faulty assumptions that get in the way of encouraging participation of nonvoluntary clients include beliefs that (1) they will not participate, (2) involving them requires pursuing impractical or unethical goals, or (3) the methods used to engage voluntary clients are not useful. You may mistakenly assume that goals nonvoluntary clients value cannot be found. You may have to restructure the problems to discover shared outcomes. Let's say that a youth is brought, by his parents and against his will, to a community mental health center. You could agree to help him reduce his parents' complaints about his behavior. The objectives involved in "getting social workers off his case" may be the same as those required to attain goals you and/or significant others value (e.g., Stein, Gambrill, & Wiltse, 1978). You often have to be creative to discover promising options. This combined with avoidance of dead ends such as jumping to the conclusion that nothing can be

done because a client is nonvoluntary will increase your chances of involving clients. Consider Mr. Ashly, who complains that because his clients are involuntary, they will not participate (see Exhibit 11.1). Is Mr. Ashly focusing on goals that are important to his client? Mr. Ashly may say (thinking that his supervisor just "isn't with it") that this is the very point, that his clients are nonvoluntary and so agreed-on goals cannot be found. Can you illustrate his faulty assumption using a Venn diagram? (See Appendix 5A). How about Ms. Wan, who complains that her clients will not follow through on seeking needed resources. Here too, there are many possibilities to consider before concluding that nothing can be done: (1) Does the client value the resources? (2) Does she need help in getting to interviews? (3) Does she believe that resources will be helpful? The more challenging the problem is, the more creative you have to be to discover options.

FACTORS THAT INFLUENCE PARTICIPATION

Client participation is a complex topic because it involves many different behaviors and many related factors, including characteristics of the client, your relationship with the client, the nature of the problem, and environmental factors (e.g., the agency, resources available, and reactions of significant others). Change is often difficult. Clients often have to act in new ways in old situations or enter unfamiliar ones. Acting in new ways usually requires effort. Typical experiences, even if painful, are at least familiar and often predictable. The new and unknown may not be. Nonvoluntary clients may be angry and suspicious—with good reason. Many medical patients do not follow the treatments prescribed for them, even when instructions are clear. Many clients forget information provided or do not read materials given to them.

Some factors related to motivation concern client variables, such as ambivalence about change. Others are related to environmental variables, such as anticipated loss of support from significant others (Gottman & Leiblum, 1974) (see Exhibit 11.2).

EXHIBIT 11.1
What Do You Think?

Mr. Ashly works in a child protection unit. All his clients are involuntary. The main reason they consent even to see him is that if they do not, their children will be taken away. He complains to his supervisor that because his clients are involuntary, there is little that he can do to involve them in a helping relationship. What do you think? How would you respond to this complaint if you were Mr. Ashly's supervisor?

Ms. Wan is a social worker attached to a homeless shelter, many of whose residents are alleged to be "mentally disturbed." She works as a case manager for some of the residents. Her job is to try to help them obtain whatever they need to ensure that their basic needs are met and also to provide other resources as available, such as substance abuse treatment programs. At the monthly staff conference, she tells the rest of the staff that there is little she can do for many of the residents, especially those who are mentally ill and do not keep the agreements she makes with them. She gives an example of making an appointment for one of the residents to visit an apartment-finding program. He did not keep it. Furthermore, this was the third appointment that he had not kept. She said that she can do little with mentally ill clients such as this client. She also reports that residents with drug abuse problems do not keep their appointments with drug treatment programs. How would you handle these complaints?

Mrs. Rodriguez, an elementary school teacher who has sought your help about a difficult-to-manage child, did not gather the data that she had agreed to collect over the past week. She tells you that she forgot. What would you do?

Mr. Johnson, a parent alleged to have abused his children, is angry and fearful that the child protective service will take them away. He claims that he has been falsely accused and resents the social worker's intrusion. How can the social worker encourage Mr. Johnson's participation in a collaborative working relationship?

Mrs. Kandice is a an elderly resident living in a single room in an inner-city hotel. Recently she has become more frail. She has difficulty getting up and down the stairs to her third-floor room, and the hotel manager reported that she seems forgetful and appears unkempt. He is worried about her and called the local protective services worker for the elderly. Mr. Jenkins, a social worker at the agency, visits Mrs. Kandice. She denies any need for help. What can be done to encourage her participation?

Ralph works at a day care center for emotionally disturbed adolescents. The staff are having increasing difficulty with an 11-year-old resident. He refuses to follow instructions, swears at the staff, and occasionally becomes violent (hits other residents). He tells Ralph to "get lost" when Ralph approaches him to discuss his behavior. What can Ralph do to encourage his participation?

These categories often overlap. For example, ambivalence about change may be due to anticipated negative reactions from relatives. Personal and social factors are especially influential in the initial stages of helping, whereas efforts to intervene (teach or confront) play an increasingly important role during the middle and later stages of intervention in influencing participation (Patterson & Forgatch, 1985). Categories of noncompliance identified by Patterson and his colleagues include "interrupt," "negative attitude," "confront," "own agenda," and "not tracking" (Patterson & Forgatch, 1985). The

EXHIBIT 11.2
Factors That Discourage Client Participation

Agency Variables

Inefficiency, unfriendly personnel.
Long waiting time.
Lack of resources (transportation, money, time).
Long time between referral and appointment.
Ineffective management practices (e.g., related to staff training and supervision).
Lack of individual appointment times.
Poor reputation of agency.
Inconvenience (e.g., location of clinic, poor transportation).

Helper Characteristics (examples)

Lack of knowledge and skill in understanding problem-related contingencies.
A focus on outcomes clients do not value.
Lack of skill in identifying obstacles to completing agreed-on tasks.
Failure to consider client's point of view about the causes of problems.

Relationship Variables

Negative transference or countertransference effects.
Errors in relating to clients (e.g., pacing, few empathic statements).

Problem-Related Variables

Competing, conflicting, or other pressing demands (poverty, unemployment).
Negative expectations and attitudes of significant others.

Intervention Variables

Overly complex recommendations.
Long duration of intervention.
Intrusiveness (e.g., interferes with other goals).
Expense.
Selection of plans that explicitly conflict with the client's point of view about the cause of problems.
Lack of continuity of care and/or lack of integration of services.

Client Characteristics

Certain diagnoses (e.g., "personality disorder").
Sensory deficits.
Lack of understanding.
Conflicting beliefs about problems and resolutions.
Negative past experiences with other helpers.
Belief that the effort, expense, and side effects outweigh potential benefits.
Embarrassment about seeing a professional helper.
Pessimism or skepticism about the value of recommended methods.
Desire to maintain control over one's life.
Impatience with degree of progress or the helping process.
Sense of fatalism.
Negative experiences that others have reported with suggested methods.
Viewing participation as interfering with values, belief system, future plans, family relationship patterns, social roles, self-concept, emotional equilibrium, or daily life patterns.
History of lack of participation.

Source: Adapted from D. Meichenbaum & D. C. Turk (1987), Facilitating treatment adherence *(pp. 43–44, 51). New York: Plenum.*

client's life circumstances must be considered (see Exhibit 11.3). These include economic and cultural factors, attitudes and behavior of family members as well as the physical environment. The nature of the problem and suggested services influence participation. Following recommended actions is greatest with acute, serious illness and least with chronic conditions. It rapidly decreases as the complexity of

EXHIBIT 11.3
One Drug-Using Mother's Story

Michelle (not her real name) was an AFDC recipient with a seven-year-old child when she found out she was pregnant. She was also a heroin addict. Determined to minimize the harm to her fetus, she contacted every agency she could think of that might be able to help her obtain drug treatment, including health and mental health clinics and the county child welfare agency. She even contacted local media, in the hope that a journalist would have information about drug treatment programs.

In Butte County, California, where Michelle lived, there was not a single treatment program available to her. She did learn, however, that methadone maintenance was the preferred treatment for pregnant heroin addicts. On the street, she heard about a methadone maintenance clinic in Sacramento, the state capitol, 65 to 70 miles away. Methadone maintenance requires daily treatments.

The Sacramento clinic had a two-year waiting list, but because Michelle was pregnant and especially because she was very persistent, she was admitted to the program. She paid the $200 monthly fee from her AFDC grant and drove every day to Sacramento, a 140-mile round trip.

After months of commuting daily, Michelle's car broke down. Still she managed to get to Sacramento nearly every day, begging family and friends to give her rides, paying people to give her rides, and on occasion even hitchhiking. These added costs out of her meager income, however, caused her to fall behind in her payments to the clinic.

Eight and one-half months pregnant, with no dependable way to get to the clinic and no way to pay its fee, Michelle gave up on the Sacramento program. Again she tried to find help closer to home. As part of the methadone treatment she had been getting regular prenatal care and was being seen at home by a student intern public health nurse, who also searched for some form of treatment for Michelle. They both came up empty-handed.

Finally, unable to get any help, Michelle did the responsible thing: she went back to using illegal drugs. This choice was in her baby's best interest, since sudden withdrawal from opiates can be deadly to a fetus.

When her baby was delivered, Michelle immediately told the doctor and other medical personnel about her drug use, so they would be able to provide appropriate treatment to the baby. The following day, Michelle was visited in the hospital by representatives of the district attorney's office and the child welfare agency. Again, she recounted her drug use, her attempts to get treatment, her inability to continue with the methadone program in Sacramento, and her return to drug use. Child Protective Services took the baby away from her.

Shortly before Michelle gave birth, the Butte County District Attorney had announced a new policy of criminally prosecuting any woman who gave birth to a baby who tested positive for drugs. According to the policy as stated by the DA, such women would not be prosecuted, however, if they went into a treatment program. Nevertheless, despite having complete information about Michelle's unsuccessful attempts to obtain treatment locally and her daily trips to Sacramento, the district attorney announced plans to prosecute her for use of a controlled substance. Following a great deal of publicity about the case, he did not pursue the charges.

Michelle's baby is still in the custody of Butte County Child Protective Services, however. Her attorney, Lucy Quacinella of Legal Services of Northern California, told *Youth Law News* that she has spoken with several pregnant women who use drugs and who will not seek prenatal care for fear of prosecution. She knows of one woman who obtained no prenatal care and delivered her baby at home alone due to this fear. She believes it likely that, absent a public statement by the DA that the policy is no longer in effect, there will be others.

Source: M. Henry (1990), *One drug-using mother's story.* Youth Law News, *11, 19.*

intervention increases. Participation increases with age, education, and socioeconomic status (SES), and is higher in white populations. However, these demographic characteristics are often confounded with other factors, such as service use (different patterns of use among different groups).

Encouraging participation requires planning and consistent attention (see Exhibit 11.4). Special arrangements must often be made. What works best depends in part on the helping stage (e.g., before you meet clients, during interviews, between sessions). For example, clarifying expected roles before initial interviews may encourage participation. Being familiar with factors related to lack of participation and skill in avoiding or lessening these should increase your success in involving clients. Exhortation (asking a person to behave in a certain manner or telling him why he should or ought to do so) is notoriously ineffective. Effective persuaders emphasize the benefits of change and prompt and support desired behaviors. They don't assume that people should or will change.

EXHIBIT 11.4
Checklist for Enhancing Participation

_____ 1. Focus on problems/outcomes that are important to clients.
_____ 2. Encourage positive expectations.
_____ 3. Enhance your credibility.
_____ 4. Clarify expectations, including time limits, and clearly describe what will be expected of clients and services offered.
_____ 5. Discourage labeling and blaming.
_____ 6. Develop instrumental views of concern (they offer guidelines for achieving desired outcomes).
_____ 7. Anticipate hesitations, including those related to cultural differences between you and your clients.
_____ 8. Prepare clients for setbacks.
_____ 9. Involve significant others.
_____ 10. Use a step-by-step approach that offers many opportunities for "small wins."
_____ 11. Offer useful assessment and intervention procedures.
_____ 12. Select tasks that result in valued outcomes.
_____ 13. Focus on strengths and build on clients' assets.
_____ 14. Seek commitment.
_____ 15. Develop a supportive relationship.
_____ 16. Tailor your interpersonal style as needed to individual and situational differences, including cultural differences.
_____ 17. Arrange helpful organizational policies and procedures.
_____ 18. Clearly describe procedures suggested and the rationale for them in a framework that makes sense and is acceptable to clients.
_____ 19. Neutralize conflicting advice.
_____ 20. Emphasize the importance of participation.
_____ 21. Empathize with reasons for reluctance to participate.
_____ 22. Form a clear agreement describing specific outcome that will be pursued and mutual responsibilities.
_____ 23. Review outcomes of assignments.
_____ 24. Arrange reminders as needed.
_____ 25. Arrange positive consequences for participation.
_____ 26. Remove or minimize negative consequences.
_____ 27. Don't rush people.
_____ 28. Don't reinforce pessimistic statements.
_____ 29. See also the Checklist for Assignments in Chapter 18.

STEPS YOU CAN TAKE TO ENCOURAGE PARTICIPATION

Participation may be enhanced by (1) educational means (offering information and instructions), (2) behavioral strategies (such as self-monitoring, reminders, reinforcement), and (3) organizational changes (such as flexibility in place and timing of contacts). Clients are more likely to participate in helpful ways if they value the goals focused on, and if services offered are compatible with their view of problems and possible solutions. Participation is related to how successful you are in encouraging clients to believe that methods will be effective. Obstacles to participation should be removed and aids offered that enhance participation (Shelton & Levy, 1981). You may identify obstacles to change by asking clients how they could stop themselves from making progress or what would be the best way to bring on a relapse.

Low participation may be related to anxiety, low motivation, lack of information, and misinformation. Clients may have interfering beliefs and attitudes, be distracted, or lack support from significant others. Life circumstances such as poverty or social isolation may be an obstacle. For example, they may interfere with observation skills and the judgments based on them that are required to track specific behaviors (Wahler & Hann, 1984). Process mistakes such as not involving clients in selecting goals and procedures, not respecting clients, and ignoring cultural differences in values, communication styles, and norms will compromise participation. Steps you can take to encourage participation are discussed in the sections that follow.

FOCUS ON CONCERNS THAT ARE IMPORTANT TO CLIENTS

Focus on outcomes that are of concern to clients whenever feasible, ethical, and legal. Problems of concern to clients are often ignored without good reason. Good reasons are that they cannot be addressed given current resources or pursuing them would be illegal or unethical or would hurt clients or significant others. Poor reasons include agency policies that get in the way, social workers' personal preferences for working on certain kinds of problems, and lack of knowledge about effective service methods. Why should clients participate in plans when the outcomes focused on are of little or no interest to them? Too often, helpers assume that they have the right to say what is and is not important for clients.

ANTICIPATE HESITATIONS

Most clients have hesitations and concerns about working with social workers. Indicators of resistance to change include attacks directed toward you, silence, intellectualizing, flooding you with details, repeated rejections of your suggestions, and yes-buts (see, for example, Block, 1981). Involuntary clients may be actively resistant. Offering information may decrease concerns and help clients become engaged. Anticipating hesitations may increase participation by (1) increasing trust and credibility since you show that you accurately recognize client concerns, (2) encouraging liking because it shows that you care about the client's concerns, (3) addressing objections before they are raised, and (4) increasing options by removing obstacles to certain alternatives. Being prepared for different kinds of objections will help you respond effectively.

Mrs. Ryan and the Greens

Mrs. Slater is a 28-year-old social worker. How will her client Mrs. Ryan (aged 87) react to her? How will Mr. and Mrs. Green, Mrs. Ryan's daughter and son-in-law (in their fifties), react? Won't they expect to meet an older person who is closer to their age? If they have concerns about this, will they express them, and how can Mrs. Slater reassure them? Mrs. Slater decided to address these questions directly by saying, "I wonder if you are concerned about whether I'll be able to understand your situation, since I am younger." They all said yes. Mrs. Slater explained why she felt that she could be of help but also said that she would be happy to refer them to an older worker if they would prefer. The Greens said no, they would like to talk to her. Mrs.

Slater's anticipatory empathy helped her respond effectively to her clients' concerns.

Hesitations About the Likelihood and Course of Change and Who Will Control This

Clients may have doubts about whether change is possible, perhaps because of lack of success with other "helpers." Describe why you think you can be of help and explain how methods you suggest differ from previous ones (see also section on encouraging positive expectations). Let clients know when they can expect to see positive changes if plans are implemented. Practice related research may provide information about this. Encouraging a collaborative relationship and involving clients in decisions will also be valuable here.

Perhaps clients have not resolved problems on their own because they do not know how to break a problem down into parts and design a step-by-step agenda. Point out and illustrate the relationship of intermediate steps (subgoals) to desired outcomes so that clients value them. For example, initiating conversations and arranging brief contacts with new acquaintances are intermediate steps to making friends. Change rarely occurs in a smooth fashion. Prepare clients for plateaus and temporary downward trends. This will increase the likelihood that clients will tell you about them when they occur. They become expected hardships rather than unexpected disappointments. Collect and review data about degree of progress to see if the overall trend is in a positive direction.

Hesitations About Confidentiality and Required Time, Effort, and Costs

Clients have concerns about how much time and effort will be involved, what they will be expected to disclose, what they may have to give up, and who will have access to material shared. Anticipate these concerns in introductory statements. Describe the number and length of meetings, mutual responsibilities, limits on confidentiality, and costs involved (if any). Just because clients don't ask about an issue does not mean that it is not a concern. You may entice a reluctant client to partici-

pate by suggesting a time-limited (e.g., 1-week) commitment.

Hesitations Related to Beliefs About Behavior and Its Causes

Clients may have hesitations about your approach clients have beliefs about behavior (e.g., how and if it can be changed). They may object to positive incentives as bribery or believe that people should not be reinforced for doing "what they should do." They may believe that bad behaviors should be punished, that all people should be treated alike, or that methods you suggest are simpleminded or mechanical. Listen carefully to and empathize with their points of view so that you can respond effectively. This does not mean that you agree with them. Nor does it mean that you should challenge them. Challenging objections is likely to increase resistance. There are more effective ways to encourage consideration of new views and approaches. Some hesitations may have been created by the very professionals from whom no help was received or harm done. You can also anticipate objections by informing clients that certain views do not represent a correct picture of your approach.

Clients may blame significant others for their problems and believe that they themselves have no part in maintaining unpleasant exchanges. In this case, you may have to help clients and significant others understand how they influence each other (how their behaviors are interrelated). You can do this by seeing clients and significant others together and suggesting assignments that demonstrate mutual influences. Helping clients understand that significant others usually have good intentions may discourage negative labels and minimize blame. New ways of acting will often feel unnatural, and clients may complain about this. Anticipate this objection by pointing out that acting differently will not feel natural at first. Emphasize that it is what happens in the long run that counts.

Hesitations About Helper–Client Differences

It may be useful to ask how a client feels about differences from you in regard to ethnicity, sexual orientation, race, age, or gender. Anticipating concerns lets clients off the hook for bringing them up, and will show that you are sensitive to these differences.

UNDERSTAND AND RESPECT DIFFERENCES (TAILORING)

Lack of participation may be related to your lack of knowledge about client values, norms, and preferred communication styles. One of the themes of this book is the importance of avoiding the "client uniformity myth" (the false belief that all clients and their environments are the same). You can do this by focusing on outcomes that clients value and matching procedures to individual preferences and suggesting methods that are compatible with the client's point of view and unique life circumstances. An awareness of class differences and animosities will help you understand negative reactions by poor and working-class clients. Ehrenrich notes: "For working-class people, relations with the middle class are usually a one way dialogue. From above come commands, diagnoses, instructions, judgments, definitions—even, through the media, suggestions as to how to think, feel, spend money, and relax" (1990, p. 139). As a 56-year-old mother of three, diagnosed as suffering from a character disorder, said of her social worker: "God I hate that woman. She makes me feel so stupid. Seems like everything that I do is wrong—the way I am with my kids, with my husband, even my sex life. She knows it all. Personally, I think her ideas are a little screwed up, but I can't tell her that" (Ehrenrich, 1990, pp. 139–140).

FOCUS ON STRENGTHS

A focus on clients' strengths has many advantages:

1. Clients may be more willing to carry out agreed-on tasks, since they will be more hopeful about achieving valued outcomes.
2. Increasing positive behaviors is often the best way to decrease disliked ones.

3. Clients may put their skills to good use.
4. Clients can take credit for success.
5. Clients develop more positive views of significant others.

Focusing on client deficiencies is not helpful. Knowing what to do less of does not necessarily provide information about what to do more of or how to go about doing it. A focus on deficiencies may encourage a client's tendency to attend to negative aspects of himself, his environment, or significant others. Avoid thinking about clients in negative terms (e.g., "he's hostile," "she's unmotivated"). This will help you focus on client strengths.

BE HONEST ABOUT COERCIVE ASPECTS OF THE SITUATION

As discussed at the beginning of this chapter, many contacts between social workers and clients have a coercive aspect. Most social work services are provided in public agencies in which the staff's principal obligation is to carry out state and federal policies (Gummer, 1997). Candid recognition of any coercive aspects of contact is important for both ethical and practical reasons. Pretending that coercive contingencies do not exist, that clients participate out of their "own free will," creates dangers for clients such as not being fully informed and being subject to decisions made for "their own good" that in fact deny people their civil and human rights (e.g., labeling a client schizophrenic and locking him up in a mental hospital rather than giving him a right to stand trial before a jury of his or her peers). Also, reasons for lack of participation may be missed. Honest recognition of coercive contingencies will help you and your clients to discuss options with a clear picture of actual and potential consequences given certain courses of action.

USE EFFECTIVE RELATIONSHIP SKILLS

Your self-presentation is more than a personal matter; it influences how much help you can offer to your clients. Communicating caring, concern, friendliness, warmth, and respect will facilitate participation (see Exhibit 11.5). Relationship behaviors and styles that may limit success are

- Distracting mannerisms or facial expressions.
- Poor attending skills.
- Difficulty following and focusing on the client's statements.
- The use of closed-end questions and an interrogative style.
- Frequent interruptions.
- Noting the surface messages of what clients say rather than their deeper-level messages.
- Relying exclusively on what is said, rather than affect or process.
- Excessive self-disclosure.
- Excessive passivity.
- Difficulty in tolerating silence.
- Appearing cool and aloof.
- Being overly friendly, seductive, or informal.
- Being aggressive or punitive. (See Kottler & Blau, 1989, pp. 80–81.)

If clients trust and like you, they are more likely to participate in effective ways. Active listening, respect for cultural differences, and validation of concerns encourage trust and liking. If staff at other agencies like you, they will be more willing to provide needed resources.

Considerable attention is given to *transference effects* in psychoanalytic practice. These refer to feelings, attitudes, or behaviors the client has toward the helper because of his or her resemblance to someone in the past. It is not surprising that clients may react to similarities between helpers and others in their past and that these reactions may influence their participation. Similarly, helpers may react to clients in certain ways based on their resemblances to people in their past. These are known as *countertransference effects*. They may affect participation by altering the helper's behaviors in positive or negative ways. Not recognizing these influences may result in errors such as mistakenly attributing a lack of progress to environmental ob-

stacles rather than to relationship factors. Kottler and Blau (1989) discuss a number of errors that may result from lack of awareness of countertransference effects, such as prematurely ending helping efforts because of an unrecognized dislike of the client. Thus, either underinvestment or overinvestment in clients may result in less than optimal decisions. Examples of errors described by Herbert Strean in one of his cases that he attributed to his negative attitude toward a client are as follows:

- He lost his objectivity and let himself be pulled into the client's manipulative ploys.
- Because of feelings of threat, jealousy, and competition, he perpetuated a continual power struggle.
- He often made the "correct" interpretation or said the "right" words, but in a tone of voice that was more hostile than empathic.
- He spent much of the time trying to prove to the client that he knew what he was doing.
- Although he was aware his counter-transference feelings were getting in the way, he could not monitor or confront them sufficiently, nor did he seek supervision or therapy to resolve them.
- He retreated behind the mask of cold, objective analyst in order to be punitive rather than adopting a posture of empathy and support. (Cited in Kottler & Blau, 1989, p. 132)

Attentive listening and empathizing with the client's perspective and the difficult situations he or she faces will help you establish a collaborative working relationship. There are many ways to encourage liking even when clients have hard-to-like characteristics. One is to keep in mind that clients are doing the best they can and that there are always two or more sides to every story. Studies of client–helper interaction show that counselors offer support to clients in about 27% of interactions during initial and middle sessions and 34% of exchanges during the last two sessions. Helpers "who do not have the skills to effectively join with and support the client will not succeed as clinicians" (Chamberlain & Baldwin, 1988, p. 155).

EXHIBIT 11.5
The Value of Just Listening

My second assignment after joining Homebuilders was a particularly difficult one for me. The presenting problems centered around 5-year-old Jason, whose mother complained that he was almost impossible to control—setting fires, destroying property, running through the neighborhood in the middle of the night, pillaging the refrigerator, etc. Jason seemed incapable of sitting still or of following a single request his mother would make of him.

But all this was not what made this family a difficult one. To all appearances Jason had been, from the beginning of his life, a neglected and abused child. As an infant, on three different occasions he had been hospitalized as a failure-to-thrive child. There had been at least eight prior CPS referrals that had faulted the parents as neglectful. Jason had been dismissed from a day-care treatment program on the grounds of noncooperation on the part of his mother.

It was difficult for me in this particular case not to cast blame on Jason's parents for these problems. I got little or no response from his mother, who seemed only to complain of Jason's behaviors, but who did not seem willing to try the suggestions I made. (Jason's dad was not living at home and was for the most part only an occasional and equally passive participant in the sessions.) To top things off, during the first week of our intervention, Jason's maternal grandmother entered the hospital for a serious operation, making it even more difficult for the mother to stay focused.

I remember so clearly the day that things shifted. I was feeling more and more frustrated and was going to confront Jason's mother on what I felt to be her lack of cooperation. What I somehow ended up doing instead was just listening to her as she told me something about her own life as a child in her family, how she had been the one in the family who was always called upon to support her mother and sisters when they had problems. As I listened, I felt touched with compassion and realized how superficial my judgments had been. All of us are just doing the very best we can.

Things changed after that—not all at once and not dramatically. I talked more with Jason's mother about her own life goals and took her one day to the local community college where she was interested in studying—of all things!—early childhood education. Jason ended up in excellent day-care and school programs. His behaviors began to fall more into the normal range. A number of months later I visited Jason's school to see another client and met Jason's teacher. She told me that he was not only doing well, but was showing signs of real leadership in the class. I also learned that Jason's parents were close to getting back together. As Jason's mother wrote in the evaluation: "Jim was very supportive. He brought us back together so that we're very close."

The lesson for me is that we really cannot judge anyone, no matter how bad the evidence looks. (Jim Poggi)

Source: J. Kinney, D. Haapala, & C. Booth (1991), Keeping families together: The Homebuilders Model *(pp. 85–86). New York: Aldine de Gruyter.*

Encouraging Quiet Clients to Talk

The client's silence may reflect underlying feelings of anger, anxiety, or confusion. Use silence as a cue to try to discover concerns clients may have.

Steps you can take to encourage quiet clients to talk include the following:

- Offer active listening (e.g., reflections, paraphrases).

- Seek out concerns clients may have.
- Avoid making critical comments.
- Respect cultural differences.
- Ask clients for suggestions.
- Reinforce clients for participating.
- Don't rush clients; respect their pace.
- Pick settings for meetings that encourage clients' involvement.
- Watch for small signals that clients want to say something and invite their comments.
- Encourage clients to share their reservations.

What is useful in encouraging clients to talk depends on why they are silent. They may say little because they don't want to see you, are not interested in goals you focus on, or don't believe that change is possible. Cultural differences should also be considered. Anticipating reluctance to share certain information and giving clients a choice about when to share this may be useful. You may say, "You might be hesitant to tell me certain details about yourself. If I were in your shoes, I might feel the same way. Don't tell me anything until you're ready." This changes the issue from whether a client will do something (share information) to when to do so. Offering a choice between alternatives is similar. A staff member at a residential center could ask a child which shower, bathroom, or color of towel he would like, rather than asking him whether he is ready to take a bath. Be alert for clues that clients would like to say something, and invite them to contribute. Encourage clients to express their reservations. If you don't know what they are, you won't be able to "fine-tune" your answers.

Calming Clients

You can use active listening skills to calm clients. Homebuilders has a rule: when in doubt, listen (Kinney, Haapala, & Booth, 1991, p. 68). Following this rule will help you avoid trying to "fix things" and take control. Just listening helps clients feel understood and respected. Active listening skills may decrease threats clients may feel and increase your influence by creating a positive working relationship.

Holding the Clients' Attention

Clients' attention may drift if they cannot follow or are not interested in what you are saying or if you talk too long. Clients may lose interest because of a monotone manner of speaking or "tune out" because of excessive affect on your part that alarms or offends them. When their attention flags, ask yourself the following:

- Is my language and speaking style compatible with my clients'? Can they understand what I am saying? Have I avoided "turn-offs" (e.g., excessive jargon or patronizing comments)?
- Is my pace too fast or too slow?
- Do we have a clear agreement on an overall service goal the client values?
- Have I avoided making critical comments?
- Do I offer a credible image (do clients believe I can help them)?
- Have I encouraged positive expectations?
- Have I encouraged a collaborative working relationship in which we share responsibility?
- Do I seek clients' feedback (invite them to respond to what I say)?

Using the Telephone

You may spend a great deal of time on the telephone (calling clients, making referrals, and returning calls). You can make this less of a burden and increase the likelihood of attaining your goals by scheduling time for these calls and preparing for them. Before you telephone, identify your goals and plan how to pursue them.

- What do I want? What is my goal?
- How can I increase the likelihood of achieving it?
- What obstacles might arise? What can I do to prevent or handle them?
- What can I do to make the call pleasant for myself and the other person?
- What reminders would be helpful?

Reminders might include

- Introduce myself.
- Describe what I want.
- Don't talk too fast.
- Wait for an answer to questions.
- Don't talk too long.
- Be positive.
- Be polite.
- Ignore hostile, curt, negative responses.
- Keep focused on my goal.
- Use active listening skills to calm people and to help others feel understood and validated.

ENCOURAGE POSITIVE EXPECTATIONS

Positive expectations are an important motivating factor (Goldstein, 1962). Research shows that they account for a substantial proportion of positive outcomes (e.g., Frank & Frank, 1991; Skrabenek & McCormick, 1992; Sloane, Staples, Cristol, Yorkston, & Whipple, 1975). This is the main element in the *placebo effect* (a favorable effect as a result of the act of treatment rather than the treatment itself) (Jarvis, 1990). Encourage positive expectations by providing estimates of success based on research findings (being honest about what is known and not known). You cannot guarantee success, but based on practice-related research you can indicate how likely it is if certain changes are made. Fulfilling the requirements for informed consent requires sharing problem-related information with clients. Competence in sharing relevant scientific research findings with clients in understandable language is a valuable skill. Beginning helpers are sometimes diffident and timid when they should be firm and confident. If you offer suggestions hesitantly, your clients may not be interested in trying them. As with all general guidelines, there are exceptions, however. Tentative descriptions may be more effective when clients are sensitive to the appearance of "being told what to do" and when your goal is to have clients make suggestions by prompts such as "Could it be that. . . ?" "Do you think that . . . might work?"

Highlight methods associated with success. For example, when describing a parenting program, prospective clients were told that successful parents required their children to earn rewards (no freebies), were satisfied with small changes leading to big ones, cooperated and worked together as a team, took scheduled breaks, and reinforced themselves as progress was made (among other things) (Kozloff, 1979, p. 159). Encourage questions and comments about what you have shared, and support optimistic statements as well as efforts to generalize new information. In offering guidelines to helpers who use parent training programs, Kozloff cautions

> Do not reinforce pessimistic statements! Get parents thinking and talking in a positive, prescriptive way. For instance, if parents indicate that they do not think that they have the skill, again stress that they are probably no different from other parents, either in their abilities or in their feelings; that other parents soon found out just how competent they could become.
>
> If parents assert that their child is somehow different from the children seen on the tapes or films (implying that the methods might not work with their children), ask them to be specific. Then, explain that no two children are alike! It is not that one "type" of child can learn whereas another "type" cannot, because the principles of learning and of good teaching are the same. Rather, the details of the teaching programs might be different for each child. In sum, using the videotapes, films, or descriptions, do your best to help the parents believe that they may well do the same thing with their children that the other parents have done (again, cautious optimism). (1979, p. 159)

Discourage negative talk about suggested methods by supporting positive expectations and enhancing your credibility. This does not mean that you should not use your active listening skills to understand and validate your clients' concerns. Rather, if you have done your best to accomplish such ends and negative talk persists, try other options. Emphasize the differences between what has been done in the past and your approach. To do this, you will need information about what clients have tried and what resulted (see Exhibit 11.6). Clients may believe that change is unlikely because they have failed in the past. They may feel hopeless and helpless. They may be in a "defeat

EXHIBIT 11.6
Setting the Stage for a New Way of Approaching a Problem

PARENT: Jane used to scratch her hands a lot.

CONSULTANT: Umm hmm. What did you do about it?

PARENT: Well, we were taking her to see Dr. Blither. He told us just to ignore it, that Jane was scratching her hands to get attention. And we did, for weeks!! But she kept it up—no more, no less than before. (Parent looks disgusted.)

CONSULTANT: Did Dr. Blither ever see Jane at home? (Consultant subtly indicates that she may question Dr. Blither's advice, because Blither was not around to conduct a behavioral analysis.)

PARENT: No.

CONSULTANT: Well, you see, attention is only one reason why Jane might have been scratching her hands. (Indicates an alternative to Blither's analysis and advice.)

PARENT: Oh?

CONSULTANT: Well, she might have scratched her hands because she had an allergy. Or, she might have been turned on or reinforced by the feelings in her hands when she scratched them. You see, before you decide what to do to handle a problem, you have to analyze the behavior and the situation—and that means that you have to examine the child, sometimes medically, and observe the child's behavior before you can really tell why the child seems to be doing the behavior. (Consultant points out that she might have offered different advice.)

PARENT: I see. And besides, she scratched her hands even when she was by herself. We never really did think that she did it just for attention.

CONSULTANT: That's good observation! (Reinforces parents.) And what about her scratching now?

PARENT: She still does it. (Gives consultant a chance to offer her own suggestion.)

CONSULTANT: See, there are several reasons why she might be scratching her hands. Allergy, attention, self-stimulation. In fact, they all may be true at the same time. So, we have to check out the possibilities and try to eliminate the ones that do not apply. It might be a good idea to have an allergist see her. If she does not have an allergy, then we can observe Jane's behavior more carefully to see what else might be causing her scratching. And, you know, even if attention has something to do with her scratching, ignoring it does not teach her other, proper ways to get attention. In addition to not rewarding or reinforcing her scratching with attention, we have to teach her alternative ways to get attention. (Presents main features of a problem-solving strategy and points out importance of teaching alternative behaviors.)

Source: M. A. Kozloff (1979), A program for families of children with learning and behavior problems *(pp. 68–69). New York: Wiley.*

state" from repeatedly submitting to others, for example, battered women (Gilbert, 1989). Only gradually, by "small wins" may hope increase. Successful assignments will encourage the belief that change is possible. Clients may overlook modest gains that show that they can have some influence over their lives. Help them identify positive changes that have occurred (see Chapter 19). When working with fatalistic clients in crisis, you may have to take major responsibility at first for identifying helpful goals and pursuing them.

ENHANCE CREDIBILITY

The more credible you appear, the more likely it is that clients will listen to what you say and participate in helpful ways. Credibility is influenced by (1) degree of expertness as indicated, for example, by professional credentials and type of agency); (2) reliability as an information source (e.g., dependability, predictability, and consistency), (3) motives and intentions—the clearer it is to clients that it is their interests toward which you are working, the greater your credibility; and (4) your dynamism—apparent confidence, forcefulness, and activity level (Goldstein, 1980, p. 31). Your credibility will be influenced by the success of your suggestions. If they decrease client distress, your credibility will improve. If they do not, it may diminish. Your suggestions are more likely to be successful if they are consistent with your client's point of views. Your similarity to clients in age, gender, ethnicity, or some other key characteristic may increase your credibility. Clients who differ in ethnicity, race, gender, age, physical abilities, or sexual orientation may have doubts about whether you can understand them and be of help. You can anticipate questions by bringing them up yourself. Helpful rules for handling challenges include

- Don't be defensive.
- Acknowledge and anticipate clients' concerns.
- Don't downplay differences.
- Describe how you can be of help despite such differences.
- Relax and listen; try to understand the client's point of view.

ENCOURAGE HELPFUL VIEWS

Help clients define problems in a way that gives them influence over their lives and a feeling of hope. The goal is to arrive at a view that points to steps clients can take to improve the quality of their lives. Clients may not accurately estimate how much influence they can have over what happens to them. They may be "stuck" in attempted solutions that maintain or worsen rather than lessen problems. They may blame significant others for problems. They may blame society. Clients may believe that they should be in complete control of what happens to them and feel guilty because they are not. Their usual attributional style (e.g., blaming others) and problem-solving approach may conflict with a view that highlights their options and responsibilities for influencing their environments. The question is, Does a particular point of view offer guidelines for attaining desired outcomes? That is, is it instrumental?

Clients with an internal locus of control (they believe that what happens to them is largely a result of their own actions) are more likely to participate than are clients who have an external locus of control (they believe that they have little or no control over what happens to them). For example, hemodialysis patients with an internal locus of control show a higher rate of adherence to dietary and medication restrictions than do patients with an external locus of control (Wenerowicz, Riskind, & Jenkins, 1978). The view that we have little or no control over what happens to us decreases our efforts to change disliked conditions, increases our anxiety, and decreases our self-esteem. Involving clients in making decisions promotes a sense of choice and freedom and increases the likelihood of collaborative efforts.

You can foster shared views by the questions you ask, interpretations you give, assessment methods you use (e.g., gathering data describing the patterns of interaction between clients and significant others), rationales you offer, and homework assignments you suggest. When you discuss data clients collect, use questions and interpretations that encourage more helpful views and highlight relationships between problem-related behaviors and their consequences. Be sure to personalize discussions by using examples from the client's own life (Jacobson & Margolin, 1979). If you find yourself saying "most people . . ." or "They say that

. . . ," you are probably not making points uniquely relevant to your clients. Emphasize positive motivations. For example, you could point out to an "overprotective mother" that it is natural for her to be concerned about her children. You can select interventions that allow this mother to continue to see herself in the role of a "good parent." Family members usually care about one another. Their behavior is usually well intended even if their actions have negative effects on significant others.

DISCOURAGE NEGATIVE LABELS AND MINIMIZE BLAME

Encouraging helpful views will often require minimizing blame and discouraging negative labels such as *drunkard*, *personality disorder*, *hostile*, and *unmotivated*. Negative labels that have no intervention guidelines and that encourage negative expectations get in the way of seeing the potential for change. They may increase hopelessness on the part of both clients and social workers, whether directed by social workers toward clients or by clients toward themselves or significant others. Negative labels do not have to be terms from the *DSM-IV* (1994) such as *personality disorder*. They can be labels such as *unmotivated* or *hostile* that you apply to clients. Graduate training often emphasizes reliance on diagnostic categories. Labels are commonly used in everyday life (e.g., "He's stupid," "I'm lazy"). Labels have an either/or quality that interferes with discovering unique patterns of behavior and related circumstances and initial steps that can be taken to attain desired outcomes. The disadvantages of labeling are described in Exhibit 11.7 (see also the discussion of labeling in Chapter 9).

BE HELPFUL

A guiding question should be, How can this meeting have some immediate payoff for this client? What concrete services can I provide? What steps can I take to reduce distress? Help clients identify specific problem-related objectives and a step-by-step agenda for pursuing them. Select plans that are efficient and effective as well as acceptable to clients. This often requires specialized knowledge of different methods that have been used to attain given outcomes. Consider cultural and developmental issues that may influence success.

ARRANGE HELPFUL ORGANIZATIONAL POLICIES AND PROCEDURES

Attitudes toward clients are shown not only by how helpers act during interviews but also by characteristics of the agency in which services are offered (see Exhibit 11.2). Organizational barriers may prevent clients from seeking services and compromise the participation of those who do. Long waiting times are associated with poor compliance and a high dropout rate (Haynes, Taylor, & Sackett, 1979). The show rates for clients given a next-day appointment were better than those for clients in a 2-week wait group (Benjamin-Bauman, Reiss, & Baily, 1984). Agency policy regarding appointment reminders affect participation (Dunbar, Marshall, & Hovell, 1979). Phone or mail reminders increase the number of appointments kept (Turner & Vernon, 1976). Attractiveness of decor, degree of privacy for interviews, and flexibility in scheduling meeting times and places indicate how the agency views its clients. The typical helping relationship may not be appropriate for many clients and/or problems, and a different format may have to be arranged. Examples are peer tutoring (parents may be trained to help other parents) and self-help groups. Participatory, community-based programs may be the best choice rather than one-on-one counseling or family-focused change. Inadequate links among or within services, such as vague referrals with no follow-up, may discourage participation. Seek changes in agency policies and procedures that would encourage participation (see Exhibit 11.8).

OTHER STEPS

Arrange reminders and incentives that increase participation. Without special prompts and incentives, clients may forget to carry out agreed-on tasks. You

EXHIBIT 11.7
Disadvantages of Negative Labels

Labels such as "unmotivated" or "resistant" define clients as adversaries with bad intentions and little common sense or desire to overcome their problems. Labels can position us to demean clients, disagree with them, and pressure them to do things "for their own good" rather than because the courses of action we recommend make sense to them. Labeling makes it harder for us to be warm and supportive, if we're thinking about coping with the negative traits we've assigned to our clients. Instead of calling clients "resistant" or "unmotivated," it's more helpful to describe them as worried about failing again, feeling hopeless, feeling helpless, lacking the skills necessary to begin thinking about the problems, or unable, at the moment, to formulate goals that seem worthwhile and obtainable.

... Once we begin to think of a client as "antagonistic" or "vindictive," we are likely to believe it, and to feel some pressure to justify our initial impressions, hindering us from being open to the whole picture and to more positive interpretations. It will be more helpful to redefine "vindictive" as "focusing on past hurts," and "antagonistic" as "afraid of being disappointed again."

Other labels such as "sociopathic," or "psychotic," can also have a tremendous impact on the client–counselor relationship. Not only do clients not like having these labels, the labels also scare us and make us think the situation is hopeless—much more hopeless than if we stuck to the specifics such as "Jerry took his grandmothers' medicine and flushed it down the toilet," or "Sometimes when Susie talks, her sentences don't make sense," or "Theron sometimes hits Judy when they fight." When clients are labeled by referring workers, it is particularly easy for us to look at the referral sheet and say, "Oh, no, a chronic psychopath, nobody can work with those!" rather than remembering that the label resulted from some specific things the client did that are not half as scary as the label might imply.

Labels can also harm our goal of helping clients feel hopeful because they imply an all or nothingness about problems. If someone *is* something, like pathological, or if they *have* something, like low ego strength, the implication is that that is the way they are, and that is the way they always will be. They have a condition. We think it's more helpful to define problems in terms of things that people do or do not do. . . . It is possible to set small goals of changing only one or a few behaviors at a time. The goals begin to seem possible. There is hope.

Source: J. Kinney, D. Haapala, & C. Booth (1991), Keeping families together: The Homebuilders Model *(pp. 84–85). New York: Aldine de Gruyter.*

may have to reframe concerns and proposed solutions to engage clients (Watzlawick, Weakland, & Fisch, 1974) (e.g., encourage perspectives that are consistent with effective methods). Enlist the support of significant others. If they understand the rationale for programs and the steps required for success and if the outcomes also will benefit them, they are more likely to work with rather than against clients.

Agreed-on tasks are more likely to be carried out if clients give their verbal and/or written commitment to do so (Levy, 1977). You should actively seek such a commitment. Forming a written service agreement and clarifying expectations may enhance participation. Be sure to review the outcomes of assignments. This will increase the likelihood that future ones will be completed. Meichenbaum and Turk (1987) recommend repeating everything as well as persistence (i.e., trying again). Lack of participation may result from rushing clients, from not respecting their pace. You may suggest a slower pace. You may have to cycle back to initial steps (see also Shelton & Levy, 1981).

EXHIBIT 11.8
Practice Example

Describe one way in which your agency's policies or procedures could be changed to encourage client participation. Clearly describe this and suggest specific changes based on a contextual assessment.

    1. What is the current practice or policy?

    _____

    _____

    _____

    2. How does it affect client participation?

    _____

    _____

    _____

    3. How should it be altered?

    _____

    _____

    _____

    4. What specific changes are possible now?

    _____

    _____

    _____

    5. What changes are possible in the future?

    _____

    _____

    _____

    6. What are intermediate steps (e.g., staff discussion)?

    _____

    _____

    _____

PREPARING FOR INTERVIEWS AS A WAY TO ENHANCE PARTICIPATION

Client participation can be enhanced by preparing for interviews. Being informed about problems of concern to clients and their life circumstances and history shows them that you care enough to be prepared. Even though you have not seen a client before and have no information about this person's problems and life circumstances, there are ways you can prepare (see Exhibit 11.9). You can arrange a place to meet that is convenient for the client and that will facilitate your exchange, empathize with the client no matter what the problem (to get his or her side of the story), and be familiar with resources that may be of value. Preparing for meetings is a

EXHIBIT 11.9
Checklist for Preparing for Meetings

_____ Prepare a tentative agenda.
_____ Review relevant information (if available).
_____ Arrange a facilitating context.
_____ If you have information about the nature of a client's problems and have little or no knowledge about them, complete necessary reading about these problems including valuable assessment, intervention, and evaluation options before seeing the client.

_____ Have useful forms available.
_____ If you have knowledge beforehand about what may be needed, gather information about resources for possible referrals as relevant.
_____ Review tasks agreed on in the previous meeting (if any).
_____ Engage in anticipatory empathy.

EXHIBIT 11.10
Case Examples of Reviewing and Updating Background Knowledge

THE LAKELANDS

Mr. Colvine had never worked with children with epilepsy, nor did he know anything about it. So when he learned over the phone that Brian had epilepsy, he decided to read about it before seeing the Lakelands. In the small agency library, he found a book describing the physical and psychological effects of epilepsy (as far as they are known), and the possible side effects of the various drugs used to control epilepsy. He learned that the recommended dosage levels varied for the same symptoms. This would be important to know, since Brian complained about the effects of the currently prescribed dosage.

MRS. RYAN AND THE GREENS

Mrs. Slater had little experience in working with what she called "old people" and did not know anyone over the age of 70. Her parents died when they were young, and she had never known her grandparents. She felt an immediate sympathy for the problems the Greens said they were having with Mrs. Ryan, their elderly relative. Her first reaction was to help the Greens locate another living arrangement for Mrs. Ryan. Clearly, she had a bias against "old people." However, she also had a rule to question her beliefs. What was known about people over 80 who lived with family members?

Mrs. Slater looked through a recent book on gerontology and found that there is wide variation in competencies, happiness, and health in old age. Many older people live with family members and get along well, although this is not to say there are no problems. Caring for an elderly relative can be a strain as well as a source of satisfaction. Mrs. Slater found that significant others often had inaccurate beliefs about their aging relatives and often acted in accord with those beliefs. For example, the differences of opinion expressed by older relatives that were considered as signs of lively interest 20 years earlier may now be viewed as stubbornness and combativeness—even senility. Mrs. Slater found that as people get older, they often have negative feelings about still being alive (since many of their friends have died) and feel guilty about being a burden to their families. Consulting the professional literature before her first interview thus helped Mrs. Slater correct her biases and appreciate environmental influences. She would have to consider the entire family situation. She could not focus solely on Mrs. Ryan in order to understand this problem.

sign of respect for clients. Excessive time pressures may make it impossible to be prepared. However, it's important not to lose sight of what is best.

Review Helpful Information

If you do have information about a client, review it before your meetings so you can be prepared with resources and anticipate obstacles. Records may contain information about the client's age, family composition, employment history, and prior experiences with other agencies. Reviewing available information will help you anticipate clients' concerns, offer clues about how to tailor your language to match your clients', and suggest cultural and value differences and the effect they may have. Be careful not to pick up negative views of clients. Records often center on what is wrong with clients, with little content on client assets. If you know what the problem is, you can collect information about helpful resources and decide what information to get in the interview. Be prepared by being up-to-date about available services, including information about potential obstacles. Familiarity with the neighborhoods and communities in which clients live often offer valuable information about problem-related conditions such as poorly maintained housing.

If you have advance information about the nature of a client's concerns and have little or no related knowledge in these areas, consult the professional literature before the interview. This may indicate related norms, helpful assessment methods, associated factors, and service options and their likely success (see Exhibit 11.10). Reviewing related literature will help you spot and counter biases and challenge inaccurate assumptions about problems and how they can be resolved. Professionals have an ethical obligation to be knowledgeable about the problems they address—about what is known and what is not. The greater the gap is between your personal knowledge and what is known—that can be of benefit to clients—the more ethically questionable it is to work with them.

Anticipatory Empathy

Anticipatory empathy refers to trying to understand another person's point of view and experiences (placing yourself in another's shoes) (Kadushin, 1990; Shulman, 1984) (see Exhibit 11.11). This will help correct stereotypes that get in the way of accurately observing people. It may be useful to recall what you thought and felt in situations similar to those of your client. However, be careful not to assume that your experiences mirror those of others. They may be quite different. Let clients tell their own story, to relate their experience as they see it. Anticipatory empathy is especially important with clients who may have committed acts such as severe child abuse. Recognizing that each person has his or her own point of view of a situation and realizing the importance of understanding that view will help you avoid messages of disapproval (Perlman, 1979).

Anticipatory empathy will help you notice subtle clues to concerns clients may have and understand reactions that may appear puzzling. For example, Julie worried that she would be asked about her sexual behavior. She decided that if Mrs. Landis brought up this topic, she would say, "I think I'll work this out on my own." Hostile statements may mask feelings of vulnerability, embarrassment, or fear. Concerns and expectations clients may have are discussed in Chapter 2. Keep this in mind when preparing to meet people. Questions that encourage anticipatory empathy are

1. What might it be like to be in this person's situation?
2. Do I have any stereotypes about this person or his or her circumstances? Am I viewing him or her as a "type" rather than as a unique human being? You can test this by completing sentences as illustrated in chapter 21 and 39.
3. Have I had a similar experience? What did I feel and think? Have I known anyone else who has? What did she think and feel?
4. How might my experience differ from her experience?
5. How should I modify my language?
6. What concerns might this person have about me?
7. What concerns might he have about coming to this agency?

EXHIBIT 11.11
Examples of Anticipatory Empathy

Julie's social worker once thought that she was pregnant at a time when she did not wish to be. She remembered the panic she felt, the feeling that things were out of control, the uncertainty about where to turn for help, the feeling that there was no good solution. Recalling her own past helped her understand Julie's concerns.

Ms. Landis knew that she tended to use big words that clients might not understand. So she reminded herself before her interview to use words that would be familiar to Julie and that would help Julie understand her. She knew that clients may not ask what a word meant even when they did not understand her. She recognized that many pregnant unmarried teenagers worried that their parents would be told about their pregnancy. (Laws about whether parental consent must be obtained before a minor may have an abortion varies from state to state. It was not a requirement in the state where Julie lived.) Ms. Landis reminded herself to describe agency rules about confidentiality: that nothing would be said to her parents without her permission and that she would not be pressured to tell her parents.

---

8. What cultural, ethnic, racial, age, sexual orientation, religious, or class differences are important here?

Arrange a Facilitating Context

Exchanges are influenced by the context in which they occur. Perhaps you work in a large public agency in which there is little privacy, high noise levels, and frequent interruptions. Try to minimize the interruptions. Involve other interested colleagues in changing dysfunctional policies, procedures, or physical arrangements. The agency is not necessarily the best place for interviews. The client's home, a playground, or a school may be a better setting. If clients are distracted by competing activities (a teacher may be trying to maintain control of her class), they may not get involved in a discussion. Taking a walk or meeting in a public place such as a fast-food restaurant may provide a better atmosphere for a talk than an office does. Try to allow sufficient time for each interview so that you and your clients don't feel rushed. If possible, allow some time between interviews to reflect on your exchange, to make required or helpful notes, and to prepare for the next interview.

Decide on a Tentative Agenda

Planning what you can accomplish during an interview will help you focus on important points and avoid drift. Agendas will differ depending on the helping phase. Some tasks, such as describing the reasons for your suggestions, are common to all meetings. Others are unique to particular phases or kinds of interviews. Agendas should be tentative and open to change as necessary. For families with many problems, crises that require attention may arise weekly (see also the discussion of structuring in Chapter 12). If pressed for time, scale down your agenda. Have helpful forms readily available.

Arrange Helpful Prompts

If you tend to forget important items, prepare a prompt list as a reminder. You could note points you want to discuss or helping behaviors you tend to forget. For instance, you may forget to "empathize" with resisters or to seek input from everyone when interviewing a family. You could jot down a word or phrase to remind yourself to do so. You could include reminders of how to handle difficult situations. For example, you may become exasperated with "Yes, but . . ." responses. A prompt will remind you to use this reaction as a cue to try to understand the function (meaning) of the "Yes, buts. . . ." You could review the checklist in Appendix 10A prior to interviews. Fade out prompts when you no longer need them.

ETHICAL ISSUES

Many of the practice skills described in this chapter are an integral part of ethical practice, such as fully informing clients of any coercive contingencies, supporting client strengths, involving clients in selecting outcomes and plans, and respecting cultural differences. You are less likely to blame clients (or yourself) unfairly for a lack of participation if you identify related environmental factors. A key ethical issue related to preparing is not having the knowledge and skills required to help clients (e.g., a gap between personal and available knowledge). Ensuring informed consent requires honestly describing what is known and not known about the effectiveness of different methods and why you think suggested methods will be useful.

Should You Use Social Psychological Persuasion Strategies?

Knowledge about social psychological persuasion strategies is useful in both resisting unwanted influences and persuading others to participate in helpful ways (see Cialdini, 1993). These strategies work through emotional associations and appeals rather than through a thoughtful consideration of arguments for and against a position (Petty & Cacioppo, 1986). Persuasion by affect comes into play when we are influenced by how attractive a person is or how confidently they present their views.

Is it ethical for helpers to use social psychological persuasion strategies with either clients or other professionals who may serve as gatekeepers to needed services? Consider the *scarcity principle*. This rests on the fact that opportunities seem more valuable when they are limited. A client may be more eager to participate in a program that is available for only a limited time. Scarcity may be a reality. If so, there is no ethical problem with noting it. However, as with other persuasion strategies, it can be used dishonestly. For example, a nursing home intake worker may tell a caller, "If you don't decide now, space may not be available" (when this is not true).

We are also influenced by the *contrast effect*, which also may be a reality. Immediately providing concrete help to a client who has not received help elsewhere may be a contrast to past experiences and so may encourage participation. Helpers also are influenced by contrast effects. After an interview with a "resistive" person, you may regard a client as very cooperative who is actually only fairly cooperative (Salovey & Turk, 1988).

The *reciprocity rule* lies behind the success of the "rejection-then-retreat technique," in which a small request follows a large one. The small request is viewed as a "concession" and may be reciprocated by a concession from the other person. For example, when college students were asked to chaperon a group of juvenile delinquents on a day trip to the zoo, 83% refused. When this was first preceded by a bigger request (to spend 2 hours a week for 2 years as a counselor to a delinquent), three times as many students agreed (Cialdini, 1984, pp. 50–51). (The contrast effect is also at work here.) Obtaining an initial concession or offering a favor may encourage participation through the reciprocity rule, because we feel obligated to return favors. The *principle of liking* is a frequently used persuasion strategy. We like to please people we know and like (i.e., to comply with their requests). Physical attractiveness, similarity, compliments, familiarity, and cooperation encourage liking. The good guy/bad guy routine takes advantage of the liking rule. We like the good guy (in contrast to the bad guy), so comply with what he wants. Persuasion strategies based on liking and authority are effective partly because of affective associations.

Another persuasion strategy is based on *the desire to be (and appear) consistent* with what we have already done. Obtaining a commitment puts the consistency rule into effect. "Commitment strategies are . . . intended to get us to take some action or make some statement that will trap us into later compliance through consistency pressures" (Cialdini, 1984, p. 75). Someone may say You already agreed to give me _____. How about _____? (which is similar). Or you may ask a person to come for "just one interview," hoping that if he does, he will attend other meetings.

The *principle of social proof* involves being influenced by what other people think is correct (consensus). Describing other clients who have overcome problems may create hope and a willingness to try suggested methods. Relying on testimonials and case examples to encourage clients to use suggested services is ethically questionable if it in-

creases the likelihood that they will rely on such weak grounds when making other life-affecting decisions (see Chapter 4). Both uncertainty and similarity heighten persuasion effects. We are more likely to go along with what other people do in ambiguous situations and when we observe others who are similar to ourselves.

The principles on which social psychological persuasion strategies are based provide convenient shortcuts that often work for us (Cialdini, 1984). But if we accept them "automatically," they can work against our best interests and the best interests of clients, and other people can exploit them for their own purposes.

SUMMARY

A contextual view requires attention to both personal and environmental factors that influence participation. Many clients are nonvoluntary and have concerns about what will be involved and what consequences will result. Clients' lack of participation may be related to agency characteristics such as inhospitable waiting rooms and long waiting times. Vague instructions and mismatches between client skills and expectations may also be responsible. Encouraging participation requires planning and effective use of practice knowledge and skills, including respecting cultural differences, focusing on clients' concerns, offering concrete help, building on clients' assets, and encouraging positive expectations. Enhancing your credibility and involving clients in making decisions make it more likely that they will participate. You can encourage participation by helping clients replace interfering beliefs and attitudes with instrumental ones, by seeking commitment, and by clarifying expectations. Arrange agency policies and procedures that maximize participation. Other steps include anticipating hesitations, individually tailoring methods to cultural differences, and preparing for meetings.

REVIEWING YOUR COMPETENCIES

Reviewing What You Know

1. Describe methods you can use to increase client participation.
2. Describe how you can increase your credibility.
3. Discuss different kinds of attributions and their relationship to participation.
4. Describe how you can encourage helpful views of problems.
5. Describe methods you can use to encourage positive expectations.
6. Discuss hesitations that clients may have about participating and how they can be addressed.
7. Describe what you can do to prepare for interviews.
8. Identify agency policies or practices that influence participation.

9. Describe relationship factors that influence participation.
10. Define the placebo effect, and give examples.
11. Discuss ethical questions about relying on testimonials and case examples to encourage client participation.
12. You can accurately identify social-psychological persuasion strategies.

Reviewing What You Do

1. Your questions and statements in interviews demonstrate advance preparation.
2. You anticipate client hesitations.
3. You clearly describe expectations.
4. You focus on client concerns.
5. You identify and support client strengths.
6. You take appropriate steps to enhance participation, as demonstrated in interviews and role plays.
7. You consider client preferences in arranging meeting times and places.
8. You can accurately describe policies and procedures in your agency that affect participation in both helpful and unhelpful ways.
9. You can carry out a contingency analysis of an agency policy or procedure that interferes with client participation and make specific recommendations for change based on this.

Reviewing Results

1. Clients share relevant information.
2. Clients accept more helpful views of problems and possible solutions.
3. Clients express hope that concerns can be resolved.
4. Clients report that interviews are helpful.
5. Clients complete agreed-on assignments.
6. Clients return.
7. Clients' knowledge and skills increase.
8. There are no physical assaults on social workers.
9. Positive expectations are encouraged.
10. Blaming statements and negative labels become less frequent.
11. Problems are resolved.

PART
IV
RELATIONSHIP SKILLS

CHAPTER 12

Interpersonal Helping Skills

OVERVIEW

This chapter describes relationship skills of value, including empathy, structuring, attentive listening, showing respect, and confronting clients. Many skills useful in everyday life will also be of value with clients, such as offering positive feedback. The term *exchange* or *meeting* is used to highlight the variety of encounters involved (e.g., with clients, significant others, and colleagues). One way to use this chapter is to select one or two skills to work on through guided practice opportunities arranged by your instructors. When reviewing the checklists in this chapter keep in mind that you may have to change some items depending on your goals and cultural differences in communication styles.

You Will Learn About

- Helping as a social influence process.
- Empathy as a key relationship skill.
- Warmth and genuineness.
- Asking helpful questions.
- Structuring interviews.
- Attentive listening.
- Encouraging helpful views and behaviors.
- Respect.
- Self-disclosures.
- Concreteness.
- Offering support and reassurance.
- Uses of humor.

- Other important social competencies.
- Improving your skills.
- Components of effective social behavior.

HELPING AS A SOCIAL INFLUENCE PROCESS

Whether we intend to or not, our actions influence how others perceive and react toward us. As the saying goes: "You cannot not communicate." The quality of your communication skills will influence client options. For example, you may obtain needed resources from another agency because you have been empathic, persuasive, and polite when talking to their staff. Exhibit 12.1 gives examples of useful relationship skills. Effective relationship skills will add to your confidence and comfort in exchanges, even difficult ones. There is a rich literature you can draw on to enhance your understanding of social behavior and to hone your relationship skills (see the references in this chapter). Knowledge about cultural differences in interactional styles may be needed to respond effectively (see Exhibit 12.2).

Effective relationship skills increase the likelihood of establishing rapport with clients, gaining their participation, and avoiding dropout (see, for example, Patterson & Forgatch, 1985). Quality of

EXHIBIT 12.1
Reviewing Your Relationship Skills

	Would Like to Work On	Fairly competent	Very competent
_____ 1. Observe and translate social signals.	_____	_____	_____
_____ 2. Recognize attitudes and feelings.	_____	_____	_____
_____ 3. Speak clearly and at an effective pace.	_____	_____	_____
_____ 4. Select appropriate social goals.	_____	_____	_____
_____ 5. Plan how to achieve specific goals.	_____	_____	_____
_____ 6. Offer an effective self-presentation.	_____	_____	_____
_____ 7. Communicate different attitudes and emotions.	_____	_____	_____
_____ 8. Use nonverbal signals consistent with your intent.	_____	_____	_____
_____ 9. Convey a friendly attitude.	_____	_____	_____
_____ 10. Ask helpful questions.	_____	_____	_____
_____ 11. Listen.	_____	_____	_____
_____ 12. Structure exchanges.	_____	_____	_____
_____ 13. Be concrete.	_____	_____	_____
_____ 14. Offer empathic responses.	_____	_____	_____
_____ 15. Offer greetings.	_____	_____	_____
_____ 16. Provide constructive feedback.	_____	_____	_____
_____ 17. Normalize concerns.	_____	_____	_____
_____ 18. Prompt, model, and reinforce helpful behaviors.	_____	_____	_____
_____ 19. Discourage unhelpful behavior.	_____	_____	_____
_____ 20. Offer encouragement.	_____	_____	_____
_____ 21. Avoid distracting revelations.	_____	_____	_____
_____ 22. Share personal information when appropriate.	_____	_____	_____
_____ 23. End exchanges in a timely and polite way.	_____	_____	_____
_____ 24. Offer compliments/express appreciation.	_____	_____	_____
_____ 25. Accept compliments.	_____	_____	_____
_____ 26. Express liking and affection without offending others.	_____	_____	_____
_____ 27. Be nonevaluative.	_____	_____	_____
_____ 28. Convey respect.	_____	_____	_____
_____ 29. Make amends (e.g., apologizing).	_____	_____	_____

EXHIBIT 12.2
Interviewing a Papago Native American

Papagos treat age and social status with a great deal of respect. And respect within the Papago culture is often expressed by silence.

Avoiding eye contact can also be of considerable importance when dealing with Papagos in any social setting, and this includes psychotherapy. Establishing and maintaining eye contact are considered to be impolite among these desert people and may be interpreted as anger.

On the desert reservation, time is treated much differently than what urban dwellers are accustomed to. Papagos may be an hour late for a meeting and think nothing of it. This, we will discover, has a considerable influence on therapy.

These several factors then are of central importance when doing therapy with the Papagos. They include the importance of the mental health technicians, the influence of the medicine man, personal secrecy, a lack of verbosity, respect for age and social status, avoidance of eye contact, and an informal orientation to time. How these variables influence the approach to therapy is considered next.

As a group, the variables just mentioned dictate that therapy done with Papagos would involve, for the most part, at least one indigenous mental health technician and that the therapy would nearly always be of a crisis intervention nature. The need for the mental health technician is obvious. Perhaps the reliance on a crisis intervention approach has reasons which aren't so obvious. First, although a medicine man often needs only one treatment session to effect a cure, this one treatment session could last several hours. The therapist must remain flexible regarding his own time orientation. Rigid adherence to the 50-minute session is simply of no value. As one graduate student extern recently pointed out when discussing marital therapy, the therapist should be willing to spend 2–4 hours with a couple and realize that this may be the only session there will be with them.

Not only does the variable of time orientation affect what will happen in one session, it also influences the execution of other sessions. That is, the client may be several hours late and the therapist must remain flexible and try to accommodate the client whenever possible.

The fact that the Papago client has had little to do when receiving other treatments (medicine man and physician) certainly affects what will happen in therapy. Quite often the Papago will present his problems (briefly) and ask "What is wrong with me?" and "What should I do?" A Rogerian reflection or question in return from the therapist may have little meaning. The therapist must be prepared to be directive—to make suggestions.

Confrontation in the therapeutic sense could be considered taboo with the Papago client. Socially, the Papago will religiously avoid confrontation. This is simply a matter of social courtesy. The therapist who confronts a Papago client in a manner that causes intense anxiety will lose the client.

Interviewing the Papago client has some unique features. The Anglo who attempts to establish direct eye contact with his client will make therapeutic rapport almost impossible. Similarly, an aggressive therapist with a loud voice will intimidate and perhaps anger the Papago client. The pace or tempo of the interview is also affected. That is, a longer period of time is needed to establish trust and rapport with the client. More time must be spent getting acquainted

(continued)

EXHIBIT 12.2 (*continued*)

with the Papago client. Questions of a personal nature should be delayed. An opening question of "What brings you here?" could stimulate anxiety and defensiveness on the part of the client.

Because of language problems, interpretations and suggestions must be made crystal clear. A client may seem to understand but not understand at all. The pretended understanding and acquiescence [*sic*] are a result of trying to show respect and social timidity.

Source: D. Lum (1992), Social work practice and people of color: A process-stage approach *(p. 128). Pacific Grove, CA: Brooks/Cole.*

the helper–client relationship was one of three qualities that Luborski and his colleagues (1985) found that distinguished more helpful from less helpful service providers. Others were (1) the helpers' adjustment, skill, and interest in helping clients and (2) the fidelity of intervention offered. Relationship enhancers such as empathy, warmth, and credibility increase liking, respect, and trust, which in turn increase openness and communication (Goldstein, 1980; see also Lambert & Bergin, 1994). Strupp contends that all forms of helping involve a relationship "characterized by respect, interest, understanding, tact, maturity, . . . a firm belief in [one's] ability to help," influence through suggestions, encouragement of open communication, self-scrutiny, honesty, interpretations of material that people are not aware of (such as self-defeating strategies in interpersonal relations), offering examples of "maturity," and "capacity and willingness to profit from the experience" (1976, p. 97). Skills identified as contributing to relationship building and helpfulness include the following (see for example Shulman, 1994):

- Sharing personal thoughts and feelings.
- Understanding clients' feelings.
- Supporting clients in taboo areas.
- Encouraging feedback concerning purpose.
- Putting clients' feelings into words.
- Partializing concerns.
- Providing data.
- Clarifying roles.
- Displaying feelings openly.
- Supporting strengths dealing with authority.

- Assessing people accurately (attending to and accurately interpreting social signals).
- Using effective verbal and nonverbal communication skills.
- Discovering how to satisfy shared interests.
- Adjusting your behavior to that of others.
- Revealing the right kinds of information.
- Making appropriate demands.

Personal barriers to communication include a lack of respect for others and a lack of relationship skills and knowledge of when to use them. Countertransference effects may result in being underprotective of clients or assuming too much responsibility for their lives (Kottler & Blau, 1989; Strupp & Hadley, 1985). The possible influences of transference and countertransference effects are discussed in Chapter 11. Examples of environmental barriers are a feeling of being rushed, high noise levels, and interruptions.

EMPATHY

Empathic responses are those that communicate that you understand what others say or experience. In *primary-level accurate empathy*, you try to let clients know that you understand what they explicitly expressed. In *advanced accurate empathy*, you comment on what clients have implied and left unstated as well as what they have expressed openly. Both *reflections of feelings* ("You feel like everyone is against you") and *paraphrases of content* (e.g., "You're not sure what to say to him") may be used to communicate to clients that you understand them. Reflections can be used for other purposes as well, including encouraging clients to talk more about their feelings, to increase awareness of feelings, and to check your understanding (Cormier & Cormier, 1991). Paraphrasing can also be used for other purposes, including guiding clients to focus on content and checking understanding.

Empathy and warmth are facilitating conditions that create a context in which other important elements of effective service are offered, such as clarifying goals and designing action programs. Empathy is positively associated with outcome (see for example Burns & Nolen-Hoeksema, 1992). Studies finding that nonprofessionals are often as helpful as professionals highlight the importance of empathy and other "nonspecific" relationship factors (Dawes, 1994a). Carl Rogers (1957) viewed the therapeutic relationship as necessary and sufficient for achieving positive outcomes and considered empathy, warmth, and genuineness to be the key ingredients of this relationship.

The goals of empathy are helping clients (1) identify their feelings associated with their experiences, (2) share relevant material, and (3) feel accepted and understood (Shulman, 1984). Empathic responses let clients know that you are listening and understand what they have said. Because you go beyond what has been explicitly stated in advanced accurate empathy, be sure to make statements tentatively. Statements intended to be empathic that confuse, frighten, or anger clients are not successful. If you put yourself "in the other person's shoes"—if you can understand the client's feelings and experiences—you are more likely to accurately observe and translate social signals (such as smiles or frowns). Empathy training has been suggested as a way to decrease errors due to biases and stereotypes (Arnoult & Anderson, 1988; see also Gladstein & Associates, 1987).

Related Behaviors

Many behaviors involved in offering accurate empathy are discussed later in this chapter. For example, if you are not a good listener, you cannot offer empathic statements. Low quality listening will give clients the impression that you are not interested in or cannot help them. Nonverbal behaviors such as eye contact, trunk lean (forward or backward), body orientation (toward or away from a person), and distance from a person account for more than twice as many judgments of empathy as verbal behaviors do (Haase & Tepper, 1972).

Common Errors

You may say nothing when you should offer an empathic comment. You may respond to content rather than to feelings and content. Reflections, paraphrases, or interpretations may distort rather than correspond to a client's feelings, beliefs, or experiences. You may offer solutions prematurely. Avoid statements like "I know what you are feeling," since you may be wrong and clients will think that you don't know what you are talking about or view you as patronizing. Examples of how to show that you appreciate someone else's experience are: "I think I'd feel the same way in your situation"; "This must be very difficult." Other errors include labeling and diagnosing (e.g., you have a dependent personality), judging and evaluating (you were really aggressive). Avoid moralizing and preaching, as in "You should respect your parents," and patronizing reactions like "You'll get over it."

Other errors are (1) telling people what they should feel (e.g., "That's not the way to feel when you see her"), (2) an interrogative interview style, (3) overinterpretation, (4) self-disclosure that distracts attention from service goals, and (5) encouragement of dependence by offering excessive help ("Call me if you ever want to talk"). Examples of physicians' poor attempts at empathy when they must deliver bad news to patients are as follows:

> One 72-year-old woman with breast cancer confided to her consultant surgeon that she did not want to lose her breast, only to be told: "At your age, what do you need a breast for?" A woman of 40 with the same disease asked a different hospital consultant if there was any way she could avoid a mastectomy. He said: "There is not much there worth keeping, is there?"

An elderly man with terminal lung cancer was asked by a junior hospital doctor why he was crying, and [he] explained that he did not want to die. The house officer's unsympathetic response was: "Well, we all have to die some time." (Collins, 1988, p. A7)

Being excessively self-preoccupied will limit empathy for others. Another way to fail to be empathic is by not giving clients the same choices you yourself would like to have (e.g., of methods that achieve what they promise and being fully informed about possible options).

WARMTH AND GENUINENESS (CONGRUENCE)

Warmth refers to the extent to which you communicate nonevaluative caring and positive regard for clients (Lambert, DeJulio, & Stein, 1978). Many of the behaviors discussed in this chapter, such as attentive listening, positive feedback, and respect, contribute to warmth. *Genuineness* can be defined as the extent to which helpers are not defensive, real, and not phony in their exchanges (Lambert, DeJulio, & Stein, 1978, p. 468). *Phoniness* refers to saying one thing and doing another. Like any other skill, being genuine involves offering some actions and avoiding others. Not hiding behind a professional role to protect yourself or to fool people or to substitute for helping clients is one aspect of genuineness discussed by Egan (1994). An example of hiding behind a professional role is saying, "I'll decide whether or not we are making progress at the proper time" in response to a question about progress. *Spontaneity* involves weighing what is said only as necessary and otherwise drawing on skills in a flexible way.

Nondefensiveness refers to responding in a non-hostile, nonaggressive, exploring fashion when confronted with disagreement or negative information about yourself; an openness to listening to criticism in which negative comments are viewed as an opportunity to explore what you can learn and/or how a service goal can be achieved (see Chapter 13 for guidelines on responding to criticism). *Consistency* means matching words, feelings, and actions.

Other aspects of genuineness include *self-disclosure*, *confrontation*, and *immediacy*. The purpose of immediacy is to help clients understand themselves better by discussing some aspect of the immediate exchange. For example, perhaps a client often interrupts you. You could point this out, discuss the effects of such behavior, and suggest alternatives. As with any other skill, effective use is demonstrated both by engaging in it when it would be helpful and by not engaging in it when it would not.

ASKING HELPFUL QUESTIONS

The questions you ask, the information you offer, and the behaviors you reinforce influence the focus of interviews. Your questions direct attention to areas that you think are important. In this sense, they indicate what you think is relevant. Questions typically progress from the general, to the specific, to feelings. Functions of questions include expressing interest, encouraging participation, arousing interest, obtaining information (e.g., clarifying problems and related circumstances), holding the client's attention, and encouraging new perspectives (Cormier & Cormier, 1991; Hargie, Saunders, & Dickson, 1981). Questions vary on a number of dimensions, including focus and allowed freedom of response. They may be open invitations (e.g., "What brings you here today?") or more direct (e.g., "Where are you employed?"). They may ask for clarification ("Can you give me an example?") or encourage new ways to view concerns (e.g., "Could it be that. . . ?"). They may direct attention to the past or present, feelings or actions, the self or others. Some questions encourage clients to offer more specific information (e.g., to move from vague to specific descriptions of problems and related situations such as "What did he do?" "What happened then?" "What did you want to happen?"). Whether you get a useful response is the key indicator of a successful question.

Ask *instrumental questions*, questions that contribute to helping clients. For example, ask yourself, "If I had this information, would it help resolve the problem?" A question may not be instrumental, for three reasons: (1) The hoped-for outcome is appropriate, but the question is asked in a way that is unlikely to achieve it (e.g., it is leading or garbled); (2) the outcome sought will not be helpful, no matter how the question is phrased; or (3) the outcome sought is appropriate, but the person cannot provide it. Common errors include

- Asking leading questions.
- Asking questions at the wrong time (they serve as distractions or interruptions).
- Asking closed-end questions calling for a yes or no answer when more information is desired.
- Asking irrelevant questions (knowing the answer will not be helpful).
- Asking more than one question at a time.
- Asking complicated questions.
- Asking a person why something occurs with the assumption that she knows the answer. (See also discussion of interviewer biases in Chapters 10 and 14.)

The order in which questions are asked and whether they are framed in terms of possible gains or losses influences how people will respond (Dawes, 1988). Unless you want to encourage a specific reply, your questions should not suggest answers. Some clients may feel uncomfortable and confused by an open invitation to talk. More focused questions may be required. Culturally preferred styles of communication will influence what is appropriate. Explaining the rationale for asking certain questions will help clients understand why you want certain information.

Use *probes* to clarify ambiguities and seek additional details (e.g., "Could you tell me more about that?"). Sensitive topics are usually best approached in a gradual fashion in which less threatening questions are first posed (e.g., asking a client how she feels about someone else engaging in a certain act). More personal questions can then be asked (asking how she feels about doing this). You can introduce questions later if they make clients uncomfortable or if they don't respond. Hypothetical questions may be of value when clients are reluctant to share their views. You could ask a client who has difficulties with her partner what she

thinks an ideal marriage would be like. Ask for clarification when a statement is unclear. You can check out your understanding by rephrasing the client's statements. The skills modeled in seeking clarification can be of value to clients.

You can ask questions in a way that will encourage clients to consider new ways of viewing problems and solutions. You could phrase them in a "Columbo" style (Meichenbaum, 1977): "Could it be that. . . .". Don't worry about asking questions in a standardized way. Let's say that you need examples of what a client refers to when she says that her son is "out-of-control." You might ask:

- Could you give me an example?
- Could you tell be about the last time this happened?
- What does he do when he is out of control?

You can use questions to regulate participation. People who hog the conversation don't ask many questions, don't bother to wait for answers to their questions, don't seem interested, and violate the question–listen–question rule, in which the conversation is turned back to the speaker. You can use the following criteria to judge the effectiveness of your questions: (1) useful outcomes result, (2) questions make sense to clients, and (3) you (or your coworkers or supervisor) can check off most of the items on the checklist in Exhibit 12.3 when reviewing an interview.

STRUCTURING EXCHANGES

Structured, time-limited approaches that are goal directed, clarify the roles of participants, and build on available assets step-by-step are more effective than less predictable approaches are, and they have fewer negative effects on clients (Paquin, 1977; see also the reviews in Bergin & Garfield, 1994). Many studies indicate that minority-group clients prefer these characteristics (e.g., see the review in Davis & Proctor, 1989). Structured frameworks avoid Haley's (1969) prescriptions for failure: Be passive, inactive, silent, and beware. Structuring interviews requires effective pacing and timing,

EXHIBIT 12.3
Checklist for Reviewing Questions

_____ 1. Do not suggest answers (unless this is your aim).
_____ 2. Ask one question at a time.
_____ 3. Use probes to clarify content and direct exchanges.
_____ 4. Reflect understanding and consideration of client's feelings and point of view.
_____ 5. Are brief and to the point.
_____ 6. Are well timed.
_____ 7. Relate to current concerns and related factors.
_____ 8. Ask what, when, where, who, and how often questions.
_____ 9. Avoid inappropriate "why" questions.
_____ 10. Reflect a sensitivity to environmental causes of problems.
_____ 11. Reflect sensitivity to individual differences (e.g., in ethnicity, class, gender, sexual orientation).
_____ 12. Describe the rationale for asking questions as necessary.
_____ 13. Use intelligible and acceptable language.
_____ 14. Avoid intrusive questions (e.g., they interrupt clients).
_____ 15. Indicators of success:
  • Clients accept more helpful views.
  • Clients use constructive problem-solving language.
  • Valued outcomes and related factors are clarified.

maintaining focus, beginning and ending interviews effectively, and making smooth transitions (see Exhibit 12.4). The functions of structuring are

• Creating a state of readiness appropriate to a task.
• Relieving anxiety due to uncertainty about what will happen.
• Gaining attention.
• Increasing motivation.
• Determining expectations and knowledge of a topic.
• Indicating objectives for a task.
• Describing expectations and responsibilities.
• Offering general information about tasks.
• Establishing links with previous meetings. (Hargie, Saunders, & Dickson, 1981.)

Structuring should be carried out in a polite and informative manner (explaining reasons for given methods). Role induction interviews, in which you review expected behaviors and the format you will follow, may encourage behaviors that "move things along." written manuals or audio and videotape presentations may be used to inform clients about what will occur (e.g., Barlow & Craske, 1990).

Maintaining Focus

One of your tasks is to help people discuss problems in a useful goal-directed fashion. It is your responsibility to maintain focus and to do so in an efficient yet comfortable way. A lack of focus results in drift. Reasons for a lack of focus include unclear goals, not identifying intermediate steps, stress (e.g., too much work), ineffective social influence skills, and a lack of preparation for the interview (see Chapter 11). A client's lack of focus may be related to fear of change or avoidance of touchy topics. If interviews are unfocused, clients will not have to consider how they contribute to problems. You can encourage focus by

• Planning an agenda.

EXHIBIT 12.4
Checklist for Structuring Interviews

_____ 1. Arrange a nondistracting environment.
_____ 2. Make a tentative agenda.
_____ 3. Offer appropriate greetings.
_____ 4. Review the results of assignments at the beginning of the interview.
_____ 5. Emphasize the purpose of the interview, and ask for the client's agreement with this.
_____ 6. Avoid irrelevant digressions.
_____ 7. Offer opportunities to clients to introduce material.
_____ 8. Make effective transitions.
_____ 9. Avoid interruptions.
_____ 10. Introduce difficult topics at appropriate times.
_____ 11. Maintain a comfortable pace (e.g., regarding sensitivity of content).
_____ 12. Use an effective speed of talking (not too slow or too fast).
_____ 13. Focus on problems of concern to client.
_____ 14. Select helpful assignments.
_____ 15. Allow time for a comfortable ending of exchanges.
_____ 16. Provide useful summaries at the end of exchanges.
_____ 17. Clarify the time and purpose of the next meeting.
_____ 18. Consider cultural differences.
_____ 19. Indicators of success:
  • Useful outcomes result (e.g., helpful tasks are agreed on, useful data are gathered).
  • Clients are as comfortable as possible.
  • Clients report that the interview was useful.
  • Clients feel more hopeful.

- Checking to see whether the agenda is compatible with service goals.
- Identifying desired outcomes.
- Using effective social influence skills.
- Summarizing at the end of the interview what was achieved and the next steps to be taken.

Focusing requires holding the clients' attention, encouraging them to talk, and refocusing the discussion when necessary in a respectful manner. Your options will depend partly on whether you are talking to clients, coworkers, or supervisors.

Clients may prefer to talk about topics that do not lead to the achievement of desired outcomes. Discomfort when discussing a topic or emergencies may require a temporary diversion from the main focus. Otherwise, you should center on service goals as efficiently and effectively as possible without unduly rushing clients, with due respect for cultural differences and attention to maintaining a collaborative working relationship. You may have to lead clients back to questions or reaffirm the purpose of the interview. The focus of an interview may change based on new information. However, if problems shift often (the "floating problem"), possible reasons should be explored. Perhaps you have not identified areas of greatest concern to clients. Clients may be reluctant to assume any responsibility for resolving complaints. They may anticipate negative consequences if outcomes are achieved. Perhaps you have not sought their commitment to pursue changes (you don't have a client—see Chapter 2). Clients may hope for instant change and be disappointed and ready to move on to another concern that can be resolved more quickly. Additional reassurance and encouragement may be required when clients are anxious or depressed. Encouragement and support may be needed to draw out quiet clients. You may have to restate questions in different ways, reexplain the reasons for your questions, and offer reassurance about the likelihood of positive outcomes.

Punctuating the Exchange

Interviews have beginnings, middles, and endings and transitions within them. Greetings and partings are social "routines" that require certain reactions from participants. The word *routine* highlights the importance of certain behaviors. Errors in greeting behaviors include mumbling (people can't hear what you say) and asking a question but not waiting for an answer.

Transitions occur within interviews such as a change from clients describing concerns in a relatively uninterrupted fashion at the beginning of an initial interview to responding to questions designed to obtain specific information. You should preface your transitions with a brief explanation of why you are guiding the discussion in a certain direction (e.g., toward specific examples of problems). *Summaries* provide an opportunity to check your understanding of what clients say and can serve as a transition to a new topic. You might say, "Mr. Rivera, let me see if I understand what you have said. You . . . . Is this correct?" Be sure to wait for an answer. Breaking silences too quickly is a common error of beginning interviewers; clients may need time to think about your question and their answer.

Endings provide an opportunity to summarize accomplishments, offer encouragement and support, agree on and practice tasks to be carried out between meetings, reaffirm the importance of carrying out agreed-on tasks, and arrange the next meeting or review steps to be taken in contacting other sources. Summaries are selective. They emphasize important points and describe what remains to be done. Plan for endings in the beginning and middle phases of your interviews (consider how much time is available, what can be accomplished in this time, and the next steps needed). People may feel rejected if you end conversations abruptly. Partings, like greetings, involve a social routine, a series of moves and options that offer opportunities for ending or extending conversations (Trower, Bryant, & Argyle, 1978).

Clients may be reluctant to end a meeting because important topics have not been discussed. They may enjoy the conversation or still have unanswered questions. How you handle their reluctance to end an interview will depend on your goals. You might say, "Let's discuss this on _____ when we meet." Or you could extend the interview if is is possible and is warranted by what has been disclosed. If you don't want to continue the exchange, remain politely firm without being harsh or rude. Don't allow yourself to be pressured into continuing conversations that you want to end. An example of a closing summary statement follows:

> Let's review what we accomplished. We've identified some changes you would like in your family and decided on a plan to get more information. Do you have any questions? (Pause for an answer. The client indicates that he has no questions.) If you have any questions when you get home, call me at the number I gave you, during the times indicated, and we'll see whether we can take care of them. We'll meet again on _____ of next week. I look forward to working with you, and I think we can make your family life a more pleasant one.

Meshing Skills and Pacing

Meshing skills ensure the continuity of content, timing, and turn taking (Trower et al., 1978). Timing refers to the smooth sequencing of speaking turns and the avoidance of interruptions and speech delays. It also refers to the point in a conversation when a certain reaction occurs. Skill in turn taking will avoid interruptions and help you take up and hand over conversations. Interviews differ in their pace (duration of pauses between questions, speed of topic transitions, pattern of sharing feelings and discussing difficult topics, and rapidity of speaking). Clients may feel rushed and not understand what you say if you speak quickly and allow few pauses. Quick topic transitions may be confusing or anxiety provoking. Be sure to allow pauses after clients stop talking so that you don't cut them off prematurely. On the other hand, try not to waste time by allowing long pauses and speaking very slowly. It usually is best to introduce difficult topics gradually. Avoid ending meetings with discussions of unsettling topics. Allow time at the end to shift to neutral content (if appropriate) and to reaffirm agreed-on tasks and the next meeting time.

Silences

Silences serve many functions. They provide transitions to new topics and allow time for clients to think about what has been said and to decide what they will say. Many silences are natural pauses in speech. Others are attempts to gain control of the interview or to avoid talking about unpleasant subjects. They may reflect uncertainty about what to say or an interest in letting others speak (Kadushin, 1990). Understanding the purpose of silences and responding correctly to them was found to be one of the three most important skills differentiating a positive skill group of social workers from a negative skill group (Shulman, 1977). When confronted with a long silence by a client, you could offer a minimal comment ("I see"), repeat or emphasize the client's last few words, or rephrase his or her last thoughts.

ATTENTIVE LISTENING

Good listeners are oriented to other people rather than to themselves. They are good observers of other people. They accurately note what others say and how they say it, as well as nonverbal cues. Good listeners are committed to listening, are physically and mentally ready to listen, wait for others to complete their statements before speaking, and use their analytic skills to supplement rather than to replace listening. These features increase the likelihood that information will be received in an undistorted form and help the speaker feel accepted and understood" (Stuart, 1980). A commitment to listening means deciding that what other people say is important, suspending your assumptions and judgments about people, not asking for additional information until people complete their statements, and making comments and questions that follow from the other persons' statements. Careful listening is aided by the assumption of ignorance (Kadushin, 1990). Thinking that we know something may prevent our hearing what is said. We tend to see what we expect to see and readily infer trait like qualities about others and overlook situational influences (Krull & Erickson, 1995). Research suggests that cultural as well as individual differences influence our tendencies to make trait or situational inferences.

Accurate paraphrases and reflections are part of

EXHIBIT 12.5
Checklist for Reviewing Listening Skills

_____ 1. Arrange a distraction-free environment.
_____ 2. Avoid interruptions and talking for clients (e.g., finishing their sentences).
_____ 3. Avoid distracting mannerisms.
_____ 4. Use facial expressions that reflect interest and concern.
_____ 5. Use postures that reflect interest and concern (relaxed but attentive, oriented toward others).
_____ 6. Use appropriate eye contact.
_____ 7. Make sure that verbal and nonverbal behaviors agree.
_____ 8. Ask questions that reflect attention and concern.
_____ 9. Use facilitating seating arrangements.
_____ 10. Take appropriate steps to avoid or remove obstacles to communication.
_____ 11. Time your paraphrases and reflections well, and communicate an understanding of what has been said.
_____ 12. Use an effective variety of responses.
_____ 13. Use minimal encourages effectively.
_____ 14. Indicators of success:
   • Clients offer more relevant material
   • Clients explore new views of concern and related events

attentive listening. They communicate that you are interested in understanding what is said and offer an opportunity to check your understanding. Meanings that are only hinted at may have to be checked out, being sensitive to clients' comfort. In addition, they help clients clarify their thoughts, focus attention on particular items and encourage further exploration, and convey concern for what clients view as important (Hargie, Saunders, & Dickson, 1981). Nonverbal behavior is important in showing that you are listening (see Exhibit 12.5). Avoid reactions that suggest disapproval (e.g., rolling your eyes, frowning). Attentive listening increases the likelihood that clients will share useful information and participate in agreed-on plans.

Common Errors

Advice giving is a common error. People often want to be heard, to be understood without being given advice, suggestions, or interpretations, and they want recognition that they have been heard. Think about your own experiences. Sometimes you may just want to share your feelings about some event without receiving suggestions about what you can or should do. Poor substitutes for listening include _responding with a cliché_, such as "That's the way the ball bounces," or _parroting_ (repeating exactly) what was said (Egan, 1994). Minimal responses (e.g., "hmm") may not be enough to communicate understanding. Egan refers to these as _inadequate responses_; others may feel that they did not say anything worth responding to. _Ignoring what has been said_ is another form of inadequate response.

Your statements may reflect inaccurate understanding, which is why you should offer paraphrases and reflections tentatively. _Tentativeness_ indicates that you are aware that you may misrepresent what has been said and are open to being corrected. You might say, "You sound like you're angry with me, but I might be wrong." Don't _pretend understanding_. If you cannot follow what has been said, ask for clarification. You might say, "I'm not sure I follow you. Could you go over that again?" Being long-winded may convey that you are more interested in talking about yourself than in understanding your clients. _Interpretations_ of why a person feels a certain way is another poor substitute for listening. _Patronizing_ comments like "You'll get over it" may offend people.

Matching a person's tone and manner of speaking can convey an understanding of his or her feelings. If someone is very sad, a happy tone will not demonstrate understanding. Avoid distracting mannerisms such as saying OK after each of your client's statements, rapidly nodding your head, or frequently gesturing with your hands. Some people jump in too quickly after others have finished speaking, thereby cutting off others who want to speak. Pausing a few seconds after someone stops speaking will give you time to decide what to say next and will avoid interrupting others.

Reflective and paraphrasing statements should be frequent enough to demonstrate understanding but not so often that they function as interruptions. A mix of paraphrasing content and reflecting feelings may be most effective. If a client stops speaking abruptly when you start to speak, it may indicate that you interrupted her. If you don't offer any feedback that you understand what has been said, clients may stop speaking because they assume that you are not interested in what they say. The percentage of time you spend listening rather than speaking will vary depending on your goals.

Criteria that you can use to judge the quality of your listening skills are that (1) clients share relevant material and participate in exploring factors related to complaints; (2) clients seem comfortable; and (3) you, your peers, or your supervisor can check many of the items on Exhibit 12.5. You could identify biases about clients that may get in the way of effective listening by noting what you think a person will say at specific points.

ENCOURAGING HELPFUL VIEWS AND BEHAVIORS

Encouraging helpful behaviors and discouraging dysfunctional ones is a key influence process during interviews (see Exhibit 12.6). For example, your questions and feedback focus clients on particular aspects of their environment, behavior, or feelings rather than others. You can support desired behaviors by reinforcing them and modeling helpful reactions. You could, for example, model constructive reactions to mistakes by pointing out that everyone makes mistakes, describing one of your own, and reframing mistakes as learning opportunities. Your influence as a model will be greater if your clients view you as competent and as similar enough to them that you can understand them. Model presentation can be used to show clients how to carry out agreed-on assignments and to develop new skills. Helping clients become more aware of what they do and why they do it is a feature of all helping approaches. Characteristics of helpful feedback include the following:

- It is descriptive rather than evaluative.
- It refers to specific behaviors.
- It focuses on positives.
- It uses process rather than terminal language (i.e., it concerns things that can be changed).
- It is offered when people are most open to receiving it.

EXHIBIT 12.6
Checklist for Encouraging Helpful Behaviors

____ 1. Model helpful behaviors.
____ 2. Prompt and reinforce helpful behaviors.
____ 3. Do not reinforce unhelpful behaviors.
____ 4. Avoid criticism and negative comments.
____ 5. Use personalized examples.
____ 6. Encourage process language.
____ 7. Avoid unnecessary confrontations.
____ 8. Avoid premature interpretations and advice.
____ 9. Avoid unsupported (or wild) speculations.
____ 10. Seek clients' reactions to views suggested.
____ 11. Use language that is intelligible to participants.
____ 12. Indicators of success
   - an increase in helpful behaviors
   - a decrease in unhelpful ones

- It is offered in an appropriate manner so that clients will be most likely to receive it. Statements should begin with "I."
- It is based on data that support it.

Be sure to reinforce clients for clearly describing problems, desired outcomes, and related factors including statements recognizing the role they play in maintaining problems. This can be done by prompts (e.g., questions) and feedback (head nods and minimal encourages such as "Go on, please."), interpretations, and reflections. You can play an active role in laying the groundwork for helpful statements by the questions you ask. A teacher may say, "I wonder if I am encouraging this annoying behavior by attending to it every time it occurs." You might say, "That's a good point, and it is a possibility." In this statement you support the teacher's efforts to be helpful and encourage her to consider the role she may play in maintaining behaviors of concern. Reactions that are not helpful can be discouraged by ignoring them (if appropriate) and by prompting and reinforcing desired alternatives. Clients often accept causal assumptions or make statements of blame that do not offer any clues to how things can be improved (e.g., "I was born this way," "You're just like your mother," "It's in my genes"). This kind of terminal language (no guidelines for removing complaints are offered) prevents the discovery of useful options and encourages negative expectations. More helpful alternative views can be suggested.

Confrontation

Gerald Egan defines confrontation as "a responsible unmasking of the discrepancies, distortions, games, and smoke screens the client uses to hide both from self-understanding and from constructive behavior change" (1975, p. 158). It is "an invitation to examine some form of behavior that seems to be self-defeating or harmful to others and to change the behavior if it is found to be so" (Egan, 1982, p. 186). One purpose of confrontation is to help clients increase their awareness of discrepancies in what they do, think, or feel. For example, a client may say his problems really don't matter but show by his demeanor and past actions that they do. A client may say she is comfortable but reveal by her nonverbal behavior (fidgeting and trembling) that she is not. Not following through on agreements is common. For example, a client may agree to carry out a task, but not do so. Possible reasons should be discussed. You might say, "Let's make sure that we both understood what was to be done and why." You can be firm and supportive at the same time. You could remind clients that they will have to shoulder some of the responsibility for achieving desired outcomes, empathize with the effort that will be involved, and reaffirm your support. Perhaps you should reassess your overall service agreement. Discussing discrepancies may encourage more helpful views of events and new ways of acting.

The term confrontation implies conflict and negative impact. Negative (compared with positive) feedback decreases risk-taking and performance (Canavan-Gumpert, 1977). Thus, be cautious in using it. Avoid criticism and lecturing. Confronting and teaching increase client resistance (Patterson & Forgatch, 1985). These behaviors are less likely to have this effect if used together with supportive or joining responses as well as reframing of problems and goals in a way that complements clients' views (Chamberlan & Baldwin, 1988). The purpose of confrontation is to help clients, and so it should be done in a manner that minimizes the likelihood of defensive reactions. It should not be accusatory but, rather, constructive. Use specific examples. Timing is important. That is, consider the client's readiness to handle the confrontation.

Examining your motives will increase the likelihood that confrontations are for the benefit of clients rather than for your benefit (to defend yourself for example). Clients may be pessimistic about the prospect of change or whether a procedure will be effective. Directly confronting negativism ("I won't" or "I can't") is *not* likely to be helpful. Clients often have good reason to think that assurances of success are empty, especially if they have a long history of failing to resolve a problem. You may learn valuable information by exploring the reasons for negative reactions. You may decide to focus on the positive aspects of your clients' statements and to ignore the negative comments. Or you could relabel or reframe negative views in a positive way. For example, the loss of a job may be viewed as an opportunity to find more rewarding employment. Clients may react to confrontation by questioning your credibility, trying to convince you that your views are wrong, minimizing the importance of what you say, seeking support elsewhere, or agreeing with your views but saying "I can't" (Cormier & Cormier, 1991). A clear focus on your purpose for confronting clients will help you handle different kinds of reactions.

Interpretations

Interpretations often refer to material expressed only implicitly. In this way, they differ from listening responses. This view of interpretation is similar to Egan's advanced accurate empathy (see the earlier discussion). Interpretations may help clients understand relationships between events, consider behavior from a different perspective, and act more effectively in real life. The emphasis of many practice approaches, including the one described here, is on current behaviors, thoughts, or feelings and related factors, not on past hidden meanings. Try to avoid premature interpretations and suggestions (those that result in negative reactions rather than enhanced understanding). Gurman and Kniskern

(1978) contend that the helper who is most likely to bring about deterioration "is one who does little to structure early sessions; uses confrontations of highly affective material early in therapy rather than reflections of feelings; labels unconscious motivation early in therapy rather than "encouraging interaction and gathering data" (1978, p. 11). Overuse of interpretations may reflect a belief that you have "an inside track" on "the real meanings" or an unwarranted belief in their potential to alter behavior, thoughts, or feelings. Service goals should guide your actions. More helpful views may occur only after behavior changes. Don't offer advice or suggestions unless you have a sound basis for doing so—unless you have the information necessary to identify options that are likely to be effective. (However, you may have to take immediate action if there is a crisis.) Clients may react to inquiries or statements not intended as suggestions as advice. To avoid this, you could preface your comments or questions with "I am not suggesting this, but. . . ." Be sure to consider cultural and educational differences when planning what to say and how to say it.

If you follow these guidelines, you will be less likely to be met with negative reactions such as clients' saying "It's not so," "It won't work," or "I won't do it," "I can't do it," or "This is a waste of time." You can judge your success in part by the absence of these responses. Keep in mind that interpretations will not change behavior if needed resources, skills, or incentives are absent. In order to resolve most complaints, clients (or other persons) must act differently in real-life settings, and additional methods usually are required to bring this about.

RESPECT

Respect includes consideration of cultural differences and not imposing values on clients. Other indicators are offering clients valid assessment and effective service methods and monitoring progress so clients can see whether their time, effort, and perhaps money have been well spent and decisions have been made in a timely manner. Avoid re-

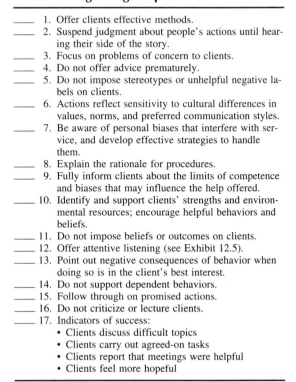

EXHIBIT 12.7
Checklist Regarding Respect

____ 1. Offer clients effective methods.
____ 2. Suspend judgment about people's actions until hearing their side of the story.
____ 3. Focus on problems of concern to clients.
____ 4. Do not offer advice prematurely.
____ 5. Do not impose stereotypes or unhelpful negative labels on clients.
____ 6. Actions reflect sensitivity to cultural differences in values, norms, and preferred communication styles.
____ 7. Be aware of personal biases that interfere with service, and develop effective strategies to handle them.
____ 8. Explain the rationale for procedures.
____ 9. Fully inform clients about the limits of competence and biases that may influence the help offered.
____ 10. Identify and support clients' strengths and environmental resources; encourage helpful behaviors and beliefs.
____ 11. Do not impose beliefs or outcomes on clients.
____ 12. Offer attentive listening (see Exhibit 12.5).
____ 13. Point out negative consequences of behavior when doing so is in the client's best interest.
____ 14. Do not support dependent behaviors.
____ 15. Follow through on promised actions.
____ 16. Do not criticize or lecture clients.
____ 17. Indicators of success:
   • Clients discuss difficult topics
   • Clients carry out agreed-on tasks
   • Clients report that meetings were helpful
   • Clients feel more hopeful

sponding mechanically (conveying a lack of interest or regard), displaying a passivity that communicates a lack of regard, and imposing values on clients. If you show respect for clients, they are more likely to discuss difficult topics, explore how they may contribute to concerns, carry out agreed-on plans, feel better about themselves, and be more hopeful (see Exhibit 12.7).

Being Nonjudgmental

There is no more important task than being nonjudgmental. This does not imply that you should not distinguish between helpful behaviors that should be supported and dysfunctional ones that should not. Indicators of judgmentalness include blaming or criticizing clients and imposing personal values about what outcomes are good or bad and ignoring cultural differences in values, norms, or preferred styles of communication. Some helpers believe (incorrectly) that because they are trying to be neutral, they are not communicating their values to clients. In fact, helpers usually do communicate their attitudes and feelings to clients, either wittingly or unwittingly (Marmor, 1976, p. 6). Being nonjudgmental is difficult, since we are often unaware of our biases and how we communicate them. Biases may be difficult to identify because they are inherent in how problems are defined in a particular society, profession, or practice framework. Judgments about what is best may be imposed on clients in the guise of "expertise" or "science" (see Chapter 7). Exploring your own reactions to specific individuals/problems/groups will help you identify biases that may affect your work.

SELF-DISCLOSURE

Sharing information about yourself can serve a number of purposes. You can use self-disclosure to encourage clients to share information or to appear less aloof and more similar to your clients. Answering personal questions can normalize concerns. Consider a developmentally disabled adolescent who asked his male social worker, "Do you masturbate?" This client had been referred because he was caught masturbating in a public men's room. The social worker's direct 'yes' conveys the message that masturbation is not something to be ashamed of. The social worker helped this client distinguish between situations in which masturbation is acceptable and those in which it is not. Clients may ask personal questions because of concerns they have or because of a desire to become closer to you. Avoid brusque refusals to answer questions, throwing questions back in a condescending manner ("I wonder why you find it necessary to ask that?") and giving overly long or involved answers that deflect attention from service goals. Sharing personal experiences can encourage a positive relationship by conveying understanding of others' experiences. You can use self-disclosure to describe new ways of viewing a situation and possible options. You may share your reactions to a client to indicate how others may respond to him

in problem-related situations. Let's say that you are helping a shy client increase her social contacts and you notice that she rarely looks or smiles at you. You may point out that if you met her in a social situation and she acted this way, you would think she wasn't interested in meeting people or was depressed.

Too little disclosure maintains distance between people. Too much may create embarrassment and reluctant reciprocation of disclosures (Derlega & Berg, 1987). Self-disclosure is dysfunctional if it takes up valuable time in non-goal-directed ways or if it is done in a "can you top this" fashion ("You think you have a problem? Let me tell you about mine"). Avoid self-disclosures that diminish your credibility. Self-disclosures that are not related to service goals are inappropriate, such as disclosures made because of a need for approval or to encourage a sexual interest. Cultural differences influence what, when, and how information is best shared.

CONCRETENESS

One of your tasks is to help clients be concrete. The term concreteness refers to the clarity of questions, statements, and information. Concreteness is necessary in regard to feelings, thoughts, behavior, and related factors as well as personal, family, and community resources. Because it is so important, it is singled out here for a separate discussion in addition to related content in Chapters 9 and 10. Concreteness encourages clients to move from vague to specific descriptions. If problems and related factors remain vague, identifying related outcomes and choosing effective plans to achieve them will be difficult. Speaking in generalities will be helpful only if you wish to avoid clear identification of an issue or concern. And, clients may not wish to do so. You can use the following criteria to explore whether questions, statements, and information are concrete:

- Specific examples of concerns and desired outcomes are obtained.

- Cues and consequences related to problem-related behaviors are clearly described.

- Plans for achieving desired outcomes are clearly described.
- Clear relevant progress indicators are identified.

OTHER IMPORTANT RELATIONSHIP SKILLS

Rewardingness has been highlighted as a key social skill (e.g., Argyle, Furnham, & Graham, 1981). If you are friendly (smile, offer attentive listening), other people are more likely to be friendly in return. These reactions contribute to empathy, which is related to outcome. On the other hand, if you act superior to others, contradict them, and "put people down" they are likely to offer you negative reactions and to dislike you. Friendly people offer attention, share information about themselves, and are supportive rather than rejecting. You can enhance your rewardingness by pointing out similarities between yourself and others, offering praise, indicating a willingness to help out of genuine concern for others, and conveying that others are worthwhile despite their shortcomings. People viewed as friendly keep criticism to a minimum and offer positive feedback. They use praise, encouragement, compliments, and sympathy. People viewed as unfriendly or anxious are not as supportive. They often turn or look away when others speak or may "look through" people. They may assume a defensive, closed posture. They might recoil or flinch when touched or approached; they frown and may be preoccupied with self-grooming and offer only brief glances.

Helping clients may require negotiating, mediating, and bargaining skills as well as skills in chairing meetings and participating in case conferences. You will often have to be persistent and should use language that is compatible with the values and language of others. You will have to learn how to handle difficult people and turn potentially negative encounters into positive ones (see Chapter 13).

Offering support and providing reassurance are key helping skills. This involves relationship skills such as attentive listening, being nonjudgmental, and showing respect, empathy, and warmth. You may validate clients' concerns and highlight client strengths (e.g., particular coping skills). Offering support and reassurance encourages clients' involvement and helps create an atmosphere of warmth and understanding. Effective helpers encourage clients to feel more hopeful and to give themselves positive feedback for useful skills and viewpoints.

Humor may lighten a difficult conversation or put matters in a more realistic, hopeful perspective. Some helpers take themselves too seriously. They may appear depressed but may not be aware of this. Humor can transform a potentially divisive exchange into a positive one. What is funny varies from person to person. Timing is important as well as similarity of values and attitudes (for more detail, see Killinger, 1977; Strean, 1994).

IMPROVING YOUR SKILLS

One of the advantages of being a professional is that you can continue to learn during your career. For any situation there is a range of options (the operant class) that may be used to attain a given outcome (see Chapter 8). This is partly what accounts for "style." You can increase your success by becoming familiar with what impressions you make on others and by acting in ways that complement your goals. There is a close relationship among self-concept (what we believe about ourselves), social identity (how we are regarded by others), and impression management (what signals we offer to others to influence our social identity) (Schlenker, 1980). The images (social signals) we offer influence how social situations are defined. For example, if a client tries to define a situation as one in which sexual advances are permitted, you can discourage this view by offering incompatible images (e.g., being task focused). Self-presentation "can go wrong in several ways—too little information, too much, bogus, too 'gray' and misleading" (Furnham & Argyle, 1981, p. 128).

COMPONENTS OF EFFECTIVE SOCIAL BEHAVIOR

Your behavior is effective if you influence the behavior and feelings of others in ways that you intend and that your profession and society expect.

EXHIBIT 12.8
Examples of Service Goals

1. *Provide support.* Provide a warm empathic environment, increase trust and rapport, and establish a positive relationship; help clients feel accepted, understood, comfortable, and reassured; give clients a chance to talk about their feelings and problems.
2. *Set limits.* Establish the relationship's goals, objectives, rules, or parameters (e.g., time, agreed-on tasks).
3. *Obtain information.* Clarify problems and related factors; identify resources.
4. *Give information.* Educate, give facts, correct misperceptions or misinformation, and explain reasons for procedures.
5. *Maintain focus.* Channel or structure the discussion.
6. *Increase hope.* Increase expectations that positive outcomes are possible and that you can help clients.
7. *Relieve distress.*
8. *Identify relevant cognitions.* Identify both helpful and unhelpful thoughts or attitudes (e.g., "I must be perfect").
9. *Identify relevant behaviors.* Identify and give feedback about behaviors of concern and/or their consequences.
10. *Increase self-management skills.* Increase clients' skills in managing their own thoughts, feelings, and/or behaviors.
11. *Identify feelings.* Help clients identify, alter, and accept their feelings.
12. *Increase clients' understanding of the causes related to complaints.*
13. *Enable change.* Enhance clients' adaptive skills, behaviors, thoughts, or feelings. Create more helpful views.
14. *Support new ways of acting.*
15. *Overcome obstacles* to valued outcomes.
16. *Prevent or resolve problems in the helping relationship.*
17. *Meet your own needs.* Protect or defend yourself; lessen your anxiety. Helpers may try to influence clients, or feel good or superior at the clients' expense.

Source: Adapted from C. E. Hill & K. E. O'Grady (1985), List of therapist intentions illustrated in a case study and with therapists of varying theoretical orientations. Journal of Counseling Psychology, 32, 8.

Exhibit 12.8 shows some possible service goals. Effective behavior avoids problematic situations and/or alters them so they are no longer worrisome and offers a maximum of positive consequences and a minimum of negative ones to you and others. Understanding the components of effective social behavior will help you plan how to improve your relationship skills and to help clients enhance their social skills.

Knowledge of Situational Requirements and Options

As with all skills, their effective use requires correct identification of when they will be of value. Effective social behavior is situationally specific. The particular behaviors required for success depend on the situation. Each situation can be considered in terms of

- *Goals* that are attainable.
- *Rules* about what may or may not be done in the situation.
- *Special skills* that are required.
- *Roles* that are required or acceptable.

Rules are shared beliefs about what reactions are permitted, not permitted, or required in certain situations. Knowledge about required or expected roles in specific situations and about typical behaviors in them will help you accurately interpret reactions and respond effectively. Roles are positions occupied by people in a situation and are associated with certain expected behaviors. Examples include parent, client, and counselor. Lack of knowledge about expected behaviors in given roles may result in inappropriate behavior and negative consequences. For example, putting your feet up on your desk when interviewing a client is not likely to create rapport and communicate respect. Power relationships between people influence options. French and Raven's (1959) classic description of different sources remains a useful one:

- Reward power (the ability to reward others).
- Coercive power (the ability to punish others).
- Expert power (others believe that you possess knowledge and/or skills that are useful to them).
- Referent power (influence based on liking).
- Legitimate power (others comply because they believe they should (e.g., a security guard asks people to leave the premises).

Goals, Plans, and Feedback

Whether you achieve your goals depends in part on whether your goals complement those of others. You are more likely to be successful if you identify your goals, plan how to achieve them, and pursue appropriate ones (e.g., Dodge, Asher, & Parkhurst, 1989). You can increase your effectiveness by paying attention to how others respond and modifying your behavior accordingly. People who are not effective often fail to pay attention to the impressions they create, misinterpret reactions, or do not change their behavior to enhance their success. Some helpers fall into *social traps* (actions that result in immediate positive effects but have long-term negative consequences). For example, a clever put-down may give you some immediate pleasure but may create negative feelings that decrease the likelihood of influencing others in the future, such as the gatekeepers of services that clients need. People differ in how much attention they pay to themselves in social situations. Low or high degrees of self-monitoring interfere with the effective use of feedback from others. Setting goals in a "must" or "should" form ("I must get this teacher to cooperate") may interfere with accurate perception and interpretation of social signals as well as with skilled reactions on your part. For example, your urgency may dampen your sense of humor.

Perception and Translation of Social Cues

You will be more effective if you accurately perceive and translate (interpret) social cues. Not only is it important to perceive that a person is smiling, it also is important to translate the meaning of this smile accurately. Is it a sign of friendliness or a sign of hostility? Skill in one area (interpreting facial expressions) does not necessarily mean that other skills are present (communicating emotions accurately). Accurate perception and translation of social cues depends in part on your knowledge of preferred communication styles of others. Communication patterns are influenced by our past experiences. African Americans' history of slavery encouraged use of indirect expressions of hostility, aggression, and fear. This history increased sensitivity to nonverbal cues and encouraged use of subordinating behaviors to avoid negative consequences. Compared with whites, African Americans place greater emphasis on nonverbal behaviors and believe that they are more accurate indicators than verbal behaviors are of how people feel and what they believe. Past experiences with oppression and discrimination may make it difficult for African–American clients to respond to a white social worker as an individual person rather than as a symbol of the establishment. Mistrust and guarded reactions are understandable. No matter how good your cross-cultural helping knowledge and skills may be, they may not alter reactions based on past experiences. Knowing the origin of reactions that make helping difficult (e.g., "testing," anger, mistrust, and/or accusations of racism) increases the likelihood of effective responses.

VERBAL BEHAVIOR (WHAT IS SAID)

The verbal behaviors discussed in this chapter include "concreteness," self-disclosure, and questions. Length of speaking also is important: You may speak too little or too much in interviews. What is "too much" or "too little" depends on your goals as well as client preferences. Your aim should be to balance talking and listening in a way that maximizes the likelihood of achieving service goals. Guidelines for increasing or decreasing participation are described in Chapter 13. Preferences about directness vary from culture to culture (e.g., regarding how to refuse requests). Gender differences in communication styles may result in misunderstandings if overlooked (e.g., Tannen, 1990, 1994). English people tend to be open, direct, and frank—even blunt in public discussion. Anglo-Americans are less so, and Asians tend to be less direct than Anglo-Americans. Many Asians view bluntness as rude, even when frank discussion is needed to make decisions.

Voice Qualities

Our attitudes are communicated more by how we speak than by the words we use. The word *par-*

alanguage refers to qualities such as voice loudness, silence, hesitations, speed of talking, and inflections (for more details, see Siegman & Feldstein, 1987).

Loudness. If you speak too softly, you might irritate others or be ignored. A soft voice volume can indicate submissiveness or sadness, whereas a louder volume can indicate confidence and dominance. Talking too loudly may offend people. Changes in voice volume can be used in conversation to emphasize points. Asians, Latinos, and Native Americans tend to speak more softly compared to Anglo-Americans.

Tone. Some people have nasal, thin voices, and others have full, resonant voices. Different tones convey different emotions. For instance, a flat, monotonous tone may give the impression of depression.

Pitch. Different combinations of pitch and loudness communicate different attitudes and emotions. People may be perceived as more dynamic if they often change the pitch of their voices during a conversation. You can increase or decrease the pitch of your voice to indicate that you would like someone else to speak.

Clarity. Some people slur their words, and others speak with a heavy drawl or accent or in a clipped or choppy manner. These speech patterns can be difficult to follow. A very clipped manner of speaking might suggest anger or impatience, whereas a drawl might suggest boredom or sadness and be difficult to understand.

Pace. If you speak very slowly, listeners may become impatient and bored. On the other hand, people may have difficulty understanding you if you speak rapidly. Slow speech can indicate sadness, affection, or boredom. Rapid speech can indicate happiness or surprise.

Speech Disturbances. Hesitations, false starts, and repetitions are common in everyday conversations. However, if they are excessive, they may detract from your effectiveness. Speech disturbances include many unfilled silences and excessive use of "filler words" during pauses (e.g., "you know" or sounds such as "ah"). A third type of disturbance includes repetitions, stammers, mispronunciations, and stuttering.

Silences. Silences have different meanings in different ethnic groups. In some Asian cultures, silence is a sign of respect for elders. Rather than a signal for someone else to take up the conversation, it may indicate an interest in continuing to speak. Effective interviewing requires a skillful use of silences (not jumping in too soon and interrupting others, not allowing long silences that make people uncomfortable).

NONVERBAL BEHAVIOR

Nonverbal signals are more important than verbal behaviors in expressing attitudes such as friendliness. We can use nonverbal behaviors to indicate how we would like a message to be viewed (as serious or funny) and to mask negative reactions. (For more details, see Siegman & Feldstein, 1987.) Make sure your nonverbal and verbal behavior match (e.g., smiling when you praise someone). If you do not, people may think you are insincere. Gestures and facial expressions can make conversations more interesting, illustrate or give emphasis to what is said, and indicate topic transitions. We use nonverbal behaviors to "frame" statements (e.g., to indicate whether we want a statement to be viewed as funny or serious) and to regulate turn taking (to indicate that we are finished speaking or would like to speak).

Nonverbal behavior reflects status differences. For example, women tend to smile more than men do and, in general, are more polite and accommodating (Rosenthal, 1979; Wilson & Gallois, 1993). Be sure to consider gender, race, class, and ethnic differences when interpreting nonverbal behavior. Overlooking such differences may result in incorrect assumptions that clients are "out of touch" with their feelings. For example, the timing and duration of shaking hands differs in different cultures. Many African–Americans believe that they can tell more about other people's attitudes and feelings by observing their nonverbal behavior than by listening to what they say, especially in regard to biases, stereotypes, and racist attitudes (Sue & Sue, 1990). Oppression, racism, and discrimination encourage sensitivity to nonverbal cues as a protection against negative consequences. One way to dismiss accurately identified biased attitudes or patronizing reactions is to claim that the person is being overly sensitive.

Facial Expression

Facial expressions are indicators of emotions and attitudes as well as "stress markers." For example, to change a statement into a question, you might raise your eyebrows as you raise the pitch of your voice at the end of a sentence. Facial expression and voice tone are the most important channels for indicating emotions and attitudes (see Ekman & Davidson, 1994). Your facial expression should be compatible with your intentions. If you look angry while trying to convey a friendly attitude, you are not likely to be successful. Norms describe standards regarding what can and should be expressed and where. The norms related to the expression of emotions (masking and neutralizing what is felt as well as regulating the intensity of emotions) vary among cultures (Derlaga & Berg, 1987). Smiling and laughter by Japanese clients may convey embarrassment, discomfort, or shyness rather than liking and positive affect. Skill in controlling emotions is valued in traditional Latino and Asian cultures. Lack of knowledge about cultural differences may result in incorrectly describing clients as inhibited or repressed or agitated and excitable.

Gaze

The term gaze refers to a person's "looking" behavior. Gaze has an important information-gathering function. Although gaze avoidance (not looking at others) deprives us of valuable information about how others respond, this may be normative in some cultures in some situations. Gaze avoidance may occur because of deference to the speaker, fear of revealing feelings, or fear of negative feedback. We use gaze to express feelings, intentions (e.g., a readiness to communicate), and attitudes. Gaze also helps us regulate turn taking. There are strong norms regarding gaze, as shown by the discomfort we feel when someone stares at us. Norms regarding gaze vary in different groups. Women gaze more than men do on almost all measures (frequency, duration, and reciprocity; see Henley, 1977).

Looking at others when they are speaking is likely to increase the amount of time they speak, although in some groups, norms may dictate that the listener not look at the speaker, especially if the listener is in a subordinate position. Looking at others while speaking adds emphasis to what is said. For whites, the average amount of time that people spend looking at others during conversations is 75% while listening and 40% while talking, and the average length of gaze is 3 seconds (Argyle & Cook, 1976). Mutual glances (eye contact) last only about 1 second and occur about 30% of the time. This differs considerably for African–American people, who make more eye contact when speaking and less eye contact when listening. Asians and Native Americans, compared with whites, have less eye contact. Head nodding and minimal responses such as "uh-hum" when listening are not as common among African–American people. Not recognizing such differences can result in inappropriate reactions, as shown in the following example:

> For instance, one Black female student was sent to the office by her gymnasium teacher because the student was said to display insolent behavior. When the student was asked to give her version of the incident, she replied, "Mrs. X asked all of us to come over to the side of the pool so that she could show us how to do the backstroke. I went over with the rest of the girls. Then Mrs. X started yelling at me and said I wasn't paying attention to her because I wasn't looking directly at her. I told her I was paying attention to her (throughout the conversation, the student kept her head down, avoiding the principal's eyes), and then she said that she wanted me to face her and look her square in the face like the rest of the girls [all of whom were white]. So I did. The next thing I knew she was telling me to get out of the pool, that she didn't like the way I was looking at her. So that's why I'm here." (Smith, 1981, p. 155)

Posture and Position

We indicate our attitudes and emotions not only by our gaze and facial expressions but also by our posture and body position. The object is to convey a relaxed and confident posture while maintaining a socially appropriate posture and position. Tightly crossing your arms over your chest may give the impression of anger or tension. A forward lean (leaning toward rather than away from others) and open arms and legs (rather than tightly crossed) communicate warmth and friendliness. Indifference may be communicated by shoulder shrugs, raised arms, and outstretched hands. Anger is conveyed by clenched fists and forward lean. Slouched shoulders may convey a lack of confidence. In contrast, good posture—with the shoulders back in a relaxed position (not "at attention")—make it more likely that others will view you as self-confident. How we position or orient our bodies (e.g., whether we face toward or away from others) communicates different degrees of intimacy or formality. The meaning of and reactions to different body orientations depend on a number of factors, including ethnic, status, and gender differences.

Proximity

Rules for proximity vary in different countries and ethnic groups. The distance zones for Americans of Northern European descent are:

- Intimate (ranging from lovemaking and comforting to the far phase of 6 to 18 inches).
- Personal (ranging from one-half to 4 feet).
- Social (ranging from 4 to 7 feet at the near phase and from 7 to 12 feet at the far phase).
- Public (12 to 25 feet or more).

Preference for spacing will influence where people sit or stand. If you remain distant from others when you speak to them, you may unintentionally communicate unfriendliness or disinterest. If you approach people too closely, they may feel uncomfortable. People who like each other tend to stand closer together than people who don't like each other.

Gestures

We use gestures such as head and hand movements to reveal or conceal feelings. We can use them to add emphasis, to illustrate points, and to manage turn taking. You can encourage others to continue talking by nodding periodically. Some gestures, such as scratching yourself, covering your eyes, picking at your clothing, tapping your feet, or wringing your hands, can, if excessive, communicate discomfort or some other negative emotion. Both regional and ethnic differences may influence the kind of gestures and the situations in which they are used.

Touch

Touch communicates and influences emotion, status, and attitudes. It takes on different meanings depending on the situation. The different types include

- Functional/professional touch, for example, a physician examining a patient.
- Social/polite touch, such as a handshake or helping someone on with a coat.
- Friendly touch, for example, putting an arm around a friend's shoulder when you say goodbye.
- Loving/intimate touch, such as kissing or handholding. (Knapp, 1980)

What kind of touch is appropriate depends on the situation and the relationship between the people involved. Norms for touching vary from culture to culture.

Touching plays a role in communicating status or dominance (Henley, 1977). High-status people engage in more touching of lower-status persons. Norms for touching between men and women reflect status differences; men touch women more than women touch men. People are more likely to touch each other when they are

- Giving information or advice (rather than receiving it).
- Giving an order (rather than responding to one).

- Requesting a favor (rather than reacting to it).
- Attempting to persuade someone (rather than being persuaded).
- Engaging in deep rather than casual conversation.
- Attending social events such as parties (rather than being at work).
- Conveying excitement (rather than receiving it from someone else).
- Receiving reactions of worry (rather than communicating them).

You can avoid misinterpretations by complementing touches with other cues that match your intentions. For example, to get someone's attention, you could touch him on the arm while saying "Excuse me." You could avoid the mistaken perception of a touch as aggressive by accompanying it with a smile and appropriate comments. Here, too, cultural differences influence what will be effective.

Physical Appearance

You can influence how others respond by offering a physical appearance that complements your goals. Components of physical appearance include facial features, hair style, skin, decorations such as jewelry, cosmetics (makeup, perfume), accessories such as hats or eyeglasses, posture, physique, hygiene, neatness, cleanliness, and style of clothing. These characteristics convey impressions to others about our attractiveness, status, degree of conformity, intelligence, personality, social class, style and taste, sexuality, and age. Many studies document the importance of physical attractiveness in initial social contacts (Calvert, 1988). Your skills, the extent to which people view you as similar or compatible to themselves, and their confidence in your ability to get things done efficiently, affect how credible and attractive you appear to others.

EXHIBIT 12.9
Troubleshooting Checklist

_____ 1. Were my goals clear?
_____ 2. Were they achievable?
_____ 3. Did I focus on common goals?
_____ 4. Did I focus on positive goals?
_____ 5. Did I have a plan? Was it likely to be effective?
_____ 6. What cues did I attend to? Were they relevant or irrelevant? Distracting or helpful?
_____ 7. Did I offer others a rewarding experience?
_____ 8. What did I do or think that was helpful?
_____ 9. What did I do or think that was *not* helpful (e.g., behaviors that occurred too often, too seldom, at the wrong time, or in the wrong form)?
_____ 10. Did I consider the perspective of others?
_____ 11. Were there special skills that I needed but don't have?
_____ 12. Was my self-presentation effective? Could it be improved?

Planning a Learning Agenda

To plan a learning agenda, first identify the skills you would like to enhance. Find out if anything is known about what behaviors contribute to or detract from achieving your goals. Take advantage of training programs and written material (e.g., Cormier & Cormier, 1991; Egan, 1994; Nelson-Jones, 1993). You could use role playing to explore your current skill levels in relation to outcomes of interest. The more clearly you describe your goals and related skills, the easier it will be to determine your current skill levels, plan a learning agenda, and monitor your progress. You could tape-record some of your interviews (with the clients' permission) and review them to discover the skills that you would like to improve. You could keep a diary of situations you find difficult, noting the situation, your goal, and suggestions for increasing success. You could arrange "prompts" to remind yourself to use new skills (e.g., placing some object on your desk as a reminder). Exhibit 12.9 is a troubleshooting checklist.

SUMMARY

Effective helpers have effective relationship skills, such as structuring meetings, attentively listening, offering constructive feedback, and being concrete, respectful, empathetic, warm, and nonjudgmental. These skills are important to use with coworkers, supervisors, and other professionals as well as with clients and significant others. Understanding the components of effective social behavior such as selecting appropriate goals, knowing the rules concerning what may and may not be done in specific situations, and accurately perceiving and translating social signals will help you determine what has "gone wrong" in a problematic social situation. Knowing what not to do is as important as knowing what to do. Whether you achieve your goals will depend not only on your skills but also on the skills of involved others and the degree to which your goals are shared. Skill in avoiding or removing barriers to communication and sensitivity to cultural differences in preferred styles of communication also are important.

REVIEWING YOUR COMPETENCIES

Reviewing What You Know

1. Clearly define your goals in specific social situations, and identify verbal and nonverbal behaviors that will help you attain them. Include behaviors you should avoid as well as those you should offer.
2. Identify components of a "friendly attitude."
3. Describe voice qualities and nonverbal behaviors that influence how others respond.
4. Identify criteria for judging the quality of questions.
5. Describe five ways to structure exchanges.
6. Describe behaviors that you should model during interviews.
7. Describe components of attentive listening as well as common errors.
8. Identify poor substitutes for empathic responses.
9. Describe the functions of self-disclosure, and give examples of situations in which this would be helpful.
10. Describe common errors in offering feedback.
11. Describe preferred styles of communication of different cultural groups.
12. Distinguish between advanced and primary accurate empathy.
13. Give examples of concrete statements and questions.
14. Describe behaviors that communicate respect.
15. Identify behaviors that should be avoided in order to be nonjudgmental.
16. Describe changes you could make in your self-presentation that would enhance your effectiveness in specific social situations.
17. Identify specific social skills you would like to improve as well as the situations in which these would be of value. Design a training program to increase your skill based on a description of specific verbal and nonverbal skills that influence success.

Reviewing What You Do

1. You offer attentive listening (you can check many items in Exhibit 12.5).
2. You can distinguish between attentive and nonattentive listening and identify related behaviors based on your observation of videotaped exchanges.

3. Your ratio of instrumental to noninstrumental questions is high (see Exhibit 12.3).
4. Your questions and comments encourage concreteness. (Rate each question and statement during an interview on a scale from 1 (not at all concrete) to 5 (very concrete).
5. You use personalized examples to support your explanations.
6. Your physical presentation increases the likelihood of attaining service goals.
7. You can distinguish between helpful and nonhelpful feedback based on examples.
8. You structure interviews effectively (see Exhibit 12.4).
9. You start and end interviews effectively.
10. You are nonjudgemental.
11. You adjust your style of communication to match the styles of your clients.
12. You offer high levels of respect (see Exhibit 12.7) and empathy.
13. You maintain a comfortable and effective pace during interviews, in both rapidness of talking and sensitivity of content discussed.
14. You accurately identify the impressions you convey to others in specific situations and also their consequences.
15. You can describe what you would do differently to create more effective impressions in specific situations.
16. You use self-disclosure effectively.
17. Your nonverbal behavior matches your verbal behavior.
18. You take advantage of opportunities to prompt and support positive behaviors.
19. You ignore irrelevant and inappropriate behaviors.
20. You give criticism in a nonthreatening, constructive manner.
21. Your paraphrases and reflective comments are accurate.

Reviewing Results

1. You attain a high percentage of your goals during social exchanges.
2. Other people succeed in attaining goals that are important to them in a high percentage of their exchanges with you.
3. Clients feel better about themselves.
4. Clients describe their exchanges with you as useful.
5. Clients carry out agreed-on tasks.
6. Clients achieve outcomes they value.

CHAPTER 13

Handling Challenging Social Situations

OVERVIEW

This chapter offers guidelines for handling challenging social situations that arise in your everyday work. These include introducing unpopular points of view, responding to criticism, and making and refusing requests. Thinking critically about decisions will involve asking colleagues to clarify points they may view as self-evident when they are not. Options for avoiding and handling emotional abuse, sexual harassment, and discrimination at work are also discussed. The guidelines in this chapter may have to be modified to consider different cultural norms for social behavior. For example, although not losing face is important in all cultures, the particular situations that result in "loss of face" may differ.

You Will Learn About

- Assertive, passive, and aggressive behavior.
- Interpersonal problem solving.
- Disagreement.
- Responding to criticism.
- Responding to put-downs.
- Refusing requests.
- Handling sexual harassment.
- Speaking more.
- Listening more.
- Obstacles.

DIFFICULT SOCIAL SITUATIONS

Social work practice requires handling difficult social situations, such as requesting changes in offensive behavior and responding to criticism. These situations may arise with colleagues, clerical staff, administrators, and professionals in other agencies as well as clients. Thinking critically about practice-related decisions requires raising questions that others may prefer to remain unasked. Examples of useful skills are shown in Exhibit 13.1. Knowledge about cultural differences will help you to respond effectively. For example, specific nonverbal behaviors have different meanings in different cultures (see Exhibit 13.2). Your feelings and actions in a situation depend largely on your past experiences in similar situations. This will influence whether you view a situation as irrelevant, positive, or stressful (one in which there is some actual or potential harm or challenge). Your past experience will also influence how you handle a situation. You could (1) seek information, (2) take direct action (change the environment and/or your own behavior), (3) do nothing, (4) com-

plain, and/or (5) use a cognitive coping strategy. The last option involves altering what you attend to or how you view events. Examples include denial, avoidance, and detachment. You could, for example, reassess an imagined slight as irrelevant. Denial is often used in everyday life (Taylor & Brown, 1988).

You can often avoid unpleasant social situations by planning ahead. For example, reinforcing valued behaviors may avoid unwanted social predicaments. Disliked behaviors often occur because positive alternatives are not reinforced (including approximations to them). So when you complain about someone, ask yourself: Am I reinforcing behaviors I want to increase or maintain? Am I inviting these behaviors? Am I reinforcing behaviors I dislike? Supervisors who complain about staff may not reinforce desired behaviors. Beliefs such as "She gets paid for this" or "She should know this" may interfere with reinforcing valued behaviors. Developing effective skills for interacting with supervisors and agency administrators will help you avoid predicaments and acquire needed training. Drury recommends: "Don't undermine their au-

EXHIBIT 13.1
Examples of Useful Social Skills

	Would Like to Work On	Fairly Competent	Very Competent
1. Raise questions about claims/point of view in a tactful manner.			
2. Request clarification (e.g., of vague concepts).			
3. Listen attentively (see Chapter 12).			
4. Communicate empathic understanding of other points of view.			
5. Prompt and reinforce desired behaviors.			
6. Remove cues for and ignore undesired behaviors.			
7. Recognize and accurately interpret social signals.			
8. Recognize and use feelings as clues to what people want.			
9. Balance talking and listening.			
10. Manage anger and anxiety.			
11. Refuse requests.			
12. Request behavior changes.			
13. Request favors.			
14. Respond constructively to criticism.			
15. Apologize when appropriate.			
16. Respond effectively to put-downs and discriminatory comments.			
17. Clearly describe expectations.			
18. Respond effectively to unwanted sexual advances.			
19. Neutralize and/or avoid hostile and violent reactions.			

EXHIBIT 13.2
The Importance of Considering Cultural Differences

Sylvia Echohawk is a 29-year-old American Indian woman who works for one of the major automobile manufacturing companies in the United States. The company has recently implemented an affirmative action program designed to open up jobs for minorities. The personnel director, a White male counseling psychologist, is in charge of it. Sylvia, who was hired under the affirmative action program, is referred to him by her immediate supervisor because of "frequent tardiness." Also, the supervisor informs the psychologist that other employees take advantage of Sylvia. She goes out of her way to help them, shares her lunches with them, and even lends them money. Several times during the lunch hours, other employees have borrowed her car to run errands. The supervisor feels that Sylvia needs to actively deal with her passive–aggressive means of handling anger (tardiness), to set limits on others, and to be able to assert her rights.

In an interview with Sylvia, the psychologist notices several things about her behavior. She is low-keyed, restrained in behavior, avoids eye contact, and finds it difficult to verbalize her thoughts and feelings. After several meetings, the psychologist concludes that Sylvia would benefit from assertion training. She is placed in such a group during regular working hours but fails to show up for meetings after attending the first one. Additionally, Sylvia's supervisor informs the psychologist that she has turned in a two-week resignation notice.

Questions

1. Is it possible that American-Indian communication styles are leading to inaccurate assumptions made by the counselor?

2. In what ways would the following values shared by American Indians affect both the work setting and counseling approach (cooperation, sharing, temporal perspective, and harmony)?

3. What does an affirmative action program mean? What does it mean to you? How do you feel about it?

4. What obligations do organizations have in adapting their practices to fit the needs of culturally different workers? What obligations does the culturally different worker have to adjust.

Source: D. W. Sue S. D. Sue (1990), Counseling the culturally different: Theory and Practice *(2nd ed.) (pp. 258–259). New York: Wiley-Interscience.*

thority; build a strong case for change (the more specific the better) and recognize norms and power dynamics in organizations" (1984, p. 255).

ASSERTIVE, PASSIVE, AND AGGRESSIVE BEHAVIOR

Some people are passive (e.g., say nothing) when they must speak up in order to attain valued outcomes. Other people are aggressive, putting people down and harshly criticizing them. Assertive behavior involves expressing preferences without undue anxiety in a manner that encourages others to take them into account and does not infringe on other people's rights (Alberti & Emmons, 1995). There is a focus on the situation or behavior rather than the person. Alternatives to aggressive reactions include calming self talk, polite requests, reframing situations (e.g., as unimportant), and em-

EXHIBIT 13.3
Comparison of Passive, Assertive, and Aggressive Styles and Their Effects

	Passive	Aggressive	Assertive
Behavior Patterns	No expression of expectations and feelings.	Critical expression of expectations and feelings.	Clear, direct descriptions of unapologetic expectations and feelings.
	Views stated indirectly or apologetically.	Blaming and judgmental criticisms. Negative intentions attributed to others.	Descriptive instead of judgmental criticisms.
	Complaints are made to the wrong person.	Problems acted on too quickly.	Persistence.
	Problems not confronted soon enough. No persistence. Unclear negotiation and compromise.	Unwillingness to listen. Refusal to negotiate and compromise	Willingness to listen. Negotiation and compromise.
Word Choices	Minimizing words. Apologetic statements. Statements made about people in general instead of to a specific person. General instead of specific behavioral descriptions. Statements disguised as questions.	Loaded words. "You" statements. "Always" or "never" statements. Demands instead of requests. Judgments disguised as questions.	Neutral language. Concise statements. Personalized statements of concern. Specific behavioral descriptions. Cooperative words Requests instead of demands. No statements disguised as. questions.
Voice Characteristics and Body Language	Pleading or questioning voice tone. Hesitation. Lack of eye contact. Slumping downtrodden posture. Words and nonverbal behavior do not match.	Sarcastic, judgmental, overbearing voice tone. Interruptions. "Looking-through-you" eye contact. Tense impatient posture.	Even, powerful voice tone. Eye contact. Erect, relaxed posture. Words and nonverbal messages that match.
Results	Rights are violated; taken advantage of. Not likely to achieve goals. Feels frustrated, hurt, or anxious. Allows others to choose for him or her.	Violates other people's rights; takes advantages of others. Achieves goals at other people's expense. Defensive, belligerent; humiliates and depreciates others. Chooses for others.	Respects own rights as well as those of others. Achieves desired goals without hurting others. Feels good about self; is confident. Chooses for self.

Source: (First three sections only) S. S. Drury (1984), Assertive supervision: Building involved teamwork *(pp. 294–295). Champaign, IL: Research Press.*

phasizing common interests. Behaviors and outcomes associated with passive, aggressive, and assertive reactions are illustrated in Exhibit 13.3. Respect for your rights and for the rights of others is integral to the philosophy underlying assertiveness. It is not a "do your own thing" approach in which you express your wishes, regardless of their effects on others, nor does it guarantee that you will achieve your goals. As with any new behavior, learning to be more assertive may feel awkward and unnatural at first. What will be effective in one social situation may not be effective in another. Draw on and expand your knowledge of cultural differences to avoid and handle social situations.

INTERPERSONAL PROBLEM-SOLVING

Your skills will be more than adequate in many situations, and you won't have to think much about what to do. In others, you may have to "problem solve" to decide what to do. Examples include:

- Staff who do not return your call.
- Clients who talk too much.
- Clients who repeatedly interrupt you.
- Supervisors who harshly criticize you.
- Clients who physically threaten you.
- Clients who are reluctant to talk.
- Supervisors who make sexual advances.
- Coworkers who put you down (e.g., make demeaning remarks).
- Coworkers who bad-mouth clients.
- Coworkers who arrive late for meetings.
- Coworkers who sleep during meetings.
- Situations that cause anxiety or anger.

The problem-solving steps described in Chapter 5 also are helpful in interpersonal problem-solving (e.g., Beyth-Marom, Fischhoff, & Quadrel, 1991; Spivak & Shure, 1974).

- Stop, calm down, and think.
- Describe the problem and how you feel.
- Select a positive goal.
- Identify options, and consider the consequences.
- Try the best plan.
- Evaluate the results.

Stop, Calm Down, and Think

Stopping, calming down, and thinking will help you avoid escalating negative emotions and selecting an ineffective option. In most situations, it is good advice. However, there are situations in which this advice is not wise, those in which quick action is called for to prevent harm and violence. Use your relaxation skills to stay calm or to calm down

(Bernstein & Borkovec, 1973; Woolfolk & Lehrer, 1993). Helpful rules for keeping interfering emotional reactions in check are

- Focus on service goals.
- When in doubt, think the best (give people the benefit of the doubt).
- Ignore minor annoyances that don't really matter.
- Be sensitive to and respect cultural differences in values, norms, and preferred communication styles.
- Catch and counter emotional "triggers" (e.g., "He is a _____," "I can't stand this").
- Reinforce behaviors you want to encourage.
- Don't reinforce behavior you want to discourage.
- Take a deep breath.
- Focus on shared interests.
- Consider other people's perspectives (cultivate empathic understanding).

Describe the Problem and How You Feel (to Yourself)

What exactly is the problem? Who is doing what (or not) to or for whom? Clearly describe the five W's: context (who, where, when), behavior (what), and effect (why). Use feelings of wanting to blame and punish others as clues to identify what you want and how you can achieve it. Being aware of how you feel in certain situations should help you understand and empathize with how others feel. Expand your vocabulary of words that describe different kinds and intensities of feelings. Larson (1993) underscores the importance of identifying your "emotional allergies" (incidents that "get under your skin" and interfere with task performance). If you know what these are and decide they do get in your way, you will be ready to ignore them when they occur and to move on to pursue service goals.

Select a Positive Goal

What do you want? What would have to be different for the problem to be solved? The more clearly you describe what you want, the more information you can offer to others. Focus on positive goals. Rather than telling your supervisor, "I was dissatisfied with our last meeting," say "I'd like more specific feedback from you about how I'm evaluating progress with Mrs. L."

Identify Options and Related Consequences

How can you achieve your goal? What are different options and the likely consequences of each? What obstacles might get in the way of promising options? What cultural differences should be considered? Ethnic and cultural factors influence what emotions people feel and how they express them. Unless you consider cultural differences, you may offend, frighten, or anger others. Indirectness is highly valued in some cultures. For example, Japanese people consider it a sign of maturity and power (Clancy, 1986). In his article "Sixteen Ways to Avoid Saying 'No' in Japan," Keiko Ueda (1974) includes the options of silence, ambiguity, and expressions of apology. Skill in carrying out on-the-spot cost–benefit analyses in which you review both potential short- and long-term consequences of an action will help you make decisions (see Exhibit 13.4). Be sure to consider both personal outcomes (effects on yourself) and social ones (effects on others). Consider what you may lose by not doing anything. For example, if you don't ask your supervisor for more specific feedback, you may lose opportunities to learn.

Try the Best Plan and Evaluate the Results

Try out the alternative that seems most promising for reaching your goals with a maximum of positive and a minimum of negative consequences to others as well as yourself. If it is successful, use it on future occasions. If not, circle back to earlier steps. Have you overlooked cultural or ethnic differences?

The Importance of Flexibility and Persistence

Establishing positive working relationships requires flexibility in adjusting your behavior to the behavior and interests of others. Decisions must be made about pacing, content to focus on, directiveness, and encouragement to offer. In some situations, taking direct action (requesting or negotiating changes) may be most effective. In others, calming self-talk or delaying a reaction may be best. What will be effective in one situation may not be in another. The actions you take or avoid to prevent predicaments with clients may differ from those you take or avoid with a colleague or supervisor. Your skills, the skills of others, the degree to which goals and values are shared, and the kinds of power people rely on (see Chapter 12) will influence options. You may decrease your success by relying on the wrong power base. For example, perhaps you have been trying to encourage an administrator to like you when demonstrating your competence would be more successful. Or you may be relying on criticism rather than praise. Agreements

EXHIBIT 13.4
Anger Cost–Benefit Analysis

Advantages of Displaying Anger	Disadvantages of Displaying Anger
1. It feels good to get it off my mind.	1. It may spoil our relationship; it will take my valuable time that could be used to pursue service goals.
2. He will know that I disapprove of him.	2. He may reject me.
3. I have a right to blow my stack if I want to.	3. I'll feel guilty and down on myself afterward.
4. He'll know I'm not a doormat.	4. He may retaliate against me and also get angry.
5. I'll show him I won't stand being taken advantage of.	5. My anger gets in the way of correcting the problem.
6. Even though I won't get what I want, I can at least have the satisfaction of revenge. I can make him feel hurt as I do.	6. This won't solve the problem; it will only make things worse. I'll get labeled as moody and immature; this distracts me from pursuit of service goals.

Source: Adapted from D. D. Burns (1990), Feeling good: The new mood therapy (p. 151). New York: Morrow.

EXHIBIT 13.5
Being Persistent in a Discussion

Situation:	Case conference.
Supervisor:	Blandy Residential Center was advertised in *Social Work*. I think this setting would be a good one for Jim.
Social Worker 1:	Yes, I've heard about the center. Other agencies also refer to Blandy.
Social Worker 2:	I've visited the center, and the staff seem very dedicated.
Social Worker 3 (you):	Do you know anything about their success in helping adolescents like Jim?
Supervisor:	Well, they've been around for 50 years. They must be doing something right.
Social Worker 3 (you):	Fifty years is a long time. I wonder if they've collected any data about how effective they have been.
Social Worker 1:	Well, let's see. Here's their brochure. It says they offer high-quality services and are sensitive to young people's needs. Sounds good to me.
Social Worker 3 (you):	Sending Jim to Blandy means removing him from his home and neighborhood. I wonder if we could think of some third or fourth alternative.
Social Worker 2:	You're new here and don't know the limitations of our resources. I think we should refer him to Blandy.
Social Worker 3 (you):	Yes, I am new to this agency, but I do think we are thinking about this in either–or terms (either leave him at home or send him to Blandy), and need information about this center's success rate.

based on affection and respect are more likely to be carried out in the absence of external control.

Often, you will have to be persistent to help your clients. Your first attempt to question a generally accepted point of view in a case conference may be ignored (see Exhibit 13.5). You may have to introduce your point more than once—and you should do so if this would be of value in helping clients and avoiding harm. For example, at a case conference the others present may recommend that a youth be sent to a residential facility they saw advertised in *Social Work* when in fact only testimonials were offered in the advertisement in support of claims of effectiveness and there are less intrusive options (e.g., working with the youth in the community). You may have to be persistent to obtain services for a client.

As a youth [Pablo] sustained a traumatic amputation of his left leg below the knee. He lived alone and worked long hours as a cook. . . . He kept himself isolated with few friends and no family. . . . He worked for cash, had little savings and, of course, no health insurance. When his prosthesis broke, he could no longer stand without crutches. He lost his job and wound up in a shelter. . . . We treated his stump, and referred him to the hospital-based clinic for a new prosthesis but learned that the "healthcare" to which shelter residents were entitled did not include prostheses. The shelter case worker deemed him ineligible for Medicaid. But an experienced social worker, new to our team, was sure that despite his alien sta-

tus he was entitled to emergency coverage. She set out relentlessly to obtain it. After six months of filing applications and placing telephone calls on his behalf, the social worker obtained approval. (Savarese & Weber, 1993, p. 4)

You may have to keep trying to contact staff at another agency. Be sure not to criticize them for not returning your calls when you do contact them. You might say "Hello, my name is _____ I am . . . I would like to talk to you about _____." Focusing on service goals will help you to handle difficult situations constructively.

DISAGREEING/QUESTIONING

Making well-informed decisions often requires a critical appraisal of different points of view (see Exhibit 13.6). Disagreements are opportunities to forward understanding. Thinking carefully about practice decisions requires raising questions such as: Have there been any critical tests of this claim? Are there any data suggesting that this method may harm rather than help clients?" Your work and learning environments may not reflect a culture of thoughtfulness in which alternative views are sought and welcomed (Gibbs & Gambrill, 1996). Disagreements may be interpreted as signs of disloyalty, impertinence, or rudeness. Some people will respond negatively to questions and differ-

EXHIBIT 13.6
An Exercise to Practice Raising Questions

Think of a practice-related situation in which questions should be raised about claims but are not. Clearly describe the situation, a claim, and questions you think should be raised, and why. Last, describe any obstacles and possible remedies.

Situation: _____

Claim: _____

_____

_____

_____

Questions that should be raised: _____

_____

_____

_____

Obstacles to raising them: _____

_____

_____

_____

Remedies for overcoming obstacles: _____

_____

_____

_____

_____

ences of opinion. They may confuse biased people with those who are expressing a point of view (and who are open to changing their minds). They may respond to questions as unwelcome challenges to their authority rather than as efforts to clarify key concepts, points of view, and associated evidence. Raising questions requires courage. Keeping service goals clearly in view (to help clients) will help you speak up (see Exhibit 13.7).

Effective Disagreement

The answer to the question, What is effective disagreement? depends on your goals, which could include the following:

- To discover options.
- To recognize shared concerns.
- To make sound decisions.
- To define problems accurately.
- To show how smart you are.
- To show people how stupid they are.

Pursuing the first four goals is more likely to foster a constructive exchange in which understanding is forwarded and sound decisions are made. Be sure you understand a position before you criticize it. You can convey understanding by paraphrasing what others say (see Chapter 12). Recognizing points of agreement lessens the likelihood of defensive reac-

EXHIBIT 13.7
To Speak or Not to Speak

You will have many opportunities during your career to protect clients from harm and ineffective service by questioning decisions and claims. Raising questions about ideas that other people take for granted requires courage, especially in environments in which disagreements are not viewed as opportunities to learn and advance understanding. You may overestimate the risk of negative consequence such as ridicule or being labeled a troublemaker. Whether or not you should speak can be guided by the following questions:

Situation (what was said, where, when, by whom):

_____

_____

_____

What I wanted (or would want) to say: _____

_____

_____

Possible positive consequences of speaking:

   For clients: _____

_____

   For colleagues: _____

_____

   For the agency: _____

_____

   For the profession: _____

_____

   For me: _____

_____

Possible negative consequences of speaking:

   For clients: _____

_____

   For colleagues: _____

_____

   For the agency: _____

_____

   For the profession: _____

_____

   For me: _____

_____

(*continued*)

EXHIBIT 13.7 (*continued*)

Possible positive consequences of not speaking:

For clients: _____

_____

For colleagues: _____

_____

For the agency: _____

_____

For the profession: _____

_____

For me: _____

_____

Possible negative consequences of not speaking:

For clients: _____

_____

For colleagues: _____

_____

For the agency: _____

_____

For the profession: _____

_____

For me: _____

_____

tions and improves the chances of discovering shared concerns and goals. You can buffer disagreement by delivering it tactfully at an appropriate time and acknowledging other points of view. You might say:

- "That's an interesting view. I like the way you. . . . Another approach might be. . . ."
- "It sounds as if we both agree that this program would be helpful, but we seem to differ in how to pursue it. . . ." "I think . . . because. . . ."

People are more likely to consider what you say if they are not offended by your style of expres-

sion. Cultural differences influence who can disagree with whom, about what, and what style is most effective. Preferred styles range from indirect to blunt. In some cultures it is important to avoid conflict. Hierarchical relationships in some families and cultures require respect for certain speaking patterns (e.g., who speaks first).

Take responsibility for points you make by using personal pronoun such as "I," or "my" and explain your reasons for your points of view. You might say, "That's an interesting point; however, I think . . . because. . . ." Disagreements that do not include elaborations may appear abrupt and do not explain the reasons for your position. Practice raising questions tactfully and responding constructively to reactions that do not foster a careful appraisal of points of view (e.g., put-downs and question begging). A constructive response results in minimal negative reactions and maximal positive reactions including forwarding service goals. Focus on service goals, and don't take things personally.

Be sure to reinforce tolerant and open-minded reactions by attending to and commenting on them. You might say, "It's great to talk to someone willing to consider other views." If you change your point of view after a discussion, tell the other person. You might say: "Your argument is a good one, and I find myself rethinking my initial ideas."

Timing

Wait until other people finish talking before starting to speak, unless you are not receiving your share of talk time. If you interrupt other people, they might react negatively to the interruption and not consider your ideas. Disagreeing with someone in front of others may be inappropriate in some cultures. This may result in a "loss of face" for the other person. Try not to violate the "pleasantness norm" during initial encounters by introducing a topic or opinion that will lead to conflict. Overlook minor differences.

What to Avoid

Avoid comments that put others down or embarrass them. Examples are: "You don't know what you're talking about," "That's a stupid idea." Such comments are likely to result in counteraggression or avoidance. Excessive negative emotion will interfere with effective disagreement, encourage defensive reactions, and increase the likelihood of unproductive conflict. Your nonverbal behavior might communicate anger or annoyance as you express an otherwise effective message. Avoid the buildup of anger by learning to identify the beginning signs of irritation (e.g., increased body tension and negative thoughts) and using constructive self-statements (e.g., "Take it easy," "What's my

goal?") and actions. Disagreeing excessively is not wise. Unrelenting questioning with the goal of changing someone's mind can be unpleasant and is not likely to be effective. Furthermore, if you disagree with many small points, your disagreement with the big points may not be taken seriously. Some people show disagreement by withdrawing their attention (for example, looking away), leaving the conversation, or avoiding future contact. Silence is not a good option if you can achieve your goals only by expressing your views.

Handling Conflict

If a discussion seems to be escalating into a conflict, you could comment on this and suggest that you move on to another topic or remind participants about service goals. You might say, "We seem to have strong feelings about this issue," "Let's keep our service goals in view," "Let's table this discussion for now and talk about. . ." (pause). You may have to bring in a mediator to move a discussion in a positive direction. Exhibit 13.8 is a checklist for disagreeing.

RESPONDING TO CRITICISM (FEEDBACK)

Responding effectively to criticism, whether from yourself or others, is essential to learning and to maintaining constructive working relationships. People may criticize claims you make, the quality of your reasoning, or your behavior. Differences provide opportunities to select well-reasoned views and to strengthen working relationships. Different kinds of criticism include teasing, blowing off steam, and attempts at problem solving (Drury, 1984). Teasing may or may not reflect a real concern that should be addressed. The techniques that Drury (1984) recommends for responding to teasing are using humor, ignoring, fogging (e.g., agreeing with some aspect of the implied criticism without agreeing with the implied judgement ("that may be"), asking the person to stop teasing, and commenting on the process (making an observation such as "I notice that . . ." and asking a question like "Is there a problem we should discuss?"). If

EXHIBIT 13.8
Checklist for Disagreeing

_____ Ignore minor differences.
_____ View disagreements and questions as learning opportunities.
_____ Acknowledge other points of view.
_____ Make sure you understand other points of view.
_____ Comment on other people's cogent points, point of agreement, and mutual concerns.
_____ Focus on common goals.
_____ Avoid derogatory critical comments and negative nonverbal reactions (e.g., scowling).
_____ Don't interrupt people.
_____ Explain why you disagree or question views/claims (use elaborated opinion statements).
_____ Express differences as they arise when appropriate; don't allow frustration to build up or time for effective action to pass you by.
_____ Reinforce others for listening.
_____ End or avoid unconstructive exchanges if possible (you could suggest another time for discussion or involve another person).
_____ Consider cultural differences in norms, values, and preferred styles of communication.

teasing reflects an underlying concern, bring this into the open and discuss it. Blowing off steam is another kind of criticism in which someone may simply want to express frustration or anger. Attempts to solve a problem comprise a third form of criticism.

Common reactions to criticism (whether of a belief or a behavior) are (1) withdrawal (avoiding the person, escaping from the situation), (2) attack (name-calling, threats), and (3) defensiveness (counteraccusations, excuses, nonverbal indicators) (see Exhibit 13.9). Criticism may reflect other people's desire to maintain their status (as an authority), sloppy thinking, unrealistic expectations, or mood, rather than the quality of your reasoning or the appropriateness of your behavior. Misunderstanding work roles may also be an obstacle. Consider the example Drury (1984) gives of the employee who accused a supervisor of being uncaring because the supervisor asked the employee to finish her work. That is, she saw the supervisor as uncaring because the supervisor was doing her job. Responding constructively to criticism can prevent unfair blame. Intense reactions to criticism (prolonged sadness, anger, or hostility) may reflect

unrealistic expectations about yourself (e.g., "I must never make mistakes") or others (e.g., "They have no right to question my behavior"). The guidelines discussed next mainly concern criticisms that are problem solving attempts. What you should do depends partly on the kind of criticism, how it is given, and your relationship with other participants.

View Feedback as a Learning Opportunity

Whether positive or negative, the reactions of others offer clues about what they want and think. Your critic may help you to discover flaws in your thinking or show you how to use a practice skill. Focus first on understanding your critic's point of view (e.g., what she wants, feels, or thinks) rather than defending yourself, making suggestions, or giving advice. Clients may "test" you to see whether you are biased or uninformed about their culture. Being prepared for such tests will help you respond effectively.

Relax and Listen (Unless Your Critic Is Abusive)

Relax and listen (unless someone is verbally abusing you or there is a danger of violence). Attend to

EXHIBIT 13.9
Signs of Defensiveness and Closed-Mindedness

- Unwillingness to listen.
- Raised voice.
- Irritable voice tones.
- Condescending comments.
- Ridicule/mockery/disgust.
- Well-placed sighs.
- "Knowing" laugh.
- Attacking/insulting person.
- Interruptions.
- Crossed arms.
- Saying no, no, no.
- Shaking the head.
- Rolling the eyes.
- Yawning dramatically.
- Ignoring comments/questions.
- Not speaking when greeted/addressed.

Source: Z. Seech (1993), Open minds and everyday reasoning (pp. 7–8). Belmont, CA: Wadsworth.

what is expressed both verbally and nonverbally. If the person is very upset (e.g., speaking loudly and fast), let him "run down" before you respond, unless he is offensive or potentially dangerous. When you do respond, avoid attacks and negative labels to avoid contributing to the emotionality of the exchange. Taking time to understand the criticism will help you learn, remain calm, and respond effectively. Other people will feel listened to. The steps that Drury (1984) recommends when criticism represents blowing off steam are (1) correcting misperceptions, (2) listening and asking for details to allow others to calm down, (3) identifying problems that should be discussed, (4) acknowledging the other person's right to their feelings, and (5) setting limits when people are violent or abusive, when the time or place is inappropriate, or when you do not want to listen.

Check Your Understanding and Ask for Clarification When Needed

Check your understanding of what has been said by paraphrasing it and reflecting the feelings expressed (see Chapter 12). This will indicate that you take the other person's concerns seriously and will allow him or her to correct any misunderstandings. You might say, "You get irritated when I don't follow through on my agreements with you," "You think I've overlooked information that shows that clients are harmed by taking this medication; is that correct?" People may tell you what they don't want but not what they do want. You might say "It sounds as if you want me to. . . . Is this right?" If the criticism is vague, ask for clarification. If a client accuses you of being rude, ask for specific examples of what you said or did (or did not say or do) so that you can clearly understand their complaint. Only if you understand what people want can you decide whether their requests or objections are reasonable and/or possible to fulfill. Your critics have a responsibility to clearly describe their criticisms, and the reasons for them.

Offer Empathic Reactions

Empathic responses may diffuse negative emotions and create a more congenial problem-solving at-

mosphere. Examples are "I can see how this would be difficult" or "I think I'd feel the same way if I thought that." You don't have to agree with criticisms to offer empathic statements. Avoid comments such as "I know how you feel," which may appear patronizing. Recognize points of agreement. Some people confuse a lack of understanding with a lack of agreement. You may understand what a person wants but not agree that it is a problem. In any case, you can demonstrate your understanding by accurately describing his or her position.

Accept Responsibility for What You Say and Do

If the criticism is sound, acknowledge it. You might say, "Yes, you're right, I did interrupt you several times." If appropriate, consider apologizing when you agree with the feedback, but don't be overly self-critical or apologetic. You could ignore unfair or abusive comments and respond only to the sound criticism. If someone says, "You interrupted me several times, and each time your remark was pointless," you could acknowledge that you did interrupt and then reintroduce your point if you still think it is a worthwhile one. If someone says, "That was a silly thing to ask," your reply might be, "There are times when I could be more on my toes, but I do think my question is a good one that still hasn't been answered. My question is. . . ."

Don't Let People Abuse or Neutralize You

Don't listen to or tolerate abuse. If you do, you will probably receive more. You could say (interrupting the person), "I can't allow you to talk to me that way." As a last resort, you could walk away (see the later section on safety). In reply to unfair criticism or to valid criticism delivered in an offensive way or at an inappropriate time, you might say, "I appreciate your suggestion, but I was embarrassed that you brought up the topic when other staff members were around. I'd prefer you to. . . ." Saying "It's difficult for me to accept criticism about this," communicates vulnerability that might encourage others to soften their approach. Don't let people neutralize you. If you do, clients may lose (see Exhibit 13.10).

EXHIBIT 13.10
Responding to Neutralizing Attempts

Criterion	Reply
• You're always questioning others.	• I question myself, too. I think we have to raise questions about our decisions. They affect clients' lives. For example . . .
• You're not working as a team member.	• I thought our purpose was to help clients and I think my questions forward this aim. For example . . .
• You're always bringing up minor points.	• I think my points are important. For example, if . . .
• We don't have time for these questions.	• My questions directly concern the quality of services we offer clients. For example, . . .
• I don't think you should be so critical of your colleagues.	• My points are directed toward ideas, not people. Only if we all are open to criticism can we learn from one another.
• You're being hardheaded. It's caring that counts.	• I think if we truly care about our clients, we will ask searching questions about whether our services help or harm them.

Seek and Offer Solutions

The best way to react to valid criticisms is to offer desired outcomes. This will satisfy your critics more than verbal assurances or excuses will. If the criticism is valid, ask for or offer suggestions to encourage people to become involved in a solution. You might say, "I do tend to interrupt you. How about giving me a signal when I do, so I can learn to stop myself?" If you say, "Since you're the one who's upset about this, you find a solution," others will feel that you don't care about or cannot respond to their concerns.

Take Time to Think If You Need It

If you feel unable to consider negative feedback or to sort out your reactions to it, arrange to discuss the criticism at another time. You might say, "I'd like to think about what you've said. How about discussing this on Friday?" Scheduling a future time to discuss concerns is important if someone introduces an issue when you have little time or privacy to discuss it. If the conversation begins to escalate into an argument or if you begin to feel confused or angry, suggest a timeout. You might say, "I think I understand and accept part of your criticism, and I've offered some solutions. However, you're repeating your original complaint and are now bringing up new ones. I'm feeling overwhelmed and would like a break."

Arrive at a Clear Agreement and Get Back on Track

If appropriate, reach a clear agreement on what will be done. Compromise and negotiation may be required to reach a mutually acceptable agreement. Focus on common goals (those shared by you and the other person), such as offering effective services (Fisher & Ury, 1983). Focus on your service goals and get back to them as soon as possible. You may have to use the "broken record" technique (repeat a statement such as "Let's get back to. . . .") (see Exhibit 13.11).

REFUSING REQUESTS

You may have to refuse requests from clients, coworkers, supervisors, or other professionals, it's best to do so in a way that maximizes positive feelings and minimizes negative ones. Be sure to consider preferred styles of communication when deciding whether to refuse a request and how to do so. Indirect ways are more acceptable in some groups (e.g., expressing regret, not using the word 'No'). People who are uncomfortable with being direct even when this is appropriate often never use the word *no*. They might say, "Well, I just don't know . . ." or "I'm sorry, I don't think so. . . ." If direct styles of refusal are appropriate, face the person, use the word *no* (as a signal that you have

EXHIBIT 13.11
Checklist for Handling Criticism

_____ View feedback as a learning opportunity.
_____ Don't take it personally.
_____ Relax and listen (unless the feedback is abusive).
_____ Check your understanding and ask for clarification as needed.
_____ Offer empathic responses (consider the other person's perspective).
_____ Avoid defensive, aggressive, and overly apologetic replies.
_____ Accept responsibility for what you say and do.
_____ Don't let people abuse or neutralize you.
_____ Seek and offer solutions.
_____ Take time to think if you need it.
_____ Arrive at a clear agreement about what will be done and get back on track.

made up your mind and have no intention of changing it), look at the person, speak loudly enough to be heard and slowly enough to be understood, and try not to stammer and hesitate. You may have to repeat your refusal. If you offer a reason for your refusal and the person rejects it, don't offer new reasons; just repeat the one you gave. The more excuses you give, the more opportunities others have to counter them. Shorter refusal statements may be more effective than long ones.

Refusing unreasonable demands from supervisors is important for your well-being. In these times of shrinking resources, staff are pushed to work longer and harder. Patronizing slogans are sometimes used such as "work smarter not harder" (as if you were not already working hard and smart). Know your rights and stick to your guns. Don't be "guilt tripped." For example, a common ploy in response to your refusal may be to say, "But this work must be done" or "Your clients need your help." You could answer, "That's a good point, but I can't do it. Perhaps you should hire some temporary help." In their book _You Don't Have to Take It!_ Ginny NiCarthy and her colleagues (1993) provide several examples of how to refuse unreasonable work requests. You as well as your clients can be exploited. Those in helping professions such as social work can perhaps be more easily guilt tripped into exploitive working conditions because of calls to elevate service to others above self-interest.

Limited resources do not mean, however, that your work climate should be punitive (e.g., complaints are punished and staff are excessively burdened).

REQUESTING BEHAVIOR CHANGES

Sometimes you will have to ask people to change their behavior. Examples include asking a supervisor for more detailed feedback, requesting a coworker to stop bad-mouthing clients, a client to stop interrupting you, and friends or coworkers to return borrowed items. Requesting behavior changes is often regarded as criticism. However, problems provide an opportunity to strengthen a relationship and should be approached from this viewpoint. Success in resolving concerns will increase your confidence that you can establish and maintain good relationships. Be sure to consider your goals. Goals such as making people feel guilty or making them pay for bad behavior carry the cost of people disliking you, and, you probably won't achieve them anyway. A reluctance to request behavior changes may be related to inaccurate or dysfunctional beliefs about social relationships (e.g., "I have no right to ask others to change") or fear of disapproval. Supervisors' rights include saying directly what they want or expect, asking employees to do the job they were hired to do, saying no when it is in the agency's best interest even if others don't like it, insisting that staff be at work for the time they are paid to work, requiring that staff keep commitments they make, confronting failure to perform even if it upsets employees, and asking employees to stop engaging in behaviors that prevent others from doing their work (Drury, 1984, p. 120).

The most positive and effective way to change offending behaviors is to reinforce positive alternatives. Suppose you dislike coworkers' dropping by your desk to chat. If they check with you before they come over, tell them you appreciate this. If indirect efforts fail (ignoring unwanted behaviors, prompting and reinforcing positive alternatives), discussing your concerns may be the next step. If you ignore your discomfort—hoping that it will go away or will magically change—you may start to dislike the person, become angry, or hopeless about the situation and may start to avoid the "culprit." We often (incorrectly) assume that other people know when their actions or inactions bother us. Or we may assume that we are helpless when we are not.

Ask: Does It Really Matter?

Is this a minor matter that should be ignored? If so, why mention it? Is it likely to happen again? If not, forget it. Is it a picky concern? If so, don't worry about it. Perhaps you are oversensitive to disapproval. You may have unrealistic beliefs (e.g., being asked a certain question by your supervisor shows disrespect or means that you are a bad person). You may confuse a problem you have with a problem you blame on someone else. On the other hand, something may matter a great deal (e.g., emotional abuse) and call for a definite request to stop (see the later section on handling emotional abuse).

Consider the Other Person's Perspective

Considering a situation from the other person's point of view will help you focus on common interests and shift from "winning" to reaching a mutually acceptable resolution. Empathy lessens anger and anxiety and also helps you estimate whether the other person can change. Two kinds of handicaps may compromise job performance: (1) personal concerns (e.g., poor training or problems at home) or (2) conditions such as large caseloads, poor supervision, and unrealistic administrative expectations. Rather than arguing about such handicaps, acknowledge them (e.g., that caseloads are large), and seek options for doing the best that can be done given the handicap and options for removing it.

Plan and Practice What to Say

Plan how to ask for changes in a positive way. You could prepare a script of what you will say and practice it. If defensive or hostile reactions are likely, despite a positive approach, rehearse constructive responses to them.

Choose the Right Time and Place

If there is time and privacy to share dissatisfactions and it is culturally appropriate to do so, express them as they arise rather than allowing them to build up. If you want to discuss a issue that occurred earlier, arrange a time to talk it over. You might say, "I'd like to talk with you about something that's been on my mind. Do you have time now?" Try not to surprise others with such requests when they might not be willing or have time to discuss them. Avoid criticizing people in front of others and talking about people behind their backs.

Start With Positive Feedback

Before you share a concern, comment on something the person does that you like or on a positive quality of your relationship. Reassure the person that you like him or her and want to maintain a positive working relationship (if this is true). An example is, "Lee, I think we work together well, but I would like to discuss. . . ." Combining a request for a change of behavior with a recognition of appreciated behaviors will help maintain these behaviors and increase the likelihood that your requests will be considered. This approach might be viewed as manipulative, if you offer positive feedback only when you give negative feedback as well.

Be Specific About What You Want and Why

Effective feedback is objective rather than judgmental. It focuses on behaviors of concern (see Exhibit 13.12). By being specific, you avoid "characterological blame" (attacks on the whole person) (Janoff-Bulman, 1979). Clearly describe what you want and why. Give specific examples and describe particular situations. When requests for change are specific, other people are more likely to respond to them as information rather than attacks. Vague complaints are likely to result in defensiveness and counterblame and do not inform people about what you want.

Be brief and to the point. Lengthy criticism can be difficult to understand and accept; people won't know what issues are most important to you and might feel overwhelmed with complaints. Limit

EXHIBIT 13.12
Checklist for Requesting Behavior Changes

_____ Ignore minor annoyances.

_____ Consider the other person's perspective. Find out if there are any handicapping conditions that get in the way and use the "given that" method.

_____ Plan and practice beforehand.

_____ Select an appropriate time and place.

_____ Give positive recognition first, as appropriate.

_____ Focus on common interests.

_____ Be specific. Describe what you want and why; give examples.

_____ Focus on the situation (the behaviors desired), not on the person. Be brief and to the point; don't overload others with criticisms.

_____ Check out the other person's understanding of what you have said, and clarify as needed.

_____ Avoid accusatory "you" statements and name-calling.

_____ Share concerns as they arise—if they are really important.

_____ Use nonverbal behaviors that communicate your seriousness.

_____ Offer specific suggestions or solutions.

_____ Remain firm when challenged (unless it is a lost cause).

_____ Use concerns as opportunities to strengthen relationships.

_____ Persist when necessary.

_____ Seek the person's commitment to follow through.

_____ Reinforce desired alternatives.

your feedback to one or two specific concerns. Recognize and focus on common interests. Examples of common goals are providing high-quality service and maintaining enjoyable and productive working relationships. Describe the positive consequences of changing and the negative ones of not doing so. This may increase motivation to alter behavior and is especially important in work situations in which the consequences may include loss of a job or negative comments in personnel records. Supervisors who have difficulty requesting behavior changes may threaten, without prior warning, a staff person with losing his or her job. This is not fair and, in fact, may be grounds for a successful lawsuit.

Personalize and Own Feedback

Use personal pronouns (I, me) rather than the accusatory you, which connotes blame. Say, "I feel uncomfortable when you criticize me in front of other students" rather than "You make me angry when you...." It's better to say, "It gives the agency a bad image when you talk so negatively about the agency in front of other people" than "You're giving the agency a bad name." Begin your comments with a personal pronoun to indicate that you take responsibility for your feelings and reactions. Including the following five components is helpful:

- I **feel** (describe your feelings, using words that refer to feelings)
- **when** (describe the specific behavior of concern),
- **because** (specify how the offensive behavior affects you).
- **I would prefer** (describe what you want),
- **because** (describe how you would feel).

The first step reminds you to use "I" statements and to express what you feel (sad, mad, happy, angry). The error you are most likely to make here is to refer to complaints or beliefs rather than feelings, as in the following comments: "I feel you should give me more feedback" or "I don't think you like me." Neither statement refers to a specific feeling. If you don't want to start off with "I feel . . . ," start with a clear description of the requested behavior change and the reasons for your request. One disadvantage of starting with a "feeling statement" is that it opens you up to attacks on your feelings (e.g., "You women are so sensitive"). If this happens, focus on what you want—don't get sidetracked. The second step calls for a clear description of your concern. The third reminds you to describe why it is a concern. The fourth involves taking responsibility for clearly describing what you want, and the last one brings you back to sharing your feelings about the desired change. Some examples are as follows:

- I **feel** frustrated
- **when** you interrupt me,
- **because** I believe my point is worth sharing.
- **I'd like you** to let me finish my statements before you speak,
- **because** then I would feel that you are really interested in what I am saying.

- I **feel** frustrated
- **when** you ask me to do extra work late in the afternoon,
- **because** often I've made plans for the evening and can't stay late.
- **I would rather** you give me new work earlier in the day,
- **because** that would help me plan my day.

People are more likely to consider your requests if you use words that communicate mild emotions (e.g., "I feel annoyed" rather than "I feel furious"). Use your feelings as clues to what you want. Avoid words such as *should*, *ought*, *have to*, and *must* that may promote guilt, anger, and defensive statements. You can share any discomfort you feel by saying, "This is difficult for me, but I do want to talk about. . . ." Knowing that you are honestly struggling with being direct might put others at ease. Self-disclosure of this kind communicates that you are vulnerable, too, and do not see yourself in a superior position. There is no need to apologize or say you're sorry. You have a right to make requests as long as you don't do so in an objectionable manner.

Avoid Negative Comments

Avoid loaded words that reflect judgments and put-downs. Statements such as "You're inconsiderate (cold, uptight, unfair)" will decrease the likelihood of a reasonable discussion. If you respect others, they are more likely to respect you and to consider your requests. Moralizing and excessive questioning (e.g., "Why did you. . . ."), giving orders, and "diagnosing" the other person ("You're doing this because you have a. . . .") will decrease your effectiveness.

Match Your Style of Presentation to Your Message

Make your request in a manner that matches your message. When asking for a change in an annoying behavior, be serious and thoughtful; do not giggle, smile, or laugh. You don't have to act out your feelings to communicate them.

Offer Specific Suggestions for Change

Before you bring up a concern, identify what changes you would like. How would you like things to be different? By offering specific suggestions for change, you share responsibility for improving the situation. Rather than saying, "You're really thoughtless," when you mean that someone interrupts you, you could say, "I'd like you to let me finish speaking before you start to speak."

Be Willing to Compromise

Demonstrating a willingness to compromise will help keep discussions on a positive note. Perhaps you had some role in an annoying event. For example, if you were kept waiting, perhaps you did not set a definite time. A willingness to share responsibility shows that you are flexible.

Offer Positive Feedback

You might say, "I'm glad we talked. I feel relieved and think we'll be able to work together better in the future. I appreciate your willingness to talk about this." You could also point out how good it is that the two of you can discuss your differences.

Avoid Sidetracks

People might try to sidetrack you by changing the subject or bringing up the past. Many informal fallacies, such as ad hominem attacks (e.g., personal criticisms), serve as distractions from addressing the real issue (such as the weakness of an argument). You can either ignore the sidetrack and repeat or elaborate your request or statement or comment on the distraction. You might say, "My point is. . . ." Don't react in kind, and don't back down when confronted with hostile or defensive reactions unless the other person is becoming very upset or threatening. Here the best option may be to "table" the discussion. You might say, "This doesn't seem like a good time to talk about this. Let's discuss it later." Try to stay calm. In some cases, you may have to take special precautions (see later discussion of safety in this Chapter).

Persist

Discussing your concerns will accomplish little unless you arrive at a clear agreement that a change will be made and describe exactly what it will be. You might have to point out that the issue remains unresolved in terms of what will be done. You might say, "I'd feel better if we reached a clear agreement about how to handle this." But you can't force people to change. If you are getting "hot under the collar" or ready to "go over the top," you probably have an expectation that this person must, ought to, or should change. Focusing on common interests rather than on winning increases the likelihood of an agreement.

When to Keep Silent

When thinking about asking people to change their behavior, consider the following:

- Does it really matter?
- Is this a matter of cultural differences that should be respected, not altered?
- Can this person change?
- Will a request encourage physical aggression?
- Will making the request have short- and long-term positive or negative consequences for your relationship?
- Are legal or ethical issues involved?

RESPONDING TO PUT-DOWNS

Put-downs are often based on stereotypes related to gender, religion, race, ethnicity, physical abilities, age, or sexual orientation. Put-downs ("zaps" as Patterson calls them) are in the eye of the beholder. They are defined by their function, not their form (i.e., they result in negative reactions on the part of the target). Regardless of the intent of the person making the remark (the person might not have intended to belittle or demean you), its effect is an important criterion for deciding whether it is a put-down. Name-calling may be used in ad homimun arguments (attacks on the person) to deflect attention from a weak argument. Whether a comment is directed toward you as a person, toward a general group, or toward someone else, you must decide whether to ignore or address it. Consider your goals in the situation and the chances of achieving them. Focusing on put-downs may get in the way of pursuing service goals. If so, ignore them and attend to service tasks. If they are recurrent in a continuing relationship, you may decide to try to change this behavior

Verbal put-downs based on race, gender, sexual orientation, age, or ethnicity are a kind of verbal harassment and could be reported to appropriate authorities (see the next section). The guidelines proposed by Naomi Gottlieb (1978) include the following (see also NiCarthy, Gottlieb, & Coffman, 1993):

- **Take time to respond in your own way.** Don't feel pressured to react immediately.
- **Avoid responding in kind** and using aggressive reactions. Use "I" statements to express your feelings and opinions.
- **Make it clear that you don't accept stereotypes.** If a person says, "Women are emotional and easily upset," show by your manner of speaking as well as by what you say that you don't accept this sexist stereotype.
- **Complement what you say with appropriate nonverbal behaviors.** Don't laugh or smile at offensive comments. You could say, "I don't think that was funny." If the reply to this is "What's the matter, no sense of humor?" you could repeat your initial comment without getting into a prolonged discussion or defense of your reaction. Look at the person; don't smile; maintain a relaxed and confident body position; don't speak in a high-pitched or whiny voice.
- **Offer and reinforce desired alternatives.** At work, in response to being called "honey" or some other inappropriate term, you might say, "I'd prefer to be called Mary."
- **Ignore the comment or put-down and focus on your goals.** At the start of a meeting, if someone says, "Hey, you look cute this morning!" You could say, "I'd like to discuss the report I've prepared."

- **Know when to stop.** If you've been "going the rounds" with someone and there is little change in unwanted behavior, introduce another topic or end the conversation.
- **Be prepared with effective reactions.** Have a few stock replies on hand to reply to put-downs (e.g., "That's in poor taste," "That sounds like a put-down to me").

HANDLING EMOTIONAL ABUSE, SEXUAL HARASSMENT, AND DISCRIMINATION ON THE JOB

Ginny NiCarthy and her colleagues define emotional abuse at work as "a pattern of intimidation, harassment, emotional manipulation, or excessive or illegitimate control of a worker" (1993, p. 5). In their book *You Don't Have to Take It!* (1993) they identify eight kinds of emotional abuse at work based on interviews and focus groups with women (see Exhibit 13.13). This book is an excellent source for raising your consciousness about work-related emotional abuse as well as options for dealing with it.

Sexual harassment or discrimination on grounds of gender, race, age, sexual orientation, pregnancy, or disability are not legal and should not be tolerated. In 1986, the U.S. Supreme Court unanimously recognized that sexual harassment is a form of sexual discrimination and that hostile environments and sex-for-jobs harassment violate the Civil Rights Act (Meritor Sav. Bank v Vinson, 477 U.S. 57 (1986). The NASW Code of Ethics states that "social workers should not sexually harass supervisees, students, trainees, or colleagues" (2.08). Forty-two percent of a sample of 10,648 women working for the federal government in 1988 said they had been harassed (cited in Petrocelli & Repa, 1992, p. 4/37). These incidents involved unwanted sexual remarks (35%), leers and suggestive looks (28%), being touched (26%), being pressured for dates and sexual favors (15% and 9%, respectively), and rape or sexual assault (8%). The sources of the reported harassment were coworkers (41%), other employees (33%), and higher-level

(19%) or immediate (12%) superiors (see also NiCarthy, Gottlieb, & Coffman, 1993). A sexual harassment policy may ban

- Verbal harassment, including making sexual comments about a person's body, telling sexual jokes or stories, spreading rumors about a coworker's sex life, asking or telling about sexual fantasies, preferences or history.
- Non-verbal harassment, such as giving unwanted personal gifts, following a person, staring at a person's body, displaying sexually suggestive material such as pornographic photos.
- Physical harassment, including touching yourself in a sexual manner in front of another person, brushing up against another person suggestively. (Petrocelli & Repa, 1992, p. 4/9)

You can recover damages if you have lost a promotion or your job because you refused sexual demands if you can prove that

- You were validly working when the harassment took place.
- The person who harassed you knew of the employment relationship.
- Your harasser intentionally and improperly interfered with your employment relationship.
- You suffered damages such as loss of your job, a demotion or a failure to get a promotion because of the interference. (Petrocelli & Repa, 1992, p. 8/16)

Concentrating on the task and not offering "mixed messages" make unwanted sexual advances less likely. Be sure your nonverbal behavior reflects the message you want to get across. Effective refusals of sexual overtures communicate a clear no without being abusive. Guidelines for refusing unwanted requests, discussed earlier, include not smiling or flirting, including the word *no* in your statement, and sticking with your explanation for refusing (if you gave one) rather than making up additional reasons or excuses. Make it clear that you choose to say no. Say, "I don't want to" rather than "I can't," "I'm not supposed to," or "I'm

EXHIBIT 13.13
Examples of Naming Emotional Abuse on the Job

1. Isolation
   - Ignore or cancel your request for meetings or feedback?
   - Stop you from joining or attending meetings of the union or professional organization?
   - Prohibit discussion of salaries or working conditions with other workers?
   - Isolate you from others who are also angry about the abuse?
2. Threats
   - Imply that you will be sorry if you don't do exactly what she or he wants down to the finest detail?
   - Warn you that if you are the first woman on this job, that you may ruin others' chances if you complain?
   - Shout, pound the desk, raise a fist, slam doors or talk nonstop to frighten you into submission?
3. Degradation and humiliation
   - Call you names like stupid or crazy?
   - Ignore your ideas and accept them from a male co-worker or someone else who has more status or power than you?
   - Criticize or ridicule you in front of other workers, customers or the public?
   - Check and recheck all your work beyond what's necessary for the job, repeatedly questioning petty details or your judgement?
4. Enforcing unreasonable demands
   - Set unnecessary, arbitrary deadlines?
   - Insist you do work that is someone else's responsibility?
   - Assign tasks he knows you haven't learned to do and refuse to provide instruction?
   - Routinely insist that work be accomplished in impossible amounts of time?
5. Occasional indulgences
   - Treat your rights to break times, vacations and so forth as if they were personal favors?
   - Respond to your intention to resign by making vague promises about how things will change?
6. Demonstrating power
   - Take credit for your production, work, or ideas?
   - Arbitrarily change agreements without consulting or negotiating with you?
   - Demand compliance and loyalty to him when you make complaints about work?
   - Become irate over issues that others find simply annoying or inconvenient?
   - Repeatedly claim that he could do your job much better than you can?
7. Monopolizing your attention
   - Feel like you are "walking on egg shells" around a supervisor or co-worker?
   - Feel anxious about your faults, even though you didn't feel that way before you took this job?
   - Worry about whether the boss or co-worker will approve of unimportant things such as the state of your desk?
   - Worry that she will yell at you or act in an angry, punishing, or unexplained critical manner?
8. Exhaustion and lowered competency
   - Work so hard to please that you feel exhausted and find it hard to recover even on days off?
   - Feel less competent to perform job tasks than you used to?
   - Often feel sick, especially on work days, even though no signs of physical illness exist?

Source: G. NiCarthy, N. Gottlieb, & S. Coffman (1993), You don't have to take it!: *A woman's guide to confronting emotional abuse at work (pp. 17–27). Seattle: Seal Press.*

sorry." Conveying that you have made the decision will make it clear that you are not a victim of constraints imposed against your will. You can say, "This [describe the behavior] offends me, and I want you to stop it now" (NiCarthy, Gottlieb, & Coffman, 1993, p. 299). You may have to persist in your refusal and directly discuss the offensive behavior, noting why it is inappropriate and undesired. If the offensive behavior persists, you could file a formal complaint through the appropriate channels, at either the state or federal level. The Civil Rights Act and the EEOC apply only to businesses with 15 or more employees (see Petrocelli & Repa, 1992, for detailed guidelines). Petrocelli and Repa also give a checklist for evaluating your case (8/13). Seek support from others who share your concerns.

SPEAKING MORE

Perhaps you rarely express your opinions or offer ideas at meetings. If so, practice speaking more often. Skill in resisting interruption and breaking into conversations is helpful. Elaborated opinion statements are useful for increasing participation (see the discussion of disagreeing). How can you tell if you talk too much or too little? The key question is, Do you meet your goals? In addition, you could ask other people what they think.

Breaking into an Ongoing Conversation

In a fast-moving conversation, you will have to speak up during brief pauses. If you wait for a long pause, the topic might change before you get a chance to share your ideas. This does not mean that you should interrupt people while they are talking but, rather, that you should speak after they finish talking. Practice coming into conversations quickly by using short sentences at first. You might say, "Yes, I think that's true." The sooner you come in, the more likely you will be viewed as an active participant. Questions, opinions, and the use of people's names are different ways to enter a conversation. You can use hand gestures or a light touch on the arm or shoulder to let people know you want to speak. Moving your body toward others, sitting forward in your chair, or standing closer might capture their attention. People are more likely to offer you an opportunity to talk if you sit in a visible location.

Resisting Interruptions

One way to resist interruptions is to raise your voice slightly when someone tries to break in. If you are with several people, direct your communication toward the receptive ones. Another technique is to pause briefly when someone tries to interrupt and then repeat what you have just said. You could ignore the interruption and continue talking. You could comment on the interruption by asking the person to wait. A hand signal or touch indicating "stop" or "hold it" could be added to a verbal request such as "just a minute." Interrupters may not be aware of their behavior or know how to change it. You could suggest a cue, such as raising your hand slightly, to alert them whenever they interrupt you. Commenting on interruptions at the time they occur may not be appropriate. You could raise the issue later.

EXHIBIT 13.14
Troubleshooting Checklist for Increasing Your Participation

_____ Do you hesitate too long before trying to enter a conversation?
_____ Can people hear you?
_____ Can people understand you; do you speak clearly?
_____ Do you use overly subtle signals to indicate that you would like to speak?
_____ Do you prepare what you want to say?
_____ Do you believe you have valuable contributions to make?
_____ Do you wait until you are angry before speaking up?
_____ Do you directly express your desire to talk after more subtle approaches fail?

Handling Monopolizers

What is best when faced with a monopolizer depends on your goals and the context. One strategy is to start speaking during a pause between the person's sentences. You could try this when waiting for a natural pause has not been successful. You could let the person know you want to speak by saying, "I'd like to respond to your first point." You could stop reinforcing his talking (e.g., not look, smile at the person) or discuss your concern with him (see the discussion of requesting behavior changes) (see Exhibit 13.14).

LISTENING MORE

Perhaps you talk too much in some situations. Pay attention to other people's nonverbal signals. Do they look bored or like they are "spacing out" when you talk? Do they fidget and tap their feet? You could use shorter, simpler sentences and limit your examples. You might mistakenly interpret a brief pause between statements as an end to a person's speech when it is a transition from one sentence to the next. To prevent this, wait a few seconds after others stop speaking before you talk. Follow the "ask–listen–ask rule" (handing back the conversation after listening to responses to a question) (Stuart, 1980). You could say, "Well, what do you think?" Be sure to offer positive feedback for other people's contributions (e.g., head nods) (see

EXHIBIT 13.15
Troubleshooting Checklist for Encouraging Others to Talk

_____ Do you follow the "ask-listen-ask" rule?
_____ Do you offer high-quality listening?
_____ Are you interested in what other people say?
_____ Do you focus too much on yourself and not enough on what other people do, feel, and think?
_____ Do you miss or misinterpret social signals that other people want to speak?
_____ Do you forget to wait a few seconds after other people finish talking before speaking?

Chapter 12 for a discussion of active listening). Perhaps other people are not as talkative as you would like because you show little interest in understanding their point of view or have been overly critical of their remarks. You may disagree too often or point out faults in what has been said in ways that offend others (see the guidelines for disagreeing). Or you may forget to point out areas of agreement (see Exhibit 13.15).

OBSTACLES TO HANDLING CHALLENGING SOCIAL SITUATIONS EFFECTIVELY

Both environmental and personal obstacles may interfere with effective social behavior (see Exhibit 13.16). Environmental factors include lack of opportunities for positive informal exchanges such as a staff lounge and an agreed on time and place for staff to discuss problems such as a support group. You may work in an agency that does not value a culture of thoughtfulness in which differences are viewed as learning opportunities. If so, you could form a support group of colleagues who share your interests. With help from others, you may be able to change your work climate and culture.

Not being familiar with the norms, values, and preferred styles of communication in different groups may get in the way. Needed skills may be absent. You may have to acquire them and prompt and reinforce their use. Skills may be available but not be used. Or you may not have needed skills or have them but not use them because they are not reinforced and/or are punished. For example, your requests for more specific supervisory feedback may have been ignored or punished. As a result, you may no longer ask, and even thinking about doing so may make you feel anxious. You can lessen anxiety by imagining the "worst-case scenario" and realizing that even this would not be a catastrophe. Your beliefs about how people should act may be an obstacle. They may not reflect real-life contingencies. Albert Ellis and Robert Harper (1975) offer examples of unrealistic expectations:

EXHIBIT 13.16
Factors Related to Ineffective Social Behavior

Problem	Remedy
1. Lack of knowledge about social rules/norms.	1. Acquire knowledge.
2. Lack of needed skills.	2. Acquire skills.
3. Interfering behavior (aggressive reactions).	3. Replace with effective reactions.
4. Inappropriate or inadequate stimulus control (e.g., skills are available but not used).	4. Develop effective stimulus control.
5. Interfering emotional reactions (anxiety, anger).	5. Identify related factors (e.g., lack of skills or knowledge, taking things personally, fear of negative evaluation, unrealistic expectations), and make needed changes.
6. Fear of negative evaluation.	6. Decrease sensitivity to social disapproval.
7. Unrealistic performance standards.	7. Moderate standards, identify unrealistic expectations (e.g., "I must please everyone") and replace with realistic ones (e.g., "I can't please everyone").
8. Lack of respect for others.	8. Increase empathic understanding.
9. A focus on winning.	9. Focus on shared goals (e.g., to help clients).
10. Few settings that encourage positive exchanges.	10. Increase access to such settings.
11. Agency culture (i.e., contingency systems in service settings).	11. Rearrange contingencies, involve coworkers.

- Everyone must like and approve of me at all times.

- I must be perfect, totally competent, and productive in order to consider myself worthwhile.

- It is a catastrophe when things are not the way I want them to be.

- Past events control my present behavior.

- Other people should act as I want, and I can and should control the behavior of those around me.

- There is always a correct and perfect solution to a problem, and it is a catastrophe if I don't find it.

- When people do something bad, they should be blamed and punished.

- My happiness is externally caused and controlled.

A belief that everyone must like you or that you must never make mistakes will get in the way of raising questions. Neither belief is likely to be confirmed and thus may result in anger if you sense disapproval, or anxiety as a result of nonreward and punishment. Use your feelings to identify your emotional "triggers" (such as unrealistic expectations), and replace them with helpful self-statements (see Exhibit 13.17). Unrealistic expectations include the belief that you must be successful with all your clients and be respected and loved by all your colleagues and clients (Ellis & Yeager, 1989). Inaccurate beliefs about conflict may also get in the way (e.g., it should be avoided at all cost, there is something wrong if you have conflicts, and there must be winners and losers).

SAFETY

Safety is an issue in some social work positions. For instance, with clients who have a history of violence, you should take special precautions, such as having direct access to an exit, leaving your office door open, having access to an alarm that is in working order, and being trained to recognize and respond effectively to the initial stages of aggressive chains of behavior (e.g., agitation, mounting tension, irritability, angry brooding, limit testing, and panic states). Insisting that clients confront negative information or refusing to meet a client's request may only make him or her more likely to become aggressive (Prins, 1988). You could try meeting in a neutral place such as a restaurant or community center. You can ask referring professionals about a client's potential for violence and past violence. Addressing outcomes of interest to clients, showing respect, and avoiding unnecessary provocations decrease the likelihood of violent behavior.

Homebuilders has a rule that if a social worker is concerned about danger, she must discuss the situation with her supervisor. (Homebuilders is an organization that offers in-home services to families in which children are at risk. In 15 years, it has reported only one incident of a worker's being slapped, despite its having had more than 5,000 clients.) Previous arrangements may be made to send help if a worker does not call at an agreed-on time. If driving, social workers are cautioned to park close to the client's home and to be alert when entering the home. If the family has a telephone, they call beforehand to set up an appointment and use active listening skills to calm angry clients. If you know that a situation may be dangerous, ask about it (e.g., "Are there guns in the house?"). The family members themselves may be worried and suggest a plan to get a potentially dangerous person out of the house.

Respect the clients' personal space and use active listening to calm people and form a collaborative relationship. If talking to an entire family is chaotic or tensions escalate, you could suggest talking to each person separately. You could talk to the most difficult person first, "to help him feel important and understood." If everyone tries to talk at once, point out that it's difficult for you to hear anyone and ask that just one person speak at a time. Inform family members of the consequences if a situation seems to be getting out of hand, as in the following example:

> The family consisted of 15-year-old Mary and her 36-year old mother, Rita. Mary had been on the run at referral and presenting problems were truancy, alco-

EXHIBIT 13.17
How to Overcome Difficulties in Being Assertive

Difficulty	How to Overcome It
Guilt	1. Become aware of guilt feelings and guilt triggers. 2. Uncover irrational beliefs, cognitive distortions, and parent messages and decide if the guilt is appropriate. 3. Develop an antidote statement.
Fear of consequences	1. Uncover your catastrophic fantasy and exaggerate it. 2. Ask yourself, "What's really likely to happen?" and be alert for irrational beliefs and cognitive distortions. 3. Weigh the risks of being assertive and the costs of not being assertive. 4. Assess what you need to do to protect yourself from negative consequences.
Fear of being taken advantage of	1. Recognize your fear and the assumptions behind it. 2. Dispute your assumptions.
Anxiety	1. Realize you can still act rationally when you're anxious. 2. Practice relaxation techniques. 3. Use deep breathing or a short meditation before confrontations.
Doubt	1. Do your homework—know what you want to accomplish and the facts of the situation. 2. Substitute positive pep talks for negative pep talks. 3. Focus on supervisory rights and responsibilities.
Anger	1. Examine negative assumptions and look for more benign alternatives. 2. Look for and dispute irrational beliefs and cognitive distortions. 3. Watch for anger triggers, especially red-flag people. 4. Empathize—put yourself in the other person's shoes.
Inflexible self-image	1. Realize that one or a few interactions will not make or break your image. 2. Remind yourself that you can act in opposing ways and still maintain your image.
Negative self-image	1. Identify and dispute ways that you undermine yourself. 2. Give yourself credit for your strengths. 3. Forgive yourself for your flaws.
Sexual and racial blocks to assertiveness	1. Dispute internal programming that keeps you from being assertive. 2. Define negative reactions as inevitable responses to changes in the traditional distribution of power. 3. Build a power base to support your assertiveness.

Source: S. S. Drury (1984), Assertive Supervision: Building Involved Teamwork *(pp. 304–305). Champaign, IL: Research Press.*

hol abuse, and sexual involvement. She and her mother had had many conflicts over these issues and sometimes became physical with one another.

During one session Rita and Mary became angry with one another. Their anger quickly escalated to the point of yelling. During this initial stage I fell back

on a rule of thumb I had learned in my training ("when in doubt: listen") and made several listening responses. However, Rita and Mary continued to scream at one another. Mary ran upstairs with Rita in close pursuit. I followed them. When they reached the top of the stairs, they began slapping one another, pulling each other's hair, and wrestling. I began expressing my concern and fear that one or both of them would be hurt. I made several statements such as "I'm afraid someone is going to get hurt," "I don't want anyone to get hurt," "I'm worried that you will hurt each other," but they continued screaming and fighting.

Next, they headed back downstairs with me close behind expressing my concern. In the living room, Mary knocked everything including the telephone off a table and yelled "I'm going to call the police" to which Rita yelled back "I'm going to call the police." In as calm a voice as I could muster at that point, I said "If you don't stop, I will call the police." They

stopped wrestling, hitting and pulling hair but continued yelling. I resumed listening to their feelings and as they began to deescalate, I was able to convince Mary to go out on the front porch. Afterward, I spent time with each of them individually and Mary said "It was weird to hear you say you would call the police." Until then, I did not know what had made the difference. (Jack Chambers). (Kinney, Haapala, & Booth, 1991, p. 51)

You could suggest a time out to get a glass of water. Other steps are calling your supervisor or the police or simply leaving.

SUMMARY

Both you and your clients will confront a variety of challenging social situations. Options for handling difficult situations such as being criticized, requesting behavior changes, and refusing unwanted requests include seeking information, taking direct action, doing nothing and changing how a situation is viewed. Interpersonal problem-solving knowledge and skills will help you plan what to do. Steps include stopping, calming down, and thinking; describing the problem and how you feel; selecting a positive goal; identifying your options and considering the consequences; trying the best plan; and evaluating the results. You can often head off unpleasant situations by planning ahead and reinforcing desired behaviors. And you can enhance your success by considering cultural differences in preferred communication styles.

REVIEWING YOUR COMPETENCIES

Reviewing What You Know

1. Identify specific social situations that are difficult for you. Select two examples and describe how you handle them and how you can increase your effectiveness.
2. Describe your "emotional allergies" that get in the way of responding effectively to difficult social situations.
3. Describe effective ways of handling problematic social situations.
4. Describe the behaviors and beliefs associated with passive, assertive, and aggressive behavior.
5. Describe helpful interpersonal problem-solving steps.
6. Give examples of the statement "Feelings are clues to contingencies."
7. Identify positive alternatives to negative social goals.
8. Suggest promising options for attaining goals in given social situations.
9. Describe factors related to ineffective social behavior.
10. Describe effective ways to overcome specific communication barriers.
11. Describe components of effective disagreement.
12. Describe helpful steps in asking others to change their behavior.

13. Describe how to react constructively to criticism.
14. Give specific examples of cultural differences in responding effectively to different social situations.
15. Give examples of work-related handicapping conditions that interfere with job performance.
16. Describe steps you can take to encourage others to talk.
17. Describe alternatives to aggressive reactions in specific situations.
18. Describe coping skills you can use to regulate your emotions.
19. Describe social signals you can use to recognize feelings and attitudes.
20. Identify indicators of emotional abuse at work (including feelings, thoughts, and actions).
21. Describe emotionally abusive work behaviors.
22. Discuss the role of power differences at work and their relationship to emotional abuse.

Reviewing What You Do

1. A review of your exchanges with clients and other professionals shows that you express disagreement, request behavior changes, respond to criticisms, and balance talking and listening in a way that increases the likelihood of attaining service goals.
2. In role plays, you can demonstrate constructive feedback and effective refusal of requests.
3. A review of your exchanges with clients and supervisors (or during staff conferences) shows that you
   • Acknowledge other positions.
   • Offer opinions effectively.
   • Avoid put-downs.
   • Raise questions about claims (as appropaite).
   • Request clarification/information/feedback.
   • Speak enthusiastically when appropriate.
   • Support your suggestions with evidence.
   • Provide specific descriptions of relevant behavior/situations.
   • Compromise when appropriate.
   • Provide and request constructive feedback.
   • Change your opinions when you have good reason to do so.
   • Accurately identify other people's emotions and attitudes.
   • Convey attitudes and emotions you intend to offer.
4. You can teach someone one of the skills described in this chapter. Criteria for success: Valued goals are attained in real-life situations.

Reviewing Results

1. Service goals are attained.
2. Sound practice decisions are made.
3. Other people like and/or respect you.
4. Few social predicaments.
5. Stress levels in exchanges are low.

6. You develop and maintain constructive working relationships.
7. You like and respect others.
8. Clients and coworkers compliment you on your knowledge of cultural differences in preferred communication styles.
9. Evaluation of specific skills you wish to improve (e.g., spotting and countering "either/or-ing" in case conferences) shows that you take advantage of an increasing number of opportunities to do so.

PART

V

GATHERING AND ORGANIZING INFORMATION

CHAPTER 14

Where to Look: Deciding How to Gather Needed Information

OVERVIEW

The framework for assessment described in Chapters 9 and 10 provides a guide to *what* data to collect. The next two chapters provide guidelines describing *how* to gather the data. Sources include self-report, standardized questionnaires, self-anchored "do-it-yourself" scales, self-monitoring, observation, physiological measures, and case records. Measures may be used to describe, screen, assess, monitor, or predict future behavior. The potential inaccuracy of any one source calls for the use of multiple sources when possible. Criteria you should consider when making choices such as reliability and validity are viewed and advantages and disadvantages of methods discussed.

You Will Learn About

- Decisions and options.
- Critically evaluating assessment methods.
- Self-report.
- Standardized measures.
- Asking clients to collect data (e.g. self-monitoring).
- Physiological measures.
- When to insist on a physical examination.
- Case records.
- Data provided by other professionals.
- Electromechanical aids.
- What to do about discrepancies.
- Keeping track of material.
- Ethical issues related to "where to look."

DECISIONS AND OPTIONS

If you provide direct services to clients, then knowledge of and skill in selecting and using feasible, informative assessment methods are essential (see Exhibit 14.1). You could, for example, talk to clients, observe them in real-life settings (if feasible and relevant), or ask them to role play situations of concern. Knowledge about the relative accuracy of different assessment frameworks and measures will help you to select referral sources and evaluate data gathered by others. Required decisions include the following:

- What data will be most helpful in making well-reasoned decisions about how to achieve valued outcomes and whether they can be achieved?

- Where can I obtain the data?

- How will I decide when I have enough information?

- What should I do if I obtain contradictory data?

- What criteria should I use to check the accuracy of data?

- How can I avoid inaccurate and incomplete accounts?

What Are Your Options?

In addition to talking to clients and significant others, you may ask clients to collect data. Sources to choose among include:

- Self-report.

- Standardized measures.

- Data gathered by clients and significant others in real-life settings (self-monitoring).

EXHIBIT 14.1
What Do You Think?

Imagine that your job includes helping residents to enhance the quality of their neighborhood. How will you go about this? What information will you gather and why?

Mr. Young, an elderly man living with his family, was referred to you because family members are concerned about what they describe as his "increasing social isolation and depression." How can you clarify these concerns? How can you discover environmental factors that influence problem-related feelings, thoughts, and behaviors (e.g., how other family members respond to Mr. Young)?

* * *

Sarah works in a community mental health center. She has just interviewed Mrs. Rivera, who described herself as "always depressed." Mrs. Rivera lives with her two small children, ages two and five. She is a divorced parent with a part-time job. Her mother helps out with the children. How can Sarah find out whether Mrs. Rivera is "always" depressed? How can she discover personal and environmental factors that influence the frequency and intensity of depression? Sarah suspects that Mrs. Rivera is not *always* depressed—that this varies depending on certain circumstances. How can she test out this assumption? Sarah's supervisor suggests that she use the Beck Depression Inventory to find out Mrs. Rivera's degree of depression as well as suicidal potential. What questions should Sarah ask about this inventory before using it with her client? What other source of information should she use?

* * *

Brian and his family have been having trouble for months. Brian complains that his parents always nag him. His parents complain that Brian is out of control (mistreats the dog, speaks in a nasty way to his parents, will not follow instructions, is doing poorly at school, and has threatened his father with violence). How can you clarify these concerns and discover related circumstances? A contextual practice perspective would lead you to guess that family members influence each other. How can you test this guess?

* * *

Imagine that you work in a neighborhood mediation center and a resident complains about his neighbor's "intrusions on his privacy" (playing loud music, throwing trash on his property, swearing at him, and so on). Are these reports accurate? How will you find out?

EXHIBIT 14.2
Guidelines for Collecting Data

Focus on gathering data that decrease uncertainty about how to attain desired outcomes.
Watch out for vivid data that may be misleading or uninformative (attend to what's *not* there as well as what is).
Use multiple sources.
Select valid methods (those that measure what they purport to measure).
Critically evaluate the accuracy of data collected.
Search for data that allow you to explore alternative views about the causes of problems.
Consider cultural differences.
Use observation in real-life settings when this is needed to clarify problems and identify related factors.
Describe behavior in its context (clearly describe problem-related behaviors as well as their antecedents and consequences).
Critically evaluate your beliefs about the cause(s) of problems. Can you offer a well-reasoned argument for them? Are alternative views likely?
Beware of the confirmatory bias (collecting only data that support preferred views).

- Observation in role plays.

- Observation in real-life.

- Physiological indicators.

- Case records.

Your decisions will be influenced by your knowledge about various methods, client preferences, your theoretical point of view, and feasibility (whether it is possible to use a method). Clients may not be willing to use certain methods. You may not have the skills required to administer and interpret a measure. Some sources such as self-report are easy to use and are flexible in the range of content provided; however, accuracy varies considerably. In addition to deciding on *sources* of data (e.g., self-report, observation) you and your clients will decide on a *type* of measure. What is best will depend on the particular outcome focused on. Options include the following:

- *Frequency:* How often a behavior, thought, or feeling occurs in a fixed period. This may be expressed as rate (number of behaviors divided by a time measure such as number of hours) or percentage (proportion of occurrences in total opportunities; e.g., percentages of conversations initiated over ten opportunities).

- *Latency:* Time interval between presentation of a cue and a behavior (e.g., time elapsing between question and an answer); time elapsing between writing to a city official and receiving an answer.

- *Duration:* Length of time over which a behavior

occurs (e.g., time spent studying); time spent arguing by family members.

- *Amount:* This involves a "how much" dimension and includes amplitude and intensity (e.g., intensity of anxiety or anger).

- *Form:* Exactly what does the behavior consist of? What criteria will be used to identify the behavior?

- *Competence:* The effectiveness of a behavior in resulting in a given outcome.

- *Variety:* Different forms resulting in a given outcome (operant class).

Helpers tend to base decisions on a small amount of data even though they collect a great deal. One problem with collecting lots of data is that decisions may be influenced by irrelevant data. Incorrect beliefs about the causes of problems may be strengthened by gathering redundant data (data that do *not* provide additional information). You can improve accuracy by using multiple methods, relying especially on those most likely to offer accurate, relevant data. You can save time and effort by focusing on material that provides the best guidelines for making practice decisions (e.g., they point to successful service plans) (see Exhibit 14.2).

**CRITICALLY EVALUATING
DIFFERENT KINDS OF DATA**

You and your clients will make life-affecting decisions based on the data collected during assess-

EXHIBIT 14.3
Reviewing Data Relied On

Select a client with whom you have recently worked. Complete the scales below and note your overall rating on each scale. If your values are low, discuss possible reasons for this. (*Suggestions for discussion:* How does your overall ratings of relevance compare with your overall ratings of accuracy and completeness? Data could be very accurate but not relevant to helping clients attain outcomes they value.)

	Accuracy[a]				Completeness[a]				Relevance[a]			
1. Client self-report.	0	1	2	3	0	1	2	3	0	1	2	3
2. Significant others' self-report.	0	1	2	3	0	1	2	3	0	1	2	3
3. Observation of clients during interview.	0	1	2	3	0	1	2	3	0	1	2	3
4. Standardized measures.	0	1	2	3	0	1	2	3	0	1	2	3
5. Projective tests.	0	1	2	3	0	1	2	3	0	1	2	3
6. Self-monitoring by clients.	0	1	2	3	0	1	2	3	0	1	2	3
7. Anecdotal observation in role plays.	0	1	2	3	0	1	2	3	0	1	2	3
8. Systematic observation in role plays.	0	1	2	3	0	1	2	3	0	1	2	3
9. Anecdotal observation in problem-related real-life contexts.	0	1	2	3	0	1	2	3	0	1	2	3
10. Systematic observation in real-life problem-related contexts.	0	1	2	3	0	1	2	3	0	1	2	3
11. Physiological measures.	0	1	2	3	0	1	2	3	0	1	2	3
12. Case records.	0	1	2	3	0	1	2	3	0	1	2	3
13. Other (please describe)[b]	0	1	2	3	0	1	2	3	0	1	2	3

Key: 0 = (not at all); 1 = (somewhat); 2 = (fairly); 3 = (very).
[a]Overall ratings may range from 13 to 39 on each scale if no other sources are noted.
[b]Are these examples of one of the items already listed? If so, do not include here.

ment. Because of this, you should critically evaluate the data on which decisions are based (see Exhibit 14.3). Have you relied on self-reports? Do these provide a sound basis for decisions? Should you check the accuracy of self-report data by observing behaviors of interest in real-life? Will this provide a sounder basis for decisions? Each source of information is subject to error. This may be random (unsystematic, varying) or systematic (biased in one direction). Sources of random error include measurement changes (observers may fluctuate in their ratings) and changes in client characteristics (for example, in mood). Sources of systematic error include *demand characteristics* (characteristics of a situation that encourage responses in one direction). For example, we tend to present ourselves in a good light. This is known as *the social desirability effect.* Both random and systematic error may interfere with discovering a client's "true score" on a measure. Common errors when gathering data can be seen in Exhibit 14.4. Many involve or result in inappropriate speculation (assuming what is can be discovered simply by

thinking about it). The question is: What method will offer information that will help you to help your clients? Criteria to consider in judging the value of data include: (1) reliability; (2) validity; (3) sensitivity; (4) utility; (5) feasibility; and (6) relevance.

Nor for Researchers Alone

Concerns about validity and factors that influence this (e.g., reliability) are not confined to researchers. They are also relevant to everyday practice. If you rely on irrelevant or inaccurate measures, you may select ineffective or harmful plans because of faulty assumptions. If you rely on an inaccurate measure of social skill you may assume incorrectly that a client has the skills required to succeed in certain situations when he does not, resulting in punishing social reactions such as rejection.

Validity concerns the question: Does the measure reflect the characteristic it is supposed to measure? For example, does behavior in a role play correspond to what a client does in similar real-life

EXHIBIT 14.4
Common Errors in Gathering Assessment Data: Being Forewarned Is Being Prepared

- Gathering irrelevant data (e.g., redundant data).
- Gathering only data that support preconceived views (see discussion of the behavioral confirmation effect in Chapter 5).
- Overlooking the role of environmental factors.
- Overlooking cultural differences that influence the validity and acceptability of given sources of data.
- Forgoing opportunities to observe behavior in real-life or role plays when needed to clarify problems and options.
- Not involving significant others in collecting data.
- Vagueness (data do not clarify problems).
- Not describing setting events, antecedents, and consequences related to behavior of interest.
- Relying on unsupported opinions of other professionals.
- Relying on unsupported data in case records.
- Not performing function tests in which antecedents or consequences are altered to determine their effects on behavior.
- Disregarding an otherwise valuable assessment tool because of a minor flaw.
- Relying on biased, unrepresentative samples (sampling too narrowly, e.g., observing behavior on only one occasion that may not provide information about what usually occurs).
- Using invalid measures (they do not measure what they are supposed to measure).

situations? *Direct* (e.g., observing teacher-student interaction) in contrast to *indirect* measures (e.g., asking a student to complete a questionnaire assumed to offer information about classroom behavior) are typically more valid. Confusion sometimes arises about issues of validity and the extent to which measures from different sources offer similar accounts. Different responses (overt behavior, thoughts) may or may not be related to certain events. Clients may report being anxious but show no physiological signs of anxiety. This does not mean that their reports are inaccurate. For these individuals, the experience of anxiety may be cognitive rather than physical. Types of *validity and reliability* include the following:

- *Predictive validity:* This refers to the extent to which a measure accurately predicts behavior at a later time. For example, how accurately does a measure of suicidal potential predict suicide attempts?

- *Concurrent validity:* This refers to the extent to which a measure correlates with a validated measure gathered at the same time; for example, do responses on a questionnaire concerning social behavior correlate with behavior in real-life contexts? Concurrent and predictive validity are sometimes referred to as *criterion validity*. In both, scores on a measure are compared to a criterion that is assumed to be accurate. For example, scores on a self-report measure of social skill

could be compared with behavior in a role-play simulation.

- *Content validity:* This reflects the degree to which a measure adequately samples the domain being assessed. For example, does an inventory used to assess parenting skills include an adequate sample of such skills?

- *Construct validity:* This term refers to the degree to which a measure successfully measures a theoretical construct—the degree to which results of a measure correspond with assumptions about the measure. The finding that depressed people report more negative thoughts on the Automatic thoughts Questionnaire (Hollon & Kendall, 1980) compared to nondepressed people adds an increment of construct validity to this measure. Evidence should be available that different methods of assessing a construct (e.g., direct observation and self-report) yield similar results and that similar methods of measuring *different* constructs (e.g., aggression and altruism) yield different results. That is, evidence should be available that a construct can be distinguished from other different constructs. For a description of different ways in which construct validity can be established, see, for example, Anastasi (1988).

- *Face validity:* This term refers to the extent to which items included on a measure make sense "on the face of it." Would you expect the items to be there given the intent of the instrument?

- *Reliability:* This refers to the consistency of results (in the absence of real change) provided by the same person at different times (time-based reliability), by two different raters of the same events (individual-based reliability as in interrater reliability), or by parallel forms or split-halves of a measure (item-bound reliability). Homogeneity is a kind of item-bound reliability assessing the degree to which all the items on a test measure the same characteristics. Homogeneity of a test is important if all items are supposed to measure the same characteristics. If a scale is *multidimensional* (many dimensions are assumed to be involved in a construct such as "loneliness" or "social support"), then homogeneity would *not* be expected.

Reliability places an upward boundary on validity. For example, if responses on a questionnaire vary from time to time (in the absence of real change), it will not be possible to use results of a measure to predict what a person will do in the future. Reliability can be assessed in a number of ways, all of which yield some measure of consistency. In test-retest reliability, the scores of the same individuals at different times are correlated with each other. Correlations may range from $+1$ to -1. The size of the correlation coefficient indicates the degree of association. A zero correlation indicates a complete absence of consistency. A correlation of $+1$ indicates a perfect positive correlation. The stability (reliability of a measure at different times) of some measures is high. That is, you can ask a client to complete a questionnaire this week and five weeks from now and obtain similar results (in the absence of real change). Other measures have low stability. Coefficients of reliability are usually sufficient if they are .80 or better. However, the higher the better (inter-rater reliability is discussed in the next chapter).

The *sensitivity* of measures is important to consider; that is, will a measure reflect changes that occur? Insensitive measures will not offer information about progress or factors related to presenting problems.

The *utility* of a measure is determined by its cost (time, effort, expense) balanced against information provided.

Feasibility is related to utility. Some measures will not be feasible to gather. For example, clients who cannot read will not be able to complete written questionnaires. Utility may be compromised by the absence of empirically derived norms for a measure.

Relevance should also be considered. Is a measure relevant to desired outcomes? Do clients and significant others consider it relevant?

Norms offer information about the typical (or average) performance of a group of individuals. You can compare your clients' results with those of similar clients. Cut points may be used to decide whether a client is in the typical range on a given characteristic or to make predictions about future behavior. Be sure to consider the representativeness of norms in relation to your client. How similar is the client to the people whose norms were obtained? Are there cultural differences? The more representative the sample is to your client, the greater the utility of the measures in relation to a client.

Relying on the criteria discussed above will help you to select useful measures. Resist the temptation to choose measures that are available and easy to use but are irrelevant or misleading. Choose those that provide accurate, relevant information in a manageable way. Compromises will often be necessary between feasibility and accuracy. You will often have to settle for measures that, although imprecise, provide helpful guidelines. You can improve accuracy by using multiple methods, relying especially on those most likely to offer accurate relevant data.

SELF-REPORT

Self-report is the most widely used source of information. As Mischel (1981) notes, "people can be excellent sources of information about themselves" (p. 482). There are many different types of self-report including verbal reports in interviews and answers on written inventories. Advantages of self-report include ease of collecting material and flexibility in the range of material that may be gathered. Some information can be gathered only through verbal reports, such as beliefs about the cause of problems, plans for the future, and many past events. Methods such as observation may not be feasible. Structured interviews have been developed for both children and adults in a number of areas. Some structured interviews provide a "psychosocial history" (description of the client's concerns and relevant current and past circumstances). Others are designed for a more specific purpose. For example, topics included in structured interviews regarding drinking problems may concern development of the problem, present drinking pattern and pattern history, alcohol-related life problems, drinking settings and associated behaviors, beverage preferences, relevant medical history, reasons for drinking, effects of drinking, other life problems, and motivation for treatment. Even if you do not use these interview schedules exactly as designed, they may be helpful to review to identify areas to explore. Many structured interviews are costly and time con-

suming to administer. Like unstructured ones, they also are subject to error.

Thinking Critically about Self-Report Data

When assessing the accuracy of self-reports consider the following questions:

• Does the situation encourage an honest answer?
• Does the client have access to the information?
• Can the client comprehend the question?
• Does the client have the verbal skills required to answer questions?
• Is the interviewer familiar with and skilled in avoiding interviewer biases?

Familiarity with sources of interviewer bias may help you to avoid them (see Exhibit 14.5). The accuracy of self-reports is influenced by questions asked and characteristics of the interviewer (see also Chapter 12).

• Questions or terms may be vague or ambiguous.

EXHIBIT 14.5
Empirical Findings Regarding Children's Suggestibility

1. There are reliable age differences in children's suggestibility, with preschoolers being more vulnerable than older children to a variety of factors that contribute to unreliable reports.
2. Although young children are often accurate reporters, some do make mistakes—particularly when they undergo suggestive interviews; and these errors are not limited to peripheral details, but may include salient events that involve children's own bodies.
3. Measures can be taken to lessen the risk of suggestibility effects. To date, the factors that we know most about concern the nature of the interview itself: its frequency, degree of suggestiveness, and demand characteristics.
   • A child's report is less likely to be distorted, for example, after one interview than after several interviews. (The term "interviews" includes any conversations between adults and children about the target event.)
   • Interviewers who ask nonleading questions, who do not have a confirmatory bias (i.e., an attachment to a single hypothesis), who do not inculcate a negative stereotype about the defendant, and who do not repeat close-ended, yes/no questions within or across interviews are more likely to obtain accurate reports from children.
   • Interviewers who are patient and nonjudgmental, and who do not attempt to create demand characteristics (e.g., by providing subtle rewards for certain responses), are likely to elicit the most accurate reports from young children.
   • Thus, at one extreme we can have more confidence in a child's spontaneous statements made prior to any attempt by an adult to elicit what they suspect may be the truth. At the other extreme, we are more likely to be concerned when a child has made a statement only after prolonged, repeated, and suggestive interviews.
4. Finally, . . . As in most areas of social science, effects are rarely as straightforward as one might wish. For example, even though suggestibility effects may be robust, they are not inevitable, nor are they ineluctably large in magnitude.

Source: Ceci, S. J., & Bruck, M. (1995). Jeopardy in the courtroom: A scientific analysis of children's testimony (pp. 271–272). Washington, D.C.: American Psychological Association.

- A particular sequence of questions may suggest certain answers.

- Too many questions may be asked (the inquisitor).

- Unwarranted assumptions may be implicit in questions asked (e.g., leading questions).

- More than one question may be embedded in a single question.

- Interviewer preferences, emotional reactions, and biases may influence what is noted.

- Answers may be misunderstood.

- Recording errors may be made.

Client characteristics also influence self-reports.

- Desire to give socially desirable answers.

- Lack of understanding of questions.

- Faulty memory.

- Anxiety.

- No true opinions/preferences.

- Distracted because of poor timing of interview.

- Misunderstandings about the purpose of the interview.

The questions asked reflect beliefs about what is and is not important. They may obscure or clarify problems. Clients' answers may reflect popular beliefs proposed in pop-psychology sources. For example, parents may inaccurately report that their child's problems started at a time suggested by certain popular psychological theories. We tend to ask questions that confirm our beliefs. This *confirmatory bias* may result in overlooking contradictory data and alternative (more accurate) problem definitions.

The response format used influences what is reported. Clients may give different reports if you ask closed-end questions calling for a "yes-no" answer than if you ask open-ended questions. Research suggests that individuals labeled "mentally retarded" have an *acquiescent response set* (a tendency to say "yes") (Sigelman, Budd, Spanhel, & Schoenrock, 1980). Use of inexact adjectives such as "often" or "seldom" can give an

illusion of precision and agreement that does not exist. We differ in our interpretation of vague terms such as "frequent" or "seldom" (Pepper, 1981). Repeated suggestions that a certain event occurred (when it did not) may result in inaccurate reports. For example, 58% of preschool children produced false stories to at least one fictitious event after 10 weeks of thinking about both real and fictitious events (Ceci, Crotteau-Huffman, Smith, & Loftus, 1994). Consider the report from Bill, a 4-year old.

> "My brother Colin was trying to get Blowtorch (an action figurine) from me, and I wouldn't let him take it from me, so he pushed me into the wood pile where the mousetrap was. And then my finger got caught in it. And then we went to the hospital, and my mommy, daddy, and Colin drove me there, to the hospital in our van, because it was far away. And the doctor put a bandage on this finger (indicating)." (Ceci & Bruck, 1995, p 219).

As this example suggests, the very process of thinking about a question may alter our memories (see also Loftus, Ketcham, 1994). Consider critiques of recovered memory therapy. Scholars such as Richard Ofshe present a compelling argument that not only may these alleged memories be false, they create havoc in people's lives, as well as in the lives of those they accuse (see Ofshe & Watters, 1994). This is not to say that all memories of past abuse are false. It is to say that some are, especially those that violate what we know about how memory works. Also, we must examine all four possible relationships between whether someone who reports being abused as a child remembers abuse, and whether it really occurred (Dawes, 1994b). This is usually *not* done, resulting in false estimates.

Often, we do not know what influences our behavior and so will not be able to identify relevant setting events, antecedents, and consequences. Incorrect accounts are not unusual (Nisbett & Ross, 1980). We often overlook environmental causes. The more specific the question as to what a person would do in a specific context, the more likely self-report is to accurately reflect real-life behavior, given that motivational factors also favor an honest reply. A client may not understand a question and so offer incorrect material. Subtle differences in how questions are asked may yield different expressions of preferences (Fishhoff, Slovic, & Lichtenstein, 1980). Thus, when inquiring about values and preferences, it is best to ask about these in different ways. Otherwise, the very process of asking about preferences may shape the responses given.

Clients may offer inaccurate reports because they are embarrassed over a lack of information, fear the consequences of offering correct accounts, or do not understand a question. If it is not in the clients' interests to share material, they are less likely to do so (Babor, Brown, & Del Boca, 1990; Faust, Hart, and Guilmette, 1988). Incorrect accounts may be given even though you do your best to put clients at ease. Descriptions offered may be related more to clients' beliefs about how they are expected to act than to what they really do. They may give incorrect descriptions about significant others because they dislike them or want to avoid responsibility for removing complaints. Social desirability influences reports given (we tend to present ourselves in a positive light). Our views about a person's current personality influence recall of past events. Confidence in the accuracy of reports may be increased by identical independent accounts. However, all observers may have been influenced by biasing factors. Examples of guidelines suggested by the National Center on Child Abuse and Neglect for interviewing parents in cases of suspected maltreatment include the following:

- Tell the parents that the child's physical condition or behavior is a matter of concern.
- Focus initially on the child's condition and its possible causes.
- Use open-ended questions (e.g., ask the parents if they know what happened).
- Don't try to prove abuse or neglect through accusations or demands.
- Don't display anger, repugnance, or shock.
- If appropriate, tell the parents that a report of suspected child maltreatment will be made and offer your continued support and assistance during the child protective investigation.

Interviewing Children

As suggested earlier, special knowledge and skills may be required when interviewing children. The importance of avoiding leading questions is demonstrated by the disregard for interview data collected in cases of alleged sexual abuse because of such questions. Guidelines for interviewing children recommended by the National Center on Child Abuse and Neglect include the following:

Do:

- Make sure the interviewer is someone the child trusts.
- Conduct the interview in private.
- Sit next to the child, not across a table or desk.
- Ask the child to indicate words or terms that are not understood.
- Tell the child if any future action will be required.

Don't:

- Allow the child to feel "in trouble" or "at fault."
- Disparage or criticize the child's choice of words or language.
- Suggest answers to the child.
- Display shock or disapproval of the parents, the child, or the situation.
- Force the child to remove clothing.
- Conduct the interview with a group of interviewers.
- Leave the child alone with a stranger (for example, a CPS worker).

Play materials, anatomical dolls, "guided imagery" or "memory work" storytelling may be used to gather data about children's feelings and experiences. As with any source of data, the validity and reliability of such methods should be explored. (See for example critiques of using anatomically detailed dolls (e.g., Ceci & Bruck, 1995.) There are both practical and ethical reasons why you should be cautious in using conjoint parent-child interviews to evaluate child allegations of sexual abuse by the parent. Faller, Froning, & Lipovsky (1991)

suggest that such interviews are potentially traumatic for children and can be misleading.

This overview should caution you against uncritical acceptance of self-reports.

STANDARDIZED MEASURES

Standardized measures have uniform procedures
for administration and scoring and are accompanied by certain kinds of information including data
concerning reliability, validity, and norms (average
scores of certain groups). Standardized measures
are used to: (1) describe populations or clients; (2)
screen clients (e.g., make a decision about the need
for further assessment or find out if a client is eligible for or likely to require a service); (3) assess
clients (a more detailed review); (4) evaluate
progress; and (5) make predictions about the likely
futures of clients.

Varieties of Standardized Measures

Thousands of standardized questionnaires have
been developed related to hundreds of different
purposes (see, for example, Bellack & Hersen,

1988; Fischer & Corcoran, Volumes I and II 1994;
Jordan & Franklin, 1995). They include personality inventories, ratings scales, checklists, questionnaires, and surveys (see, for example, Exhibit 14.6).
Some require only yes or no answers, others call
for longer responses as in paper-and-pencil analogs
in which clients note what they would do or say in
specific situations. Many require little time and expense and are useful when direct methods such as
observation are not possible. Others, such as structured interview schedules, may require considerable time to collect and interpret data. Some provide an overview of many areas. Others focus on
one particular kind of situation.

Questionnaires can be used to gather demographic information (e.g., family composition, income, work history, and age), to explore attitudes,
or to assess knowledge (e.g., of effective behavior
in specific situations). Many provide information
from the client's perspective. You can compare the
responses of your client to normative data (responses of others who complete the same measure)
to see if they fall in the typical range for similar
individuals. Be sure to explain the purpose of a
measure before asking clients to complete it, and
encourage clients to be as accurate and honest as

EXHIBIT 14.6
Examples of Standardized Measures

Measure	Purpose
Anger Inventory (Novaco, 1975)	Determine degree of anger aroused by 80 different situations.
Automatic Thoughts Questionnaire (Hollon & Kendall, 1980)	Identify negative thoughts associated with depression (37 items).
Knowledge of AIDS Risk Behavior (Kelly, St. Lawrence, Hood, & Brasfield, 1989)	Evaluate knowledge about AIDS risk behavior.
Pleasant Events Schedule (MacPhillamy & Lewinsohn, 1982)	Identify pleasant activities engaged in over the past month and degree of enjoyment for each (320 items). Used to identify activities that may function as reinforcers for depressed clients.
Social Support Inventory (Barrera, Sandler, & Ramsey, 1981)	Assess perceived social support.
Abusive Behavior Inventory (Shepard & Campbell, 1992)	Assess domestic violence (30 items).
Knowledge of Child Development Inventory (Larsen & Juhasz, 1986)	Assess knowledge of child development. (A 56-item multiple-choice test containing items relevant from birth to age to three years in areas of emotional, cognitive, physical, and social development).
Attributional style questionnaire (Peterson et al 1982)	Assess attributions.
Fear Survey Schedule for Children (see Ollendick 1983)	Assess specific fears. (There are 80 items on the revised scale for younger and middle-aged children.)

possible. Consider reading levels required to complete a measure as well as cultural differences that may influence the appropriateness of items. If a client cannot read, you could present items out loud.

Objective tests include specific questions, statements, or concepts and respondents are asked to reply with direct answers, choices, or ratings. Some focus on one area. Others review many dimensions. Julian Rotter's (1966) locus of control scale is an example of the former, and the MMPI is an example of the latter. Personality tests such as the MMPI (Minnesota Multiphasic Personality Inventory) offer data that are used as signs. Inferences are made about underlying dynamics, traits, or future behavior that may be determined by those traits. Other measures seek information about specific behaviors in specific situations. In the latter approach, it is assumed that the more specific the items, the more helpful the answers. The distinction between these approaches is known as the sign versus sample approach to assessment. A sample approach is preferred in contextual practice, because this offers more specific data about behaviors and related cues and consequences compared to sign approaches.

Projective tests such as the Thematic Apperception test, incomplete sentences test, and the Rorschach Inkblot test are purposefully vague and ambiguous. It is assumed that each person will impose on this unstructured stimulus presentation unique meanings that reflect his or her perceptions of the world and responses to it. Psychoanalytic concepts underlie use of most projective tests. These tests focus on assessing general personality characteristics and uncovering unconscious personality processes. Projective tests have little predictive validity and provide little guidance about what methods will be most helpful in resolving complaints. Little or no information is provided about environmental factors that may influence problems.

Checklists and rating scales consist of a series of items, for example, a list of behaviors. Respondents indicate which ones are descriptive of themselves or of significant others. Responses may call for a simple yes or no, or a scale may be used. For example, the Assertion Inventory (Gambrill & Richey, 1975) lists 40 behaviors, such as "resisting pressure to drink," and the respondent is asked to indicate degree of discomfort on a scale ranging from 1 (none) to 5 (a great deal) and the likelihood of engaging in the behavior if the situation arose on a scale from 1 (always do it) to 5 (never do it). Scores on given item clusters can be used to discover areas of concern. More specific information about these areas can then be gathered. Rating scales are easy to score and take little time to complete. Responses on checklists are subject to the same type of demand characteristics as other types of self-report data. Items included are often vague (for instance, "impertinence"). Another disadvantage is the tendency to use overall scores to describe a person, which may obscure the situational variability in behavior. Many checklists emphasize problems rather than assets.

Paper and pencil analogs are designed to offer a sample of behavior that is assumed to reflect what a person would do in real-life. They may be presented in a written form (paper-and-pencil analogs) in which specific situations are described and the client indicates what he would do in each one. Notice that this is a form of self-report and so subject to sources of inaccuracy in self-report data. Clients may write down what they would do in each situation or select an option from a list of alternatives. Paper-and-pencil analogs tap "content" knowledge. Content knowledge (knowing what) may not reflect performance skills (knowing how). Such measures may underestimate or overestimate what clients can do.

Criteria for Selecting a Standardized Measure

As always, a key question is: "Is the measure valid?" Does it measure what it claims to measure (see Exhibit 14.7)? Is a person who has a high score on the Beck Depression Inventory (Beck et. al. 1961) really depressed? Do items included represent the domain of interest? Is there any evidence that scores on a measure will allow you to predict future behavior? What about concurrent validity? Do scores correlate in expected ways with other measures that are accepted as a criterion? For

EXHIBIT 14.7
Checklist For Reviewing Standardized Measures

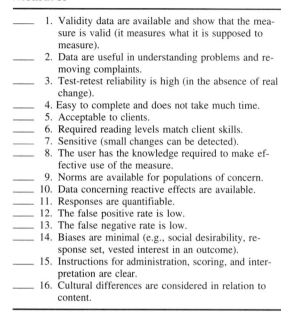

_____ 1. Validity data are available and show that the measure is valid (it measures what it is supposed to measure).
_____ 2. Data are useful in understanding problems and removing complaints.
_____ 3. Test-retest reliability is high (in the absence of real change).
_____ 4. Easy to complete and does not take much time.
_____ 5. Acceptable to clients.
_____ 6. Required reading levels match client skills.
_____ 7. Sensitive (small changes can be detected).
_____ 8. The user has the knowledge required to make effective use of the measure.
_____ 9. Norms are available for populations of concern.
_____ 10. Data concerning reactive effects are available.
_____ 11. Responses are quantifiable.
_____ 12. The false positive rate is low.
_____ 13. The false negative rate is low.
_____ 14. Biases are minimal (e.g., social desirability, response set, vested interest in an outcome).
_____ 15. Instructions for administration, scoring, and interpretation are clear.
_____ 16. Cultural differences are considered in relation to content.

example, do scores on a social skills inventory correlate with behavior during role plays? How high is the correlation? Can a measure be used to discriminate between people who have a certain characteristic and those who do not? For example, do scores on the Beck Depression Inventory help you to predict who will attempt suicide in the next six months and who will not? What about construct validity? Does a scale designed to assess altruism positively correlate with measures used to assess similar characteristics and negatively correlate with measures used to assess quite different characteristics (e.g., stinginess)? Direct measures (observing people in real-life situations) are often more valid than indirect ones (asking people what they do). Reliability should also be considered. How stable are responses on a measure given a lack of real change? Reliability should be .80 or better. Unstable measures are not likely to be valid. With unidimensional scales (those that include only one dimension in assessing a concept), find out about homogeneity (correlation between items). A measure may not be valid because only one dimension of a multidimensional concept is included on a scale. For example, caregiver burden may be related to a number of different factors. Reliance on a scale that taps only one dimension may not offer an accurate view.

Will a measure detect change that occurs in problem-related behaviors? The cruder the measure in scoring options (e.g., yes/no compared to a continuum of ratings), the less sensitive the measure may be. Utility is also important to assess. Can the measure be used? Is it feasible? Is it easy to administer? Is it easy to score and interpret? Will it offer you what you want to know? For example, some measures may be satisfactory for assessing pre-post change but not detect day-to-day changes in behaviors of interest. Are norms available describing the scores of similar individuals? If there were no norms for the Beck Depression Inventory, you could not determine whether a client's score indicates an unusual level of depression. Norms may be available but not for people like your client. For example, your clients may be Latino, and available norms may be for Caucasians. These norms may not represent responses of Latinos. (Norms should not necessarily be used as a guideline for selecting outcomes for individual clients because outcomes they seek may differ from normative criteria).

Limitations of Standardized Measures

As with verbal reports, responses on standardized measures may not offer an accurate picture. One disadvantage of standardized measures is overconfidence in the accuracy of a measure because of the appearance of rigor. Sources of error and bias that influence verbal reports also influence written measures. Factors that influence accuracy include response biases on the part of respondents (e.g., the tendency to answer in socially desirable ways); reactivity (completing the measures creates changes); and clarity of items (the more vague the questions the more likely clients will interpret them in different ways). Questionnaires should be designed to avoid a yes/no response set by varying how items are worded (some in a positive direction and some in a negative one). Questions may be leading (suggest answers). Responses will be influenced by demand characteristics (pressures in a situation to offer a certain type of report). For example, clients may exaggerate problems when seeking help and exaggerate positive change following intervention. The language used may be biased. Words may be incomprehensible to respondents or have a different meaning than the one intended. Normative data may not be available allowing comparison of a client response with other similar individuals. Measures differ in the percentage of *false positives* (respondents incorrectly assumed to possess a certain characteristic) and *false negatives* (respondents incorrectly assumed not to possess a certain characteristic) (see Chapter 17 on evaluating test accuracy).

Measures may have to be altered to increase their relevance for different groups. Don't discard an otherwise valuable measure because of the inappropriateness of one or two items. Change the wording or omit the items. Keep in mind, however, that if you alter a measure, available data about reliability, validity, and norms may no longer apply.

Standardized personality inventories lack the detail necessary to plan for behavior change. Answers usually do not offer information about specific behaviors and related events. The use of such inventories may be helpful in choice of plan if there is evidence of correlations between certain traits and service outcomes. Criteria suggested for reviewing assessment instruments for elderly clients are shown in Exhibit 14.8.

Special Precautions When Using Screening Measures. Standardized measures can be used to screen clients (e.g., to decide which clients are most at risk for a problem such as abuse or most likely to benefit from a service). Unless some decision rests on screening, it should not be done. Important characteristics of screening tools include brevity, lack of expense, and ease of use by staff with little or no training. Accuracy in identifying those who do and those who do not have a certain characteristic of problem is a crital concern. For ex-

EXHIBIT 14.8
Criteria for Reviewing Assessment Measures Used with Elderly Clients in Need of Care

- It offers comprehensive information about the client and the client's situation providing the basis for an individualized understanding of problems and selection of a service plan.
- It helps providers to make decisions with and on behalf of a client by providing information about functional abilities and suggesting the cause of observed problems and how they might be remedied. Information about potential to attain valued outcomes is offered.
- It is sensitive to changes in functional status over time.
- It is keyed to thresholds with practical significance for the client's well-being or independence.
- It provides an equitable way of making decisions about eligibility for services.
- It distinguishes small changes allowing distinctions among different levels of functioning at the lower end of the continuum where slight improvement or worsening might be significant.
- It provides information about both performance and opportunity. Performance is influenced by motivation and opportunity. For example, in some nursing homes residents are not allowed to bathe themselves. Case managers and caregivers need to determine capabilities apart from environmental constraints to select plans that maximize functional potential.
- It is acceptable to clients.
- It is acceptable to providers. The purposes of the questions are clear, the instrument is streamlined, and raters are capable of making accurate judgments.
- Costly or bulky equipment are not needed.
- A branching procedure is used so that it is suitable for clients whose functional status varies widely without requiring respondents to answer questions that are too difficult, too simple, or irrelevant.
- A branching format is used that allows exploration of areas of particular concern for individual clients.
- It produces categories of need that satisfy equity requirements in initiating and ending services across clients.
- It is supplemented with a brief screening procedure to determine the need for full-scale assessment. The initial intake assessment can be streamlined, with branching for reassessments and monitoring that emphasize collection of specific data at specific intervals, depending on the nature of desired outcomes.
- Decision rules are described to decide when the client is an appropriate informant and when reliable information should be sought elsewhere.

Source: Adapted from Kane R. A., and Kane, R. L. (1981). Assessing the elderly: A practical guide to measurement *Lexington, MA: Lexington Books, pp. 248–249.*

ample, what are the false positive and false negative rates (see discussion of using tests to make decisions in Chapter 17)?

Two purposes of screening can be easily confused: (1) case finding; and (2) describing a population. These two purposes require different methods for selecting samples and tests and interpreting results. With case finding, the measure should be keyed to appropriate thresholds (e.g., cut-points on measured scores) for identifying cases and the sampling should focus on specific populations at risk. Using data derived from screening to estimate the prevalence of a problem in a population will result in overestimates of the prevalence (base rate). The higher the prevalence of some characteristic in a population (the higher the *base rate*), the higher the sensitivity threshold should be set; otherwise, most of the population would be screened in. A representative sample is needed to describe a population as well as a measure that offers relevant data about areas of concern.

ASKING CLIENTS TO COLLECT DATA (E.G., SELF-MONITORING)

Clients often gather valuable information (see Exhibit 14.9). Benjamin Franklin kept track of his daily successes and failures in relation to virtues such as temperance (eat not to dullness, drink not to elevation), silence (avoid trifling conversation), order (keep things in order), resolution (meet goals set), frugality (avoid waste), industry (lose no time), tranquility (be not disturbed by trifles), and chastity (rarely use venery but for health or offspring; never to dullness, weakness, or the injury of your own or another's peace or reputation) (Silverman, 1986, pp. 91–92).

> I determined to give a Week's strict Attention to each of the Virtues successfully. Thus in the first Week my great Guard was to avoid even the least Offense against Temperance, leaving the other Virtues to their ordinary Chance, only marking every Evening the Faults of the Day. Thus if in the first Week I could keep my first Line marked T clear of Spots, I suppos'd the Habit of that Virtue so much strengthen'd and its opposite weaken'd, that I might venture extending my Attention to include the next, and for the following Week keep both Lines clear of Spots. (Silverman, 1986, p. 94)

As with any other source, not all clients will be able or willing to participate. Extensive education, training, or time are *not* required to gather data in real-life settings. Consider recent work with single

EXHIBIT 14.9
Monitoring the Behavior of Others—Case Examples

Brian kept track of the number of times his parents praised and criticized him and noted what happened right before and afterward on an ABC form. His parents also kept track for one week of how often they praised and criticized Brian and what happened right before and afterward on a similar form. Mr. Colvine (the social worker) showed Brian and his parents how to use the form and offered practice opportunities in recording before they left the office. Mr. Colvine thought that what was noted in the before columns would help the clients to identify relationships between their own behavior and that of other family members. He was familiar with the research showing that desired behaviors are often ignored and annoying ones reinforced in families experiencing problems. An excerpt from Brian's mother's form is shown in Exhibit 14.10. Mr. Colvine calculated the mean rate for praise and criticism and reviewed what happened right before and after to identify related factors. Data were converted to rates since behavior was observed for different time periods. His summary was as follows:

Mrs. Lakeland's hourly rate of praise was .23 compared with an average rate of criticism 1.5. Mr. Lakeland's average rate of praise was .24 and his average rate of criticism was .62. Mrs. Lakeland offered six times more criticism than praise and her husband offered over two times as much criticism compared to praise. The data indicated a low rate of interaction between Brian and his parents, with Mr. Lakeland having an especially low rate. This low level was also reflected in statements Brian made during the interview and in observation of the family during interviews.

A review of antecedents suggested that Mr. Lakeland intervened when he thought that "things were getting out of hand" (he waited until high level aversive behaviors occurred before taking some action, usually a punitive one). Criticism rarely resulted in positive changes. Brian's response to praise was usually silence. Praise offered tended to be vague and mixed with criticism. Many reactions recorded as praise probably did not serve this function. This was supported by Brian's data recorded the same week. He noted only one incident of praise from his father and one from his mother and he reported more criticism.

mothers following divorce (Patterson & Forgatch, 1990). Fifty-five percent of these mothers received public assistance. The mothers kept track of daily pleasant and unpleasant events in structured diaries. Data were summarized over 6 days to determine the mean proportion of negative to total events. An irritability measure was also gathered. The mothers rated their mood twice a day on a 7-point scale ranging from irritable to calm. The mean of 12 scores over 6 days was used as an overall measure. The mothers also rated their anger each day on a 5-point scale. In addition, the sum of five items that made the mother angry that day was obtained. Social isolation was assessed based on three items: feeling lonely, without anyone to talk to, and without anyone to share experiences with. Percent of positive contacts was also obtained. The data provided valuable case planning guidelines as well as the basis on which to evaluate progress.

Advantages of self-monitoring include lack of intrusion by outside observers, and an educational function in helping clients learn a useful skill; clients gain practice in clarifying concerns and identifying related factors. Attending carefully to the details of problems increases the likelihood that related circumstances will be discovered. The frequency of some events, such as thoughts and urges, can only be determined by self-monitoring. An abusive mother could monitor her urges to hit her child; self-monitoring may be a first step in helping her to recognize and control such feelings. Identification of urges and engaging in alternative behaviors at this early point may alter usual ways of reacting. A daily record of dysfunctional thoughts and constructive responses may be kept.

Decisions

You and your clients will have to decide the following:

- What to observe and record.
- Who is to do it.
- When and where it is to be done.
- How it is to be done.
- Where the recording form is to be kept.

- Who has access to the form.
- What prompts to arrange.
- What incentives to arrange.
- Over how many days information is to be gathered.
- What to do if difficulties arise.
- How to summarize data collected.

In choosing who is to observe and record, keep two criteria in mind. (1) Can the person provide reasonably accurate information? (2) How easy will it be to do so? Clients may collect useful information about exchanges with significant others. Whether they will collect data and how accurate they will be depend in part on whether you help them to design a recording method that is easy to use and provides helpful data. You will have to decide *how* events of interest are to be recorded. Your decisions will depend on information you need, how frequently related events occur, and practical considerations such as time available. If a behavior occurs frequently, you could select one representative period to explore contingencies. If behaviors of interest vary in different situations, you may have to collect data in each one. You will have to decide on the daily length of the sampling period. Select recording assignments that are easy to complete and that provide valuable case planning information.

Increasing the Likelihood That Clients Will Gather Useful Data

Designing successful self-monitoring tasks is a skill that develops with practice. You may discover valuable, easy to use recording forms by consulting practice-related literature. Select methods that do not intrude unduly on daily activities. Review points noted in Exhibit 14.11 before clients start to gather data. What is often blamed on clients or on limitations of self-monitoring as a source of information is often due to lack of skill on the part of helpers in selecting relevant, feasible procedures. Methods selected should match each client's unique skills and interests. Design or have on hand recording forms that permit easy, accurate collection of data. Codes may be used on recording forms to make recording easier (e.g., S = social situation; W = work).

Be sure that forms are easy to fill out and readily accessible. Self-monitoring assignments are more likely to be carried out if obstacles are identified and arrangements made to overcome them. A form may be too cumbersome or times selected to observe too intrusive. If so, design an easier form and select more convenient times. Vague instructions or failure to make sure that clients know how to collect data will decrease the likelihood that useful information will be collected. Be sure to show clients how to record and to provide practice opportunities before they try to collect data in real-life settings. Encourage clients to record observations as soon as possible after behaviors of interest occur as memory is fallible. Clients could audiotape relevant exchanges. You may have to arrange cues to remind clients to observe and record behavior. They could use a kitchen timer, parking-meter timer, or watch alarms. And you may have to arrange special incentives to encourage data collection. You can make recording easier for children by using drawings such as faces indicating different moods or stick figures indicating different actions. They can circle the face that represents their mood or place a check next to the appropriate stick figure to indicate their responses. Clients may ask you to accept their recollections in lieu of recorded data. These recollections may be inaccurate and are often vague. You could make access to training contingent on receiving needed data. If data is really necessary to plan wisely, this makes good sense.

Prearranged telephone calls provide an opportunity to collect data, to support clients for their efforts, and to troubleshoot (catch and correct problems at an early point). Clients who do not have phones could mail in data using prepared postcards. (See Chapter 18 for additional guidelines concerning assignments.) If clients have difficulty, you may have to arrange additional practice and provide more detailed instructions. Further contact could be made contingent on receiving needed data. Support clients for initial efforts, no matter how far removed from the ideal. If they bring in *any* data at all, praise them for this and review how this is of value. If it is not feasible for clients to gather data, or if this

is tried and is unsuccessful, other methods will have to be used.

Exploring Contingencies: Narrative Recording

This form of recording describes behavior and related events (what happens before and after specific behaviors of interest) (see Exhibit 14.10). It is used to identify events that cue and maintain behaviors of concern. Information about the frequency or rate of behavior is often provided at the same time. Teenagers who have problems managing aggressive responses to provocation could keep track of these as well as antecedent provoking events, consequences, and self-ratings of anger. Feelings and thoughts as well as behavior could be monitored. An ABC recording form can be used in which three columns are listed: (1) what happened right before; (2) the behavior thought or feeling; and (3) what happened right afterward. Common errors in using narrative recording include the following:

- Not noting events that happen *immediately* before and after behaviors, thoughts, or feelings of concern.

- Concentrating on feelings and thoughts rather than behaviors.

- Recording too little data about specific behaviors of concern.

- Not being clear about what to record.

You could use code categories for frequently related situations to make recording easier. The recorder enters the relevant code to indicate what he was doing when a behavior occurred. For example, the categories (R) reading, (E) eating, and (W) working are some that have been used when keeping track of smoking. A chart can be made with days along the top and times along the sides (e.g., 7–8 A.M., 8–9 A.M.). The appropriate code can be noted when the behavior occurs. This information will indicate times and situations when a behavior is most and least likely. Be sure to clearly define what is to be recorded. A depressed client could record the date, time, mood rating on a scale ranging from 1 (very low) to 100 (elated), as well as

EXHIBIT 14.10
Example of Narrative Recording

Date	Time	What Happened Right Before	Behavior	What Happened Right Afterward
10/15	4 P.M.	Brian lying on couch	I said "get up and do something useful."	Brian said "Ah, shut up—you do something useful."
10/15	5 P.M.	Brian refused to come to dinner	I said "You give me such aggravation—this is the last time I'm calling you."	Brian said "who cares?"
10/15	5:15 P.M.	Brian teasing his sister	I said "Stop. You are impossible."	Brian said "Don't be an old nag."

what happened at that time. Data can be categorized in terms of intensity of mood ratings (0–25, 26–50, 51–75, and 76–100) and records examined to identify events related to different mood levels. Information about factors related to social situations of concern could be collected by using a form with the following categories: date, time, situation, who was present, what I wanted, what I did, and what happened. Thoughts could also be noted to identify unhelpful and helpful self-statements. You could ask clients to write down what they *could* have done, said, or thought to assess their knowledge of effective reactions. Clients may prefer to record data in a diary.

Exploring How Often Problem-Related Behaviors Occur

Data describing the frequency or magnitude of relevant behaviors, thoughts, or feelings collected

EXHIBIT 14.11
Checklist for Reviewing Self-Monitoring Tasks

1. The client knows what, when, where, and how to record.
2. Clients understand the purpose of self-monitoring.
3. Data gathered will be of value in case planning.
4. An easy-to-use recording method is used.
5. Positive behaviors are emphasized.
6. Practice opportunities have been arranged.
7. Prompts and incentives are arranged as necessary.
8. Clients are coached to continue acting as they normally would.
9. Recording will not interfere with daily activities.
10. An agreed-on date when data are to be shared is set.
11. Decisions have been made about who is to have access to records.

prior to intervention offer information about the seriousness of a behavior and provide a baseline comparison point for evaluating progress. Data may be collected by clients, or by significant others depending on interest, time, and skills. A variety of aids are available for making recording easy and even fun. These include wrist counters, timers, and biofeedback devices. Many items are inexpensive and can be loaned to clients. Audiotape recorders are useful for recording exchanges. Videotape recording may offer a valuable adjunct to assessment. Behavior can be monitored in many different ways, including frequency recording (sometimes called event recording), in which the number of times a behavior occurs is counted; time samples, interval recording, and duration measures that are based on units of time rather than on discrete behaviors; and measures of behavior products, magnitude, and distance.

Ease of collecting data and the likelihood that relevant, representative information will result are key criteria to consider in making selections. These criteria should be considered when deciding what to record, in what situations, how long observation periods will be, and who will collect data. Well-designed forms and readily available aids such as wrist counters can increase the ease and accuracy of recording. If a client feels anxious only in certain kinds of social situations, data can be gathered only in these situations. If a mother has trouble at bedtime with her child, she can collect data only at this time. Clients could collect data about what happens before and after behaviors of interest at the same time they note data concerning frequency (see prior discussion of narrative recording). For example, a father who had physically abused his child while drinking kept track of what he drank, the situation, how much he drank, the time, as well as his thoughts and feelings before and afterward (Stein, Gambrill, & Wiltse, 1978). This provided baseline data related to drinking as well as information about related cues and consequences.

Frequency (Event) Recording. This refers to a count of the number of times a behavior, thought, or feeling occurs during a period of time (for example, hour, day, or week). This method is valuable when behaviors or events of interest have clear beginnings and endings. The rate must be low enough to count and individual instances relatively similar in duration. Thoughts or feelings may be recorded. For example, a client may be asked to note when she has an urge to eat. Behaviors can be listed along the top of a page and days down the left and a check made in the appropriate square each time a behavior occurs. This form is often called a Behavior Checklist. It could be small in size (e.g., to place in a pocket) or large (if it is to be posted so that clients can easily see it). Recording forms should be readily accessible and behaviors to be noted clearly described. If only one behavior is counted, a wrist counter can be used.

Total frequency counts are often too troublesome to obtain. An alternative is to record how often a behavior occurs during some time period focusing on periods in which behavior is of particular concern. Recording responsibilities could be divided among significant others (e.g., staff and residents, family members). A disadvantage of recording only during selected periods is that the frequency of a behavior may vary in different situations. So recording only in one may not offer accurate accounts of the frequency in other situations. If behaviors of interest occur often and regularly, sampling periods can be short while still offering a reasonable estimate of frequency. Time periods must be selected carefully if a behavior occurs only under certain situations or varies in different contexts.

Rate of Behavior. If observation periods differ from day to day, then you will have to use the rate of behavior as a measure. Divide the number of hours or minutes of observation into the number of behaviors that occurred. Let's say that a mother keeps track of how often she praises her son. On Saturday, she was home for seven hours, and praised her son three times and on Thursday she was home for three hours and praised her son once. Her hourly rate of praise was .43 on Saturday and .33 on Thursday. If saying pleasant things was monitored over a seven-hour day, and the frequency was 5, the rate per hour would be 5 divided by 7, or about .7 per hour. Finding the rate of behavior in terms of some common index, such as number per day or hour, allows comparison of different behaviors. A convenient recording form includes room for the date, time (start and stop), total time, number of behaviors, and daily rate. Daily rate can be graphed for review.

One-shot Recording. Some behaviors can occur only once in a given period. The behavior either does or does not occur during this time, which can be a month, week, day, or hour. Examples include making breakfast for children before they go to school and being on time for work. The behavior check sheet or a recording form allowing room to note the date and whether the behavior occurred can be used. The percentage of days on which the behavior occurred can be found by dividing the number of days in which behavior was checked into the number in which it occurred.

Time Samples. Clients may not have time to record the frequency of a behavior even during a selected period. Or this may be difficult because what is of interest may not have a definite beginning and ending or may last for varying times (e.g., wearing an orthodontic device). Time sampling, in which behavior is sampled at fixed or random times, provides an alternative. Select times that offer representative information about behavior and related events. Preselected times can be written down on a form and a yes or no recorded for each, depending on whether the behavior occurred or not. Ideally, random times should be selected so that clients will not be able to predict when behavior will be checked. A cue may be needed to remind clients to check on behavior. Random times can be preselected and a timer set for each.

Time samples may be gathered without selecting particular times. The observer simply records behavior when she happens to remember to do so or does so an agreed-on number of times during the day. Julie used time sampling to note whether she was worrying about her decision or not, the time she noted this information, and what she was thinking. You can find the daily percentage of times in which the behavior occurred by dividing the number of times the behavior was checked into the number of times it was observed. If a parent checked on her son's behavior five times and recorded only one instance, the daily percentage for that day would be .20.

Gathering information on an hourly basis may be helpful in discovering factors related to complaints. Schwartz and Goldiamond (1975) asked a client to record the following every hour during the day: what he was doing (work); the setting (sitting at desk); who was there (self); what he wanted (to get work done); what happened (little accomplished); and comments (sat and daydreamed). These records revealed events related to difficulty in completing work, such as going to other people's offices rather than having clients come to him.

Duration. Measures of duration are useful when behaviors are continuous rather than discrete and when the objective is to alter the length of time a behavior occurs. The total length of time a behavior occupies either for a single occurrence (duration of a temper tantrum) or over a certain time period such as a day (for instance, daily time spent doing chores) could be measured. Make sure that the onset and ending of a behavior is easy to determine. Use of duration allows you to set approximations to a desired outcome rather than using an either/or criterion as in the one-shot method. Duration is not necessarily the method of choice for behaviors that vary in length of time, such as tantrums, because recording this may be too time consuming. A time sample could be used instead. A client could check whether the behavior is occurring at random times and find out the percentage of instances in which it did occur, or a required time lapse could be imposed between behaviors before recording another instance. If observation pe-

riods differ in length, the proportion of time in which the behavior occurred can be determined.

Magnitude/Intensity. Magnitude (e.g., intensity of pain or anxiety) may be the most relevant measure. Noise level could be recorded by using a decibel counter. Self-anchored scales are often used to rate magnitude of emotional reactions. For example, anxiety could be rated on a scale ranging from 1 (complete calmness) to 100 (extreme discomfort). Clients could rate their mood on a scale ranging from $+3$ (very good) to -3 (very bad) using the scale shown below.

+3	+2	+1	0	−1	−2	−3
		some-what		some-what		
very happy	happy	happy	neutral	blue	depressed	very depressed

Self-Anchored Scales. Self-anchored scales are often used to measure thoughts, feelings, and behaviors. These are individually tailored for each client. Advantages include flexibility in designing a scale that matches the unique circumstances of each client. Self-anchored scales can be used to assess events (such as urges and negative thoughts) that cannot be determined by other means. Disadvantages include lack of norms. Because these are individually constructed, no norms are available allowing comparison of the client's responses with those of others. In addition, no information may be available about reliability and validity. Steps recommended by Bloom, Fischer, and Orme (1995) when creating self-anchored scales include the following:

1. Help clients define problems and desired outcomes using their own words.
2. Decide on the number of scale points. Clients could rate their anxiety on a scale that includes ratings from 1 (none), 2 (a little), 3 (moderate), 4 (anxious), and 5 (very anxious).
3. Encourage a client to view scale values as equally distant from each other. A thermometer analogy is sometimes used.
4. Design scales with one dimension.

5. Give clear examples of scale values. Examples of values used to rate social anxiety may be as follows:

    25   Mild anxiety that does not interfere with behavior.

    50   Uncomfortable anxiety that affects concentration but does not disrupt behavior.

    75   Uncomfortable preoccupying anxiety (it is hard to concentrate and the client has thoughts of leaving the situation).

    100   The highest anxiety ever experienced or that the client can imagine feeling.

6. Decide how often the client will complete the scale and where.

Other Measures. Recording behavior products may be useful when other forms of observation may affect the frequency of the behavior being observed or when it is too time-consuming to observe behavior directly. Examples include empty beer cans, problems completed, meals prepared, and weight. *Latency* may be the most appropriate measure. Examples include time elapsing between a parent's request and a child's compliance and time between lying down and falling asleep. Use of latency as a measure requires clear description of a cue (e.g., a request) and when a behavior starts and stops. *Distance* will be the choice for some valued outcomes (e.g., when a client wants to travel farther from home without fear).

Reactive Effects of Self-Monitoring

Self-monitoring draws attention to particular behaviors and so may influence their form or frequency. Such changes are called *reactive effects*. They may be negative or positive. Positive effects include an increase in desirable behaviors or decrease in problematic behaviors. Students who monitored their study time had significantly higher grades than those who did not (Johnson & White, 1971). Negative reactive effects include an increase in problematic behavior or a decrease in desired behavior. The effects of self-monitoring usually fade over time.

Factors That Influence Reactivity

Factors that influence the "reactivity" of self-recording (whether self-recording results in a change in the frequency of behaviors, thoughts, or feelings) are described below (for more detail see Ciminero, Nelson, & Lipinski, 1986).

1. *Motivation.* Self-monitoring may result in greater reactivity if clients are motivated to change their behavior. For example, Lipinski et al. (1975) found that self-monitoring decreased smoking only for people who were motivated to stop smoking. Monitoring resisted urges to smoke decreased smoking, whereas recording number of cigarettes smoked increased it (McFall, 1970). Clients tend to underestimate their undesirable behaviors and overestimate desirable ones.

2. *Setting goals and offering feedback.* Reactivity is greater if specific goals are set and clients receive incentives for attaining them. Feedback on performance increases reactivity.

3. *Timing.* Recording a behavior before it occurs interrupts the usual chain of reactions and provides an alternative to an undesired reaction (e.g., hitting).

4. *The recording method.* Intrusive methods are more reactive. A wrist counter may function as a cue that influences behavior.

5. *Schedule of self-monitoring.* Recording behavior at the end of the day or periodically during the day seems to be less reactive than continuous recording. Clients who monitored their mood and recorded their activities hourly reported an increase in pleasant activities and a decrease in depressed mood (Harmon, Nelson, & Hayes, 1980). Self-monitoring was cued by a timer set on a variable-interval (1-hour) schedule. Such effects have not been found for clients who recorded their mood or activities once a day.

6. *Other factors.* Instructions may influence reactivity. If you suggest that a client's worrisome thoughts will decrease, they may. The more be-

haviors that are monitored the less the reactivity (and the less likely that the client will monitor them). Reactivity seems to be greater for nonverbal than for verbal behaviors.

Accuracy of Self-Monitoring

Variables that enhance reactivity will decrease accuracy. There are many ways you can increase accuracy. If clients object to recording "negative" behaviors (e.g., yelling at children), ask them to track positive alternatives. Clearly describe behaviors so clients can easily identify them. Use unintrusive recording methods and encourage clients to record data right after relevant behaviors occur. Clients will not gather data if recording interferes with their daily life activities. Training and practice increase accuracy. Be sure to consider the potential negative effects of monitoring. For example, monitoring inaccurate solutions on a mathematics task resulted in decreased self-reward and accuracy, and lowered self-evaluations (Kirschenbaum & Karoly, 1977). Asking a depressed client to write down negative thoughts may increase these, and clients should be prepared for this. Individually tailor recording tasks for each client. A particular method may be easy for some clients and difficult for others.

The observer's behavior may change as a result of watching someone else. For example, parents may decrease their use of criticism as a result of using narrative recording in which they note the frequency of their child's annoying behaviors as well as what they do before and after. Check on the representativeness of data by asking clients and significant others whether exchanges noted are typical of what usually occurs. You will have to decide whether to tell significant others they are being observed. Not telling them may have ethical problems. Telling them may result in changes in their behavior. A child who bullies other children on a playground may not do so when he knows he is being watched by a teacher. The effects of observation typically decrease over time as the usual real-life contingencies take precedence. The main concern is to obtain a reasonably accurate account of behaviors and related events.

PHYSIOLOGICAL MEASURES

Measures include heart rate, respiration rate, skin conductance, muscle tension, and urine analysis. Although some measures require expensive equipment, others do not, such as pulse and respiration rate. Physiological measures are useful when verbal reports may be inaccurate. Other examples include measuring blood pressure of clients with hypertension, breathing function of asthmatics, and breathalyzer tests to determine blood alcohol levels. The field of behavioral medicine has mushroomed over the past years, bringing with it increased interest in the use of physiological measures.

WHEN TO INSIST ON A PHYSICAL EXAMINATION

Problems may be related to physical causes. Examples include anxiety, aggression, depression, headaches, and sexual problems. In such instances, a physical examination may be wise. Without this, physical causes may be overlooked. Consider the inaccurate diagnosis of people who have Wilson's disease. Symptoms of this illness include various psychological changes as well as trembling. Wilson's disease is a result of failure to absorb copper, and it can be diagnosed by a blood test as well as by certain indications in the eye. Misdiagnosis of associated symptoms as due to psychological causes has resulted in the unnecessary death of clients. Nutritional deficiencies may result in psychological changes as may prescribed medication.

CASE RECORDS

Advantages of reliance on archival and case records include savings in time and cost, unobtrusiveness, and availability. Examples of archival records include school grades, police reports, and hospital records. Disadvantages include missing data (see Exhibit 14.12). Records may not contain clear descriptions of problems, desired outcomes, or related contingencies. Vague obscure language may con-

EXHIBIT 14.12
Common Problems with Case Records

Assumed pathology of clients and significant others is focused on; assets are ignored.

Descriptions of problems, desired outcomes, and related circumstances are vague; they do not provide case planning guidelines.

Environmental causes are overlooked.

Important demographic information is missing (e.g., age, household members).

Irrelevant content is included.

Unsupported speculations are offered (conclusions based on insufficient data); theory is presented as fact.

Jargon (psychobabble) is used.

Conclusions are drawn based on small biased sample.

Descriptions and inferences are confused; descriptive terms are used as explanatory terms (see Chapter 15).

Assessment procedures are not clearly described.

Services provided are not clearly described.

Service goals are vague.

Up-to-date information is missing.

---

fuse and mislead rather than enlighten. Assessment methods and services offered may be vaguely described, as may claims about progress. Information about current life circumstances may be missing. It is sometimes even hard to discover what the presenting problems were. A further concern is a focus on pathology rather than on assets. The accuracy of archival data such as school or police records is influenced by the biases of those who record data and by policy changes about what and how to record. Material may be hard to find because it is scattered through a lengthy record. Negative conclusions are often drawn on vague grounds and alternative accounts are too rarely suggested. Often no information is given about the basis for inferences or how they may be helpful in resolving problems. We may read "This client is paranoid" with no details presented as to why this conclusion was reached or what help it will be. Inferences made may be based on one of the questionable criteria described in Chapter 14. The sources on which claims are based should be critically examined no matter who prepares a report. Key questions include: Are claims well-reasoned? What evidence is presented for inferences? Are alternative possibilities noted? Do suggested causal accounts provide clear service guidelines about what to do next? (See Tallent, 1993.)

DATA PROVIDED BY OTHER PROFESSIONALS

Clients may be referred to other professionals, for example, to evaluate special skills or abilities. Whether data provided are helpful (or misleading) will depend on the questions asked, the knowledge and skills of the involved professional, and the knowledge that exists related to the task involved. Potential sources of information that other professionals may draw on are the same as those you and your clients may use. Critically review data they provide using the same questions you would use to review material from any source: "How valid are tests used?" "Are inferences well reasoned?" Are claims made on questionable grounds (e.g., what's usually done)? Don't be intimidated by credentials and degrees. If you are working with people who are indeed professionals, they will welcome questions about their assumptions and will take the initiative in telling you about any limitations of tests used and assumptions made.

WHAT TO DO ABOUT DISCREPANCIES

What if reports from different sources provide contradictory data? Certain kinds of discrepancies are common and may provide useful assessment data. Verbal reports of anxiety often lag behind performance measures. For example, clients may report more fear than they show in real-life situations. Lack of agreement may occur because clients differ in their reaction patterns. Some clients have measurable physiological changes in anxiety-provoking situations. Other clients may experience anxiety mainly cognitively (have anxious thoughts).

Differences between verbal self-reports and responses on written measures may be a result of different wording or response formats. Overall scores on a measure that reviews behavior in a variety of situations may not reflect reactions in particular situations. Consider the Assertion Inventory, which measures anxiety in a wide variety of social situations (Gambrill & Richey, 1975). Discrepancies between verbal reports of anxiety and overall scores may occur because a client experiences anxiety only in some (or one) of the situations described on the inventory. Only one subscale (cluster of items) on an inventory may be correlated with behavior in certain situations—not the overall score. A client may be anxious when initiating conversations and arranging future meetings but not when refusing unwanted requests and responding to criticism.

KEEPING TRACK OF MATERIAL

There are many ways to keep recording minimally time consuming and maximally useful, including use of computers (see for example Nurius & Hudson, 1993). Well-designed forms will make it easy to record and organize data. Assignments can be written down using a carbon copy or paper that automatically makes a copy (NCR paper); the client can be given one copy and the other copy placed in your records. You may have to take notes during interviews to keep track of material. Note taking does not have to interfere with attentive listening. Be sure to explain what you are noting and who will have access to your notes. If possible,

schedule time between interviews to keep up with recording. You could audiotape interviews for later review with the client's permission. If you do, explain your purpose for taping interviews and inform the client about who will have access to taped material and when tapes will be erased. Typing notes directly into a computer could save time.

ETHICAL ISSUES

Select measures that are valid and relevant (they provide information that will help you and your clients to make well-reasoned decisions about what to do next). Avoid unnecessary tests that waste the client's time and tests and questions that pathologize or stigmatize clients. Be sure to consider possible negative effects of contacting collateral sources. Contacting a supervisor at work with whom a client is having trouble is not a good idea if it would make things worse for the client. You should use only methods you are competent to use (e.g., know how to interpret data collected). Resist temptations to use methods that are easy to use and at hand, but offer few or no guidelines about how to help clients.

SUMMARY

You and your clients will have to decide how to clarify problems and options for resolving them (if any). You should only be as precise as you have to be to clarify problems and options. Sources of data to choose among include self-reports in the interview, written measures, self-monitoring, role play, observation in real-life settings, case records, and physiological measures. Each source is subject to error. The function test (altering circumstances to determine their influence on behavior) is the final arbiter of whether data gathered and assumptions made are accurate. Social workers tend to rely too much on verbal reports, neglecting self-monitoring, role play, and observation in real-life. Being informed about the advantages and disadvantages of different sources of data will help you and your clients to make well-reasoned decisions whether you offer direct services or whether you refer clients elsewhere. Focus on gathering useful data—data that decrease uncertainty about how to help and if you can. Some sources will not be feasible. For example, some clients will not be able to provide needed information in the interview. Some clients will refuse to gather data at home. What is often blamed on clients (they will not or cannot collect data) is often due to lack of care, creativity, and flexibility on the part of helpers in discovering or designing feasible, relevant measures. What is needed is a representative picture, not a totally accurate account—data that will guide next steps (e.g., be of value in selecting service plans). If possible, combine self-report data with data collected in the natural environment.

REVIEWING YOUR COMPETENCIES

Reviewing What You Know

1. Describe sources of assessment information and the advantages and disadvantages of each.
2. Describe conditions under which verbal reports are likely to be accurate.
3. Identify helpful criteria for assessing measures.
4. Define the term "reactivity" and give an example.
5. Describe the difference between a frequency count and a time sample and give an example of each.
6. Given examples of specific problems, describe feasible means that clients or significant others could use to collect valuable data.
7. Define the terms *reliability* and *validity* and give examples of different kinds of reliability and validity. Describe why each is important.
8. Describe steps you can take to increase the accuracy of self-monitoring.
9. Identify characteristics of helpful self-monitoring assignments.
10. Describe steps you can take to increase the likelihood that clients will gather useful data.
11. Describe how rate of behavior is determined.
12. Identify questions that should be asked about standardized measures.
13. Given specific examples describe reasons why a data collection method was not successful.
14. Give examples of the value of norms.

Reviewing What You Do

1. You design feasible, relevant self-monitoring assignments.
2. You complement indirect sources (e.g., self-report) with direct ones (e.g., observation) when possible and important.
3. You can accurately evaluate the quality of evidence in case records.
4. You make effective use of written questionnaires.
5. You gather valuable case planning information in role plays.
6. You include graphed baseline data relevant to desired outcomes in clients' case records.

Reviewing Results

1. Clients collect useful data.
2. Clients report that collecting data was helpful.
3. Data collected result in selection of successful plans.
4. Clients acquire a useful problem-solving skill (attending closely to the details of a problem).

CHAPTER 15

Observation: Learning to See

OVERVIEW

This chapter offers guidelines for observing behavior in real-life settings and for evaluating data gathered by others. Evaluating observational reports and observing are valuable practice skills. Common sources of error are described as well as suggestions for avoiding them.

You Will Learn About

- The value of seeing for yourself.
- Observation in the natural environment.
- Thinking critically about observation.
- Attending to the physical environment.
- The value of observation in task analysis.
- Keeping track of data collected.

THE VALUE OF SEEING FOR YOURSELF

Observation in real-life settings may be required to clarify problems and identify related circumstances (see Exhibit 15.1). Without a fine-grained (detailed) description of problem-related contingencies based on careful observation, you may make inaccurate assumptions about maintaining conditions (see Exhibit 15.2). You may overlook problem-related behaviors and misapplied and unapplied contingencies. Each individual and each environment is unique. Only through careful observation may interaction patterns between clients and significant others be understood. As the designers of one observational form note, "It is more respectful of a person's dignity and autonomy to assume that functional reasons exist for challenging behavior rather than to think that it occurs because of some major 'trait or [personality] characteristics' " (O'Neill, Horner, Albin, Storey, & Sprague, 1990, p. 28). Sherlock Holmes emphasized the importance of "observing" what others merely "see" (Truzzi, 1976, p. 60).

EXHIBIT 15.1
The Value of Observation

At age 11, Sam Brown burned down his neighbor's garage and was sent to a residential youth facility. Two years later he returned home. The adjustment wasn't easy. Sam fought with his two younger brothers, and their mother (Anne) had difficulty handling them. Sam's father worked at night and was reluctant to discipline the children, fearing he would lose his temper. With all three boys home during summer vacation, tensions mounted. One afternoon, while playing outside, Sam and his 9-year-old brother Frank got into a violent fight. A neighbor called the police when Sam began choking Frank. The police took Sam, accompanied by his mother, to a psychiatric emergency room. The hospital called in a social worker from the Home-Based Crisis Intervention Program, who drove Sam and his mother home. The next morning the social worker returned to talk to them.

Over the next 6 weeks, the worker spent almost every other day with the family and was able to observe their daily routines at first hand. He discovered that Sam was not always the instigator of fights with his brothers. In fact, his brother Frank often started a brawl and then blamed it on Sam. (Frank had assumed the role of "number one son" while Sam was away and was upset about giving it up.) The worker brought this to their mother's attention and encouraged her to discipline all three boys and not just Sam. "Anne had good parenting skills," the worker recalls. "What she needed was a lot of reassurance that she could handle them." They worked on building her confidence in her parenting skills and her ability to take charge when a fight broke out.

Source: Adapted from S. Leavitt & B. McGowan (1991), Transferring the principles of intensive family preservation services to different fields of practice. In E. M. Tracy, D. A. Haapala, J. Kinney, & P. Pecora (Eds.), Intensive family preservation services: An instructional sourcebook (pp. 61–62). Cleveland: Case Western Reserve University, Mandel School of Applied Social Sciences.

Overlooking the value of observation contributes to the fundamental attribution error in which problems are incorrectly attributed to clients' personal characteristics and related environmental circumstances are overlooked. No matter how good your reasoning skills are, if you base your decisions on inaccurate data, you will be less likely to help your clients. The money and time saved by not observing problem-related behaviors in real-life settings when necessary for accurate assessment may be wasted many times over in lost opportunities to help clients because of incorrect definitions of problems. Observing behavior during interviews may offer clues about how other people respond to clients and how clients feel about topics discussed. You may note that family members interrupt one another and offer few positive comments. Keep in mind however, that behavior during interviews may not correspond to what occurs in real-life (e.g., at home).

Given the possible lack of agreement between self-report and observational data, gather both when needed and possible (see Exhibit 15.3). If observa-

EXHIBIT 15.2
Common Errors Related to Observation in Real-Life Settings

- Not believing it is important when feasible and relevant (guessing how many teeth a horse has rather than looking in to see).
- Overlooking preconceptions that interfere with accurate observation (e.g., stereotypes).
- Not describing behaviors in their context (setting events, antecedents, and consequences related to behaviors of concern are not described);
- Descriptions are vague.
- Assuming that what is observed in one setting reflects what occurs in others.
- Offering inferences rather than descriptions.
- Assuming that agreement between observers indicates accuracy.

EXHIBIT 15.3
Using Multiple Sources of Information

Elsie Pinkston and her colleagues used observation of problem-related exchanges as well as other sources of information such as self-monitoring and self-report in their work with elderly clients and their caregivers. "Very often an observation session follows the initial interview. During this session the practitioner spends an hour or more at the client's home, observing interactions and activities. When possible, another observer besides the practitioner participates. . . . **Anecdotal observations** are usually recorded in three columns: antecedent events, client behaviors, and consequent events with all client behaviors being recorded in the center column. . . . The arrangement provides the groundwork for a preliminary functional analysis of the client's interaction with the environment and a more accurate guess at appropriate and inappropriate behaviors to be measured. Thus, behaviors of others in the client's environment, as well as the client's behaviors, are included.

. . . Mr. Young was referred to a home health care social worker because the family and the home care nurse were concerned about his low activity level, his refusal to converse or socialize, and his general depression. His severe cardiac condition placed some limitations on active behaviors. During a preliminary anecdotal observation, the practitioner found that Mr. Young was not responsive to efforts by family members to converse with him (he mumbled or answered in very brief sentences). The practitioner also observed that family members had the required prompting and praising abilities to encourage behaviors and that Mr. Young's activities were indeed very low level and nonsocial in form. The assessment helped the practitioner and the family select some target behaviors for further assessment and intervention: positive statements by Mr. Young, responses of more than three words, praise by family members, and increasing out-of-home activities."

Source: E. Pinkston & N. L. Linsk (1984), Care of the elderly: A family approach *(p. 24). New York: Pergamon.*

tion in real-life is not possible, observation during role plays may be a good alternative. The question is, which method offers accurate information about behaviors of concern and related events. **The function test** (altering specific antecedents or consequences to determine their influence on behavior) can help you and your clients test your guesses about the reasons for behaviors of interest. Only by rearranging the environment in certain ways and observing the effects of these changes may you and your clients detect influential contingencies.

When Observation Is Needed But Is Not Possible

Observation, although needed to clarify problems and discover options, may not be possible, perhaps because your agency does not allow time for it or provide the requisite training. You may have to "shoot from the hip" (make inferences about problems and related circumstances without the minimally needed information to do so (let alone optimal). Deciding on plans without a careful assessment may result in ineffective or unnecessarily intrusive interventions. Consider the following example that one of my students noted in her critical thinking log:

Situation: Case conference at a day care center for clients alleged to have Alzheimer's disease. The staff wanted to ask Mrs. L. to leave because she yells loudly, "because of her dementia."

What you did: I raised the possibility that yelling may not be a result of her dementia but might be maintained by positive consequences such as attention from volunteers and escaping unwanted situations. I noted that as a result of yelling, Mrs. L. had been assigned a one-to-one volunteer and did not have to participate in a group that she did not like. I suggested that we examine the contingencies related to yelling by observing what happens before and after yelling. **What happened:** The other staff said, "Look, we know that Mrs. L. is demented. That's why she yells. She does not know what she is doing." I persisted. I pointed out that if Mrs. L. left the day care center, she would be sent to a nursing home, which was an intrusive plan, since she now lived at home. I reintroduced the idea of gathering systematic data that we could then examine.

What should you do in such a situation? First, remember what you are trying to accom-plish; otherwise you may forget about or aban-don sound assessment guidelines and label clients (e.g., as demented) rather than help them maintain or enhance the quality of their lives. Second, involve interested colleagues in altering agency policies and practices that prevent collection of needed data. Third, you could collect data regarding problem related contingencies and share this information with staff.

EXHIBIT 15.4
An Example of Using Role Playing to Assess Communication Styles

Expressing negative feelings was one situation of concern to Mrs. Ryan and the Greens. Mrs. Ryan, aged 89, lived with her daughter and son-in-law (Mr. and Mrs. Green) and their children. They all were asked to enact how they usually spoke to one another when they tried to share their feelings. Mrs. Ryan chose "feeling left out" at the dinner table. The social worker asked her clients to pretend they were at home talking about this. The following exchange took place:

MRS. RYAN: I never seem to get a chance to talk during supper. All the attention goes to the children.

MR. AND MRS. GREEN (together): Well, the children . . . (Mr. Green stopped and Mrs. Green continued) Well, we don't get a chance to talk to the children except at dinner.

MRS. RYAN: I don't feel that anyone cares about what I have to say.

MR. GREEN: The kids aren't interested in that old stuff—they get tired of that.

MRS. RYAN (at the words old stuff noticeably flinches): Yes, "old stuff"; I guess I am just old stuff, to be stuffed away in a corner.

MR. GREEN: Don't be ridiculous. You know we care about you.

MRS. RYAN: If you cared about me, you'd listen to me more. But you don't care, either, about "old stuff."

MRS. GREEN: It just seems that you are never interested in what we are doing or in what the children are doing, that you are interested only in your past times, your old friends, people we don't even know.

The conversation continued along these lines with accusations and counteraccusations and a noticeable lack of eye contact, empathic statements, paraphrases of the other person's point of view, or proposed solutions. The social worker praised the clients for taking part in the role play, reaffirming that the criterion for success was acting as they usually did at home. This role play suggested objectives to focus on to enhance positive communication among family members.

EXHIBIT 15.5
Examples of Using Role Play for Assessment

Purpose	Task	Possible Measurement
1. Assess couple's communication skills.	Discuss situations they disagree about. Record interactions.	Identify rate of specific behaviors (e.g., questions asked).
2. Assess conflict resolution skills of parents and children.	Discuss conflicts.	Record frequency of certain verbal behaviors.
3. Assess parenting skills.	Request parent and child to interact in a free-play situation in which parent sets rules (parent's game) and then shift and have child set the rules (child's game).	Determine rate of positive feedback or sequential child–parent behavior (e.g., following instructions).
4. Assess social skills of psychiatric patients.	Respond to tape-recorded situations.	Review behavior in terms of previously identified, explicit criteria.

ROLE PLAY (ANALOGUE SITUATIONS)

Analogue situations are designed to simulate real-life conditions. You can use role plays to find out whether clients have needed skills and to identify changes in behavior needed to attain outcomes clients value as well as related cues and consequences (see Exhibit 15.4). It is hoped that clients' reactions during role play reflect what clients and/or significant others do (or could do) in real life. Let's say that a father and son argue about who is to do household chores. Audiotaping or videotaping exchanges (with the clients' permission) permits a detailed review. Role plays used to review the communication skills of parents and children or of couples last about ten minutes. Situations may be presented by film, audiotape, or videotape. An example of a situation of concern to "delinquent" adolescents together with possible reactions is as follows.

> "It is 1:30 at night, and you're walking along a street near your home. You're on your way home from your friend's home, and you know it is after curfew in your town. You weren't doing anything wrong. You just lost track of time. You see a patrol car cruising along the street and you feel scared, because you know you can get into trouble for breaking curfew. Sure enough, the car stops next to you, the policeman gets out, and he, says, 'You there, put your hands on the car. Stand with your feet apart.' What do you say or do now? Score:
> 8 Either the youth does it without saying anything OR he asks a brief general question respectfully.

Example: 'What's wrong, officer?' 'Is something the matter?' OR he explains honestly and convincingly where he was.

6 The youth explains where he was, etc., but in a less assertive or less convincing manner. Examples: 'I just got out of Pete Jones' house. You can call him if you want to.'

4 No specific criteria . . . midway between responses scores 6 and 2.

2 The youth is antagonistic or flippant or insolent.

0 Either the youth hits the policeman OR he runs away. (Freedman, Donahoe, Rosenthal, Schlundt, & McFall, 1978, p. 1452)

Compared with paper-and-pencil analogues (see Chapter 14), behavioral role plays offer more accu-rate and more detailed information about problem-related behaviors, including valuable skills that are not used to advantage. Exhibit 15.5 gives examples of using role plays for assessment. Role plays have been used to evaluate the quality of care that respite providers give to handicapped children (Neff, Parrish, Egel, & Sloan, 1986) and the telephone con-versational skills of socially isolated, impaired nurs-ing-home residents (Praderas & MacDonald, 1986). Some coding systems designed to assess interaction patterns may not be feasible for you to use because of the time required to learn how to use them reliably and to gather and summarize the data. For example, the Couples Interaction Coding System contains 31 code cate-

EXHIBIT 15.6
Examples of Communication Problems

Overtalk. Speaking much more than others.

Rapid latency. Speaking very quickly after the speech of another.

Affective flatness. Speaking without the vocal characteristics usually associated with the content of what is being said.

Obtrusions. Making frequent utterances while others are speaking. Such intrusions become interruptions if they result in an immediate and premature end of the speech by the other.

Quibbling. Efforts to explicate, clarify, or dispute minor, tangential, and irrelevant details.

Underresponsiveness. Saying too little in answer to a question or comment.

Dogmatic statements. Making a statement in a categorical, unqualified, all or none, "black or white" manner.

Overgeneralization. Misrepresenting the frequency or pervasiveness of behaviors or other events (e.g., claiming a behavior "always" occurs in a situation when it occurs only sometimes).

Presumptive attribution. Misrepresenting the motivations, feelings, and thoughts of others (mind-reading).

Topic avoidance. Avoiding opportunities to talk about a topic.

Vague descriptions. Being general and abstract.

Temporal remoteness. Dwelling excessively on the past or hypothetical future.

Positive talk deficit. Failing to compliment or say nice things about the other as a person or about what the other says or does.

Acknowledgment deficit. Failing to admit or give credit when the other person is correct or failing to recognize other points of view.

Opinion deficit. Failing to express a preference or an opinion when the discussion calls for one.

Excessive disagreement. Disagreeing excessively with others.

Negative talk surfeit. Frequent or lengthy negative comments about others, events, or one's surroundings.

Source: Adapted from E. J. Thomas, C. L. Walter, & K. O'Flaherty (1974), A verbal problem checklist for use in assessing family verbal behavior. *Behavior Therapy, 35, 238–239.*

gories, such as mind reading, proposing a solution, agreement, and disagreement (Notarius & Markman, 1989).

You could ask your clients to act out exchanges with significant others or with some other person. Exhibit 15.6 shows some of the common communication problems of couples identified during role-played discussions. Notice that some reflect a lack of critical thinking (e.g., not acknowledging other points of view, vague descriptions, and overgeneralizing). You could ask clients to imagine situations of concern and to act out how they would respond in each; be sure to allow them time to clearly imagine the situation. People differ in their skills in clearly imaging situations.

Advantages and Disadvantages of Role Playing

The advantages of role playing are convenience and efficiency. Exchanges can be tape-recorded or videotaped for later review to identify problem-related behaviors, cues, and consequences. Gains of efficiency must be balanced against concerns about validity. Does the behavior represent what occurs in real life? Clients may be more (or less) anxious during role plays than they would be in similar real-life situations. Role plays may reveal that a client does have the skills needed to achieve valued outcomes. However, these skills may not be used in real life. Current environments may provide neither opportunities nor incentives.

Making the Most of Role Playing

To make the most of role playing, focus on situations that are directly related to desired outcomes. You may have to sample behavior in a variety of contexts to discover situations in which changes would be desirable. For example, if a client has trouble making friends, the social situations of concern include initiating conversations, introducing topics of conversation, sharing personal information, asking questions, and arranging future meetings (Gambrill & Richey, 1988). Take advantage of what is known about the situations of concern to different groups. Clearly explaining the purpose of role playing and criteria for success will help put clients at ease. Reassure them that most people feel awkward and uncomfortable at first. You could ease clients into role playing by asking them to play a role that is comfortable and that will not reflect negatively upon them. They could play themselves with the criterion for success being how well they do so. Another way to relax clients is to use yourself as a model. You could select a neutral situation and participate yourself, asking the client to play a less active role. Support client participation with generous use of praise.

The more similar that role plays are to real-life circumstances, the more likely it is that behaviors observed will represent what usually takes place. It therefore is important to clearly describe specific situations related to valued outcomes. You may have to assume the role of a significant other yourself if only the client is present. If so, find out first how this person usually responds in the situation. You could discover this by asking the client to play the role of the significant other or to describe how this person usually reacts. Use props to make the scene more realistic. If telephone conversations are involved, use a phone as a prop. Start the role play

based on what occurs in real life. For example, if you are role-playing a job interview, begin by having the client enter the room so that you can see her posture, eye contact, facial expression, and gait.

Be sure to clearly describe behaviors related to desired outcomes. Descriptions like "participate actively" or "communicates well" are too vague to be helpful. The specific behaviors referred to by these general terms as well as the specific situations in which they can be used with success must be identified. Be sure to attend to nonverbal as well as verbal behaviors. Nonverbal behaviors such as eye contact, posture, and facial expression influence how we affect others. Check to see whether the client's nonverbal behavior matches his or her verbal behavior. For example, smiling while telling someone bad news is usually not appropriate. How something is said (e.g., tone, loudness, fluency) is as important as what is said. Are statements made loudly enough to be heard? Are facial expressions appropriate? You can use checklists or rating scales to assess behavior.

One reason for using role plays during assessment is to identify valuable skills clients and significant others could use in problem related situations. This highlights the importance of discovering what clients could do as well as what they usually do in situations of concern. After role-playing a typical exchange, Mrs. Ryan and the Greens were asked to replay the same situation, doing the "best they could." This time they made some empathic statements and paraphrased other points of view. But they did not offer any ideas for resolving their concerns, nor were any requested. Discovering client's assets is a key assessment goal. If skills are available, they will not have to be developed, although cues and incentives may have to be arranged to encourage their use. Ask clients what they are thinking at certain times during role plays to identify both helpful and unhelpful self-statements. An example of the former is "Good for me for trying." Examples of self-handicapping thoughts are negative labels ("that was stupid") and negative expectations ("I'll fail again").

You can use structured role plays to assess interaction patterns. Forehand and McMahon (1981)

EXHIBIT 15.7
Checklist for Using Role Playing
for Assessment

_____ 1. Situations are related to client concerns.
_____ 2. The purpose of using role play is clearly described to clients.
_____ 3. Role plays are structured to tap available skills as well as typical reactions in situations of concern.
_____ 4. The role the client is to assume is clearly described.
_____ 5. Criteria for success are clear and clients can meet them (e.g., act as you typically do in the situation).
_____ 6. Props are used to increase realism.
_____ 7. Situations selected closely resemble those in real life.
_____ 8. Clients will be fairly comfortable during role plays.
_____ 9. Exchanges are recorded for later review.
_____ 10. Praise is offered following each role play.
_____ 11. Specific changes that would be helpful are identified.

---

designed a parents' game and a child's game to explore parenting behavior under different conditions. Parents could be asked to make their child look as good as possible to observe their child-management skills. Some parents who have problems with their children do have effective parenting skills, as is shown by studies that found no differences between mothers of problem children and mothers of nonproblem children in altering their child's compliance or in the behaviors they used to obtain compliance and noncompliance (Green, Forehand, & McMahon, 1979). Other studies have found that parents who have difficulty with their children can make them look worse but not better. Use the checklist in Exhibit 15.7 to remind yourself of important points to consider when using role playing for assessment. Common errors are

- Not using role plays when they would offer valuable information.

- Vaguely describing situations of concern and related behaviors.

- Not recording exchanges (as appropriate and feasible) for detailed review.

- Allowing role plays to last too long.

- Giving punishing rather than positive feedback.

OBSERVING IN THE NATURAL ENVIRONMENT: SEEING FOR YOURSELF

You may have to observe clients and significant others in real-life settings to identify problem-related behaviors and related antecedents and consequences, with your client's permission. You and your clients will have to decide: (1) who will observe, (2) what to observe, (3) when to observe, (4) how long to observe, (5) how to minimize intrusiveness, and (6) how to keep track of data you collect. Observation in real life is a valuable complement to interview data. This may indicate that a client's views about the causes of problems are incomplete or inaccurate (for detailed examples, see Carr et al., 1994). Observation often reveals that appropriate behaviors are ignored and undesired ones are reinforced. For instance, the staff in a residential center may complain about the residents' behavior. Observa-tion may show that staff ignore desired behaviors (e.g., polite requests and greetings) and reinforce (with attention) disliked behaviors (e.g., shouting). In addition to discovering influential consequences related to behaviors of concern, it also is important to identify related setting events and antecedents. Only when the staff have ignored several requests by the residents may they resort to inappropriate behaviors such as shouting. Only when a child has had a fight with his parents at home may he be aggressive and hit other children at school.

You may use initial observation periods to identify relevant behaviors and related events. Since behavior often differs in different situations, you may have to collect data in more than one setting. For example, a child may act quite differently on the playground and in a classroom. You may have to collect data over a few days to allow time for people to become accustomed to being observed and for their behavior to return to its usual pattern. Observation periods often last about 30 minutes. How much time you will need depends on whether the contingencies of interest are clear. O'Neill and colleagues (1990) recommend that data be gathered for 2 to 5 days or until a minimum of 10 to 15 occurrences of the behavior have been observed. If no consistent patterns emerge, specific antecedents and consequences can be altered and the effects noted. You can use prompts to encourage certain reactions. The disadvantages of observation include cost and inconvenience, restriction to overt behavior, intrusiveness, and reactive effects (i.e., your presence may alter behavior). The guidelines discussed next suggest how to minimize these disadvantages.

Guidelines for Observation

The guidelines for making recording easy for clients apply to you as well. Count behaviors only after they have been clearly defined and can be reliably coded. It is frustrating to try to count behaviors when you are not ready to do so. If you are not prepared, this will become obvious when exchanges occur faster than you can record them. Take advantage of observational systems that have been developed (e.g., Reppe & Karsh, 1994; Tyron, 1996). Hand-held computers provide immediate feedback about interaction patterns between clients (e.g., students) and significant others (teachers) (Sugai & Lewis, 1989). Well-designed forms and thorough training increase the likelihood of gathering accurate data. Success in collecting relevant, accurate data will depend on

- The observer's skill in identifying specific problem-related behaviors (including positive alternatives to disliked behaviors) and related setting events, antecedents, and consequences (e.g., misapplied and unapplied contingencies).
- The availability of helpful tools such as recording forms/counters/computers.
- Ease of access to relevant contexts.
- Preparation of clients to facilitate the observation of relevant contingencies (or their absence).

Be sure to describe clearly the purpose of observation to clients and significant others. If you are observing in agencies, hospitals, or residential centers, review the procedures with staff members as ethically and practically necessary before collecting data, and follow the agency's rules and policies. Helpful rules during home observation of fam-

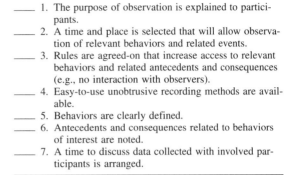

EXHIBIT 15.8
Checklist for Observing Interaction in Real-Life Settings

_____ 1. The purpose of observation is explained to participants.
_____ 2. A time and place is selected that will allow observation of relevant behaviors and related events.
_____ 3. Rules are agreed-on that increase access to relevant behaviors and related antecedents and consequences (e.g., no interaction with observers).
_____ 4. Easy-to-use unobtrusive recording methods are available.
_____ 5. Behaviors are clearly defined.
_____ 6. Antecedents and consequences related to behaviors of interest are noted.
_____ 7. A time to discuss data collected with involved participants is arranged.

ily interaction are not speaking to the observer, not permitting TV or phone calls, requesting clients to remain in the room, removing items that might be distracting to small children (such as handbags), and sitting or standing in an unobtrusive place. Observation takes time and effort. Prepare carefully so that you can make good use of these opportunities (see Exhibit 15.8).

The distinction between _descriptions_ and _inferences_ is important. Let's say you observe a mother and her son and write in your case record, "She is hostile." This is an inference based on behaviors you observed rather than a description of what you saw. Be sure to include descriptive accounts relevant to your inferences. Clear descriptions of what is referred to by inferences allows others who review your records to understand what you mean by certain terms. (see Exhibit 15.9).

Sequential Recording

Making sound practice decisions may require detailed information about problem-related contingencies, including interactions between clients and significant others to determine who reinforces whom, when, and for what. Sequential recording systems have been developed to observe interactions in a variety of settings, including group homes, geriatric nursing facilities, institutional settings, classrooms, nursery schools, and community

EXHIBIT 15.9
Distinguishing Inferences from Descriptions

Check those items that you believe are inferences.
1. She is a good parent.
2. She hit her child when he called her "old nag."
3. He is an alcoholic.
4. My supervisor likes me.
5. He fell and hit his head.
6. Mrs. Rivera is a battered spouse.
7. She says that her neighbor hates her.
8. He told her to get lost.
9. Her son is out of control.
10. Mr. Monk is mentally ill.

settings such as supermarkets. Systems differ in the number and type of code categories included and in the training required (Foster, Bell-Dolan, & Burge, 1988). For example, the Patterson Coding System for observing family interaction contains 29 categories (Reid, 1978). Examples include hit, talk, command, request, and cry. Interactions are coded sequentially by concentrating on one family member for 5-minute periods and noting his or her behavior as well as the reactions of other family members to it. One way to gather sequential data is to describe each interaction (including the context, the behavior, and the consequences) on a separate index card (see Exhibit 15.10). You can also

EXHIBIT 15.10
Three Cards For Gary

Three cards for Gary grouped according to the common theme of response to a request to perform a nonpreferred task within the category of escape-motivated behavior.

Name: Gary	Observer: Rob	Date: 3/10/87
General Context: Gathering work materials		Time: 9:30 A.M.

Interpersonal Context: Cal asked Gary to bring over a wheelbarrow full of potting soil to the workbench.
Behavior Problem: Gary punched Cal in the chest and tried to punch him a second time in the face but Cal ducked.
Social Reaction: Cal told Gary to "keep cool" and moved away from him. After a few minutes, Cal got the wheelbarrow himself.

Name: Gary	Observer: Bob	Date: 6/25/88
General Context: Lunch		Time: 12:30 P.M.

Interpersonal Context. Gary had just finished eating his lunch. Mrs. Ibsen was very busy trying to get a number of things done so that she and Gary could keep a doctor's appointment. Because she was so busy, she asked Gary to clean the table and put away the dishes. She had to make several requests to get Gary moving.
Behavior Problem: Gary responded by biting his hand, spitting, and trying to slap his mother.
Social Reaction: Mrs. Ibsen backed away. When Gary had calmed down, she quickly cleaned up the table and put the dishes in the sink.

Name: Gary	Observer: Bob	Date: 4/11/87
General Context: Shaving		Time: 7:30 P.M.

Interpersonal Context: Gary's father asked him to go into the bathroom and shave.
Behavior Problem: Gary shouted, "Go away!" and bit himself.
Social Reaction: Gary's father walked away and Gary did not shave.

Source: E. G. Carr, L. Levin, G. McGonnachie, J. I. Carlson, D. C. Kemp, & C. E. Smith (1994), Communication-based Intervention for Problem Behavior: A User's Guide for Producing Positive Change *(p. 85). Baltimore: Paul H. Brookes.*

EXHIBIT 15.11
Practice in Observation

Make 10 copies of the following form. Choose a behavior you are interested in, and describe 10 related interactions based on your observation. Review this information, and suggest possible function(s) of the behavior.

Name: _____ Observer: _____ Date: _____

General Context: _____ Time:_____

Antecedents (who was present, what happened right before): _____
_____
_____

Behavior (what the person did): _____
_____
_____

Social Consequences (how others responded): _____
_____
_____

Hypothesis (The behavior's probable function): _____
_____
_____

write down your guesses about the function (meaning) of behaviors noted. (Behaviors of interest may have more than one function.) After you record a number of critical incidents, you can review the data collected to explore possible functions (e.g., escape from unwanted attention or tasks, attention from peers or teachers, gaining a valued item). Consider Michael, whose behaviors of concern were slapping and pinching. The initial data suggested that these behaviors were maintained by escape from less familiar, more difficult tasks. His teachers decided to explore this by varying the difficulty of teaching tasks over sessions. Michael's aggressive behavior was consistently higher in conditions requiring difficult tasks. Try the practice exercise in Exhibit 15.11.

Interval Recording

Interval samples are a form of time sampling in which a period is broken into smaller units of time, such as 15-second intervals. Then, for each interval, the observer notes with a check mark whether the behavior occurred. Not every instance of the behavior is recorded—only whether it occurred during the selected time period. Thus, interval recording provides an estimate of the true frequency or duration of behaviors. The maximum frequency of a behavior is determined by the size of the time unit selected, which should be related to the frequency with which the behavior occurs. If a 10-second interval is used, the maximum rate of behavior will be 6 per minute. With a frequent behavior, the unit should be smaller in order to reflect its rate more accurately. Using intervals that are too long underestimates the behavior's frequency. Whenever you use small time intervals, be sure to use an audible timing device so you will know when to start recording. Intervals can be programmed on a cassette tape by saying "one," "two," "three," and so forth, at every 10-second interval.

You also may record behaviors *at* the interval

rather than within an interval. For example, Goodwin and Coates (1976) developed a procedure for simultaneously recording both behavior and its consequences. Their codes for students include on-task behavior, scanning, social contact, and disruptive behavior. The teacher consequences included instructing, rewarding, neutral behavior, and disapproval. The observer notes at each 5-second interval what the student is doing and the teacher's response and checks the appropriate space. To evaluate the progress, the percentage of intervals in which a behavior occurred during baseline can be compared with the percentage after intervention.

Time Sampling

Both time sampling and interval recording depend on units of time rather than discrete behaviors. Both estimate the frequency of a behavior. *Time sampling* refers to recording procedures with a much longer span of time between intervals compared with those of interval recording. Time sampling is useful when a behavior may occur over a long time span and when it does not have a definite beginning or end. For example, ward staff could monitor residents' social exchanges by making 20 observations of each resident every day. *Prompting* is often used when behaviors of interest are under strict stimulus control, such as responding to someone initiating a conversation (e.g., walking up to a person and saying hello). In such cases, it would be a waste of time to wait around until the behavior occurred.

You can use time sampling to discover the range of behaviors that occur in a particular situation. Data can be summarized by counting the total number of times a person was observed and the total number in which each behavior occurred, and dividing the former into the total for each behavior. If behavior were observed at 17 intervals during one shift in a residential setting, and a resident were found to be sleeping during 10 and talking during 2, you could determine what percentage of 17 that each of these behaviors occupies. Time sampling can be helpful in discovering antecedents related to behaviors of concern (Touchette, MacDonald, &

Langer, 1985). The observer notes whether or not the behavior occurred in each time block and may also note whether it occurred frequently. The resulting scatterplot indicates the times when there is a high frequency of the behavior and a low frequency of the behavior.

Other Measures

Total frequency counts may be feasible to gather (e.g., number of cigarettes smoked, number of bottles of beer consumed). You can also note related cues and consequences. You may use rate or percentage (see Chapter 14). Sometimes a *duration measure* will be most appropriate (e.g., length of conversation, duration of pain). Latency has been used to measure the time between when an instruction is given and when it is followed. Behavior products may be noted, such as amount of litter, energy used, empty beer cans.

Data Describing a Group

At times a group measure may be best. If you know the rate of positive and negative exchanges between clients during group meetings (see Exhibit 15.12), you can compare different groups or a behavior of one group over many sessions. If the size of the group differs on different occasions, divide the number of behaviors by the number of people, and then divide this figure by a time measure to obtain the rate of behavior (see Rose, 1989, for other examples). You can use a time sample with fixed or random intervals to observe residents' behavior. A form for the observer to note location, position, whether the person was awake or asleep, facial expression, social orientation, and activities was reliably used by mentally retarded residents of a state school and hospital (Craighead, Mercatoris, & Bellack, 1974). You can summarize the data by counting the number of residents engaged in each behavior over all intervals. Let's say that you observed 10 residents for 17 intervals and that a total of 35 were watching television. The number of intervals multiplied by the number of residents yields the total number of opportunities for any one

EXHIBIT 15.12
Positive and Negative Exchanges and the Rate of On-Task Behavior Observed in a Mutual-Aid Group

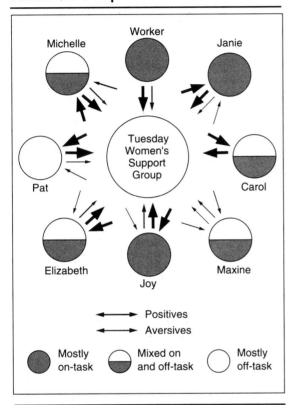

Source: M. A. Mattaini (1993), More Than a Thousand Words: Graphics for Clinical Practice *(p. 97). Washington, DC: National Association of Social Workers.*

behavior over all intervals. To find the percentage contribution of any one behavior, divide the number of people engaging in this behavior by the total number possible. This example illustrates how you can gather observational data that may be valuable in enhancing the residents' quality of life.

THINKING CRITICALLY ABOUT OBSERVATION

Like other sources of data, observation is subject to error (see Exhibit 15.13). Observation is theory laden. We see what we expect to see and may miss what we do not expect to see. Unless you take special precautions, you may miss what is there to be seen and see things that aren't there. Knowledge of sources of bias and error as well as skill in avoiding them will help you to make effective use of observation. Be sure to consider reliability and validity when reviewing data (see Chapter 14). Basing decisions on small, biased samples may result in poor decisions. Social workers often address "highly charged" problems. Consider possible differences of opinion among neighborhood residents about what problems should be given greater priority and what should be done to resolve them, or the different views of staff and youth about the causes of fights in a residential setting. The staff may blame the residents, and the residents may blame the staff. Preconceptions about how people will behave based on stereotypes may influence what is seen and reported. Observers of an event may have quite different views about what occurred (see for example, Ross, Read, & Toglia, 1994). Observers may be inconsistent in their use of behavior defi-nitions. Recording methods may be cumbersome. Observers are more accurate when they think that their results will be checked. Vague definitions of behavior is a common cause of error. Behavior may change because it is being observed.

Reactive Effects

Like self-monitoring, observation may also have reactive effects. For example, when parents knew they were being observed, they played more, offered more positive verbal reactions, and structured their children's activities more than when they were not aware of being observed (Zegiob, Arnold, & Forehand, 1975). Reactive effects may be temporary. That is, over time, clients may become accustomed to the observer's presence and their behavior may return to its natural patterns and rates. The purpose of observation is to obtain a representative picture of behavior and related events. Only if reactive effects are so severe that what is seen is quite unrepresentative of what usually occurs, should there be concern.

EXHIBIT 15.13
Sources of Error in Observational Data

Type of Error	Description
1. Central tendency error.	Observers tend to select subjective midpoints on rating scales when judging a series of events.
2. Tendency to be generous or lenient.	Observers tend to be lenient or generous when using scales requiring "yes," "sometimes," "rarely," or "no."
3. Primacy or recency effects.	Initial impressions distort later judgments.
4. Logical errors (informal or formal)	Judgment errors due to assumptions (e.g., that because a teacher is warm, she or he is also instructionally effective).
5. Overlooking vested interests and values of observer.	Judgments are influenced by personal biases or expectations.
6. Classification of observations.	Fine distinctions are lost when general categories are used.
7. Faulty generalizations about behavior.	Judgments are based on data from an unrepresentative sample, resulting in false conclusions or incorrect classifications of people or events.
8. Failure to consider the perspective of those observed.	Overlooking participants' perspectives may result in inaccurate accounts.
9. Poorly designed observation methods.	Recording forms may be cumbersome, resulting in low reliability and validity. Recording methods may be vaguely described.
10. Failure to consider the rate of exchanges.	Observers can't keep up with what's happening, resulting in missing data.
11. Reactions of those observed.	Teachers may behave differently when being observed than they otherwise would.
12. Failure to consider the situation or context	Contextual differences that influence behavior are overlooked. Incorrect assumptions of functional equivalence (e.g., assuming that reading time 1 = reading time 2 may result in overlooking the effects of changes in activities or variations in obligations in different situations).
13. Overlooking the function of behavior.	Incorrect conclusion that a behavior lacks stability because differences in contingencies that influence behavior are overlooked.
14. Overlooking the simultaneity of behaviors of interest.	Errors due to failure to account for multiple activities occurring at one time. For example, more than one message may be sent at a time through different channels (verbal and nonverbal). A message may have more than one function at a time.
15. Assuming that a behavior has only one function.	A behavior may serve many functions (e.g., escape from unwanted tasks, attention). Focusing on one alone will decrease success.
16. Inattention to observer drift.	Errors caused by changes in uses of a coding system over time, resulting in descriptions that do not match the original categories or that vary from one another.

Source: Adapted from C. M. Evertson & J. L. Green (1986), Observation as Inquiry and Method. In M. C. Wittrock (ed.), Handbook of Research on Teaching *(3rd ed.) (p. 183). New York: Macmillan.*

Reviewing Reliability and Accuracy

How reliable are observations? Do observers agree with one another? You can explore reliability by finding out how closely two or more observers independently agree on what they observe. You can calculate interobserver agreement in a number of ways. One is to divide the number of agreements by the number of agreements plus disagreements and multiply this by 100. Or you could determine the correlations between two raters. Percentage agreement, however, can be misleading because some agreement will occur purely by chance and agreement percentage scores do not correct for this. Point-by-point agreement, in which an agreement is counted only when both observers identify the same behaviors at the same time, provides more accurate estimates than do procedures that do not require point-by-point agreement. When using interval recording, you should not count those intervals in which neither observer recorded a code, since including them artificially inflates the index of reliability. Reliability can be increased through training. Records can be compared right after observation, disagreements discussed, and rules developed to resolve them. Observers should be familiar with

EXHIBIT 15.14
Reviewing the Quality of Observational Data

- Are reliability data presented? Are they adequate?
- Are validity data presented? Are they adequate?
- How was the sample of observed interactions selected? Are there biases of concern?
- Does the sample of observed exchanges comprise a representative sample?
- Do data collected help you and your clients make sound decisions?

behavioral definitions used, the data sheet, and any timing devices. If an independent assessment of reliability is not possible (i.e., using two observers), the accuracy of response definitions can be checked by periodically gathering examples of relevant behaviors and seeing whether they match agreed-on definitions.

Observer accuracy refers to the extent to which the observer's ratings match the coding of a criterion. Observer's reliability may be high but the observer's accuracy may be low. Even if observers agree on how to describe a behavior, their ratings may not reflect the "meaning" (function) of behavior for those occurrences observed. For example, an observer may score the interruptions of one person by another as having a negative consequence when in reality it does not. What is a positive or negative consequence for one person may not be to others. Accuracy can be determined by having observers periodically code a criterion tape (an audiotape or videotape of situations of concern) to find out whether coding matches agreed-on definitions. You can detect **observer drift** (changes in recording over time) by comparing data collected with data based on a criterion observer. Exhibit 15.14 suggests questions to ask when reviewing observational data.

OBSERVING THE PHYSICAL ENVIRONMENT

You may discover valuable options by carefully observing the physical environments in which clients live, work, and play. Advantages of altering the physical environment include low cost in terms of training, time, money, and interference with routines and policies. Once in place certain kinds of physical alterations tend to remain. Concerns about continued staff participation are not as problematic. Questions to ask include the following:

- In what ways do physical arrangements encourage valued behaviors?
- In what ways do they discourage valued behaviors?
- In what ways do they encourage undesired reactions?
- How could the physical setting be altered to enhance desired outcomes?
- Who would benefit from changes made?
- Who would experience negative consequences?
- Are there hazards that should be removed (e.g., faulty electrical wiring, unprotected windows that people could fall out of)?

Observing Neighborhoods and Communities

Information about different aspects of neighborhoods and communities (e.g., physical such as transportation, political such as who holds office, and social such as who talks to whom, where, when, and about what) may be needed to plan how to resolve concerns (see also Chapter 24). A visit to a client's neighborhood and community may provide valuable information. Computer programs allowing notation of the geographical location of given types of services can aid in rapidly finding accessible services for a client. In her classic book *The Death and Life of Great American Cities* ([1963] 1993), Jane Jacobs eloquently describes the importance of detailed knowledge about neighborhoods, their links with people with influence in their districts, and the links of these individuals to people in city-wide power positions. The fields of environmental and community psychology suggest valuable ways of describing neighborhoods and communities (e.g., Stokols & Altman, 1987).

Examining Residential Environments

The Staff-Resident Interaction Chronograph (Paul, Licht, Mariotto, Power, & Engel, 1987a) and the

EXHIBIT 15.15
Physical Features in Middleton Nursing Home

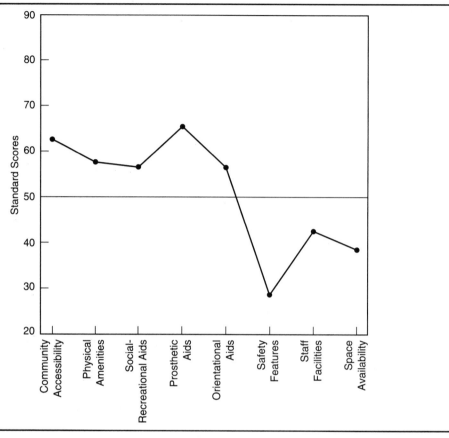

Source: R. H. Moos & S. Lemke (1994), *Group Residences For Older Adults: Physical Features, Policies, and Social Climate* (p. 5). New York: Oxford University Press.

Time-Sample Behavioral Checklist (Paul et al., 1987b) are designed for use in residential settings. Rudolph Moos and Sonne Lemke (1994) designed a series of scales to describe residential settings. Areas included in description of physical features can be seen in Exhibit 15.15. Assessment of the social climate includes scales for cohesion, conflict, independence, self-disclosure, resident influence, and physical comfort. Assessment of policies and services uses scales for expectations of functioning, acceptance of problem behavior, resident control, policy clarity, provision for privacy, health services, daily living assistance, and social-recreational activities. Environmental characteris-

tics that should be assessed in residential settings for elderly persons include structural barriers to wheelchairs and walkers, distance barriers, prompts and cues indicating where and when activities are to take place, type of furniture and arrangement, lighting, content of activities and materials used, and scheduling conflicts (Hussian & Davis, 1985). Do the residents have sufficient privacy? If not, how can it be increased? Are the residents allowed to personalize their rooms? Is the setting free of hazards (are railings in place on all stairs)? Are the beds comfortable? Are the toilet facilities clean and accessible? Are recreational areas available. Are these sufficient? Chairs could be repositioned to increase social exchanges (Peterson, Knapp, Rosen, & Pither, 1977). Food could be served family style rather than institutional style to encourage verbal exchanges (VanBiervliet, Spangler, & Marshall, 1981). Stores could be placed in the lobby of a nursing home to increase social and leisure time participation (McClannahan & Risley, 1973). Participation of residents in recreational activities could be enhanced by making materials readily available and prompting their use (McClannahan & Risley, 1975). Risley and Twardosz (1976) explored variations in the physical design of preschool settings.

Examining the Physical Characteristics of Organizational Environments

Physical arrangements in an agency influence work climate and effectiveness. Noise pollution, poor lighting, lack of privacy, and few phones may adversely influence the staff's behavior, which in turn compromises the services that clients receive. The agency's physical characteristics may reflect staff's attitudes toward their work and/or citizens' attitudes toward the particular client group. For example, a center serving homeless people and families may be in need of paint and have few decorative amenities. Use your observational skills to identify low-cost improvements that could be made and involve interested colleagues in getting them done.

THE VALUE OF OBSERVATION IN TASK ANALYSES

The purpose of a task analysis is to identify the behaviors required to attain a valued outcome. Examples of behaviors involved in putting on a pullover shirt are

1. Pick up a shirt/holding at bottom.
2. Open shirt/holding at sides.
3. Place over head.
4. Pull shirt until head emerges.
5. Put right arm in right sleeve.
6. Right arm emerges completely.

7. Put left arm in left sleeve.
8. Left arm emerges completely.
9. Pull shirt down to waist. (Young, West, Howard, & Whitney, 1986)

This information serves as a training guide to develop needed skills. Many helpers ignore the need for a task analysis and in its place often use questionable substitutes such as armchair speculation—perhaps abetted or hindered by personal experience. Central to task analysis is observing behaviors in the contexts in which they occur. If behavior by the residential staff is of interest, then their behaviors and the effects on the residents' behavior would be observed. If ordering food in a fast-food restaurant is of concern, then that is the place to observe behavior (see van den Pol, Iwata, Ivancic, Page, Neef, & Whitley, 1981). Videotapes of behaviors of interest in real-life situations may be useful for discovering effective behaviors as well as problematic points and options for handling them.

All the questions and concerns that arise with observation of behavior in real-life settings come into play here. Are there reactive effects? That is, does behavior change as a result of being observed? How many different people should be observed to obtain a representative account? Redundancy is one criteria that could be used (i.e., observation ceases when no additional information is provided). Sometimes it will be obvious that certain behaviors must occur to attain a given outcome. For example, you have to remove the toothpaste cap before you can squeeze out the toothpaste. At other times, the required behaviors are not obvious. For example, without careful observation, the relationship between a social behavior and its effects on the environment may not be clear. Or the future effects of certain social behaviors may not be known. A person who talks a great deal at a senior center may get the attention of others at the time but be avoided on future occasions. There may be a variety of ways in which a desired outcome can be achieved. The more accustomed we are to one way of acting in a situation, the harder it may be to think of alternatives. You or your clients could collect data in real-life settings to discover options. Most task analyses provide information about what most people do in a specific situation. Thus a task analysis may not offer information about creative variations that may result in similar (or valued) outcomes.

The task is broken down into teachable components describing what the learner is expected to do. Each step should be numbered and clearly described. Responsibility for the learner acquiring the task is placed on the trainer. You (as the trainer) must decide on the size of the components into which a sequence of behavior is divided and the alternatives that are acceptable at each point. In training to a criterion, you should accept (and encourage) all behaviors in an *operant*. (The term "operant" refers to a class of behaviors all of which have a similar effect on the environment.) For example, if you don't hold out your hand with the palm turned up when getting change in a fast-food restaurant, the chain of behavior required to order food successfully may be disrupted at this point. However, you could hold out your left rather than your right hand or ask the person to put the change on your tray.

Obstacles

Obstacles for observation include overconfidence that you can discover needed information just by "thinking about it" (i.e., speculation). You may overlook sources of bias that enter the picture when just "thinking about it", such as stereotypes and unrepresentative personal experiences. Another obstacle is accepting other people's reports without questioning them. Instead, you should ask, what evidence is there that behaviors said to be important

are required to achieve desired outcomes in real life? Five psychologists may rate a behavior effective in a role play, but does their rating correlate with the behavior's effectiveness in real life? The sole criterion used to justify the selection of judges may be a professional degree (e.g., they are psychologists), but what evidence is there that these individuals can accurately judge the importance of specific behaviors? For all we know, they may be the least likely to correctly identify behaviors required for success. Underestimating the training required to become an expert "task analyzer" is an obstacle. Cost in time, money, and effort is an issue. Observation in real life is time-consuming. However this must be balanced against the cost of less than hoped-for success if plans are not based on a task analysis.

KEEPING TRACK OF DATA

Be sure to record clearly and concisely what you observe. You can use special recording forms. Clearly describe behaviors of interest and related setting events, antecedents, and consequences. Base your hunches about causes on descriptive data when suggesting next steps. Next steps depend on your responsibilities and what the scientific literature suggests is important. Whoever is responsible for providing services can check the accuracy of your written descriptive analyses by carrying out a functional analysis (rearranging setting events, antecedents, or consequences presumed to influence behaviors of interest and determining the effects).

SUMMARY

Observation is a valuable skill at all levels of practice. An accurate assessment may require systematic observation in real-life settings and/or role plays to identify specific behaviors of concern, associated setting events, antecedents and consequences, and resources that can be used. You may discover changes in the physical environment that can contribute to positive outcomes. The time taken to "see for yourself" is usually more than compensated by the value of the data obtained. Sound training in observational methods as well as knowledge about sources of bias and how you can minimize them will help you to take advantage of this valuable source of information.

REVIEWING YOUR COMPETENCIES

Reviewing What You Know

1. Describe how you can make role plays more realistic.
2. Describe steps you can take to increase the likelihood of gathering accurate data by observing problem-related contingencies in real-life settings.
3. Give examples of the following measures collected while observing in real-life settings: sequential, frequency, duration, rate, time samples, interval recording.
4. For various practice examples describe the observational data that would be valuable to collect and design easy-to-use recording methods that would yield helpful data.
5. Describe the difference between a descriptive and a functional analysis.
6. Describe the purposes of a task analysis and its components.
7. Describe the errors commonly made in observation and how to avoid them.

Reviewing What You Do

1. You collect valuable data from role plays.
2. You supplement self-report data with observational data when relevant and feasible.
3. You correctly identify inferences when given a list of both descriptions and inferences.
4. The data you collect facilitates case planning.
5. Your inferences are based on accurate descriptive data.
6. Given a filmed or videotaped presentation of a behavior to be decreased, you can clearly define the behavior, as well as alternative behaviors to increase and describe a useful recording procedure.
7. You identify valuable ways in which a client's physical environments could be rearranged.
8. Based on observations, you make well-reasoned guesses about the functions of problem-related behaviors.
9. You accurately identify reliability and validity problems in samples of data collected.
10. Your case records contain accurate clear, concise summaries of data.
11. Your inferences in case records are based on relevant descriptive data.
12. You can carry out an accurate task analysis.

Reviewing Results

1. Plans result in valued outcomes.
2. Data collected result in well-reasoned decisions not to intervene (e.g., the data show that there is no way to influence problem-related contingencies).

CHAPTER 16

Reviewing Resources and Obstacles

OVERVIEW

This chapter provides guidelines for reviewing resources and obstacles. Personal resources include motivation to resolve problems and supportive significant others. Family resources include mutual caring and helpful neighbors. Agency resources include a culture of thoughtfulness and policies that facilitate the use of services. Neighborhood and community resources include convenient public transportation, and recreational opportunities. Societal resources include economic, educational, and health policies that help residents enhance the quality of their lives. Obstacles may include the absence of these characteristics. Your options to help clients will often be limited by a lack of resources.

You Will Learn About

- A contextual approach to thinking about resources and obstacles.
- Organizational resources and obstacles.
- Community and service system resources and obstacles.
- Social networks and social support systems.
- Significant others as resources and obstacles.
- Personal resources and obstacles.

THINKING CONTEXTUALLY ABOUT RESOURCES AND OBSTACLES

Problems involve a gap between a current and a desired situation. Only by reviewing resources and obstacles can the potential for closing the gap be estimated. The nature of the problem influences the particular resources and obstacles focused on. Perhaps only a distant approximation to closing the gap is possible. Your only alternative may be to offer support to help clients tolerate difficult situations and to take steps at other levels (e.g., community organization) to increase future resources. Resources and obstacles are often in the eye of the beholder: that is, what at first may seem to be an obstacle may, when creatively viewed, turn out to be a resource. The very starkness of many clients' needs calls for a creative and energetic search for resources. You may have to create new resources. What you do will depend on whether you are a case manager and so arrange, coordinate, and evaluate services provided by other agencies or whether you offer the services yourself. Guidelines for reviewing resources and obstacles are suggested in Exhibit 16.1. Relevant questions are

- What resources are needed?
- What resources are available?
- Which resources are most likely to offer needed services?
- What efforts have been made to obtain them, and to what effect?
- What factors facilitate or hinder access to and use of resources? (e.g., eligibility requirements)
- What are obstacles?
- What can be done to overcome them?
- What resources could be created?

EXHIBIT 16.1
Guidelines for Reviewing Resources and Obstacles

- Use a contextual approach (a wide-angle lens).
- Identify and build on clients' strengths.
- Involve significant others.
- Take advantage of options for rearranging the physical environment.
- Keep informed about community resources and unmet needs.
- Help clients to take advantage of self-help and support groups.
- Consider cultural differences that affect resources and obstacles.
- Involve other professionals and community residents in creating services.
- Alter agency procedures and policies that interfere with service.
- Alter service system interrelationships that interfere with service.

Here, as in other phases of helping, focusing only on the individual or family may get in the way of discovering resources and obstacles. We live in a society that emphasizes psychological causes of problems. Those who use a "deficiency model" rivet on people's defects, their disabilities, and what they cannot do—as if people are made up of only their problems (Sarason & Lorentz, 1979, p. 128). A contextual view directs attention to both environmental and personal characteristics. Attaining needed resources may require influencing legislation and helping community members with a common interest organize to pursue valued goals. A variety of steps may be needed to help a client locate and use a resource. For instance, a single parent who wants to enroll in a job-training program may need day care services. First find out whether the client has tried to find day care and why she was not successful. Help her locate and review the possibilities and decide which one is best for her in regard to hours, cost, and location. You may find one that meets her needs but then discover that her child must be toilet trained in order to be eligible. A next step is to locate a toilet-training program. If no such program is available, alternatives must be pursued (e.g., a mutual help group for single parents in which they share their skills).

Obstacles include: (1) lack of resources, (2) a lack of knowledge about resources, (3) organizational and service system barriers, (4) poor management of resources, and (5) an unwillingness to use resources. Clients may not know about valuable resources or have located a resource but encountered barriers. People in need of medical care may not realize that they are eligible for Medicare. One of your tasks is to inform clients about helpful resources. Clients may not be willing to use benefits to which they are entitled. Cultural values and norms influence the kind of help that is acceptable. Understanding the reasons for objections will help you respond effectively.

RESOURCES AND OBSTACLES RELATED TO SERVICE SYSTEMS AND AGENCIES

Ineffective marketing, long and confusing application forms, and poor links among services hinder service, sometimes with tragic results (see Exhibit

EXHIBIT 16.2
An Example of the Harmful Effects of Uncoordinated Services

In 1986, Shulamis Riegler beat her 8-year-old son Israel so badly that he was hospitalized in a coma. Doctors noticed human bite marks on his shoulder.

When the boy recovered, he and his two little brothers spent several years in foster care before going home in 1988 and 1989.

Then, barely a year later, Mrs. Riegler beat another son, Yaakov. She twisted his leg so viciously that she heard his thigh bone crack. The retarded boy, 8 years old, 3-feet-8 and 48 pounds, was taken to the hospital in a coma and never woke up.

KNOWN AS ABUSIVE

Yaakov was one of seven children who died in 1990 after repeated beatings and whose families were known to New York City's child welfare system as abusive or neglectful, a recent city report found.

In the report, the only public accounting of how the city's Human Resources Administration handled such cases, Yaakov was an anonymous statistic, unnamed because of strict state confidentiality laws that protect the privacy of informants and families, even, as in Yaakov's case, when the mother has pleaded guilty to killing her child. Mrs. Riegler will be sentenced Monday to $7^1/_2$ to 15 years in prison.

Yaakov's story, pieced together through interviews and medical, school, and court records, is about an affectionate if sometimes demanding boy, who could speak only in monosyllables, but whose bruises and broken bones would later tell of his pain. It is about a mother who married at 19, had children quickly and was overwhelmed by the unending tasks of homemaking.

AGENCY'S SCATTERED WORK

And it is about a child welfare system that was unable, despite repeated warnings, to help the child. The work the agency did was so scattered and uncoordinated that at one point a city worker was ending the supervision of Mrs. Riegler—because she supposedly had learned to be a nonviolent parent—on the same day that another worker was investigating a new report that Yaakov was being abused. And confidentiality laws also played a part, preventing Mrs. Riegler's probation officer from finding out about new reports of abuse in her home.

Lastly, it is a story about a pediatrician who, though he knew of Mrs. Riegler's abusive history and was called on several times to treat Yaakov's wounds, said he recognized in the Riegler household only a harried mother, not a battered child.

When Mrs. Riegler pleaded guilty in State Supreme Court in Brooklyn last month, Judge Francis X. Egitto condemned the city's child protection system—a system whose goal is, where possible, to reunite children with their natural parents—and the boy's doctor for not saving Yaakov's life.

"It's not just Mrs. Riegler who is guilty of the death of Yaakov," the judge said.

Source: C. W. Dugger (1992, February 10). As mother killed her son, protectors observed privacy (pp. A1, A16). *New York Times.*

16.2). Staff may not be dedicated to designing policies and procedures that maximize service quality. They may not regularly review the impact of their agency's policies and procedures on goal attainment based on ongoing tracking of relevant indicators. Service agencies can suffer from all the problems possible in any organization:

- Vague goals.
- Lack of an agreement on goals.
- Ineffective technology.
- Insufficient resources (e.g., money/staff/clerical help).
- Pursuit of goals that do not benefit and/or harm clients.
- Lack of support for valuable practice behaviors.
- Lack of supervision.
- Lack of staff training to develop practice skills and knowledge.
- An informal communication structure that undermines the attainment of goals.
- Trying to satisfy too many constituencies.

Howitt (1992) argues that many studies of child sexual abuse so confound client and system abuse that it is impossible to tell whether negative consequences found are a result of the alleged perpetrators (e.g., a parent) or the intrusion of social service personnel into the family's lives was responsible. Clients may be given incorrect information (e.g., be told they are not eligible for services when they are). They may be expected to conform to a service delivery pattern that is difficult for them (e.g., be required to come to the agency even when transportation is difficult). Agencies may compete with one another for clients resulting in fragmented services, withholding of information about other resources, or complicating access to resources. These problems require changes in the service delivery system, such as improving links with, within, and among agencies (Pincus & Minehan, 1973). For further discussion of overcoming organizational obstacles see Chapter 24.

Social workers often refer clients to residential centers and/or work in them. These settings differ in the extent to which they offer and achieve what they claim. They differ, in how much control residents have over decisions that affect them (see Exhibit 16.3), and in their physical characteristics. Contingencies may erode rather than enhance and maintain competencies needed in real-life. Consider nursing homes. Observational studies show that residents' independent behavior is often discouraged and their dependency reinforced (Baltes, 1988). Some scholars suggest using clients' engagement as an indicator of the quality of life in a setting. This refers to clients' active participation in the activities provided in their living environment. "High levels of engagement denote high levels of reinforcement" (Favell & McGimsey, 1993, p. 27.) "People have a right to live in an environment that is interesting and appropriate for them. . . . One of the clearest and most basic indicators of an impoverished unresponsive environment is the lack of activity of its inhabitants" (p. 28). Beneficial effects of engagement include a decrease in unwanted behavior because there is abundant reinforcement of desired behaviors and natural teaching, practice and play opportunities.

If a client is to be moved from one place to another (e.g., from a mental hospital to a halfway house), you should explore the extent to which this new environment will support valued behaviors. What behaviors will be reinforced? What behaviors will be punished? Will the behaviors encouraged in day care and residential settings increase clients' opportunities for reinforcement in real-life environments? You should be familiar with the contingencies in settings of interest (e.g., what behaviors are reinforced, punished, or ignored and when, where, and by whom) and with clients' current repertoires to maximize the match between behaviors that will be supported and valued outcomes.

NEIGHBORHOOD AND COMMUNITY RESOURCES AND OBSTACLES

Neighborhoods and communities differ in the opportunities they offer to residents. Characteristics that influence residents include:

- Informal support systems.

EXHIBIT 16.3
Policies and Services in Middleton Nursing Home

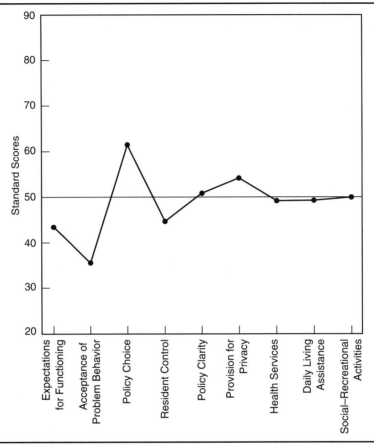

Source: R. H. Moos & S. Lemke (1994), *Group residences for older adults: Physical features, policies, and social climate*
(p. 80). New York: Oxford Press.

- Contexts for positive social exchanges.

- Freedom from crime.

- Opportunities for privacy.

- Quality of educational opportunities.

- Quality of housing.

- Access to health care.

- Access to public transportation.

- Recreational opportunities.

- Employment opportunities.

Communities' characteristics influence problems such as substance abuse, delinquency, and child abuse or neglect (Garbarino, Stocking, & Associates, 1980). Guidelines for assessing communities are suggested in Chapter 24.

Neighborhoods and communities differ in their range and quality of settings and in the overlap among settings in terms of participation. Using the least intrusive methods will require working with clients in the community whenever possible. Take advantage of natural reinforcing communities (real-life settings) that support valued behaviors. What settings encourage valued behaviors? What settings discourage them? Supported employment has replaced sheltered workshops as the best option for persons with severe disabilities (Rusch, 1990). This consists of paid employment in an integrated work setting (i.e., persons without disabilities also are employed). An employment specialist helps the employees perform expected tasks and provides follow-up services. Data gathered from job analyses and each client's specific social and vocational skills are considered when arranging placements and training programs. Placing a person in a group of people with adaptive behaviors provides opportunities for constructive modeling and reinforcement of valued behaviors. Group homes may be a good option. Here, too, find out whether the contingencies and programs provided are likely to enhance or erode the quality of life for residents.

SOCIAL NETWORKS AND SOCIAL SUPPORT SYSTEMS

Assessing social support systems and social networks is often an important part of assessment. The term **social network** refers to people with whom an individual interacts. Social networks differ in structure, function, and perceived value. **Social support system** refers to social exchanges that offer some resource such as emotional support or material aid. (See Payne & Jones, 1987, for a discussion of conceptual and methodological problems in assessing support.) Rook (1985, 1990) distinguishes between the exchange of problem-focused aid and companionship (shared leisure and other activities undertaken mainly for enjoyment) and argues that the latter plays an important (and often unrecognized) role in sustaining emotional well-being. Networks differ in the number of people in different domains (e.g., work, family, neighbors). They also differ in perceived availability of different kinds of support (e.g., mutual help, information, emotional, problem-solving) and in their stability (how long people have known each other) and frequency of contact. They differ in reciprocity (extent to which help goes both ways).

The distinction between social network and social support highlights the fact that *social exchanges* (interactions among people in a network) may not be supportive. They can be a source of stress as well as joy and support. It is not the quan-

tity but the quality of interaction that influences satisfaction (see Sarason, Sarason, & Pierce, 1990, for more details). Negative (compared with positive) interactions weigh especially heavily in influencing personal relationships (Rook, 1984a). Inadequate, stress-producing, and/or unwanted deviance-supporting social exchanges are related to many problems. Depression, for instance, may be related to a lack of significant others. An elderly widow may be socially isolated and lack skills in forming friendships and so may start to drink alcohol because this lessens her loneliness.

Sources of Social Support

Sources of social support range from voluntary associations to intimate, confiding relationships with friends. Social experiences in one area may influence those in others. For example, there is an association between a parent's social exchanges outside the home and how they respond to their children. On high friendship days for the parent, they were less negative toward their children, and their children showed improved behavior (Wahler, 1980). Friends, relatives, neighbors, acquaintances, or "community caretakers" such as bartenders, hairdressers, and waitresses may provide support. Neighborhoods differ in the number and variety of settings in which informal meetings are possible. One goal of the Community Networks Strategies (Horner, Meyer, & Fredericks, 1986) was to enhance the social support of severely disabled persons, by increasing their access to others and the amount of contact (by decreasing barriers such as inflexible amounts of time allotted to certain social activities) and maximizing the disabled persons' social contributions to the social network (e.g., acknowledging birthdays and feeding pets).

Social network diagrams can be used to identify supportive persons (see for example Tracy and Whittaker, 1993) or you could identify the frequency of supportive activities by asking clients to complete "The Inventory of Socially Supportive Behaviors" (Barrera, Sandler, & Ramsey, 1981). You may help a client distribute support among providers so that no one person is overburdened. Social agencies may provide mediators, such as Big

Brothers and Big Sisters. Settings such as senior centers offer opportunities for supportive social contacts. The level of intervention (e.g., individual, family, or community) required to increase social support depends on each person's skills and circumstances, including the characteristics of the community in which she or he lives. Possible options are

- Increasing the social skills of clients and/or significant others.
- Creating self-help groups.
- Establishing neighborhood exchanges/block organizations.
- Rearranging the physical environment in order to increase opportunities for positive social exchanges (e.g., increasing recreational space, establishing a community center).

The Functions of Social Support

Social support is related to both psychological and physical well-being. For example, participation in a weekly support group increased the survival time of patients with metastatic breast cancer (Spiegel, Bloom, Kraemer, & Gottheil, 1989). Positive effects of social support include:

- Reducing the stress of relocating from one place to another.
- Encouraging adherence to health care regimes.
- Encouraging persistence in coping with problems.
- Decreasing vulnerability to physical illness.
- Maintaining positive family relationships.
- Decreasing stress.
- Encouraging constructive problem-solving.
- Encouraging a positive outlook.

Informal social support may provide both tangible (e.g., money) and intangible goods (e.g., emotional support). Valued outcomes include financial or physical resources, information, guidelines for fulfilling roles (e.g., as a parent), and opportunities for nurturance and reassurance of one's worth. Additional functions are social integration (feeling part of a valued group) and attachment to others. A study of the kinds of informal help that single mothers exchanged with one another revealed 26 separate behaviors (Gottlieb, 1978), including emotionally sustaining behaviors (listening, encouragement, reassurance, and companionship) and problem-solving behaviors (offering information or a new perspective; providing suggestions, material aid, or direct service). The kind of resource needed will help determine the provider (Foa & Foa, 1980). Some resources can be provided by many different people, whereas others have fewer potential providers.

Obstacles

Personal obstacles include a lack of required skills (e.g., initiating conversations) as well as interfering behaviors (e.g., aggressive reactions, physiological reactions such as anxiety and/or negative self-statements (e.g., no one will like me). Little time may be available to make friends. Care givers may be over burdened (see Novak & Guest, 1989). Neighborhoods differ in the variety and number of settings that offer opportunities for positive social exchanges. The residents of poor communities, may have few if any extra resources to offer to others in need. A long-term resident of a mental hospital or prison inmate may no longer have any contacts in the community. This situation led Fairweather and his colleagues to establish a network of social contacts among people in the hospital and to move an entire group into a community home (Fairweather, Sanders, Cressler, & Maynard, 1969). Their program remains a classic and underused model, given its success in keeping people in the community (see also Fairweather & Fergus, 1993). A needs assessment is useful in identifying the kinds of support valued and needed as well as the stressors (anticipated or actual) that may accompany transitions such as returning from residential care to the community.

SIGNIFICANT OTHERS AS RESOURCES AND OBSTACLES

Significant others (mediators) are people (e.g., teachers, peers, parents, partners) who have an on-

EXHIBIT 16.4
Attending to Cultural Differences: The Hmong

More than 100,000 Hmong (pronounced "Mung") refugees live in the United States. To the Hmong, the family encompasses all relatives who belong to an extended family known as the *clan*. The clan serves as the locus for resolving problems and making decisions and also provides a sense of belonging. There are 18 Hmong clans, and the leader of each clan is the head of all the families belonging to that clan. Clan leaders serve as liaisons between Hmong communities and outsiders.

Working with Hmong children in the school, social service, or health care system may involve decision-making by clan leaders as well as parents and professionals. For example, if a child is referred by a teacher to a school social worker for behavior problems, the social worker may find the Hmong family uncooperative in developing a plan. The family may prefer to seek a clan leader's advice. Hmong families may rely on their own system of foster care. For example, a child may be sent to live with a relative on the clan leader's suggestion. Trying to circumvent clan involvement may result in alienation and withdrawal of a family from any contact with social service personnel.

Source: Adapted from K. McInnis (1991), Ethnic-sensitive work with Hmong refugee children. Child Welfare, 70, 571–580.

going relationship with the client. They may be the main cause of the client's problems, as when an elderly person is abused or robbed by her own grown children. The value of working with significant others lies in their continuing interaction with clients, as part of their real-life circumstances. If a client's complaints are related to how significant others respond, these significant others should be involved when useful and possible. They become the mediators of change. You enhance their knowledge and skills in interacting with their significant others (e.g., children, students, residents). To be effective, mediators must have access to reinforcers of value to clients, as well as the motivation, knowledge, skills, and opportunities to offer them contingently and consistently. In deciding which significant others to involve, you will have to assess each one's capabilities to support valued behaviors.

Finding Significant Others

Teachers, parents, and residential staff often consult social workers about problems with children, youths, or adults. These individuals are significant others for those they are troubled by. If significant others are not cooperative or available, you may locate others who can support valued behaviors. For example, foster grandparents may help train severely handicapped children (Fabry & Reid, 1978). Peers provide an important source of reinforcement in many contexts (e.g., classrooms). Preschool children have been enlisted to help parents educate their handicapped children (Cash & Evans, 1975). Knowledge of cultural differences will help you identify significant others (see Exhibit 16.4).

Overcoming Obstacles to the Participation of Significant Others

Obtaining the cooperation of significant others may not be easy. Significant others may not possess effective reinforcers or be willing or able to offer them contingent on desired behavior. Problems that may occur and suggestions for resolving them are discussed in the next section.

Significant Others May Not Possess Reinforcers. Significant others cannot be used as mediators unless they have access to effective reinforcers. One goal of intervention might be to increase the reinforcing potential of mediators by pairing attention with consequences that already function as reinforcers. For example, parents' attention could be strengthened as a reinforcer by pairing it with access to desired activities (see Chapter 8).

Lack of Skill and Knowledge.

Many intervention programs involve helping significant others acquire the contingency management skills needed to attain valued outcomes (see Chapter 22). If reinforcers are not offered following desired behaviors and withheld following undesired ones in a consistent fashion, it is unlikely that change will occur. Significant others may not understand (or may deny) that they influence behaviors they complain about. Family members often do not realize how they influence one another. That is, they may not believe they are "significant." They may protest, "It's her fault" or "If only he wouldn't. . . ." Parents and teachers may believe that a child's problems are his own fault and expect you to correct them by seeing him alone. A teacher may be surprised to hear that you would like to observe her exchanges with students in her classroom. Self-monitoring methods you can use to help people understand how they support disliked behaviors are discussed in Chapter 14.

Clients may lack skills in reinforcing desired behaviors and withholding reinforcement following undesired behaviors. Parents may be unable to contain their angry outbursts when a child engages in annoying behaviors and so may reinforce such behavior. Special procedures such as desensitization may be needed to help mediators tolerate annoying behaviors so that they can refrain from reinforcing disliked reactions while reinforcing desired behaviors. Significant others may be either underinvolved (offer little aid or support to clients) or overinvolved (e.g., reinforce dependent behaviors). Relatives with high levels of expressed emotion tend to be self-sacrificing in "a noncontingent overinvolved manner" (Falloon, Boyd, & McGill, 1984, p. 48). Training programs designed to help family members alter their expression of emotion may be needed.

Fear of Failure.

Significant others may be wary of trying anything else because previous efforts were not successful. Arranging some immediate payoff will encourage hope that different methods can be successful.

Reluctance to Offer Positive Reinforcers.

If significant others are reluctant to offer positive incentives, find out why. Further discussion may be needed to convince them that encouraging competence by offering positive consequences contingently is a caring act. You may have to explain the difference between bribery and the use of positive reinforcement, pointing out the advantages of positive incentives and the benefits of new ways of acting to mediators. Bribery refers to giving someone something to induce him to do something illegal or wrong (Webster's New World Dictionary, 1988). Thus, the use of positive incentives to increase behaviors valued by mediators could not accurately be called bribery. A staff member may object to offering rewards for tasks that "clients should do anyway." Point out that acting in new ways requires finding out that new behaviors have a payoff. You could point out that "unless we reinforce our children with praise while they are struggling with the hard task of learning to read, they may not stick to it long enough to find out that it is enjoyable and beneficial" (Kozloff, 1979, p. 75).

Significant others may worry that clients will become dependent on positive reinforcers and so demand them in the future. Point out that artificial reinforcers (e.g., points or tokens) are only a temporary measure and that as behavior stabilizes, they will be faded out and natural consequences such as praise, approval, and self-reinforcement relied on to maintain behavior. Significant others may feel that it is unfair to offer special incentives to only one person. This view assumes that all persons are identical and they are not. "To deny them those [special] environmental conditions in the name of equality may mean that they are denied the very conditions that could help them to be more equal in terms of their behaviors and, hence, in their control of their own future" (Kozloff, 1979, p. 78).

A relationship may have become so negative that it is unpleasant for family members to offer one another positive feedback. Rather, they may get pleasure from hurting one another. In such instances, try to find an acceptable approximation, such as removing attention contingent on undesired reactions. For example, a husband who is unwilling to reinforce his wife for behaviors he likes may be willing to leave the room when she acts in disliked ways. We must start "where the client is." Backup reinforcers can be offered at home if a teacher is not willing (or able) to offer them at school.

Fear of Loss of Valued Outcomes. Anticipated negative consequences of participation may pose a barrier.

> Our staff strongly urged a widowed mother to call the juvenile authorities when next her daughter, Annie, sneaked out of the house at night. The mother was unable to do so, because this might have resulted in the daughter's being adjudicated delinquent. If the daughter were confined to a detention or correction home, the mother would have lost the pension that she administered for the daughter, and that was the family's major support. It was economically unfeasible for the mother to behave in her daughter's best interest. (Tharp & Wetzel, 1969, pp. 130–131)

> A very seriously predelinquent adolescent boy had repeatedly engaged in fist fights with his stepfather. The stepfather had hated the child for years. After four weeks of a closely proctored intervention plan, the boy's misbehavior was rapidly decreasing. The father, fearful that the boy might stay in the home if he reformed, disobeyed every instruction that our staff gave him. The case disintegrated; the boy ran away. It was very clear that the boy's continued presence in the home was so punishing to the father that the rewards our staff offered him—praise, encouragement, attention—were swamped. (Tharp & Wetzel, 1969, pp. 131–132)

A student may worry that his peers will hassle him if his grades improve. Worries about negative consequences should be discussed and steps taken to prevent them or to prepare clients for handling them. A cost–benefit analysis of seeking changes (or not) may be useful. The advantages and disadvantages are written down and reviewed.

A Preference for Aversive Control. Significant others may continue to use punishment, even

though it is ineffective in the long-run and even though you have pointed out its limitations. In this case, you may have to offer incentives to mediators to use positive consequences. Seeing the benefits of positive contingencies may overcome a preference for aversive control.

Overlooking Cultural Differences. A woman's desire to become more assertive with her husband may not be compatible with her culture's norms, and she may be criticized by her husband, children, friends, and other family members for doing so. Consult clients and significant others, and also the literature describing cultural differences, for information about differences that may influence mediating potential (e.g., Gibbs, Huang, & Associates, 1989; Sue & Sue, 1990).

Other Problems. Mediators may have trouble identifying desired changes. Helping clients clearly describe how they would like their lives to change is a key assessment task. If personal problems such as marital discord, poor health, substance abuse, or depression interfere with the consistent use of new contingencies, you will have to address them. Perhaps the caregivers of an elderly relative are overburdened. If so, try to find a way to lessen their responsibilities and/or to accommodate plans into their schedule. Respite care may be needed. A reluctance to try new methods may be overcome by making minimal demands.

PERSONAL RESOURCES AND OBSTACLES

You may discover resources by finding out what's going well and what concerns have been resolved successfully. Helpful attitudes, knowledge, and skills may be available but not used in problem-related situations. For example, a client may use effective anger-management skills at work but not at home. Interfering thoughts, behaviors, or physiological reactions may contribute to problems. Clients may not be motivated to address problems. Guidelines for encouraging participation are discussed in Chapter 11.

Problem-Solving Styles and Skills

People have different problem-solving styles and skills. A review of past problem-solving efforts may reveal useful skills. Examples of coping strategies are

- Using confrontive coping (remaining in the situation and pursuing valued goals, such as requesting behavior changes).
- Regulating emotions (becoming more aware of increasing tension, using relaxation skills).
- Seeking social support (talking to someone).
- Employing escape avoidance (leaving the situation).
- Planful problem solving (reviewing coping resources and planning how to use them in anticipation of demands; gathering information; planning how to avoid or reduce stressors, for example, clearly describing the problem, identifying alternatives for resolving it and the likely consequences of each, trying out the best option, and evaluating the results).
- Using positive reappraisal (reframing situations (e.g., viewing a social slight as irrelevant in the long term) or altering one's view of self-efficacy.

Attempted solutions may create more problems. For example, clients may avoid feared situations which close off options for control. Clients may try to problem solve when they are tired, angry, or anxious. They may skip important problem-solving steps (e.g., not clarify goals) or not consider alternatives and their consequences. Examples of "self-handicapping" strategies are a lack of persistence and a low tolerance of failure. Clients may have a pessimistic outlook and feel helpless; they may believe that because their problems cannot be solved, there is no use trying. As some authors point out, self-handicapping behaviors can be self-serving (e.g., protect us from failure). If we don't try, we can't fail. (See Higgins, Snyder, & Berglass, 1990.)

Attributions/Beliefs

The term *attribution* refers to beliefs about the cause(s) of behavior and outcomes. Understanding clients' attributions for problems provides a guide

for redirecting them in a constructive direction.

For example, aggressive and nonaggressive boys differ in their altributions as well as in their processing of social cues, social problem solving, affect labeling, outcome expectations, and perceived competence (Lochman & Dodge, 1994). In *Lay Theories* (1988) Adrian Furnham reviews people's beliefs about the causes of problems such as "alcoholism," "depression," "mental illness," and "crime." Examples of attributional biases are shown in Exhibit 16.5. Attributions influence whom we hold responsible for given behaviors or outcomes, how much control we think we (or others) have over outcomes, and how we view our own or others' intentions. Some people believe that the world is basically a "just place," that events and the relationships among them are regular and predictable and can be discovered. This view encourages the belief that there are right and wrong ways to act, so it makes sense to act responsibly (Lerner, 1980). Others believe that the world is basically an unjust place, that events occur randomly and cannot be predicted or understood. An implication of this view is that there are no right and wrong ways to act, so there is little point in trying to understand the world or what is wrong or right. An "unjust" worldview may result in apathy and the failure to acknowledge responsibility for one's actions, since it makes little sense to try anything.

Attributions may be global or specific, stable or unstable, personal or external (Abramson, Seligman, & Teasdale, 1978). A supervisor may attribute a student's quiet demeanor to a passive–aggressive personality, a stable internal trait over which the student has little control. This is quite different from attributing such behavior to the effects of a new situation (a new field internship) (an external, changeable, specific attribution). Women who are victims of rape and who attribute the cause to their own stable, internal, unchangeable personality characteristics take longer to recover from this experience (Janoff-Bulman, 1979; see also Janoff-Bulman & Thomas, 1989). Men who are violent toward their partners are more likely, compared to nonviolent men, to attribute negative intentions to their wives (Holtzworth-Munroe & Hutchinson, 1993). How much control we think we have influences whether

EXHIBIT 16.5
Attributional Biases

Ignore Consensus Information

We tend to ignore information about what most people do in a situation (we ignore base rates).

Attend to Available Data (Salience)

We are influenced by vivid, available data.

Fundamental Attribution Error

We tend to overlook environmental causes and focus on dispositional characteristics (e.g., alleged personality characteristics).

An Actor's (Versus an Observer's) Bias

We explain our own behavior as related to situational factors more often than we do in relation to other peoples' behavior. Scott Plous sums this up in the phrase "My situation is your disposition" (1993, p. 181).

More Likely to Accept Responsibility for Success Than Failure

We have a self-serving bias in our attributions, due partly to motivational factors (we want to look good).

Egocentric Biases

We tend to accept more responsibility for group outcomes (whether good or bad) than other people attribute to our contributions.

Positive Effect

We tend to attribute positive behaviors to dispositional factors and negative ones to situational factors.

We Tend to Ascribe Less Variability to Others Than to Ourselves

We view our own behavior as more variable over situations than our friends' behavior. We see ourselves as more complex and less predictable than others. As a result, stereotypes flourish.

Debiasing Methods

Ask what you would have done in the situation.
Pay attention to what most people do in a situation.
Search for less obvious causes.

Source: Based on S. Plous (1993), The psychology of judgment and decision making. *New York: McGraw-Hill.*

we will try to attain valued goals and how long we will persist. We are more likely to persist in trying to achieve our goals if we assume responsibility for our behavior and attribute our successes to our efforts rather than to luck (Dweck, 1975).

Clients may blame themselves for events that cannot be uncontrolled or assume no responsibility for events over which they do have influence. They may continue to believe something, despite contradictory evidence, or have negative self-fulfilling prophecies. They may use defenses such as projection (e.g., attributing unacceptable thoughts and behaviors to other sources) or denial (see Freud, 1967). Recently, greater attention has been given to the positive effects of denial (Lazarus, 1982; Taylor & Brown, 1988). That is, sometimes it is best to over-

look risks or potential for failure. Attributing disliked reactions to dispositional traits ("he's moody") and overlooking environmental circumstances (being asked to work late) may create ill feelings between partners. People diagnosed as "paranoid" may falsely believe that people want to harm them.

Self-Statements

Our beliefs and attributions are reflected in what we say to ourselves about ourselves. This in turn influences what we feel and do. Negative self-statements and self-labels may interfere with problem solving. Mrs. Ryan thought of herself as "an old lady," "no longer useful" (see case example in Chapter 2), and wondered why she was still alive when so many of her friends had already died. She believed she was in the way, useless. These thoughts interfered with improving the quality of her life. Both Mr. and Mrs. Lakeland thought of themselves as "bad parents," and Brian thought that something was "wrong" with him, since he got into so much trouble. Popular—compared with aggressive or withdrawn—children make significantly more facilitating than inhibiting self-statements (Stefanek, Ollendick, Baldock, Francis, & Yaeger, 1987). Self-efficacy (our beliefs about what we can do and what outcomes will result) is reflected in what we say about ourselves. People with a negative self-concept and low self-esteem say many more negative things about themselves and their potential than do people who have a positive self-concept and high self-esteem. Our self-concept, self-esteem, and self-efficacy are influenced by our experiences. (past and current environmental contingencies). Consider a client I saw for depression and suicidal attempts who had a "very low self-image." A review of her past revealed many years of being told by her parents that she was limited intellectually and would never amount to much. Pessimistic thoughts may reflect a lack of success in achieving valued outcomes and may discourage efforts to change a troubling situation. Written questionnaires such as the Automatic Thoughts Questionnaire (Hollon & Kendall, 1980) can be used to explore what clients say to themselves.

Clients' problems may be related to unrealistic beliefs such as "Everyone must like me," "I should never make mistakes," "I should never feel frustrated or anxious," or "People should be the way I expect them to be." These reflect incorrect "rules" about real-life contingencies (Poppen, 1989). They may think in terms of "musts" and "shoulds" rather than "wants" and "desires." Albert Ellis (1962–1996) has long suggested that people's automatic irrational beliefs stem from their core philsophies related to life's adversities. Aaron Beck and his colleagues suggest that unrealistic expectations and inaccurate attributions contribute to anxiety and depression (e.g., Beck, Rush, Shaw, & Emery, 1979; Beck & Emery, 1985). Clients may jump to conclusions, overgeneralize, or think in ei-

EXHIBIT 16.6
Examples of Cognitive Distortions

Overgeneralizing	Generalizing from single examples (e.g., about your overall competence).
Negative scanning	Attending only to negative events/circumstances.
Assuming excessive responsibility	Assuming you are responsible for all negative events.
Catastrophizing	Thinking the worst.
Dichotomous thinking	Thinking in terms of extremes (e.g., "this will be either _____ or _____").
Emotional reasoning	Assuming your feelings reflect reality.
Magnifying	Overestimating the significance of an event.
Minimizing	Underestimating the significance of an event.
Personalizing	Assuming events are related to you when they are not.
Selective abstraction	Attending to only part of the picture and drawing conclusions based on this (discounting positive events/attributes).

ther/or terms (see Exhibit 16.6). Such tendencies may be related to attributional biases shown in Exhibit 16.5. A history of punishment in a situation may result in a vigilance for negative outcomes and a neglect of positive ones. Positive alternatives to dysfunctional thoughts can be discovered by asking clients to note them in a daily log.

Problem-Related Knowledge

Parents may not be informed about children's typical behavior at different ages. Adolescents may not know about effective birth-control methods. Both youths and adults may not know how AIDS can be transmitted. Clients may have incorrect beliefs about behavior. Client knowledge about problem-related behaviors may be a valuable aspect of helping (see Chapter 21).

Intellectual Functioning

The term *intelligence* refers to performing certain tasks at certain levels of competence. Intelligence is a "hypothetical construct" (i.e., it is assessed indirectly by certain measures presumed to reflect intelligence). Scholars such as Perkins (1995) criticize traditional ways of measuring intelligence as being too narrow and suggests that there are many kinds of intelligence, including artistic and social. Individual differences in different kinds of intelligence may influence what outcomes can be attained. It is important not to deny that people can achieve different outcomes because that can result in inappropriate expectations, and, at the same time, not to underestimate what they can achieve. A contextual assessment, with its emphasis on exploring environmental and personal factors and constructing repertoires, is less likely to err in either direction. Perhaps this is why a behavioral approach has been so useful in devising helpful programs for children and adults with developmental disabilities (e.g., Meyer, Peck, & Brown, 1991).

Self-Management Skills

Self-management refers to altering our behavior and/or environment to increase the likelihood of attaining goals we value. For example, you may turn off your phone to avoid being distracted while studying. Related skills include:

1. Setting specific goals (clarifying the question "What do I want?").
2. Gathering information about how to attain your goals.
3. Forming a plan.
4. Arranging prompts and incentives.
5. Monitoring progress.
6. Altering plans as necessary. (Watson & Tharp, 1993)

Clients may have some self-management skills such as arranging reminders, identifying specific goals, and collecting useful information but lack others (e.g., rewarding progress). Skills are required to break large tasks into a series of small achievable steps, arrange access to needed tools (such as a telephone), and provide reminders and incentives. Hyperactive, impulsive children do not use self-instructions that help maintain their attention, such as setting response standards, noting when their attention is drifting, producing motor reactions (such as shaking their head) to increase vigilance, and playing cognitive games to make the task more interesting (Meichenbaum & Goodman, 1971). You may help clients respond to problems by first clearly describing them. For example, a client may believe she is not receiving promotions as rapidly as other workers are who are "more assertive." What does she mean by "more assertive"? What do these other women do (and not do) that makes them "more assertive"? Only if the behavioral referents for this term are identified, can clients discover if they have related skills and if they do not, whether they want to acquire them.

Clients have different patterns of self-reinforcement. Depressed compared to nondepressed, people offer fewer positive self-statements or reinforcers for accomplishments. They have a high frequency of self-critical statements like "How could I do such a stupid thing?" You should make separate assessments of positive and negative self-statements because they have been found to be relatively independent.

Stress-Management Skills

Problems may be related to a lack of stress-management skills. Physical complaints such as headaches, ulcers, or high blood pressure may be related to stress. Anxiety or anger may prevent a client from learning and using helpful skills. The skills that will be of value in decreasing stress depend in part on its source. Stress may result from unresolved problems or the absence of hoped-for positive consequences. Clients often struggle with stresses such as poor housing or a lack of money. Clients may benefit from learning how to replace stress-inducing thoughts with task-focused ones. For example, they may be more successful in job interviews when they learn how to manage their reactions to rejections and slights.

Additional social skills may be needed to avoid conflicts and to obtain emotional support and needed material resources. You may discover helpful skills by asking clients how they usually handle stress. Folkman and Lazarus (1980) investigated the ways people coped with daily life. Both problem- and emotion-focused coping were used in 98 percent of episodes. Emotion-focused coping skills included trying to forget an unpleasant experience, joking about it, concentrating on something good that could result, or talking to someone about your feelings. Problem-focused coping skills included concentrating on the next step, making and following a plan of action, drawing on past experiences, and coming up with some different solutions (see also the section on problem-solving skills). Clients also differ in their skills in forming intimate relationships that may buffer the effects of stress.

Beliefs About the Helping Process

Beliefs about the helping process (for example, who will have to change and how) may be an obstacle. Clients may believe that you will do all the work, that you will make decisions for them. They may be searching for an "instant" cure or believe that change will come about with little or no effort on their part. They may feel hopeless that nothing can be done. You can encourage accurate beliefs about the helping process by clearly describing both your and your client's role. David Burns (1995) asks his clients to complete a self-help questionnaire describing what is expected (e.g., complete weekly questionnaires). You can set the stage for viewing concerns in a contextual perspective by seeing clients and significant others together (e.g., parents and children) and providing introductory information.

Relationship Skills

Presenting problems often involve social behaviors. For example, not having an intimate relationship is a precursor to depression (Brown & Harris, 1978). Social behaviors are required for getting along with coworkers, making and keep-

ing friends, relating to family members, and acquiring resources such as support and validation. Interpersonal skills are needed to interact effectively with service providers, clerks, and phone operators. Behavior deficits such as a lack of cooperative and friendship skills may be related to behavior surfeits such as aggressive behavior. Explosive anger reactions may result when behavior changes are not requested and feelings are not expressed in appropriate ways. People may lose or not get a job because of disliked social behaviors (e.g., sarcasm).

Beliefs about rights are related to aggressive behavior. For example, an abusive husband may believe that he has a right (he is entitled) to hit his wife. Anger may be fueled by reliving imagined slights. A lack of social skills may result in loneliness, which in turn contributes to depression or substance abuse. For recently separated or divorced mothers, a lack of relationship competence is a high-risk factor for entering a spiral of negative interactions (Patterson & Forgatch, 1990).

Clients may lack skills in planning enjoyable activities and encouraging others to talk about interesting topics. They may approach people who do not share any of their interests and rely on punishment to influence others. Negative self-statements ("I'm really stupid"), unrealistic expectations ("I have to please everyone"), and excessive concern about negative evaluations may contribute to ineffective social behavior. Role plays are valuable in assessing social behaviors (see Chapter 15). You may include situations that are important to address, even though the client did not think of them. For example, psychiatric patients may not realize the value of stigma-reduction skills.

Physical Assets and Obstacles

Skill in certain sports, a high energy level, and good health may contribute to removing problems. On the other hand, preexisting medical problems and/or limitations in physical functioning may present obstacles. Physical problems may or may not be changeable. Even with an unchangeable situation such as confinement to a wheelchair, resources may be located that maximize opportunities for reinforcement and minimize negative consequences. Examples are a motorized wheelchair that allows greater freedom and independence or a specially designed computer terminal that offers easy access to friends. In his classic article "Geriatric Behavioral Prosthetics" (1964), Ogden Lindsley highlights the importance of arranging "prosthetics" that allow elderly people to maintain access to valued reinforcers (e.g., railings in bathrooms, response amplifiers in case of physical weakness or sensory deficits, and prompting devices to remind a person to take required medication).

Reinforcer Profile

A reinforcer profile lists events that function as reinforcers for an individual. Helping clients often requires rearranging contingencies (the relationships between behaviors and their consequences). An interest in increasing client skills and using positive change methods highlights the importance of identifying feasible reinforcers. Reinforcers are relative; that is, what functions as a reinforcer for one person may not for another, and what functions as a reinforcer for a person in one situation may not in others. Deprivation level, competing contingencies, and past history influence whether an event will serve as a reinforcer. Thus, each person's reinforcer profile is somewhat different.

The range and kinds of events that function as reinforcers may present an obstacle. A study of car theft from the offender's perspective showed that the main reason for initial involvement were friends' influence (31%), boredom (18%), excitement (18%), a laugh (10%), and money (10%). The main reasons for persisting were money (42%), a buzz (24%), nothing else to do (10%), somewhere to go (5%), a desire to drive (5%), and a laugh (2%) (Nee, 1993). A client's feelings about significant others may be either an asset or an obstacle. For instance, residential staff who have trouble with residents they like may be more willing to reinforce valued behaviors than may staff who dislike the residents. If children like to help others, such opportunities can be used as a reinforcer (Strain, 1981; Strain, Kohler, & Goldstein, 1996).

Types of Reinforcers

There are many different types of reinforcers, including social (approval), activity-oriented (bike riding), edible (cake, ice cream), tangible (marbles), informative feedback (grades), and self-reinforcers (positive self-statements). Clients who complain about other people's behavior often rely on punishment to change it, by criticizing them or withdrawing privileges.

Social reinforcers include physical contact (hugs, kisses), proximity (sitting or standing near someone), verbal statements (approving comments), nonverbal expressions of approval (looking, smiling, laughing), and shared activities (talking or playing a game together). Parents and teachers use social approval to establish and maintain a range of behaviors. Social reinforcers have many advantages: They don't take much time to offer and are part of the natural environment. No prior preparation is required, as may be needed to arrange access to an activity, and satiation is not as much of a problem as it is with reinforcers such as food. Social reinforcers typically do not distract recipients from desired behaviors, as does consuming a sweet.

Examples of **activity-oriented reinforcers** are going to the movies, having lunch with friends, and playing a game. Behaviors that have a high probability can be used to reinforce behaviors that have a low probability (Premack, 1965). If Behavior A (drinking a cup of coffee) is more probable than Behavior B (completing case reports), in a situation, you can increase the rate of B by making A contingent on B, so that in order to drink a cup of coffee, you must first complete a portion of the report. High-probability behaviors share many of the advantages of social reinforcers. They are readily available and can be used both to maintain and to establish behaviors. They are more distracting than social reinforcers in that engaging in an activity often precludes other behaviors and some activities require preparation. Many high-probability behaviors involve social exchanges. The following examples can be seen in the list that follows.

Behaviors Involving Social Interaction

Walking with someone	Introducing people who like
Talking about old times	each other
Visiting friends	Visiting relatives
Meeting someone new	Playing basketball
Going to the movies with	Helping someone
someone	Singing in a choir
Playing cards	
Doing something nice for	
someone	
Attending a club meeting	

Other Behaviors

Listening to music	Taking a trip
Playing with a cat	Going to the library
Watching television	Swimming
Looking at beautiful scenery	Visiting a museum
Playing the guitar	Running
Shopping	Visiting garage sales
Gardening	Reading a book
Working on a crossword	
puzzle	
Writing letters	
Cooking	
Watching people	

Preferences	Freedom From Tasks
For vacation days	Child care
Choice of dinner	Sleeping late
Choice of clothing to wear	Somebody doing the dishes
For a night's entertainment	Longer lunch hour
Staying out later	
Staying up later	

Consumables (e.g., food) can be used as reinforcers. Consequences such as food are valuable when social approval does not function as a reinforcer. Possible disadvantages are satiation and the possibility that consuming food or beverages may distract people from engaging in desired behaviors. Some of these problems can be avoided by using small amounts, which are easy to carry around and do not take long to consume, and by offering them for only a limited time.

Using **material items** such as books and magazines, tools, records, and toys as reinforcers usually involves engaging in an activity. If clothes are reinforcers, related activities may be looking at clothes, wearing them, or showing them to others. The behaviors associated with a given item may not be immediately apparent, however, so it may be helpful to look for the items first and then to think of related

activities. The advantages and disadvantages of material items as reinforcers are similar to those for high-probability behaviors. Some reinforcers function as **generalized reinforcers.** They allow access to a wide range of reinforcers. Examples are money, approval, and tokens. Money can be used to purchase many items or to gain access to a variety of activities, and tokens or points can be traded for a range of items on a reinforcer menu. If we have someone's approval, many different positive consequences may be available from that person.

Feedback may function as a reinforcer. It has two components: evaluative or approval and informative (about progress). Informative feedback can be used when performance criteria are clear, such as when staff are expected to carry out specific tasks in a residential center. Feedback may not enhance performance. For example, some studies have found that offering feedback to staff regarding clients' outcomes does not have any effect on staff behavior (Pommer & Streedbeck, 1974). On the other hand, feedback has been successfully used to encourage some behaviors (e.g., approaching a feared object) (Leitenberg, Agras, Thompson, & Wright, 1968). Other examples of informative feedback are time spent in an activity, problems completed correctly, number of cigarettes smoked, tasks completed, calories consumed, or pounds lost. Some writers believe that feedback always entails an evaluative (good/bad) judgment component (Kanfer, 1970).

Self-reinforcers are consequences that are self-presented contingent on certain achievements. They include self-statements (e.g., "It worked—I did it," "Good for me") as well as social, material, or activity reinforcers that are contingent on carrying out a task. For example, you may make an agreement with yourself that after you read 10 pages of this book, you can call a friend on the telephone.

How to Locate Reinforcers

You can find reinforcers by using verbal or written reports or observation or by trying out different consequences in real life. Verbal reports may not be as accurate as information gained from observation. That is, although clients may say that they do not want anything, observation may reveal reinforcing events. Self-reports point to possible reinforcers. Not until items or opportunities are made contingent on behavior and a future increase in behavior is found can we be sure that a reinforcer has been identified and is being used effectively. The next section describes methods you can use to identify reinforcers.

Observe Behavior. You can observe behavior in real life to identify behaviors exchanged among significant others and also other sources of reinforcement. Pace and his colleagues (1985) developed a method for assessing reinforcer preferences among clients with profound retardation by measuring approaches, avoidance, smiling, vocalizations, and compliance with instructions. Only by observing clients at a variety of times and in a number of contexts may reinforcers be discovered.

Ask Clients. Ask clients what they do and with whom they spend their time. What would they like to do more or less often? What did they do in the past that they no longer do? If general terms are used, such as have fun, the referents for these terms as well as mediators of these events can be identified by asking questions such as "Can you give me an example?" and "Whom do you have fun with?" Items can be ranked in terms of desirability. Pictorial displays have been developed for children. They can look through these and point to valued activities.

Ask Significant Others. You can ask parents what their children like to do, with whom they spend time, and what they do at different times of the day. Significant others may be surprisingly uninformed about what events please family members. They may rely on aversive control. Check out the value of suggested reinforcers by asking the person involved and/or by making the reinforcers contingent on behavior and seeing whether behavior changes.

Reinforcer Sampling. You can use reinforcer sampling to identify or prime (increase) the use of reinforcers. This involves offering a reinforcer noncontingently and allowing people to sample it. Their behavior will reveal whether the item is of

interest. For example, when I asked my sister during her illness whether she would like to hear some music, she said no. When I asked her if she would mind if I played some, she said, "Not at all." Her next response was "That sounds wonderful. Let's hear some more."

Vary Reinforcers. You can offer variations of a reinforcer, and note selections. For example, different magazines or games could be made available to residents of an old age home. Different kinds of groups could be offered or different individuals could approach a resident to start a conversation.

Use Written Schedules. The Pleasant Events Schedule (MacPhillamy & Lewinsohn, 1982) can be used to identify events that may function as a reinforcer. This schedule lists events that may function as reinforcers, such as taking a walk, reading a book, or talking to a friend. One version lists 160 items. Respondents rate how pleasurable each item is on a 3-point scale, as well as how often each event occurred in the past month. A list can be made of enjoyable items, ranked in terms of importance. Self-report measures include the Leisure Questionnaire, on which women with developmental disabilities noted hobbies and their use of a recreation center (Johnson & Bailey, 1977), and the Uplifts Scale, on which respondents indicate how often they experience each of 135 items (Kanner, Coyne, Schaefer, & Lazarus, 1981).

Identify States of Deprivation. Current states of deprivation influence whether a consequence will function as a reinforcer. For instance, if a client lives alone and has little contact with others, social contacts may be a powerful reinforcer.

WHEN NEEDED RESOURCES ARE NOT AVAILABLE

Lack of needed resources is perhaps the most frequently heard complaint by social workers who work in public agencies. For example, although poor single parents (overwhelmingly women) are encouraged to work, jobs may be scarce, and day care services may be in short supply and costly. Parents are often unable to afford them. Problems such as depression may be related to stressful, impoverished environments in which clients have little control over daily events. You may have to fill in service gaps by creating (often with the aid of other interested people) new services or improving the existing services' accessibility and integration. Or you could help residents form community groups to address or prevent problems.

Lack of resources is often a direct result of public policy decisions regarding how resources are distributed, which in turn reflect dominant cultural values and economic interests. Unemployment is related to decisions made by businesses to relocate. Understanding the "big picture" will help you to identify factors related to resource distribution and discover options for increasing social and economic opportunities. This may require action on many different levels—organizational, community, policy, and legislative.

SUMMARY

Helping clients requires reviewing resources and obstacles. A lack of resources such as job-training programs, housing, and health care is often an obstacle. Agency policies and procedures may interfere with helping clients. Viewing clients and significant others in terms of their strengths rather than their deficiencies will increase your chance of discovering resources. Clients differ in their pattern of coping and reinforcer profile (what they like and dislike). These differences will influence options. Their attributions for problems (beliefs about causes) and beliefs about how they can be resolved may help or hinder planning. An emphasis on supporting positive alternatives to problematic behaviors requires a search for reinforcers that will maintain valued behaviors. The contextual nature of problems emphasizes the value of involving significant others such as family members as mediators when possible. Considering their values, worries, knowledge, and skills will increase the likelihood that they will participate in helpful ways. You may have to create new resources to help clients.

REVIEWING YOUR COMPETENCIES

Reviewing What You Know

1. Identify procedures and policies that contribute to high-quality service in your agency.
2. Identify procedures and policies that interfere with service in your agency.
3. Identify the agencies in your community and the problems they address.
4. Identify county, state, and federal programs relevant to certain types of problems.
5. Given specific examples, describe how a setting's physical characteristics may influence behavior.
6. Explain what is meant by the term *significant other* (mediator), and give examples.
7. Identify required characteristics of mediators.
8. Describe obstacles to involving significant others and options for preventing or overcoming them.
9. Discuss the role of significant others in case examples given in class.

10. Describe the difference between social networks and social support systems.
11. Describe common deficiencies in social networks.
12. Give examples of cognitive coping skills.
13. Give examples of specific social skills and settings in which they could be useful.
14. Explain what is meant by the term *reinforcer profile*.
15. Describe how to find out if a given consequence will function as a positive reinforcer.
16. Explain what is meant by the *relativity of reinforcers*.
17. Identify four methods of locating reinforcers.
18. Give examples of using high-probability behaviors as reinforcers.
19. Explain what is meant by the term *attribution*, and give examples of common attributional biases.

Reviewing What You Do

1. You can describe your social network and the "social provisions" (resources) you receive and help another person to do so.
2. You identify feasible reinforcers and significant others who offer these contingent on valued behaviors.
3. You design effective ways to overcome obstacles with mediators.
4. You identify the personal assets of clients and significant others.
5. You take advantage of community resources such as self-help groups.
6. You arrange valuable rearrangements of the physical environment.
7. You create resources when necessary.
8. You overcome obstacles to using resources.
9. You identify neighborhood and community resources and obstacles related to presenting problems.

Reviewing Results

1. Desired outcomes are achieved.
2. Significant others participate in agreed-on plans.
3. New resources are created.

CHAPTER 17

Putting It All Together

OVERVIEW

This chapter offers guidelines for organizing and interpreting data and selecting outcomes. Errors that may occur and guidelines for avoiding them are described. A key question is, Does your problem definition provide guidelines for achieving valued outcomes? Helping clients is a cumulative process. Success in earlier phases sets the stage for success in later ones. Disappointing results in later stages may require circling back to earlier phases.

You Will Learn About

- Choosing among causes as problem definition.
- Thinking about causes.
- Guidelines for discovering causes.
- Reviewing your inferences.
- Ideals and actualities.
- Using tests to make decisions.
- Ethical issues in selecting outcomes.
- The value of records.

ORGANIZING AND INTERPRETING DATA

Problem-solving requires making decisions about how to organize and interpret data. What does it add up to? Is there a problem? What kind of a problem is it? You will think about concerns as you work with clients (see Exhibit 17.1). Your beliefs about behavior and its causes will influence what data you collect and how you organize it. This in turn influences selection of objectives (outcomes to pursue), change agents (whom to involve), and settings (where to intervene). The criteria you use to

EXHIBIT 17.1
Thinking About Problems: Mrs. Ryan and the Greens

I think this family could learn to live together and have a more enjoyable family life. I think it's premature to place Mrs. Ryan in an old-age home, and from what I can see, the Greens are not ready for this, nor is Mrs. Ryan. I think we should work on the problems they've mentioned and see if this improves the situation. But what if I'm wrong? Maybe the family will break down if Mrs. Ryan is not moved. The marriage could become strained. The children could start to act out. But I don't think that will happen. The Greens seem to love each other and to love Mrs. Ryan. The children's concerns seem typical for their age. If problems start, we can catch them at an early point.

evaluate claims and arguments will influence what data you search for and when you stop searching. Your task environment (e.g., time pressures) also will affect the search.

The data collected should indicate the probable difficulty of achieving outcomes that clients value and the feasibility and likely effectiveness of different approaches. Discovering all influential factors is not necessary and usually impossible. What you need is information that decreases uncertainty about how to help clients or to determine that little or no help is possible. Information about resources will indicate whether obstacles can be overcome and, if so, how and to what degree. Reviewing resources and obstacles will offer information about

- Who should and can be involved (including other service providers).
- Who has access to behaviors of concern and is willing and able to support desired behaviors.
- Whether clients will participate in helpful ways.
- Whether obstacles can be overcome.

If You Get Stuck

If you have difficulty clarifying problems and discovering related factors, use this as a cue to gather additional data, unless a crisis is at hand and you have to act quickly despite having little information. Assessment may be incomplete (see Exhibit 17.2). You may have to observe clients in real-life, problem-relevant contexts in order to clarify complaints and discover related contingencies (see Chapter 15). Helpful questions include the following:

- Have I listened carefully to clients about what they want?
- Have I discussed clients' concerns about the helping process?
- Have I ignored important contingencies?
- Have I overlooked helpful sources of information?
- Can the practice-related scientific literature help me?
- Am I doing the best that can be done under the circumstances?
- Have I overlooked benefits clients gain from complaints?

EXHIBIT 17.2
Examples of Incomplete Assessment

- Problem-related behaviors are not clearly described.
- The functions (meaning) of behaviors of concern are unknown.
- Cultural factors are overlooked.
- Clients' assets (strengths) are overlooked.
- Positive alternative behaviors to undesired behaviors are not identified.
- Baseline data are not available (i.e., description of the frequency/duration of behaviors, thoughts, or feelings before intervention).
- The cause of behavior (e.g., aggression) is assumed to be another behavior (e.g., low self-esteem).
- Higher-level contingencies are overlooked (e.g., loss of welfare payments).

- Are my feelings about the clients and/or significant others getting in the way? (Am I over- or underinvolved?)

- Have I made a process error (e.g., tried to move too fast)?

- Have I considered cultural differences in values, norms, and preferred communication styles?

CHOOSING AMONG CAUSES AS PROBLEM DEFINITION

Problem-solving requires making inferences about causes. Just as the expert detective searches for clues, you and your clients also do so. Questions include:

- What are possible causes?

- What's the most likely account?

- Can I make a sound argument for my theory?

- Is my view compatible with what is known about behavior?

- Have I considered the problem-related scientific literature?

- Have I left out anything important? (Is my view incomplete?)

- Does my account provide service guidelines?

- Does my view account for all the information at hand?

- Can you make a stronger argument for an alternative view?

The particular causes focused on depend partly on how advanced knowledge is in an area. Few, if any, helpers today would rely on examination of the bumps on someone's head as Lombroso did long ago. Choosing among different views involves reviewing data collected and considering alternative accounts in the light of these data. Both a microscopic and wide angle lens will be useful. Observation in real-life settings may be needed to identify behaviors of concern and related antecedents and consequences. Two questions should be asked about any view: 1) does it offer leverage in re-

EXHIBIT 17.3
Reviewing Alternative Accounts: The Lakeland Family

Brian's parents believed that his behavior resulted from epilepsy and that if the epilepsy could be controlled, the problem behaviors would disappear. What evidence do they have for this conclusion? How complete is this view? Are alternative accounts more likely? Perhaps Brian has problems at school that have caused his problems at home. Negative interactions with teachers and other students can serve as "setting events" that increase the likelihood of aggressive behaviors at home. Data suggesting that Brian's parents reinforce behaviors they do not like and ignore behaviors they do like suggest that Brian's epilepsy is not the sole cause. Brian may have low self-esteem because of past childhood experiences. Here, too, we should ask, Have we overlooked important causes? Does this view provide intervention guidelines? Are there other factors that we should consider?

Perhaps the Lakelands' problems with Brian are due to marital problems that Mr. and Mrs. Lakeland have hidden from the social worker. Some family systems theories assume that if there is a problem in one subsystem (between parents and child), there must be problems in others as well. No such assumption is made in other family system approaches, such as behavioral perspectives. It is assumed that only through assessment can you discover who is involved and in what way. There were no indications that there were problems in the marriage. Mr. and Mrs. Lakeland seemed to work well together to raise their family on a modest income.

solving problems?; and (2) would an alternative account offer more? Consider the Lakeland family. You could suggest that problems are related to Brian's characteristics, his parents' reactions or characteristics, experiences in other settings (e.g., school), interactions between Brian and his parents, economic stresses on the family, or a mix of these possibilities (see Exhibit 17.3).

Reviewing assessment data with clients provides an opportunity to involve them in making decisions about outcomes and how to pursue them. Be selective to highlight key points and use language that is intelligible to clients. Illustrate your points using examples related to clients' lives. Encourage positive expectations as appropriate, and note the clients' assets and environmental resources that can be put to good use. Exhibit 17.4 gives examples of "putting it all together."

THINKING ABOUT CAUSES

Identifying the causes of behavior is difficult because (1) they may be unknown, (2) they occur at different levels (e.g., physiological, psychological, sociological), (3) they interact in complex or simple ways, (4) they change over time, and (5) they are influenced by chance occurrences (Haynes, 1992). A given cause may affect behavior differently at different times and places. The organization of knowledge by discipline and profession encourages a fragmented view. The glossary in Exhibit 17.5 shows the complexity of causes.

Clues to Causality

Clues to causality include the following:

- Contiguity (events occur close together).

EXHIBIT 17.4
Case Examples

MRS. RYAN AND THE GREENS

Developmental Considerations
The Greens' initial interest was to discuss the possibility of finding other living accommodations for Mrs. Ryan. There was a span of 74 years between Mrs. Ryan and the Greens' youngest daughter, who was 15. As Mrs. Ryan grew older, the relationship between her and her daughter and son-in-law changed. They assumed the role of provider. This required adjustments for all of them. The children, too, were experiencing many changes in their lives. Jean, the daughter, was having difficulty freeing herself from her mother's control in order to be able to go out with boys. After the family's move to the suburbs where no transportation was available except by car, Jean spent most of her time watching television, gaining a great deal of weight in the process. She and Mrs. Ryan had many clashes. Mrs. Ryan could not become accustomed to what she considered vast differences in how children were raised today compared with how she was raised almost 80 years ago. Mrs. Ryan also was confronted by her own increasing age and feeling of helplessness and uselessness.

A Review of Contingencies and Related Effects
Based on the information she collected in interviews, in structured role plays in the office, and by observing the family at home, Mrs. Slater, the social worker, arrived at the following views. In the past, her daughter and son-in-law considered Mrs. Ryan to be an independent, self-sufficient woman and a pleasant companion. Indeed, it was they who insisted that she live with them after Mrs. Ryan's

(continued)

EXHIBIT 17.4 (*continued*)

husband died, and they bought a house that was large enough for Mrs. Ryan to have her own bedroom. But this move made a drastic change in her life: Mrs. Ryan never replaced the valuable social contacts in her life when she moved in with the Greens, and she now found herself stranded in the suburbs and dependent on others for transportation. This was quite different from her previous home, which was just half a block away from the main street of a small town filled with friends. Thus Mrs. Ryan lost many of her reinforcers. She also developed a serious heart condition a year after she moved in with the Greens and was told that she must severely limit her activities, in order to decrease the likelihood of another heart attack. Many friends with whom she had corresponded had died. These losses resulted in a depression of varying intensity that was influenced by how much attention she received from her daughter, son-in-law, and their children. In turn, Mrs. Ryan's behavior influenced how her relatives responded to her.

As Mrs. Ryan offered fewer positive events to the Greens, they offered fewer to her. As the children grew older, the differences in their way of life from Mrs. Ryan's caused further conflict. She began to spend more and more time alone in her room and developed the habit of sleeping most of the day and staying up at night doing chores such as the dishes, which kept the family awake. Not Mr. or Mrs. Green or Mrs. Ryan had effective communication skills for discussing and resolving their differences. Mrs. Green was a classic negative thinker: "Nothing can be done"; "Things won't change, but if they do, it will be for the worse"; "What can we do? This is a terrible situation"; and so on. Mrs. Ryan was overly sensitive to criticism, interpreting requests for behavior changes as slaps in the face, no matter how carefully they were worded. Family members offered too lean a schedule of positive reinforcement to one another and too many aversive events.

A review of desired outcomes indicated that many were interrelated: The Greens' wish to have more time alone was related to Mrs. Ryan's interest in being more active outside the house. Deciding where Mrs. Ryan would live involved many steps, including sharing feelings and getting information about Medicare and aging.

In Summary

The Greens are considering having Mrs. Ryan move because of a decrease in shared positive events and increase in unpleasant exchanges. This change is related to the family members' lack of communication skills and Mrs. Ryan's failing to replace lost sources of enjoyment with new ones. Mrs. Slater reframed the presenting concern from making a decision about where Mrs. Ryan would live to gathering information to make this decision. The question now was, could positive events be increased. A review of the resources available to Mrs. Ryan and the Greens revealed many, perhaps the most important being that Mrs. Ryan, the Greens, and their teenaged children liked one another. This increased their willingness to participate in case plans. Community resources such as a local senior center were available. Although the Greens and Mrs. Ryan had to budget their money carefully, they did have enough to get along on, especially if they took advantage of Medicare.

Intermediate Steps

Almost all outcomes of interest to these clients were intermediate steps to deciding where Mrs. Ryan would live. Mrs. Slater discussed the relationship of these steps to this decision and suggested that discussion of that decision be temporarily put aside until the desired changes were perused over a 2-month period. They identified outcomes related to each area. Baseline data made it possible to select appropriate intermediate steps. One of Mrs. Ryan's goals was to increase her contacts with other people. Other than going to a lunch meeting of retired civil servants twice a year, she saw only her relatives. Assessment information indicated that she did have skills for meeting and talking to other people; she had had many friends in the community where she had lived. Mrs. Slater joined Mrs. Ryan on a brief walk one day and had an enjoyable conversation with her. She was interested in current events and liked talking about a variety of topics.

Mrs. Ryan's reluctance to participate in the activities at the local senior center was partly due to her reluctant to trouble anyone to drive her there. She refused to allow this, even when she learned that the center had a van and would pick up people at their homes. (It was too far for her to walk there.) As a first step, Mrs. Slater suggested that they visit the center together and get a monthly bulletin describing its activities. After some hesitation, Mrs. Ryan agreed. Other intermediate steps included the following:

- Review the monthly bulletin and select two activities each month that you might enjoy.
- Read the description of the transportation service and arrange for the van to pick you up to attend two events.
- Initiate one conversation at each meeting.
- Obtain the telephone numbers of people you want to contact.
- Telephone one person each week.
- Attend three activities each month at the center.
- Telephone two people each week.
- Invite one person over every other week for tea, or arrange a brief outing such as a shopping trip or lunch.

Intermediate objectives were set for other outcomes as well.

BRIAN AND THE LAKELANDS

Developmental Considerations

The Lakelands were a family shifting from raising small children to learning how to handle adolescents. Some of their current difficulties were related to Brian's desire for greater independence. Even though he was 14 and their daughter Joan was only 11, the Lakelands were looking forward to an easing of child-rearing responsibilities.

A Review of Contingencies and Related Effects

This family was typical of many families experiencing parent–child problems: Undesired behaviors were reinforced and desired behaviors were ignored. The Lakelands' lack of positive parenting skills resulted in an escalation of aversive exchanges. Brian and his parents had fallen into the habit of looking for disliked behaviors rather than reinforcing one another for valued behaviors.

(continued)

EXHIBIT 17.4 (continued)

Mrs. and Mrs. Lakeland used threats that they did not enforce and that were either too severe and/or threatened positive activities, such as Brian's paper route. They nagged Brian to try to get him to comply with their requests, repeating their requests over and over, but often they just gave in to his wishes. They offered reinforcers noncontingently rather than contingent on desired behaviors. For example, Brian's allowance was not contingent on any specific behaviors. Contributing factors included both parents' working too much, so they were tired and more vulnerable to stress. Family members did not have negotiation skills to resolve conflicts. Mr. Colvine, their social worker, had looked into the possible relationship between epilepsy and the behaviors Brian displayed and found that there was no evidence that they resulted from the epilepsy per se. This conclusion was supported by a conversation with the family doctor.

In Summary

Brian's inappropriate behavior was maintained by attention from parents and siblings. Desired behaviors were not reinforced. Family members exchanged few positive events, such as outings together, and did not possess effective problem-solving skills. Brian had no study schedule, so his homework often remained undone, which contributed to his poor grades. It also seemed that he could use tutorial help in mathematics and a more suitable place to study. Contingencies would have to be rearranged and constructive problem-solving skills increased.

JULIE

Developmental Considerations

Julie was in a stage of rebellion against her parents, who were very strict. She felt overwhelmed by the pressures that seemed suddenly to descend on her, such as deciding what to do about sex, how far she should push her parents, and what she wanted to do with her life.

A Review of Contingencies and Related Effects

Julie's decision was easy for her to put off, since the ultimate aversive consequences were distant. These would have to be made more current through identification of alternatives and the advantages and disadvantages of each. Her stress interfered with careful considerations of different options. This would have to be decreased. This stress also interfered with Julie's enjoyment of her everyday life. Assessment indicated that Julie had inferiority feelings about her looks, was easily pressured into sexual intercourse even though she did not want it, had little information about birth control, and had ambivalent feelings about having sex.

* Temporal order (the presumed cause occurs before the presumed effect).

* Covariation (as one changes, the other changes).

* Alternative explanations can be ruled out.

* There is a logical connection between the variables; a sound argument can be made for the link.

Attention to only one of the conditions may result in the incorrect belief that because an event follows another, it is caused by it. Haynes (1992) argues that *constant conjunction* (two events always occurring together) is not applicable to the social sciences because of the complexity of causes related to behavior.

EXHIBIT 17.5
Glossary Related to Concepts of Causality

> **Causal model:** Assumptions about the cause(s) of behavior.
> **Critical periods:** The effects of a variable depend on age or developmental stage.
> **Equilibrium time:** Time required for the effects of a causal variable to stabilize.
> **Latency of causal effects:** How long it takes for a cause to affect behavior.
> **Mediating variable:** A variable that can strengthen or weaken the relationship between two other variables.
> **Necessary cause:** Y never occurs without X.
> **Necessary and sufficient cause:** Y occurs whenever X occurs, and Y never occurs without X.
> **Parameter:** Dimensions of a variable (e.g., depression) that can be measured (e.g., magnitude or duration). This term also is used to describe the characteristics of a population, in contrast to the characteristics of a sample.
> **Probabilistic nature of prediction:** Predictions are always imperfect, some are more probable than others.
> **Sufficient cause:** Y occurs whenever X occurs.
> **Temporal precedence:** X must precede Y if X is a cause of Y.
> **Vulnerability:** The probability that a causal variable will result in a behavior; the magnitude of the variable that is necessary to create the behavior (p. 123).

Source: *Based on S. N. Haynes (1992),* Models of causality in psychopathology: Toward dynamic, synthetic and nonlinear models of behavior disorders. *New York: Macmillan.*

Necessary and Sufficient Causes

Variables related to problems may be *necessary* (a condition that must be present if the effect occurs), *sufficient* (a condition that by itself will bring about change), or *necessary* and *sufficient* (a condition that must be present for an effect to occur and one that by itself will bring about an effect). Rarely can we point to necessary and sufficient conditions related to problems.

Interrelated Causes

Explanations differ in the system level(s) to which they appeal (e.g., biological, psychological, sociological) and how integrative they are (the extent to which relationships among different causes are recognized). Contributory causes often come into play that help to create the total set of conditions necessary and sufficient for an effect. Social problems are usually related to factors at many interconnected system levels. For example, poor funding of schools, combined with modest or low income, influences students' opportunities to do well academically. These opportunities, in turn, affect other outcomes such as employability. Consider Brian and his parents. If more money were available for special-education programs and related assessment services, smaller classes, and better preparation of teachers, Brian's grades might be better. Temperamental dispositions may increase the likelihood of certain kinds of behavior, which in turn influence how others respond. A contextual framework will help you avoid incomplete accounts that recognize only one cause of a problem.

Individual Differences in the Strength of Causal Variables

The strength of causal variables differs among individuals with the same problem-related behaviors. People differ on

- The number of variables of which their behavior is a function.

- Which variables influence the onset, magnitude, and duration of behavior.
- The relative strength of individual causal variables.
- The role of mediating variables.
- Predispositions and vulnerability to particular events.
- The setting generality of causal relationships.
- The paths through which causal effects occur. (Haynes, 1992, p. 108)

The variation in causal relationships highlights the importance of a contextual, multifocused assessment. Ideally, intervention should focus on the key causal variables. This requires estimating the weights of different variables before intervening (Haynes, 1992, p. 109).

Causes and Explanations

Causes differ in their explanatory completeness. Identification of causes is not necessarily explanatory. For example, the cause of an illness (such as cancer) and its symptoms and associated pathology may be known, but the etiology may not be understood. People use different criteria to decide when an explanation is at hand (e.g., it allows accurate prediction, it "makes sense"). What's best depends on your purpose. The goal of helping clients highlights the value of explanations that yield intervention guidelines.

Compatibility with What Is Known About Behavior

Beliefs about causes differ in the extent to which they are compatible with what is known about behavior; for instance, claims of "levitation" (the ability to float in the air) are not compatible with the laws of gravity. Lack of generalization of positive outcomes over settings and time is a major problem in helping clients. Thus, a plan that does not take this into account is not compatible with what is known about behavior.

The Fallacy of False Cause

In the *fallacy of false cause*, we inaccurately assume that one or more events cause another.

Consider Clever Hans, the wonder horse. Clever Hans supposedly could solve mathematical problems. When presented with a problem by his trainer, he would tap out the answers with his hoof. Many testimonials were offered in support of his amazing ability. But then a psychologist, Oskar Pfungst, decided to study the horse's ability. He systematically altered conditions to search for alternative explanations. This exploration revealed that Clever Hans was an astute observer of human behavior. He watched the head of his trainer as he tapped out his answer: His trainer would tilt his head slightly as Hans approached the correct number, and Clever Hans would then stop (reported in Stanovich, 1992). *Confounding factors* (variables that are related to both some characteristic and an outcome) are one reason for the spurious appearances of causation.

Underestimating Coincidences and the Play of Chance. We tend to underestimate the frequency of chance events. What do you think the odds are that in a class of 23 people, two will have their birthday on the same day? The odds are over 50–50. One reason behavior is so difficult to predict is that chance (accidental events) plays a role in our lives. That is, the occurrence of important causal events may not be predictable because such events may not be under our control and may be unexpected. Consider fires, earthquakes, and many illnesses. One of the subjects of great literature are the ways in which individual lives are affected by historical events (wars, famines). Unexpected deaths or meetings may change our lives dramatically.

Mistaking Causes and Their Effects. Is depression a cause of marital conflict, or is marital conflict a cause of depression? Is cognitive disorientation a result of being homeless, or does being homeless cause cognitive disorientation? Tavris (1992) argues that the depression that many women complain of is often a result of gender role expectations (e.g., that women be the major caretaker of children) that limit women's opportunities for well-paid work. Can you think of any other examples?

The fundamental attribution error may result in

mistaking effects for causes. Consider for example, Jimmy, a 12-year-old black student, who was referred because of apathy, indifference, and inattentiveness to classroom activities (Sue & Sue, 1990, p. 44). The counselor believed that Jimmy harbored repressed rage that needed to be ventilated and dealt with. He believed that Jimmy's inability to express his anger led him to adopt a passive–aggressive means of expressing hostility (i.e., inattentiveness, daydreaming, falling asleep) and recommended that Jimmy be seen for intensive counseling to discover the basis of his anger. After 6 months of counseling, the counselor realized the basis of Jimmy's problems. He came from a home of extreme poverty, where hunger, lack of sleep, and overcrowding sapped his energy and motivation. That is, his fatigue, passivity, and fatalism were more a result of poverty than some innate characteristic.

Mistaking Correlations and Causation.

The fallacy of false cause may occur because correlations are mistaken for causes. We may assume that because two variables (brain and foot size) covary, one causes the other. Although we may scoff at the idea that brain size causes foot size, other mistaken assumptions based on confusions between correlations and causation may not be so obvious. The history of the professions provides many illustrations of the confusion between correlation and causation. For example, people used to think that tuberculosis was inherited because people who lived together often got it. Consider also the common assumption that low self-esteem causes problems such as depression. In fact, both low self-esteem and depression may be related to other variables (e.g., a high frequency of punishing experiences and a low frequency of positive feedback in the past and the present). Our tendency to overestimate correlations heightens our susceptibility to this error.

Dead-End and Incomplete Accounts

Dead-end accounts are those that do not provide guidelines for achieving valued outcomes. They may get in the way of discovering promising options. "After-the-fact" accounts describing what people did (and why) may sound profound but may not provide "before-the-fact" information that help you and your clients select effective plans. Dead-end accounts may be incomplete (omit crucial causes). *Incomplete accounts* include only some pieces of a puzzle. They may focus on thoughts without relating them to what people do in specific situations. Another kind of incomplete account is assuming that behavior causes another behavior without asking about the causes of both. For example, self-esteem is often accepted as a cause of behavior. But where does self-esteem come from? You may assume that your success in a job interview is due to high self-efficacy (an expectation that you will succeed). A more complete account would include information about your history in related situations. Rather than self-efficacy (or self-esteem) being the cause of doing well, it may be a product of past successful experiences. We feel confident in situations in which we do well.

Confusing Form and Function.

Focusing on the form of behavior (hitting) and overlooking its function (removing demands) may result in incomplete accounts. This error is less likely if practice theories emphasize the distinction between form (the typology of behavior) and function (what maintains the behavior—why it occurs). Simply describing behavior does not provide information about its function (why it occurs). The context in which behavior occurs must also be explored. If you know the circumstances in which a client is likely to engage in certain behaviors, you have information about how you might alter the environment to influence these behaviors. Ignoring the context encourages excessive focus on psychological causes. For example, individual counseling may be recommended for an adolescent having problems at school that are related to the reactions of her peers and teachers as well as to the economic stress experienced by her single parent. A problem-oriented curricular design (e.g., aging, health, family) may encourage the confusion of form and function. It may discourage recognition of similar kinds of contingencies of reinforcement that apply to different problems.

GUIDELINES FOR DISCOVERING CAUSES

The following guidelines should help you avoid common errors in thinking about causes such as the confirmatory bias. Many errors involve partiality in the use of evidence (looking at only part of the picture) (see Exhibit 17.6). The "shortcuts" we use to make decisions (e.g., relying on what's available, such as a familiar practice theory) may lead us astray. Once we have accepted a view, it may bias our subsequent search (what we look for and discover). Overlooking the inaccuracy of data may result in unwise practice decisions.

Clearly Describe Problems and Related Factors

Vague descriptions of problems make it difficult (or impossible) to discover related factors. Another way to get bogged down is to focus on problems rather than related factors. Rather than focusing on elder or child abuse per se, identify factors related to the abuse and address them.

Watch Out for the Fundamental Attribution Error

We tend to focus on attributes of the person and to overlook environmental variables (i.e., fall into the fundamental attribution error). This, combined with the greater vividness of negative behaviors, often results in pathologizing clients. To avoid doing this, be sure to consider the context in which the behaviors or conditions of concern occur. The more clearly you describe this, the more information you will have about problems and related factors. You may overlook environmental influences because you focus on psychological characteristics and rely solely on self-report data that may not reflect what is really happening. Our thoughts and feelings in problem-related situations are often more vivid than associated environmental contingencies, and so it is easy to focus on them as causes and to overlook environmental influences.

Be Data Focused

Speculative thinking may be relied on "to solve problems which can only be solved by the obser-

vation and interpretation of facts. . . . The belief that one can find out something about real things by speculation alone is one of the most long-lived delusions in human thought" (Thouless, 1974, p. 78). We often are guilty of the contrary-to-fact hypothesis in which we state "with an unreasonable degree of certainty the results of events that might have occurred that did not" (Seech, 1993, p. 131). An example is, "She felt sad because of her neighbor's family problems. If only she hadn't gotten married at such an early age, she would be a happier woman today" (p. 131). Speculation is valuable in discovering new possibilities but, it does not offer information about whether these insights are correct. What **is** cannot be deduced from what **ought** to be. Speculation is not without its effects, since theories influence what we look for.

Chapman and Chapman (1969) reviewed the reports of 32 practicing clinicians who analyzed the Rorschach protocols of homosexual men. These clinicians listed signs that had face validity but were empirically invalid as responses characteristic of homosexual men. They selected signs based on "what seemed to go together"—on what "ought" to exist—rather than on empirically determined associations between signs and criteria. Clinicians were more likely than naive observers to report illusory correlations. Such studies illustrate that expectations based on theories and semantic associations overwhelm the influence of data that do not match these expectations or even refute them. This tendency is encouraged by the **confirmatory bias** (seeking data that confirm our beliefs and overlooking data that do not). For example, we often attend to only the positive-positive cell of a four-cell contingency table (see later discussion in this chapter.

There is nothing odd or negative about weighing data in relation to available theories. The problem arises when we invent ad hoc accounts for the purpose at hand and overlook points-of-view (causes) that would have predicted other events or relationships and never reconsider them when our initial beliefs are shown to be incorrect (Einhorn, 1980). This tendency may be heightened in eclectic practice in which we use ad hoc theories or notions that may actually contradict each other.

EXHIBIT 17.6
Sources of Error That May Result In Inaccurate or Incomplete Problem Structuring

Source	Description
1. Partiality in the use of evidence.	Overlooking, distorting, or discounting contradictory evidence. Giving favored treatment to favored beliefs. (see for example items 2 to 7.)
2. Rationalizing rather than reasoning (justifying rather than critiquing).	Focusing on building a case for a position rather than gathering information impartially. This is an example of item 1.
3. Focusing on irrelevant or incorrect reasons (fallacy of false cause).	Selecting irrelevant or marginally relevant reasons or "evidence" to support beliefs or actions. The conclusion may have nothing to do with the reasons provided.
4. Jumping to conclusions.	Failing to treat a belief or conclusion as a hypothesis requiring scrutiny.
5. Unwarranted persistence.	Not changing your mind even when there is compelling evidence to do so.
6. Categorical rather than probabilistic reasoning.	Reducing options to two possibilities (either _____ or _____).
7. Confusing naming with explaining (e.g., "diagnosing" rather than contextually assessing).	Assuming that giving something a name (e.g., bipolar personality disorder) explains it and offers intervention leverage.
8. Confusing correlation with causation.	Assuming that an association between two or more events indicates causation.
9. Confusing shared with distinguishing characteristics.	Focusing on characteristics that may not distinguish among different groups/causes.
10. Faulty generalization.	Relying on small or biased samples; assuming that what is true of the whole is true of the parts, or vice versa.
11. Stereotyping.	Incorrectly estimating the degree of variability in a group.
12. Influence by consistent data.	Being influenced by data that do not offer any new information but are merely consistent with data already available.
13. Lack of domain-specific knowledge.	Not having information needed to clarify and understand problems (e.g., facts, concepts, theories). This source of error is related to many others in this list.
14. Confusing form and function.	Mistakenly assuming that similar forms of behavior have similar functions and different forms of behavior reflect different functions.
15. Simplistic accounts.	Relying on accounts that ignore important causes and/or overlook uncertainties.
16. Vagueness.	Vaguely describing problems and/or causes.
17. Uncritical acceptance of explanations.	Accepting explanations without evaluating them and comparing them with alternative accounts; not checking whether a belief is consistent with known facts; selecting untestable beliefs.
18. Assuming that a weak argument is not true.	Assuming that because you cannot offer a convincing argument, a claim is false.
19. Reliance on ad hoc explanations.	Making up explanations as you go along, even though they may contradict one another or be circular (explain nothing).
20. Incorrect weighing of different contributors.	Not weighing contributing factors in relation to their importance.
21. Misuse of speculation	Believing that you can find out what is going on just by thinking about it.
22. Overcomplex accounts.	Relying on needlessly complicated accounts that obscure causes.
23. Ecological fallacy.	Assuming that an association between two variables on a group level is also true on an individual level.
24. Confusing correlations and baserates.	Incorrectly assuming that a correlation reflects the base rate.
25. Relying on questionable criteria for evaluating the accuracy of claims.	Examples include consensus, authority, and tradition (see Exhibit 4.5)
26. Using a general rule that is not applicable to a particular situation.	Assuming that because agency administrators are usually fair that a particular administrator was fair on a certain occasion.

Note: The sources of error described may be (and usually are) not related to intentions. Caring about people is not enough to avoid them.

Being data focused rather than theory focused will help you to avoid premature and excessive reliance on dubious accounts (Einhorn, 1980). The more tenuous a theory is, the less you should rely on it when assessing data, and the more attention you should pay to the data. What exactly is the problem? Exactly how is it manifested? What factors have been observed to be associated with it?

Focus on Informative Data

The data you have gathered could be (1) relevant (help you and your clients select effective intervention methods), (2) irrelevant, or (3) misleading. Focus on relevant data. Irrelevant data may lead you astray. A few worthless items can dilute the effect of one helpful item. Consider the study in which social work graduate students were asked to estimate the likelihood that some people were child abusers. Being told that the person "fixes cars in his spare time" and "once ran away from home as a boy" decreased the effects of the description of this man as having "sado masochistic sexual fantasies" (see Nisbett & Ross, 1980, p. 155). There is no research showing that people who fix cars in their spare time and once ran away from home as a boy are more (or less) likely to abuse their children. Irrelevant material about this person tended to make him less "similar" to someone who might abuse his child. When irrelevant data are given about a case, we often rely on this and ignore data describing what is "normative" (typical behavior) in a situation. That is, in thinking about what a particular person might do in a situation, we tend to disregard data that describe how people usually act (i.e., consensus data) even though this may help us predict what an individual would do. Ask: "Is this data relevant here?" How so?

We tend to focus on vivid events and to overlook those that are important but not vivid. We tend to recall vivid examples that may mislead us about factors related to a problem. In trying to explain why negative exchanges weigh so heavily in basically positive relationships (they may ruin a friendship), Rook (1984a) suggested that the positive behaviors exchanged became the expected background and so are less vivid than the rare negative events.

Assess Rather Than Diagnose, or Explain Rather Than Name

Problem solving can be likened to walking along an unknown path with many dead ends. One kind of dead end is simply naming (e.g., labeling) something (a problem or behavior of interest). Suppose that you see a homeless person on the street gesturing oddly and talking to himself. You may think, "He is mentally ill." Is this label helpful? Does it decrease uncertainty about how you could help him? If behavior is multidetermined, using a vague label (e.g., depression, anxiety, attention deficit disorder) is of little or no value.

> Intervention programs cannot be based solely on a diagnostic or classification category such as "depression" or "attention-deficit disorder" because such topographically based [form] diagnoses do not identify which of many possible determinants are operational for a particular client. Diagnoses typically provide only an array of possible causal factors. The generalizability of the suggested variables and weights to a particular client cannot be presumed.

> Diagnosis can facilitate the design of intervention programs only if any of three conditions are met: (1) specific causal paths are invariably associated with specific diagnostic categories, (2) a hierarchy of the most probable paths or their weights is associated with specific diagnostic categories, and/or (3) effective interventions are available for specific diagnostic categories regardless of within-category variance in causality. These conditions are seldom met. (Haynes, 1992, p. 109)

Assessing rather than diagnosing will help you avoid explanatory fictions (terms that seem to offer information but do not). Pseudoexplanations (circular accounts) are prime examples. In a circular account, we use a behavior to infer an explanation and appeal to the same behavior to support our explanation (no additional information is provided). For example, a teacher may "explain" a student's hitting other children by stating that he is aggressive and, when asked how she knows, may say, "Because he hits other children." Failing to elaborate the "problem space" (to complete a contextual analysis) is a principal cause of ineffective problem solving (Nickerson, Perkins, & Smith, 1985).

Avoid the Single-Cause Fallacy: Ask "What's Missing?"

Just as an explanation may be overly complex and obscure options, it also may be incomplete (overlook causes) and obscure options. We may assume (incorrectly) that different problems have one cause. Rarely is behavior related to one cause. For example, recent investigations of relapse in depression suggest many related factors, such as age, gender, past history of depression, current stresses, and availability of a social support (Krantz & Moos, 1988). Simplistic accounts in which the cause of complex problems such as family violence is attributed to one factor (e.g., past history of violence) can be misleading. Thinking in either/or terms and relying on the "best-guess strategy" (simplifying complex situations by ignoring or discounting uncertainties) encourage selection of simplistic accounts. Ask yourself, Does my account consider major influences? Have I left out important influences?

Avoid Unnecessarily Complex Accounts

Just as an account may be overly simple (overlook causes related to a problem), it may be overly complex (unnecessary concepts may be used that get in the way of discovering causes). This is why parsimony is emphasized in science (see Chapter 4). Although general sensitizing concepts can be helpful in the exploratory stage of problem solving, they must be clarified to obtain a detailed understanding of problems and options for resolving them. We tend to believe that vague, jargon-filled accounts are more profound than clearly stated ones (Armstrong, 1980).

Watch Out for Illusory Correlations

Mistaken assumptions about causes may be due to incorrect estimates of the degree to which two or more events covary. Covariations (and thus causal relationships) are often assumed between certain characteristics (e.g., personality traits or recent life changes) and problems or between certain symptoms and diagnostic categories (e.g., vigilance for danger and generalized anxiety disorder). "Everyone possesses what might be called 'data' on the degree of covariation between various socially relevant dimensions and behavior dimensions, but the data are usually skimpy, hit-or-miss, vague, and subject to bias and distortion in both encoding and recall" (Nisbett & Ross, 1980, p. 98). Covariations may be assumed on the basis of a belief that causes are similar to their effects (our old friend the representativeness heuristic). We tend to overestimate the size of correlations between factors that we believe "go together" and to underestimate the degree of covariation when we do not have any particular preconceptions about the relationship between two or more factors (Jennings, Amabile, & Ross, 1982). Incorrect estimates often persist despite disconfirming information. For example, a clinician may insist that a woman is schizophrenic because she was once labeled a schizophrenic, even though there is no current evidence to support this diagnosis.

Expectations of consistency encourage illusory correlations. We tend to assume that people behave in trait-consistent ways when, in fact, correlations between personality traits and behavior are often relatively low (e.g., Mischel, 1968). One reason for this is that "we tend to see most people in a limited number of roles and situations and thus are exposed to a more consistent sample of behavior than we would obtain from a true random sample of a person's behavioral repertoire" (Nisbett & Ross, 1980, p. 107). Apparent discrepancies are readily explained away. Subjective feelings of control are enhanced by the belief that other people are consistent in their traits and thus are predictable.

How do we get through a day if our power to deduct covariations is so poor? As Nisbett and Ross (1980) note, we may be better able to detect covariations in more specific domains. Consider the consequences of turning the steering wheel when driving a car: each movement has an immediate effect; that is, each change has an immediate feedback. Such direct experience offers an opportunity to correct misleading beliefs about what "ought" to go together. However, if our preconceptions are rigid and the feedback is vague or irrelevant, experience may do little to alter incorrect beliefs.

Examine All Four Cells. We tend to focus on our "hits" when estimating covariation. This encourages false estimates that may result in incorrect beliefs about causes. For example, parents often worry that their teenaged children will have a car accident. Let's say that a mother worries, and her son then is in an accident (Jensen, 1989). The parent may attribute this to "clairvoyance" or some other mystical power. Only the "hits" (worry followed by accident) receive attention; false alarms, misses, and correct rejections are ignored (see Exhibit 17.7). The tendency to ignore negative instances encourages beliefs in suspect causes such as psychic powers. People who say that their prayers are answered usually do not consider the times they prayed and their prayers were not answered. That is, they do not keep track of all the times they prayed, noting the outcome for each. "Answered prayers" are more vivid. The confirmatory bias (our tendency to search selectively for evidence that supports our preconceptions) en-

courages a focus on hits. We must examine all four cells in a 2×2 contingency table.

Sometimes people make inferences based on only one row in a 2×2 table. Consider reports of being abused as a child and whether or not an individual was in fact abused. We must examine all four cells in a 2×2 table (Dawes, 1994). We must consider those who have and have not reported abuse and those who have actually been and those who have not been abused. In everyday practice, only one row of a four cell contingency table is available to counselors. Consider people who have or have not been caught for abuse and whether they are or are not abusers. We don't know who would be represented in the other row (not caught). As Dawes points out, often, we do not think in comparative terms. "We match (often from memory) rather than compare," (p. 4). Statements that sound convincing may in fact be quite inaccurate." The only way to avoid these kinds of errors, as Dawes notes, is to make it a habit to elaborate joint probabilities (i.e., draw a 2×2 contingency table). (See also, Dawes 1982, 1993.)

Pay Attention to Base Rates

Base rates indicate the prevalence of a behavior or event in a population. Only some parents who were abused as children abuse their own children (estimates range from 40 to 60%). We tend to rely on data about a particular case and to ignore base rate probabilities. Imagine that you have just left a staff position in a shelter for battered women where 90% of the clients seeking services had been abused. You are now working in a community mental health center in which the base rate of battered women is much lower, say 10%. Ignoring these different base rates may result in incorrect assumptions that clients have been battered when they have not been. Base rate data are not as vivid as characteristics of the client whom you see during interviews. It thus is easy to overlook this information, even though it is important to consider when making decisions. If we rely on resemblance criteria (similarity) to evaluate probability, we may overlook prior probability (base rate data) (Tversky & Kahneman, 1974, p. 1124). We can use Bayes's

EXHIBIT 17.7
Contingency Table

	Worry	
	Yes	No
Accident Yes	Hit	Miss
Accident No	False Alarm	Correct Rejection

theorem to consider base rate data (prior odds) (for further details, see Gibbs, 1991).

Watch Out for Sample Bias

Practice decisions are made on the basis of samples of behavior or conditions. Helpers often make generalizations about what clients do in real-life contexts based on how they act during interviews. Inaccurate assumptions may result from **overgeneralizations** based on small, biased samples. We often overlook **selection bias.** Consider the assumption that since students' achievement in private—compared with public—schools is superior, private schools are better. What do you think?

Watch Out for Anchoring Effects

We tend to be influenced by what we first see or think of. This influences later judgments. Make it a habit to question initial impressions.

Search for Alternative Accounts

We tend to seek data that confirm our views and not to look for evidence against them. This is known as the *confirmatory bias* or *self-fulfilling prophecy*. This style of search often results in faulty judgments (Einhorn & Hogarth, 1978). Studies of medical decisions show that overinterpretation is a key source of error (contradictory evidence is ignored or is incorrectly assumed to support preferred views) (Elstein et al., 1978). We use different standards to criticize evidence against our views when we use to evaluate evidence that supports them. Evidence that is mixed (it provides some support for and some against favored views) increases the confidence of believers of both views (Lord, Ross, & Lepper, 1979). We readily think up causes. We have an investment in understanding and predicting what happens around us. A premature focus on one possibility will get in the way of considering alternative views. Unless your assumptions about causes provide guidelines for removing complaints or unless you must act quickly ("shoot from the hip"), you should consider alternative possibilities.

Enhance Your Understanding of Probabilities

Misunderstanding regarding probabilities may result in faulty problem structuring. Different kinds of probabilities include: (1) *compound* (probability of X *and* Y), (2) *conditional* (probability of X *given* Y), and (3) *simple* (X). In the conjunction fallacy, we overlook the fact that the probabilities of A and B *both* occurring must be less than the simple probability of A or the simple probability of B. Consider the example given by Tversky and Kahneman (1983) in which subjects received the following facts about Linda, a 31-year-old single, outspoken, bright student who majored in philosophy. She was very concerned with issues regarding discrimination and social justice and took part in antinuclear demonstrations. Subjects were asked to evaluate the following:

a. Linda works in a bookstore and takes Yoga classes

b. Linda is active in the feminist movement

c. Linda is a psychiatric social worker

d. Linda is a bank teller

e. Linda is an insurance salesperson

f. Linda is a bank teller and is active in the feminist movement

Statement (f) is the conjunction of (b) and (d). The probability of (f) cannot be greater than either (b) or (d). However most subjects believe that (f) is more probable than (d) (perhaps because of the representative heuristic (see Chapter 5). Because we are influenced by representativeness (the similarity of events) we often make inferences with no reference to known or estimated base rates of the characteristic in question. Dawes (1988) gives the example of assuming that low self esteem (c) results in problems (P) because people who consult counselors regarding problems have low self-esteem. This confuses P $(c|S)$—the probability of low self-esteem given problems and $(p$ $S|c)$—the probability of problems given low self-esteem. As Dawes points out, we do not know $(p$ $S|c)$ is high "because clients come to [counselors] because they have problems" (p. 76). The counselors' experience is conditional on S. Also, as Dawes points out, peoples' self-esteem may be poor *because* they have problems. (See also Appendix 5A illustrating that conditional probabilities are not symmetric.) Readers of books on sexual abuse are often asked to review a length list of symptoms to see if they have indicators of sexual abuse. One problem here is assuming that the probability of a symptom (e.g., suicidal thoughts) is the same as the probability of an underlying problem or experience (e.g., sexual abuse as a child) (Ofshe & Watters, 1994). Symptoms such as depression are much more common than any one underlying cause. When we do not consider this, we are subject to illusory correlations (e.g., between symptoms and presumed causes).

Watch Your Language

The role of language is discussed at many points in this book. Language influences how successful we are in communicating with ourselves as well as with clients and colleagues. Some uses of language have an almost magical quality, as when we label a behavior and think that we have explained it when we have not (see the earlier discussion of naming versus explaining). It is easy to slip from describing someone (She complains about being lonely) to a causal inference that provides little or no intervention leverage (She has a dependent personality). We tend to convert trait names (e.g., aggressive) into presumed causes (e.g., aggressive personality) that get in the way of searching for problem-related factors. Psychobabble (vague, obscure, excessively abstract concepts) obscures rather than clarifies.

Acquire Domain-Specific Knowledge and Skills

You may need domain-specific knowledge to understand and resolve a problem and so may have to read problem-related scientific literature. Many helpers are unaware of the influence of schedules of reinforcement on behavior and so mistakenly attribute the cause of problems to personal charac-

teristics (low self-esteem), overlooking the role of scheduling effects (see Chapter 8). Lack of knowledge about the effects of certain physical illnesses or drugs may result in incorrect assumptions about the cause of an elderly client's "depression."

Be Aware of What You Don't Know

Be honest about what you know and do not know. Knowledge about how to help clients is usually incomplete. Source of uncertainty include potential effectiveness of different methods, the accuracy of assessment and evaluation measures, and the future course of certain behavior patterns. Recognizing uncertainty in problem solving can help you avoid overconfidence and make better decisions. Witte, Witte, and Kerwin (1994) offer a course on medical ignorance at the University of Arizona School of Medicine to highlight the importance of knowing what is not known as well as what is.

Watch Out for Redundant Data

Our tendency to collect redundant information encourages a false sense of overconfidence. You may, for example, ask a client who complains of depression about her past history of depression. In selectively scanning for depression, you may overlook periods of happiness and related factors.

Take Advantage of Helpful Tools

Making practice decisions often requires combining different kinds of data (e.g., self-report and observational data). Let's say you have to decide whether to remove a child from his home. You may want to consider the probability of further abuse, steps that can be taken to avoid it, the safety provided in other settings (foster homes), and so on. Integrating different kinds of data is difficult. You should consider both new information and information you already have. Two kinds of odds should be considered: (1) prior odds (odds before additional material is available) and (2) posterior odds (odds after considering additional data). The addition of more information should change prior odds.

EXHIBIT 17.8
Bayes's Theorem

New information should be considered together with information you already have. Let's assume that you think there is a 90% probability that Brian's behavior is due to poor parenting skills but decide to check out your views by asking his parents to complete a test of parenting skills. What if they receive a high score on appropriate parenting behaviors? How will you combine this information with data already available (e.g., observation of family interaction)? You should consider two kinds of odds (Arkes, 1981). One kind is prior odds—odds before additional material is available. Obtaining more information (data that decrease uncertainty) should change these prior odds. Bayes's theorem can help you combine different sources of data (e.g., your observations and a score on a test) in a way that makes use of multiple sources of information. Without this, we tend to disregard information (e.g., beliefs based on observation of family interaction). We can use Bayes's theorem to consider base-rate data (prior odds) that we tend to ignore (see Gibbs & Gambrill, 1996). You may need to use both astute intuitive judgments and Bayes's theorem to make accurate estimates.

Bayes's theorem can help you combine different sources of data. Without this, we tend to disregard prior information (see Exhibit 17.8).

You could use computer programs that are based on practice-related research as a decision making tool (for example, to assess risk or allocate services such as homemaker chore time (Clark, Miller, & Pruger, 1980; Schuerman, 1995). Different weights could be assigned to different sources to reflect their importance. Using such programs can enhance both the accuracy and equity of decisions (clients with similar needs receive similar services). More than 100 studies show that empirically based actuarial methods are superior to clinical judgments in making decisions in a number of areas, including the diagnosis of medical and psychiatric disorders, the prediction of treatment outcome, and the length of hospitalization (Dawes, 1994a; Dawes, Faust, & Meehl, 1989). Statistical or actuarial judgment involves the systematic combination of data from many sources, including life history, test scores, ratings of behavior, and subjective judgments based on interviews. It draws on both expert opinion and empirical data describing the relationship between certain outcomes (e.g., hospitalization) and "predictors" (e.g., severity of diagnosis). Visual models such as flowcharts and decision trees may be useful (see Exhibit 17.9).

Be Rational (Flexible)

One definition of rationality is changing your mind when the data indicate that you should. Our tendency to be overconfident of our judgments and to look for data that confirm our views (the confirmatory bias) encourages unwarranted persistence. Change your mind when you have good reason to do so.

Avoid False Dilemmas

We often think in either/or terms when searching for causes and selecting service plans. We may think it must be either _____ or _____ when in fact there may be a number of possibilities.

REVIEWING YOUR INFERENCES

Can you make a well-reasoned argument for your assumptions? Guidelines for presenting arguments are as follows:

- Clearly identify your conclusion and premises.
- Separate evidence and inferences.
- Use accurate premises.
- Avoid overstating inferences.

EXHIBIT 17.9
Example of a Tree Diagram

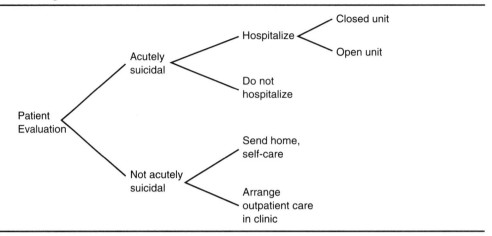

Source: T. G. Gutheil, H. J. Bursztajan, A. Brodsky, & V. Alexander (1991), *Decision making in psychiatry and the law* (p. 44). Baltimore: Williams & Wilkins.

• Review your argument for fallacies.

• Search for alternative accounts.

Can you make a well-reasoned argument that the objectives you and your clients have decided to pursue will resolve the problem? Is there a clear relationship between assumptions about causes and selection of outcomes? Is your account compatible with what is known about behavior and about this particular problem? Can a stronger argument be made for some other account?

The main point of critiquing an argument is to show that some inconsistency or implausibility is involved in accepting the premises and rejecting the conclusion (Scriven, 1976, p. 32). Focus on criticisms that are relevant to the main thrust of an argument (strong criticisms) rather than nitpick (use weak criticisms). Are there hidden assumptions? What are they? Consider both the factual soundness of an argument and its logical soundness. An argument can be logically sound but lead to false conclusions because of one or more false premises. The steps involved in getting from the premises to the conclusion may be obscure because steps have been left out. Inaccuracies are easier to spot if you put an argument into visual or diagrammatic form. Consider the argument that smoking marijuana im-

plies with high probability using hard drugs such as heroin (see Chapter 5, Appendix A). This argument is an example of the confusion of the inverse (the confusion between the probability of using heroin if you smoke marijuana and the probability of smoking marijuana if you use hard drugs). The two probabilities are quite different.

On the Use and Misuse of Intuition

Although intuition is an invaluable source of ideas about what may be true or false, it is not a sound guide for testing those beliefs, as discussed in Chapter 4. There are over 100 studies showing that actuarial methods are superior to intuition in making decisions in a variety of fields (Dawes, Faust, & Meehl, 1989). Jonathan Baron defines intuition as "an unanalyzed and unjustified belief" (1994, p. 26) and argues that because beliefs based on intuition may be either sound or unsound, basing beliefs on intuition may result in consequences that harm people. Attributing sound judgments to "intuition" decreases opportunities to teach helping skills (one has "it" but doesn't know how or why "it" works). Relying on intuition, or what "feels right," is not wise if it results in ignoring information about problems, causes, and remedies, including possible consequences of given courses of action. There is no doubt that knowledge is fragmentary, forcing you to rely on questionable beliefs to fill in the gaps. What is ethically questionable is relying on intuition when other grounds—including a critical examination of intuitively held beliefs—will result in sounder decisions.

IDEALS AND ACTUALITIES

The purpose of assessment is to find out what is needed and what can be offered. Think of a balance scale. The balance will often reveal many problems and few resources. An "impossible job" is one in which you do not have the resources (e.g., time) to solve the problems you confront or can only minimally address them. Case management, for example, will not substantially change structural and fiscal problems that limit the kinds of outcomes that can be achieved (Austin, 1992).

When a Contextual Framework Is Not Preferred

Adequate assessment may not be possible because your supervisor or agency relies on practice frameworks that yield incomplete accounts of problems and related circumstances. Some of my students want to use effective methods but cannot do so. They may not be permitted (or may not have the time) to gather observational data needed to clarify problems, outcomes, and related factors. Their options for speaking up and changing inadequate and/or harmful practices and policies may be limited. Supervisors may favor an interview style emphasizing individual states and conditions and background information and inferences not closely tied to observational data.

Contextual in Name Only

Practice may be contextual in name only. Staff may say they use a contextual approach but reveal by their actions that they do not. Multiple services may be offered with little integration to avoid duplication and working at cross-purposes.

When a Contextual Approach Is Favored But Is Not Possible

A contextual approach may be preferred but not be possible. Obstacles include heavy caseloads, lack of resources, and time pressures. As resources shrink, "speed-ups" (having to cover more cases in the same amount of time) have become common. You may have neither time nor opportunity to clarify problems and discover related factors. You may have to make recommendations hastily, with little time for critical reflection. Required assessment skills may not be available.

What Can You Do in Such Circumstances?

You can do whatever you can to address your clients' needs and explore what can be done to create additional resources. Dysfunctional responses to imbalances between ideals and actualities include focusing on areas of little interest to clients and becoming a natterer (merely complaining). You can be aware of the limitations of your assessment (what you know and don't know) (be your own best constructive critic). This will help you to accurately appraise the evidence on which you base your assumptions. If you accurately acknowledge the limitations of your assessment, you are more likely to avoid overconfidence (unwarranted belief in assumptions) and to keep your assessment skills well honed. Avoiding overconfidence does not mean that you do not act in spite of uncertainty; as Thouless (1974) points out, this would be the height of "crooked thinking." It means that you take what actions you must, bearing in mind associated uncertainty.

Do What You Can. The concept of "successive approximations" is valuable not only in helping clients, but in helping you to focus on what can be done even in dismal circumstances. Perhaps you can complete some of the steps in a sound assessment. Do what you can. Complete the closest approximation to a contextual assessment.

Keep Your Eye on the Gold Standard. The gold standard is that we have sufficient data to make sound decisions. It is not that assessment data be complete. This is usually impossible. Plans must typically be made based on incomplete data. However, there are degrees of incompleteness, ranging from totally inadequate (no clear description of problems, outcomes, or related factors) to excellent (clear description of problems, outcomes, and related factors).

When we cannot do what we think we should do, we may change our mind about what is "best." Suppose that you work in an agency in which you have to make hasty decisions. You may gradually change your beliefs about what should be done. You could form a support group of colleagues with similar values to prevent drifting away from standards you value. Without this, ideals, possibilities, and actualities may be confused.

Change Questionable Policies and Procedures.
Talk to others who share your concerns, and work together to seek changes. Don't assume that policies and procedures that interfere with services cannot be changed.

USING TESTS TO MAKE DECISIONS

Professionals often use tests to understand clients or problems or to predict how people are likely to respond in the future. Social workers often assess risks (e.g., of elder or child abuse). Thousands of children are on "at risk" registers on the assumption that they are at a continuing risk of abuse. Tests should be used to revise subjective estimates, to change a decision about what should be done. Otherwise, why bother? Let's say you suspect (based on an interview) that an elderly client has Alzheimer's disease and you obtain psychological test results as well. You should then use the test results to choose among different options in light of your new estimate based on the results. That is, you may revise your estimate of the probability that the client has Alzheimer's disease (see Exhibit 17.10). Clients should not be asked to take tests simply to satisfy the curiosity of professionals or because the tests are available. This wastes time and provides an illusion of "work being done." Inform clients about the costs and benefits of any recommended test so they can participate in a meaningful way in making decisions. A balance sheet describing benefits and risks, together with their likelihood (if

known) and the subjective value for each, can help clients make decisions (Eddy, 1990). This sheet should include information about the accuracy of the test (e.g., false positive and false negative rates). Someone may request a test even though it is not very accurate and is costly in money, time, discomfort, likelihood of misdiagnosis (a false positive or a false negative), or harm from the test itself. We differ in the risks we are willing (or eager) to take.

The predictive accuracy of test results is often overestimated. Incorrect estimates of a test's predictive accuracy may result from confusing two different conditional probabilities. We tend to confuse **retrospective accuracy** (the probability of a positive test given that the person has a condition) and **predictive accuracy** (the probability of a condition given a positive test result). Retrospective accuracy is determined by reviewing test results after the true condition is known. For example, an autopsy may show that a woman who had a positive mammogram indeed did have breast cancer. Predictive accuracy refers to the probability of having a condition given a positive test result and the probability of not having a condition given a negative result. A physician may ask a patient to have a mammogram and, if it is positive, may infer that she has breast cancer and recommend a biopsy. It is predictive accuracy that is important when considering a test result for an individual (see Eddy, 1982).

Inaccurate estimates based on invalid tests may harm clients. Both test sensitivity and test specificity should be considered as well as prevalence (base rate) for the problem of concern. **Test sensitivity** refers to a test's accuracy in correctly identifying the proportion of people who have a problem or will engage in a certain behavior (see the Glossary in Exhibit 17.11). **Test specificity** refers to the accuracy of a test in correctly identifying the proportion of people who do not have a disorder (or will not engage in a behavior). Both are calculated by examining the columns in a 2×2 table as shown in Exhibit 17.12. Neither permit predictions about individuals. Test sensitivity is often incorrectly equated with the predictive value of a positive test result, and test specificity is often incorrectly equated with the predictive value of a negative test result resulting in gross overestimates of the predictive value. See Beck, Byyny, &

EXHIBIT 17.10
Should A Test Be Used?

Suppose that the social worker seeing Mrs. Ryan and the Greens discusses this family at a staff conference and the attending psychologist suggests that Mrs. Ryan is in the beginning stages of dementia and wants to give her some tests. Ask him why he thinks this. What indicators is he using? What is the correlation between each indicator and an accurate diagnosis of dementia? Suppose that the psychologist believes that Mrs. Ryan has "loose associations" and that these are an indicator. Exactly what are "loose associations?" What are examples? What percentage of people her age have similar "loose associations"? That is, what is the base rate? What is the correlation between "loose associations" and dementia?

What is the probability that "loose associations" are predictive of dementia? And if they are, would this change what you would do now or in the future? What is the cost of the tests to the clients in money, possible anxiety, and stigma? Would family members start to pathologize Mrs. Ryan if additional assessments were recommended? Would positive results on additional "tests" give family members an excuse to "get rid" of Mrs. Ryan, even though they offer no additional information about whether her current complaints could be resolved and, if so, how?

Adams, 1981; Elstein, 1988, Dawes, 1988). The positive predictive value of a test depends on the prevalence rate, specificity, and sensitivity. The probability that a client with a positive (or negative) test result for dementia really has dementia depends on the prevalence (base rate) of dementia in the population from which the person was selected (on the pretest probability that the person has dementia). Because there is little appreciation of this point, predictive accuracy is often overestimated. Thus, test accuracy varies depending on whether a test is used as a screening device in which

EXHIBIT 17.11
Glossary

False negative rate: Percentage of persons incorrectly identified as not having a characteristic.

False positive rate: Percentage of persons inaccurately identified as having a characteristic.

Predictive accuracy: The probability of a condition given a positive test result.

Predictive value of a negative test: The proportion of those with a negative test result who do not have a problem.

Predictive value of a positive test: Proportion of those with a positive test result who actually have a problem.

Prevalence rate (base rate, prior probability): The frequency of a problem among a group of people. The best estimate of the probability of a problem before carrying out a test.

Retrospective accuracy: The probability of positive test, given that a person has a condition.

Test sensitivity: The proportion among those known to have a problem who test positive.

Test specificity: The proportion among those known to not have the problem who test negative.

True negative rate: Percentage of persons accurately identified as not having a characteristic.

True positive rate: Percentage of persons accurately identified as having a characteristic.

EXHIBIT 17.12
Elements for Judging a Prediction Instrument's Value

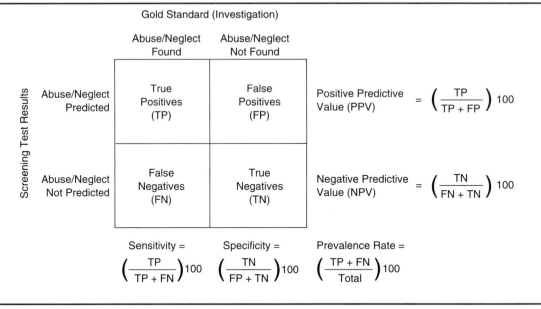

Source: L. Gibbs (1991), *Scientific reasoning for social workers* (p. 225). New York: Macmillan.

there are large numbers of people who do not have some condition of interest (e.g., depression) or whether it is used for clients with known signs or symptoms. In the latter case, the true positive and true negative rates are much higher, and so there will be fewer false positives and false negatives. Overlooking this difference results in overestimates of test accuracy in screening situations, resulting in a high percentage of false positives.

ETHICAL ISSUES IN THE SELECTION OF OUTCOMES

Ethical practice requires involving clients in selecting outcomes, forming a clear agreement about what outcomes will be pursued, considering the interests of all involved parties, and focusing on functional objectives (those that are of value to clients in real-life environments). A clear service agreement highlights your responsibility to work toward agreed on objectives and decreases the likelihood of hidden agendas (goals you pursue but do not

share with clients). The influence of professionals is often obscured by the vagueness of objectives pursued. Labeling may be used to obscure questionable decisions. For example, labeling a client mentally ill may legitimize the use of intrusive methods that would otherwise be considered unethical. The fuzzier the goal is, the greater the chance that an outcome will be pursued that is not of interest to clients.

You may help clients recognize the influence of social norms and values on their selection of outcomes and thus expand their options. For example, consumerism is a hallmark of American culture, but buying unnecessary consumer items may result in strained family relationships because of financial worries. Stereotypes and a lack of knowledge may result in incorrect assumptions that a particular problem is related to race, gender, sexual orientation, or age. Differences of opinion about objectives may concern who the target of change is to be, in addition to what is to be altered. Until fairly recently, seeking to change a homosexual orientation to a heterosexual one was readily accepted as an outcome by many professionals (and still may be by some). Many now argue against this on the grounds that it reflects and supports societal biases and the resulting oppression of and discrimination against gay and lesbian people.

Empowering Clients

Expanding freedom is a key criterion in selecting objectives. This includes freedom from restrictions that result from a lack of skills, freedom to gain outcomes that do not harm others, and freedom to avoid unfairly imposed or unnecessary negative consequences. You can expand clients' freedom by focusing on **functional objectives**; those that enhance opportunities for reinforcement in real-life settings. A focus on objectives that are valuable only in artificial contexts such as a day treatment center violates legal regulations intended to ensure effective services to persons with developmental disabilities (see for example Positive Behavioral Intervention Regulations, 1993). To arrive at ethical decisions, you must consider the interests of your clients and also those of involved others. When interests conflict, ethical practice calls for helping all parties to identify possible options and the advantages and disadvantages of each. Focusing on common goals will help you to identify mutually acceptable outcomes.

If you have authority over people in a supervisory or monitoring role (as in child welfare or correctional settings), you should be especially careful when selecting outcomes. Questions to ask yourself are (1) Is there a legitimate reason for intervening? Will the outcomes sought benefit both clients and significant others? Does the behavior occur often enough to justify intervening? (2) Are my judgments free of bias for example in relation to gender, sexual orientation, ethnicity, age, or race?

THE VALUE OF RECORDS

Records can help you plan cases, think about the causes of problems, decide on intervention, and review your clients' progress. Records protect clients from unnecessarily repetitive questions and help you avoid mistakes based on faulty assumptions and recollections. They serve as a guide for others who take over a case and allow supervisors and administrators to review the quality of services provided. Review should be based on clear agreed-on criteria related to effective planning. Are objectives clearly defined? Do they address outcomes of concern to clients? Are service methods clearly described? Are records up-to-date? Asking "Is this material useful in planning what to do?" can help you decide what to record. You can save time by eliminating redundant forms and using standardized forms that allow easy recording and review. Common deficiencies of case records and psychological reports include missing data, overly general or unsupported speculations, and vague or overly technical language (Tallent, 1993). Writing tips include the following:

- Be precise.
- Get rid of unnecessary words.
- Never use a long word when a short one will do.
- Use active verbs.
- Clearly define key terms.
- Focus on main points.
- Clearly identify your conclusions and the premises on which you base them.
- Support your inferences with descriptive data.

Problem-oriented recording keeps the presenting problems in view. Try to record the problems in the client's (or referral source's) own words. A log of contacts noting the date, people present, purpose, and type of contact can save time when preparing court reports. Note the sources of data used (see Exhibit 17.13). Describing current and desired levels of behaviors and/or environmental conditions and intermediate steps provides an "agenda" for change tailored to each client. Clearly describe plans, including the settings that will be used, who will be involved, what they will do, and the reasons for selections made. Also describe progress indicators and plans for maintaining gains. Ethical issues regarding records include protecting clients' rights to confidentiality (e.g., not sharing

EXHIBIT 17.13
Checklist for Reviewing Case Records

	Not at All	A little	Fair Amount	Ideal
1. Route to agency is clearly noted.	0	1	2	3
2. Presenting problems are described.	0	1	2	3
3. A problem (outcome) profile is included.	0	1	2	3
4. Demographic data are complete.	0	1	2	3
5. Relevant historical data (e.g., work history) are included.	0	1	2	3
6. Current life circumstances are clearly described	0	1	2	3
7. Problem-related behaviors are clearly described.	0	1	2	3
8. Sources of data relied on are noted.	0	1	2	3
9. Valid assessment sources are used.	0	1	2	3
10. Self-report data are supplemented by observational data.	0	1	2	3
11. Baseline data are available.	0	1	2	3
12. Contingencies related to behaviors of concern are clearly described.	0	1	2	3
13. Client assets are noted.	0	1	2	3
14. Relevant assets of significant others are noted.	0	1	2	3
15. Environmental resources are described.	0	1	2	3
16. Uninformative labels are avoided.	0	1	2	3
17. Objectives, including intermediate steps, are clearly described.	0	1	2	3
18. Inferences about the causes of problems are supported by evidence and are compatible with what is known about behavior.	0	1	2	3
19. Meeting objectives will remove complaints.	0	1	2	3
20. Intervention methods are clearly described.	0	1	2	3
21. Plans selected have an empirically tested track record of success.	0	1	2	3
22. Clear relevant progress indicators are noted.	0	1	2	3
23. Graphs showing degree of progress are included and are up-to-date.	0	1	2	3
24. There is little irrelevant material.	0	1	2	3
25. A log of contacts is included.	0	1	2	3

Key: 0 = not at all, 1 = a little, 2 = a fair amount, 3 = ideal. Total scores may range from 0 to 75.

records with other people unless you must because of legal regulations or you have the client's permission), avoiding irrelevant negative material, and using records as a tool in planning and evaluating services. For more discussion of case records, see Kagle, 1991.

SUMMARY

Helping clients requires deciding how to organize and interpret data. You have to make guesses about how to help clients attain valued outcomes. Depending on the time available and the reasoning used, these guesses may be informed or off-the-cuff. Ideally, objectives are selected that involve a change in problem-related circumstances and build on personal assets and environmental resources. Common errors in this helping stage include acting on hasty assumptions, selecting vague objectives, overlooking the client's strengths, and offering incomplete accounts (ignoring environmental causes such as lack of jobs in the community). We tend to be overconfident of our beliefs, to focus on data that support them, and to ignore data that do not. Helpful rules-of-thumb for avoiding errors include searching for alternative accounts, questioning initial assumptions, and asking what is missing. Flowcharts and decision trees may be useful in organizing information and seeing what is missing.

REVIEWING YOUR COMPETENCIES

Reviewing What You Know

1. Recognize and give examples of incomplete assessment.
2. Give examples of common errors in organizing and interpreting data.
3. Give examples of naming rather than explaining.
4. Describe helpful rules for avoiding errors in organizing and integrating data.
5. Describe important questions to ask when deciding whether to use a test to make predictions.
6. Explain why it is important to consider base rate data when interpreting test results, and give an example.

Reviewing What You Do

1. The inferences you make are compatible with what is known about behavior/problems.
2. Descriptions, causal analyses, and predictions are supported by evidence and suggest feasible plans.
3. The objectives you select are relevant to outcomes of most concern to your clients.
4. Given case examples, you can detect incomplete accounts and missing information.
5. Given case examples, you can spot faulty arguments and accurately describe why they are faulty.

Reviewing Results

1. Plans selected are effective.
2. Situations in which there are no effective options are accurately identified.

SELECTING PLANS AND ASSESSING PROGRESS

CHAPTER 18

Selecting and Implementing Service Plans

OVERVIEW

This chapter describes decisions in selecting plans, options you may consider and guidelines for selecting among them. Service methods differ in their track record of success and the resources needed to implement them successfully. The data collected during assessment should help you and your clients decide whether and how to pursue valued outcomes. Problems that may arise when trying to implement plans are reviewed and suggestions for handling them offered. See Chapters 21 to 24 for additional details about working with individuals, families, groups, organizations, and communities.

You Will Learn About

- The relationship between assessment and intervention.
- Factors related to success.
- Decisions involved in selecting plans.
- Options (system levels, roles).
- Guidelines for thinking critically about plans.
- Implementing plans.
- Ethical issues.

THE RELATIONSHIP BETWEEN ASSESSMENT AND INTERVENTION

The distinction between assessment and intervention is somewhat arbitrary, in that assessment may produce change (e.g., clients may become more or less hopeful), and additional assessment data may emerge during intervention. The distinction is not arbitrary, however, in that you should not pursue plans unless you and your clients have good reason to believe they will be successful. If initial plans fail, clients may be less willing to "try again" and feel more hopeless. Tailoring plans for each client (whether an individual, family, group, community, or organization) and their unique circumstances is a hallmark of a contextual approach. Conditions must be arranged so that people act, think, or feel differently in relevant situations. Assessment should suggest problem-related outcomes, how to attain them, and the likelihood of success given available resources.

Different views of problems have different service implications (see Exhibit 18.1). You will match available resources against what is needed to judge the feasibility of different options. The goal is to discover *leverage points* at different system levels. Altering behavior and/or circumstances at one level (e.g., helping citizens participate effectively in community board meetings) will often be needed to achieve valued outcomes at other levels (e.g., change policies). Options will be limited by the influence you have or can bring to bear on different players in varied systems. They will de-

pend on the number and complexity of problems, the strength of contingencies that compete with those you and your clients try to introduce or maintain, the resources available, and agency policy.

Your knowledge of problem-related scientific literature will help you identify promising options. We know more today than we did years ago about how to attain certain outcomes. This makes your task more difficult in that there is more to learn and easier in that better guidelines are available. Although the equivalence hypothesis (the belief that all methods are equally effective) is true for some problems, it is not true for many. There is evidence that for some problems, certain methods are more effective than others (e.g., Giles, 1993). Build on client strengths by involving them in suggesting and reviewing options. Treatment fidelity influences success. This refers to the extent to which what is offered matches what is required for success. Because of this, professional associations such as the American Psychological Association

EXHIBIT 18.1

Different Accounts Have Different Intervention Implications: The Lakeland Family

Account	Intervention Implications
1. Brian's troubling behaviors are due to his epilepsy. (B)[a]	1. Control epilepsy. Contact family doctor to adjust prescription.
2. The medication Brian takes is responsible. (B)	2. Change medication. Contact family's physician.
3. Developmental changes are responsible. (D)	3. Educate family members about developmental changes; help them acquire skills for handling changes.
4. Brian's behavior is maintained by reinforcement from his parents. (E/F)	4. Alter patterns of reinforcement; teach family members to reinforce desired behaviors and to ignore undesired ones.
5. Problems at home are due to stress at school. (E)	5. Refer to school social worker to address problems at school.
6. Mother's personality disorder is responsible for family's problems. (P)	6. Refer to community mental health center for individually focused counseling.
7. Worry about money and fatigue, coupled with the lack of effective conflict resolution skills, increases stress, which decreases the use of effective parenting skills. This results in a high frequency of problem behaviors and a low frequency of desired behaviors. (E/P)	7. Relieve fatigue and economic worries (if possible), alter patterns of reinforcement among family members, and enhance conflict resolution skills.
8. Actions by siblings prompt and reinforce Brian's problem behavior. (E/F)	8. Alter siblings' behavior.
9. Family's life developmental stage is the cause of problems. (F/D)	9. Help family members understand the influence of family's life cycle on current experiences.
10. An "enmeshed subsystem" between Brian and his mother is responsible. (F)	10. Help family members, especially Brian and his mother, establish appropriate boundaries.
11. Increased cost of living forces both parents to work full time, creating strains due to stress and worry. (E)	11. Create changes in the tax system that redistribute income downward to economically struggling families.

[a]The letter following each account reflects the kind of account: B = biological, D = developmental, E = environmental, E(F) = family environment, F = family, P = psychological.

have developed protocols for a number of problem areas.

FACTORS THAT INFLUENCE SUCCESS

Variables associated with success that are common to many helping methods include: (1) support (e.g., relief of isolation, positive helping relationship, trust), (2) learning (e.g., advice, exploring new frameworks, feedback, insight, corrective emotional experiences, changed expectations for personal effectiveness, assimilation of troubling experiences), and (3) action (e.g., change behavior, face fears, have successful experiences, reality test) (Lambert & Bergin, 1994). The degree of match between helpers' and clients' views of problems, different parties' expectations, timing of service, and support offered in real life influence outcome. Helper empathy is related to outcome. (see e.g., Burns & Nolen-Hoeksema, 1992). However, there is little relationship between outcome and years of experience or professional degrees and licenses (Dawes, 1994a). Indeed, research shows that empathic paraprofessionals can be as effective as professionally trained helpers with a range of complaints. Consider the study by Strupp and Hadley (1979), in which they randomly assigned clients either to professors with no background in psychology or to professional helpers. The professors achieved the same results as did the professionally trained helpers. Does this mean that training and experience make no difference? Yes and no. Training would make little difference if positive effects could be achieved without it. On the other hand, if specific competencies are needed to help clients, and training is required to attain them than programs that provide such knowledge and skills have something to offer. Thus we should ask, (1) Are special competencies needed to help clients attain certain outcomes? (2) What are they? (3) Are they learned in a training program? (4) Are knowledge and skills used successfully on the job? and (5) If not, why not? It is not hours spent in training that is critical but the demonstrated relationship between the knowledge and skills acquired and success in helping clients achieve outcomes they and

significant others value. Offering clients effective methods requires knowledge of such methods and skill in maximizing their effectiveness. Understanding how behavior is influenced by the environment, developmental changes, and the relationship between personal troubles and social issues will help you to identify options.

DECISIONS INVOLVED IN SELECTING PLANS

Decisions must be made about whether to (1) change thoughts or feelings, (2) change how people act, (3) alter the environment in which they live, or (4) use several approaches (Gottman & Lieblum, 1974). Decisions must be made about level of intervention (individual, family, group, organization, neighborhood, community, service system, policy), what to focus on within levels, whom to involve, what settings to use (e.g., home, classroom, community), what particular methods to use, and how to encourage generalization and maintenance (see Exhibits 18.2 and 18.3). Familiarity with possible options provides a "menu" from which to choose. You will be less likely to overlook valuable options. Altering the environment may involve changing the behavior of significant others and making linkages with other service providers. Depression may be related to negative self-statements and a procedure designed to alter what clients say to themselves (their cognitive ecology) may be helpful. Or, it may be related to lack of money, an unhappy marriage, or sexual and physical abuse. This suggests a different approach.

Flowcharts of the steps involved in selecting or using a plan can guide decision making (see Exhibit 18.4) by highlighting decision points, options, and criteria for reviewing them. Decision trees or balance sheets may help you and your clients weigh the likelihood of different outcomes and balance the risks and benefits. People differ in the risks they are willing to take and a balance sheet allows inclusion of these preferences (Eddy, 1990). Plans usually involve a number of steps. It may be critical to success to clearly describe and order them. Your preferred practice theory will influence what

EXHIBIT 18.2
Decisions and Possible Options

Decision	Options

What intervention level(s) to focus on
- Individual.
- Family.
- Group.
- Agency.
- Neighborhood.
- Community.
- Service system (e.g., policy legislation).

What to focus on
- Offer support.
- Clarify problems and their causes.
- Rearrange contingencies.
- Provide concrete services.
- Provide information.
- Enhance skills.
- Enhance support system.
- Enhance support and communication channels.
- Alter physical environment.
- Redistribute resources via changes in policy.

What helping role(s) to use
- Broker.
- Mediator.
- Advocate.
- Enabler.
- Teacher.
- Planner.

What to focus on at the individual level
- Enhance skills in gaining access to needed material resource.
- Attributions (e.g., views about self and/or others).
- Vocational skills.
- Relationship skills.
- Recreational skills.
- Self-management skills.
- Emotional/affective patterns.

What kind of skills are needed
- Vocational.
- Resources acquisition.
- Relationship.
- Recreational.
- Problem solving.
- Self-management.
- Emotion management.

What relationship skills are needed
- Friendship.
- Parenting.
- Negotiation.
- Assertive.
- Partnership.
- Caregiving.
- Self (relationship with).

What to focus on at the family level
- Communication styles.
- Intergenerational conflicts.
- Decision-making styles.
- External resources.
- Rules.
- Shared activities.

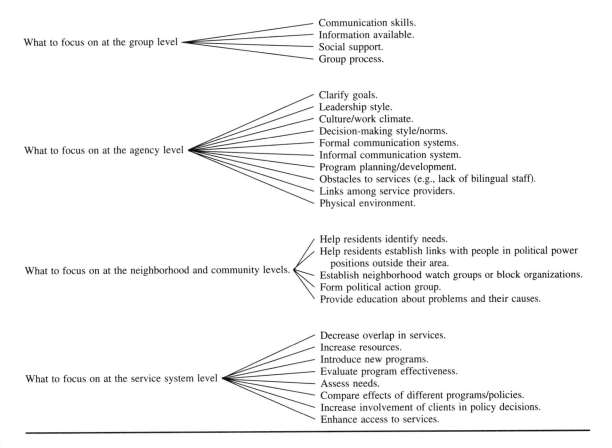

What to focus on at the group level
- Communication skills.
- Information available.
- Social support.
- Group process.

What to focus on at the agency level
- Clarify goals.
- Leadership style.
- Culture/work climate.
- Decision-making style/norms.
- Formal communication systems.
- Informal communication system.
- Program planning/development.
- Obstacles to services (e.g., lack of bilingual staff).
- Links among service providers.
- Physical environment.

What to focus on at the neighborhood and community levels.
- Help residents identify needs.
- Help residents establish links with people in political power positions outside their area.
- Establish neighborhood watch groups or block organizations.
- Form political action group.
- Provide education about problems and their causes.

What to focus on at the service system level
- Decrease overlap in services.
- Increase resources.
- Introduce new programs.
- Evaluate program effectiveness.
- Assess needs.
- Compare effects of different programs/policies.
- Increase involvement of clients in policy decisions.
- Enhance access to services.

problems you and your clients focus on, how they are defined, and what plans are selected. The decisions made will influence the likelihood of success.

What System Level(s) to Focus On

System levels include: individual, family, group, neighborhood, community, organization, and service systems. Success often requires work at several levels with many different people, including significant others and other professionals. Helping clients with problems such as a lack of paid employment may require planned changes at the community, city, state, country, or international level. Attention to both social and economic development is integral to social developmental perspectives (Midgley, 1995). A key question is: Are the levels focused on likely to result in successful outcomes.

Keeping track of discrepancies between what is needed and what can be done will provide a record that you can use to advocate for needed changes in service patterns and policies.

Intervention Roles: How Will You Intervene?

Helping clients often involves one or more of the following helper roles:

- Broker: Link clients with needed services. Example: Refer a client to a senior center.

- Mediator: Resolve disputes/conflicts. Example: Help community members resolve a conflict.

- Enabler: Help clients identify and make effective use of their knowledge and skills (offer support).

- Teacher: Provide information and teach new

EXHIBIT 18.3
Presumed Causes, Service Focus, and Role

Service Focus	Presumed Causes					
	Individual	Family	Group	Neighborhood, community	Agency	Service System
Individual						
Family						
Group						
Neighborhood/ Community						
Agency						
Service/ System						

Focus of Intervention	Possible Intervention Role
1. Provide concrete services.	1. Broker, advocate.
2. Offer support.	2. Enabler.
3. Rearrange contingencies.	3. Enabler, teacher.
4. Provide information or advice.	4. Enabler, teacher.
5. Increase understanding.	5. Teacher, enabler.
6. Enhance skills.	6. Mediator, teacher, enabler.
7. Improve social support systems.	7. Teacher, enabler, mediator, planner.
8. Improve communication.	8. Teacher, broker.
9. Alter physical environment.	9. Teacher, advocate, mediator.
10. Alter agency policies and procedures.	10. Advocate, broker, planner.
11. Alter interactions among agencies.	11. Advocate, mediator, planner.
12. Alter policies affecting resource distribution.	12. Advocate, mediator, planner.
13. Influence legislation.	13. Advocate, mediator, planner.
14. Create new services/programs.	14. Advocate, planner.

skills. Example: Help a youth acquire skills for making and keeping friends.

- Advocate: Argue, mediate, negotiate, alter contingencies on behalf of clients. Example: Accompany a client to a social service agency to help her obtain benefits.

- Planner: Create new resources, improve service programs, create new programs, evaluate programs.

Carrying out one role may involve other roles. For example, helping clients find and use resources (a broker role) may require accompanying clients to an agency and speaking up in their behalf (advocacy), helping clients acquire skills in requesting services (teaching) and identifying and supporting the skills that clients already possess (enabling). Skill in discovering problem-related contingencies is valuable in all these roles (see Chapters 9 and 10).

EXHIBIT 18.4
Analysis of Routine Stressors

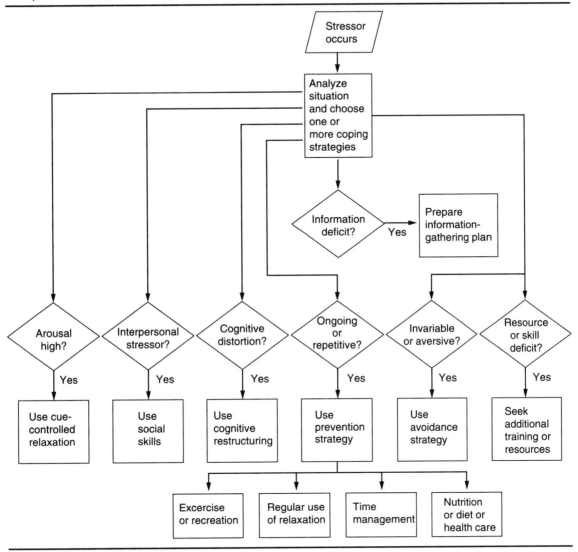

Source: R. Tolman & S. Rose (1985), Coping with stress: A multimodel approach. *Social Work, 30,* 156.

Broker and Mediator. Offering help may require improving links with, within, or among agencies; coordinating services; creating better outreach programs; and designing new services (Pincus & Minahan, 1973). Often, many different services are needed to help a client (see Exhibit 18.5). You may have to refer clients to other sources for money, clothes, housing, or medical or legal services. A knowledge of problem-related scientific research and familiarity with available services will help you make successful referrals. Whenever possible, rely on track records of success in achieving valued outcomes. Gaining needed help requires familiarity with both formal and informal resources and a commitment to involve "indigenous helpers" such as significant others and neighbors. Required compe-

EXHIBIT 18.5
Involvement of Multiple Service Agencies in Helping Clients

A custodian of a neighborhood tenement reported that one of the tenants spent nearly all her days crying, locked in her apartment. Upon investigation it was realized that . . . a Vietnam refugee with four children, aged 6 to 14, was the person reported about. This woman had lost her husband and youngest son in Vietnam. She had no relative or friend in this country and did not speak English. Her small apartment was completely bare except for two beds. The allotment she received from public assistance was not sufficient to buy furniture or clothing and no special allowance had been provided for these purposes. The situation was potentially dangerous—all the family possessed was warm weather clothing and winter was approaching.

The children, because of their home situation and inability to communicate, had problems in school. The fact that the family had been affluent in Vietnam compounded the difficulties that they were experiencing. The mother felt that she might be on the verge of a breakdown. Five major problem areas were isolated:

1. Financial—more money required for family's basic needs
2. Socialization—human contact needed particularly by the mother
3. Language—need by all family members to learn English
4. Health—children's teeth particularly in need of work
5. Housing—need for a larger apartment.

A staff worker monitored the provision of services and participation of the client. The following services have been provided to the family as of this date:

1. International Rescue Committee supplied $600 for furniture, $275 for winter clothing and $80 for a sewing machine.
2. A neighbor agreed to help the mother shop and along with the worker provided some of the human contact that was needed.
3. The mother and children were enrolled in special English classes provided by the Board of Education and Immigration services.
4. Governeur Hospital gave all members of the family physical checkups and provided the dental work required by the children.
5. A local agency contracted to work with the family in finding more appropriate housing.

It is obvious that this woman could not be helped by merely providing emotional insight. Five or six organizations, besides the focal agency that took on her case, had to provide services. Some person had to see to it that all the needed services were arranged for, that they were actually provided, and that they were sufficient to help this woman provide for herself and her family. The role this type of worker plays is the case manager role.

Source: H. Weissman, I. Epstein, & A. Savage (1983), *Agency-based social work: Neglected aspects of clinical practice* (pp. 74–75). Philadelphia: Temple University Press.

tencies include familiarity with agency policies and operating procedures and information about barriers to service use. Follow up to make sure effective links have been made. Effective social skills will be of value including bargaining and negotiating obstacles in a nonabrasive manner, making specific requests, and compromising when necessary (see Chapter 13). Skills of value as a mediator include clarifying problems, bargaining, and negotiating.

Advocate. Advocacy can be defined as the "act of directly representing or defending others, championing the rights of individuals or communities through direct intervention or through empowerment" (Barker, 1995, p. 11). In *case advocacy*, you act on behalf of individuals. In *cause advocacy*, you help a group or community achieve a valued goal such as receiving more timely services from an agency or gaining access to mandated services. Social workers should always be case advocates. For example, you may accompany a client to an agency, telephone a worker who has denied a request, or contact an administrator. Advocacy may be needed when clients are refused benefits to which they are entitled or when services are provided in a dehumanizing manner. Denial of civil or legal rights (e.g., discrimination based on ethnicity, race, age, or gender) may require advocacy. Agency policies and procedures that impede the delivery of services may have to be changed.

Effective advocacy requires a knowledge of clients' legal and civil rights, appeal processes, resources, and methods that may be used to attain valued outcomes. Knowledge and skills described in earlier chapters such as clearly describing problems will be needed. Contingency analysis skills will help you identify resources and obstacles, including vested interests of involved others. Confrontation may be necessary to advocate for clients. You may have to "blow the whistle" to make headway or lobby legislators. Advocating for clients often involves asking people to do something they would not do voluntarily and questioning the decisions and power of others. Be prepared for negative reactions. Emphasizing common goals, thinking the best about others, and em-

pathizing with other points of view (intellectual empathy) will increase your success. Stay focused on your goal (helping clients). This will help you manage your emotions.

Brokering, advocating, and mediating require a familiarity with agency policies, regulations, and administrative structures and how different service systems are connected. Not understanding other approaches and being biased against them may hamper the coordination of services. And there may be little agreement about how to pursue goals because different criteria are used to select knowledge.

Enabler and Teacher. You may also help clients make effective use of their own resources and help them acquire information and skills (see Chapters 21 and 22).

Planner. Planning (e.g., deciding what to do, reviewing and creating options) is often a part of other helping roles and may be the key service focus, such as when you help agencies or community residents identify needs, set priorities, review current service programs, and plan new ones. Depending on your job responsibilities, you may be heavily or only slightly involved in program planning (e.g., offering suggestions about needed programs to agency administrators).

Another Way to Think About Service Roles

Being a broker, advocate, enabler, teacher, mediator, or planner may involve (1) talking to clients and significant others, (2) planning and carrying out assignments in real life, (3) practicing relevant behaviors, or (4) directly influencing behavior in real-life settings such as the home or school (Kanfer & Phillips, 1969). Specific procedures are selected within these roles. Considering options in relation to different roles highlights the requisites for successful use of each as well as their advantages and disadvantages.

Hundreds of different kinds of intervention methods are available that may use one or more of the roles described. *Enactive* methods, in which clients carry out behaviors in real-life contexts (or those similar to them), tend to be more effective than *symbolic* methods, in which clients imagine situations or talk about them (Bandura, 1986). Enactive—versus symbolic—methods provide realistic feedback about what can be accomplished and greater changes in self-efficacy, which influence what we attempt and how long we persist in our efforts. *Self-efficacy* refers to beliefs about whether we can carry out certain behaviors and their likely success in gaining valued outcomes. If it is not possible to use enactive methods at first (perhaps because of anxiety), you could start with symbolic procedures in which events and reactions are imagined and then move on to enactive methods. Successful performance does not automatically result in increased confidence. Attributing success to external factors such as luck rather than to personal competency may discourage this.

Talking to Clients. Helpers and clients talk to each other. Requirements include verbal facility and the use of "insights" and support gained in interviews to alter behavior, thoughts, or feelings in real-life contexts. Clients may form more helpful views of their problems and identify new options. Generalization and maintenance of positive effects may be a problem, since intervention does not occur in the clients' natural environment.

Using Assignments. Here clients carry out agreed-on tasks in real-life settings such as the home, school, or community. A range of behaviors can be addressed with agreed-on assignments, including those that are private (e.g., thoughts) or occur in contexts unavailable to social workers. This role also depends on verbal exchanges and thus relationship skills are also important here. Clients have to remember to carry out tasks and be willing to do them and to share the results. Your support and positive outcomes that result from completing assignments will encourage clients' continued participation. Select assignments that address the clients' concerns and match their skill and comfort levels. Exhibit 18.6 shows important characteristics of assignments. Initial tasks often involve collecting assessment data. Selecting feasible, relevant assignments is a skill that develops with practice. You may have to arrange cues to remind clients to act in new ways and provide incentives to support desired behaviors. Generalization and maintenance are not as problematic as in a ver-

EXHIBIT 18.6
Checklist for Reviewing an Assignment

	Not at all	A Little	Satisfactory	Ideal
1. It addresses outcome(s) of concern to clients.	0	1	2	3
2. It is clearly described.	0	1	2	3
3. There is empirical evidence that if completed, it will contribute to outcome(s) sought.	0	1	2	3
4. Participants value hoped-for consequences.	0	1	2	3
5. Clients understand and accept the reasons for it.	0	1	2	3
6. Participants can accurately describe what is to be done, by whom where, and when.	0	1	2	3
7. Clients can carry it out.	0	1	2	3
8. It focuses on positive behaviors.	0	1	2	3
9. Clients practice tasks before trying them out in real life.	0	1	2	3
10. Real-life opportunities are available to carry it out.	0	1	2	3
11. Needed cues are arranged.	0	1	2	3
12. Needed incentives are arranged.	0	1	2	3
13. Needed tools are provided.	0	1	2	3
14. Possible obstacles are identified and plans made to overcome them.	0	1	2	3
15. Intrusiveness is low.	0	1	2	3
16. It has a high probability of being correctly completed.	0	1	2	3

**This scale can be used in a variety of ways. You could determine the overall score for an assignment. Possible values range from 0 to 39. You could note the percentage of criteria satisfied. You could find the average score for a number of assignments. You could keep track of task completion using the following scale: 0 = not at all, 1 = some, 2 = most, and 3 = all.

bal role, since agreed-on tasks are carried out in real life. You can increase the likelihood of assignment completion by telephoning clients between meetings to "trouble-shoot" and collect data.

Practicing. In this role behaviors of interest, such as offering positive feedback are practiced in simulated environments. Efforts are made to "replicate" real-life conditions. This role may also be used during assessment, as described in Chapter 15. A parent may practice new ways of praising her child. Community members may practice effective ways of introducing issues on community boards. Research suggests that exposure to feared situations is the key contributor to success in cognitive–behavioral programs designed to decrease anxiety and anger (Barlow, 1988). Practice is a step closer to real life than simply talking about events. Skills and comfort levels can be assessed more accurately than with verbal methods alone, and constructive feedback can be offered. New ways of reacting can be practiced in a safe environment. Disadvantages include the possibility that relevant situations may not be selected, behavior may not represent what happens in real life, and generalization may be a problem. Because behaviors are practiced in an artificial setting (the office), arrangements must be made to encourage their use in real life.

Influencing Behavior in Real-Life Contexts. In this role, you enter the natural environment and directly influence behavior. If a parent is not able to follow instructions to act in new ways with her children, you could cue the mother when she is home with her children to use different consequences, such as praise (see for example the classic study by Hawkins, Peterson, Schweid, & Bijou, 1966). You could accompany a client who has difficulty obtaining food stamps to the office and "prompt" effective responses. This role is useful when it is difficult for clients to change their behavior without on-the-spot guidance. Clients can see the effects of new ways of acting, and procedural errors are less likely because an expert trainer is present. The trainer's help should be faded out as clients acquire skills. Disadvantages of this role include cost in time (visiting real-life settings), intrusiveness of the trainer, and need to fade out help to maintain gains under natural conditions.

OFFERING SUPPORT

Offering support is an important aspect of all phases of work with clients. Support is the context in which other kinds of help are offered. Functions of support include reducing stress, restoring hope, and enhancing recognition of resources, both personal and environmental. Normalization of concerns is one aspect of support. Clients learn that their feelings, behaviors, or thoughts or the situations they experience are not odd or pathological but common for many people. Related helper skills include attentive listening, structuring, presenting a helpful model, being concrete and respectful, reinforcing helpful behaviors, and being nonjudgmental, empathetic, warm, and genuine (see Chapter 12). Helping clients understand environmental factors related to problems will decrease tendencies to blame themselves for outcomes over which they have little control. Support will not be enough when clients need material resources such as money, housing, food, clothing, jobs, or health services or do not have the knowledge and required skills to attain valued outcomes.

Lack of resources may leave you with little but support to offer. If clients value this, then your time is well spent. However, keep your eyes open for opportunities to change policies, procedures, and programs that leave you with so little to offer. Pursuing vague objectives may encourage undue reliance on support. When social workers say they are using support to help a client, I ask, "What are the client's goals?" The answer often reveals that more than support is needed (see Exhibit 18.7). Although clients may feel better if support is provided, they may be even more pleased if they also achieve concrete goals.

THINKING CRITICALLY ABOUT PLANS

Sources of error when deciding on plans that may result in choosing ineffective or harmful methods are shown in Exhibit 18.8. Perhaps you have not

EXHIBIT 18.7
Support as a Poor Substitute for Needed Services

Joyce works in a community center offering services to poor families. She has been asked to work with a group of parents to help them with any problems they may have. I asked her what she was working on. Let's take a look at the discussion:

EG: How many times does the group meet?
ST: The group meets for 10 sessions.
EG: What are the group's goals?
ST: To get support. To get help for their concerns.
EG: What are you working on now?
ST: Really nothing specific. My goal is to support and help these parents increase their self-esteem. We let the mothers talk about whatever they want to talk about.
EG: Have they mentioned any problems that concern them?
ST: Yes, they want better relations with the school.
EG: What would be different if they had better relations with the school?
ST: I don't know.
EG: Did they give you any clues?
ST: They want to be treated with respect.
EG: What would be different if they were treated with respect?
ST: They would feel better about themselves and the school.
EG: What changes would help them feel better?
ST: The teachers would involve them in the decisions made about their children. They would ask for their opinions at meetings.
EG: Are they invited now?
ST: No.
EG: Do the teachers ever ask the parents for their opinions? *Note:* The interview progressed in this way with two additional specific changes identified by the parents that would help them "feel respected."
EG: Well, it seems that you do have some specific information about what these parents would like. Do they want to work toward these changes?
ST: I don't know. The group changes from week to week in who comes. I don't really know what they want to work on.
EG: Have they mentioned any other areas?
ST: No, they keep mentioning the school situation.
EG: *Note:* Is this method of working the best that can be done here? Are attentive listening and empathy enough? What do you think?

involved clients in selecting outcomes to focus on and so are trying to pursue outcomes of little or no interest to them. Pursuing vague objectives is a major obstacle because you and your clients are not sure about what you are trying to accomplish and thus have only vague guidelines to follow to discover what might be helpful. You are on a voyage with no clear destination. Overlooking the client's assets may result in selecting unnecessarily intrusive methods and wasting time. Incomplete assessment is a cause of many errors (e.g., overlooking environmental contingencies). Lack of resources and time pressures may limit options. You may want to use methods that have been shown to be effective but not be able to because of agency policy and procedures. The **client uniformity myth,** the belief that plans can be used without regard for

situational and individual differences (Kiesler, 1966) can be avoided by matching client and environmental characteristics and plans. Plans differ in the extent to which they increase skills that are valuable in a range of settings and prevent future problems. They differ in the likelihood of immediate results, their complexity, and in the amount of training required for competent use. You can use the checklist in Exhibit 18.9 to review your plans.

Clearly Describe Plans and the Reasons for Them

Review assessment data and suggested plans with clients, and discuss the relationship between what was discovered and the plans proposed. Be sure to use clear language that clients understand. Clearly

EXHIBIT 18.8
Sources of Error in Deciding on a Plan

- Faulty problem structuring (the problem has not been correctly defined).
- Incomplete assessment.
- Overlooking lack of needed resources.
- Incorrect beliefs about a plan's effectiveness due to reliance on weak criteria such as popularity or tradition.
- Incorrect estimates about a plan's potential effectiveness because of lack of knowledge about problem-related scientific literature or ignoring this knowledge.
- Time pressures that require "shooting from the hip" and create interfering emotional reactions (e.g., anxiety).
- Social pressures (to agree with colleagues).
- Low tolerance for uncertainty/ambiguity.
- Overlooking clients' strengths.
- Overlooking opportunities to rearrange the physical environment.
- A "one-size-fits-all" approach (the same plan is offered to all clients regardless of likely effectiveness).
- Underestimating the knowledge, time, and skill required to implement a plan successfully.
- Trying to do too much.
- Not involving clients and significant others in selecting plans.
- Overlooking cultural differences that influence preferences and success.

describe plans including intermediate steps. Otherwise, it will be difficult (if not impossible) to estimate their feasibility and the possibility of side effects or to implement them in a planned way. The description should provide information needed for informed consent (e.g., description of risks, benefits, possible side effects and alternative methods). The plan should include a clear description of:

- Problem-related objectives, intermediate steps, and a projected timetable for attaining them.

- Who will be involved and how (responsibilities of each participant).

- What situations, prompts, and reinforcers will be used.

- What progress indicators will be used.

- The changes to be made dependent on degree of progress and criteria used to introduce them.

Many plans require a series of steps. For example, changes in what people think may lay the groundwork for changing what they do. Helping clients relabel problems as challenges and accept more realistic expectations provides a "cognitive" framework for acting differently and for viewing these changes positively. A timetable for attaining subgoals provides timely feedback so that you and your clients can change approaches that are not working. Describing the relationship between each component of the plan and each goal will help you to check that you have a plan to meet each objective and protect clients against excessive or insufficient service. Identify those people responsible for carrying out each part of the plan, and make sure they are qualified to do so.

Review agreements about records to be kept (if any) and how progress will be evaluated to make sure expectations are clear. Ask your clients if they have any questions about the plans and the reasons for them. Give them copies of agreed-on tasks so they can refer to them at home as needed. You can highlight important points as reminders. Exhibit 18.10 illustrates a program worksheet used in helping a client. The client wanted to learn to drive a car and then buy one (see item one). The second item concerned career choice. The third concerned both independence and weekend depression resulting from lack of pleasant events on weekends. The fourth addressed loneliness and shyness with women. Plans should be reviewed and updated as needed in accord with degree of progress. This is another way you are accountable to your clients.

Select Plans That Are Acceptable to Participants

A plan may not be feasible because clients and/or significant others do not like it. Agency staff may not like your recommendations for changes in their service programs. An adolescent who wants to meet more people may not want to join a group designed to achieve this outcome. If so, explore other options. Children, their parents, as well as staff in a psychiatric ward, considered reinforcement of incompatible behavior more acceptable, appropriate, fair and reasonable in handling child behavior problems, compared to time out or drug therapy (Kazdin, French & Sherick, 1981). Procedures differ in how much discomfort they en-

EXHIBIT 18.9
Checklist for Reviewing Service Plans*

	Not at All	A Little	Satisfactory	Ideal
1. Assessment data support selection.	0	1	2	3
2. Problem-related circumstances are addressed.	0	1	2	3
3. Requisites can be provided.	0	1	2	3
4. Plans and the rationale for them are acceptable to participants.	0	1	2	3
5. Plans are clearly described, including intermediate steps.	0	1	2	3
6. Positive methods are used.	0	1	2	3
7. Plans allow for the incremental acquisition of skills in accord with baseline levels.	0	1	2	3
8. Plans are not too intrusive.	0	1	2	3
9. Plans are efficient in cost, time, and effort.	0	1	2	3
10. Plans selected offer the greatest likelihood of success.[a]	0	1	2	3
11. Positive side effects are likely.	0	1	2	3
12. Negative side effects are unlikely.	0	1	2	3
13. Significant others are involved.	0	1	2	3
14. Cues and reinforcers for desired behaviors are arranged.	0	1	2	3
15. Cues and reinforcers for undesired behaviors are removed.	0	1	2	3
16. Plans encourage generalization of valued outcomes.	0	1	2	3
17. Settings used maximizes the likelihood of success.	0	1	2	3
18. Cultural differences are considered.	0	1	2	3
19. Multiple services are well integrated.	0	1	2	3
20. A written description of plans is given to participants.	0	1	2	3
21. Plans meet legal regulations and ethical standards.	0	1	2	3
22. The probability of success is high	0	1	2	3

Reviewing Plans That You Do Not Think Will Be Effective

Total score can range from 0 to 66. If this is low, or you rate the probability of success low (item 22), review the following questions:

Is there anything more you could do?   _____ Yes   _____ No
If no is this because
_____ I don't know how to offer effective methods.
_____ I know how but don't have the time.
_____ Needed resources are unavailable.
_____ Agency policies pose an obstacle.
_____ Client is unwilling.
_____ There is no practice-related research that provides guidelines about what to do.
_____ Other.
If yes, what could you do? (Describe):

_____

_____

_____

*Questions to review when answering item 10:
• There is scientific evidence that your plan will achieve outcomes focused on.
• There are empirically based principles that suggest that the plan will be effective with this client.
• There is scientific evidence that this plan is likely to be more effective than other plans.

tail. What is comfortable varies from person to person. Describing plans in a way that compliments the beliefs and values of clients and significant others will increase their appeal. For example, Mrs.

Slater presented the suggestion to include Mrs. Ryan in meetings in a framework her clients valued; they were a family and families work together to resolve concerns.

EXHIBIT 18.10
Program Worksheet: Robert Jones, June 28

Available Assets	Intermediate Steps
1. Passed written test for driver's license.	1. Pay tuition at auto school. Take at least *one* lesson.
2. Received catalogues from art school.	2. Discuss with professors X and Y about next steps.
3. Spent last Sunday in Loop.	3. Plan and carry out activity for Saturday and Sunday in downtown Chicago (or Hyde Park).
4. Had coffee with Jean two times.	4. Ask Jean to lunch.

Program Notes
1. A great step forward toward eventual "independence."
2. Career choice.
3. Break the weekend "depression," also tied to "independence."
4. A step toward decreasing loneliness.

Source: A. Schwartz & I. Goldiamond (1975), Social casework: A behavioral approach *(p. 120). New York: Columbia University Press.*

Select Plans That Are Effective and Efficient

Research by O'Donahue and his colleagues suggests that clients want their helpers to select methods based on past successful personal experience and research. As they note, personal experience is important "because even therapies that are in principle effective can become ineffective when incompetently delivered" (1989, p. 403). However, basing decisions solely on experience may result in incorrect estimates of effectiveness (see Chapter 4). Although research about the comparative effectiveness of different methods is often unavailable, research is available in many areas indicating the greater success of some methods than others (see for example, Barlow, 1988; Patterson, Dishion, & Chamberlain, 1993; Hibbs & Jensen, 1996; Kazdin, 1991).

Not much is known about the efficiency of many methods in relation to cost and time. However, data are available in some areas. When possible, offer clients the choice of efficient programs that have a track record of success (see the later discussion of ethical concerns). Arrange environments that enhance functional skills and resolve problems (See Favell & McGimsey, 1993). Avoid complex methods when simpler, less costly ones (in time, effort, or money) will be effective. Offering permission may be all that is required. For example, a client's reluctance to accept needed financial assistance may be overcome by pointing out that this is a right, not a handout. Worries about being "abnormal" because of some behavior, thought, or feeling can be dampened by normalizing behaviors. A socially anxious client may not realize that most people are shy in some situations and that most people sometimes worry about being rejected. Estimate the likely success of a plan in helping clients attain outcomes they value (10%, 90%). If this is low, is another plan more likely to succeed (see Exhibit 18.11).

Select Feasible Plans

How feasible are proposed plans? Can they be carried out in ways that maximize success, or is only some diluted version possible? Review personal and environmental resources and constraints to evaluate feasibility.

- Are needed material resources available?
- Can eligibility requirements be met?
- What helpful contexts and services are available?

EXHIBIT 18.11
Estimated Impact of Plans

+3	*Maximal:*	Clients receive valued services at levels that maximize the likelihood of success with minimal or no negative side effects.
+2	*Moderate*	Partially addresses concerns.
+1	*Minimal:*	Band-Aid services offered on crisis basis only. More intensive or varied services are needed to help clients attain outcomes they value.
0	*No Effect:*	No change
−1	*Slight Harm:*	Minimal negative effects
−2	*Moderate Harm:*	Moderate harmful effects
−3	*Significant Harm:*	For example, client is stigmatized as being mentally ill or is forced to take medications that have long-term negative side-effects.

- Can significant others (e.g., parents, teachers) be consistent mediators?
- Do participants have the skills required to carry out the plans?
- Do significant others have access to effective reinforcers?
- Can significant others be created?
- Can needed resources be created?
- Do helpers have needed skills?

Are those who will be responsible for offering services competent to do so? How do you know? Recent research shows that competence in applying a method does not necessarily reflect competence to teach others (e.g., parents) (McGimsey, Greene, & Lutzker, 1995). Consultation skills are required to teach others successfully such as providing a rationale for methods used, demonstrating the steps while describing them, arranging role plays of each step, providing verbal praise for efforts, accurately describing errors and desired behaviors, and repeating the process of describing, modeling, and role playing as needed (see Chapter 21). Can clients be their own managers of change? Which of their skills can be used to advantage? Do they have any physical conditions that limit the use of certain plans? You can use role playing to find out whether clients have needed skills. If skills are not available, you will have to help clients acquire them or choose other plans. What can be used as reinforcers? Review possible intervention settings (e.g., home, school, work). Perhaps a group would be best. Your list of possible plans will usually be shortened when you consider the requisites for each and the resources available. Current service patterns may limit options. You may have to redefine the problem from helping clients attain needed resources to helping them to bear up under the strain of not having them or involve clients with similar concerns in social action efforts (see Chapter 24).

Select the Least Restrictive Plan

Restrictiveness is a legal, ethical, and practical concern. It is a practical concern because the more that circumstances during intervention differ from those in real life, the more effort will be required to generalize and maintain gains in the natural environment (see Chapter 20). Restrictiveness is an ethical and legal concern because the more intrusive a procedure is, the more it affects people's lives. Many state laws require demonstration that positive procedures were tried and failed before punishment-based methods can be used. Proce-dures involving punishment are more intrusive than those that rely on positive reinforcement. They create negative emotional reactions and, unless combined with other procedures, do not encourage alternative desired reactions.

Intrusiveness may involve irreversibility of effects, the extent to which program effects can be voluntarily resisted, or duration of change efforts. Plans that remove people from real-life environments (institutionalizing them or placing them in foster care) are more intrusive than those that do not. It is less intrusive to work with a child and his parents in the home than to move him to a community halfway house and the latter is less intrusive than placing him in an institution. Avoid offering incentives that undermine natural reinforcing systems. Be sure to encourage clients and/or their significant others to consider the long-term consequences of not using an intrusive method in the short term. For example, not doing so may result in outcomes that require the ongoing institutionalization of an individual (e.g., Goldiamond, 1984). The items suggested by Axelrod and his colleagues (1993) for review when considering a plan's restrictiveness include the following:

- The urgency with which the behavior must be changed.
- The speed with which the procedure works.
- The likely side effects of the procedure, a prediction of which should be based on the individual's past history and the history of the procedure and behavior with other people.
- The amount of embarrassment, deprivation, or discomfort the procedure causes.
- The likelihood that the procedure can be applied correctly in normalized environments.
- The social acceptability of the procedure.

- The potential for harm to the individual and program implementers when applying the procedure.

- The degree to which the procedure removes the individual from educational, social, and vocational opportunities.

Axelrod and his colleagues argue that

> in the case of dangerous behaviors, people are entitled to the least restrictive effective treatment from the outset. People should not be exposed to a hierarchy of treatments that are likely to be ineffective when there are treatments available that are likely to be effective. A hierarchical decision-making model stating that a number of "nonrestrictive" procedures be used first fails to hit the target, because it implies that there is nothing wrong with several failures before an effective procedure is identified. This does not make sense in cases of serious self-abuse and aggression. There is an urgency to eliminating some problems, therefore, finding effective procedure from the outset is crucial. (1993, pp. 189–190)

Select Plans That Are Likely to Have Positive Side Effects and Avoid Negative Side Effects

What positive side effects are likely? Are any negative side effects likely? A positive change in some behaviors may lead to both positive and negative changes in other behaviors. Encouraging assertive behavior of staff may result in punishing consequences at work from supervisors and administrators. Carefully consider both short- and long-term potential side effects. A decrease in an annoying behavior (e.g., bedwetting) usually increases positive reactions on the part of significant others such as parents. Positive changes in the behavior of siblings have been found in programs in which parents acquire more effective child-management skills with one of their children (Arnold, Levine, & Patterson, 1975).

Rely on Positive Methods

Use positive methods (e.g., positive reinforcement and prompting) when possible (see Chapter 22). Usually, the most effective way to decrease undesirable behaviors is to increase desired alternatives.

Punishing behavior does not necessarily increase any other particular behavior. Other disadvantages include modeling aggressive behavior, creating anger and anxiety, and avoiding the "punisher" (e.g., teachers or parents) (see also Chapter 8).

Avoid Harmful Plans, Programs, and Policies

Professionals often assume that they must do something. The ethical obligation to do no harm requires balancing the risks and benefits of doing something against the risks and benefits of doing nothing. Offering ineffective methods may increase client demoralization or may raise false hopes that change will be easy. Improving students' school performance, for example, may require restructuring the entire school system, with heavy involvement from parents and other local residents. Examples of service plans are illustrated in Exhibit 18.12.

IMPLEMENTING PLANS AND PROGRAMS AND TRYING AGAIN

The best-laid plans may go awry, and you may have to try again (see Exhibit 18.13). Obstacles may continue to get in the way, or new ones may be revealed. Significant others or clients may not complete agreed-on tasks; agencies may not offer services; emergencies may arise. Initial plans are a best guess as to what will work. Often they will have to be altered. Success in earlier stages influences success in later ones. The more carefully you consider procedural requirements, clients' preferences, resources, and obstacles, the more likely it is that plans will succeed. Clients won't carry out agreements that they don't want to complete or don't know how to complete.

You may have to offer more prompts and incentives for desired behaviors, remove competing contingencies, and provide additional opportunities to use valued skills or simplify procedures. You may have to involve other change agents or settings. Perhaps you have not involved all significant others (e.g., supervisors, staff on all shifts who work with residents) or arranged regular reviews of progress. If a teacher refuses to participate, parents

18.12 CASE EXAMPLES
Case Example 1: Brian and His Parents

Brian's social worker, Mr. Colvine, considered different plans as he and the Lakelands gathered assessment data. He made sure to hold initial assumptions tentatively. He knew that it was important to select a plan that would yield some benefits fairly rapidly, since the Lakeland family's relationships were strained. Although the parents had not mentioned removing Brian from their home, they seemed likely to do so, especially after a bad day. Brian was very unhappy with his life at home and at school. The family showed some of the effects of receiving little help in the past: they were discouraged, weary, and leery of the possibility of improvement. But they were willing to make another attempt. Any plan selected would have to fit the parents' busy schedule. Mr. Colvine's review of possible plans was influenced by his knowledge of methods that had been effective with similar families. He was familiar with research showing that simply talking about new ways of acting was usually not enough to alter a family's interactions. He suggested a point program and negotiation training. After three assessment sessions, one of which took place in the Lakeland Home, Mr. Colvine and the Lakelands had 13 more meetings.

POINT PROGRAM

A point or token program is a motivational system for altering behavior. Points or tokens are awarded for behaviors to be increased. A loss of tokens may also be agreed on for undesired behaviors. Bonuses may be included as a special reward for high levels of positive behavior. Points are exchanged for backup reinforcers. They are gradually faded out as natural reinforcers, such as praise, take effect. Token and point programs have been used in many contexts, including the classroom, the home, day care facilities, and residential settings (Kazdin, 1988). They are useful when

- Few naturally occurring reinforcers are available.
- Reinforcers are available, but it is doubtful that they will be applied consistently in an unambiguous form.
- It is difficult to arrange for the immediate presentation of reinforcers.
- Establishing some consequence (e.g., parental approval) as a reinforcer is a goal.
- Significant others must be "prompted" to reinforce desired behaviors.

Since points can be exchanged for a variety of reinforcers, their effectiveness is independent of any specific deprivation. In addition, points provide a visible record of achievement. Although natural reinforcers, such as social approval, were available in the Lakelands' home, it was unlikely that they would be used consistently and likely that any approval would be mixed with criticism. It was not possible to immediately reinforce all behaviors due to the different schedules of Brian and his parents and because some backup reinforcers (e.g., going fishing with his father), could occur only on days when Mr. Lakeland did not have to work. The point program was completed at the third meeting and was carried out over the following 6 weeks. Sessions 4 through 12 included discussion of the point program, readjustment as necessary, and fading of this.

A reinforcer menu was created that identified reinforcers and their point values. Some items selected as reinforcers could be earned daily, such as money (up to $5 each week), a special dessert, and 30 minutes of help from his brother Bob on his homework. Others could be earned less frequently because they were more costly (e.g., a fishing trip with his father and being driven around by Mr. Lakeland to collect paper-route money). The agreement of all involved parties was obtained before any item was included. For example, Bob agreed to help Brian with his homework. Mr. Colvine made a chart listing behaviors down the left-hand side and days across the top. Behaviors included straighten room, take out the garbage, cut the grass, speak politely to parents, take medication three times a day, inform his parents before going out, and play nicely with dog. Points were also awarded for improvement in grades. The reinforcer menu, definitions of behaviors, and the point values of each behavior or behavior product, such as grades were listed on the chart. A copy of the chart was given to Brian and to his parents, and they were asked to note, with a check mark, each behavior performed. They were urged to avoid criticism, and Mr. and Mrs. Lakeland were reminded to praise Brian for desired behaviors and to ignore behaviors such as Brian's teasing his sister. During the interview, they practiced offering praise, taking care to identify statements that both Brian and his parents considered positive.

All participants should be involved in the design of point or token programs, to ensure the relevance of behaviors and reinforcers selected. Their involvement also serves an educational function, since they gain practice in clearly describing behaviors and in balancing responsibilities and costs, and increase their understanding of what other family members value. Programs should be adjusted to reflect the client's progress. For example, as desired behaviors increase and stabilize, points for them can be faded out and new ones added. Initial requirements are set at or just slightly above baseline levels so that they can be readily achieved and so reinforced. When these are met, next steps are required until desired outcomes are attained. In the Lakeland family, point values had to be adjusted when they disagreed about them. A major problem was reminding Mr. and Mrs. Lakeland not to criticize Brian but, rather, to praise him for desired behaviors. One function of the point program was to accomplish this change. A second concern was supporting family members until they could see some progress. Mr. Colvine telephoned them every other day to check how the point program was progressing, to find out how many points had been earned, to offer support, and to discuss any problems with the program. By asking for data, he could find out whether the Lakelands were carrying out the program. These calls lasted about 15 minutes. (Calls can be kept brief by agreeing beforehand on their purpose.)

NEGOTIATION TRAINING

Mr. Colvine involved his clients in negotiation training during sessions 4 through 7, for 40 minutes. The purpose of negotiation training is to enhance the clients' skills in resolving conflicts, such as suggesting options, identifying issues, and offering complete communications, and to minimize behaviors that discourage helpful discussions, such as countercomplaining and interrupting (Patterson & Forgatch, 1989). **Complete communications** are statements that indicate a position regarding a topic (what you think or want) and include a request for the other person to state or respond to a position. An example is "I want to spend

(continued)

18.12 CASE EXAMPLES (*continued*)

my summer-job money on a bike. Is that OK with you?" (Kifer, Lewis, Green, & Phillips, 1974, p. 359). **Identification of issues** refers to "statements that identify the point of conflict in a discussion. Such statements may contrast two opposing positions, clarify a position, or identify what someone thinks a conflict is about. An example is 'You want me to buy clothes, but I want to buy a bike' " (p. 359). **Suggestion of options** refers to "statements that suggest a course of action to resolve a conflict, but not merely statements of an original position. An example is 'How about if I spend some on clothes and use the rest to buy a bike if you'll help pay for it?' " (pp. 359–360).

Brian and his parents were asked to identify troublesome situations. Brian chose not having a desk of his own, and his parents chose "his being mean to the dog." These were positively rephrased as having a desk of his own and playing nicely with the dog (lightly stroking the dog and refraining from tail pulling and rough pulling or pushing). The first 5-minute role play was used to identify specific behaviors to increase conflict resolution skills (i.e., for assessment). This showed that Brian and his parents made many statements of blame and hopelessness and did not suggest options or compromises, solicit opinions, or check to see whether others understood their position.

Specific behaviors to increase and decrease were identified and the rationale for altering them was described. Mr. Colvine played an audiotape for the clients that offered a model of a teenager and his parents discussing issues in a constructive manner. The Lakelands then practiced more effective behaviors. Three behaviors (complete communications, statement of issues, and suggestions of options) were focused on. Mr. Colvine offered constructive feedback after each role play. Family members gradually assumed more responsibility for noting helpful behaviors, offering support, and identifying desired changes. Their "homework" assignments were to carry out the point program and practice their negotiation skills twice a week at a prearranged time. Mr. Colvine lent them a tape recorder and asked them to record their practice sessions and to bring in the tapes so he could review them.

COLLATERAL CONTACTS

Mr. Colvine contacted the school counselor—with Brian's and his parents' permission—to discuss how he might help improve Brian's grades and make life more pleasant for Brian at school. The counselor agreed that Brian's math teacher did not like him but felt that the teacher was justified, although he could not give any reasons to support his belief. The counselor was critical of Brian and seemed wedded to the belief that epilepsy caused behavior problems and that little could be done to improve the situation. He foresaw a dismal future for Brian and doubted whether he would complete high school. Mr. Colvine did not think that it would be of any use to challenge these negative views. Instead, he described positive changes that had taken place and asked if he could talk with him again later.

This example illustrates that some of your most frustrating contacts will not be with clients but with other professionals. Not all professionals are professional in the sense of being well informed and knowledgeable about how to help clients. It is not helpful to "bad-mouth" clients, as Brian's counselor did. This discourages a search for and support of client assets. As with clients, it will be of little value to tell these people what you think is correct in a confrontative fashion. Rather, emphasize shared goals, and provide data that support your arguments (e.g., data showing progress).

Mr. Colvine also contacted Brian's doctor to find out what she thought about changing Brian's medication level, since Brian had complained of drowsiness. This time Mr. Colvine did meet a professional. The doctor reviewed Brian's medical chart and concluded that it would be a good idea to lower the dosage, and she said she would have her secretary telephone the family and tell them about the change.

OFFERING SUPPORT

Mr. Colvine offered sustained optimism that the Lakelands could achieve their goals if they carried out the program. He praised them for completing agreed-on tasks and for the progress they made, and he helped make this progress visible. He was an attentive listener and created an atmosphere in which his clients felt accepted and respected. He helped Brian and his parents discover strengths in their family, such as their love for one another, the Lakelands' wish to be good parents, and the skills they already had. This was important in decreasing their belief that they were "bad parents" who had a "bad kid."

OFFERING INFORMATION

Mr. Colvine provided normative data concerning conflict between parents and their children, pointing out that this was the norm rather than the exception. The Lakelands learned how to describe their problems more clearly and learned a useful problem-solving process.

Case Example 2: Julie

Outcomes of concern to Julie included deciding what to do about her unplanned pregnancy, learning more effective decision-making methods, increasing control over worrisome thoughts, becoming informed about birth-control methods, and acquiring and using effective refusal skills. Ms. Landis (the social worker) and Julie saw each other four times before she had an abortion and four times afterward. As with many decisions, time limited how long Julie could consider alternatives. Julie vacillated among options, all of which seemed unsatisfactory. She seemed to believe that a solution would magically reveal itself. Ms. Landis drew on guidelines available to help people make difficult decisions. These encourage the counselor to refrain from giving advice about which alternative to select and avoid suggesting that certain choices are good or bad but, instead, to help clients use their own resources to select an optimizing decision compatible with their values (Janis & Mann, 1977, p. 368; Wheeler & Janis, 1980). Helpful questions are, What steps have I taken so far to make a decision? Have I considered both the negative and the positive consequences of each option?

A client may believe that a decision must be made when it may not have to be. For example, an imagined slight may be exaggerated in importance (rather than ignored), creating unnecessary worry about whether to confront the "slighter"

(*continued*)

18.12 CASE EXAMPLES (*continued*)

about this. Julie had to make a decision. Not making a decision was in itself a decision. Ms. Landis used her relationship skills (e.g., empathy) to encourage Julie to share information and to discourage her from misrepresenting situations because of a desire to please her, to avoid anxiety (and use platitudes to hide conflicts), or to justify her actions with rationalizations (Janis & Mann, 1977, p. 370). Honest statements can be encouraged by avoiding value judgments about what should be done. Ms. Landis suggested where to go for information and provided a way to consider alternatives.

Thoughtful decision making involves a number of steps (Janis & Mann, 1977; Wheeler & Janis, 1980):

- Clarifying the decision to be made.
- Reviewing options (choices).
- Weighing the advantages and disadvantages of each (considering consequences).
- Choosing the alternative with the most benefits and the least cost.
- Implementing the decision.
- Enhancing commitment.
- Evaluating the outcome.

Beliefs that are helpful to explore are the following: Does the client believe that the risks of taking (or not taking) a course of action are serious? If Julie continued to put off making a decision, having an abortion would no longer be an option. Does the client believe that there is a satisfactory alternative? Julie did not. Such disbelief may lead to avoidance, as it did with Julie. Does the client believe that there is enough time to search for and review information and advice?

When thinking about problems, people often do not identify choices and review consequences and/or take time to gather, and review information that can aid this process, and they may not use the decision-making skills they use in other contexts. A first step in helping clients make a decision is to identify possible alternatives. Brainstorming may be useful at this point (listing alternatives without considering whether they are realistic). In this way, you are less likely to overlook options. Julie listed three alternatives: (1) having an abortion, (2) having her baby and giving it up for adoption, and (3) having her baby and taking care of it herself. She had not identified potential gains and losses associated with each alternative.

Ms. Landis suggested that Julie write down each alternative on a separate sheet of paper and list the possible consequences, including tangible gains or losses and anticipated approval or disapproval, from both herself and significant others. Like the choice of alternatives, gains and losses are a personal matter. In the daily log that Julie kept for a week, she suggested factors to consider in making her decision. She wanted to be a nurse. Having a baby might mean that she would have to drop out of school to take care of it. Noting potential gains and losses related to each alternative is helpful and may reveal overlooked consequences. Julie discovered that she had not considered her boyfriend's reactions. They had been going together for a year, and she wanted to continue to see him and believed that if he found out about her pregnancy, he would still want to see her. Now, however, she realized, for the first time, that he might not want to have anything to do with her. Overlooking the losses associated with a chosen alternative increases the client's vulnerability to negative feedback after decisions are acted on (Janis & Mann, 1977, p. 378). Julie thought that having an abortion might interfere with having children in the future, and she felt guilty about not involving her parents but knew that they would be furious if they found out. Here, too, Julie had overlooked some points—that excluding her parents may make her feel more distant from them.

After listing the pros and cons of each alternative, Ms. Landis helped Julie weigh her options. Julie decided to have an abortion and not tell her boyfriend or parents. Ms. Landis helped Julie put her decision into effect and prepared her to stick with her decision despite negative feedback. The methods suggested by Janis and Mann (1977) for bolstering commitment to a course of action include exaggerating favorable feedback and minimizing unfavorable consequences. Clients can be prepared for setbacks by making sure they consider the possible risks and losses beforehand and by helping them acquire reassurance skills (e.g., reminding themselves that they carefully considered alternatives). Ms. Landis gave Julie a written copy of the steps involved in making a decision so she could refer to it when making other decisions.

OFFERING INFORMATION

Julie was not well informed about birth-control methods. Ms. Landis described various methods and their advantages and disadvantages. Julie decided on a diaphragm, and Mrs. Landis arranged for her to see a doctor.

INCREASING ASSERTIVE BEHAVIOR

Julie had difficulty refusing her boyfriend's advances. She did not know what to say to him and was afraid of making him angry. She wanted to learn alternative methods for handling this kind of situation. Ms. Landis encouraged Julie to explore her right to say no and identified beliefs related to her reluctance to express her feelings. She then modeled alternative ways to refuse unwanted requests, and they role-played them.

CONTROLLING WORRISOME THOUGHTS

Ms. Landis helped Julie learn how to catch worrisome thoughts and to replace them with constructive thoughts or activities. She wrote down her instructions so that Julie could refer to them as needed. Weekly assignments gave her opportunities to practice her new skills.

OTHER INTERVENTION PROCEDURES

Ms. Landis was supportive by being an attentive and nonjudgmental listener, offering Julie hope that she could resolve her concerns, respecting her, helping her discover her assets, celebrating her successes, and helping her evaluate her progress.

(*continued*)

18.12 CASE EXAMPLES (*continued*)
Case Example 3: Mrs. Ryan and the Greens

One important decision that social workers make is whom to involve in assessment and intervention. Mr. and Mrs. Green originally contacted Mrs. Slater about their concern with Mrs. Ryan. Mrs. Slater urged the Greens to include Mrs. Ryan in their work together, for both practical and ethical reasons. She pointed out that Mrs. Ryan also was dissatisfied with her living situation and that it was only fair to include her in planning for her own future. Mrs. Slater emphasized that decision making is a process and noted that the changes the Greens desired were related to the very decision they were trying to make. She suggested the intermediate goal of pursuing desired changes in their family life, and this was acceptable to the Greens. They felt relieved that they would no longer be discussing Mrs. Ryan "behind her back." The Greens then spent some time discussing with Mrs. Slater how they could encourage Mrs. Ryan to participate.

The second interview was with both the Greens and Mrs. Ryan, in which Mrs. Ryan spelled out specific changes that she would like. Then Mrs. Slater visited their home after dinner one night. This visit was followed by eight more meetings, some of which were outside the agency, for example, at the senior center. Mrs. Slater telephoned the Greens to collect information concerning progress and to offer support.

DECREASING BOREDOM AND DEPRESSION

Objectives related to this goal included increasing contacts with other people, taking more walks, writing more letters, doing more household chores, and having more enjoyable conversations with family members.

Increasing Social Contacts. Mrs. Slater had determined (based on Mrs. Ryan's past history, her verbal reports, and from observation) that Mrs. Ryan did have skills to make new acquaintances (she could, for example, initiate and maintain enjoyable conversations) and that she enjoyed social contacts. On the rare occasions that she attended social gatherings (twice a year), it "made her week." She would talk cheerfully about the coming event for days beforehand, reported that she had a splendid time afterward, and complained in between about how seldom these events occurred. Incentives used to gradually introduce Mrs. Ryan to a local senior center included support from Mrs. Slater and from family members, as well as the natural consequences of enjoyable social contacts.

Taking More Walks. Mrs. Ryan took one walk a week for about 10 minutes, but she said that she would like to get out every day and that her doctor had recommended she exercise daily. She agreed to take a daily walk in the late afternoon right before dinner. A chart to record her walks was used as a reminder and to offer feedback on progress. Mrs. Ryan posted the chart on the wall in her room.

Writing Letters. Mrs. Ryan used to be a prolific letter writer, but over the past 2 years, her letters had dwindled to about one a week. She set a goal of six letters a week. Intermediate steps were, first, two letters a week, then three a week, and so on. She used the same chart (see above) to record the number of letters she wrote.

Household Chores. Three chores that Mrs. Ryan could help with were identified. The Greens would not agree to vacuuming, since her doctor had said that this was too strenuous.

Increasing Enjoyable Conversations with Family Members. When Mrs. Slater visited the family, she noticed that Mrs. Ryan tended to tell long, involved stories about the past and did not ask the children anything about their lives. Mrs. Ryan agreed to ask the children more often about their interests: what happened at school and so forth. Only Mrs. Ryan seemed to enjoy talking about current events, so she agreed to talk about them with her contacts at the senior center and to join a group that discussed current events.

INCREASING FREE TIME FOR THE GREENS

Mr. and Mrs. Green rarely went out because Mrs. Green felt that either she or her husband should be home in case anything happened to Mrs. Ryan. They and Mrs. Slater explored the need for this, and Mrs. Green agreed that she was overly concerned and that as long as someone was home, she would consider having a night out with her husband once every 2 weeks.

SHARING FEELINGS

Family members either did not request changes they would like or they shared their feelings in a negative, critical manner. Mrs. Slater identified specific changes that would be helpful based on her observation of their interaction and on their own reports. One objective was to increase their use of "I" statements. For example, Mrs. Ryan could say, "I'd like to do more chores around the house." Mrs. Ryan had made such requests in the past, but when Mr. and Mrs. Green criticized her (telling her why she shouldn't do more chores), she no longer shared her desires. They would tell her why she shouldn't have more chores; that is, defend their position. Mrs. Slater suggested that they first let Mrs. Ryan know that they heard what she said and understood how she felt. Mrs. Slater offered examples of empathic statements they could make. Although the Greens did not want to practice making such statements in the office, they did agree to try to use them at home, to listen to an audiotape illustrating expression of feelings, and to read selected portions of *Talking It Out* (Strayhorn, 1977).

GAINING INFORMATION

Mrs. Slater referred Mrs. Green to an agency where she could get information about Medicare. The Greens also wanted information about aging. Mrs. Slater suggested two sources, a support group for couples living with older relatives and some reading material. They were not interested in joining the group but did want to read something, so Mrs. Slater recommended a book. This information was valuable to the Greens in a variety of ways: They felt guilty when Mrs. Ryan spoke about being old and useless; they took these comments personally rather than recognizing that many older people have such thoughts and feelings. They acknowledged that they themselves were threatened by Mrs. Ryan's greater closeness to death, as it reminded them of their own mortality. The children's bids for independence got in their way of viewing Mrs. Ryan as a person in her own right

(continued)

18.12 CASE EXAMPLES (*continued*)

rather than an "old fogy" whom they did love but who tried to bind them to disliked rules and customs.

OTHER METHODS

Mrs. Slater offered support in a variety of ways, one of which was validating each person's point of view. Remember, you don't have to agree with someone's point of view to empathize with it. Mrs. Slater also involved all the family members. Weekly assignments and arrangements for feedback concerning progress were additional components of the intervention.

---

could offer backup reinforcers at home. On-going evaluation of progress will help you and your clients make "timely" decisions. If plans succeed, they can be continued or next steps implemented. If progress is nil or limited, or negative effects are found, explore related reasons (see Chapter 19).

Mutual Responsibilities

The responsibilities of clients and significant others include participating in agreed-on plans and reporting any difficulties (Pinkston, Levitt, Green, Linsk, & Rzepnicki, 1982). If possible, clients should also collect information about progress. Each client's responsibilities must be tailored to his or her values, knowledge, and skills, as well as available resources. Your responsibilities are to

• Select plans that are likely to help clients achieve outcomes they value.

EXHIBIT 18.13
What Can Go Wrong: Everything and Anything

• *Clients do not carry out agreed-on assignments* (explore why—review Chapter 11).
• *Agencies do not offer services sought.* Find out why. What is the source of the problem? (e.g., how the client approached staff, cumbersome application procedures, burned-out staff). Maybe your book of services is out-of-date. You may have referred a client to an agency that no longer offers that service.
• *Services are not available.* Perhaps you can create resources, like self-help groups, community advocacy groups.
• *Emergencies arise that must be addressed.*

• Ensure that clients have the knowledge and skills required to carry out plans.
• Arrange needed prompts and incentives.
• Arrange opportunities for desired behaviors to occur.
• Offer service methods in a way that maximizes the likelihood of success.
• Identify and remove obstacles when possible.
• Arrange on-going feedback about progress.
• Arrange for the generalization and maintenance of gains.
• Modify plans as necessary (try again).

If you are a case manager and other professionals are providing services, they will be responsible for these tasks. However, as a case manager, you should review the soundness of plans and progress.

Increasing the Likelihood of Success

Guidelines for encouraging participation are given in Chapter 11. Clients are more likely to participate in helpful ways if they have been involved in all decision-making steps, if you focus on outcomes they value, and if they understand and agree with the rationales for plans. In his cognitive–behavioral program for depression, David Burns (1995) asks clients to complete a self-help questionnaire before the first interview, in which clients indicate whether they are willing to complete each week three brief questionnaires regarding anxiety, depression, and helper empathy and whether they are willing to carry out agreed-on tasks in real life. Most clients agree. Burns uses the weekly scores to review his clients' progress and to catch discrepancies between how his clients look (great) and what they are feeling (e.g., suicidal). If you believe (as Burns does) that this information is essential to helping, then you should ask for it. Progress may be hampered by a lack of match in problem-solving approaches, by choosing tasks that are too difficult, and by not describing the relevance of tasks to valued outcomes.

Arrange Prompts and Opportunities to Use Valued Skills. Prompts (reminders) may be needed to encourage new behaviors. For instance, Ms. Landis suggested that Julie wear a special bracelet or ring to remind her to redirect her attention from worrisome thoughts to constructive tasks or thoughts. Tokens or points can be used to remind significant others to attend to desired behaviors, and timing devices and recording forms can be used as prompts. Parents' attendance at training sessions increased from 17 to 77% when they were telephoned 2 days in advance of the meeting to remind them of the session (Ayllon & Roberts, 1975). Clearly describing tasks increases the likelihood that they will be carried out as planned. Collecting information by phone may remind clients to complete assignments (knowing that you will call at a certain time to collect information may remind clients of agreed-on tasks). These calls also provide an opportunity to support clients for their efforts and to catch problems at an early point. Desired behaviors will not occur if there are no opportunities to use them. Be sure to arrange access to situations in which valued skills can be put to good use. For example, you may help a client who wishes to make more friends to select promising situations in which to initiate conversations.

Arrange Supporting Contingencies. Special contingencies may be required to involve clients. Reinforcers should be individually selected in accord with incentives that are meaningful to each participant. Reinforcers are relative; what is reinforcing to some people is not to others. Parenting salaries reduced drop-out among low income single-

parent families (Fleischman, 1979). Paying a deposit equal to the total program fee at the beginning of intervention resulted in a higher rate of attendance and assignment completion by parents (Eyberg & Johnson, 1974). Portions of the fee were refunded contingent on attendance and task completion. A promise to work on a problem of concern in another setting, such as school, may be made contingent on progress in altering behavior at home.

Try to minimize any negative consequences associated with participation. You may have to enhance clients' anxiety-management skills or select assignments that are less stress provoking. Lack of participation may be related to negative reactions from significant others. Be sure to consider the effects of plans on significant others as well as clients. If both clients and significant others value the goals being pursued, believe that agreed-on plans will work, have the skills and comfort levels required to complete tasks, have access to opportunities to use skills as well as prompts and incentives to do so, agreed on tasks are likely to be completed. They are more likely to be completed if environmental stressors are muted (e.g., worries about money, child care, medical care). If participation is a problem, explore possible reasons why (see Chapter 11).

Pay Attention to the Integrity of Plans. Research describing effective plans offers guidelines about how to maximize the likelihood of positive outcomes. Consult problem related treatment manuals for help (e.g., Barlow, 1993; Carr et al., 1994; LeCroy, 1994; Koegel, Koegel, & Dunlap 1996; VanHasselt & Hersen, 1996). In addition, you could provide a manual for clients (see for example, Greenberger & Padesky, 1995; Patterson, 1975). If a plan is not implemented correctly it is not suprising if little or no progress occurs. If clients keep records, review them to see what they did and what resulted. Ineffective implementation is a major cause of failure. Case records may offer information about the fidelity of methods used and progress made. Reviewing what was done when there is little or no progress may reveal what went wrong.

Track Progress. Tracking progress allows you and your clients to make timely changes and also provides motivating feedback. Clients are more likely to collect information about progress if they understand its value; have the required knowledge, skills, and tools to do so; and use unintrusive methods. Be sure to (1) explain the purpose of evaluating progress, (2) select indicators that are meaningful to clients, (3) provide needed skills and tools, and (4) encourage clients to report any difficulties. If clients don't keep agreed-on records, it may be because you did not explain their purpose and did not choose an easy recording method.

ETHICAL ISSUES IN SELECTING PLANS

Ethical concerns to consider when selecting plans include the following:

1. Clients are fully informed about the track record of different methods for attaining outcomes they value.
2. Clients help select plans.
3. The scientific literature suggests plans agreed on will result in valued outcomes.
4. Clients and significant others agree with their selection.
5. Plans do not harm clients or significant others.
6. Plans increase knowledge and skills that will help clients enhance the current and future quality of their lives.
7. They are the least restrictive possible (e.g., they maximize the clients' integration in real-life contexts).
8. You and your clients can implement the plans in a way that maximizes the likelihood of success.

Empowering interventions include action-oriented, community-based practice in which residents learn how to help themselves (e.g., form coalitions and self-help groups).

Allocating Scarce Resources

You may not have enough resources to help your clients. How will you allocate scarce resources, in-

cluding your time, skills, and knowledge? What criteria will you use? Social work scholars, such as Burt Gummer (1997) and Russell Hardin (1990), have highlighted the allocation of scarce resources as a major ethical problem, about which the NASW Code of Ethics has had little to say. Do the staff in your agency discuss this challenging problem? If so, have they arrived at criteria for distributing scarce resources, or is this distribution left to chance and the individual discretion of each staff member? If so, is this the best way to operate?

Fully Informing Clients

Informed consent is an ethical requirement of professional practice. Honoring this entails informing clients about what is known about the track record of success of different methods in achieving outcomes clients value. Procedures recommended as well as alternative options should be clearly described to clients and significant others and decisions about continuing or ending programs should be based on clear outcome criteria. Clients are sometimes said to be "free to participate or not" when in fact if they don't, they may suffer significant negative consequences (their children may be removed by child protective services). Fully informing clients requires a candid discussion of any coercive contingencies. Your clients may be on prescribed medications of various kinds. For example, neuroleptic medication is often prescribed for people alleged to be mentally ill. Clients should be informed about the potential negative side effects of these medications such as irreversible neurological damage (see for example, Breggin, 1990).

Questionable Criteria

Examples of questionable criteria are personal preferences (unsupported by empirical research) or, simply, what is available. Consider a discussion I had with a social worker who was using narrative therapy with a 9-year-old boy diagnosed as having ADD (attention deficit disorder). She had not told the boy and his family what other options were available and their track record of success (e.g., Hinshaw, 1994). Although practice-related litera-

EXHIBIT 18.14
Popular But Problematic Ideas that Impair Treatment Decisions and Suggested Replacement Views

- *Existing scientific research is not relevant to practice decisions.*
  Replacement. The relevance of research lies on a continuum. It may or may not be directly relevant. In the latter case, view this as an open empirical question about generalizability.
- *Drawing on findings from the scientific literature is a waste of time because there are usually conflicting results.*
  Replacement. Research shows consistently effective interventions for some problems. Where this consistency has not been found, guidelines may be available to assist in selecting a subset of methods with the best empirically tested record of success.
- *Research shows that all methods are equally effective, so it doesn't matter what I use.*
  Replacement. Meta-analytic studies related to some problem areas suggest differences between various types of intervention and in relapse rates. Dismantling studies have shown that adding or subtracting components of an intervention result in differential effectiveness and many treatments have no evidence regarding their effectiveness. Therefore it is important to accurately analyze the research record to identify which method would be the most effective for a particular person because they are not all equivalent.
- *Clinical judgment and intuition can be more useful than the results of scientific research.*
  Replacement. Clinical judgment is subject to a variety of errors that scientific research methods help to avoid (see Chapter 4). Thus, it is important to supplement assumptions about what may be effective with findings of scientific research.
- *Becoming familiar with relevant research is expensive and time-consuming.*
  Replacement. Locating problem-related scientific literature is easier now with computerized data bases and it is cost-beneficial in terms of possible payoffs for clients.
- *Ignoring problem-related scientific literature does not harm my clients or me.*
  Replacement. Ignoring this harms my clients, myself, and my profession.
- *Practitioners who make poor treatment decisions should be tolerated and condoned.*
  Replacement. Poor practice decisions that result in harm to clients or forgoing effective methods should be criticized and those who make them should be educated regarding sound criteria for decision making. Appropriate escalation should be conducted with individuals who continue to make poor decisions.
- *I am usually correct and can point to my successes to confirm this.*
  Replacement. Feedback from experience offers an incomplete picture. More systematic observations are needed to test assumptions. (See discussion of experience in Chapter 4).

Source: Adapted from W. O'Donohue & J. Szymanski (1994). How to win friends and not influence clients: Popular but problematic ideas that impair treatment decisions. *The Behavior Therapist, 17,* 29–33.

ture suggests that cognitive–behavioral methods in a small group format are useful in altering related behaviors, she did not tell the family about this option. How, then, could they give their informed consent? Beliefs that get in the way of drawing on problem-related scientific literature are illustrated in Exhibit 18–14.

What should you do if you cannot offer methods that are most effective and that clients would select if given a choice? Is this a sound and ethical reason to withhold information from them? I don't think so. I suspect that if you were making an important medical decision, you would like to know about the track record of different methods even when (or perhaps especially when) your physician offers only a remedy that is unlikely to be effective (and that may harm you in the process). Shouldn't we inform clients as we ourselves would like to be informed? We have found that the crite-

ria on which social workers base decisions about their clients differ from those they would like their physicians to rely on when making recommendations or from the criteria they ideally would like to use (Gambrill & Gibbs, 1996). They rely on questionable criteria such as intuition and their experience with a few cases in making decisions about clients. In the other two situations criteria preferred were controlled experimental studies and demonstrated track record of success.

Research by Batson and his colleagues suggests that selection of methods may be based on what is available (what resource an agency has to offer) rather than what is needed to resolve problems (Batson, Jones, & Cochran, 1979) (see Exhibit 18.15). The reasons may be economic (the agency will lose money if clients are referred elsewhere) or a lack of knowledge about effective methods. Resources influence rates of hospitalization and in-

EXHIBIT 18.15
Basing Resources on What Is Available: A Questionable Practice

The case involved a 6-year-old boy (Lin) who had just migrated to the United States from Thailand to live with his father and his father's woman friend Jian. The boy's mother had died when he was an infant, and he had been raised by an aunt in Thailand. The family was referred to the agency because Lin was having problems at school. He spoke little English. He did not follow instructions at school and was said to be aggressive with his peers. He did not follow instructions at home, especially from Jian. The social worker was using play therapy with Lin. When I asked her why, she told me, "Because that's what my agency offers." She had not observed interactions between the boy and his teacher and peers and had not seen the family members together, even though they were willing to come to the agency and/or to have the social worker visit their home.

Further details about the family suggested that helping the father and Jian improve their child-management skills would be useful. They were willing to participate in whatever way the agency recommended making parent training likely to be a success. Additional information would be needed to see what was happening at school. It is possible that Lin was having trouble in school because the teacher did not speak his language and because her skills in child management and curricular planning were deficient. But the social worker had not looked into any of these possibilities.

stitutionalization. For example, the juvenile confinement rate is related to the number of beds available (see Schwartz, 1989). Basing decisions about plans on such criteria is ethically questionable when relying on other criteria would offer clients a better chance of attaining outcomes they value

and avoiding or minimizing negative ones. Because helpers and clients may use different criteria to select plans, O'Donahue and his colleagues (1989) recommend that helpers tell clients what criteria they are using (e.g., personal preference, testimonials, results of experimental studies).

SUMMARY

Successful plans change problem-related circumstances. A sound assessment will help you and your clients select promising plans or to discover that there are no promising plans. The steps in choosing plans include reviewing options, selecting a plan that is acceptable to clients and significant others and is likely to be effective, and describing how plans will be implemented and results evaluated. You and your clients must decide whom to involve, what they will do, and what settings to use. You may have to arrange prompts and incentives to encourage valued behaviors. Mutual responsibilities should be clearly described. Success may require use of multiple helping roles at a variety of system levels (e.g., individual, group, community, service system). You may have to broker, mediate, advocate, teach, and enable, and to do so, you may have to talk to clients, agree on assignments to be carried out in real-life settings, practice skills in role plays, and/or directly intervene in the natural environment. You often have to work with, within, and among agencies and coordinate services provided by a number of agencies.

The criteria for evaluating plans include feasibility, probable effectiveness, efficiency, intrusiveness, and likelihood of positive and negative side effects. The plan's acceptability to clients and significant others and the likelihood of generalization and durability of positive outcomes also are important to consider. Compromises must often be made among what would be ideal, what is feasible, and what is acceptable to the participants. Being informed about the relative effectiveness of different methods as suggested by scientific research, and the reasons that they cannot be offered (e.g., lack of resources) will help you make sound decisions and avoid unfairly blaming yourself (or your clients) for limited success. Ongoing tracking of progress will allow you and your clients to make timely changes as needed. Clear descriptions of what was done and what happened will help you to discover obstacles and decide on next steps. Anticipating problems will make setbacks less likely. However, unanticipated obstacles often arise and, you will need creativity, knowledge, and flexibility to address them.

REVIEWING YOUR COMPETENCIES

Reviewing What You Know

1. Describe the criteria that should be considered when selecting plans.
2. Describe major intervention roles and the requisites for each.
3. Describe the advantages of involving significant others.
4. Distinguish between enactive and vicarious methods, and discuss their relative effectiveness.
5. Describe steps you can take to increase the likelihood that clients will complete agreed-on tasks.
6. Given case examples, you can describe feasible options for overcoming obstacles.
7. Describe the responsibilities of social workers in implementing plans.
8. Describe the responsibilities of clients in carrying out plans.
9. Describe the important characteristics of assignments.
10. Identify correct and incorrect use of specific procedures based on videotaped or written descriptions.
11. Accurately critique the clarity and potential effectiveness of proposed plans.

Reviewing What You Do

1. Based on the available resources and problem-related scientific literature, the methods you select have the greatest possibility of success.
2. The plans you select are closely linked to your assessment data.
3. Plans involve minimal use of artificial procedures and are minimally intrusive.
4. Plans build on client assets and community resources.
5. Plans are tailored to characteristics of clients and their environments.
6. Opportunities are taken to rearrange the physical environment in useful ways.
7. Your plans clearly describe intermediate steps.
8. The rationale for suggested methods are described to clients.
9. You seek your clients' agreement to participate.

10. You involve significant others in plans.
11. You effectively coordinate multiple services.
12. You honor your commitments to clients and other staff.
13. You clearly describe plans in writing.
14. You give your clients written descriptions of plans.
15. You arrange prompts and incentives as necessary.
16. You implement intervention methods with a high degree of fidelity.
17. You arrange collateral services as needed.
18. Your plans consider cultural differences in values and norms.
19. You anticipate and avoid obstacles when possible.
20. You put aside systematic intervention efforts only as necessary.
21. Assignments are relevant, feasible, and clearly described.
22. You refer your clients to programs that use effective methods and track progress.

Reviewing Results

1. Agreed-on assignments are completed.
2. Completion of assignments results in outcomes that clients and significant others value, as judged by their self-reports and by observation in real life.
3. Clients feel better when they leave your office than when they came in.
4. Effective referrals are made. (Clients use and benefit from services provided by referral agencies).
5. Valued outcomes are achieved.
6. Probable success of plans is accurately predicted.

CHAPTER 19

Evaluating Outcomes as Integral
to Problem Solving

OVERVIEW

Guidelines for evaluating policies, programs, and plans are described in this chapter as well as sources of error that result in incorrect estimates of outcome and incorrect assumptions about the role of services in relation to outcome. Questions that arise and options for answering them are described, as well as steps to take when plans are successful and steps to take when they are not. Practical and ethical advantages of ongoing evaluation of the outcomes of service are highlighted. Compared to the money involved in implementing policies, programs, and practices, the money spent for evaluating outcome is modest and the information gained invaluable for learning how to enhance services.

You Will Learn About

- The value of timely corrective feedback.
- Questions, options, and decisions.
- Advantages and disadvantages of careful evaluation.
- Misconceptions.
- Sources of error.
- The value of visual feedback.
- Options for finding out if there is any change.
- Options for exploring whether intervention was responsible for outcomes.
- Next steps when plans are successful.
- Next steps when there is no progress or things get worse.
- Program evaluation.
- Obstacles to corrective feedback.

- Ethical issues.
- Evaluating your progress.

THE VALUE OF TIMELY CORRECTIVE FEEDBACK

Evaluating outcomes is essential for problem solving. Policies, programs, and service plans for individuals are hypotheses (guesses) to be tested against reality and corrected in the light of experience. Relying on inaccurate measures may result in unwise decisions, such as referring clients to agencies that use ineffective methods or continuing policies and programs that harm rather than help clients. Only if we discover whether there is a need for improvement can we take steps to improve programs in a timely manner.

QUESTIONS AND DECISIONS

Evaluation concerns discovering the outcomes of policies, programs, and practices. Do they help, harm, or make no difference? Consider the example in Exhibit 19.1. Evaluation research often starts with a policy question (e.g., what are policy issues, how can we improve programs, what is their impact (compared with what), how cost effective is the program, and what resources are needed to implement it effectively?). Positive outcomes include an increase in those clients and significant others value (e.g., increased social support, learning additional skills), and a decrease in outcomes they dislike (e.g., harassment at work), positive collateral effects, and less need for restrictive services (e.g., residential care). Measures used by agency administrators may include a 20% increase in the percentage of yearly goals attained, a 40% increase in staff morale, a 20% increase in funding, and more positive views of the agency by external groups. Measures on a community organization evaluation scale included the following:

- Community residents recognize the group as a route to social change.
- There is an agreed-on, clearly defined structure containing rules, operating procedures, and a known way for participants to hold one another accountable.
- Individual members have a greater sense of community.
- Group members have a sense of solidarity.
- A fund-raising plan has been designed.
- Success in recruiting and retaining indigenous leaders.
- Success in maintaining a steady funding level.
- Success in forming coalitions with other organizations. (Shields, 1992)

EXHIBIT 19.1
What Would You Do?

Jean works with seniors and their families. She helps caregivers of elderly relatives arrange for respites from caregiving and helps family members alter behaviors that prevent frail elderly people from continuing to live with their relatives. There are many ways she and her clients could evaluate services. She could rely on her "off-the-wall" opinion: Do her clients seem to feel better off? She also could ask her clients what they think. She could ask family members to keep track of behaviors of interest. For example, perhaps behaviors valued by significant others, such as housekeeping chores, are no longer completed. Here, too, the frequency of chore completion could be tracked.

If a teacher tells you that a student's behavior has improved, will you be satisfied and leave it at that? Will you also ask the student? Should you go to the school and see for yourself or ask the teacher to collect data on the degree of progress?

As in other helping phases, many decisions are involved such as deciding: (1) the purpose of evaluating outcomes, (2) what measures to use, (3) level of outcomes viewed as a success, (4) how often to gather data, (5) how to summarize data, and (6) when and how to share data with clients. You and your clients must decide what to do if progress is less than hoped for or if things get worse. The purpose of evaluating progress will suggest the kind of data that will be useful. Possible goals include the following:

- Get a rough estimate of progress.
- Get an ongoing, accurate estimate of progress so that plans can be made in a timely way based on accurate feedback.
- Be accountable to clients.
- Prevent harm.
- Motivate clients to continue their participation.
- Provide data for supervisory review.
- Provide data for administrative review.
- Add to knowledge base of social work.
- Explore the role of intervention in outcomes achieved.
- Enhance clients' understanding of themselves.
- Provide feedback to other service providers.
- Provide data to third-party payers (insurance companies).

Some questions are important to all work: Does a plan achieve hoped-for outcomes? Are complaints improving, getting worse, or staying the same? Do the outcomes noted make a difference in the quality of clients' lives? Has a policy achieved what it was intended to achieve? Are service programs reaching clients? If so, to what degree? How can we increase the acceptability of effective plans? Are outcomes a result of services provided? Which kinds of service are most effective? Which method

does a client like best? Other questions, such as Was the intervention responsible for the change? are important in knowledge building and may sometimes be critical in making practice decisions. Exploring what method offered by whom is most effective for what person with what problem under which circumstances requires the gradual accumulation of knowledge over time. Asking whether psychotherapy or social work is effective is not helpful. This is like asking if medicine is effective. With some problems it is. With others it is not. The question "How do you know?" applies to all of the questions above. (See Baer, 1988.)

OPTIONS

All social workers evaluate their practice. They differ in how they evaluate it. Some use process measures such as the number of sessions attended and services offered. Some use outcome measures such as self-reports by clients and significant others, opinions of social workers, standardized self-report measures, and observation in role plays or in real life. Different choices have different opportunity costs (e.g., not discovering early on that services have harmful effects). "All genuine evaluations produce findings that are better than speculation" (Berk & Rossi, 1990, p. 34). Your aim should be to gather accurate, timely information to inform your decisions about services. The less precise your answers need to be to evaluate progress, the rougher your estimates can be.

You can evaluate progress in a vague, haphazard manner relying on unsatisfactory surrogate measures or in a systematic way that allows you and your clients to make well-informed, timely changes in plans based on ongoing, accurate feedback or in some variation in between these. Some evaluation methods are more likely than others to avoid biases that get in the way of accurately estimating progress and what was responsible for it (see Exhibit 19.2). Your knowledge, skills, and resources as well as those of clients and significant others will influence how you evaluate outcomes. You will often have a choice between feedback that can improve the soundness of future decisions and

EXHIBIT 19.2
Ten Ways to Fool Yourself and Your Clients About Degree of Progress

1. Focus on vague outcomes.
2. Rely on testimonials.
3. Rely on your intuition.
4. Select measures because they are easy to use, even though they are not related to the client's problem and are not sensitive to change.
5. Do not gather baseline data (discover the frequency of behaviors, thoughts, or feelings of concern to client before service).
6. Assess progress only in artificial settings such as the office.
7. Under no circumstances, graph data.
8. Use only pre-post measures (do not track progress in an ongoing manner).
9. Use only post measures.
10. Do not gather follow-up data.

feedback that prevents "de-bugging" (identifying and remedying errors) (Bransford & Stein, 1984). Careful evaluation requires clear descriptions of expected outcomes and plans and identification and monitoring of relevant, feasible, sensitive progress indicators. These should be

Relevant: Meaningful to clients and significant others.
Specific: Clearly described.
Sensitive: Reflect changes that occur.
Feasible: Possible to obtain.
Unintrusive: Not interfere with service provision.
Valid: Measure what they are supposed to measure.
Reliable: Show consistency over different measurements in the absence of change.
Cost-effective

Any time we claim that a plan, program, or policy was successful, we assume that we know what it was supposed to accomplish. If desired outcomes are vague, we neither know what we are trying to achieve or when we have done so. Evaluation should include clear descriptions of process (what was done), so that the integrity of services can be evaluated, accurate estimates of outcome, so that results can be known, and assessments of social va-

lidity (see later discussion). In professions such as social work, clients have real-life problems. We can find out whether they are getting worse or better or are staying the same. Inaccurate estimates of progress will result in poor decisions about what to do next. Unless you track progress in an ongoing way using valid measures, you may believe progress has been made when it has not or miss improvement when there has been some.

Indirect Measures

Indirect measures include verbal reports by clients and significant others about progress. This offers information about **social validity:** Do the outcomes attained make a difference to clients and significant others (Wolf, 1978)? Social validity is always important to explore, and indirect measures usually are easy to gather. For example, you can ask your clients to rate the helpfulness of each session on a scale from 1 (not at all) to 5 (very). Social workers' opinions about progress is another kind of indirect measure. The problem is that they are not unbiased reporters. Reports of clients are subject to the *hello–goodbye effect* (reporting conditions as worse than they really are at the beginning of contact and as better than they really are following intervention) (Hathaway, 1948). For example, Schnelle (1974) found that 37% of parents reported that their children's school attendance had improved when it had decreased. Measures of consumer satisfaction seem to encourage a "congratulatory" reaction. Most consumers of therapy report that they are satisfied with the services provided (between 76 and 83%) (Lebow, 1983). Global ratings of satisfaction do not offer information about what service components contributed to progress.

Process measures—also indirect measures—refer to how service is delivered. Examples are the number of sessions attended, methods used, and assignments completed. Process measures do not provide information about whether any changes occurred in real life (e.g., a change in parenting behaviors at home). Ideally, both process (descriptions of what was done) and outcome (what happened) should be described. The former provides a check of the quality of service. The latter provides information about results. The higher the correlation between process and outcome measures, the more you can rely on process measures as a guide to outcome. (See also Patterson et al., 1993.)

Direct Measures

Direct measures assess change in real-life settings. Examples are the number of conversations initiated, daily rate of positive feedback to children, percentage of clients receiving food stamps, and percentage of desired outcomes attained by a neighborhood council. The importance of using both indirect and direct measures is highlighted in studies showing that parental attitude is more predictive of the referral of a child to a clinic than is the child's rate of deviant behavior, which may not differ from that of his peers or siblings (Arnold et al., 1975). A lack of agreement between direct and indirect measures may indicate that problems of most concern to clients have not been addressed. Progress measures used may not be sensitive to change.

Assessment of Social Validity and Invalidity

The purpose of social validity assessments is to evaluate the acceptability or viability of a program. Questions regarding social validity concern the following three areas: (1) are the goals of the procedures important and relevant to desired changes? (2) are the methods used acceptable to consumers and the community, or do they cost too much (e.g., in terms of effort, time, discomfort, ethics, etc.)? and (3) are the consumers satisfied with the outcome, including predicted changes as well as unpredicted effects? (Wolf, 1978). Social validity data provide an important supplement to measuring clear, valid, reliable outcome measures.

As Schwartz and Baer (1991) emphasize, the key purpose of such assessments is to anticipate the rejection of a program before that happens and for this reason, they should include feedback from *all* relevant consumers of a program. These include: (1) *direct consumers*, the main recipients of a program; (2) *indirect consumers*, those who purchase a program or are strongly affected by the changes pursued in the program but are not its recipients;

(3) *members of the immediate community*, people who interact with direct and indirect consumers on a regular basis; and (4) *members of the extended community*, people who live in the same community but who do not directly know of or interact with the direct or indirect consumers. Consider a group home for juveniles. The juveniles would be the direct consumers; the referring agency an indirect consumer; the neighbors would be members of the immediate community; and readers of newspaper articles about the group home would be members of the extended community.

Only if the right questions are asked of the right people (e.g., the four consumer groups discussed above), at the right time, and the results are used to enhance the acceptability of programs are social validity assessments useful. Information gathered should be used to improve the acceptability of services, otherwise as Schwartz and Baer (1991) note, such assessments are in some sense fraudulent. This emphasizes the value of information about social *in*validity (e.g., complaints about specific aspects of a program) as well as social validity. The point is not to encourage false praise and fake positive reports, but to identify specific sources of trouble (which program aspects are liked and which ones are not liked) that can then be addressed. Too often consumer satisfaction ratings are used merely to obtain continued funding or to provide vague assurance that all is well when in fact there may be many complaints and effective programs may not be used. Complaints provide valuable information about how to improve services. Some successful service businesses view unsolicited complaints as free gifts they can use to enhance services and increase profits.

Settling for Approximations, Being Creative

Concerns about cost, acceptability to clients, and feasibility will limit options. Clients or significant others may be unwilling to gather data, or you may not have time to carefully evaluate outcome. Still, you can do the best you can under given circumstances. Let's say you are facilitating a bereavement group. You and your clients could identify valued outcomes (e.g., a positive outlook toward the future), and participants could rate them on a scale ranging from 1 (not at all) to 5 (very much) at the beginning and end of each group meeting. The clients could keep a journal and review it for indicators of progress. You will have to decide whether it is ethical to proceed without ongoing data about degree of progress. Some reasonably accurate measure of progress is needed to make informed decisions about what to do next. Keep in mind that every decision has an **opportunity cost,** certain options are foreclosed as a result. An opportunity cost of not accurately assessing progress is not having the benefit of finding out what can be improved and taking steps to do so.

PRACTICAL AND ETHICAL ADVANTAGES OF CAREFUL EVALUATION

As always, we should consider our purpose. Why should we carefully evaluate the effects of programs and practices? Answers may differ depending on whose perspective we consider (e.g., clients, significant others, service providers, the public, legislators who make funding decisions).

Practical Advantages

Testing guesses about the effects of services has many advantages, whether working with individuals, families, groups, communities, or organizations: (1) Both staff and clients receive ongoing feedback about degree of success; (2) plans can be changed in a timely manner depending on outcomes; (3) positive feedback increases clients' motivation; and (4) the relationship between services and outcomes can be explored. Evaluation helps you and your clients make informed decisions about the next steps you should take and to avoid faulty decisions based on incorrect estimates of progress and related factors. Timely corrective feedback is essential to catching and correcting harmful unintended effects at an early point. Careful evaluation takes some of the guess work out of practice. Also helping clients often requires many intermediate steps. Recognizing small wins will help you and your clients to keep going (Weick, 1984).

Careful evaluation can help you decide when to introduce a plan, whether to continue it, and whether to combine it with other methods. For example, one of my students had her field placement in a hospital. She discovered that a young girl with beta thalassemia (an inherited chronic illness) was not doing well, even though she was following her prescribed treatment regime. The student discovered this because she monitored both the girl's compliance and the results of her lab tests. The lack of expected match between compliance and the lab results led to the discovery that a treatment change recommended a year before had never been implemented, a discovery that may have saved this girl's life. If you and your clients don't know whether things are getting better or worse or staying the same, you don't have the information you need to plan next steps. You are "working in the dark."

The more rapid and continuous the feedback is, the more sensitive and valid the outcome measures are, and the more clearly outcomes are described, the more opportunities there are to make timely changes. Many social workers see clients over a number of sessions and so will have many opportunities to alter decisions. Programs and policies may be in effect for months and years, providing many opportunities for corrective feedback. The ease of evaluation is related to the clarity of the outcomes pursued. Ideally, the same measures used to gather baseline data should be used to monitor progress. For example, Julie continued to monitor her worry-free time (see the case examples later in this chapter). The point is to select an evaluation method that offers reasonably accurate ongoing feedback in a feasible way.

Ethical Advantages

Clients have a right to know whether they benefit from or are harmed by services. They have a right to know whether their effort, time, and (often) money are well spent. Preventing avoidable harm is an ethical obligation of professionals. This can only be done if outcomes are tracked on an ongoing basis using valid measures rather than uninformative surrogates (e.g., harmful programs can be stopped). Court rulings highlight the role of evaluation in providing services in residential programs:

> The courts have identified regular evaluation of client progress, periodic reevaluation of treatment or educational plans, and removal from a course of treatment that worsens one's condition as clients' rights that require ongoing evaluation by the residential treatment program. . . . It is only through evaluation that a program can be accountable, and only through accountability that it can continue to be legally safe, much less functional and effective. (Christain & Romanczyk, 1986, p. 145)

Decisions about continuing or ending programs should be based on clear outcome criteria (not on guesses), and all involved parties should help select service plans and outcome measures.

REASONS GIVEN AGAINST CAREFUL EVALUATION

Objections to obtaining corrective feedback often are related to misconceptions about careful evaluation. Given the potential benefits of corrective feedback for problem solving (e.g., altering harmful practices at an early point and fully informing clients about the outcomes of service), if you subscribe to any of these views, you should think twice about them. The alternative to collecting data describing the outcome of plans is basing decisions on "guesstimates" (uninformed guesses).

It Requires Selecting Trivial Outcomes or Measures

Some people believe that rigor requires rigor mortis, that evaluation requires selecting trivial or irrelevant outcomes and measures of them. Hundreds of reports in the professional literature demonstrate that outcomes can be assessed in a relevant, informative way. It is true that evaluating progress in a relevant, nonintrusive manner requires creativity, flexibility, knowledge, and skill. It also is true that there has been too much emphasis in the professional literature on being objective and rigorous and not enough emphasis on describing the rela-

tionship of these characteristics to accountability to clients and case planning. This has resulted in ritualistic practices such as using a measure simply because it is available, with little regard for whether it provides a meaningful measure of outcome. If your purpose is to find out whether you are helping clients, outcome measures must be relevant, and clients and significant others should be involved in selecting them.

It Interferes with Offering Services

You may believe that evaluation interferes with offering services (e.g., clients don't like it, it interferes with the helping relationship). As with any other helping phase, evaluation can be implemented either well or poorly. The aim is to use evaluation to fulfill the ethical requirement of accountability to clients and also the practical goal of making timely, well-reasoned practice decisions. Keeping these purposes clearly in view will help you and your clients select evaluation methods that contribute to, rather than detract from, helping. Evaluation does not require adhering to rigid arbitrary schedules. To the contrary. **Practice concerns come first**. Flexibility is one of the advantages of the single-case designs described later in this chapter. Research shows that clients like the feedback they receive from careful evaluation (Campbell, 1988). In a quality assurance review program that graphed the progress toward each goal for more than 2,000 psychiatric patients, clients reported that they appreciated the careful evaluation of progress (Bullmore, Joyce, Marks, & Connolly, 1992). Rather than interfering with services, evaluation facilitates this aim.

It Is Not Possible

Some people believe that careful evaluation is not possible because of conceptual difficulties (e.g., no one knows how to measure progress). However, clients have real-life problems, so why not determine how well they have been resolved? In their survey of 296 social workers, Penka and Kirk (1991) found that many social workers believed that change often occurs too long after services have ended to measure it. This belief should be tested. And, even if desired outcomes occur after contact, related changes that could be measured may take place during contact. Some social workers believe that evaluating real-life outcome is unnecessary because the quality of the helping relationship determines effectiveness (Penka & Kirk, 1991). This guess also needs to be tested. The nature of the client–helper relationship does influence outcome, but research shows that it is not the sole influence.

It Requires Using Behavioral Methods

No matter what your theoretical preferences, hoped for outcomes can be clearly identified and progress monitored. Hundreds of studies illustrate that progress can be assessed within many different practice approaches (see for example Fonagy & Moran, 1990).

It Requires a Lot of Extra Time

Identifying clear problem-relevant objectives is a key assessment task that may take time. However, identifying clear problem-related objectives is not solely for the purpose of evaluating progress. This key task serves many other functions such as accurately defining problems and wisely selecting service plans. Careful evaluation will save effort and time in the long run by allowing timely changes in ineffective methods and ending unnecessary services.

It Is the Same as Research

My students often are told by their supervisors that they cannot keep track of progress because this is research and requires the approval of the agency's human subjects committee. This confusion between research and evaluation may occur because identifying clear objectives and progress indicators and tracking them on an on going basis is not a typical agency practice. Research and evaluation have different goals, although they may overlap. Progress is evaluated for both ethical and practical reasons related to effective case management. By providing

timely feedback about gains and harms, evaluation offers guidelines to what to do next so that service is not continued beyond what is necessary, so that harmful methods can be removed, so that additional methods can be added as needed, and/or so that consultation can be sought in a timely manner. Thus, evaluation is for service purposes. Consider the example of the youth with beta-thalassemia major described earlier. Only through careful monitoring of both outcomes and adherence to a medical regime was a medication error detected that could be corrected. The purpose of research is to yield new knowledge. Applied research has a dual goal—to discover knowledge and to help clients. The growth of knowledge requires methods that critically test theories. Although some evaluation methods involve such tests, many do not (see the later discussion in this chapter). Evaluating practice does not necessarily add to the knowledge base of practice, nor do poorly designed research efforts.

SOURCES OF ERROR IN MAKING JUDGMENTS ABOUT PROGRESS AND RELATED CAUSES

Biases that may lead us astray in estimating progress and what was responsible for it are shown in Exhibit 19.3. (Reviews of related research can be found in Dawes, 1988; Hogarth, 1987; and Plous, 1993.) If you are familiar with them, you have a greater chance of avoiding these sources of error and their unwanted effects, such as continuing harmful or ineffective plans or programs. Many of these biases also affect decisions in other helping phases (e.g., defining problems). Ignoring feedback or relying on incomplete or irrelevant feedback may result in incorrect judgments. You may confuse correlation and cause or chance and cause. The vaguer the outcome measures are, the more likely that bias will creep in because there is less chance for corrective feedback.

Hindsight Bias

We have a tendency to say that we "knew it all along" when a certain outcome occurs, especially

EXHIBIT 19.3
Sources of Error in Estimating Progress and Identifying Related Factors

- Being swayed by hindsight bias.
- Being overconfident.
- Engaging in wishful thinking.
- Having an illusion of control.
- Overlooking the role of chance (coincidences).
- Overlooking confounding causes such as regression effects.
- Attributing success to your own efforts and failure to other factors.
- Being swayed by confirmation bias (attending only to successes, seeking only data that support preferred views or hoped-for outcomes).
- Relying on observed rather than relative frequency.
- Overlooking the interaction between predictions and their consequences.
- Mistaking correlation for causation.
- Relying on misleading criteria (e.g., testimonials).

when it is consistent with our preconceptions. In fact, we often cannot recall what we predicted before an outcome is known or missrecall in a biased direction. This encourages overestimates of predictability (e.g., overestimating the relationship between returning a child to the home of his biological parents and subsequent child abuse). Knowledge of an outcome encourages the view that it was inevitable, that we should have known what it would be, even though there was no way we could have known the outcome beforehand. We tend to assume a direct relationship between an outcome and certain causes when no evidence is offered for or against such an assumption. We can easily come up with explanations, so possible accounts are readily at hand. Hindsight bias often results in blaming people for what appear to be errors that could have been avoided. For example, you may unfairly blame or praise yourself for what were lucky guesses. Looking back, you may assume "I should have known." (See Fischhoff, 1975.)

Overconfidence

We tend to be overconfident in the accuracy of our judgments. This is common among experts as well as among lay people. Hindsight bias encourages overconfidence by inflating estimates of the relationship between certain causes and outcomes. This

overconfidence may get in the way of accurately estimating the effects of a program.

Wishful Thinking

We tend to see what we want to see. Helpers and clients want positive outcomes. This "set" encourages biased estimates (see the discussion of confounding causes).

The Illusion of Control

Our need to feel in control of what happens to us and to make sense of our lives encourages biased perceptions of progress and false estimates of the strength of the relationship between variables (such as a service plan and an outcome).

Overlooking the Role of Chance

What you believe is a result of your services may have occurred by chance. We underestimate the role of chance and can easily come up with explanations. Underestimating the role of chance and coincidences is one result of our interest in making sense of the world.

Overlooking Confounding Causes

What you think is a result of services may be the result of a confounding factor such as maturation or history (see Exhibit 19.4). Positive outcomes may be due to the **act of treatment** rather than the treatment itself (i.e., a placebo effect). Negative as well as positive placebo effects may occur. The former have a negative impact on outcome and/or result in negative side effects. These may be related to subtle signs of inattention or a raised eyebrow. One or more of the following reactive effects may contribute to the placebo effect:

- **Hello–goodbye effect.** Clients present themselves as worse than they really are when they seek help and as better than they really are when the service has ended. This leads to overestimating progress.

EXHIBIT 19.4
Possible Confounding Causes (Rival Explanations) for Change

1. *History.* Events that occur between the first and second measurement, in addition to the experimental variables, may account for changes (e.g., clients may get help elsewhere).
2. *Maturation.* Simply growing older or living longer may be responsible, especially when long periods of time are involved.
3. *Instrumentation.* The way that something is measured changes (e.g., observers may change how they record).
4. *Testing effects.* Assessment may result in change.
5. *Morality.* There may be a differential loss of people from different groups.
6. *Regression.* Extreme scores tend to return to the mean.
7. *Self-selection bias.* Clients are often "self-selected" rather than randomly selected. They may differ in critical ways from the population they are assumed to represent and differ from clients in a comparison group.
8. *Helper selection bias.* Social workers may select certain kinds of clients to receive certain methods.
9. *Interaction effects.* Only certain clients may benefit from certain services, and others may even be harmed.

Source: D.T. Campbell & J.C. Stanley (1963), Experimental and quasi-experimental designs for research. Chicago: Rand McNally.

- **Hawthorne effect.** Improvements may result from being the focus of attention. Going to a well-known clinic or being seen by a famous therapist may result in positive outcomes.

- **Rosenthal effect.** We tend to give observers what we think they want—to please people we like or respect.

- **Observer bias.** The observer's expectations may result in biased data.

- **Social desirability effect.** We tend to offer accounts viewed as appropriate. For example, clients may underreport drinking.

Extreme values tend to become less extreme on repeated assessment. If you do unusually well on a test, you are likely to do less well the next time around. Conversely, if you do very poorly, you are likely to do better the next time. These are called *regression effects.* There is a regression (a return) toward the mean (your average performance level). Overlooking these effects can lead to faulty judgments. A supervisor may say, "Joe did unusually

well the first time he took our employee evaluation test but did not do well the second time. I don't think he wants the promotion."

Attributions for Success and Failure

We tend to attribute success to our skills and failure to chance. Use of vague or irrelevant feedback obscures the true relationship (or lack thereof) between our judgments and outcomes.

Confirmatory Bias

Partiality in the use of evidence is a common source of bias. We look at only part of the picture. We tend to focus on data that support our assumptions and may even recall data that were not present that support our views. Feedback may be ignored, especially if it contradicts hoped-for outcomes. Trying to recall events is an active process in which we often reconstruct accounts (i.e., revise memories) (see Loftus & Ketchum, 1994). This reconstruction may involve a selective focus (confirmatory bias) that encourages overconfidence in judgments.

Rely on Observed Rather Than Relative Frequency

We tend to focus on our "hits" and overlook our "misses." Anecdotal experience may give a slanted view because we focus on successes and overlook failures. For example, you may recall clients with whom you were successful and ignore those with whom you were not (there was no change, or problems increased). To accurately estimate your track record (or anyone else's), you must examine both "hits" and "misses" as well as what would have happened without intervention (see Chapter 17).

Overlooking the Interaction Between Predictions and Related Actions

The interactive nature between the actions we take as a result of the predictions we make may obscure the true relationship between the effects of our actions and outcomes (Einhorn, 1988). We tend to forget that actions taken as a result of predictions influence the outcomes. Consider the prediction that the banks will fail, followed by a "run on the banks" and their subsequent failure. If you believe you can help a group, you may extend greater effort, which may increase the probability of a positive outcome. If an applicant is accepted for a job, opportunities on the job may ensure future success. Those who are rejected do not have these opportunities.

Relying on Misleading Criteria

Relying on questionable criteria such as testimonials and case examples will give false estimates of "what works," as discussed in Chapter 4.

THE VALUE OF VISUAL FEEDBACK

A picture is worth a thousand words. Graphed data provide a valuable source of feedback (see Exhibits 19.5 and 19.6). Progress shown may enhance motivation to continue to pursue difficult goals. Only if a graph is effective in communicating information is it useful (e.g., the relationship between depression and positive social contacts). Data should be clearly and accurately represented, and graphs should be readily accessible to clients and signifi-

cant others. You will have to decide how to aggregate the data (e.g., daily or weekly) and how many graphs to use to describe best what is happening. If many measures are plotted on one graph or if the graphs are sloppy, discovering trends will be difficult or impossible. Mrs. Ryan kept track of the number of social contacts she had each day and then combined daily figures into a weekly total (see Exhibit 19.6). A social contact was defined as a social exchange with someone other than a relative which lasted at least ten minutes.

How to Construct Graphs

Some time measure (days or weeks) is represented along the horizontal axis and a response measure (number, rate, duration, or percentages) is noted on the vertical axis. Be sure to label your graphs so that what is recorded (the time periods involved, and the different phases, such as different service methods) are clear. You could note days on which a behavior could not occur by not connecting the data points on either side of this day (or week). If a student is monitoring a classroom behavior that can occur only on weekdays, he can plot only weekdays. If the behavior could have occurred but was not monitored, you could draw a dotted rather than a solid line between the days on either side. Include

EXHIBIT 19.5
Percentage of Julie's "Worry-Free Periods" Before and After Intervention

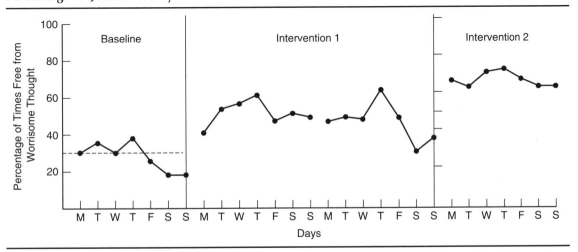

EXHIBIT 19.6
Frequency of Mrs. Ryan's Social Contacts Before and After Intervention

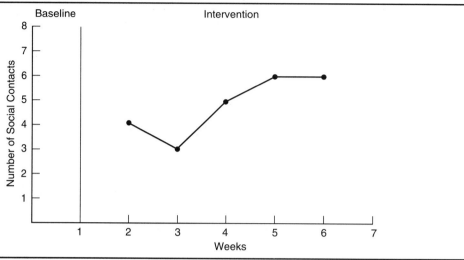

data gathered after intervention on the same graph that presents baseline information, so that degree of change can be readily seen. Different phases can be indicated by dropping a vertical line between phases and by not connecting the data points between phases. If a behavior can seldom occur, such as making a bed each morning, you can group the data collected daily by week in order to see trends more clearly.

Measures of duration, magnitude, or a behavior product, such as number of points earned could be graphed. In **criterion-referenced graphs**, the desired level of performance (e.g., writing one letter each day), is noted on the graph by drawing a line from this value horizontally across the chart. Whether performance met, exceeded, or fell below the criterion level is noted for each day (or week). In a **cumulative graph**, the number of behaviors on any day is added to the number on previous days. The slope of the line between data points indicates the rate of change. The higher the slope, the higher the rate of behavior. A cumulative graph can only go up; it cannot go down because values are added to each other. Thus if you try to construct such a graph and the line between data points goes up and down, you have not succeeded. Bar graphs (or histograms) can be useful for summarizing data. A re-

sponse measure is noted to the left, and one of a variety of measures may be indicated along the bottom, such as different people or groups.

Other Kinds of Visual Representations

Mark Mattaini (1993) provides many examples of different kinds of visual representations. An example is shown in Exhibit 19.7. Changes in group interaction over time can be graphically displayed (see Exhibit 19.8). (See Tufte, 1983, for a superb book on graphics and also Butterfield, 1993.) These books discuss such valuable concepts as "the lie factor" and "chart junk."

Visual Inspection and Statistical Analysis

Changes that are important to clients should be obvious from looking at the data. You can see how many data points during intervention overlap with those during baseline and examine trends in different phases. You can supplement visual inspection with statistical analysis to determine whether there have been statistically significant changes. You can find out whether the mean level of behavior during intervention falls above the mean level during baseline. Remember, however, that

EXHIBIT 19.7

Intake and 4-, 8-, and 12-Week Ecomaps Describing Changing Life Circumstances and Depression (Using the Beck Depression Inventory).

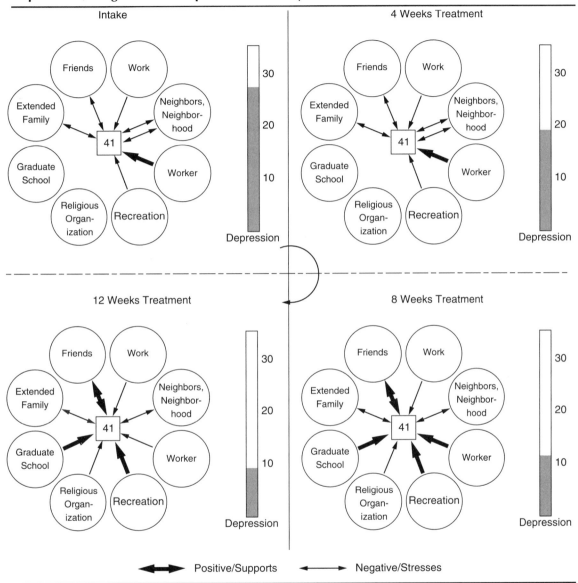

Source: M. A. Mattaini (1993), *More than a thousand words: Graphics for clinical practice* (p. 159). Washington, DC: National Association of Social Workers.

statistical significance is not necessarily correlated with clinical significance. That is, there may be no change of value to clients, even though statistical analysis shows a significant change. Ongoing re-

view of data allows timely alterations in plans (unlike post hoc statistical analysis of effects). Those who favor statistical analysis point out that "eyeballing" may not reveal changes and so lead to

EXHIBIT 19.8
Graphic Representations of Group Process over Time

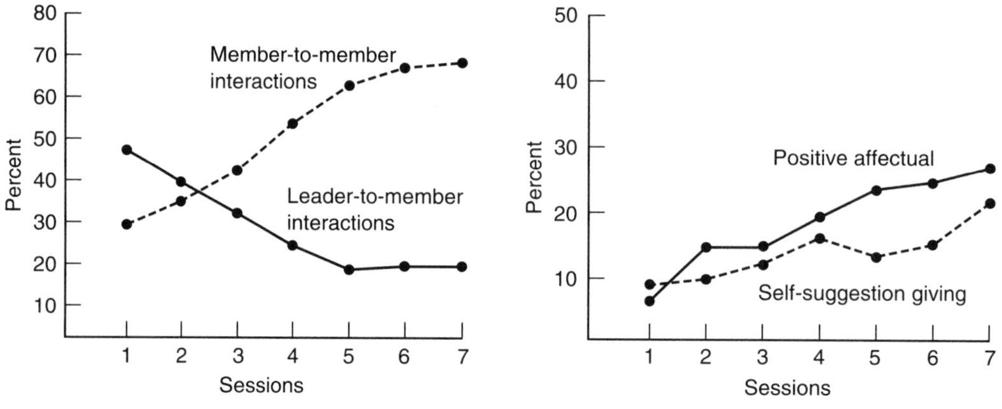

A. Direction of Interaction   B. Type of Interaction

Source: S. D. Rose (1977), *Group therapy: A behavioral approach* (p. 49). Englewood Cliffs, NJ: Prentice-Hall.

abandoning promising procedures and that inconsistent decisions are made on the basis of visual inspection. This does not have to be an either/or decision; you can use both visual inspection and statistical analysis. A number of easy-to-use statistical tests, such as the celeration line, have been developed to analyze data from single-case studies (e.g., Bloom, Fischer, & Orme, 1995).

A CLOSER LOOK AT OPTIONS FOR REVIEWING PROGRESS

The next section offers more detailed descriptions of how you and your clients could evaluate the outcomes of service. Clients may ask you to accept their self-reports in the interview about degree of progress and refuse to collect data regarding outcomes via self-monitoring or observation that may be needed to check accuracy and plan next steps. In this case, you will have to ask: "Can we make informed decisions without this information?" If the answer is "No," then you will have to discuss this with your clients. Perhaps there are ways to collect needed data that you both can agree on. If you cannot reach an agreement, you may have to inform a client that you cannot proceed without this

information. Keep in mind that we are talking about information needed to make informed decisions about what to do next (e.g., to continue a plan or to change a plan if it has negative effects). The alternative is to forge ahead without the necessary data, that is, to make uninformed decisions based on questionable grounds.

Goal Attainment Scaling

This involves identifying a series of objectives in terms of their desirability (Kiresuk, Smith, & Cardillo, 1994). You can use baseline levels as a reference point. The expected level is the one considered most likely. Outcomes that represent more and less than this are indicated above and below this level.

Task Completion

You can review the completion of tasks using the following scale suggested by Reid and Epstein (1977):

4. **Complete.** Tasks are fully accomplished (e.g., a job has been found, a homemaker secured). If the goal was to reduce quarreling, a rating of (4)

could be given if hostile interchanges seldom occur, no longer present a problem, and clients see no need for further work.

3. **Substantial.** The task is largely accomplished, though further action may be needed.

2. **Partial.** Progress has been made, but considerable work remains to be done.

1. **Minimal (or not at all).** No progress has been made, or progress is insignificant or uncertain.

You can calculate the percentage of success for each task. Let's say that 10 tasks were agreed on, so complete success would be 10×4, or 40. A key question here concerns the relationship between task completion and achievement of valued outcomes.

Probes

This involves occasional assessment of an outcome. Probes provide a convenient alternative to ongoing tracking of progress. Mr. Colvine used probes to review the Lakelands' progress in improving their negotiation skills. He tape-recorded their discussions while they were trying to resolve a conflict during a baseline period lasting 10 minutes as well as at the end of the fourth training session and at a follow-up meeting. A supervisor can randomly select cases from each staff member's caseload to review various indicators of service.

Social Comparison

One student's level of unacceptable classroom behavior can be compared with that of students who behave acceptably in class. Problems with using normative data include undesirable normative standards (e.g., low rates of positive feedback) and difficulty identifying a normative group. What is normative is not necessarily desirable.

Critical Incidents Can Be Recorded

Events or exchanges of concern can be identified and noted in a diary. Suppose that women staff are concerned about emotional abuse. They could record related incidents and then group them by

type, such as humiliation (e.g., checking and rechecking work beyond what is necessary), isolation (e.g., ignoring requests for meetings), or demonstrating power (e.g., taking credit for your work, demanding compliance and loyalty when you make complaints) (NiCarthy, Gottlieb, & Coffman, 1993).

Reviewing Pre/Post Change

You can collect global client satisfaction ratings before and after service and compare them with client ratings of progress in particular areas. For example, Mrs. Lakeland emphasized the importance of the decline of Brian's nasty talk, whereas Brian related improvement mostly to a decrease in his parents' nagging. You can compare your ratings with those of your clients. You also can supplement these measures with other measures. For example, you can review daily mood ratings in addition to scores on the Beck Depression Inventory before and after a 5-week group program. If possible, you should use objective measures of change to supplement global ratings.

Pre/post measurement does not provide ongoing feedback about progress. Ongoing evaluation is more helpful, since it allows timely changes in plans as needed. Also, because of rival hypotheses that may account for change, we cannot assume that service was responsible for outcomes observed (see Exhibit 19.4). Since there is no control group, we do not know if clients who did not receive service would have done as well or better. Regression effects are another problem (e.g., people who do very poorly at first tend to do better later, and people who do very well at first tend to perform more poorly later).

SINGLE-CASE DESIGNS

Single-case designs are a kind of interrupted time-series design involving repeated measurement of some outcomes of interest over time. They range from B designs (tracking progress only during intervention, so there is no baseline) to designs that are complex and allow exploration of the role of service in relation to outcome (i.e., experimental single-case designs). They differ from case studies and anecdotal reports in carefully tracking clearly described outcomes of interest over time. Requirements for using single-case designs include: (1) description of measures, (2) different phases (such as baseline and service or different kinds of service, and (3) repeated measurement of outcomes of interest in each phase. At least three data points should be included in each phase. If there are fewer than three, you won't be able to distinguish a trend and variability around a trend. Variability, level, and trend in behavior within each phase are evaluated in relation to variability, level, and trend in other phases. Different single-case designs offer different information. Some provide information about whether change occurred but not whether intervention was responsible. There are too many rival explanations (see Exhibit 19.4). Single-case designs can be used to answer questions such as, "Is there progress?" For example, Julie wanted to increase "time out from worry." (Her self-monitoring assignment is described in Chapter 14.) A daily percentage was calculated of the number of 1-hour periods in which she was free of worry out of all the 1-hour periods that she monitored each day. These percentages were then graphed (see Exhibit 19.5).

There are many variations between anecdotal case reports characterized by unsystematic data collection and vague outcome measures and systematic single-case studies that differ in accuracy of feedback and threats to internal validity (rival assumptions about the role of service in relation to outcome). On-going tracking of progress allows timely changes in plans. This provides feedback that can correct inaccurate views of progress due to one or more of the biases discussed earlier. Some single-case designs offer information about the comparative effectiveness of different methods or the relative importance of components of a procedure that contains many components, such as parent training.

Pros and Cons

First we should distinguish among different kinds of single-case designs. Key requisites of A-B (base-line followed by service) and B (service) designs, such as a clear description of objectives and on-going tracking of progress using clear relevant progress indicators are also practical and ethical requirements for case management and accountability. Thus A-B or B designs should always be used because they provide the information needed to make informed, timely, case-management decisions. Single-case designs attend to individual variations in problem-related behavior and circumstances. They provide a way to respect the uniqueness of each client's particular problem related circumstance and degree of progress. They can help you and your clients to test your hunches. Baseline data (information about the frequency of behaviors of interest before intervention) can often be gathered and, may be needed to define problems accurately and discover promising options. For example, critical assessment data regarding what happens right before and after behaviors of concern often are gathered along with data regarding the frequency of a behavior as described in Chapter 14. This information provides information about the functions of problem-related behaviors and alternative positive behaviors that may be critical in planning service programs. If baseline data are available, outcomes can be compared with these initial levels providing accurate estimates of progress, so that well-informed decisions about next steps can be made. Opportunities may arise to use a more informative design (one that provides information about the role of service in outcome seen) with little extra effort or cost, either to you or to your clients. Selection of a design will be an evolving process depending on what information is needed to provide informed service, what is possible, and degree of progress. **Practice and ethical concerns come first.** This is the very reason for carefully evaluating outcome.

What's the downside? Gathering information needed to make timely, informed practice decisions takes time and effort and may require special training for both you and your clients. Helpers tend to rely on irrelevant standardized measures rather than on measures uniquely suited to each client's concerns. You will have to forgo relying on unexamined hunches, and you and your clients will have to candidly confront less than hoped-for success or harms that result from intervention.

Single-Case Compared to Group Designs

Single-case in contrast to group designs involve the careful study of the variability of behavior of individuals. Practice considerations "drive" what is done. For example, you and your clients may decide to try another plan if progress is minimal. In group designs, a prearranged protocol is often followed. Group means are compared. Lack of attention to individual differences in prearranged protocols (even those that have been found to be effective) may compromise success. Allowances are not made for individual differences that, if attended to, would enhance success. In contrast, single-case designs are flexible. Experimental group designs require the random distribution of clients to different groups, which often is impossible in practice. Even if there is no evidence that the usual agency practices are effective, staff may object to randomly placing some clients in those groups offering the usual agency practice and assigning the others to a new method whose effectiveness may or may not have been tested.

Baselines

Baselines describe preintervention levels of problem-related behaviors. Needed information about problem-related circumstances is often gathered at the same time. Baselines can be used to estimate the frequency of problem-related behaviors in the future if the client's life-circumstances remain stable. A baseline allows you to estimate what the variability, trend (slope), and level of behavior would have been if service had not been introduced. In variable baselines, behavior varies considerably, and there is no clear trend. Ideally, to explore the role of service in relation to outcome, the baseline should be stable or be changing in a direction opposite to that desired. **Practice concerns come first.** These will indicate whether it is feasible or ethical to gather baseline data. These will also indicate whether it is unethical not to do so (e.g., problems may be inaccurately defined, progress can not be accurately assessed).

How Long Should Baselines Be? If possible, baselines should be continued until the pattern of behavior is fairly clear. If monitoring results in positive effects, it could be continued. Baseline data may reveal a lower than expected frequency of problem related behaviors. If so, you and your clients can renegotiate the focus of service or review the adequacy of baseline measures. Perhaps they do not reflect the client's concerns. The severity of a problem may have been overestimated.

When Should You Change Phases? Examine the pattern, trend, and stability of data in earlier phases to decide when to shift phases (e.g., from one kind of program to another). If the data are unstable, you have several options: (1) seek the source of variability, (2) wait until a more stable pattern emerges, (3) try out different temporal units of analysis (e.g., weeks instead of days), or (4) go on anyway to the next phase. If there is good progress and behaviors have stabilized at desired levels, you and your clients can implement plans for generalizing and maintaining gains, as described in Chapter 20. Variability in a baseline may be a result of the measurement or unrecognized extraneous variables such as fatigue or motivational changes. The clearer the criteria for deciding when valued outcomes have been reached, the easier it will be to decide what to do next. Also, keep in mind that unchanging data may be influenced by a number of variables that cancel out each other (Barlow, Hayes, & Nelson, 1990).

What If Change Occurs Slowly?

Change may occur only slowly. A change in self-image may result only over a long period. Involving more community members in a neighborhood action group may require varied plans that take a year. Many skills may be needed to attain desired outcomes. You could keep track of percentage of skills learned over time. Although single-case designs often trace changes that occur over a relatively short period, this is by no means required. Rather than plotting days along the time dimension, you could plot weeks, months, or even years. For example, you could track over months the percentage of community residents involved in a neighborhood action group. You also could note on a graph the different steps taken to encourage resident participation. You can make an estimate of when change might occur based on a practice theory.

A-B Designs

A-B designs require the repeated measurement of some behavior, thought, or feeling during baseline (the A phase) and also during intervention (the B phase). The B phase may consist of any type of intervention. The data collected are examined to determine changes in stability, trend, or level over phases. It is assumed that the trend, level, or variability seen in the initial phase would continue if nothing were done. A sharp change in the level of behavior or a reversal of a trend offers more confidence that service may have been responsible than does a change of trend in a similar direction. A change in level refers to a discontinuity in graphed data at the point of phase change. A change in slope refers to a difference in trend across phases. The A-B design offers information about whether a change occurred and describes its magnitude. It does not provide information as to whether the change was a result of service; there are too many rival hypotheses (see Exhibit 19.4).

An increase in desired behavior during baseline may be due to a **positive surveillance effect** (a change due to monitoring). Baseline data may reveal a decreasing trend. If the desired outcome is to decrease behavior, then here too there is a positive surveillance effect: monitoring behavior has decreased negative behaviors. If the trend is great enough, you may want to continue monitoring. Remember, though, that the effects of self-monitoring are usually temporary (see Chapter 14). An increasing trend in desired behavior during baseline—although good from a practice perspective—is not good for determining whether intervention was responsible for the change, since the behavior is already increasing. You also may find **negative surveillance effects** (behavior changes in an undesired way). For example, negative thoughts may increase if they are monitored. A-B designs are often feasible to use in every day practice. If one procedure is not effective, others can be added.

B Designs and Their Variations

You may not have time to gather baseline data. However, even in "crisis" situations, you can still track progress. If intervention is successful, you will not need to introduce other procedures. If it is not, other plans may be selected. Earlier procedures may or may not be continued depending on progress. For example, a social skills training program (B) may be only partially successful in increasing social contacts. You and your clients may decide to add other procedures, such as relaxation training (C) and reevaluation of unrealistic expectations (D). Each new method may offer additional gains. One procedure may be ended when another is introduced if the first one had few or no effects.

EXPLORING WHETHER INTERVENTION WAS RESPONSIBLE FOR OUTCOMES

Sometimes it is important to find out not only whether the intervention is working but also whether it was responsible for change. For example, it may be important to rule out medical causes (Gardner, 1967). The degree of confidence that can be assumed in relation to an observed change depends on a number of factors, including the length of time that baseline data were gathered, their stability, and whether multiple data sources indicate similar changes. A sharp change in slope or level when intervention is introduced offers greater confidence than a gradual change does. You can use brief planned withdrawals of intervention as probes to find out whether behavior is maintained under real-life contingencies. Natural withdrawals as a result of vacations or illness also are opportunities to see whether gains are maintained without special procedures. The **changing-criterion design** is useful when a goal is pursued in a series of steps and when changes in behavior can be expected fairly soon after each new criterion is introduced (see for example Bigelow, Huynen & Lutzker, 1993). A baseline is first taken, and then a criterion level is selected. The consequences for reaching or not reaching this level are usually arranged beforehand. If behavior changes, a new criterion is set (e.g., Foxx & Rubinoff, 1979).

Multiple Baseline Designs

You may have opportunities to use *multiple baseline designs*, in which you introduce the same intervention following baselines of different lengths. In multiple baselines across behaviors, a baseline is taken for different behaviors, and intervention is applied to one at a time while continuing to track all behaviors (see Exhibits 19.9 and 19.10). Behaviors may involve different behaviors by the same person in the same situation or the same behavior by one person in different situations (e.g., sharing toys on the playground, at lunch, and during recess). In each case, the intervention is applied to one behavior at a time. If a change occurs in its frequency and no change takes place in the other behaviors, then the intervention is applied to the next behavior. As the number of behaviors increase that

change in frequency only after the intervention is introduced, confidence grows that change is related to intervention. If behaviors are influenced by similar factors (i.e., they are not independent), changes in other behaviors will occur when intervention is introduced. Multiple-baseline designs across settings can be valuable in reviewing the quality of care staff provide to residents. Schnelle and Traughber (1983) used a multiple-baseline across different nursing homes to assess the effects of training in both nursing homes. This offered information about the external validity of the training methods (the extent to which they can be used with success in different settings).

Seekins, Mathews and Fawcett (1984) worked with the executive board of a low-income, self-help center to develop and implement a training procedure for chairing meetings. The role of the chairperson at board meetings provided an opportunity for poor people to achieve success in a leadership position. The role of chair rotated among

EXHIBIT 19.9
A Multiple Baseline Across Behaviors Evaluating Assertion Training

A multiple-phase design across behaviors was used to evaluate assertion training with a 56-year-old carpenter who was hospitalized after an explosive argument with his supervisor at work (Foy, Eisler, & Pinkston, 1975). He reacted to what he considered "unreasonable demands from others" with verbal abuse and physical assaultiveness. His marriage had been described as full of strife, and he was physically abusive toward his wife. Baseline data were collected during seven work-related role plays that involved situations such as "you are blamed for making a mistake that is not your fault." Each scene was described first, and then the counselor (playing the role of supervisor) introduced the prompt; for example, "I am not sure that you deserve a raise" (p. 135).

A review of the client's behavior during role plays revealed the following concerns: hostile comments, compliance to unreasonable requests, irrelevant comments, and not requesting changes in behavior. These were addressed within a multiple-baseline design. The effectiveness of different procedures was explored. The first procedure (modeling alone) was applied to all four behaviors at once. Modeling plus instructions was then introduced in a staggered fashion (see Exhibit 19.10).

The addition of instructions enhanced the effects of model presentation. Gains were maintained at a 6-week follow-up. The client reported that his relationship with his supervisor had improved. He used less verbal abuse and made more appropriate requests. As a result, his supervisor had made positive changes in the client's working conditions. The client also reported that his new skills had improved his relationship with his son.

EXHIBIT 19.10
Target Assertive Behaviors During the Four Phases

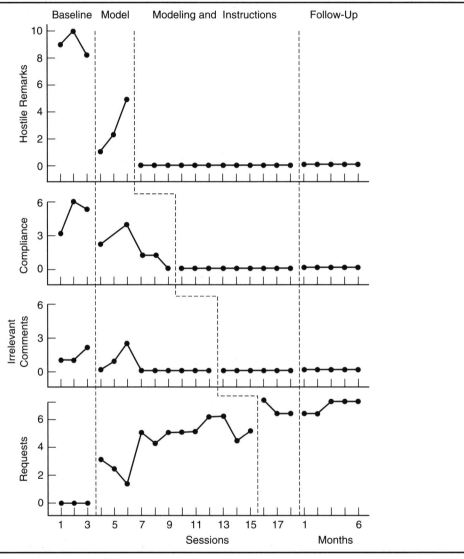

Source: D. W. Foy, R. M. Eisler, S. Pinkson (1975), Modeled assertion in a case of explosive rages. *Journal of Behavior Therapy and Experimental Psychiatry,* **6,** p. 136.

the members. A review of the literature and discussions with people who conducted good meetings suggested 40 specific chairperson behaviors under categories such as opening and closing meetings, leading discussions, and solving problems. A combination of behavioral specifications, examples, rationales, study guides, practice, and feedback were used to teach these behaviors. A multiple baseline design allowed exploration of the effects of training on the directly observed behaviors of persons serving as chairperson. There were marked increases in desired activities—to near

EXHIBIT 19.11
Mean Rates of Daily Incidents of Verbal Aggression for Two Groups of Adolescents During Baseline, Intervention, and Follow-up Conditions

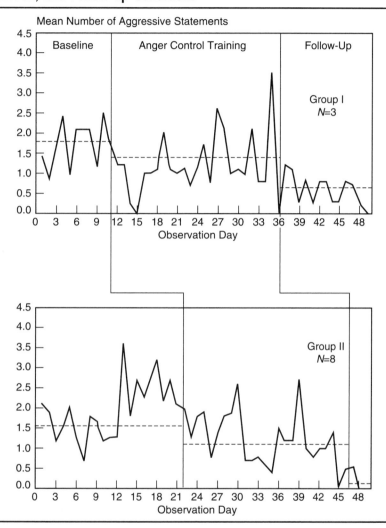

Source: R. F. Dangel, J. P. Deschner, & R. R. Rasp (1989), Anger control training for adolescents in residential treatment. *Behavior Modification, 13,* 454.

mastery levels. The percentage of agenda items on which closure was reached rose from an average of 30% to more than 85%.

Multiple baseline design can be used across groups. For example, Richard Dangel and his colleagues (1989) used anger-control training in a group context to decrease verbal aggression. The dotted lines in Exhibit 19.11 represent the mean

rate in each phase. You could plot data for individuals in a group if you want to explore whether some improved more than others.

Cautions About Assumption of Effects

A number of factors—such as the questionable reliability and validity of measures, variations in how measures are used, and short unstable baselines—may limit confidence in whether a procedure was responsible for a change. You may not be able to offer and withdraw plans at will. Conditions that covary with intervention may make it impossible to determine the role of intervention alone. For example, different instructions often accompany different reinforcement procedures. External validity (the degree to which results can be generalized to other behaviors, people, or situations) may be compromised by the effects of observers on outcome or by use of a certain sequence of procedures (i.e., generalization may be limited to situations in which the same sequence is used).

The Role of Replication

There are many ways to increase confidence in the effectiveness of a procedure. Effects can be replicated with other clients (**intersubject replication**). For example, many A-B or B-C designs with clients with similar problems can be gathered using similar interventions. If problem levels have been stable for a long time and you successfully resolve many clients' complaints, you can more confidently discard rival hypotheses (e.g., that measurement changes were responsible for outcomes; see Exhibit 19.4). You could use **intra-subject replication**. That is, you could replicate the effects of an intervention with one client by repeatedly introducing and removing a procedure. Let's say that your clients want to find out whether stress-management skills or programming of other activities is more effective in decreasing family arguments. You could help your clients acquire related skills and ask them to use them alternate weekends. (See also Busse et al., 1995.)

SEEKING ANSWERS TO OTHER QUESTIONS

You can explore whether one method is more effective than another by using experimental group designs or certain types of single-case designs. Practice constraints often rule out group designs, but you may have opportunities to use single-case designs to explore whether one method is more effective than another. In **simultaneous-treatment designs**, two or more interventions are simultaneously available. In a classic study by Browning and Stover (1971), observation of interaction in a residential center among a boy, the staff, and his peers revealed that three contingencies were in effect for bragging: positive attention, being ignored, and verbal admonishment. Three groups of two staff each simultaneously and successively used the three conditions for 3 weeks following a baseline period. This comparison showed that ignoring bragging was most effective.

You or your clients may want to know whether combining two or more methods improves outcome. You may want to explore whether self-reinforcement is a useful adjunct to social skills training. You could use both procedures at first and then withdraw self-reinforcement training. If gains are maintained, then additional self-reinforcement training may not add anything. You could use a **periodic treatment design** to explore the effects of interventions that take place during interviews, as separate from methods used between interviews. For example, Ms. Landis saw Julie once a week for 8 weeks. To explore the effects of these 1-hour sessions separately from use of thought stopping during the week, Julie and Ms. Landis could examine the graph of worry-free periods to see if they increased right after their meetings. You could explore changes within sessions (e.g., in anxiety, social skills, or group interaction).

If you are using a procedure with many components and suspect that one or more may not be necessary, you could omit some and assess the effects. Most procedures consist of many components. Consider parent training, which includes discrimination training (parents learn to identify specific behaviors), training in how to monitor behavior and observe contingencies, introduction of a new vocabulary to describe behaviors and related events, and enhancing effective use of instructions, positive reinforcement, extinction, and time-outs. You and your clients will also make decisions about service level (e.g., weekly or biweekly meetings). You could explore the effects of varying levels on outcome.

NEXT STEPS WHEN PLANS ARE SUCCESSFUL

If intervention is successful, gradually remove any parts of the program that are not part of the client's real-life environments. For example, the point program designed for the Lakeland family was gradually faded out (see Exhibit 19.12). You could gradually withdraw your involvement in community programs as residents acquire needed skills. Group leaders should gradually phase out their involvement as group members assume leadership responsibilities. Ongoing evaluation of outcomes will indicate whether gains are maintained at desired

EXHIBIT 19.12
Case Examples

BRIAN AND HIS PARENTS

The point program was successful in increasing the number of chores that Brian completed, from a baseline of one per week to eight per week during the fourth week of the program. Teasing the dog decreased and addressing Mrs. Lakeland in a polite fashion increased from zero to once a day during the fourth week. Brian's quiz grades increased from C− to B− in two of his courses over a 3-month period. Both he and his parents reported that they were pleased with these changes. Comparison of the baseline rates of praise and criticism of Brian by his parents, with those during the fourth week of intervention indicated an increase in praise (from .23 per hour to .5 per hour for Mrs. Lakeland, and from .24 to .42 per hour for Mr. Lakeland) and a decrease in criticism (from 1.5 per hour during baseline to .13 for Mrs. Lakeland, and from .62 to .07 per hour for Mr. Lakeland). Brian gained access to reinforcers, such as fishing trips with his father.

Mr. Colvine used both direct and indirect measures to evaluate negotiation training. He asked the Lakelands whether they had noticed any change in how they resolved conflicts. In addition, Mr. and Mrs. Lakeland kept track of the percentage of conflicts successfully resolved. A review of tape-recorded exchanges between Brian and his parents (one at baseline and one during the fourth training session) indicated that the clients increased their frequency of complete communications (from zero to five) and also made gains on statement of issues (from two to six) and suggestions of options (from one to seven). Brian and his parents said that they had fewer arguments at home and that they were able to settle disagreements more easily. The percentage of conflicts successfully resolved at home increased from zero to 70%. All three measures indicated that positive changes had been made.

The Lakelands reported that they got along better, and neither Mr. nor Mrs. Lakeland indicated any interest in having Brian removed from their home. But they wondered how long these gains would last, since the family did "have its ups and downs." Mr. Colvine also spoke to Brian's older brother and his sister to get their view of how things were. They agreed that the household was calmer. Brian said that he no longer got sleepy at school since the dosage of his medication had been lowered and that he did not mind taking it now. He still had difficulty with some of his teachers and still found it irresistible at times to tease his sister. However, his parents now ignored this, and his sister also paid less attention to Brian. The school counselor, however, was not impressed with Brian's progress and made a gloomy forecast of what was to come.

(continued)

EXHIBIT 19.12 (*continued*)
Case Examples

MRS. RYAN AND THE GREENS

Mrs. Slater used graphs to review progress with her clients. Mrs. Ryan thought the graphs were wonderful: "What a good idea. I wish I had known about that long ago. I can see how I am doing, right on the wall of my own room." Mrs. Ryan increased the number of her social contacts from a baseline level of one per week to six per week at the end of the fifth week of intervention. She noted the enjoyment value of these in a diary that she kept, which also included brief, positive descriptions of her new acquaintances. As Mrs. Slater predicted, based on her assessment of Mrs. Ryan's social skills, Mrs. Ryan soon made friends at the center and was receiving invitations from others. Indeed, Mrs. Ryan "bloomed" amidst her increased social contacts, which Mrs. Slater saw at first hand during a visit with Mrs. Ryan to the center during the fifth week. Four people enthusiastically greeted Mrs. Ryan when she entered the building. Mrs. Ryan confessed that she had originally had a very inaccurate view of what went on at senior centers. She had thought that there would be dull people sitting around doing "dull things like working with beads."

Mrs. Ryan's letter writing increased from one letter per week to five per week, and by the fifth week she had started to receive more mail. She did not do too well with her daily walks, though. At first, they increased from a baseline of almost zero to once a day, but by the fifth week, they had fallen back to twice a week. Mr. and Mrs. Green had agreed on three chores that Mrs. Ryan could do: straighten up the living room each day in the late afternoon or evening, take the dishes out of the dishwasher each evening, and clean the washbasin in the bathroom twice a week. She had agreed to keep track of these chores so that she could see whether she did them more often, but she did not. She did report, however, that she "helped out more," and Mr. and Mrs. Green confirmed this. Mrs. Slater decided not to ask her to record questions about her grandchildren's activities and talking less about "old times" at dinner, but she did ask Mrs. Ryan what her grandchildren were doing during their meetings. Other family members reported that Mrs. Ryan now talked more about her social outings.

Both Mr. and Mrs. Green reported that their meeting with the social worker concerning Medicare and the book Mrs. Slater had suggested had been helpful. Mrs. Slater asked them if they could describe a couple of ways the book had been of value. They said that it helped them understand some of the changes that people go through when they are Mrs. Ryan's age, such as wondering why they are still alive, even feeling guilty, and worrying about who will take care of them if they become disabled. They seemed to be better able to put themselves into Mrs. Ryan's shoes. They also acknowledged that having more time to themselves was really up to them and did not have anything to do with Mrs. Ryan, that they had simply fallen into some bad habits of not planning evenings out. They had gone out twice in the past 4 weeks and had had a good time.

The outcomes shared by Mrs. Ryan and Mr. and Mrs. Green were learning to express their feelings more constructively and deciding where Mrs. Ryan would live. They were not interested in using behavior rehearsal to practice sharing their feelings in a more positive way, but they did read the book and had listened to the tape Mrs. Slater had lent them. The tape illustrated effective and ineffective ways to share feelings. Mrs. Slater helped them think about the last discussion they had had at home and to compare this with the tape. Mrs. Green chose re-acting empathetically rather than defensively; Mrs. Ryan chose not blaming oth-ers; and Mr. Green chose paraphrasing statements (see Chapter 12). Mrs. Green had thought up a strategy of counting to five before she said anything except "hmmm" following a statement by Mrs. Ryan. One important topic that came up during their meetings was that Mr. and Mrs. Green said they felt guilty about not spending more time with Mrs. Ryan. But Mrs. Ryan assured them that she liked having time to herself and did not expect more time with them. The Greens seemed to feel relieved after this discussion. Mrs. Ryan said that she did not have concerns "on her mind" to share with the Greens, but she did share her plea-sure with her new social life.

What about deciding where Mrs. Ryan should live? At the last session, after they discussed their progress in other areas, Mrs. Slater reminded them of this question. After a moment's silence, Mrs. Green said, "I wouldn't think of having my mother living anywhere else unless she's unhappy living with us." Mr. Green agreed and noted that everyone seemed happier now. Mrs. Ryan also stated that she wanted to continue living "with her family."

JULIE

Julie's baseline data showed that she was free of worry on 28% of the occasions on which she checked this. Her thought stopping and self-instruction training was only partially successful. The percentage increased to 46% over a 2-week period. Ms. Landis suggested using a cue to remind Julie to use her new skills, asked her to practice these skills for 15 minutes each evening, and arranged an agreed-on reinforcer that Julie would receive if the percentage decreased by 20 or more. These additional procedures increased the percentage of worry-free pe-riods to 61% at the end of the third week, where they remained.

Ms. Landis's assessment suggested that three factors seemed to be related to Julie's unplanned pregnancy: (1) Julie's lack of information about birth-control methods, (2) her lack of assertive skills, and (3) her low self-esteem. Ms. Landis evaluated Julie's newly acquired information concerning birth control in a dis-cussion. Julie discarded her belief in the rhythm method as an effective birth-control procedure and decided that she would like to be fitted for a diaphragm. She said that she had decided not to have intercourse but thought she should be prepared, just in case. Skill in refusing unwanted sexual overtures was eval-uated in role plays. A comparison of Julie's behavior during assessment with her behavior during these role plays revealed that Julie now had different ways to respond to such pressure that were acceptable to her. Change in self-esteem was assessed by comparing Julie's expectations of doing well (2), fair (1), or poorly (0) in five situations each day. The average daily rating increased from three during baseline to seven during the fifth week. Julie reported that she "liked her-self better." Notice that Ms. Landis did not focus on self-esteem. Low self-es-teem is often considered to be the cause of problems such as poor performance at school or lack of assertive behavior, and intervention is focused directly on changing self-esteem, perhaps by altering what clients say to themselves (i.e., decreasing negative self-statements and increasing positive self-statements). In a behavioral approach, self-esteem is assumed to be related to success experi-ences in everyday life, and so the focus of intervention is on increasing such contingencies.

levels as service is phased out. Further planning may be needed to maintain desired outcomes and generalize valued behaviors to other contexts (see Chapter 20). Keep in mind that success does not necessarily indicate that services offered were responsible. Focusing on vague outcomes, not tracking progress using valid measures and not taking a baseline will get in the way of determining degree of progress and exploring the role of intervention in contributing to outcome. Follow-up data will allow you and your clients to see if outcomes are maintained. Gathering this provides an opportunity to support clients and to offer additional service as needed. One way to gather data is to mail postage-paid, self-addressed postcards to clients that they return after supplying the information you want. Your agency's policy will influence whether you can obtain follow-up data. For example, your agency may have a policy against continued contact with clients.

WHEN THERE IS NO PROGRESS

Options when there is no improvement include waiting longer, adding or subtracting components, trying a different plan or changing goals (Barlow, Hayes, & Nelson, 1990). Problems such as incorrectly using plans can be identified early on by staying in frequent contact with participants by telephone or postcard between meetings. The initial plan selected should be the one most likely to work, with the most comfort and acceptability to clients and significant others in the most efficient manner with the fewest negative and most positive side effects, given available resources and constraints. Considerable thought should have been devoted to choosing it and you and your clients should not lightly discard it. Exhibit 19.13 suggests questions to ask before deciding that a plan was a flop. Setting realistic goals increases opportunities for success. Be sure to consider the typical success rate with a given problem when evaluating your success. Social workers tackle many kinds of problems. Opportunities for success is minimal for some.

EXHIBIT 19.13
Questions to Raise When There Is No Improvement

1. Is the plan acceptable to clients and significant others?
2. Was the program carried out as planned? How do I know?
3. Does the plan address clients' concerns? Are the outcomes pursued socially valid (important to clients and significant others)?
4. Does the plan address key problem-related factors? Have I overlooked related problems?
5. Is there empirical evidence that indicates that this plan will be successful in achieving outcomes sought with this client?
6. Is there empirical evidence that suggests that another plan would be successful?
7. Does the plan include requisites known to be related to success?
8. Have I used specific, relevant, sensitive progress measures to monitor progress?
9. Did I arrange needed prompts?
10. Are positive incentives sufficiently strong and frequent and given in appropriate contexts?
11. Are there competing contingencies (e.g., negative reactions from significant others)?
12. Should other mediators be involved? Who? How?
13. Do clients fear negative consequences of change?
14. Do participants have the required skills, resources, and time to carry out agreed-on tasks? How do I know?
15. Have you allowed enough time for change to occur?
16. Are helper–client relationship factors interfering with progress?
17. Do participants believe the plan will work?
18. Would another method of graphing or data summary reveal change?
19. Would other methods be feasible and successful?
20. Should I seek consultation?
21. Should I end service?
22. Should I refer the client elsewhere?

Was the Plan Used?

Staff in other agencies to which you referred your clients may have been overburdened, resulting in limited or no services. Maybe the programs or plan was not even implemented. Be sure to check this before assuming that your plan was a flop. If your plan was never tried, find out why.

Was the Plan Used as Agreed?

Perhaps the plan carried out differed from the one originally decided on. Program integrity is important to review. Find out exactly how the plan was implemented.

Was Progress Monitored?

Clients may ask you to accept their "guestimates" about progress. They may say, "I know what is happening without keeping track of changes." Actually, no one knows what is happening if progress is not monitored. Explore objections to suggested ways to assess progress, and make changes as necessary. Keep in mind that evaluation methods must be feasible as well as meaningful to clients.

Are Measures Used Sensitive to Change?

Measures used may not be sensitive to change. Perhaps you selected a measure based on its availability rather than on its accuracy in reflecting change. Perhaps the units you and your clients used in collecting or graphing data (e.g., weeks rather than days) obscure change.

What About Treatment Integrity?

Treatment integrity refers to the degree to which plans match those known to be effective. Review the requirements for procedures used to see if important ones were included. Find out whether tasks were carried out as agreed on in a consistent manner. What percentage of assignments were adequately completed? A review of records kept by clients may indicate that a procedure was not used at all, or was not implemented appropriately. A plan that is not used will not be effective. The frequency of reinforcement and practice is related to degree of behavior change. If there is little practice, it should not be surprising if there is little progress. A user-friendly record-keeping procedure will help you review a program's fidelity and progress.

Not following recommended guidelines is common. Strayhorn (1988) uses the term "Dilution Effects (A Drop in the Bucket)" to refer to two ways in which progress may be compromised: (1) many skills are required to achieve outcomes but only some are addressed and (2) many influences affect whether skills can be attained and maintained but only some are considered. You may not have time to implement a plan properly, and so may have

to offer an approximation. Effective use of a method may require 10 group meetings, but you may be able to offer only four. A client may need five different skills to achieve a valued outcome (e.g., making more friends), but your program provides training on only two. It is not surprising if there is little progress. Progress may be limited if many environmental characteristics affect whether a client uses skills, and you address only some of them. Perhaps you do not have time to help a client decrease her social anxiety or to alter unrealistic expectations (e.g., "I have to please everyone") that hamper the use of her skills.

Explore the possible reasons for not following agreed-on plans. Plans may deviate from what is optimal because of interfering beliefs, a lack of knowledge or skill on your part, or a lack of required resources or because clients and significant others do not carry out agreed-on plans, perhaps because of lack of reminders and incentives. Progress may be hindered by overly rigid use of a method. Cultural differences requiring service alterations may be ignored. Effective use of a program may drift over time. You may believe that you know best how to implement a procedure, even though research shows that your method is not effective. Helpers who are well trained in a method are less likely to deviate from recommended methods. The more complex an intervention program is, the greater the need for thorough training. Perhaps you have tried to do too much with too few resources or too little knowledge about what is needed to achieve certain outcomes. Trying to address too many problems may compromise treatment fidelity and decrease chances for success in areas of most concern to clients.

Other Points to Check

Perhaps your plan is not feasible. Perhaps you neglected to give clients practice in required skills. Perhaps outcomes focused on are of little interest to clients and significant others. Plans may be too complex or intrusive. Perhaps you dislike a client and so were not as warm and supportive as usual. You may have underestimated environmental obstacles such as high-crime neighborhoods and health problems. If progress has been monitored and plans carried out as agreed and there is little or no progress, check to see whether you arranged adequate cues and incentives. You may have to arrange prompts for valued behaviors. Ms. Landis suggested that Julie use a cue (a special bracelet or ring) to remind her to use self-instructions. Additional services may be required or other change agents may have to be involved (e.g., parents, neighbors). Perhaps you expected change to occur in too brief a time. Your review of possible reasons will indicate needed changes. You could add or subtract service components. If no other plans are feasible or other methods have also failed, seek consultation or refer clients elsewhere if other options are available. Also keep in mind that people have a right to participate on their own terms. "The individual's right to fail is something that professionals have extraordinary difficulty comprehending" (Sarason & Lorentz, 1979, p. 116).

Dealing with Discrepancies

What if there are discrepancies between different measures? For example, during the first 2 weeks of intervention, Mr. and Mrs. Lakeland said that they didn't feel very much was changing, even though review of data they collected showed that Brian had completed more chores and had engaged in other desired behaviors more often. It seemed that one fight during the week was enough to discourage Mr. and Mrs. Lakeland. The disrupting effect of emotional reactions on discrimination is an important reason for keeping an objective record of progress. If a discrepancy between measures persists, explore the reasons for this. Perhaps you are not addressing outcomes of most concern to clients. Perhaps progress measures are not sensitive to change.

WHAT IF COMPLAINTS GET WORSE?

If things are getting worse, explore possible reasons. Is it the result of intervention? Would this have happened anyway? For example, maybe a gang expanded its territory into a neighborhood,

disrupting efforts to increase the residents' involvement in citizen's groups. Perhaps matters have to get worse before they get better. If you believe this, can you make a sound argument for this view (one that is consistent with what is known about behavior)? Is there something wrong with your progress measures? If it seems that the intervention is responsible for deterioration, it should be stopped unless research shows that things do get worse before they get better. You may have to circle back to assessment to review assumptions. Plans selected may have little chance of success because that's the best that can be done under the current conditions (see the previous discussion of the dilution effect). They may fail, leaving clients more hopeless than before. The causes of some problems clients confront cannot be addressed by social workers. Without keeping "the big picture" in view, you may blame clients and/or yourself and become a contributor to empty promises and problem mystification (see Chapter 7).

PROGRAM AND POLICY EVALUATION

Guidelines for program and policy evaluation are similar to those for evaluating progress with individuals, groups, families or communities. Significant others (stake holders) must be considered (e.g., who will benefit and lose in what ways from given methods of evaluation; what program components are liked and disliked by whom as well as resources and validity of measures. (See earlier discussion of social validity.) Here, too, data regarding outcomes allows timely informed decisions. Here too, the potential for evaluation differs. For example, if goals are vague, careful evaluation is not possible. Here too we should ask "Compared with what?" in relation to a program (e.g., no program, a different program, or a different intensity of the same program). Goals, including hoped for level of success, should be clearly described as well as clear, sensitive, relevant progress measures. Questions are:

- **Whom** is the information for, and who will use the findings?
- **What** kinds of information are needed?

- **How** is the information to be used? For what purposes?
- **When** is the information needed?
- **How** much will it cost to get?
- **What** resources are available to gather needed data (what evaluations are feasible)?
- **How** accurate are different data sources? What systematic errors may be present? (Berk & Rossi, 1990; p. 39)

Here too, program implementation and service integrity is important to review, especially if there is little progress or harmful effects are found. An accountability checklist for agencies is suggested in Exhibit 19.14.

Program evaluation, compared with evaluation with individuals, families and groups is usually more complex and may be more conflictual depending on the number of involved individuals and groups inside and outside the agency or organization. It may be even more impossible to please everyone. Questions of equity and access may be vital to review (see for example Munton, Mooney, & Rowland, 1995). Questions of concern suggested by Richard Berk and Peter Rossi (1990) include the following:

1. Is the program reaching the appropriate beneficiaries?
2. Is the program being properly delivered?
3. Are the funds being used appropriately?
4. Can effectiveness be estimated? What is the evaluability potential? "Evaluability assessments essentially determine whether there are program goals that are sufficiently well articulated, whether the program is sufficiently clear and uniformly delivered and whether the requisite resources are available" (p. 74).
5. Did the program work? How good is good enough? Unless the size of the program effect required is clearly noted, "evaluators are shooting at a moving target" (p. 76).
6. Was the program worth it? Answering this question requires comparing cost with effectiveness.

EXHIBIT 19.14
Accountability Checklist for Agencies and Institutions

- Goals are clearly defined and agreed on.
- Intermediate steps required to attain goals are described.
- Models of successful service are provided.
- Accurate feedback regarding both process and outcome is available to clients, staff, and the public.
- Competent performance is reinforced.
- Harmful and ineffective methods are discarded.
- Procedures are in place and are used to find out how all facets of the agency or institution affect service quality.
- Regular reviews of progress are conducted based on clear relevant criteria.
- Staff receive needed training and attain required competency levels, as shown by tests of knowledge and skills.
- Potential negative and positive outcomes are monitored.
- A system is in place that allows administrators to find out if something is going wrong.
- A high percentage of those in need of service receive it, and a high percentage benefit.
- All staff receive feedback on their performance from both those above (e.g., administrators) and those below (e.g., supervisees), based on clear agreed-on criteria.
- Staff evaluate progress in an ongoing manner using relevant, sensitive progress indicators.
- Significant others are involved in assessing progress.
- Indirect measures of change are compared with direct measures.
- Case records clearly describe procedures used and outcomes achieved.
- The evaluation methods used enhance services and suggest opportunities for improving service.

Here, too, critical discussion and thinking are key skills. Berk and Rossi suggest that "evaluation research should not be undertaken by persons who prefer to avoid controversy, or who have difficulty facing criticism. Often, moreover, the criticism is 'political' and not motivated by scientific concerns" (1990, p. 14). Possible reasons for a program's failure include (1) excessive staff discretion in providing service, resulting in variations that decrease success; (2) minimal, watered-down programs (the dilution effect); (3) what works when used by well-trained, motivated staff does not when used by others; (4) what works for some clients doesn't work for others; and (5) clients refuse to participate. Perhaps programs were not implemented at all. Practices such as "creaming" (offering services only to clients who are most likely to benefit) will artificially inflate estimates of success. Costs, services and outcomes provided can be reviewed over time (e.g., in a time series design) to get an overall view (see Burchard & Schaefer, 1992).

Program outcomes may be compared with

1. the outcomes of similar programs.
2. the outcomes of the same program the previous year.
3. the outcomes of model programs in the field.
4. the outcomes of programs known to have difficulty.
5. the stated goals of the program.
6. external standards of desirability as developed by the profession.
7. standards of minimum acceptability (e.g., basic licensing standards).
8. ideals of program performance.
9. guesses made by staff or other decision makers about what the outcomes should be.

The "compared with what" question is critical. Are you comparing a program with the lack of a program, comparing two different programs, or exploring the effectiveness of different levels of a program (e.g., follow-up services for 6 months and 3 months)? "Success or failure is always related to some benchmark" (Berk & Rossi, 1990, p. 76).

Ongoing Evaluation and Assessment as Integral to Service

Quality assurance systems should be in place to assess the quality and consistency of services provided and improve staff performance and service quality. Identifying areas for improvement is a key aspect of any sound management system. Lower than hoped for standards of service provide opportunities for improvement. The periodic service review (PSR) described by Gary LaVigna and his colleagues contains four integrated elements:

1. **Performance standards** consisting of operational descriptions of desired processes and outcomes, the sum total of which define the quality to which the agency aspires.

2. **Performance monitoring** refers to the methods by which the agency verifies whether or not it is carrying out the process intended and is achieving its desired outcomes. The results of such monitoring set the stage for supervisory and management feedback.

3. **Supervisory and management feedback** are provided based on the results of performance monitoring to improve and maintain quality of services. Specific feedback is offered based on graphed data.

4. **Staff training** is provided to ensure that staff can competently carry out the procedures required to achieve the desired outcomes of the agency. (1994, pp. 15–16)

A focus on *systems* (e.g., how a group home is operating rather than on individual staff performance) encourages cooperative involvement of all staff. Individual feedback should also be provided by each supervisor to each staff member. Clear guidelines should be described regarding who is responsible for carrying out expected tasks and how task completion will be verified. Fairness to staff is one advantage of identifying clear performance standards for all job categories. Staff know what is expected. The criteria should be realistic and may be based on average or best past performance. Staff at all levels should help set standards, monitor progress, and decide on objectives. Their acceptance of monitoring can be encouraged by focusing on standards met and acknowledging the effort and good work this represents. Clear performance standards provide a guideline for the design of training programs. Competency-based criterion referenced training should be provided as needed. This refers to training based on what is known about how to achieve valued outcomes (what competencies are required) and which includes specific criteria that can be used to determine whether desired skill levels have been achieved. Sampling of relevant staff behaviors make quality assurance programs workable. For further discussion of program evaluation, see Berk & Rossi, 1990; Patton, 1986, 1987; Rossi & Freeman, 1993; Scriven, 1991.)

OBSTACLES TO EVALUATION

If we agree that ongoing tracking of outcomes is needed both for practical and ethical reasons, we should explore what stands in the way. Reasons given by social workers include not knowing methods well enough to use them, no encouragement from agencies, and insufficient time (Penka & Kirk, 1991).

Overlooking Ethical and Practical Benefits

Staff may not appreciate the importance of clearly describing outcomes and tracking them in order to improve plans, or the ethical problems raised by pursuing vague outcomes and relying on vague outcome measures such as not detecting unintended negative effects. Pursuit of vague outcomes give helpers wide discretion to explore areas that are of little interest to clients.

It's Scary and Threatening

A clear description of outcomes and services increases the visibility of what was done with what result. People can see what you are up to. Vague goals and "guesstimates" about outcomes make it easy for you to assume that you are helping clients when you may not be. Embarrassing and threatening questions are avoided, such as How do we know that our services help clients? Evaluation can be especially threatening if you have received punishing feedback. Feared negative consequences that may result from a poor showing (e.g., a decrease in funding) may discourage evaluation of service outcomes. Recognizing the ethical and practical benefits of evaluation for problem solving and viewing less than hoped-for success as an opportunity for improvement will encourage you to seek rather than avoid data regarding outcome.

Management Policies and Practices Do Not Encourage It

Clients may be shifted from one service provider to another, with little time to coordinate their efforts. Prompts and incentives that encourage evaluation may not be available. The administrators' first interest may be in maintaining funding sources, not in candidly reviewing the outcomes of programs. Authority rather than critical inquiry may be relied on in making decisions. It is up to management to encourage a culture that views evaluation as an essential part of problem solving, a culture that values truth over ignorance and prejudice.

Lack of Creativity, Skill, and Knowledge

You may not know how to identify clear problem-related outcomes or valid, feasible, outcome measures and arrange for their ongoing tracking. It takes creativity to come up with easy-to-use valid outcome measures. (See for example, Favell, Realon, & Sutton, 1996.) Consult problem-related scientific literature to get ideas. This describes many innovative, ways to evaluate outcome. For example, high-risk mothers used a cardsort to evaluate 32 program services (Pharis & Levin, 1991). Items rated high in importance included "Helped you learn more about how children develop and what they need to grow up healthy and happy," "Helped you have more confidence in yourself," "Helped you understand yourself better," and "Gave you a person to talk to who really cared about you."

Trying to Do Too Much

You may select outcome measures that are relevant but not feasible. Progress measures do not have to be "perfect" and rarely can be. Ask "Is there an easy yet valid way we can assess outcome?" You should only be as precise as you need to be. Stay focused on what is needed for case planning. The "so what?" question is always important (e.g., "How will I use this information?"). Lack of resources may limit options. Keep track of obstacles to evaluating outcome (e.g., excessive caseloads, fragmented service delivery systems) in order to discover possibilities for reducing them.

Competing Beliefs, Values, and Styles

Staff may assume incorrectly that setting clear goals and monitoring outcome interferes with establishing a working relationship (see earlier discussion). Caring enough to look requires courage and a commitment to clients to fully inform them. This may be absent. Evaluation may be viewed as unnecessary rather than integral to problem solving. Staff may rely on poor substitutes such as appeals to tradition (what's been done in the past) or testimonials. They may rely on intuition to test guesses about outcome. Although intuition is essential for coming up with good ideas about what may be true or false and for discovering ways to test them, it is only critical discussion and testing that can yield corrective feedback. Even when behaviors occur in public places, staff may object to collecting data that could improve services. For example, I suggested to a student in a research course that she base her project on staff behavior during hospital rounds, in which she participated. She could keep a critical incident record of staff behavior that encouraged helpful patient behavior and also staff behavior that seemed to discourage such behavior. But her supervisor refused to allow her to collect this information because it might make staff members uncomfortable. The supervisor ignored the potential benefits to patients and opportunities for staff to improve their skills.

TAKE ADVANTAGE OF HELPFUL TOOLS

You can make evaluation easier by taking advantage of helpful tools such as graphs. Standardized, user-friendly, valid measures and computer programs to graph and summarize data may save time (see Bloom, Fischer, & Orme, 1995; Mattaini, 1993a; Nurius & Hudson, 1993). Edward Bullmore and his colleagues (1992) designed a computerized quality assurance program that allows entry of up to four goals for each client, with four objectives for each. Both helpers and clients rate problem severity, goal difficulty, and present level of social functioning. Problem severity and goal difficulty may not be related. That is, a problem may be severe but reaching related goals may be easy, or a problem may be only moderately severe but attaining related goals may be difficult. Clients and helpers also rate clients' present mood and quality

of life (work, home, and social). The data are graphed for review.

EVALUATING YOUR PROGRESS

One of the advantages of being a professional is continuing to enhance your skills over your career. Self-directed learning skills are needed to make the most of this advantage. Helpful questions are

- What skills would I like to acquire?
- What value would these skills have for my clients?
- What exactly would I do (and not do) if I had this skill?
- What approximations take me closer to my goal?
- What criteria would most accurately reflect mastery of skills?
- Is this skill of value in other situations?
- What training programs would be most effective in helping me learn this skill?

One of your goals may be to increase the variety of service options you consider. If you have only one option and it fails, you and your clients will be stuck. Mark Mattaini (1989) found that students who used eco-mapping paid more attention to higher-level systems than did students who did not use it. You could use the contextual analysis form in Exhibit 8.3 to see if it makes a difference in outcomes. It takes courage and commitment to clients to candidly review the match between your values, knowledge and skills and what is needed to help clients and avoid harm. This review will help you to spot learning opportunities. You are more likely to continue to enhance your professional knowledge and skills if you are open to new ideas and can plan or select effective training programs. So, evaluation is not just for clients, it is for you, too. It also is for supervisors and administrators so that they can be informed about the quality of services provided by their staff and use this information to improve services. In what areas do staff do well? In what areas do they not do so well? This information is needed to select training programs (e.g., McClanaghan & Krantz, 1993).

SUMMARY

The proof of the pudding concerning the effects of policies, programs, and plans is whether or not hoped for outcomes result. The history of the helping professions clearly shows that caring (a good heart) is not enough to protect clients from ineffective or harmful "service." Even a benevolent fox may have difficulty fulfilling his guard duties. No one really knows if a program is harming or helping clients or making no difference at all unless the outcomes are carefully explored. The more vague the assessment of progress, the greater the opportunities for the unrecognized play of self-interest that may harm clients. Our preferences influence what we see and do unless we have strategies for avoiding bias. Key questions you should ask include (1) What information is needed to make well-informed decisions about what to do next? (2) What data would provide accurate estimates at the least cost (e.g., in time, effort, money)? and (3) how can the acceptability of effective methods be increased?

Accountability is a requirement of ethical practice. Clients have a right to know whether services help or harm or are irrelevant. Does parent training affect the frequency of child abuse? Do staff members in an agency acquire and use more effective conflict resolution skills? To answer these questions, hoped-for outcomes must be clearly described, and relevant, feasible, sensitive outcome measures must be identified and monitored. Careful evaluation serves an important case-planning function. Self-reports of clients and significant others about progress provide important information. Direct measures such as observation allow you and your clients to see whether changes did occur. Both are important. Myths about evaluation include the belief that it requires selection of trivial outcomes and that it interferes with the helping relationship. Ongoing review of progress allows timely changes in plans based on degree of success. It will help you and your clients avoid common sources of error such as overconfidence and hindsight bias that result in inaccurate estimates of progress and the role of services. Feedback about positive outcomes provides an incentive to continue the hard work often needed for success.

A lack of resources and time may limit opportunities for careful evaluation. You and your clients will often have to choose an approximation. Keeping your eye on the purpose of your work with clients will help you make well-reasoned decisions. Clear descriptions of services offer valuable information to review if plans are not successful (treatment fidelity can be assessed). You can use your skills in evaluating progress with clients to assess and upgrade your practice skills.

REVIEWING YOUR COMPETENCIES

Reviewing What You Know

1. Describe the relationship between evaluation and case planning.
2. Identify criteria that can be used to evaluate progress, and critique each.
3. Describe sources of bias that may result in incorrect estimates of progress, and give examples.
4. Describe sources of bias that may result in an incorrect assumption that services were responsible for outcomes.

5. Describe what is meant by the term *social validity* and give examples of ways to assess this.

6. Discuss the relationship between clarity of objectives and evaluation of outcome.

7. Accurately critique different kinds of evaluation methods.

8. Give examples of multiple-baseline designs.

9. Describe questions to raise when services offered are not successful.

10. Describe confounding factors in different types of single-case and group designs related to the assumption that outcomes resulted from services offered.

11. Accurately describe your knowledge and skill levels related to specific assessment and intervention methods, and identify relevant, feasible, sensitive progress measures to evaluate enhancement of these competencies.

12. Discuss the importance of clearly describing level of progress hoped for in program evaluation.

13. Identify and critique different criteria against which a program could be evaluated.

14. Describe the characteristics of a well-designed quality assurance program.

15. Describe the role of management practices in influencing services provided by line staff.

16. Discuss the ethical and practical problems of not evaluating progress.

17. Describe how goals may differ in evaluation and research.

18. Identify obstacles to careful evaluation, and suggest steps to overcome them.

19. You can accurately describe the purpose of assessing social validity and identify consumer groups that should be involved.

Reviewing What You Do

1. When possible, you evaluate progress in an ongoing manner using valid, unintrusive measures, and write clear, accurate summaries of outcomes in case records. Criteria: objectives and progress indicators are clear and relevant (e.g., meaningful to clients); accurate graphed summaries of data are available.

2. You identify valid measures of progress in specific situations and design appropriate visual representations.

3. You can accurately plot data on a graph.

4. You can accurately and concisely summarize graphed data and make sound recommendations about next steps.

5. Given an example of graphed data, you can determine the average value within different phases (e.g., baseline, intervention) and draw correct inferences about the effects of service.

6. Given examples of claims about progress and/or the role of services in outcome, you can accurately identify alternative hypotheses and fallacies in reasoning.

7. You use both direct (e.g., observation) and indirect (self-report) measures to evaluate progress when feasible.

8. You involve significant others as well as clients in selecting progress measures.

9. You clearly describe to clients the reasons for evaluating progress (e.g., as determined by review of audiotaped interviews).

10. You carefully review your clients' progress in each interview.

11. You ask helpful questions and take appropriate steps when there is no progress.

12. Given examples, you accurately identify sources of bias that result in incorrect estimates of progress.

13. When possible, you refer clients to agencies in which staff use valid progress measures and assess social validity.
14. You make effective use of probes to determine the need for continued service.
15. You gather baseline data when possible.
16. You assume increasing responsibility for identifying specific personal learning goals, for selecting accurate ways to assess performance levels, and for arranging effective training opportunities.
17. You help a fellow student to clearly define a personal learning goal and design a way to monitor progress.
18. You use practice-related scientific literature to evaluate the quality of service methods.
19. You design sound program evaluations.
20. You gather accurate data regarding specific liked and disliked aspects of service programs and use this information to increase service acceptability.

Reviewing Results

1. You make timely changes in service plans based on evaluation of progress.
2. Program acceptability increases.
3. You avoid faulty claims about service effectiveness.

CHAPTER 20

Planning for Endings

OVERVIEW

Both planned and unplanned endings are discussed in this chapter. Reasons for unplanned endings are described as well as components of planned endings and steps you can take to increase the probability that positive outcomes occur in real-life contexts and are maintained.

You Will Learn About

- How to plan for endings.
- Contributors to unplanned endings.
- The importance of planning for generalization and maintenance.
- Strategies for encouraging generalization and maintenance.
- Ethical issues.

Only some endings will be planned (objectives are met and arrangements are made to maintain positive outcomes) or appropriate referrals are made. You will also have unplanned endings in which clients may not return even though agreed-on goals have not been met. Some clients may benefit from a single meeting (Talmon, 1990). Others may require continued support over a long period. The dropout rate is about 50% in typical practice settings. It should be noted, however, that not all dropouts are failures (see review in Pekarik, 1993).

HOW TO PLAN FOR ENDINGS

It should be obvious, to you as well as to your clients, when you will hold your last meeting: Agreed-on outcomes have been achieved and plans to maintain gains are in place (see Exhibit 20.1). Or you may have been able to offer only an approximation to what is needed, perhaps because of lack of resources, and next steps must be decided on, such as a referral. Planning for endings should begin during initial interviews. Endings will be

EXHIBIT 20.1
Checklist For Planned Endings

1. Desired outcomes are clearly described.
2. Clear, agreed-on criteria for evaluating progress are identified.
3. Expectations of clients are clearly described.
4. Responsibilities of helpers are clearly described including what can be offered and what cannot.
5. A specific number of meetings is agreed on in the first interview.
6. Progress is evaluated on an ongoing basis.
7. Arrangements are made for generalization and maintenance.
8. Feelings about ending are discussed.
9. Gains made are noted and supported.
10. Clients' contributions are described and supported.
11. Helpful next steps (e.g., referrals, follow-up meetings) are planned.

planned to the extent to which you and your client: (1) clearly describe outcomes to focus on and criteria to evaluate progress and levels of progress hoped for; (2) clearly describe expectations and responsibilities; (3) monitor progress; and (4) plan for generalization and maintenance of gains. It does little good to develop needed skills if these are not used in (do not generalize to) real-life situations of concern to clients. Preparing for endings will avoid negative emotional reactions such as anger, frustration, or guilt that may result from unfocused work. Even if you are not successful in helping clients attain valued outcomes, if you have used "state-of-the-art" methods to pursue clear relevant objectives, or have done what can be done in an impossible job, you have given your best. Review your beliefs and feelings about endings to make sure they encourage planned endings. You may have difficulty ending because you assume more responsibility for the well-being of clients than is realistic (or good for clients) or try to solve unsolvable problems. Keep in mind that clients make decisions about their degree and kind of participation. They as well as you are responsible for choices made.

Limiting service to a set number of interviews is increasingly common under managed care and may motivate clients to become involved at an early point. Research suggests that many clients prefer brief compared to long-term treatments and that most clients attain most benefit during the first few sessions (see review by Pekarik, 1993). However, as Pekarik (1993) notes, truly consumer-oriented services would require offering what is needed and wanted. You can remind clients of time limits by occasional statements such as "Well, we have _____ more meetings." Unnecessarily extending meetings may have negative effects, for example increase dependency (Cummings, 1977). Contacts may stop when an involuntary arrangement such as probation or parole ends. If you have not been of help, both you and your client will probably feel relieved when the last meeting arrives. If you have been of help, ending interviews provide an opportunity to celebrate successes, to support clients for their contributions, and to help clients plan how to maintain gains. If success has been limited, "small wins" can be noted, work that remains to be accomplished discussed, and helpful next steps decided on (perhaps a referral). Examples of planning for endings can be seen in Exhibits 20.2 to 20.4.

CONTRIBUTORS TO UNPLANNED ENDINGS

Clients will usually not continue contact if they receive little or nothing of value, or feel misunderstood, ignored, patronized, or "put down." Unplanned endings are more likely under the following circumstances:

1. The purpose of meetings is not clearly identified.

2. Expectations are not clearly described.

3. Progress is not monitored.

4. Outcomes focused on are not important to clients or do not complement their values.

5. A time frame is not agreed on.

6. Plans suggested and/or the rationale for them are not acceptable to clients and/or significant others.

7. There are problems in the helping relationship such as mistrust.

EXHIBIT 20.2
Examples of Planning for Endings

In all three of the examples that follow, the social workers paid careful attention to significant others and focused on behaviors that would continue to be reinforced after services ended. Artificial reinforcers and schedules were removed and procedures were selected that clients could apply themselves, thus decreasing dependence on the social worker. The rationales for plans were explained, conditions that might present future obstacles identified, and coping skills developed to use in such situations. Clients were given written descriptions of plans to take home with them.

CASE EXAMPLE 1: BRIAN AND HIS PARENTS

Mr. Colvine helped Brian and his parents to develop more positive ways of talking to each other in the office. He asked his clients to practice the skills they had learned twice each week as one effort to generalize use of effective problem-solving skills to the home. He selected specific topics to be discussed to make sure these could be handled with their new skills. The second week he asked the clients to assume more responsibility for choosing topics. He used prompts to encourage them to identify issues and gradually faded them out as the clients acquired skill. Knowing that Mr. Colvine would ask them about their practice sessions served as a reminder to practice new skills at home.

Brian now received a weekly allowance of up to ten dollars, contingent on carrying out specific chores and obtaining certain grades. Two extra bonus dollars were offered for "a good week." This was defined as completing all scheduled chores, doing an extra "thoughtful deed" for a family member, or getting a very good grade on a test or assignment, or as a final grade. Examples of thoughtful deeds included taking the dog out for a walk even though this was not his job, and helping his mother unload the groceries. All artificial reinforcers were removed before the last session. Brian had joined a woodworking class at the local recreation center and had made two acquaintances through this class. Mr. Colvine helped his clients to identify situations that were likely to lead to backsliding, such as fatigue on the part of the parents, and to identify methods they could use to counter downward trends and maintain positive gains, such as occasionally monitoring praise given to Brian. Mrs. Lakeland said that this helped her to remember to focus on "the good" rather than "the bad."

Mr. Colvine gradually faded out contacts with his clients from once a week to one in-person contact every other week and biweekly telephone contact, to one in-person contact every three weeks and biweekly phone contacts, and then to once-a-month phone contacts. Booster sessions were scheduled every three months for a year. Brian and his parents reported that they looked forward to these meetings, because they provided an opportunity to review successes as well as to discuss concerns that had been raised. They reported that having written copies of steps to follow when discussing differences helped them to remember what to do. Brain made no physical threats against his parents over the one-year follow-up period. His grades hovered at about a B− average, and his school counselor still waited for what he believed would be the inevitable backsliding. The family still had its ups and downs and its arguments, as most families do. The difference was that now family members had more control over them.

CASE EXAMPLE 2: JULIE

Arranging prompts (reminders) for new behaviors in the natural environment was an important aspect of Ms. Landis' work with Julie. Special cues were arranged to remind Julie to use her new skills when she started to worry. Ms. Landis did not fade her contacts with Julie but let it be known that her door was open in case Julie wanted to consult her after the last planned session. The last session was used to review progress and to offer positive feedback to Julie for her contributions. Julie said that she felt more "sure of herself" and that she thought she would be able to refuse unwanted overtures. Ms. Landis reminded her to review the tape of various ways to refuse unwanted requests if she became uncertain in the future. She reminded Julie to consult her copy of instructions for decreasing worrisome thoughts and increasing self-confidence if she found herself slipping. She and Julie agreed to speak together within six months.

At a six-month follow-up Julie reported that she was enjoying school more and things were "going OK" with her boyfriend. She wasn't sure she wanted to confine her social activities to "only him." She did feel sad at times about the abortion, but if this lasted too long, she reminded herself about the commitment-enhancing methods she had learned from Ms. Landis. She believed that she had made the right decision and said she would not put herself in this position again. She was not using any birth control procedures except "not doing it."

CASE EXAMPLE 3: MRS. RYAN AND THE GREENS

Mrs. Slater made arrangements to get in touch with Mrs. Ryan and the Greens within six months and extended an open-door policy to them. When she spoke to the clients she learned that Mrs. Ryan had a mild heart attack three months after the last session but that she was recovering well and was gradually resuming visits to the senior center. The Greens had been very helpful during her recovery. Mrs. Ryan's letter writing had decreased during her illness but was now picking up again. The Greens had decided that they liked getting out of the house occasionally. Little seemed to have changed in discussions at the dinner table except that family members seemed more tolerant of each other.

THE FUTURE

What does the future hold for these clients? Base-rate data could be consulted to gain some idea. Mrs. Landis knew that there was a good probability that Julie might get pregnant again. Is there anything else Ms. Landis could do other than having an open-door policy and sharing information with Julie about the possible consequences of certain courses of action or inaction?

There is a high probability that Mrs. Ryan will have another heart attack within the next few years. Her greatest fear was that she would linger in a debilitated condition at great financial and psychological expense both to herself and to her significant others. Could this be avoided? What steps can she take to prevent this such as completing a "living will"? Mrs. Slater provided information about legal rights and suggested sources of information to her clients. She also provided information about financial resources. Although the Greens were still worried about

(*continued*)

EXHIBIT 20.2 (*continued*)
finances if Mrs. Ryan became chronically ill, her age and fragility increased their
sense of closeness to and warmth for her. This was indeed a family in transition—the children were getting older and Mrs. Ryan's health was not good.

The Lakeland family was also a family in transition. One son was in college
and would probably be off on his own in a couple of years. Brian would enter
high school soon. Given the lack of aggressive behavior in Brian's early history
and the absence of aggressive behavior over the past year, there was a good
chance that troublesome behaviors of this kind would not recur if reinforcement
for positive behaviors was maintained.

Unplanned endings may occur because clients move or become ill.

Some clients will return, not because they have benefited from meetings with you but because they still hope to do so. Or they may have received some benefit, but not as much as hoped for. Clients may feel angry or frustrated if there is no progress. If you have not helped clients to identify specific valued outcomes and steps to achieve them you may feel guilty or frustrated and are in an embarrassing spot—so embarrassing that you may choose not to recognize it. If you have not followed a helping process that permits planned endings, you may start to feel uncomfortable with clients and even start to dislike them. Use your feelings as a cue to explore related reasons. You will not be able to help all your clients. Success in altering behavior of anti-social children older than 12 is not as great (30%) as it is for children under 12 (70%) (Bank, Patterson, & Reid, 1987). Overestimating the potential for progress may result in frustration as well as a tendency to overlook limited success. Candid appraisal of degree of progress will help you and your clients to take appropriate next steps.

EXHIBIT 20.3
Ending Sessions of a Group

"During the final phase, the emphasis was placed on reviewing the skills that
had been taught and planning for dealing with stress after the group ended. In
session nine, Lydia [the facilitator] suggested some extra group tasks that would
help members think of how they could maintain the skills they had learned during the previous 8 weeks." She noted that without planning for maintenance, the
benefits of training may dwindle. Each group member discussed the principles
of transfer and maintenance. Lydia suggested that they use the principles to develop a personal maintenance plan that would be the focus of the last session.
Everyone agreed to try it out. During the 10th session group members reviewed
each other's plan. Jim planned to read some books on assertiveness and stress
management. . . . Ellen was going to . . . keep a diary of stress situations and how
she handled them and to continue walking 2 miles a day, and Susan would accompany her. Susan had joined a church group in which she hoped to use the
assertive techniques she learned in the group. Janet was going to join a yoga
class to improve her relaxation.

A booster session was planned in 3 months. "They could discuss how they
had used their stress management skills, refresh any skills that had been forgotten, and do problem solving. Most of the members were willing to attend, and
Lydia noted that she and the agency would be happy to cooperate with such a
plan." The main purpose of the booster session would be to see how well they
were carrying out their maintenance plans.

Source: Adapted from Rose, S. D. (1989). Working with adults in groups. San Francisco: Jossey-Bass., pp. 325–326.

EXHIBIT 20.4
Planning the Last Group Session

SESSION SIX: REVIEW, LOOKING AHEAD, AND ENDING

I. Objectives

To support and consolidate what has been learned.

To identify and support suggestions for building and maintaining support networks and maintaining hope.

To discuss feelings about ending.

To discuss issues related to future contact.

To briefly address issues not covered.

To evaluate the group experience.

II. Preparation

Review information on group dynamics with special focus on endings. Gather information about other support services.

Review follow-up forms from previous sessions to identify specific incomplete areas of discussion and information not distributed.

Be prepared for the following content and group process:

Session is seen as last chance to "get it all out."

Members may pressure others to maintain contact.

Feelings of abandonment.

Fear of endings.

Select role plays for review (e.g., "Meeting each other in person"; "Continuing contact"). An example is:

Your telephone support group has ended and you want to find another type of group in your area. You are unsure who may provide this information and are concerned about telling people what kind of group you are looking for. How can you get the information you want? Who will you ask? What will you ask?

III. Suggested Activities

"Check-in" (brief reports from members about how they have been since last session).

Ask group members to summarize what has been covered in previous sessions and give input as necessary. Ask if there is any subject they want to discuss briefly.

Review strategies for getting help and available resources.

Raise the issue of ending and how everyone is feeling about this.

If group members want to continue contact, discuss a way to do this (e.g., exchange phone numbers and addresses. Do this carefully so no one feels pressured to maintain contact.

IV. Ending the Session

Ask for feedback about group members' experience in the group.

Source: Galinsky, M., Rounds, K., Montague, A., & Butowsky, E. (1993). Leading a telephone support group for persons with HIV disease. School of Social Work, University of North Carolina at Chapel Hill: pp. 44–46.

THE IMPORTANCE OF PLANNING FOR GENERALIZATION AND MAINTENANCE

Arranging for generalization and maintenance of positive outcomes is an important part of planned endings. "Generalization involves the occurrence of valued behaviors under different, nontraining conditions (i.e., across subjects, settings, people, behaviors, and/or time) without the scheduling of the same events in those conditions as had been scheduled in the training conditions" (Stokes & Baer, 1977, p. 350). It may occur across behaviors (response generalization), time (maintenance), or across individuals or situations (stimulus generalization). Behaviors that are similar in form to those focused on are likely candidates for generalization, although if diverse behaviors serve the same function (they are in the same operant) a change may occur in very different behaviors. Lack of generalization is a common problem. Preventing a downward drift in positive outcomes often requires careful planning. A concern for the durability of positive outcomes should also be a consideration when selecting assessment and intervention methods. Whenever intervention does not take place in real-life settings, a program should be designed to arrange for the generalization of desired behaviors to real-life environments. Different procedures may be needed to encourage generalization or transfer of changes than to maintain changes. Not arranging for the maintenance of positive outcomes may be related to a belief that methods used and outcomes attained will inoculate clients against the effects of environmental changes. Lack of generalization may be due to a train and hope approach—providing training and hoping that new ways of responding will occur in real-life situations. This approach is not likely to be effective.

If an outcome is valued (such as receiving positive feedback from others, e.g., compliments, active listening, requests for meetings), one aim may be to increase the range of situations in which this occurs. This could be accomplished by decreasing obstacles (e.g., fatigue), broadening the stimulus control (see Chapter 22), and/or reminding significant others to reinforce the behavior. If new ways of acting may result in changes in how others react, clients should be prepared for this. If a client wants other people to be more responsive, learns new social behaviors that result in more friendly overtures, and does not know how to handle them, finds them anxiety provoking, or wonders if he deserves them, he is not likely to continue using his new skills. "Probes" for generalization can offer information about whether changes of behavior in one situation result in changes of behavior in other situations or other behaviors in the same context. (If effects on other behaviors are of interest, their baseline frequency should be determined.) They are most effective when they do not occur too frequently and are nonreactive (for further detail see Horner, Dunlap, & Koegel, 1988).

Maintenance programs will be required whenever reinforcement for new behaviors will not be naturally provided in real-life settings or when reinforcement may decrease over time. Lack of maintenance of valued outcomes is a major problem. Mothers who are insular (who have few contacts with friends and whose contacts with relatives and personnel from social agencies tend to be unpleasant) tend not to maintain gains made in parent training (Wahler, 1980). Often, there is a drift toward less frequent use of positive contingencies and more frequent use of punishment. Poor housing, insufficient income, high crime rates, and poor health may increase stress, which, in turn, may compromise use of effective parenting skills. If we are under emotional stress, it is harder to make discriminations (e.g., identify positive behaviors to support). Positive behaviors may be ignored and parents may fall back into the reinforcement trap (reinforcing undesired behavior because this is followed by some immediate peace at the cost of increasing unwanted behavior in the future).

STRATEGIES FOR ENCOURAGING GENERALIZATION AND MAINTENANCE

You cannot count on generalization. Instead, careful planning is required based on assessment. You may, for example, ask clients to carry out assignments in real life to encourage generalization and maintenance. Stokes and Osnes (1986) describe three general principles of programming for generalization: (1) take advantage of natural communities of reinforcement; (2) train diversely; and (3) incorporate functional mediators (e.g., self-instruc-

EXHIBIT 20.5
Guidelines for Encouraging Generalization and Maintenance

1. Focus on behaviors that will be reinforced in real-life settings.
2. Train to a proficiency level that makes behaviors of value functional (i.e., they occur in real-life settings, and valued outcomes follow).
3. Prompt and reinforce behaviors; involve significant others.
4. Recruit natural communities of reinforcement and teach clients how to do so.
5. Use varied stimuli and responses (train loosely).
6. Make learning situations similar to real-life circumstances. When possible, train in real-life settings in which skills will be used and train in other settings as necessary.
7. Choose methods that clients can make use of on their own.
8. Remove artificial cues, reinforcers, and schedules.
9. Encourage beliefs about the causes of problems that contribute to persistence.
10. Identify high-risk situations for relapse and help clients to acquire coping skills to prevent and handle them.
11. Give clients written descriptions of plans.
12. Arrange follow-up contacts.
13. Arrange needed supports on an ongoing basis.
14. Use similar contingencies.
15. Offer opportunities for overlearning.
16. Reinforce unprompted generalizations.

tions) (see Exhibit 20.5). Maintenance can be enhanced by changing the frequency or magnitude of reinforcement, the locus of reinforcement, or the form of reinforcement. Understanding the principles of generalization programming and their relationship to environmental contingencies (e.g., what behaviors are reinforced or punished) will help you to approach planning from a conceptual as well as a technological basis. Decisions will have to be made about what components of plans should be continued.

Focus on Relevant Behaviors

New behaviors created in one context may generalize to others, but whether they are maintained (continued over time) will depend on whether they are reinforced in these other contexts. Honoring the **relevance-of-behavior rule** (teaching behaviors that will continue to be reinforced after helping efforts end) provides the greatest assurance of maintenance (Ayllon & Azrin, 1968). If there is little possibility that new ways of responding will be supported in real life, think twice about progressing on to intervention. The purpose of a task analysis is to accurately identify behaviors needed to attain a certain outcome such as influencing decisions made at community board meetings (see Chapter 15). Satisfying the relevance-of-behavior rule may require creating new reinforcers. For example, social approval from adults may not function as a reinforcer for some children. Given that this is involved in the socialization of children, a program may be designed to establish this consequence as a reinforcer by pairing social approval with events that are reinforcing. New activities may acquire reinforcing functions. If learning new skills is reinforced, learning itself may become rewarding. Tracking use of new behaviors (e.g., coping skills) as well as progress will indicate the relationship between the new behaviors and valued outcomes. A review of daily mood ratings and daily number of pleasant activities may show a relationship between mood and frequency of pleasant events. Keeping track of frequency of positive feedback offered to staff and staff morale may show a relationship between feedback and morale.

Prompt and Reinforce Valued Behaviors; Involve Significant Others

Arrange for prompts and reinforcement of valued behaviors as needed. The rationale for involving significant others is their continuing influence on clients. Whenever possible, make arrangements to ensure that new behaviors on their part will continue to be supported. One way to do this is to follow the relevance-of-behavior rule (see preceding discussion). You could include significant others in group or family meetings. Rose and Edleson (1987) invite the parents of adolescents to attend group meetings after youth feel confident in their use of new skills. The purpose of many community organization programs is to enhance the effectiveness of residents' skills in seeking valued outcomes. Changes in the behavior of a significant other (such as a parent, teacher, or supervisor) that result in desired changes in a client's behavior may create a chain reaction in which, due to positive changes, the mediator reacts to the client in a more positive way, which results in further positive changes on the part of the client. In such cases, maintenance is likely. At other times, additional support will have to be arranged, for example, from other family members. Mrs. Slater included Mrs. Ryan in her work with Mr. and Mrs. Green and also spoke to Mrs. Ryan's grandchildren who lived with her. Mr. Colvine saw Brian and his parents together and involved all three in case planning. He also spoke to Brian's older brother.

Peer-mediated interventions have been successful in establishing, maintaining, and generalizing children's behavior changes (Fowler, 1988). Involvement of peers has many advantages. They are readily available and provide a natural resource. Variations of peer-mediated interventions include involving the child in need of behavior change as a peer counselor to one or more classmates. For example, rather than receiving points for his improved performance, the child could award points to classmates when they offer desired behaviors. Or peers could be recruited to prompt and reinforce his behavior. You could help clients learn how to prompt and reinforce their own behaviors to generalize behaviors to situations in which they will be useful and to maintain them. (See later section on choosing methods that clients can make use of on their own).

Recruit Natural Communities of Reinforcement

Take advantage of natural reinforcing communities in which clients can learn to "recruit" reinforcement for valued behaviors (Stokes, Fowler, & Baer, 1978). Community resources such as recreation centers may be available that will help clients maintain and increase valued skills and opportunities for reinforcement. Mrs. Slater introduced Mrs. Ryan to the local senior center and her social skills were amply supported in this setting. Peers are a valued source of reinforcement in the neighborhood, school, or playground as described earlier. There is a rich literature describing the recruitment of peer reinforcement.

Use Varied Stimuli and Responses

You can encourage generalization by including multiple trainers and models (so that new behaviors will not be influenced by one person only); multiple settings (so that behaviors will not be limited to one setting); and multiple types and sources of reinforcement (so behaviors will not be influenced only by one kind of reinforcement) (see Exhibit 20.6). Let's say you have been asked to help community residents acquire "canvassing

skills" to encourage resident participation in local community groups. Training should include a variety of different kinds of reactions they may encounter. If the goal is for a child to follow instructions from both parents, both parents should be involved in training. Mr. Colvine encouraged his clients to practice negotiation skills when discussing a variety of conflicts. Ms. Landis and Julie rehearsed refusing different kinds of requests in different situations. Offer a variety of examples of behaviors of interest during training (e.g., different

EXHIBIT 20.6
An Example of Plans for Generalization and Maintenance

Steven [was] a mildly retarded autistic boy with Tourette syndrome. He engaged in frequent aggression, destruction, and self-abuse. These problems precluded continuation of placement in a school for deaf and blind individuals. Assessment of the functional environment revealed likely contingencies of coercion and escape.

Intervention involved differential reinforcement of behaviors other than self-abuse or self-stimulation. Reinforcing consequences included praise, talk, affectionate touch, edibles, and activities such as listening to music. Self-abuse was followed by loss of access to a preferred ongoing activity. The program also included extinction contingencies for demands and threats and physical guidance following noncompliance, so that Steven could not escape from demands.

One issue at the outset of training included whether to carry out training in the regular classroom or in a separate room. The classroom was preferable but not practical. Therefore, a "classroom" arrangement in the gym was used. The program then proceeded from training in the gym to in-classroom training and the incorporation into training of any other setting that would be a regular part of Steven's routine (e.g., cafeteria). Multiple settings and trainers were involved as training progressed. Variations in appropriate responding were considered acceptable, and more children were added to the responsibility of the staff member working with Steven so that more distractions/stimuli were provided under more natural situations. The intrusiveness of the program was faded as quickly as possible, and behaviors of adaptive value (e.g., self-help) were taught.

Steven's teachers and parents came to the residential facility and were taught by the staff to implement Steven's program in a manner consistent with the specialized treatment. After Steven's transfer back to the school for deaf and blind persons, the program staff initially implemented the program in that setting along with the teachers. As the teachers demonstrated mastery of the program, school visits were decreased, systematically fading residential program involvement based on the teachers' mastery and continuation of the programming. Steven's improvements maintained well under these conditions, to the extent that he was later described as a model student.

Source: Stokes, T. F., & Osnes, P. G. (1988). The developing applied technology of generalization and maintenance. In R. H. Horner, G. Dunlap, & R. L. Koegel (Eds.), Generalization and maintenance: Life-style changes in applied settings. Baltimore, Maryland: Paul H. Brookes, pp. 13–14.

ways to refuse unwanted requests). This provides clients with different response options. Training loosely (including varied training conditions) will decrease the likelihood that real-life variations interfere with generalization and maintenance.

Make Learning Conditions Similar to Real-Life Conditions

If possible, intervention should be carried out in real-life settings and should involve significant others who influence behaviors of concern. For example, when training was given in a one-to-one training session, skills acquired by autistic children did not generalize to a group setting, even when groups as small as two children with one teacher were used (Koegel & Rincover, 1974). A gradual increase in group size together with "thinning" of the reinforcement schedule did improve performance in a classroom of eight children with one teacher. This was important, because the aim was to find out whether autistic children could be integrated into a regular classroom.

Choose Methods That Clients Can Make Use of On Their Own

Gains are more likely to be maintained if clients learn skills they can use on their own. Institutionalized girls labeled delinquent were taught how to increase positive feedback from staff members who rarely reinforced appropriate behaviors (Seymour & Stokes, 1976). Residents learned how to call good work to the attention of staff. Clients can learn self-instructions that function as cues for desired behaviors. Helping children acquire self-instruction skills such as "slow down" can increase task engagement (Hinshaw, 1995). Examples of coping statements youth were encouraged to use when they did not succeed in controlling their anger included the following (Feindler & Ecton, 1986, p. 111):

- Uh-oh, made a mistake. Next time I'll think ahead.
- Some of this control stuff is tough, but I'll keep practicing.

- This is new for me. Everyone makes mistakes.
- I gotta remember that I used to really "lose it," but now I'm much better controlled.
- It's okay to feel really angry. I just have to concentrate on not letting it take over.
- Some situations are just gonna be harder than others.

Self-reinforcement may be used to maintain gains. This involves observation of behavior, evaluation of behavior based on some criteria, and feedback indicating whether performance meets criteria selected (Kanfer, 1970). Examples of self-reinforcing consequences used by children with handicaps include points recorded on a counter, tokens, marks such as + on a piece of paper, and self-praise. The former three consequences could be traded for back-up reinforcers such as money, free time, food, or special privileges.

Occasional self-monitoring may help to maintain positive changes. For example, if a client believes that her rate of positive self-statements is decreasing, she could keep track of their frequency for a few days. If positive statements have decreased, procedures could be temporarily reintroduced, such as written reminders to replace negative self-statements with positive ones. Periodic tracking of pleasing and displeasing events can be used to catch and reverse the beginning stages of a downward trend in positives. Self-monitoring can remind clients about the relationship between self-management (e.g., exercising) and valued outcomes (e.g., maintaining a certain weight or encouraging a positive mood). Clients can be given postcards to return to the agency at agreed-on times as a reminder to monitor behavior. Self-management training has been successful with a range of clients in maintaining valued behaviors (see for example Koegel, Frea & Surratt, 1994; Koegel & Koegel, 1990). Helping clients to acquire problem-solving skills may encourage maintenance (see Chapter 21). For example, teachers may learn to gather data as a first step when confronted with annoying behavior on the part of a child. An employee may learn to ask her supervisor to clarify vague criticisms before responding.

Remove Artificial Cues/Reinforcers/ and Schedules

Gradually remove artificial components of plans unless they are needed on an ongoing basis to support behavior. Your praise and attention should become less important as natural reinforcers become more important. Strupp and Hadley (1985) argue that one of the causes of negative outcome in psychotherapy is failing to be aware of and to discourage excessive dependency. If artificial reinforcers, such as points or tokens, have been used, fade them out and arrange for natural reinforcers such as social approval to reinforce behavior. Or you could increase the value of self-reinforcement. The point is to return to real-life schedules.

Most behavior in real-life is maintained on intermittent schedules of reinforcement (reinforcement is not offered after every response) (see Chapter 8). If "artificial" schedules of reinforcement have been used (such as continuous reinforcement—every response is reinforced), these should be changed to resemble those in real life. Reinforcement can be gradually thinned. Higher performance criteria can be required for a given number of points or fewer and fewer points can be given as natural reinforcers take effect. Tracking progress on an ongoing basis will let you know whether you are "thinning" a schedule too rapidly. Training that involves failure as well as success increases durability of change. Children who only had success experiences on math problems showed deterioration in performance when confronted with failure, whereas children who had failure as well as success and who received attribution training in which they were encouraged to try harder following a failure (a message that this resulted from too little effort rather than lack of skill) maintained or improved their performance following failure (Dweck, 1975). The importance of beliefs about learning and persistence in problem solving was noted in Chapter 5. Persistence of behavior can be en-

hanced by increasing the delay between behavior and its consequences.

Develop Helpful Attributions

How we attribute the outcomes of our behavior influences its durability. We are more likely to continue to use skills if we see the connection between them and outcomes we value. If we believe that success is a result of our efforts, we will persist longer when confronted with adversity (Dweck, 1975). You can explore clients' understanding of the rationale for methods suggested by asking them to describe this. Mr. Colvine helped Brian and his parents to learn three behaviors of value in discussing conflicts (see Chapter 18). To check on clients' understanding and the clarity of his explanation, he asked each family member to describe skills focused on in their own words, the situations in which each was of value, and the rationale for using each skill. Focus on changes that are compatible with clients' beliefs. If we succeed in new endeavors, but feel like impostors, we are less likely to continue new ways of acting. Developing helpful attributions sets the stage for use of valuable skills. Studies of successful programs designed to help people stop smoking suggest that earlier steps lay the groundwork for later ones (see Exhibit 20.7).

Offer Relapse Training

Another way to maintain gains is to help clients and significant others to identify situations that may result in relapse (loss of gains) and to develop constructive reactions to "slips." Maintenance programs may only forestall rather than prevent relapse. The persistence of effects will depend on the stability of environmental conditions (do contingencies continue to support desired behaviors), and the client's skills in catching and countering downward drifts and developing new skills that will be required in novel situations. The term "relapse training" is used to refer to helping clients acquire skills for catching and reversing downward trends in valued outcomes. Clients learn to view these as slips requiring corrective actions rather than as

EXHIBIT 20.7
A Stage Model of Self-Change

1. *Precontemplation.* Precontemplators are unaware, unwilling, or discouraged about changing the behavior. They engage in few or no efforts to change and may be defensive about the behavior. They are unconvinced that the negative effects of the behavior outweigh the positive ones. They are not considering changing in the foreseeable future and would be least responsive to change activities. To move ahead, precontemplators must become interested in changing. They may, for example, increase their awareness of the negative effects of current behavior patterns and evaluate the likelihood of changing more positively.
2. *Contemplation.* Here prospects of change are considered. Contemplators seek information and begin to reevaluate themselves in light of the behavior (e.g., smoking) and evaluate the losses and rewards change would bring. But they are not prepared to take action.
3. *Preparation.* Individuals in this stage intend to change in the near future and have learned valuable lessons from past change attempts.
4. *Action.* There is a change in problem-related behavior. Behavior change skills are acquired (e.g., in stimulus control and contingency management) to interrupt usual patterns of behavior and to adopt desired patterns. People become aware of the pitfalls that may undermine continued effective action including abstinence-violation beliefs, tempting settings and peer pressure. Effective strategies are needed to prevent lapses or slips from becoming complete returns to the problem behaviors (relapse).
5. *Maintenance.* This involves sustained behavior change activities for periods of 6 months to 3 or more years.

Source: Prochaska, J. O., & DiClemente, C. C. (1992). Stages of change and the modification of problem behaviors. In M. Hersen, R. M. Eisler, & P. M. Miller (Eds.), Progress in behavior modification. *Vol. 28. New York: Academic, pp. 185–187.*

signs of failure or hopelessness of ever succeeding. Marlatt included a relapse prevention phase in his program for problem drinkers (Marlatt & Gordon, 1985). High-probability situations for drinking are described as decision points in terms of whether to drink or not and clients acquire coping skills to handle such situations. For example, they may weigh the ultimate aversive consequences of drinking against the immediate positive effects and learn how to resist pressure from others to drink. Relapse training is now a part of many programs (see for example Falloon & others, 1990; Wilson, 1992).

Discussing problems that might arise in maintaining progress forewarns clients that setbacks will occur and that they are not a sign of failure. This discussion sets the stage for learning how to deal constructively with setbacks. David Burns (1995) reported that the likelihood of dips in positive moods following cognitive behavioral intervention for depression is 100%, perhaps within three weeks. Clients are forewarned of this. Stuart (1980) offered couples "what-if" exercises as part of a maintenance program. These involved situations that commonly arose but may not have been discussed. An example is shown below.

> Several months after she and Rob finished their marriage therapy, one of Maxine's old boyfriends turned up in town sporting a recent divorce. He invited Maxine to have dinner with him to "talk over old times." It was her discovery of Rob's relationship with another woman that prompted Maxine to suggest that they both get outside help.
> a. What should Maxine do now?
>   1. Meet her old beau for lunch and possibly have an affair with him just to balance the books with Rob?
>   2. Tell Rob about the call and ask if he would mind her meeting her friend just to hash over old times, calling him back to make certain he knows her feelings?
>   3. Just tell Rob about the call without asking approval, also calling to clarify her intentions with her friend?
>   4. Have just a friendly lunch without mentioning it to Bob?
>   b. What principle(s) guide(s) this action? (Stuart, 1980, p. 378)

Some of these exercises were used as probes during final sessions to evaluate skills and to offer practice opportunities to enhance them. Clients were required to gradually assume more responsibility for discussing situations on their own.

Give Clients Written Descriptions of Methods Used

Written or audiotaped descriptions of methods used and related skills can serve as useful reminders.

Clients can review them as an aid to maintaining gains. Stuart (1980) gave each couple a written summary of intervention. This included a description of the nature of the presenting concern, a reformulation of this request as a set of positive change goals, and a summary of the assignments used during each service phase. Clients were asked to review this whenever they felt uneasy about their relationship, as well as during a monthly review of success in maintaining valued outcomes. In the rehabilitation program designed by Anthony et al. (1980; 1990) clients receive copies of plans together with check steps for each part of the plan. These consist of questions that should be asked before, during, and after each task to increase the likelihood of success.

Plan Follow-Up Contacts

Follow-up sessions offer information about the effectiveness of services as well as opportunities to catch downward drifts at an early stage. Anticipation of follow-up meetings may remind clients to use new skills. Periodic telephone calls can be used to support new skills. Decisions must be made about what data to gather at follow-up, how to collect it, and who to involve.

What about booster sessions? Booster sessions refer to periodic meetings following more frequent contact to support useful skills and troubleshoot. Booster sessions were built into Stuart's (1980) relationship counseling program. Clients were asked to spend one hour each month reviewing written statements of steps each person took to maintain gains and identifying additional desired changes. Results concerning the usefulness of booster sessions are mixed (see Lambert & Bergin, 1994). The sheer persistence of a behavior or thought such as a high frequency of negative self-statements over many years may make it necessary to periodically reintroduce special programs to maintain changes. A contextual analysis will suggest the likelihood of maintenance of valued behaviors. Without supporting contingencies, there is no reason to expect lasting change. The futility of expecting short-term solutions to problems that require long-term efforts suggests the value of additional periodic service.

Arrange Ongoing Services as Needed

There may be a continuing need for supportive services. Volunteers may be recruited to provide ongoing services. Children could participate in enriching day-care programs to make up for lack of parenting skills in encouraging children's cognitive development. Prosthetic devices such as railings in bathrooms and easy-to-use devices that allow people to signal for help may allow clients to remain in their homes. Ongoing support groups could be arranged. Maintaining participation in social action efforts will require ongoing support. Hoped-for changes may be in the distant future. Only by valuing and recognizing the small wins may needed efforts continue. Joining a consumer advocacy group may provide a way to gain the support and ideas needed to make a difference.

Other Methods

You can increase the probability of generalization by reinforcing unprompted generalizations, by overlearning (providing additional practice after mastery of a skill) and by clearly describing principles related to use of new skills. Using similar contingencies decreases the likelihood that valued behaviors are confined to a narrow range of situations. You could arrange delays between behaviors of interest and their reinforcement as well as omission of cues for this purpose. Following the rule to use the least intrusive intervention will also facilitate generalization and maintenance. Gradually fading contacts may facilitate maintenance. You and your clients could change meetings from twice a week to once a week, then to biweekly contact and then to monthly meetings or telephone contact. This pattern of contact will be useful in discovering problems that arise in maintaining positive outcomes. Managed care regulations will limit your options. Exhibit 20.8 provides an opportunity for you to plan a maintenance program.

EXHIBIT 20.8
Practice Example

Identify a valued behavior of your own or one of a client and describe a plan for maintaining it.

Situation:

_____

_____

Behavior:

_____

_____

Current maintaining contingencies:

_____

_____

_____

Remote maintaining contingencies:

_____

_____

_____

Maintenance plan:

_____

_____

_____

_____

ETHICAL ISSUES

Whenever clients need help with real-life problems, generalization and maintenance is a key concern; ". . . there is an ethical obligation, if not a responsibility, to make sure that generalization programming is incorporated into every program that endeavors to make important social and lifestyle changes for clients" (Stokes & Osnes, 1988, p. 16). This suggests an ethical mandate to inform clients about the likelihood of generalization and maintenance. To do this, you will have to be informed about the likelihood of durable change given specific circumstances and have the knowledge and skills needed to plan as effectively as possible for generalization and maintenance. If you work in an agency in which little or no attention is given to generalization and maintenance, you should raise this as a concern. You could start by sharing research findings showing the lack of generalization and maintenance of valued outcomes.

SUMMARY

Some endings will be planned. Others will not. Final meetings should allow time to discuss feelings about ending, to review progress, to celebrate successes, and to plan next steps. Planned endings are more likely if you focus on specific outcomes clients value and track progress on an ongoing basis so you can compare outcomes to progress hoped for. Planned endings require arranging for the generalization and maintenance of positive outcomes and support for the clients' contributions to progress. You can encourage generalization by making training conditions as similar as possible to those in the natural environment, arranging practice in a variety of settings and with a variety of trainers, explaining the rationale for methods used, and arranging cues and reinforcers to encourage generalization. To maintain valued outcomes you can involve significant others, encourage behaviors that will continue to be supported in real-life, develop helpful attributions, arrange community supports, remove artificial procedural components, and select methods that give clients personal control (they are self-mediated). You can identify situations in which slips may occur and help clients acquire skills for preventing and handling them. Some clients will require ongoing services. What is needed will depend on the unique characteristics of each client and his or her circumstances.

REVIEWING YOUR COMPETENCIES

Reviewing What You Know

1. Describe characteristics of planned endings.
2. Identify reasons for unplanned endings.
3. Define the term *generalization* and give examples.
4. Given specific examples, you can identify feasible, effective ways to enhance generalization.
5. Given specific examples, you can identify feasible effective ways to increase the durability of valued outcomes.
6. Describe attributions that enhance the durability of positive outcomes.
7. Describe what is meant by relapse training and give examples of what this involves.
8. Discuss the ethical obligations of helpers regarding generalization and maintenance.

Reviewing What You Do

1. Observation of your ending interviews demonstrates that important components of planned endings are included such as sound plans for maintaining valued outcomes.
2. You plan for generalization of change.
3. You plan for the maintenance of change both in early and later phases.
4. You train clients in relapse prevention.

Reviewing Results

1. Generalization of positive outcomes occurs.
2. Desired outcomes are maintained.
3. Clients use relapse prevention skills with success.

INTERVENTION
OPTIONS

CHAPTER 21

Education and Skill Building

OVERVIEW

The value of helping clients acquire positive behavior change skills is highlighted in Chapter 22. Clients may also benefit from acquiring additional information and other kinds of skills (see for example Linsk, Hanranan & Pinkston, 1991). Guidelines for achieving these goals are described in this chapter. Viewing behavior as a result of unique learning histories and current contingencies lays the groundwork for a knowledge and skill-building emphasis. Reframing problems as related to a lack of learnable skills (e.g., rather than to unchangeable personality traits) will encourage positive expectations and help people to view each other in more positive ways. Options for developing new behaviors include shaping, prompting and fading, and social skills training. Cognitive-behavioral methods designed to alter thoughts, feelings, and behavior are also described.

You Will Learn About

- Guidelines for providing information.
- Options for developing new behaviors.
- Shaping: A key practice skill.
- Prompting and fading.
- Social skills training.
- Enhancing useful cognitive skills.
- Enhancing skills in managing emotions.

EXHIBIT 21.1
Kinds of Information Clients May Benefit from Having

- How to obtain certain kinds of information.
- Available resources related to a particular goal.
- Relationships between personal troubles and social, political, and economic conditions.
- Different options for increasing community/neighborhood resources.
- Relationship of emotional reactions to evolutionary history.
- About others who share their concerns.
- Developmental norms.
- Life transitions.
- The consequences of different patterns of behavior.
- New options for attaining valued goals.
- How they influence others.
- How others influence them.
- How they can alter their social environment (e.g., change how other people think, feel, or act).
- How they can alter their physical environment to achieve valued goals.

PROVIDING INFORMATION

Clients may benefit from learning about available services or norms describing typical patterns of behavior in different developmental phases (see Exhibit 21.1). Paublo Freire (1973) argues that "op-

pression comes from within the individual as well as from without; and hence that felt needs must be . . . questioned as to their causes if people are to be freed from blind adherence to their own world views as well as to the world views of others which they have uncritically internalized" (p. 89). Group work with clients often has a dual role of providing information and support (see Exhibit 21.2). Guidelines for offering information suggested by Donald Meichenbaum and Dennis Turk (1987) are shown in Exhibit 21.3. Provide clear rationales about why information is of value and check clients' understanding of what you describe. Also, anticipate and remove possible obstacles to using information. For example, make sure clients have the skills required to make use of information. Write down important points and give a copy to clients. Helpers sometimes overestimate clients' interest in information.

Insight as Information

You may help clients to understand how their behavior is influenced by their environment and how they influence their environment. This may be a first step to changing behaviors, thoughts, or feel-

EXHIBIT 21.2
Methods of Coping with the Medical Care System and Social Service Agencies

1. *Acquire information about treatments:* Clients can request appointments with their physician to explain their treatment in more detail. They can take a list of questions to their appointments and ask doctors to write down important information. They can meet with a nurse or hospital social worker to discuss their concerns or read on their own about the various options. They can talk to each other or other individuals who are HIV positive. They can call the National AIDS Hotline (1-800-342-2437). In seeking and providing information, it is important that group members keep in mind that illness progression and reactions to treatment vary among individuals.
2. *Become informed about patients' rights:* Group members can learn about their rights as patients by:
    Sharing information with each other and with the group leader.
    Finding out who the patient advocacy persons and social workers are at their hospital or clinic and talking to them.
    Calling or writing AIDS advocacy groups.
3. *Acquire effective assertion skills:* Group members may find it difficult to request services or speak up when they feel they are not treated properly. They could practice valuable skills in role plays.
4. *Increase support:* Family members and friends can help group members cope with the medical and social care systems by providing emotional support, assisting with red tape, being advocates, and visiting group members when they are in the hospital. Group members can increase support by educating significant others about HIV, and how to interact with medical social service personnel.
5. *Other options:*
    Going to appointments with a supportive person who takes notes
    Asking for a number to call if a problem arises.

Source: Adapted from M. Galinsky, K. Rounds, A. Montague, & E. Butowsky (1993), Leading a telephone support group for persons with HIV disease *(pp. 24–25). Chapel Hill: School of Social Work, University of North Carolina.*

EXHIBIT 21.3
Guidelines for Giving Information

- Be selective. The fewer the instructions given, the greater the recall.
- Organize material. We have greater recall of information presented in the first third of an exchange and of the first instruction given.
- Prepare the client in advance for what you are about to say (e.g., "First, I am going to describe _____, then I will describe _____").
- Be specific, clear, detailed, and simple in giving instructions. Use short words and sentences. Use down-to-earth, nontechnical language. Give concrete illustrations.
- Attend to cultural differences (e.g., in manner of presenting information, meaning of concepts).
- Give small amounts of information at each visit. Do not overload clients with details. Individually pace and tailor content given.
- Different clients need different kinds of information at different points. Check for receptivity and understanding.
- Involve clients and significant others in planning.
- Do not oversell programs.
- Describe the rationale for suggested plans (e.g., how they relate to goals clients value), the specific behaviors involved, and the possible consequences of following or not following recommendations.
- Tie to personal experience.
- Explore whether the information is compatible with the client's beliefs about the problem and what should be done about it. Review the client's view of agreed-on methods at the time they are initiated as well as at later points.
- Help clients develop strategies to recall material (e.g., summaries and outlines).
- Supplement verbal descriptions with audio-visual material and visual graphic aides (diagrams, charts, audiotapes, videotapes, films, brochures). Be sure that clients can comprehend written material.
- Emphasize the importance of following agreed-on plans.
- Check comprehension. Ask questions and request feedback. Encourage clients to raise questions and take notes or write summaries.
- Ask the clients to describe the information given in their own words.
- Be sure that clients have the skills required to follow recommendations.
- Individualize instructions and give feedback and praise for efforts.
- Build up the client's self-confidence that he or she can be successful in using information.
- Help clients diminish or remove barriers caused by the procedures themselves.
- Supplement education with other methods (e.g., planned phone calls to troubleshoot).

Source: Adapted from D. Meichenbaum & D. C. Turk (1987), Facilitating treatment adherence. *(pp. 131–132) New York: Plenum.*

ings. However, insight is neither a necessary or sufficient condition for improvement (Hobbs, 1962; Frank, 1976, p. 84). For example, if clients do not have the skills required to act in effective ways, insight will not alter behavior in real-life settings. Gilbert's work suggests that battered women may benefit from understanding their reactions within an evolutionary perspective in which defeat states (e.g., helplessness) are typical ways of avoiding further aggression. The kind of insight emphasized differs in different practice approaches, and different people may value different kinds. In *Psychoanalytic Terms and Concepts* (1990), Moore and Fine define insight as "the capacity or act of apprehending the nature of a situation or one's own problems" (p. 99). Within a psychoanalytic perspective insight is assumed to have two significant components: affective and cognitive. Clients may benefit by learning about the process of learning.

Some people believe that they have little influence over what they learn, perhaps because of nonrewarding and punishing experiences at home and school. Pessimistic beliefs highlight the importance of careful selection of assignments and sound training so that efforts are successful and clients will see that they can make a difference in the quality of their lives.

Formats for Providing Information

You could provide information verbally, in written form, via interactive computer programs, videotape, or audiotape. The term "bibliographic methods" is a fancy way to describe asking clients to read material (see Scogin, Jamison, & Gochneaur, 1989). You will have to be familiar with relevant sources to select appropriate material. Be sure to consider required reading level and language preferred so you select content that matches clients' skills. Client manuals are available for some programs (see for example Craske, Barlow, & O'Leary, 1992; Greenberger & Padesky, 1995; Otto, Pollack & Barlow, 1995; Patterson, 1975). Self-help manuals have been developed to help parents handle challenging situations (see for example Clark and others, 1977; Loitz & Kratchowill, 1995; Forgatch & Patterson, 1989). Review content beforehand to make sure that it informs (rather than misinforms) and that content will not "turn off" readers because of sexist, homophobic, racist, or classist content. Written self-help programs are available related to many concerns as well as guidelines for evaluating them (Gambrill, 1992; Rosen, 1981; 1987). Careful selection of material will increase the likelihood that it helps rather than harms. Mailing monthly newsletters has been explored as a way to enhance parenting skills of teenage parents (Cudaback, Darden, Nelson, O'Brien, Pinsky, & Wiggins, 1985). Written handouts may be used to supplement other training methods (see for example the description of a program to help parents acquire effective skills for communicating with professionals, Kohr et al, 1988). Wandersman, Andrews, Riddle, and Fawcett (1983) used bibliographic approaches to establish neighborhood block organizations. As they note, providing knowledge about how behavior is influenced by the environment can help clients to create, select, and transcend their environments. Educational programs may be offered to newly arrived refugees to increase their understanding of their environments.

Information, Advocacy, and Consciousness Raising

Helping clients understand the relationship between personal troubles and political, social, and economic factors is a key part of radical, structural, and feminist practice (see, for example, Mullaly, 1993; Rose & Black, 1985). It is key to Pablo Friere's critical pedagogy in which the role of the teacher is to help others to penetrate false consciousness—to help others to understand how "dominant social and economic groups impose val-

ues and methods that legitimize their own power and policies of control" (Brookfield, 1995, p. 208). Education in this sense is viewed as a discussion among equals—an experience in cooperative learning. B. F. Skinner (1953; 1971) advocated wide distribution of knowledge about the principles of behavior so that we understand how our behavior is influenced by our environments and can be more effective in resisting unwanted influence and seeking valued change. Information is a resource. Embarrassing information is closely guarded by organizations and governmental agencies, and ire and punishing consequences may be heaped on whistle-blowers. Consider the attempts to smear and discredit Ralph Nader when he exposed lethal defects in the Pinto automobile. The suppression of information is one of the major ways in which politicians and the media influence citizens (see for example, Bagdikian, 1992; Jensen, 1994). Providing information about problems/causes and possible solutions is a powerful adjunct to social action efforts. Simply informing citizens about a problem may mobilize them to participate in advocacy efforts. Relevant information may be found in a variety of sources including the Social Worker's Almanac (Ginsberg, 1995).

> Information is the key to effective advocacy. It comes in many forms. Some pieces of information are numbers—the answers to questions like: How many children live here? How many are in school? How much money is available? But data include much more than numbers. Answers to questions like: What kind of services are there for physically handicapped children? Where can you find them? Who's in charge of them? Are they any good? Do parents know about them? involve valuable facts that go beyond numbers. You'll need to know officials' names, addresses, phone numbers and responsibilities. You'll want to know who your allies are and who is likely to oppose what you want. You'll need to know about relevant rules, laws, guidelines, policies, and regulations. You'll want to see budgets, program activity reports, statements of priorities and plans, and evaluations of programs affecting individuals you're concerned with.
>
> Gathering information will enable you to reveal officials' evasions, question their assumptions, and, if necessary, counter their figures. (Shur & Smith 1980, pp 1–3)

Community Education. Broad-based community involvement is emphasized in community education. If citizens are to work together to resolve shared problems, they must have access to helpful information. What problems are shared? What are related contingencies at different system levels? A needs assessment may be needed to identify shared problems (see Chapter 24). David Mathews (1990) suggests that an effective community has the following characteristics:

1. It educates itself as a *whole*, in all of its subdivision and groups, about the *whole* of its interests.

2. It has more than just facts; it knows what the facts mean in the lives of the people in the community and helps people to think and use those facts effectively.

3. It talks through issues to develop shared knowledge.

4. It knows the difference between mass opinion and "public judgments."

5. It makes a distinction between government officials and public leaders.

Larry Decker (1992) highlights the importance of community education as a process. He suggests four components of community education:

1. Provision of diverse educational services to meet the varied learning needs of community residents of all ages;

2. Development of interagency cooperation and public-private partnerships to reduce duplication of efforts and improve overall effectiveness of the delivery of human services;

3. Encouragement of community improvement efforts that make the community more attractive to both current and prospective residents and businesses; and

4. Involvement of citizens in community problem solving and decision making" (p. 263).

Community schools provide a key resource in facilitating community education:

"A community school reflects the fact that people's learning needs are both full-time and lifelong. In contrast to the traditional school, a community school serves all ages and functions 12 to 18 hours a day, 7 days a week, 12 months a year" (p. 265).

DEVELOPING NEW BEHAVIORS

Clients and significant others may benefit from enriching their behavioral repertoires. Clients may lack self-care, social, vocational, and/or recreational skills. Skills focused on may include work related skills (Mathews & Fawcett, 1984; Chadsey-Rusch, 1986; Hall, Sheldon-Wildgen, & Sherman, 1980), respite care skills (Neef Parrish, Egel, & Sloan, 1986), skills for parents with children with disabilities (Kirkham & Schilling, 1989), leisure skills (Schlein, Meyer, Heyne, & Brandt, 1995), and integration skills for students with disabilities (Gaylord-Ross, 1989). Neighbors may not know how to use positive methods to request changes in annoying behaviors. Community residents may not know how to form coalitions to seek change. Participants on community boards may not know how to influence group process. Aggressive children may not know now to make friends. A superviser may not know how to listen attentively to staff complaints. Arnold Goldstein et al. (1980) describe 50 different skills in their book *Skillstreaming the Adolescent* under six different categories including dealing with feelings, alternatives to aggression, dealing with stress, planning skills, beginning social skills (e.g., starting a conversation), and advanced social skills (e.g., asking for help, joining in). Skill training is an important component of psychiatric rehabilitation programs (see for example, Liberman, DeRisi, & Mueser, 1989).

Most procedures designed to develop new skills, such as social skills training, consist of a number of components including shaping, chaining, prompting and fading, model presentation, and rehearsal. Creating a distraction-free environment will increase the effectiveness of training sessions as will assessment of each client's entry level competencies and a task analysis in which behavioral objectives and intermediate steps are clearly described (See Chapter 15). In this way you can "start where the client is" and pursue a planful agenda that includes positive feedback for each step along the way. "*Access behaviors*" should be identified and encouraged. This term refers to behaviors that increase access to reinforcing environments and provide opportunities for additional skill acquisition (Hawkins, 1986). If you are responsible for helping clients to acquire new skills, you will need competencies in developing new behaviors. You can also use this knowledge to assess skill training programs provided by other agencies.

SHAPING

Shaping involves the differential reinforcement of successive approximations to a desired behavior. Successive approximations are variations of behavior that increasingly resemble the final behavior desired. Shaping takes advantage of the variability of behavior, selecting variations that are closest to desired behavior and reinforcing them, and ignoring others. One way or another, we are all involved in shaping behavior (and, are being shaped by others). Helping clients to acquire positive shaping methods is a common goal. Skilled negotiators and mediators are skilled shapers. Shaping can be used when instructions and model presentation cannot be relied on alone. It is often used to develop self-care, social, recreational, academic, and vocational skills of both children and adults with developmental disabilities.

Positive and Punitive Approaches

There are both positive and negative ways to shape behavior. Skilled athletic coaches are expert shapers as are effective drama coaches. Skill in the use of positive methods to shape behavior is one of the most valuable repertoires you can possess. Positive compared to negative methods are more effective and more pleasant for all involved parties. They make learning enjoyable (even fun) and are less likely to create resistance and negative feelings. Reliance on positive methods requires work and creativity to identify suitable positive reinforcers. People often

rely on aversive methods (yelling, threatening, or removing privileges) because they lack positive shaping skills. Preferences for positive rather than negative means of influence are related to one's values as well as skills. Caring and respect for others encourage positive methods that make people's day brighter rather than dimmer. The discussion of evolutionary influences in Chapter 8 illustrates the difference between societies in which status and order is maintained through fear and intimidation and those in which they are maintained through positive consequences (e.g., caregiving and signals of reassurance). We live in a society in which fear and intimidation are rife. Many people learn neither positive skills for influencing their environment nor values that encourage their use (Sidman, 1989).

What Is Involved

Two procedures are used in shaping: positive reinforcement for successive approximations and operant extinction for other behaviors. In the latter, reinforcement is withheld; behavior occurs but is no longer reinforced. Shaping relies on the use of positive feedback and builds on current repertoires (starts where the client is). The concept of successive approximations is a key one. Shaping involves the following steps:

1. Select the target behavior.
2. Select the initial behavior that the client currently performs that resembles the target behavior in some way.
3. Select powerful reinforcers with which to reinforce the initial behavior, successive approximations of the target behavior, and the target behavior.
4. Reinforce the initial behavior until it occurs frequently.
5. Reinforce successive approximations of the target behavior each time they occur.
6. Reinforce the target behavior each time it occurs.
7. Reinforce the target behavior on an intermittent schedule of reinforcement. (Foxx, 1982, pp. 72–73)

First, establish a conditioned reinforcer so you can immediately reinforce approximations. You could pair a clicker with a reinforcer such as food, or tokens or points established as a reinforcer. When an approximation occurs, the conditioned reinforcer (e.g., clicker) can be immediately presented as a signal that reinforcement is available. You can use prompts (verbal instructions, gestures, physical guidance, or environmental changes) to encourage closer approximations. Prompts are gradually removed so behavior will occur without reminders. Additional reinforcement may be provided for close approximations (e.g., three tokens rather than one). Select reinforcers that can be delivered immediately and are nondistracting and nonsatiating (they do not quickly lose their reinforcing potential). Skill is required in deciding when to reinforce only a closer approximation, in recovering from backsliding toward more distant approximations, and in withholding reinforcement for behaviors that do not approximate desired outcomes (see Exhibit 21.4). *Don't Shoot the Dog: The New Art of Teaching and Training* (1984) by Karen Pryor provides a sound, clear, entertaining description of shaping.

If You Are Not Successful

Indicators of poor shaping skills include lack of success in altering behavior in desired ways, attempts to escape from the situation, and negative emotional reactions (e.g., anger and anxiety). Common errors include:

- Vague descriptions of entering repertoires, desired outcomes, and intermediate steps so it is difficult to decide what to reinforce and what not to.

- Selecting performance requirements that are too difficult.

- Giving too much or too little reinforcement for approximations.

If an approximation is reinforced too often, variability of behavior will decrease and closer approximations will occur less often. Remember, shaping takes advantage of the natural variability of behav-

---

EXHIBIT 21.4
Skills Involved in Shaping

- Obtain the person's attention.
- Determine the operant level (the closest approximation).
- Demonstrate the desired behavior.
- Start with the correct step (reinforcing the closest approximation).
- Proceed to the next step appropriately.
- Return to an earlier step when necessary.
- Ignore undesired behavior.
- Prepare the context correctly (providing needed props and removing distraction).
- Train for one task at a time.

REWARDING
- Find an effective reinforcer.
- Give the reinforcer right after the approximation.
- Pair verbal reinforcement with material reinforcers.
- Offer verbal reinforcement enthusiastically.
- Offer physical reinforcers such as hug enthusiastically.
- Pair physical reinforcement with the material reinforcer (e.g., hugging a child and offering him a bite of food).
- Use praise to establish chains of behavior (so material reinforcement can be faded out).
- Alter the reinforcer as necessary (for example, if satiation occurs).
- Withhold reinforcement correctly.

COMMUNICATING
- Get acquainted before training.
- Give the correct emphasis to key words when providing instructions.
- Use correct verbal instructions.
- Use the person's name before the instruction.
- Use gestures that supplement verbal cues.
- Use physical prompts effectively.
- Fade prompts and gestures as soon as possible.
- Show patience, interacting in a respectful manner.

Source: Adapted from J. M. Gardner, D. J. Brust, & L. S. Watson (1970), A scale to measure proficiency in applying behavior modification techniques to the mentally retarded. American Journal of Mental Deficiency, *74, 633–636.*

---

ior. So the more often one variation is reinforced, the fewer variations are likely to occur. If an approximation is not reinforced often enough, behavior may drift back to a more distant one. If you are not successful, review the points described above as well as others noted in the discussions of positive reinforcement and operant extinction in Chapter 22.

Verbal instructions and manual guidance may be needed, or they may have been included when no longer necessary, preventing the person from independently carrying out a chain of behavior. Perhaps you reinforced an awkward way of performing an approximation that makes next steps difficult. You may have to reinforce an earlier approximation, increase verbal prompts, use physical guidance, or reduce requirements. Satiation or fatigue may intensify as work progresses. If so, reinforce a successfully performed response and end the training session.

Distractions such as other people in the learning environment may encourage behaviors that get in the way.

Chaining and Shaping

Shaping and chaining are closely related. Behaviors that are shaped often involve a chain of behaviors. The term *behavior chain* refers to a sequence of responses in which specific cues signal behavior in a sequence that ends with a reinforcer. One useful feature of chaining is the possibility of breaking down any component behavior into a more detailed set of behaviors. This allows you to tailor training to the unique skill levels and progress of each client. A task analysis may be needed to identify the specific behaviors and their sequence that are involved in a chain (e.g., ordering food in a fast food restaurant) (see Chapter 15). Nine behaviors are included in the sequence described below for teaching a child how to put on a pair of slacks.

1. Taking the slacks from the dresser drawer.
2. Holding the slacks upright with the front facing away from the individual.
3. Putting one leg in the slacks.
4. Putting the other leg in the slacks.
5. Pulling the slacks to the knees.
6. Pulling the slacks to the thighs.
7. Pulling the slacks all the way up.
8. Doing up the button or snap.
9. Doing up the zipper.

Process task analysis involves the design of strategies for teaching content (e.g., certain concepts such as "besides," "on-top"). Examples include *matching to sample* (presenting an object and asking the learner to select from a group of objects the one that matches) and *oddity* (the learner selects from a group of objects the one that does not belong). Skill in designing and conducting such training are important for teachers of individuals with developmental disabilities.

Some chains of behavior such as shoe tying are more easily established by starting from the end of the chain. In *backward chaining*, the last part of the task is taught first, then the next to last, and so on. In *forward chaining*, the first part of a task is taught first, then the next, and so on. In total task presentation, the entire task is presented and reviewed. Feedback (to let the learner know what is wanted and if he is achieving it) may be offered before, during, and/or after practice. This may be verbal (e.g., praise), nonverbal (a symbol, for example, a smiling face), or consist of direct guidance. The term *criterion* refers to a predetermined point at which it is decided that learning has taken place (e.g., repeated observation of the behavior under the conditions in which it is expected to occur).

Without an understanding of chaining you may skip necessary steps resulting in lack of progress and/or backsliding, not reinforce each step along the way, or steps may be "out-of-order" making learning difficult. Chaining and shaping are additional ways in which individual differences are considered. We each have a different *"entering repertoire"* in relation to a skill. Without knowledge about each client's unique repertoire and the steps required to achieve an outcome, frustration and failure may result rather than success and pleasure in accomplishment. Chains of behavior are easier to interrupt in the early parts of the chain that are furthest removed from the final reinforcer. Some chains of behavior are more difficult to disrupt than are others. For example, couples who are dissatisfied with their relationships have a more difficult time stopping dysfunctional conversations about their communication problems than do satisfied couples. For distressed couples such discussion seems to be an "absorbing state" (Bakeman & Gottman, 1986, p. 209).

Prompting and Fading

Prompting and fading can be used to provide additional guidance or cues for valued behaviors.

Prompting refers to use of a cue (a prompt) to signal someone to carry out a certain behavior. Prompts are discriminative stimuli (cues) that are not part of the natural environment. They may be verbal, gestural, or physical. Fading involves the gradual removal of a prompt. This ". . . is used to foster independence by reducing or eliminating the control that the prompter (instructor) and prompts have had over the student's behavior" (Foxx, 1982, p. 83). You could, for example, decrease the number of words in an instruction or reduce the size of gestures. Prompting and fading can be used to prevent backsliding of valued behaviors that may result in an intrusive intervention such as institutionalization.

MODEL PRESENTATION

Model presentation is used in many ways in everyday practice. You may model helpful problem-solving steps to your clients. Model presentation was used to demonstrate effective communication skills to Brian and his parents (see Chapter 18). Mrs. Slater loaned an audiotape to Mrs. Ryan and the Greens illustrating effective and ineffective ways to share feelings. She also modeled useful skills in the office and gave her clients written descriptions. Ms. Landis used model presentation with Julie to enhance her skills in resisting unwanted sexual overtures. Group leaders model behaviors that group members may benefit from learning. Supervisers and managers should model communication methods they would like their staff to use. Components involved in the effective use of modeling include:

- Clear description of specific behaviors to be altered.
- Presentation of a model.
- Observation of the model.
- Practice of modeled behaviors.
- Corrective feedback.
- Repeat as needed.

Modeling will be more effective if attention is drawn to particular behaviors that are valued. For example, you could point out the effect of empathic comments on decreasing anger. A mediator may model requests for solutions and suggestion of compromises. Modeling of valued behaviors is an integral part of social skills training. Strayhorn (1994) encourages parents to read stories to their children that present models of valued behaviors and to avoid modeling negative behaviors. In his competency-based program for young children and their parents he explains the importance of parents modeling valued behaviors and of omitting models of violence, sarcasm, and hostility. He encourages parents to ". . . raise their consciousness about the degree of violence in entertainment. A useful exercise is counting the violent acts in even G-rated Disney classics, and pondering the consequences of injury and death if those acts were carried out in real life. A slapstick blow on the head could result in concussion and permanent seizure disorder" (p. 59). He encourages parents

> not to present the boycott of violent entertainment as the withdrawal of a good thing that should be a privilege and a pleasure for everyone. The parent takes some time to explain that violence is a big problem in our society, that violent entertainment promotes this problem, and that the family is trying to boycott violent entertainment out of a spirit of not wanting to "vote" for the continuation of a major cause of such a bad problem. In other words, the parent attempts to convert the child to a social activist stance rather than to attribute to the child a high vulnerability to violent behavior. (p. 60)

He also encourages parents to use plays, songs, and dances that model valued attitudes, feelings, thoughts, and actions. Additional guidelines for making effective use of models are described in the next section.

SOCIAL SKILLS TRAINING

Social skills training is designed to enhance effective social behavior. It is used to "empower" people by increasing their influence over their environments. For example, people with physical

disabilities learned how to identify and report issues at group meetings (Balcazar, Seekins,
Fawcett, & Hopkins, 1990; Sievert, Cuvo &
Davis, 1988). Training may be carried out either
in individual or group meetings. Groups provide
a number of advantages and seem to be an optimal setting for some clients such as children diagnosed as having an attention deficit disorder
(Hinshaw, 1994). Social skills training has been
used to help clients develop a wide variety of behaviors related to a wide variety of goals
(O'Donohue & Krasner, 1995). Programs have
been developed to enhance the quality of care
provided to residents in institutional settings
(Risley & Favell, 1979), to enhance friendship
skills among women at risk for child maltreatment (Richey, Lovell, & Reid, 1990), to help children make friends, (Asher & Coie, 1990), to enhance social skills of clients with a psychiatric
diagnosis (Liberman, DeRisi & Mueser, 1989)
and to enhance options for youth and adults with
developmental disabilities (Meyer, Peck, &
Brown, 1991). The main goal of enhancing social skills may be to prevent problems (see
Gilchrist & Schinke, 1985; Gilchrist, Schinke &
Maxwell, 1987; Wurtele, and others, 1986;
Schinke & Gorden, 1992). You can help clients
acquire relationship skills they can use to enrich
the quality of their social networks (their social
cultures) (see for example Mueser, Valenti-Hein,
& Yarnold, 1987). Examples of relevant behaviors include offering positive feedback to others
(empathy and listening), expressing feelings, personal disclosure, requesting behavior changes,
negotiating, and refusing requests (see Chapters
12 and 13). Natural contexts provide many opportunities to enhance valued skills (see for example Gaylord-Ross, Stremel-Campbell, &
Storey, 1986). Broadly speaking, parent training
programs and programs designed to enhance
communication among family members can also
be viewed in part as social skills training programs because they involve social behaviors (see
for example Dangel, & Polster, 1988). Assertion
training is a form of social skills training (see for
example, Gambrill, 1995c; Rakos, 1991; Wilson
& Gallois, 1993).

Assessment Comes First

Social skills training should be preceded by a contextual assessment. Helpers sometimes jump into
training too soon without clear descriptions of
client goals and how to attain them. Only through
a careful assessment can you determine if a lack of
social skills is an issue. Clients may have skills but
not use them. Research related to children alleged
to have ADHD (attention deficit-hyperactive disorder) suggests that these children do have required
social skills but do not use them (Hinshaw, 1995).

Identify Situations of Concern. Exactly what situations are involved, who is involved, and where
do relevant exchanges occur? What are the client's
goals? Social behavior is situationally specific in
terms of what is effective. A behavior that is effective in achieving a given outcome in one situation may not be successful in another. This highlights the importance of clearly describing
situations of concern.

***Clearly Describe Behaviors Required for
Success.*** What behaviors are required for success?
The behaviors that make up an effective reaction
differ in different situations. Definitions of socially
effective behavior differ in the extent to which personal outcomes (effects on oneself) as well as social outcomes (effects on others) are considered.
Most definitions emphasize providing reinforcing
consequences in a way that is socially acceptable
and does not harm others. How can you find out
what behaviors are required to achieve certain outcomes in a situation? Let's say a client does poorly
in job interviews. What do people do who succeed?
What is success? Practice-related literature may offer guidelines about what is effective. Situations of
concern as well as effective response options have
been identified for many groups including psychiatric patients, adolescents, the elderly, and individuals with different kinds of physical disabilities.
Task analyses of behaviors of interest may be available. These provide an empirically based training
guide. Willner et al. (1977) asked youth residing in
a halfway house to rate specific staff behaviors on
a scale ranging from A to F. Examples of highly

rated behavior included joking and doing what was promised. Disliked behavior included criticism and not following through on promises. Degree of success in real-life will offer feedback about whether relevant skills have been identified and were used. Be cautious about using your experience as a guide. It may be limited or unusual. You may discover what is effective and what is not in a specific situation by engaging in related activities and generating skill lists. You could ask clients to observe people in similar roles who are effective and to note the situation, what was done (including both verbal and nonverbal behaviors), and what happened.

Normative criteria may be used as a criterion (what most people do in a situation). A concern here is that the norm may not reflect what is desirable. For example, school teachers may give low rates of praise and high rates of criticism. You would not want to encourage this pattern. Another disadvantage of norm-referenced objectives is lack of information about the specific behaviors required to attain an objective.

Clearly Describe Clients' Entering Repertoires.

This step requires identifying what skills clients already possess. The gap between current skill levels and required skills can then be accurately assessed. Role plays are valuable for this purpose as described in Chapter 15.

Identify Possible Obstacles.

What obstacles (e.g., negative thoughts or feelings) interfere with success? Does anxiety or anger get in the way? If so, is it related to negative self-statements (e.g., I'm no good) or inappropriate expectations (I should always get my way)? Be sure to find out how clients feel about altering their behavior in specific situations. Unique socialization patterns may get in the way of changing behavior in positive directions. Beliefs such as "I must please everyone" that pose obstacles to acting in new ways may have to be identified and re-evaluated. (see Chapter 16.) Clients may have inappropriate goals (those that cannot be met or are met at a high cost such as social rejection). For example, children who have difficulty making friends may value dominance over cooperation. Poor choice of goals may result in poor choice of social behaviors (those that result in punishing rather than positive consequences). Aggressive compared to nonaggressive boys differ in their social-cognitive processes (Lochman & Dodge 1994).

Steps Involved in Training

An explain-demonstrate-practice-feedback-model is used in which explanations are first offered about why certain skills are of value and situations in which they can be used are identified (see Exhibit 21.5). Training should be individually tailored to each persons's unique entry level skills and obstacles that may interfere with acquiring and using skills. An effective training orientation may increase participation (see for example, Liberman et al., 1989). Repeated practice and feedback are key in developing mastery and enhancing comfort with new skills. Preceed practice by model presentation of effective responses and identification of specific behaviors (both verbal and nonverbal) to be increased, decreased, or varied. Overt behavior includes both verbal (what is said) and nonverbal (smiles, facial expression, eye contact) components. Other skills include rewardingness, (offering friendly reactions such as smiling and positive verbal statements) self-presentation, and empathy (ability to take the role of others).

Model Presentation.

Model presentation is an important component of social skill training. The more extensive the lack of skills, the more likely model presentation, rehearsal, feedback, and instructions will be needed to develop skills. In other cases, practice or instructions alone may be sufficient to achieve desired outcomes. Model presentation is used in parent training (see for example, Dongel & Polster, 1988). For example, videotaped presentations of problem situations and demonstrations of parents successfully handling them were shown to parents who abused their children as one part of a program to enhance positive parenting skills (Denicola & Sandler, 1980). (For another example of the use of videotape modeling see Haring, Breen, Weiner, Kennedy, et al., 1995.) Models can be presented in many different ways

EXHIBIT 21.5
Steps Involved in Social Skills Training

ASSESSMENT

_____ Describe specific social situations of concern.
_____ Identify specific goals in each. Review for appropriateness.
_____ Identify behaviors required in each situation to attain goals sought.
_____ Review clients entering repertoire (what they can now do).
_____ Identify additional skills needed as well as when to use them to good effect.
_____ Identify obstacles to using skills (e.g., anxiety, unrealistic expectations).
_____ Encourage positive expectations.

SOCIAL SKILLS TRAINING

_____ Model effective alternatives.
_____ Engage clients in practice (behavioral rehearsal).
_____ Prompt and cue participants as needed during role plays.
_____ Provide constructive feedback following each role play (e.g., identify and encourage improvements in relevant verbal and nonverbal skills in small, attainable increments).
_____ Repeat model presentation, practice, and feedback as necessary (until skill levels required for success are met).
_____ Discourage behavior that gets in the way (e.g., joking in groups). For example, you could ignore it.
_____ Address obstacles to success (e.g., interfering thoughts and feelings).
_____ Help clients to identify relevant homework assignments and seek their commitment to carry these out.
_____ Review results of homework assignment.
_____ Provide additional training as necessary.
_____ Help clients develop self-management skills that will help to maintain valued skills (e.g., periodically keep track of particular skills and outcomes).

including written scripts, audiotape, videotape, film, or live. One advantage of written descriptions is that they can be referred to as needed. Clients can be coached to carefully observe effective models in real-life contexts to learn new behaviors and to increase knowledge about when certain behaviors can be used with success. Their observations can be discussed, noting effective reactions as well as other situations in which specific behaviors could be of value. Drawing attention to important behaviors through verbal prompts will encourage acquisition of new skills. For example, you could coach a client to notice the model's eye contact and body orientation. Model helpful self-statements

during role plays if negative thoughts interfere with success. They can first be spoken out loud by the client when imitating the model's behavior and then, by instruction, moved to a covert level.

If an attempt to use model presentation fails, check to determine whether the requisites for use of the procedure have been satisfied. Specific behaviors may have to be individually established before they can be combined in a complex chain of behavior; you may have to break steps down into smaller units. Perhaps the client did not attend carefully to the modeled behavior. You may have to prompt attention and/or offer incentives to encourage imitation. When working with children or adults with severe behavior deficits, a first step is to teach them to imitate behaviors. You could use physical guidance to encourage desired behaviors. Modeling effects can be enhanced if observers have an opportunity to practice the observed behavior and if they are asked to identify relevant behaviors and to describe rules for using them.

Behavior Rehearsal (Role Playing). Behavioral rehearsal involves the practice of behaviors. For example, a client who has difficulty during job interviews can practice effective ways of acting after watching a model. Analogue situations include those in which clients interact with significant others in an artificial environment such as the office, as well as situations in which clients participate in role plays with someone other than a real-life significant other (e.g., a social worker). Role playing offers a safe environment to practice new behaviors, given that tasks and criteria for success are clearly defined, and constructive feedback is used that is tailored to each person's unique skill levels.

Participation in role plays may change attitudes. Brian and his parents were more willing to listen to what each other had to say after negotiation training. Mrs. Lakeland reported that she could now see how they would all have to work together to make things better at home and that it wasn't all Brian's fault. Role reversal in which a client assumes the role of a significant other may increase awareness of what it is like to be in someone else's shoes. Be sure to clearly describe situations used in role plays, as well as how they relate to client concerns. You can encourage participation in role plays by:

- Asking clients to read from a prepared script.
- Decreasing the length of role plays.
- Clarifying the purpose of role plays.
- Identifying clear, achievable criteria for success.
- Reinforcing participation.
- Pointing out that initial discomfort is usual.
- Selecting easier situations.
- Coaching clients during role plays.

You could give clients control over prompts. Let's say you are working with a teenager who wants to learn new ways to maintain conversations. You could ask him to start off by himself and to draw written prompts from a box suggesting topics only as necessary. You can decrease a client's anxiety by modeling behaviors to be practiced, offering reassurance, and clearly describing procedures to be used. You could ask for volunteers if you are using a group. A group provides a valuable context for role playing because many models and varied sources of feedback are available (see Rose & Edleson, 1987).

Coaching and Prompting. Take advantage of coaching and prompting to encourage desired behaviors. You could give clients a list of written prompts related to specific verbal and nonverbal behaviors. You could use hand signals to coach clients during role plays. Fade out prompts and guidance as skills increase. Keep a training record to track progress. You could list behaviors of interest to the left and leave room along the top for successive role plays. You and your clients can assess progress by evaluating skills at the beginning and end of each session.

Programming Change. Identify initial skill levels and build on them in a step-by-step manner that complements degree of mastery. You and your clients should decide on specific goals for each training session. Only one or two behaviors may be focused on during a session. Or, initial skill levels may allow practice of all required behaviors. You and your clients can use the data collected during assessment from role plays or observation in real-life contexts to describe available skills. Repeat model presentation, rehearsal, prompts, and feedback as needed until desired skill and comfort levels are demonstrated. Be sure to identify clear criteria to determine when a skill has been mastered. Including difficult situations that may arise in role plays will help clients practice handling them. Emphasize coping with, rather than mastery of challenges. Distractions and provocations by people playing the role of clients were built into scenes in which child welfare workers role played interviewing clients (Greene, Kessler, & Daniels, 1996). A "parent" would interact inappropriately with "her children" (yell, ridicule, threaten, or make inappropriate physical contact) or the client would tell the social worker "These AA meetings you're making me go to are stupid."

Provide Constructive Feedback

Be sure to provide constructive feedback after each role play. First note specific positive aspects of the performance, then give specific suggestions for improvement. Be sure to give praise for improvement in relation to each client's unique baseline repertoire rather than in comparison with other people. Note and praise improvements, even small ones. Avoid critical comments such as "You can do better," or "That wasn't too good." *Specific* feedback based on clearly defined criteria will help clients to identify what to do to enhance their effectiveness. Also, using constructive feedback offers a model for participants to follow. Enthusiasm will encourage positive feelings and participation. You can encourage involvement of all group members by using a structured format in which specific behaviors related to a goal are written down in a checklist format and each group member rates each role play guided by the criteria on the checklist. They could rate each behavior as needing work, improved, or good. Examples of nonverbal behavior may include eye contact, posture, and facial expression. Content may include relevance to situation. Paralinguistic components may include voice loudness, tone, and fluency. A recording sheet used in training parents how to use "planned ignoring" included the following entries (Hall & Hall, 1980, p. 25).

1. Look away from child.
2. Move away from child (at least 3 feet).
3. Impassive face.
4. Ignore all requests.
5. If necessary, leave room.

Homework Assignments

Select homework assignments that offer clients real-life practice opportunities after criterion level skill and comfort levels have been achieved in role plays. Encourage behaviors that will result in positive outcomes for both clients and significant others and that have a high probability of success at a low cost in discomfort. You could write down important components on cards and give a copy to clients that they can review as necessary (e.g., prior to employment interviews). Remind clients that new ways of acting may not immediately alter the behavior of others in desired directions. Change may be slow and new reactions may initially create negative feelings and consequences. For example, attempts to initiate conversations may be ignored. Job interviewers may be rude. If such reactions may occur, help clients to develop coping skills for handling them before they try out new behaviors in real life. A contextual understanding of the situations involved will help you to prepare clients for or avoid negative outcomes. When possible, involve significant others in role plays. Behaviors in real-life settings may not be an exact replica of those rehearsed. The purpose of skill training is to help clients acquire the essential elements of effective behavior. They may combine new knowledge with their own unique effective styles.

If You Are Not Successful

There are many ways a training program can go wrong. You may go too fast or too slow. The more behaviors that must be learned, the more complex they are, the greater the needed training competencies on your part. Needed prompts and coaching may be missing. Homework assignments may be too few or too difficult. A common mistake is spending too much time talking about what to do and not enough time on modeling, practice, and feedback. Valued behaviors may be punished in real-life settings and/or not reinforced. If progress is disappointing, check out these possibilities (see also Chapter 20). Helping clients acquire new skills requires many skills on the part of the trainer.

Particular kinds of information are needed. Developing new skills often requires a task analysis in which behaviors needed to attain valued goals are identified, including immediate steps. Entering repertoires (what clients can already do) must be discovered and an "agenda" for change planned. Without finding out what clients can now do and what they cannot, you may skip necessary steps or move too slowly. Conducting skills training in a group will require preparation and planning to maximize effectiveness. Special arrangements may be needed to encourage generalization as described in Chapter 20. Shooting from the hip in skill training is not a good idea; you may set clients up for failure and overlook opportunities to help them.

ENHANCING SELF-MANAGEMENT SKILLS

Self-management training has been used to pursue a wide variety of goals with a wide variety of clients including decreasing stereotypic behavior of students with autism (Koegel & Koegel, 1990), decreasing drinking in adults (Sobell & Sobell, 1993), decreasing pain (Hanson & Gerber, 1990), and decreasing impulsive behavior of children and adults (Meichenbaum & Goodman, 1971). (See also Gardner & Cole, 1989; Koegel, Frea, & Surratt, 1994.) Self-management skills are involved in helping students study and helping people to maintain and enhance good health by eating a more nutritious diet, maintaining an exercise regime and stopping smoking. Self-management skills are used to pursue goals we would like to obtain. Essentially, we manage our behavior in the here and now to achieve desired goals such as making more friends or getting our work done. Steps include: (1) identifying a goal; (2) identifying the steps needed to attain the goal; (3) designing a plan to monitor related behaviors in a consistent way; and (4) arranging consequences that will maintain related behaviors. We may either rearrange cues and consequences related to behavior of interest or acquire skills such as relaxation that offer us greater influence over our environments (see Watson & Tharp, 1993). Self-management skills have been discussed at many points in this book including Chapter 20 under the section on choosing methods that clients can make use of on their own. Self-instruction training is a kind of self-management training. We learn to prompt and reinforce valued

behaviors (see later discussions of problem-solving training and programs designed to help clients to manage their emotions). Enhancing self-reinforcement skills is valuable when support will not be offered in real-life. Clients could increase positive self-statements as well as access to specific reinforcers contingent on desired behaviors. Positive self-statements should reward accomplishment, be specific, and be acceptable to clients. Written prompts may be needed to remind clients of important steps (e.g., questions such as "Is my goal clear?").

HELPING CLIENTS CHANGE THEIR COGNITIVE ECOLOGY

What clients say to themselves (their self-statements) may contribute to problems. For example, how youth interpret the social behavior of others influences their reactions (see for example Dodge, 1993; Lochman & Dodge, 1994). Clients may have dysfunctional rules about how to act or what consequences to expect in certain situations. A client may believe that if she does not get what she wants in a situation "It is a disaster." Changing cognitive ecology may involve changing **equivalence relations** either among stimuli or functions. You may for example help a client no longer equate between being rejected and viewing one's self as a failure). Changing what people say to themselves may involve decreasing excessive rule governance (e.g., "I must please everyone"), or increasing rule governance (e.g., following through with choices we have made). People who have angry outbursts may relive imagined slights and exaggerate their importance. What we say to ourselves is influenced by our learning histories. The term "cognitive restructuring" refers to methods that focus on changing what people say to themselves. Albert Ellis, Aaron Beck, and Donald Meichenbaum have taken a leading role in highlighting the role of thoughts in problem-related feelings and behaviors (see for example, Beck, Rush, Shaw, & Emery, 1979; Ellis & Dryden, 1996; Meichenbaum, 1977). **Reframing** can be used to alter views of problems. This refers to encouraging a different way of viewing events/

behaviors (Watzlawick, Weakland, & Fisch, 1974). For example, you may encourage a client to view a disliked characteristic as an asset. **Thought stopping** is designed to decrease the frequency of persistent thoughts. This consists of helping clients to identify thoughts to be decreased and increased and arranging practice in stopping negative thoughts via self-instructions (e.g., saying "stop" covertly or overtly). This is combined with helping clients to focus on constructive thoughts or tasks (see for example, DeBortali-Tregerthan, 1979).

Cognitive-behavioral methods have been used to address a wide range of problems including depression, aggression, pain, substance abuse, anger, and "personality disorders." Such methods address both overt and covert (thoughts), behaviors related to problems (see for example, Craighead, Craighead, Kazdin, & Mahoney, 1994; Dobson, 1988; Hollin, 1989; Kendall, Ronan & Epps, 1991; Linehan, 1993; Steketee & Foa, 1987). One component of cognitive-behavioral programs for depression involves clients learning to identify negative thoughts and related cognitive distortions and to replace them with positive self-statements (see for example, Burns, 1990; Nezu, Nezu, & Perri, 1989). Cognitive-restructuring may require identifying the "themes" (e.g., beliefs), underlying negative self-statements (e.g., "I am worthless"). Without this, change efforts may be of little value because core beliefs remain untouched (see also Chapter 16). Methods such as systematic desensitization (a procedure designed to decrease anxiety) and problem-solving training also address thoughts. Checklists have been developed for some programs to assess the correctness with which methods are used.

PROBLEM-SOLVING TRAINING

Effective problem-solving skills are valuable at all levels of intervention. Clients are encouraged to clearly identify problems, alternative ways to resolve them, and the consequences of each (see case example concerning Julie in Chapter 18 as well as Chapter 5, Exhibit 4). Community residents may be unsuccessful in attaining valued goals because they do not clearly define problems of concern or because they choose a path that aggravates rather than mitigates problems. Community board members may benefit from enhancing their problem-solving skills (see for example, Briscoe, Hoffman, & Bailey, 1975). Pablo Freire (1973) used a mix of organizing and educational approaches to enhance group solidarity and social action organizations via a problem-solving process (for further discussion of community level interventions see Chapter 24). Community living for clients with developmental disabilities may require solving a variety of problems (see Foxx & Bittell, 1989). Problem solving is a key parenting skill (see Forgatch & Patterson, 1989). A variety of programs have been developed to help children and adolescents to acquire effective social problem-solving skills, most of which have a self-management component involving self-instructions (see Baron & Brown, 1991; Elias & Tobias, 1996; LeCroy, 1994). Imagined rehearsal and modeling may be used in addition to actual practice and modeling. A social problem-solving curriculum, used with learning disabled and low-achieving youth labeled delinquent, designed by Larson and Gerber (1987) involved three lessons in verbal self-instruction. These encouraged youth to covertly (via thoughts) cue themselves to stop and think before responding to situations in which impulsive reactions might result in negative consequences. Nine lessons in social metacognitive awareness guided youth in what to consider when facing a social problem. They learned how to identify salient "self" and "other" variables and how to evaluate the usefulness of information about these variables to assess problem difficulty and identify response requirements. During ten lessons in social metacognitive influence skills, participants learned a seven-step problem-solving strategy for using social information: (1) clearly describe the problem; (2) propose solutions; (3) decide on the best one; (4) be ready with a back-up alternative; (5) anticipate obstacles and plan step-by-step procedures to carry out chosen options; (6) carry out the plan; and (7) review results. Both trainer and youth read lessons aloud. Each lesson plan was organized around cartoon-like posters to encourage focus and attention. Problem situations were presented daily and youth practiced applying new skills. Group activities included: (1) sharing experiences in applying skills; (2) reading lesson plans aloud; (3) discussing questions presented; (4) practicing steps and problem-solving methods; (5) modeling specific skills; and (6) assigning "homework" tasks to practice a skill. To maximize generalization, trainers illustrated the usefulness of each skill; focused on problems similar to those in real-life; reminded youth to use skills; gave homework assignments, and involved youth as active participants.

Using the phrase "choices and consequences" highlights individual responsibility in making choices and considering consequences. In acceptance and commitment counseling clients are encouraged to accept responsibility for their choices and to accept and get beyond things they cannot change (see for example, Hayes, Jacobson, Follette, & Dougher, 1994; Nelson-Jones, 1987). Examples include events that occurred in the past (e.g., our past behaviors and behaviors of others over which we have no control), events that really don't matter, and our emotional reactions to everyday events. For example, rather than saying "I am too anxious to approach that person to start a conversation even though I want to," you might say, "I want to approach that person to start a conversation *and* I feel anxious approaching him." In the second example we acknowledge our feelings but act anyway. When we focus on getting rid of an unpleasant feeling such as anxiety or depression, this may only make matters worse (we may feel more depressed) and it gets in the way of acting in spite of our feelings. Clients may benefit from learning how to carry out mini cost-benefit analyses as a guide to how to act. You could help clients prepare crisis cards on which they note specific behaviors they could engage in at times of stress to prevent undesired reactions such as hitting their children (Kinney, Haapala, & Booth, 1991). Examples they describe on a card may be pet the cat, take a walk, and call a friend.

ENHANCING SKILLS IN MANAGING EMOTIONS

Feelings can be altered by changing related overt and covert (i.e., thoughts) behaviors. As Leonard Berkowitz (1994) notes, our emotions are often from the bottom up (i.e., from our automatic arousal to certain events such as being criticized or rejected) and it is our topdown cognitive use of rules and self-instructions by which we learn to think before we act. Programs have been developed to help clients with anger, panic attacks, social anxiety, pain, and post-traumatic stress reactions (see for example, Barlow, 1993; Gatchel & Turk, 1996; Heimberg & Others, 1995; Leitenberg, 1990; Novaco, 1995; Steketee & Foa, 1987; Wolpe, 1990). An anger control training example is shown in Exhibit 21.6. Some authors use the term emotional intelligence to refer to recognizing our feelings, managing our emotions, and recognizing emotions in others (Goleman, 1995; Salovey, Hesse, & Mayer, 1993). Education is a component of cognitive-behavioral programs designed to help clients manage their emotions. Clients learn how feelings and thoughts influence their behavior and how their behavior influences what they think and feel. These programs may help to "inoculate" us against unpleasant and dysfunctional levels of emotions (e.g., anxiety or anger). Skills focused on in school-based programs designed to increase social competence included the following:

- Identifying and labeling feelings.
- Expressing feelings.
- Assessing the intensity of feelings;
- Managing feelings.
- Delaying feelings.
- Controlling impulses.
- Reducing stress.
- Knowing the difference between feelings and actions.

Related cognitive skills included: (1) self-talk; (2) interpreting social cues; (3) problem solving and

EXHIBIT 21.6
An Anger Control Training Example

		Definition	Example
Step 1:	Identify triggers	External events and internal self-statements that provoke anger and aggression	Being close to a particular co-worker or having one's space suddenly invaded by anyone
Step 2:	Identify cues	Individual physical events such as clenched fists, raised hand, flushed face, particular vocal sounds, and so forth, that let someone know he or she is angry	Becoming red in the face and starting to vocalize loudly
Step 3:	Using reminders	Self-statements such as "Calm down" or "Relax" or nonhostile explanations of others' behaviors	Saying to oneself, "Take a break," or "Talk quiet," (using a trained sign, symbol, or vocalization)
Step 4:	Using reducers	Techniques designed to lower the individual's level of anger, such as deep breathing, counting backward, imagining a peaceful scene, or thinking about the long-term consequences of one's behavior	Walk to a designated quiet area in the room and listen to music using headphones and a portable tape deck
			Taking out a wallet and looking at pictures of 3–4 favorite scenes or activities that took place that week
Step 5:	Using self-education	Reflecting on how well the situation was handled	Initially being told by a favorite staff person that he or she did very well and later, saying to self "Good job"

Source: L. H. Meyer & I. M. Evans (1989), Nonaversive intervention for behavior problems *(p. 138). Baltimore: Paul H. Brookes.*

decision making (e.g., to control impulses, set goals, identify alternative actions, and anticipate consequences); (4) understanding the perspective of others; (5) understanding norms (what is and what is not acceptable behavior); and (6) self-awareness (e.g., identifying realistic expectations about oneself). Behavioral skills include both nonverbal and verbal behaviors such as making clear requests, responding effectively to criticism, resisting negative influences, listening to others, and helping others.

In stress management training, clients learn to identify feelings and thoughts associated with emotional reactions such as anxiety and anger and to use them as cues for constructive thoughts and actions. They learn how to carry out a situational analysis of arousal-provoking thoughts. The relationship between thoughts, feelings, and behavior is emphasized. For example, stress experienced in unexpected traffic delays could be avoided by allowing more time to complete journeys and by having interesting activities available (e.g., listening to "books-on-tape"). Clients are encouraged to view emotions as reactions they can influence rather than

as feelings that are out of their control. They are encouraged to identify low levels of unpleasant arousal so they can use mood-altering skills at an early point to prevent escalation. Stress-producing situations are broken down into four stages (preparing for the stressor, controlling a stressor, coping with feelings of being overwhelmed, and reinforcing self-statements) and constructive self-statements are developed for each stage (Meichenbaum, 1977). (See Exhibit 21.7.) Viewing situations from the other person's perspective and focusing on common goals will help clients maintain constructive levels of arousal. Goals such as "telling the _____ off" are not likely to result in positive outcomes. Research on anger has shown that such goals encourage negative feelings and counterattacks and are not likely to be achieved (Averill, 1982). Clients may benefit from acquiring relaxation skills that help them handle stressful situations (see for example, Burish, Snyder, & Jenkins, 1991). Relaxation training is a part of systematic desensitization methods for reducing anxiety (Wolpe, 1990). (For descriptions of relaxation methods see Bernstein & Borkovec, 1973; Woolfolk & Lehrer, 1993.)

EXHIBIT 21.7
Examples of Coping Self-Statements Rehearsed in Stress Inoculation Training

Preparing for a stressor
    What is it I have to do?
    I can develop a plan to deal with it.
    Think about what I can do about it.
    No negative self-statements; just think rationally.
    Don't worry; worry won't help.
    Maybe what I think is anxiety is eagerness.
Confronting and Handling a stressor
    Just "psych" myself up—I can meet this challenge.
    You can convince yourself to do it. You can reason your
        fear away.
    One step at a time; I can handle the situation.
    Think about what I want to do.
    Anxiety is a reminder to use my coping skills.
    This tenseness can be an ally; a cue to cope.
    Relax. Take a slow deep breath.
Coping with the feeling of being overwhelmed
    When fear comes, just pause.
    Focus on the present; what's my goal?
    Don't try to totally eliminate fear, just keep it manageable.
    Even if fear increases, it's no big deal.
Reinforcing self-statements
    It worked; I did it.
    It wasn't as bad as I expected.
    It's getting easier each time.

Source: Adapted from D. Meichenbaum (1977). *Cognitive Behavior Modification: An Integrative Approach.* New York: Plenum

Forming a Stimulus Hierarchy

Practice (behavior rehearsal) is often used to alter emotional reactions such as anxiety or anger. Research suggests that exposure to feared cues is the key ingredient in overcoming fear reactions (see Barlow, 1988; Marks, 1987). First, make a list of anxiety-provoking situations based on identification of cues for anxiety (or anger). Then develop a hierarchy arranged in terms of degree of anxiety related to each situation. Start rehearsal with situations that create only a small amount of discomfort and, as anxiety decreases, introduce more difficult ones. In vivo systematic desensitization was used to decrease anxiety of an 18-year-old adolescent to men (Meyer & Evans, 1989). She avoided male staff members in her new group home and tantrumed whenever they approached her. She also refused to see professionals, such as an optometrist, who were men. Although her foster mother suspected that her fear resulted from sexual abuse, the cause was unknown. Examples from the hierarchy of situations developed to provide opportunities for direct experiences with men include the following:

1. On outings into the community, such as to a fast food restaurant, staff will try to select a table near a group of men. Donna can sit in the middle of her own group.

2. On similar occasions it will again be arranged to be near men, and Donna will sit on the outside.

3. When the opportunity arises to interact with a male in an official role (e.g., delivery person, store assistant), Donna is to make eye contact and smile.

4. Staff will try to select stores, banks, and so forth, that have male service personnel; Donna has to approach a man, with one of her friends, and ask for something.

5. Male staff in the home will sit on the other side of the room from her and talk to other female clients, not Donna (p. 141)

Care was taken to protect her from realistic dangers. Donna learned not to talk to male strangers unless other people were around or unless they had some official role and received counseling in the dangers of sexual abuse.

MIXED AND MULTISYSTEM PROGRAMS

A contextual assessment will often indicate that a multicomponent program is needed. Consider children diagnosed with ADHD (attention-deficit hyperactive disorder). Research suggests that social skills training is of limited value. Programs include both self-management training (e.g., in self-monitoring) and anger management training in a group setting (Hinshaw, 1995). Points are awarded for appropriate behaviors to give immediate positive feedback for desired behaviors. Helping people who are depressed often involves multiple kinds of intervention carefully geared to a contextual assessment (see Nezu, Nezu, & Perri, 1989). This may include changing environmental stressors, as well as what people say to themselves, and what they do (i.e., activity planning). Changing social interactions may also be required (see for example, Frank & Spanier, 1995).

Multisystem intervention programs will often be required to address concerns. Programs designed to reduce AIDS risk activities usually comprise a variety of methods including education, sexual assertion training, self-management training, and enhancing social support (see for example Helquist, 1987; Kelly, St. Lawrence, Hood, & Brasfield, 1989). Consider also the community reinforcement approach (CRA) that Azrin and his colleagues developed to decrease alcohol abuse (Azrin, 1976; Sisson & Azrin, 1989). This multisystem approach includes attention to family relationships, helping clients to find jobs, establishing a non-drinking social network, and developing recreational opportunities. A buddy system was developed and a social club arranged that provided social opportunities without drinking alcohol. In addition the program included drink refusal training, training in controlling urges to drink and an antiabuse program. A key feature of the CRA is altering client's social networks to create a non-drinking culture. This kind of multicomponent program has also been used to decrease drug abuse (see for example, Budney, Higgins, Delaney, Kent, & Bickel, 1991). Ecobehavioral programs with families involve multisystem interventions (Lutzker & Campbell, 1994; Wesch & Lutzker, 1991). Helping clients to obtain jobs often requires a multilevel intervention program attending to both individual and environmental characteristics (see for example, Azrin, Philip, Thienes-Hontos, & Besalel, 1980; Drake & others, 1996; Murphy & Rogan, 1995). The same applies to working with youth who belong to gangs (see Goldstein, & Huff, 1993). Dan Olweus (1993) developed and evaluated a multilevel program for de-

creasing bullying at school (see also Olweus, 1994). Intervention is conducted at the school, class, and individual levels (see Exhibit 21.8). This program has been successful in reducing bullying. Charles Borduin and his colleagues found that multisystem intervention was more effective than individual therapy in the long-term prevention of violence among juvenile offenders (Borduin et al., 1995).

EXHIBIT 21.8
Overview of Multilevel Intervention Programs to Reducing School Bullying

Overview of Intervention Program

General Prerequisites
• Awareness and involvement

Measures at the School Level
• Questionnaire survey
• School conference day on bully/victim problems
• Better supervision during recess and lunch time
• More attractive school playground
• Contact telephone
• Meeting staff—parents
• Teacher groups for the development of the social milieu of the school
• Parent circles

Measures at the Class Level
• Class rules against bullying: clarification, praise, and sanctions
• Regular class meetings
• Role playing, literature
• Cooperative learning
• Common positive class activities
• Class meeting teacher—parents/children

Measures at the Individual Level
• Serious talks with bullies and victims
• Serious talks with parents of involved students
• Teacher and parent use of imagination
• Help from "neutral" students
• Help and support for parents (parent folder, etc.)
• Discussion groups for parents of bullies and victims
• Change of class or school

Source: D. Olweus (1993), Bullying at school: What we know and what we can do *(p. 64). Oxford: Blackwell.*

SUMMARY

Helping clients may require increasing their knowledge and skills. Giving people more options for influencing their environment is key to empowerment. Providing information can help clients to understand problems, to identify promising options, and to reframe problems in constructive ways. Information is a key resource in advocacy efforts to mobilize community members and to suggest strategies to seek valued outcomes. Options for helping clients to acquire new skills include shaping, modeling, and social skills training. If your job involves helping clients to learn new skills, you should develop expert skill-building competencies. A variety of cognitive-behavioral methods are available to alter thoughts, emotions, and behaviors in helpful ways.

REVIEWING YOUR COMPETENCIES

Reviewing What You Know

1. You can describe key skills involved in shaping.
2. You can describe components of social skills training.
3. You can describe why careful assessment is a prerequisite to successful skills training.
4. You can accurately describe guidelines for giving information.
5. Given examples of social skills training you can describe how to improve the likelihood of success.
6. Given examples of shaping you can accurately describe how to enhance success.
7. You can describe how to maximize the effectiveness of model presentation.
8. You can accurately describe the characteristics of constructive feedback.
9. You can describe intervention options for helping clients change their cognitive ecology and their emotional reactions.

Reviewing What You Do

1. You can teach someone how to use shaping.
2. Review of your interviews shows that you take advantage of opportunities to offer clients valuable information and do so in a way that maximizes the likelihood that the client will use it successfully.
3. You can demonstrate your shaping skills by shaping a behavior of your instructor, peer, or significant other.
4. Review of skills training programs you use show that you effectively implement component methods.
5. You help clients identify obstacles that get in the way of using effective skills.
6. You can use cognitive-behavioral methods to alter one of your own behaviors.
7. You can design a multi-intervention program for specific problems.

Reviewing Results

1. You help a group of parents acquire accurate knowledge about child development.
2. You help citizens gather and disseminate information that exposes a serious community problem.
3. You help a client to acquire self-care skills.
4. You help teenagers learn effective skills for refusing invitations to drink.
5. You help a teacher communicate more effectively with her students.

6. You help a parent acquire positive parenting skills.

7. You help a depressed single parent learn more effective cognitive coping skills.

8. You help residential staff control their anger when confronted with annoying behaviors on the part of residents.

9. You help a client control angry outbursts.

10. You help a client with chronic pain to maximize "time-outs" from thinking about the pain.

11. You help community members to participate effectively at local board meetings.

CHAPTER 22

Helping Clients Learn Positive Behavior Change Skills

OVERVIEW

This chapter describes positive methods for helping clients to rearrange problem-related contingencies. Disliked situations may occur because of a lack of positive behavior change skills. Options for altering what happens before behavior are described as are options for rearranging consequences. Clients may be parents, students, teachers, community residents, members of support groups, staff in residential settings, or agency managers. Assessment will indicate whether it is possible to alter contingencies, if so how, and at what levels (e.g., individual, family, group, community, organization, or service system) and in what settings within each level.

You Will Learn About

- The value of positive behavior change skills.
- Myths and misconceptions about contingency management.
- Increasing behavior.
- Decreasing behavior.
- Positive alternatives to the use of punishment.
- Rearranging antecedents.

THE VALUE OF POSITIVE BEHAVIOR CHANGE SKILLS

Resolving problems involves altering behavior (see Exhibit 22.1). If you are a community organizer trying to encourage people both to register to vote and to vote, these are behaviors. People have to do something. For example, they have to go to the polls on election day and vote. A focus on changing the behavior of individuals is often confused with a psychological focus. There is a confusion between means (methods) and outcomes (goals).

EXHIBIT 22.1
Examples of Behaviors Related to Different Intervention Levels

Political/ Legislative	• Vote yes on legislation that increases services.
	• Write letters to legislators to encourage them to fund community-based service centers.
	• Register to vote.
	• Attend hearings regarding proposed policies/programs.
	• Distribute a face-sheet about a problem/situation (e.g., health care).
Service System	• Arrange regular meetings with staff in all agencies concerned with a specific problem to integrate services.
	• Design common face-sheet used by interlinked agencies.
	• Design an information management system compatible across agencies.
	• Select and pursue one legislative goal of mutual interest.
Organization	• Reinforce staff for desired behaviors.
	• Clarify goals.
	• Establish an ombudsman service for clients/staff.
	• Arrange for the participation of all staff in decisions that concern them.
Community	• Help neighbors.
	• Attend parent-teacher meetings.
	• Raise issues of concern to community boards.
	• Form a neighborhood block organization.
Group	• Suggest solutions to problems.
	• Offer to help others.
	• Reinforce other group members for valued behaviors.
	• Clarify desired outcomes of group.
Family	• Share mutually enjoyable activities.
	• Care for an elderly relative.
	• Provide proper nutrition to children.
	• Use positive parenting skills.
Individual	• Positive self-statements.
	• Accurate attributions for behaviors/outcomes.
	• Request services (e.g., food stamps, medical help, tutoring for children).
	• Initiate conversations.
	• Complete expected work on time.

This confusion may result in discounting individually focused methods that result in valued changes at other levels (e.g., in groups, schools, communities, organizations, or legislation) (see Exhibit 22.2). The question is: What is the purpose of altering the behavior of individuals? At what system level(s) are changes in behavior directed toward?

(see Exhibit 22.2.) The relationship skills described elsewhere in this book such as active listening, empathy, and warmth—as well as consultation skills such as arranging practice opportunities and providing corrective feedback (see McGimsey, Greene, Lutzker, 1995)—are valuable complements to knowledge and skills required to help clients and significant others rearrange contingencies.

Knowledge and skill in rearranging contingencies (relationships between behavior and the environment) are valuable at all levels of intervention. The principles of behavior described in Chapter 8 offer guidelines for altering behavior through rearranging contingencies. A contingency is the complete description of a specific operant. It includes a clear description of the behaviors that result in certain consequences (the operant class) as well as related antecedents and setting events (situations in which certain consequences influence related behaviors). Positive reinforcement and many forms of stimulus control (rearranging antecedents) rely on positive methods, removing the need for negative methods such as criticizing, removing privileges, and blaming. Once clients acquire valuable skills, they can help other clients learn these skills (see for example Neef, 1995).

MYTHS AND MISCONCEPTIONS ABOUT CONTINGENCY MANAGEMENT

Misconceptions and misinformation about the rearrangement of contingencies that may get in the way of drawing on valuable methods are discussed next.

1. Altering Contingencies Dehumanizes People

For both practical and ethical reasons goals pursued should be selected by clients and significant others, and a collaborative working relationship should be established that emphasizes client involvement in selecting methods. A contextual assessment in which problem-related environmental contingencies are explored decreases the likelihood

EXHIBIT 22.2
Examples of Focus and Outcomes

Focus	In Order To	Which Will
• Increase job-related social skills.	• Maintain employment.	• Maintain or enhance, independence.
• Encourage community members to register to vote and to vote.	• Influence what politicians are elected.	• Increase likelihood of passing certain legislation.
• Form self-help groups of parents who care for an elderly relative.	• Provide respite, validation, information and problem-solving assistance.	• Prevent institutionalization; enhance positive family relationships.
• Help clients acquire employment skills.	• Get a job.	• Enhance or maintain independence and self-esteem, support family.
• Help community residents form a social action group.	• Acquire funds to establish a shelter for battered women.	• Provide services to abused women and their children.

of "victim blaming"—viewing the victim of a problem as the cause of the problem. Helping clients acquire positive behavior change skills will increase their influence over their environments in ways that maximize positive consequences. As the creators of Homebuilders say, "We want [our clients] to learn how to get by with less pain, less punishment, more accomplishment, more love (!) and more fun" (Kinney, Haapala, & Booth, 1991, p. 93). This is a laudable goal for others as well, including supervisers, students, and administrators.

2. Contingencies Are All Powerful

This is not so. Often it is not an easy matter to change someone's behavior without his or her awareness. If we do not want our behavior altered, it is unlikely that others can do so unless they have access to influential contingencies. Other limiting factors include unique biological boundaries (see Chapter 8).

3. Underlying Causes Are Not Addressed

In contrast to the belief that contingencies are all powerful is the belief that they have little influence and, that if we focus on them, we ignore underlying causes such as feelings and thoughts. In fact, thousands of studies both in laboratory and applied settings have demonstrated the effects of consequences on our behavior (see references cited in Chapter 8). This does not imply a belief in radical environmentalism (the belief that our behavior is

determined by environmental events). Many other influences come into play (see Chapter 8). Any approach, including contingency analysis, can be carried out in a superficial manner in which contingencies related to problems are ignored. A thorough analysis of both self-presented and environmental contingencies, is required to "understand" problems and options. If this is carried out and related plans implemented, unwanted negative effects are less likely to occur.

4. Thoughts and Feelings Are Not Considered

Thoughts and feelings are considered in contingency analysis and management. They provide clues about contingencies (e.g., our experiences with certain individuals) and cognitive-behavioral programs focus directly on altering them (e.g., increasing helpful self-statements as described in Chapter 21). They are integrally involved in "rule-governed" behavior (verbal description of contingencies that may or may not reflect those in real-life). However, focusing solely on thoughts and feelings (as in "He hit her because he was angry") provides *incomplete* accounts. For example, we don't know the antecedents to "anger" nor the consequences of related behaviors such as hitting that may maintain them.

5. Individual Differences Are Ignored

Attention to individual differences is a hallmark of contingency analysis. Individuals, families, groups, organizations, and communities differ in their reinforcer and punisher profiles (what is valued and what is disliked) and related contingencies. Only if the unique value of different consequences to different individuals, groups, organizations, or communities is understood can successful programs be implemented. For a classic example of the failure of economic development programs due to lack of attention to cultural differences, see Kunkel (1970). Each individual has a unique learning history molded by his or her unique culture as well as by unique genetic and physiological differences. Individual learning histories create unique "meanings" for events for each individual, group, organization, or community. Cultures differ in their reinforcer profile.

6. The Helper-Client Relationship Is Unimportant

The client-helper relationship is considered to be important in contingency management. Warmth, respect, and empathy contribute to mutual understanding and a collaborative working relationship. However, the relationship is not viewed as the only or even key source of change. And, there is an effort to clearly identify specific relationship behaviors that contribute to valued outcomes. Candid recognition of the social influence effects in the helping process decreases the likelihood that they will be used (knowingly or not) in unethical and ineffective ways. Ignoring such influences does not make them go away. Rather it allows their use in an unsystematic or undercover way. It has been argued that nondirective counseling in which objectives remain vague and progress is not monitored is the most controlling of all approaches because sources of influence are unrecognized (see for example, Jurjevich, 1974).

7. People Learn How to Manipulate Each Other

Manipulation refers to influencing others in an unfair or fraudulent way for one's own profit (*Webster's New World Collegiate Dictionary*, 1988). Helping clients attain specific outcomes

they value is hardly manipulative. The contextual approach described in this book emphasizes the importance of involving significant others in choosing goals, outcomes and methods. We inevitably influence each other. As the old saying goes, "We cannot not communicate." There may be situations when an ethical argument could be made for showing some individuals how to change the behavior of other individuals without the awareness of the latter. For example, residents in institutional settings could learn how to gain more positive feedback from staff reluctant to provide this. Students aged 12 to 15 were taught how to increase their teachers' positive statements and to decrease their negative statements (Graubard, Rosenberg, & Miller, 1971). If residents or students have no other way to alter the behavior of their significant others (e.g., staff or teachers), isn't it unethical to withhold such knowledge from them? What do you think? Helping clients acquire effective behavior change skills does increase their influence over their environments (a large part of which may be provided by other people), but it does not teach them to manipulate this environment in an insidious or unfair way. So too with social skills training in which clients acquire more effective relationship skills that offer benefits both to themselves as well as to others (see Chapter 21).

8. Control Is Imposed Where None Exists

This incorrect belief overlooks sources of influence already present. Influencing others is an inescapable part of life. People have been trying to change other people's behavior throughout the centuries. They often try to do so by rearranging the consequences of behavior. Parents may admonish their children to eat their dinner or they will have to go to their room, or tell them that if they eat their dinner they can go out and play. Many people either do not possess or do not use positive behavior change skills and rely instead on negative methods (e.g., criticism, nagging, hitting). Much unhappiness and misery results. Problems are often aggravated by use of punitive methods. Not only may this be ineffective, it creates bad feelings as well as counteraggression as described in Chapter 8.

People don't like to be punished even if it is "for their own good." Both punishing and nonreinforcing environments contribute to burnout among professional helpers and are related to a variety of problems including depression and social anxiety (see for example Trower, Gilbert & Sherling, 1990).

It is true that preexisting contingencies may not be "planned." This does not mean that they are without influence. Viewing people as totally free encourages misplaced blame on families and individuals for problems such as poverty; political and economic causes are overlooked. Denying the influence of environmental contingencies no more negates their effects than would the law of gravity be suspended if we did not believe it. However, denial of such influence does permit those in privileged positions to blame poverty, discrimination, and oppression on those who experience them.

9. Contingencies That Already Exist Are More Natural

It is sometimes said that the contingencies that already exist are "more natural," meaning that no one has arranged them to attain given ends and that they do more good than harm. Actually, many contingencies that influence our behavior are deliberately arranged by, for example, governmental agencies. The advertising industry is in business to influence our behavior and to make a profit in doing so. Ethical problems raised by the influence of behavior cannot be avoided by refusing to recognize influence and its implications (Skinner, 1953). The question is: "Who benefits and who loses from ignorance about influential contingencies?" If knowledge about and skill in altering real-life contingencies provide freedom from unwanted influences, isn't this a benefit rather than a harm?

10. I'm Already Doing It

One way to discount something new is to say: "I already know that"; "I already do it." We rearrange contingencies every day. This does not mean that we do so in a systematic way in pursuit of specific outcomes. It is the systematicness and complete-

ness with which contingencies are analyzed and altered in relation to specific objectives and the ongoing monitoring of degree of progress that is key to success. Consider the poor track record of following New Year's resolutions. Occasional unevaluated use of positive incentives to change vaguely defined or even well-defined behaviors is not likely to be successful. Or, success will be less than would be possible. (See Watson and Tharp [1993] for a helpful guide to self-change experiments.) Malott (1994) suggests that we often resort to unconscious motivational explanations to understand why we and others do not follow through with actions that correspond with our values because we have such limited understanding of the causes of poor self-management.

11. Extrinsic Reinforcers Undermine Intrinsic Ones

Some people argue that using reinforcement to alter behavior (e.g., increase study behavior) undermines the intrinsic reinforcing value of behaviors. Phillip Hineline (1995) argues that this is a destructive half-truth. It is true that using contrived reinforcers may reflect the user's rather than the client's values and that one must be vigilant that this is not the case. It is also true that it is of little value to rely on reinforcers that will not maintain behavior after the trainer leaves. It is also true that offering reinforcers that are functionally superfluous (not needed to maintain behavior) may decrease intrinsic reinforcement. The destructive half-truth is arguing that contingent consequences should not be used or are of no value in educational and helping contexts. In fact, research shows that external reinforcers that are not functionally superfluous can be used to increase intrinsic motivation (see for example, Dickinson, 1989; Lepper & Hodell, 1989). They should not be introduced when intrinsic ones are present unless the latter result in injury to self or others. Contrived reinforcers should only be used when natural consequences are not feasible. And, new repertoires "should be made functional by bringing them into contact with reinforcing consequences that are natural to the situation" (Hineline, 1995, p. 1). Avoid incentives that are not already part of the natural en-

vironment when possible. If it is necessary to introduce artificial reinforcers such as tokens or points,
plan their removal so that behavior is maintained
by real-life contingencies (also Eisenberger &
Cameron, 1996.)

12. Rearranging Contingencies Takes Little Skill

There are a relatively small number of key concepts
related to rearranging contingencies, however, their
application to real-life problems is often complex
(see for example Exhibit 8.5). Unless you understand
the complexities of rearranging internested contingencies related to real-life problems, they may seem
simpleminded. You might say everyone knows that
consequences affect behavior. Rearranging contingencies in a way that maximizes the likelihood of
success (attaining outcomes valued by clients and
significant others) requires knowledge and skill.
Knowledge and accompanying procedural skills are
needed to translate problems into observable behaviors, to discover maintaining conditions, and to select and implement effective plans.

13. Contingency Management Is Only Useful at the Individual Level

Understanding and rearranging contingencies are
key aspects of work at all system levels including
community organization and policy planning.
Many examples have already been given in this
book. This is required to discover misapplied and
unapplied contingencies related to situations of
concern. Arranging management systems in service
agencies that ensure high quality services is of concern not only to professionals, but to clients as well.
Quality performance can be encouraged by identifying clear standards of performance, arranging
needed training and feedback, and involving all
staff in setting standards and selecting feedback
methods (LaVigna et al., 1994). Contingency
analysis is also useful at the cultural level to explore how contingencies at different levels (individual, family, group, organization, community,
and policy) influence problem-related behaviors
(see Chapter 8, Exhibit 3).

EXHIBIT 22.3
Options for Decreasing Undesired Behavior and Increasing Desired Behavior

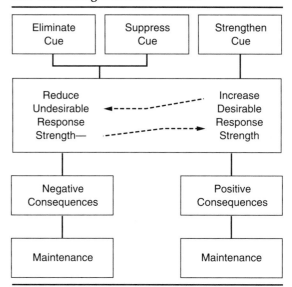

Source: R. B. Stuart & B. Davis (1972), *Slim chance in a fat world* (p. 76). Champaign/Urbana, IL: Research Press. Reprinted with permission.

INCREASING BEHAVIOR

Some problems involve behaviors that do not occur often enough. A superviser may seldom provide positive feedback to her staff. A parent may
seldom praise her children. A legislator may seldom vote for proposals to increase accessibility of
health care for all citizens. You may seldom offer
yourself positive feedback for behaviors you value.
Teachers may seldom seek the opinion of parents
of the children they teach. Options for increasing
behavior include rearranging consequences, antecedents and setting events (see Exhibit 22.3).

POSITIVE REINFORCEMENT

The term positive reinforcement refers to a procedure in which an event (a reinforcer) is presented
following a behavior and there is an increase in the
future likelihood of that behavior. Positive reinforcement provides a way to increase behavior that

is already occurring. It plays a key role in developing new behaviors (see Chapter 21).

Making Effective Use of Positive Reinforcement

Requisites for effective use of positive reinforcement include:

- Identify an observable, countable behavior.
- Select an event that will function as a reinforcer (see Chapter 16).
- Arrange for the behavior to occur.
- Make sure the reinforcer follows the behavior immediately.
- Use an appropriate criterion for reinforcement (e.g. it is achievable).
- Reinforce often.
- Reinforce immediately.
- Reinforce behavior across multiple behaviors, settings, and time.

Reinforcers are relative. They are known not by their physical characteristics but by their function (their effects on behavior). Many programs fail because the relativity of reinforcers is ignored. Each individual has a unique history of reinforcement. This refers to the frequency, schedule, intensity, and/or duration with which particular behaviors have been reinforced in particular situations. Because of different learning histories, an event that functions as a reinforcer for one person, may not for another. On the other hand, because of similar learning histories in a given society, the same reinforcer may have identical functions for many people. An event that functions as a reinforcer in one situation may not do so in another. Significant others, such as parents, spouses, or teachers often assume that what is reinforcing for them is reinforcing for others. This may not be so. Such events could, however, be developed as reinforcers. For example, teacher approval could be established as a reinforcer by pairing it with consequences that already function as a reinforcer. Some reinforcers are substitutable (they may satisfy the same or similar

needs). Others are not. Different reinforcement patterns in different cultures create different reinforcer profiles. Considering the relativity of reinforcers is part of what it means to be multiculturally sensitive.

Whenever possible, use "natural" rather than artificial reinforcers and reinforce behaviors that will continue to be supported in real-life environments. Positive reinforcement is often combined with operant extinction of undesired behaviors (see later discussion of differential reinforcement).

Variables That Influence the Effectiveness of Reinforcement

Timing, schedule, amount, and frequency influence the effectiveness of reinforcement (see Chapter 8). An ideal reinforcer:

1. Can be presented immediately following behavior with little trouble to the person providing it.
2. Can be presented in a consistently effective form (critical dimensions of the reinforcer can be kept constant).
3. Does not lose effectiveness through satiation.
4. Is a strong influence on behavior.
5. Delivery can be accurately recorded.

Reinforcement should encourage task completion rather than time spent on a task. Increasing time spent on a task such as cleaning or studying may not result in an increase in task completion. Guidelines for discovering reinforcers are described in Chapter 16. Deprivation of a reinforcer increases the likelihood of all behaviors that may result in its acquisition (see discussion of establishing operations in Chapter 8). If children are deprived of social contacts, they are more likely to engage in behaviors that result in such contacts. If they are "satiated," there will be a cessation of responding. Satiation involves providing a reinforcer in such quantity and frequency that it no longer functions as a reinforcer. This is one way to decrease behavior. It is usually not used because of the practical limitations of providing large quantities of a reinforcer; the temporary nature of satiation effects with reinforcers such as food; the negative effects of providing large quantities of some reinforcers, such as food; and, the gradualness of change. Both reinforcer exposure (observing another person using a reinforcer) and reinforcer sampling (a reinforcer is sampled) may increase the effectiveness of a reinforcer.

Frequency refers to how often a behavior is reinforced. Many people make the mistake of waiting for a low-frequency behavior to occur rather than reinforcing approximations (see discussion of shaping in Chapter 21). Selecting small steps to reinforce makes frequent reinforcement possible. The more often a behavior is reinforced, the more rapidly it will be established.

Timing is important. A reinforcer should follow desired behaviors immediately. If it does not, it may follow some other behavior and increase this instead of the one of interest. Errors in timing are one of the main reasons people are not successful in using reinforcement. For example, reinforcement may be provided too long after the behavior of interest. As Karen Pryor points out, "The dog sits, but by the time the owner says 'good dog' the dog is standing again" (1984, p. 27). Delays between a behavior and later consequences can be "bridged" in older children and adults by reminders about the contingency (e.g., if I don't study for this test I might fail the course). If a mother tells her child that, because he broke a plate, his father will spank him when he comes home, this interim may be filled with anticipated unpleasant events ("thinking about the punishment to come") if such threats have been followed up in the past. If a child is very young, no connection may be made between later punishment and earlier behaviors. Tokens or points may be used to "bridge" delays in access to back-up reinforcers.

We may also offer reinforcers too soon. Karen Pryor suggests that saying "That's the way to go, you almost got it right" may reinforce trying rather than successful performance and encourage saying "I can't." Considering the long-term as well as the short-term consequences of behavior can be difficult as illustrated by the many people who continue to smoke even though they are aware of the health risks.

Amount of reinforcement influences the effects of reinforcement. Too much may result in satiation, too little in no change in behavior. How big a reinforcer should you use? "The answer is as small as you can get a way with" (Pryor, 1984, p. 30). This decreases waiting time because of distractions by the reinforcer (e.g., playing with a toy, eating food). Richard Malott (1994) argues that we often fail in our efforts to alter our own behavior or that of others because related contingencies have inconsequential effects. Consider seat belt use and teeth flossing. He argues that the immediate consequences of these behaviors are inconsequential (e.g., a slight reduction in fear of injury, less chance of loosing one's teeth in twenty years) and so of little or no influence. Only if we arrange circumstances to heighten consequences are such behaviors likely to occur on a regular basis.

Schedule refers to the particular pattern that describes the relationship between behavior and its consequences. Schedules influence the rate of behavior, the maintenance of behavior, and resistance to extinction (how difficult it is to decrease a behavior) (see Chapter 8). Continuous reinforcement schedules provide for the fastest acquisition of behavior and for the most rapid decrease of behavior when reinforcement is no longer provided. Maintenance of behavior in real-life settings usually requires shifting to an intermittent schedule after behavior stabilizes at a desired level. Transition from a low variable-ratio schedule in which small outputs are sometimes reinforced, to a large fixed-ratio schedule may disrupt behavior. This may account in part for lower output when a person is promoted from a job where tasks are reinforced on a variable schedule to one where behavior is reinforced only after a set high number of behaviors. Thus, a disinterest in initiating an activity may be due to too thin a schedule of reinforcement. Fixed-ratio strain is a unique property of high ratio schedules; we may be disinclined to work if too much behavior is required for reinforcement.

A special history is needed to develop behavior maintained on large fixed- or variable-ratio schedules. Many small and intermediate schedules must first be used. Expected behaviors may not occur because this process of approximating larger ratios has not been completed. Without an understanding of the role of schedules, lack of success may be mistakenly blamed on individual characteristics of clients (he is lazy). Occasional reinforcement may maintain behavior. Parents who try to decrease behavior by no longer reinforcing it often do this only part of the time. They provide periodic reinforcement, which will establish behavior that is difficult to decrease.

Other Factors. Quality of a reinforcer refers to its reinforcing potential relative to other reinforcers. The higher the quality, the more reinforcing potential it may have. For example, you may like certain kinds of ice cream better than others. Novelty also influences the effectiveness of reinforcers. The more varied, the more reinforcing they may be, perhaps because satiation is less likely. Karen Pryor (1984) recommends the use of "jackpots" (giving a much bigger reward than the usual—the reinforcer comes as a surprise). Describing contingencies may increase the effects of new reinforcement patterns; however, it is not essential. Relationships between behavior and consequences can be highlighted by describing the contingency before as well as when it occurs.

If You Are Not Successful

Lack of success is related to misapplied and unapplied contingencies. Perhaps there is an overly narrow focus on one system level. For example, you may work with a child to alter her behavior and ignore problem-related contingencies in her family. You may involve supervisors in an agency but overlook contingencies administrators provide to supervisors. You and your clients may arrange contingencies that result in small inconsequential effects. Use the form in Chapter 18, Exhibit 18.3 to review what you focus on in relation to what seems to be needed. Review the following possibilities if your efforts to use positive reinforcement are not successful and take appropriate action:

- The consequence used as a reinforcer does not fill this function perhaps because there is no motivating condition (see Chapter 8). It may be too

small to make a difference or of poor quality. The consequence selected may not be a reinforcer for this individual (See e.g., Green et. al., 1988).

- Behavior is not reinforced often enough. An easier approximation may have to be selected.
- The reinforcer can be obtained via other behaviors.
- The reinforcer is delayed too long.
- The reinforcer is not presented consistently following the behavior (perhaps because relevant behaviors are not clearly described).
- Competing behaviors receive richer schedules of reinforcement.
- Satiation occurs because of lack of variation of reinforcers.
- A behavior seldom occurs so there is little opportunity to reinforce it.
- Punishment and/or response cost is mixed with positive reinforcement.
- Insufficient time has been allowed for change.
- Prompting may be required (see later section on rearranging antecedents).

Advantages and Disadvantages

Positive reinforcement "feels good." We like people who offer us positive consequences and are likely to continue behaviors in the absence of external surveillance (e.g., threats and nagging). Unlike punishment, positive reinforcement does not encourage escape and avoidance. Quite the opposite. It encourages approach. One disadvantage of positive reinforcement is its "seductiveness." We are less likely to "rebel" against it (exert counter control) because it "feels good." Advertisers and politicians take advantage of this fact. This was one of Skinner's (1971) major points in *Beyond Freedom and Dignity* (perhaps his most misunderstood book). Another disadvantage is that people may become dependent on a narrow range of positive reinforcers and the individuals who provide them (Balsam & Bondy, 1983). For example, clients may become overly dependent on their therapists. You can avoid this by using a variety of reinforcers, involving significant others, and encouraging self-reliance. A third disadvantage is that it usually takes a while for positive reinforcement to effect behavior in contrast with punishment, which may have an immediate (though temporary) effect. This is one reason people often rely on aversive means of influence. A fourth disadvantage is that it often takes more effort and creativity to identify positive consequences that will function as positive reinforcers without unwanted side effects than to identify negative ones.

Myths and Misunderstandings about Positive Reinforcement

Some people object to the use of positive reinforcement on the grounds that this is bribery. In *Webster's New World Collegiate Dictionary* (1988) a bribe is defined as "anything, especially money, given or promised to induce a person to do something illegal or wrong." Thus, the use of positive reinforcement to increase desired behaviors cannot accurately be considered bribery. People are often willing to punish undesired behavior but unwilling to offer positive incentives contingent on desired behaviors. (See also earlier section on myths and misconceptions.)

DIFFERENTIAL REINFORCEMENT

Differential reinforcement of alternative behavior (DRA) is widely used to decrease undesired behavior and to increase desired behavior. Reinforcement is withheld following behaviors to be decreased (operant extinction) and presented following desired behaviors (positive reinforcement). Behavior surfeits (behaviors that occur too often and create problems such as hitting) are often related to behavior deficits (lack of desired behaviors such as sharing toys). In differential reinforcement of other behaviors (DRO), reinforcement is offered if a certain time passes in which a behavior does not occur. A child may receive a reinforcer if he is not accused of stealing for an entire day. Reinforcement can be offered contingent on a specific low rate of behavior (DRL). For example, a student may receive points if he talks out

of turn only once every hour. In differential reinforcement of incompatible behaviors (DRI) a behavior incompatible with one to be decreased is reinforced. Techniques designed to decrease anxiety such as desensitization and stress-management training, involve increasing alternative behaviors such as calming self-instructions.

NEGATIVE REINFORCEMENT

Behavior can be increased by delaying, preventing, or removing unwanted consequences contingent on behavior. Like the definition of positive reinforcement, the definition of negative reinforcement also includes two parts: (1) *description of a procedure* (the removal of an event contingent on a behavior); and (2) *a behavioral effect* (a subsequent increase in the future probability of the behavior). As with positive reinforcers, the classification of an event as a negative reinforcer depends on its effects on behavior. In both positive and negative reinforcement, behaviors are followed by a change in the environment. In the former, something is presented. In the latter, something is removed. Both procedures *increase* the future probability of behavior and both involve contingencies (relationships between behavior and the environment). Negative as well as positive reinforcement play a key role in the development and maintenance of behaviors. The same factors that are important with positive reinforcement (immediacy, amount, schedule, and frequency) are important with negative reinforcement.

Making Effective Use of Negative Reinforcement

Requisites for using negative reinforcement are the same as those for using positive reinforcement except that a negative consequence is removed, delayed, or prevented following a behavior. It is important that desired behavior results in the removal of the aversive event. Because it is often the form of escape or avoidance behavior that is problematic (not the function), desirable alternatives could be reinforced. The same parameters that influence the effectiveness of positive reinforcement influence the effectiveness of negative reinforcement (see earlier discussion). If negative reinforcement is not effective it may be because one of the requisites for effective use of punishment is not satisfied (see later discussion of punishment).

Advantages and Disadvantages

Both negative and positive reinforcement increase behavior. Many self-managed contingencies are maintained by negative reinforcement (e.g., studying removes guilt and worry). The close relationship between punishment and negative reinforcement (aversive events must be presented or threatened if they are to be removed) is a disadvantage of relying on negative reinforcement. However, punishment is a daily part of real-life environments. Donald Baer (1984) points out that "Many of our most useful skills, like walking or driving a car, are skills that were learned and are maintained under severe, consistent punishment for almost any small error. Yet we do not consider that our interactions with the surface of the planet or with automobiles are problems in need of intervention, despite the pervasively aversive nature of the contingencies surrounding them" (p. 557). All contingencies including punishment and negative reinforcement provide us with information (e.g., clues about how we could alter our behavior to increase positive outcomes and to decrease negative ones). Malott (1994) suggests that we should make greater use of negative reinforcement to encourage outcomes we value (e.g., learning, wearing seat belts, exercising).

Myths and Misunderstandings

Negative reinforcement is often confused with punishment. Although punishment and negative reinforcement both involve aversive events, they differ in their effects (one increases behavior and may be associated with positive emotional reactions such as relief; the other decreases behavior and is associated with negative emotional reactions such as fear and anxiety). Many highly adaptive behaviors are maintained by negative reinforcement (e.g.,

EXHIBIT 22.4
Levels of Intrusiveness of Intervention

LEVEL 1. DIFFERENT REINFORCEMENT

- Of low rates of behavior (DRL).
- Of other behavior(s) (DRO).
- Of incompatible behavior (DRI).
- Of alternative behavior(s) DRA).

LEVEL 2. EXTINCTION

LEVEL 3. REMOVAL OF DESIRED STIMULI

- Response-cost.
- Time-out.

LEVEL 4. PRESENTATION OF AVERSIVE STIMULI

- Unconditioned aversive stimuli.
- Conditioned aversive stimuli.
- Overcorrection.

Source: P. A. Alberto & A. C. Troutman (1990), Applied behavior analysis for teachers. *Columbus, OH: Merrill.*

turning the wheel of a car to avoid an accident, wearing protective gloves to decrease risk of HIV infection among nurses).

DECREASING BEHAVIOR

Many problems involve unwanted behaviors, behaviors that occur too often, at the wrong time, or in the wrong form. There are many options for decreasing behavior (see Exhibit 22.4). Some are more effective with less hassle and negative effects than are others.

EXTINCTION

In operant extinction, the consequences that usually follow a behavior no longer occur.

Making Effective Use of Extinction

Only if reinforcers are consistently withheld will extinction be effective. If they are not or if the re-

inforcer maintaining a behavior cannot be identified, the behavior will be occasionally reinforced,
which will maintain the behavior. Questions suggested when considering the use of extinction include the following (Alberto & Troutman, 1990, p.
264):

1. Can the behavior be tolerated temporarily?
2. Can an increase in the behavior be tolerated?
3. Is the behavior likely to occur?
4. Are the reinforcers known?
5. Can reinforcement be withheld?
6. Have alternative behaviors been identified that
   can be reinforced?

If it is not possible to withhold reinforcement following a behavior, other procedures must be used.
You can only be certain that the reinforcers have
been identified after they are no longer provided,
and a subsequent decrease in behavior occurs.

Advantages and Disadvantages of Extinction

Extinction is not as aversive as some other means of
decreasing behavior such as punishment. It may be
easy to implement and effective provided that all involved parties are consistent and persistent in withholding reinforcement. Disadvantages of extinction
when used alone include an initial increase in the intensity, severity, and frequency of the behavior being extinguished that may be aversive to others. Even
when extinction is combined with positive reinforcement of desired behaviors it may take a few days
to see a change in behavior. There may be periods
of "spontaneous recovery" of the behavior.
Occasional reinforcement may undo an extinction
procedure. Also, keep in mind that no specific desired responses may be increased. In fact, other undesirable behaviors may occur because of negative
emotional reactions. Aggressive reactions may occur
as well as negative emotional effects. Withholding
reinforcement elicits aggressive attack behavior in a
range of species. Feelings of discouragement, failure,
and helplessness and depression may accompany extinction. Social anxiety may be due not only to punishing consequences, but to a lack of positive rein-

forcement in social situations (i.e., nonreward). Being
ignored in social situations is not emotionally neutral
for most people. It is unpleasant.

If You Are Not Successful

You may not be successful because reinforcement
was not consistently withheld. Resistance to extinction is influenced by the reinforcement schedule that has maintained a behavior (see discussion
of schedules of reinforcement in Chapter 8). It is
also influenced by the amount, number, and quality of reinforcers, number of previous extinction
trails, and effort required to engage in a behavior.
Extinction should be combined with the positive
reinforcement of desired behaviors. This will avoid
the initial increase in undesired behavior, increase
a specific other desirable behavior, and avoid negative emotional effects that accompany extinction.

Myths and Misconceptions

Successful use of extinction requires withholding
reinforcement for all instances of a behavior.
Occasional, sporadic withholding of reinforcement
will not be effective. We have seen that extinction
creates negative emotional reactions. Thus, it is not
without emotional effects. And, as noted above, extinction does not increase any other particular behavior.

RESPONSE COST

In response cost a positive reinforcer is removed
contingent on a behavior. This is often combined
with positive reinforcement of desired behaviors.
Response cost may be used as a part of token or
point programs. Tokens or points could be deducted
contingent on certain behaviors (or their lack).
Removal of tangible items such as a candy bar is
often difficult and involves attention that might reinforce inappropriate behavior.

Making Effective Use of Response Cost

Select an observable, countable behavior, as well
as a positive reinforcer to be removed, and arrange

the consistent removal of this event following the behavior. Be sure to combine response cost with positive reinforcement of desired behaviors. Arrange the precise cost beforehand (e.g., how many days will use of a car be lost?). The loss should match the severity of the behavior, be consistently and immediately applied, and the contingency should be verbally described. Time out involves response cost (see later discussion).

If You Are Not Successful

Perhaps the consequence removed is not a reinforcer. Not enough reinforcement may be offered for alternative behaviors (see also discussion of punishment).

Advantages and Disadvantages

Advantages of response cost include ease of combining it with other methods (e.g., positive reinforcement of desired behaviors) and rapid effects on behavior. Disadvantages are similar to those of punishment (e.g., increased aggression, avoidance of the response cost enforcer and contexts in which positive consequences are removed, and focus on negative behaviors).

Myths and Misunderstandings

Response cost decreases behavior. It does not necessarily increase any other behavior despite beliefs and hopes that "He should know what to do." And, it creates negative emotional reactions.

PUNISHMENT: THE LEAST DESIRABLE ALTERNATIVE

Punishment is a procedure in which an aversive event is presented following a behavior and there is a subsequent decrease in that behavior (see also Chapter 8). Behaviors maintained on "thin schedules" of reinforcement are especially likely to be disrupted by punishment. Aversive events differ in their intensity ranging from a mild verbal rebuke to a slap in the face. Aversive events, like positive ones, are relative. That is, what functions as aversive events varies from person to person and from time to time for the same person depending on each person's unique history and current situation. Some argue that it is never necessary to use aversive methods. They argue that other procedures are available for decreasing behavior including differential reinforcement of other behavior or positive reinforcement combined with time out (Sailor & Carr, 1994). Others argue that there is no way to avoid the use of punishment if we want to enhance freedom, which requires individual responsibility, which, in turn, requires sharing the costs and pain that result from behavior (Birnbrauer, 1990; 1994). They argue that to insist that socialization or self-management can occur without any use of punishment (e.g., verbal reprimands) is simply wrong. With some behaviors, such as head banging, it may not be possible to withhold reinforcement for the behavior, and so operant extinction cannot be used. The frequency of a behavior may be so high that it interferes with desired behavior and so these cannot be reinforced. Punishment may be necessary to reduce this high frequency so that positive behaviors can be reinforced. Positive consequences are not always successful in altering behavior in desired directions. In certain instances, for example, with severe self-destructive behavior, it may be more humane to use punishment combined with positive reinforcement than to combine the latter with planned ignoring because the former is more rapidly effective. Carr and his colleagues (1990) believe that the question "Should aversives be used?" is the wrong question. They believe that the right question is "What does a functional assessment indicate is necessary to accomplish valued outcomes with minimal use of aversives and maximum reliance on positive methods?"

Birnbrauer (1990) suggests that the "solution is to institute and maintain contingencies that maximize positives and minimize negatives for each member of the group" (p. 232). Thus, both the individual and the group must be considered in relation to costs and benefits. Because the effects of offensive behavior are usually positive for the offender and only negative to others ". . . planning priorities should be placed upon instituting and maintaining contingencies of reinforcement, both positive and negative, so that (a) the need for punishment is diminished, (b) the unsystematic use of aversives is diminished, and (c) aversives are employed only in contexts that maximize effectiveness in the shortest period of time" (p. 233) (see also Sailor & Carr, 1994).

Making Effective Use of Punishment

Requisites for the effective use of punishment include:

- Identify specific behaviors
- Withhold positive reinforcement for these behaviors
- Select an event that will function as a punishing consequence that elicits as little aggression as possible.
- Arrange the consistent presentation of this immediately following the behavior
- Reinforce desired alternatives.

If punishment is used, it should be combined with reinforcement for desired behaviors (e.g., alternate ways to gain desired consequences). Criticism can be decreased by identifying and reinforcing desired behaviors. Unwanted escape from the contingency must be prevented and, if possible, every instance of behavior to be decreased should be followed by the punishing event. Make sure that the punishing event is not associated with positive reinforcement; otherwise, it may serve as a cue that valued consequences will follow and undesired behaviors may increase. They become cues that reinforcement will follow. It is more effective to punish early rather than later components in a chain of behavior. Early components are more easily disrupted, and reinforcement of undesired behaviors that may occur if the behavior chain is completed is avoided. Remove cues and reinforcers for undesired behavior; otherwise, the effects of punishment will be diluted by continued reinforcement. In everyday life, many undesired behaviors are followed by both reinforcement and punishment. As long as the amount of reinforcement exceeds the amount of punishment, the behavior will continue, especially if no alternative source of rein-

forcement is provided. You can bring behavior under the influence of verbal cues such as "No" or "Stop that" by pairing such statements with punishment. Behavior can then be influenced by the verbal cue alone. Providing reasons why certain actions should be avoided or taken may be helpful.

Variables That Influence the Effectiveness of Punishment

The same variables that influence the effectiveness of reinforcement influence the effectiveness of punishment, including the immediacy with which a negative event follows behavior, the intensity of this event, the schedule of punishment and the proportion of responses punished. Punishment is more effective if initially introduced at an intense level than if it is introduced at moderate or mild levels. If punishment is mild, habituation to the punishing event may occur, resulting in a decrease in the effect of the aversive consequence. That is, stronger levels of punishment may be required to achieve the same behavioral effect. Continuous, in contrast to intermittent, punishment is more effective.

If undesired behaviors are still being reinforced, the effects of punishment will be influenced by the schedule of reinforcement in effect. For example, tantrums may be reinforced by attention delivered on a variable-ratio schedule. This will decrease the effects of punishment. However, if an alternative way is provided to obtain a reinforcer, punishment can be very effective in decreasing unwanted behavior and increasing desired behaviors. Deprivation decrease the effects of punishment. If a person is deprived of a reinforcer, such as social approval, punishment of behaviors that result in this reinforcer will not be as effective. Punishment will be ineffective if escape from the contingency is possible. If a mother tells her son that because he was late for dinner he will receive no dinner that evening, and if he can go out and have dinner with a friend, her words may have little impact.

If You Are Not Successful

Check the following possibilities and rearrange plans as needed:

- The consequence used is not aversive.
- The behavior is being positively reinforced.
- There are no alternative routes to obtain positive reinforcers.
- Escape is possible.
- One of the other requisites for the effective use of punishment has not been satisfied.

Disadvantages of Reliance on Punishment

Avoid use of punishment when possible. The many disadvantages of punishment are described in Chapter 8. Punishment only teaches what not to do and leaves the development of desirable behaviors to chance. It does not eliminate reinforcement for undesired behavior. Aversive consequences, especially moderate or high-level ones, should only be used under extreme circumstances (e.g., behaviors that pose a great danger to self or others), and, only when positive and less aversive methods have not been effective. Guidelines suggested by Alberto and Troutman (1990) include the following:

1. Demonstrated and documented failure of alternative nonaversive methods to alter behavior.
2. Informed written consent of the client and significant others (e.g., legal guardians) through due process procedures and assurance of their right to withdraw their consent at any time.
3. A decision to use an aversive procedure made by a designated body of qualified professionals.
4. A prearranged timetable to review the effectiveness of the method and to ensure its discontinuance as soon as possible.
5. Periodic observation to ensure consistent and reliable use of the method.
6. Documentation of the effectiveness of the method as well as evidence of increased accessibility to instruction.
7. Use of the method only by designated staff member(s) who have had prior instruction in its use, have reviewed published studies in its use, and who are familiar with procedure-specific guidelines and possible negative effects.

8. Arranging positive reinforcement of incompatible behavior whenever possible. (pp. 276–278)

Myths and Misconceptions

Many people rely on punishment because they believe it is effective. Although it may be temporarily effective, no other particular desired alternative is encouraged, which may be the main goal of the "punisher." Punishment teaches what not to do, not what to do.

Why Do So Many People Rely on Punishment?

Use of punishment is encouraged by its immediate effects, lack of knowledge and skill in positive behavior change methods, and a low tolerance for undesirable behavior. For example, staff in a residential center may neither know about or be skilled in using positive contingencies. They may know about them but not have the skills required to implement them effectively. Use of positive methods requires creativity to discover or create positive reinforcers. It usually doesn't take much thought to identify what can be taken away from a client or what can be presented that will be unpleasant. Staff may be concerned that their physical safety and/or that of others cannot be assured unless aversive methods are used. Research suggests that in most cases, safety can be maximized via use of positive methods (see for example, Lavigna et al., 1994).

Overcorrection

This method can be used to decrease inappropriate behaviors and to provide practice of desired alternatives. It involves the use of aversive events. In restitutional overcorrection, the person is required to correct the results of his behavior by restoring the situation to an improved state compared to that which existed before the behavior. For example, a youth who spits on the floor may be required to wash the entire floor. Positive-practice overcorrection involves the practice of correct behaviors. A youth who throws trash around could practice placing trash in wastebaskets. (See other sources for more detailed descriptions (Martin & Pear, 1996).

Time Out

In time out an individual is removed to a less reinforcing environment for a *brief* period contingent on undesired behavior or lack of a desired behavior. A person is removed from one environment (the "time-in" environment) to another that is less reinforcing (the time-out environment), contingent on a behavior (or its lack). This procedure is often used with young children and can be very effective especially when combined with positive reinforcement of desired behaviors. Time-out contingencies involve a variety of components, including: (1) response cost (removal of positive reinforcers, the "time-in" environment); (2) negative reinforcement (time out is ended only after inappropriate behavior has ended); (3) punishment (isolation itself may be unpleasant); and (4) positive reinforcement (valued behaviors are reinforced following the end of time-out). Time-out should be combined with positive reinforcement of desired behavior and time-out duration should be brief, about 5 to 15 minutes. Time out will not be effective if undesired behavior is reinforced during time out.

Effective use of time out requires specialized knowledge and training. You must identify specific behavior(s), select a time-out area that does not contain positive reinforcers, and arrange for the removal of the person to this area contingent on specific behavior(s) (or their lack). Time will be needed to train significant others how to use time out correctly, and arrangements should be made to monitor its use and provide corrective feedback as necessary. Questions to review include the following:

1. Have I overlooked use of more positive procedures such as differential reinforcement?

2. Have I considered both nonseclusionary and seclusionary time-out methods?

3. Can time-out be used with minimal client resistance? Can significant others handle possible resistance?

4. Have the rules for desired behavior and the results of undesired behavior been clearly explained and understood?

5. Have the rules for behavior while in time out been clearly explained and understood?

6. Have regulations concerning use of time-out been reviewed and complied with?

7. Will appropriate behavior be reinforced in conjunction with the use of time-out? (Alberto & Troutman, 1990, p. 275)

Common errors in attempting to use time-out include providing reinforcing attention and physical contact on the way to time-out. In such cases, time-out may function as a positive reinforcer. Time-out may function as a positive reinforcer if the time-in environment is not positive. Other possibilities you should consider if time out is not effective include the following: The time-out area is reinforcing; time-out is not consistently enforced; time-out periods are too long (e.g., not allowing opportunities for reinforcement of appropriate behaviors); or time-out may not be immediately implemented following undesired behavior. Positive alternatives may not be reinforced. Time-out periods may be ended even though inappropriate behavior is occurring.

POSITIVE ALTERNATIVES TO THE USE OF PUNISHMENT

There are a variety of alternates to the use of punishment that focus on increasing desired behaviors and avoid the negative effects of punishment.

Reinforcing Desired Behaviors

Reinforcing desired behaviors is a positive alternative to punishment (see prior discussion of differential reinforcement). Positive quality assurance programs emphasize use of positive consequences and involve all staff in discovering opportunities to improve the quality of services (LaVigna et al., 1994). Agreement among staff that certain service standards are not up-to-par are viewed as opportunities to enhance services. You can discover alter-

EXHIBIT 22.5

Source of Motivation, Possible Communicative Messages, and Related Interventions

Motivational Source	Possible Communicative message(s)	Teach Replacement Response	Functionally Related Alt-R Procedures	Change Antecedents
I. *Positive reforcement* Attention maintains behavior	"Pay Attention to me" "Look at me," "Play with me" "Help me" "Play," "Help"	Teach a variety of means for requesting attention (e.g., tap on arm, greeting sign, "Play," "Help")	Use attention to reinforce already occurring alternative responses Direct instructions + social reinforcement of new alternative behaviors.	Alter environment to provide non-contingent attention
Material reinforcers (e.g., food, objects)	"I want _____"	Teach manual sign for desired consequence.	Use desired materials to reinforce already occurring alternative behaviors. Direct instruction + social reinforcement of new, alternative responses.	Alter environment to provide non-contingent access to material reinforcers (stimulus satiation).
II. *Negative reenforcement.* Termination of an aversive stimulus or situation.	"I don't want to do this anymore" "Stop!" "No" "I don't understand" "I want out!"	Teach manual/gestural/ sign/end activity, escape.	Reinforce alternative escape behaviors.	Alter context to decrease/ eliminate aversiveness; simplify tasks; increase preference value of tasks; decreases or alter instructional demands; alter instructional procedures.
III. *Extinction frustration* Previously available reinforcers are no longer available.	"Help me" "I'm frustrated" "Why can't I have . . ." "You used to give me _____"; "I want it now"	Teach communication skills to obtain desired reinforcers; and/or to enlist aid to obtain reinforcers.	Reinstate previously available reinforcers contingent on occurrence of alternative responses.	After environment to provide previously available reinforcers; alter instructions, provide richer reinforcement schedule, etc.
IV. *Arousal induction* Behavior provides sensory stimulation that is intrinsically reinforcing.	"I'm bored" "I'm not getting the input I want"	Teach how to obtain sensory input, e.g., request for sensory activity.	Provide reinforcing sensory input through alternative activities. Direct instruction + reinforcement of alternative behaviors.	Alter environment to provide more stimulation
V. *Arousal reduction* Behavior is maintained by termination of aversive overstimulation (e.g., it "blocks out" excess sensory input)	"I'm anxious/ excited/overwhelmed" "Help me"	Teach alternative means for expressing distress/enlisting aid. effects of	Provide and reinforce alternative means of removing the aversive overstimulation; vigorous exercise Relaxation Response	Alter environment to decrease stimulation and demands

(continued)

EXHIBIT 19.12 (*continued*)

Motivational Source	Possible Communicative message(s)	Teach Replacement Response	Functionally Related Alt-R Procedures	Change Antecedents
VI. *Respondent conditioning* Behavior originated from a traumatic event (e.g., loud noise, pain) that triggers the behavior. Behavior is then maintained by positive or negative reinforcement.	"I'm afraid" "This is a bad habit that I can't control" "I want _____ to stop" "Help"	Teach how to express distress or enlist assistance	Reinforce gradual tolerance of trigger stimulus; systematic desensitization; Direct instruction + reinforcement of alternative responses to trigger stimulus	Alter environment to preclude trigger stimulus
VII. *Physiological* Behavior is the product of a physiological process"	"I hurt" "I tired"	Teach communicative means to express distress.	Not applicable	Not applicable

Source: Adapted from Donnellan, A. M., Mirenda, P. L., Mesaros, R. A., & Fassbender, L. L. (1984). Analyzing the communicative functions of aberrant behavior. In Journal of the Association for Persons with Severe Handicaps, *9, 207, 206–207.*

natives to punishment by considering the *communicative intent* of behaviors (by discovering the cues and consequences related to behaviors of interest in real-life settings) as suggested in Exhibit 22.5. Undesired behaviors may have an escape function maintained by negative reinforcement. For example, if unrealistic work standards are imposed on staff they may find ways to show these are being met (when they are not) to avoid loss of pay or other positive feedback. A key assessment goal is to discover the *functions* of problem-related behaviors. The goal of *communication training* is to teach people language that allows them to convey messages in a manner that results in desired consequences. The basic idea is that valued behaviors will increase when they are functional (when they result in valued consequences). These methods are designed to increase motivation to communicate in effective ways. You can enhance motivation to engage in desired behaviors by making sure that behaviors: (1) have utility for those involved; (2) are acquired in the context in which they will be used; (3) are age appropriate for participants; and (4) are generalizable to other situations (Sailor, Goetz, Anderson, Hunt, & Gee, 1988). Objectives pursued should have *functional relevance* for clients. They should make a difference in real-life settings.

You can replace disruptive behaviors maintained by attention or by gaining assistance by developing appropriate alternatives to obtain these consequences. For example, helping students with severe disabilities initiate and maintain conversations with nondisabled peers decreased inappropriate social behaviors (Hunt, Alwell, & Goetez, 1988). Teaching children how to prompt feedback by asking "How is my work?" will increase teacher attention. Young adults with severe disabilities in integrated work settings learned how to recruit feedback for their performance (Mank & Horner, 1987). They learned how to monitor a target behavior, to evaluate their performance in relation to a specific criteria, and then to request feedback from supervisers. Improved work rate was related to self-recruited feedback. This kind of program increases the influence people have over the quality of their work environments. Pictorial communication systems can be used to help people who cannot speak clearly (or at all) to communicate more effectively with others. For example, pictures of various food items could be placed on a chart and clients can point to desired items when ordering food in fast food restaurants.

Other Positive Options

Incidental teaching takes advantage of naturally oc-curring training opportunities. For example, to en-courage requests you could place a desired item out of reach and wait for the student to request it. Natural reinforcers are used, and functionally sig-nificant behaviors are increased without use of prompts (Carr, 1985). Time delay methods are de-signed to decrease errors and thus increase success experiences and to allow clients to decide when to continue a task. For example, significant others may wait a few seconds before prompting desired behavior. Relaxation and exercise provide non-aversive methods to alter behavior. For example, relaxation training resulted in a decrease in hyper-ventilation and seizures in a profoundly retarded epileptic child (Kiesel, Lutzker & Campbell, 1989). Exercise has been found to decrease aggressive and hyperactive behaviors of adults with severe and profound disabilities (McGimsey & Favell, 1988). Giving clients small frequent requests that can be easily followed can be used to increase request fol-lowing. Positively reinforced pretask requests ease transitions from less demanding and more rein-forcing settings (recess) to more demanding and less reinforcing ones (academic work). Chains of behavior can be disrupted by removing links, es-pecially those that occur early in the sequence (see also next section and Lavigna & Donnellan, 1986).

REARRANGING ANTECEDENTS

Another way to alter behavior is to rearrange an-tecedents. This is known as stimulus control. Cues for desired behaviors are enhanced and cues for undesired ones muted or removed. Removing a discriminative stimulus (S^D) for a behavior or pre-senting an S^Δ (stimulus delta) will decrease asso-ciated behaviors. A problem in stimulus control exists whenever instructions (including self-in-structions) are given and hoped for behavior does not occur. Teachers often label children "disobe-dient" who do not follow their instructions. Perhaps the children do not understood or do not have the knowledge or skills to comply with the instructions. Perhaps behavior has not been brought under the influence of particular cues. Teachers may have "too many" rules. "There's no point in surrounding ourselves with unnecessary rules and regulations that only breed resistance" (Pryor, 1984).

Stimulus control is a key aspect of any skilled activity (e.g., playing in an orchestra, dancing). Most of our behavior consists of *discriminated op-erants* (behaviors that occur only in certain situa-tions, those in which they are reinforced). Antecedent events acquire influence over our be-havior through their association with reinforcing consequences. For example, we ask certain kinds of questions ("How do you feel?", "How are you?") only in certain situations. We are more likely to engage in particular behaviors in situa-tions in which they have been reinforced in the past and less likely to perform them in situations in which they have been punished or not rein-forced. Characteristics of situations unrelated to whether or not behavior is reinforced but that are usually present may also influence behavior if they change radically. Trying to "problem solve" when this is not possible because of fatigue or compet-ing goals such as completing work, is a waste of time. A specific future time to think about a topic could be selected (unless a crisis is at hand). Goldiamond (1965) suggested setting up a "sulk-ing stool" where a client could go and sit when he brooded. The purpose was to decrease negative thoughts about his partner by narrowing the range of situations in which they occurred. Ms. Landis used stimulus control to help Julie remember to use thought stopping to decrease worrisome thoughts (see Chapter 18).

You may rearrange the physical environment to encourage desired patterns of behavior. For exam-ple, placing chairs around tables (rather than against walls) increased talking among residents (Peterson, Knapp, Rosen, & Pither, 1977). Stimulus control is often used in behavioral medicine. You could, for example, help a client to associate a spe-cific cue (e.g., yellow gown) with painful but nec-essary procedures (such as changing burn dress-ings), decreasing anxiety reactions in other contexts (when the yellow gown is not worn) (Shorkey & Taylor 1973). Home safety for children can be en-hanced by altering physical conditions at home

(Barone, Greene & Lutzker, 1986). You can encourage desired behaviors by removing cues for
competing behaviors. For example, to increase
studying you could remove cues for writing letters,
talking on the telephone, or daydreaming. You in
effect "purify" the stimulus situation by allowing
only desired behaviors to occur in that setting. You
remove cues for undesired reactions and enhance
cues for desired ones. Altering the meaning (the
cueing function) of feelings and environmental
events (making these cues for constructive
thoughts, feelings, or actions rather than for dysfunctional ones) is the goal of cognitive-behavioral
methods such as anxiety management training.

Making Effective Use of Stimulus Control

"To establish stimulus control, you shape a behavior and then in effect shape the offering of this behavior during or right after some particular stimulus. This stimulus then becomes the cue, a signal,
for the behavior" (Pryor, 1984, p. 85). Behavior is
reinforced in the presence of the cue that will influence the behavior and not reinforced in its absence. As Karen Pryor (1984) emphasizes, the discipline required to achieve stimulus control via
positive means (many people rely on coercion) is
on the part of the trainer or coach. In errorless discrimination learning or fading, a discrimination is
established without the occurrence of errors and
with minimal disruption of behavior by starting out
with large differences between two or more stimuli
that are easily distinguishable and then gradually
making these more similar. This method is useful
when people have intense negative reactions when
they make errors. Fading compared to extinction
and punishment do not result in escape behavior.

Factors That Influence the Effectiveness of Rearranging Antecedents

Reinforcement history will influence the degree to
which a cue affects the frequency of a behavior.
Other influences include the number and intensity
of competing cues for other behaviors and the particular schedules of reinforcement in effect for each.
The "learner" must "recognize" the signal and be ca-

pable of carrying out hoped-for behaviors. Options
for rearranging cues differ in different settings.

Advantages and Disadvantages of Stimulus Control

As Karen Pryor notes in her wonderful book, *Don't
Shoot the Dog* (1984), stimulus control yields "cooperation without coercion." This captures the
main advantage of stimulus control.

> "People who have a disciplined understanding of
> stimulus control avoid giving needless instructions,
> unreasonable or incomprehensible commands, or or-
> ders that can't be obeyed. They try not to make re-
> quests they're not prepared to follow through on; you
> always know exactly what they expect. They don't
> fly off the handle at a poor response. They don't nag,
> scold, whine, coerce, beg, or threaten to get their way,
> because they don't need to. And when you ask them
> to do something, if they say yes, they do it. When
> you get a whole family, or household, or corporation
> working on the basis of real stimulus control—when
> all the people keep their agreements, say what they
> need, and do what they say—it is perfectly amazing
> how much gets done, how few orders ever need to be
> given, and how fast the trust builds up. Good stimu-
> lus control is nothing more than true communica-
> tion—honest, fair communication. (105–106)

Disadvantages of altering behavior via rearrangement of antecedents include prelearning
dips and related temper tantrums. Prelearning dips
refer to a discouraging decrease in hoped-for behaviors during learning. They can be frustrating for
both teachers and learners. Karen Pryor calls this
reaction a temper tantrum and suggests that this
phase is related to attending to the signal (cue) that
interferes with responding.

If You Are Not Successful

Lack of success may be due to relying on cues that
are difficult to distinguish and/or to unsystematic
use of reinforcement with the result that behavior
does not come under the influence of particular
cues. Lack of patience is an obstacle. Bringing behavior under new stimulus control takes time.

SUMMARY

Helping clients learn positive behavior change skills is a common practice goal. This often entails helping clients to shift from use of punishment (e.g., criticism, hitting, removing privileges), to use of positive methods (e.g., praise for accomplishments, asking for what one wants). Clients learn that intent is not necessarily related to outcome. For example, a superviser may intend to help a student by her critical feedback; however, if this feedback decreases desired behaviors, it is punishing not reinforcing. There are many positive shortcuts for altering behavior including rearranging antecedents (changing what happens before behaviors of interest). Options for rearranging contingencies will vary in different circumstances.

REVIEWING YOUR COMPETENCIES

Reviewing What You Know

1. Describe the requisites for use of positive reinforcement.
2. Describe the advantages of using positive reinforcement.
3. Describe common errors in attempting to use positive reinforcement.
4. Describe parameters that influence the effectiveness of reinforcement.
5. Distinguish between negative and positive reinforcement and give examples of each.
6. Describe two lost-cost methods that can be used to increase behaviors.
7. Describe procedures that can be used to decrease behaviors and give an example of each.
8. Describe the disadvantages of using punishment.
9. Give two examples from your own experience of rearranging antecedents to alter behavior.
10. Describe situations in which it would be appropriate to use artificial reinforcers such as tokens or points (see Chapter 18).
11. Describe the different emotional effects of positive and negative contingencies.

Reviewing What You Do

1. You effectively use positive reinforcement to increase behavior.
2. You effectively use stimulus control to alter behavior.
3. You can show another person how to use positive reinforcement to attain a valued outcome.
4. You can show another person how to use stimulus control to achieve a desired outcome.
5. Reinforcement plans are carried out with a high degree of fidelity.
6. Methods selected have the best chance of success, given available resources.

Reviewing Results

1. Positive outcomes are achieved.
   - You help parents learn positive behavior change (or maintenance) methods.

- You help staff in a residential setting shift from reliance on punishment to reliance on positive methods that support accomplishments and increase independence of residents.
- You help community members to increase opportunities for positive informal exchanges.
- You help participants of a support group to increase behaviors they want to see more of and decrease behaviors they want to see less often.
- You help administrators to provide more positive feedback to staff for valued behaviors.
- You help caregivers to increase use of positive methods to maintain self-care skills of their elderly relatives.

2. Clients feel better when they leave the office than when they came in.
3. Clients acquire positive skills for altering the behavior of others.
4. Clients acquire positive skills for altering their own behavior.
5. Clients understand the difference between intent and outcome.

CHAPTER 23

Working with Groups and Families

OVERVIEW

This chapter provides additional guidelines for working with families and groups. Many examples throughout this book involve families. The guidelines in previous chapters are relevant to families and groups as well as to individuals, organizations, and communities. The relationship skills described in Chapters 12 and 13 are of value in group settings including case conferences, team meetings, and meetings with community residents. The critical thinking skills described throughout this book will be of value in avoiding problem-solving styles that get in the way of making sound decisions.

You Will Learn About

- What is a family?
- Assessing families.
- Intervention options.
- Working with groups.
- Making decisions in groups.
- Self-help groups.

WHAT IS A FAMILY?

This is a controversial question that has implications for the way resources are distributed. For example, same sex (or cohabiting heterosexual) couples living in long-term relationships are usually not entitled to employer-provided medical cover-

age for their partner. Families may be defined by biological relatedness and/or living arrangements. There are many kinds of families including stepfamilies, nuclear families, extended families, gay/lesbian families, single-parent families, families without children, families with grown children, and bicultural families (see for example, Booth &

Dunn, 1994; Hetherington & Arasteh, 1988; Laird & Greene, 1996). Many children now grow up in blended families because of divorce and remarriage. Families serve many functions both for society and the individual including raising children, regulating sexual relations, socializing family members into social roles valued by society or by a particular cultural group, economic maintenance, and household management. Functions of families have changed over time.

ASSESSING FAMILIES

Each person has a family history, which may be more or less positive or negative (see for example, Hinde & Stevenson-Hinde, 1988). It is always unique. Families are influenced by the community and society in which they live. Feminist critics argue that family theories do not recognize historic, social, economic, and political influences on the family that encourage and maintain subordination of women to men in access to resources. They argue that we live in a patriarchal social order that encourages oppressive gender-typed family roles and results in blaming women for problems such as battering, rape, and incest. This societal and historic level of understanding is also important in a contextual view. Acceptance of oppressive gender-based roles may pose a significant obstacle to changing interaction patterns including spouse battering and child abuse. A contextual approach to families suggests the questions included in Exhibit 23.1. Both family structure (e.g., who is in the family, how often they see each other) and function (e.g., who reinforces whom for what) may relate to problems. Exhibit 23.2 describes goals that are often of interest in work with families.

Who you decide to see gives messages to clients about who is involved in a problem. Both assessment needs and feasibility will influence your decisions (e.g., are all family members willing to participate?). Seeing all family members together provides opportunities to observe interaction styles and to model positive styles during meetings. You may decide to see children separately as well as with parents to allow opportunities for them to talk

without other family members present. Be sure to clarify your rules about confidentiality. Otherwise, you may be in the awkward position of not being able to share problem-related information with other family members.

Family Stresses

Families involved in the public social welfare system often experience many environmental stressors such as lack of money, poor quality housing, lack of health care, and lack of day care for children. These stresses are important to review as they influence problems families confront. Separation may create a spiraling series of negative effects that persist over time (Patterson & Forgatch, 1990). Families may have unique caregiving burdens requiring special support (see Singer & Irvin, 1991).

Living Situation

What is the family's living space like? How much space is available? How is space used? What effect does the living space have on family relationships? Are there health hazards such as exposed wires (see Tertinger, Greene, & Lutzker, 1984)? What's the neighborhood like? How does this neighborhood affect family life.

Composition and Extended Networks

Who lives in this family? Is there an extended family network and if so, what role(s) does it play in this family?

Power

Families differ in who can influence whom to do what. Questions to ask include the following:

- Who makes what decisions in the family?
- Who's preferences are usually followed?
- Who does most of the talking?
- Who speaks for others?
- Who controls whom by covert means (e.g., complaints)?

EXHIBIT 23.1
Questions to Ask about Families

A. LIVING ENVIRONMENT

- How much space is available?
- Are safe play spaces available for children?
- Are neighbors available for aid?
- Are there physical hazards in the home (e.g., exposed wires)?
- How safe is the neighborhood?
- Is transportation easily accessible?
- Are contexts available for informal exchanges?

B. COMPOSITION AND EXTENDED NETWORKS

- What is the family composition?
- Who else lives in the family?
- Is there an extended family?
- What stage of the life cycle is this family in?
- What subsystems exist in this family (coalitions/alliances)?
- Who spends time with whom in this family?
- How much contact do family members have with the outside world? Are family boundaries too rigid or too permeable?

C. FAMILY STRESSES

- What caregiving responsibilities do family members have?
- Are economic resources sufficient?
- What external strains does the family experience?
- Have typical family supports been removed (refugees and immigrants)?
- Has this family had to deal with any recent stresses such as illness or unemployment?
- Are one or more family members depressed?
- Are there generational differences in acculturation?
- Are caregiving burdens unusually heavy?
- What outside support does this family have?

D. FAMILY STRENGTHS/RESOURCES

- What are strengths of this family?
- Do family members like each other?
- Can relatives help out in times of need?
- Is there enough money to cover basic needs?
- What positive events do family members share?
- Who helps whom with what and in what ways?

E. COMMUNICATION STYLES AND INTERACTION PATTERNS

- What are preferred communication styles?
- Who reinforces whom for what in what context?
- Is the interaction style reciprocal or coercive?
- What is the level of violence in this home?
- How effective are family members' conflict resolution and problem-solving skills?
- How effective are parenting skills?
- What is the level of intimacy in this family? Who is attached to whom? Are attachments positive or conflicted? Who shares what information with whom?
- Who is responsible for what in this family? What are family roles?

F. RULES, BELIEFS, AND VALUES

- What are rules in this family?
- What cultural norms and values are important in the family?
- What role does religion play in this family?

G. POWER

- Who makes decisions about what in this family?
- Who can influence whom to do what?

- Are positive or negative consequences usually relied on?

Cultural norms and values influence power structure. Power balances may shift over the life cycle of families and in response to changes such as illness, unemployment or relocation. For example, a woman who usually stays home may be the only one able to get a job when a family moves to a new location. This may change the family power structure. Power is not always obvious. Family members may control each other through illness or depression. For example, family members may remove pressures on wives who complain of depression. Complaints may be

negatively reinforced (demands are removed following complaints). Family members may be satisfied or unhappy with current power structures. The power structure may be stable or unstable. Families with antisocial children have coercive interaction styles in which family members rely on punishment and negative reinforcement to alter behavior (Patterson, Reid, & Dishion, 1992).

Decision Making

Who makes what decisions in a family about disciplining children, handling finances, dealing with relatives, distributing household chores, and so on?

EXHIBIT 23.2
Common Goals in Family/Couple Counseling

- Enhance problem-solving/conflict resolution skills. Help
  clients to communicate more effectively, to:
  - Clearly describe problems/desired outcomes.
  - Avoid blame and critical comments.
  - Listen without interrupting others.
  - Paraphrase what others say.
  - Validate concerns/interests of other family members.
  - Suggest options.
  - Suggest and accept compromises.
  - Neutralize escalating negative exchanges.
  - Reinforce each other for valued behaviors.
  - Avoid unnecessary confrontations.
- Alter misconceptions and distorted views of significant
  others.
- Alter family alignments.
- Help family members acquire needed material resources.
- Help family members cope with caregiving responsibilities.
- Enhance positive parenting skills.
- Enhance positive behavior change skills
  - Decrease punishment.
  - Decrease reliance on negative reinforcement.
  - Increase positive reinforcement for valued behaviors.
  - Help family members understand cultural differences
    among family members of different generations.

Decision making is related to power structure. Dissatisfaction with how decisions are made may be a presenting problem. Some family members may feel that they are excluded from the decision-making process. Decision-making patterns may be related to presenting problems such as an "unmanageable child" (parents may argue about how to discipline children).

Caregiving Skills

Families often have caregiving responsibilities for children. Are these responsibilities fulfilled? Are parenting skills adequate? Examples include monitoring, involvement, discipline, problem solving, and positive reinforcement (Bank, Patterson, & Reid, 1987). Family members may also care for elderly or sick relatives. What is the quality of care provided? What supports are needed (e.g., respite care)?

Rules, Beliefs, and Values

Families have rules about who can do what to whom and what may or may not be discussed by whom in what context. They have rules about how family members should act with people outside the family. Rules are often implicit rather than explicit. They may be helpful or harmful in relation to responsibilities of family members such as raising children. They may conflict with rules followed by other community residents. Families differ in the flexibility of rules and in sanctions imposed for rule violation. Cultural differences between family members may create clashes between children and parents, or between partners from different cultural backgrounds.

Communication Styles

Families differ in their preferred modes of communication and in their problem-solving and conflict-resolution skills. They differ in what they argue about. They differ in what they talk about. Examples of problematic communication styles can be seen in Chapter 15, Exhibit 15.6. Problems may involve "receiver" skills (listening, validating) and/or "sender" skills (owning feelings, communicating approval). Enhancing problem-solving and conflict management skills of family members is a common goal. Family members may be occupied with defending their positions rather than listening to others and validating their concerns. Helping clients to listen to each other and to recognize other points of view are common goals (see case example in Chapter 18).

Patterns of Interaction and Affection

Do family members like each other? They may not. The family is the most common site of violence of all kinds (see for example, Van Hasselt, Morrison, Bellack, & Hersen, 1987). What subsystems exist in the family? Minuchin (1974) emphasizes the importance of attending to particular coalitions and alliances that may be based on interest, gender, generation, or responsibilities (such as meal preparation). He highlights the importance of clear, well-defined boundaries between spouse, parental, and sibling subsystems that allow family members to carry out required functions but yet are flexible enough to permit resource exchange among subsystems. Family rules (which are influenced by cultural norms and values), influence the boundaries between subsystems. The concept of "enmeshment" is a key one in structural family therapy. This refers to excessive closeness in which family members think and feel alike; there is little opportunity for independent functioning and what happens to one family member immediately affects others. In enmeshed families, one subsystem (for example, a mother and son) may form a coalition against another family member (a father). Or, a mother may act as a sister (rather than a parent) to a daughter. Identifying and managing alliances (including those between yourself and family member(s) is important so that dysfunctional ones are not encouraged. Enmeshed families can be contrasted with "disengaged" families in which family members have little emotional involvement with one another. Triangulation is a concept used in Bowian family therapy. This refers to a dysfunctional relationship among three people. For example, a third person may be involved in a relationship to act as an ally or distraction when one person feels powerless, pressured, or distressed.

What is the level of trust in the family? Who trusts (and distrusts) whom in relation to what? Do family members support each other or do they do their best to tear each other down and compromise each other's self-esteem? Do family members help each other to enhance their skills and positive experiences? Or do they hinder growth and enjoyment? Do they support dysfunctional behavior of one or more family members? For example, does a spouse contribute to her partner's alcohol abuse? Who reinforces whom for what? Do family members control each other mainly by punishment and negative reinforcement? Or do they rely on positive feedback for encouraging valued reactions? Family members may rely on punishment as a way to maintain dominance. Status hierarchies are a significant aspect of our evolutionary heritage (Gilbert, 1989, 1992).

Connection with Outside World

How connected is the family to the outside world? Many families in which abuse/neglect occur are isolated. Isolation decreases opportunities for social support and corrective feedback.

Family Life Stage

Families progress through developmental stages. Both predictable (retirement) and unpredictable life events (illness) influence families. Relationships change over time (see for example Gottman, 1990; Parkes, Stevenson-Hinde & Marris, 1991). A given event may have a different effect in different life stages. For example, severe illness of a new mother will have a different effect than illness when a child is older. Stages of family development include:

- Unattached young adult.
- New couple.
- Family with young children.
- Family with adolescents.
- Family with grown children.
- Family much later in life.

Cultural norms and values influence behavior in each stage. Myths about different stages may be functional or dysfunctional (see Hunter & Sundel, 1989).

Family Strengths

What are family assets? These may include emotional (caring about each other), material (a comfortable home or stable source of income), or interactional (positive conflict-management skills) strengths. Families, like individuals, are made up of more than their problems.

Shared Beliefs

Families differ in their shared beliefs about life and the world. Some families believe that most people are benevolent (try to do the right thing). Other families believe that people are basically out for themselves and will try to do you in given half a chance. These beliefs and related contingencies influence both behavior and emotions. For example, they may influence relationships with neighbors and service providers. They may function as self-fulfilling prophecies. Here, too, unique cultural experiences influence what we think, feel, and do.

Some groups tend to be fatalistic—to believe in luck or God's will. Norms for interacting with authority figures will influence how family members interact with service providers. Family members may believe that they should know what other family members want without being told. Clients may not be aware of unrealistic expectations that create and maintain problems.

Family Roles

The term role refers to the behaviors expected of a person in a certain position, such as a parent, sibling, or employer. Families differ in how roles are distributed among family members, in how satisfied family members are with this arrangement, and in how open family members are to changing roles. Role distribution may facilitate or hinder attainment of valued goals. Family members may have distorted views about their responsibilities. A mother may expect to meet all the needs of her family. Cultural norms and values influence how roles are distributed, how easy it is to alter them, and how clearly roles are defined. Families differ in degree of outside support (or interference) for preferred role allocations. Changes in a family such as illness of a family member or need to care for an elderly relative may create burdens. Family roles change over the life of a family. Stepparenting usually requires a rearrangement of family roles.

Expression of Feelings

Families, like individuals, differ in the range and intensity of feelings expressed. Positive emotions such as happiness may prevail in families in which behavior is maintained mainly by the exchange of positive reinforcers. Negative emotions such as anger, anxiety, and sadness may prevail in families in which there is little interaction or in which family members rely on punishment and negative reinforcement. Cultural norms and values influence what emotions can be expressed when and to whom. They influence whether feelings are expressed indirectly (e.g., by doing a chore for another family member to show liking and appreciation) or directly (by verbally expressing caring).

Family Goals

Families differ in the goals they have and whether these are shared. Examples of family goals include increasing material comfort, moving closer to relatives, or keeping the yard looking good to impress the neighbors. Goals may be implicit or explicit and functional or dysfunctional in their effects. For example, a parent's interest in keeping the house immaculate may interfere with a teenager's wish to have friends visit.

INTERVENTION OPTIONS

A wide spectrum of service options is available including working with the partners of uncooperative substance abusing partners (see for example Thomas & Ager, 1993; Thomas, Yoshioka, & Ager, 1996) with couples, with all family members, and with extended families. Many examples of working with families are given in earlier chapters. Here too, the roles of broker, mediator, enabler, educator, and/or advocate may be required. There is extensive literature describing how to increase positive parenting skills (see for example, Dangel & Polster 1988; Fleischman, Horne, & Arthur 1983; Patterson, 1975; Sanders & Dadds, 1993). There is rich literature describing assessment, intervention, and evaluation methods with couples, most of which focuses on heterosexual couples (e.g., Gottman, 1994; Jacobson & Margolin, 1979; Jacobson & Gurman, 1995). Enhancing positive communication skills is a key focus in many family therapy approaches (see for example Robin & Foster, 1989). Clients learn how they communicate with each another, explore what kind of family relationships they would like, and develop more effective ways of communicating. Structural approaches emphasize alliances within families, boundary disputes, and patterns of communication (see for example, Szapocznik & Kurtines, 1988). An example of instructions for encouraging "feeling talk" suggested by Gottman, Notarious, Gonso, & Markman (1976) is the following: To engage in feeling talk, the speaker must: (1) get in touch with what he is feeling; (2) put the feelings into words; (3) edit the words so they can be heard by the listener; and (4) the listener must hear and validate what is said. Like most skills, it requires practice. Feeling talk is not a license for total candor. Few relationships could withstand the effects of total honesty. Simply prefacing nasty remarks with "I feel . . ." does not remove the destructive potential of fully uncensored communication. Distressed compared to nondistressed couples engage in a higher frequency of negative statements.

- *Use "I" statements.* Statements that begin with you sound like an accusation and run the risk of creating defensiveness. Those that begin with it, we, others, some people permit avoidance of personal responsibility.
- *Use statements rather than questions.* Questions are often an indirect way of making a point or an accusation. If questions are required, "how" are preferable to "why" questions as they are less accusatory.
- *Be present oriented.* Saying "I feel angry when . . ." is better than saying "It used to upset me when . . . ," which may leave the listener unsure of how things stand now. (Gottman, Notarious, Gonso, & Markman, 1976)

Sue and Sue (1990) suggest that both the communication and structural approaches to family therapy are appropriate in working with minority groups because they highlight the importance of the family as a unit and focus on the resolution of concrete issues. Behavioral family therapies share these emphases (see Falloon, 1988; Thyer, 1989; Turkowitz, 1984). Szapocznik and his colleagues (1988) have developed a systems approach to working with Latino families in which adolescents are suspected of or were observed using drugs. Patterns of family interaction that interfere with change are restructured to encourage participation of family members (see also Szapocznik & Kurtines, 1989; Szapocznik & others, 1988).

WORKING WITH GROUPS

Social group work is a traditional part of social work practice. (For recent references see for example,

Edleson & Tolman, 1992; Garvin, 1987; Greif & Ephross, 1996; Rose, 1989; Rose & Edleson, 1987; Subramanian & Ell, 1989; Toseland, 1990). A group can be defined as two or more individuals who meet together to address a shared task or problem or enjoy a shared interest.

Different Kinds of Groups

Helping clients requires participation in many different kinds of groups. Committees are an inescapable aspect of organizations. Some groups are time-limited and deal with a particular task (e.g., a task force created to decide how to decrease teenage pregnancy). Other groups meet on a regular basis to attend to certain functions such as coordinating work between intake and other staff. Case conferences and multidisciplinary team meetings may be held regularly. Community organization may involve setting up social action groups. Many different kinds of interventions are provided in a group setting. Aims may include education, skill building, or providing support and companionship (for example, Foster, Stevens, & Hall, 1994; Martin & Neyowith, 1988; Pence & Paymar, 1993; Tutty, Bidgood & Rothery, 1993). Social workers often facilitate self-help groups.

Advantages of Group Settings

Groups have many advantages:

- They provide varied models of how to handle certain situations/roles.
- They provide a sense of community.
- They offer opportunities to normalize and validate concerns.
- They provide opportunities to learn new skills.
- They provide an opportunity for catharsis, confession, and criticism.
- They provide opportunities to meet new people.
- They provide "partners" for carrying out assignments outside the group.
- They provide many sources of support.
- They save time and expense.

- They may be less threatening for some people compared to individual exchanges.
- They provide diverse opportunities for role plays.

The advantages of group settings provide guidelines about when to consider using a group. Decisions required when using groups include the following:

- What is the purpose of the group?
- What criteria should be used to decide who to include in the group?
- What rules (if any) should be agreed on?
- How often should the group meet?
- Should more people be allowed to join the group anytime?
- How will time be structured?
- Will there be a group leader? If so, how active will he or she be? Will there be one or two?
- Will participants have assignments outside the group?
- How will success be evaluated?
- What activities (if any) will be used for what purpose?

Goals may be shared or diverse. For example, all members may share the goal of finding a job, or enhancing problem-solving skills. Each person may apply skills learned to his or her own unique situation. The goals of the group will provide guidelines about group size and composition.

Group Structure and Process

Components of group structure include: (1) patterns of attraction and rejection among group members; (2) communication (who talks to whom about what); (3) roles (a status with certain associated behaviors such as leader); (4) division of labor (how tasks are allocated); and (5) power (patterns of influence) (Garvin, 1983; Thibaut & Kelley, 1987). Roles evolve over time as the group continues. Questions that may be relevant to consider depending on goals include the following:

- Who speaks for whom?
- Who influences whom?
- Who feels close to whom?
- Who dislikes whom?
- How do group members feel about the "leader"?
- Who assumes what kind of role(s) (e.g., placater, jokester, naysayer).
- Who offers whom positive support?
- Who offers whom punishing consequences?

Graphic representations can be useful in describing group process (see examples in Mattaini, 1993). Groups differ in how power is shared and who has power (who can influence whom to do what and/or who has access to valued resources outside the group). People differ in the roles they prefer and/or are assigned. Some enjoy the role of maintaining a constructive group process. They may encourage others to participate, diffuse rising tensions, suggest compromises, and emphasize common interests. Roles may be functional or dysfunctional. Helpful roles include:

- Educator
- Compromiser
- Encourager
- Seeker of information
- Questioner of dubious assertions
- Validator
- Attentive listener
- Diffuser of tension

Dysfunctional roles include:

- Ridiculer
- Dominator
- Complainer
- Scapegoat
- Attention seeker

Methods used should build on client assets (individual skill levels) in a step-by-step manner that

EXHIBIT 23.3
Example of Helpful and Dysfunctional Behaviors in Groups

Helpful	Dysfunction
• Offering useful suggestions • Validating other people's comments • Active listening • Maintaining focus • Participating in group tasks • Owning feelings ("I" feel . . .) • Considering others people's views and preferences • Asking others for their opinions • Encouraging others to participate • Supporting other people's assets • Using humor effectively • Following group norms • Responding positively to feedback • Identifying clear progress indicators • Participating in discussions • Accurately perceiving and translating social signals • Cooperating with others	• Interrupting • Belittling, sarcastic remarks • Blaming, attacking, namecalling • Excessively loud talking • Barely audible speech • Distracting mannerisms, noises • Excessive joking around • Making fun of others • Giving advice excessively • Sidetracking to irrelevant topics • Punishing valuable behaviors • Disregarding agreed-on norms • Encouraging group-think by discouraging consideration of other points-of-view

provides opportunities for practice, feedback, and coaching (see discussion of skills training in Chapter 21). This will require description of each person's current skill levels as well as skills required to attain outcomes clients value.

Groups, like individuals, communities, or organizations, develop a culture with unique norms, values, and rules. Examples of helpful and unhelpful behaviors can be seen in Exhibit 23.3. Process variables will influence what conflicts occur, how they are handled, and who suggests ideas. Group process is influenced by the particular activities introduced. One of the group leader's responsibilities is to structure group process in a way that helps group members achieve goals they value. Effective group workers are knowledgeable and skilled in selecting activities that contribute to valued outcomes. These may be games or plays. What is appropriate will depend on the age of the participants and their goals. Conflict is common in groups due to different interests, values, and preferred styles of communication.

Group Phases

Groups move through different phases. Here too, as when working with individuals and families,

there are beginnings, middles, and endings. The pregroup phase includes planning before a group meets. Goals in the beginning phase include negotiating the purpose of the group, dealing with ambivalence about participation, beginning to develop a group structure, starting to form relationships among participants, establishing norms, and deciding on plans. Obtaining resources may also be part of this phase (Garvin, 1987). Tasks in initial meetings include the following:

- Describe the purpose of the group.
- Discuss confidentiality.
- Describe group format.
- Explain content to be covered.
- Describe your role.
- Acknowledge awkwardness/anxiety/ambivalence.
- Build group cohesiveness and encourage relaxation (e.g., use an "ice breaker" such as asking people to introduce themselves to each other).

Group norms should be established to maximize effectiveness (see Exhibit 23.4). They may concern agreements about confidentiality, expectations about attendance, being polite, and so on. A final

EXHIBIT 23.4
Developing Group Norms

GL: So it's not like we want to come up with a lot of rules, but you know, having some idea about how we as a group want to handle certain things is good because it helps create an environment in which we all feel safe to talk. So, for example, something I think we should talk about and well, is always important in support groups, is confidentiality. People in the group should know that anything they say here is going to stay right here with us. It's real easy to want to share stuff with your wife or a good friend but you know, even if you don't use the person's name, well, they might piece things together and decide they know the person. So, does that make sense, I mean, do we all agree that that's a good norm to have?

B: Well, yeah, I feel more comfortable knowing that we all agree to that.

C: Yeah, me too. I mean you just don't know who knows who, so yeah, that suits me.

GL: Another idea that I wanted to present has to do with the way our conversations are handled. Because we're on the phone I can't see your faces to tell if someone is quiet because they're sad, or they are just getting a lot out of listening that day. But because of this, sometimes I'll ask like, "A, do you have anything you want to add?" You can either answer or just say "I pass." That's fine if you just want to pass.

(laughter)

GL: (CONTINUES): So, if that's OK I'll move on.

(All respond affirmatively).

Source: M. Galinsky, K. Rounds, A. Montague, & E. Butowsky (1993). *Leading a telephone support group for persons with HIV disease*, pp. 58–59. Chapel Hill: School of Social Work, University of North Carolina

phase includes planning for maintenance and ending. Exhibit 23.5 provides an example of objectives, preparation for, role plays used in, suggested activities, and guidelines for ending a group session.

Roles Social Workers Play in Groups

Roles of value when working on other levels (e.g., individual and community) are also of value when working with groups. These include broker, enabler, mediator, educator, and facilitator. You may, as a broker, refer group members to helpful resources. As a mediator, you may help group members resolve problems and handle conflicts. As an educator, you may enhance participants' conflict resolution skills and inform them about constructive approaches to problems. As a facilitator, you may encourage participation from all members, re-mind the group of its agenda, and review what has been accomplished. Groups differ in the extent to which leadership is shared. One of the very purposes of a group may be to transfer leadership skills to group members. Roles and tasks of the group leader can be seen in Exhibit 23.6. Preparation is a key leader responsibility. Group leadership skills include:

- Planning agendas/setting goals.
- Encouraging participation.
- Regulating participation.
    Handling hostile participants.
    Handling reluctant participants.
    Handling monopolizers.
    Handling apathy.
- Offering positive feedback.

EXHIBIT 23.5
Preparing for a Group Session

Session 4: Coping with feelings and beliefs related to being HIV positive.

The purpose of this session is to provide members with a safe environment where they can openly discuss personal issues, including sexuality and sexual behavior. By the end of Session 4 group members will have begun to identify and explore uncomfortable feelings related to their illness; shared their experiences and ways of coping with changes in sexual behavior; identified new and helpful ways of coping with these changes; and reinforced and expanded knowledge of safer sex practices.

These subjects may prove somewhat difficult for both group members and the group leader to discuss. They are left until Session 4 so that group members' level of confidence and trust in one another will be high, facilitating an open discussion.

Objectives

- To help members recognize troubling feelings and beliefs related to having HIV disease.
- To help members understand that these feelings are common.
- To learn ways of coping with troubling feelings and beliefs.
- To share experiences in coping with changes in sexual behavior.
- To gain information about safer sex practices.
- To encourage and reinforce the practice of safer sex.

II. Preparation

- It may be helpful for you to review some of the salient feelings and beliefs that each group member has expressed in previous sessions.
- You may want to review some of the literature to increase your understanding of AIDS prevention and your knowledge of safer sex practices. You may also need to explore your own feelings and prepare for an open discussion of sensitive issues and materials. It is important that you are familiar with your state laws regarding an individual's responsibility to disclose his or her HIV status. You should consider your feelings and concerns regarding personal and professional ethics regarding disclosure issues.

This session is primarily focused on HIV transmission as it relates to sexual activity. However, if group members are participating in or are associated with injection drug use, you may want to review literature on ways to minimize the risk of transmission by needles.

- The following is a list of potentially difficult content and group process issues that may arise during this session:
  Extreme mood swings of members
  Severe depression of members
  Members may feel upset hearing about others' troubling feelings
  Suicidal thoughts and how to handle them
  Misunderstandings about HIV transmission
  Different levels of interest in sex and different levels of sexual activity
  Concerns about how to tell a partner or potential partner about diagnosis
  Member may reveal that s/he is practicing unsafe sex
  Member may reveal that s/he has been unable to tell partner(s) about diagnosis
  Members may be of different sexual orientations and experience discomfort because of this
  Reluctance to discuss sexual behavior
  Legal and ethical obligations to tell others about HIV diagnosis

Role Plays

Feelings and Beliefs
- Lately you have been feeling depressed. You lack motivation, and even though you're still fairly healthy and mobile, you don't enjoy your favorite activities anymore. You've been trying to conceal your feelings but you've decided it may be good to talk to a friend.
- Have group members think about some of the strong, troubling feelings they have had, when they have them, and who they were with when they had them. Ask if they would like to role play these types of situations to see if there are ways of handling the situation that make them feel better.

Changes in Sexual Behavior
- You found out this week that you are HIV positive. You have been dating a man for a few weeks and recently the two of you have become sexually involved. The two of you have been practicing safer sex and have been honest about your personal histories and concerns about contracting AIDS. Tonight is the first time you have seen him since your diagnosis.
- You were diagnosed HIV positive about six months ago, but, until you met Jane last week, you thought you would never have sex again. Both of you are very attracted to each other, and you feel you must tell her about your diagnosis now because sex seems inevitable. She has just arrived at your house.

(continued)

- Since learning your diagnosis, you have been very careful to practice safer sex through the use of condoms. You have been seeing a man for several weeks and you decide to sleep together for the first time. When you pull out a condom, he says to you "I never use those things. I hate the way they feel. Let's just do it natural."

III. Suggested Activities

- "Check-in" with each group member by asking for brief reports on the previous week.
- Before beginning the discussion, ask members if there are any topics/subjects they would like to add to this week's session.
- To begin the discussion have members name any feelings they have had related to having HIV disease.
- Encourage a discussion of how the members handle these feelings. Group members may be able to make suggestions to one another on methods of coping with different feelings related to having HIV disease.
- Certain troubling feelings may relate directly to changes in sexual behavior. Examples are: frustration, guilt, and depression. To make the transition from talking about feelings and beliefs to changes in sexual behavior, you might ask members if they have experienced any troubling feelings because of changes in sexual behavior. Ask members if they would be willing to share any of these changes in sexual behavior and related feelings with the group. It may be helpful to use vignettes to initiate the discussion. The vignettes will allow group members to talk about changes in sexual behavior in the third person until they feel comfortable enough to bring up their own issues.
- Ask members to share ways they cope with changes in sexual behavior and sexual frustrations. You may need to offer suggestions for coping with these changes. Strategies for coping with troubling feelings and changes in sexuality include: learning safe ways to express sexuality such as massage, masturbation, fantasy, caresses, and hand holding. Other techniques for feeling better include refocusing, reframing, spending time on enjoyable activities and meditation, positive thinking tapes, and similar activities. Stress and anxiety can be lowered by getting involved in non-HIV related activities, getting out of the house when able to walk, exercising or just sitting and enjoying a favorite spot, watching movies, reading, meditating, and learning relaxation techniques.
- A discussion of safer sex practices and prevention is important, particularly for individuals who may have been given information but never had the chance to ask specific questions. Begin this discussion by asking what preventive measures members are taking. It is likely that this subject will follow naturally from the discussion on changes in sexual behavior. The discussion will include information giving as well as facilitation of mutual support and encouragement among members. The amount of information you need to give will vary depending on group members' knowledge.
- Initiate a discussion about informing sexual partners if the members do not bring it up. Group members will need to explore their fears about telling others and to understand that it is normal to have these fears. You can help frame disclosure in terms of taking control of the situation. Group members may want to rehearse potential disclosure scenes from their own lives.

IV. Ending the Session

- Summarize some of the main themes of the discussion emphasizing ways of coping with troubling feelings and changes in sexual behavior. Support members' beliefs that they can cope with these feelings and situations.
- Remind group members that any pending issues can be brought up again next week and that the next session will be about issues surrounding living with a life-threatening illness, as well as practical matters related to insurance, legal assistance, and wills.

Source: M. Galinsky, K. Rounds, A. Montague, & E. Butowsky (1993), Leading a telephone support group for persons with HIV disease (pp. 32–37). Chapel Hill: School of Social Work, University of North Carolina.

- Anticipating obstacles.
- Identifying common interests.
- Avoiding premature closure on an option.
- Effective pacing.
- Summarizing skills.

Lack of Preparation as a Key Obstacle

Trying "to wing it" will dilute effects that can be achieved and may result in harm (participants who could benefit leave the group and become more discouraged). Being familiar with activities (how can they be introduced to encourage helpful behaviors and discourage those that get in the way of attain-

ing valued goals) is important. Skill training in groups requires many competencies (see Chapter 21). Facilitating groups requires certain skills (Larson, 1993). Consider what could be offered by someone well trained compared to what you could offer. If this gap is large, consider whether you should take on related tasks. Do a cost benefit analysis of harm and benefits to potential participants (and yourself).

MAKING DECISIONS IN GROUPS

Decisions are often made in groups. Community residents may discuss shared concerns and decide

EXHIBIT 23.6
Roles and Tasks of the Group Leader

ENCOURAGE MUTUAL HELP AND SUPPORT

Ask open-ended questions.
Aim for balanced participation.
Make connections between what group members say; find common threads.
Turn questions and comments directed toward you back to the group, when possible.
Respect clients' abilities to offer each other support while intervening to build the group process.
Encourage clients to raise issues they want to discuss.

MAINTAIN FOCUS

Keep group members from drifting off-track. Bring discussion back to the "here and now," "so how does this affect us personally, now?"
Remind participants at the start of each session about the topics for that session, and at the end of each session about topics for the next one.

EDUCATE/GIVE INFORMATION

Try not to take on the burden of being the only one who provides information. Clients may have the latest information about some questions.
Encourage members to teach each other new skills.
Encourage accurate information. Do reality testing when you hear inaccurate information, for example, around how AIDS is transmitted.
Call in "experts" when appropriate.

MODEL USEFUL BEHAVIOR

Model acceptance, support, and encouragement, and expression of feelings.
Recognize the strengths and achievements you see in group members.
Break tasks into component behaviors and model them (e.g., how to ask for help).

ENHANCE SELF-EFFICACY

Support clients' beliefs that they take actions that will help them live with their illness.
Provide opportunities to practice new behaviors (e.g., discuss one's illness with a family member).

Source: Adapted from M. Galinsky, K. Rounds, A. Montague, & E. Brutowsky (1993), Leading a telephone support group for persons with HIV disease *(pp. 11–12). Chapel Hill: School of Social Work, University of North Carolina.*

which one(s) to focus on. Decisions that influence clients are made in multidisciplinary case conferences and staff meetings. The process used to make decisions will influence their soundness. Guidelines for encouraging effective discussion include the following:

- Avoid getting side-tracked on minor issues.
- Encourage brevity.
- Encourage members to listen attentively to each speaker.
- Combine wise control of time and size of problem.
- Sum up often and keep members informed where they are in a discussion.
- Secure equal sharing of responsibility
- Provide facilitating physical conditions (Edwards, 1938).

Groups differ in their preferred decision-making style. Some are authoritarian. The opinion of one or a few individuals wins the day rather than the most well-reasoned argument. An intuitive style may be used in which feelings are emphasized. The opinion of alleged experts who are brought in may weigh heavily.

Group Process Variables That Interfere with Sound Decision Making

Observation of case conferences shows that decisions may be made, not through careful consideration of evidence, but on the basis of influence by pitches and/or denunciations on the part of influential group members (Dingwall, Eekelaar, & Murray, 1983). In his classic article "Why I do not attend case conferences," Meehl (1973) identified characteristics of case conferences and group meetings that decrease the quality of decisions such as rewarding everything, "gold and garbage" alike. That is, no matter what anybody says it is regarded as profound and informative. "The prestigious thing to do is to contribute ideas to the conference . . . whether or not the quality of evidence available is adequate to support the view offered"

(Meehl, 1973, p. 235). Participants may be reluctant to criticize other views (even though they may be uninformative or inaccurate) because of the "buddy-buddy syndrome" (not criticizing friends). The value of high quality data is often disregarded. The tendency to be impressed by plausible-sounding, but uninformative explanations is encouraged by not asking questions such as: "What evidence is there for this view?" or "How does this help us understand and know what to do about this problem?"

Trivial statements that are uninformative because they are true of all people may be made (Kadushin, 1963). This is called the Barnum effect. Examples are "She has intrapsychic conflicts" or "He has problems with object relations" or "There is a contingency management problem here." Unreliability of and lack of validity of measures may be overlooked resulting in dubious conclusions. Another obstacle is the belief that hard headed means hard hearted. Regard for rigorous examination of a topic may be viewed as cold, unemotional, and unfeeling whereas a disregard for vagueness, non sequiturs, and tolerance of fallacies may be considered a mark of caring and compassion. Participants may use different standards to review the quality of disliked arguments than to review their own argument. Other sources of errors that may get in the way of arriving at reasoned judgments are described in Chapter 5. Use the culture of thoughtfulness scale in Chapter 5, Exhibit 5.8 to review your work environments including case conferences and team meetings.

Group think "refers to deterioration of mental efficiency, reality testing, and moral judgments that result from in-group pressures" (Janis, 1982, p. 9). Indicators include:

- An illusion of invulnerability that results in over-optimistic and excessive risk taking.
- Belief in the group's inherent morality.
- Pressure applied to any group member who disagrees with the majority view.
- Collective efforts to rationalize or discount warnings.
- A shared illusion of unanimity.

- Self-appointed "mind guards" who protect the group from information that might challenge the group's complacency.
- Self-censorship of deviation from what seems to be the group's consensus.
- Stereotypical views of adversaries as too evil to make negotiating worthwhile, or too stupid or weak to pose a serious threat (Janis, 1982).

Methods Janis suggests to discourage group think include the following:

1. The leader should assign the role of critical evaluation to each member. Every member should be encouraged to air objections and doubts and to look for new sources of information.
2. The leader should not state his or her own judgments or preferences at the outset.
3. Several independent policy planning groups should be established, each with a different leader.
4. The group should divide into subgroups and meet separately and then later come together to work out differences.
5. Members should discuss deliberations of the group with qualified outsiders.
6. Qualified outsiders should be invited in for group deliberations.
7. One member of the group should be assigned the role of devil's advocate. (Assigning just one devil's advocate in a group may not be effective because of the strong tendencies of groups to persuade a lone dissenter (see for example, the classic study by Asch, 1956).
8. After the group has reached an agreement, another meeting should be held in which every member is encouraged to express any doubts and to rethink the issue.

Enhancing Your Effectiveness in Case Conferences

There are many steps you can take to improve the quality of case conferences. One is to prepare for meetings. If you plan to present a point of view at a case conference, prepare beforehand by rehearsing what you will say, and by reviewing your argument and related evidence. Anticipate and be prepared to respond to disagreements and counter proposals. Effective skills in entering conversations and expressing opinions will be valuable (see Chapter 13). Present your ideas clearly in a way that links your view to a shared goal. Don't take things personally. If you do, your emotional reactions will get in the way of constructive participation. Focus on service goals. Be sure to reinforce others for valuable contributions. Valuing truth over winning will help you to contribute to a culture of inquiry. Distinguish between strong opinions and bias (see Chapter 6) so that you do not mistakenly assume that a person with a strong opinion is not open to considering different points of view. Guidelines emphasized by Fisher and Ury (1983) include focusing on the problem not the people, focusing on interests not positions, using objective criteria, and seeking options that benefit all parties.

Knowledge about group process and structure will help you to anticipate and avoid problems. If possible, know who you are dealing with (be familiar with the goals and preferred interaction styles of participants). Although it may not be possible to totally change styles that compromise the quality of decision making, they can be muted in a number of ways (e.g., by agreeing on group norms, focusing on the problem not the person, and reinforcing alternative positive behaviors). Agree on an agenda to clarify the goals of a meeting and increase the likelihood that they are met. This prior step offers an opportunity to reaffirm decisions to pursue agreed-on goals if people get off the track. Helpful norms include: (1) not interrupting other people; (2) not hogging the floor; (3) holding speakers responsible for accompanying claims with evidence; and (4) avoiding personal attacks (see also code of conduct for discussing controversial issues in Chapter 6). Be familiar with propagandistic strategies such as distorting arguments, dragging in a red herring, appealing to self-interest or fear, and develop skills to counter them effectively (e.g., focus on service goals). This will help you to keep anger and anxiety in bounds even with people who are skilled in aggravating others. Intellectual empathy will encourage listening to and understanding other points of view (see Chapter 6 Exhibit 6.3).

SELF-HELP AND MUTUAL HELP GROUPS

Self-help groups are based on the assumption that people with similar problems can help one another. A self-help group can be defined as a small group of individuals who meet together voluntarily for mutual aid in the accomplishment of a specific purpose (Katz & Bender, 1976). Examples include the following:

- Depressives Anonymous
- Neurotic Anonymous
- Narcotics Anonymous
- Adoptees' Liberty Movement Association (for adopted children seeking their natural parents)
- Parents Anonymous (for parents who abuse their children)
- Overeaters Anonymous
- Gamblers Anonymous

Mutual helping programs offer the best of all worlds in that both givers and recipients benefit (see for example, Exhibit 23.7). Self-help groups serve many functions. Benefits include support, information, insight, acquiring coping skills, validation, sense of community, and normalization. Participants may even live longer (Spiegel & others, 1989). They provide affiliation with people who are similar in some way and who are sympathetic to concerns shared by all members.

> Bringing people together who share the same problems, feelings, and experiences overcomes the tendency to ostracize one's self. The negative value placed on the uniqueness of one's situation is reduced when the individual discovers that others have been there. Probably the most common reaction of relief that is reported in mutual assistance groups and probably in all group therapy is the sense that "I am not the only one. I am not crazy. I am not alone!" The

EXHIBIT 23.7
Examples of People Helping Other People

Foster grandparent	Low-income individuals aged 60 and older work with children (e.g., in hospital pediatric wards, institutions for people alleged to be the mentally and emotionally disturbed, correctional facilities, homes for dependent and neglected children, public school classrooms for exceptional children, day-care centers, and private homes). (Bowles, 1976)
Senior Companion	People 60 and older provide services to adults with special needs, especially older individuals. They work in private homes as well as hospitals, nursing homes, and senior centers.
Big Brothers and BigSisters	Adults are matched with children or teenagers to provide support/ recreation/models/validation to these children.

unique personal, previously defined as deviant and isolating, become social. Under some conditions, the discovery that the problem is social and not personal can be a stimulus for members of the group to undertake social and political action to change social conditions that come to be defined as oppressive or to encourage the larger society to devote resources to the group's central interest. (Levine, 1988, p. 171)

Unique characteristics of self-help groups that make them an attractive alternative (and perhaps a better one) to professional services include the following (see for example Katz, 1993):

- Ease of communication because members are peers.

- Opportunities for socialization.

- Individual differences can be eased by group discussion and confrontation.

- More natural contexts compared to professional relationships or institutional settings.

- Status is defined in terms of group goals and needs; each person's status in the group is relatively clear.

- Opportunities for learning from others.

- Multiple sources of support.

- Normalization of concerns and experiences.

- Avoidance of one-down status inherent in professional contact.

- Inexpensive.

- Opportunities to help others, increasing self-esteem.

Levine and Perkins (1987) describe five types of self-help groups. In one, members have some characteristics that may result in social isolation, stigmatization, scorn, pity, or social rejection (some characteristic that disqualifies them as "normal" and results in discrimination that limits opportunities). Examples include people labeled as mentally ill, exconvicts, gamblers, people who are gay or lesbian, the elderly, and overweight people. Some groups accept society's definition of a behavior/characteristic as wrong and seek to decrease associated behaviors while emphasizing the worthwhileness of participants. The aim of other groups is to change public attitudes about a problem/characteristic. Society's definition of a "problem" is rejected. Examples include civil rights organizations and gay rights groups.

In a second type, those who are related to individuals with a stigmatizing characteristic are involved (e.g., parents of antisocial children, Al-Anon for partners of substance abusers). A third kind of self-help group is comprised of individuals who tend to be socially isolated, not because of a particular characteristic but perhaps because of lack of public resources. Examples include widows groups, parents without partners, and parents of children with cancer. Ethnicity, religion, or race are the basis for a fourth kind of self-help group. Such groups may provide education, recreational opportunities, and cultural preservation. Pursuit and preservation of specific interests such as opposition to school busing is the basis of a fifth kind of quasipolitical group. Other purposes may be to limit taxation, to preserve the character of a neighborhood, and to develop a community. Any one group may have a mix of purposes.

Increasing skills in gaining support is a focus of many self-help groups. For example, one of six group sessions provided to clients with HIV is devoted to helping participants to enhance social support (Galinsky, et al., 1993). A group formed in

EXHIBIT 23.8
Examples of Self-Help Groups Noted in Newsletter

Ads in this column are free to nonprofit self-help groups. Announce upcoming events. Request information from other groups. Reach out for new members. Submit two or three lines to Self-Helper, California Self-Help Center, UCLA, 2349 Franz Hall, 405 Hilgard Avenue, Los Angeles, CA 90024-1563.

Los Angeles County

"New Outlook" is a self-help group for ostomates in their 20s–50s. It's for eleostomates, colostomates, and urostomates as a result of ulcerative colitis, Crohn's disease, cancer or other reasons. We offer support, information, tips, positive role models, speakers and friendship. The group meets every two to three months informally: it's free and open. Please call (310) 826-8330 for more information.

The Los Angeles HPV Support Group offers mutual support to those with HPV (genital warts). For more information contact Joann Woodward at The Los Angeles HPV Support Group, 820 Manhattan Avenue, Suite 102, Manhattan Beach, CA, 90266 or call (310) 798-CARE (2273).

Orange County

Two **Herpes Support Groups** meet in Orange County. The first Friday group meets monthly at 6:15 p.m. in Tustin. The third Sunday group meets quarterly in Mission Viejo. Meetings include discussion group, multi-media presentation, question and answer session and often, medical speakers. They are free to everyone. For free information, write the HELP chapter, P.O. Box 4326, Orange, CA, 92613-4326 or call (714) 669-4454, 24 hrs.

The Orange County unit of the **American Cancer Society** has a list of ongoing support groups for cancer patients. For further information, contact the Patient Services and Education Department at (714) 556-7804. *The following four groups are sponsored as a free community service by the **Adult Day Health Care Center**, 2021 Calle Frontera, San Clemente, CA, 92672. Call (714) 498-7671.* **Alzheimer's Support Group** for the family and caregivers of those with Alzheimer's Disease and other memory-related disorders. A **Parkinson's Support Group** uses an educational as well as a mutual sharing format. **Joint Efforts** is an arthritis exercise class. The **Adult Children of Aging Parents Support Group** provides help specifically for the caregiver adult child.

The following three groups are sponsored by the John Henry Foundation. For information call Otty at (714) 542-4377.
Psychosis Free is a weekly peer-led support group to target people suffering from psychotic illnesses. **Multi-Family Support Group** is a weekly professionally-facilitated meeting emphasizing what a powerful resource the family can be in the treatment process and as advocates involved in seeking better care for their ill family members. **Obsessive-Compulsive Support Group** is a new peer-led support group.

San Diego County

The San Diego Phobia Foundation is a non-profit organization that serves all of San Diego County. The foundation currently sponsors four free weekly self-help support groups for people suffering from phobias, anxiety, and panic attacks. For more information and group locations, call or write: San Diego Phobia Foundation, 2037 San Elijo Avenue, Cardiff-by-the-Sea, CA, 92007, (619) 944-6334.

Ventura County

The Thousand Oaks Satellite Ostomy Group, United Ostomy Association, meets the third Monday of each month. Medical professionals are guest speakers. No fee. All are welcome. For further information, please call Dottie at (805) 379-9622.

Statewide

Freedom 1st, a project of Community Connection Resource Center, was designed by ex-offenders for ex-offenders and is committed to helping with the transition from jail or prison to a successful re-entry into the community. The meetings are held at three locations from 6:00 to 7:30 p.m. on Fridays.
• 2144 El Cajon Blvd., San Diego, 92104, (619) 294-3900
• 429 J Street, Plaza Level, Sacramento, 95814, (916) 442-1484
• 140 W. Park Avenue, #100, El Cajon, 92020, (619) 440-7316

International

Register now for the **International Conference on Self-Help/Mutual Aid in Ottawa, Canada, September 2–4, 1992.** For more information contact the Canadian Council on Social Development, 55 Parkdale Avenue, Ottawa, Canada, K1Y 4G1.

Announcement: I am in the process of starting a newsletter specifically for partners, friends and family members who are living and dealing with people who have **Multiple Personality or Dissociative Disorders.** Please write to SHARE, P.O. Box 88722, Tukwila, Washington, 98138-2722 for information. Seth E. Cawthra, Publisher/Editor.

Third International Convention of People Who Stutter will be held August 13–16, 1992 at the Cathedral Hill Hotel in San Francisco. All people who stutter, speech pathologists, parents, friends and loved ones are welcome. For further information call the National Stuttering Project at (415) 566-5324.

Source: Self-Helper: The California Network Quarterly for Support Group News *(1992), Spring 7(2), p. 5.*

Raleigh, NC, in an African-American poor, neighborhood met once a month for both social and service aims (Korte, 1983). This group identified neighbors in need of services and assumed responsibility for offering assistance. Recipients of services could offer one of many services the club valued. Support groups for caregivers are widely used (e.g., for family members of persons with AIDS (Kelly & Sykes, 1989). Social support and mutual aid groups can be used as a preventative strategy for people in transition from one life stage to another (e.g., prospective parents, people about to retire, those at risk due to loss of a significant other because of death, divorce, or separation (Gitterman & Shulman, 1994; Gottlieb, 1988). Personal growth groups are another kind of self-help group. The aim of some groups is to provide support and to help members resolve a problem (e.g., Alcoholics Anonymous). Be familiar with different kinds of groups available in your community so you can suggest relevant ones. Take advantage of newsletters and daily newspapers to stay informed about options (see Exhibits 23.8 and 23.9).

The Limits and Potentials of Self-Help

Do self-help groups help people? Do they have harmful effects? As with any method, claims of effectiveness should rest on critical tests. Some writers believe that professionals are the least likely to succeed or be interested in creating self-help resources because of vested interests in maintaining an elite status and tendencies to focus on client deficiencies. They argue that these characteristics conflict with those of successful resource exchanges (e.g., the assumption that everyone has something to offer and that everyone has equal rights in decision making) (Sarason & Lorentz, 1979). Be sure that programs developed support rather than undermine the competencies of indigenous helpers by creating dependencies on professionals. Peer-led support groups have been found to be as effective as professional-led groups (Toseland, Rossiter, & Labrecque, 1989).

EXHIBIT 23.9
Examples of Self-Help Groups Advertised in Local Newspapers

Miscarriage/Infant Death United Inc, support group for parents grieving death of child through miscarriage, stillbirth or infant death. 1st Tue of month, 7:30 p.m., Kennedy Gerontology Center, 30 E Laurel Rd, Stratford. Information: Susan Wagner, 346-7883 or 582-2883.

American Chronic Pain Assn. Self-help group for people with chronic pain. Meets 1st Tue of month, 7:30–9 p.m., 122 Kings Hwy, Maple Shade. Next meeting this Tue. Information: 235-0860.

Groups for Widowed To Live Again support group for newly widowed people meets every Tue, 7–8:30 p.m. lower hall of Queen of Heaven Church, Rte 70, Cherry Hill. Also, regular meeting for all widowed people held 2nd Mon of month, 7:30 p.m., St Peter Celestine Church, Kings Hwy, Cherry Hill, Nondenominational, 779-9438.

Adult Children of Alcoholics For adults who are recovering from having been child in dysfunctional family. Every Tue, 8 p.m., Unitarian Church, Religious Education Building

Incest Free support group for women survivors of incest. Meetings held every Tue evening in Cherry Hill. Information: 428-8388.

Lyme to Lyme Support Group of Marlton. 1st & 3rd Wed of month. 7:30 p.m., call for location. Information: 988-1515.

Widows and Widowers Support Group Marlton THEOS "Healing and Recovery Group." Meets 1st & 3d Weds of month, 7:30 p.m., RAP Room, 15A E Main St, Marlton. All widows and widowers invited. Information: 983-2189.

Spousal Caregivers Support group for spouses caring for husbands/wives at home; sponsored by Promise Alternative Day Care for Adults, Cherry Hill, 1st Wed of month, 11 a.m.–12:30 p.m., call for location. Information: 662-3555.

Step-Parent Support Group Sponsored by the Parents Project. Meets 1st and 3d Weds of month, call for time and location. Information: 662-2751.

Depressive/Manic Depressive Support Group Meets 1st & 3d Weds of month, 7:30 p.m., Temple Sinai, New Albany Rd near Rte 130, Cinnaminson. Information: 871-1142.

Special-Needs Children Support group for parents who have child with special emotional needs. Meets 1st Wed of month, 7 p.m., at new location: Burlington County YMCA, Marter Ave, Mt Laurel. Information: 231-7562.

The '90s Mom Support group for mothers with young children and for mothers-to-be. 1st Wed of month, 7:30–9:30 p.m., Women's Center at Rancocas Hospital, 218-A Sunset Rd, Willingboro. Information: 835-3399.

Phobia Support Group For anyone who suffers panic and phobia disorders. 1st Thu of month, 6:30 p.m., Cranberry Hall, Charles St, Medford.

Group for Widowed "Reach Out," support group for recently widowed people. Thu, 7 p.m., Maple Shade Municipal Complex, 200 Stiles Ave, Maple Shade. Regular monthly meeting of To Live Again is held 4th Mon at 7:45 p.m., same location. Information: 779-0659.

Chronic Pain Self-help group for anyone over 50 who suffers who chronic pain. Register in advance for meeting, Fri, 10:30–11:30 a.m., Kennedy Gerontology Center, 30 E Laurel Rd, Stratford. Discuss concerns, share information, apply coping strategies. Information: 800-522-1965.

Herpes Anonymous support group for herpes sufferers. 2d Fri of month, 7 p.m., Kennedy Memorial Hospital.

Compassionate Friends Self-help support group for people (parents and others) who have experienced loss of child. 2d Fri of month, 7:30 p.m., First United Methodist Church, 25 Brainerd St, Mt Holly. Information: 871-9711.

South Jersey Stroke Club Group to help stroke victims and their families get back into social activities. Jan meeting changed to this Sat, 1 p.m., Homestyle Restaurant, Blackwood-Clementon Rd, Blackwood. Information: 939-4639.

Violent Crime "Victims No More" support group for survivors of violent crime. Confidentiality respected. New group will begin meeting Sat, 1:30 p.m., Starting Point Inc, Sentry Office Plaza, 216 Haddon Ave, Suite 608, Westmont. Information: 875-8213.

Caregiver Support Group Seeks to promote well-being and address emotional needs of those who care for elderly. Registration required for meeting. 1/11, 1–2:30 p.m., Kennedy Gerontology Center, 30 E Laurel Rd, Stratford. Information: 346-7777.

Recently Widowed H.O.P.E. (Helping Other People Evolve Inc), support and information program for recently widowed men and women of all ages, will begin its winter season in Burlington County in Jan. Ten-week program consists of lectures, discussions, workshops and guest speakers. Day and evening sessions available.

Source: Philadelphia Inquirer, *January 3, 1993, BR8.*

Self-help, like any form of intervention, has limits on what can be achieved. For example, in *Complaints and Disorders: The Sexual Policies of Sickness* (1973), Ehrenrich and English point out that "Self help is not an alternative to confronting the medical system with the demands for reform of existing institutions" (p. 85). They also note that the problems that confront women differ in different economic classes and emphasize the importance of recognizing these differences in self-help efforts. Because it seems unlikely that there will be considerable redistribution of economic resources into the service sector, the creation of mutual help and self-help groups may become more common. (For further discussion see Gartner & Riesman, 1984; Powell, 1990).

SUMMARY

Working with families and groups is an integral aspect of social work. The diversity of families calls for knowledge about different kinds of families and how these differences may influence problems and options. Families include those that are blended (including stepparents), single parent, gay/lesbian, and nuclear.

Group work is a traditional aspect of social work practice. Knowledge about group process, composition, structure, and development as well as skills in using this knowledge to facilitate group goals will help you to work effectively with groups of clients and colleagues. Valuable skills include offering helpful models, planning agendas, reinforcing constructive behaviors, regulating group process, involving participants in helpful activities identifying common interests and transferring leadership skills to group members. Encouraging a culture of thoughtfulness will be valuable in avoiding "group think" that may result in poor decisions. Advantages of group settings include opportunities to enhance a sense of community, validation, and normalization of concerns and opportunities to learn new coping skills from a variety of individuals. Support groups and self-help groups provide valuable options.

REVIEWING YOUR COMPETENCIES

Reviewing What You Know

1. Describe how family composition has changed over the past years.
2. Describe some cultural differences regarding families.
3. Identify major dimensions that can be of value in understanding families.
4. Discuss the influence of economic resources on family life.
5. Describe different kinds of groups social workers participate in.
6. Describe different group phases and important tasks in each.
7. Identify factors you should consider in composing groups.
8. Identify problems that may arise in group process and suggest helpful remedies for them.
9. Describe preparations that should be made for each group session and why they are important.
10. Describe indicators of group think.
11. Describe what can be done to discourage group think.
12. Identify major indicators of a culture of thoughtfulness.

Reviewing What You Do

1. You accurately describe power relations in families and groups.
2. Observation of your work with families shows that you model and support valuable behaviors.
3. Observation of your behaviors in groups shows that you are well prepared and exercise good leadership.
4. You accurately spot and counter weak appeals in case conferences.
5. You raise important questions in case conferences and introduce valuable points of view.
6. You accurately identify problems in group process and suggest valuable remedies based on practice-related literature.

Reviewing Results

1. Family members achieve effective problem-solving skills.
2. Family members report that they are happier.
3. Intergenerational differences at home work to strengthen family cohesiveness.
4. Groups attain goals they value.
5. Sound decisions are made at group conferences.

Organizations and Communities

OVERVIEW

This chapter provides an overview of social work practice with organizations and communities. Helping clients may require intervention at the organizational and community levels. Skill in identifying and rearranging contingencies related to behaviors of interest at these levels will help you to discover options.

You Will Learn About

- Understanding and changing organizations.
- Working at the community level.
- Social planning and program development.
- Prevention.
- Offering consultation to other professionals.

UNDERSTANDING AND CHANGING ORGANIZATIONS AND SERVICE SYSTEMS

Most social work practice takes place in an organizational context. Many people spend part of their lives in an institutional setting. It is estimated that one third of elderly people will spend some time in a nursing home. Our prisons and jails are overflowing. Residential settings for youth are thriving businesses. Services are influenced by the contingency systems that operate both within and exter-

nal to agencies and institutions. For example, funding patterns may discourage effective services (see for example, Meinhold & Mulick, 1990). Skill in being a good bureaucrat (negotiating the stresses, opportunities, and constraints in organizational life) will help you to prevent burnout and maximize service provision (Pruger, 1973). Organizational diagnostician and reformer are two of the ten roles highlighted as important by Weissman, Epstein, and Savage (1987). You may help staff to:

- Clarify agency goals.
- Distinguish between objectives that are means and those that are ends.
- Identify the conditions required to accomplish valued outcomes.
- Help staff prioritize goals.
- Estimate the likelihood of attaining goals.
- Offer suggestions for evaluating outcome(s).
- Help the agency to develop or maintain a culture of thoughtfulness (see Exhibit 5.8).
- Overcome barriers to communication.
- Suggest funding sources.
- Design an effective information management system.
- Enhance decision-making styles.
- Develop programs to attain valued outcomes.
- Evaluate resources.
- Translate legal regulations and/or directives from a board of directors into specific policies, programs, and practices.
- Identify organizational obstacles to fulfilling agency mission (e.g. in communication styles and channels, authority structure, personnel policies).
- Identify and alter obstacles in the agency's external environment.
- Describe clear performance standards.
- Create positive feedback systems to maintain performance standards.

You may help an agency to decide where to focus change efforts for example, on policy (e.g., eligibility requirements), programs or practices (how services are offered), or personnel (e.g., hire bilingual staff, involve volunteers).

Like individuals, families, groups, and neighborhoods, agencies are influenced by their external environment including other service organizations, funding sources, and vested interests of political groups and client groups. Access to service may be limited by agency policies and procedures, lack of coordination among agencies, and limited agency resources. Goal displacement may limit services.

This occurs when an agency's means become its ends. For example, an agency may use process measures such as number of client interviews to evaluate outcomes. Number of client interviews does not provide information about outcomes. Both efficiency and effectiveness of service may be compromised by inadequate monitoring of the extent to which staff performance standards are met and lack of incentive systems that support valued staff behaviors. Operative goals reflected in staff activities and their outcomes may differ from those officially described, to the detriment of clients.

Knowledge about how organizations and service systems function as well as external constraints and options (e.g., funding patterns) will be useful in discovering options and obstacles (see for example, Davis & Newstrom, 1989; Hasenfeld, 1992; Netting, Kettner, & McMurty, 1993; Roberts & Hunt, 1991; Whetten & Cameron, 1995). Knowledge and skill in carrying out a contextual assessment will be valuable in identifying options. Consider the following questions when thinking about options:

- What physical characteristics of relevant settings influence service delivery?
- Who has power over whom?
- What are influential communication channels?
- What contingencies support valued behaviors and outcomes?
- What contingencies compete with achieving valued outcomes?
- Who should be involved in change efforts?
- What incentives can be used to support desired behaviors?
- What obstacles exist (e.g., limited time, skill, or other resources, negative attitudes, funding sources, competition for clients)?
- How can obstacles be decreased?
- What resources are available?
- What format(s) will be most successful in involving staff (e.g., formal training for all staff, informal on-site coaching, training one person who would then train others)?

EXHIBIT 24.1
Framework for Analyzing Human Service Organizations

Focus	Tasks
A. Identifying the agency's task environment	1. Identify funding sources 2. Identify sources of noncash revenues 3. Identify clients and client sources 4. Identify other constituents
B. Recognizing the dynamics of agency/environment relations	5. Observe relationships with clients 6. Observe relationships with resource sources 7. Observe relationships with competitors
C. Analyzing the organization	8. Identify corporate authority and mission 9. Understand organizational structure 10. Understand administration, management, and leadership 11. Recognize the organization's culture 12. Assess the organization's programs and services 13. Assess organizational technology 14. Evaluate personnel policies and procedures 15. Recognize how the organization deals with community relations 16. Recognize methods of financial management and accountability 17. Identify facilities, equipment, computer utilization, and records management

Source: F. E. Netting, P. M. Kettner, & S. L. McMurty (1993), Social work macro practice (p. 160) New York: Longman.

You could visually describe the interrelationships among staff to explore how they influence services (e.g., draw a series of circles on a piece of paper, write in the names of particular staff or note staff level in each, and use arrows of different colors to note who interacts with whom and the nature of the exchange—basically positive, negative, or neutral (Tichy & Sherman, 1993). Both formal and informal communication links could be noted. Exhibit 24.1 provides a framework for analyzing organizations.

Organization Culture and Climate

Organizations develop cultures and climates (see Glossary in Appendix A). Certain values are preferred, and certain norms and rules are followed. Components of culture include history, contingencies in effect, patterns of communication, decision-making styles, philosophy, myths, and stories. Dimensions of communication style described by Rudi Klauss and Bernard Bass (1982) as valuable include the following (p. 47):

- Careful transmitter (chooses words carefully).

- Open and two-way (considers other points of view, follows up conversations with feedback).

- Frank (levels with others).

- Careful listener (attends to what the speaker is saying, lets others finish speaking before commenting).

- Informal (relaxed, natural).

Credibility dimensions they identified are trustworthiness (just, kind), informative (well informed on issues concerning areas of responsibility), and dynamic (energetic). Review your communication style by completing Exhibit 24.2. Indicators of a well-functioning organization are suggested in Exhibit 24.3.

Although status (ranking) is important in all organizations the criteria on which it is based differ in different organizations, for example, longevity of service, charisma, expertise, positive incentives, and/or coercive power. Contingencies may or may not

EXHIBIT 24.2

Complete the items below to review your organizational style. Review your ratings to discover options for enhancing your effectiveness. Add other items you think are important.

1. I offer positive feedback to my colleagues for behaviors that contribute to effective services.	0	1	2	3	4
2. I involve my colleagues in seeking changes in policies and programs that affect service quality.	0	1	2	3	4
3. I value learning about my colleagues' points of view.	0	1	2	3	4
4. I seek feedback that will help me to enhance my skills and knowledge.	0	1	2	3	4
5. When I have a complaint I discuss it with the person involved rather than talk about it behind his or her back.	0	1	2	3	4
6. I involve others in arranging opportunities to discuss practice/policy issues/topics.	0	1	2	3	4
7. I write notes of congratulations to others regarding professional or personal events/accomplishments.	0	1	2	3	4
8. I come prepared for team meetings and case conferences.	0	1	2	3	4

Key: 0 (not at all); 1 (a little); 2 (a fair amount); 3 (a great deal); 4 (best that could be).

support patterns of behavior that benefit clients and bring out the best in staff (Daniels, 1994). Valued behaviors may be punished or ignored and undesired behaviors reinforced. Bureaucratic propaganda may obscure policies and practices (Altheide & Johnson 1980). Organizations differ in the clarity with which their philosophy, mission, goals, and related objectives are clearly described and the extent to which all staff are involved in making decisions. The clearer the description of goals, related objectives, and expected success levels, the easier it will be to evaluate the extent to which valued outcomes are attained and to detect negative and positive side effects. Style, philosophy, and competencies valued as part of agency culture at Spectrum, a Bay Area agency providing services to children, families, and schools, include the following:

Style	Philosophy	Competencies
Open, honest	Social action	Behavior analysis
Humor	Integration	Education
Assertiveness	Nonaversive	(of self/clients)
Independence	Data-guided	Communication
Flexibility	Outcome	Problem solving
Reinforcing	oriented	Consultation
Hard working	Vision	Writing skills
Ability	Responsibility for	Computer literacy
to accept	learning	Evaluation
feedback	Behavioral	
Team work	Scientific	
Passion		
Integrity		
Pragmatic		

Organizations differ in the extent to which they engage in strategic planning within their own agency and together with other agencies. Advantages of such planning include the following (see for example, Quinn, et al., 1996):

• Provides a sense of identity.

• Helps staff see what they are doing in a wider context (e.g., consider remote as well as current contingencies).

• Decisions are made in light of the future.

• Requires discussion of mission, aims, goals, and resource allocation.

• Creates a network of information.

• Forces the system to take stock of all resources, both internal and external.

• Encourages and gives direction to long-term studies that contribute to sound decisions.

• Provides a forum for critical discussion.

• Provides options for alternative directions. Alternative paths become clearer.

Decision-Making Styles

Organizations have different ways of making decisions and handling conflict and uncertainty and less-than-hoped-for success. Agencies differ in the extent to which they seek clear, accurate informa-

EXHIBIT 24.3
Indicators of a Well-Designed Organization

1. All staff are involved in deciding on agency philosophy, mission, and related objectives.
2. Performance standards are clearly described for each staff position. Checklists are available that can be used as a guide to competent performance.
3. Performance is monitored for all staff positions based on agreed-on criteria. There is an emphasis on less-than-hoped-for success and mistakes as opportunities for improvement.
4. Feedback is provided to all staff at agreed-on intervals based on performance monitoring and feedback from staff both below and above them in administrative positions.
5. There is an emphasis on how well the agency or specific unit within it are doing as well as on how well individual staff are meeting agreed-on performance standards. This encourages a sense of team involvement, a sharing of responsibility.
6. Training is provided as needed and is criterion referenced and competency-based (i.e., knowledge and skills to be acquired are clearly described and are related to outcomes pursued and are assessed via clear, relevant written and performance tests).
7. Staff are open about problems/mistakes/shortcomings and seek remedies for avoiding them in the future. They experiment with new approaches, and staff feel free to point out difficulties because they expect problems to be addressed and are optimistic that they can be solved.
8. Staff act in a planful manner. Practices and policies are improved based on systematic feedback. Staff think problems through and make changes to improve services. They consider both long-term and short-term consequences of procedures and policies.
9. In addressing problems, staff are not preoccupied with status, territory, or second-guessing higher management. It is OK to challenge the boss. Nonconformity is tolerated.
10. Knowledge, skills, interests, work load, and timing influence assignment of responsibilities rather than organizational level.
11. Input from all staff levels is sought and valued. Staff are encouraged to critically examine suggestions.
12. Problems addressed include personal needs of staff and their interrelationships.
13. Staff request help/seek advice when needed.
14. Staff work together to address frustrations and crises. They support and offer constructive feedback for other people's ideas.
15. Differences of opinion are viewed as important to problem-solving decision making, troubleshooting, and growth and critical discussion and testing is valued as a way to arrive at sound decisions.
16. Staff help each other to enhance their skills. On-the-job learning is a routine part of work. Resources are shared.
17. Staff value and care about one another. Individuals do not feel isolated.
18. Staff work hard but enjoy and value their work. People trust each other. There is a sense of freedom and mutual responsibility.
19. Leadership is flexible, changing as needed in style and person.
20. Organization structure, procedures, and policies are designed to help staff get the job done and to strengthen the organization. They are changed as needed. There is a sense of order coupled with a high rate of innovation.
21. The organization adapts to opportunities and changes in its external environment.
22. Staff take reasonable risks when this would improve service.
23. Red tape is minimized.
24. Yearly reviews of outcomes achieved by staff are held in light of agency philosophy, mission, and related objectives and changes made as necessary.

Sources: See LaVigna et al. (1994), The periodic service review. Baltimore: Paul H Brookes; R. W. Weinbach (1990), The social worker as manager (pp. 316–319). New York: Longman: I. J. Fordyce & R. Weil (1979), Managing with people (pp. 11–14). Reading, MA: Addison-Wesley.

tion about service outcomes and use this information to improve services. They differ in the extent to which they value a culture of thoughtfulness in which critical discussion of different options is valued (see Exhibit 5.8). This kind of culture will increase the likelihood of sound decisions. It will discourage group think (see Chapter 23) and rule by cliques.

Different styles of decision making discussed in the literature on organizations include an *incremental model* in which decisions are made in small steps. For example, policy is changed a little at a time. In a *rational model*, decision makers define problems and then search for alternative solutions. "Once the search is complete, they assess the probability that each alternative will result in some desired outcomes, assign values to the different outcomes, and select the alternative that produces the outcome with the highest value" (Roberts & Hunt, 1991, p. 327). It is assumed that decision makers:

• Are aware of their values.

• Possess all information about alternatives.

• Understand all possible outcomes of any alternative.

- Know the likelihood of each alternative resulting in a valued outcome.
- Can evaluate accurately the extent to which each alternative will contribute to overall values.
- Choose the alternative that maximizes value. (p. 327)

In an *administrative model*, bounded rationality is emphasized in which constraints such as lack of time and cognitive biases are recognized. Here it is assumed that:

- We are willing to (or must) settle for less than the best.
- We search for only a limited set of alternatives and continue our search only until a good solution is reached.
- We do not consider all consequences.
- We consider probability only in a rough way if at all.
- Our choice may be influenced by one major factor.

Judgment models focus on how judgments are made and what influences them such as cognitive biases that result in overlooking important factors. As discussed in Chapter 5 we tend to:

- Underestimate the effect of environmental influences on behavior (especially other people's behavior).
- Are influenced by vivid events.
- Perceive consensus when there is none.
- Overlook the informational value of events that do not take place.
- Are influenced by the roles people occupy (e.g., by authority).

Technology Relied on and Criteria Used to Select It

Agencies differ in the service methods they use and the criteria they use to select them (e.g, scientific, tradition) (see Exhibit 2.4). This affects services. Your agency may rely on methods that focus on changing people's behaviors, thoughts or feelings, people processing techniques (e.g., giving people labels that increase their access to certain services), or methods that focus on changing the environments in which people live. They differ in the extent to which they draw on the scientific literature to select policies, programs, and practices that have a track record of success and the extent to which they do so over all service areas. For example, an institutional setting may draw on this literature in designing programs inside the institution but not do so in providing transitional services to the community. Agencies differ in the extent to which criteria used to select methods are candidly discussed and the degree to which service outcomes are reviewed.

Administrative Tasks

Management tasks include budgeting, coordinating activities, resolving conflicts, encouraging compliance with expected standards, and coordinating agency needs and goals and external requirements from regulatory or funding sources (Hasenfeld, 1987). Providing effective staff training is a key administrative role and administrators are responsible for ensuring trainers' expertise (McClannahan & Krantz, 1993). Maintenance roles are key ones for administrators. These include harmonizer (solving disagreements and reducing tension), consensus tester (checking whether a group is nearing a decision), encourager (being friendly and warm), and compromiser (e.g., changing a position when called for) (Resnick, 1982). Administrators also serve a reality tester role (to see if a suggestion would work). Administrators rely on different power bases. Some form valuable alliances and encourage reciprocity via positive social exchanges. Others rely on coercive power. Some have a consensual style of management. They involve staff in decisions. Others have an authoritarian style—they make the decisions with little staff input. Leary (1989) suggests that men and women differ in ways that may influence their behavior as leaders including:

(a) the public images they tend to value (e.g., women tend to value interpersonal relationships, whereas men value task accomplishment); (b) their self-perceived competencies in fostering certain impressions (e.g., men are more confident in their ability to appear authoritative, whereas women are more confident in appearing socioemotional); (c) their expectations regarding how others would respond to certain public images (e.g., behaviors that others regard as "assertive and tough" in a male leader may be seen as "bitchy" in a woman. . . . (p. 370)

Administrators can encourage an effective working environment by:

- Modeling and promoting tolerance for diversity, conflict, expression of grievances, and constructive approaches to conflict resolution.

- Encouraging and facilitating unit or program interdependency and team approaches to tasks that cut across programs and professions.

- Minimizing the "height" of the organizational hierarchy ("flat" hierarchies tend to promote communication and improve staff morale).

- Delegating authority and responsibility to all levels of the hierarchy, particularly in those areas that directly affect job performance.

- Providing opportunities and rewards for participating, planning, and decision making.

- Establishing effective formal channels for sharing information across all levels and programs—memos and reports should flow in all directions.

- Clarifying and promoting understanding of organizational goals, ethics, and ideology.

- Clarifying staff roles and responsibilities. (Crowell, 1982, p. 27)

The Self-Learning Organization

An increased emphasis on accountability to clients, advances in information technology (e.g., computer processing of data), and decreasing resources all point to the value of self-learning organizations—those that seek and use corrective feedback about how they can improve services and adapt to changing circumstances (e.g., in funding) (see for example, Hasenfeld, 1996; Schwartz & Baer, 1991). As Hasenfeld (1996) notes, no longer will agencies be able to rely on anecdotal accounts to obtain funding sources. (See also Argyris & Schon, 1996.)

OBSTACLES TO ORGANIZATIONAL CHANGE

Environmental obstacles may include funding patterns, vested interests in current power networks, and related contingencies, limited resources, and preferred ideologies (Meinhold & Mulick, 1990; Netting, Kettner, & McMurty, 1993). There may be conflicts between professional values and agency practices. Personal obstacles include a belief that change is not possible, a view of conflict as inappropriate, and a high need for social approval. Inertia and feared losses as a result of proposed changes may contribute to resistance. The vaguer the proposed changes, the more anxiety staff may experience. People may disagree over goals or simply not like each other. Strained personal relationships or friendships between staff and management may get in the way. For example, staff may not express their concerns because they are afraid of offending friends or have been criticized by supervisers for doing so. Decisions will have to be made about how to handle disagreements among staff who advocate for change and administrators who oppose it.

Staff may underestimate options for altering harmful or ineffective practices and policies or be reluctant to discuss known problems (Block, 1981). A search for ideal solutions may breed dissatisfaction and get in the way of making small but valuable improvements. We may expect "too much too soon" and so forego opportunities to support successive approximations. The concept of successive approximations highlights the gradual nature of change, whether working with individuals, families, groups, agencies, communities, or social service systems. Seeking approximations to valued goals may pose less of a threat to those who fear changes. Valuing and recognizing small wins will help staff to persist in long-term change efforts (Weick, 1984). A belief that administrators don't care about clients may interfere with collaborative pursuit of common goals. What appears to be non-caring on the part of administrators may reflect pressures they experience. Perhaps the timing of a proposed change is not good. Perhaps staff have just gone through many changes.

The organizational culture and climate (e.g., beliefs, norms, values, contingencies) will influence options for change. Noting facilitating and constraining factors is valuable in reviewing options (see Exhibit 24.4). Other factors include preferred criteria for selecting service methods, the competencies of and relationships among staff, legal and administrative factors, and information and communication channels (Levine & Perkins, 1987). Preferred styles of communication and problem solving may be an obstacle. Feminist writers note that women prefer win-win rather than win-lose approaches; they prefer collaborative styles in which interpersonal relationships are valued in and of themselves, not merely as a means to an end. Valuing critical discussion as a route to improving services will encourage a work climate in which clashing points of view are valued. New roles in public services suggested by Raven (1984) include critic, muckraker, whistle-blower, organizational invader, prophet, and visionary (p. 79).

The Importance of Political "Savvy"

Political knowledge and skills are of value in understanding and dealing with constraints. Conflict is inevitable in all spheres of life including organizations. It is how conflicts are viewed and handled that is critical to outcome. (See discussion of the value of culture clashes in Chapter 6.) Forming a coalition of interested parties is often a useful step to take. A group of individuals seeking change will have more clout than an individual. Learn to recognize political ploys used to avoid change such as denying that a proposed change merits serious consideration and mobilizing biased others to exclude consideration of opposing viewpoints. The denial of conflict is one of the more underhanded uses of power (Bachrach & Baratz, 1971). Other ploys include stonewalling (e.g., assurances of change unaccompanied by any effort to bring them about or flat out refusal to consider changes) and stalling (forming endless committees). Be prepared to handle what Austin (1988) calls "intimidation rituals" used to "cool out" troublemakers such as discounting, isolation, defamation (attacking the individual's character), and/or dismissal.

Involving Clients

Limited options for changing agencies and service systems may require helping residents/clients to alter staff behavior (see Seymour & Stokes, 1976). Willner and his colleagues described how to run an effective halfway house for delinquent youth in which self-government is encouraged and res-

EXHIBIT 24.4
Reviewing Facilitating Factors and Constraints

Desired outcome: Establish a committee of students and faculty that would meet once a month for an hour to discuss integration of field and class content.

Facilitating Factors	Constraints
_____ 1. Students who favor this	_____ 1. Passing of time (students who want this change graduate; other students too busy.
_____ 2. Faculty who favor this.	_____ 2. Faculty who oppose it.
_____ 3. A rationally based decision-making climate in which students are encouraged to think for themselves	_____ 3. An authority-based decision-making climate in which students are expected to accept what faculty says is best.
_____ 4. An available meeting room.	_____ 4. No meeting room available.
_____ 5. A set student meeting time.	_____ 5. No set student meeting time.
_____ 6. An information network allowing polling of students.	_____ 6. No way to get information to all students/faculty.

idents evaluate staff (see for example, Willner and others, 1977). Resident rights groups should be created in all residential settings to work with staff to enhance service quality and protect client rights.

WORKING IN TEAMS

Social workers often work as part of an interdisciplinary team. A physician, social worker, physical therapist, occupational therapist, and nurse may all contribute to serving frail elderly clients. Social workers and nurses work closely together in hospice work. Management skills required of team leaders include motivating staff, resolving conflicts, setting up information networks and disseminating information, making decisions, allocating resources, developing positive working relationships, and facilitating team meetings. The involvement of different professionals with different helping approaches, and perhaps interests, highlights the potential for misunderstandings and conflict. Shared goals and values will contribute to success including valuing a culture of thoughtfulness in which everyone participates, agreed-on tasks are clear, differences of opinion are viewed as learning opportunities, and there is a sincere interest in understanding other points of view (people listen to each other) (see Exhibit 5.8). Suggestions for encouraging effective group meetings given by Edwards (1938) include:

- Avoid getting sidetracked on minor issues.
- Encourage brevity.
- Invite all members to listen attentively to each speaker.
- Combine wise control of time and size of problem.
- Sum up often and keep members informed just where they are in the discussion.
- Pause when helpful.
- Secure equal sharing of responsibility.
- Provide facilitating physical conditions for discussion.

Dimensions suggested by Resnick (1982) to evaluate team effectiveness include the following: (1) degree of mutual trust; (2) degree of mutual support; (3) communication (e.g., guarded to open); (4) team objectives (not understood to clear); (5) handling conflict (deny, avoid to confront with threats); (6) use of member resources; (7) control methods (imposed to self-influence); and (8) organizational environment (pressure to conform to free). Good will as well as relationship skills will be valuable in negotiating differences and distributing responsibilities. (For further discussion see Bailey, 1991; Tropman, 1996).

WORKING AT THE NEIGHBORHOOD AND COMMUNITY LEVELS

Helping clients will often require working on multiple system levels including the neighborhood and community. Neighborhood types described by Warren (1980) vary from anomic neighborhoods in which there is an absence of a shared value system to integral neighborhoods in which there is a high potential for problem solving. A community can be defined as that combination of social units and systems that perform the major social functions that meet residents' local needs. Important functions include support, social control, socialization, social participation, and production, distribution and consumption related to food, shelter, transportation, medical care, sanitation, and recreation. Varieties of community organization practice include community development, social planning, and social action (see for example, Rothman & Tropman, 1987).

These three models of community organization differ along a number of dimensions including goal categories of community action. Community development stresses self-help and developing community capacity whereas a social planning model emphasizes problem solving regarding community problems and social action has the goal of shifting power relationships and resources. These three models also differ on the following dimensions (see Rothman & Tropman 1987): (1) assumptions about community structure and problem definitions; (2) basic change strategy; (3) characteristic change tactics and techniques; (4) salient practitioner roles; (5) medium of change; (6) orientation toward power structures; (7) boundary definition of the community-client system; (8) assumptions regarding interests of community groups; (9) view of client population; and (10) conception of client roles. Some work through consensus. In others, disagreement and conflict are expected and may even be encouraged (see for example Hardcastle, Wenocur & Powers, 1996; Kahn, 1991; Netting, Kettner, & McMurty, 1993; Rothman, Erlich, & Tropman, 1995; Tropman, et al., 1995; Warren, & Warren, 1977). The satisfactions of helping community residents can be rich. "I don't think anything equals the feeling you get in seeing people take real control of their lives, which grass-roots organizing allows for," says Irma Rodrigues, a social worker and currently associate director of the multiservice Forest Hills Community House in New York City (Hiratsuka, 1990). Skills in networking and coalition building may be needed to help clients attain resources. Service characteristics that enhance neighborhood and community influence include the following (Fawcett, Mathews, & Fletcher, 1980):

- Inexpensive
- Effective
- Decentralized
- Flexible
- Sustainable
- Simple
- Compatible with existing customs, beliefs, and values

Vested interests in maintaining the status quo as well as funding needs and patterns may limit options.

COMMUNITY DEVELOPMENT

Community development emphasizes self-help and voluntary cooperation to achieve valued goals. Key helping roles include enabler, coordinator, and supporter of problem-solving skills. Citizens are viewed as participants in a shared problem-solving process (Fawcett & others, 1996). A collection of community groups may seek help. Identifying shared concerns may be a first step. Involving community members in all steps along the way will help to mobilize residents and ensure that their values are respected. Valued goals such as preserving neighborhoods, removing tax assessments, increasing safety, and decreasing crime may be pursued through neighborhood block organizations (Prestby, Wandersman, Florin, Rich, & Chavis, 1990; Unger & Wandersman, 1983; Chavis & Wandersman, 1990). To empower citizens we should give them more than a "feeling" that they are empowered. We should help them to increase the influence they have over decisions that affect the quality of their lives. Examples include teaching community board members to speak effectively at board meetings (Briscoe, Hoffman, & Bailey, 1975), helping people decide on agendas (Seekins & Fawcett, 1987), enhancing advocacy skills of people with physical disabilities (Balcazar & others, 1994; Balcazar, Seekins, Fawcett, & Hopkins 1990; Fawcett & others, 1994), involving community residents in identifying community needs (Schriner & Fawcett, 1988), enhancing leadership skills (Seekins, Mathews, & Fawcett, 1984), helping community members to disseminate information to funding sources resulting in additional money for valued services (Seekins & Fawcett, 1987), lowering utility rates (Seekins, Maynard-Moody, & Fawcett, 1987), and extending community control of new methods through study circles (see Exhibit 24.5). Meredith Minkler (1992) views empowerment as operating on two levels in community organization. First, people may gain increased social support and sense of control, which may enhance personal confidence, coping capacity, and certain benefits (e.g., access to health care). Secondly, a community may become more effective in participating in shared efforts to gain valued outcomes. Self-directed change and resources are seen as important in their own right. Pablo Friere (1973) emphasized involving community members in developing their own programs for learning and changing oppressive conditions. Potential for empowering clients will be influenced by: (1) knowledge of problems and solution alter-

EXHIBIT 24.5
Extending Community Control of New Technologies Through Study Circles

Problem. Each year a number of innovative programs and procedures emerge from various sources. Many potentially useful programs are rejected or fail to produce the promised results. One cause of such failures is the lack of involvement in adoption decisions by those who must implement the program or those who are affected by it.

Study circle method. A study circle worksheet was prepared to present a sequence of prompts to be followed by potential adopters in considering innovative solutions to problems. The worksheet consists of 28 steps involved in problem analysis, program design, and evaluation. Each step describes an activity to be performed by the group considering the adoption of an innovation (e.g., defining the problem). It also provides prompts in the form of questions to be answered by the group responsible for the activity (e.g., What has been done in the past about this problem?).

During meetings of a study circle, one member acts as a proctor by reading the prompts for each step, encouraging comments from all, and recording statements that show a consensus. The innovation is considered in the context of the problem it is intended to address and in the context of other options. The outcome of the use of the study circle worksheet is a written analysis of a problem, an outline of a program designed to address it (including the innovation—perhaps in modified form), a list of actions to be taken, publicly accepted responsibilities, and standards for evaluation determined by those responsible for implementing the solution.

Outcomes. The study circle procedures were used in both an adult education program considering the adoption of a living skills program and in an afterschool project operated by a community center considering the adoption of a basic skills program. In both settings the respective programs had been available for at least two years and training in their use had been provided, but neither program had been implemented. Following the study circle procedures, modified programs were initiated in both settings. However, the adult education setting directly adopted only two components from the model innovation while modifying four, rejecting eleven, and adding two completely new components. The afterschool program adopted six components directly from the Follow Through model, modified six, rejected five, and added four new components.

Dissemination. The worksheet itself has been modified and distributed to community leaders and agencies in Kansas during a series of community problem solving workshops conducted in centrally located cities. In addition, the worksheet has been used in conjunction with applications of the concerns report method described earlier.

Implications. The study circle process provides an opportunity for people to participate actively in decisions about the design and implementation of technologies that will affect them. In addition, it recognizes the uniqueness of their situation by providing an opportunity for individuals to use the information and skills they have acquired through their intimate familiarity with local conditions. Insofar as this technology gives local groups the power to adapt social and educational innovations to their own needs and circumstances, it extends indigenous control over technology designed by people outside the community.

Source: S. B. Fawcett, T. Seekins, P. L. Whang, C. Muiu, & Y. Suarez de Balcazar (1984), Creating and using social technologies for community empowerment. In J. Rappaport, C. Swift, & R. Hess, (Eds) Studies in empowerment: Steps toward understanding and action (Vol. 3, pp. 154–156). New York: Haworth.

natives; (2) skill in presenting issues, leading groups, and using related strategies; (3) degree of influence over consequences for critical actors in the system; and (4) environmental and structural variables (e.g., access to agendas of meetings of elected officials).

Understanding Communities and Neighborhoods

Just as it may be impossible to understand an individual's environment and how he or she influences it without seeing for yourself, it may be impossible to understand what a neighborhood or community is like and how residents influence it without observing this yourself. The fields of community psychology (Levine & Perkins, 1996), environmental psychology (Stokols & Altman, 1987), and community organization (see previous citations) provide a rich source of information about neighborhoods and communities including how to accurately describe and understand them. Guidelines for assessing communities are suggested in Exhibit 24.6.

Conducting needs assessment is an important practice skill. Questions include: "What are the needs in a community? Who should be involved in identifying them? What criteria should be used

EXHIBIT 24.6
Framework for Assessing Communities

A. *Community boundaries and demographic characteristics*
   • What are the geographical boundaries of relevance?
   • Describe groups that live in the community and their demographic profiles.
   • Identify neighborhoods in the community and describe how people in each influence each other (if they do).
   • To what extent do jurisdictional boundaries of health and human service programs match that of the community?
B. *Dominant values*
   • What cultural values, traditions, or beliefs are important to different community groups?
   • Which ones are generally shared?
   • What values and styles conflicts exist?
C. *Profile of resources/needs*
   • Describe existing community agencies and volunteer groups that provide services. What services do they provide to which residents?
   • What are the primary sources of funding for services?
   • Are there strong indigenous leaders within the community?
   • What stores are available/needed.
   • What police protection is available/needed.
   • What transportation services are available/needed.
   • What health services are available/needed?
   • What recreational resources are available/deeded.
D. *Profile of problems*
   • Describe problems that affect residents (including frequency and variety, percentage of residents affected by each).
   • Are some subgroups affected more than others?
   • What contingencies influence each problem of concern?
   • What kind of information is available concerning social problems, how accurate is it, and how is it used in the community?
   • Who collects the data, and is this an ongoing process?
   • What are options to better track problems and their frequency?
   • Are there barriers that interfere with residents becoming integrated into the community?
   • What forms of discrimination are common?
E. *Service Delivery*
   • How is resource distribution influenced by neighborhood and community characteristics?
   • How is resource distribution influenced by extracommunity characteristics?
   • What potential exists to organize residents to advocate for changes they value?
   • What service programs are needed?
   • What barriers exist to organizing residents to advocate for changes they value.

Source: Adapted from F. E. Netting, P. M. Kettner, & S. L. McMurty (1993), Social Work Macro Practice *(pp. 91–92). New York: Longman*

to identify them? You could: (1) compare what exists with an expert's standard; (2) ask residents what they want (i.e., perceived need); (3) determine service use (expressed need); or (4) determine the gap between those who use a service and similar others who do not. Each method has advantages and disadvantages in relation to accuracy (Bradshaw, 1972; Rossi & Friedman, 1993). Counting the number of people who need a given kind of service may be useful in planning services. Some efforts involve community residents at all stages of data collection. For example, Sarri and Sarri (1992) involved youth in low-income neighborhoods in Detroit in gathering data about community needs. Schriner and Fawcett (1988) developed a community concern report method that involved all residents in completing a survey about community needs. Involving residents is consistent with the philosophy and tradition of empowerment. It emphasizes influence by citizens in contrast to control by experts (Rappaport, 1987). First, items were identified that related core human values to the basic functions of community: (1) freedom; (2) general welfare; (3) dignity or self-esteem; (4) justice; and (5) security or survival. These values were placed in relationship with 18 community functions and institutions including local government, citizen participation, community services, education, and employment opportunities. For example, the value of security was related to the community function of entertainment and recreation in the survey item "Community parks and recreation areas are safe." The value of dignity or self-esteem was related to the function of local government in the item "The individual is treated with respect by local government officials." Items were added, modified, or deleted based on a search of the community development literature and extensive interviews with approximately 25 community leaders, city government officials, and other residents commonly recognized as experts in one or another aspect of community functioning (pp. 307–308). Community representatives developed a 30-item survey based on items identified. This survey was then given to all community residents. For each

item, respondents indicated how important it was and how satisfied they were. Strengths identified included the following:

1. Good fire protection (90% satisfied; 97% important).
2. Availability of ambulance service (85% satisfied; 97% important).
3. Far East Lawrence Improvement Association involvement in community improvement (83% satisfied; 96% important).
4. Overall quality of the neighborhood (78% satisfied; 96% important).
5. Safety of community (70% satisfied; 95% important).
6. Availability of recreational facilities for children (66% satisfied; 84% important).

Problems identified included the following:

1. Availability of an affordable grocery store (22% satisfied; 85% important).
2. Well-managed bus or transit system (27% satisfied; 88% important).
3. Adequate dog control in the neighborhood (29% satisfied; 88% important).
4. New homes on lots of adequate size (36% satisfied; 84% important).
5. Enforcement of speeding and muffler regulations (38% satisfied; 88% important).
6. People care for the appearance of their homes (62% satisfied; 94% important).

This information provided the basis for informed selection of objectives to focus on.

Organizing and Disseminating Information

After you collect information about community needs, a next step is to organize and disseminate it. Education about community needs can be empowering as eloquently argued by Pablo Friere (1973) in his concept of "education for critical consciousness." This will require listening to others, understanding issues, and critical discussion. Be sure to consider your audience. Some will be allies. Others include the uninvolved and ambivalent and active opponents. Questions suggested by Richan (1991) include the following:

1. Are you dealing with one audience or several? If the latter, are some more important to reach than others?

2. What concerns are uppermost in members' minds? It is these concerns you want to tap into right at the beginning. . . .

3. What do members know about the topic, and what do they "know" (presume) in advance? What they know is what you build upon to further understanding. What they presume may be a barrier to further learning. . . .

4. How do they feel about the subject? If the subject involves a particular risk population, are members of the audience positively disposed toward that population? If a government program, is the audience inclined to favor such a role of government? Richan notes that research is particularly important here because of your own tendency to stereotype audience reactions.

5. How do they feel about you or people like you? You have an identity—age, sex, race, and ethnic, class, religious, educational, and occupational, even height and weight. It will influence how your message is received. . . .

6. How do you feel about people like them? Honest answers only.

You could prepare a problem/policy analysis that includes the following:

1. A clear description of the problem and groups that are affected by it.

2. A description of likely causes of the problem and what these guesses are based on (e.g., a review of related research).

3. A description of public and private programs concerned with the problem.

4. Possible options for decreasing the problem.

5. Estimated costs and impacts of current programs and of other options for resolving the problem.

6. Objectives that might be met by action designed to remedy the problem.

7. Criteria that might be used to track progress in resolving the problem (e.g., decrease in problem related complaints).

8. Description of obstacles to reducing the problem.

9. A description of additional study and analysis needed and an estimate of the cost and duration.

Be sure to identify critical assumptions, clarify key terms and concepts, and isolate key issues that need to be resolved.

Media outreach. Distributing information to newspapers, television, and radio is another key way to bring problems to the attention of a wider audience and/or to educate people about it. A good example is offered by AIDS advocacy groups (see also later section on social action).

Enhancing Social Support

Enriching social support systems may prevent and/or remove complaints. Take advantage of natural support systems (see for example, O'Brian, 1987; Tracy, 1990). Powell and his colleagues (1987) designed a program to strengthen supports to families with young children by enhancing family members' use of social networks and neighboring resources. Fawcett and his colleagues (1976) developed a low-cost community education system to increase self-help and mutual assistance skills among residents in low-income communities (see also Fawcett & Fletcher, 1977; Mathews & Fawcett, 1977). Skill areas included: how to handle legal aid referrals and how to handle emergency medical requests. They designed learning units and trained low-income residents who worked at a neighborhood service center to administer standardized learning units to their peers. This program was effective in training low-income community residents to serve as proctors for a community education system. The Support Development Groups designed by Gottlieb and Todd (1979) provided information about social support, developed network maps of relationships, and discussed social support issues. D'Augelli (1989) describes the development of a helping community for lesbian and gay men. (For other sources see Gitterman & Shulman, 1994; Gottlieb, 1988).

Residents may be reluctant to participate in groups designed to enhance social support. Meredith Minkler (1985; 1992) used an innovative indirect approach to increasing social support and developing collective problems-solving groups. Elderly residents of single room occupancy hotels were offered blood pressure screenings, coffee, and refreshments in the hotel lobby. The interactions that occurred around the check station resulted in the formation of an informal discussion group. Seven additional groups were formed in other inner-city hotels. Environmental approaches to prevention and habilitation, such as building networks via shared activities and restructuring social settings are often ignored (Rook, 1984b). Rural indigenous trainers including ministers, housewives, hairdressers, merchants, teachers, and local service workers were involved in the Community Helpers Project (D'Augelli, Vallance, Danish, Young, & Gerdes, 1981) in which participants acquired: (1) helping skills (e.g., nonverbal attending); (2) life development skills (e.g., decision making, assessing risk of change); and (3) crisis resolution skills (e.g., assessing precipitating factors and developing a problem-solving strategy). Following training, pairs of trainers co-lead small group sessions for local residents. Guidelines for exploring opportunities to enhance positive social exchanges are suggested in Exhibit 24.7.

Neighbors may provide resources and support. The advantages of help from neighbors over professional help are their concrete, practical, experience-based, common sense-oriented, spontaneous, and caring aspects (Bulmer, 1986, p. 43). Care must be taken to augment these aspects of help among neighbors, not train them out. Encouraging positive links with neighbors and enhancing social skills for meeting people and making friends may decrease social isolation that is associated with child maltreatment (Richey, Lovell, & Reid, 1990). You

EXHIBIT 24.7
Describing the Ecology of Social Opportunities

A. *Settings that provide opportunities for positive social exchanges.*
   1. Their nature, variety, and rate of availability.
   2. Kinds of individual who participate including available models.
   3. Positive social consequences available, their schedule, and the probability of maximizing positive outcomes given needed skills.
   4. Negative social consequences likely and their schedule given high/moderate/low skill levels (e.g., lack of positive outcomes, aversive outcomes).
   5. Knowledge and skills required to obtain valued social outcomes in each setting.
   6. How often each can be sampled with positive effects and considering competing activities (e.g., work, sleep, child care).
   7. Current obstacles to taking advantage of opportunities.
      a. interfering responses such as social anxiety, aggression
      b. lack of social skills
      c. lack of self-management skills
      d. lack of transportation, money
      e. competing contingencies (work, child care)
      f. cultural norms/taboos
      g. competing cultural contingencies (to make money rather than provide social opportunities for citizens)
B. *Settings that could be created* (same questions as above).
C. *Obstacles to both A and B that could be removed and plan for doing so* (e.g., lack of skills, social anxiety, lack of correct information).

could help neighborhood residents to design a proactive neighboring program in which behaviors are encouraged that may prevent future problems.

Neighboring potential is related to unique characteristics of each neighborhood (who lives there, the physical arrangements, stores [e.g., their variety], the daily hassles and crises that affect social interactions, and political and economic factors related to these events). Programs designed to increase helpful neighboring behaviors should be based on a contextual assessment. Assessment should include identification of behaviors neighbors value and the circumstances in which residents can offer them with positive results as well as identification of behaviors and events that annoy neighbors and interfere with well-being (Gambrill & Paquin, 1992). This provides information about the actual and potential social relationships among individuals in a neighborhood. Obstacles to a proactive stance toward neighboring include ambivalence about offering, asking for, and receiving help, misunderstanding of different cultures, and limited resources. The greater the diversity of the community, the more difficult it may be to discover common interests and norms that transcend differences. Care must be taken not to overburden already stressed families.

Limits to Community Development

Limits to community development include need for changes at higher levels. Unless neighborhood residents have links with people outside their neighborhood and unless these individuals have links to city-wide political groups, little may be gained (Jacobs, 1993c; 1961). Communities may be so impoverished that residents have no cushion of time or energy to devote to improving community conditions. Profit-making concerns of corporations often assume precedence over local community interests. This becomes more common as corporate headquarters are located far away, perhaps even in another country. Administrative staff may be moved in and out of communities, decreasing opportunities for business people to take an ongoing leadership role in addressing community problems. Some studies have found negative effects of professional involvement in volunteer programs (Wolf, 1985). Policy-makers could view increased helping among neighbors as an excuse to make cuts in statutory service programs. The ideologies of self-help and social support may encourage "blaming the victim." Funds available will limit options. Use the contingency diagrams in Exhibits 8.3 and 8.5 to explore options (see also Exhibit 24.6).

SOCIAL PLANNING AND PROGRAM DEVELOPMENT

Social workers plan and evaluate programs and analyze policies. Weissman, Epstein, and Savage (1987) view program developer as one of ten key social work roles. New programs may be developed to meet unmet needs or to overcome bureau-

cratic obstacles. Developmental planning programs related to a certain problem/population may be pursued over many years as in Jack Rothman's (1991) work with runaway youth and the research of Edwin Thomas and his colleagues with partners of substance abusers (see for example, Thomas & Ager, 1993). Unlike the community development model in which clients are involved as active participants in all stages, here they are viewed as consumers or recipients of services. Key helper roles include fact gatherer, analyst, and implementer. Planning phases include analysis, design of programs, implementation, and evaluation. Program development steps recommended by Hasenfeld (1987) include the following:

1. Describe the problem and translate it into what clients need.
2. Marshall support for program development.
3. Allocate responsibilities to a board or advisory council.
4. Describe the purpose (or overall goal) of the program.
5. Identify clear subgoals or objectives.
6. Carry out a feasibility study.
7. Seek needed financial resources.
8. Describe how the program will provide services.
9. Get the program going.
10. Plan how services will be effectively provided on an ongoing basis.

Criteria that should be considered when reviewing options include cost, manpower requirements, facilitating and competing contingencies, needed facilities and equipment, and anticipated support of goals by other agencies and the community.

COMMUNITY-BASED SOCIAL ACTION

Community-based social action programs usually address specific issues and populations such as providing services to rape victims, the homeless, or runaway youths. Clients are viewed as co-participants. Kinds of groups that engage in social action include the following:

- Pressure groups that seek to advance a particular legislative issue.
- Citizen participation groups designed to influence policies and actions.
- Citizen action groups (e.g., welfare rights groups).
- Community groups that want to improve local or personal conditions.
- Social movements (groups that seek relatively large-scale changes).
- Improvement associations (e.g., league of women voters, Sierra Club) (Zander, 1990).

Questions of interest include:

- What do we think should be changed? How?
- How should we organize ourselves? Who will do what?
- Who should we approach for help?
- How shall we try to convince these people to develop this innovation?
- What methods should we use? Why?
- How can we maximize the likelihood of success?
- How can we get ready to take action and keep up our morale? (Zander, 1990, p. 2)

Agencies, professionals, and/or community members may acquire expertise in specific issues and form coalitions with other community organizations and agencies that share concerns. They may participate in both local and national voter registration drives and endorse and support candidates viewed as sympathetic to their interests. An example of successful social action can be seen in Exhibit 24.8.

Social action includes a consciousness raising goal (increasing awareness of problems, related factors, and what could be done to alter or prevent them). Alinsky (1972) viewed low-income communities as disenfranchised in comparison to those "with money and power." He emphasized enhanc-

ing the problem-solving skills and resources of a community, including fostering indigenous leadership. Encouraging discomfort with the "status quo" was one method used to encourage resident participation. Nancy Amidei (1982) suggests the value of "truth squads." She correctly notes that misinformation that goes unchallenged often becomes accepted.

> Wild charges appear in newspapers, small and large, and are repeated by ill-informed people on radio talk shows. These charges get the stamp of truth when television news programs and newspapers present information inaccurately or in ways that reflect public prejudices. . . .
>
> We can do something to solve this problem. . . . [This] will require a conscious effort to set the record straight whenever misinformation about social programs or those who depend on them appears; it means joining with others to form "truth squads" of people who view winning a better understanding of social programs as part of their civic or professional responsibility. . . . Concerned people, armed with good information, need to divide up the media in their states and communities, and use information at their command to present a more accurate picture of public benefits and those who use them. (p. 38)

You may have to lobby, persuade, bargain, teach, inform, advise, and analyze formal and informal power structures. Mobilizing voters, forming coalitions, and gaining access to the media to educate or expose problems may be required. You will have to decide whether to rely on politicians or to mobilize independent advocacy groups. Contingency analysis skills will come in handy for describing the "power ecology" in settings of interest (see Chapters 8 and 9). Compatibility of interests between clients and professionals cannot be assumed.

Achieving change will often require involving many people at varied system levels. Coalitions are of value not only in community work, but in seeking change in your own agency as well. Characteristics that weaken coalitions include elitism, hidden agendas, and processes that waste time. Characteristics that strengthen them include reminding members of the benefits of seeking shared goals (see Dluhy, 1990). Resources that are needed

EXHIBIT 24.8
Public Efforts Make a Difference: DES

Background: DES (diethylstilbestrol) was hailed as a great achievement offering enormous practical value in preventing miscarriages, facilitating growth in cattle, treating problems of menopause, acne, gonorrhea in children, and certain types of cancer. Early on, research raised concerns about carcinogenic effects of DES. Early results showed "the first known human occurrences of transplacental carcinogenesis—the development of cancer in offspring due to exposure in utero to a substance that crossed the mother's placenta." The following quote illustrates the role of social action groups in informing people about the dangers of DES.

The origins of DES Action go back to 1974, when Pat Cody and a few other women in Berkeley, California, dismayed at the continuing lack of information and resources for DES victims, decided that something had to be done. They formed a group to work on the problem and developed an informational pamphlet. This pamphlet circulated widely through informal networks and, as the information spread, so did concern and commitment. By 1978, at least five other DES groups had formed around the country. They agreed to establish a national network, with a common name and common objectives. Their motto: "Don't Mourn, Organize!!!"

This motto could hardly have been more apt. By 1987, there were over sixty DES Action groups around the country and throughout the world. Their activities have been manifold, ranging from public and professional education, to the development of technical resources such as audiovisual materials and physician referral lists. Two national DES newsletters provide current information on medical, legal, and legislative developments. Largely as a result of lobbying by DES groups, more than fourteen states have considered or passed bills or resolutions dealing with DES, and at least three (New York, California, Illinois) also appropriated funds. One of the most effective laws was New York's, passed in 1978, which set up special DES-screening centers around the state and a DES registry for research and follow-up. An intensive media campaign mandated by the N.Y. legislation almost doubled public awareness of DES in the state.

DES advocates have been active nationally as well, testifying at various congressional hearings. DES Action lobbyists were instrumental in getting HEW to form federal task forces on DES in 1978, and again in 1985. Letters from local DES action groups helped convince Congress to declare a "National DES Awareness Week" in 1985. The efforts of DES Action may also have helped sensitize judges to the special legal problems of DES victims. Starting with the *Sindell* decision in California [Dutton, Chapter 8], a number of courts have allowed DES daughters to sue major DES manufacturers without having to identify the specific brand that caused the injury—in effect, shifting the burden of proof from the victim to the manufacturer. In California, several industry-sponsored attempts to overturn the *Sindell* ruling were defeated, and press coverage gave credit for these defeats to "DES victims," in particular the opposition of DES Action. In New York, six years of lobbying by DES Action finally led, in 1986, to the passage of a law adopting a three year "discovery rule" for filing DES lawsuits, thereby removing an important obstacle to recovery by DES victims.

A crucial factor in DES Action's success has been the intense commitment of the women involved, many of whom have been personally affected by DES. The consequences of DES exposure are frightening and potentially lethal. Ties to the women's health movement helped transform these personal fears into political action. Women's health activists, all too familiar with being marginal to mainstream medicine, financially threatening to the drug industry, and low priority for the federal government, have schooled DES advocates in the tactics of self-help through collective action, sharing resources and contacts. DES Action has also benefited greatly from the involvement of compassionate physicians. But it has been DES Action's ties to its local constituents that are its greatest source of strength. This community base has kept the organization publicly accountable while allowing it to flourish entirely outside any formal structure of government, academia, or industry. With this base, DES Action has shown growing numbers of women how to take political as well as personal control of their medical destinies.

Source: D. B. Dutton (1988), Worse than the disease: *Pitfalls of medical progress (pp. 339–340) New York: Cambridge University Press.*

include: (1) money; (2) energy; (3) facilities; (4) political legitimacy; (5) expertise and knowledge; and (6) political mobilization (Siporin, 1987). Intermediate steps may include raising issues in a community and getting an issue on the formal agendas of policy-setting groups. You will have to decide whether to focus on a single issue (e.g., voter registration) or to pursue broader consciousness-raising efforts. Focusing on a single issue may get in the way of seeing "the big picture." Clearly describing goals and objectives and concentrating on

those of greatest concern will focus efforts. (For further detail see for example, Bobo, Kendall, & Max, 1991; Richen, 1991.)

INFLUENCING LEGISLATION

Helping clients may require changing legislation (see Moore, 1991). Legislators may have to be contacted and their support obtained. Understanding the legislative process will help you to approach this goal in an informed manner. You can increase your impact by mobilizing concerned others. Involve interest groups that share your goals. Writing skills include drafting legislation and amendments, summarizing bills, and documenting need. You may prepare letters of support/opposition, legislative reports, or press releases. Speaking skills include testifying at special hearings on committees and speaking to civic groups as well as speaking during informal exchanges.

ECONOMIC AND SOCIAL DEVELOPMENT

Economic development is concerned with increasing access to paid employment. Social development goals (helping people to work collaboratively together) are often required and pursued at the same time (Midgley, 1995). There is a rich literature describing economic development projects in countries around the world as well as in the United States (see for example, citations related to employment in Chapter 22). Some programs eliminate middle men (e.g., give sewing machines to women so they do not have to pay rent for them). Given the concerns with poverty in social welfare, pursuing such possibilities has a high priority. Success will require expertise in identifying and developing employment related skills, identifying and developing employment opportunities and many core social work skills such as helping people to work collaboratively together to achieve mutually valued outcomes. We can draw on the extensive literature describing how to create and maintain jobs for people with developmental disabilities in seeking options (see for example, Murphy & Rogan, 1995; Rusch 1990). Descriptions of recent employment development programs can also be found in Drake & Others (1996) and Raheim (1995).

PREVENTION

Primary prevention refers to preventing problems from arising in the first place. For example, all children are required to get a polio vaccination.

Secondary prevention efforts focus on identifying those at risk of a problem (e.g., child abuse, AIDS, behavior labeled delinquent), so special efforts can be devoted to this at-risk population to prevent problems. Garvin, Leber, and Kalter (1991) provided an 8-week intervention program for fourth- and fifth-graders of divorced parents (n = 53). Goals were to:

- Normalize common experiences.
- Clarify divorce-related issues and terms.
- Provide a supportive forum in which children could experience and rework potentially stressful aspects of postdivorce life.
- Develop coping strategies for difficult feelings and situations.
- Involve parents in the concerns of their children.

Children identified as at risk for adjustment problems (their scores suggested a clinical depression) showed especially significant gains. Group discussions, activities, and role playing were used. *Tertiary prevention* refers to providing services after problems have occurred, for example, preventing them from becoming worse. Offering clients skills that can be used in a range of situations may prevent future problems (see Chapter 20).

Although there is a great deal of talk about prevention in social work, opportunities to offer related services are limited by a lack of resources. Most prevention efforts are tertiary or secondary at the individual or group level. Social workers have little control over political and economic factors related to many problems that clients confront such as homelessness, lack of medical care, poor housing, and unemployment. This does not mean that they can have no influence over these conditions. You can, for example, write to legislators in support of proposed bills, form a coalition of like-minded people to lobby for a change, and seek changes in agency policies, procedures, and programs. (See other sources for further detail, e.g., Edelstein & Michelson, 1986; Felner & Felner, 1989; Felner, Jason, Moritsugu, & Farber, 1983; Gilchrist & Schinke, 1985; Gilchrist, Schinke, & Maxwell, 1987).

SUMMARY

Acquiring needed services for clients may require rearranging agency practices, programs, and policies. Knowledge about how organizations function as well as effective communication skills will be useful assets in seeking valued outcomes. Community efforts include both cooperative development efforts as well as conflictual social action. Here too, as with individuals, education can be vital—informing residents about problems and related factors. Here too, political skills and knowledge will be valuable in identifying competing interests of different actors involved and possible options. Contingency analysis skills will help you and your clients to identify leverage points at different system levels. Although many bemoan the lack of community as contributing to a decline in the quality of our lives, too seldom are jobs available to pay social workers to engage in the kind of community organization and development efforts that would encourage a sense of community and the positive consequences this may bring. Although prevention is more often discussed than practiced in social work, this provides the most proactive level of intervention.

REVIEWING YOUR COMPETENCIES

Reviewing What You Know

1. You can describe agency characteristics that influence services clients receive.
2. You can identify important aspects of agency culture.
3. You can accurately describe group think and suggest effective remedies for avoiding it.
4. You can describe different kinds of administrative decision-making styles and their advantages and disadvantages.
5. You can give examples of the influence of external funding sources and political interests on the services agencies offer.
6. You can describe hallmarks of a well-designed agency.
7. You can describe the philosophy and preferred technologies of your agency and the implications for clients.
8. You can identify characteristics of teams that contribute to and detract from effective decision making.
9. You can draw an accurate force-field analysis of constraining and facilitating factors related to a particular change in agency practices or programs or in a community.
10. You can accurately describe community characteristics that influence specific problems of concern to residents.
11. You can identify people outside a community who can help to attain outcomes residents value.
12. You can describe valuable characteristics of coalitions.
13. You can describe the skills required of community organizers.

Reviewing What You Do

1. You can draw an accurate diagram of the organizational structure of your agency.
2. You can draw an accurate diagram describing formal and informal communication channels in your agency.

3. You can draw an accurate diagram describing the relationship of your agency with other agencies and community groups that influence agency services.
4. You can accurately identify helpful changes in group meetings that will enhance their quality and suggest a feasible method for doing so.
5. You can prepare a concise report describing the effects of an agency policy, program, or practice and make sound feasible recommendations based on your analysis.
6. You facilitate group discussions effectively (e.g., prompt behaviors that encourage critical discussion).
7. You prepare contingency diagrams describing community-related factors that influence a problem of concern to residents.
8. You carry out accurate needs assessment of a community.
9. You can prepare a budget for an agency program.
10. You identify ways to provide more positive feedback to staff for valued behaviors.
11. You make effective presentations at community meetings (e.g., people listen to your presentation and consider your points-of-view/facts in making decisions).
12. You identify community residents who are most likely to be of help in pursuing desired changes.
13. You use a systematic problem-solving process in trying to resolve organizational or community concerns.
14. You help others to use a systematic problem-solving process to address concerns.

Reviewing Results

1. You help an organization to improve relationships between staff and administrators.
2. You decrease obstacles to effective service provision in an agency.
3. You help an agency to establish clear staff performance standards as well as an efficient, accurate system for tracking performance.
4. You help an agency to shift from an authoritarian decision-making style to a rational style.
5. You help a community lobby politicians for resources.
6. You help community residents to form a neighborhood block association.
7. You improve interagency linkages resulting in increased client access to services.
8. You help community residents to gain access to public school facilities for community meetings.
9. You help minority group members to participate more effectively at board meetings.
10. You help community residents to identify and prioritize needs.
11. You help community members become effective fundraisers to pursue goals they value.

APPENDIX A GLOSSARY

Autocratic model: Reliance on power, authority, and obedience.

Boundary spanners: People with communication links both with people in their neighborhood (or agency or department) as well as with people outside (e.g., with people in other units and in the wider community).

Bureaucracy: Large, complex administrative systems operating with impersonal detachment from people.

Charisma: Leaders who have a great influence on their followers by force of their personal characteristics.

Clique: A group of people who are linked often by friendship.

Coalition: Temporary alliances among people to pursue a shared aim.

Coercive power: Based on fear and reliance on response cost, punishment, and negative reinforcement.

Cohesiveness: The extent to which people stick together, rely on each other, and desire to be a member of a group.

Collegial model: Reliance on teamwork to build employee responsibility.

Community empowerment: "Process of increasing control by groups over consequences that are important to their members and to others in the broader community" (Fawcett et al., 1984, p. 146) (e.g., forming a tenant's rights organization in a public housing project to obtain improvements in housing conditions).

Conflict: Disagreement over what goals to pursue and/or how to pursue them.

Conformity: Following what others do without independent thinking.

Consensus: Agreement on the part of most people of a group.

Consultive management: A management focus in which employees are encouraged to contribute ideas before decisions are made.

Credibility gap: Difference between what a person says and what he does.

Cultural distance: Degree of difference between two contingency systems.

Expert power: Influence based on a person's knowledge of and skills related to certain tasks/problems.

Grievance system: An established procedure for discussing complaints.

Informal organization: The pattern of social relationships that arise spontaneously as people associate with one another in an organization.

Legitimate power: Based on the authority of one individual to influence another (e.g., as given within an agreed-on social structure). Those in position to use legitimate power may also use coercive and/or reward power.

Management by objectives (MBO): A system in which managers and staff agree on clear employee objectives as well as on the criteria used to assess accomplishment.

Mediator: An outside person who helps parties in a dispute to come to an agreement.

Mentor: Someone who serves as a role model to others (e.g., to give advice and model valuable behaviors).

Morale: Level of job satisfaction.

Neighborhood: People who live near each other and share certain common spaces.

Source: *Some items based on K. Davis & J. W. Newstrom (1989),* Human behavior at work: Organizational behavior *(pp. 109–123). New York: McGraw-Hill; K. H. Roberts & D. M. Hunt (1991).* Organizational behavior *(p. 41). Boston: PWS-Kent.*

Nominal group technique: A method to arrive at a group decision.

Network: Linkage among a defined set of people. Networks differ in degree of connectedness and reciprocity.

Normative (legitimate) power: Based on the belief in the right of others to control our behaviors.

Ombudsperson: An individual who mediates conflicts among people.

Organization: Roberts and Hunt (1991) define this as "A social invention for accomplishing tasks or goals" (p. 9).

Organizational climate: The atmosphere in an organization (e.g., happy/stressed, connected/isolated). Climate is influenced by organizational culture.

Organizational culture: Assumptions, beliefs, and values shared among members; kinds and patterns of contingencies in effect.

Organizational politics: Actions taken by staff to acquire and use power and other resources to attain desired outcomes.

Overmanning: A setting that has more people in it than it can accommodate.

Performance standards: Description of expected levels of knowledge, skills, and outcomes.

Position: A person's place in the social system.

Power: Influence over others.

Referent power: Influence based on admiration/respect.

Reward power: Influence based on positive reinforcement.

Role: A set of behaviors expected of an occupant of a position (e.g., superviser).

Role ambiguity: Vague expectations concerning expected behaviors in a given position.

Role conflict: This may refer to competition among roles or differences in opinion about how a role is to be fulfilled.

Role models: Leaders who serve as examples for their followers.

Role perceptions: How people think they are supposed to act in their own roles and others should act in their roles.

Sanctions: Rewards and penalties that a group uses to persuade persons to conform to its norms.

Satisficing: Arriving at a solution that is acceptable but probably not optimal.

Sociogram: A diagram representing feelings among people in a group (e.g., who likes or dislikes whom).

Status: Rank or prestige accorded an individual (this may be achieved or ascribed).

Undermanning: Insufficient people to carry out essential program and maintenance tasks.

Utilitarian power: Power as a result of control over contingencies.

Values: Our view of the desirability of certain goals (psychological, social, or economic).

PART
VIII

THE LONG RUN

CHAPTER 25

Maintaining Skills and Staying Happy in Your Work

OVERVIEW

This chapter describes steps you can take to continue to enjoy your work and maintain effective practice skills. Enhancing and maintaining critical thinking skills will help you to view uncertainty and setbacks as learning opportunities, and continue to learn. Considering the context of practice (e.g., the agency in which you work, your profession, and the society in which you and your clients live) will help you to avoid blaming either clients or yourself for limited options and to identify promising directions for altering service systems. You can avoid self-handicapping strategies such as blaming others for your problems and read useful material and seek further training to keep your knowledge and skills up to date.

You Will Learn About

- Developing effective skills for handling uncertainty.
- Recognizing limits on your ability to help.
- Responding to setbacks as opportunities for improvement.
- Considering the context of practice.
- Developing alternatives to self-handicapping reactions.
- Being an activist.
- Maintaining and enhancing knowledge, skills and attitudes that contribute to success.
- Preventing burnout/job stress.

Some options for enjoying your work will benefit clients. Others will not, though they may contribute to your satisfaction. The latter include relying on questionable criteria to evaluate service outcomes and select assessment and intervention methods, and complaining without taking steps to alter disliked situations. Your philosophy of practice will influence your job satisfaction as well as the services you provide. The suggestions discussed in this chapter will help you to use experience and educational opportunities to increase your effectiveness and to maintain a solid identity as a social worker. Many, such as questioning beliefs, responding to setbacks as learning opportunities, and recognizing limits, involve critical thinking skills emphasized throughout this book.

DEVELOP CONSTRUCTIVE SKILLS FOR HANDLING UNCERTAINTY

Practice decisions are made in the face of uncertainty about their likely effects. As one social worker said: "And how do we know we're right? That's the frightening bit—have I made the right decision? This is one of the things that tires you out" (Fineman, 1985, p. 70).

> In this job you never know whether you've done anything right—especially with kids. How can you decide that the decision you've made (albeit with other people) is the right one? You don't know until that child is grown up. The choices are more clear cut with the elderly—you can see the results when you put in a home help for an old person, or move an old person from a grotty house to a decent one. But with children and teenagers you just don't know. Maybe some initial improvement, and then it will go back. (Fineman, 1985, p. 70)

You will only be able to gather so much information due to time constraints. You may have to decide on plans even though you have little information about their effectiveness. "Practitioners are asked to solve problems everyday that philosophers have argued about for the last two thousand years and will probably debate for the next two thousand. Inevitably, arbitrary lines have to be drawn and

hard cases decided" (Dingwall, Eekelaar, & Murray, 1983, p. 244). Uncertainty breeds a temptation to deny it, perhaps fearing that recognizing it would stifle needed action. For example, child welfare workers may put off making decisions because of the risks associated with different options. They may ignore the consequences of not making timely decisions.

Recognizing uncertainty is an advantage if it increases the soundness of practice decisions. Use uncertainty as a cue to see if you can decrease it. For example, you may be able to gather additional information by consulting the scientific literature. And, you and your client can rely on an assessment framework that is likely to provide accurate problem analyses. Another way to decrease uncertainty is to arrange for ongoing tracking of progress so that you and your clients know what is happening and can make timely decisions based on what you discover. You can estimate your degree of confidence in your predictions. You may predict that there is an 80% chance that a program will increase positive exchanges among family members. If your estimate is low, you may want to consider other plans. Making clear estimates and comparing them with results, offers more precise feedback than vague estimates (e.g., "I think it will be effective") and so may improve the accuracy of future predictions.

RECOGNIZE THE LIMITS OF THE HELP THAT CAN BE PROVIDED

You won't be able to help all the people you see. No one may be able to help clients attain some outcomes such as housing in a particular neighborhood. Policies, laws, or lack of resources may limit options. Literature, art, and music throughout the ages show that life is often not an easy place. Life brings misery as well as happiness. Young children die, the elderly linger on in great physical discomfort, lovers leave, and friends betray us. People may lose their jobs through no fault of their own. Karl Popper has argued that trying to make people happy is not only futile, but results in imposing allegedly better policies on citizens even if against their will.

Social workers cannot solve the world's problems. Yet often they have promised to do so (e.g., remove poverty). The pursuit of utopian goals distracts us from working in many small ways to minimize avoidable miseries and may encourage a drift into dysfunctional reactions (see later discussion). You can do no more than give your best. Giving your best includes making well-reasoned practice decisions (e.g., using effective methods), helping clients use their own resources, and taking whatever steps possible to improve service systems. Some of your efforts to redress inequities may not benefit today's clients but may help others in the future.

RESPOND TO SETBACKS AS LEARNING OPPORTUNITIES

Some argue that we learn more from our mistakes than from our successes. We learn by acting ("risking") and responding to the resulting feedback. This allows us to discover what we understand and what we do not, what we can do and what we cannot, and what is effective and what is not. Effective troubleshooting skills are characteristic of experts. You may not have time to correct a mistake at the time you make it. Review and rethinking may have to come later. At other times you can correct an error immediately. If you ask a confusing question, you could say, "Let me start again . . ." and restate the question.

CONSIDER THE CONTEXT OF PRACTICE

Professional practice is influenced by the societal context in which it occurs. Taking occasional time-outs to reflect on the ecology of practice will help you to keep the larger picture in mind and resist the wearing down effect of difficult work environments. Understanding the helping professions (how they develop, what constraints influence them) will help you to work toward changes in your professional organization that will improve services. Contingency analysis skills will help you to explore who benefits or loses from given ideologies, poli-

cies, laws, programs, and practices. Ignoring political and economic influences may result in offering clients ineffective methods and inappropriately blaming yourself or your clients for lack of success and not taking steps to change policies and practices that compromise services. Keeping the "big picture" in view will remind you that change can occur, and that it usually takes effort and time. Consider Ignas Semmelweiss who around 1840 discovered that the death rate of mothers from childbed fever could be decreased from 25% to 2% if surgeons washed their hands before delivering babies (see Sinclair, 1909). Not until the end of that century did the medical profession act on his recommendations. Women won the vote in the United States only in 1920. Slavery was declared illegal in the United States only in 1865. Only recently did the Equal Employment Opportunity Commission declare that employers cannot refuse to hire people with disabilities because of concerns about their effect on health insurance costs. We prepare the way, well or poorly, for the next generation of clients and social workers.

DEVELOP POSITIVE ALTERNATIVES TO DYSFUNCTIONAL REACTIONS

Work in many agencies requires learning how to deal constructively with difficult situations (see Exhibit 25.1). Often, there is a discrepancy between what is needed and what can be offered. Money may not be available for in-home services, requiring elderly clients to enter residential care. Many social workers who work in public agencies feel frustrated.

> "Nobody in the headquarters sees the pressure here; nobody wants to see it! They just don't seem to understand that we can't keep piling on more cases for social workers—they'll stop functioning." (Fineman, 1985, p. 74)

> "It's so frustrating. At times I've taken action in the best interests of a client which has been blocked by bureaucratic action—or I've been making demands on the wrong budget at the wrong time. I give up in these circumstances." (Fineman, 1985, p. 73).

EXHIBIT 25.1
Options for Coping with Difficult Situations

Self-Handicapping Strategies	Constructive Strategies
• Become fatalistic, focus on problems and the absence of solutions. (Complain without taking action to correct disliked situations.)	• Seek positive alternatives. Identify the exact changes you would like, as well as how they could be attained and take steps in that direction.
• Blame others/Blame yourself.	• Same as above.
• Decide there is little help that can be offered and do your job in a "routinized" uncaring manner.	• Offer whatever help you can to clients and meet with others to explore what changes could be made to improve services.
• Congratulate yourself on services offered even though few are provided or no one knows what is accomplished.	• Accurately evaluate progress and be honest about your degree of success.
• Claim you do not make decisions.	• Recognize the decisions you make, identify factors that limit options, and meet with others to see how these could be altered.
• Struggle on by yourself.	• Involve others in seeking positive alternatives; form coalitions; a group has more power than an individual.

Scientific evidence related to problems and their causes may not match service approaches favored in your agency. When our skills and resources do not match the challenges we confront, we seek reasons. We may assume that what is must be (become fatalistic that nothing can be done to improve conditions). We may fall into the "cult of curability" in which we overestimate what we can achieve or have achieved. We may focus on concerns that are not of key importance to clients (e.g., recommend that a client participate in counseling even though this will not address problem-related environmental circumstances). We may overlook harm done in the name of help. We may deny that we make decisions. We may accept excuses that preserve self-esteem and help us to live with limitations, but do not address problems (Higgins, Snyder, & Berglas, 1990). We may fall into quackery (see Exhibit 25.2). Reasons given by social workers for limited success such as lack of resources and high caseloads often do reflect reality. Objectives may be difficult or impossible to attain. Excuses, like any other behavior, serve different functions, which at first may not be obvious. So, when you offer an excuse ask, "Does this work for or against me and my clients?" "Does this increase or decrease the probability of providing needed services and enjoying my work?" To the extent to which excuses relieve you from assuming undue responsibility for the welfare of your clients and encourage reasonable risk taking, they are helpful. They are self-handicapping if they reduce options

for achieving goals (if they get in the way of recognizing obstacles that could be removed). They are dysfunctional when they interfere with offering effective services and avoiding harm and making changes that could enhance success and work satisfaction. Nattering (defined here as complaining with no intention to do anything about the situation) will not result in change.

Simply complaining that "caseloads are too high" may forestall lobbying efforts to lower caseload size. A constructive way to handle discrepancies between services needed and those available is to provide whatever help you can to clients while taking steps to decrease mismatches (e.g., talk to other staff; bring them to the attention of administrators and legislators, form a coalition of interested parties to pursue change). Even when resources are cut reactions may be constructive or dysfunctional. Positive strategies include expanding volunteer services, seeking innovative models others have used to handle cuts and maintain service quality, exploring how resources could be shared, involving other interested parties in problem solving and lobbying to regain resources.

BE AN ACTIVIST

An understanding of the "big picture" coupled with a genuine concern for the hardships clients confront will encourage advocacy efforts to decrease these hardships. An activist stance can be taken at the

EXHIBIT 25.2
Why Professionals Become Quacks

Quackery refers to promoting services known to be ineffective, or which are untested, for a profit. Given that social workers get paid for what they do whether they work in public agencies or are in private practice, they profit from their work. Why is it that some professionals start to act like quacks? In *Dubious Dentistry* (1990), William Jarvis suggests a number of reasons.

POSSIBLE REASONS

- *Boredom.* Daily work can become humdrum. Pseudoscientific ideas can be exciting.
- *Low esteem.* Social work is not the most highly regarded profession. Dissatisfaction with a limited scope of practice may encourage pursuit of grandiose goals and unwarranted claims of effectiveness.
- *Reality shock.* Social workers regularly see very troubling situations. This requires making psychological adjustments. Some helpers are simply not up to it.
- *Belief encroachment.* Science is limited in its methodology to dealing with problems that are possible to solve. This constraint may become burdensome and additional aims embraced such as helping people with religious questions.
- *The profit motive.* Quackery can be lucrative.
- *The Prophet motive.* Some clients experience uncertainty, doubt and fear about the meaning and purpose of life. Others confront difficult situations that may seem hopeless. The power over people provided by the Prophet role is awesome. Egomania is commonly found among quacks. They enjoy the adulation and discipleship their pretense of superiority evokes. By promoting themselves, they project superiority to their colleagues and to their professional community.
- *Psychopathic traits.* Psychopaths exhibit glibness and superficial charm, grandiose sense of self-worth, pathological lying, conning/manipulative behavior, lack of guilt, proneness to boredom, and lack of empathy often seen in quacks.
- *The conversion phenomenon.* Many professionals who become quacks have gone through emotionally difficult experiences such as a practice failure, midlife crisis, divorce, or life-threatening illnesses.

Source: Based on William Jarvis (1990), Dubious dentistry. Loma Linda, CA: Loma Linda University.

agency level as well as at other levels. Social action may include conducting a needs assessment to document situations that require attention, writing to legislators advocating passage of a bill, volunteering time to help elect socially conscious representatives, participating in public hearings, or organizing a group to seek a specific change. Understanding how bills are developed, introduced, and guided through passage will help to demystify the legislative process (see for example, Nader, 1983). Both students and faculty can lobby for greater attention to be given to community organization courses in schools of social work. You can push for course content about discriminatory practices based on sexual orientation, race, gender, ethnicity, age, and class.

Other Steps

You can honor valued goals and focus on steps you can take to achieve them by making goals and decisions explicit and reviewing your values in difficult times. Discouragement often comes from not setting clear goals and not monitoring progress.

Evaluating practice in an ongoing manner will allow you and your clients to recognize and celebrate "small wins." You can use effective interpersonal skills to avoid unnecessary social predicaments, encourage client participation, obtain needed resources, and negotiate differences of opinion. Critical thinking skills will help you to get out of loops and avoid "dead end accounts" (those that do not offer intervention knowledge) and excuses that detract from work satisfaction and service quality.

Take advantage of opportunities to add to the knowledge base of social work. Effective practice and sound research require many overlapping attitudes, skills, and knowledge. Data from individual cases can be collected resulting in a series of AB designs related to a problem. You may develop a new service. Both qualitative and quantitative methods have much to offer depending on the questions asked (Gambrill, 1995a). Reid (1987) has described guidelines for encouraging staff to participate in research. Computers can be used to ease the burden of case recording, evaluating progress, and locating helpful literature (Nurius & Hudson, 1993; Schoech, 1990).

MAINTAINING AND ENHANCING KNOWLEDGE, SKILLS, AND ATTITUDES

How will you enhance and maintain valuable practice knowledge and skills? Will good intentions be enough? Studies of physicians indicate that even though many said they intended to carry out recommended procedures, they did so only 10% of the time (Cohen, Weinberger, Hui, Tierney, & McDonald, 1985). Can you count on supervisers, fellow social workers, and agency administrators to support effective practice skills? Or will agency incentive systems erode these? If you want to enhance your knowledge and maintain effective skills and upgrade your competencies, you will have to assume responsibility for this yourself. Arrange prompts and incentives that encourage valuable skills. Ongoing evaluation of progress with clients provides a valuable source of feedback. Seek support for knowledge, skills, and outcomes that contribute to success from colleagues and supervisers. If this is not possible in your agency, locate other professionals who share your values and goals and form a support/consultation group. You could meet monthly to share successes, seek options for handling setbacks, and discover new methods. Seek out first rate critical reviews of service effectiveness and rely on rigorous criteria to review claims (see for example, Jacobson & Christensen, 1996). Take advantage of visual representations of problems, options, and data (e.g., Venn diagrams, graphed data describing progress). A picture is worth a thousand words. If competencies drift downward, use your contingency analysis skills to find out how you can reverse this trend (see Chapters 8 and 9). What prompts and consequences support use of valued skills? Are valued behaviors punished? How can you rearrange your environment to increase positive feedback for skills that contribute to effective service? Can additional prompts be arranged? Are necessary tools available? Are competing behaviors reinforced?

PREVENTING BURNOUT/JOB STRESS

The term "burnout" refers to feelings of stress, boredom, depression, depersonalization, or fatigue related to work as well as a sense of helplessness and hopelessness among people who work with others (Maslach, 1982; Schaufeli, Maslach, & Merek, 1993). There is a loss of concern for clients. Some social workers lose sight of why they chose social work as a career such as wanting to help clients improve the quality of their lives. Depersonalization means a lack of feelings or callous or negative reactions toward clients. Clients are treated in a detached, mechanical manner. Job stress and burnout contribute to poor quality services for clients and high job turnover.

Causes of burnout are complex including personal, organizational, and social factors. Personal causes could be not getting enough sleep, ineffective planning and goal setting skills, unrealistic expectations, and lack of assertion. Inflexibility and intolerance of ambiguity are related to stress (Hellman, Morrison, & Abramowitz, 1987). Just as positive emotions encourage generosity toward others and contribute to effective problem solving, negative emotions have the opposite effect (Isen, 1993). You may be overinvolved or underinvolved with your clients (Larson, 1993). Organizational factors related to burnout include unsupportive peer and supervisory relationships, high caseloads, limited clerical help, vague expectations, lack of positive feedback, and conflicting role demands. Societal factors include individual competitiveness and shrinking resources. Social workers usually work with clients who are distressed, perhaps due to injustice and even cruelty. To continue to care requires effective handling of what some have called the "vicarious trauma" that results from empathizing with many people who are hurting.

You can take steps to prevent burnout even if you work in an agency that encourages it (e.g., form a support group to pursue valued changes). Viewing mistakes as learning opportunities, recognizing the limits of help you can provide, accepting the uncertain nature of practice decisions, and using methods that contribute to success will help. Burnout is less likely if you pursue clear, agreed-on objectives and evaluate progress. Use stress and dissatisfaction as cues to identify related causes. Perhaps you take your work home with you (see also Matteson & Ivancevich, 1987). Perhaps you have lost sight of the decisions you do make on the job and feel unnecessarily helpless. You may accept unreasonable assignments because you have difficulty refusing requests. You may have to enhance your time management skills. You may blame yourself for limited resources rather than recognizing the role of social, political, and economic patterns.

Learning as a Journey

Becoming a skilled social worker is like a journey with many potential sidetracks and pitfalls; a kind of social work dungeons and dragons. In spite of good intentions, many potential paths lie ahead besides your destination—to enjoy your work and offer high quality services to clients, a professional who not only believes that she helps clients, but really does. As with all journeys there will be detours

and setbacks. One of the aims of this book is to encourage you to view mistakes and setbacks as inevitable and as learning opportunities. Setbacks and detours are quite different from dead ends. Dead ends refer to getting permanently sidetracked at a destination that you do not like and did not plan on (although you may kid yourself that this is what you really wanted). For example, you may offer service in a routinized uncaring manner, blame clients for lack of success or continue to rely on a practice framework that does not provide intervention knowledge. Antiscience, pseudoscience, and quackery abound as does a justification approach to knowledge (see Chapter 4). Maintaining social bonds will be more important to many than discovery of new knowledge and authorities may punish those who raise probing questions highlighting the need for courage for discovery (Sternberg & Lubart, 1995).

SUMMARY

The quality of becoming rather than of being characterizes a professional. This requires a commitment to enhance and maintain values, knowledge, and skills that maximize the likelihood of increasing the personal welfare of clients and involved others and avoiding harm. Responding to mistakes as learning opportunities and recognizing the limits of your ability to help as well as the uncertainty involved in everyday practice, will help you to avoid the dissatisfaction and negative emotional reactions reflected in burnout. Avoiding self-handicapping excuses will also serve this end. Understanding how agencies and professional organizations function as well as social, political, and economic causes of problems will be useful in identifying constraints and options. Other steps you can take to maintain high quality service include evaluating practice, selecting practice knowledge and skills based on what has been found to be effective, and setting clear relevant service goals. Developing a guiding philosophy of practice and reviewing this in times of stress and discouragement will help you to focus on valued goals. If you develop the skills discussed in this chapter, you will not allow your vision of the potential of practice to be limited by what "is."

REVIEWING YOUR COMPETENCIES

Reviewing What You Know

1. Identify steps you can take to decrease the uncertainty involved in your work.
2. Describe factors related to burnout and what you can do to avoid them.
3. Identify specific changes that could be made in your agency to increase your work satisfaction and the quality of service.

4. Identify self-handicapping excuses and suggest constructive alternatives.
5. Describe helpful steps you can take to maintain valued skills.
6. Describe steps you can take to enhance valuable skills.

Reviewing What You Do

1. You welcome opportunities to examine the accuracy of your beliefs as shown in discussions with colleagues and clients (e.g., you seek constructive criticism).
2. Given an example of a setting in which staff experience "burn-out," you collect useful data and offer helpful recommendations.
3. You can help a colleague design methods to maintain valued skills.

Reviewing Results

1. You rate yourself high on work satisfaction and personal efficacy.
2. Clients, supervisers, and administrators give you high competency ratings.
3. Your practice skills increase each year as assessed by a review of methods used and service goals attained.

References

Abbott, A. (1988). *The system of professions: An essay on the division of expert labor*. Chicago: University of Chicago Press.

Abercrombie, M. L. J. (1960). *The anatomy of judgment*. New York: Basic Books.

Abramovitz, M. (1988). *Regulating the lives of women: Social welfare policy from colonial times to the present*. Boston: South End Press.

Abramson, L. Y., Seligman, M. E. P., & Teasdale, J. D. (1978). Learned helplessness in humans: Critique and reformulation. *Journal of Abnormal Psychology, 87*, 49–74.

Adams, J. L. (1986). *Conceptual blockbusting: A guide to better ideas* (3rd Ed.). Reading, MA: Addison-Wesley Publishing Co.

Adler, R. (1988). The placebo effect as a conditioned response. In R. Adler, H. Weiner, & A. Baum, *Experimental foundations of behavioral medicine: Conditioning approaches* (pp. 47–66). Hillsdale, NJ: Lawrence Erlbaum.

Alberti, R. & Emmons, M. (1995). *Your perfect right: A guide to assertive living* (7th Ed.). San Luis Obispo, CA: Impact.

Alberto, P. A. & Troutman, A. C. (1990). *Applied behavior analysis for teachers*. Columbus: Merrill.

Alessi, G. (1988). Diagnosis diagnosed: A systemic reaction. *Professional School Psychology, 32*, 145–151.

Alinsky, S. D. (1972). *Rules for radicals*. New York: Random House.

Altheide, D. L. & Johnson, J. M. (1980). *Bureaucratic propaganda*. Boston: Allyn & Bacon.

American Federation of State, County and Municipal Employees. (1990). *Guidelines for evaluating suspected sexual abuse in young children*. American Professional Society on Abuse of Children.

American Psychiatric Association. *Diagnostic and statistical manual of mental disorders* (4th Ed.). Washington, D.C.: American Psychiatric Association.

Amidei, N. (1987). How to be an advocate in bad times. *Public Welfare, 40*(3), 108–109.

Amir, Y. (1969). Contact hypothesis in ethnic relations. *Psychological Bulletin, 71*, 319–342.

Anastasi, A. (1988). *Psychological testing* (6th Ed.). New York: Macmillan.

Angel, R. & Thoits, P. (1987). The impact of culture on the cognitive structure of illness. *Culture, Medicine, and Psychiatry, 11*, 465–494.

Anthony, W. A., Cohen, M. R., & Farkas, J. R. (1990). *Psychiatric rehabilitation*. Boston, MA: Center for Psychiatric Rehabilitation, Boston University.

Anthony, W. A., Pierce, R. M., Cohen, M. R., & Cannon, J. R. (1980). *The skills of diagnostic planning: Psychiatric rehabilitation practice series. Book 1*. Baltimore: University Park Press.

Argyle, M. & Cook, M. (1976). *Gaze and mutual gaze*. London: Cambridge University Press.

Argyle, M., Furnham, A., & Graham, J. (1981). *Social situations*. Cambridge, England: Cambridge University Press.

Argyris, C. & Schon, D. A. (1996). *Organizational learning II: Theory, method, and practice*. Reading, MA: Addison Wesley.

Arkes, H. (1981). Impediments to accurate clinical judgment and possible ways to minimize their impact. *Journal of Consulting and Clinical Psychology, 49*, 323–330.

Armstrong, J. C. (1980). Unintelligible management research and academic prestige. *Interfaces, 10*, 80–86.

Arnold, J. E., Levine, A. G., & Patterson, G. R. (1975). Changes in sibling behavior following family intervention. *Journal of Consulting and Clinical Psychology, 43*, 683–688.

Arnoult, L. H. & Anderson, C. A. (1988). Identifying and reducing causal reasoning biases in clinical practice. In D. C. Turk & P. Salovy (Eds.), *Reasoning, inference and judgment in clinical psychology* (pp. 209–232). New York: Free Press.

Asch, S. E. (1956). Studies of independence and conformity: Minority of one against a unanimous majority. *Psychological Monographs, 70* (9, Whole No. 416).

Asher, S. R. & Coie, J. D. (Eds.). (1990). *Peer rejection in childhood.* New York: Cambridge University Press.

Asher, S. R., & Hymel, S. (1986). Coaching in social skills for children who lack friends in school. *Social Work in Education, 8,* 205–218.

Asimov, I. (1989). The relativity of wrong. *The Skeptical Inquirer, 14,* 35–44.

Austin, C. (1992). Have we oversold case management as a "quick fix" for our long-term care system? *Journal of Case Management, 7,* 61–65.

Austin, M. J. (1988). Managing up: Relationship building between middle management and top management. *Administration in Social Work, 12,* 29–46.

Averill, J. (1982). *Anger and aggression: Implications for theories of emotion.* New York: Springer-Verlag.

Axelrod, S., Spreat, S., Berry, B. & Moyer, L. (1993). A decision-making model for selecting the optimal treatment procedure. In R. Van Houten & S. Axelrod (Eds.), *Behavior analysis and treatment* (pp. 183–202). New York: Plenum Press.

Ayllon, T. & Azrin, N. H. (1968). *The token economy: A motivational system for therapy and rehabilitation.* New York: Appleton-Century-Crofts.

Ayllon, T. & Roberts, M. D. (1975). Mothers as educators for their children. In T. Travis & W. S. Dockens (Eds.), *Applications of behavior modification.* New York: Academic Press.

Azrin, N. H. (1976). Improvements in the community-reinforcement approach to alcoholism. *Behavior Research and Therapy, 14,* 339–348.

Azrin, N. H. & Holz, W. L. (1966). Punishment. In W. K. Honig (Ed.), *Operant behavior: Areas of research and application* (pp. 380–447). New York: Appleton-Century-Crofts.

Azrin, N. H., Philip, R. A., Thienes-Hontos, P., & Besalel, V. A. (1980). Comparative evaluation of the job club program with welfare recipients. *Journal of Vocational Behavior, 16,* 133–145.

Babor, T. F., Brown, J., & Del Boca, F. K. (1990). Validity of self-reports in applied research on addictive behaviors: Fact or fiction. *Behavioral Assessment, 12,* 5–31.

Bacharach, S. B. & Lawler, E. J. (1981). *Bargaining: Power, tactics and outcomes.* San Francisco: Jossey-Bass.

Bachrach, P. & Baratz, M. S. (1971). *Power and poverty: Theory and practice.* London: Oxford University Press.

Baer, D. M. (1982). Applied behavior analysis. In G. T. Wilson & C. M. Franks (Eds.), *Contemporary behavior therapy: Conceptual and empirical foundations* (pp. 277–309). New York: Guilford.

Baer, D. M. (1984). Future directions?: Or, is it useful to ask, "Where did we go wrong?" before we go. In R. F. Dangel & R. A. Polster (Eds.), *Parent training: Foundations to research and practice* (pp. 547–557). New York: Guilford Press.

Baer, D. M. (1987). Weak contingencies, strong contingencies, and many behaviors to change. *Journal of Applied Behavior Analysis, 20,* 335–337.

Baer, D. M. (1988). If you know why you're changing a behavior, you'll know when you've changed it enough. *Behavior Assessment, 10,* 219–223.

Baer, D. M. (1991). Tacting "to a fault." *Journal of Applied Behavior Analysis, 24,* 429–432.

Baer, D. M., Wolf, M. M., & Risley, T. R. (1968). Some current dimensions of applied behavior analysis. *Journal of Applied Behavior Analysis, 1,* 91–97.

Baer, D. M., Wolf, M. M., & Risley, T. R. (1987). Some still current dimensions of applied behavior analysis. *Journal of Applied Behavior Analysis, 20,* 311–327.

Bagdikian, B. H. (1992). *The media monopoly* (4th Ed.). Boston: Beacon Press.

Bailey, D. (1991). Designing and sustaining effective organizational teams. In R. L. Edwards & J. A. Yankey (Eds.), *Skills for effective human services management* (pp. 145–146). Silver Spring, MD: NASW.

Bailey, R. & Brake, M. (Eds.). (1975). *Radical social work.* New York: Pantheon.

Baines, C. T., Evans, P. M., & Neysmith, S. N. (1991). *Women's caring: Feminist perspectives on social welfare.* Toronto, Ontario: McClelland & Stewart.

Bakeman, R. & Gottman, J. M. (1986). *Observing interaction: An introduction to sequential analysis.* Cambridge, MA: Cambridge University Press.

Baker, P. J., Anderson, L. E., & Dorn, D. S. (1993). *Social problems: A critical thinking approach* (2nd Ed.). Belmont, CA: Wadsworth.

Balcazar, F., Hopkins, B. L., & Suarez, Y. (1986). A critical, objective review of performance feedback. *Journal of Organizational Behavior Management, 7,* 65–89.

Balcazar, F. E., Mathews, R. M., Francisco, V. T., Fawcett, S. B. and others. (1994). The empowerment process in four advocacy organizations of people with disabilities. *Rehabilitation Psychology, 39*, 189–203.

Balcazar, F. E., Seekins, T., Fawcett, S. B. & Hopkins, B. L. (1990). Empowering people with physical disabilities through advocacy skills training. *American Journal of Community Psychology, 18*(2), 281–296.

Balsam, P. D. & Bondy, A. S. (1983). The negative side effects of reward. *Journal of Applied Behavior Analysis, 16*, 283–296.

Baltes, M. M. (1988). The etiology and maintenance of dependency in the elderly: Three phases of operant research. *Behavior Therapy, 19*, 301–319.

Bandura, A. (1986). *Social foundations of thought and action.* Englewood Cliffs, NJ: Prentice-Hall.

Bandura, A., Blanchard, E. B., & Ritter, B. (1969). Relative efficacy of desensitization and modeling approaches for inducing behavioral, affective, and attitudinal changes. *Journal of Personality and Social Psychology, 13*, 173–199.

Bank, L., Marlowe, J. H., Reid, J. B., Patterson, G. R., & Weinrott, M. R. (1991). A comparative evaluation of parent training for families of chronic delinquents. *Journal of Abnormal Child Psychology, 19*, 15–33.

Bank, L., Patterson, G. R., & Reid, J. B. (1987). Delinquency prevention through training parents in family management. *The Behavior Analyst, 10*, 75–82.

Banta, H. D. (1984). Embracing or rejecting innovations: clinical diffusion of health care technology. In S. Reiser & M. Anbar (Eds.). *The machine at the bedside* (pp. 65–92). Cambridge, MA: Cambridge University Press.

Barker, R. L. (1987). *The social work dictionary.* Silver Spring, MD: National Association of Social Workers (3rd Ed., 1995).

Barlow, D. H. (1988). *Anxiety and its disorders: The nature and treatment of anxiety and panic.* New York: Guilford.

Barlow, D. H. (1993). *Clinical handbook of psychological disorders: A step-by-step treatment manual* (2nd Ed.). New York: Guilford.

Barlow, D. H. & Craske, M. G. (1990). *Mastery of your anxiety and panic (MAP).* Graywind Publications, c/o 1535 Western Ave. Albany, NY 12203.

Barlow, D. H., Hayes, S. C., & Nelson, R. O. (1990). *The scientist practitioner: Research and accountability in clinical and educational settings.* New York: Pergamon.

Baron, J. (1985). *Rationality and intelligence.* New York: Cambridge University Press.

Baron, J. (1994). *Thinking and deciding* (2nd Ed.). New York: Cambridge University Press.

Baron, J. & Brown, R. V. (Eds.). (1991). *Teaching decision making to adolescents.* Hillsdale, NJ: Lawrence Erlbaum.

Barone, V. J., Greene, B. F., & Lutzker, J. L. (1986). Home safety with families being treated for child abuse and neglect. *Behavior Modification, 10*, 93–114.

Barrera, M., Sandler, I. N., & Ramsey, T. B. (1981). Preliminary development of a scale of social support: Studies on college students. *American Journal of Community Psychology, 9*, 435–447.

Barrows, H. S. (1994). *Practice-based learning: Problem-based learning applied to medical education.* Springfield, IL: Southern Illinois University School of Medicine.

Barth, R. P. & Gambrill, E. (1984). Learning to interview: The quality of training opportunities. *The Clinical Supervisor, 2*, 3–14.

Bartley, W. W., III (1984). *The retreat to commitment.* LaSalle, IL: Open Court.

Bates, P., Morrow, S. A., Pancsofar, E., & Sedlak, R. (1984). The effect of functional vs non-functional activities on attitudes/expectations of non-handicapped college students: What they see is what we get. *Journal of the Association for Persons With Severe Handicaps, 9*, 73–78.

Batson, C. D., Jones, C. H., & Cochran, P. J. (1979). Attributional bias in counselors' diagnosis: The effects of resources on perception of need. *Journal of Applied Social Psychology, 9*, 377–393.

Batson, C. D., O'Quin, K., & Pych, V. (1982). An attribution theory analysis of trained helpers' inferences about clients' needs. In T. A. Wills (Ed.), *Basic processes in helping relationships* (pp. 59–80). New York: Academic Press.

Beck, A. T., Rush, A. J., Shaw, B. F., & Emery, G. (1979). *Cognitive therapy of depression.* New York: Guilford.

Beck, A. T. & Emery, G. (1985). *Anxiety disorders and phobias: A cognitive perspective.* New York: Basic.

Beck, A. T., Freeman, A. & Associates. (1990). *Cognitive therapy of personality disorders.* New York: Guilford.

Beck, A. T., Ward, C. H., Mendelson, M., Mock, J., & Erbaugh, J. (1961). An inventory for measuring depression. *Archives of General Psychiatry, 4*, 561–571.

Beck, P., Byyny, R. L., & Adams, K. S. (1981). *Case exercises in clinical reasoning.* Chicago: Yearbook Medical.

Bellack, A. S. & Hersen, M. (Eds.). (1987). *Research and practice in social skills training* (3rd Ed.). New York: Plenum.

Bellack, A. S. & Hersen, M. (Eds.). (1988). *Behavioral assessment: A practical handbook* (3rd Ed.). New York: Pergamon.

Bellah, R., Madsen, R., Sullivan, W., Swidler, A., & Tipton, S. (1985). *Habits of the heart: Individualism and commitment in American life.* New York: Harper.

Belle, D. (1989). *Children's social networks and social supports.* New York: John Wiley.

Belle, D. (1990). Poverty and women's mental health. *American Psychologist, 45,* 385–389.

Benjamin-Bauman, J., Reiss, M. L., & Bailey, J. S. (1984). Increasing appointment keeping by reducing the call-appointment interval. *Journal of Applied Behavior Analysis, 17*(3), 295–301.

Bennett, E. M. (Ed.). (1987). *Social intervention: Theory and practice.* Lewiston, NY: Edwin Mellen Press.

Benson, H. (1967). *Dollars and sense: Ideology, ethics, and the meaning of work in profit and non-profit organizations.* New York: Macmillan.

Bergan, J. R. & Kratochwill, T. R. (1990). *Behavioral consultation and therapy.* New York: Plenum.

Berger, P. L. & Luckman, T. (1966). *The social construction of reality.* New York: Doubleday.

Bergin, A. E. & Garfield, S. L. (Eds.). (1994). *Handbook of psychotherapy and behavior change* (4th Ed.). New York: John Wiley.

Berk, R. A. & Rossi, P. H. (1990). *Thinking about program evaluation.* Newbury Park: Sage.

Berkowitz, L. (1994). Is something missing? Some observations prompted by the cognitive-neo associationist view of anger and emotional aggression. In L. R. Huesmann (Ed.), *Aggressive behavior: Current perspectives* (pp. 35–57). New York: Plenum.

Berliner, A. K. (1989). Misconduct in social work practice. *Social Work, 34,* 69–72.

Berndt, T. & Ladd, G. (Eds.). (1989). *Peer relationships in child development.* New York: John Wiley & Sons.

Bernstein, D. A. & Borkovec, T. D. (1973). *Progressive relaxation: A manual for the helping professions.* Champaign, IL: Research Press.

Berry, J. W. (1991). Refugee adaptation in settlement countries: An overview with an emphasis on primary prevention. In F. L. Ahearn, Jr. & J. L. Athey, *Refugee children: Theory, research, and services* (pp. 19–38). Baltimore: The Johns Hopkins University Press.

Besharov, D. J. (1985). *The vulnerable social worker: Liability for serving children and families.* Silver Spring, MD: National Association of Social Workers.

Best, J. (1988). Missing children, misleading statistics. *Public Interest, 92,* 84–92.

Beyerstein, B. L. (1990). Brainscams: Neuromythologies of the new age. *International Journal of Mental Health, 19,* 27–36.

Beyth-Marom, R., Fischhoff, B., & Quadrel, M. J. (1991). Teaching decision making to adolescents: A critical review. In J. Baron & R. V. Brown (Eds.), *Teaching decision making to adolescents* (pp. 19–59). Hillsdale, NJ: Lawrence Erlbaum.

Bigelow, K. M., Huynen, K. B., & Lutzker, J. R. (1993). Using a changing criterion design to teach fire escape to a child with developmental disabilities. *Journal of Developmental and Physical Disabilities, 5,* 121–128.

Biglan, A. (1987). A behavior-analytic critique of Bandura's self-efficacy theory. *Behavior Analyst, 10,* 1–15.

Biglan, A. (1996). The need for a science for changing cultural practices. Paper presented at the 22nd Annual Conference, Association for Behavior Analysis, San Francisco, CA, May 25.

Biglan, A., Hops, H., Sherman, L., Friedman, L., Arthur, J. & Osteen, V. (1985). Problem-solving interactions of depressed women and their husbands. *Behavior Therapy, 16,* 431–451.

Biglan, A., Lewin, L., & Hops, H. (1990). A contextual approach to the problem of aversive practices in families. In G. R. Patterson (Ed.), *Depression and aggression in family interaction* (pp. 103–129). Hillsdale, NJ: Lawrence Erlbaum and Associates.

Birnbrauer, J. S. (1990). Responsibility and quality of life. In A. C. Repp & N. N. Singh (Eds.), *Perspectives on the use of non-aversive and aversive interventions for persons with developmental disabilities* (pp. 231–236). Sycamore, IL: Sycamore Press.

Birnbrauer, J. S. (1994). Should only positive methods be used by professionals who work with children and adolescents? No. In M. A. Mason & E. Gambrill (Eds.), *Debating children's lives: Current controversies on children and adolescents* (pp. 237–242). Newbury Park: Sage.

Blalock, H. M., Jr. (1984). *Basic dilemmas in the social sciences.* Newbury Park, CA: Sage.

Blenkner, M., Bloom, M., & Nielsen, M. (1971). A research and demonstration project of protective service. *Social Casework, 52,* 483–499.

Block, P. (1981). *Flawless consulting: A guide to getting your expertise used.* San Diego, CA: Pfeiffer & Co.

Bloom, M., Fischer, J., & Orme, J. G. (1995). *Evaluating practice: Guidelines for the accountable professional* (2nd Ed.). Englewood Cliffs, NJ: Prentice-Hall.

Bobo, K., Kendall, J., & Max, S. (1991). *Organizing for social change: A manual for activists in the 1990s.* Cabin John, MD: Seven Locks Press.

Bond, L. A. & Compas, B. E. (Eds.). (1989). *Primary prevention and promotion in the schools.* Newbury Park: Sage.

Booth, A. & Dunn, J. (Eds.). (1994). *Stepfamilies: Who benefits? Who does not?* Hillsdale, NJ: Lawrence Erlbaum.

Borduin, C. M., Mann, B. J., Cone, L. T., Henggeler, S. W., Fucci, B. R., Blaske, D. M., & Williams, R. A. (1995). Multisystemic treatment of serious juvenile offenders: Long-term prevention of criminality and violence. *Journal of Consulting and Clinical Psychology, 63,* 569–578.

Boring, C. C., Squires, T. S., & Heath, C. W. (1992). Cancer statistics for African Americans. *CA—A Cancer Journal for Clinicians, 42,* 7–17.

Bosk, C. L. (1979). *Forgive and remember: Managing medical failure.* Chicago: University of Chicago Press.

Bowles, E. (1976). Older persons as providers of services: Three federal programs. *Social Policy,* Nov-Dec., 81–88.

Boyer, R. O. & Morais, H. H. (1994). *Labor's untold story* (3rd Ed.). Pittsburgh, PA: United Electrical, Radio and Machine Workers of America. (Originally published in 1974.)

Boyle, M. (1990). *Schizophrenia: A scientific delusion?* London: Routledge.

Bradshaw, J. (1972). The concept of social need. *New Society, 30,* 640–643.

Bransford, J. D. & Stein, B. S. (1984). *The IDEAL problem solver: A guide for improving thinking, learning, and creativity.* New York: W. H. Freeman.

Bransford, J. D., Vye, N. J., Adams, L. T., & Perfetto, G. A. (1989). Learning skills and the acquisition of knowledge. In A. Lesgold & R. Glaser (Eds.), *Foundation for a psychology of education* (pp. 199–250). Hillsdale, NJ: Lawrence Erlbaum.

Breggin, P. R. (1990). Brain damage, dementia, and persistent cognitive dysfunction associated with neuroleptic drugs: Evidence, etiology, implications. *Journal of Mind and Behavior, 11,* 425–463.

Breggin, P. R. (1991). *Toxic psychiatry.* New York: St. Martin's Press.

Breton, M. (1988). The need for material aid groups in a drop-in for homeless women: The sistering case. *Social Work With Groups, 11,* 47–61.

Brickman, P., Rabinowitz, V. C., Karuza, J., Jr., Coates, D., Cohn, E., & Kidder, L. (1982). Models of helping and coping. *American Psychologist, 37,* 368–384.

Briscoe, R. V., Hoffman, D. B., & Bailey, J. S. (1975). Behavioral community psychology: Training a community board to problem solve. *Journal of Applied Behavior Analysis, 8,* 157–168.

Brody, L. R. & Hall, J. A. (1993). Gender and emotion. In M. Lewis & J. M. Haviland (Eds.), *Handbook of emotions* (pp. 447–460). New York: Guilford Press.

Bronfenbrenner, U. (1979). *The ecology of human development: Experiments by nature and design.* Cambridge, MA: Harvard University Press.

Brookfield, S. D. (1987). *Developing critical thinkers: Challenging adults to explore alternative ways of thinking and acting.* San Francisco: Jossey-Bass.

Brookfield, S. (1995). *Becoming a critically reflective teacher.* San Francisco: Jossey-Bass.

Brown, G. W. & Harris, T. (1978). *Social origins of depression: A study of psychiatric disorders in women.* New York: Free Press.

Brown, P. & Funk, S. C. (1986). Tardive dyskinesia: Barriers to the professional recognition of an iatrogenic disease. *Journal of Health and Social Behavior, 27,* 116–132.

Browning, R. M. & Stover, D. O. (1971). *Behavior modification in child treatment: An experimental and clinical approach.* Chicago: Aldine.

Budney, A. J., Higgins, S. T., Delaney, D. D., Kent, L., & Bickel, W. K. (1991). Contingent reinforcement of abstinence with individuals abusing cocaine and marijuana. *Journal of Applied Behavior Analysis, 24,* 657–665.

Buege v Iowa, No. 20521 (Allamakee, Iowa, 30 July, 1980).

Buie, J. (1987, December). Newspaper's tone, errors irk sources. *APA Monitor, 18,* 23.

Bullmore, E., Joyce, H., Marks, I. M., & Connolly, J. (1992). A computerized quality assurance system (QAS) on a general psychiatric ward: Towards efficient clinical audit. *Journal of Mental Health, 1,* 257–263.

Bulmer, M. (1986). *Neighbors: The work of Phillip Abram.* Cambridge, England: Cambridge University Press.

Bunge, M. (1984). What is pseudoscience? *The Skeptical Inquirer, 9*(1), 36–47.

Burchard, J. D. & Schaefer, M. C. (1992). Improving accountability in a service delivery system in children's mental health. *Clinical Psychology Review, 12,* 867–882.

Burish, T. J., Snyder, S. L., & Jenkins, R. A. (1991). Preparing patients for cancer chemotherapy: Effects of coping preparation and relaxation interventions. *Journal of Consulting and Clinical Psychology, 59,* 518–525.

Burnham, J. C. (1987). *How superstition won and science lost: Popularizing science and health in the United States.* New Brunswick: Rutgers University Press.

Burns, D. D. (1990). *Feeling good: The new mood therapy.* New York: William Morrow.

Burns, D. (1995). Workshop on anxiety and depression. Emeryville, CA.

Burns, D. D. & Nolen-Hoeksema, S. (1992). Therapeutic empathy and recovery from depression in cognitive-behavioral therapy: A structural equation model. *Journal of Consulting and Clinical Psychology, 60,* 441–449.

Busse, R. T., Kratochwill, T. R., & Elliott, S. N. (1995). Meta-analysis for single-case consultation outcomes: Applications to research and practice. *Journal of School Psychology, 33,* 269–285.

Butterfield, W. H. (1993). Graphics. In L. Beebe (Ed.), *Professional writing for the human services* (pp. 105–150). Washington, D.C.: National Association of Social Workers.

Bynum, W. F., Browne, E. J. Porter, R. (Eds.). (1985). *Dictionary of the history of science.* Princeton: Princeton University Press.

California State Department of Consumer Affairs. (1990). *Client bill of rights.* (p. 16). Sacramento, CA.

Calvert, J. D. (1988). Physical attractiveness: A review of reevaluation of its role in social skill research. *Behavioral Assessment, 10,* 29–42.

Campbell, D. T. & Stanley, J. C. (1963). *Experimental and quasi-experimental design for research.* Chicago, IL: Rand McNally.

Campbell, J. A. (1988). Client acceptance of single-system evaluation procedures. *Social Work Research and Abstracts, 24,* 21–22.

Canavan-Gumpert, D. (1977). Generating reward and cost orientations through praise and criticism. *Journal of Personality and Social Psychology, 35,* 501–513.

Caplow, T. (1994). *Perverse incentives: The neglect of social technology in the public sector.* Westport, CT: Praeger.

Carkhuff, R. R. & Anthony, W. A. (1979). *The skills of helping.* Amherst, MA: Human Resource Development Press.

Carr, E. G. (1985). Behavioral approaches to language and communication. In E. Schlopler & G. B. Mesibov (Eds.), *Communication problems in autism* (pp. 35–57). New York: Plenum.

Carr, E. G. & Durand, M. V. (1985). The social-communicative basis of severe behavior problems in children. In S. Reiss & R. R. Bootzin (Eds.), *Theoretical issues in behavior therapy* (pp. 219–254). New York: Academic Press.

Carr, E. G. & Durand, V. M. (1985). Reducing problem behaviors through functional communication training. *Journal of Applied Behavior Analysis, 18,* 111–126.

Carr, E. G., Levin, L., McConnachie, G., Carlson, J. I., Kemp, D. C., & Smith, C. E. (1994). *Communication-based intervention for problem behavior: A user's guide for producing positive change.* Baltimore: Paul H. Brookes.

Carr, E. G., Robinson, S., & Palumbo, L. W. (1990). The wrong issue: Aversive versus nonaversive treatment. The right issue: functional versus non-functional treatment. In A. C. Repp & N. N. Singh (Eds.), *Perspectives on the use of nonaversive and aversive interventions for persons with developmental disabilities* (pp. 361–379). Sycamore, IL: Sycamore Press.

Cash, W. M. & Evans, I. M. (1975). Training preschool children to modify their retarded siblings' behavior. *Journal of Behavior Therapy and Experimental Psychiatry, 6,* 13–16.

Ceci, S. J. & Bruck, M. (1993). Suggestibility of the child witness: A historical review and synthesis. *Psychological Bulletin, 113*(3), 403–439.

Ceci, S. J. & Bruck, M. (1995). *Jeopardy in the courtroom: A scientific analysis of children's testimony.* Washington, D.C.: American Psychological Association.

Ceci, S. J., Crotteau-Huffman, M., Smith, E., & Loftus, E. W. (1994). Repeatedly thinking about non-events. *Consciousness and Cognition, 3,* 388–407.

Censored, The news that didn't make the news—and

why. Carl Jesnon & Project Censored. New York: Four Walls Eight Windows.

Chadsey-Rusch, J. (1986). Identifying and teaching valued social behavior. In F. R. Rusch (Ed.), *Competitive employment: Issues and strategies* (pp. 273–287). Baltimore: Paul H. Brookes.

Chamberlain, P. & Baldwin, D. V. (1988). Client resistance to parent training: Its therapeutic management. In T. R. Kratochwill (Ed.), *Advances in school psychology* (Vol. 6 of a series) (pp. 131–171). Hillsdale, NJ: Lawrence Erlbaum.

Chamberlain, P. & Patterson, G. R. (1995). Discipline and child compliance in parenting. In M. H. Bornstein (Ed.), *Handbook of Parenting, Vol. 4: Applied and Practical parenting* (pp. 205–225). Mahwah, NJ: Laurence Erlbaum.

Chapman, L. J. & Chapman, J. P. (1969). Illusory correlation as an obstacle to the use of valid psychodiagnostic signs. *Journal of Abnormal Psychology, 74*, 271–280.

Chavis, D. & Wandersman, A. (1990). Sense of community in the urban environment: A catalyst for participation and community development. *American Journal of Community Psychology, 18*, 55–82.

Chi, M. T. H., Glaser, R., Farr, M. J. (Eds.), (1988). *The nature of expertise*. Hillsdale, NJ: Lawrence Erlbaum.

Christian, W. P. & Romanczyki, R. G. (1986). Evaluation. In F. J. Fucco & W. P. Christian (Eds.), *Behavior analysis and therapy in residential programs* (pp. 145–193). New York: Van Nostrand.

Cialdini, R. B. (1984). *Influence: The new psychology of modern persuasion*. New York: Quill.

Cialdini, R. B. (1993). *Influence: Science and practice* (3rd Ed.). New York: Harper.

Ciminero, A. R., Calhoun, K. S., & Adams, H. E. (Eds.). (1986). *Handbook of behavioral assessment* (2nd Ed.). New York: John Wiley.

Ciminero, A. R., Nelson, R. O., & Lipinski, D. P. (1986). Self-monitoring procedures. In A. R. Ciminero, K. S. Calhoun, & H. E. Adams (Eds.), *Handbook of behavioral assessment* (2nd Ed.) (pp. 195–232). New York: John Wiley.

Clancy, P. (1986). The acquisition of communication style in Japanese. In B. R. Schieffelin & E. Ochs (Eds.), *Language acquisition and socialization across cultures* (pp. 213–250). Cambridge: Cambridge University Press.

Clark, C. L. & Asquith, S. (1985). *Social work and social philosophy: A guide for practice*. London: Routledge & Kegan Paul.

Clark, H. B., Greene, B. F., Macrae, J. W., McNees, M. P., Davis, J. L., & Risley, T. R. (1977). A parent advice package for family shopping trips: Development and evaluation. *Journal of Applied Behavior Analysis, 10*, 605–624.

Clark, M., Miller, L. S., & Pruger, R. (1980). Treating clients fairly: Equity in the distribution of in-home supportive services. *Journal of Social Service Research, 4*, 47–60.

Cloward, R. A. & Epstein, I. (1965). Private social welfare's disengagement from the poor: The case of family adjustment agencies. In M. Zald (1st Ed.), *Social welfare institutions* (pp. 623–644). New York: John Wiley & Sons.

Coates, T. J. (1990). Strategies for modifying sexual behavior for primary and secondary prevention of HIV disease. *Journal of Consulting and Clinical Psychology, 58*, 57–69.

Cohen, L., Sargent, M., & Sechrest, L. (1986). Use of psychotherapy research by professional psychologists. *American Psychologist, 41*, 198–206.

Cohen, S. J., Weinberger, M., Hui, L. S., Tierney, W. M., & McDonald, C. J. (1985). The impact of reading on physicians' nonadherence to recommended standards of medical care. *Social Science and Medicine, 21*, 909–914.

Cohen, S. & Syme, S. L. (Eds.). (1985). *Social support and health*. New York: Springer.

Collins, R. (1988). Lessons in compassion for student doctors. *Sunday New York Times*, Aug. 7, A7.

Colman, A. M. (1987). *Facts, fallacies and frauds in psychology*. London: Hutchinson.

Comstock, G. D. (1991). *Violence against lesbians and gay men*. New York: Columbia University Press.

Conrad, P. & Schneider, J. W. (1992). *Deviance and medicalization: From badness to sickness*. Philadelphia: Temple University Press.

Cooper, J. O., Heron, T. E., & Heward, W. L. (1987). *Applied behavior analysis*. Columbus: Merrill.

Cormier, W. H. & Cormier, L. S. (1991). *Interviewing strategies for helpers: Fundamental skills and cognitive behavioral interventions* (3rd Ed.). Monterey, CA: Brooks/Cole.

Corteen, R. S. & Williams, T. (1986). Television and reading skills. In T. Williams (Ed.), *The impact of television: A natural experiment in three communities* (pp. 39–86). Orlando, FL: Academic.

Craighead, L. W., Craighead, W. E., Kazdin, A. E., & Mahoney, M. J. (1994). *Cognitive and behavioral interventions: An empirical approach to mental health problems*. Boston: Allyn and Bacon.

Craighead, W. E., Mercatoris, M., & Bellack B. (1974). A brief report on mentally retarded residents as behavioral observers. *Journal of Applied Behavior Analysis, 7,* 333–340.

Craske, M. G., Barlow, D. H., & O'Leary, T. (1992). *Mastery of your anxiety & worry.* Albany, NY: Graywind Publications.

Crowell, J. (1982). Understanding clinical staff's views of administration. In M. J. Austin & W. E. Hershey (Eds.), *Handbook on mental health administration* (pp. 18–35). San Francisco, CA: Jossey-Bass.

Cudaback, C., Darden, C., Nelson, P., O'Brien, S., Pinsky, D. & Wiggins, E. (1985). Becoming successful parents: Can age-based newsletters help? *Family Relations, 4,* 271–275.

Cummings, N. A. (1977). Prolonged (ideal) versus short-term (realistic) psychotherapy. *Professional Psychology, 2,* 491–501.

Curtis, R. C. (1989). *Self-defeating behaviors: Experimental research, clinical impressions, and practice implications.* New York: Plenum.

Daly, M. & Wilson, M. (1988). *Homicide.* New York: Aldine de Gruyter.

Damer, T. E. (1995). *Attacking faculty reasoning: A practical guide to fallacy free arguments* (3rd. Ed.). Belmont, CA: Wadsworth.

Dangel, R. F., Deschner, J. P., & Rasp, R. R. (1989). Anger control training for adolescents in residential treatment. *Behavior Modification, 13,* 447–458.

Dangel, R. F. & Polster, R. A. (1988). *Teaching child management skills.* New York: Pergamon.

D'Augelli, A. R. (1989). The development of a helping community for lesbian and gay men: A case study in community psychology. *Journal of Community Psychology, 17,* 18–29.

D'Augelli, A. R., Vallance, T. R., Danish, S. J., Young, C. E., & Gerdes, J. L. (1981). The community helpers' project: A description of a prevention strategy for rural communities. *Journal of Prevention, 1,* 209–224.

Daniels, A. C. (1990). *Performance management: Improving quality productivity through positive reinforcement.* Tucker, GA: Aubrey Daniels & Associates.

Daniels, A. C. (1994). *Bringing out the best in people.* New York: McGraw Hill.

Daniels, A. K. (1973). How free should professions be? In E. Freidson (Ed.), *The professions and their prospects.* Beverly Hills, CA: Sage.

Davis, K. & Newstrom, J. W. (1989). *Human behavior at work: Organizational behavior* (8th Ed.). New York: McGraw-Hill.

Davis, L. E. & Proctor, E. K. (1989). *Race, gender and class: Guidelines for practice with individuals, families, and groups.* Englewood Cliffs, NJ; Prentice Hall.

Dawes, R. M. (1982). The value of being explicit when making clinical decisions. In T. A. Wills (Ed.), *Basic processes in helping relationships* (pp. 37–58). New York: Academic Press.

Dawes, R. M. (1988). *Rational choice in an uncertain world.* Orlando: Harcourt, Brace Jovanovich.

Dawes, R. M. (1993). Prediction of the future versus an understanding of the past: A basic asymmetry. *American Journal of Psychology, 106,* 1–24.

Dawes, R. M. (1994a). *House of cards: Psychology and psychotherapy built on myth.* New York: Free Press.

Dawes, R. M. (1994b). On the necessity of examining all four cells in a 2×2 table. *Making better decisions.* 1(2), pp. 2–4. Pacific Grove, CA: Brooks/Cole.

Dawes, R. M., Faust, D., & Meehl, P. E. (1989). Clinical versus actuarial judgement. *Science, 243,* 1668–1674.

Day, W. (1983). On the difference between radical and methodological behaviorism. *Behaviorism, 11,* 89–102.

de Anda, D. (1984). Bicultural socialization: Factors affecting the minority experience. *Social Work, 29*(3), 101–107.

Deacon, J. R. & Konarski, E. A., Jr. (1987). Correspondence training: An exampleof rule-governed behavior? *Journal of Applied Behavior Analysis, 20,* 391–400.

Dean, G. (1986–1987). Does astrology need to be true? Part 1: A look at the real thing. *The Skeptical Inquirer, 11*(2), 166–185.

Dean, G. (1987). Does astrology need to be true? Part 2: The answer is no. *The Skeptical Inquirer, 11*(3), 257–273.

DeBortali-Tregerthan, G. J. (1979). Behavioral treatment of child abuse: A case report. *Child Behavior Therapy, 1,* 287–294.

Decker, L. E. (1992). Thinking and acting from a broad perspective: Community education. In C. Collins & J. N. Mangieri (Eds.), *Teaching thinking: An agenda for the twenty-first century* (pp. 257–268). Hillsdale, NJ: Erlbaum.

Demott, B. (1990). *The imperial middle: Why Americans can't think straight about class.* New York: William Morrow.

Denicola, J. & Sandler, J. (1980). Training abusive parents in cognitive-behavioral techniques. *Behavior Therapy, 11,* 263–270.

Derlaga, V. J. & Berg, J. H. (Eds.). (1987). *Self-disclo-*

sure: Theory, research and therapy. New York: Plenum.

DeVos, G. (1985). Dimensions of the self in Japanese Culture. In A. J. Marsella, G. Devos, & F. L. K. Hsu (Eds.), *Culture and self* (pp. 141–184). New York: Tavistock Publications.

Dewey, J. (1933). *How we think: A restatement of the relation of reflective thinking to the education process.* Boston: Heath.

Dickinson, A. M. (1989). The detrimental effects of extrinsic reinforcement on "intrinsic motivation." *The Behavior Analyst, 12,* 1–15.

Dingwall, R., Eekelaar, J., & Murray, T. (1983). *The protection of children.* Oxford, England: Basil Blackwell.

Dishion, T. J., Patterson, G. R., & Griesler, P. C. (1994). Peer adaptations in the development of antisocial behavior: A confluence model. In L. R. Huesmann (Ed.), *Aggressive behavior: Current perspectives* (pp. 61–95). New York: Plenum.

Dishion, T. J., Patterson, G. R., & Kavanagh, K. A. (1992). An experimental test of the coercion model: Linking theory, measurement, and intervention. In J. McCord & R. E. Tremblay (Eds.), *Preventing antisocial behavior: Interventions from birth through adolescence* (pp. 253–282). New York: Guilford Press.

Dixon, S. (1987). *Working with people in crisis* (2nd ed.). Columbus, OH: Merrill.

Dluhy, M. J. (1990). *Building coalitions in the human services.* Newbury Park: Sage.

Dobson, K. S. (Ed.). (1988). *Handbook of cognitive-behavioral therapies.* New York: Guilford.

Dodge, K. A. (1993). Social-cognitive mechanisms in the development of conduct disorder and depression. *Annual Review of Psychology, 44,* 559–584.

Dodge, K. A., Asher, S. R., & Parkhurst, J. T. (1989). Social life as a goal-coordination task. In R. Ames and C. Ames (Eds.), *Research on motivation in education.* New York: Academic.

Domjan, M. (1983). Biological constraints on instrumental and classical conditioning: Implications for general process theory. In G. H. Bower (Ed.), *The psychology of learning and motivation* (pp. 215–277). New York: Academic.

Donnellan, A. M., Mirenda, P. L., Mesaros, R. A., & Fassbender, L. L. (1984). Analyzing the communicative functions of aberrant behavior. *Journal of the Association For Persons With Severe Handicaps, 9 ,* 201–212.

Douglas, M. S. & Mueser, K. T. (1990). Teaching conflict resolution skills to the chronically mentally ill. *Behavior Modification, 14,* 519–547.

Dovidio, J. F. & Gaertner, S. L. (1986). *Prejudice, discrimination, and racism.* Orlando, FL: Academic Press.

Drake, R. E., McHugo, G. J., Becker, D. R., Anthony, W. A., and others. (1996). The New Hampshire study of supported employment for people with severe mental illness. *Journal of Consulting and Clinical Psychology, 64,* 291–399.

Dreyfus, H. L. & Dreyfus, S. E. (1986). *Mind over machine: The power of human intuition and expertise in the era of the computer.* New York: Free Press.

Druckman, D. & Bjork, R. A. (Eds.). (1991). *In the mind's eye: Enhancing human performance.* Washington, D.C.: National Academy Press.

Drury, S. S. (1984). *Assertive supervision: Building involved teamwork.* Champaign, IL: Research Press.

Duck, S. (Ed.). (1990). *Personal relationships and social support.* London: Sage.

Duffy, K. G., Grosch, J. W., & Olczak, P. V. (Eds.). (1991). *Community mediation: A handbook for practitioners and researchers.* New York: Guilford.

Dugger, C. W. (1992). As mother killed her son, protectors observed privacy. *New York Times,* 2/10/92, A1/16.

Dunbar, J. M., Marshall, G. D., & Hovell, M. F. (1979). Behavioral strategies for improving compliance. In R. B. Haynes, D. W. Taylor, & D. L. Sackett (Eds.), *Compliance in health care* (pp. 174–190). Baltimore, MD: John Hopkins Press.

Dutton, D. B. (1988). *Worse than the disease: Pitfalls of medical progress* (pp. 339–340). New York: Cambridge University Press.

Dweck, C. S. (1975). The role of expectations and attributions in the alteration of learned helplessness. *Journal of Personality and Social Psychology, 31,* 674–685.

Dweck, C. S. (1989). Motivation. In A. Lesgold & R. Glaser (Eds.), *Foundation for a psychology of education* (pp. 87–135). Hillsdale, NJ: Lawrence Erlbaum.

Eddy, D. M. (1982). Probabilistic reasoning in clinical medicine: Problems and opportunities. In D. Kahneman, P. Slovic, & A. Tversky (Eds.), *Judgment under uncertainty: Hueristics and biases.* New York: Cambridge University Press.

Eddy, D. (1990). Clinical decision making: From theory to practice: Comparing benefits and harms: The balance sheet. *Journal of the American Medical Association, 263,* 2493–2505.

Edleson, J. L. & Tolman, R. M. (1992). *Intervention for men who batter: An ecological approach.* Newbury Park: Sage.

Edelstein, B. A. & Michelson, L. (Eds.). (1986). *Handbook of prevention.* New York: Plenum.

Edwards, V. (1938). *Group leader's guide to propaganda analysis.* New York City, NY: Institute for Propaganda Analysis (p. 28).

Egan, G. (1975). *The skilled helper: A model for systematic helping and interpersonal relating.* Monterey, CA: Brooks/Cole.

Egan, G. (1994). *The skilled helper: A problem-management approach to helping* (5th Ed.). Pacific Grove, CA: Brooks/Cole.

Ehrenreich, B. (1990). *Fear of falling: The inner life of the middle class.* New York: Harper Collins.

Ehrenreich, B. & English, D. (1973). *Complaint and disorders: The sexual politics of sickness.* Glass Mountain Pamphlet #2. The Feminist Press.

Ehrenreich, J. H. (1985). *The altruistic imagination: A history of social work and social policy in the United States.* Ithaca: Cornell University Press.

Einhorn, H. J. (1980). Overconfidence in judgement. In R. A. Shweder (Ed.), *New directions for methodology in social and behavioral science: No. 4. Fallible judgment in behavioral research* (pp. 1–16). San Francisco: Jossey-Bass.

Einhorn, H. J. (1988). Diagnosis and causality in clinical and statistical prediction. In D. C. Turk & P. Salovey (Eds.), *Reasoning, inference and judgment in clinical psychology* (pp. 51–70). New York; Free Press.

Eisenberg, J. M. (1986). *Doctors' decisions and the cost of medical care.* Ann Arbor, MI: Health Administration Press Perspectives.

Eisenberg, R. & Cameron J. (1996). Detrimental effected reward: Reality or myth? *American Psychologist, 51,* 1153–1166.

Ekman, P. (1994). All emotions are basic. In P. Ekman & R. J. Davidson (Eds.), *The nature of emotion: Fundamental questions* (pp. 15–19). New York: Oxford University Press.

Ekman, P. & Davidson, R. J. (Eds.). (1994). *The nature of emotion: Fundamental questions.* New York: Oxford University Press.

Elias, M. J. & Tobias, S. E. (1996). *Social problem solving: Interventions in the schools.* New York: Guilford.

Elliott, A., O'Donohue, W. T., & Nickerson, M. A. (1993). The use of sexually anatomically detailed dolls in the assessment of sexual abuse. *Clinical Psychology Review, 13,* 207–221.

Ellis, A. (1962). *Reason and emotion in psychotherapy.* New York: Carol Pub.

Ellis, A. (1996) *Better, deeper, and more enduring brief therapy: The rational-emotive behavior therapy approach.* New York: Brunner/Mazel.

Ellis, A. & Dryden, W. (1996). *The practice of rational-emotive therapy* (2nd Ed.). New York: Springer.

Ellis, A. & Harper, R. A. (1975). *A new guide to rational living.* North Hollywood, CA: Wilshire Book Company.

Ellis, A. & Yeager, R. J. (1989). *Why some therapies don't work.* Buffalo: Prometheus Books.

Ellul, J. (1965). *Propaganda: The formation of men's attitudes.* New York: Vintage.

Elstein, A. S. (1988). Cognitive processes in clinical inference and decision making. In D. C. Turk & P. Salovey (Eds.), *Reasoning, inference and judgement in clinical psychology* (pp. 17–50). New York: The Free Press.

Elstein, A. S., Shulman, L. S., Sprafka, S. A. and others. (1978). *Medical problem solving: An analysis of clinical reasoning.* Cambridge, MA: Harvard University Press.

Engel, S. M. (1994). *With good reason: An introduction to informal fallacies* (5th ed.). New York: St. Martin's Press.

Ennis, R. H. (1987). A taxonomy of critical thinking dispositions and abilities. In J. B. Baron & R. J. Sternberg (Eds.), *Teaching thinking skills: Theory and practice* (pp. 9–26). New York: W. H. Freeman.

Entwistle, N. (1987). A model of the teaching-learning process. In J. T. Richardson, M. W. Eysenck, & D. W. Piper (Eds.), *Student learning: Research in education and cognitive psychology* (pp. 13–28). Society for Research into Higher Education and Open University Press. England: Milton Keynes.

Epling, W F. & Pierce, W. D. (1988). Applied behavior analysis: New directions from the laboratory. In G. Davey & C. Cullen (Eds.), *Human operant conditioning and behavior modification* (pp. 43–58). New York: John Wiley.

Ericsson, K. A. & Smith, J. (Eds.). (1991). *Toward a general theory of expertise: Prospects and limits.* New York: Cambridge University Press.

Erickson, E. H. (1968). *Identity, youth and crisis.* New York: Norton.

Evans, R. L. & Jaureguy, B. M. (1982). Phone therapy outreach for blind elderly. *The Gerontologist, 22,* 32–35.

Evertson, C. M. & Green, J. L. (1986). Observation as inquiry and method. In M. C. Wittrock, *Handbook of research on teaching* (3rd Ed.). AERA: Macmillan.

Eyberg, S. M. & Johnson, S. M. (1974). Multiple assessment of behavior modification with families:

Effects of contingency contracting and order of treated problems. *Journal of Consulting and Clinical Psychology, 42,* 594–606.

Fabry, P. L. & Reid, D. H. (1978). Teaching foster grandparents to train severely handicapped persons. *Journal of Applied Behavior Analysis, 11,* 111–123.

Fairweather, G. W. & Fergus, E. O. (1993). *Empowering the mentally ill.* Austin, TX: G. W. Fairweather Publishing.

Fairweather, G., Sanders, D., Cressler, D. & Maynard, H. (1969). *Community life for the mentally ill.* Chicago: Aldine.

Faller, K. C. (1996). *Evaluating children suspected of having been sexually abused.* Thousand Oaks, CA: Sage.

Faller, K. C., Froming, M. L., & Lipovsky, J. (1991). The parent-child interview: Use in evaluating child allegations of sexual abuse by the parent. *American Journal of Orthopsychiatry, 61,* 552–557.

Falloon, I. R. H. (Ed.). (1988). *Handbook of behavioral family therapy.* New York: Guilford.

Falloon, I. R. H., Krekorian, H., Shanahan, W. J., Laporta, M., & McLees, S. (1990). The Buckingham Project: A comprehensive mental health service based upon behavioral psychotherapy. *Behaviour Change, 7,* 51–57.

Falloon, I., McGill, C., Boyd, J., & Pederson, J. (1987). Family management in the prevention of morbidity in schizophrenia: Social outcome of a two-year longitudinal study. *Psychological Medicine, 17,* 59–66.

Faust, D., Hart, K., & Guilmette, T. J. (1988). Pediatric malingering: The capacity of children to fake believable deficits on neuropsychological testing. *Journal of Consulting and Clinical Psychology, 56,* 578–582.

Faust, D. & Ziskin, J. (1988). The expert witness in psychology and psychiatry. *Science, 241,* 31–35.

Favell, J. E. & McGimsey, J. F. (1993). Defining an acceptable treatment environment. In R. Van Houten & S. Axelrod (Eds.), *Behavior analysis and treatment* (pp. 25–45). New York: Plenum.

Favell, J. E., Realon, R. E., & Sutton, K. A. (1996). Measuring and increasing the happiness of people with profound mental retardation and physical handicaps. *Behavioral Interventions, 11,* 47–58.

Fawcett, S. B. (1991). Some values guiding community research and action. *Journal of Applied Behavior Analysis, 24,* 621–636.

Fawcett, S. B. & Fletcher, R. K. (1977). Community applications of instructional technology: Training writers of instructional packages. *Journal of Applied Behavior Analysis, 10,* 739–746.

Fawcett, S. B., Mathews, R. M., & Fletcher, R. K. (1980). Some promising directions for behavioral community technology. *Journal of Applied Behavior Analysis, 15,* 505–518.

Fawcett, S. B., Mathews, R. M., Fletcher, R. K., Morrow, R., & Stokes, T. F. (1976). Personalized instruction in the community: Teaching helping skills to low-income neighborhood residents. *Journal of Personalized Instruction, 1,* 86–90.

Fawcett, S. B., Paine, A. L., Francisco, V. T., & Vliet, M. (1993). Promoting health through community development. In D. S. Glenwick & L. A. Jason (Eds.), *Promoting health and mental health in children, youth and families* (pp. 233–255). New York: Springer.

Fawcett, S. B., Paine-Andrews, A., Francisco, V. T., Schultz, J. A., Richter, K. P., Lewis, R. K., Harris, K. J., Williams, E. L., Berkley, J. Y., Lopez, C., M. & Fisher, J. L. (1996). Empowering community help: Initiatives to evaluation. In D. M. Fetterman, S. J. Kaftarian, and A. Wandersman (Eds.), *Empowerment evaluation: Knowledge and tools for self-assessment and accountability* (pp. 161–187). Thousand Oaks, CA: Sage.

Fawcett, S. B., Seekins, T., Whang, P. L., Muiu, C. & Suarez de Balcazar, Y. (1984). Creating and using social technologies for community empowerment. In J. Rappaport, C. Swift, & R. Hess (Eds.), *Studies in empowerment: Steps toward understanding and action* (pp. 145–171). New York: Haworth.

Fawcett, S. B., Seekins, T., Whang, P. L., Muiu, C., & Balcazar, Y. S. (1982). The concerns report method: Involving consumers in setting local improvement agendas. *Social Policy, 13,* 35–41.

Fawcett, S. B., White, G. W., Balcazar, F. E., Suarez-Balcazar, Y., Mathews, R. M., Paine-Andrews, A., Seekins, T., & Smith, J. (1994). A contextual-behavioral model of empowerment: Case studies involving people with physical disabilities. *American Journal of Community Psychology, 22*(4), 471–496.

Federico, R. C. (1990). *Social welfare in today's world.* New York: McGraw Hill.

Feindler, E. L. & Ecton, R. B. (1986). *Adolescent anger control: Cognitive-behavioral techniques.* Elmsford, NY: Pergamon.

Feinstein, A. R. (1967). *Judgement.* Baltimore, MD: Williams & Williams.

Felner, R. D. & Felner, T. Y. (1989). Primary prevention programs in the educational context: A transactional-ecological framework and analysis. In L. A. Bond & B. E. Compas (Eds.), *Primary prevention and promotion in the schools* (pp. 13–49). Newbury Park: Sage.

Felner, R. D., Jason, L. A., Moritsugu, J. N., & Farber, S. S. (Eds.). (1983). *Preventative psychology: Theory, research and practice.* New York: Pergamon.

Ferster, C. B. (1972). The experimental analysis of clinical phenomenon. *The Psychological Record, 22,* 1–16.

Ferster, C. B., Culbertson, S. & Boren, M. C. P. (1975). *Behavior Principles* (2nd ed.). Englewood Cliffs, NJ: Prentice Hall.

Fineberg, S. A. (1949). *Punishment without crime: What you can do about prejudice.* Garden City, NY: Doubleday.

Fineman, S. (1985). *Social work stress and intervention.* Aldershot Harts, England: Gower.

Fingarette, H. (1988). *Heavy drinking: The myth of alcoholism as a disease.* Berkeley: University of California Press.

Finkielkraut, A. (1995). *The defeat of the mind.* New York: Columbia University Press. Translated by J. Friedlander.

Fiorentine, R. & Grusky, O. (1990). When case managers manage the seriously mentally ill: A role-contingency approach. *Social Service Review, 64,* 79–93.

Fischer, J. & Corcoran, K. (1994). *Measures for clinical practice: A sourcebook* (2nd Ed.), *Vol. 1: Couples, families, and children. Vol. 2: Adults.* New York: Free Press.

Fischoff, B. (1975). Hindsight does not equal foresight: The effect of outcome knowledge on judgement under uncertainty. *Journal of Experimental Psychology: Human Perception and Performance, 1,* 288–299.

Fischoff, B., Slovic, P., & Lichtenstein, S. (1980). Knowing what you want: Measuring labile values. In T. S. Wallsten (Ed.), *Cognitive processes in choice and decision behavior* (pp. 117–141). Hillsdale, NJ: Lawrence Erlbaum.

Fisher, R. & Ury, W. (1983). *Getting to yes: Reaching agreement without giving in.* New York: Penguin.

Fleishman, M. J. (1979). Using parenting salaries to control attrition and cooperation in therapy. *Behavior Therapy, 10,* 111–116.

Fleishman, M. J., Horne, A. M., & Arthur, J. L. (1983). *Troubled families: A treatment program.* Champaign, IL: Research Press.

Flew, A. (1985). *Thinking about social thinking.* Oxford: Blackwell.

Foa, E. B. & Foa, U. G. (1980). Resource theory: Interpersonal behavior as exchange. In K. J. Gergen, M. S. Greenberg, & R. H. Willis (Eds.), *Social exchange: Advances in theory and research* (pp. 77–101). New York: Plenum.

Fogler, H. S. & LeBlanc, S. E. (1995). *Strategies for creative problem solving.* Englewood Cliffs, NJ: Prentice Hall.

Folkman, S. & Lazarus, R. S. (1980). An analysis of coping in a middle-aged community sample. *Journal of Health and Social Behavior, 21,* 219–239.

Fonagy, P. & Moran, G. S. (1990). Studies on the efficacy of child psychoanalysis. *Journal of Consulting and Clinical Psychology, 58,* 684–695.

Fordyce, J. & Weil, R. (1979). *Managing with people* (pp. 11–14). Redding, MA: Addison-Wesley Publishing Co.

Forehand, R. L. & McMahon, R. J. (1981). *Helping the noncompliant child: A clinician's guide to parent training.* New York: Guilford.

Forgatch, M. S. & Patterson, G. R. (1989). *Parents and adolescents living together. Part 2: Family problem solving.* Champaign, IL: Research Press.

Foster, S. L., Bell-Dolan, D. J., & Burge, D. A. (1988). Behavioral observation. In A. S. Bellack & M. Hersen (Eds.), *Behavioral assessment: A practical handbook* (3rd ed.). (pp. 119–160). New York: Pergamon.

Foster, S. V., Stevens, P. E., & Hall, J. M. (1994). Offering support group services for lesbians living with HIV. *Women & Therapy, 15,* 69–83.

Foster, W. S. (1978). Adjunctive behavior: An under-reported phenomena in applied behavior analysis. *Journal of Applied Behavior Analysis, 11,* 545, 546.

Fowler, S. A. (1988). The effects of peer-mediated interventions on establishing, maintaining, and generalizing children's behavior changes. In R. H. Horner, G. Dunlap, & R. L. Koegel (Eds.), *Generalization and maintenance in applied settings* (pp. 143–170). Baltimore: Paul H. Brookes.

Foxx, R. M. (1982). *Increasing behaviors of severely retarded and autistic children* (p. 104). Champaign, IL: Research Press.

Foxx, R. M. & Bittel, R. G. (1989). *Thinking it through: Teaching a problem-solving strategy for community living.* Champaign, IL: Research Press.

Foxx, R. M., Fall, J. D., Taylor, S., Davis, P. K., et al. (1993). "Would I be able to ...": Teaching clients to assess the availability of their community living lifestyle preferences. *American Journal on Mental Retardation, 98,* 235–248.

Foy, D. W., Eisler, R. M. & Pinkston, S. (1975). Modeled assertion in a case of explosive rages.

Journal of Behavior Therapy and Experimental Psychiatry, 6, 135–137.

Frank, E. & Spanier, C. (1995). Interpersonal psychotherapy for depression: Overview, clinical efficacy and future directions. *Clinical Psychology: Science and Practice, 2,* 349–369.

Frank, J. D. (1976). Restoration of morale and behavior change. In A. Burton (Ed.), *What makes behavior change possible.* New York: Brunner/Mazel.

Frank, J. D. (1978). Expectation and therapeutic outcome—The placebo effect and the role induction interview. In J. D. Frank, R. Hoehn-Saric, S. D. Imber, B. L. Liberman, and A. R. Stone. *Effective ingredients of successful psychotherapy* (pp. 1–34). New York: Brunner/Mazel.

Frank, J. D. & Frank, J. B. (1991). *Persuasion and healing: A comparative study of psychotherapy* (3rd Ed.). Baltimore: John Hopkins Press.

Frankl, V. (1967). *Psychotherapy and Existentialiam.* Harmondsworth: Penguin.

Frankl, V. (1969). *The doctor and the soul.* Harmondsworth: Penguin.

Freedman, B. J., Donahoe, C. P., Rosenthal, L., Schlundt, D. G. & McFall, R. M. (1978). A social-behavioral analysis of skill deficits in delinquent and nondelinquent adolescent boys. *Journal of Consulting and Clinical Psychology, 46,* 1448–1462.

Freire, P. (1973). *Education for critical consciousness.* New York: Continuum.

Freire, P. (1993). *The pedagogy of the oppressed* (rev. ed.). New York: Continuum.

French, J. R. P., Jr. & Raven, B. (1959). The bases of social power. In D. Cartwright (Ed.), *Studies in social power.* An Arbor: University of Michigan, Institute for Social Research.

Freud, A. (1967). *The ego and the mechanisms of defense* (rev. ed.). New York: International Universities Press.

Freud, S. (1924). *Collected papers of Sigmund Freud.* Vol. I. E. Jones (Ed.). London: Hogarth Press.

Friedson, E. (1973). Professions and the occupational principle. In E. Freidson (Ed.), *The professions and their prospects.* Beverly Hills, CA: Sage.

Friedson, E. (1986). *Professional powers: A study of the institutionalization of formal knowledge.* Chicago: University of Chicago Press.

Fromm, E. (1963). *Escape from freedom.* New York: Holt, Rinehart & Winston.

Furnham, A. (1985). School leavers' self-reported attributions. Unpublished manuscript. Reported in Furham (1988).

Furnham, A. F. (1988). *Lay theories: Everyday understanding of problems in the social sciences.* New York: Pergamon.

Furnham, A. & Argyle, M. (1981). The theory, practice and application of social skills training. *International Journal of Behavioral Social Work and Abstracts, 2,* 125–144.

Gagne, R. M. (1985). *The conditions of learning and theory of instruction* (4th ed.). Fort Worth: Holt, Rinehart & Winston.

Gagne, R. M. (Ed.). (1987). *Instructional technology: Foundations.* Hillsdale, NJ: Lawrence Erlbaum.

Gahagan, J. (1984). *Social interaction and its management.* London: Methuen.

Galinsky, M., Rounds, K., Montague, A., & Butowsky, E. (1993). *Leading a telephone support group for persons with HIV disease.* Chapel Hill, NC: School of Social Work, University of North Carolina.

Galper, J. H. (1975). *The politics of social services.* Englewood Cliffs, NJ: Prentice Hall.

Gambrill, E. (1990). *Critical thinking in clinical practice: Improving the accuracy of judgments and decisions about clients.* San Francisco: Jossey-Bass.

Gambrill, E. (1992). Self help books: Pseudoscience in the guise of science. *Skeptical Inquirer, 16*(4), 389–399.

Gambrill, E. (1995a). Less marketing and more scholarship. *Social Work Research, 19,* 38–47.

Gambrill, E. (1995b). Helping shy, socially anxious and lonely adults: A skill-based contextual approach. In W. O'Donohue & L. Krasner (Eds.), *Handbook of psychological skills training: Clinical techniques and applications* (pp. 247–286). Boston: Allyn and Bacon.

Gambrill, E. (1995c). Assertion skills training. In W. O'Donohue & L. Krasner (Eds.), *Handbook of psychological skills training: Clinical techniques and applications* (pp. 81–118). Boston: Allyn and Bacon.

Gambrill, E. D. (1997). Social work education: Current concerns and possible futures. In M. Reisch & E. Gambrill (Eds.), *Social work in the 21st century* (pp. 317–327). Thousand Oaks, CA: Pine Forge Press.

Gambrill, E. D. & Gibbs, L. (1996). Is what's good for the goose good for the gander? Unpublished manuscript, University of California, Berkeley, CA.

Gambrill, E. D. & Paquin, G. (1992). Neighbors: Their role and potential. *Children and Youth Services Review, 14,* 353–372.

Gambrill, E. D. & Richey, C. A. (1975). An assertion inventory for use in assessment and research. *Behavior Therapy, 6,* 547–549.

Gambrill, E. D. & Richey, C. A. (1988). *Taking charge of your social life*. Berkeley, CA: Behavioral Options.

Gambrill, E. D., Thomas, E. J. & Carter, R. D. (1971). Procedure for socio-behavioral practice in open settings. *Social Work, 16*, 51–62.

Gans, H. (1980). *Deciding what's news*. New York: Vintage.

Garbarino, J. (1992). *Children and families in the social environment* (2nd Ed.). New York: Aldine de Gruyter.

Garbarino, J., Stocking, S. H., & Associates. (1980). *Protecting children from abuse and neglect: Developing and maintaining effective support systems for families*. San Francisco: Jossey-Bass.

Gardner, J. E. (1967). Behavior therapy treatment approach to a psychogenic seizure case. *Journal of Consulting Psychology, 31*, 209–212.

Gardner, J. M., Brust, D. J. & Watson, L. S. (1970). A scale to measure proficiency in applying behavior modification techniques to the mentally retarded. *American Journal of Mental Deficiency, 74*, 633–636.

Gardner, M. (1981). *Science: Good, bad and bogus*. Buffalo: Prometheus.

Gardner, R., III, Sainato, D. M., Cooper, J. O., Heron, T. E., Heward, W. L., Eshleman, J. W., & Grossi, T. A. (1994). *Behavior analysis in education: Focus on measurably superior instruction*. Pacific Grove, CA: Brooks/Cole.

Gardner, W. I. & Cole, C. L. (1989). Self management approaches. In E. Cipani (Ed.), *The treatment of severe behavior disorders* (pp. 19–36). Washington, D.C.: American Association on Mental Retardation.

Garland, D. F. (1916). The municipality and public welfare. *Proceedings of the National Conference of Charities and Corrections* (pp. 306–316). 43rd session. Indianapolis, Indiana, May. Chicago,IL: Hildman Printing Co.

Gartner, A. & Riessman, F. (1984). *The self-help revolution*. New York: Human Sciences.

Garvin, C. D. (1983). Theory of group approaches. In A. Rosenblatt & D. Waldfogel (Ed.), *Handbook of clinical social work* (pp. 155–175). San Francisco: Jossey-Bass.

Garvin, C. (1987). Group theory and research. In *Encyclopedia of Social Work* (pp. 682–696). Silver Spring, MD: National Association of Social Workers.

Garvin, C.D. (1987). *Contemporary group work* (2nd Ed.). Englewood Cliffs, NJ: Prentice Hall.

Garvin, V., Leber, D., & Kalter, N. (1991). Children of divorce: Predictors of change following preventive intervention. *American Journal of Orthopsychiatry, 61*, 438–447.

Gatchel, R. J. & Turk, D. C. (1996). *Psychological approach to pain management: A practitioner's handbook*. New York: Guilford.

Gaylord-Ross, R., Stremel-Campbell, K., & Storey, K. (1986). Social skill training in natural contexts. In R. H. Horner, L. H. Meyer, & H. D. B. Frederick (Eds.), *Education of learners with severe handicaps: Exemplary service strategies* (pp. 161–187). Baltimore: Paul H. Brooks.

Gaylord-Ross, R. (Ed.). (1989). *Integration strategies for students with handicaps*. Baltimore: Paul H. Brookes.

Gelles, R. J. (1982). Applying research on family violence to clinical practice. *Journal of Marriage and the Family*. Feb. 9–20.

Gelman, S. R. (1992). Is Tarasoff relevant to AIDS related cases? No. In E. Gambrill & R. Pruger (Eds.), *Controversial issues in social work* (pp. 350–354). Boston: Allyn & Bacon.

Gelman, S. R. (1997). Should clients have access to their mental health records? YES. In E. Gambrill & R. Pruger (Eds.), *Controversial issues in social work ethics, values and obligations* (pp. 1–5). Boston: Allyn & Bacon.

George, V. & Wilding, P. (1984). *The impact of social policy*. London: Routledge & Kegan Paul.

Giacalone, R. A. & Rosenfeld, P. (Eds.). (1989). *Impression management in organization*. Hillsdale, NJ: Lawrence Erlbaum.

Gibbs, J. T., Brunswick, A. F., Conner, M. E., Dembo, R., Larson, T. E., Reed, R.J., & Solomon, B. (Eds.). (1988). *Young, black, and male in America: An endangered species*. Dover, MA: Auburn House.

Gibbs, J. T., Huang, L. H., and Associates. (1989). *Children of color: Psychological interventions with minority youth*. San Francisco: Jossey-Bass.

Gibbs, L. E. (1991). *Scientific reasoning for social workers: Bridging the gap between research and practice*. New York: Macmillan.

Gibbs, L. & Gambrill, E. (1996). *Critical thinking for social workers: A workbook*. Thousand Oaks, CA: Pine Forge Press.

Gibelman, M. & Schervish, P. (1996). *Who we are: A second look*. Washington, D.C.: NASW Press.

Gilbert, P. (1989). *Human nature and suffering*. New York: Guilford Press.

Gilbert, P. (1992). *Depression: The evolution of powerlessness*. New York: Guilford Press.

Gilbert, P. (1993). Defense and safety: Their function

in social behaviour and psychopathology. *British Journal of Clinical Psychology, 32,* 131–153.

Gilbert, P. (1994). Male violence: Toward an integration. In J. Archer (Ed.), *Male violence.* London: Routledge.

Gilchrist, L. D. & Schinke, S. P. (Eds.). (1985). *Preventing social health problems through life skills training.* Seattle, WA: Center for Social Welfare Research, School of Social Work.

Gilchrist, L. D., Schinke, S. P., & Maxwell, J. S. (1987). Life skills counseling for preventing problems in adolescence. *Journal of Social Service Research, 10,* 73–84.

Giles, T. R. (1993a). *Handbook of effective psychotherapy.* New York: Plenum.

Giles, T. R. (1993b). *Managed mental health care: A guide for practitioners, employers, and hospital administrators.* New York: Allyn & Bacon.

Gilligan, C. (1982). *In a different voice.* Cambridge, MA: Harvard University Press.

Gilliland, B. E. & James, R. K. (1993). *Crisis intervention strategies* (2nd Ed.). Pacific Grove, CA: Brooks/Cole.

Ginsberg, L. (1995). *Social work almanac* (2nd Ed.). Washington, D.C.: National Association of Social Workers.

Gitterman, A. & Shulman, L. (Eds.). (1994). *Mutual aid groups, vulnerable populations, and the life cycle* (2nd Ed.). New York: Columbia University Press.

Gladstein, G. A. & Associates. (1987). *Empathy and counseling: Explorations in theory and research.* New York: Verlag.

Glattborn, A. A. & Baron, J. (1991). The good thinker. In A. L. Costa (Ed.), *Developing minds: A resource book for teaching thinking* (rev. ed.). Vol. I. (pp. 63–67). Alexandria, VI: Association for Supervision and Curriculum Development.

Glazer, M. P. & Glazer, P. M. (1989). *The whistleblowers: Exposing corruption in government and industry.* New York: Basic Books.

Glenn, S. S. (1991). Contingencies and metacontingencies: Relations among behavioral, cultural and biological evolution. In P. A. Lamal (Ed.), *Behavioral analysis of societies and cultural practices* (pp. 39–73). New York: Hemisphere.

Goldenberg, I. I. (1978). *Oppression and social intervention: The human condition and the problem of change.* Chicago: Nelson Hall.

Goldiamond, I. (1965). Self-control procedures in personal behavior problems. *Psychological Reports, 17,* 851–868.

Goldiamond, I. (1984). Training parent trainers and ethicists in nonlinear analysis of behavior. In R. F. Dangel & R. A. Polster (Eds.), *Parent training: Foundations of research and practice* (pp. 504–546). New York: Guilford.

Goldsmith, J. B. & McFall, R. M. (1975). Development and evaluation of an interpersonal skill-training program for psychiatric patients. *Journal of Abnormal Psychology, 84,* 51–58.

Goldstein, A. P. (1962). *Therapist-patient expectancies in psychotherapy.* Elmsford, NY: Pergamon.

Goldstein, A. P. (1980). Relationship enhancement methods. In F. H. Kanfer and A. P. Goldstein (Eds.). *Helping people change: A textbook of methods* (pp. 18–57). Elmsford, NY: Pergamon.

Goldstein, A. P. & Huff, C. R. (1993). *The gang intervention handbook.* Champaign, IL: Research Press.

Goldstein, A. P., Sprafkin, R. P., Gershaw, N. J., & Klein, P. (1980). *Skillstreaming the adolescent: A structured learning approach to teaching prosocial skills.* Champaign, IL: Research Press.

Goldstein, R. S. & Baer, D. M. (1976). R.S.V.P.: A procedure to increase the personal mail and number of correspondents for nursing home residents. *Behavior Therapy, 7,* 348–354.

Goleman, D. (1995). *Emotional intelligence: Why it can matter more than I. Q.* New York: Bantam Books.

Gomory, T. (1997). Does the goal of preventing suicide justify placing suicidal clients in care? NO. In E. Gambrill & R. Pruger (Eds.), *Controversial issues in social work ethics, values, and obligations* (pp. 70–74). Boston: Allyn & Bacon.

Gondolf, E. W. & Fisher, E. R. (1988). *Battered women as survivors: An alternative to treating learned helplessness.* Lexington, MA: Lexington Books.

Goode, W. J. (1960). Encroachment, charlatanism, and the emerging professions: Psychology, sociology, and medicine. *American Sociological Review, 25,* 902–914.

Goode, W. J. (1978). *The celebration of heroes: Prestige as a control system.* Berkeley, CA: University of California Press.

Goodwin, D. L. & Coates, T. J. (1976). The teacher-pupil interaction scale. *Journal of Applied Behavior Analysis, 9,* 114.

Gorenstein, E. E. (1992). *The science of mental illness.* New York: Academic Press.

Gottlieb, B. H. (1978). The development and application of a classification scheme of informal helping behaviors. *Canadian Journal of Behavioral Science, 10,* 105–115.

Gottlieb, B. H. (1988). *Marshalling social support: Formats, processes and effects*. Newbury Park, CA: Sage.

Gottlieb, B. H. & Todd, D. M. (1979). Characterizing and promoting social support in natural settings. In R. F. Munoz, L. R. Snowden, J. G. Kelly & Associates (Eds.), *Social and psychological research in community settings* (pp. 183–242). San Francisco: Jossey-Bass.

Gottlieb, N. (1978). Helpful hints for responding to sexist put-downs. Unpublished manuscript. University of Washington, School of Social Work, Seattle, WA.

Gottman, J. M. (1990). How marriages change. In G. R. Patterson (Ed.), *Depression and aggression in family interaction* (pp. 75–101). Hillsdale, NJ: Lawrence Erlbaum.

Gottman, A. (1994). *Why marriages succeed or fail*. New York: Simon and Schuster.

Gottman, J. M. & Leiblum, S. R. (1974). *How to do psychotherapy and evaluate it: A manual for beginners*. New York: Holt, Rinehart and Winston.

Gottman, J., Notarius, C., Gonso, J., & Markman, H. (1976). *A couples guide to communication*. Champaign, IL: Research Press.

Gould, S. J. (1995). Ladders and cones: Constraining evolution by canonical icons. In R. B. Silvers (Ed.), *Hidden histories of science* (pp. 36–67). New York: New York Review Books.

Graubard, P. S., Rosenberg, H., & Miller, M. B. (1971). Student applications of behavior modification to teachers and environments or ecological approaches to social deviancy. In E. A. Ramp and B. L. Hopkins (Eds.). *A new direction for education: Behavior analysis* Vol. 1. (pp. 80–101). Lawrence, KS: University of Kansas, Department of Human Development.

Gray, J. (1987). *The psychology of fear and stress* (2nd Ed.). Cambridge: Cambridge University Press.

Gray, W. D. (1991). *Thinking critically about new age ideas*. Belmont, CA: Wadsworth.

Green, C. W., Reid, D. H., White, L. K., Halford, R. C., Brittain, D. P., & Gardner, S. M. (1988). Identifying reinforcers for persons with profound handicaps: Staff opinion versus systematic assessment of preferences. *Journal of Applied Behavioral Analysis, 21*, 31–43.

Green, J. (Ed.). (1992). *Cross-cultural social work: Cultural awareness in the human services*. Englewood Cliffs, NJ: Prentice-Hall.

Green, K. D., Forehand, R. & McMahon, R. J. (1979). Parental manipulation of compliance and noncompliance in normal and deviant children. *Behavior Modification, 3*, 245–266.

Greenberger, D. & Padesky, C. A. (1995). *Mind over mood: A cognitive therapy treatment manual for clients*. New York: Guilford.

Greene, B. F., Kessler, M. L., & Daniels, M. E. (1996). Issues in child welfare: Competency training family preservation and reunification service personnel. Unpublished manuscript. Carbondale, IL: Southern Illinois University, Psychology Department.

Greeno, J. G. (1989). A perspective on thinking. *American Psychologist, 2*, 134–141.

Greenwood, E. (1957). Attributes of a profession. *Social Work, 2*, 45–55.

Greif, J. L. & Ephross, P. H. (1996). *Group work with populations at risk*. New York: Oxford University Press.

Gresham, F. M. (1988). Social skills: Conceptual and applied aspects of assessment, training, and social validation. In J. C. Witt & S. N. Elliot (Eds.), *Handbook of behavior therapy in education* (pp. 523–546). New York: Plenum.

Gross, P. R., & Levitt, N. (1994). *Higher superstition: The academic left and its quarrels with science*. Baltimore, MD: Johns Hopkins University Press.

Gummer, B. (1997). Is the Code of Ethics as applicable to agency executives as it is to direct service practitioners? NO. In E. Gambrill & R. Pruger (Eds.), *Controversial issues in social work ethics, values and obligations* (pp. 143–148). Boston: Allyn & Bacon.

Gummer, B. (1990). *The politics of social administration: Managing organizational politics in social agencies*. Englewood Cliffs, NJ: Prentice Hall.

Gurman, A. S. & Kniskern, D. P. (1978). Deterioration in marital and family therapy: Empirical, clinical, and conceptual issues. *Family Process, 17*, 3–20.

Gutheil, T. G., Bursztajan, H., J., Brodsky, A., & Alexander, V. (1991). *Decision making in psychiatry and the law*. Baltimore, MD: Williams and Wilkins.

Gutierrez, L. M. (1990). Working with women of color: An empowerment perspective. *Social Work, 35*, 149–153.

Haase, R. F. & Tepper, D. T. (1972). Nonverbal components of empathic communication. *Journal of Counseling Psychology, 19*, 417–424.

Hadley, R., Cooper, M., Dale, P., & Stacey, G. (1987). *A community social worker's handbook*. London: Tavistock.

Haley, J. (1969). The art of being a failure as a therapist. *American Journal of Orthopsychiatry, 39,* 691–695.

Hall, A. S. (1974). *The point of entry: A study of client reception in the social services.* London: Allen & Unwin.

Hall, C., Sheldon-Wildgen, J., & Sherman, J. A. (1980). Teaching job interview skills to retarded adults. *Journal of Applied Behavior Analysis, 13,* 433–442.

Hall, E. T. (1966). *The hidden dimension.* Garden City, NY: Doubleday.

Hall, R. V. & Hall, M. C. (1980). *How to use planned ignoring.* Lawrence, KS: H. H. Enterprises.

Hannah, G. T., Christian, W. P., & Clark, H. B. (1981). *Preservation of client rights.* New York: Free Press.

Hanson, R. W. & Gerber, K. E. (1990). *Coping with chronic pain: A guide to patient self-management.* New York: Guilford.

Hardcastle, D. A., Wenocur, S. & Powers, P. R. (1996). *Community practice: Theories and skills for social workers.* New York: Oxford University Press.

Hardin, R. (1990). The artificial duties of contemporary professionals. *Social Service Review, 64,* 528–541.

Hare-Mustin, R. T., Marecek, J., Kaplan, A. G., & Liss-Levinson, N. (1979). Rights of clients, responsibilities of therapists. *American Psychologist, 34,* 13–16.

Hargie, O., Saunders, C. & Dickson, D. (1981). *Social skills in interpersonal communication.* London: Croom Helm.

Haring, T. G. & Breen, K. G. (1992). A peer-mediated social work network intervention to enhance the social integration of persons with moderate and severe disabilities. *Journal of Applied Behavior Analysis, 25,* 319–333.

Haring, T. G., Breen, K. G., Weiner, J., Kennedy, C. H., et al. (1995). Using videotape modeling to facilitate generalized purchasing skills. *Journal of Behavioral Education, 5,* 29–53.

Harmon, T. M., Nelson, R. O., & Hayes, S. C. (1980). Self-monitoring of mood versus activity by depressed clients. *Journal of Consulting and Clinical Psychology, 48,* 30–38.

Harrison, D. F., Wodarski, J. S., & Thyer, B. A. (Eds.) (1992). *Cultural diversity and social work practice.* Springfield, IL: Charles Thomas.

Hart, B. & Risley, T. R. (1995). *Meaningful differences in the everyday experience of young American children.* Baltimore: Paul H. Brookes.

Hasenfeld, Y. (1987). Program development. In F. M. Cox, J. L. Erlich, J. Rothman & J. E. Tropman, *Strategies of community organization: Macro practice* (4th ed.). Itasca: F. E. Peacock.

Hasenfeld, Y. (Ed.). (1992). *Human services as complex organizations.* Newbury Park: Sage.

Hasenfeld, Y. (1996). The administration of human services—What lies ahead? In P. R. Raffoul & C. A. McNeece (Eds.), *Future issues for social work practice* (pp. 191–202). Boston: Allyn and Bacon.

Hathaway, S. R. (1948). Some considerations relative to nondirective counseling as therapy. *Journal of Clinical Psychology, 4,* 226–231.

Hawkins, R. P. (1986). Selection of target behaviors. In R. O. Nelson & S. C. Hayes (Eds.), *Conceptual foundations of behavioral assessment* (pp. 331–385). New York: Guilford Press.

Hawkins, R. P., Peterson, R. F., Schweid, E., & Bijou, S. W. (1966). Behavior therapy in the home: Amelioration of problem parent-child relations with the parent in a therapeutic role. *Journal of Experimental Child Psychology, 4,* 99–107.

Hawthorne, L. (1975). Games supervisors play. *Social Work, 20,* 179–183.

Hayek, F. A. (1976). *Law, legislation and liberty, Vol. 2: The mirage of social justice.* Chicago: University of Chicago Press.

Hayes, S. C. (1989). *Rule-governed behavior: Cognitions, contingencies and instructional control.* New York: Plenum.

Hayes, S. C. & Brownstein, A. J. (1987). Mentalism, private events, and scientific explanation: A defense of B. F. Skinner's view. In S. Modgil & C. Modgil (Eds.), *B. F. Skinner: Consensus and controversies* (pp. 207–218). New York: Falmer Press.

Hayes, S. C., Jacobson, N. S., Follette, V. M., & Doegher, M. J. (Eds.). (1994). *Acceptance and change: Content and context in psychotherapy.* Reno, NV: Context Press.

Hayes, S. C., Kohlenberg, B. S., & Melancon, S. M. (1989). Avoiding and altering rule-control as a strategy of clinical intervention. In S. C. Hayes (Ed.), *Rule-governed behavior: Cognition, contingencies, and instructional control* (pp. 359–385). New York: Plenum.

Haynes, R. B., Taylor, D. W., & Sackett, D. L. (1979). *Compliance in health care.* Baltimore, MD: John Hopkins.

Haynes, S. N. (1992). *Models of causality in psychopathology: Toward dynamic, synthetic and nonlinear models of behavior disorders.* New York: Macmillan Publishing Co.

Health Letter. Published by Public Citizen Health Research Group, Editor Sidney M. Wolfe. 2000 P St. N. W., Washington, D. C. 20036.

Healy, J. F. (1995). *Race, ethnicity, gender and class:*

The sociology of group conflict and change. Newbury Park, CA: Pine Forge Press.

Heimberg, R. G., Dodge, C. S., Hope, D. A., Kennedy, C. R., Zollo, L. J., & Becker, R. E. (1990). Cognitive behavioral group treatment for social phobia: Comparison with a credible placebo control. *Cognitive Therapy and Research, 14,* 1–23.

Heimberg, R. G., Liebowitz, M. R., Hope, D. A., & Schneider, F. R. (1995). *Social phobia: Diagnosis, assessment and treatment.* New York: Guilford.

Hellman, I. D., Morrison, T. L., & Abramowitz, S. I. (1987). Therapist flexibility/rigidity and work stress. *Professional Psychology, 18,* 21–27.

Helms, J. E. (1990). *Black and white racial identity: Theories, research and practice.* Westport, CT: Greenwood Press.

Helquist, N. (1987). *Working with AIDS: A resource guide for mental health professionals. AIDS Health Project,* University of California, San Francisco, pp. 14–17.

Henley, N. M. (1977). *Body politics: Power, sex and non-verbal communication.* Englewood Cliffs, NJ: Prentice-Hall.

Henry, M. (1990). One drug-using mother's story. *Youth Law News, 11,* 19. 114 Sansome St., Suite 900, San Francisco, CA 94104.

Henry, M. (1996). Plaintiffs ask for receivership as Utah child welfare agency gets worse. *Youth Law News, 18*(2), 1–7.

Hepler, J. B. (1991). Evaluating the clinical significance of a group approach for improving the social skills of children. *Social work With Groups, 14*(2), 87–104.

Herbert-Jackson, E., O'Brian, M., Poterfield, J., & Risley, T. R. (1977). *The infant center—A complete guide to organizing and managing infant day care.* Baltimore: University Park Press.

Herek, G. M., Janis, I. L., & Huth, P. (1989). Quality of U.S. decision making during the Cuban missile crisis: Major errors in Welsh's reassessment. *Journal of Conflict Resolution, 33,* 446–459.

Hetherington, E. M. & Arasteh, J. D. (Eds.). (1988). *Impact of divorce, single parenting, and stepparenting on children.* Hillsdale, NJ: Lawrence Erlbaum.

Hetherington, E. M. & Blechman, E. (Eds.). (1996). *Stress, coping, and resiliency in children and families.* Hillsdale, NJ: Lawrence Erlbaum.

Hibbs, E. D., & Jensen, P. S. (Eds.). (1991). *Psychosocial treatment for child and adolescent disorders: Empirically based strategies for clinical practice.* Washington, D.C.: American Psychological Association.

Higgins, R. L., Snyder, C. R., & Berglas, S. (1990). *Self-handicapping: The paradox that isn't.* New York: Plenum Press.

Hilgartner, S. & Bosk, C. L. (1988). The rise and fall of social problems: A public arenas model. *American Journal of Sociology, 94,* 53–78.

Hill, C. E. & O'Grady, K. E. (1985). List of therapist intentions illustrated in a case study and with therapists of varying theoretical orientations. *Journal of Counseling Psychology, 32,* 3–22.

Hillard, J. R. (1995). Predicting suicide. *Psychiatric Services, 46,* 223–225.

Hinde, R. A. & Stevenson-Hinde, J. (1988). *Relationships within families: Mutual influences.* Oxford: Clarendon Press.

Hineline, P. N. (1995). President's column: External reinforcers, entrance reinforcers and awards. *Division 25, Recorder, 30*(2), Summer, 1–2.

Hinshaw, S. P. (1994). *Attention deficits and hyperactivity in children.* Newbury Park: Sage.

Hinshaw, S. P. (1995). Enhancing social competence: Integrating self-management strategies with behavioral procedures for children with ADHD. In E. D. Hibbs, & P. S. Jensen (Eds.), *Psychological treatment for child and adolescent disorders: Empirically based strategies for clinical practice* (pp. 285–309). Washington, D.C.: American Psychological Association.

Hiratsuka, J. (1990). Social work "stepchild" awaits resurgence. Community organizing: Assembling power. *NASW News, 35,* p. 3 (Sept.).

Ho, M. K. (1987). *Family therapy with ethnic minorities.* Newbury Park: Sage.

Hobbs, N. (1962). Sources of gain in psychotherapy. *American Psychologist, 17,* 741–747.

Hobbs, N. (1975). *The futures of children.* San Francisco: Jossey-Bass.

Hoff, L. A. (1995). *People in crisis: Understanding and helping* (4th Ed.). San Francisco: Jossey-Bass.

Hogarth, R. M. (1987). *Judgement and choice* (2nd ed.). New York: John Wiley.

Hokenstad, M. C., Khinduka, S. K., & Midgley, J. (Eds.). (1992). *Profiles in international social work.* Washington, D.C.: NASW Press.

Holden, C. (1991). Depression: The news isn't depressing. *Science, 254,* 1450–1452.

Holland, J. H., Holyoak, K. J., Nisbett, R. E. & Thagard, P. R. (1986). *Induction: Processes of inference, learning, and discovery.* Cambridge: MIT Press.

Hollandsworth, J. G., Jr. (1990). *The physiology of psychological disorders: Schizophrenia, depression, anxiety and substance abuse.* New York: Plenum.

Hollin, C. R. (1989). *Cognitive-behavioral interventions with young offenders*. De Moines, IA: Longwood Division, Allyn and Bacon.

Hollon, S. D. & Kendall, P. C. (1980). Cognitive self-statements in depression: Development of an automatic thoughts questionnaire. *Cognitive Therapy and Research, 4*, 109–143.

Holmes, S. A. (1996). Income disparity between poorest and richest rises. *New York Times*, June 20, A1/10.

Holtzworth-Munroe, A. & Hutchinson, G. (1993). Attributing negative intent to wife behavior: The attributions of maritally violent versus nonviolent men. *Journal of Abnormal Psychology, 102*, 206–211.

Homel, R. & Burns, A. (1989). Environmental quality and the well being of children. *Social indicators research, 21*, 133–158.

Hops, H., Sherman, L. & Biglan, A. (1990). Maternal depression, maritaldiscord, and children's behavior: A developmental perspective. In G. R. Patterson (Ed.), *Depression and aggression in family interaction* (pp. 185–208). Hillsdale, NJ: Lawrence Erlbaum.

Horner, R. H., Dunlap, G., & Koegel, R. L. (1988). *Generalization and maintenance: Life-style changes in applied settings*. Baltimore: Paul H. Brookes.

Horner, R. H. & Meyer, L. H. & Fredericks, H. D. (1986). *Education of learners with severe handicaps: Exemplary service strategies* (pp. 161–187). Baltimore: Paul H. Brookes.

Houts, A. C. (1984). Effects of clinical, theoretical orientation and patient explanatory bias on initial clinical judgments. *Professional Psychology: Research and Practice, 15*, 284–293.

Houts, A. C. & Galante, M. (1985). The impact of evaluative disposition and subsequent information on clinical impressions. *Journal of Social and Clinical Psychology, 3*, 201–212.

Howitt, D. (1992). *Child abuse errors: When good intentions go wrong*. New York: Harvester Wheatsheaf.

Huck, S. W. & Sandler, H. M. (1979). *Rival hypotheses: Alternative interpretations of data based conclusions*. New York: Harper & Row.

Hunt, P., Alwell, M., & Goetz, L. (1988). Acquisition of conversation skills and the reduction of inappropriate social interaction behaviors. *JASH Journal, 13*, 20–27.

Hunter, S. & Sundel, M. (Eds.). (1989). *Midlife myths: Issues, findings, and practice implications*. Newbury Park: Sage.

Hussian, R. A. & Davis, R. L. (1985). *Responsive care: Behavioral interventions with elderly persons*. Champaign, IL: Research Press.

Illich, I., Zola, I. K., McNight, J., Caplan, J. A., & Shaiken, H. (1978). *Disabling professions*. New Hampshire: Marion Boyers.

In court: Duty to warn vs. confidentiality. *NASW News* (1990), 35, p. 16.

In re Gault, 387 US1, 87 S. Ct. 1428 L.ED, 527 1967.

In re Fisher, 643, P.2d 887 (Wash. App. 1982).

Isen, A. M. (1987). Positive affect, cognitive processes, and social behavior. In L. Berkowitz (Ed.), *Advances in experimental social psychology*, Vol. 20. (pp. 203–253). New York: Academic Press.

Isen, A. M. (1993). Positive affect and decision making. In P. Lewis & J. M. Haviland (Eds.), *Handbook of emotions* (pp. 261–277). New York: Guilford Press.

Iwata, B. A. (1987). Negative reinforcement in applied behavior analysis: An emerging technology. *Journal of Applied Behavior Analysis, 20*, 361–378.

Jacobs, J. (1993). *The death and life of great American cities*. New York: Random. (Originally published in 1963.)

Jacobson, J. W., Mulick, J. A., & Schwartz A. A. (1995). A history of facilitated communication: Science, pseudoscience, and antiscience working group on facilitated communication. *American Psychologist, 50*, 750–765.

Jacobson, N. S. & Christensen, A. (1996). Studying the effectiveness of psychotherapy: How well can clinical trials do the job? *American Psychologist, 51*, 1031–1039.

Jacobson, N. S., Holtzworth-Munroe, A., & Schmaling, K. B. (1989). Marital therapy and spouse involvement in the treatment of depression, agoraphobia, and alcoholism. *Journal of Consulting and Clinical Psychology, 57*, 5–10.

Jacobson, N. S. & Gurman, A. S. (1995). *Clinical handbook of couple therapy*. New York: Guilford Press.

Jacobson, N. S. & Margolin, G. (1979). *Marital therapy strategies based on social learning and behavior exchange principles*. New York: Brunner/Mazel.

Jacobson, R. B. & Humphrey, R. A. (1979). Families in crisis: Research and theory in child mental retardation. *Social Casework, 12*, 597–601.

Janis, I. L. (1982). *Group think: Psychological studies of policy decisions and fiascos* (2nd Ed.). Boston: Houghton Mifflin.

Janis, I. L. & Mann, L. (1977). *Decision making: A psychological analysis of conflict, choice and commitment*. New York: Free Press.

Janoff-Bulman, R. (1979). Characterological versus behavioral self-blame: Inquiries into depression and rape. *Journal of Personality and Social Psychology, 37*, 1798–1809.

Janoff-Bulman, R. & Thomas, C. E. (1989). Toward an understanding of self-defeating responses following victimization. In R. C. Curtis (Ed.), *Self-defeating behaviors: Experimental research, clinical impressions, and practice implications* (pp. 215–234). New York: Plenum Press.

Jarvis, W. T. (1990). *Dubious dentistry: A dental continuing education course.* Loma Linda University School of Dentistry, Loma Linda, CA 92350.

Jennings, D. L., Amabile, T. M., & Ross, L. (1982). Informal covariation assessment: Data-based versus theory-based judgements. In D. Kahneman, P. Slovic, & A. Tversky (Eds.), *Judgement under uncertainty: Heuristics and biases* (pp. 211–230). New York: Cambridge University Press.

Jensen, C. & Project Censored. (1994). *Censored, the news that didn't make the news—and why.* New York: Four Walls Eight Windows.

Jensen, D. D. (1989). Pathologies of science, precognition, and modern psychophysics. *The Skeptical Inquirer, 13,* 147–160.

Johnson, M. S. & Bailey, J. S. (1977). The modification of leisure behavior in a half-way house for retarded women. *Journal of Applied Behavior Analysis, 10,* 273–282.

Johnson, S. M. & White, G. (1971). Self-observation as an agent of behavioral change. *Behavior Therapy, 2,* 488–497.

Jones, J. M. (1986). Racism: A cultural analysis of the problem. In J. F. Dovidio & S. L. Gaertner. *Prejudice, discrimination, and racism* (pp. 279–314). New York: Academic Press.

Jordan, C. & Franklin, C. (1995). *Clinical assessment for social workers: Quantitative and qualitative methods.* Chicago: Lyceum.

Jurjevich, R. M. (1974). *The hoax of Freudism: A study of brainwashing the American professionals and laymen.* Philadelphia: Dorrance.

Kadushin, A. (1963). Diagnosis and evaluation for (almost) all occasions. *Social Work, 8,* 12–19.

Kadushin, A. (1968). Games people play in supervision. *Social Work, 13,* p. 23.

Kadushin, A. (1990). *The social work interview: A guide for human service professionals* (3rd Ed.). New York; Columbia University Press.

Kadushin, A. (1992). *Supervision in social work* (3rd Ed.). New York: Columbia University Press.

Kadushin, A. & Martin, J. A. (1981). *Child abuse: An interactional event.* New York: Columbia University Press.

Kagan, J. & Reznick, J. S. (1989). Shyness and temperament. In W. H. Jones, J. M. Cheek, and S. R. Briggs (Eds.), *Shyness: Perspectives on research and treatment* (pp. 81–90). New York: Plenum.

Kagle, J. D. (1991). *Social work records* (2nd Ed.). Belmont, CA: Wadsworth. Kagle, J. D. & Kopels, S. (1994). Confidentiality after Tarasoff. *Health and Social Work, 19,* 217–222.

Kagle, J. D. & Kopels, S. (1994). Confidentiality after Tarasoff. *Health and Social Work, 19,* 217–222.

Kahane, H. (1995). *Logic and contemporary rhetoric: The use of reason in everyday life* (7th Ed.). Belmont, CA: Wadsworth.

Kahn, M. W., Williams, C., Galvez, E., Lejero, L., Conrad, R., & Goldstein, G. (1975). The Papago Psychology Service: A community mental health program on an American Indian Reservation. *American Journal of Community Psychology, 3,* 91–93.

Kahn, S. (1991). *Organizing: Guide for grassroots leaders.* Silver Spring, MD: NASW Press.

Kahneman, D. & Tversky, A. (1973). On the psychology of prediction. *Psychological Review, 80,* 237–251.

Kamerman, S. B. & Kahn, A. J. (1992). *Social services in the United States: Policies and programs.* Philadelphia: Temple University Press.

Kamerman, S. B. & Kahn, A. J. (Eds.). (1989). *Privatization and the welfare state.* Princeton, NJ: Princeton University Press.

Kane, R. A. & Kane, R. L. (1981). *Assessing the elderly: A practical guide to measurement.* Lexington, MA: Lexington Books.

Kanfer, F. H. (1970). Self-monitoring and clinical applications: Methodological limitations. *Journal of Consulting and Clinical Psychology, 35,* 148–152.

Kanfer, F. H. & Phillips, J. S. (1969). A survey of current behavior therapies and a proposal for classification. In C. M. Franks (Ed.). *Behavior therapy: Appraisal and status* (pp. 445–475). New York: McGraw-Hill.

Kanner, A. D., Coyne, J. C., Schaefer, C. & Lazarus, R. S. (1981). Comparison of two modes of stress measurement: Minor daily hassles and uplifts versus major life events. *Journal of Behavioral Medicine, 4,* 1–40.

Kanner, A. D., Kafry, D., & Pines, A. (1978). Conspicuous in it's absence: The lack of positive conditions as a source of stress. *Journal of Human Stress, 4,* 33–39.

Kantrowitz, R. E. & Ballou, M. (1992). A feminist critique of cognitive-behavioral theory. In L. Brown & M. Ballou (Eds.), *Personality and psychopathology: Feminist reappraisals* (pp. 70–79). New York: Guilford.

Karger, H. J. (1983). Science, research and social work: Who controls the profession? *Social Work, 28*, 200–205.

Karger, H. J. & Stoesz, D. (1994). *American social welfare policy: A structural approach* (2nd Ed.). New York: Longman.

Karls, J. M. & Wandrei, K. E. (Eds.). (1994). *Person-in-environment system: The PIE classification system for social functioning problems.* Annapolis Junction, MD: NASW Press.

Kassirer, J. P. & Kopelman, R. I. (1991). *Learning clinical reasoning.* Baltimore: Williams and Wilkins.

Katz, A. H. & Bender, E. I. (1976). *The strength in us: Self-help groups in the modern world.* New York: New Viewpoints.

Katz, A. H. & Bender, E. I. (1976). Self-help groups in Western society: History and prospects. *Journal of Applied Behavioral Science, 12*, 265–282.

Katz, A. H. (1993) *Self-help in America: A social movement perspective.* New York: Twayne.

Katz, M. B. (1989). *The undeserving poor: From the war on poverty to the war on welfare.* New York: Pantheon.

Katz, S. H. (1995). Is race a legitimate concept for science? AAPA Revised Statement on Race: A Brief Analysis and Commentary. Philadelphia, PA: University of Pennsylvania.

Kazak, A. E. & Marvin, R. S. (1984). Differences, difficulties and adaptation: Stress and social networks in families with a handicapped child. *Family Relations, 33*, 67–77.

Kazdin, A. E. (1988). The token economy: A decade later. In G. Davey & C. Cullen (Eds.), *Human operant conditioning and behavior modification* (pp. 119–137). New York: John Wiley.

Kazdin, A. E. (1991). Effectiveness of psychotherapy with children and adolescents. *Journal of Consulting and Clinical Psychology, 59*, 785–798.

Kazdin, A. E., French, N. H., & Sherick, R. B. (1981). Acceptability of alternative treatments for children: Evaluations by inpatient children, parents, and staff. *Journal of Consulting and Clinical Psychology, 49*, 900–907.

Kazdin, A. E. & Marvin, R. S. (1984). Differences, difficulties, and adaptations: Stress and social networks in families with a handicapped child. *Family Relations, 33*, 67–77.

Kelly J. & Sykes, P. (1989). Helping the helpers: A support group for family members of persons with AIDS. *Social Work, 34*, 239–242.

Kelly, J. A., St. Lawrence, J. S., Hood, H. V. & Brasfield, T. L. (1989). An objective test of AIDS risk behavior knowledge: Scale development, validation and norms. *Journal of Behavior Therapy and Experimental Psychiatry, 20*, 227–234.

Kelly, J. A., St. Lawrence, J. S., Hood, H. V., & Brasfield, T. L. (1989). Behavioral intervention to reduce AIDS risk activities. *Journal of Consulting and Clinical Psychology, 57*, 60–67.

Kendall, P. C. (Ed.). (1991). *Child and adolescent therapy: Cognitive-behavioral procedures.* New York: Guilford Press.

Kendall, P. C., Ronan, K. E., & Epps, J. (1991). Aggression in children and adolescents: Cognitive behavorial treatment perspectives. In D. J. Pepler & K. H. Rubin (Eds.), *The development and treatment of childhood aggression* (pp. 341–360). Hillsdale, NJ: Lawrence Erlbaum.

Kennedy, N. J. & Sanborn, J. S. (1992). Disclosure of tardive dyskinesia: Effect of written policy on risk disclosure. *Pharmacology Bulletin, 28*(1), 93–100.

Kerr, P. (1992a). Centers for head injury accused of earning millions for neglect. *New York Times*, Feb. 16, A1. Profits from trauma: A special report.

Kerr, P. (1992b). Mental hospital chains accused of much cheating on insurance. *New York Times*, Nov. 24, p. 1, 28.

Keyworth, R. (1990). Performance pay-An evolving system at Spectrum Center. *Performance Management Magazine, 8*, 6–10.

Kiesel, K. B., Lutzker, J. R. & Campbell, R. V. (1989). Behavioral relaxation training to reduce hyperventilation and seizures in a profoundly retarded epileptic child. *Journal of the Multihandicapped Person, 2*, 179–190.

Kiesler, D. J. (1966). Some myths of psychotherapy research and the search for a paradigm. *Psychological Bulletin, 65*, 110–136.

Kifer, R. E., Lewis, M. A., Green, D. R., & Phillips, E. L. (1974). Training pre-delinquent youths and their parents to negotiate conflict situations. *Journal of Applied Behavior Analysis, 7*, 357–364.

Killinger, B. (1977). The place of humor in adult psychotherapy. In A. J. Chapman & H.C. Foot (Eds.), *It's a funny thing humor.* Elmsford, NY: Pergamon.

Kinney, J., Haapala, D., & Booth, C. (1991). *Keeping families together: The Homebuilders model.* New York: Aldine de Gruyter.

Kinzie, J. D. (1985). Overview of clinical issues in the treatment of Southeast Asian refugees. In T. C. Owan (Ed.), *Southeast Asian mental health treatment prevention services, training and research.* Washington, DC: National Institute of Mental Health.

Kiresuk, T. J., Smith, A., & Cardillo, J. E. (Eds.). (1994). *Goal attainment scaling: Applications, theory and measurement.* Hillsdale, NJ: Erlbaum.

Kirigin, K. A., Braukmann, C. T., Atwater, J. D., & Wolf, M. M. (1987). An evaluation of teaching-family (Assessment Place) group homes for juvenile offenders. *Journal of Applied Behavior Analysis, 15,* 1–16.

Kirk, S. A. & Kutchins, H. (1988). Deliberate misdiagnosis in mental health practice. *Social Service Review, 62,* 225–237.

Kirk, S. A. & Kutchins, H. (1992a). *The selling of DSM: The rhetoric of science in psychiatry.* New York: Aldine de Gruyter.

Kirk, S. A. & Kutchins, H. (1992b). Five arguments for using DSM-III-R and why they are wrong. In E. Gambrill & R. Pruger (Eds.), *Controversial issues in social work* (pp. 146–154). Boston: Allyn & Bacon.

Kirk, S. A. & Kutchins, H. (1994). The myth of the reliability of DSM. *The Journal of Mind and Behavior, 15,* 71–86.

Kirkham, M. A. & Schilling, R. F. (1989). Life skills training with mothers of handicapped children. *Journal of Social Service Research, 13,* 67–87.

Kirmayer, L. J. (1994). Is the concept of mental disorder culturally relative? Yes. In S. A. Kirk & S. D. Einbinder (Eds.), *Controversial issues in mental health* (pp. 2–9). Boston: Allyn Bacon.

Kirschenbaum, D. S. & Karoly, P. (1977). When self-regulation fails: Tests of some preliminary hypotheses. *Journal of Consulting and Clinical Psychology, 45,* 1116–1125.

Kitchener, K. S. (1986). The reflective judgment model: Characteristics, evidence and measurement. In R. A. Mines & K. S. Kitchener, *Adult cognitive development: Methods and models* (pp. 76–91). New York: Praeger.

Klauss, R. & Bass, B. M. (1982). *Interpersonal communication in organizations.* San Diego: Academic.

Knapp, M. L. (1980). *Essentials of nonverbal communication.* New York: Holt, Rinehart and Winston.

Knapp, S. & VandeCreek, L. (1987). *Privileged communication in the mental health profession.* New York: Van Nostrand Reinhold.

Knitzer, J. (1978). Responsibility for delivery of services. In J. S. Mearig and Associates. (Eds.). *Working for children* (pp. 74–89). San Francisco: Jossey-Bass.

Koegel, L. K., Koegel, R. L., & Dunlap, G. (1996). *Positive behavioral support: Including people with difficult behavior in the community.* Baltimore: Paul H. Brookes.

Koegel, L. K., Koegel, R. L., Kellegrew, D., & Mullen, K. (1996). Parent education for prevention and reduction of severe behavior problems. In L. K. Koegel, R. L. Koegel, & G. Dunlap (Eds.), *Positive behavioral support: Including people with difficult behavior in the community.* Baltimore, MD: Paul H. Brookes.

Koegel, R. L. & Koegel, L. K. (1990). Extended reductions in stereotypic behavior of students with autism through a self-management treatment package. *Journal of Applied Behavior Analysis, 23,* 119–127.

Koegel, R. L. & Rincover, A. (1974). Treatment of psychotic children in a classroom environment: I. Learning in a large group. *Journal of Applied Behavior Analysis, 7,* 45–59.

Koegel, R. L., Frea, W. D., & Surratt, A. V. (1994). Self-management of problematic social behavior. In E. Schopler, G. B. Mesibov (Eds.), *Behavioral issues and autism: Current issues in autism* (pp. 81–97). New York: Plenum Press.

Kohlberg, L. & Lickona, T. (1986). *The stages of ethical development: From childhood through old age.* New York: Harper.

Kohr, M. A., Parrish, J. M., Neef, N. A., Driessen, J. R., & Hallinan, P. C. (1988). Communication skills training for parents: Experimental and social validation. *Journal of Applied Behavior Analysis, 21,* 21–30.

Koertge, N. (1995). How feminism in now alienating women from science. *The Skeptical Inquirer, 19,* 42–43.

Kopta, S. M., Newman, F. L., McGovern, M. P., & Sandrock, D. (1986). Psychological orientations: A comparison of conceptualizations, interventions, and treatment plan costs. *Journal of Consulting and Clinical Psychology, 54,* 369–374.

Korte, C. (1983). Help-seeking in the city: Personal and organizational sources of help. In A. Nadler, J. D. Fisher, & B. M. DePaulo (Eds.), *New directions in helping.* Vol. III, Applied perspectives on help seeking and receiving (pp. 255–271). New York: Academic Press.

Kottler, J. A. & Blau, D. S. (1989). *The imperfect therapist: Learning from failure in therapeutic practice.* San Francisco: Jossey-Bass.

Kozloff, M. A. (1979). *A program for families of children with learning and behavior problems.* New York: John Wiley.

Kozol, J. (1990). *The night is dark and I am far from home*. (Rev. Ed.) New York: Simon & Schuster.

Krantz, S. E. & Moos, R. H. (1988). Risk factors at intake predict nonremission among depressed patients. *Journal of Consulting and Clinical Psychology, 56*, 863–869.

Krull, D. S. & Erickson, D. J. (1995). Inferential hopscotch: How people draw social inferences from behavior. *Current Directions in Psychological Science, 4*, 35–38.

Kuhn, T. S. (1970). *The structure of scientific revolutions* (2nd. Ed.). Chicago: University of Chicago Press. (Originally published in 1962.)

Kunkel, J. (1970). *Society and economic growth: A behavioral perspective of social change*. New York: Oxford University Press.

Laird, J. & Green, R. J. (Eds.). (1996). *Lesbians and gays in couples and families: A handbook for therapists*. San Francisco: Jossey-Bass.

Lambert, M. J., & Bergin, A. E. (1994). The effectiveness of psychotherapy. In A. E. Bergin & S. L. Garfield (Eds.), *Handbook of psychotherapy and behavior change* (pp, 143–189). New York: John Wiley.

Lambert, M. J., DeJulio, S. S., & Stein, D. M. (1978). Therapist interpersonal skills: Process, outcome, methodological considerations, and recommendations for future research. *Psychological Bulletin, 85*, 467–489.

Lane, H. L. (1992). *Mask of benevolence: Disabling the deaf community*. New York: Knopf.

Lang, P. (1988). What are the data of emotion? In V. Hamilton, G. H. Bower, & N. H. Frijda (Eds.), *Cognitive science perspectives on emotion, motivation, and cognition* (pp. 173–191). Boston: Kluwer Academic Pub.

Langer, E. J. (1975). The illusion of control. *Journal of Personality and Social Psychology, 32*, 311–328.

Langer, E. J. (1989). *Mindfulness*. Reading, MA: Addison-Wesley.

Langer, E. & Rodin, J. (1976). The effects of choice and enhanced personal responsibility: A field experiment in an institutional setting. *Journal of Personality and Social Psychology, 34*, 191–198.

Lappe, F. M., & DuBois, P. M. (1994). *The quickening of America: Rebuilding our nation, remaking our lives*. San Francisco: Jossey-Bass.

Larson, D. G. (1993). *The helpers' journey: Working with people facing grief, loss, and life-threatening illness*. Champaign, IL: Research Press.

Larsen, J. J. & Juhasz, A. M. (1986). The knowledge of child development inventory. *Adolescence, 21*, 39–54.

Larson, K. A. & Gerber, M. M. (1987). Effects of metacognitive training for enhancing alert behavior in learning disabled and low achieving delinquents. *Exceptional Children, 54*, 201–211.

Lasch, C. (1977). *Haven in a heartless world*. New York: Basic Books.

LaVigna, G. W., Willis, T. J., Schaull, J. F., Abedi, M., & Sweitzer, M. (1994). *The periodic service review: Total quality assurance system for human services in education*. Baltimore, MD: Paul H. Brookes.

LaVigna, G. W. & Donnellan, A. M. (1986). *Alternatives to punishment: Solving behavior problems with non-aversive strategies*. New York: Irvington.

Layng, T. V. J. & Andronis, P. T. (1984). Toward a functional analysis of delusional speech and hallucinatory behavior. *The Behavior Analyst, 7*, 139–156.

Lazarus, R. S. (1982). The costs and benefits of denial. In S. Breznitz (Ed.), *The denial of stress*. New York: International Universities Press.

Lazarus, R. S. & Launier, R. (1978). Stress-related transactions between person and environment. In L. A. Pervin & M. Lewis (Eds.), *Perspectives in interactional psychology* (pp. 287–327). New York: Plenum.

Lazarus, R. S., Kanner, A., & Folkman, S. (1980). Emotions: A cognitive-phenomenological analysis. In R. Plutchik & H. Kellerman (Eds.). *Theories of emotion*. New York: Academic Press.

Leahey, T. H. & Leahey, G. E. (1983). *Psychology's occult doubles: Psychology and the problem of pseudoscience*. Chicago: Nelson Hall.

Leary, M. R. (1989). Self-presentational processes in leadership emergence and effectiveness. In R. A. Giacalone & P. Rosenfeld (Eds.), *Impression management in the organization* (pp. 363–374). Hillsdale, NJ: Lawrence Erlbaum.

Leary, M. R. (1995). *Self-presentation, impression management and interpersonal behavior*. Madison, WI: Brown & Benchmark.

Leavitt, S. & McGowan, B. (1991). Transferring the principles of intensive family preservation services to different fields of practice. In E. M. Tracy, D. A. Haapala, J. Kinney, & P. J. Pecora (Eds.), *Intensive family preservation services: An instructional sourcebook* (pp. 51–69). Mandel School of Applied Social Sciences: Case Western Reserve University.

Lebow, J. (1983). Research assessing consumer satisfaction with mental health treatment: A review of findings. *Evaluation and Program Planning, 6,* 211–236.

LeCroy, C. W. (1994). *Handbook of child and adolescent treatment manuals.* New York: Lexington Books.

Lee, J. A. B., & Swenson, C. R. (1978). A community social service agency: Theory in action. *Social Casework, 59,* 359–369.

Leichtman, M. D. & Ceci, S. J. (1995). The effects of stereotypes and suggestions on preschoolers' reports. *Developmental Psychology, 31,* 568–578.

Leitenberg, H. (Ed.). (1990). *Handbook of social and evaluation anxiety.* New York: Plenum.

Leitenberg, H., Agras, W. S., Thompson, L. E. & Wright, D. E. (1968). Feedback in behavior modification: An experimental analysis in two phobic cases. *Journal of Applied Behavior Analysis, 1,* 131–137.

Lemerise, E. A. & Dodge, K. A. (1993). The development of anger and hostile interactions. In M. Lewis & J. M. Haviland (Eds.), *Handbook of emotions* (pp. 537–546). New York: Guilford.

Lemert, E. M. (1967). *Human deviance, social problems and social control.* Englewood Cliffs, NJ: Prentice Hall.

Lennon, T. M. (1993). *Statistics on social work education in the United States, 1992.* Alexandria, VI: Council on Social Work Education.

Lenrow, P. & Cowden, P. (1980). Human services, professionals, and the paradox of institutional reform. *American Journal of Community Psychology, 8,* 463–484.

Lepper, M. R. & Hodell, M. (1989). Intrinsic motivation in the classroom. In C. Ames and R. Ames (Eds.), *Research on motivation in education. Vol. 3: Goals and cognitions.* New York: Academic.

Lerman, H. (1992). The limits of phenomenology: A feminist critique of humanist personalities. In M. Ballou & L. Brown (Eds.), *Personality and psychopathology: Feminist reappraisals* (pp. 8–19). New York: Guilford.

Lerner, M. (1980). *The belief in a just world: A fundamental delusion.* New York: Plenum.

Levine, M. (1988). An analysis of mutual assistance. *American Journal of Community Psychology, 16,* 167–189.

Levine, M. & Perkins, D. V. (1996). *Principles of community psychology: Perspectives and trends* (2nd Ed.). New York: Oxford.

Levy, R. L. (1977). Relationship of an overt commitment to task compliance in behavior therapy.

Journal of Behavior Therapy and Experimental Psychiatry, 8, 25–29.

Lewin, J. (1990). Neglect at nursing home: In a first, suits are won. *New York Times,* A-1/14 7/12/90.

Lewis, M. & Haviland, J. M. (Eds.). (1993). *Handbook of emotions.* New York: Guilford Press.

Lewis, R. G. & Ho, M. K. (1975). Social work with Native Americans. *Social Work, 20*(5), 379–382.

Lewontin, R. C. (1991). *Biology as ideology: The doctrine of DNA.* New York: Harper Collins.

Lewontin, R. C. (1994). *Inside and outside: Gene, environment, and organism.* Clark University Press.

Lewontin, R. C. (1995). In R. B. Silvers (Ed.), *Hidden histories of science.* New York: New York Review Books.

Lewontin, R. C., Rose, S., & Kamin, L. J. (1984). *Not in our genes.* New York: Pantheon.

Liberman, R. P., DeRisi, W. J., & Mueser, K. T. (1989). *Social skills training for psychiatric patients.* New York: Pergamon.

Lidz, C. W., Meisel, A., Zerubavel, E., Carter, M., Sestak, R. M., & Roth, L. H. (1984). *Informed consent: A study of decision making in psychiatry.* New York: Guilford.

Lindsey, D. (1994). *The welfare of children.* New York: Oxford University Press.

Lindsley, O. R. (1964). Geriatric behavioral prosthetics. In R. Kastenbaum (Ed.). *New thoughts on old age* (pp. 41–60). New York: Springer-Verlag.

Linehan, M. M. (1993). *Cognitive-behavioral treatment of borderline personality disorder.* New York: Guilford.

Linney, J. A. (1990). Community psychology into the 1990's: Capitalizing on opportunity and promoting innovation. *American Journal of Community Psychology, 18,* 1–17.

Linsk, N. L. & Hanrahan, P. & Pinkston, E. M. (1991). Teaching the use of community services to elderly people and their families. In P. A. Wisocki (Ed.), *Handbook of clinical behavior therapy with the elderly client* (pp. 479–504). New York: Plenum.

Lipinski, D. P., Black, J. L., & Nelson, R. O. and others. (1975). Influence of motivational variables on the reactivity and reliability of self-recording. *Journal of Consulting and Clinical Psychology, 43,* 637–646.

Lipman, M. (1991). *Thinking in education.* Cambridge: Cambridge University Press.

Lipsky, M. (1983). *Street-level bureaucracy: Dilemmas of the individual in public services.* New York: Russell Sage.

Lipton, J. P., & Hershaft, A. M. (1985). On the widespread acceptance of dubious medical findings. *Journal of Health and Social Behavior, 26,* 336–351.

Lochman, J. E. & Dodge, K. A. (1994). Social-cognitive processes of severely violent, moderately aggressive, and nonaggressive boys. *Journal of Consulting and Clinical Psychology, 62,* 366–374.

Lochman, J. E., Wayland, K. K., & White, K. J. (1993). Social goals: Relationships to adolescent adjustment and to social problem solving. *Journal of Abnormal Child Psychology, 21,* 135–151.

Lock, M. (1987). DSM-III as a culture-bound construct: Commentary on culture-bound syndromes and international disease classifications. *Culture, Medicine & Psychiatry, 11,* 35–42.

Lock, M. (1993). *Encounters with aging: Mythologies of menopause in Japan and North America.* Berkeley, CA: The University of California Press.

Locke, E. A., Cartledge, N., & Koeppel, J. (1968). Motivational effects of knowledge of results: A goal setting phenomenon? *Psychological Bulletin, 70,* 474–485.

Lockwood, S. E. (1990). What's known- and what's not known-about drug-exposed infants. *Youth Law News, 11,* 15–19.

Lofland, J., & Lofland, L. H. (1995). *Analyzing social settings: A guide to qualitative observation and analysis* (3rd Ed.). Belmont, CA: Wadsworth.

Loftus, E. (1979). *Eyewitness testimony.* Cambridge, MA: Harvard University Press.

Loftus, E. (1993). The reality of repressed memories. *American Psychologist, 48,* 518–537.

Loftus, E. F. & Christianson, S. (1989). Malleability of memory for emotional events. In T. Archer & L. Nilsson (Eds.), *Aversion, avoidance and anxiety: Perspectives on aversively motivated behavior* (pp. 311–322). Hillsdale, NJ: Lawrence Erlbaum.

Loftus, E. & Ketcham, K. (1994). *The myth of repressed memory: False memories and allegations of abuse.* New York: St. Martin's Press.

Loitz, P. A. & Kratochwill, T. R. (1995). Parent consultation: Evaluation of a self-help manual for children's homework problems. *School Psychology International, 16,* 389–396.

Lord, C., Ross, L., & Lepper, M. R. (1979). Biased assimilation and attitude polarization: The effects of prior theories on subsequently considered evidence. *Journal of Personality and Social Psychology, 37,* 2089–2109.

Luborsky, L., McClellan, A. T., Woody, G. E.,

O'Brien, C. P., & Auerbach, A. (1985). Therapist success and its determinants. *Archives of General Psychiatry, 42,* 602–611.

Luiselli, J. K., Matson, J. L., & Singh, N. H. (Eds.). (1992). *Self-injurious behavior: Analysis, assessment, and treatment.* New York: Springer-Verlag.

Lum, D. (1992). *Social work practice and people of color: A process-stage approach.* Pacific Grove, CA: Brooks/Cole.

Lutzker, J. R. & Campbell, R. V. (1994). *Ecobehavioral family interventions in developmental disabilities.* Pacific Grove: Brooks Cole.

Lynch, E. W. & Hanson, M. J. (1992). *Developing cross-cultural competence: A guide for working with young children and their families.* Baltimore, MD: Paul H. Brookes.

Lytton, H. & Roney, D. M. (1991). Parents' differential socialization of boys and girls: A meta-analysis. *Psychological Bulletin, 109,* 267–296.

MacKenzie-Keating, S. E. & McDonald, L. (1990). Overcorrection: Reviewed, revisited and revised. *The Behavior Analyst, 13,* 39–48.

MacLean, P. D. (1993). Cerebral evolution of emotion. In M. Lewis & J. M. Haviland (Eds.), *Handbook of emotions* (pp. 67–83). New York: Guilford Press.

MacPhillamy, D. J. & Lewinsohn, P. M. (1982). The pleasant events schedule: Studies on reliability, validity, and scale intercorrelation. *Journal of Consulting and Clinical Psychology, 50,* 363–380.

Magee, J. (1985). *Philosophy in the real world.* LaSalle, IL: Open Court.

Mager, R. F. (1972). *Goal analysis.* Belmont, CA: Fearson.

Mager, R. F. & Pipe, P. (1970). *Analyzing performance problems.* Belmont, CA: Fearon.

Malott, R. W. (1989). The achievement of evasive goals: Control by rules describing contingencies that are not direct acting. In S. C. Hayes (Ed.), *Rule-governed behavior: Cognition, contingencies and instructional control* (pp. 269–322). New York: Plenum.

Malott, R. W. (1994). *Rule-governed behavior, self-management, performance management.* Kalamazoo, MI: Western Michigan University, Department of Psychology.

Malott, R. W., Whaley, D. L. & Mallott, M. E. (1993). *Elementary principles of behavior* (2nd Ed.). Englewood Cliffs, NJ: Prentice Hall.

Maluccio, A. N. (1979). *Learning from clients.* New York: Free Press.

Manderscheid, R. W. & Sonnenschein, M. A. (Eds.).

(1993). *Mental health, United States, 1992.* Rockville, MD: U. S. Department of Health and Human Services.

Mank, D. M. & Horner, R. H. (1987). Self-recruited feedback: A cost-effective procedure for maintaining behavior. *Research in Developmental Disabilities, 8,* 91–112.

Manning, N. (Ed.). (1988). *Social problems and welfare ideology.* Brookfield, VT: Gower.

Margolin, L. (in press). *Under the cover of kindness: The invention of social work.* Charlottesville, VI: University Press of Virginia.

Marks, I. M. (1987). *Fears, phobias and rituals: Panic, anxiety, and their disorders.* New York: Oxford University Press.

Marlatt, G. A. & Gordon, J. R. (Eds.). (1985). *Relapse prevention: Maintenance strategies in the treatment of addiction.* New York: Guilford.

Marmor, J. (1976). Common operational factors in diverse approaches to behavior change. In A. Burton (Ed.), *What makes behavior change possible?* New York: Brunner/Mazel.

Martin, G. & Pear, J. (1996). *Behavior modification: What it is and how to do it* (5th ed.). Upper Saddle River, NJ: Prentice-Hall.

Martin, M. A. & Neyowith, S. A. (1988). Creating community: Group work to develop social support networks with homeless mentally ill. *Social Work With Groups, 11,* 79–93.

Martin, R. (1975). *Legal challenges to behavior modification: Trends in schools, corrections, and mental health.* Champaign, IL: Research Press.

Maslach, C. (1982). *Burnout: The cost of caring.* Englewood Cliffs, NJ: Prentice Hall.

Masson, J. M. (1984). *The assault on truth: Freud's suppression of the seduction theory.* New York: Farrar, Straus & Giroux.

Mathews, D. (1990). Effective communities are different. In L. Decker & Associates (Eds.), *Community education: Building learning communities* (pp. 1–11). Alexandria, VI: National Community Education Association.

Mathews, R. M. & Fawcett, S. B. (1977). Community applications of instructional technology: Training low-income proctors. *Journal of Applied Behavior Analysis, 10,* 747–784.

Mathews, R. M. & Fawcett, S. B. (1981). *Matching clients and services: Information and referral.* Beverly Hills, CA: Sage.

Mathews, R. N. & Fawcett, S. B. (1984). Building the capacities of job candidates through behavior in-

struction. *Journal of Community Psychology, 12,* 123–129.

Mattaini, M. A. (1989). Eco-mapping in family assessment: Preliminary empirical support. Unpublished manuscript. School of Social Work, Columbia University (described in Mattaini, 1993, p. 250.)

Mattaini, M. A. (1991). Choosing weapons for the war on "crack": An operant analysis. *Research on Social Work Practice, 1*(2), 188–213.

Mattaini, M. A. (1993). *More than a thousand words: Graphics for clinical practice.* Washington, D.C.: NASW Press.

Matteson, M. T. & Ivancevich, J. M. (1987). *Controlling work stress: Effective human resource and management strategies.* San Francisco: Jossey-Bass.

Mayer, J. E. & Timms, N. (1970). *The client speaks: Working class impressions of casework.* New York: Atherton Press.

Mayfield, M. (1994). *Thinking for yourself: Developing critical thinking skills through reading and writing* (3rd Ed.). Belmont, CA: Wadsworth.

Mays, D. T. & Franks, C. M. (Eds.). (1985). *Negative outcome in psychotherapy and what to do about it.* New York: Springer.

M'Cagg, E. B. (1879). The charities of Chicago. In F. B. Sanborn (Ed.), *Proceedings of the sixth annual Conference of Charities*, Chicago, June (pp. 145–152). Boston: Williams & Co.

McClanahan, L. E., & Krantz, P. J. (1993). On systems analysis in autism intervention programs. *Journal of Applied Behavior Analysis, 26,* 589–596.

McClannahan, L. E. & Risley, T. R. (1973). A store for nursing home residents. *Nursing Homes, 7,* 26–31.

McClannahan, L. E. & Risley, T. R. (1975). Design of living environments for nursing home residents: Increasing participation in recreational activities. *Journal of Applied Behavior Analysis, 8,* 261–268.

McCulloch, O. C. (1880). Associated charities. In R. B. Sanborn (Ed.), *Proceedings of the seventh annual Conference of Charities* (pp. 122–135). Cleveland, June & July, 1879. Boston: Williams & Co.

McCullough, J. P., Cornell, J. E., McDaniel, M.H., & Mueller, R. K. (1974). Utilization of the simultaneous treatment design to improve student behavior in a first-grade classroom. *Journal of Consulting and Clinical Psychology, 42,* 288–292.

McDermott, C. J. (1989). Empowering the elderly nursing home resident: The resident rights campaign. *Social Work, 34,* 155–157.

McDowell, J. J. (1988). Matching theory in natural human environments. *The Behavior Analyst, 11,* 95–109.

McFall, R. M. (1970). The effects of self-monitoring on normal smoking behavior. *Journal of Consulting and Clinical Psychology, 35,* 135–142.

McGimsey, J. F. & Favell, J. E. (1988). The effects of increased physical exercise on disruptive behavior in retarded persons. *Journal of Autism and Developmental Disorders, 18,* 167–179.

McGimsey, J. F., Greene, B. F., & Lutzker, J. R. (1995). Competence in aspects of behavioral treatment and consultation: Implications for service delivery and graduate training. *Journal of Applied Behavior Analysis, 28,* 301–315.

McGrath, E., Keita, G. P., Strickland, B. R., & Russo, N. F. (Eds.). (1990). *Women and depression: Risk factors and treatment issues.* Washington, D.C.: American Psychological Association.

McGregor, D. (1960). *The human side of enterprise.* New York: McGraw Hill.

McInnis, K. (1991). Ethnic-sensitive work with Hmong refugee children. *Child Welfare, 70,* 571–580.

McLaugh, L., Irby, M. A., Langman, J. (1994). *Urban sanctuaries: Neighborhood organizations in the lives and futures of inner-city youth.* San Francisco: Jossey-Bass.

McMurty, S. L. (1993). *Social work macro practice.* New York: Longman.

McReynolds, P. (1989). Diagnosis and clinical assessment: Current status and major issues. In M. R. Rosenzweig & L. W. Porter (Eds.), *Annual Review of Psychology, 40,* 83–108.

Meehl, P. E. (1973). Why I do not attend case conferences. *Psychodiagnostic Papers* (pp. 225–302). Minneapolis, MN: University of Minnesota Press.

Meichenbaum, D. (1971). Examination of model characteristics in reducing avoidance behavior. *Journal of Personality and Social Psychology, 17,* 298–307.

Meichenbaum, D. (1977). *Cognitive behavior modification: An integrative approach.* New York: Plenum.

Meichenbaum, D. H. & Goodman, J. (1971). Training impulsive children to talk to themselves: A means for developing self-control. *Journal of Abnormal Psychology, 77,* 115–126.

Meichenbaum, D. & Turk, D. C. (1987). *Facilitating treatment adherence: A practitioner's handbook.* New York: Plenum.

Meinhold, P. & Mulick, J. A. (1990). Counter-habilitative contingencies for mentally retarded people: Ecological and regulatory influences. *Mental Retardation, 28,* 67–73.

Melin, L. & Gotestam, K. G. (1981). The effects of re-arranging ward routines on communication and eating behaviors of psychogeriatric patients. *Journal of Applied Behavior Analysis, 14,* 47–51.

Merelman, R. M. (1975). Social stratification and political socialization in mature industrial societies. *Comparative Education Review, 19*(1), 13–30.

Meritor Sav. Bank v. Vinson (1986). 477. US. 57.

Meyer, D. (1988). *The positive thinkers: Popular religious psychology from Mary Baker Eddy to Norman Vincent Peale and Ronald Reagan.* (Rev. Ed.). Middletown, CT: Wesleyan University Press.

Meyer, L. H., Peck, C. A. & Brown, L. (Eds.). (1991). *Critical issues in the lives of people with severe disabilities.* Baltimore: Paul H. Brookes.

Meyer, L. H. & Evans, I. N. (1989). *Nonaversive intervention for behavior problems: A manual for home and community.* Baltimore, MD: Paul H. Brookes.

Meyers, R. J. & Smith, J. E. (1995). *Clinical guide to alcohol treatment: The community reinforcement approach.* New York: Guilford.

Michaels, J. L. (1993). *Concepts and principles of behavior analysis.* Kalamazoo, MI: Society for Advancement of Behavior Analysis.

Midgley, J. (1995). *Social development: The developmental perspective in social welfare.* Thousand Oaks, CA: Sage.

Military whistleblowers receive PD support. (1990). *Psychological Practitioner, 4*(2), Summer, p. 5. Washington, D.C.: American Psychological Association.

Millenson, J. R. & Leslie, J. L. (1979). *Principles of behavioral analysis* (2nd Ed.). New York: Macmillan.

Miller, D. (1994). *Critical rationalism: A restatement and defense.* Chicago: Open Court.

Miller, D. C. (1990). *Women in social welfare: A feminist analysis.* New York: Praeger.

Miller, J. D. (1987). The scientifically illiterate. *American Demographics, 9,* 26–31.

Miller, D. J. & Hersen, M. (1992). *Research fraud in the behavioral and biomedical sciences.* New York: John Wiley.

Miller, L. S., Pruger, R., & Clark, M. (1979). Referral: Technology and efficiency. *Journal of Social Service Research, 3,* 175–186.

Mills, C. W. (1959). *The sociological imagination.* New York: Oxford University Press.

Mindel, C. H. & Haberstein, R. W. (Eds.). (1981). *Ethnic families in America: Patterns and variations* (2nd Ed.). New York: Elsevier.

Minkler, M. (1985). Building supportive ties and sense

of community among the inner-city elderly: The Tenderloin Senior Outreach Project. *Health Education Quarterly, 12*, 303–314.

Minkler, M. (1992). Community organizing among the elderly poor in the United States: A case study. *International Journal of Health Services, 22*, 303–316.

Minuchin, S. (1974). *Families and family therapy.* Cambridge, MA: Harvard University Press.

Mirowsky, J. & Ross, C. E. (1989). *Social causes of psychological distress.* New York: Aldine de Gruyter.

Mischel, W. (1968). *Personality and assessment.* New York: Wiley.

Mischel, W. (1981). A cognitive-social learning approach to assessment. In T.V. Merluzzi, C. R. Glass, & M. Genest (Eds.), *Cognitive assessment* (pp. 479–502). New York: Guilford.

Moncher, M. & Schinke, S. P. (1994). Group intervention to prevent tobacco use among Native American youth. *Research on Social Work Practice, 4*, 160–171.

Moore, E. D. (1991). Influencing legislation for the human services. In R. L. Edwards and J. A. Yankey, *Skills for effective human services management* (pp. 76–89). Silver Spring, MD: National Association of Social Workers.

Moore, B. E. & Fine, B. D. (Eds.). (1990). *Psychoanalytic terms and concepts* New Haven and London: The American Psychoanalytic Association and Yale University Press.

Moore, T. E. (1996). Scientific consensus and expert testimony: Lessons from the Judas Priest Trial. *The Skeptical Inquirer, 20*, 32–38.

Moos, R. H. & Lemke, S. (1994). *Group residences for older adults: Physical features, policies, and social climate.* New York: Oxford University Press.

Morales v. Turman case (383F. Supp. 53) (E.D. tex 1974).

Morris, R. (1986). *Rethinking social welfare: Why care for the stranger?* White Plains, NY: Longman.

Morrow, B. (1990). Early intervention programs may help drug-exposed children. *Youth Law News, 11*(1), 31–32.

Morrow-Bradley, C. & Elliot, R. (1986). Utilization of psychotherapy research by practicing psychotherapists. *American Psychologist, 41*, 188–197.

Moses, A. E. & Hawkins, R. O., Jr. (1981). *Counseling lesbian women and gay men: A life issues approach.* St. Louis, MO: C. V. Mosby.

Mueser, K. T., Valenti-Hein, D., & Yarnold, P. R. (1987). Dating-skills groups for the developmentally disabled. *Behavior Modification, 11*(2), 200–228.

Mulick, J. A. & Meinhold, P. M. (1992). Analyzing the impact of regulations on residential ecology. *Mental Retardation, 30*, 151–161.

Mullaly, R. (1993). *Structural social work: Ideology, theory, and practice.* Toronto: McClelland & Stewart.

Munakata, T. (1989). The socio-cultural significance of the diagnostic label "Neurasthenia" in Japan's mental health care system. *Culture, Medicine, and Psychiatry, 13*, 203–213.

Munton, A. G., Mooney, A., & Rowland, L. (1995). Deconstructing quality: A conceptual framework for the new paradigm in day care provision for the under eights. *Early Childhood Development and Care, 114*, 11–23.

Munz, P. (1985). *Our knowledge of the growth of knowledge: Popper or Wittgenstein.* London: Routledge & Kegan Paul.

Munz, P. (1987). Philosophy and the mirror of Rorty. In G. Radnitzky & W. W. Bartley, III (Eds.), *Evolutionary epistemology, rationality, and the sociology of knowledge* (pp. 345–398). LaSalle, IL: Open Court.

Munz, P. (1992). What's postmodern, anyway? *Philosophy and Literature, 16*, 333–353.

Murphy, S. T. & Rogan, P. M. (1995). *Closing the shop: Conversion from shelter to integrated work.* Baltimore: Paul H. Brooks.

Murray, C. (1984). *Losing ground: American social policy 1950–1980.* New York: Basic Books.

Mydans, S. (1995). Should dying patients be told? Ethnic pitfall is found. *New York Times*, Sept. 13, A/13.

Nader, R. (1983). *A citizen's guide to lobbying.* New York: Dembner.

Naftulin, D. H., Ware, J. E. & Donnelly, F. A. (1973). The Doctor Fox lecture: A paradigm of educational seduction. *Journal of Medical Education, 48*, 630–635.

Natale, J.A. (1988). Are you open to suggestion. *Psychology Today, 22*, 28–30.

National Association of Social Workers. (1996). *Code of ethics.* Silver Spring, MD: NASW. (Adopted 8/15/96.)

Nay, W. R. (1979). *Multimethod clinical assessment.* New York: Gardner.

Nay, W. R. (1986). Analogue measures. In A. R. Ciminero, K. S. Calhoun, & H.E. Adams (Eds.),

Handbook of behavioral assessment (pp. 223–252). New York: Wiley.

Nee, C. (1993). Car theft: The offender's perspective. *Home Office Research and Statistics Department, Research Findings, 3,* Feb. Home Office, 50 Queen An's Gate, London, SW 1H 9AT, Information Department, Research and Planning Unit.

Neef, N. A. (1995). Pyramidal parent training by peers. *Journal of Applied Behavior Analysis, 28,* 333–337.

Neef, N. A., Parrish, J. M., Egel, A. L., & Sloan, M. E. (1986). Training respite care providers for families with handicapped children: Experimental analysis and validation of an instructional package. *Journal of Applied Behavior Analysis, 19,* 105–124.

Neifert, J. (1995). field work report. Unpublished paper, University of California at Berkeley.

Neighbors, H., Jackson, J., Bohman, P., & Gurin, G. (1982). Stress, coping, black mental health: Preliminary findings from a national study. *Prevention in Human Services, 2,* 5–29.

Nelson-Jones, R. (1987). *Personal responsibility counseling and therapy: An integrative approach.* New York: Hemisphere.

Nelson-Jones, R. (1993). *Practical counseling and helping skills: How to use the lifeskills helping model* (3rd Ed.). New York: Cassell.

Netting, F. E., Kettner, P. M., & McMurty, S. L. (1993). *Social work macro-practice.* New York: Longman.

Nezu, A. M., Nezu, C. M., & Perri, M. G. (1989). *Problem-solving therapy for depression: Theory, research, and clinical guidelines.* New York: Wiley.

Nicarthy, G., Gottlieb, N., & Coffman, S. (1993). *You don't have to take it!: A woman's guide to confronting emotional abuse at work.* Seattle: Seal Press.

Nickerson, R. S. (1986). *Reflections on reasoning.* Hillsdale, NJ: Lawrence Erlbaum.

Nickerson, R. S. (1988–89). On improving thinking through instruction. In E. Z. Rothkopf (Ed.), *Review of research in education* (pp. 3–57). Washington, DC: American Educational Research Association.

Nickerson, R. S., Perkins, D. N., & Smith, E. E. (1985). *The teaching of thinking.* Hillsdale, NJ: Lawrence Erlbaum.

Nisbett, R. & Ross, L. (1980). *Human inference: Strategies and shortcomings of social judgement.* Englewood Cliffs, NJ: Prentice-Hall.

Notarious, C. I. & Markman, H. J. (1989). Coding marital interaction: A sampling and discussion of current issues. *Behavioral Assessment, 11,* 1–11.

Novaco, R. W. (1975). *Anger control: The development and evaluation of an experimental treatment.* Lexington, MA: Heath-Lexington.

Novaco, R. W. (1995). Clinical problems of anger and assessment and regulation through a stress coping skills approach. In W. O'Donohue & L. Krasner (Eds.), *Handbook of psychological skills training: Clinical techniques and applications* (pp. 320–338). Boston, MA: Allyn & Bacon.

Novak, M. & Guest, C. (1989). Application of a multi-dimensional caregiver burden inventory. *The Gerontologist, 29,* 798–803.

Nurius, P. S. & Hudson, W. W. (1993). *Human services: Practice, evaluation, and computers.* Pacific Grove, CA: Brooks/Cole.

Oakley, A. (1976). *Women's work: The housewife, past and present.* New York: Vintage.

O'Brien, J. (1987). A guide to life-style planning: Using natural support systems. In B. Wilcox, G. T. Bellamy, *A comprehensive guide to the activities catalogue: An alternative curriculum for youth and adults with severe disabilities* (pp. 175–189). Baltimore: Paul H. Brookes.

O'Donohue, W. & Krasner, L. (Eds.). (1995). *Handbook of psychological skills training: Clinical techniques and applications.* Boston: Allyn & Bacon.

O'Donohue, W. & Szymanski, J. (1994). How to win friends and not influence clients: Popular but problematic ideas that impair treatment decisions. *The Behavior Therapist, 17*(2), 29–33.

O'Donohue, W., Fisher, J. E., Plaud, J. J. (1989). What is a good treatment decision? The client's perspective. *Professional Psychology: Research and Practice, 20,* 404–407.

Ofshe, R. & Watters, E. (1994). *Making monsters: False memories, psychotherapy, and sexual hysteria.* New York: Charles Scribner's.

Ohman, A. (1993). Fear and anxiety as emotional phenomena: Clinical phenomenology, evolutionary perspectives, and information-processing mechanisms. In M. Lewis & J. M. Haviland (Eds.), *Handbook of emotions* (pp. 511–534). New York: Guilford.

Ollendick, T. H. (1983). Reliability and validity on the Revised Fear Survey Schedule for Children (FSSC-R). *Behavioral Research & Therapy, 21,* 685–692.

Ollendick, T. H., Matson, J. L., & Helsel, W. J. (1985). Fears in children and adolescents: Normative data. *Behavioral Research and Therapy, 23,* 465–467.

Olweus, D. (1993). *Bullying at school: What we know and what we can do.* Oxford: Blackwell Press.

Olweus, D. (1994). Bullying at school: Long-term outcomes for the victims and an effective school-based intervention program. In L. R. Huesmann (Ed.), *Aggressive behavior, current perspectives* (pp. 97–130). New York: Plenum.

O'Neill, R. E., Horner, R. H., Albin, R. W., Storey, K., & Sprague, J. R. (1990). *Functional analysis of problem behavior: A practical assessment guide.* Sycamore, IL: Sycamore Press.

Opulente, M. & Mattaini, M. A. (1993). Toward a welfare that works. *Behavior and Social Issues* (pp. 17–34).

Ortiz de Montellano, B. (1992). Magic melanin: Spreading scientific illiteracy among minorities: Part II. *Skeptical Inquirer, 16*, 162–166.

Otto, M. W., Pollack, M. H., & Barlow, D. H. (1995). *Stopping anti-anxiety medication: A workbook for patients wanting to discontinue benzodiazepine treatment for panic disorder.* Albany, NY: Graywind Publications.

Pace, G. M., Ivancic, M. T., Edwards, G. L., Iwata, B. A., & Page, T. J. (1985). Assessment of stimulus preference and reinforcer value with profoundly retarded individuals. *Journal of Applied Behavior Analysis, 18*, 249–255.

Pacey, A. (1983). *The culture of technology.* Cambridge, MA: MIT Press.

Paquin, M. J. (1977). The status of family and marital therapy outcomes: Methodological and substantive considerations. *Canadian Psychological Review. 18*, 221–232.

Parkes, C. M., Stevenson-Hinde, J., & Marris, P. (Eds.). (1991). *Attachment across the life cycle.* New York: Routledge.

Patterson, C. J. (1995). Lesbian and gay parenthood. In M. H. Bornstein, (Ed.), *Handbook of parenting, Vol. 3: Status and social conditions of parenting* (pp. 255–274). Mahwah, NJ: Erlbaum.

Patterson, G. R. (1975). *Families: Applications of social learning to family life.* Champaign, IL: Research Press.

Patterson, G. R. (1982). *A social learning approach, Vol. 3, Coercive family process.* Eugene, OR: Castalia.

Patterson, G. R. & Chamberlain, P. (1994). A functional analysis of resistance during parent training therapy. *Clinical Psychology: Science and Practice, 1*, 53–70.

Patterson, G. R. & Chamberlain, P. (1988). Treatment process: A problem at three levels. In L. C. Wynne (Ed.), *State of the art in family therapy research: Controversies and recommendations* (pp. 189–223). New York: Family Process Press.

Patterson, G. R., DeBaryshe, B. D., & Ramsey, E. (1989). A developmental perspective on anti-social behavior. *American Psychologist, 44*, 329–335.

Patterson, G. R., Dishion, T. J., & Chamberlain, P. (1993). Outcomes and methodological issues relating to treatment of antisocial children. In T. R. Giles, *Handbook of effective psychotherapy* (pp. 43–88). New York: Plenum.

Patterson, G. R. & Forgatch, M. S. (1985). Therapist behavior as a determinant for client noncompliance: A paradox for the behavior modifier. *Journal of Consulting and Clinical Psychology, 53*, 846–851.

Patterson, G.R. & Forgatch, M. S. (1987). *Parents and adolescents living together. Part I: The basics.* Eugene, OR: Castalia.

Patterson, G. R. & Forgatch, M. S. (1989). *Parents and adolescents living together. Part I. The basics.* Eugene, OR: Castalia.

Patterson, G. R. & Forgatch, M. S. (1990). Initiation and maintenance of process disrupting single-mother families. In G. R. Patterson (Ed.), *Depression and aggression in family interaction* (pp. 209–245). Hillsdale, NJ: Lawrence Erlbaum.

Patterson, G. R., & Reid, J. B. (1970). Reciprocity and coercion: Two facets of social systems. In C. Neuringer & J,. L. Michael (Eds.), *Behavior modification in clinical psychology.* New York: Appleton-Century-Crafts.

Patterson, G. R., Reid, J. B., & Dishion, T. J. (1992). *A social learning approach: IV. Antisocial boys.* Eugene, OR: Castalia.

Patton, M. Q. (1986). *Utilization focused evaluation* (2nd Ed.). Beverly Hills, CA: Sage.

Patton, M. Q. (1987). *Creative evaluation* (2nd Ed.). Newbury Park, CA: Sage.

Paul, G. L. & Lentz, R. J. (1977). *Psychosocial treatment of chronic mental patients: Milieu versus social-learning programs.* Cambridge, MA: Harvard University Press.

Paul, G. L., Licht, M. H., Mariotto, M. J., Power, C. T., & Engel, K. L. (1987a). *The staff-resident interaction chronograph: Observational assessment instrumentation for service and research.* Champaign, IL: Research Press.

Paul, G. L., Licht, M. H., Mariotto, M. J., Power, C. T., & Engel, K. L. (1987b). *The time-sample behavioral checklist: Observational assessment instrumentation for service and research.* Champaign, IL: Research Press.

Paul, G. L. & Menditto, A. A. (1992). Effectiveness of inpatient treatment programs for mentally ill adults in public psychiatric facilities. *Applied and Preventive Psychology: Current Scientific Perspectives, 1,* 44–63.

Paul, R. (1992). *Critical thinking: What every person needs to survive in a rapidly changing world* (2nd Ed.). Sonoma, CA: Foundation for Critical Thinking.

Paul, R. (1993). *Critical thinking: What every person needs to survive in a rapidly changing world* (3rd Ed.). Sonoma, CA: Foundation for Critical Thinking.

Pavlov, I. P. (1927). *Conditioned reflexes* (G.V. Anrip, Trans.). New York: Liveright.

Payne, R. L. & Jones, J. G. (1987). Measurement and methodological issues in social support. In S. V. Kasl & C. L. Cooper (Eds.), *Stress and health: Issues in research methodology* (pp. 167–206). New York: Wiley.

Pedersen, P. B., Draguns, J. G., Lonner, W. J. & Trimble, J. E. (Eds.). (1996). *Counseling across cultures* (4th Ed.). Thousand Oaks, CA: Sage.

Peed, S., Roberts, M., & Forehand, R. (1977). Evaluation of a standardized parent training program in altering the interaction of mothers and their noncompliant children. *Behavior Modification, 1,* 323–350.

Pekarik, G. (1993). Beyond effectiveness: Uses of consumer-oriented criteria in defining treatment success. In T. R. Giles (Ed.), *Handbook of effective psychotherapy* (pp. 409–436). New York: Plenum.

Pelton, L. H. (1989). *For reasons of poverty: A critical analysis of the public child welfare system in the U.S.* New York: Praeger.

Pence, E. & Paymar, M. (1993). *Education groups for men who batter: The Duluth Model.* New York: Springer.

Penka, C. & Kirk, S. (1991). Practitioner involvement in clinical evaluation. *Social Work, 36,* 513–518.

Pepper, C. (1984). *Quackery: A $10 billion scandal.* Subcommittee on health and long-term care of the Select Committee on Aging. U.S. House of Representatives. No. 98–435. U. S. Government Printing House.

Pepper, S. (1981). Problems in the quantification of frequency expressions. In D. W. Fiske (Ed.), *New directions for methodology of social and behavioral science. No. 9. Problems with Language Imprecision* (pp. 25–41). San Francisco: Jossey-Bass.

Perkins, D. (1992). *Smart schools: From training memories to educating minds.* New York: The Free Press.

Perkins, D. (1995). *Outsmarting IQ: The emerging science of learnable intelligence.* New York: The Free Press.

Perlman, H. H. (1957). *Social casework: A problem-solving process.* Chicago: University of Chicago Press.

Perlman, H. H. (1976). Believing and doing: Values in social work education. *Social Casework, 57,* 381–390.

Perlman, H. H. (1979). *Relationship: The heart of helping.* Chicago: University of Chicago Press.

Peterson, C., Maier, S. F., & Seligman, M. E. P. (1993). *Learned helplessness: A theory for the age of personal control.* New York: Oxford University Press.

Peterson, C., Semmel, A., von Baeyer, C., Abramson, L. Y., & Seligman, M. E. P. (1982). The attributional style questionnaire. *Cognitive Therapy and Research, 6,* 287–299.

Peterson, D. R. (1987). The role of assessment in professional psychology. In D. R. Peterson & D. B. Fishman (Eds.), *Assessment for decisions* (pp. 5–43). New Brunswick: Rutgers University Press.

Peterson, R. F., Knapp, T. J., Rosen, J. C. & Pither, B. F. (1977). The effects of furniture arrangement on the behavior of geriatric patients. *Behavior Therapy, 8,* 464–467.

Petrocelli, W. & Repa, B. K. (1992). *Sexual harassment on the job.* Berkeley, CA: Nolo Press.

Petty, R. E. & Cacioppo, J. T. (1986). The elaboration likelihood model of persuasion. In L. Berkowitz (Ed.), *Advances in experimental social psychology,* Vol. 19. New York: Academic.

Pharis, M. E. & Levin, V. S. (1991). "A person to talk to who really cared": High-risk mothers' evaluations of services in an intensive intervention research program. *Child Welfare, LXX,* 307–320.

Phillips, D. C. (1987). *Philosophy, science and social inquiry: Contemporary methodological controversies in social science and related applied fields of research.* New York: Pergamon Press.

Phillips, D. C. (1990). Subjectivity and objectivity: An objective inquiry. In E. W. Eisner & A. Peshkin (Eds.), *Qualitative inquiry in education: The continuing debate* (pp. 19–37). New York: Columbia University Press.

Phillips, D. C. (1992). *The social scientist's bestiary: A guide to fabled threats to, and defenses of, naturalistic social studies.* New York: Pergamon.

Phillips, K. (1990). *The politics of rich and poor: Wealth and the American electorate in the Reagan aftermath.* New York: Random House.

Piaget, J. (1976). *Piaget sampler: An introduction to Jean Piaget through his own words.* New York: Wiley.

Pincus, A., & Minahan, A. (1973). *Social work practice: Model and method.* Itasca, IL: Peacock Publishers.

Pinkston, E. M. & Linsk, N. L. (1984). *Care of the elderly: A family approach.* New York: Pergamon.

Pinkston, E. M., Levitt, J. L., Green, G. R., Linsk, N. L., & Rzepnicki, T. L. (1982). *Effective social work practice: Advanced techniques for behavioral intervention with individuals, families, and institutional staff.* San Francisco: Jossey-Bass.

Piven, F. F. & Cloward, R. A. (Eds.). (1993). *Regulating the poor: The functions of public welfare.* New York: Random.

Plato. *The last days of Socrates.* Translation by H. Tredennick & H. Tarrant. New York: Penguin (1954). 1993.

Plous, S. (1993). *The psychology of judgement and decision making.* New York: McGraw-Hill.

Pommer, D. A. & Streedbeck, D. (1974). Motivating staff performance in an operant learning program for children. *Journal of Applied Behavior Analysis, 7,* 217–221.

Ponterotto, J. G., Casas, J. M., Suzuki, L. A. & Alexander, C. M. (Eds.). (1995). *Handbook of multicultural counseling.* Thousand Oaks, Sage.

Poppen, R. L. (1989). Some clinical implications of rule-governed behavior. In S. C. Hayes (Ed.), *Rule governed behavior: Cognition, contingencies and instructional control* (pp. 325–357). New York: Plenum.

Popper, K. R. (1972). *Conjectures and refutations: The growth of scientific knowledge* (4th Ed.) London: Routledge & Kegan Paul. (Originally published in 1963.)

Popper, K. R. (1992). *In search of a better world: Lectures and essays from thirty years.* London: Routledge & Kegan Paul.

Popper, K. R. (1994). *The myth of the framework: In defense of science and rationality.* Edited by M. A. Notturno. New York: Routledge.

Popple, P. R. & Leighninger, L. (1993). *Social work, social welfare, and American society* (2nd Ed.). Allyn & Bacon.

Positive Behavioral Intervention Regulations. California Department of Education, July, 1993. 721 Capitol Mall, P.O. Box 944272, Sacramento, CA 94244–2720.

Powell, D. (1987). A neighborhood approach to family support groups. *Journal of Community Psychology, 15,* 51–62.

Powell, T. J. (1990). *Working with self-help.* New York: NASW.

Praderas, K. & MacDonald, M. L. (1986). Telephone conversational skills training with socially isolated, impaired nursing home residents. *Journal of Applied Behavior Analysis, 19,* 337–348.

Pratkanis, A. R. & Aronson, E. (1991). *Age of propaganda: The everyday use and abuse of persuasion.* New York: W. H. Freeman and Company.

Premack, D. (1965). "Reinforcement theory." In D. Levine (Ed.), *Nebraska Symposium on Motivation* (pp. 23–80). Lincoln: University of Nebraska Press.

Price, R. H. (1989). Bearing witness. *American Journal of Community Psychology, 17,* 151–167.

Prestby, J., Wandersman, A., Florin, P., Rich, R., & Chavis, D. (1990). Benefits, costs, incentive management and participation in voluntary organizations: A means to understanding and promoting empowerment. *American Journal of Community Psychology, 18,* 117–150.

Prins, H. (1988). Dangerous clients: Further observations on the limitations of mayhem. *British Journal of Social Work, 18,* 593–609.

Prochaska, J. O. & DiClemente, C. C. (1992). Stages of change and the modification of problem behaviors. In M. Hersen, R. M. Eisler, & P. M. Miller (Eds.), *Progress in behavior modification.* Vol. 28 (pp. 183–218). New York: Academic.

Proctor, E. K., Morrow-Howell, N., & Lott, C. L. (1992). Classification and correlates of ethical dilemmas in hospital social work. *Social Work, 38,* 166–177.

Professional therapy never includes sex. (1990). California State Department of Consumer Affairs.

Pruger, R. (1973). The good bureaucrat. *Social Work, 18,* 26–32.

Pryor, K. (1984). *Don't shoot the dog.* New York: Bantam Books.

Pyszczyuski, T. & Greenberg, J. (1987). Toward an integration of cognitive and motivational perspectives on social inference: A biased hypothesis-testing model. In L. Berkowitz (Ed.), *Advances in experimental social psychology* (Vol. 20) (pp. 297–340). Orlando, FL: Academic Press.

Quinn, R. E. et al. (1996). *Becoming a master manager: A competency framework.* New York: John Wiley & Sons.

Rachlin, H. (1980). *Behaviorism in everyday life.* Englewood Cliffs, NJ: Prentice Hall.

Rachlin, H. (1989). *Judgment, decision, and choice: A cognitive/behavioral synthesis.* New York: W. H,. Freeman.

Rago, W. V., Jr., Parker, R. M., & Cleland, C. (1978). Effect of increased space on the social behavior of institutionalized retarded male adults. *American Journal of Mental Deficiency, 82,* 554–558.

Raheim, S. (1995). Self-employment training and family development: An integrated strategy for family empowerment. In P. Adams & K. Nelson (Eds.), *Reinventing human services: Community-and family-centered practice: Modern applications of social work* (pp. 127–143). New York: Aldine de Gruyter.

Rakos, R. F. (1991). *Assertive behavior: Theory, research and training.* London: Routledge.

Rappaport, J. (1987). Terms of empowerment/exemplars of prevention: Toward a theory for community psychology. *Journal of Community Psychology, 15,* 121–148.

Raven, J. (1984). *Competence in modern society: Its identification, development and release.* London: H. K. Lewis & Co.

Rawls, J. (1971). *A theory of justice.* Cambridge, MA: Harvard University Press.

Reamer, F. G. (1990). *Ethical dilemmas in social services* (2nd Ed.). New York: Columbia University Press.

Reamer, F. G. (1992). Is Tarasoff relevant to AIDS related cases? Yes. In E. Gambrill & R. Pruger (Eds.), *Controversial issues in social work* (pp. 342–349). Boston: Allyn and Bacon.

Reamer, F. G. (1994). *Social work malpractice and liability.* New York: Columbia University Press.

Reamer, F. G. (1995). *Social work values and ethics.* New York: Columbia University Press.

Redd, W. H. (1980). Stimulus control: An extension and extinction of psychosomatic symptoms in cancer patients in protective isolation. *Journal of Consulting and Clinical Psychology, 48,* 448–455.

Reid, D. H. (1987). *Developing a research program in human service agencies: A practitioner's guidebook.* Springfield, IL: Charles C. Thomas.

Reid, D. H., Parsons, M. B., & Green, C. W. (1989). *Staff management in human services.* Springfield, IL: Charles C. Thomas.

Reid, D. H., Parsons, M. B., McCarn, J. E., Green, C. W., Phillips, J. F., Schepis, M. M. (1985). Providing a more appropriate education for severely handicapped persons: Increasing and validating functional classroom tasks. *Journal of Applied Behavior Analysis, 18,* 289–302.

Reid, J. B. (1978). *A social learning approach to family interaction. Vol. 2. A manual for coding family interactions.* Eugene, OR: Castalia.

Reid, W. J. & Epstein, L. (1977). *Task centered casework.* New York: Columbia University Press.

Rene, A. A. (1987). Racial differences in mortality: Blacks and whites. In W. Jones & M. Rice (Eds.), *Health care issues in Black America: Policies, problems and prospects.* New York: Greenwood.

Renstrom, L., Andersson, B., & Marton, F. (1990). Students' conceptions of matter. *Journal of Educational Psychology, 82,* 555–569.

Repp, A. C. & Singh, N. N. (1990). *Perspectives on the use of nonaversive and aversive interventions for persons with developmental disabilities.* Sycamore, IL: Sycamore Press.

Repp, A. C. & Karsh, K. G. (1994). Laptop computer system for data recording and contextual analysis. In T. Thompson & D. B. Gray (Eds.), *Destructive behavior in developmental disabilities: Diagnosis and treatment* (pp. 83–101). Sage Focus Education, Vol. 170. Thousand Oaks, CA.

Rescola, R. A. (1988). Pavlovian conditioning: Its not what you think it is. *American Psychologist, 43,* 151–160.

Resnick, H. B. (1982). Facilitating productive staff meetings. I. M. Austin & W. E. Hershey (Eds.). *Handbook of mental health administration* (pp. 196–197). San Francisco: Jossey-Bass.

Richan, W. C. (1991). *Lobbying for social change.* New York: Hayworth.

Richey, C. A., Lovell, M. L., & Ried, K. A. (1990). Interpersonal skill training to enhance social support among women at risk for child maltreatment. *Children and Youth Service Review, 13,* 41–60.

Richmond, M. E. (1917). *Social diagnosis.* New York: Russell Sage Foundation.

Riley, M. W. (1988). On the significance of age in sociology. In M. W. Riley (Ed.), *Social structures & human lives* (pp. 24–45). Newbury Park, CA: Sage.

Risley, T. R. & Favell, J. (1979). Constructing a living environment in an institution. In L. A. Hammerlynck (Ed.), *Behavioral systems for the developmentally disabled: II. Institutional, clinic, and community environments* (pp. 3–24). New York: Brunner/Mazel.

Risley, T. R. & Twardosz, S. (1976). The preschool as a setting for behavior intervention. In H. Leitenberg (Ed.), *Handbook of behavior modification and behavior therapy* (pp. 453–474). Englewood Cliffs, NJ: Prentice-Hall.

Roberts, K. H. & Hunt, D. M. (1991). *Organizational behavior*. Boston: PWS-Kent Publishing Co.

Robin, A. L. & Foster, S. L. (1989). *Negotiating parent adolescent conflict: A behavioral-family systems approach*. New York: Guilford.

Robinson, D. N. (1974). Harm, offense, and nuisance: Some first steps in the establishment of an ethics of treatment. *American Psychologist, 29,* 233–238.

Rodin, J. & Langer, E. J. (1977). Long-term effects of a control relevant intervention with the institutionalized aged. *Journal of Personality and social psychology, 35,* 897–902.

Rogers, C. R. (1957). The necessary and sufficient conditions of therapeutic personality change. *Journal of Social Issues, 21,* 95–103.

Rogers, R. (1988). *Clinical assessment of malingering and deception*. New York: Guilford.

Rogler, L. H., Malgady, R. G., Giuseppe, C., & Blumenthal, R. (1987). What do culturally sensitive mental health services mean? The case of Hispanics. *American Psychologist, 42,* 565–570.

Rook, K. S. (1984a). The negative side of social interaction: Impact on psychological well being. *Journal of Personality and Social Psychology, 46,* 1097–1108.

Rook, K. S. (1984b). Promoting social bonding: Strategies for helping the lonely and socially isolated. *American Psychologist, 39,* 1389–1407.

Rook, K. S. (1985). The functions of social bonds: Perspectives from research on social support, loneliness, and isolation. In I. G. Sarason & B. R. Sarason (Eds.), *Social support: Theory, research and application* (pp. 243–268). Boston: Martinus Nijhoff.

Rook, K. S. (1990). Social relationships as a source of companionship: Implications for older adults' psychological well-being. In B. R. Sarason, I. G. Sarason, & G. R. Pierce (Eds.), *Social support: An interactional view* (pp. 219–250). New York: Wiley.

Rose, S. D. (1977). *Group therapy: A behavioral approach*. Englewood Cliffs, NJ: Prentice Hall.

Rose, S. D. (1989). *Working with adults in groups: A cognitive behavioral approach*. San Francisco: Jossey-Bass.

Rose, S. D. & Edleson, J. L. (1987). *Working with children and adolescents in groups*. San Francisco: Jossey-Bass.

Rose, S. M. & Black, B. L. (1985). *Advocacy and empowerment: Mental health care in the community*. Boston: Routledge & Kegan Paul.

Rosen, G. M. (1981). Guidelines for the review of do-it yourself treatment books. *Contemporary Psychology, 26,* 189–191.

Rosen, G. M. (1987). Self-help treatment books and the commercialization of psychotherapy. *American Psychologist, 42,* 46–51.

Rosenau, P. M. (1992). *Post-modernism and the social sciences: Insights, inroads, and intrusion*. Princeton: Princeton University Press.

Rosenfeld-Schlichter, M. D., Sarber, R. E., Bueno, G., Greene, B. F. & Lutzker, J. R. (1983). Maintaining accountability for an ecobehavioral treatment of one aspect of child neglect: Personal cleanliness. *Education and treatment of children, 6,* 153–164.

Rosenhan, D. (1973). On being sane in insane places. *Science, 179,* 250–258.

Rosenthal, R. (Ed.). (1979). *Skill in nonverbal communication: Individual differences*. Cambridge, MA: Oelge-Schlager, Gunn, & Hain.

Rosenthal, R. (1994). Interpersonal expectancy effects: A 30-year perspective. *Current Directions in Psychological Science, 3,* 176–179.

Rosenthal, R. & Jacobson, L. (1992). *Pygmalian in the classroom: Teacher expectations and pupils' intellectual development*. New York: Irvington. (Originally published in 1968.)

Ross, D. F., Read, J. D., & Toglia, M P. (Eds.). (1994). *Adult eyewitness testimony: Current trends and developments*. New York: Cambridge University Press.

Rossi, P. H. & Freeman, H. E. (1993). *Evaluation: A systematic approach* (5th Ed.) Newbury Park, CA: Sage.

Rosswell, V. A. (1988). Professional liability: Issues for behavior therapists in the 1980s and 1990s. *The Behavior Therapist, 11,* 163–171.

Rothman, J. (1980). *Social R & D: Research & development in the human services*. Engelwood Cliffs, NJ: Prentice-Hall.

Rothman, J. (1991). *Runaway and homeless youth: Strengthening services for families and children*. New York: Longman.

Rothman, J., Erlich, J. L., & Tropman, J. E. (1995). *Strategies of community intervention: Macro practice* (5th Ed.). Itasca, IL: F. E. Peacock.

Rothman, J., & Thomas, E. J. (Eds.). (1994). *Intervention research: Design and development for the human services*. New York: Hayworth.

Rothman, J. & Tropman, J. E. (1987). Models of community organization and macro practice perspectives: Their mixing and phasing. In F. M. Cox, J. L. Erlich, J. Rothman and J. E. Tropman (Eds.), *Strategies in community organization: Macro practice* (pp. 3–26). Itasca, IL: Peacock.

Rotter, J. B. (1966). Generalized expectancies for internal versus external control of reinforcement. *Psychological Monographs*, *80*, (No. 609).

Rudovsky, D., et al. (1988). *Rights of prisoners* (4th Ed.). Southern Illinois University Press.

Ruggiero, V. R. (1988). *Teaching thinking across the curriculum*. New York: Harper and Row. (See also 3rd Ed., 1991).

Rusch, F. R. (Ed.). (1990). *Supported employment: Models, methods and issues*. Sycamore, IL: Sycamore Press.

Rusch, F. R., DeStefano, L., & Chadsey-Rusch, J. (Eds.). (1991). *Transition from school to work for youth and adults with disabilities*. Sycamore, IL: Sycamore Press.

Rutter, M. (1995). Maternal deprivation. In M. H. Bornstein (Ed.), *Handbook of parenting, Vol. 4: Applied and practical parenting* (pp. 3–30). Mahawah, NJ: Laurence Erlbaum.

Ruzek, S. K. & Daniels, A. K. (1971). Descriptions of ethical problems presented by social workers. In Final Report, NIMH, Grant HI02775–02, A. Daniels.

Ryan, W. (1976). *Blaming the victim*. New York: Vantage.

Sagan, C. (1987). The burden of skepticism. *The Skeptical Inquirer*, *12*, 38–74.

Sagan, C. (1990). Why we need to understand science. *Skeptical Inquirer*, *14*, 263–269.

Sailor, W. & Carr, E. G. (1994). Should only positive methods be used by professionals who work with children and adolescents? Yes. In M. A. Mason & E. Gambrill (Eds.), *Debating children's lives: Current controversies on children and adolescents* (pp. 225–227). Newbury Park: Sage.

Sailor, W. Goetz, L, Anderson, J., Hunt, P., & Gee, K. (1988). Research on community intensive instruction as a model for building functional generalized skills. In R. Horner, G. Dunlap, & R. Koegel (Eds.), *Generalization and maintenance in applied settings* (pp. 67–98). Baltimore: Paul Brookes.

Salovey, P. & Mayer, J. D. (1990). Emotional intelligence. *Imagination, Cognition, and Personality*, *9*, 185–211.

Salovey, P. & Turk, D. C. (1988). Some effects of mood on clinician's memory. In D. C. Turk & P. S. Salovey (Eds.), *Reasoning, inference, and judgment in clinical psychology* (pp. 107–123). New York: Free Press.

Salovey, P., Hesse, C. K., & Mayer, J. D. (1993). Emotional intelligence and the self-regulation of affect (pp. 258–277). In D. M. Wegner & J. W. Pennebaker (Eds.) *Handbook of mental control*. Englewood Cliffs, NJ: Prentice Hall.

Samantrai, K. (1990/91). MSWs in public child welfare: Why do they stay, and why do they leave? *NASW California News*, *17*, 10.

Sanders, M. R. & Dadds, M. R. (1993). *Behavioral family therapy*. Boston: Allyn & Bacon.

Sarason, B. R., Sarason, I. G. & Pierce, G. R. (Eds.) (1990). *Social support: An interactional view*. New York: John Wiley.

Sarason, S. B. & Lorentz, E. (1979). *The challenge of the resource exchange network: From concept to action*. San Francisco: Jossey-Bass.

Sarber, R. E., Halasz, M. M., Messmer, M. C., Bickett, A. D., & Lutzker, J. R. (1983). Teaching menu planning and grocery shopping skills to a mentally retarded mother. *Mental Retardation*, *21*, 101–106.

Sarri, R. & Finn, J. (1992). Child welfare policy and practice: Rethinking the history of our uncertainties. *Children and Youth Services Review*, *14*, 219–236.

Sarri, R. & Sarri, C. (1992). Participatory action research in two communities in Bolivia and the United States. *International Social Work*, *35*, 267–280.

Savarese, M. & Weber, C. M. (1993). Case management for persons who are homeless. *Journal of Case Management*, *2*, 3–8.

Schaufeli, W. B., Maslach, C., & Marek, T. (Eds.). (1993). *Professional burnout: Recent developments in theory and research*. Washington, DC: Taylor & Francis.

Scheff, T. J. (1984). *Labeling madness* (2nd ed.). Englewood Cliffs, NJ: Prentice-Hall.

Scheper-Hughes, N. & Lovell, A. M. (Eds.). (1987). *Psychiatry inside out: Selected writings of Franco Basaglia*. New York: Columbia University Press.

Schilling, R. F., El-Bassel, N., Serrano, Y., & Wallace, B. C. (1992). AIDS prevention strategies for ethnic-racial minority substance users. *Psychology of Addictive Behaviors*, *6*(2), 81–90.

Schinke, S. P. & Gordon, A. N. (1992). Innovative approaches to interpersonal skills training for minority adolescents. In R. J. DiClemente (Ed.), *Adolescents and AIDS: A generation in jeopardy* (pp. 181–193). Newbury Park: Sage.

Schleien, S. J., Meyer, L. H., Heyne, L. A., & Brandt, B. B. (1995). *Lifelong leisure skills and lifestyles for persons with developmental disabilities*. Baltimore: Brooks/Cole.

Schlenker, B. R. (1980). *Impression management: The self-concept, social identity, and interpersonal relations*. Monterey, CA: Brooks/Cole.

Schnaitter, R. (1986). Behavior as a function of inner states and outer circumstances. In T. Thompson &

M. D. Zeiler (Eds.), *Analysis and integration of behavioral units* (pp. 247–274). Hillsdale, NJ: Erlbaum.

Schneider, W. H. (1965). *Danger: Men talking*. New York: Random House.

Schnelle, J. F. (1974). A brief report on invalidity of parent evaluations of behavior change. *Journal of Applied Behavior Analysis, 7,* 341–343.

Schnelle, J. F. & Traughber, B. (1983). A behavioral assessment system applicable to geriatric nursing facility residents. *Behavioral Assessment, 5,* 231–243.

Schoech, D. (1990). *Human services computing*. New York: Haworth Press.

Schon, D. (1987). *Educating the reflective practitioner*. San Francisco: Jossey-Bass.

Schrader, C. & Levine, M. (1994). *PTR: Prevent, teach, reinforce* (2nd Ed.). 454 Gallinas, San Rafael, CA 94903: Behavioral Counseling and Research Center. 415–499–8455.

Schriner, K. F. & Fawcett, S. B. (1988). Development and validation of a community concerns report method. *Journal of Community Psychology, 16,* 306–316.

Schuerman, J. R. (1995). Research, practice, and expert systems. In P. M. Hess & E. J. Mullens (Eds.), *Practitioner-researcher partnerships: Building knowledge from, in, and for practice* (pp., 253–263). Washington, D.C.: National Association of Social Workers.

Schultz, R. (1976). Effects of control and predictability on the physical and psychological well-being of the institutionalized aged. *Journal of Personality and Social Psychology, 33,* 563–573.

Schwartz, A. & Goldiamond, I. (1975). *Social casework: A behavioral approach*. New York: Columbia University Press.

Schwartz, I. M. (1989). *(In)justice for juveniles: Rethinking the best interests of the child*. Lexington, MA: Lexington

Schwartz, I. S. & Baer, D. M. (1991). Social validity assessments: Is current practice state of the art? *Journal of Applied Behavior Analysis, 24,* 189–204.

Scogin, F., Jamison, C., & Gochneauer, K. (1989). Comparative efficacy of cognitive and behavioral bibliotherapy for mildly and moderately depressed older adults. *Journal of Community and Clinical Psychology, 57,* 403–407.

Scriven, M. (1976). *Reasoning*. New York: McGraw-Hill.

Scriven, M. (1991). *Evaluation thesaurus* (4th Ed.). Newbury Park, CA: Sage.

Seech, Z. (1993). *Open minds and everyday reasoning*. Belmont, CA: Wadsworth Publishing Co.

Seekins, T. & Fawcett, S. B. (1987). Effects of a poverty-clients' agenda on resource allocations by community decision makers. *American Journal of Community Psychology, 15*(3), 305–320.

Seekins, T., Fawcett, S. B., & Mathews, R. M. (1987). Effects of self-help guides on three consumer advocacy scales: Using personal choices to influence public policy. *Rehabilitation Psychology, 32,* 29–38.

Seekins, T., Mathews, R. M., & Fawcett, S. B. (1984). Enhancing leadership skills for community self-help organizations through behavioral instruction. *Journal of Community Psychology, 12,* 155–163.

Seekins, T., Maynard-Moody, S. & Fawcett, S. B. (1987). Understanding the policy process: Preventing and coping with community problems. In L. A. Jason, R. E. Hess, R. D. Felner, & J. N. Moritsugu (Eds.), *Prevention: Toward a multidisciplinary approach*. Vol. 5. Issue 2 (pp. 65–89). New York: Haworth Press.

Self-Help Sourcebook. (1992). A national guide to finding & forming self-help support groups (4th Ed.). St. Claires: Riveside Medical Center. American Self-Help Clearing House, Denville, NJ.

Seligman, M. E. P. (1975). *Helplessness: On depression, development and death*. San Francisco: W. H. Freeman & Co. Pub.

Seligman, M. E. P., Abramson, L. Y., Semmel, A., & von Baeyer, C. (1979). Depressive attributional style. *Journal of Abnormal Psychology, 88,* 242–247.

Seymour, F. W. & Stokes, T. F. (1976). Self-recording in training girls to increase work and evoke staff praise in an institution for offenders. *Journal of Applied Behavior Analysis, 9,* 41–54.

Shapiro, E. S. & Cole, C. L. (1994). *Behavioral change in the classroom: Self-management interventions*. New York: Guilford.

Shapiro, E. S. & Kratochwill, T. R. (1988). *Behavioral assessment in schools: Conceptual foundations and practical applications*. New York: Guilford.

Shapiro, M. H. (1974). Legislating the control of behavior control: Autonomy and the coercive use of organic therapies. *Southern California Law Review, 47,* 237–356.

Shearer, D. E., & Loftin, C. R. (1984). The Portage Project: Teaching parents to teach their preschool children in the home. In R. F. Dangel & R. A. Polster (Eds.), *Parent training: Foundations of research and practice* (pp. 93–126). New York: Guilford.

Shelton, J. L. & Levy, R. L. (1981). *Behavioral as-

signments and treatment compliance. Champaign, IL: Research Press.

Shepard, M. F. & Campbell, J. A. (1992). The Abusive Behavior Inventory: A measure of psychological and physical abuse. *Journal of Interpersonal Violence, 7*, 291–305.

Shields, J. J. (1992). Evaluating community organization projects: The development of an empirically based measure. *Social Work Research and Abstracts, 28*, 15–20.

Shorkey, C. T. & Taylor, J. E. (1973). Management of maladaptive behavior of a severely burned child. *Child Welfare, 52*, 543–547.

Shotton, A. (1990). State appellate courts move toward definitions of "reasonable efforts." *Youth Law News, 11*(3), 1–6.

Shulman, L. (1977). *A study of the helping process*. Vancouver, BC, Social Work Department: University of British Columbia Press.

Shulman, L. (1984). *The skills of helping: Individuals and groups* (2nd Ed.). Itasca, IL: F.E. Peacock.

Shulman, L. (1992). *The skills of helping: Individuals, families, and groups* (3rd Ed.). Itasca: IL: Peacock.

Shulman, L. (1991). *Interactional social work practice: Toward an empirical theory*. Itasca, IL: F. E. Peacock:

Shur, J. L. & Smith P. V. (1980). *Where do you look? Whom do you ask? How do you know?: Information resources for child advocates*. Washington, DC: Children's Defense Fund.

Shure, M. B. & Spivak, G. (1988). Interpersonal cognitive problem solving. In R. H. Price, et al., *Fourteen ounces of prevention: A casebook for practitioners* (pp. 69–82).

Shweder, R. A. & Bourne, E. (1982). Does the concept of the person vary cross-culturally? In A. J. Marsella & G. White (Eds.), *Cultural conceptions of mental health and therapy* (pp. 129–130). Boston: Reidel.

Sidman, M. (1989). *Coercion and its fallout*. Boston: Authors Cooperative.

Sidman, M. (1994). *Equivalence relations and behavior: A research story*. Boston: Authors Cooperative.

Siegman, A. W. & Feldstein, S. (1987). *Nonverbal behavior and communication* (2nd ed.). Hillsdale, NJ: Erlbaum.

Sievert, A. L., Cuvo, A. J., & Davis, P. K. (1988). Training self-advocacy skills to adults with mild handicaps. *Journal of Applied Behavior Analysis, 21*, 299–309.

Sigelman, C. K., Budd, E. C., Spanhel, C. L., & Schoenrock, C. J. (1980). When in doubt say yes: Acquiescence in interviews with mentally retarded persons. *Mental Retardation, 4*, 53–58.

Silverman, K. (1986). *Benjamin Franklin: Autobiography and other writings*. New York: Penguin.

Simon, B. L. (1994). *The empowerment tradition in American social work: A history*. New York: Columbia University Press.

Simon, R. (1989). Social worker stabbed to death by patient in Santa Monica clinic. *NASW California News, 15*(7), P. 1/S.

Sinclair, W. J. (1909). *Semmelweiss, his life and his doctrine: A chapter in the history of medicine*. Manchester, England: University Press.

Singer, G. H. S. & Irvin, L. K. (1991). Supporting families of persons with severe disabilities: Emerging findings, practices, and questions (pp. 271–312). In L. H. Meyer, C. A. Peck, & L. Brown (Eds.), *Critical issues in the lives of people with severe disabilities*. Baltimore: Paul H. Brookes.

Siporin, M. (1987). Resource development and service provision. In A. Minahan (Ed.), *Encyclopedia of social work* (18th Ed.). Vol. 2 (pp. 498–503). Silver Spring, MD: National Association of Social Workers.

Sirota, A. D. & Mahoney, M. J. (1974). Relaxing on cue: The self-regulation of asthma. *Journal of Behavior Therapy and Experimental Psychiatry, 5*, 65–66.

Sisson, R. & Azrin, N. (1989). The community reinforcement approach. In R. K. Hester & W. R. Miller (Eds.), *Handbook of alcoholism treatment approaches* (pp. 242–258). New York: Pergamon.

Skinner, B. F. (1953). *Science and human behavior*. New York: Macmillan.

Skinner, B. F. (1969). *Contingencies of reinforcement: A theoretical analysis*. New York: Appleton-Century-Crofts.

Skinner, B. F. (1971). *Beyond freedom and dignity*. New York: Knopf.

Skinner, B. F. (1974). *About behaviorism*. New York: Knopf.

Skinner, B. F. (1981). Selection by consequences. *Science, 213*, 501–504.

Skinner, B. F. (1984). The operational analysis of psychological terms. *The Behavioral and Brain Sciences, 7*, 547–581.

Skinner, B. F. (1987). *Upon further reflection*. Englewood Cliffs, NJ: Prentice Hall.

Skinner, B. F. (1988). The operant side of behavior therapy. *Journal of Behavior Therapy and Experimental Psychiatry, 19*, 171–191.

Skrabanek, P. (1990). Reductionist fallacies in the theory and treatment of mental disorders. *International Journal of Mental Health, 19*, 6–18.

Skrabanek, P. & McCormick, J. (1992). *Follies and fallacies in medicine* (2nd Ed.). Chippenham: Tarragon Press. (Also available from Prometheus Press).

Sloane, R. B., Staples, F. R., Cristol, A. H., Yorkston, N. J., & Whipple, K. (1975). *Psychotherapy versus behavior therapy*. Cambridge, MA: Harvard University Press.

Slovic, P., Fischhoff, B., & Lichtenstein, S. (1982). Facts versus fears: Understanding perceived risk. In D. Kahneman, P. Slovic, & A. Tversky (Eds.), *Judgement under uncertainty: Heuristics and biases* (pp. 463–489). Cambridge, England: Cambridge University Press.

Smith, E. J. (1981). Cultural and historical perspectives in counseling blacks. In D. W. Sue (Ed.), *Counseling the culturally different: Theory and practice* (pp. 141–185) New York: John Wiley.

Smith, L. B. & Thelen, E. (Eds.). (1993). *A dynamic systems approach to development: Applications*. Cambridge, MA: M.I.T. Press.

Snyder, M. & Swann, W. B. (1978). Behavioral confirmation in social interaction: From social perception to social reality. *Journal of Experimental Social Psychology, 14*, 148–162.

Snyder, M. & Thomsen, C. J. (1988). Interactions between therapists and clients: Hypothesis testing and behavioral confirmation. In D. C. Turk & P. Salovey (Eds.), *Reasoning, inference, and judgement in clinical psychology* (pp. 124–152). New York: Free Press.

Sobell, M. B. & Sobell, L. C. (1993). *Problem drinkers: Guided self-change treatment*. New York: Guilford.

Sox, H. C., Blatt, M. A., Higgins, M. C., & Marton, K. I. (1988). *Medical decision making*. Boston: Butterworth-Heinemann.

Specht, H. (1990). Social work and the popular psychotherapies. *Social Service Review, 64*, 345–357.

Specht, H. & Courtney, M. (1994). *Unfaithful angels: How social work has abandoned its mission*. New York: Free Press.

Spector, M. & Kitsuse, J. I. (1987). *Constructing social problems*. New York: Aldine De Gruyter.

Spiegel, D., Bloom, J. R., Kraemer, H. C., & Gottheil, E. (1989). Effect of psychosocial treatment on survival of patients with metastatic breast cancer. *Lancet*, 1989, Oct. 14, pp. 888–891.

Spivak, G. & Shure, M. B. (1974). *Social adjustment of young children: A cognitive approach to solving real-life problems*. San Francisco: Jossey-Bass.

Stanovich, K. E. (1992). *How to think straight about psychology* (3rd Ed.). New York: Harper Collins.

Stearns, C. Z. (1993). Sadness. In M. Lewis & J. M. Haviland (Eds.), *Handbook of emotions* (pp. 547–561). New York: Guilford.

Stefanek, M. E., Ollendick, T. H., Baldock, W. P., Francis, G., & Yaeger, N. J. (1987). Self-statements in aggressive, withdrawn and popular children. *Cognitive Research and Therapy, 11*, 229–239.

Stein, T. J., Gambrill, E. D. & Wiltse, K. T. (1978). *Children in foster homes: Achieving continuity of care*. New York: Praeger Special Studies.

Steketee, G. (1987). Behavioral social work with obsessive-compulsive disorder. *Journal of Social Service Review, 10*, 53–72.

Steketee, G. S., & Foa, E. B. (1987). Rape victims: PTSD responses and their treatment. *Journal of Anxiety Disorders, 1*, 69–86.

Sternberg, R. J. (1986). *Intelligence applied: Understanding and increasing your intellectual skills*. San Diego: Jovanovich.

Sternberg, R. J. (1987). Teaching intelligence: The application of cognitive psychology to the improvement of intellectual skills. In J. D. Baron and R. J. Sternberg, *Teaching thinking skills: Theory and practice* (pp. 182–218). New York: W. H. Freeman.

Sternberg, R. J. & Davidson, J. E. (Eds.). (1995). *The nature of insight*. Cambridge, MA: The MIT Press.

Sternberg, R. J. & Lubart, T. I. (1995). *Defying the crowd: Cultivating creativity in a culture of conformity*. New York: The Free Press.

Stoesz, D. (1997). The end of social work. In M. Reisch & E. Gambrill (Eds.), *Social work in the 21st century* (pp. 368–375). Thousand Oaks, CA: Pine Forge Press.

Stokes, T. F. & Baer, D. M. (1977). An implicit technology of generalization. *Journal of Applied Behavior Analysis, 10*, 349–367.

Stokes, T. F., Fowler, S. A. & Baer, D. M. (1978). Training preschool children to recruit natural communities of reinforcement. *Journal of Applied Behavior Analysis, 11*, 285–303.

Stokes, T. F. & Osnes, P. G. (1988). The developing of applied technology of generalization and maintenance. In R. H. Horner, G. Dunlap, & R. L. Koegel (Eds.), *Generalization and maintenance: Life-style changes in applied settings* (pp. 13–14). Baltimore, MD: Paul H. Brookes.

Stokes, T. F. & Osnes, P. G. (1989). An operant pursuit of generalization. *Behavior Therapy, 20*, 337–355.

Stokols, D. & Altman, I. (Eds.). (1987). *Handbook of environmental psychology*. New York: John Wiley.

Stone, G. C. (1979). Patient compliance and the role of the expert. *Journal of Social Issues, 35*, 34–59.

Strain, P. H. (Ed.). (1981). *The utilization of classroom peers as behavior change agents*. New York: Plenum.

Strain, P., Kohler, F. W., & Goldstein, H. (1996). Learning experiences, an alternative program: Peer-mediated interventions for young children with autism. In E. D. Hibbs & P. S. Jensen (Eds.), *Psychosocial treatments for child and adolescent disorders: Empirically based strategies for clinical practice* (pp. 573–587). Washington, D.C.: American Psychological Association.

Strayhorn, J. M. (1977). *Talking it out: A guide to effective communication and problem solving*. Champaign, IL: Research Press.

Strayhorn, J. M. (1988). *The competent child: An approach to psychotherapy and preventive mental health*. New York: Guilford.

Strayhorn, J. M. (1994). Psychological competence-based therapy for young children and their parents. In C. W. LeCroy (Ed.), *Handbook of child and adolescent treatment manuals* (pp. 41–91). New York: Lexington Books.

Strean, H. S. (Ed.). (1994). *The use of humor in psychotherapy*. Northvale, NJ: Jason Arsonson.

Strupp, H. (1976). The nature of therapeutic influence and its basic ingredients. In A. Burton (Ed.), *What makes behavior change possible*. New York: Brunner/Mazel.

Strupp, H. H. & Hadley, S. W. (1979). Specific versus nonspecific factors in psychotherapy. *Archives of General Psychiatry, 36*, 1125–1136.

Strupp, H. H. & Hadley, S. W. (1985). Negative effects and their determinants. In D. T. Mays & C. M. Franks (Eds.), *Negative outcome in psychotherapy and what to do about it* (pp. 20–55). New York: Springer.

Stuart, R. B. (1980). *Helping couples change: A social learning approach to marital therapy*. New York: Guilford Press.

Stuart, R. B. & Davis, B. (1972). *Slim chance in a fat world: Behavioral control of obesity*. Champaign, IL: Research Press.

Subramanian, K. & Ell, K. O. (1989). Coping with a first heart attack: A group treatment model for low-income Anglo, black, and Hispanic patients. *Social Work With Groups, 12*(4), 99–117.

Sue, D. W. & Sue, D. (1990). *Counseling the culturally different: Theory and practice* (2nd Ed.). New York: Wiley-Interscience.

Sugai, G. & Lewis, T. (1989). Teacher/student interaction analysis. *Teacher Education and Special Education, 12*, 131–138.

Sulzer-Azaroff, B., & Mayer, G. R. (1991). *Behavior analysis for lasting change*. Fort Worth: Holt, Rinehart and Winston.

Sundel, S. S. & Sundel, M. (1993). *Behavior modification in the human services: A systematic introduction to concepts and applications* (3rd Ed.). Newbury Park: Sage.

Swann, W. B., Jr., & Guiliano, T. (1987). Confirmatory search strategies in social interaction: How, when, why, and with what consequences. *Journal of Social and Clinical Psychology, 5*, 511–524.

Swartz, R. J. & Perkins, D. N. (1990). *Teaching thinking: Issues and applications*. Pacific Grove, CA: Critical Thinking Press and Software, P.O. Box 448, 93950, 408–375–2455.

Swiezy, N. B. & Matson, J. L. (1993). Coordinating the treatment process among various disciplines. In R. Van Houten & S. Axelrod (Eds.), *Behavior analysis and treatment: Applied clinical psychology* (pp. 203–227). New York: Plenum Press.

Sykes, C. J. (1993). *A nation of victims: The decay of the American character*. New York: St. Martin's Press.

Szapocznik, J. & Kurtines, W. (1989). *Breakthroughs in family therapy with drug abusing & problem youth*. New York: Springer.

Szapocznik, J., Perez-Vidal, A., Brickman, A. L., Foote, F. H., Santisteban, D. & Hervis, O. (1988). Engaging adolescent drug abusers and their families in treatment: A strategic structural systems approach. *Journal of Consulting and Clinical Psychology, 56*, 552–557.

Szapocznik, J., Rio, A., Murray, E., Cohen, R., Scopetta, M., Rivas-Vazquez, A., Hervis, O., Posada, V., & Kurtines, W. (1989). Structural family versus psychodynamic child therapy for problematic Hispanic boys. *Journal of Consulting and Clinical Psychology, 57*, 571–578.

Szasz, T. S. (1970). *The manufacture of madness: A comparative study of the inquisition and the mental health movement*. New York: Harper and Row.

Szasz, T. S. (1987). *Insanity: The idea and its consequences*. New York: John Wiley & Sons.

Szasz, T. S. (1994). *Cruel compassion: Psychiatric control of society's unwanted*. New York: John Wiley.

Szasz, T. S. (1995). *Our right to drugs: The case for a free market*. New York: Praeger.

Tallant, S., Rose, S. D. & Tolman, R. M. (1989). New evidence for the effectiveness of stress management training in groups. *Behavior Modification, 13*, 431–446.

Tallent, N. (1993). *Psychological report writing* (4th ed.). Englewood Cliffs, NJ: Prentice-Hall.

Talmon, M. (1990). *Single-session therapy: Maximizing the effect of the first (and often only) therapeutic encounter*. San Francisco: Jossey-Bass.

Tannen, D. (1990). *You just don't understand: Women and men in conversation*. New York: Ballantine Books.

Tannen, D. (1994). *Talking from 9–5: Women and men in the workplace: Language, sex and power*. New York: Avon.

Tapper, T. & Salter, B. (1978). *Education and the political order*. New York: Macmillan.

Tarasoff v Regents of the University of California. (1974), 17, Cal 2d 425.

Tavris, C. (1989). *Anger: The misunderstood emotion* (rev. ed.). New York: Simon & Schuster.

Tavris, C. (1992). *The mismeasure of women*. New York: Simon & Schuster.

Tavris, C. (1994). The illusion of science in psychiatry. *Skeptic, 2*(3), 77–85.

Taylor, R. J., Neighbors, H. W., & Broman, C. L. (1989). Evaluation by Black Americans of the social service encounter during a serious personal problem. *Social Work, 34*, 205–211.

Taylor, S. E. & Brown, J. D. (1994). Positive illusions and well-being revisited: Separating fact from fiction. *Psychological Bulletin, 116*, 21–27.

Taylor, S. E. & Brown, J. D. (1988). Illusion and well being: A social psychological perspective on mental health. *Psychological Bulletin, 103*, 193–210.

Teger, A. I. (1980). *Too much invested to quit*. New York: Pergamon.

Tertinger, D. A., Greene, B. F., & Lutzker, J. R. (1984). Home safety: Development and validation of one component of an ecobehavioral treatment program for abused and neglected children. *Journal of Applied Behavior Analysis, 17*, 159–174.

Tharp, R. G. & Wetzel, R. J. (1969). *Behavior modification in the natural environment*. New York: Academic.

Thibaut, J. W. & Kelley, H. H. (1987). *Social psychology of groups* (2nd ed.). New York: John Wiley and Sons.

Thomas, E. J. & Ager, R. D. (1993). Unilateral family therapy with spouses of uncooperative alcohol abusers. In T. O'Farrell (Ed.), *Treating alcohol problems: Marital and family interventions*. New York: Guilford Press.

Thomas, E. J. & Walter, C. L. (1973). Guidelines for behavioral practice in the open community agency: Procedure and evaluation. *Behavior Research and Therapy, 11*, 193–205.

Thomas, E. J., Walter, C. L., & O'Flaherty, K. (1974). A verbal problem checklist for use in assessing family verbal behavior. *Behavior Therapy, 35*, 235–246.

Thomas, E. J., Yoshioka, M. & Ager, R. D. (1996). Spouse enabling of alcohol abuse: Conception, assessment, and modification. *Journal of Substance Abuse, 8*, 61–80.

Thompson, J. B. (1987). Language and ideology. *Sociological Review, 35*, 517–536.

Thouless, R. H. (1974). *Straight and crooked thinking: Thirty-eight dishonest tricks of debate*. London: Pan Books.

Thyer, B. A. (Ed.). (1989). *Behavioral family therapy*. Springfield, IL: Charles C. Thomas.

Tichy, N. M. & Sherman, S. (1993). *Handbook for revolutionaries*. New York: Doubleday.

Todd, J. T. (1992). Case histories in the great power of steady misrepresentation. *American Psychologist, 47*, 1441–1453.

Todd, J. T. & Morris, E. K. (1983). Misconception and miseducation: Presentations of radical behaviorism in psychology textbooks. *The Behavior Analyst, 96, 153–160.*

Tolman, R. & Rose, S. D. (1985). Coping with stress: A multimodal approach. *Social Work, 30*, 151–158.

Torrey, E. F. (1995). Outpatient commitment to ensure treatment of seriously mentally ill people. *Health Letter, 11*(9), 3–4. (Public Citizen Health Research Group.)

Toseland, R. W. (1990). *Group work with older adults*. New York: New York University Press.

Toseland, R. W., Rossiter, C. M., & Labrecque, M. S. (1989). The effectiveness of two kinds of support groups for caregivers. *Social Service Review, 63*, 415–432.

Touchette, P. E., MacDonald, R. F., & Langer, S. N. (1985). A scatter plot for identifying stimulus control of problem behavior. *Journal of Applied Behavior Analysis, 18*, 343–351.

Tracy, E. M. (1990). Identifying social support resources of at-risk families. *Social Work, 35*, 252–258.

Tracy, E. M. & Whittaker, J. K. (1993). The social network map: Assessing social support in clinical practice. In J. B. Rauch (Ed.), *Assessment: A sourcebook for social work practice* (pp. 295–300). Milwaukee, WI: Families International, Inc.

Tropman, J. E. (1996). *Effective meetings: Improving group decision making.* (2nd Ed.). Thousand Oaks, CA: Sage.

Tropman, J. E., Erlich, J. L., & Rothman, J. (Eds.) (1995). *Tactics and techniques of community intervention* (3rd Ed.). Itasca, IL: F. E. Peacock.

Trower, P., Gilbert, P., & Sherling, G. (1990). Social anxiety, evolution, and self presentation. In H. Leitenberg (Ed.), *Handbook of social and evaluation anxiety* (pp. 11–45). New York: Plenum.

Trower, P., Bryant, B., & Argyle, M. (1978). *Social skills and mental health.* London: Methuen.

Truax, C. (1966). Reinforcement and nonreinforcement in Rogerian psychotherapy. *Journal of Abnormal Psychology, 71,* 1–9.

Truzzi, M. (1976). Sherlock Holmes: Applied social psychologist. In W. B. Sanders (Ed.). *The sociologist as detective: An introduction to research methods* (2nd Ed.). New York: Praeger.

Tsui, P. & Schultz, G. L. (1985). Failure of rapport: When psychotherapeutic engagement fails in a treatment of Asian clients. *American Journal of Orthopsychiatry, 55,* 561–569.

Tuchman, B. W. (1985). *The march of folly: From Troy to Vietnam.* New York: Ballantine.

Tufte, E. R. (1983). *The visual display of quantitative information.* Cheshire, CT: Graphics Press.

Tullock, G. (1986). *The economics of wealth and poverty.* Washington Square, NY: New York University Press.

Turkowitz, H. (1984). Family systems: Conceptualizing child problems within the family context. In A. W. Meyers & W. E. Craighead (Eds.), *Cognitive behavior therapy with children* (pp. 69–98). New York: Plenum.

Tutty, L. M., Bidgood, B. A., & Rothery, M. A. (1993). Support groups for battered women: Research on their efficacy. *Journal of Family Violence, 8,* 325–343.

Tversky, A. & Kahneman, D. (1971). Belief in the law of small numbers. *Psychological Bulletin, 76,* 105–110.

Tversky, A. & Kahneman, D. (1973). Availability: A heuristic for judging frequency and probability. *Cognitive Psychology, 5,* 207–232.

Tversky, A. & Kahneman, D. (1974). Judgment under uncertainty: Heuristics and biases. *Science, 185,* 1124–1131.

Tversky, A. & Kahneman, D. (1981). The framing of

decisions and the psychology of choice. *Science, 211,* 453–458.

Tversky, A. & Kahneman, D. (1983). Extensional versus intuitive reasoning: The conjunction fallacy in probability judgment. *Psychological Bulletin, 90,* 93–315.

Tyron, W. W. (1996). Observing contingencies: Taxonomy and methods. *Clinical Psychology Review, 16,* 215–230.

Ueda, K. (1974). Sixteen ways to avoid saying "No" in Japan. In J. C. Condon & M. Saito (Eds.), *International encounters with Japan; Communication—Contact and conflict* (pp. 184–192). Tokyo: Simul.

Unamuno, M. (1972). *The tragic sense of life in men and nations.* Princeton: Princeton University Press.

Unger, D. G. & Wandersman, A. (1983). Neighboring and its role in block organizations: An exploratory report. *American Journal of Community Psychology, 11,* 291–300.

Valenstein, E. S. (1986). *Great and desperate cures: The rise and decline of psychosurgery and other medical treatments for mental illness.* New York: Basic Books.

VanBiervliet, A., Spangler, P. F., & Marshall, A. M. (1981). An ecobehavioral examination of a simple strategy for increasing mealtime language in residential facilities. *Journal of Applied Behavior Analysis, 14,* 295–305.

Vance, L. (1992). *Treatment of a child with thalassemia.* Unpublished manuscript, School of Social Welfare, University of California at Berkeley. E-13.

van den Pol, R. A., Iwata, B. A., Ivancic, M. T., Page, T.J., Neef, N. A., & Whitley, F. P. (1981). Teaching the handicapped to eat in public places: Acquisition, generalization, and maintenance of restaurant skills. *Journal of Applied Behavior Analysis, 14,* 61–69.

VanHasselt, V. B. & Hersen, M. (Eds.). (1996). *Sourcebook of psychological treatment manuals for adult disorders.* New York: Plenum.

VanHasselt, V. B., Morrison, R. L., Bellack, A. S., & Hersen, M. (1987). *Handbook of family violence.* New York: Plenum.

VanHouten, R., Axelrod, S., Bailey, J. S., Favell, J. E., Foxx, R. M., Iwata, B. A., & Lovaas, O. I. (1988). The right to effective behavioral treatment. *Journal of Applied Behavior Analysis, 21,* 381–384.

Vollmer, T. R. & Iwata, B. (1992). Differential reinforcement as treatment for behavior disorders: Procedural and functional variations. *Research in Developmental Disabilities, 13,* 393–417.

Voss, J. F. (1989). Problem solving and the educational process. In A. Lesgold & R. Glaser (Eds.), *Foundations for a psychology of education.* Hillsdale: Lawrence Erlbaum.

Wahler, R. G. (1980). The insular mother: Her problems in parent child treatment. *Journal of Applied Behavior Analysis, 13,* 207–219.

Wahler, R. G. & Fox, J. J. (1981). Setting events in applied behavior analysis: Toward a conceptual and methodological expansion. *Journal of Applied Behavior Analysis, 14,* 327–338.

Waitzkin, H. (1991). *The politics of medical encounters: How patients and doctors deal with social problems.* New Haven: Yale University Press.

Wakefield, J. C. (1988). Psychotherapy, distributive justice, and social work. Part 2: Psychotherapy and the pursuit of justice. *Social Service Review, 62,* 353–382.

Wakefield, J. C. (1992). Why psychotherapeutic social work don't get no re-Specht. *Social Service Review, 66,* 141–151. (See also reply by Specht, pp. 152–159.)

Wakefield, J. C. (1994). Is the concept of mental disorder culturally relative? NO. In S. A. Kirk & S. D. Einbinder (Eds.), *Controversial issues in mental health* (pp. 11–17). Boston: Allyn Bacon.

Walker, S. (1994). *Sense and nonsense about crime and drugs: A policy guide* (3rd Ed.). Belmont: Wadsworth.

Wandersman, A., Andrews, A., Riddle, D., & Fawcett, C. (1983). Environmental psychology and prevention. In R. Felner, L. Jason, J. Moritsugu, & S. Farber (Eds.), *Preventive psychology: Theory, research and practice* (pp. 104–127). Elmsford, NY: Pergamon.

Warren, D. I. (1980). Support systems in different types of neighborhoods. In J. Garbarino, S. H. Stocking, and Associates. *Protecting children from abuse and neglect: Developing and maintaining effective support systems for families* (pp. 61–93). San Francisco: Jossey-Bass.

Warren, R. B. & Warren, D. I. (1977). *The neighborhood organizer's handbook.* Notre Dame, IN: University of Notre Dame Press.

Watkins, S. A. (1989). Confidentiality and privileged communication: legal dilemma for family therapists. *Social Work, 34,* 133–136.

Watson, D. L., & Tharp, R. G. (1993). *Self-directed behavior: Self-modification for personal adjustment* (6th ed.). Monterey, CA: Brooks/Cole.

Watzlawick, P., Beavin, J. H., & Jackson, D. D. (1967). *Pragmatics of human communication—A study of interactional patterns, pathologies, and paradoxes.* New York: W. W. Norton & Co., Inc.

Watzlawick, P., Weakland, J., & Fisch, R. (1974). *Change: Principles of problem formation and problem resolution.* New York: W. W. Norton & Co.

Webster's New College Dictionary. Third College Edition (1988). New York: Webster's New World.

Webster, Y. O. (1992). *The racialization of America.* New York: St. Martin's Press.

Weick, K. E. (1984). Small wins: Redefining the scale of social problems. *American Psychologist, 39,* 40–49.

Weinbach, R. W. (1990). *The social worker as manager: Theory and practice.* New York: Longman.

Weisberg, R. (1986). *Creativity, genius and other myths.* New York: W. H. Freeman.

Weissman, H. H., Epstein, I. E., & Savage, A. (1983). *Agency-based social work: Neglected aspects of clinical practice* (pp. 74–75). Philadelphia: Temple University Press.

Weissman, H. H., Epstein, I. E., & Savage, A. (1987). Expanding the role repertoire of clinicians. *Social Casework, 68,* 152–155.

Weisz, J., Suwanlert, S., Chaiyasit, W., & Walter, B. R. (1987). Over- and undercontrolled referral problems among children and adolescents from Thailand and the United States: The *Wat* and *Wai* of cultural differences. *Journal of Consulting and Clinical Psychology, 55,* 719–726.

Wenerowicz, W. J., Riskind, J. H., & Jenkins, P. G. (1978). Locus of control and degree of compliance in hemodialysis patients. *Journal of Dialysis, 2,* 495–505.

Wesch, D. & Lutzker, J. R. (1991). A comprehensive 5-year evaluation of Project 12-Ways: An ecobehavioral program for treating and preventing child abuse and neglect. *Journal of Family Violence, 5,* 17–35.

Westermeyer, J. (1987). Cultural factors in clinical assessment. *Journal of Consulting and Clinical Psychology, 55,* 471–478.

Weston, A. (1992). *A rule book for arguments* (2nd Ed.). Indianapolis: Hackett Publishing Co.

Wexler, R. (1990). *Wounded innocents: The real victims of the war against child abuse.* Buffalo: Prometheus.

Wheeler, D. D. & Janis, I. L. (1980). *A practical guide for making decisions.* New York: Free Press.

Whetten, D. A. & Cameron, K. S. (1995). *Developing management skills* (3rd Ed.). New York: Harper Collins.

White, A. D. (1993). *A history of the warfare of science with theology in Christendom.* Vols. I and II. New York: Prometheus. (Originally published in 1896.)

Whitree v. New York State (290 N.Y.S. 2d. 486 (ct. Claims). 1968.

Wilbern, Y. (1984). Types and levels of public morality. *Public Administration Review, 44*, 102–108.

Willner, A. G., Braukmann, C. J., Kirigin, K. A., Fixen, D. L., Phillips, E. L., & Wolf, M. M. (1977). The training and validation of youth-preferred social behaviors of childcare personnel. *Journal of Applied Behavior Analysis, 10*, 219–230.

Wills, T. A. (1978). Perceptions of clients by professional helpers. *Psychological Bulletin, 85*, 968–1000.

Wills, T. A. (1982). Nonspecific factors in helping relationships. In T. A. Wills, (Ed.), *Basic processes in helping relationships* (pp. 381–404). New York: Academic Press.

Wilson, E. O. (1975). *Sociobiology: The new synthesis.* Cambridge, MA: Harvard University Press.

Wilson, K. & Gallois, C. (1993). *Assertion and its social context.* New York: Pergamon Press.

Wilson, P. H. (Ed.). (1992). *Principles and practice of relapse prevention.* New York: Guilford.

Wilson, S. J. (1978). *Confidentiality in social work: Issues and principles.* New York: Free Press.

Winchester-Vega, M. (1997). Should clients have access to their mental health records? NO. In E. Gambrill & R. Pruger (Eds.), *Controversial issues in social work ethics, values, and obligations* (pp. 6–9). Boston: Allyn & Bacon.

Witt, J. C., Elliott, S. N., & Gresham, F. (1988). *Handbook of behavior therapy in education.* New York: Plenum.

Witte, C. L., Witte, M. H. & Kerwin, A. (1994). Suspended judgment: Ignorance and the process of learning and discovery in medicine. *Controlled Clinical Trials, 15*, 1–4.

Wolf, M. M. (1978). Social validity: The case for subjective measurement or how applied behavior analysis is finding its heart. *Journal of Applied Behavior Analysis, 11*, 203–214.

Wolf, J. H. (1985). Professionalizing volunteer work in a black neighborhood. *Social Service Review, 59*, 423–434.

Wolf, M. M., Braukmann, C. J., & Ramp, K. A. (1987). Serious delinquent behavior as part of a significantly handicapping condition: Cures and supportive environments. *Journal of Applied Behavior Analysis, 20*, 347–359.

Wolpe, J. (1986). Individualization: The categorical imperative of behavior therapy practice. *Journal of Behavior Therapy and Experimental Psychiatry, 17*, 145–154.

Wolpe, J. (Ed.). (1990). *The practice of behavior therapy.* Elmsford, NY: Pergamon.

Wong, S. E., Terranova, M. D., Bowen, L., Zarate, R., Massel, H. K., & Liberman, R. P. (1987). Providing independent recreational activities to reduce stereotypic vocalizations in chronic schizophrenics. *Journal of Applied Behavior Analysis, 20*, 77–81.

Woolfolk, R. L. & Lehrer, P. M. (1993). *Principles and practice of stress management* (2nd Ed.). New York: Guilford.

Wurtele, S. K., Saslawsky, D. A., Miller, C. L., Marrs, S. R., & Britcher, J. C. (1986). Teaching personal safety skills for potential prevention of sexual abuse: A comparison of treatments. *Journal of Consulting and Clinical Psychology, 54*, 688–692.

Wyatt v. Stickney decision (344F. Supp. 387 (MD Ala, 1972).

Wyatt, W. J. (1990). Radical behaviorism misrepresented: A response to Mahoney. *American Psychologist, 45*, 1181–1184.

Wyllie, I. G. (1954). *The self-made man in America: The myth of rags to riches.* New Brunswick, NJ: Rutgers University Press.

Yoshioka, M. R., Thomas, E. J., & Ager, R. D. (1992). Nagging and other drinking control efforts of spouses of uncooperative alcohol abusers: Assessment and modification. *Journal of Substance Abuse, 4*, 309–318.

Young, J. H. (1992). *American health quackery.* Princeton: Princeton University Press.

Young, K. R. & West, R. P., Howard, V. F., & Whitney, R. (1986). Acquisition, fluency training, generalization, and maintenance of dressing skills of two developmentally disabled children. *Education and Treatment of Children, 9*, 16–29.

Yourdon, E. (1989). *Modern structured analysis.* Englewood Cliffs, NJ: Prentice-Hall.

Zander, A. (1990). *Effective social action by community groups.* San Francisco: Jossey-Bass.

Zegiob, L., Arnold, S., & Forehand, R. (1975). An examination of observer effects in parent-child interactions. *Child Development, 46*, 509–512.

Ziskin, J. & Faust, D. (1988). *Coping with psychiatric and psychological testimony.* Vols. 1–3 (4th Ed.). Los Angeles: Law and Psychology Press.

Zuniga, M. E. (1992). Families with Latino roots. In E. W. Lynch & M. J. Hanson (Eds.), *Developing cross-cultural competence.* Baltimore, MD: Paul H. Brookes.

Zuriff, G. E. (1985). *Behaviorism*: A conceptual reconstruction. New York: Columbia.

Index